THE CAMBRIDGE
ANCIENT HISTORY

VOLUME XIII

THE CAMBRIDGE
ANCIENT HISTORY

VOLUME XIII
The Late Empire, A.D. 337–425

Edited by

AVERIL CAMERON
Warden of Keble College, Oxford

PETER GARNSEY
*Professor of the History of Classical Antiquity
in the University of Cambridge, and Fellow of Jesus College*

CAMBRIDGE
UNIVERSITY PRESS

Published by the Press Syndicate of the University of Cambridge
The Pitt Building, Trumpington Street, Cambridge CB2 1RP
40 West 20th Street, New York, NY 10011–4211, USA
10 Stamford Road, Oakleigh, Melbourne 3166, Australia

© Cambridge University Press 1998

First published 1998

Printed in the United Kingdom at the University Press, Cambridge

A catalogue record for this book is available from the British Library

Library of Congress Catalogue card number: 75–85719

ISBN 0 521 30200 5 hardback

CONTENTS

List of maps   *page* xi

List of text-figures   xii

Preface   xiii

PART I   CHRONOLOGICAL OVERVIEW

1   The successors of Constantine   1
     by DAVID HUNT, *Senior Lecturer in Classics and Ancient History at the*
     University of Durham

          I   The dynastic inheritance, 337–40   1
          II   Constans and the west, 340–50   5
          III Constantius and Persia, 337–50   11
          IV   Magnentius, Vetranio and the recovery of the west, 350–3   14
          V   Athanasius, Gallus and Julian, 353–6   22
          VI   Constantius in Rome, 357   29
          VII Sirmium and the search for a creed, 357–9   32
          VIII Constantius in Constantinople, 359–60   37
          IX   Sapor and Julian, 360–1   39

2   Julian   44
     by DAVID HUNT

          I   The early years   44
          II   Caesar in Gaul   49
          III Proclamation at Paris   56
          IV   Constantinople   60
          V   Antioch   67
          VI   Persia   73

3   From Jovian to Theodosius   78
     by JOHN CURRAN, *Lecturer in Classics at The Queen's University of*
     Belfast

          I   Jovian   78
          II   Valentinian and Valens: accession   80

v

III   Religion, magic and treason at Rome   82
IV   Valentinian and the north-west frontier   83
V   Valentinian and Britain   86
VI   Valentinian and Africa   87
VII   Valens and the revolt of Procopius   89
VIII   Valens and Persia   91
IX   Valens and the Goths   94
X   Theodosius: the Gothic war   101
XI   Theodosius and Christianity   103
XII   The usurpation of Maximus and the fall of Gratian   104
XIII   The fall of Valentinian II and the usurpation of Eugenius   108

4   The dynasty of Theodosius   111
    by R. C. BLOCKLEY, *Professor of Classics, Carleton University, Ottawa*
    I   Introduction   111
    II   The empire divided, 395–404   113
    III   The German onslaught on the west, 400–8   118
    IV   Alaric in Italy, 408–10   125
    V   The early years of Theodosius II, 408–14   128
    VI   Barbarian settlements in the west, 411–18   129
    VII   The ascendancy of Pulcheria, 414–23   133
    VIII   The last years of Honorius and the usurpation of John, 419–25   135

PART II   GOVERNMENT AND INSTITUTIONS

5   Emperors, government and bureaucracy   138
    by CHRISTOPHER KELLY, *Lecturer in Classics in the University of
    Cambridge, and Fellow of Corpus Christi College*
    I   Introduction   138
    II   The emperor in the later Roman world   139
    III   Bureaucracy   162
    IV   Conclusions   180

6   Senators and senates   184
    by PETER HEATHER, *Lecturer in Early Medieval History,
    University College London*
    I   Institutional change   184
    II   Senatorial careers   191
    III   Senators and emperors   197
    IV   Senators and local politics   204
    V   Conclusion   209

7   The army   211
    by A. D. LEE, *Lecturer in Classics and Ancient History at the
    University of Wales, Lampeter*
    I   Organization and deployment   213

II   Resources and manpower   219
III The army, politics and society   224
IV   Military effectiveness   232

8   The church as a public institution   238
    by DAVID HUNT

    I   Introduction: bishops at court   238
    II   Organization and hierarchy   240
    III A Christian environment   250
    IV   Wealth   257
    V   The church as a career   262
    VI   Bishops and the community   269
    VII Bishops and the law   272

PART III   THE EMPIRE: ECONOMY AND SOCIETY

9   Rural life in the later Roman empire   277
    by C. R. WHITTAKER, *Fellow of Churchill College, University of
    Cambridge and* PETER GARNSEY

    I   Rural production   277
    II   Labour and property owners   287
    III The organization of the countryside   304

10 Trade, industry and the urban economy   312
    by PETER GARNSEY *and* C. R. WHITTAKER

    I   Introduction   312
    II   State intervention and its limits   316
    III Expanding estates, declining cities   322
    IV   The city economy   328
    V   Conclusion   335

11 Late Roman social relations   338
    by ARNALDO MARCONE, *Professor of the Economic and Social
    History of the Ancient World, University of Parma*

    I   Introduction   338
    II   The sources   339
    III   A society in transition   340
    IV   The regional reality   351
    V   The emperor   352
    VI   The upper classes   354
    VII   The lower classes   356
    VIII Other social distinctions   359
    IX   From patronage to *patrocinium*   361
    X   Social mobility   363
    XI   Social marginalization   366
    XII   Conclusion   369

12 The cities   371
    by BRYAN WARD-PERKINS, *Fellow of Trinity College, Oxford*

        I   What is a *civitas* and what is a city?   371
        II   The decline of the *curiae* and the 'end of the classical city'   373
        III The new structures of power and loyalty   382
        IV   Military needs   389
        V   The impact of Christianity   392
        VI   The size and wealth of cities   403
        VII Conclusion   409

    PART IV   FOREIGN RELATIONS AND THE
              BARBARIAN WORLD

13 Warfare and diplomacy   411
    by R. C. BLOCKLEY

        I   War, diplomacy and the Roman state   411
        II   Sources   414
        III   The defence of the empire to Constantine   416
        IV   From Constantine's death to the treaty of 363   419
        V   The Pannonian emperors   424
        VI   Theodosius I: the aftermath of Adrianople   426
        VII   The reigns of Arcadius and Honorius   429
        VIII Theodosius II: the emergence of diplomacy   433

14 The eastern frontier   437
    by BENJAMIN ISAAC, *Professor of Ancient History at Tel Aviv University*

        I   Rome and Persia   437
        II   Arabs and desert peoples   444
        III Regional and local unrest   452
        IV   Military organization   455
        V   Conclusion   460

15 The Germanic peoples   461
    by MALCOLM TODD, *Principal of Trevelyan College and Professor of Archaeology at the University of Durham*

        I   Introduction   461
        II   Gaul, the Germanys and Raetia   464
        III The northern coastlands and Holland   472
        IV   Britain   474
        V   Scandinavia and the western Baltic   478
        VI   The eastern territories and the Danube lands   482

16 Goths and Huns, *c.* 320–425   487
    by PETER HEATHER

        I   Sources   487

    II   The Goths to *c.* 370   488
    III Goths and Huns beyond the Roman frontier, *c.* 370–425   499
    IV   Goths and Romans, *c.* 376–425   507

17 The barbarian invasions and first settlements   516
    by I. N. WOOD, *Professor of Early Medieval History at the University*
    of Leeds

PART V   RELIGION

18 Polytheist religion and philosophy   538
    by GARTH FOWDEN, *Centre for Greek and Roman Antiquity,*
    National Research Foundation, Athens

    I   Repression and compromise, 337–61   539
    II   Julian, philosopher and reformer of polytheism   543
    III Jovian to Theodosius II: the attrition of polytheism   548
    IV   Polytheist resistances   554
    V   Polytheism and Christianity   558

19 Orthodoxy and heresy from the death of Constantine to the eve
    of the first council of Ephesus   561
    by HENRY CHADWICK, *Professor Emeritus of the University of*
    Cambridge

20 Asceticism: pagan and Christian   601
    by PETER BROWN, *Professor of History, Princeton University*

21 Christianization and religious conflict   632
    by PETER BROWN

PART VI   ART AND CULTURE

22 Education and literary culture   665
    by AVERIL CAMERON

    I   Introduction   665
    II   Christianity and traditional education   667
    III   Literary education as a path to advancement   673
    IV   Neoplatonism   680
    V   Legal and other studies   682
    VI   History-writing and its context   684
    VII   High literary culture   691
    VIII Epistolography and literary networks   696
    IX   Christian writing   698
    X   Biography, Christian and pagan   699
    XI   Ascetic literature   700
    XII   Theological works   702
    XIII Conclusion   704

23*a* Syriac culture, 337–425   708
    by SEBASTIAN BROCK, *Reader in Syriac Studies in the University*
    of Oxford

         I   Introduction   708
        II   Literary genres   712
       III   The threefold inheritance   712
        IV   Interaction between Syriac and Greek culture   714
         V   Syriac into Greek and Greek into Syriac   717

23*b* Coptic literature, 337–425   720
    by MARK SMITH, *University Lecturer in Ancient Egyptian and Coptic,*
    University of Oxford

         I   Magical texts   722
        II   The Bible and Apocrypha   722
       III   Patristic and homiletic works   725
        IV   Monastic texts and martyrologies   727
         V   The Nag Hammadi library and related tractates   730
        VI   Manichean writings   733

24   Art and architecture   736
    by JAŚ ELSNER, *Lecturer in the History of Art at the Courtauld*
    Institute, University of London

         I   Introduction   736
        II   The modern critical context   739
       III   Art and architecture, 337–425   742

Chronological table   762

                          BIBLIOGRAPHY

Abbreviations   768
Frequently cited works   771
Part I: Chronological overview (chapters 1–4)   778
Part II: Government and institutions (chapters 5–8)   784
Part III: The empire: economy and society (chapters 9–12)   799
Part IV: Foreign relations and the barbarian world (chapters 13–17) 809
Part V: Religion (chapters 18–21)   818
Part VI: Art and culture (chapters 22–24)   826

Index   846

MAPS

1   The Roman empire in the late fourth century A.D.   18
2   Gaul and the German frontier   52
3   The Balkans and the Danube region   96
4   The Alps and northern Italy   119
5   Greece and Asia Minor   243
6   Asia Minor and the eastern provinces   440
7   North Africa   584
8   Egypt   615
9   Syriac centres in the Middle East   711

TEXT-FIGURES

1 The cities discussed in chapter 12   372
2 The comparative size of fourteen walled towns and cities in
the Roman empire, c. A.D. 350–450   374
3 From colonnaded street to souk: Sauvaget's hypothesis   383
4 Trier in the fourth century   385
5 Constantinople in the later fifth century   387
6 Rome at the death of Constantine, A.D. 337   397
7 Major barbarian peoples and Roman frontiers: late fourth–
fifth centuries   462
8 Warrior burials in northern Gaul and the German provinces:
late fourth–early fifth centuries   466
9 Fifth-century Germanic burials in Britain   476
10 Settlements and cemeteries of the Černjachov culture   489
11 The arrival of the Huns c. A.D. 370–95   501
12 The crisis of A.D. 405–8 and Huns west of the Carpathian
mountains   504

PREFACE

The new edition of *The Cambridge Ancient History* includes two volumes additional to the twelve of the original version, of which the present volume, covering the period A.D. 337 to 425, is the first. Together they extend the scope of the series to the end of the sixth century A.D., and thus to the eve of the Arab invasions. In so doing they reflect the remarkable growth of interest in the period after Constantine that has taken place since the first edition appeared. The reasons for choosing the end of the sixth century as a final terminus will be explored in the preface to Volume XIV, but a few words may be appropriate here about the conception and scope of the new volumes. In one sense any choice of terminus is arbitrary. We did not adopt this framework out of any desire to revive the 'Pirenne thesis' or to imply that alternative chronological divisions such as the period from the fourth to the seventh centuries adopted in several recent publications were necessarily less desirable. These volumes were first planned before the decision was taken to produce a new edition of the first volume of *The Cambridge Medieval History*; however, while there will inevitably be some overlap between them, readers are likely to notice a distinct difference in treatment and perspective.

Since the appearance in 1939 of the final volume of the original edition (which concluded at A.D. 324, thus deliberately excluding the reign of Constantine as sole emperor, and perhaps in particular the foundation of Constantinople), conceptions of the period from Diocletian (A.D. 284–305) to the end of the sixth century have been transformed for English-speaking readers by the appearance in 1964 of A. H. M. Jones's magisterial work, *The Later Roman Empire 284–602. A Social, Economic and Administrative Survey*. A further major development has been the popularization of the concept of late antiquity as an object of study in itself; the publications of Peter Brown, in the first instance *The World of Late Antiquity* (1971), were highly influential in bringing this about. But while Jones remains unsurpassed in his presentation of the evidence for the workings of late Roman government, law and administration, the last generation has seen an explosion of interest in the archaeology of the period, and in religious and cultural history, while the study of the 'barbarian' peoples has also been completely transformed, not least by a new interest in ethnogenesis. Much of this had already been prefigured in European scholarship, notably in the works of O. Seeck, E. Stein and A. Piganiol; more recently it has been expressed in such important collective works as the *Storia di Roma*, vol. III, *L'Età tardoantica*, ed. A. Carandini, L. Cracco Ruggini and A. Giardina (1993), the four volumes of *Società romana e impero tardoantico*, ed. A. Giardina (1986), and the French volume *Hommes et richesses dans l'Empire byzantin I, IVe–VIIe siècle*, ed. C. Morrisson and J. Lefort (1989), to which we must now add the comprehensive survey of the period provided by A. Demandt, *Die Spätantike: römische Geschichte von Diocletian bis Justinian 284–565 n.Chr.* (1989); the differing titles to some extent reflect differences in national tradition.

One of the features observable in recent work on this period has been a move away from older historical categories towards a more nearly 'total' view of the period. The effects of this tendency can also be observed within individual chapters in the volume, and it added to the difficulties experienced by the editors in determining the division of chapters. Nevertheless, this volume begins with a series of narrative chapters, thereafter grouping the material in broad sections. Not everything could be included that we would have liked, even in a volume of this size; on some topics, therefore, the reader should refer to the preceding or following volumes.

Volume XIII covers the fourth century A.D., from the death of Constantine in A.D. 337, to the early fifth, and concludes *c.* A.D. 425, during the reign of Theodosius II (408–50). Within that span of time came the division of the empire into eastern and western halves on the death of Theodosius I in A.D. 395. The disastrous defeat of the Roman army by the Goths at Adrianople in A.D. 378 and the invasion of Italy and sack of Rome by Alaric in A.D. 410 have been seen both by contemporaries and by later generations as marking the first stages in the break-up of the Roman empire in the west. With the reign of Theodosius II in Constantinople, a more distinctly eastern style of government evolved; the ability of this government, based on an impressively expanding capital city, to harness the resources of the east enabled Justinian in the sixth century to launch a 'reconquest' of the west. Crucial to this development, whereby the east was able to escape the fragmentation experienced in the contemporary west, were the events of *c.* A.D. 400 in Constantinople, to which several chapters make reference. By the end of the period covered here, therefore, barbarian settlement was well established in the west; in A.D. 430 the Vandals, having crossed into North Africa from Spain, were in a position to attack Augustine's town of Hippo Regius. Yet the long reign of Theodosius II in the east saw a period of civilian government and a degree of civic prosperity.

Culturally, the period from the death of Constantine to the reign of Theodosius II was one of the most vigorous in antiquity. It saw the development of the church as a public institution under imperial patronage, and the rise of such powerful bishops as Ambrose of Milan. The monastic movement, part of a much wider ascetic tendency not confined to Christian contexts, also took root now. But the late fourth century was also a great age of literary and artistic patronage; moreover, new local literary and linguistic cultures emerge in these years, especially in the east, as we see in the chapters by S. P. Brock and M. Smith in Part VI. Older conceptions of 'decline' and rigidity in the late Roman social and economic structure are challenged by Peter Garnsey and C. R. Whittaker in chapters 9–10, while Christopher Kelly in chapter 5 analyses the bureaucratic system and the level of imperial ceremonial in terms of negotiation and shifting allegiances rather than according to the traditional categories of corruption and state control. The visual art of the fourth century has too often been viewed as necessarily either 'pagan' or 'Christian'; in chapter 24 Jaś Elsner questions the value of such a dichotomy and shows the interconnection of themes and patronage. Part IV, with its treatment of the 'barbarian' world, demonstrates how far scholarship has moved in this field towards a better understanding of the processes of settlement and acculturation since the publication of the first edition.

As in other volumes of this *History*, individual chapters may represent differing points of view. We have not attempted to impose uniformity, though authors were asked to indicate, so far as possible, matters on which they were themselves diverging from currently accepted views. Again as in the case of other volumes, this one has been long in the making, and scholarship has not stood still meanwhile. We must thank the contributors for their co-operation and in many cases for their willingness to update and revise their chapters in the light of new publications or editorial comment. We have adopted a different procedure in this volume in relation to the bibliographies: works of central importance, or to which reference is frequently made throughout the volume, have been listed separately by author and short title, following which there is a bibliography arranged by author and title for each of the six parts into which the volume is divided, some works appearing for convenience in more than one of these lists. We hope that this may make it easier for readers to find the references they need.

Readers will notice that a variety of spellings and transliterations have been employed for proper names in this volume, according to the specialist preference of each contributor. Latin place names and their modern equivalents are cross-referenced in the index, as are personal names such as Sapor and Shapur or Arsak and Arsaces which come in two or more different forms.

John Matthews played an important role in the planning and early stages of this volume as a member of the original editorial troika; we are also indebted to a number of other colleagues, especially Peter Heather, for assistance with individual chapters. We are grateful to the staff of Cambridge University Press, particularly to Pauline Hire and Paul Chipchase, for their various skills in preparing the volume for publication. The maps were drawn by David Cox and the index compiled by Barbara Hird.

A.M.C.
P.D.A.G.

CHAPTER 1

THE SUCCESSORS OF CONSTANTINE

DAVID HUNT

I. THE DYNASTIC INHERITANCE, 337–40

Newly baptized into the faith which he had professed and fostered in the Roman empire for twenty-five years, Constantine died in an imperial villa on the outskirts of Nicomedia at Pentecost (22 May) in 337. Amid public expressions of grief, soldiers of the guard laid the body in a golden coffin and bore it, draped in a pall of imperial purple, into Constantinople, where the dead ruler lay in state in his palace surrounded by brightly burning candles on gold candlesticks, guarded day and night by palace officials. Adorned with the diadem and other symbols of the imperial office, Constantine in death continued to receive the rituals of homage which military and civilian leaders normally addressed to a living emperor – he still reigned in his city (Eus. *V. Const.* iv.66–7). Of the other members of the ruling dynasty, it was Constantine's middle son, Constantius, who arrived from Antioch (where he was preparing for imminent conflict with Persia) to assume control of the funeral arrangements; although summoned at the news of his father's illness, he came too late to find him still alive (Jul. *Or.* 1.16c–d, 11.94b; Zon. XIII.4.28). With Constantius at their head, soldiers and people accompanied the coffin to Constantine's recently completed mausoleum; but here the Caesar and his troops withdrew, and it was left to the 'ministers of God' and a thronged congregation of the faithful to conduct the final obsequies. Raised on a lofty catafalque, Constantine was laid to rest, as he had intended, in the midst of memorials of the twelve apostles, and now in company with them in God's kingdom he received the prayers of his Christian subjects (*V. Const.* iv.60, 70–1). In eastern Christianity Constantine remains to this day the 'equal of the apostles'.[1]

For Eusebius, to whose praises of the Christian Constantine we owe these details of his funeral, this seamless web of ritual and piety was the only fitting climax to Constantine's earthly existence. Yet the ceremonies evoked by the death of the first Roman emperor to espouse Christianity

---

[1] For Constantine's funeral, see Kaniuth (1941), who notes (pp. 7–9) the separation of the religious ceremony from the rest of the proceedings. For the date of the Church of the Holy Apostles next to the mausoleum, see below, p. 38.

were more an amalgam of traditional and novel components. As throughout Constantine's rule, the deposit of past practice and symbolism was
tenacious, and had not yet had time to give way (indeed, there is no reason
to expect it) to exclusively Christian forms of expression. Hence the strictly
Christian aspect of the proceedings was confined to the funeral service
proper in church – and here Eusebius' rhetoric manages to conceal a significant innovation: gone was the huge pyre of great imperial cremations
of the past, to be replaced now by Christian burial. The state ceremonial,
on the other hand, the homage of leaders and people, the military escort,
retained features inherited from previous imperial funerals (despite
Eusebius' predictable insistence on the uniqueness of the Constantinian
occasion).[2] Nor did Constantine escape the overtly pagan fate of deifica-
tion. Some sources (Aur. Vict. *Caes.* XLI.16; Eutr. X.8.2) report the traditional appearance of a comet in the skies portending his death and
apotheosis, while even Eusebius – somewhat disingenuously, in the context
of Christian devotion – acknowledged the issue of posthumous coinage
depicting Constantine rising to the heavens in a chariot to be received by
the hand of God, and (at Rome) pictures of the dead emperor dwelling
above the globe of the world (*V. Const.* IV.69.2, 73). Both these images
derived from the traditional store of pagan iconography:[3] panegyrists, for
example, had spoken of Constantine's father being carried to the skies in
the sun's chariot, to be received there by the outstretched right hand of
Jupiter. While Christians could, and did, reinterpret them in their own
terms (referring them respectively to the Old Testament ascent of Elijah
and to the eternal rule of Christ over the earth), their appearance to honour
the dead Constantine owes more to previous usage than to the new faith.
It is not hard to credit the story reported by Philostorgius (II.17) that
Constantine's statue in the forum of Constantinople became the object of
pagan rituals aimed at warding off misfortune: Constantine in death was
not, *pace* Eusebius, solely the preserve of Christian religious observance.

Eusebius' tableau of Constantine's uninterrupted transition from earth
to heaven also hides from view the political and dynastic dislocation which
ensued at his death. It is necessary to revert briefly to the last years of his
reign.[4] In their final form Constantine's intentions for the succession had
embraced both his own three surviving sons (the youngest of whom,
Constans, had become a Caesar in 333) and the descendants of his step-
mother Theodora: her grandson, Constantine's nephew Dalmatius, was
made a fourth Caesar on 18 September 335, and the following year a granddaughter was married to the Caesar Constantius; while Dalmatius' brother
Hannibalianus, honoured as a *nobilissimus* and accorded the title 'king of

---

[2] See Price (1987) 99ff.   [3] See MacCormack, *Art and Ceremony*, 121–32.
[4] Constantine's dynastic arrangements are conveniently summarized in Barnes, *CE* 250–2.

kings' (in the context of threatened hostilities against Persia), was given Constantine's daughter Constantina in marriage. Constantine had evidently envisaged that the two families would share the inheritance of his empire. This was not how Eusebius came to portray the succession. For him Constantine's heirs were exclusively his own three sons, no less by the will of God than by that of their father, and it was because of their (temporary) absence at the time of his death that Constantine 'continued to rule' from the grave; when he was translated to the company of the apostles, his empire on earth carried on in the persons of his three sons. This posthumous rule of Constantine, which is reflected in a surviving law of 2 August 337 issued still in his name (*C.Th.* XIII.4.2), was in reality a far cry from the unbroken continuity hymned by Eusebius. Not for the first time in the succession politics of Roman imperial history a dead emperor was kept 'alive' until the resolution of dynastic conflict. It was only in fact on 9 September 337 (*Chron. Min.* I, 235), more than three months after Constantine's death, that his sons Constantine II, Constantius II and Constans formally succeeded him as Augusti. Eusebius' picture thus reflects the situation as it stood after that date, and the interests of the new rulers in presenting themselves as the heaven-sent and exclusive claimants of their father's inheritance.

Meanwhile, in an episode consigned to diplomatic silence by Eusebius, the descendants of Theodora had been violently displaced from the share in the succession which Constantine had destined for them. The summer of 337 saw what Gibbon famously termed a 'promiscuous massacre'.[5] The future emperor Julian, at the time a child of six years or so, later looked back on the murders of nine of his relatives (*Ep. ad Ath.* 270c–d): his father and uncle (Julius Constantius and Flavius Dalmatius, the sons of Theodora), six of his cousins (including Dalmatius Caesar and Hannibalianus) and his oldest brother (unknown). Another victim is likely to have been the Caesar's tutor, the eminent Gallic rhetor Aemilius Magnus Arborius.[6] Julian himself and his older half-brother Gallus, who was seriously ill at the time and expected to die in any event, proved to be the sole survivors of this family bloodletting (Greg. Naz. *Or.* IV.21; Lib. *Or.* XVIII.10). Julian recalled these unsavoury events in 361, when he was a usurping emperor embarked on civil war against Constantius II: small wonder that in such circumstances he should accuse Constantius of the murders. But even in the context of an earlier panegyric, Constantius could not entirely escape censure: Julian acknowledged that in the sequel to Constantine's death he had been 'forced by circumstances and reluctantly failed to prevent others doing wrong' (*Or.* 1.17a). It is hard not to conclude that Constantius had some part in this

[5] *Decline and Fall* (ed. Bury), vol. 2, p. 236. For summary narrative, Barnes, *CE* 261–2; more detailed discussion in Olivetti (1915), Klein (1979a).
[6] Ausonius, *Profess.* XVI.13ff. (with R. P. H. Green *ad loc.*).

brutal overturning of his father's dynastic plans. He was the Caesar first to appear after Constantine's death and seize the initiative in Constantinople – to the displacement, it would appear, of Dalmatius, of whose whereabouts we hear nothing, but who as Caesar in Moesia and Thrace ought to have been closest at hand to the affairs of the capital. The actual agents of the destruction were the troops in and around Constantinople, who staged a military coup against Dalmatius and the rest of Theodora's clan (the survival of the two boys Gallus and Julian may owe something to the fact that Constantius was married to their sister); if Aurelius Victor is to be believed, the soldiers had already voiced their dissent at Dalmatius' elevation as Caesar in 335.[7] This uprising effectively resolved the dynastic rivalries, as the troops were made to proclaim their allegiance to 'no ruler other than the sons of Constantine' (Zos. II.40.3; for Eusebius (*V. Const.* IV.68) such pronouncements only served to confirm his image of seamless continuity from father to sons); and their conduct was later provided with a semblance of justification, as an act of revenge, by the circulation of a rumour that Constantine had actually been poisoned by his half-brothers.[8] Even bathed in the language of Julian's panegyric, Constantius had 'failed to prevent' these murders; another source has him *sinente potius quam iubente* (Eutr. *loc. cit.*; cf. Socr. *HE* II.25.3). Whatever his precise role, the soldiers delivered him the outcome which served his interests, and a determination to keep the military under control was, with good reason, a hallmark of his rule (Amm. Marc. XXI.16.1–3). In the early stages he may already have faced a reaction from some of his father's establishment figures, for he soon found it convenient to remove the powerful and long-serving praetorian prefect Flavius Ablabius, and the following year (338) had him and some associates killed amid accusations of attempting to seize power.[9]

Constantius' two brothers, elsewhere in the empire at the time of their father's death, apparently took no part in the events which secured the removal of their rival dynasts. In the autumn of 337 the three new Augusti conferred in Pannonia and agreed on the division of their empire:[10] Constantius retained the whole of the east, where he had been serving as Caesar, to which was added the diocese of Thrace (formerly in the control of Dalmatius); the remainder of Dalmatius' domain (Moesia) went to Constans, who controlled the rest of Illyricum, Italy and Africa; while Constantine, the senior of the three, was left with the region where he had been Caesar, the western prefecture of Gaul, Spain and Britain. It was not

---

[7] *Caes.* XLI.15 (reading '*obsistentibus*'). For this military uprising, see also Eutr. X.9.1; *Epit. de Caes.* XLI.18; Jer. *Chron. s.a.* 338 (ed. Helm, 234); Greg. Naz. *Or.* IV.21.

[8] A story unique to Philostorgius (II.16), the one ecclesiastical historian sympathetic to Constantius.

[9] Jer. *Chron. s.a.* 338 (Helm, p. 234). For the pagan view of the Christian Ablabius' fate see the narrative of Eunap. *V. Soph.* 464 (Loeb, pp. 388–90), and Zos. II.40.3.

[10] Jul. *Or.* I.19a. For the movements of the new rulers, see Barnes, *Athanasius* 218ff.

long before all three were advertising their imperial credentials by embarking on military campaigns. From Antioch in 338, amid mounting tensions with Persia, Constantius intervened to secure a friendly ruler in Armenia; while around the same time Constantine claimed a victory over the Alamanni, and Constans took the field against the Sarmatians across the Danube (*ILS* 724). All these were tasks which reflected a continuity of concerns inherited from Constantine's last years.

But events were soon to prove that the dynastic competition had still not run its course. Constantine II, the oldest of the heirs and longest serving of his father's Caesars, had already seized the initiative of seniority as early as June 337 (before the three were named as Augusti) to order the return of the exiled bishop Athanasius to Alexandria, claiming the authority of the unfulfilled intentions of his late father.[11] After the formal division of autumn 337 Constantine continued to assert a senior authority over his youngest brother's share of the empire (Constans was still only in his early teens in 337): according to some accounts he sought to extend his control into Italy and Africa (*Epit. de Caes.* XLI.21; Zos. II.41), an allegation given some support by his addressing a law from Trier on 8 January 339 to the proconsul of Africa (*C.Th.* XII.1.27). Early in 340, not content with merely legislative intervention in Constans' territory, Constantine led an army across the Alps from Gaul and invaded northern Italy.[12] Constans, based at Naissus in Moesia, sent troops to confront his brother; these led Constantine's army into a disastrous ambush near Aquileia, and Constantine himself was killed, his body cast into the river Alsa (Ausa) (*Epit.* XLI.21; Zon. XIII.5.7–14). His failed territorial ambitions thus provided the opportunity for Constans to gain possession of the entire western empire. By April Constans had himself reached Aquileia, and on 29th of that month the praetorian prefect of Italy received a law repealing some of the acts of the *publicus ac noster inimicus* (*C.Th.* XI.12.1). The official record was soon to obliterate the memory of the younger Constantine: when Libanius came to compose a panegyric of the emperors (*Or.* 59) in the later 340s it was as if he had never been. Constantius, now embroiled in a dogged confrontation with the Persians in Mesopotamia, had no cause to intervene in the fraternal strife in the west: Julian (*Or.* II.94c–d) was later to commend him for seeking no territorial advantage from the conflict.

II. CONSTANS AND THE WEST, 340–50

The provinces of the west which had briefly owed allegiance to Constantine II appear to have been largely unmoved by his downfall, and

---

[11] See letter cited by Athan. *Apol. c. Ar.* LXXXVII.4–7.
[12] On the pretext of advancing eastwards to aid Constantius: Zos. II.41.

readily transferred their loyalties to Constans. The only hint of reprisals lies in the persuasive conjecture that Constantine's praetorian prefect in Gaul, Ambrosius (father of a famous son), was a victim of the change of regime.[13] For most of the next decade Constans divided his residence between Trier, the capital in Gaul which his family had made their own, and the north of Italy. He may, too, have visited Rome.[14] The most obvious opportunity for a rare imperial *adventus* into the ancient capital might have been provided by the occasion of Rome's eleventh centenary in 348, a date which passed without celebration, we are told (at least by comparison with the millennium a century earlier), but which Constans duly marked with the issue of the new FEL TEMP REPARATIO coinage.[15] While still in northern Italy in the summer of 340, after the overthrow of his older brother, Constans had received a delegation from Rome headed by the city prefect, Fabius Titianus (*Chron. Min.* 1.68), which presumably presented appropriate congratulations on his victory: it was a timely gesture of loyalty by Titianus, who the next year became Constans' long-serving praetorian prefect of Gaul.

For the Gauls, Constans' government was marked, at least in its early years, by his adherence to the vigorous stance against barbarians across the Rhine which he inherited from his dynastic predecessors who had held court at Trier: the fear which the Alamanni had of Constans, claims Ammianus (xxx.7.5), was eclipsed only by their later respect for the successes of Julian. Of actual campaigning, all we hear is of two expeditions against the Franks, an inconclusive contest in 341 followed by a victory for Constans the following year, when the enemy were forced into submission and a peace treaty.[16] In the early months of 343 Constans crossed the English Channel for a brief foray into Britain (he was back in Trier by June), an episode sufficiently celebrated for Libanius to devote several chapters of his panegyric to expounding it (*Or.* LIX.137ff.), and for Ammianus to have made it the occasion for a digression in one of his lost books on the geography of Britain (xxvII.8.4). What in fact captured the interest of writers was the emperor's perilous winter crossing of the Channel[17] – Ammianus had spoken of 'the movements of the rising and falling Ocean' – and not his exploits in Britain, which appear to have been minor. We may infer from Libanius (ch. 141) that this British expedition was not forced upon Constans by revolt or disorder in the island; furthermore, he was reportedly accompanied by a retinue of only one hundred men (ch. 139). It was evidently not a military campaign, and may have had a more administrative purpose: the only hint of its object perhaps lies in Ammianus' remark

[13] *PLRE* 1.51 'Ambrosius 1'.   [14] T. D. Barnes, *HSCP* 79 (1975) 327–8.

[15] J. P. C. Kent, *RIC* 8 (1981) 34–5. For the comparison with the proceedings of 248, see Aur. Vict. *Caes.* xxvIII.2.   [16] See Jer. *Chron. s.a.* 341, 342 (Helm, p. 235); Lib. *Or.* LIX.127ff.; Socr. *HE* II.13.4.

[17] Cf. Firm. Mat. *De errore prof. relig.* xxvIII.6, with Turcan (Budé) *ad loc.*

(XXVIII.3.8) that his account of Constans in Britain had made mention of an obscure corps of couriers known as *areani*. It is rash to attribute to this brief and little-known episode, as some have tried, a wholesale reorganization of the northern frontier in Britain, or the building of certain Saxon shore forts (Pevensey?).[18]

If Constans inherited from his father's era the need for the emperor of the west to show himself an effective bulwark against the barbarians, he could also not forget that he was a scion of the first Christian dynasty to rule the empire; and he ruled, unlike his father or his fellow emperor Constantius, as one already baptized in the faith (Athan. *Apol. ad Const.* VII). It is to a law of Constans, issued in 341 to the *vicarius* of Italy, that we owe the earliest general condemnation of pagan cult preserved in the Theodosian Code: *cesset superstitio, sacrificiorum aboleatur insania* (*C.Th.* XVI.10.2: significantly, Constans was careful to invoke the precedent of a law of his father's, *divi principis parentis nostri*). The next year (XVI.10.3) he conceded to the prefect of Rome the preservation of temple buildings outside the walls as the points of origin of many of the public entertainments of the capital, though with the inevitable proviso that pagan rites were debarred. In dealing with the established institutions of Rome, where Constantine had already charted the pragmatic course which would be followed by his Christian successors through the century, the emperor faced constraints against the thoroughgoing eradication of paganism which the will of God ideally required – and of which Constans and his brother were eloquently reminded about this time in Firmicus Maternus' pamphlet *On the Error of Profane Religions*: 'only a little of the task remains before the devil will be utterly cast down and laid low by your laws, in order that the deadly contagion of past idolatry may perish' (xx.7).

A more definitive legacy of Constantine's was the transformation of ecclesiastical politics into affairs of state.[19] Not only did the Christian ruler believe himself called to forge unity among church leaders, but the bishops now found themselves blessed with privileged access to the imperial court and 'appeal to Caesar'. In the 340s a Roman empire shared between two servants of God redoubled the possibilities of episcopal lobbying, as Constans' heartlands of Italy and Gaul played host to bishops who had fallen foul of their fellows in the east, and had been banished on the orders of his fellow emperor.[20] The amnesty signalled by Constantine II's restoration of Athanasius in 337 had proved short-lived, and it was not long before the political dominance of Athanasius' opponents reasserted itself:

---

[18] See e.g. Frere (1987) 336–8; Johnson (1980) 93–4.

[19] See the concise summary in Barnes, *Athanasius* 165–75.

[20] Note the complaint of western bishops at the council of Sardica about 'bishops who do not cease going to the court' (Can. 8 Hess). On the ecclesiastical politics of the 340s, see e.g. Frend (1984) 528ff.; on the role of Constans, Barnard (1981), Barnes, *Athanasius* 63ff.

the bishop of Alexandria and others who had succeeded in returning (including Marcellus of Ancyra, whose contentious views on the indivisibility of the divine nature had led to his condemnation before Constantine in 336) were re-exiled from their sees. Athanasius was ousted from Alexandria in March 339. The first port of call for these dislodged easterners was Rome, where they were received into the fold by bishop Julius (Athan. *Apol. c. Ar.* xxxiii). Although the western emperor cannot have been unaware of these arrivals in Rome, it was to be three years before Athanasius was summoned to a meeting with Constans in Milan (*Apol. ad Const.* iv). Perhaps it was the confidence of military success over the Franks which induced the emperor to turn his attention to healing the divisions of the church – to say nothing of the influence of bishops close to the court, like Maximinus of Trier, who favoured the cause of the exiles (whose number now included Paul, the ousted bishop of Constantinople).[21] Like his father before him, Constans was confronted by a world of disaffected bishops and doctrinal differences which invited the intervention of a Christian ruler aware of his responsibilities to his God. He took the initiative with his brother in convoking what was intended to be a general council of western and eastern bishops at Sardica, on the eastern border of his empire – at their meeting in Milan he told Athanasius that he had already communicated with Constantius on the subject – and it was from his court at Trier the next year (343) that Athanasius and the venerable Ossius of Cordova set out for the council (*Apol. ad Const.* iv). Sardica was to be Constans' Nicaea.

Some 170 bishops (with the westerners in the majority) came at the imperial bidding to Sardica;[22] but the two factions stayed apart, and the council failed amid mutual recriminations and excommunications. While the western group held their own gathering, the eastern bishops found an excuse to withdraw in the summons to celebrate a Persian victory by Constantius (*Hist. Ar.* xvi.2): so interlocked by now were matters ecclesiastical and secular. In these years around the council of Sardica imperial diplomacy between west and east was dominated by the subject of bishops banished by one ruler only to have their causes taken up by the other. In the spring of 344 Constans despatched a delegation to Antioch (*Hist. Ar.* xx.2; Theod. *HE* ii.8.54), consisting of two bishops (Vincentius of Capua and Euphrates of Cologne) and a general, his *magister equitum* Flavius Salia, to press his brother for the return of Athanasius to Alexandria, and he had further meetings with Athanasius in Italy and Gaul on the question of his reinstatement (*Apol. ad Const.* iv). This diplomatic offensive mounted by

[21] For Maximinus' reception of Paul and support of the exiles, see the complaints of the eastern bishops at Sardica: *CSEL* lxv, pp. 66–7.

[22] For the number 'about 170', see Athan. *Hist. Ar.* xv. On the council, see Barnes, *Athanasius* 71–81.

the western emperor, aided perhaps by the fact that Constantius continued to have pressing preoccupations on the Persian front, eventually bore fruit in consent to Athanasius' return (his see was in any case vacant since the death of his 'replacement' Gregory in June 345): the bishop of Alexandria triumphantly reclaimed his city on 21 October 346.[23] The degree to which Athanasius later (in his *Apology to Constantius*) protested his innocence of fomenting fraternal strife between the emperors suggests that these ecclesiastical differences had placed real strain on the *concordia* of Constantine's heirs – even to the extent that Constans was apparently ready to threaten military intervention against his brother.[24] Their political estrangement is confirmed by the fact that their joint consulship of 346, the last year in which they shared the office, went unrecognized in Constans' half of the empire.[25] The eulogy, in Libanius' panegyric of the imperial brothers (*Or.* LIX.152ff.), of the fellow-feeling which united the two rulers of separate territories may have a more than conventional significance.

Yet another Constantinian legacy came to haunt the government of Constans. In 347 two imperial officials, Paul and Macarius (tradition, but no ancient evidence, calls them *notarii*), arrived in Carthage on a mission to distribute funds for the churches of Africa and for almsgiving (Optatus, III.3). The divisions of African Christendom, Catholic and Donatist, which Constantine had despairingly abandoned to the 'judgement of God', made their task a minefield; but from the perspective of Donatus and his followers they were perceived to behave with undisguised partisanship for Catholic congregations.[26] It was these agents of Constans who first provoked the outraged question, *quid est imperatori cum ecclesia?* As they travelled into Numidia, Donatist resistance was roused: the bishop of Bagai summoned up bands of circumcellions and confronted the officials, who replied by sending in soldiers – the bishop was among the victims (Optatus, III.4). Other Donatist martyrs soon followed, while in Carthage on 15 August 347 the proconsul of Africa issued a decree of Constans, in response to the violence, ordering the unity of all the churches under the Catholic bishop of Carthage. This made Constans 'religiosissimus' in the eyes of the Catholics of Africa, and Paul and Macarius 'servants and ministers of the holy work of God';[27] yet to the Donatists the age of persecution and martyrdom had returned, and Constans was the reincarnation of his pagan predecessors. They would have found it difficult to credit the

---

[23] *Festal Index* 18; cf. Greg. Naz. *Or.* XXI.27–9. For Constantius' agreement to his return, see Athan. *Apol. c. Ar.* LI.4
[24] A threat implied in Constans' letter cited by Socr. *HE* II.22; for further discussion, Barnes, *Athanasius* 89ff.   [25] See Bagnall *et al.* (1987) 226–7.
[26] Frend, *Donatist Church* 177–82. For a narrative based on Donatist sources, see Grasmück (1964) 112ff.
[27] So the documents of the subsequent council of Carthage: Munier (ed.), *Concilia Africae (CCSL* 149), p. 3.

claims later put to Constantius by Ossius of Cordova, that Constans never used violence against bishops, nor had his officials exercised coercion (Athan. *Hist. Ar.* XLIV.6).

Constans' Donatist subjects in Africa might have had more sympathy with the judgement of Eutropius (x.9.3) that he was 'intolerabilis provincialibus'. Even the population of Gaul, where Constans could bask in the credit of successes against the Germans, doubtless came to resent the financial impositions demanded to sustain a vigorous military effort – and on the part of an emperor who seems increasingly to have deserted them for other parts of his domain;[28] while military discipline also began to take its toll of the soldiers' loyalty, to such an extent that by the end Constans was equally unpopular with the army, *militi iniucundus*. He surrounded himself, it is alleged, with bad company, and failed to listen to wise counsel (cf. Amm. Marc. XVI.7.5) – but that is a conventional charge to level at fallen rulers. Certainly he had his rapacious subordinates, like the *magister officiorum* Eugenius;[29] yet the allegation that he kept a coterie of captive barbarians to gratify his homosexual tastes sounds more like hostile folklore.[30] Revealing, though, of the extent of disaffection from Constans is the fact that the ringleaders of the coup which overthrew him represented both the military and civilian echelons of his court: Fl. Magnus Magnentius was commander of the leading field army regiments, the Joviani and Herculiani, and his chief lieutenant, Marcellinus, was Constans' *comes rerum privatarum*. The desertion of Magnentius has added significance in that his service to the imperial house went back to Constantine, and he owed a debt of loyalty to Constans, who had once rescued him from a military mutiny (Zos. II.46.3, Zon. XIII.5.16). Another notable deserter was Fabius Titianus, who had served Constans throughout the 340s as praetorian prefect of Gaul, only to throw in his lot with Magnentius and return to Rome for a second tenure of the city prefecture (February 350). It may have been in the same context of alienation from Constans that the elder Gratian, father of future emperors, retired from a distinguished military career to his home in Pannonia (where Magnentius was later to be a guest: Amm. Marc. XXX.7.3). The regime of Constans evidently forfeited the allegiance of some of its most prominent members.

The setting for Magnentius' coup was Autun, a city which looked back to a time when it had been rebuilt by Constans' grandfather and further honoured by his father, but which was now overshadowed by the primacy which Trier had come to enjoy as the favoured imperial residence in Gaul:

[28] The evidence is scanty, but Constans is last attested in Gaul in 345: Barnes, *Athanasius*, 225.

[29] Lib. *Or.* XIV.10; for Eugenius' presence at court, cf. Athan. *Apol. ad Const.* III.

[30] E.g. Aur. Vict. *Caes.* XLI.24; Zos. II.42.1; Zon. XIII.5.15, 6.7–9 (the most detail). In this context it is ironic that Constans was the author of a notably strident pronouncement against homosexuality: *C.Th.* IX.7.3.

in Magnentius' usurpation Autun at last found its own emperor.[31] Here on 18 January 350 (*Chron. Min.* 1, 237), while Constans was reportedly diverted by a hunting expedition, the associates of Magnentius gathered ostensibly to celebrate the birthday of Marcellinus' son (Zos. 11.42; *Epit. de Caes.* XLI.22; Zon. XIII.6). At the chosen moment Magnentius left the dinner party, shortly to reappear clothed in imperial purple and acclaimed by the assembled company; his proclamation was quickly taken up by the citizens of Autun and the surrounding region, and by the army regiments. So widespread was the revolt that Constans could rally no resistance – only flee south towards the Mediterranean. Abandoned at the last by all but one junior officer (Amm. Marc. XV.5.16), he was captured and killed in the town which bore the name of his grandmother, Helena (Elna); the officer in command of this successful mission, Gaiso, was rewarded for his services by sharing the consulship of 351 with Magnentius.

III. CONSTANTIUS AND PERSIA, 337–50

From the meeting in Pannonia in the autumn of 337 which confirmed the division of the empire with his brothers, Constantius II had returned to take up residence in Antioch (where he had already been based as Caesar during his father's last years) – but not before attending to one further political task in Constantinople. He secured the transfer of Eusebius from Nicomedia to the disputed bishopric of the capital (Socr. *HE* II.7). Eusebius had baptized his dying father, and may have played a role in smoothing the path for Constantius through the dynastic turmoil of summer 337:[32] it was due time for services rendered to the imperial house to receive their reward. For the few remaining years of his life (he was dead before the end of 341) Eusebius and his associates were to dominate the ecclesiastical politics around Constantius II. Although too late to prevent the restoration of Athanasius in Alexandria instigated from Gaul by Constantius' older brother, the next year (338) – in the first of a series of councils convened in Antioch to coincide with the residence of the imperial court[33] – they once again achieved his deposition: by spring 339, as we have seen, a new bishop (Gregory) was being escorted to his see by the prefect of Egypt on the emperor's order, and Athanasius was again on his way to exile in the west.[34] The repercussions of this *cause célèbre* continued to resound at Constantius' court. In January 341 the dedication of Constantine's 'golden' church in Antioch, in the presence of Constantius,

---

[31] Thévenot (1932) 98–100.   [32] According to the version of Philostorgius, 11.16.

[33] E. Schwartz, *Gesammelte Schriften* (Berlin, 1959) III.279. On these events, see Barnes, *Athanasius* 36ff.

[34] The events associated with the 'intrusion' of Gregory are colourfully recounted in Athan. *Ep. Encycl.* 2ff.

was attended by ninety-seven eastern bishops (Athan. *De Syn.* xxv.1; Hil. *De Syn.* xxviii) who used the occasion to shift the doctrinal ground away from the Nicene *homoousios* towards the language of 'similarity' of substance between Father and Son, and begin the process of creed-making which would loom large in Constantius' later efforts to bring unanimity to the faith;[35] and it was to Antioch, as we have seen, that Constans' envoys came to urge the return of Athanasius after the council of Sardica. When matters were finally settled, eastern emperor and returning bishop met in Antioch in 346 (*Apol. ad Const.* v), and Constantius was ready to commend their pastor to the Christian people of Alexandria (*Apol. c. Ar.* lv).

Yet the quarrels of bishops, even matters of faith, could not monopolize the concerns of the Augustus of the east.[36] As Caesar, Constantius had attended to the building of new fortifications in northern Mesopotamia in the face of renewed aggression from the Persian empire, and he had seen his father before his death preparing for a military offensive against the armies of Sapor II: expectations of a triumphant Christian victory are implicit, for instance, in Aphrahat's contemporary application of the biblical prophecies of Daniel.[37] To Constantius fell the task of accomplishing these heady hopes raised by his father's war plans (Lib. *Or.* lix.60). And the task was pressing. Already Armenia, under the successors of Rome's long-ruling ally Tiridates, had come under the control of pro-Persian factions; and Mesopotamia was subject to Persian raids – it may have been as early as the summer of 337 that the fortress town of Nisibis, the Roman headquarters of the region, endured the first of the three sieges which were to beset it in the coming years (this was the occasion which gave rise to its bishop Jacob's legendary exploits in summoning forth plagues of gnats to torment the Persians' animals, notably their fearsome elephants).[38] Armenia and Mesopotamia were the two regions which the Persian ruler coveted as historically part of his empire, which had in recent times been lost to the Romans in the treaty enforced by Diocletian and Galerius in 299; presumably they were the subject of the embassy 'arguing over boundaries' which Sapor sent to Constantine before his death (Lib. *Or.* lix.71), as they would be of later diplomatic exchanges in the 350s. As for Armenia, Constantius appears to have succeeded quickly (338) in restoring the Roman interest, without a military conflict, by establishing the loyalty of the new king Arsaces: through the allusiveness of Julian's panegyric (*Or.* 1.20c–21b) we can discern the return of an exiled monarch and his supporters, and a change of allegiance on the part of those who had favoured

---

[35] See Hanson (1988) 284–92.

[36] For what follows on Constantius' dealings with Armenia and the Persians, see Blockley (1989), summarized in Blockley, *Foreign Policy* 12–24. For source material (translated): Dodgeon and Lieu, *Eastern Frontier* 164ff.   [37] Barnes (1985).

[38] For date, see Barnes (1985) 133. On bishop Jacob, Peeters (1920) 285–312.

Persia, all facilitated by liberal Roman gifts and honours. Through these traditional means of diplomacy, Constantius ensured that Armenia remained in the Roman fold throughout the 340s.

It was for Mesopotamia that Constantius reserved his military response to the Persian offensive. Based in Antioch between 338 and 350, he presided over a protracted war against Sapor's repeated incursions across the Tigris into the east of Roman Mesopotamia. Although his generals mounted some counterattacks into Persian territory, enough for Constantius to claim the title *Adiabenicus* (*ILS* 732) and for Libanius (*Or.* LIX.83) to single out the capture of one (unnamed) city in Persia, this was overwhelmingly a defensive war. Constantius set out to maintain control of Mesopotamia by holding on to its fortified towns, which were the key to the possession of the province: it was a conflict of Persian sieges (Nisibis was invested again in 346 and 350), successfully withstood by Roman defenders; large field army deployments and full-scale battles were generally avoided.[39] In the one notable exception, the massed conflict before the fortress of Singara in 344 (?),[40] a Roman victory was lost through the troops' over-enthusiasm to prolong the fighting into the night, and to pursue the enemy in disarray against the emperor's orders (Eutr. x.10). Even so, the Romans could claim Sapor's son Narses as a casualty of this battle (Jul. *Or.* 1.24d; Lib. *Or.* LIX.117). Another Roman success prompted the victory celebrations in Antioch which were the occasion of the eastern bishops' withdrawal from the council of Sardica in 343. But Constantius' strategy, while conspicuously successful in denying the Persians their objective of controlling eastern Mesopotamia, was not destined to generate glamorous victories. It was a striking departure from the traditional Roman reaction to Persian aggression, the major offensive into Persian territory: this is the tactic implied by Constantine's own extensive war preparations at his death, and it was of course to be resumed in Julian's ill-fated intervention in Persia in 363 – the disastrous results of which would only confirm the wisdom of Constantius' holding-operation. Not surprisingly it was to be apologists for Julian who were most vocal in denouncing Constantius' strategy as cowardly and morale-breaking for the soldiers ('it was just as though he had sworn to fight alongside the enemy': Lib. *Or.* XVIII.206).[41] It may have been a caution partly pressed upon him by lack of sufficient troops for any more adventurous plan,[42] but it was evidently also a calculated intention to

---

[39] On this defensive strategy, see Warmington (1977).

[40] 344 is the date implied by Jul. *Or.* 1.26b ('six years' before the overthrow of Constans), but many have argued for 348 (following Jer. *Chron*): for discussion, Barnes, *Athanasius*, app. 9, n. 19. For accounts of the conflict, see Dodgeon and Lieu, *Eastern Frontier* 181ff.

[41] Cf. the standard accusation of Constantius' lack of success in foreign (as opposed to civil) wars. Eutr. x.15.2; Amm. Marc. XVI.10.2, XXI.16.15.

[42] So Blockley, *Foreign Policy* 13–14. Jul. *Or.* 1.18c implies that Constantius did not have the resources for a major offensive.

discard the reckless expectations of conquest in Persia which he inherited from the last months of Constantine – even *c.* 340 the so-called *Itinerarium Alexandri* was reminding Constantius of the exploits of Alexander and Trajan, and evoking the prospect of great victories.[43]

If the adherents of Julian did not admire this strategy, then certainly the citizens of Nisibis were grateful for Constantius' dogged defence of Mesopotamia (cf. Ephr. Syr. *C. Iul.* II.20, IV.15). Ammianus records the pointed reflection of one of them, witnessing the pitiful surrender of his city to the Persians after Jovian's treaty of 363, that Constantius had lost no Roman territory (xxv.9.3). The Nisibenes had all the more reason for gratitude since by the summer of 350, when the city had to endure the third and most celebrated of Sapor's sieges (which included the flooding of the river Mygdonius to force a breach in the walls),[44] Constantius had already received news of the overthrow of Constans and the loss of the western provinces to Magnentius; yet he had given the continued defence of Mesopotamia a higher priority than the challenge of a usurper (Jul. *Or.* 1.26b–d).[45] Only when the Persian army had been driven back after a four-month siege, and when the reconstruction of Nisibis had been undertaken (Zon. XIII.7.14), did Constantius begin the withdrawal of troops for the coming confrontation with Magnentius. It was safe, as it turned out, for Constantius to direct his attention westwards, for Sapor's army did not return in 351. He was diverted, it appears, by uprisings of his own among the peoples to the east of the Persian empire in Afghanistan, but equally, we may suspect, deterred by heavy losses and failure over many years to make headway into Roman Mesopotamia. Hostilities on Sapor's western front at the Tigris were scaled down to the opportunistic raids of local satraps.[46]

IV. MAGNENTIUS, VETRANIO AND THE RECOVERY OF THE WEST, 350–3

Constans' destroyer, Fl. Magnus Magnentius, was representative of a new breed of *capaces imperii* springing up in the western provinces in the fourth century: a man of barbarian origins (one tradition surviving in *scholia* on Julian gives him a Frankish mother and a 'Breton' father) whose family settled on Roman lands, and who rose to the high command after a career of service in the army.[47] He may be compared with his fellow officer

---

[43] Barnes (1985) 135.   [44] On the various accounts of this siege, see Lightfoot (1988).

[45] Although Constantius was not himself present at the relief of Nisibis: Ephr. Syr. *Carm. Nisib.* 11.2 (Theod. *HE* 11.30 has him at Antioch). The officer in command was Lucillianus: Zos. III.8.2 (in wrong context).

[46] The situation prevailing at the opening of the surviving portion of Ammianus (353–4): (e.g.) XIV.3.1.

[47] On Magnentius' origins, see Zos. II.54.1, with Paschoud *ad loc.* (Budé), and L. Fleuriot, *Études Celtiques* 19 (1982).

Silvanus, another Roman general of Frankish descent, who would himself
– after a timely desertion of Magnentius – briefly aspire to be emperor in
355. Magnentius' contemporary credentials for empire, against the background of widespread disaffection among the erstwhile adherents of
Constans, quickly secured him the allegiance of the Gallic prefecture (Gaul,
Spain and Britain). Africa and Italy were not far behind: by the end of
February 350 Magnentius' men were both praetorian prefect of Italy
(Anicetus) and prefect of Rome (Titianus). Yet Rome itself was reluctant
to acknowledge the usurper, for the city was to be the scene of a short-
lived, but violent, dynastic reaction against Magnentius' uprising. Its central
figure was Julius Nepotianus, son of Constantine's half-sister Eutropia, and
hence a descendant of that branch of the imperial clan massacred in the
summer of 337 (Nepotianus' father may have been among the victims). In
June 350, supported by a motley following variously described as 'gladiators' and 'desperate men', Nepotianus raised a rebellion in Rome serious
enough to force a diplomatic withdrawal by the urban prefect and to defeat
the resistance organized by his praetorian counterpart, who was killed.[48]
Only when Magnentius sent a force against him under the command of his
chief collaborator and now *magister officiorum*, Marcellinus, was Nepotianus'
coup brought to an end after a mere twenty-eight days in power, and his
severed head paraded before the population of Rome (Jer. *Chron. s.a.* 350
(Helm, p. 238), Eutr. x.11.20). Confiscations and purges among the capital's
nobility followed, including the killing of Eutropia and others (it is alleged)
from the imperial family.[49] Such reprisals make it clear that the episode had
amounted to more than an outbreak of popular disorder: it was a warning
to Magnentius that he could not count on the support of the Roman
establishment, and that – however unpopular Constans may have become
in court and military circles in Gaul – the house of Constantine remained
a potent focus of loyalty.

With Constantius, now sole representative of the Constantinian succession, still preoccupied in Syria, Magnentius naturally looked to extend his
empire to include the remainder of what had been Constans' domain – that
is, the Danube lands as far east as the borders of Thrace. In this, however,
he was forestalled by the action of troops at Mursa in lower Pannonia, who
on 1 March 350 (*Chron. Min.* 1, 237) proclaimed as Augustus their elderly
and long-serving general Vetranio, formerly Constans' *magister peditum*.
Vetranio, we are told, made up for what he lacked in cultural attainments
by his military success and popularity with his soldiers.[50] As with
Nepotianus, it is difficult not to see these developments at Mursa as a

[48] Zos, 11.43.2–4; Aur. Vict. *Caes.* XLII.6; *Epit. de Caes.* XLII.3; Eutr. x.11.2; Socr. *HE* 11.25.10.
[49] On Marcellinus' eminent Roman victims, see Jul. *Or.* 11.58c–d, with Athan. *Apol. ad Const.* VI.
[50] Eutr. x.10.2; cf. Aur. Vict. *Caes.* XLI.26. On Vetranio's proclamation, see also Zos. 11.43.1, Jul. *Or.*
1.26c, and other refs. in *PLRE* 1.954.

loyalist move aimed at countering any extension of Magnentius' empire. We may attribute a crucial role to the distinguished and influential figure of Vulcacius Rufinus, who had long been Constans' praetorian prefect in Illyricum and continued in that capacity throughout this turbulent period (until later transferred to the prefecture of Gaul by Constantius). Rufinus, it should be observed, was a relative of the imperial house.[51] The dynastic dimension of Vetranio's *coup* also emerges from the report of one source (Philost. III.22, Bidez/Winkelmann, p. 49) not only that the action was encouraged by Constantina, the sister of Constantius, but that Constantius himself actually acknowledged Vetranio as an imperial colleague by sending him the diadem.[52] Any such recognition by Constantius will have served to install Vetranio temporarily as a convenient bulwark against Magnentius until the time when he himself could safely leave the east. It is apparent in all of this that Magnentius' imperial pretensions were met by a strong showing of dynastic solidarity – Constantius reportedly dreamed of his father calling on him to avenge the death of Constans (Pet. Patr. fr. 16) – which even transcended the bloodstained divisions of 337: for Constantina was also the widow of the murdered Hannibalianus, and Vulcacius Rufinus an uncle of Gallus.

In the face of such opposition, Magnentius mounted a complex propaganda and diplomatic offensive. He presented himself in the traditional terms of 'restorer' and 'liberator' (*ILS* 742), while courting both Constantius and Vetranio. From the former he sought legitimacy and recognition as an imperial colleague – a conciliatory front reflected in some of his coin types and surviving inscriptions[53] – although for safety's sake his emissaries did not neglect to call upon potential opponents of Constantius, like bishop Athanasius at Alexandria, who might prove useful allies (Athan. *Apol. ad Const.* IX; Athanasius, not for the first time, was drawn into the empire's political divisions). Magnentius' attempts equally to win over Vetranio met with more success, and the Danubian pretender was temporarily weaned away from his pact wth Constantius (Jul. *Or.* I.30c–d, II.76c). But this diplomatic interlude was abruptly ended by the arrival of Constantius and his troops in the Balkans in the last weeks of 350. Vetranio swiftly came back into line, and went to the eastern border of his territory to greet Constantius at Sardica (Zon. XIII.7.22); when the two armies united at Naissus on 25 December, both rulers shared the tribunal, but it was Constantius who addressed them, and at the end of his speech the soldiers 'in a new and unaccustomed fashion' (Eutr. X.11.1) clamoured for the deposition of Vetranio. The veteran general was peacefully and ceremoni-

---

[51] On this eminent figure, see *PLRE* 1.782–3. He served as an envoy between Vetranio and Constantius: Pet. Patr. fr. 16 (*FHG* IV.190).

[52] For Constantius' initial encouragement of Vetranio, see Jul. *Or.* 1.30b–c.

[53] For coins, see *RIC* 8, p. 40; inscriptions, *CIL* 8, 22552, 22558 (Africa).

ously divested of his imperial regalia, and pensioned off to six years of comfortable 'exile' at Prusa in Bithynia.[54] This bizarre outcome reinforces the impression that Vetranio hardly deserves the label of 'usurper' at all: for most of its nine-month duration, his rule had served as a convenient instrument of the dynasty, holding Magnentius at bay until the real conflict could begin. With the advent of Constantius in Europe he had served his purpose, and it was fittingly in Constantine's birthplace that Vetranio's removal from office signalled the outbreak of the 'holy war' (Jul. Or. 1.33c) which would defend the imperial inheritance against Constans' murderer. The inheritance was further advertised at Sirmium on 15 March 351 (Chron. Min. 1, 238), when the childless Constantius named his cousin Gallus as Caesar, and married him to Constantina (Zos. 11.45.1): he was despatched to Antioch to maintain the imperial presence in the east. Magnentius, any hope of rapprochement now over, countered by elevating his kinsman Decentius as his own Caesar in Gaul (Zos. 11.45.2).[55] The battle lines were drawn, and Constantius was in the ascendant: as he had recently passed through Ancyra he had heard Themistius, in his first essay in imperial panegyric, saluting the virtues which had defeated the Persian king (Or. 1.12a);[56] and he was soon to be further assured of God's blessing on his rule and support against his foes in a letter from the bishop of Jerusalem, reporting the miraculous appearance of a cross of light over the holy city on 7 May 351 (PG xxxiii.1165ff.). Against such marks of divine approbation Magnentius stood little chance: the God who had sent his sign to Constantine before the Milvian Bridge now championed Constantine's son, and coins from Danubian mints took up the victory signals (and the Constantinian echo) with the legend HOC SIGNO VICTOR ERIS.[57]

The emperor who so advertised God's protection for the coming conflict with Magnentius was also careful to show a proper concern for matters of the faith, even amidst the preoccupations of war. While resident at Sirmium in the early months of 351 Constantius received an appeal from the controversial local bishop Photinus against the condemnation of his beliefs (he was a disciple of the outlawed Marcellus of Ancyra). The emperor's response was to summon a council to Sirmium, which went on to reaffirm Photinus' condemnation and depose him from the see; but not before Constantius had first appointed a commission of eight eminent Christian laymen (all of them senior court figures, and among them several future praetorian and urban prefects), served by notarii and other palace

---

[54] On the peaceful end to Vetranio's rule, see Jul. Or. 1.30d–32a, 11.76d–77c; Them. Or. iv.56b; Zos. 11.44.3–4; Jer. Chron. s.a. 351 (Naissus) For Prusa, Socr. HE 11.28.20.

[55] Most sources make Decentius a brother of Magnentius (e.g. Eutr. x.12.2; Aur. Vict. Caes. xlii.9), although Epit. de Caes. xlii.2 has 'cousin'.

[56] On the dating of Themistius' first oration, see Barnes, Athanasius, app. 9, n. 21.

[57] See RIC 8, pp. 344–5 (Siscia, an issue begun under Vetranio), 386 (Sirmium), 399 (Thessalonica).

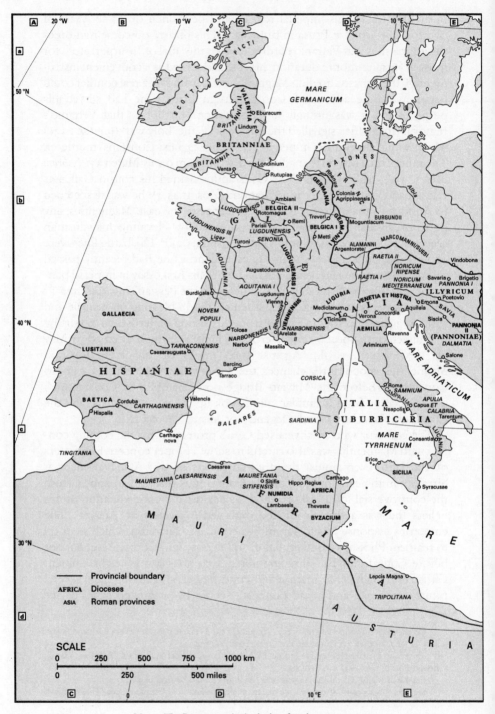

Map 1 The Roman empire in the late fourth century A.D.

officials, to listen to Photinus' defence of his faith under cross-examination, and ensure a correct record of it, as a preliminary to the full council.[58] It is a striking indication of the mix of demands at the court of Constantius that in the midst of civil war against a usurper the emperor should assemble men of the rank of counts and patricians to deliberate, not on prosecuting the war, but on the doctrinal views of the local bishop.

The summer of 351 saw a series of 'Balkan campaigns'.[59] The vanguard of Constantius' army tried to force a way into Italy through the Julian Alps at Atrans, only to be repulsed; Magnentius' forces countered by advancing along the river Save into Pannonia and capturing the town of Siscia. From here they made for Mursa, and it was on the plains before this city, near the confluence of the Drave and the Danube, that they were confronted by Constantius. In the course of these military manoeuvres Constantius sent his eastern praetorian prefect, Flavius Philippus, to urge Magnentius' withdrawal to Gaul (Zos. 11.46.2ff.); and it may have been the prefect's persuasiveness which encouraged one of Magnentius' commanders, Silvanus, to lead his men over to join Constantius.[60] The clash came on 28 September 351 (*Chron. Min.* I, 237). Although both contenders had left substantial forces behind in Gaul and the east, Mursa became renowned as an epic encounter, one of the great conflicts of the age (Zos. 11.50.4; *Epit. de Caes.* XLII.4): Eutropius (X.12.1) pointedly remarked on the huge losses of Roman manpower more properly employed in fighting external foes. If we are to believe the figures preserved by Zonaras (XIII.8.17), Magnentius lost two-thirds of his men, and Constantius nearly half of his. To Christian observers, and not least to the emperor himself – who left the battlefield to pray at a nearby martyr's shrine – Constantius' victory was further confirmation of the heavenly approval already denoted by events in Jerusalem; and Valens, the bishop of Mursa, was careful to foster this celestial atmosphere by announcing that he had heard news of the outcome 'from an angel' (Sulp. Sev. *Chron.* 11.38.5–7). Although more earthbound minds would attribute Constantius' victory to the superiority in the field of his mailed cavalry (Jul. *Or.* 1.37b–38a, 11.57b–d), Valens was nicely attuned to the emperor's appreciation of the special talents that bishops might provide in war (Eusebius of Emesa, for example, had been favoured for the 'miracles' he had worked against the Persians: Socr. *HE* 11.9.10), and he would use his advantage to considerable effect in the ecclesiastical politics of the coming years.

---

[58] Epiphan. *Pan.* LXXI.1 (ed. Holl, III, p. 250), Sozom. IV.6.15. On this council of Sirmium, see Brennecke (1984) 91ff., and (for a date later in 351) Barnes, *Athanasius* 109.

[59] Narrated (problematically) by Zos. 11.45.3ff.; see Paschoud's notes *ad loc.* for discussion of the manoeuvres.

[60] On this celebrated desertion, see Jul. *Or.* 1.48b, 11.97c; Aur. Vict. *Caes.* XLII.15; Amm. Marc. XV.5.33; Zon. XIII.8.9.

Magnentius escaped the carnage of Mursa (where his colleague Marcellinus was lost without trace: Jul. *Or.* 11.58c–59b) and withdrew to Aquileia to guard the approach to Italy. Here he spent the winter, at least as hostile report has it, indulging in the pleasures of the city (Jul. *Or.* 1.38d). Constantius, in no hurry for pursuit, remained at Sirmium into the summer of 352. When the offensive was resumed, Magnentius was driven out of Aquileia and eventually, after a rally near Ticinum, back across the Alps into Gaul.[61] By the autumn Italy was recaptured, and in November Constantius was in Milan, abrogating the decisions of the 'tyrant' in an edict addressed to 'all the provincials and people' (*C.Th.* xv.14.5: 3 November 352). The prefect of Rome was now Naeratius Cerealis, who had taken up office on 26 September. As a brother of Vulcacius Rufinus and uncle of Gallus Caesar, this man was indubitably a loyalist of the dynasty: in Rome he would honour Constantius as *restitutor urbis Romae atque orbis et exstinctor pestiferae tyrannidis*.[62] Even before these clear indications of Constantius' victory in Italy, however, Magnentius had been losing ground. The murderous aftermath of Nepotianus' uprising can have won him few friends, and the uncertainties of his hold on Rome are reflected in his difficulty in securing city prefects: in an unusually rapid succession – no less than five between March 351 and September 352 – he had to call on several to hold office for a second time.[63] Significantly, Celsinus Adelphius, prefect from June to December 351, was accused by a subordinate of plotting rebellion against Magnentius (Amm. Marc. xvi.6.2); we may suspect the influence of his wife, the aristocratic poetess Faltonia Betitia Proba, whose compositions included (besides her *Cento Vergilianus de laudibus Christi*) an epic poem celebrating Constantius' war against Magnentius.[64] News of the victory of Mursa, it appears, encouraged the usurper's opponents in the capital: loyal senators, even erstwhile adherents of Magnentius enticed by the timely offer of an amnesty, fled to Constantius in Pannonia – Julian's panegyric pictures him welcoming refugees who had sailed across the Adriatic (*Or.* 1.38b–c, 48b; cf. *Or.* 11.97b). It is perhaps against this background of defection that we should set Magnentius' permission for the resumption of nocturnal sacrifices in Rome (soon repealed by Constantius in a law addressed to Cerealis in 353: *C.Th.* xvi.10.5), a gesture less of religious conviction – for it is only a 'hostile press' which makes Magnentius an inveterate pagan and lover of magic[65] – than of political expediency in the face of the

---

[61] Jul. *Or.* 1.39b–d. For Ticinum, see *Epit. de Caes.* xlii.5.

[62] *ILS* 731. See *PLRE* i, 'Cerealis 2'. For his kinship with Rufinus and Gallus, Amm. Marc. xiv.11.27.

[63] On Magnentius' unpopularity in Rome, see Zos. 11.53.2. For the succession of prefects, Chastagnol, *Fastes* 131–5.

[64] *PLRE* i, p.732. On the political context of Proba's poem, see Matthews (1992) 291–9.

[65] See e.g. Athan. *Apol. ad Const.* vii; Philost. iii.26 (in contrast to the divine protection shown to Constantius by the appearance of the cross over Jerusalem). On Magnentius and Christianity, see Ziegler (1970) 53–69.

uncertain loyalties of the Roman establishment. Even so, Constantius' recovery of Italy was an anxious and delicate moment for a senate which had perforce, after Nepotianus' overthrow, recognized the rule of the usurper. Diplomatic delegations were sent to conciliate the victorious emperor. Among the envoys in these 'difficult times' was Vitrasius Orfitus, a man well chosen for the task in that he had already shown himself a loyal adherent of Constantius by sharing in the fighting against Magnentius: he would eventually succeed Cerealis in the prefecture.[66]

Meanwhile Orfitus also served in the next phase of the erosion of Magnentius' empire, the reconquest of Africa: he was Constantius' first proconsul in the province. Control of Italy had given Constantius command of fleets, which could now be deployed to aid the recovery of Africa and Spain (Jul. Or. 1.40c). In the summer of 353 the last stage of the land war, the 'third bout' of Julian's panegyric (Or. 1.40b, II.74c), saw Magnentius driven back from the passes through the Cottian Alps and defeated at Mons Seleucus;[67] although even before this there are signs that his hold on the region which had made him emperor was slipping. His Caesar Decentius, left to guard the Rhine, had failed to resist the incursions of the Alamanni (Amm. Marc. xvi.12.5);[68] and in response the imperial city of Trier, in a demonstration of loyalty to the dynasty whose capital it had so often been, had closed its gates to the rebel Caesar (Amm. Marc. xv.6.4).[69] The end came on 10 August 353 (Chron. Min. 1, 238), when Magnentius committed suicide at Lugdunum, and Decentius followed suit (Epit. de Caes. XLII.6–8). The usurper's severed head, in customary fashion, was paraded in conclusive evidence of Constantius' victory (Amm. Marc. xxii.14.4). With Constans avenged, Constantine's surviving son was now sole ruler of the Roman world; he spent the winter at Arles providing lavish celebrations of his triumph and – by happy coincidence – of the thirtieth anniversary of his first elevation as Caesar.[70]

V. ATHANASIUS, GALLUS AND JULIAN, 353–6

To the writers of panegyric, Constantius' reconquest of the west was the occasion for an appropriate display of clemency towards defeated enemies (Jul. Or. 1.48a–b, II.95d ff.). That was not the way it appeared to the histo-rian Ammianus, whose rich narrative of imperial affairs now becomes our principal source. In his eyes the pathologically suspicious Constantius,

[66] Chastagnol, Fastes 141–2.

[67] For the location, see Socr. HE II.32.6; Soz. IV.7.3. The place is named as a mansio in the Bordeaux Itinerary (555, 3).

[68] Constantius, it was claimed, had instigated barbarian raids (a tactic which would be alleged again in 361, see pp. 58–9 below): Zos. II.53.3; Lib. Or. xvIII.33.   [69] On this incident, see Wightman, Trier 61.

[70] Amm. Marc. xiv.5.1, where the month should read 'November' (Constantius had been made Caesar on 8 November 324).

encouraged by obsequious and over-mighty courtiers, conducted a witch-hunt against former associates of the usurper, and encompassed their downfall through the unscrupulous activities of his agents (XIV.5) – chief among them the *notarius* Paul (known as the 'Chain' because of his facility in ensnaring victims with his accusations). Through Ammianus' highly coloured rhetoric it is possible to discern here the political realities of Constantius' first winter as emperor in Gaul and the western provinces: the reassertion of legitimate dynastic rule had to be accompanied by effective 'internal security' against the remains of a regime which had governed the region for nearly four years. That Ammianus names a military (?) *comes* and the civilian *vicarius* of Britain as victims of these purges is some indication of the scrutiny of officials being carried out, and it was presumably in connection with securing a submissive establishment in these newly won provinces that the loyalist praetorian prefect Vulcacius Rufinus was about this time transferred to Gaul.[71]

Ammianus' secular narrative is naturally silent about another aspect of Constantius' assertion of authority during these months at Arles. While there, he summoned a council of bishops.[72] The matter at issue, and one which threatened the unanimity of Constantius' victory, again focused on Athanasius, who was once more at the centre of the political stage after he had received a delegation from Magnentius, and was accused of corresponding with the usurper (Athanasius later asserted the letters to be forgeries: *Apol. ad Const.* XI). An eastern synod at Antioch (probably in 352) had already formally deposed him from his see and named the Cappadocian George as his successor (Sozom. IV.8.4);[73] and in May 353 Constantius sent a palace official from Milan to summon Athanasius to Italy – but the bishop, perhaps sensing his vulnerability at the moment of Magnentius' downfall, contrived to evade the summons.[74] But this was not all. Magnentius' delegation had included two bishops from Gaul (Athan. *Apol. ad Const.* IX): the usurper, we may conclude, had sought the support of the ecclesiastical, as well as the secular, establishment. Against such an incriminating background (not unlike the position of the Roman senate) the Gallic bishops came to Arles at the bidding of the victorious Constantius, and doubtless to share in the festivities of his *tricennalia*: as with the secular leadership, they were being brought into line. The test of loyalty was to endorse the condemnation of Athanasius. Ecclesiastical sources speak of an 'edict' imposing obedience (Sulp. Sev. *Chron.* II.39.1),

---

[71] First attested March 354: *PLRE* I.783.

[72] On the council of Arles, see Brennecke (1984) 135ff., and Barnes, *Athanasius* 115–16.

[73] For the possibility that Athanasius' deposition occurred as early as 349, see Barnes, *Athanasius* 97–100.

[74] On the mission of the *silentiarius* Montanus, see *Festal Index*, 25; *H. Aceph.* 1.8. For Athanasius' defence against the charge of disobedience, *Apol. ad Const.* XIX–XXI.

but it was more likely the familiar combination of deference and threats inherited from his father's methods of handling bishops which secured their compliance[75] – with one exception: Paulinus, Maximinus' successor at Trier, alone among the bishops at Arles refused to subscribe against Athanasius and was ordered into exile.[76]

In the spring of 354 Constantius moved north from Arles and led an army through snowbound passes to confront the Alamanni opposite the fort of Kaiseraugst (Amm. Marc. xiv.10.6ff.). This was the territory of the most southerly canton of the tribe, the Brisigavi, ruled by the brothers Gundomadus and Vadomarius, who had been raiding unchecked into Roman territory (like their counterpart Chnodomarius, whose incursions had proved too much for Magnentius' Caesar Decentius). Constantius was able to restore some prestige for his newly established rule by cowing the enemy into submission, and striking a treaty with the Alamannic kings, before returning south into Italy and establishing his court at Milan. More success followed in 355, when his *magister equitum* Arbitio had the best of an encounter further to the east, leading his troops around the shores of Lake Constance to confront another group of Alamanni, the Lentienses (Amm. Marc. xv.4).

But if Constantius was thus confirming his hold on the western empire, the arrangements which he had set in place in 351 to watch over the east had proved less than durable. On the military front, to be sure, the Caesar Gallus served his purpose by keeping Persian marauders at bay:[77] the satrap Nohodares, for example, was deterred by a show of strength from attacking the important trading centre of Batnae in Osroene (Amm. Marc. xiv.3); and with the aid of the eastern *magister equitum*, Ursicinus, Gallus' forces also successfully dealt with an outbreak of Jewish disorder which destroyed three towns in Galilee.[78] The intelligence which reported such successes to Constantius – the praetorian prefect Thalassius and others made it their business to inform him (Amm. Marc. xiv.1.10,7.9) – will also have kept him apprised of the kind of regime maintained by Gallus and Constantina in Antioch, a regime which showed increasing signs of waywardness and independence. Constantius may have found little to complain of in his Caesar's popular Christian zeal, reflected, for instance, in his promotion of the local martyr cult of Babylas (Sozom. v.19.12–13); nor necessarily in his (and his wife's) reputation for acts of savagery – which even Gallus' brother

---

[75] According to Athanasius (*H. Ar.* xxxi, referring to councils both at Arles and Milan), court officials were despatched far and wide to enforce signatures, and local magistrates ordered to compel bishops to comply.   [76] See *CSEL* lxv, p. 102; Sulp. Sev. *Chron.* ii.39.3.

[77] Amm. Marc. xiv.7.5 alludes to an eastern campaign; for his reputed success against the Persians, cf. Philost. iii.28; Zos. iii.1.1.

[78] Jer. *Chron. s.a.* 352 (Helm, p. 238) names Diocaesarea, Tiberias and Diospolis; Socr. *HE* ii.33 mentions only Diocaesarea. For the rebel leader Patricius, see Aur. Vict. *Caes.* xlii.11. Ursicinus' role is established from Talmudic sources. On this rebellion, see J. Arce, *Athenaeum* 65 (1987) 109–25.

Julian had to concede (*Ep. ad Ath.* 271d) – when they were deployed in enforcing administrative decisions to relieve famine in the city against the recalcitrance of Antioch's *curia* (Amm. Marc. XIV.7.2). But acquiescence in the lynching of the provincial governor was a different matter; as was the challenging of senior officials despatched by Constantius himself. When a new praetorian prefect, Domitianus, was sent to the east in 354, he arrived with orders for Gallus to join Constantius in Italy (XIV.7.9). Gallus' response to these instructions was to send troops to arrest the prefect. The quaestor Montius, who owed his appointment and patrician rank to Constantius,[79] warned the soldiers that they might as well be overturning the statues of the emperor (XIV.7.12) – to no avail, for he and Domitianus were murdered by troops loyal to Gallus, and subsequently two of Domitianus' relatives were victims of treason accusations. Such actions are indicative of more than tensions between the Caesar and the emperor's officials: from Constantius' vantage point in the west they were interpreted (as Montius realized they would be) as treasonable.[80] A succession of subordinates was sent to Antioch during 354 to erode Gallus' military support and recall him to Italy; when eventually prevailed upon to leave, the disgraced Caesar caused more outrage to his superior through courting popularity by holding races in Constantinople (XIV.11.12–13). As he neared Italy, in October 354, Gallus was arrested and deposed at Poetovio, and shortly afterwards executed on the emperor's orders – the charge was the deaths of Constantius' men in Antioch.[81]

Constantius' first experiment with a dynastic deputy was thus abruptly ended, in Gallus' twenty-ninth year. Others were caught up in his downfall. Even before Gallus was prised away from Antioch, the eastern *magister equitum* Ursicinus was recalled to Constantius' court in Milan (the *protector* Ammianus was one of his retinue: XIV.11.4–5). He had been awkwardly caught between allegiance to the emperor who appointed him and the more immediate orders of the Caesar who placed him in charge of the trials of Domitianus' relatives; and there were those around Constantius, including the *mag. equitum* at court, Arbitio, who were ready to accuse Ursicinus and his family of disloyal intent (XV.2).[82] It was also a dangerous time for Gallus' younger half-brother Julian, who was summoned to court and detained for seven months at Comum, before the intercession of Constantius' empress Eusebia secured his escape to the lecture rooms of Athens.[83]

The court's residence in Italy in the mid 350s continued to be dogged by

---

[79] Constantius had sent Montius to Antioch in Gallus' retinue: *Artemii Passio*, 12 (see Philostorgius (ed. Bidez/Winkelmann), p. 52).

[80] The political background to Gallus' downfall is explored by Thompson (1947) 56–71; Blockley (1972); Matthews, *Ammianus* 34–6, 406–8.

[81] For the accusation, Amm. Marc. XIV.11.21, XV.3.1. On the date of Gallus' death, T. D. Barnes, *HSCP* 92 (1989) 416.   [82] On the domestic politics of Constantius' generals, see Blockley (1980a).

[83] See p. 47 below.

the issue of Athanasius: to the emperor the glory of an empire reunified by the defeat of Magnentius and the assent of the bishops at Arles still appeared tarnished by the defiance of the bishop of Alexandria and his supporters.[84] These included Liberius, Julius' successor as bishop of Rome. In Italy Constantius was readily accessible to the approaches of Liberius appealing for a council to settle the *negotium Athanasii*. In a letter conveyed by his emissaries to the court in Milan (*CSEL* LXV.89–93) Liberius held out to the emperor the prospect of emulating the anti-Arian unity which with God's favour his father had achieved by the gathering of so many bishops at Nicaea; for him, as for Athanasius' other western allies, the issue extended beyond the bishop of Alexandria to the *causa fidei* itself (since the council of Sardica they had labelled Athanasius' detractors as Arian heretics).[85] Constantius, on the other hand, while receptive to the Constantinian precedent and careful to advertise his tireless concern ('night and day') for matters of the faith,[86] focused more starkly on the person of Athanasius: he it was who, accused of dabbling with Magnentius and already disowned by a succession of church councils, stood out as the persistent obstacle to the unity to which Constantius' Christian empire aspired. Thus in acceding to the request for a council he was aiming to reinforce the already repeatedly expressed (most recently at Arles) condemnation of the Alexandrian bishop.[87] The ecclesiastical historians make vastly exaggerated claims for the size of the gathering at Milan ('over 300 bishops': Socr. *HE* II.36, Sozom. IV.9): in fact it was a mere thirty or so, mostly from Italy, who joined Dionysius of Milan in his church in the city in the summer of 355.[88] Their proceedings are obscured from history by the *tendenz* of pro-Athanasian sources, although it does emerge through the polemic that the later stages of the council were transferred to the imperial palace (where the emperor could place himself quite literally 'in the wings'), and that the newly influential Valens of Mursa was a prime mover in engineering the desired outcome[89] – such imperial manipulation of ecclesiastical gatherings was an aspect of the Nicaean precedent which might have appealed less to Liberius. The tally of those among the bishops who refused to disavow Athanasius – and incurred the emperor's penalty of exile – was in the end just three: Dionysius of Milan, Eusebius of Vercellae and Lucifer of Cagliari.[90] Liberius of Rome had sent only delegates, but before long

[84] See Brennecke (1984) 147ff.; Barnes, *Athanasius* 115ff. For the general context of Constantius' dealings with western bishops, Frend (1984) 534ff.
[85] Cf. Liberius' letter to Eusebius, bishop of Vercellae: *CCSL* IX, p. 121.
[86] As he stressed to Eusebius of Vercellae: *ibid.*, p. 120.
[87] As implied in the same letter to Eusebius: *ibid.*, p. 121.
[88] See Brennecke (1984) 164ff.; Barnes, *Athanasius* 117.
[89] For the active participation of bishop Valens, see *CSEL* LXV, p. 187. On the emperor's proximity to the gathering in the palace, Lucif. Cal. *Moriendum esse*, 1 (*CCSL* VIII.266), 4 (272).
[90] Jer. *Chron. s.a.* 355 (Helm, p. 239); Sulp. Sev. *Chron.* II.39.3–6.

Constantius was sufficiently confident of success to order his arrest, with the aid of a compliant city prefect (the same Leontius who had in 351 been among those eminent Christians called in by Constantius to listen to Photinus' defence); later in 355 Liberius was brought to the court in Milan, only to follow the others into exile when he refused to toe the line.[91] Meanwhile in Alexandria itself, after a further unsuccessful attempt to dislodge the bishop through the intervention of an imperial *notarius*, a show of force by the military commander Syrianus finally expelled Athanasius from the city to make for the cover of the desert (February 356: *H. Aceph.* 1.9–11, *Apol. ad Const.* XXII–XXV) – he was not to return during Constantius' lifetime. Though it would appear differently to bishops banished from their cities, from the perspective of an emperor eager to lay claim to a unified Christian empire God's judgement would have seemed at last to have been accomplished.

Even as Constantius was seeing the bishops assembled in Milan reaching (virtual) unanimity over the condemnation of the troublesome bishop of Alexandria, news from across the Alps brought a sharp reminder of the fragility of his reunited empire. On (most probably) 11 August 355 the *magister peditum* in Gaul, Silvanus, was clothed in makeshift imperial purple and proclaimed Augustus by troops in Cologne (Amm. Marc. xv.5.16).[92] It was news all the more unwelcome in the light of Silvanus' recent demonstration of loyalty to the dynasty by his conspicuous desertion of Magnentius before the conflict at Mursa, a move which had earned him the high command in Gaul from the victorious Constantius. The emperor reacted urgently to the report of Silvanus' rebellion. A night-time meeting of the *consistorium* was summoned to the palace in Milan (were the bishops still in residence?). Its deliberations at last found a use for the eastern *magister equitum* Ursicinus, who was still detained at court after his suspect involvement with the fallen Caesar Gallus. Ursicinus was to be sent post-haste to Cologne with a select entourage of officers to engineer the recall of Silvanus to Italy, or failing that – if the *coup* was already too far advanced – to accomplish his downfall (Ursicinus' rivals were reportedly encouraged by the thought that, even if he were unsuccessful in bringing down Silvanus, he would at least destroy himself). Ammianus, who accompanied Ursicinus on this evidently dangerous mission and describes its progress, coolly recounts the devious means of deception and treachery by which Silvanus was undermined and his followers suborned, to the point when the usurper was dragged from the refuge of a

---

[91] For Liberius' arrest, Amm. Marc. xv.7.6–10; on the date, Barnes (1992) 134. On the whole episode, see Brennecke (1984) 265ff.; Pietri, *Roma Christiana* 237–68.

[92] The date derives from an old suggestion by Seeck, that the occasion on which Silvanus demonstrated his loyalty 'four days before' his usurpation (Amm. Marc. xv.6.3) was Constantius' birthday, i.e. 7 August. On the whole episode as recounted by Ammianus (xv.5), see Matthews, *Ammianus* 37ff.

Christian church and slaughtered (xv.5.31).[93] His rule had lasted less than a month.[94]

Panegyric lauds Constantius for resisting those courtiers who demanded reprisals against Silvanus' supporters;[95] yet Ammianus, as in the sequel to the defeat of Magnentius, more realistically reports otherwise, and catalogues the purge (xv.6). One victim insisted under torture that Silvanus had been driven to seize power by necessity, not ambition; and such a view is reflected in Ammianus' own version of the court intrigues and rivalries which had forced Silvanus to take the initiative in the interests of self-preservation. Others have argued that it was the soldiers, backed by the provincials of Gaul, who made Silvanus their emperor;[96] and whatever the precise background of his proclamation, it was this local dimension which was uppermost in Constantius' reaction to it. For most of the century, from the first Constantius onwards, Gaul had seen a resident Augustus or Caesar from the imperial dynasty. The notion of a 'Gallic' emperor on the spot was deep-rooted in the region, as was the potential resentment against a more remote ruler in Italy or further afield: the interlude of Magnentius, for example, owes something to the fact of Constans' increasing absence from Gaul in the later 340s, and it was after Constantius' own withdrawal to Italy in 354 that Gaul was once again denied its resident emperor. What is more, despite his success against the Alamanni in that year, it is clear that the frontier regions of Gaul continued to be badly affected by barbarian incursions: it would be claimed that by the end of 355 forty-five towns had had their fortifications destroyed, let alone numerous other lesser outposts, and that raiders were ranging freely deep into Roman territory.[97] Such conditions were easily blamed on the failure of commanders like Silvanus, but it is more to the point that they focused attention precisely on the absence of an effective ruler, and encouraged the prospect of usurpation. Constantius' answer to this instability and danger in Gaul – to avoid another Magnentius or Silvanus – was, inevitably, to restore the tradition of a resident representative of the house of Constantine. Hampered by his own lack of offspring, and the demise in the previous year of the failed Caesar Gallus, his only choice was his cousin, Gallus' half-brother Julian. Out of such political calculations ensued the summons which recalled Julian from the academe of Athens to the imperial court at Milan, to be invested by Constantius with the imperial regalia and named as Caesar before the assembled troops on 6 November 355 (Amm. Marc. xv.8). Shortly after-

[93] For Silvanus' fate, cf. Jul. *Or.* 1.48c, 11.98d.
[94] Jul. *Or.* 11.99a; '28 days' acc. to Jer. *Chron. s.a.* 354 (Helm, p. 239), Aur. Vict. *Caes.* XLII.16, *Epit. de Caes.* XLII.10 (a duration suspiciously identical to that recorded for Nepotianus' rule).
[95] Jul. *Or.* 1.48d–49a, 11.99b, singling out clemency towards Silvanus' son.
[96] E.g. den Boer (1960).
[97] Jul. *Ep. ad Ath.* 278d–279b (a source, admittedly, with an interest in exaggerating adverse conditions in Gaul); cf. Lib. *Or.* XVIII.33–5.

wards he was given Constantius' sister Helena in marriage, and (on 1 December) escorted by the emperor on his way to Gaul. He spent his first winter as Caesar in Vienne. It was a timely arrival, for the news had come in – as if in confirmation of Gaul's need of an imperial saviour – that Cologne, the base of Silvanus' brief usurpation, had fallen to Frankish raiders (xv.8.18–19).

Forewarned by the precedent of Gallus' all too independent disregard for the emperor's officials, Constantius was careful to define and circumscribe his new Caesar's role.[98] Julian was allowed a very modest personal court and a small contingent of soldiers for his immediate entourage; military command lay with the generals appointed by Constantius, and the civilian administration remained the responsibility of the praetorian prefect. Although five years later, when Julian had himself turned into a rebel Augustus, he would write of these limitations with resentment and claim that he had been forced to contend against malicious obstructiveness on the part of the emperor and his subordinates, the fact remains that from the moment in November 355 when he was taken up by Constantius to share the imperial carriage, and received into the palace (Amm. Marc. xv.8.17), Julian was consistently cast as a dynastic *partner*, married to the Augustus' sister, and sharing with him the consulship of 356. The practical results of this partnership were seen in military collaboration: while Julian was energetically engaged on his first campaigns for the recovery of Gaul in 356, Constantius was leading a (less publicized) assault on the Alamanni from the south; and the emperor acted decisively in support of his Caesar by retiring the general Marcellus after he had failed to send reinforcements to Julian at Sens (Amm. Marc. xvi.7.1). Julian was likewise the dutiful Caesar. Although already a secret apostate from Christianity (he had been seduced by the exotic theurgy of Maximus of Ephesus in 351), he found time amid the offensive against the Alamanni to be an agent of Constantius' continuing crusade against dissident bishops: it was Julian who convoked the synod at Béziers in 356 which resulted in the deposition and exile of bishops Hilary of Poitiers and Rhodanus of Toulouse.[99]

VI. CONSTANTIUS IN ROME, 357

The securing of the western empire against usurpers, successful stirrings against the Alamanni, and the enforcement of ecclesiastical conformity, all might appear to Constantius to denote a climax of unity within the empire and success beyond it. The moment was ripe for a symbolic imperial visit to Rome, Constantius' first and only appearance in the ancient capital of his

---

[98] For what follows, see, in more detail, pp. 49–51 below.
[99] The role of Julian is alluded to by Hilary, *Liber ad Const.* 2 (*CSEL* LXV, p. 198). On Béziers, see Brennecke (1984) 239ff., and Barnes (1992).

empire. A more specific occasion beckoned in the celebration of his own
vicennalia as Augustus, an imperial milestone which had also brought his predecessors Diocletian and Constantine in state to Rome.[100] Towards the end
of April 357 the court moved from Milan to Rome (Amm. Marc. XVI.10).
Not only was Constantius accompanied by his empress Eusebia, but they
were also joined in Rome by his sister (and wife of his Caesar) Helena
(XVI.10.18): the imperial anniversary was an occasion for dynastic display.
Constantius entered the city seated in a golden carriage, and surrounded on
all sides by a military guard in gleaming armour, to be hailed by the echoing
shouts of senators and people. This majestic *adventus*, famed from
Ammianus' exceptionally vivid description of the emperor's statuesque
demeanour ('figmentum hominis': XVI.10.10) – the look fixed straight ahead
'as though his neck were in a clamp', the head and hands held motionless –
has become the classic portrayal of the late Roman ruler.[101] But although
such distant grandeur may have become the normal expression of the
emperor's comings and goings 'in his provinces' (XVI.10.9), Rome still
demanded some reversion to the style of a former age on the rare occasions
when it now saw its emperor: and so, once in the city, in an assiduous re-
enactment of more traditional expectations of imperial conduct in the
capital, Constantius paid court to the senators in their meeting-house, and
deferred to the populace at the games (XVI.10.13–14). These will have been
unfamiliar concessions for a ruler used to thinking of himself as 'lord of the
whole world' (XV.1.3) – and unfamiliar surroundings: the emperor could
only gaze in admiration at the sight of Rome's monumental reminders of its
past, and ask inquisitive questions of his guides (XVI.10.14–17, cf. Symm.
Rel. III.7). The emperor of Rome had become a stranger to his heritage.

Although this Roman visit was far from being an old-style imperial
triumph – Constantius' father had put paid to that tradition when he had
abandoned the practice of worshipping Jupiter on the Capitol – none the
less the military defeat of Magnentius could not but be recalled (if nothing
else, the prefect of the city was again Vitrasius Orfitus, Constantius' loyal
supporter in the recovery of Italy in 352).[102] Sufficient time had now
elapsed to heal the embarrassments of senatorial recognition of the
usurper, and panegyrists could openly proclaim the victory over a 'barbarian' tyrant – it was conveniently forgotten that a few years earlier
Magnentius had been emperor of Italy and the west.[103]

---

[100] For *vicennalia* as context see *Chron. Min.* I, 239. Among discussions of this Rome visit, see Duval
(1970); Klein (1979b).

[101] See Matthews, *Ammianus* 231ff. On the literary background, C. J. Classen *Rhein. Mus.* 131 (1988)
177–86 and pp. 142–3 below.

[102] On the transformation of the victory context, see MacCormack, *Art and Ceremony* 39–45;
McCormick (1986) 84–91.

[103] Jul. *Or.* 1.42a; Them. *Or.* III.43a (a speech composed to honour this Rome visit). Ammianus, by
contrast, would accuse Constantius of triumphing over 'Roman blood' (XVI.10.1).

His background of service against Magnentius and his usefulness in confirming the senators' allegiance to Constantius are perhaps more pertinent to the recall of the pagan Orfitus to a second prefecture in 357 than any supposed concessions to traditional religion associated with Constantius' Roman visit.[104] In tune with the confident optimism of these months, Constantius had issued a flurry of anti-pagan laws from Milan in the winter of 356–7 (C.Th. IX.16.4, 5; XVI.10.4, 6) – outlawing divination, closing temples and banning sacrifices – and a volte-face on his arrival in Rome seems improbable. The arguments surrounding the displaced altar of Victory in the 380s would claim that Constantius had preserved Roman paganism, in that he had not interfered with traditional institutions and ceremonies, and would exploit the fact that he made appointments to priesthoods; but such actions spring from the diplomatic requirements of an emperor's dealings with the Roman establishment ('when in Rome . . .'), and not from an intention to favour the old gods.[105] Nor should it be forgotten that it was Constantius on this Roman visit who first ordered the removal of that same pagan altar from its powerfully symbolic place in the senate house (Symm. Rel. III.4–6; Ambr. Ep. XVIII.32).

The seemingly smooth interaction between Christian emperor and pagan senators (their response to the short-lived removal of the altar can only be guessed at) may be contrasted, ironically, with the hostility encountered from a Christian congregation resentful at the arrest and exile of their bishop Liberius and his replacement by Constantius' nominee Felix: the echo of popular liberties from a former age brought with it the opportunity of protest no less than of acclaim.[106] After two years of exile, when he had subscribed to the approved statement of faith, Liberius would be allowed to return; more immediately Constantius could demonstrate himself the dutiful Christian heir of his father by completing the building of the church on the Vatican hill over the tomb of St Peter.[107] Another culmination of a project inaugurated by Constantine was the erection of an Egyptian obelisk in the Circus Maximus (it now stands before the basilica of St John Lateran).[108] The inscription on its base (ILS 736) returned to the theme of Magnentius: this was Constantius' victory trophy to hail the recovery of the west from the defeated 'tyrant'. Christian basilica and triumphal obelisk were to be the permanent reminders of what was only a

[104] For dismissal of arguments associating Orfitus' prefecture with a pagan resurgence, see Salzman, Roman Time 212ff.

[105] Symm. Rel. III.7. On my (religiously 'neutral') interpretation, cf. Edbrooke (1976), and Salzman, Roman Time 218ff.

[106] For popular protest demanding the return of Liberius, see Sozom. IV.11.12, Coll. Avell. (CSEL xxxv) 1.3; Theod. HE II.17 places the complaints on the lips of senators' wives.

[107] ILCV 1753, discussed by Krautheimer (1987).

[108] For Constantius completing a project begun by his father, see Amm. Marc. XVII.4.12ff., with Fowden (1987).

brief Roman interlude for Constantius. After a mere thirty days in the city, the emperor and his court set off on 29 May northwards through Italy to take up residence in Pannonia, on the news that Suebi, Quadi and Sarmatians were disturbing the peace of the Danube frontier (Amm. Marc. XVI.10.20). In the face of such present emergencies Rome exerted only a passing claim on the emperor's attention.

VII. SIRMIUM AND THE SEARCH FOR A CREED, 357–9

For the next two years (357–9) Constantius established his court at Sirmium. From here he deployed a traditionally Roman amalgam of military offensive and diplomatic negotiation against the Sarmatians and Quadi who were threatening Pannonia. In the early summer of 358 Constantius led an army across the swollen waters of the Danube and campaigned successfully to force the raiders into submission. One by one, separate groups of Sarmatians and Quadi were defeated and isolated, their rulers granted peace terms in return for the recovery of Roman prisoners and the provision of hostages; the young prince Zizais was installed as leader of the so-called 'free' Sarmatians, while their former slaves the Limigantes were forced back into remote areas away from the Danube plains (Amm. Marc. XVII.12–13). Constantius was acclaimed *Sarmaticus* (for the second time),[109] and hailed by his victorious soldiers as invincible: the return from the front to winter quarters at Sirmium amounted to a triumphal procession.[110] Triumph, though, nearly turned to disaster the next year when some of the Limigantes who had contrived to be admitted to the empire rebelled and stormed the emperor's tribunal, forcing him to flee – and even abandon his golden chair to be plundered (XIX.11.10–12). The troops reacted swiftly and conclusively to avenge this insult to Roman majesty.

Such military emergencies demanded Constantius' time alongside the continuing quest for a unified Christendom in his empire. In the aftermath of his Roman *vicennalia*, and amid news of Julian's successful exploits in his name in Gaul, the time might have seemed opportune – particularly now that the disruptive voices of Athanasius and his leading supporters appeared to have been quelled. The abortive council of Sardica had shown the impossibility of approaching common ground on doctrine while dispute about individuals remained unresolved; with the latter now seemingly settled, the way lay open to come to a consensus of faith. This process naturally thrust into prominence those bishops closest to the court and most accessible to the emperor: with the court resident at Sirmium, the local bishop Germinius, Photinus' replacement, was best placed to seize

[109] Amm. Marc. XVII.13.25; for the first occasion, cf. *ILS* 724.
[110] Amm. Marc. XVII.13.33. Contrast Julian's belittling of Constantius' activities on the Danube front at *Ep. ad Ath.* 279d.

the initiative, along with the neighbouring Balkan bishops Valens of Mursa (who already enjoyed a privileged place in Constantius' esteem) and Ursacius of Singidunum. As former allies of Eusebius of Nicomedia,[111] Valens and Ursacius afforded some continuity with the series of influential councils which had accompanied the early years of Constantius' residence in Antioch; it was now the turn of imperial Sirmium to host the creed-making process. Hostile report portrays the emperor in this process as a puppet of over-mighty bishops cast in the guise of influential courtiers (*familiares amici*);[112] but to take such a view is to reckon without Constantius' own serious commitment, as his father's son, to doctrinal consensus. His rule would avail him nothing, Constantine is said to have advised Constantius, if God were not worshipped with one voice (Sozom. III.19.5); and in a famous observation on Constantius' Christianity, even the secular Ammianus (xxI.16.18) noted his preoccupation with the finer points of belief. Already at Sirmium in 351, in the midst of war with Magnentius, Constantius had involved himself in condemning the views of bishop Photinus. When in 357 Germinius, Valens, Ursacius and some other like-minded bishops at Sirmium produced a creed enunciating for the first time the principle that the non-scriptural terminology of 'substance' was best avoided in statements of faith, the emperor is likely to have seen this as offering a welcome prospect of cutting through the seemingly intractable arguments over the divine nature.[113]

These arguments had assumed fresh complexities with the emergence in the east of a radical viewpoint linked to the names of the deacon Aetius at Antioch and his disciple Eunomius, who adopted the extreme position (theologically opposite to that of Photinus) of declaring that the substance of the Son was 'unlike' (*anomoios*) that of the Father.[114] It was to counter this view that a delegation from a small council at Ancyra arrived at court in Sirmium in the summer of 358 (Sozom. IV.13.4ff.) advancing the belief that the Son was 'like the Father in substance' (*homoiousios*). Constantius was at least temporarily persuaded of the validity of this formula, which he would recognize as having a respectable 'mainstream' pedigree among eastern bishops deriving from the Antioch 'dedication council' of 341 (where he had been present) – and its principal advocate, Basil of Ancyra,

---

[111] Demonstrated, for example, by their serving on the commission sent by the council of Tyre to investigate Athanasius' activities in Egypt (Athan. *Apol. c. Ar.* LXXII.2ff.), and subsequently accompanying Eusebius to Constantinople (*ibid.*, LXXXVII.1).

[112] The phrase is from Lucif. Cal. *De non conveniendo*, 7 (*CCSL* VIII, p. 175); at *Moriendum esse*, VII (p. 281), he dubs them 'satellites'. Cf. Sulp. Sev. *Chron.* II.38.4 on the bishops' 'occupation' of the palace, and (more colourfully) Athan. *Hist. Ar.* LII.

[113] For Constantius' general objective of ecclesiastical harmony, see Sozom. IV.11.2. The Sirmium creed: Athan. *De Syn.* XXVIII; Hil. *De Syn.* XI. For the view that the document was not the product of a formal 'council', see Barnes, *Athanasius* app. 10.

[114] Barnes, *Athanasius* 136–8. For fuller treatment of Aetius and Eunomius see e.g. Hanson (1988) 598–636.

came to enjoy a brief court ascendancy which for a few months eclipsed that of the Danubian bishops.[115] It is a measure of Basil's influence that, throughout all the bewildering debates and negotiations about right doctrine which were to follow, Constantius voiced a consistent opposition to the views of the 'anomoean' faction.

The emperor's sense of a mission to forge consensus out of this doctrinal ferment directed him towards a new general council, one which would be more genuinely universal than Nicaea in embracing both east and west, yet avoid the stillborn fate of Sardica. The council was to convene in two separate geographical halves, each of which would transmit its agreed conclusions to the imperial court via small delegations of ten bishops,[116] who would then under the emperor's eye together contrive the desired universal outcome. With hindsight, this strategy was to be denounced as a ploy of Valens of Mursa and the other bishops around Constantius at Sirmium to manipulate the proceedings in favour of their own views (Sozom. IV.16.19–22); in reality, though, it must have seemed to the emperor an attractive mechanism for imperial management of the conciliar process. Writing to the bishops assembling for the western council at Rimini, Constantius made a point of instructing them not to concern themselves with the easterners[117] – there was, in other words, to be no repeat of the irreconcilable collision which had occurred at Sardica. The emperor was interested in more than the mechanics of this extended and divided council: he also shared with the bishops the preparation of a doctrinal statement produced at Sirmium on 22 May 359 to serve as the basis for the discussions. The heading of this statement named not only the 'religious and victorious' Constantius but also the consuls who gave their names to the year, thus notoriously provoking the outrage of Athanasius at a 'dated creed' which presumed to determine in the present day the age-old faith of the church.[118] Yet the naming of the emperor did no more (and no less) than attach his authority to the creed, just as the *homoousios* formula at Nicaea had carried Constantine's personal support. In the case of Constantius the authority was rather more than nominal, for he is reported to have stayed with the bishops long into the night as they argued, and insisted on a compromise formula – the Son was not simply 'like' (*homoios*) the Father, but 'like *in all respects*' – to accommodate the objections of Basil

[115] Basil's ascendancy over imperial policy emerges most clearly from the hostile account of Philostorgius (IV.8–9), alleging as many as seventy banishments among the 'anomoeans'. Constantius gave imperial endorsement to the *homoiousios* formula in a letter to the church of Antioch: Sozom. IV.14.4.
[116] As Constantius himself instructed the western gathering at Rimini: *CSEL* LXV, p. 94. Cf. Sozom. IV.17.1.   [117] *CSEL* LXV, p. 94.
[118] Athan. *De Syn.* III; for the text of the document, see *De Syn.* VIII.3–7. On this creed, and the ensuing councils of Rimini and Seleucia, see Barnes, *Athanasius* 144–9; Hanson (1988) 362–80; Brennecke (1988) 23ff.

of Ancyra to what was proposed by Valens of Mursa.[119] Even so, the principle of the 357 Sirmium creed, eschewing mention of the non-biblical term 'substance', was adhered to: 'we say that the son is like the Father in all things, as the Scriptures say and teach'. In propounding a statement of faith which spoke only in terms of the similarity of Father and Son, and avoided the theological niceties of 'substance', Constantius might well hope to have found the lowest common denominator politically capable of producing a consensus of doctrine, west and east.

The western portion of the council assembled first. In the early summer of 359 over 400 bishops, the largest such gathering yet seen, were summoned by imperial officials to Rimini on Italy's Adriatic coast – conveniently close at hand for those Pannonian bishops who had controlled the preliminary stages at Constantius' court, but a more troublesome journey, and one demanding all that the *cursus publicus* could provide, for the three attending from far-off Britain.[120] The logistics and direction of affairs at Rimini fell to Fl. Taurus, then praetorian prefect of Italy and a loyal Christian associate of the emperor (he had been among those senior laymen who had listened to the investigation of Photinus in 351).[121] The council was to drag on into the winter, with the bishops detained away from their sees for over six months, until the prefect was able to secure endorsement of the Sirmium formula.[122] The majority had first rejected this creed presented to them by Valens of Mursa and his allies, even denying them communion; but the tactics of delay were effectively deployed by the emperor's managers, while the plenary council was stalled awaiting the return of the delegations which the two factions sent to Constantius, and these delegations in turn were obliged to take second place to imperial campaigning on the Danube front (Athan. *De Syn.* LV.3) – an interval exploited (even engineered?) with the intention of changing minds among the majority delegates. On 10 October, at the *mansio* of Nike in Thrace, the Rimini envoys rescinded the condemnation of bishop Valens and his associates, and endorsed the Sirmium doctrine that the Son was 'like the Father, as the Scriptures say and teach';[123] the bishops still left at Rimini, anxious to return home before the depth of winter, proceeded to follow their delegates' lead. When the council finally came to a conclusion in December, envoys were despatched, in accordance with the planned procedure, to the imperial court (which by now had moved to Constantinople), conveying the news of unanimity which Constantius wanted to hear (Sulp. Sev. *Chron.* II.43ff.).

[119] See Epiphan. *Pan.* LXXIII.22.5ff., with *CSEL* LXV, p. 163.

[120] Sulp. Sev. *Chron.* II.41.1–3. The number is confirmed by Athan. *Syn.* VIII.1; Sozom. IV.17.1.

[121] According to Sulp. Sev., *loc. cit.*, Taurus' reward for a successful council was to be the consulship (which he achieved in 361, only to have his career disrupted by the challenge of Julian).

[122] Sulp. Sev. *Chron.* II.44.1; cf. the complaints of the detained bishops at Athan. *De Syn.* LV and *CSEL* LXV, p. 84.   [123] *CSEL* LXV, pp. 85–6; for the text agreed at Nike, see Theod. *HE* II.21.3–7.

That tradition would portray this as an outcome secured only by the 'trick-ery' of Valens of Mursa was not something to occupy the mind of an emperor who sensed that the elusive unity of the faith was at last within his grasp.[124]

The eastern 'half' of the council meanwhile had convened on 27 September 359 at Seleucia, the ancient harbour town on the shore of Cilicia and suitable meeting-point for Asia and the east (Theod. *HE* II.26.4). The original intention of a gathering at Nicomedia, handy for Basil of Ancyra's 'homoiousian' bishops in Asia Minor, had been thwarted by the ruinous earthquake of August 358. The *cursus publicus* brought 160 bishops from the eastern provinces to Seleucia, where the task of fulfilling the emperor's charge to find an agreed statement of belief was entrusted to the *comes* Leonas.[125] Leonas had the assistance of the local provincial governor, and fellow *comes*, Lauricius: as a man of 'diplomatic prudence', who used his particular talents ('threats rather than severity') to check the inroads of Isaurian raiders, Lauricius might appear a useful ally in handling the argu-ments of bishops.[126] But Leonas encountered only schism. After a mere four days, the synod of Seleucia dissolved in factional in-fighting, princi-pally between the majority who favoured the 'homoiousian' statement of Basil of Ancyra and his supporters, and others led by Acacius of Caesarea who adhered to the principles of the Sirmium declaration. Each party sent its representatives to the court, as had earlier happened at Rimini. In Constantinople Constantius personally presided over last-ditch efforts – in company with other senior laymen in the capital, including its first urban prefect Honoratus – to gain assent to the creed to which he had given his name at Sirmium in May.[127] The extreme views of Aetius were again out-lawed on the emperor's authority; but even Aetius' principal opponent, Basil of Ancyra, was by now outmanoeuvred (his qualification 'in all respects' had been dropped from the credal formula).[128] Deep into the night on the last day of 359 the emperor laboured among the delegates from Seleucia to gain their acquiescence to the 'homoios' creed which the western council had now endorsed, to the end that the inauguration of his tenth (and destined to be his last) consulship could be accompanied, at the start of the new year, by the proclamation of true belief unified in east and west, and his father's unfinished legacy could be at last accomplished. It was

---

[124] For the 'dolus' of Valens, see Sulp. Sev. *Chron.* II.44.7, Sozom. IV.19.9–12 (applying the term to the manoeuvring at Nike).

[125] The principal narrative of the council is found in Socr. *HE* II.39ff. (followed by Sozom. IV.22ff.); cf. also Athan. *De Syn.* XII; Hil. *C. Const.* XII–XV (Hilary was present at Seleucia).

[126] For Lauricius' secular activities, see Amm. Marc. XIX.13.2.

[127] For what follows, see esp. Sozom. IV.23.3ff.

[128] See the creed cited at Athan. *De Syn.* XXX (cf. the Nike declaration, p. 35 above). On the rejection of Aetius, Philost. IV.12 (Bidez/Winkelmann, p. 65) and Theod. *HE* II.27.10ff. For Constantius' change of attitude towards Basil, Theod. *HE* II.27.5.

left to a further council of seventy-two local bishops who assembled in Constantinople in January under the presidency of Acacius of Caesarea to affirm the approved doctrine, and with the emperor's blessing remove from office those (Basil of Ancyra and his 'homoiousian' followers) unreconciled to what was now the official orthodoxy.[129]

VIII. CONSTANTIUS IN CONSTANTINOPLE, 359–60

It was fortuitous that the city of Constantine should see the culmination of his son's inherited pursuit of credal uniformity. For Constantius, obliged by the demands of the eastern front to reside chiefly in Antioch, only ever spent brief sojourns as emperor in Constantinople – and one such visit, in 342, was made in anger, to restore order in the city after factional riots over contenders for the bishopric had resulted in the murder of the *magister equitum* Hermogenes (on this occasion the inhabitants were punished by having their grain rations reduced).[130] Yet despite such passing acquaintance with the city, Constantius had a symbolic tie with Constantinople, for it had been on the day of its formal inauguration (8 November 324) that he, as a seven-year-old boy, had first been raised to the rank of Caesar (Them. *Or.* IV.58b). Themistius chose the occasion of Constantius' *vicennalia* in Rome, which he attended as an emissary of the Constantinople senate, to remind the emperor that, although named after Constantine, 'the city is really yours rather than your father's' (*Or.* III.40c): Constantius had nurtured and adorned his father's fledgling foundation into a place fit for 'both god and emperor' (*Or.* III.48a). For Themistius' Roman listeners, such sentiments must have placed Constantius' short-lived display of traditional regard for their city in a more realistic perspective: for the predominant focus of the emperor's civic attentions lay on the Bosphorus.[131] Besides completing the building of Constantinople's circuit wall (Jul. *Or.* I.41a), he continued the development of its interior: Themistius, for instance, looks forward to the beauty of the vast 'Constantian' baths which he saw being constructed (they were not completed until 427).[132] Constantius, too, founded the great imperial library and its associated *scriptorium* which would immortalize in Constantinople the glories of the Greek cultural heritage (Them *Or.* IV.59ff.).

Besides being the new showpiece of the Greek world, Constantius' Constantinople also saw the growth of the institutions of a Roman capital – which his father had established merely in embryo. Under Constantius

---

[129] Socr. *HE* II.41ff.; Sozom. IV.24ff.; note Sozomen's outburst at iv.26.aff. against the emperor's 'persecution' of fellow Christians. On the number attending the Constantinople council, see *Chron. Pasch.* (ed. Dindorf), 543.   [130] See Socr. *HE* II.13; Sozom. III.7.5–7; Lib. *Or.* LIX.94ff.

[131] For Constantius' contribution to Constantinople, see Dagron, *Naissance* 89, 94–5; Ruggini (1989) 202–11.   [132] Them. *Or.* IV.58c; for their inauguration in 345, see *Chron. Pasch.* (ed. Dindorf), 534.

the senate of Constantinople became a body to match that of Rome, transformed from mere local curia into an order of *clarissimi* numbering some 2000 by the end of the reign: again it was pointedly for his Roman audience that Themistius evoked the enthusiasm of new senators flocking to the eastern capital and readily undertaking the expenses of office (*Or.* III.48a).[133] He himself was the principal agent of this recruitment, given the task by Constantius after being adlected to the Constantinople senate in 355. In his letter recommending Themistius Constantius called it the fusion of 'Hellenic wisdom' and 'Roman dignity', although the bulk of the influx was probably achieved merely by the administrative device of transferring to Constantinople existing Roman senators resident far away from Rome in the eastern prefecture.[134] It was Constantius who thus gave the eastern empire its 'own' senate – and in a comprehensive law of 3 May 361 proceeded to define the obligations and privileges of the new order.[135] To accompany this enlarged body the number of Roman-style praetorships in Constantinople, which entailed the main financial burdens which went with being a senator, was increased from two in 337 to five by 361. Constantius used the occasion of his residence in 359–60 to provide the eastern capital with its own city governor, the prefect of Constantinople (again on the Roman model), who would come to rank second only to the praetorian prefect in the eastern pecking-order. The first holder of the office was Honoratus (Socr. *HE* II.41), an experienced public figure who had already served as *comes Orientis* and praetorian prefect of Gaul.[136] For an emperor said by Ammianus (XXI.16.1) to have been responsible for few administrative innovations, Constantinople affords a notable exception.

Nor was Constantius' physical and institutional enhancement of Constantinople confined to the secular sphere. On 15 February 360 Constantius attended the dedication, by the newly installed bishop Eudoxius, of the new 'great' church near the imperial palace which later generations would know as 'Holy Wisdom'.[137] Constantius had initiated this building in the 340s and richly endowed it, overshadowing the old church of Holy Peace alongside (which his father had reconstructed). With the embellishment of his father's tomb (Jul. *Or.* 1.16c), Constantius had also provided Constantinople with its first 'apostle'. Later, in 356–7, came the first arrivals in the city of relics of an earlier apostolic generation – Timothy, Andrew and Luke – and Constantius began the reconstruction of his father's mausoleum to transform it into a shrine for Constantinople's

---

[133] On the Constantinople senate, see Dagron, *Naissance* 124ff., with modifications by Chastagnol (1976). For numbers, Them. *Or.* XXXIV.13.

[134] For Constantius' letter, see Teubner edn of Themistius, vol. III. Arrangements about the transfer of senators in the east are implied by *C.Th.* VI.4.11 (357); for an example, *PLRE* I.643–4 'Olympius 3'.   [135] See Dagron, *Naissance*, 133–5.   [136] Dagron, *Naissance*, 215ff.; *PLRE* I.438–9 'Honoratus 2'.

[137] Socr. *HE* II.43.11, with *Chron. Pasch.* (ed. Dindorf), 544.

accumulating apostolic heritage.[138] By the late 350s, as new senators were
arriving to give substance to Constantinople's status as capital of the east,
new apostles were being imported to provide the city with a Christian
history to equal that of Rome (to say nothing of Antioch and Alexandria).
Constantius emerges as the real creator of Christian Constantinople, as he
was of its secular institutions.

IX. SAPOR AND JULIAN, 360–1

Constantius had come to Constantinople late in 359 *en route* from Pannonia
to the eastern front, where news of a Persian emergency was again
demanding the emperor's presence. Sapor and his forces had successfully
besieged and destroyed the upper Tigris fortress of Amida. It was a site
familiar to Constantius from many years past, for when still Caesar he had
rebuilt its fortifications after a previous attack (Amm. Marc. XVIII.9.1). This
renewed Persian aggression reflects a change of circumstances since
Constantius had entrusted Gallus with the defence of the east in 351.[139]
Then Sapor's main army was engaged in wars at the other end of his
empire, and Roman Mesopotamia was left to contend with only minor
offensives from the neighbouring Persian satraps: by 357 the praetorian
prefect Musonianus even judged the moment right to tempt the Persian
king with offers of peace. But the next year, having come to terms with his
eastern enemies in Afghanistan (the 'Chionitae and Gelani') and made them
his allies (XVII.5.1), Sapor was strongly placed to resume the campaigns on
his western front against Roman territory.[140] Envoys came to Constantius
restating the Persian claim to Armenia and Mesopotamia (Themistius saw
the delegation passing through Antioch: *Or.* IV.57b), which was countered
in turn by Roman insistence on a peace which preserved existing boundaries; these Roman ambassadors returned without peace, bringing only
reports of Sapor's eagerness to resume the fight. In 359 the Persian king
and his army were on the move. In response to intelligence reports –
including a secret mission into Corduene by the *protector* Ammianus (now
back on the eastern front with his commander Ursicinus) – the Roman high
command in Mesopotamia embarked on a 'scorched earth' policy to
hamper the Persian offensive; but Sapor's army, reputedly on the advice of
a prominent Roman deserter (XVIII.7.10–11), outflanked the defenders of
Mesopotamia by taking a more northerly detour in the direction of
Armenia – and thus reached the fortress of Amida. After the experience of
his failures at Nisibis and elsewhere in the 340s, Sapor did not at first intend

---

[138] Dagron, *Naissance* 401ff.; Mango (1990).
[139] For this phase of operations in the east, see Blockley (1989), 478ff., and Blockley, *Foreign Policy*
17–24. Source material conveniently assembled (in translation) by Dodgeon and Lieu, *Eastern Frontier*
ch. 8.   [140] See Matthews, *Ammianus* 39ff.

to risk a siege (XVIII.6.3), especially since the Roman garrison was swollen by extra regiments rushed to its defence; but he was provoked into investing the fort after the son of his new-found ally, the king of the Chionitae, was killed before the walls. Although ultimately successful – Amida was stormed and destroyed, and its surviving population led into captivity – the seventy-three-day siege was costly for the Persians, and they took advantage of the lateness of the season to return across the border.[141]

For Constantius it was disturbing news. In over twenty years of defending Roman territory in the east, Amida was the first place to fall to the Persians. At Constantinople he ordered an investigation into the disaster, which resulted in Ursicinus' being retired from his command (Amm. Marc. XX.2). The prospect of more widespread Persian aggression in the coming year forced a change from the cautious 'holding operation' which had previously characterized his military policy in the region: Constantius now saw the need not only to return to the front himself but to amass a larger fighting force for a counter-offensive. Against this background he despatched the *notarius* Decentius to the commanders of Julian's forces in Gaul, ordering reinforcements to be moved eastwards (XX.4.2). Military logic might appear to dictate such a transfer of resources. In 357 Julian had defeated a massed confederation of the Alamanni near Strasbourg, and duly delivered their ruler Chnodomarius as a prisoner to Constantius; he had followed this up with campaigns into German territory which had forced the submission of a succession of Alamannic kings, and with the physical reconstruction of the Rhine frontier. The military task in Gaul appeared accomplished, and forces could surely be spared for the east. Nor was it an isolated demand for troops, but part of a concerted effort at strengthening Roman defences against Persia (XX.8.1). This included securing the alliance with Arsaces of Armenia (XX.11.1–3, XXI.6.8),[142] whom Constantius had first installed as a friendly ruler in 338; as part of a continued diplomatic offensive to counter Sapor's designs on Arsaces, some time after 350 the emperor had provided the Armenian ruler with a Roman consort – in the person of Olympias, the daughter of the former praetorian prefect Ablabius and once betrothed to Constans.[143] None the less, although explicable in such a context, the summoning of troops from Gaul may also have had other political motives: this eastern emergency provided Constantius with an opportunity to rein in his increasingly ambitious and overweening Caesar – it did not require a long memory to observe that the manoeuvres which led to the deposition of Gallus in 354 had begun with the gradual removal of his troops.[144]

In the spring of 360, without awaiting the arrival of any reinforcements

---

[141] On Ammianus' account (XIX.1–9) of the siege of Amida, see Matthews, *Ammianus* 57–66.
[142] For the privileged status of Arsaces and his family, cf. *C.Th.* XI.1.1 (360).
[143] Cf. Athan. *Hist. Ar.* LXIX; for conjectural dating (354), see Baynes (1955) 193.
[144] See further pp. 55–6 below.

from Gaul (which could not in any case have reached the east in time for the start of campaigning), Constantius set off from Constantinople for the eastern front. As expected, the Persian army had returned to Mesopotamia. Avoiding the principal fortress of Nisibis where the Roman defence was concentrated, and which was the scene of three unsuccessful sieges in the past, Sapor made instead for the smaller garrison of Singara, which suffered the same fate which had befallen Amida the previous autumn: the place was destroyed and its population evacuated to captivity (xx.6). The Persians then moved to attack the hilltop fort of Bezabde on the bank of the Tigris. It was a naturally defensive site, protected by a garrison of three legions; but the enemy breached a weak spot in the walls and stormed inside. Once more the inhabitants, including Bezabde's Christian bishop, were taken prisoner; but unlike Amida and Singara, this Tigris border fortress was rebuilt and occupied by a Persian force – it was Sapor's first foothold in Roman Mesopotamia.[145]

Constantius meanwhile was approaching through Asia Minor. At Caesarea in Cappadocia he received Arsaces of Armenia with the ceremony and munificence befitting a crucial ally in the conflict with Persia – a welcome which contrasted dramatically with the anger he displayed to emissaries who arrived from Julian (xx.9.2). The substance of their message Constantius will already have learned from other reports from the west: how the troops being assembled at Julian's winter camp in Paris had forestalled their transfer to the east by investing him as Augustus, and Julian had signalled his assent with the traditional promise of a donative. Constantius' rule was once more challenged by a usurpation in the west, and again (as in 350) at a moment when Roman territory was threatened from Persia. As ten years previously, Constantius gave the military priority to the eastern front, safely concluding that at this stage Julian was more concerned with negotiation than going to war, and contented himself with a diplomatic riposte to his Caesar's pretensions – sending his quaestor Leonas, the official who had recently managed the council of Seleucia, to warn Julian of his rightful place. In another demonstration that he recognized no change in his Caesar's position, and no loss of his own authority in the western provinces, Constantius appointed a new praetorian prefect of Gaul in succession to Florentius (xx.9.4–5).[146] In the meantime he continud his advance towards Mesopotamia. It was autumn before he left Edessa, where the main body of the army had been ordered to assemble (xx.11.4). From there he moved to inspect the ruins of Amida, then

---

[145] Amm. Marc. xx.7.8–9 hints at treachery on the part of the Christian bishop negotiating with the Persians, but the Syriac martyr acts present him as a fellow victim with the rest of the population: see Dodgeon and Lieu, *Eastern Frontier* 215.

[146] Nebridius: for his loyalty to Constantius, cf. Amm. Marc. xxi.5.11–12; Jul. *Ep. ad Ath.* 283c; Lib. *Or.* xviii.110.

advanced to the fortress of Bezabde to attempt to recapture it from the occupying Persians; but hampered by the newly reconstructed fortifications and the onset of winter, the Roman besiegers were unable to dislodge the defenders, and Bezabde remained in enemy hands. The emperor withdrew to Antioch before the end of the year (xx.11.32).

To add to the Persian threat and the news from Gaul, Constantius encountered in Antioch a faction-ridden church which belied the ecclesiastical unity so confidently asserted in Constantinople.[147] After Eudoxius' translation to the see of Constantinople, the troubled bishopric was eventually filled by Meletius, who in a test of faith in the emperor's presence satisfied Constantius of his adherence to the new 'homoian' orthodoxy.[148] But Meletius lasted only a month in the ferment of Antioch before he was deposed – in circumstances for ever obscured by the idealized portrayal which the historical tradition accords him.[149] His opponents evidently found accusations which struck home with the emperor, whose presence was an aid to his prompt removal (Epiphan. Pan. LXXIII.34.1). The new choice was Euzoius, once a companion of Arius in Alexandria. His imperial credentials must have been satisfactory, for we may take it that it was Euzoius who presided at Constantius' wedding in Antioch to his new empress Faustina (Amm. Marc. xxi.6.4); and it was from Euzoius that Constantius would at last receive his Christian baptism (Socr. HE ii.47; Philost. vi.5). During this winter at Antioch Constantius made preparations to confront the expected 'spring offensive' of Sapor: new levies were ordered and the eastern provinces placed on a war footing; nor was there any let-up in courting alliances among local rulers vulnerable to the approaches of the Persian king (Amm. Marc. xxi.6.6–8). But he was increasingly obliged to look westwards as well, for the beginning of 361 saw the diplomatic stalemate with Julian deteriorate into an overt challenge. Julian was confidently playing the Augustus in Gaul, and the armies which the previous year had been ordered to send reinforcements to Constantius were now being prepared to march against him.[150] To pre-empt Julian's gaining control of Africa, Constantius despatched the notarius Gaudentius to organize the local commanders against the usurper; and amidst other measures he might take some satisfaction from the news that a raid into Roman territory by king Vadomarius of the Alamanni was temporarily diverting Julian's attention.[151]

As Julian's army was taking possession of Illyricum in the summer of 361, Constantius was again at Edessa (Amm. Marc. xxi.7.7, 13.1) where the

---

[147] On Antiochene factions, see Sozom. iv.28.1–2. For what follows, Brennecke (1988) 66–81; Hanson (1988) 382–4.

[148] For Constantius' role, see Theod. HE ii.31; on Meletius' exposition, Epiphan. Pan. LXXIII.29ff.

[149] John Chrys. In Melet. (PG L.516).   [150] See pp. 58–9 below.

[151] Jul. Ep. ad Ath. 286a–b, for this and other obstacles to Julian's progress.

forces were massed awaiting news of Sapor's expected crossing of the Tigris. In an uncanny repetition of the circumstances of 351, word came that the Persian king, instead of invading Mesopotamia, had withdrawn his army (XXI.13.8). We may suspect the reason was less the unfavourable auspices claimed by Ammianus than the prospect of continuing heavy losses in the hard siege warfare entailed in gaining control of eastern Mesopotamia – the occupation of Bezabde was all the Persians had to show for two years of costly offensives into Roman territory. Whatever the motives of Sapor's retreat, however, Constantius was freed to confront his rebel cousin, as he had Magnentius ten years earlier. The defence of Mesopotamia was scaled down to its regular garrison, while the bulk of the army accompanied Constantius back towards Antioch. At Hierapolis he rallied his troops against Julian. All were confident that he would repeat the victory he had gained over Magnentius; indeed one eminent citizen of Hierapolis enthusiastically predicted that Julian's severed head would soon be on show (XXII.14.4). An advance force was sent ahead to hold the pass of Succi in Thrace, while Constantius himself passed through Antioch for the last time – and was baptized by bishop Euzoius. This was perhaps more in response to the providential removal of the Persian threat than an anticipation of his coming death, although he had reportedly begun to receive premonitions of the end, and told his closest associates that he sensed his guardian spirit had deserted him (XXI.14.2). He was first taken ill at Tarsus, but continued his journey as far as the edge of Cilicia in the foothills of the Taurus mountains. He had reached the *mansio* of Mopsucrenae when he died of a high fever on 3 November 361, aged 44.[152] Julian, who received the news while he was still at Naissus in Moesia, would see the hand of the gods at work in giving him the mastery of the Roman world without the need for war; but more mundane reflections pointed to the fact that Constantius was still childless at his death (his only child, a daughter, was born posthumously) and that, almost by default, the dynastic inheritance had come to rest with Julian alone. The young survivor of the 'promiscuous massacre' of 337 was the sole heir of the house of Constantine.

---

[152] Amm. Marc. XXI.15.2–3 (reading 'November'); Socr. *HE* II.47, III.1.1; *Chron. Min.* I, 240. For the place, cf. *It. Burd.* 579, 2, and *It. Eg.* 23.6.

CHAPTER 2

JULIAN

DAVID HUNT

I. THE EARLY YEARS

Despite Julian's success in convincing himself that the gods had set him on an imperial mission against the Christian dynasty of Constantine, his assumption of empire on the news of Constantius' death in November 361 could scarcely have been predicted by the young boy who survived the massacre of his relatives in 337.[1] As the sons of Constantine monopolized the empire, and control of the east fell to Constantius, Julian and his older half-brother Gallus were excluded from the public life of the court. While in later years Julian would look back affectionately on his early introduction to the Greek classics, 'after my seventh year', at the hands of his family tutor, the eunuch Mardonius (*Misop.* 351a–353a; *Or.* VIII.241c–d), he chose to keep silent about another of his early mentors, his kinsman bishop Eusebius of Nicomedia.[2] As with Mardonius (who had been the tutor of Julian's mother Basilina), Eusebius' connection with the young Julian was essentially a domestic one; yet it could not escape notice that the bishop was also a powerful political ally of the new emperor Constantius, who had an interest in encouraging his supervision of Julian and Gallus as they emerged into adulthood.

After bishop Eusebius' death Constantius had the brothers transferred to the confines of the imperial estate in Cappadocia known as Macellum, not far from the city of Caesarea, where they were to reside for six years (342–8).[3] This extensive property, comprising a grand palace surrounded by gardens and fountains (Sozom. v.2.9), ought to have provided a comfortable existence for the teenage princes; but Julian came to regard their spell there as nothing short of imprisonment ('we were watched as

---

[1] On Julian's sense of divinely inspired mission, see the 'autobiographical myth' in his *Or.* VII (*To the Cynic Heracleius*), 227c–234a.

The modern bibliography on Julian is headed by the classic work of Bidez (1965). See also Browning (1975), with rev. by Brown, *Society and the Holy* 83–102; Bowersock, *Julian*; Athanassiadi, *Julian*. On Julian's administrative measures, Pack (1986). There is much valuable information compactly presented in Lieu (1989). [2] For bishop Eusebius as a relative of Julian, see Amm. Marc. XXII.9.4.

[3] *Ep. ad Ath.* 271b–d. On the location of Macellum, Hadjinicolaou (1951). For Julian at Macellum, see further Bouffartigue (1992) 29–39.

though we were captives of the Persians'). The truth about this formative period of his life is beyond recall, lost in the polemic of Julian's admirers and detractors; from the perspective of Gregory of Nazianzus, for example, the sojourn at Macellum could be presented as the work of a humane Constantius bent on educating the young men for a future share in the empire (*Or.* IV.22). Certainly Julian, for his part, has exaggerated the isolation of these years of his 'glittering servitude'. Macellum was close by the main thoroughfare across Asia Minor linking Constantinople and Antioch, and is likely to have played host to a succession of officials and courtiers while the emperor was on the eastern front during the 340s; on one occasion Constantius himself stayed at Macellum while Julian was resident there (*Ep. ad Ath.* 274a). Nor was Julian, as he later asserted, 'excluded from all serious study'. It was a time when, inspired by Mardonius' teaching, he immersed himself in books: works of classical oratory and philosophy, as well as Christian writings, borrowed (and copies of them made) from the extensive library of George of Cappadocia, the churchman who would later be Athanasius' replacement as bishop of Alexandria. Julian did not forget the treasures of this library, and when later George met a violent end at the hands of a lynch-mob in Alexandria he sent orders to acquire George's books for himself (*Epp.* 106–7 Bidez). George, we may suggest, was bishop Eusebius' successor in the role of imperial 'minder', charged with the oversight of Julian's adolescence. The brothers' Christian upbringing – and instruction in the scriptures – extended to their being ordained into the junior ranks of the clergy as lectors (Greg. Naz. *Or.* IV.23); and they were also encouraged to appropriate displays of Christian piety, including the dedication of a new shrine to the local martyr St Mamas (Greg. Naz. *Or.* IV.24ff.; Sozom. V.9.12–13: a lesson in imperial patronage not lost on Gallus, who later as Caesar did the same for St Babylas at Antioch).

By 348 the brothers had returned to Constantinople, and Julian's educational horizons came to encompass the schools of grammar and rhetoric burgeoning in the new capital and in nearby Nicomedia.[4] It was at Nicomedia that Julian first encountered the teaching of Libanius (Lib. *Or.* XVIII.13; Socr. *HE* III.1.13). Libanius' own claim is that Julian was moved to Nicomedia on the orders of the emperor, for fear of his growing popularity in 'court circles' in the capital. There is no need, though, to invoke the suspicions of Constantius, when it is sufficient to conclude that the imperial pupil was most likely a target of fierce competition between the various luminaries of the schools, and moved from the capital just as Libanius himself had earlier been driven out to Nicomedia by his rivals. One of these, Hecebolius, pursued his vendetta to the point of endeavouring to deny Julian access to Libanius' teaching in Nicomedia – a pro-

---

[4] See e.g. Athanassiadi, *Julian*, 27ff.; Bouffartigue (1992) 39–42.

hibition which he circumvented by paying a copyist to make daily transcriptions of the lectures.

Julian remained at Nicomedia when his older brother was elevated to imperial rank in March 351; the two met as the new Caesar passed through the city *en route* to taking up his residence at Antioch (Lib. *Or.* XVIII.17). From his family's new-found public recognition – and from the fact that Constantius had other pressing preoccupations in the west – Julian gained more freedom of movement, and the opportunity to pursue his life of study further afield: he graduated to the schools of Neoplatonist philosophy which flourished in the cities of western Asia Minor.[5] He was first attracted to Pergamum by the reputation of the venerable Aedesius, who had himself been a pupil of Iamblichus and stood in direct continuity with the founding fathers of Neoplatonism in the previous century, Plotinus and Porphyry. The talk among Aedesius' own students was of the spectacular talents of one of their number, Maximus of Ephesus, who was a leading exponent of the supernatural version of contemporary Neoplatonism known as theurgy;[6] Julian listened in admiration to stories of the magical and miraculous means by which Maximus demonstrated his communion with the gods – how he so revered the goddess Hecate that he had brought her statue to life, made it smile and laugh, and even prevailed on the torches in her hands to burst into flames. Despite warnings against such showmanship from Aedesius' more rationally-minded students, Julian was captivated: 'farewell and devote yourselves to your books; you have shown me the man I was in search of'. He travelled to Ephesus, and found what was to be his true spiritual home among the protégés of Maximus, where he was initiated into the heady mix of religion, magic and spectacle which made up their exotic world. In retrospect, for Julian personally, it was to be his decisive break with Christianity, the moment when, in his own words, at the age of twenty he had begun to 'follow the right path in the company of the gods' (*Ep.* 111.434d Bidez). Opponents and adherents alike recognized that this was the occasion of his conversion: for Gregory of Nazianzus, Asia was the 'school of his impiety' (*Or.* IV.31), while Libanius interpreted Julian's introduction to the Neoplatonists as the time when 'with philosophy as his guide to truth he recognized the real gods instead of the false one' (*Or.* XII.33). Yet it remained a secret commitment, shared only with an intimate circle of devotees like Maximus. Libanius is carried away with the enthusiasm of hindsight when he goes on to claim that Julian's conversion was the 'beginning of freedom for the world' (*Or.* XII.34), and that pagans far and wide began to look forward to Julian's future rule 'with hidden prayers and

---

[5] For the narrative which follows, see Eunap. *V. Soph.* 473–5 (Loeb, pp. 428–34), with Bidez (1965) 67ff.; Athanassiadi, *Julian* 32ff.; Fowden (1982) 40–3; Matthews, *Ammianus* ch. 7; Bouffartigue (1992) 42–5. [6] See Dodds (1947); Bidez (1965) ch. 12; Fowden, *Egyptian Hermes* 126–31.

secret sacrifices' (Or. XIII.14).[7] In fact, in 351, although the movements of the emperor's cousin in Asia must have been public knowledge, there can have been no widespread awareness of his private apostasy, nor indeed any expectation of his imperial succession. To all appearances he returned to his functions as a lector in the church at Nicomedia (Socr. HE III.1.20), attending the lectures of his mentors and giving no inkling of any intention to follow his brother to a share of the throne.

If Julian harboured any such thoughts, then Gallus' deposition and execution late in 354 must have provoked some hesitation. There is no reason to disbelieve his protestations that he had no part in the events which led to his brother's downfall (Ep. ad Ath. 273a). They had exchanged letters, and Julian had received visits from Gallus' Christian emissary Aetius (despatched, it is said, because of the Caesar's growing concern about his younger brother's religious leanings),[8] but they were not in close contact – the imperial court at Antioch was a long way from the lecture halls of Nicomedia or the schools of Pergamum and Ephesus. Nevertheless Julian found himself summoned to Constantius in Milan to face accusations of complicity with the fallen Caesar. Seen from Constantius' perspective, the insubordination of Gallus inevitably cast suspicion around his surviving brother, and after arriving in Milan Julian was held 'under guard' (his own expression) for seven months, mostly in the nearby town of Comum; only once was he able to penetrate the protective wall of courtiers for an audience with the emperor.[9] His guardian angel in these anxious days turned out to be Constantius' empress Eusebia. At her intercession he was at last given safe conduct home and then, after a change of plan, granted permission to travel to Athens in the summer of 355 to resume his studies. It was a destination calculated both to be congenial to Julian's intellectual interests and to remove him to a safe distance from the political fall-out of Gallus' overthrow.

Julian's stay in Athens lasted only a matter of weeks ('a little while': Ep. ad Ath. 273d), yet it was to acquire for him a symbolic significance out of all proportion to its brevity.[10] Athens emerged as his 'true fatherland' (Or. III.118d), for which the years of study in the cities of Asia Minor had been mere preparation. When in 361 he came to compose a defence of his rebellion against Constantius, he would write to the Athenians as the 'fellow citizens of all the Greeks', proclaiming his special regard for their

---

[7] The once popular notion of a 'pagan underground' supporting Julian is dismissed by Drinkwater (1983) 348–60.

[8] So Philostorg. III.27 (ed. Bidez/Winkelmann, 53). For the letters, Lib. Or. XII.35, XVIII.25. (Philostorgius' mention of Aetius' missions generated a fictitious correspondence between Gallus and Julian: Ep. 82 Loeb.)

[9] Julian's own narrative is at Ep. ad Ath. 272d–274b. For the role of Eusebia, cf. Or. III.118b–c, and Amm. Marc. XV.2.8.

[10] See Bidez (1965) ch. 20; Athanassiadi, Julian, 46–51; Bouffartigue (1992) 45–8.

city (*Ep. ad Ath.* 287c–d). Back in 355 Julian was one of the throng of his social peers, Christian and non-Christian alike, who were 'finishing' their higher education in rhetoric and philosophy in Athens, and enjoying the camaraderie of the university city.[11] Among Julian's contemporaries in Athens were future Christian bishops (Basil of Caesarea, Gregory of Nazianzus), and many others destined for distinguished careers in secular office.[12] In such company the emperor's cousin was inevitably a focus of attention ('there was always a swarm to be seen around him': Lib. *Or.* XVIII.29). He was certainly noticed by Gregory of Nazianzus, whose hostile portrait of Julian as emperor (*Or.* v.23) owed much to the impression of his wild intensity which Gregory had gained from their student encounters in Athens. Julian also sought out those likely to be sympathetic to the kind of religious commitment he had undertaken at Ephesus. At Athens this led him into a lasting friendship with Priscus, another of Aedesius' pupils who, like Maximus, would come to share Julian's company at the imperial court and on his final campaign;[13] meanwhile the attractions of ritual initiation sampled at Ephesus now brought Julian to the great shrine at Eleusis, where the chief priest admitted him to the sacred mysteries of Demeter (Eunap. *V. Soph.* 475–6, Loeb pp. 436–8). We may readily believe that in Julian's case this counted as rather more than a conventional gesture.

These opportunities to indulge his religious tastes in the company of like-minded souls in Athens were cut short by a further summons to Constantius' court in Milan. The floods of tears and supplications to Athene which Julian poured out on his departure (*Ep. ad Ath.* 275a–b) were perhaps no more than the normal ritual of student farewells (Basil of Caesarea left Athens in tears too: Greg. Naz. *Or.* XLIII.24). Yet there were also real grounds for anxiety about returning to face an emperor and his court who – forewarned by the experience with his brother – had so far preferred to isolate him in the garb of a student rather than recognize his imperial status. Nor was Julian's situation, it might seem, made any easier in the autumn of 355 by the tense atmosphere in Milan resulting from Silvanus' recent short-lived rebellion across the Alps. But this second rebellion in Gaul, following soon after that of Magnentius, proved also to be Julian's opportunity. The childless emperor now found a use for his young cousin, as a dynastic lieutenant to win over insecure provinces and restore breached frontiers – and there was no need this time for the intercessions

---

[11] On the intellectual life of Athens in this period, see (briefly) Fowden (1982) 43–5. For camaraderie, cf. Greg. Naz. on the experience of Basil: *Or.* XLIII.14–16.

[12] e.g. Libanius' pupil Celsus, future governor of Cilicia and Syria: Amm. Marc. XXII.9.3, with *PLRE* 1.193–4.

[13] See Julian's correspondence with Priscus, *Epp.* 11–13 Bidez; and Lib. *Or.* XII.55 on the 'philosopher from Athens'.

of Eusebia.[14] Julian and his admirers might be at pains to stress his reluctance to forsake a life of study ('his intention was to live and die in Athens': Lib. *Or.* XVIII.31) to assume the burdens of the Caesarship in dutiful obedience to his emperor; nevertheless it was this moment of 'yielding' (*Ep. ad Ath.* 277a) which was Julian's passport into imperial office, and set him on the road which he came to believe the gods intended him to follow.[15]

II. CAESAR IN GAUL

Julian arrived at Vienne for his first winter in Gaul with a modest personal entourage (only four attendants, on his own testimony, besides his close friend and physician Oribasius: *Ep. ad Ath.* 277b–d) and a military escort of 360 soldiers (Zos. III.3.2).[16] His initial campaigning season of 356 took him northwards via Autun (which he reached on 24 June), Auxerre and Troyes to Rheims, where he met the main Gallic field army under the command of the *magister equitum* Marcellus (Silvanus' destroyer, Ursicinus, also remained for the time being seconded to the high command in Gaul). As the emperor's deputy, Julian now took the field on the march eastwards to the territory along the Rhine which was in the hands of the Alamanni – and his forces were able to recapture Brumath (north of Strasbourg) after inflicting a military defeat on the barbarians (XVI.2). This was followed up by a bold advance down river and the successful recovery of Cologne from the Franks (XVI.3), only some ten months (Jul. *Ep. ad Ath.* 279b) after it had been seized. Julian returned to the interior of Gaul to winter at Sens, having distributed the majority of the troops around other towns to provide local protection from the continuing barbarian raids (XVI.4.1, cf. *Ep. ad Ath.* 278b). In so doing, the Caesar, it transpired, left himself exposed to attack, and he and the small force he retained had to endure a month-long siege within the walls of Sens. When report reached Constantius of the danger in which his Caesar had been placed, and the generals' failure to send reinforcements, Marcellus and Ursicinus were ordered back to Milan, and a new *magister equitum*, Severus, was posted to the Gallic command (XVI.10.21).

Such a bare narrative has to be extracted from a 'Julianic' source tradition which dwells with heavy emphasis on the undue restrictions which Constantius laid upon his Caesar, and on the uncooperativeness of the emperor's commanders, as well as making the most of barbarian inroads into Roman territory (to enhance the glory of Julian's initial successes).

---

[14] Julian is explicit that on this occasion he did not approach Eusebia: *Ep. ad Ath.* 273b–d, cf. *Or.* III.121b. [15] For Julian's investiture as Caesar, see pp. 28–9 above.

[16] For a brisk account of Julian's activities in Gaul, see Bowersock, *Julian* 33–45, together with Matthews, *Ammianus* 87ff. (Unattributed references from this point on in the text are to the books of Ammianus.)

Certainly Julian was harried by many enemy raids when he first moved
north from Vienne, and the area of Sens was evidently vulnerable to attack;
but the impression that the Germans were rampaging unchecked and – as
he later affirmed – had 'created a desert' (*Ep. ad Ath.* 279a–b) deep into
Gaul surely betrays some rhetorical exaggeration. More significant, though,
is Julian's misrepresentation of his position as Caesar in relation to
Constantius and the existing military establishment in Gaul. Parading the
emblems of imperial rule – a task which Julian presented as a restrictive
limitation of his activities (*Ep. ad Ath.* 278a, d; cf. Lib. *Or.* XVIII.42) – was
in fact the very *raison d'être* of his presence beyond the Alps: in Constantius'
eyes Julian's role was, precisely, to personify the ruling dynasty in a fractious
region of the empire. Moreover, the ill-fated experience of Gallus had
given Constantius every reason to issue precise instructions to circumscribe the conduct of the untried Julian, and reinforce the authority of his
own military commanders – they were sent letters with orders to watch
over him (*Ep. ad Ath.* 277d), and Constantius even despatched a *libellus* in
his own hand (XVI.5.3) specifying such details as the amount to be spent on
the Caesar's food (a document likely to have provided less congenial reading for Julian than the 'books of philosophers, historians, orators and
poets' (*Or.* III.124a) which the empress Eusebia gave him on his departure
for Gaul). The actions which Julian dismissed as obstructiveness on the
part of Marcellus and others in fact represented their attempts at obeying
the emperor's orders, coupled with resentment at what they perceived as
Julian's usurping of their established authority. It was this personal and
institutional tension between Caesar and generals which resulted in Julian
being left to withstand the siege of Sens unaided. Constantius, it should be
noted, actually accepted his Caesar's version of this episode, and went on
to make changes to the high command in Gaul which met with Julian's
approval. Julian probably exaggerates in claiming that from 357 he was
accorded full command of the army (*Ep. ad Ath.* 278d), since Constantius
continued to appoint the generals; none the less, the new *magister equitum*
Severus evidently had a much more harmonious relationship with the
Caesar than his predecessor had enjoyed (XVI.11.1).

However much Constantius' interests dictated that his Caesar's independence should be curbed, the whole logic of Julian's appointment was
that emperor and Caesar had to be seen to be dynastic partners in rule, and
co-operating in the defence of Gaul.[17] While Julian presided over an attack
on the Alamanni from the west, Constantius' generals also bore down upon
them over the Alps from northern Italy. Some such 'pincer' manoeuvre had
already occurred in 356, but is more fully documented for the following

---

[17] Cf. Bowersock, *Julian* 39: 'there can be no doubt that outwardly the emperor and his Caesar were
working harmoniously together'.

year, when the *magister peditum*, Barbatio, amassed an army of 25,000 at Kaiseraugst to attack the enemy from the south in concert with Julian's resumed offensive from the interior of Gaul. In the event, the two armies failed to co-ordinate the assault, and Barbatio's forces were driven back by the Alamanni (XVI.11; cf. Lib. *Or*. XVIII.49ff.). So much is apparent from accounts which again betray the distortions of a Julianic viewpoint, blaming Barbatio's supposed inbuilt resentment against the Caesar for the failure to combine their forces. Some resentment in fact may not have been out of place, for it was Julian, it appears, who, by diverting his troops against other enemy targets elsewhere on the Rhine, left the *magister peditum* isolated and exposed to attack.[18]

This high-handed neglect of co-operative strategy paved the way (perhaps was intended to) for Julian's 'finest hour' in Gaul – his victorious confrontation with the massed confederation of Alamanni, under their leader Chnodomarius (together with six other kings), at the battle of Strasbourg. Without Barbatio's 25,000 men, he faced an enemy confident in their numerical superiority (Julian was said to have an army of 13,000, facing 35,000 of the Alamanni: XVI.12.2, 26) and encouraged by the defeat newly inflicted on Barbatio. It was a reckless move, and even Julian contemplated the wisdom of delay, only to be overruled by the enthusiasm of his men and the eagerness of the senior officials around him. The claim that Julian had to be persuaded into an encounter which he had done so much to provoke carries little conviction – but the glory of victory was all the greater for seeming to stem from the urgings of others, and not least from the favour of the gods (XVI.12.13–14). Yet the battle of Strasbourg was undeniably a personal triumph for the Caesar with only one year's campaigning experience behind him. Julian's own account of the conflict is lost to us, and the principal surviving narrative in the pages of Ammianus is an epic vehicle for the heroic exploits of the central character, at the expense of a clear record of the conflict (or of the activities of the other commanders).[19] But the outcome is clear. Routed on the field of battle, the defeated Alamanni were driven back into the Rhine, their casualties numbered in thousands in stark contrast to the tally of 243 victims precisely recorded for the Roman side (XVI.12.63).

Nor was this the end of the year's campaigning (XVII.1–2). Julian now moved down river and took the fight into Alamannic territory opposite Mainz, forcing the surrender of three more kings. His return to winter quarters was then delayed by a diversion to dislodge a band of Franks who had seized possession of two disused forts on the river Meuse. It was not until January of 358 that these hectic operations were brought to an end

---

[18] The interpretation of Austin (1979) 56–60, favoured by Matthews, *Ammianus* 299.

[19] See Blockley (1977). For Julian's βιβλίδιον, see Eunap. fr. 17 Blockley (Lib. *Or*. XIII.25 and *Ep*. 38.6 Loeb allude more generally to narratives of the Gallic campaigns).

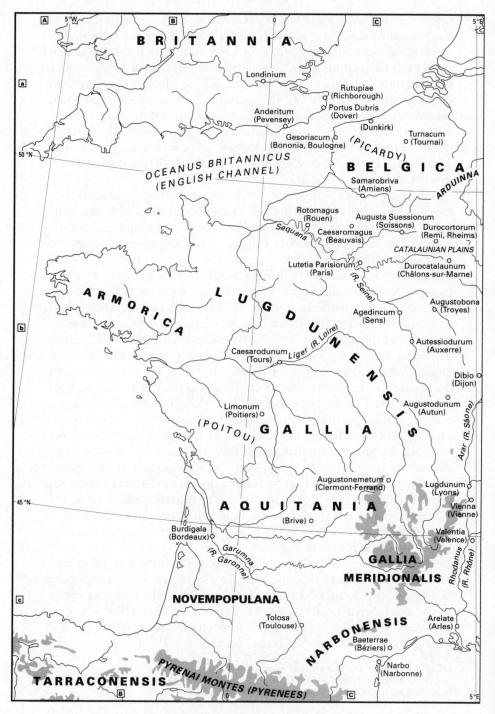

Map 2 Gaul and the German frontier

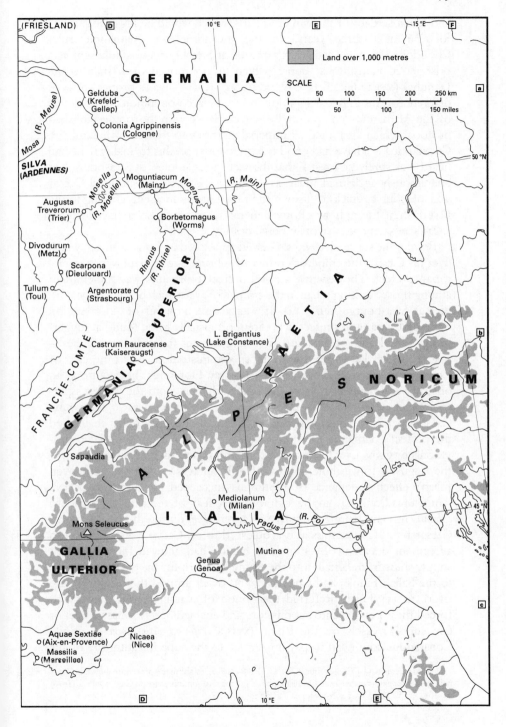

(FRIESLAND)

GERMANIA

Land over 1,000 metres

SCALE
0   50   100   150   200   250 km
0   50   100   150 miles

Mosa (R. Meuse)

SILVA (ARDENNES)

Gelduba (Krefeld-Gellep)

Colonia Agrippinensis (Cologne)

Moguntiacum (Mainz)

Moenus (R. Main)

Mosella (R. Moselle)

Augusta Treverorum (Trier)

Borbetomagus (Worms)

Divodurum (Metz)

Scarpona (Dieulouard)

Rhenus (R. Rhine)

Tullum (Toul)

Argentorate (Strasbourg)

GERMANIA SUPERIOR

FRANCHE-COMTÉ

Castrum Rauracense (Kaiseraugst)

L. Brigantius (Lake Constance)

RAETIA

ALPES

NORICUM

Sapaudia

Mediolanum (Milan)

ITALIA

Padus (R. Po)

Mons Seleucus

GALLIA ULTERIOR

Genua (Genoa)

Mutina

Aquae Sextiae (Aix-en-Provence)

Nicaea (Nice)

Massilia (Marseilles)

and Julian settled for the winter at Paris, which would be his headquarters for the next three years. In the meantime the Alamannic ruler Chnodomarius, who had been captured at Strasbourg, was duly sent as a prisoner to Constantius' court (which in 357 moved from Italy to the Danube) (XVI.12.66; cf. Lib. *Or.* XVIII.66). It was Julian's proper show of deference to his imperial superior and to their 'co-operation' in the defeat of the Alamanni – and pointedly in accordance with the long-established protocol which attributed all imperial victories to the senior incumbent. Constantius will have had good reason to insist on this formality if he had heard – as surely he must – that the victorious soldiers at Strasbourg had unanimously acclaimed Julian as Augustus (XVI.12.64). The loyal Caesar was, of course, quick to disown the title; but the incident, coming in the first flush of triumph over Rome's enemies, can hardly fail to have fostered Julian's awakening sense of imperial destiny.

Besides the successive *magistri militum* appointed by Constantius to watch over his Caesar, the emperor's principal subordinate in Gaul was the praetorian prefect. The recently arrived prefect Florentius was pre-eminent among those advising Julian in the council of war which preceded the conflict at Strasbourg (XVI.12.14). It was a rare moment of co-operation between Caesar and prefect, who are more usually to be found at loggerheads over levels of taxation or arrangements for military supplies – matters which lay within the prefect's administration. As in the case of Constantius' generals, Julian would portray Florentius' behaviour as an obstructive vendetta (*Ep. ad Ath.* 282c); whereas from the prefect's perspective it is not hard to imagine a sense of resentment at the young Caesar's perceived interference in his sphere of authority. Julian challenged the prefect's demands for supplementary taxation from the Gallic provincials by going over his head to Constantius, and successfully persuading the Augustus to withhold approval for the increases (XVII.3);[20] moreover, Julian's effective defiance of Florentius succeeded, if we are to believe Ammianus (XVI.5.14), in the 'extraordinary feat' of reducing the standard *capitatio* in Gaul from twenty-five to seven *solidi* during the period of his Caesarship.[21] Constantius also acquiesced in his Caesar's disregard of an agreement drawn up by Florentius which had allowed the passage of supply ships from Britain into the Rhine in return for the payment of fees to the Salian Franks and Chamavi (who dwelt around the mouth of the river): in 358 Julian preferred the option of a military offensive which forced these peoples into submission, and enabled him to amass a fleet of 600 supply vessels on the Rhine (XVII.8; *Ep. ad Ath.* 280a–c). While Constantius continued to pay lip-service to the superior authority of his

---

[20] Two recent laws of Constantius, *C.Th.* XI.16.7–8 (356–7), establish the procedure requiring imperial consent for extra tax demands. On all aspects of Julian's civil administration in Gaul, see Pack (1986) 62–103.   [21] The phrase is from Jones, *LRE* 120.

praetorian prefect over the civilian administration of Gaul,[22] he had his own experience of earlier campaigning against the Alamanni to tell him of the supply difficulties inherent in the division of responsibilities between military commanders and the praetorian prefecture (XIV.10.2–5); and in any event a clash of authority between Caesar and prefect might have been predicted from Gallus' ill-fated regime at Antioch. The tone of the Julianic record should not, then, be allowed to obscure the fact that, in these conflicts with Florentius, Constantius sided with his Caesar (as in the confrontations with the generals) in the interests of a united imperial front. Nor was the lesson lost on the praetorian prefect: at least by the campaigning season of 359 Florentius was co-operating in the war-effort, and ensuring plentiful supplies for Julian's troops (XVIII.2.4).

After the triumphant Strasbourg campaign, the following years (358–9) saw Julian mount two further expeditions across the Rhine to ravage the land and villages of the Alamanni, and force the submission of more of their rulers (XVII.10, XVIII.2). Roman captives were restored, and Rhine forts destroyed only a few years previously were rebuilt with the aid of wagons and materials supplied by the newly defeated kings. By 359 Julian's forces were able to penetrate deep into enemy territory, reaching the remnants of the old *limes* which had marked the extent of Roman power in its Antonine heyday, and providing an unfamiliar sight of Roman arms for more distant cantons of the Alamanni: one of their rulers, Macrianus, 'was amazed at the variety and splendour of the weapons and forces' (XVIII.2.17). Over four years of warfare against the Germans, Julian claims the recapture of 'almost forty' towns, and the taking of 10,000 prisoners (*Ep. ad Ath.* 280c–d); while his panegyrists applaud the civic revival of Gaul occasioned by the combination of frontier reconstruction and a benevolent tax regime (Lib. *Or.* XVIII.80–1; *Pan. Lat.* III(XI).4–5). For them, Julian's presence in Gaul was the incarnation of all the martial and civilian virtues – and an accumulation of success which aroused only envy in the senior emperor, contemplating renewed Persian inroads into Mesopotamia and the loss of Amida at the very time when his Caesar's achievements were reaching their climax.[23] Yet it would be false to regard the attitude ascribed to Constantius, and supposedly encouraged by his subservient courtiers, as merely a literary foil to the eulogizing which attended Julian's role in Gaul. In reality the Caesar's successful, perhaps too successful, accomplishment of the imperial task in the west was a mixed blessing for Constantius. Although, as we have seen, he had publicly maintained support for his precocious deputy, none the less he had also sought to restrict Julian's access to funds to reward his victorious soldiers (significantly the one area where

---

[22] He advised Julian 'not to interfere so as to seem to discredit Florentius' (XVII.3.5).

[23] For Constantius' 'envy', see Lib. *Or.* XVIII.90; Zos. III.5.3; the same reaction is implied by Ammianus, XX.4.1.

the Augustus does seem to have obstructed the actions of his Caesar:
XVII.9.6, XXII.3.7) – a prudent precaution in a region of the empire which
had already produced two imperial pretenders in a decade. For his part
Julian in a speech (358) ostensibly praising Constantius had given voice to
a Hellenic ideal of kingship capable of being read as a programme for his
own rule;[24] and he shared with members of his immediate entourage (led
by Oribasius) his intimations that he himself was destined some day to sup-
plant Constantius.[25] In contrast to the emperor's subordinates with whom
Julian crossed swords in Gaul, his own inner circle of pagan associates –
together with the local military élite whose loyalties came to focus on their
successful Caesar[26] – were given encouragement to look to future
prospects under a Julianic regime. Not surprisingly, Julian's destiny was hastened on its way by those who stood to profit most from its fulfilment.

III. PROCLAMATION AT PARIS

These submerged currents were brought to the surface by the arrival in
Gaul, in February 360, of Constantius' *notarius* Decentius, with orders for
the removal to the east of substantial numbers of troops (xx.4.2–3): four
auxiliary regiments, together with contingents of 300 men from the rest of
the units in the field army, and the best men from two of the guard corps
serving with Julian – in all, perhaps as much as a third to a half of the army
in Gaul.[27] Such projected troop movements need to be seen in the context
of Constantius' heightened response to the renewed Persian aggression in
Mesopotamia; yet they cannot but recall the similar withdrawal of soldiers
which had been the prelude to the deposition of the Caesar Gallus, and
reflect a concern on the part of the senior emperor at his Caesar's increasingly independent power-base in Gaul. Constantius' officials, chiefly the
prefect Florentius, had not neglected to keep the emperor informed of
develoments in Gaul, so much so that Julian and his apologists were later
to blame Florentius directly for the order to transfer the troops (*Ep. ad Ath.*
282c; xx.4.2, 7). The arrival of Decentius was a sharp reminder of the subordinate nature of Julian's rank as Caesar. Despite four years as the imper-

[24] On Julian's second panegyric to Constantius, see Athanassiadi, *Julian* 63–6.
[25] So Julian's confiding to Oribasius the details of a dream portending the overthrow of Constantius: *Ep.* 14.384a–c Bidez. Oribasius' name also occurs prominently in Eunapius' tale of secret rites aimed at 'the destruction of the tyranny of Constantius': *V. Soph.* 476 (Loeb, pp. 438–40). Cf. *V. Soph.* 498 (Loeb, p. 532), where Eun. declares that Oribasius 'made Julian emperor'.
[26] Drinkwater (1983) 370ff. highlights the role of the pagan entourage – and the suspicions being aroused are reflected in Constantius' recall of Julian's associate Salutius in 359 (*Ep. ad Ath.* 282c; Lib. *Or.* XVIII.85–6; Zos. III.5.3) – but it was no less the Gallic commanders who stood to gain from Julian's seizure of power.
[27] For discussion of numbers, see Szidat (1977) 141. On the whole episode of the usurpation, see Matthews, *Ammianus* 93–100; Drinkwater (1983) 370ff. For varying details in the sources, see Bowersock, *Julian* ch. 5.

ial representative in the west at the forefront of success against the
Alamanni, he was still at the mercy of reports passing between prefect and
emperor; and when the order for troop movements arrived, it was
addressed not to Julian in his quarters at Paris but to those of Constantius'
commanders who had direct charge of the soldiers concerned – the *magister equitum* Lupicinus (who had recently succeeded Severus) and one of the
palatine officers, Sintula. Disregarding Julian's protests, Sintula obeyed his
emperor's instructions and set off eastwards with his picked men from the
guards; the transfer of the field army troops, on the other hand, was
delayed by the absence of Lupicinus (with some of the regiments involved)
on campaign in Britain. Julian professes that he dutifully sought to facilitate compliance with Constantius' orders, and emphasizes his deference to
the authority of both Lupicinus and the prefect Florentius (*Ep. ad Ath.*
283a, c):[28] it was an inconvenient coincidence, on this version of events,
that when Decentius arrived, both men were elsewhere, Lupicinus in Britan
and Florentius (ostensibly organizing supplies) in Vienne (xx.4.6, 8.20). Yet
Julian's insistence on his efforts at this juncture to co-operate with
Constantius' senior personnel lacks some credibility, when he was more
often given to complaining of their obstructiveness; and there is a hint of
suspicion surrounding the absence of Florentius, who previously appears
regularly at Julian's side.[29] At any event, in the absence of the high
command, Julian himself made a show of hastening the despatch of
troops, to forestall (so it was claimed) a growing mood of disaffection being
fuelled by the circulation of anonymous letters among the rank and file
(xx.4.10; cf. *Ep. ad Ath.* 283b; Zos. iii.9.1): the regiments to be transferred
were massed at the outskirts of Paris to hear an address from Julian urging
them on their way, and their senior officers shared his dinner-table
(xx.4.13). Far from obedience to the emperor's orders, however, the
outcome was rebellion. Soldiers clamouring for Julian surrounded his quarters during the night and acclaimed him their Augustus. At daybreak Julian
emerged in an ineffective show of resistance, eventually consenting to their
demands (in contrast to his refusal after Strasbourg). Amid the shouts, he
was raised aloft on a shield, and a standard-bearer of the Petulantes
contributed his torque as a makeshift imperial diadem. The first act of their
new-found ruler was the traditional promise of his accession donative, five
gold *solidi* and a pound of silver for each man (xx.4.17–19).

This Paris proclamation displays some of the classic ingredients of a late
Roman usurpation – the fomenting of discontent, the assembling of
troops, the officers' dinner party, the parading in imperial garb. Julian was

[28] It was not, it is fair to observe, the first occasion on which he had contributed reinforcements to
Constantius: *Ep. ad Ath.* 280d.
[29] Ammianus (xx.4.6, 8.20) sees Florentius' absence as a tactical withdrawal forced on him by the
prospect of a military uprising.

hardly the innocent bystander that he protested himself to be, swept along by spontaneous and uncontrollable forces. His profession of innocence and his reference to the 'work of the gods' are naturally designed to conceal any responsibility of his own for what happened (*Ep. ad Ath.* 282d, 284b); but even if the initiative did not lie directly with Julian himself, Oribasius and that intimate circle with whom he was in the habit of sharing his divine communications surely took the hint,[30] while loyal officers seized the opportunity afforded by the advent of Decentius and his controversial orders. Julian would be confirmed in the conviction that he was merely executing the will of the gods by the 'breathing-space' which Constantius' preoccupations in the east conveniently provided. His attempts at negotiation met with no more than diplomatic rebukes from the senior emperor in the months which followed (xx.8–9), allowing him the freedom to play the role of Augustus in Gaul. The guard units which had earlier set off eastwards were recalled, and the rest of the army stayed put under its new emperor (xx.5.1). Of Constantius' erstwhile subordinates, Lupicinus found himself isolated in Britain and arrested when he set foot back in Gaul (xx.9.9; cf. *Ep. ad Ath.* 281a), while Florentius, confronted by a new ruler in his prefecture, fled across the Alps (xx.8.21). Julian took the opportunity to reward his Gallic supporters ('whose deserts and loyalty he knew': xxi.8.1) by making his own senior appointments, regardless of replacements made by Constantius (xx.9.8, xxi.1.4). The summer of 360 saw a three-month campaign across the lower Rhine against the Atthuarian Franks ('who recalled that no previous emperor had ever invaded their territory'), followed by a march up river as far as Kaiseraugst, before Julian returned to winter at Vienne (xx.10; cf. Jul. *Ep.* 26.414b Bidez). Here, in the city which had first acclaimed his arrival in Gaul as Caesar, he provided games in celebration of the *quinquennium* of his rule (6 November 360), now openly parading the regalia of a reigning Augustus (xxi.1.4). One facet alone of Julian's rebellion remained hidden from public view: still in the guise of the Christian ruler which he had maintained throughout his years in Gaul (only his closest associates were party to his apostasy), he led the celebration of the feast of Epiphany at Vienne in January 361 (xxi.2.4–5).

This provocative display as Augustus in Gaul signalled the end of the diplomatic stalemate with Constantius. It was an open challenge to his superior, further aggravated in the spring of 361 by Julian's arrest of the Alamannic ruler Vadomarius (xxi.3–4), who could lay claim to an earlier treaty of alliance with Constantius (struck in 354). Julian accorded much propagandist publicity to the allegation that Constantius was encouraging Vadomarius' Alamanni to raid the borders of Raetia, producing letters

---

[30] Note Ammianus' report (xx.5.10) of Julian's vision 'in the night before he was proclaimed Augustus' of a figure representing the *genius* of the Roman state, an experience which he shared 'with his most intimate friends'.

purporting to be those exchanged between emperor and barbarian chieftain.[31] It was the prelude to the military advance against Constantius. After the action against Vadomarius, Julian rallied the troops at Kaiseraugst, and sent them off eastwards into Pannonia under his own newly appointed commanders from Gaul. The advance was split into three divisions, the bulk of the forces forming two columns through the north of Italy and through Raetia/Noricum, while Julian himself with a retinue of 3000 men took boats down the Danube (xxi.8; Zos. iii.10.1–2). By the middle of the summer a triumphant reception was welcoming him to the city of Sirmium (xxi.10.1).[32] To the orator Mamertinus, a member of Julian's entourage, this progress down river was one continuous and stately *adventus* (*Pan. Lat.* iii(xi).7). In fact it was a hurried and, where possible, secret advance which bypassed the main strongholds and gave Julian the advantage of speed and surprise over those of Constantius' forces left to defend Illyricum (xxi.9.5–7).[33] Pausing only to entertain the grateful populace of Sirmium with a day's races, Julian moved on to establish a vanguard at the pass of Succi on the borders of Thrace (xxi.10.2). With the pass secured under the command of his *magister equitum* Nevitta, he returned to base himself at Naissus, and await news of Constantius' movements further east.

This apparently effortless occupation of Illyricum, the triumphal progress of the new Augustus, was merely the veneer of a more insecure reality. For Julian, now embarked on civil war, Illyricum was 'enemy territory', which only two years previously had seen Constantius himself resident at Sirmium and successfully campaigning on the Danube front. Two legions which Constantius had left at Sirmium Julian now ordered back to Gaul, only to have them seize possession of Aquileia in Constantius' name and threaten a blockade of the Julian Alps, which would have isolated Julian from his support in the west. Troops had to be diverted to lay siege to Aquileia (xxi.11–12). At Naissus Julian was caught between this emergency and the prospect of his rival's armies advancing from the east (Constantius left Antioch in late autumn) to confront him at Succi.[34] Nor was it only a matter of doubtful military loyalties, for the civilian population around Aquileia, led by some of the city's *curiales*, also joined in the uprising against Julian (xxi.11.2, 12.20). Against such a threatening background, Julian used his stay at Naissus, the city of Constantine's birth and the place which in more recent days had witnessed the overthrow of the pretender Vetranio and the launch of the war against Magnentius, to engage in a diplomatic

---

[31] *Ep. ad Ath.* 286a; Lib. *Or.* xviii.107. Socr. *HE* iii.1.38 reports that the letters were 'read in the cities'.

[32] On the chronology of Julian's advance to Sirmium, see Paschoud's discussion in his Budé edition of Zosimus, iii, pp. 92–4, and Nixon (1991).

[33] The speed of Julian's advance is also stressed by Lib. *Or.* xviii.111 and Greg. Naz. *Or.* iv.47; for the secrecy, note Amm. Marc. xxi.9.2.

[34] For Julian's military dilemma, see Amm. Marc. xxi.12.21–2, and Greg, Naz. *Or.* iv.48.

and propaganda offensive aimed at legitimizing his rule: in this strongly dynastic context Julian stressed his own imperial legacy, into which the gods were summoning him.[35] From Naissus he penned a group of letters in defence of his conduct, addressed to various cities in Greece (of which only that to the Athenians survives in its entirety), and to the senators of Rome: this latter communication, when read in the senate house, provoked a hostile reaction, demanding respect for Constantius (XXI.10.7). It was probably, then, more than conventional courtesy which impelled Julian to pay court to two senior senators (one of them the elder Symmachus) who passed through Naissus on their way back from an embassy to Constantius (XXI.12.24). Whatever Julian's confidence in the outcome of the expected contest, the military and diplomatic odds as he waited in the Balkans were not on his side.

IV. CONSTANTINOPLE

In November two imperial *comites* arrived at Julian's headquarters bearing the news of Constantius' death in Cilicia. With his dying words, so report had it, he had named his cousin as his successor, thus saving the Roman empire from the civil war which threatened.[36] Fate's intervention transformed a usurper into the sole Augustus, and a march which had begun with secret offerings to the old gods (XXI.5.1) now proceeded under the public auspices of restored pagan worship: 'we openly honour the gods', Julian triumphantly declared to his mentor Maximus (*Ep.* 26.415c Bidez), inviting him to join the imperial retinue. In thus confirming his destiny, the gods, Julian might well reflect, had opportunely rescued him from a military clash he was unlikely to have won, and with Constantius safely dead he could afford a magnanimous display of loyalty.[37] The new emperor was now at liberty, as the protocol of orderly succession demanded, to project the appropriate image of respect for his predecessor which the Roman senate had urged on him. Thus, after the formalities of his ceremonial *adventus* into Constantinople on 11 December (XXII.2.4), Julian's first political act (despite the apostasy which he had publicly displayed before the army at Naissus) was to preside at Constantius' Christian burial: humbly divested of his imperial regalia, he escorted the body from the harbour to its resting-place alongside Constantine at the Church of the Apostles.[38]

[35] On this background to Julian's stay in Naissus, see Kaegi (1975).

[36] Ammianus attributes the designation of Julian as Constantius' successor both to rumour (XXI.15.2, 5) and to the official announcement by the *comites* (XXII.2.1); it is legitimate to suspect that the report emanated from Julian's camp.

[37] As in the letter written at this time to his uncle Julianus (*Ep.* 28 Bidez), affirming that he had gone to war against Constantius only because the gods ordained it.

[38] On Julian's participation in Constantius' funeral, see *Pan. Lat.* III(XI).27.5; Lib. *Or.* XVIII.120; and, from a less generous perspective, Greg. Naz. *Or.* V.16–17.

Such a display of dynastic solidarity was calculated not only to advertise Julian's new-found legitimacy, but also to help dispel some of the ambiguities surrounding his arrival in Constantinople. To his admirers, and on the lips of the customary embassies of congratulation from elsewhere in the east, Julian's advent was that of a god-given ruler.[39] Yet he was entering a capital which, although his own birthplace,[40] had come to embody the legacy of Constantine: Constantius had added significantly to its buildings, and had given Constantinople its new and largely Christian ruling élite; and now Julian's *adventus* as Augustus risked being overshadowed by that of Constantius' body, accompanied by the troops who had been following him in expectation of victory against a usurper, and greeted by a population in mourning.[41] It was a situation which demanded from Julian more than a mere display of legitimacy; he had actively to cultivate the support of military and civilian classes in the east who clung to the memory of his dead rival.

Soon after Julian's arrival in Constantinople a judicial tribunal was constituted at Chalcedon across the Bosphorus, which proceeded to convict a succession of high-ranking figures from Constantius' regime (XXII.3). The victims included not only the more notorious agents of the previous government – such as Constantius' seemingly all-powerful chamberlain Eusebius – but also some of its most senior personnel: two former praetorian prefects (Taurus and Florentius), the current *magister officiorum* (another Florentius), and both the *comes rei privatae* (Evagrius) and *comes sacrarum largitionum* (Ursulus). Julian's apologists were hard put to defend such reprisals: the fate of Ursulus, in particular, caused Ammianus to bemoan the denial of justice to a finance minister who had actually stood out against Constantius' attempts to deny funds to Julian in Gaul (XXII.3.7).[42] But Ursulus' condemnation, as that of the other civilian ministers of Constantius, was really determined (Ammianus was forced to admit) by the hostility of the military hierarchy, who had occasion to resent Ursulus' well-publicized views on the high costs of the army (cf. XX.11.5). Faced by a soldiery and senior officers whom he needed to conciliate, Julian was not his own master at Chalcedon.[43] Significantly, for an emperor normally eager to involve himself in the administration of justice, he was not even present, leaving the proceedings to be watched over by his newly appointed praetorian prefect (and old ally in Gaul) Secundus Salutius. Yet of Salutius' five assistants only one was another civilian, Mamertinus

[39] For congratulatory embassies, see Eunap. fr. 24 Blockley, with *Misop.* 367c–d.

[40] XXII.9.2, with Zos. III.11.2–3: on Zosimus' exaggeration of Julian's interest in Constantinople, see Paschoud *ad loc.*

[41] Greg. Naz., *loc. cit.*, stresses the compulsion on Julian to honour the dead emperor.

[42] Lib. *Or.* XVIII.153 attempts to exonerate Julian.

[43] A point stressed by sources hostile to Julian: Greg. Naz. *Or.* IV.64; Socr. *HE* III.1.43ff. On the political background to the Chalcedon trials, see Thompson (1947) 73–9, and Kaegi (1967).

prefect of Illyricum; the rest were generals, including Constantius' two most senior military men, Arbetio and Agilo, and the trials took place in the presence of officers from palatine regiments (XXII.3.2). In remaining aloof from Chalcedon, Julian was in fact seeking to distance himself from a military court bent on vengeance against the previous government, and over which he had little control. One of the judges, Mamertinus, in his speech of thanks for his consulship in January 362, counted it among the praises of Julian that he was held in affection by the entire army (*Pan. Lat.* III(XI).24.6); but the Chalcedon episode suggests that any credit gained with Constantius' former troops in the east came only at the price of acceding to the will of their commanders.

There were constraints, too, on Julian's religious measures in the city of Constantine, and across eastern provinces which had become acclimatized to two generations of Christian rule. In the confines of the imperial palace he was at liberty to indulge his personal enthusiasm for participation in pagan sacrifices and have his own domestic shrine to the sun god (Lib. *Or.* XII.80–2, XVIII.127), as well as surround himself (as he had begun to do in Gaul) with a retinue of like-minded associates: invitations went out to religious intimates and intellectual peers to join him at court.[44] But the world beyond could not so easily be reshaped in Julian's image. The emperor issued orders to restore and reopen temples and lift the ban on sacrifices, and dismantle the privileged status which Christians had come to enjoy (XXII.5.2, Lib. *Or.* XVIII.126);[45] while imperial communications with the provinces now showed favour to those cities which demonstrated a commitment to the old gods, and penalized communities which were predominantly Christian.[46] Julian loudly proclaimed his preference for persuasion over the use of force in his dealings with Christians;[47] yet this philanthropy was surely a virtue born of necessity. It is hard to see what other course was open to him in a world where there were in practice severe limitations on the enforcement of any emperor's will, let alone one set on overturning the religious legacy of his predecessors in the heartlands where it was most entrenched. His much-vaunted 'toleration' in granting an amnesty to bishops exiled by Constantius, and exhorting Christian factions in Constantinople to settle their differences, offers an instructive revelation of the realities of Julian's position.[48] Clothed in lofty sentiments of religious freedom, the amnesty no doubt concealed an underlying intention to weaken the standing of Christianity in eastern cities with congregations

---

[44] So *Epp.* 26, 29, 33, 34, 41, 46 Bidez.

[45] The order arrived in Alexandria on 4 February 362; *H. Aceph.* IX.

[46] Sozom. *HE* v.3.4, citing instances from Nisibis and Maiuma (near Gaza).

[47] *Ep.* 83, and *Ep.* 115.424c Bidez: a stance applauded by Lib. *Or.* XVIII.121 ff., but accorded ulterior motives by Greg. Naz. *Or.* IV.57.

[48] *Epp.* 110.398d, 114.436a–b. Ammianus, XXII.5.3–5, is alone in referring specifically to Constantinople.

riven by factional division (although Julian nowhere expressed this aim as explicitly as Ammianus' celebrated observation that he was exploiting the Christians' animal-like tendency to internecine strife: xxII.5.4).[49] Yet, equally, the amnesty was dictated by more mundane political demands, clearly expressed, for example, by the church historian Socrates (III.1.43): Julian was out to 'appropriate' to himself those sections of the population which had most grievance against the previous regime. Like the generals alienated by the dominance of Constantius' civilian ministers, dissident Christian leaders who had fallen foul of Constantius were a natural constituency to be cultivated by the new emperor as he sought to build support for his rule.[50]

Julian took care to distance himself from unwelcome features of what had preceded him. The new order conspicuously set aside the perceived luxury of Constantius' court, as Julian ejected large numbers of palace servants and minor officials in favour of a simpler, more accessible imperial lifestyle (xxII.4; Lib. Or. xvIII.130ff.). It was a gesture which appealed to the conventions of panegyric, and both Mamertinus (Pan. Lat. III(XI).11) and Libanius (Or. xvIII.190) lauded a new ruler who divested himself of the extravagant trappings of majesty ('he did not measure the happiness of his reign by the depth of his purple') and made himself the equal of his subjects. Yet the Roman empire of the fourth century had grown accustomed to a different demeanour in its rulers: it is again Socrates (III.1.53) who effectively deflates the eulogy with the realistic observation that by diminishing the sense of 'wonder' engendered by the wealth of the court Julian was risking his monarchy falling into contempt. The point is confirmed by Ammianus' reaction to Julian's reported behaviour on the occasion when the philosopher Maximus eventually arrived in Constantinople from Ephesus: the emperor 'so forgot who he was' that he rushed out of the senate to greet his spiritual mentor in an undignified and ostentatious display of affection (xxII.7.3).[51]

It was characteristic of Julian's stay in Constantinople that Maximus should arrive to find him occupied in the senate. The emperor was frequently to be seen in the curia, participating as a senator in the debates and delivering speeches which he would sit up all night composing.[52] In a law of February 362 (C.Th. IX.2.1) aiming to protect senators from unjust accusations in court, he voiced his respect for the institution: 'the rights of senators and the authority of that order in which we number ourselves also

[49] For the attribution of similarly ulterior motives, see Sozom. HE v.5.7 and Philost. vII.4.
[50] A process already begun by Julian in Gaul in 360: Brennecke (1984) 360-7. On Julian's cultivation of exiled bishops, see further Barnes, Athanasius 153-4.
[51] Contrast Libanius' (Or. xvIII.155-6) commendation of Julian's deference to the philosopher.
[52] Socr. HE III.1.54. For Julian's involvement with the senate, cf. Amm. Marc. xxII.7.3; Pan. Lat. III(XI).24.5; Lib. Or. xvIII.154.

must be defended from all outrages'. The eastern capital witnessed a striking display of this old-fashioned imperial deference at the consular
inaugurations of January 362, when the new consuls Mamertinus and
Nevitta, duly seated in their curule chairs, were escorted through the
crowds by the emperor preceding them on foot from palace to *curia*.[53] To
see this behaviour in its full perspective, it should be recalled that the majority of the senators to whom Julian displayed this exaggerated respect would
belong to Constantius' recent new influx to the order, stemming from predominantly Christian circles among the cities of the east – they were the
political establishment whose loyalty Julian needed to 'appropriate'. His
success was mixed: some observers commended his conduct at the consular ceremonies, Ammianus comments, but others criticized it as 'cheap
affectation' (XXII.7.1). After the remote imperial grandeur favoured by
Constantius and his entourage, Julian's impulsive informality might well
seem an uncomfortable experience.

The austere style of Julian and his court harked back to an age when
Roman emperors cultivated the image of themselves as fellow citizens,
living the simple life, respectful of the dignities of the senate and open to
the will of their subjects. It reflected a growing obsession with the 'revolution' of the Christian Constantine, who was accused by Julian (and the rest
of the pagan tradition) of creating an overblown and extravagant imperial
entourage: the Constantine of Julian's *Caesars* is the ruler who amasses
wealth to spend on himself and his friends.[54] In blaming Constantine,
Julian cast him as the hate-figure who had overturned the traditions of the
past (XXI.10.8): he rejected Constantinian laws, for example, as innovations
which subverted *ius antiquum* (*C.Th.* II.5.2, III.1.3), and it was because of
Constantine and the 'folly of the Galilaeans' that 'everything had been
overturned' (*Ep.* 83 Bidez). The purging of the court, then, cannot be dis-
entangled from this broader aim of undoing the malevolent work of
Constantine, and returning the Roman empire to what, in Julian's perception, was its purest condition. As one who had come into his imperial inheritance from the schools of Hellenism, his vision was grounded in the Greek
world of the eastern Mediterranean, and his view of the empire was as a
union of healthy, well-ordered cities, taking pride in their great heritage and
honouring their gods.[55] Seen in this light, the pruning of the court was the
complement of efforts to relieve the cities of financial burdens and revive
their institutions, against a recent background which had seen the proliferation of central government and its demands, accompanied by a growing
trend of privileged exemptions from civic *munera*.[56]

[53] The proceedings are admiringly described by Mamertinus in his surviving speech of thanks: *Pan. Lat.* III(XI).28–30.
[54] *Caes.* 335b; cf. Ammianus' criticism of Constantine for 'opening the jaws of those closest to him' (XVI.8.12).   [55] For Julian's civic ideals, see Athanassiadi, *Julian* 98ff.   [56] See Millar, 'Empire and city'.

Julian's interest in reducing the scale of imperial government did not stop at the doors of the imperial palace: it extended to all the tentacles of the administration. A series of laws addressed to the prefect Mamertinus, for example, aimed to restrict the issue of permits for the *cursus publicus* (*C.Th.* VIII.5.12–14); and there were reportedly substantial reductions to the corps of *agentes in rebus*, principal users of the *cursus* as they carried information between the palace and its functionaries around the empire.[57] Apart from a backward glance at the perceived abuses of Constantius' government, such measures were directed at the relief of the cities, where the burdens of maintaining this machinery of empire fell most heavily.[58] Concern for the cities also involved Julian in the task of rebuilding and regulating the local *curiae*:[59] Libanius commended the rescript ('worthy of all praise') in which the emperor cancelled invalid exemptions and recalled those who had evaded their civic responsibilities ('the lifeblood of the city is a strong council': *Or.* XVIII.147–8). The Theodosian Code preserves sections of a comprehensive law on the subject of *curiales* addressed to the eastern praetorian prefect in March 362, in which Julian both restricted the categories of immunity (Christian clergy were specifically denied exemption: *C.Th.* XII.1.50) and yet at the same time laid compulsion on civic leaders to meet their public obligations (XI.16.10, XI.23.2); to improve their financial position he ordered public estates (which would include temple properties) to be restored to the cities as a source of revenue (X.3.1),[60] and exempted *curiales* from the requirement to make up arrears of the 'gold and silver' tax levied on tradesmen (XII.1.50). A further law in April (XII.13.1; cf. Lib. *Or.* XVIII.193) rendered voluntary the contributions of 'crown gold' which city councils had become obliged to send to the emperor to mark significant imperial occasions (and had lately sent to Julian on his accession).[61] Measures such as these held out before the eastern cities the benevolent tax regime which Julian had earlier displayed to the communities of Gaul.[62] 'Our aim is not to accumulate as much as we can from our subjects, but to provide for them the most benefits', he proclaimed in responding to a petition for tax reductions from the people of Thrace (*Ep.* 73.428c Bidez); and he was later to remind the Antiochenes of his generous tax remissions to their city (*Misop.* 365b, 367d). Predictably, *liberalitas* ranked among the virtues which a favourable historical tradition lavished on Julian (Amm. Marc. XXV.4.15).

Ammianus was markedly less complimentary about other aspects of

---

[57] Lib. *Or.* XVIII.135ff. Little credibility attaches to Libanius' claim elsewhere (*Or.* II.58) that the corps was reduced to a mere seventeen!

[58] For Julian's administrative measures in relation to civic policy, see Pack (1986) 115ff., who discusses in detail the laws summarized in this paragraph.   [59] Pack (1986) 224ff.

[60] For the reconfiscation of temple properties in 364, see *C.Th.* X.1.8.   [61] Cf. above, p. 61.

[62] Cf. his insistence (*C.Th.* XI.16.10) that no unauthorized tax burdens should fall upon his subjects in the east.

Julian's regulation of the cities, complaining of the 'harshness' and 'injustice' of his attempts to limit curial exemptions (XXI.12.23, XXII.9.12, XXV.4.21); and the emperor himself would need to look no further than the failure of his efforts to increase the strength of the *curia* at Antioch (by removing immunity from those serving as financial officials at court: *Misop.* 367d–368b) to be reminded of the obstacles in the way of reform.[63] Although there is no reason to question Julian's sincere belief in the need to bolster the city councils, he could not in practice counter the opposite trends represented by competition with the enlarged demands of central government and the avenues to immunity which it provided.[64] In the context of the Code, his curial legislation assumes only modest significance as part of a long series of (unsuccessful) imperial attempts to enforce civic responsibilities: even the denial of immunity to the clergy had already been voiced by his Christian predecessors. Julian was, too, sufficiently a creature of his times to confirm the curial exemption of those who had served in the imperial *scrinia* and in the reduced corps of *agentes* (*C.Th.* VI.26.1, 27.2).[65] What is more, Julian's dealings with the *curiales* were hardly conducted in a manner conducive to a sense of civic independence – the councillors of Antioch, for example, discovered that the emperor expected to intervene directly in the nomination of suitable candidates (*Misop.* 368b; cf. *C.Th.* XII.1.53). Realistically, Julian's professed goal of strong and effective city councils was at odds with the centralized nature of imperial autocracy in the late Roman empire.

The degree to which imperial involvement encroached upon local independence is also reflected in the best known of Julian's civic measures, the pronouncement of 17 June 362 which ordained procedures for the appointment of suitably qualified teachers in the cities.[66] The selection of teachers, who were to be eminent 'first in character, then in eloquence', was delegated to the decision of local councils – but only because it was impossible for the emperor 'to be present in person in all the cities'. He still required the cities' nominations to be referred to him for final approval, so that they might take up their appointments 'with added prestige'. Julian thus left no doubt that he regarded the choice of suitable teachers for the cities of the empire as his business. Right learning, παιδεία, was central to Julian's Hellenic programme,[67] as he made clear in the surviving letter which expands his thinking on the 'good character' to be demanded in his teachers (*Ep.* 61 Bidez). They are to be morally

---

[63] On Julian's regulation of the *curia* at Antioch, see Pack (1986) 345ff.

[64] Cf. Millar, 'Empire and city' 95.

[65] Note also his liberal extension of the facilities of the *cursus* to the friends invited to join him at court: see above, p. 62, n. 44.

[66] *C.Th.* XIII.3.5. For full discussion, see Pack (1986) 261ff.; Klein (1981).

[67] See, in general, Athanassiadi, *Julian* ch. 4.

upright, capable of distinguishing right from wrong, and sincerely practise what they preach. Only towards the end of the document is Julian's target made explicit, as he impugns the behaviour of those teachers who do not believe in the true worth of their subject: 'they should either show piety towards the gods, or withdraw to the churches of the Galilaeans to expound Matthew and Luke' (423d). There was to be no place for Christian teachers in Julian's reordered cities, where true learning was inseparable from devotion to the old gods (cf. Lib. *Or.* xviii.157). The implication that the common educational curriculum and the monopoly of learning were the preserve of paganism caused understandable alarm to Julian's Christian contemporaries, since by 'paganizing' culture – and hence access to public careers – it posed potentially the most serious threat to their social standing in the empire:[68] Gregory of Nazianzus made it his central accusation against the apostate emperor that he had sought to equate their shared Hellenic learning with the practice of pagan cult (*Or.* iv.5, 100ff.), and in the longer term Julian's law provoked much intellectual heart-searching in the Christian tradition about the proper relationship between education and religion.[69] But its immediate impact was less pervasive. As with the rest of Julian's regulation of city affairs, there were practical limits to the effectiveness of imperial exhortations, especially when accompanied by official disclaimers of any punitive intent ('I think foolish men should be educated, not punished': 424b). Some prominent Christian teachers – Prohaeresius at Athens, Marius Victorinus in Rome – abandoned their posts,[70] but many who enjoyed a lower profile must have carried on without interference. It is some indication of the degree of reluctance to give effect to Julian's measure that the pagan Ammianus famously dismissed it as a 'harsh act which should be buried in lasting oblivion' (xxii.10.6, cf. xxv.4.20), and even the admiring Libanius conspicuously failed to mention it among his praises for the emperor's patronage of true learning (*Or.* xviii.157ff.).

V. ANTIOCH

When the law on the qualifications of teachers was issued in June 362, Julian may already have embarked on the journey from Constantinople to Antioch, with the intention of assembling an army to resume the war against Persia which Constantius had left unfinished. He might reflect on the political advantage to be gained, especially among the eastern military, from a prestige expedition which would invite comparison with his earlier

---

[68] On the political significance of the measure as a move to create a pagan ruling élite, see Klein (1981) 90ff. [69] See e.g. Markus (1974).

[70] Prohaeresius: Eunap. *V. Soph.* 493 (Loeb, p. 512); Jer. *Chron. s.a.* 363 (ed. Helm, 242–3). Victorinus: August. *Conf.* viii.5.

successes against German tribes.[71] Meanwhile, the route across Asia Minor provided an opportunity to observe the impact of his Hellenic crusade at close quarters. The protocol of loyal speeches and receptions by local dignitaries which accompanied any such imperial *adventus* (Lib. *Or.* XVIII.159) could do little to conceal the reality that the cities were falling far short of the pagan revival which Julian had enjoined on them. He was met by a combination of civic inertia and Christian resistance.[72] From Ancyra in Galatia he made a special detour to visit Pessinus, home of the cult of Cybele, Mother of the Gods (XXII.9.5), only to discover that the shrine there was neglected by the community and the object of Christian abuse (*Ep.* 84.431d Bidez; Greg. Naz. *Or.* v.40). He did not, it appears, travel through Cappadocian Caesarea, but when reports reached him of the failure of its pagan minority to prevent violence against temples, he took fiscal reprisals against the Christian population and demoted Caesarea from its civic status (Sozom. *HE* v.4.1–5). Even without active Christian opposition to the restoration of pagan worship, the repossession of property previously in temple hands will have been a disruptive process, in the face of which Julian's vocabulary of persuasion increasingly made way for the more familiar repertoire of imperial punishments. Few areas are likely to have seen the reopening of the temples accomplished with such diplomacy as that reputedly exercised by Chrysanthius of Sardis, Julian's high priest in Lydia, who is said to have so avoided offence to Christians that 'there did not seem to be any great and universal change' (Eunap. *V. Soph.* 501, Loeb, p. 546). These provincial priesthoods, where Julian could place sympathetic associates, were key appointments in the programme of pagan reform:[73] the holders would receive instructions from the emperor, in which Julian in the role of *pontifex maximus* lectured his priestly subordinates on the proper conduct of their office, much as he did the cities about the qualifications of teachers. After passing through Galatia, for example, and seeing for himself the strength of the church and its network of charitable institutions, he addressed a didactic epistle to the high priest of the province, Arsacius, on ways of furthering the pagan cause: 'that Hellenism does not yet prosper as it should is the fault of those who profess it' (*Ep.* 84.429c Bidez). Arsacius 'and all the priests of Galatia' (430a) are urged to follow a thoroughgoing programme of personal moral example and public actions to outdo the Christians at their own game, including the establishment in their cities of charitable hostels (ξενοδοχεῖα) to rival those of the Christians, for which the emperor made available supplies of grain and wine: 'for it is disgraceful that none of the Jews is a beggar, and the impious

---

[71] He had already reportedly rejected an expedition against the Goths across the Danube, in favour of a 'better enemy': Amm. Marc. XXII.7.8.

[72] On Julian's passage through Asia Minor, see Mitchell (1993) 88–95.

[73] 'The shock troops of Julian's religious reform': Athanassiadi, *Julian* 181ff.

Galilaeans provide support for our people as well as their own, yet ours are seen to lack aid from us'. Hospitality, Julian impressed on Arsacius, had been a virtue of the Greeks since Homer (430b–431b).

The emperor reached Antioch on 18 July, his expectations high for the pagan revival in this leading city of the east, whose inhabitants he called 'sons of Greeks' (*Misop.* 367c). He had already given orders to his uncle (and namesake), the *comes Orientis*, for rebuilding the famous temple of Apollo at nearby Daphne; and he was later to tell Libanius that he had intended, in an echo of Augustus' plans for Rome, to make Antioch a 'city of marble'.[74] It might have been a source of satisfaction that his formal arrival in the city coincided with a pagan festival, the ancient cult of Adonis, except that the accompaniment of orchestrated displays of grief at the young lover's fate seemed to some an ill omen for Julian's advent (xxii.9.15). The Adonis festival was one of a range of such occasions which Antioch and its environs offered to suit Julian's religious tastes, and to test the results of his reforming zeal in what he might have thought fruitful territory.[75] But for the Antiochenes their habitual round of festivals survived now more as occasions of communal feasting and civic entertainments than as opportunities for fervent pagan ritual (*Misop.* 346c, 362d): Julian's preference for earnest attendance at the temples, and 'drenching the altars with too much blood from excessive repetition of sacrifices' (xxii.12.6), found little sympathetic response,[76] especially at a time when (as we shall see) extravagant slaughtering of animals for sacrifice compared ill with a pressing food shortage in the city. As the citizens were jestingly to remind Julian, theirs was a city which looked with favour on 'the *chi* and the *kappa*' (*Misop.* 357a, 360d) – an allusive way of affirming that Christianity had become the dominant form of religious expression, and that his rival Constantius had greater claim on the loyalties of Antioch: it had, after all, been Constantius' principal place of residence during the long years of campaigning in northern Mesopotamia, and it had been from Antioch only the previous autumn that Constantius had set out for his expected victory against Julian. The new emperor's hopes of the people of Antioch were to prove dramatically misplaced: far from enthusiastically embracing the old gods, they would accuse Julian of 'turning the world upside down' (*Misop.* 360d) – of being precisely the revolutionary force that he himself blamed Constantine for being.

It was Julian's favoured shrine of Apollo at Daphne which became the focus of the quarrel between the emperor and his new subjects in

---

[74] Lib. *Or.* xv.52. For the rebuilding of Daphne, see Jul. *Ep.* 80 Bidez, with Amm. xxii.13.2 ('a magnificent colonnade'). On Julian's stay in Antioch, see Downey, *Antioch* 380–97; Pack (1986) 301–77.

[75] For continuing pagan ceremonies in Antioch see the survey in Liebeschuetz, *Antioch*, 228–31.

[76] 'Who will put up with an emperor who goes to the temples so often?' (*Misop.* 346c).

Antioch.[77] In August he hastened there from the temple of Zeus on Mt Kasius for the traditional annual festival (*Misop.* 361d ff.), expecting to participate in fitting religious ceremonies ('sacrifices, libations, dances in honour of the god, incense, youths surrounding the shrine . . . adorned in white and splendid raiment') – only to find the local priest alone with a solitary offering of a goose brought from his own home, who reported that 'this time' the city had made no other arrangements. It is hard not to interpret this as the city authorities' snub to Julian's unwelcome pagan enthusiasm. That was evidently how it appeared to the emperor, who proceeded to deliver a moral discourse to the assembled *curiales* of Antioch on their duty to uphold the priests in the proper performance of local cults, and not to devote resources to feasting and celebration, nor to the rival demands of Christian charity. Julian had also harboured the intention of reviving Apollo's oracular powers (Amm. Marc. xxii.12.8; Sozom. *HE* v.19.15–16), and to this end he ordered the removal of the polluting presence of the body of a local Christian martyr Babylas (whose remains Gallus Caesar had earlier had interred in a new tomb at Daphne). Antioch's Christians duly exhumed their saint, but turned the public ceremony of reburying him in his old resting-place in the city into a defiant display of solidarity against the pagan emperor: 'shame on all those who worship graven images, and who put their trust in idols' (Sozom. *HE* v.19.17–19). This dangerous level of tension was soon exacerbated even further by the outbreak of a mysterious fire on 22 October, which damaged the roof of the temple and destroyed the cult-statue of Apollo (xxii.13.1). In the atmosphere of conflict there was no room for accidental explanations.[78] While the Christians saw the fire as God's response to the petitions of their uprooted martyr, Julian detected the human agency of arson: when a tribunal of investigation[79] failed to yield names (even the priest of Apollo under interrogation could identify no one: Sozom. *HE* v.20.6), he fell back on communal reprisals against the Christians, ordering the closure of the principal church in Antioch and the seizure of its goods. It was the climax of a hectic deterioration of relations between the emperor and the Christian population of Antioch, and of Julian's own descent into the role of persecuting ruler. Nor was it only at Antioch that imperial tolerance of Christian resilience was severely tested, as reports continued to reach him of the halting progress of pagan revival. Christian leaders in other cities found themselves accused of fomenting disorder to thwart the opening of the temples. At the time of the Daphne fire, bishop Athanasius was ordered out of Alexandria as an 'enemy of the gods': the principal source of Julian's

---

[77] For a valuable survey of the evidence about Julian and Daphne, see Lieu (1989) 46ff.

[78] Amm. Marc. (xxii.13.3) alone among the sources introduces the possibility ('although on the slightest rumour') of stray sparks from candles lit in front of the statue by a pagan devotee of Julian's.

[79] For details of this tribunal, and the likely involvement of Libanius, see Lieu (1989) 51.

anger against him was that he 'dared to baptize' pagan women of distinction in the city.[80] Athanasius' fate as an opponent of Julian's paganism was also shared by the bishop of Cyzicus, Eleusius (Sozom. *HE* v.15.4ff.); elsewhere, the property of the church at Edessa was confiscated (Jul. *Ep.* 115 Bidez), while the Christians of Bostra were directly challenged by the emperor to eject their own bishop as the only means of ending civil strife (*Ep.* 114, esp. 438a). It did not need the direct involvement of the emperor to unleash local violence against Christian leaders who had resisted the old gods, as bishop Marcus and his followers discovered in the Syrian town of Arethusa.[81] Both in Antioch and elsewhere in the east the most obvious outcome of the attempt to implement Julian's religious programme was turning out to be polarized communities and social disorder.

The divisive impact of Julian's presence in Antioch was not confined to matters of religion. When the imperial court arrived in the city, the ritual lamentations for Adonis were soon drowned out by more pressing cries of protest in the theatre at the high costs of food ('everything plentiful, everything dear!').[82] Recent crop failures and drought were encouraging the profiteering habits of local landowners and merchants, and the advent of Julian offered a timely opportunity to invoke a display of imperial philanthropy, especially from an emperor eager to project an image of civic benevolence. His first instincts, typically, were towards moral persuasion (in contrast to his brother Gallus' more violent reaction to a similar crisis):[83] Julian summoned the leading citizens to hear a homily on the threat to public harmony posed by the evils of unjust profit. For three months they failed to put their house in order, until in October Julian intervened directly in the workings of Antioch's market: he ordered price-controls on all foodstuffs, and had extra supplies of corn brought in from surrounding cities, subsequently supplemented by deliveries from nearby imperial estates, and even the diversion to Antioch of corn supply-vessels from Alexandria (originally destined for Constantinople). Yet even this range of measures was ineffective against the profit-making tendencies of Antioch's well-to-do, who apparently retained their own corn stocks for sale at a high price in the countryside, thus forcing country-dwellers to flock into the city and exaggerate the strain on the food supply (*Misop.* 369c–d; Lib. *Or.*

---

[80] So Julian's angry letter to the prefect of Egypt, *Ep.* 112 Bidez. On the timing of Athanasius' expulsion, see *H. Aceph.* x–xi.

[81] An episode which soon entered the Christian demonology on Julian: Greg. Naz. *Or.* iv.88–91; Sozom. *HE* v.10.8–14. Marcus' persecution was reportedly seen as counter-productive by Julian's supporters: Greg. Naz. *Or.* iv.91; Lib. *Ep.* 103.6 Loeb. For full details of persecution of Christians (and list of martyrs) under Julian's rule, see Brennecke (1988) 87–157.

[82] *Misop.* 368c ff.; cf. Lib. *Or.* xviii.195; Amm. Marc. xxii.14.1. On Julian and economic crisis in Antioch, see (among older discussions) Petit, *Libanius* 105–22, and more recently, Pack (1986) 363–77, Matthews, *Ammianus* 409–14.

[83] The comparison with Gallus is explicitly drawn by Ammianus (xxii.14.2), who is unsympathetic to Julian's handling of the problem.

xviii.195). At the root of these economic difficulties, but barely hinted at
in Julian's complaints of the obstructive behaviour of Antioch's city
fathers, was the massive influx of the army being assembled in and around
the city for the invasion of Persia[84] – a considerable additional market with
disposable resources, and offering lucrative prospects for the local landowners. The sight of well-fed soldiers carousing through the streets of
Antioch (xxii.12.6) while its inhabitants were unable to buy corn was
further graphic evidence of the contradictions surrounding the presence
of Julian and his court in the city: despite a much-heralded concern to
promote well-ordered civic life in all its aspects, the emperor's increasingly
impatient incursions into the affairs of Antioch, whether religious or economic, led only to more social tension.

On 1 January 363 Julian assumed his fourth consulship in Antioch. The
ceremonies were ominously marred by the sudden death of one of the
(elderly) officiating priests (xxiii.1.6), and though the emperor could take
comfort from the flattering sentiments in praise of his devotion to the gods
which marked Libanius' oration for the occasion, Julian's unrestrained reaction to the priest's death represented another undignified lapse of imperial
deportment.[85] But the New Year festivities were also a traditional opportunity for voicing protests with relative impunity.[86] The people of Antioch
seized their chance to ridicule Julian's physical appearance (notably his
beard) and ascetic personal habits – his dislike of the theatre and horse
races; nor did the Christian populace spare his eccentric displays of religious enthusiasm, 'calling him *victimarius*, "slaughterer", instead of high
priest, with many mocking his frequent sacrifices' (xxii.14.3). Julian's satirical response to such criticisms, the *Misopogon*, was posted outside the palace
in Antioch, some time later in January.[87] Although to some extent belonging to a tradition of imperial ripostes to disobedient subjects, it is also a
document very personal to Julian, burning with resentment at the failure of
the populace and *curiales* of Antioch to conform to the image of Hellenic
harmony in which he had cast them.[88] If the licence of the New Year ceremonies was intended to ease tensions, it was of no avail. By the time Julian
left for the Persian campaign on 5 March, he had appointed a notoriously
savage governor of Syria 'as a fitting judge for the greedy and abusive

[84] Socr. *HE* iii.17.2–4, alone among the ancient sources (although Julian twice alludes to the arrival
of 'foreigners' in the city: *Misop.* 368d, 370b), makes the connection between the corn crisis and the military presence in Antioch. Libanius would blithely claim that Antioch had sufficient resources to
support imperial court and army: *Or.* xv.16–17.

[85] So Lib. *Or.* 1.129. The speech in question is *Or.* xii.

[86] For what follows on the circumstances of the composition of the *Misopogon*, see Gleason (1986).

[87] The 'seventh month' after his arrival in Antioch: *Misop.* 344a. For the posting of the text, see
Malalas, *Chron.* p. 328.

[88] Note Julian's pointed contrast between his favourable reception among the 'Celts' of Gaul and
his rejection by the 'Hellenes' of Antioch: *Misop.* 360c–d.

Antiochenes', and the crowd escorting him on his way were told of his intention to return for the winter, not to Antioch, but to a new headquarters at Tarsus in Cilicia (XXIII.2.3–5).[89] In a world accustomed to savage reprisals, such official anger was understandably a source of real fear among the leading Antiochenes. Libanius was an obvious spokesman to attempt to appease the emperor,[90] but even so 'most' of the *curiales* felt it necessary to follow Julian as far as Chalcis in a vain effort to restore their city to favour (Jul. *Ep.* 98.399c Bidez).

VI. PERSIA

By now the emperor's quarrels with the Antiochenes and the faltering of the reform programme were dwarfed by the even loftier design of war against the Persians. This had been the grand idea which had brought Julian to Antioch in the first place, and it was a preoccupation which vied with the campaign against the Christians in claiming his attention. Besides the polemic of the *Contra Galilaeos* (Lib. *Or.* XVIII.178), the winter nights at Antioch late in 362 also saw the composition of the satirical tract known as the *Caesars*.[91] In this mock portrayal of a contest of Roman emperors before the gods (which concludes with the disgrace of the Christian Constantine), Julian introduced a significant additional participant in the person of Alexander, whose claim to inclusion is specifically his defeat of the Persians (323d ff.) – an objective which (among Julian's Roman predecessors) Trajan shared with him (333a).[92] The memory of Trajan – and of other emperors who had successfully invaded Persian territory: Verus, Severus and the ill-fated Gordian – is also invoked in the speech which Ammianus gives to Julian as he rallies his forces in Mesopotamia; here the emperor contrasts earlier successes with recent disasters inflicted by the Persians, alluding to Sapor's offensives in the last years of Constantius' rule (XXIII.5.16ff.).[93] Summoning up Alexander and Trajan as exemplars, Julian thus advertised a return to 'old-style' Roman aggression against the great enemy to the east, to the discredit of the cautious war of attrition in northern Mesopotamia waged by his predecessor.[94] It was a version of recent

---

[89] Cf. Lib. *Or.* 1.132, xvi.53. Already in the *Misopogon* (370b) Julian had announced his intention of moving his court elsewhere.

[90] For Libanius' 'frankness', see *Or.* 1.126, xv.12. *Or.* xv was composed as a plea to the emperor for the city's forgiveness.

[91] For the composition of the *Caesares* as a companion-piece to the *C. Galil.*, see Baldwin (1978).

[92] On the Alexander motif as a key factor in Julian's thinking prior to the Persian war, see Athanassiadi, *Julian* 192ff.

[93] For the theme of past defeats awaiting revenge, cf. XXII.12.1.

[94] For an explicit statement of this Julianic criticism of Constantius' war, see Lib.*Or.* XVIII.205–11. The most recent precedent for Julian's reversion to a more aggressive strategy was, ironically, Constantine: Kaegi (1981). On the 'traditional' context of Julian's projected campaign, Blockley, *Foreign Policy* 24ff.

history which defied the true nature of Constantius' legacy on the eastern front, where by 361 only one captured fortress (Bezabde) remained in Persian hands and Sapor's army had finally been deterred from further incursions into Roman territory. Precise considerations of the military context, however, were not the real reason for a major offensive expedition: much more to the point was the emperor's own ambition for a glorious and 'traditional' war, and an objective which would redeem the increasing sense of domestic failure typified by events in Antioch. Julian was bent on conflict, ostentatiously rejecting diplomatic overtures, and boasting to the cities of Mesopotamia that he would 'lay bare Persia'.[95]

An expedition which owed so much to the emperor's own intensity of purpose was not without its critics, especially among an eastern military hierarchy not yet entirely reconciled to the advent of Julian. Several army officers who met their deaths under Julian, and whom the Christian tradition was to claim as martyrs at the hands of his pagan regime, may well owe their fate to discontent about the projected Persian adventure – even Libanius was obliged to admit the existence of military plots against the emperor (*Or.* XVIII.199).[96] Many of Julian's own immediate associates sought, unsuccessfully, to dissuade him from the enterprise, not least the emperor's fellow consul Sallustius, praetorian prefect of Gaul, who wrote 'begging that the expedition be abandoned' (XXIII.5.4): the prefect had good reason to fear for Julian's own hard-won security in Gaul if Roman military resources were to become over-concentrated on a major war in the east.

Julian was not, though, to be diverted from his Persian mission. By the time Sallustius' letter arrived, the emperor was at Cercusium on the edge of Sapor's territory, marshalling his forces as they crossed the river Abora (XXIII.5.1, 4; cf. Zos. III.13.1).[97] He had reached there at the beginning of April, having led the march south to Callinicum on the Euphrates from Carrhae, where he had earlier divided the Roman forces for a double offensive: Julian himself headed the main advance down the Euphrates, an army 65,000 strong accompanied by some 1000 transport vessels which assembled in Callinicum; while a second force (perhaps numbering as many as 30,000) under the command of his kinsman Procopius and the *comes* Sebastianus continued the eastward route from Carrhae towards the Tigris, to open a second front against the Persians in conjunction with the movements of Rome's ally Arsaces of Armenia (XXIII.3.5, cf. Lib. *Or.*

---

[95] Ephr. Syr. *C. Iul.* II.15. For rejection of diplomacy, see Lib. *Or.* XVIII.164.

[96] For military martyrs of Julian's reign, see Bowersock, *Julian* 107, and Brennecke (1988) 144–5 (Iuventinus and Maximinus).

[97] Julian's movements are traced through the complexities of overlapping source material by Dodgeon and Lieu, *Eastern Frontier* ch. 9; see also the compact summary in Lieu (1989) 89–93. Detailed points of geography are often clarified by Paschoud's notes to the Budé edition of Zosimus. For extensive discussion of the whole campaign from a variety of perspectives, see Matthews, *Ammianus* ch. 8.

XVIII.214–15; Zos. III.12.4–5).[98] Despite the fact that Julian is said to have disclosed nothing of his military plans (Lib. *Or.* XVIII.213), it is apparent that this second offensive was conceived as a diversionary tactic to mislead the Persians about the direction of the Roman march, while the main expedition headed for the principal objective of Ctesiphon on the lower Tigris, the ancient Parthian capital and traditional prize of Roman emperors who invaded Mesopotamia. Speed was of the essence, as it could hardly be expected that Persian leaders would be deceived for long by the Romans' movements; but the advance to Ctesiphon in fact proved slow and hazardous. To remain in close order with the ships, Julian's large army was forced to hug the banks of the Euphrates,[99] and enemy fortresses *en route* had either to be bypassed after negotiations or besieged and captured; and there were still Persian forces (and their Saracen allies) left to defend the approaches to Ctesiphon in sufficient numbers to lay ambushes for Roman reconnaissance parties (XXIV.2.4–5, 3.1–2). The problems were magnified as the army reached the area criss-crossed by numerous waterways between the Euphrates and Tigris in the hinterland of Ctesiphon: a route already waterlogged by spring floods was made even more difficult by the enemy's tactic of deliberately breaching the canal dykes (XXIV.3.10; cf. xxiv.8.2). The impression that the Romans were ill-informed about the terrain and unprepared for its problems is confirmed by the fact that, in order to give his fleet access to the Tigris, Julian had first to open up a long-disused channel the whereabouts of which were only discovered 'from books'.[100] When Ctesiphon was at last in sight, the emperor defied his generals' caution and ordered troops to be ferried across at night to the far bank of the river; in an encounter before the gates they successfully drove the Persian defenders back into the city, but had to be restrained from risking all by undisciplined pursuit (XXIV.6; cf. Lib. *Or.* XVIII.248–55; Zos. III.25).

There was seemingly no strategy beyond an assault on Ctesiphon. Now that Julian's army was before the walls, the reality of the city's impregnability forced a dramatic reconsideration, 'like the sand shifting beneath his feet' (Greg. Naz. *Or.* v.10). A council of war decided on an advance into the Persian interior east of the Tigris, in the hope (it may be suggested) of a rendezvous with the second force under Procopius and Sebastianus.[101] It was a change of plan which carried with it a drastic corollary – the order for the destruction of the 1000-strong fleet, which would have been

[98] For discussion of numbers, see Paschoud (1979) 109–11 (army), 113–14 (ships).

[99] Extending over a distance of 'almost ten miles': Amm. Marc. XXIV.1.3 (Zos. III.14.1 has '70 stades').

[100] Lib. *Or.* XVIII.245; cf. Amm. Marc. XXIV.6.1–2. On the conflicting testimony about the ancient canal (Naarmalcha, or 'Royal River') linking Euphrates and Tigris, see Paschoud (1979) appendix B, and Matthews, *Ammianus* 149ff.

[101] The movements of this second army are clouded in mystery, not least because some material appears to have fallen out of Ammianus' text: XXIV.7.8.

virtually impossible to drag back upstream with the river in full flood. A mere dozen boats necessary for bridge-building were saved from the flames, and the 20,000 men who had been occupied with the fleet were now freed to serve with the main army (XXIV.7.4; Lib. *Or.* XVIII.262). Whatever strategic arguments prevailed for burning the ships, they could do little to allay the catastrophic damage done to the morale of Julian's soldiers, faced with the full horror of their predicament:[102] isolated in enemy territory in the heat of the summer, on the 'wrong' side of the Tigris, and with no obvious means of retreat – it was an atmosphere ripe for rumours of Persian infiltrators dictating Roman policy.[103] Their circumstances were rendered even more desperate by the knowledge that the main body of Sapor's army was drawing closer (XXV.1.1), and thus cutting off any prospect of reunion with Procopius' force. Yet Julian, still mindful of Alexander (Lib. *Or.* XVIII.260), is reported to have rebuffed the Persian king's offers of peace (*ibid.* 257–9) – an exhibition of imperial bravado which the Roman leaders would soon come to regret.

On 16 June, abandoning plans to strike further into Persia, Julian and his army set off northward in the direction of Corduene (XXIV.8.5), in the hope of eventually re-entering Roman territory.[104] The fertile lands north of Ctesiphon which might have offered abundant supplies were burnt dry by the enemy's ruthless 'scorched earth' policy (XXIV.7.7; XXV.1.10, 2.1). Denied these crops, they were hard-pressed by the heat and lack of food, and slowed even further by the need to transport what had previously been carried on the ships. They were also constantly harried by attacks from Persian forces and Saracen bands. On 26 June, when the rear of the column was suddenly attacked as they drew near to Samarra (some fifty miles to the north of present-day Baghdad), Julian rushed from his tent to rally Roman resistance, neglecting – with typical impulsiveness – to don his full armour (XXV.3.3).[105] In the chaos of the skirmish he was felled from his horse by a spear which passed through his ribs. The sight of the emperor being carried to his tent was the signal for a fierce battle which claimed the lives of high-ranking personnel on both sides, including fifty leading Persians and Julian's *magister officiorum* Anatolius; the praetorian prefect Salutius only narrowly escaped death (XXV.3.13–14). But the day's principal casualty was still to come. The attentions of his faithful doctor Oribasius, who had been in attendance on Julian since the years in Gaul, could not save the emperor,

---

[102] Ammianus' account wavers between the strategic justification and the desperation of the troops: Austin (1972b).
[103] Exploited most by Julian's Christian opponents (Greg. Naz. *Or.* v.11–12; Ephr. Syr. *C. Iul.* II.18; etc.), but cf. also Amm. Marc. XXIV.7.5; Fest. *Brev.* 28. For discussion of the part played by Persian deserters, see Paschoud (1979) 182–4.   [104] On the itinerary of the retreat, see Paschoud (1979) 186ff.
[105] Christian sources were quick to claim that Julian in desperation deliberately courted death: Ephr. Syr. *C. Iul.* III.16; Greg. Naz. *Or.* v.12. Libanius on the other hand surmised over-confidence: *Or.* XVIII.268. On the location of the fatal conflict, see Paschoud (1979) 201–2; Matthews, *Ammianus* 181.

and he died of his wounds during the ensuing night (xxv.3.23).[106] That he spent his last hours discoursing with his philosophical mentors Maximus and Priscus 'about the nobility of the soul' is probably the stuff of legend; for the facts of Julian's death were soon to be submerged in a war of words between Christians and pagans, principally over the source of the fatal spear (most likely it was thrown by a Saracen fighting with the Persians).[107] The thought that Julian might have died by the hand of one of his own side (xxv.6.6; Lib. Or. xviii.274–5) was a godsend to a Christian tradition eager to have the apostate emperor accorded his just deserts.[108] Yet such a rumour was not solely the product of religious polemic. It had its roots in the broader trail of disaffection which Julian left in his wake: among his soldiers trapped beyond the Tigris, as in the empire's divided cities, there were many who had some cause to resent their emperor's ill-fated zeal.

[106] Only Philostorgius (vii.15: Bidez/Winkelmann, p. 103) specifically mentions the presence of Oribasius at Julian's deathbed.
[107] For the variant traditions, see Bowersock, *Julian* 116–18, and Paschoud (1979) 204–6.
[108] Julian's assassin was destined for Christian sainthood: Baynes (1937).

CHAPTER 3

FROM JOVIAN TO THEODOSIUS

JOHN CURRAN

I. JOVIAN

At dawn on 27 June 363, after Julian's body had been carefully stowed away for the long journey back to the west, the senior officers of his Persian expedition met to elect a new emperor.[1] A heated debate took place and factions emerged. Arintheus and Victor, who had been much favoured by Constantius II, clashed with a knot of Gallic officers, led by Nevitta and Dagalaifus, who had accompanied Julian from Gaul. No agreement was reached until the name of Saturninus Secundus Salutius, praetorian prefect of the East, was proposed. Like Julian, the elderly Gallic general was a Christian apostate with a taste for philosophy. But the attempt of the conclave to settle on a compromise candidate failed when Salutius declined the offer on grounds of age and ill health.

Elsewhere in the camp, where the extreme danger of the army's situation was not lost on the legionaries, 'a few hot-headed soldiers' proclaimed Jovian, a thirty-two-year-old *primicerius domesticorum*, emperor. Jovian's only distinction was to have escorted the body of Constantius II to Constantinople for burial in 361. But his father Varronianus, a soldier from Singidunum in Moesia, was well known as a successful commander. Jovian was swiftly provided with a purple robe and led before the eyes of the troops, strung out in a column for four miles along the road from Ctesiphon. Some, hearing the emperor's name acclaimed by their comrades, believed that Julian had recovered and burst into tears of disappointment at the sight of the stooping Jovian.

The new emperor's first task was to extricate the expeditionary force, and on his behalf the entrails of sacrificial animals were favourably inspected by *haruspices*. The great army moved off slowly along the right bank of the Tigris, heading north-east towards Sumere. On 1 July it arrived at Dura where the Persians closed in, detaining the Romans in the heat and dust for four days. Discipline in the Roman army deteriorated and although a bridge-head was established on the far bank of the Tigris, rough waters

---

[1] Amm. Marc. xxv.5. See von Haehling (1977); Solari (1933).

78

on 6 and 7 July prevented a crossing and the supply situation became critical.

With considerable shrewdness, Sapor opened peace negotiations. He sent the Surena, his most senior minister, to the Roman camp. In difficult negotiations, Sapor demanded the return of lands which Maximianus Augustus (286–305) had taken from him. Five Roman provinces to the east of the Tigris were to be handed back to Persia: Arzanena, Moxoeona, Zabdicena, Rehimena and Corduena. Fifteen fortresses in the same region were to be given up along with the cities of Nisibis, Singara and Castra Maurorum. Jovian agreed, with the exception that Nisibis, Singara and the fifteen Roman fortresses were to be handed over without their citizens.

Sapor also extracted from Jovian a promise that no help would ever again be given to Arsaces, king of Armenia. The two sides exchanged hostages to seal the peace, which was to last thirty years.[2]

Jovian gave orders for the Tigris to be crossed, and the legions limped back to Hatra. At Ur, trusted officials were despatched to Illyricum and Gaul to announce the details of Jovian's elevation. The messengers were instructed to give the impression that the Persian expedition, Julian's death aside, had been a complete success.

At Thilsaphata Jovian met the forces of Procopius and Sebastianus, which Julian had stationed in the area for the defence of Mesopotamia. The armies merged and began the long march to the doomed city of Nisibis.

The citizens of Nisibis had been devastated by rumours that their city was to be handed over to the Persians. Jovian pitched his camp outside their walls, and the day after his arrival, the Persian king's representative made an appearance. Having secured the emperor's approval, he raised Sapor's standard over the battlements of Nisibis. In accordance with the terms of the peace, the people of Nisibis who had successfully withstood the arms of Persia in 337, 346 and 350 were given three days to gather up such property as they could transport. The episode prompted a bitter denunciation from Ammianus who declared (erroneously) that Rome had never voluntarily surrendered territory won by force of arms.[3] But Jovian had little time to ponder Roman history; mindful of the proclivity of the northern legions for choosing emperors of their own, he was most anxious to proceed westwards.

The army was divided into two parts: the larger force accompanied Procopius to Tarsus with the body of Julian, and Jovian took the smaller to Antioch, diplomatically visiting the largest city of the eastern empire, where he hoped to make a better impression than Julian had done. His

---

[2] On the peace: Amm. Marc. xxv.7.9–14; Zos. III.31.1–2. Also Matthews, *Ammianus* 185–7. For Romano–Persian relations in the period: Blockley, *Foreign Policy* 26–30; Blockley (1985); Baynes (1910). For geography, see Fontaine's commentary 4.2, 257–9 (nn. 646–8) and for excellent photographs: Kennedy and Riley (1990).   [3] xxv.9.9–10.

arrival in Antioch was accompanied by events which were later regarded as portentous. The statue of Maximianus Augustus dropped from its hand the bronze orb of the world, the symbol of an emperor's authority; comets were seen and the roof beams of the hall in which the emperor convened his *consistorium* were heard to creak ominously.

Difficulties within the Christian community detained the emperor. One of Jovian's first acts had been to declare Christianity the official religion of the empire again.[4] With Athanasius, he had made a triumphant return to Antioch in 363. But when they reached the city, they found that three rival bishops were vying for the episcopate. Paulinus and Meletius were both Nicenes but disagreed over the *hypostases* of the deity; Euzoius offered an Arian alternative. Athanasius was anxious to heal the rift between the Nicene bishops, but in recognizing Paulinus as legitimate he drew upon himself the vituperation of churchmen suspicious of candidates favoured in the west. At the end of 363, a synod of twenty-five bishops was convened in Antioch which reaffirmed the Nicene creed but added an Origenist gloss, thereby creating the so-called 'New Nicenes'.[5]

By late October 363, Jovian's work in Antioch was completed and he set off for Constantinople. At Tyana in Cappodocia, he encountered the first of his returning messengers, who brought details of how his accession had been received in the west. Certain senior ministers had accepted commissions but others had turned down Jovian's offers.

All things considered, the information gave Jovian cause for satisfaction; late in December he reached Ancyra, where he made preparations for his installation as consul on 1 January 364. He took as his colleague his infant son Varronianus, who wailed infelicitously throughout the ceremony. But at Dadastana, on the last leg of his journey to Constantinople, Jovian was found dead in his quarters. The circumstances were not investigated and it was widely believed that he had been asphyxiated in his sleep by fumes from a charcoal brazier heating his room. Ammianus implies, however, that like Scipio Aemilianus, Jovian had been strangled.[6]

II. VALENTINIAN AND VALENS: ACCESSION

Jovian's body was embalmed and sent to Constantinople. The legions moved on to Nicaea and there, among the many distinguished military and civilian personnel, a new emperor was sought. Januarius, a relative of Jovian

[4] *H. Aceph.* XII.

[5] A powerful group of Cappadocian theologians, clustered around Basil of Caesarea, supported Meletius. Basil had hopes that Athanasius and Meletius might resolve the differences between them, but they were never realized and the former died on 2 May 373 unreconciled to the bishop of Antioch. See Frend (1984) 630–4.

[6] Amm. Marc. xxv.10.13. For a general assessment of Jovian: Wirth (1984).

serving in Illyricum, was considered qualified but too distant. Aequitius, on the other hand, commander of the first division of *scutarii*, was rejected as too rough and boorish. Agreement was reached when the name of Flavius Valentinianus was put forward. Recently promoted to the command of the second division of *scutarii*, Valentinian was stationed some distance away in Ancyra, and the generals in Nicaea spent a tense ten days with the army while news of his elevation was communicated to the new emperor.[7]

Valentinian arrived in the city on 25 February 364. Since the day was the intercalated *bisextum*, a day of ill-omen, he went straight to his quarters. On the evening of the 25th, the praetorian prefect of the East issued an order that no person of high rank was to appear in public the next morning; the stage was to be left to Valentinian and the troops. But the carefully stage-managed ceremony was disturbed by the unanticipated demand of the soldiers for the appointment of a second Augustus to rule jointly with Valentinian. The memory of near-fatal dissension in the scorching wastes of Persia was too fresh among the legionaries. Valentinian displayed admirable authority in calming his men but he wisely undertook to provide a colleague.

With his accession confirmed, Valentinian and his staff retired to consider the choice of an imperial partner. Every officer knew that the emperor had a brother, Valens, languishing as a *protector domesticus*, but only the *magister equitum* Dagalaifus had the courage to voice what many thought: if Valentinian loved the state, he should ignore family loyalty and seek a colleague of the highest standing elsewhere. The emperor was embarrassed and angered by the frank advice, but nevertheless on 28 March Valens was proclaimed emperor in a suburb of Constantinople.

Valentinian was an orthodox Nicene Christian. His tolerance in religious matters impressed pagans, many of whom had expected a violent response to Julian's michievous religious policy.[8] But the emperor's professed laicism did not prevent him from promulgating legislation hostile to certain heretical sects and attacking the fraudulence of unscrupulous clerics.[9] The new emperor Valens, on the other hand, was not orthodox. He responded to disputes by upholding the canons of Ariminum (Rimini) and Seleucia, councils held in the final years of Constantius' reign which had promulgated Arian declarations of faith.

Almost immediately after Valens' elevation, the two emperors fell ill. A rigorous enquiry was launched but no evidence of sorcery was discovered. When the emperors recovered, Valentinian took the opportunity to settle some old scores. The philosopher Maximus, a close friend of Julian who had previously indicted Valentinian on religious grounds, was unceremoniously exiled.[10]

---

[7] See Neri (1985).   [8] Amm. Marc. xxx.9.5.
[9] Clerics: *C.Th.* xvi.2.20 (370); Manichees: *C.Th.* xvii.5.3 (372).
[10] Zos. iv.2.2. For Julian and Maximus, see Matthews, *Ammianus* 122ff.

In the spring of 366, the emperors formally shared out the legions, the praetorian prefects and the imperial residences, and assumed consulships; Valentinian thereupon set off for Milan and Valens returned to Constantinople.

III. RELIGION, MAGIC AND TREASON AT ROME

At Rome, the increasing influence and wealth of the episcopate attracted candidates who did not scruple to use violence to achieve it.[11] On the death of Liberius (xxiv.9.366), two of his deacons, Damasus and Ursinus, struggled violently to take over the leadership of the Christian community. One pitched battle between the rivals at a church on the Esquiline in October 366 left over one hundred people dead.[12] Damasus' victory ushered in a controversial papacy, marked by accusations of clerical corruption and compromise.[13] But under Damasus' leadership, the Roman community laid powerful claim to a rich martyrial tradition, saw the influence of Christianity spread unprecedentedly among the Roman aristocracy, and attracted the immense literary skills of Jerome to the side of the papacy.[14]

Sometime during 368, a senator and his wife reported to the prefect of Rome that an attempt had been made to poison them.[15] Several lowly suspects were detained but the trial was delayed because the prefect fell ill. The accusers used their influence to secure the appointment as judge of Maximinus, prefect of the Annona and former vice-prefect of Rome. A Pannonian by birth, he had little time for senatorial sensibilities and investigated the matter vigorously. He quickly unearthed evidence of illicit magical practices and scandalous immorality among the ancient aristocracy of Rome. When Valentinian was informed of Maximinus' preliminary findings, he ordered the use of torture on suspects, as in the case of treasonable offences. Trials involving adultery and corruption prompted executions, exiles and fines, but charges of magic were examined with particular ruthlessness. So concerned were the senators of Rome that they sent a special embassy to Valentinian, requesting leniency in sentencing and an end to the use of torture in the investigations. The emperor denied all knowledge of the latter, but a courageous court official reminded him that

---

[11] Ammianus contrasted Roman and regional clergy at xxvii.3.14–15. The prominent pagan Vettius Agorius Praetextatus is reported by Jerome to have declared jokingly that he would become a Christian immediately, if he could have the power and wealth of the bishop of Rome: *Against John* 8 = *PL* xxiii.361.

[12] Amm. Marc. xxvii.3.12. See Lippold (1965); Greenslade (1964). Coleman-Norton (1966) 1.311ff. collects and translates the important texts.

[13] Most notoriously that pope Damasus was 'the ear-tickler of matrons': *Collectio Avellana* 1.10. See Piétri, *Roma Christiana* 407–431.   [14] See Kelly, *Jerome* 80–90.

[15] For what follows, see Amm. Marc. xxviii.1. Also, Alföldi (1952); Hamblenne (1980) 198ff.; Matthews, *Ammianus* 209–17.

he had indeed issued the instructions, which were now dropped. The enquiries, however, did not cease and continued into the early 370s. Some of the most eminent men in the senate underwent the ignominy of investigation, and Aginatius, a former vice-prefect of the city of Rome, was executed for adultery and black magic. Relations between emperor and senate were badly soured and even the winding-up of the investigations was announced grudgingly.[16]

IV. VALENTINIAN AND THE NORTH-WEST FRONTIER

Late in 364, a party of Alamanni had visited Valentinian's headquarters to receive the placatory gifts which had customarily been paid by his predecessors.[17] But they were offered cheap and inferior items, and their disdain was indelicately handled by Ursatius, the *magister officiorum*. They resolved to avenge the slight by raiding the Roman provinces across the Rhine.

In January 365, operating in several large bands, they broke into Gaul. The Roman defences were overwhelmed; standards belonging to two *auxilia palatina* were taken, and Charietto, the *comes per utramque Germaniam*, was killed. Valentinian received news of the Alamannic incursion and Procopius' usurpation on the same day.[18] He briefly considered marching eastwards, but court advisers and deputations from various Gallic cities dissuaded him from leaving Gaul by pointing out the certainty of disaster in his absence. Swayed by a noble pragmatism, Valentinian 'followed the view of the majority, often repeating that Procopius was his own and his brother's enemy, but the Alamanni were enemies of the whole Roman world'.[19]

After a series of frustrating and unsuccessful campaigns, Jovinus, *magister equitum* in Gaul, was sent against the Alamanni. He annihilated one force near Scarpona (Dieulouard), and at Catalauni (Châlons-sur-Marne) the enemy suffered losses of 6000 killed and 4000 wounded, while Jovinus lost not more than 1200 men. The remaining barbarians retired to their homes.

The emperor remained in Gaul, and at Amiens in the summer of 367 he fell ill again. The names of likely candidates for the imperial succession began to circulate at court. A clique of Gallic officers was known to favour Rusticus Julianus, at that time *magister memoriae*, but they were vigorously opposed by the supporters of the *magister peditum* Severus. However, before a serious breach could occur, Valentinian recovered sufficiently to make his own arrangements. On 27 August 367 the legions were assembled on a plain outside the city. Valentinian was helped on to a tribunal by his senior officers and presented his eight-year-old son Gratian to the troops. As men

---

[16] *C.Th.* IX.38.5 (May 371).   [17] For the Alamanni: Todd (1992) 207–10; Müller (1973).
[18] For Procopius, see pp. 89–91 below.
[19] Amm. Marc. XXVI.5.13. For the campaigns, see Demandt (1972) 82ff.

spared the horrors of another dynastic contest, they acclaimed the new emperor by clashing their weapons loudly on their shields. Significantly, Valentinian dispensed with the protocol of nominating such a young emperor as Caesar, but bestowed on him the title of Augustus from the outset.

The new emperor did not have to wait long before being introduced to the military responsibilities of his position. Intelligence reports confirmed an unexpected *coup d'état* in Alamannic territory, where king Vithicabius, a frail but determined enemy of Rome, had been assassinated. In the summer of 368, Valentinian, accompanied by Gratian and a large army, crossed the Moenus (Main) and pushed into Alamannic territory.[20] The Romans contented themselves with destroying crops and other useful resources which the retreating Alamanni had left unguarded, but at Mount Pirus (Spitzberg, near Rottenburg) Valentinian, recklessly reconnoitring the position himself with a small bodyguard, was ambushed by a group of Alamanni and barely escaped with his life, losing a trusted attendant and a ceremonial helmet. The fierce battle which ensued was only won when the Roman reserves were committed on the barbarian flank. Valentinian led his army back to their winter quarters before travelling on to Trier.

Expeditions in force constituted only part of Valentinian's defensive work. He also undertook the fortification of the borders of Roman authority from Raetia to the Belgic Channel.[21] One outpost was at Mount Pirus, scene of Valentinian's resounding success in 368. A deputation of Alamanni complained to the officers in charge of construction but, finding their entreaties brushed aside, they returned in force and massacred the engineers.

Frustrated by the continual drain on Roman manpower, Valentinian decided to break Alamannic power by exploiting the rivalries between them and their neighbours. In 369 or early in 370 the emperor contacted the Burgundians, who were in dispute with the Alamanni over boundaries and salt mines.[22] A joint operation was planned, but when the Burgundians sent a host of their warriors to the Rhine to rendezvous with their allies, they found the Roman bank deserted. Incensed and dismayed, the Burgundians retired again into the interior of Germany, killing the hostages whom Rome had offered as a sign of good faith. Valentinian's *magister equitum* Theodosius, however, attacked the disordered Alamanni through Raetia, and at Valentinian's request prisoners were settled as farmers in northern Italy, in the fertile valley of the Po.

Central to Alamannic effectiveness was the competence of their various kings. In Macrianus, they possessed a particularly tenacious and resource-

---

[20] See Gerland (1930).   [21] Von Petrikovits (1971).
[22] For the Burgundians, see Todd (1992) 211–15.

ful leader. In 372, acting on reports from barbarian deserters, Valentinian attempted to seize the king in a daring but unsuccessful raid on Alamannic territory. In 374, following disturbing reports from Illyricum, Valentinian finally nullified the threat by making peace with Macrianus. The king was summoned to a point across the Rhine near Mainz. Valentinian and his guard crossed cautiously, and protracted discussions resulted in an oath of friendship to which Macrianus remained loyal until his death.[23]

The reason for peace had been the growing danger from the Quadi and Sarmatians.[24] The cause of the unrest was Valentinian's decision to establish a garrison across the Danube on their land. In 374, representatives of the Quadi opened negotiations with Roman regional commanders, but Gabinius, their king, was treacherously cut down at a banquet given by his Roman hosts. In response, the Quadi crossed the Danube in the autumn of 374 and plundered the Danubian provinces before the harvests could be brought in. One band of warriors almost intercepted Constantia, the daughter of Constantius II, who was travelling westwards to celebrate her marriage to Gratian. The situation deteriorated further when a band of Sarmatians made common cause with the Quadi. The veteran legions Pannonica and Moesiaca were badly mauled by the barbarians. When they reached the threshold of Moesia, however, news reached them of a dynamic general (Theodosius) operating there who had recently crushed a Sarmatian army. The barbarians sued for peace and were allowed to withdraw unhindered.

In the spring of 375 Valentinian moved his court from Trier to Illyricum. A deputation from the Sarmatians contacted him *en route* and begged him to believe that their people had not been involved in outrages, but Valentinian replied that the matters must be investigated carefully where they had occurred.

Valentinian's subsequent campaign of August 375 against the Quadi was a punitive operation. One corps was despatched to plunder barbarian territory from the north-west, while the emperor himself took a force to Aquincum (Budapest), where he bridged the Danube and attacked the Quadi from the south-east. Valentinian's army slaughtered every person it encountered, in an act of savage reprisal for Quadic participation in the raids of 374. In the autumn of 375, the emperor led his men back to Aquincum without loss and then proceeded to Brigetio.

Curious portents foretold some dire event. Comets were seen; a bolt of lightning was reported to have struck the imperial palace at Sirmium; and most disturbing of all, on the night before he died, Valentinian dreamed that he saw his own wife, then in Gaul, dishevelled and in mourning. When the emperor called for his horse early next day, the animal refused to let

[23] Amm. Marc. xxx.3.4–6.   [24] On the Sarmatians: Bichir (1977); Sulimirski (1970).

Valentinian mount him, occasioning a particularly ill-tempered response from the emperor, who ordered the stableboy's hand to be cut off.

Despite Valentinian's gloomy mood, official business on his last day began encouragingly. The Quadi had come to beg forgiveness and pledged recruits for the Roman army. Before Valentinian, the barbarians explained that the raid of the previous year had been the action of uncontrolled elements. But when the envoys justified that invasion by referring to the unlawful construction of a fortress on their land, Valentinian exploded with rage at their insolence. A torrent of abuse was directed at the ambassadors. When the emperor appeared to have calmed a little, he was suddenly struck speechless and began to choke. He was rushed away from barbarian eyes to an inner chamber but nothing could be done to save him. After a characteristically vigorous struggle, he died on 17 November 375, aged 55.

Plans for the campaign against the Quadi were suspended as Valentinian's body was made ready for despatch to Constantinople. His leaderless soldiers became restive and Gratian was far away in Trier. The *magister militum* Merobaudes, who had distinguished himself in the campaign of 375, was summoned to Brigetio by Valentinian's staff, while his fellow commander Sebastianus, a popular general, was sent to a distant posting in order that the succession should be uncomplicated. The decision was taken to maintain the Pannonian dynasty and promote Valentinian's four-year-old son Valentinian (II). The spontaneous choice of the Pannonian legions irritated Gratian and Valens; but there was no alternative to accepting the elevation of another colleague backed by powerful military factions.

V. VALENTINIAN AND BRITAIN

In June 367, reports reached Valentinian of co-ordinated barbarian activity on the north-west frontier.[25] The Picts, Attacotti and Scots had broken into the provinces of Britain and the security of the lower Rhine had been threatened by Frankish and Saxon incursions into coastal areas.[26] A succession of commanders despatched to contain the incursion proved unable to restore order, so Valentinian turned to one of his Spanish officers, Flavius Theodosius, then *comes rei militaris*, to solve the problem.[27]

In the sprng of 368, Theodosius embarked his vanguard at Bononia (Boulogne) and crossed the Channel to Rutupiae (Richborough). A swift attack led to the capture of London. Shrewdly, Theodosius issued an amnesty for deserters, and within months order had been restored.

---

[25] Date: Blockley (1980b); Tomlin (1974).
[26] Amm. Marc. XXVII.8.5. See Frere (1987) 339ff. For Saxons in this period: Todd (1992) 216–24; Bartholomew (1984).   [27] See Demandt (1972) 84ff.

Early in 369, Theodosius broke out from London. The progress of his campaign was jeopardized, however, by the ambitions of Valentinus, an exiled Pannonian general who had taken advantage of the chaos in Britain to attract forces to himself and may have been contemplating imperial promotion. Theodosius had Valentinus' camp infiltrated and apprehended the renegade and his staff, who were executed.

With Valentinus removed, Theodosius turned his attention to the restoration of the defences of the chief towns in Britain. The *arcani*, an intelligence-gathering community which had collaborated during the invasions, were disbanded. Advance posts and watchmen were placed on the frontier and a new province of Valentia was established. Theodosius sent an official despatch to Valentinian, informing the emperor that peace had returned, before himself returning to court, where he was promoted to the position of *magister equitum*.

VI. VALENTINIAN AND AFRICA

During Jovian's reign, the small but warlike tribe of the Austoriani cut a violent swathe through the province of Africa Tripolitania.[28] The alleged reason for the outbreak of unrest was the execution by the imperial authorities of a tribesman who had been convicted of conspiracy to betray the province. The Austoriani ravaged the territory of Lepcis Magna for three days. But Romanus, the *comes per Africam*, demanded that the citizens supply his men and spent forty idle days in the region when they proved unable to do so.

Several months later, in 365, the citizens of Lepcis Magna chose two representatives to take accession gifts to Valentinian I. Owing, however, to Romanus' contacts at Valentinian's court, the citizens' embassy was prevented from presenting their grievances to Valentinian and was ordered instead to submit any complaints to the *comes per Africam*.

When a further upsurge of unrest occurred in 365, Valentinian sent Palladius, a military tribune and *notarius*, to pay the legions in Africa and ascertain the situation. But when Palladius confronted Romanus, he found himself neatly blackmailed by the *comes* for accepting bribes. The two men came to an agreement: Palladius returned to Valentinian with a version of events which exonerated Romanus, while the unfortunate citizens who had shown Palladius around Lepcis had their tongues cut out.

Shortly after Palladius' return to Gaul, a second embassy from Lepcis reached Valentinian. The unsuspecting emperor sent his *notarius* to Africa again. This time, Romanus' agents bribed certain citizens of Lepcis to bring trumped-up charges against their own ambassadors. Allegations were

---

[28] See Matthews, *Ammianus* 383ff.; Demandt (1968a; 1968b); Warmington (1956).

made that they had exceeded their instructions, and the surviving member of the delegation himself confessed to having lied to the emperor. He and a number of 'accomplices' were condemned to death. Ruricius, the *praeses* of Africa Tripolitania, was executed at Sitifis because he had submitted what the emperor thought was a false report on the invasion of the Austoriani. Valentinian believed that order had been restored.

In 372, a dynastic dispute broke out within the Iubaleni tribe in the Roman provinces of North Africa.[29] Through murder and intrigue, Firmus, a personal enemy of Romanus, became chieftain. Romanus' despatches to Valentinian were filled with hostile reports, and when Firmus attempted to put his own case to the emperor, his efforts were frustrated by allies of Romanus at court. Fearful of summary arrest and execution, Firmus rebelled, taking the title of Augustus.[30]

Early in the summer of 373, Theodosius, then *magister equitum* in Gaul, was ordered to suppress the revolt in Africa. Romanus was reproached for his inactivity and placed in custody in Sitifis. When his private papers were examined, his collusion with Palladius was uncovered. Palladius committed suicide rather than respond to a summons to court, and Remigius, Romanus' agent at the emperor's court, also killed himself.[31]

Roman military operations commenced with a drive into the coastal plain of Mauretania Caesariensis. After two unsuccessful attempts to open negotiations, Firmus parleyed with the Roman general. Theodosius' observation of the truce, however, was entirely a matter of expediency. As Ammianus remarked, it was 'in the public interest' at the time; the Romans had paused only to gather their strength.[32]

When fighting resumed, it marked Theodosius' attempts to subdue the scattered tribal groups which had supported Firmus. The campaigning was arduous and the loyalty of some troops uncertain. But by February 374, Theodosius was able to launch a diplomatic initiative. Envoys were sent to the African tribes offering amnesties in return for renewed allegiance to Rome. The strategy eroded Firmus' support and drove him into hiding. He was treacherously detained by Igmazen, king of the Isaflenses, but committed suicide. Nevertheless, the body was brought to Theodosius' camp at Subicara, and the Roman army returned to Sitifis in 374.

Theodosius' success in Africa confirmed him as one of the foremost generals in Roman service. But with the conclusion of war in Africa, he was himself placed under investigation. It is possible that his prominence and popularity endangered him following the death of Valentinian I. The enquiries were rapidly and secretly completed; late in 375 or early in 376, Theodosius was executed at Carthage.[33]

---

[29] Amm. Marc. XXIX.5.   [30] Title: *CIL* 8, 5338. See Kotula (1970).
[31] Romanus himself was subsequently acquitted: Amm. Marc. XXVIII.6.29. See *PLRE* 1.768 'Romanus 3'.   [32] XXIX.5.16.   [33] Jer. *Chron. s.a.* 376. See Demandt (1969).

VII. VALENS AND THE REVOLT OF PROCOPIUS

Procopius was a native of Cilicia and a kinsman of the emperor Julian.[34] Educated, reserved and strict, he had enjoyed success under Constantius II, and when Julian set out on his fateful Persian campaign in the spring of 363, he instructed Procopius and his fellow *comes* Sebastianus to station their forces along the northern sector of the Mesopotamian frontier to secure the flank of the imperial army or to suggest a feint.

News of Jovian's accession reached Procopius late in 363, along with a new commission to accompany Julian's remains to their final resting-place in the suburbs of Tarsus. The change of emperor signalled dangers for Procopius, whose relations with Julian had been close. Rumours circulated, one alleging that Julian had nominated Procopius secretly as his successor before setting out on his last campaign, and another that Julian had uttered Procopius' name with his last breath. Sensing the danger, Procopius performed the obsequies for Julian and slipped quietly from view.

Procopius did not, however, consider himself to be unsuitable for the throne, and imperial pretensions mingled with his fears. At first, he lived anonymously at Chalcedon, but making discreet visits to Constantinople, he ascertained the extreme unpopularity of Valens' regime there. The emperor's anxiety about war with Persia had transmitted itself to the urban officials, who were attempting to recover moneys owed to the imperial purse even from the reign of Aurelian. Torture was employed, and quadruple fines alienated the propertied classes in Constantinople.

In the spring of 365, Valens set off for Antioch, from where he hoped to direct operations in the east. But reports of an imminent Gothic invasion of Thrace forced him to divert the corps of Divitenses and Tungricani back westwards to bolster the defences on the Danubian frontier. At Constantinople, Procopius made contact with a number of acquaintances serving as officers in these legions. Subverted by extravagant promises, they welcomed him into their camp. A desultory acclamation, perhaps engineered by Procopius' bodyguard, swelled to become a rousing acceptance. The new emperor's entourage then made its way to the senate house but, finding no *clarissimi*, it proceeded on to the imperial palace, where on the evening of 28 September 365 Procopius took up residence.

News of the revolt reached Valens as he was preparing to leave Caesarea in Cappadocia. He was advised not to continue his march eastwards, as Galatia was likely to go over to the usurper. Faced by a renascent Persia in the east, a Gothic threat in Thrace and the prospect of a difficult civil war in Asia, Valens considered abandoning everything, but his advisers urged

---

[34] See Matthews, *Ammianus* 191–203; Austin (1972c); Blockley, *Ammianus* 55–61. For the problem of usurpation generally: Wardman (1984).

him to send two legions (Jovii and Victores) against the rebels at once; other units could be summoned from the eastern provinces as required. The emperor recovered his composure and decided to fight for his throne.

Procopius lost no time in establishing his own government. He recalled the generals Gomoarius and Agilo, whom Julian had passed over.[35] The *comes* Julius, commanding a powerful corps in Thrace, was tricked into coming to Constantinople by forged orders, and his troops were quickly subverted. Procopius also produced 'messengers' who affirmed the death of Valentinian. He located Constantia Postumia, Constantius II's infant daughter, and used her as a powerful symbol of legitimacy; a letter was even despatched to the Goths asserting Procopius' connection with Constantine the Great, an emperor so impressive in barbarian memory that 3000 warriors were sent to help the usurper.

Not every initiative succeeded, however. Mellifluous messengers sent to Illyricum, their packs stuffed with coins showing Procopius' head, were detained and executed by Aequitius, *magister militum per Illyricum*, who sealed the communicating passes between east and west.[36]

Late in 365, the Jovii and Victores intercepted Procopius and his forces at Mygdus on the river Sangarius. But as the armies closed together, Procopius dashed between the lines and hailed an old comrade-in-arms who was standing in the first rank of Valens' legionaries. The usurper violently denounced the Pannonian occupation of the imperial throne and turned the allegiance of the troops, who declared for Procopius.

Territorial successes followed. Blocked in the west, Procopius extended his empire in the east by capturing Nicaea. When Valens attempted to recover nearby Chalcedon, the defenders of the city berated the emperor as a 'sabaiarius' or 'beer-drinker', and a sudden sally made by Procopius' forces in Nicaea drove him back to Ancyra in disorder. Virtually the whole of Bithynia fell into the usurper's hands.

Thus far, Valens' response to Procopius' usurpation had been conditioned by the need to take action quickly; he had been compelled to make what use he could of the limited forces he had available and his own modest military talent. In the spring of 366 Valens, bolstered by the *magister militum per Orientem* Lupicinus and his troops, marched west to confront Gomoarius, who was operating in Lydia.[37] Procopius' general had brought Constantia Postumia with him and was using her presence to sway popular support towards the usurper. As a highly effective counter-measure,

[35] The former had had experience of usurpation before; he had betrayed Vetranio to Constantius II in 350.

[36] For Procopius' coins, see J. W. E.Pearce, *RIC* ix, 209–16 (Constantinople); 192–3 (Heraclea); 239–41 (Cyzicus); 250–2 (Nicomedia).

[37] Amm. Marc. xxvi.9.2 has 'Lycia' but modern scholars have doubted that Procopius' forces could have been so widely dispersed. See Fontaine 5, 227 (n. 121); Paschoud II.2, 347 (n. 121).

however, Valens succeeded in persuading Flavius Arbitio, the veteran general of Constantine I, to come to his camp. Procopius, who had plundered the old man's house in Constantinople, was denounced as a common brigand. The usurper's troops began to waver, and Gomoarius, deserting a usurper for the second time in his distinguished career, led his forces into Valens' camp at Thyatira in March or April 366.

Valens pressed on into Phrygia, where he engaged Procopius at Nacolia. As the emperor gained the upper hand, Agilo defected. His men inverted their shields and hastened across the field into the emperor's lines.

Procopius realized that his military foundation had been destroyed. He fled with Florentius, his commander in Nicaea, and a trusted tribune, Barchalba. But his companions, seeing the only hope of saving their own lives, suddenly seized and bound him and brought him to the camp of Valens. There he was at once beheaded, and Barchalba and Florentius, to their dismay and Ammianus' disapproval, were also executed.

VIII. VALENS AND PERSIA[38]

Sapor's persistent interference in the affairs of Armenia finally violated the treaty which he had signed with Jovian in 368.[39] King Arsaces, invited to meet Persian agents on the pretext of re-establishing friendship, was imprisoned and then murdered. The government of Armenia was placed in the hands of Cylaces and Arrabanes, both agents of the Persian king. But Pharandzem, Arsaces' wife, and Papa, his son, remained at large in the treasury city of Artogerassa. When Sapor's forces besieged the city, Papa was smuggled out to the court of Valens at Neocaesarea in Pontus Polemoniacus, where he received a state welcome. Encouraged by the reception given to Papa, Cylaces and Arrabanes requested that Valens restore him to the Armenian throne. The emperor, however, was anxious not to infringe the treaty with Persia by king-making, so he returned Papa to Armenia in 369 without royal status but supported by the dux Armeniae Terentius.

Sapor now determined to conquer the whole of Armenia. Extensive Persian military activity forced Papa, Cylaces and Arrabanes into hiding for five months. The city of Artogerassa also fell into Sapor's hands, along with Arsaces' widow and the considerable treasures of the former royal family. In these circumstances, with the kingdom tottering on the brink of Persian

[38] Grousset (1973) 140f.; Baynes (1910).
[39] Amm. Marc. XXVII.12. Date: Fontaine, 5, 270 n. 301. Ammianus says that Sapor's activities were in contravention of the treaty with Jovian but his own account of the treaty does not fully support this. In 363 Rome promised not to give aid to Armenia but Persia did not undertake any similar obligation. Nevertheless, the spirit of the treaty was broken. See Them. Or. VIII (translated in Heather and Matthews, 1991).

overlordship, Valens ordered his *magister peditum* Arintheus to undertake the defence of Armenia and provided him with a force to complement Terentius' legions. He thus forestalled a second full-scale Persian invasion of Armenia, but the ever-resourceful Sapor sued for peace directly with Papa, who was induced to execute his two closest advisers as a gesture of good will. Sapor contacted Valens and reminded him of the promise made by Jovian not to defend Armenia. Valens, however, pressed on with his arrangements in the east. In 370, a vigorous campaign conducted by Terentius restored a pretender, Sauromaces, to half of Iberia, a mountainous kingdom in the Caucasus mountains, north-east of Armenia. The area to the east of the river Cyrus was left in the hands of Aspacures, a Persian protégé.

The Persian king now realized that Valens had no intention of observing the terms of Jovian's treaty and in the spring of 371 he crossed into Roman territory. Trajanus and Vadomarius, a former king of the Alamanni, met a powerful collection of Persian cataphracts, archers and infantry at Vagabanta, but the outcome was inconclusive, and at the end of the season Sapor retired to Ctesiphon, Valens to Antioch.

There, the praetorian prefect of the Orient uncovered details of magical practices in high places, using information supplied by Palladius, a humble poisoner, and Heliodorus, an expert in horoscopy.[40] It was claimed that a certain ex-governor, Fidustius, assisted by two accomplices, had actually sought and ascertained the name of the emperor's successor through supernatural agencies. This man, the inquisitors were informed, was to be one Theodorus, an educated and charismatic *notarius* of the second rank from Gaul.

Theodorus was summoned from Constantinople and investigations were carried out into the affairs of a large number of men of high rank living throughout the eastern provinces. The atmosphere of fear and danger was increased by an attempt made on Valens' life by a *scutarius* as he was resting on the road between Antioch and Seleucia. Ammianus, an eyewitness of the trials, explains that the emperor's natural bad temper was compounded by his gullibility to make him the most unbending of judges.[41]

Tortures were employed against men of distinction, and further details of the divinatory activity emerged. Hilarius, a palace officer, had made a small imitation of the Delphic tripod and placed on it a round dish, on the edges of which were marked the twenty-four letters of the Greek alphabet. A ring was suspended over the dish in an elaborate ceremony recalling the rites of Pythian Apollo. Upon consultation, the suspended ring moved over the letters, spelling out hexameter verses. One of the questions which

---

[40] Amm Marc. xxix.1.4ff. For what follows, see Zos. iv.13.2–15.2. Also Matthews, *Ammianus* 219–26 and for the survival of magic in the period: Barb (1963).   [41] Amm. Marc. xxix.1.20.

the consulters put to the magical machine was 'What man will succeed the present emperor?' The ring began to spell out the letters: theta (TH), epsilon (E), omicron (O) and delta (D) before the meeting broke up in excitement as each man realized the prediction. A letter written in Theodorus' own hand and seeking further details of the prediction was found, sealing his fate. Valens, in response to a request from the court judges for advice, issued a single order that all those convicted should die.[42] More trials followed, as a result of which many men of all ranks perished.[43] Suspect books were seized and burned in a frenzy of investigation.

Relations between Rome and Papa, meanwhile, had been badly damaged by the latter's attempted *rapprochement* with Sapor. In 373, the *dux Armeniae* and his fellow officers contacted Valens and complained that Papa was behaving cruelly and arrogantly. They advised Valens to find a more suitable king for Armenia. The emperor courteously summoned Papa to the imperial court, but at Tarsus he was placed under house arrest. The artful prince staged a spectacular escape, putting to flight a full legion and evading a force of 1000 *scutarii* before regaining his kingdom.

Armenia itself was still occupied by Trajanus' army, and Valens issued instructions to his *dux* to assassinate Papa. Slowly and carefully, Trajanus won the confidence of the fugitive, showing him conciliatory letters from Valens and attending banquets given by the king. During a feast hosted by the Romans, Trajanus absented himself from the table when the hospitality was most pleasant and sent in a barbarian *scutarius* who ran the Armenian king through.[44]

Sapor, fearing the resurgence of an aggressive and expansionist Roman policy towards Armenia, sent his envoy to Valens in 373 to demand the withdrawal of Roman forces from the country or at least the evacuation of the portion of Iberia which they occupied. Valens flatly refused to comply and declared that he was determined to stand by Jovian's treaty, thus ushering in a period of complex and fruitless diplomacy.

In spring 378 an exasperated Sapor attempted to justify his claim to Armenia and asserted that most of the signatories of Jovian's peace were now dead. But Valens, who clearly held the initiative, delivered a final ultimatum: the king's claim on Armenia was unjust; the Armenians had been guaranteed independence, and Sapor must observe it. The Roman soldiers whom Sapor had taken when he campaigned against Sauromaces were to be returned within one year.

---

[42] Amm. Marc. XXIX.1.38. All were strangled except Simonides, who was burned alive.

[43] Maximus the philosopher, a former confidant of the emperor Julian, was convicted of having knowledge of the verses which prophesied Theodorus' *regnum*. He was beheaded at Ephesus: Amm. Marc. XXIX.1.42. Other executed philosophers named by Zosimus: IV.15.1: Hilarius of Phrygia, Simonides, Patricius of Lydia, Andronicus of Caria. Ridley (1982) 188 n. 40 says that the trials virtually wiped out the remaining pagan philosophers of the east.   [44] Amm. Marc. XXX.1.20.

Valens' ambassadors performed impressively at Sapor's court but they had unwisely accepted the allegiance of certain Armenian kingdoms as they travelled to the king's headquarters. When the Surena visited Valens and made a conciliatory offer of the same kingdoms, the emperor responded by declaring that they were not the king's to give. Gravely insulted, the Persians retired to prepare for war. Sapor ordered his Surena to recover the whole of Armenia. But as the respective empires anticipated a great conflict, news began to reach Valens of a terrible disaster in the western portions of his territory. Within months his belligerence towards Sapor had vanished and his power was extinguished in a manner quite unforeseen.

IX. VALENS AND THE GOTHS

In 366, Valens declared that the decision of the Goths to aid Procopius was a breach of the treaty which they had signed with Constantine in 332, but in reality trouble with Gotho–Roman relations had been developing since the reign of Julian. In 362, Julian had dismissed them contemptuously, declaring that only through war would they secure better conditions. And Procopius had intercepted and subverted units already making their way to Thrace to counter a perceived threat. Thus, in 366, when the Goths defended themselves by claiming that Procopius had demonstrated his kinship to Constantine, their excuse was of little importance; Valens had already decided to undertake pre-emptive military action to secure the Danube frontier.

In a series of campaigns between 367 and 369, Valens penetrated Gothic territory, causing widespread disruption among the Tervingi and also making contact with the more distant Greuthungi.[45] But the successes were unconvincing, and Valens' failure to subdue the Goths decisively made news from the east more unwelcome.

Sapor had toppled the kings of Armenia and Iberia and was threatening to upset the balance of power on the eastern frontier. Valens would himself have to move east and direct operations. With some reluctance, therefore, he was forced to abandon his aggressive policy towards the Goths and negotiate peace.

The treaty of 369 superseded the peace of 332. King Athanaric had bound himself by a solemn oath to his father never to set foot in Roman territory, and the signatories were transported to a boat moored in the centre of the Danube. Henceforth, the Goths were no longer to receive subsidies from the emperors and they undertook not to cross the Danube.

---

[45] For these peoples and the difficulty in identifyng them: Todd (1992) 147–91; Heather, *Goths and Romans* 12–18; Wolfram, *Goths* 24–6.

The privilege of uninterrupted trade with the Romans was lost; commercial relations were to continue at only two points on the Danube.[46]

Despite the confident rhetoric which issued from court panegyrists, the peace which Rome concluded with the Goths in 369 marked her failure to solve the problems which the Gothic presence posed. But Valens was given little time to reassess the situation because of an utterly unforeseen crisis developing far beyond the Gothic kingdoms.

The ancient sources identify the Huns as the cause of a remarkable migration of northern peoples.[47] Living a nomadic life on the steppes beyond the Maeotic Sea (Sea of Azov), the Huns had survived by developing superb skills of horsemanship and a ferocious fighting spirit. Moving westwards, they had overwhelmed the Halani, living in Asia just beyond the river Tanais. They then crossed into Europe and attacked the Greuthungi, killing two kings and pushing a mass of refugees on to the banks of the Dniester.

The advance of the Huns brought them inexorably into contact with the Tervingi. Their king, Athanaric, put up stout resistance in an attempt to keep the invaders beyond the Dniester, but a savage and unexpected night attack broke Tervingian resistance. The Huns' insatiable appetite for booty gave the Tervingi time to contemplate a desperate solution to their threatened destruction. The Roman province of Thrace lay just beyond the Danube and their own recent history provided them with evidence of the vigour of Rome's armies. Only the proud Athanaric, loyal to his father's memory and fearful of Valens, refused to consider so dishonourable a plan and retired into the Carpathian mountains.

Early in 376 the Tervingi, now led by Alavivus, sent envoys to Valens at Antioch. The barbarians promised to conduct themselves peacefully and supply Rome with recruits if the emperor would grant them admission to the empire and lands in Thrace.[48] It was pointed out to Valens that such a plentiful resource of recruits would leave Roman farmers free to work the land, thereby increasing the revenue to the imperial treasury. Thus, in the autumn of 376, Valens decided to allow the Tervingi to cross into Thrace. The Greuthungi, however, were denied access to Roman territory.[49] The final demand made of the Goths may have been that they convert to Arian Christianity.[50]

[46] See Amm. Marc. xxvii.5; Them. Or. x.135 (trans. in Heather and Matthews (1991)); Zos. iv.11.4; Heather, Goths and Romans 115–16.
[47] Amm. Marc. xxxi.2.1ff. with Richter (1974). Cf. Zos. iv.20.3–7; Jordanes,Getica 121–3; Eunap. fr. 41, 42 Blockley. For Huns, see Diesner (1982) 71–85 (for the Goths, see: 90–123); Maenchen-Helfen, Huns; Altheim (1959 6z) vols 1 and z, Thompson, Attila. Also, Heather, Goths and Romans 135ff.
[48] Amm. Marc. xxxi.4.1; 5; 8; Zos. iv.20.5. No formal treaty: Orosius vii.33.10. The terms of settlement, see Heather, Goths and Romans 124ff.; Wolfram, Goths and Romans 117ff.; Chrysos (1973).
[49] For the story of a Gothic 'oath', see Heather, Goths and Romans 139ff.
[50] See Heather, Goths and Romans 127–8; Heather (1986); Rubin (1981).

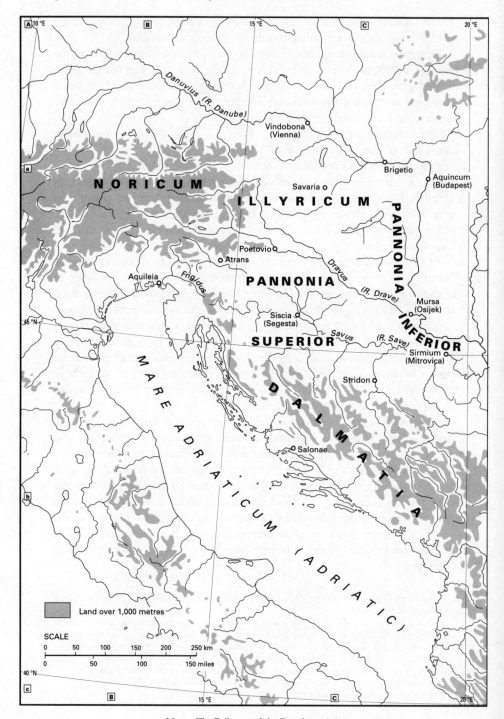

Map 3 The Balkans and the Danube region

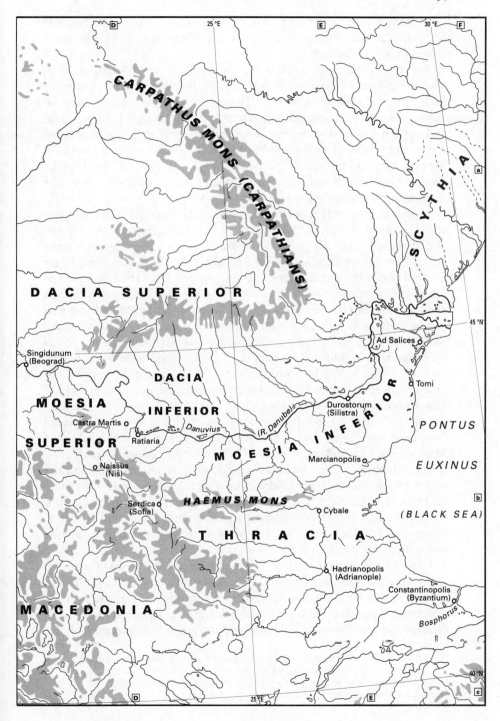

Estimates of the number that crossed the Danube vary between Eunapius' unreliable figure of 200,000 warriors and modern projections of 90,000 people of all ages.[51]

The Goths had expected a swift dispersal to their allotted lands in Thrace but found themselves detained on the Roman bank and cheated by Lupicinus, the *comes rei militaris* in Thrace, who bargained dog meat for slaves. Their relief at escaping the Huns was quickly replaced by distrust and apprehension. The Roman commanders, realizing that their own forces were dwarfed by the Gothic horde, issued the order to move off towards Marcianopolis. But the departure of troops from the Danube allowed the Greuthungi, who had earlier been denied admission, the opportunity to make their way secretly into Thrace.[52]

Lupicinus, meanwhile, invited the leading Gothic chieftains Fritigern and Alavivus to his camp as a gesture of good will. But troops were stationed between Marcianopolis and the barbarians, and permission to enter the city and secure supplies was refused. Driven to desperation by hunger and exasperated by Roman tactlessness, a group of Goths became involved in a pitched battle with some of the townspeople. Lupicinus was informed and he immediately massacred the guards whom Fritigern and Alavivus had brought with them, seizing the kings as hostages. The Goths were incensed, and Fritigern convinced Lupicinus that war could only be averted if he was freed to return to his people.[53] The Tervingi, however, were now convinced that Valens had no intention of honouring his promises and under Fritigern's leadership they began looting villages in the vicinity of Marcianopolis.

Lupicinus realized that his attempt to manage the crossing and avoid hostilities had failed. He drew up his forces nine miles west of Marcianopolis and advanced on the Goths. The Roman army was met by a furious barbarian attack which swept it away; its standards were captured by the enemy and the commander himself only survived after a disgraceful flight from the field. The defeat left Thrace wide open to attack from the north, and numerous barbarians in Roman employment deserted, bringing to the Goths valuable intelligence on Roman military dispositions and settlements ripe for plunder.

News of the disaster reached Valens at Antioch late in 376. Victor, his *magister equitum*, was despatched to Sapor's court to negotiate a settlement over Armenia. Crossing into Europe in the spring of 377, the Romans hemmed a large band of Goths into the defiles of the Haemus mountains. Gratian had sent his *dux* Frigiderius and the *comes domesticorum* Richomer

---

[51] Eunap. fr. 42 Blockley; Schmidt (1969) 403. Cf. Burns (1978) and Paschoud 2.2, 376 n. 143.

[52] For the theory that the Tervingi and Greuthungi co-operated, see Heather, *Goths and Romans* 138ff.

[53] Alavivus is not heard of again. For the possibility that the kings represented rival Gothic factions: Heather, *Goths and Romans* 137.

with legions from Pannonia and Gaul in response to an appeal from Valens. At Salices, the western and eastern armies met within sight of the laager of wagons which the Goths had drawn about their camp. The subsequent battle was bloody but the heavy losses on both sides failed to produce a decisive result. The Romans, however, could ill afford their casualties; the generals were so anxious to withdraw to Marcianopolis that all but the highest-born dead were left unburied.

When the Romans returned to the site of the battle some seven days later, they were surprised to find the Gothic army still there and block-aded it again. The barbarians finally made contact with bands of Huns and Alans who had crossed the Danube and, offering them huge quanti-ties of booty, secured their alliance. The Romans drew back from the powerful coalition, and within weeks the barbarians had ravaged the province of Thrace from the Hellespont to the Rhodope mountains, causing huge loss of life.

Fleeing one large band of Goths, Frigiderius fell upon a force made up of Taifali and Goths in Illyricum. The Romans won a resounding victory and the barbarians who survived were settled by Gratian in Mutina, Regium and Parma.[54]

Gratian was anxious to help his uncle personally, but in February 378 the Lentienses were apprised of his preparations to leave the west and crossed the frozen Rhine. Between forty and seventy thousand warriors entered Raetia. Gratian was forced to recall the legions he had sent to Pannonia and stage a lightning campaign across the Rhine, losing valuable weeks while the Goths overran Thrace.

Valens, meanwhile, had shifted his court from Antioch to Constantinople in the spring of 378. Intelligence reports reached the court that disparate Gothic forces were coming together at Cybale and moving on Adrianople. A letter from Gratian also arrived, assuring Valens that the western emperor was marching with all speed to meet him. The letter also mentioned the recent victory over the Lentienses, and the reference dis-turbed Valens. He felt pressurized to match the success of his nephew and his own generals. Thus, late in July, when news reached him of a force of 10,000 Goths moving towards Nice, Valens could wait no longer; he formed his army into a massive square and took it to Adrianople. There, Richomer arrived to tell Valens that only days separated the forces of the two emperors; Gratian's army had been attacked by Alans at Castra Martis and he himself had been afflicted with fever, but Valens was advised to wait until the armies had been combined. Valens, believing himself to be on the brink of a resounding victory which would restore the security of the Danube, did not wish to share his glory. Only one of the generals, a

---

[54] Amm. Marc. xxxi.9.4.

Sarmatian named Victor, advised delay, but the rest, including the usually cautious Sebastianus, urged the emperor to engage the enemy.

The Goths retained some hope that combat could be avoided, or at least delayed. Fritigern sent a Christian presbyter to Valens and made a formal demand that Thrace, with its flocks and stores, should be ceded. A private letter for Valens alone requested that the emperor move his force to within clear sight of the Goths so that Fritigern could use its impressive appearance to dampen the belligerence of his people. Valens refused to hand over so vital a territory as Thrace, and he may also have suspected a subterfuge by which the Goths could gauge the size of the Roman army.

On the morning of 9 August 378, the emperor deposited his imperial seal and his field treasury in Adrianople. He then led his soldiers out into the plain in a north-westerly direction towards the Gothic camp. At about two o'clock in the afternoon the legionaries caught sight of the wagons of the Goths drawn into a huge circle around the perimeter of their camp. In battle order, with the right wing of cavalry pushed slightly ahead of the main body, the army advanced.[55]

The Goths, who were awaiting the arrival of a large force of Greuthungi cavalry, stalled, but Valens dismissed an embassy contemptuously, as it did not include any Gothic kings. Fritigern responded by giving the impression that he was summoning more senior representatives while his men lit fires up-wind of the Roman army, which waited in the baking heat. Valens was presently contacted again with the offer that Fritigern would curb the aggression of his soldiers if the emperor would despatch some noble hostages to him. Aequitius, one of the palatine tribunes and a relative of the emperor, refused to go, remembering a previous incarceration. Richomer volunteered for the task, and collecting up proofs of his rank, set off for Fritigern's headquarters. But as he left the Roman lines, a fierce skirmish erupted between some over-eager archers and the barbarian guards. The combat was observed by the returning cavalry of Alaethus and Saphrax, who charged their men into the Roman ranks.

The massed forces surged together with a violent impact. The left wing of the Roman army pressed forward and almost reached the enemy camp, but contact with supporting cavalry was lost and the flank was violently thrown back. Desperate hand-to-hand fighting ensued and missiles rained down on the densely packed ranks. By the early afternoon, the Roman forces were exhausted; they had marched to the battlefield and been in full armour under the blazing sun since dawn. Under fierce pressure from the Gothic assault, their lines broke and the great army disintegrated; units lost their shape and a headlong flight from the field followed. Valens attempted to rally his men but his auxiliary reserve, the Batavi, was nowhere to be

---

[55] Amm. Marc. xxxi.12.11. See Wolfram (1977); Burns (1973); Pavan (1979).

found. The Goths, realizing that the day was won, pressed home their attacks. Only dusk brought an end to the carnage.

Valens himself, escaping among a throng of common soldiers, was killed by an arrow, although the failure to recover his body gave rise to vivid stories of his end. Ammianus recorded one version in which the emperor was carried, wounded, to a peasant's cottage by bodyguards and eunuchs. A band of Goths surrounded the house and burned it, without knowing whom they had killed.[56]

Barely one-third of Valens' army escaped the battle. A large number of *viri illustres* were killed, most notably Trajanus and Sebastianus; Valerianus, *curator stabuli*, Aequitius the *curator palatii* and Potentius the tribune of the *promoti* were lost; thirty-five tribunes fell; numerous *rectores* and *vacantes* perished. Modern scholars suggest that between fifteen and thirty thousand Roman soldiers died.[57] Ammianus considered Adrianople to be the worst defeat suffered by Rome since Cannae (216 B.C.).

X. THEODOSIUS: THE GOTHIC WAR

Although Gratian grieved little for his uncle, he could not rule the empire alone.[58] Moesia and Thrace had been devastated by the Tervingi and Greuthungi; Gaul was threatened by Alamanni and Franks. He therefore moved to Sirmium to consider the credentials of imperial candidates, while the government of Valens' dominions devolved upon the generals appointed before his death. Some desperate measures were taken. Julius, *magister equitum et peditum per Orientem*, assembled a larger number of Goths in Roman service outside Constantinople. When the barbarians had been disarmed, they were butchered to a man.

In his nineteen years, Gratian had not acquired the nerve and military experience needed to reverse Roman fortunes. There was, however, a general of outstanding skill who had been living in retirement since the dramatic downfall and execution of his father in 374. An urgent appeal brought Flavius Theodosius from his family's Spanish estates to take up the post of *magister equitum*, and on 19 January 379 Gratian crowned him emperor at Sirmium.

The disaster at Adrianople had ravaged the ranks of the legions. To make good the losses, Theodosius sponsored stern and comprehensive conscription laws.[59] Edicts threatened those who furnished unfit recruits, and even self-mutilation did not secure an exemption from service. But the depth of

---

[56] Amm. Marc. XXXI.13.14–16. Some Catholics considered his death a punishment for his Arianism: Ambrose, *De Fide ad Gratianum* 2, 16; Orosius, *Historiae adversus Paganos* VII.33.15–19.

[57] Amm. Marc. XXXI.13.19. See Heather, *Goths and Romans* 147 for a discussion of the Roman losses.

[58] See Heather, *Goths and Romans* 147–56 and Appendix B; Wolfram, *Goths* 131–9.

[59] *C.Th* VII.13.8; 9 (380); 10 (381); 11 (382).

Roman distress was most vividly illustrated by the decision to admit non-Romans to the army in unprecedented numbers. The hostile Zosimus claimed that there was no longer any distinction between Roman and barbarian in the ranks. Even deserters from barbarian armies beyond the Danube were admitted.[60]

Although the source material will not sustain a coherent narrative of the first years of Theodosius' reign, there is sufficient evidence to sample something of the chaos and hardship of the early campaigns which the emperor conducted from Thessalonica.

After the victory at Adrianople, the Gothic army attempted unsuccessfully to capture the city. The subsequent fragmentation of the Gothic host enabled Theodosius to win victories over a number of individual bands of barbarians.[61] One group making for Constantinople itself was foiled by Arab archers of queen Mavia and by the city's impressive walls.[62]

By the spring of 380, two particularly powerful Gothic concentrations had emerged. One, led by Fritigern, made for Macedonia and Thessaly. The other, under the command of Allortheus and Saphrax, the guardians of king Viderich, threatened Pannonia. In the summer of 380, the latter collided with Gratian's forces.[63] The barbarians' advance was checked and late sources hint at a separate peace between Gratian and the invaders, who were settled as federate allies in Pannonia II, Savia and Valeria.[64]

An engagement between Theodosius and the Goths ended in a serious defeat for the Romans.[65] In the winter of 380–1, Theodosius fell seriously ill and baptism was administered in anticipation of his death. He recovered, however, in time to receive the king Athanaric, who had originally refused to enter Roman territory, but fled from domestic intrigues to the court of Theodosius at Constantinople in January 381.[66] The king was in poor health, and when he died two weeks later, a magnificent funeral was held and Athanaric was interred in a grand mausoleum. Many of the Tervingi in Roman service were deeply impressed by Theodosius' gesture.

Elsewhere, beyond the common desire for booty, the invaders had no guiding strategy and the emperors were able to exploit their inconstancy and lack of cohesion. On 3 October 382 Theodosius' *magister militum* Saturninus signed a treaty with the remaining Goths.[67] Only the scantiest

---

[60] Zos. IV.31.1.

[61] The official calendar of the eastern empire records celebrations on 17 November 379 held to mark victories over Goths, Alans and Huns: *Cons. Const. (Chron. Min.* 1.243, 379, 2ff. and 380, 1).

[62] Amm. Marc. XXXI.16.5–6 to be preferred to Zos. IV.22.1–3.

[63] Heather, *Goths and Romans* 155 thinks this campaign is to be dated to 381.

[64] See Heather, *Goths and Romans* Appendix B; Wolfram, *Goths* 132 with n. 92.

[65] Zos. IV.31.3–5. For more details of fighting, see Eun. fr. 50 M; Jord. *Getica* 139–40.

[66] Zos. IV.34.1ff.; *Cons. Const. s.a.* 381 (*Chron. Min.* 1.243, 381, 1 and 2). See also Jord. *Getica* 143ff.

[67] *Chron. Min.* 1, 243. According to Wolfram, *Goths* 133: 'Probably the most momentous *foedus* in Roman history'. Gratian may already have made peace with the Greuthungi. See n. 64 above and cf. Heather, *Goths and Romans* ch. 5; Wolfram, *Goths* 133–4.

details of the agreement survive. In January 383, the orator Themistius praised Theodosius for the new settlements of men in Thrace, settlements made up of former enemies, not relocated easterners.[68] It would seem, therefore, that Theodosius' peace of 382 made provision for the settlement of large numbers of barbarians on Roman territory, most probably along the Danube in Lower Moesia, Thrace, Dacia Ripensis and Macedonia. Barbarians had been admitted to the empire and armies of Rome before but they had been required to submit themselves to Roman command and discipline.[69] Those settled by Theodosius retained their native military structure and followed their own chieftains into battle on the Roman side. Thus the barbarians lived as discrete nations within the frontiers and served as allies (*foederati*) when Rome called upon them in war.[70]

XI. THEODOSIUS AND CHRISTIANITY

After his accession Theodosius took time to understand fully the complexity of Greek Christianity. In February 380 he issued an edict which indelicately defined orthodoxy as 'the form of religion handed down by the apostle Peter to the Romans and now followed by bishop Damasus [of Rome] and Peter of Alexandria'.[71]

When he took possession of his capital on 24 November 380, one of his first acts was to depose the Arian bishop Demophilus. A council sitting in Antioch, for the purpose of suppressing the followers of Apollinaris and discussing reconciliation with Rome, extended an invitation to Gregory of Nazianzus to take up the vacant see. Theodosius hoped that Gregory's appointment might bridge the divisions in the Christian community, and his desire for unity was reflected in a law of 10 January 381 which again defined orthodoxy, but in terms which studiously avoided reference to Rome or Alexandria.[72] Gregory, for his part, was happy to leave his isolated diocese at Sasima in Cappadocia. Constantinople was in a ferment over the theological credentials of the candidates. In a memorable sermon, Gregory of Nyssa, another Cappadocian bishop, described the atmosphere in the city: 'If you ask anyone for change, he will discuss with you whether the Son is begotten or unbegotten. If you ask about the quality of bread, you will received the answer that "the Father is greater, the Son is less." If you suggest that you require a bath, you will be told that "There was nothing before the Son was created."'[73]

In the summer of 381, Theodosius summoned a great council at

---

[68] *Or.* XVI.211.   [69] See de Ste Croix, *Class Struggle* 509ff.
[70] Cf. Heather, *Goths and Romans* 159 who thinks the term inappropriate because the Goths surrendered (*deditio*) and did not therefore have a *foedus* with Rome.
[71] *C.Th.* XVI.1.2. See Piganiol, *Empire chrétien* 237–8.   [72] *C.Th.* XVI.5.6.
[73] *De Deitate Filii et Spiritus Sancti* (*PG* XLVI.557–8).

Constantinople to confirm the decisions of Nicaea and formally elect Gregory of Nazianzus bishop. The wording of the Nicene creed was reviewed and all dissenting groups anathematized. Gregory was welcomed but by leaving his diocese at Sasima he had laid himself open to the charge of violating canon fifteen of the council of Nicaea which prohibited epis-copal translation. He himself proceeded to misjudge the feelings of suspi-cion towards the Latin church when he recognized Paulinus, favoured by pope Damasus, as the legitimate bishop of Antioch. Confronted by the rising tide of indignation, Gregory resigned his position, leaving the court to engineer the elevation of Nectarius, an unblemished diplomat, to the patriarchate.

Not all the decisions of Constantinople went the way of the oriental bishops. Canon three was revised to read: 'The bishop of Constantinople shall have primacy and honour *after* the bishop of Rome, for Constantinople is the New Rome.'[74] The formula ultimately satisfied few present. Most Constantinopolitan churchmen felt no inferiority to Rome; Damasus was disappointed at the absence of any reference to the Petrine tradition; and the Alexandrians were not mentioned at all. While the council of Constantinople sealed the fate of Arianism, it perpetuated and deepened the distrust between the major Christian communities of the Mediterranean.

XII. THE USURPATION OF MAXIMUS AND THE FALL OF GRATIAN

Since the spring of 381, Gratian had regularly resided in northern Italy, usually at Milan.[75] There, a strong influence over the boy emperor came to be exercised by Ambrose, the bishop.[76] Although Gratian had at his acces-sion, like all his predecessors, happily accepted the title and functions of *pontifex maximus*, in 382 he refused to receive the pontifical robe from a delegation of senators who had travelled from Rome.[77] At the same time, he finally removed state subsidies from the pagan ceremonies and deprived the *vestales* of their stipends.[78] The altar of Victory, so swiftly restored after Constantius had ordered its removal in 356 or 357, was taken from the senate house.[79] An immediate appeal from Rome was refused access to the emperor at Milan, largely through the agency of Ambrose.[80]

[74] Mansi (1759–98) 3, 560 C.
[75] See Baldus (1984); Rodgers (1981); Matthews, *Western Aristocracies* 173–82, 223–38; Palanque (1965) 255–63.
[76] Ambrose, the former governor of Aemilia Liguria, was consecrated bishop on 7 December 373. He was rushed through all the clerical grades in only eight days, a violation of Canon 9 of the council of Nicaea. For Ambrose's career, see now McLynn (1994).
[77] Zos. iv.36.5. See Cameron, Alan (1968); Matthews, *Western Aristocracies* 203–4; Croke and Harries (1982) 29–30.   [78] *C.Th.* 16, 10, 20 (dated 30 August 415 but containing much of Gratian's measures).
[79] Symm. *Rel.* iii.15.
[80] Ambrose, *Ep.* 17.10. He claimed that the delegation from the senate did not represent the body. Cf. Symm. *Rel.* iii.1; xx.

In June 383, Gratian took an army through the Brenner Pass into Gaul to face an Alamannic invasion. Gratian had little liking for the arduous military life, preferring the classes of Ausonius and the pseudo-militarism of athletics. He was dazzled by the archery skills of one of his auxiliary regiments of Alans and fêted the barbarians, to the chagrin of some of the legionaries. This imperial diversion coincided with an outbreak of unrest among the notorious legions of Britain, where the *comes Brittaniarum* Magnus Maximus had barely concealed a smouldering discontent since the elevation of Theodosius. In the spring of 383, his men declared him Augustus.[81] Although Maximus was warmly welcomed by the tough corps on the Rhine, the Gallic legions retained their loyalty to Gratian. In five days of skirmishing near Paris, however, the emperor's conduct of operations so undermined the confidence of the soldiers that his leading general, Merobaudes, defected to the enemy. Gratian turned and fled with a small bodyguard of cavalrymen towards the Alps but was apprehended crossing the Rhône at Lugdunum (Lyons). On 23 August 383 he was executed along with his senior ministers.

When he had overrun Gratian's territories, Maximus showed no inclination to turn on Valentinian II. Instead, he invited Valentinian to come to Trier where they could live 'as father and son'.[82] Ambrose interceded, claiming that the court could not make the journey in winter but giving Valentinian time to fortify the Alpine passes separating him from Maximus.

An embassy was also sent by Maximus to Theodosius. The new emperor did not claim responsibility for Gratian's death and arrogantly demanded recognition, or war. Theodosius reflected that Valentinian's territories remained unassailed and he knew that the barbarians would not fail to note his own departure from the Danube should he attempt to attack Maximus. There was, in addition, the excellence of Maximus' military reputation; a war with him would by no means result in certain victory.[83] In the summer of 384, Theodosius therefore formally recognized the usurper. The names of the emperors were commemorated on inscriptions and their images displayed together in public.[84]

The death of Gratian (383) and the appearance of Magnus Maximus convulsed the delicate arrangements made after the death of Valentinian I. The altar of Victory had become a symbol for high-born pagans and with Gratian's untimely death many pagan senators hoped for a more

---

[81] 'A vigorous and honest man, worthy to be Augustus had he not risen by usurpation contrary to his oath of allegiance' (Oros. VII.34.9).

[82] Ambrose, *Ep.* 24.7. Diplomatic activity also involved Maximus' son, Victor, travelling at least once to Milan.

[83] Them. *Or.* XVIII.220d–221a, cf. 224c, seems to refer to some kind of military activity against the west in summer 384. Its nature is unknown and it was certainly not successful.

[84] Inscriptions: *CIL* VIII.27. Statues: Zos. IV.37.3 (at Alexandria). Gratian's acts remained in force: Ambrose, *Ep.* 17.

sympathetic attitude in Valentinian II. In 384, the senate's leading orator, Q. Aurelius Symmachus, conveyed an elegant and passionate plea to the young emperor for the return of the altar. Once again, however, Ambrose's influence over the throne proved to be decisive, although he himself had to compose two long letters to secure the rejection of Symmachus' request.[85]

But as the displaced emperor's stay in Milan became prolonged, tensions between Valentinian, Justina and Ambrose emerged. In the spring of 385 Valentinian's praetorian prefect requested that the bishop hand over the Portian basilica in Milan for the use of an Arian community in the emperor's army. Ambrose refused to have anything to do with the demand and a tense confrontation took place on 9 April 385, when Ambrose was ordered to surrender the building.[86] Popular opinion in the city was firmly behind the bishop, and the court was forced to back down, but the cooling of relations between bishop and emperor enabled the Arians at court to pass a law which was favourable to the creed of Ariminum.[87] At the beginning of 386 Auxentius, an Arian bishop, was received by Valentinian and Justina. Ambrose was again ordered to surrender a church to the Arians in Milan. Once more, however, he resisted. Refusing to obey an order to leave the city, he occupied the basilica and denounced the perfidy of heretics.

In the eastern empire, Theodosius took no direct action against the pagan cults during the first twelve years of his reign. But if Theodosius was commendably moderate, some of his subordinates were notably less so. The praetorian prefect of the Orient, Maternus Cynegius, took the opportunity during his tour of eastern dioceses and Egypt in 385 to oversee the destruction of temples in the region.[88]

The first real test of the Gothic peace of 382 occurred in 386, when a force of Greuthungi appeared on the Danube. But Promotus, *magister peditum per Thracias*, had saturated the Roman bank of the river with troops and prevented a crossing. On 12 October 386 a magnificent triumph was held at Constantinople and an impressive column was erected in the Forum Tauri.[89]

Probably in the same year (386), peace was made between Rome and Persia. Armenia was divided up and six satrapies between the upper Euphrates and Tigris (about one-fifth of the kingdom) came into Roman hands. The satraps remained as governors of the strategically vital areas, but their installation was formally handled by Rome and their symbols of office came henceforth from the emperor himself.[90]

---

[85] Documents collected in Wytzes (1977) and translated in Croke and Harries (1982) 28–51.

[86] Ambrose *Ep.* 20.8. See Gottlieb (1985); Piganiol, *Empire chrétien* 271–2; McLynn (1994) 173–5.

[87] *C.Th.* XVI.1.4 (January 386); for what follows, McLynn (1994) 187–96.

[88] Zos. IV.37.3 alleges that Theodosius had issued orders. Cf. Lib. *Or.* XXX. See Fowden (1978).

[89] See Zos. IV.38–9, a confused passage. *Cons. Const. (Chron. Min.* 1.244, 386) attributes the victory to Arcadius and Theodosius.   [90] See Baynes (1955) 207; Blockley, *Foreign Policy* 39–45.

In the spring of 387, complex circumstances conspired to bring together a contested bishopric and increased financial impositions in Antioch. In response, the populace made a concerted attack on the images of the emperor and his family. Twenty-four days after the disturbance, Theodosius published his verdict: Antioch's metropolitan status was abolished; henceforth she came humiliatingly under the jurisdiction of the village of Laodicaea. Her baths and circus were closed and corn distributions to the citizens ceased. A tribunal was established under senior imperial officials, and trials, tortures and executions followed. The Antiochenes lodged an appeal, which was made at Constantinople early in April. To the delight of the citizens, a pardon was granted and was celebrated magnificently on Easter Sunday 387.[91]

Maximus, meanwhile, was not long satisfied with his annexation of Gratian's dioceses. In 386 or 387, he launched a sudden attack on Valentinian II's dominions, sending the latter and his court fleeing to Thessalonika, safely within Theodosius' portion of the empire.

Maximus arrived in Milan in time to take the consulship of 388, the occasion of a characteristically fulsome speech by the senate's foremost orator, Q. Aurelius Symmachus.

After consulting the senate of Constantinople, Theodosius undertook the liberation of the west. Anticipating a naval attack, Maximus' troops were surprised by Theodosius' swift overland march, and advance elements apprehended Maximus himself at Aquileia. Theodosius' officers tore off Maximus' imperial insignia and brought him bound to their commander. The eastern emperor upbraided him for his crimes before executing him on 28 August 388.[92]

On 18 June 389, Theodosius visited Rome, displayed his second son, the four-year-old Honorius, and conciliated the senators who had supported Maximus. Symmachus, who had taken refuge in a church, was publicly pardoned.[93] This exhibition of clemency encouraged pagan senators at Rome to hope that the altar of Victory might yet be restored to the senate house. Symmachus again journeyed to the court at Milan. But he and his supporters had badly misjudged the emperor; enraged by the request, Theodosius gave orders that the orator was to be unceremoniously removed from the city to a distance of a hundred miles.[94]

In Milan, Theodosius no less than Gratian encountered the formidable personality of Ambrose. Sometime during Theodosius' war of liberation in the west, the fortress town of Callinicum on the Euphrates frontier

[91] Lib. Or. Antioch, Chrysostom Homiliae de Statuts (PG XLIX.1–222); Downey, Antioch 419–33; Browning (1952); further, pp. 154–5 below.

[92] Date of execution: Cons. Const. (Chron. Min. 1.245, 388, 2).   [93] Socr. HE v.14.

[94] Ambrose Ep. 57.4. For Symmachus' removal: Ps.-Prosper, De Promissionibus et Praedictionibus Dei III.38.41 (PL LI.834).

witnessed a short but violent outbreak of sectarian fighting, during which
a Catholic mob destroyed a Jewish synagogue and a Valentinian church.[95]
Theodosius ordered the local bishop to repair both structures and to
punish those who had caused the damage. But in a sermon preached before
Theodosius himself, Ambrose argued that it was inappropriate of the
emperor to favour Jews and heretics in this way. Theodosius relented,
thereby strengthening the moral force which prominent churchmen could
bring to bear on imperial business.

In 390, Butheric, the garrison commander of Thessalonica, was lynched
by a mob of citizens in a dispute over the detention of a charioteer.
Theodosius decided that a clear demonstration of his anger was required
and in April 390, when the citizens of Thessalonica had gathered in the
circus of their town, the emperor's troops were let loose. The slaughter was
frightful; 7000 men, women and children were massacred in three hours.[96]
Ambrose withdrew in horror from the emperor's court. He denounced
Theodosius' wickedness and banned him from receiving communion until
he had repented.[97] The emperor sought absolution and was readmitted to
communion on Christmas day 390, after an eight-month penance.[98]

Within weeks of being received back into communion, Theodosius
drafted laws which constituted an unprecedented attack on the ancient
cults. On 24 February 391 the prefect of Rome received instructions to
close all temples and enforce a complete ban on all forms of sacrifice.[99] In
November of the same year the ban was officially extended to the households of the empire, with the stipulation of fines for those detected worshipping the *lares* or *penates*. Penalties were also set down for state officials
who did not perform their enquiries with sufficient alacrity.[100] Henceforth,
any act of pagan cult was illegal.

XIII. THE FALL OF VALENTINIAN II AND THE USURPATION OF EUGENIUS[101]

Valentinian II had been restored by Theodosius in 388. The young
emperor's regime had been bolstered by the appointment of two Frankish
officers, Bauto and Arbogast, as advisers. Following the death of the

---

[95] Ambrose, *Ep.* 40.6 and 16; 41, esp. 26–8. See Matthews, *Western Aristocracies* 233–4; McLynn (1994) 298ff.

[96] Ambrose, *Ep.* 51; Aug. *De Civ. Dei* v.26; Paulin. *V. Ambros.* xxiv; Sozom. *HE* vii.25; Theod. *HE* v.17. Zosimus, amazingly, passes over the incident. A purple passage in Gibbon's *Decline and Fall* 3, ed. Bury, 172–4; McLynn (1994) 315ff.   [97] Ambrose, *Ep.* 51.

[98] Ambrose, *De obitu Theodosii* 34; Rufinus xi.18; Aug. *De Civ. Dei* v.26; Paulin. *V. Ambr.* xxiv; Soz. *HE* vii.25 (in wrong year, 392); Theod. *HE* v.17 (caution needed).   [99] *C.Th.* xvi.10.10.

[100] *C.Th.* xvi.10.12.

[101] See Matthews *Western Aristocracies* 238–50; Szidat (1979); Straub (1966). A very useful selection of translated sources in Croke and Harries (1982) 52–72.

former, Arbogast assumed the rank of *magister militum* without the consent of Valentinian himself. Angry and humiliated, Valentinian thrust a letter of dismissal before Arbogast sometime in the spring of 392. The *magister militum* coolly declared that since Valentinian had not appointed him to his command, he could not deprive him of it.[102] On 15 May 392, the young emperor was found dead at Vienne in Gaul.[103]

Arbogast could harbour no pretensions about occupying the throne himself; he therefore turned to a pliant professor of rhetoric at Valentinian's court. On 22 August 392 Flavius Eugenius became Augustus.[104] It was probably hoped that his Christianity would help conciliate his eastern partner. New coins bearing the names of Theodosius and his son Arcadius were minted at Trier and Milan;[105] Valentinian's body was sent to Milan and unsuccessful attempts were made to enlist the city's bishop, Ambrose, as a go-between.

Theodosius did not offer recognition, but denunciation was muted.[106] In January 393, however, Theodosius dashed Eugenius' remaining hopes by making his son Honorius Augustus at Constantinople.[107]

Eugenius' anxiety for support led him to restore the altar of Victory to the senate house at Rome, although he had turned down the same request twice before.[108] Ambrose was informed that when Eugenius had won success on the battlefield, he would return to make the bishop's cathedral a stable and his priests soldiers.[109]

The armies met at the river Frigidus in September 394. Eugenius, released from the need to placate Christian opinion, had a great statue of Jupiter clutching golden bolts of lightning set up to overlook the field, and his soldiers followed an image of Hercules into battle.[110] When battle was joined (6 September 394), a violent tempest disordered Eugenius' troops and enabled Theodosius to rout the enemy.[111] Eugenius was executed and Arbogast took his own life; the Christian order had visited a crushing defeat upon its pagan enemies.

After the battle of Frigidus, Theodosius moved to Milan.[112] His health deteriorated suddenly, and Honorius was summoned from the eastern

---

[102] Zos. IV.53. See also Paschoud 2.2, nn. 200–1.

[103] Date: Epiphanius, *De Mensuris et Ponderibus* 20. Identity of murderer as Arbogast: Zos. IV.54.3 but cf. Ambr. *De Obitu Theodosii* 39–40. See Paschoud's commentary 2.2, 455–8 and Croke (1976).

[104] *Chron. Min.* 1.298, 517. See *PLRE* 1.293 'Fl. Eugenius 6'.   [105] *RIC* IX, 32f.; 80f.

[106] Eunap. fr. 59 Blockley.

[107] *Chron. Min.* 1.298, 521. Cf. Seeck (1919) 281. Honorius was not recognized in the west.

[108] Ambrose, *Ep.* 57.6. Full status of cults not restored: Matthews, *Western Aristocracies* 240–1.

[109] Paulin. *V. Ambr.* XXXI.

[110] For the pagan dimension to Eugenius' revolt, see Croke and Harries (1982) 52–72; Bloch (1945), and Bloch (1963) in Momigliano, *Conflict.*

[111] For details of the war and this battle see Paschoud's commentary, appendix C (pp. 474–500).

[112] According to Zos. IV.59.1 Theodosius made a visit to Rome. See Paschoud's commentary 2.2, n. 213.

capital. Stilicho, Theodosius' *magister utriusque militiae*, was appointed as his tutor. During games held in Milan to celebrate the imperial presence, Theodosius was forced to retire; he died on 17 January 395.[113] Ambrose, who had deftly ingratiated himself again with Theodosius before the latter's death, made a great oration over the body.[114]

---

[113] Socr. *HE* v.26; Philost. xi.2.

[114] Rehabilitation: *Epp.* 61; 62. The oration: *De Obitu Theodosii.* The body was interred in Constantinople on 8 Nov. 395: Socr. *HE* vi.1; Marcellinus, *Chron. Min.* ii.64, 395, 2.

CHAPTER 4

THE DYNASTY OF THEODOSIUS

R. C. BLOCKLEY

I. INTRODUCTION

The years from 395 to 425, during which the Roman world was ruled by
Arcadius and Honorius, the sons of Theodosius I, and by Theodosius II,
his namesake's grandson, stand at the fulcrum of the series of events that
transformed the Roman empire of antiquity into the European kingdoms,
the Byzantine empire and the Islamic states of the Middle Ages. At the
beginning of this period the two parts of the Roman empire, still constitu-
tionally undivided, came close to hostilities as the result of the ambitions
of those who controlled the governments. In the east, political dissensions
and an inability even to put an army in the field against foreign enemies
placed the state in grave danger, while in the west the firm and able guidance of the *magister utriusque militiae* Stilicho appeared to offer a respite from
the turmoil of the fourth century. At the end of the period, harmony
between the two parts of the empire had been restored. But by now it was
the west that was headlong into its final process of political disintegration,
while in the east the twenty-four-year-old emperor Theodosius II, almost
half-way into a long reign, was presiding over a recovery of stability and
strength that both laid the foundations of the Byzantine state and gave it
the resiliency necessary to weather the storms of the fifth-century invasions, the grandiose schemes of Justinian, and the onslaught of the armies
of Islam.

In both parts of the empire the developments during this crucial thirty
years both crystallized what had gone before and shaped what followed. In
the west the barbarization – mostly Germanization – of the Roman army
accelerated, and with the emergence of one *magister utriusque militiae* superior to the other military *magistri*, the emperor was to become little more than
a puppet in the control of an often German 'generalissimo'. Honorius
appears for most of his reign to have been complaisant, and those of his
successors who attempted to assert their independence failed, so that little
really changed when in 476 (or, better, 480 when Nepos was killed) the
western emperor was eliminated and the *patricius* Odovacer began to rule
Italy as the representative of the eastern court. The Germanization of the

Roman army was matched by a massive movement of mainly German tribes into Roman territory and the beginning of legalized settlement, first in Gaul by the Visigoths and Burgundians. Britain was abandoned, and, most ominous of all, at the very end of the period the Vandals began their movement into Africa. In the face of these pressures, as early as the beginning of the century the western Roman government began to behave like the government of Italy, for which the sack of Rome in 410, while of profound significance to individuals throughout the empire, was merely one amongst many setbacks. Under these circumstances the western provinces turned more to self-help and, where possible, accommodation with the invaders. In Spain both recourses brought little relief to the devastated Roman population, and in Britain the respite was only temporary. But in Gaul, agreements with the more Romanized Visigoths and Burgundians led first to the survival of the Gallo-Roman élite and later their co-optation, via the civil government, into the élite of the emergent German kingdoms. For the western Romans in a period of collapsing institutions, the Christian church, Nicene in creed at the insistence of Theodosius I, offered, together with Roman law, the guarantee of their identity, the more so since the invaders usually clung to their Arianism. The next stage – assimilation, with its greater potential – lay far in the future with the conversion of the Franks to orthodoxy at the beginning of the sixth century.

In the east the Germanization of the army and the militarization of government were both averted by the consolidation of a civilian administration which, especially under the *praefectus praetorio* Anthemius, was able to make timely and effective reforms. Timely, too, was the extended period of peace on the eastern border made possible by a succession of ephemeral and weak Persian kings, followed by Yezdegerd I (399–420), who was willing to cultivate good relations; the development in this context of mechanisms for Roman–Persian dialogue as an alternative to war laid the foundations for the effective and widely admired Byzantine diplomacy of the Middle Ages. Two further 'Byzantine' characteristics emerged during this period: the centralization of government in Constantinople and its environs, which soon led to the formation of state policy in the interests of 'The City'; and the insistence of the emperor and his ministers that the population of the empire accept a form of orthodox Christianity, Nicene in origin but after 451 Chalcedonian by definition.

The legacy of Theodosius I to the Roman world contained three elements of capital importance. First, his insistence that the Nicene version of Christian orthodoxy prevail routed Arianism from its strongholds in the Balkans and in Constantinople itself and laid down the lines of development for Roman Christianity, both east and west. Second, his settling as autonomous federates the barbarian peoples who had crossed into the Roman empire both before and after Adrianople, his greatly increased use of federate troops in the Roman armies, and his cultivation of the chieftains of the barbarians, especially the Visigoths, all led to an influx of such peoples not subject to the traditional controls, who were, however, drawn into the political process of the Roman state. Alaric was one result of this policy, Stilicho another: the former battling for lands for his followers and a position in the Roman military hierarchy for himself, the latter co-opted into the imperial family through marriage to Theodosius' niece and adopted daughter Serena, advanced through the military commands to the position of *magister utriusque militiae* of the western Roman armies, and established as guardian of the child emperor Honorius. Finally, Theodosius' determination that his dynasty should rule the whole Roman world led to a costly civil war against Eugenius and, at his own death shortly thereafter, the division of the empire between his two young and incapable sons, controlled by ministers whose rivalries split the resources of the state at a time when they needed to be united.

II. THE EMPIRE DIVIDED, 395–404

Theodosius died on 17 January 395, leaving his two sons already Augusti, Arcadius since 383, Honorius since 393. Arcadius, now aged seventeen or eighteen years, had been left at Constantinople when his father marched west against Eugenius; Honorius, now ten, was installed at Mediolanum as the emperor of the west. Arcadius was of an age himself to exercise the imperial authority, but his own inadequacies ensured that he would be under the control of others. At the beginning of 395 this control was exercised by the *praefectus praetorio* Rufinus, an able and unscrupulous Gaul who had every intention of maintaining his position. Honorius needed a guardian, and the promotion of Stilicho, already a member of the imperial family by marriage, made Theodosius' intention clear. Stilicho himself claimed that at his death Theodosius had appointed him guardian not only of Honorius but of Arcadius also. This appointment, at best undocumented and unofficial, was underpinned by Stilicho's claim to be the senior member of the imperial family (a claim emphasized by Claudian's description of him as *parens*), and it gained plausibility from Theodosius' obvious desire to keep the empire united under his dynasty. In the face of these claims, of arguable legitimacy but undoubtedly strong, Rufinus could only marshal his ascendancy over Arcadius and the emperor's apparent unwillingness to submit to the *parens*, though one source does allege that Rufinus planned to enter the imperial family also by marrying his daughter to Arcadius.[1] The plan, if it existed, fell through when on 27 April Arcadius

---

[1] Zos. VI.1.4–5.3; Jo. Ant. fr. 190 (both from Eunapius). Had this been Rufinus' plan, it is hard to believe that he would have been hoodwinked by Eutropius as easily as the sources suggest.

married Eudoxia, a Frankish general's daughter who, after the death of her father, had been raised in the household of Promotus, an enemy and allegedly a victim of Rufinus. The broker of this marriage was the eunuch chamberlain (*praepositus sacri cubiculi*) Eutropius, the emergent challenger to Rufinus' ascendancy.

Stilicho was able immediately to act in conformity with his claims. At or before the death of Theodosius, the Visigothic federates settled in Lower Moesia, angered perhaps by the use made of them at the battle of the river Frigidus, which caused them disproportionate losses, and by the lack of rewards from the campaign, rose in revolt under the leadership of Alaric and attacked Thrace and Macedonia. The eastern government, the bulk of its battlefield troops still in the west, was helpless against the Visigoths, as it was later in the same year against a Hunnic incursion from Transcaucasia into Asia Minor and Syria. Rufinus' attempt to negotiate in person with Alaric led only to a suspicion of collusion with the Goth for his own ends. The situation called for intervention from the west. Stilicho, after securing the borders of Noricum and Pannonia against raiders, marched at the head of the eastern and western forces to confront Alaric in Thessaly. According to Claudian (*In Ruf.* 11.186–96), Stilicho was on the point of engaging and destroying the Visigoths when a letter arrived from Arcadius ordering him to send on the eastern troops to Constantinople and himself leave Illyricum. Now, probably for the first time, Stilicho was made forcibly aware that Arcadius rejected his claim to guardianship. Nevertheless, legitimist on this occasion as throughout his career, he obeyed the command, encouraged no doubt by the presence, as potential hostages, of his wife and children at Constantinople, where they had gone for the funeral of Theodosius. Why he did not destroy Alaric before sending on the eastern forces has been much discussed. There is evidence of unrest in his army, probably the result of animosity between the eastern and western soldiery; it is also possible that Stilicho was nowhere as near to the decisive encounter as Claudian's dramatic account suggests, so that to have pursued Alaric to that point would have shown too obvious contempt for Arcadius' orders.[2]

The eastern troops proceeded to Constantinople under the command of count Gainas, a Goth. When Rufinus came out with the emperor from the city to greet them, he was surrounded and hacked to death (November 395). The deed was perhaps of Stilicho's planning, but the chamberlain Eutropius, who replaced Rufinus as Arcadius' favourite, profited from it. Although relations wth the west remained good for a short while, Eutropius was no more willing than Rufinus to yield power, and during 396

[2] The best discussion of the evidence for the campaigns of 395 and 397 and the many problems of interpretation is by Cameron, Alan, *Claudian* 156–80. Basic also for the narrative of this chapter are Heather, *Goths and Romans* and Liebeschuetz, *Barbarians and Bishops*; see also pp. 429–30 below.

he consolidated his position by engineering the exile of two of Theodosius' senior military *magistri*, Abundantius and Timasius, the latter by the kind of plot, involving blackmail and treachery, that was all too often ascribed to the eunuch chamberlains of the later empire. Eutropius also had some of the duties of the *praefectus praetorio* transferred to the *magister officiorum*, an obvious attempt to limit the former.

After Stilicho's withdrawal, Alaric plundered Greece at his leisure, only Thebes and Athens of the major cities escaping the devastation; the theory that he intended to settle there permanently remains merely that. In the spring of 397, however, Stilicho, having spent the previous year rebuilding his army mainly, it appears, with barbarian allies, crossed by sea to Greece, probably expecting that by now the eastern government would welcome his arrival. After some fighting, Alaric was blockaded but permitted to retreat to Epirus, and Stilicho withdrew to Italy. Again there has been much discussion of why Stilicho allowed Alaric to escape a second time if he had him at his mercy, as Claudian seems to claim (*IV Cons. Hon.* 479–83). On this occasion, too, the poet might have exaggerated his patron's success, since there is some indication that the rebuilt western army again proved unreliable; but, again, an order from Arcadius to withdraw is alleged (Claud. *Bell. Get.* 516f.) and cannot be discounted. At all events, Alaric continued his rampage in Epirus until the eastern government, probably in 398, appointed him *magister militum per Illyricum*, giving him the Roman command that he desired and a licence to plunder legally the cities and arsenals of the region and therefrom to resupply and rearm his followers.[3]

A serious deterioration in relations between the eastern and western governments followed the expedition to Greece. Perhaps now the senate at Constantinople declared Stilicho a public enemy, and when in late 397 Gildo, the count of Africa and master of the soldiers there, proposed to transfer Africa from the western to the eastern empire, his initiative was welcomed in the east. Grain was withheld from Rome; starvation threatened the city, and was averted by the importation of supplies from Gaul and Spain. Gildo, however, received no material assistance from Constantinople, and in spring 398 he was easily destroyed by a small force which sailed from Italy under his brother Mascezel. Africa having been restored to the west, the victorious general returned to Italy, where he soon perished by drowning, at the instigation, an eastern source alleges (Zos. v.11.4), of the jealous Stilicho. During the African crisis Stilicho had worked to secure his position both by courting the Roman senate (and involving it in difficult political decisions) and by marrying his elder daughter Maria to Honorius.

---

[3] Cameron, Alan, *Claudian* 177–80, argues (correctly in my opinion) against the view that there was also a pact between Stilicho and Alaric.

In the east, meanwhile, Eutropius determined to deal with the Hunnic raids from Transcaucasia by taking the field in person, apparently with success, beating back the enemy and pursuing it through Armenia (397); no subsequent attack from that quarter is recorded until a raid into Persia in 425. In the next year, at the height of his pre-eminence, which was confirmed by the title *patricius*, Eutropius made what turned out to be a capital error by having himself nominated consul for 399. The revulsion in the west at a eunuch-consul appears to have been matched by that in the east, and the chamberlain's enemies prepared their move. A revolt in early 399 by Ostrogothic federates settled in Phrygia, whose leader Tribigild held a grudge against Eutropius, provided the opportunity. Gainas, sent out in command of the Roman forces against the rebels, failed to pursue the war and, probably at this juncture entering into collusion with Tribigild, urged Arcadius to accede to the rebels' main demand, that Eutropius be removed. The resistance of the emperor, who appears to have been genuinely fond of his chamberlain, was broken by the intervention of the empress Eudoxia with her little daughters, who complained of Eutropius' insults towards her. When he realized that Arcadius was willing to sacrifice him, Eutropius fled to the altar of St Sophia, where the bishop of Constantinople, John Chrysostom, himself appointed with Eutropius' support in the previous year, gave him asylum. Eutropius finally agreed to come out on promise of his life. He was deprived of his titles and property, banished to Cyprus, and later recalled and executed on a trumped-up charge.

If Gainas expected to replace Eutropius in control of the government, he was disappointed. The empress Eudoxia, in alliance with members of the senatorial élite, moved to take over power, installing one of their number, Aurelian, as *praefectus praetorio* by August 399. At this, Gainas joined Tribigild in open rebellion and, advancing upon Chalcedon, in an interview with Arcadius compelled the emperor to confirm him as *magister utriusque militiae in praesenti* and to surrender to him Aurelian and other allies of Eudoxia; after a sham execution, they were exiled. Although Gainas entered Constantinople as master of the government before the end of 399, at the beginning of the next year Eudoxia, despite the loss of her main allies, was able to consolidate her own position through elevation to the rank of Augusta. Furthermore, Gainas, faced by opposition both from the court and from the bishop of Constantinople, proved himself completely ineffectual in power and, pleading illness, suddenly quit the city, having arranged with his barbarian supporters that they follow him. As the barbarians were leaving, the populace of the city began to attack them and slaughtered those whom they trapped within. Gainas, now declared a public enemy, turned to plundering Thrace and then, when the *magister militum per Orientem*, Fravitta, thwarted his attempt to re-cross to Asia Minor, retreated north of the Danube, where he was killed by a Hunnic king, Uldin, in late 400.

Eudoxia and her allies, Aurelian and his fellows having returned from exile, were now re-established firmly in control of the government. In this context, of the expulsion of Gainas and his supporters and the restoration of a 'Roman' government, a speech *On Kingship* delivered before the emperor himself by Synesius of Cyrene, who was on an embassy from his city to Constantinople, has been widely regarded as the political manifesto of the 'anti-German' party that now controlled the government. Certainly, amongst other proposals, Synesius advocates the elimination of barbarians from all positions, except servile, within the Roman world, and especially from the army. Furthermore, in 400 Fravitta, who, advancing what was probably the Theodosian and Stilichonian argument that division engendered weakness, had apparently criticized the government's refusal to restore relations with the west, was put to death. Even if his execution was caused primarily by a determination to continue resisting Stilicho's ambitions in the east, the rejection of the Theodosian policy of co-operation with and use of barbarian peoples is clearly shown by the lack of any German name after Fravitta's amongst the eastern military *magistri* until the Goth Plintha in 419. On the other hand, a recent protest against the application to the history of the late empire of the anachronistic notion of parties with ideologically motivated programmes has pointed out that the politics of the period were mainly driven by the ambitions and manoeuvres of individuals.[4] This view, which carries force, also has the merit of emphasizing that the most important result of the expulsion of Gainas was not the elimination of barbarians but the removal of the threat of military rule and the consolidation of civilian government in the east.

Eudoxia and her allies dominated the government of the east for the next four years. During this period, as the sedentary nature of Arcadius' court led to the emergence of Constantinople as the true capital of the east, one of the characteristics of life in the city – religious turbulence – appeared in the conflict between the empress and court, on the one hand, and the bishop, John Chrysostom, on the other. Appointed in 398 with the support of Eutropius, Chrysostom, eloquent, aggressive, self-righteous and uncompromising, set out to advertise the primacy of his see (itself recognized only in 381) and expand its power, and to establish the dominance of his church over the life of the city itself. Chrysostom's crude interference in sees outside his immediate jurisdiction aroused enmities, while his fulminations against the extravagances of the élite of the city, which he

---

[4] Holum, *Theodosian Empresses* 67f. (actually discussing another of Synesius' writings, *De Providentia*). See also on Synesius, Liebeschuetz, *Barbarians and Bishops* and Cameron and Long, *Barbarians and Politics*; further pp. 140–1 and 162–3 below. Liebeschuetz also provides a detailed account of the fall of John Chrysostom.

contrasted in his sermons with the miseries of the poor, brought him into conflict with the empress and her circle, against whom much of the censure might appear to be directed. His early relations with the court were good, and, indeed, his determined resistance to Gainas' demands for an Arian church within the city was an element in the latter's discomfiture. But by 403 relations between empress and bishop, which had fluctuated for the previous two years, were so bad that Eudoxia, working through Theophilus, bishop of Alexandria, who had himself been summoned to Constantinople to answer a charge of heresy, was able to bring Chrysostom before a synod on various charges. When Chrysostom refused to appear, he was deposed by the judges and subsequently exiled by imperial decree. After delivering two inflammatory sermons to his flock, he allowed himself to be escorted from the capital. But widespread anger at his departure, coupled with an earthquake, persuaded the superstitious empress to have him recalled. Although Chrysostom was brought back and a temporary reconciliation effected, by the end of the year further attacks on a court festival, which the bishop denounced as heathenish, and upon the empress herself determined Eudoxia again to rid herself of the troublesome prelate. A second synod was summoned early in 404 to try Chrysostom on the charge of illegally reoccupying his see. The bishop was confined to his palace in the interim, and when his followers tried to assemble, they were twice dispersed by troops with loss of life. The synod was unable to reach a decision, and in June 404, in order to end the continuing disturbances, Arcadius himself ordered Chrysostom to be taken from the city and banished permanently to Roman Armenia. Despite attempts by Honorius and Innocent, the bishop of Rome, to intervene on his behalf, Chrysostom was kept in exile until his death in 407. Eudoxia, however, did not long survive her victory, dying of a miscarriage in October 404.

III. THE GERMAN ONSLAUGHT ON THE WEST, 400–8

In the year 400, while the east was in turmoil, Claudian was celebrating the virtues and achievements of his patron, who was in his first consulship. In that year Stilicho was at the height of his power and prestige. The borders of the western empire seemed secure. He himself enjoyed the support of the Theodosian officials, in whose hands the civil government largely remained, and commanded the attentions of the Roman senators. Nevertheless, clouds were visible: Constantinople had resisted his attempts to interfere in the east; Alaric, though probably not yet perceived as a serious threat, was at large in Epirus; and the western army, dependent upon its barbarian allies, had proved unreliable. In 401 the storm broke that swept away first Stilicho and finally the Roman government of the west. In late summer of that year Alaric, his forces rearmed and resupplied in

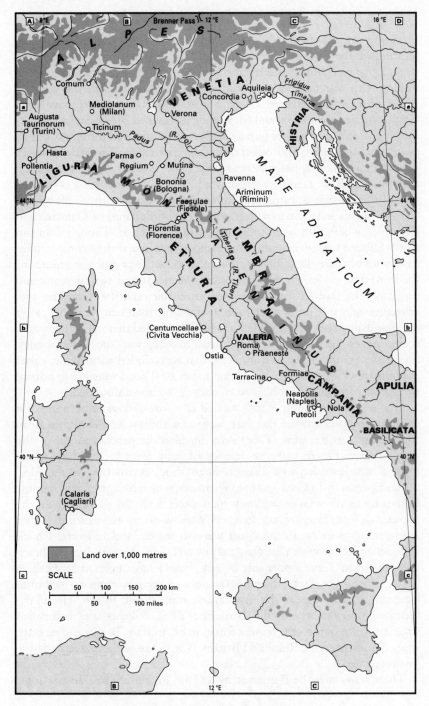

Map 4 The Alps and northern Italy

Illyricum, entered north Italy, presumably to the relief and perhaps with the blessing of the eastern government, and defeated a Roman force at the river Timavus. During the winter Stilicho was in Raetia and Noricum dealing with Vandal and Alan raids and recruiting troops; the walls of Rome were hastily repaired. Alaric, whose objective seems to have been Gaul, marched westwards and for a while threatened Mediolanum, until at Easter 402 Stilicho brought him to battle at Pollentia. The result was a draw costly to both sides, and Stilicho, whose barbarian allies had yet again behaved unreliably, apparently permitted Alaric to disengage on condition that he withdraw eastwards from Italy. When the retreating Visigoths turned northwards towards the Alpine passes, two defeats, at Hasta and Verona, persuaded them to withdraw into the borderlands of Dalmatia and Pannonia, where they seem to have remained until 407. Though Claudian extols Stilicho's achievements in the campaign of 402 as the saving of Italy, he cannot obscure the criticisms that his conduct, especially his failure for the third time to destroy Alaric, aroused. As in 395 and 397, his army, and especially the barbarian allies, proved unreliable; and the Visigoths, too, after their stay in Epirus, were more formidable than before. Hence, after the bloodshed at Pollentia, Stilicho probably decided that minimal engagement, never popular with the Roman public, was the safest policy. Suspicions, both ancient and modern, that he colluded with Alaric, either in conformity with the pro-Visigothic stance of Theodosius I or in pursuit of imperial ambitions for his son Eucherius, appear unfounded.[5]

One result of this war, which carried far more serious implications for the long-term security of the west, was the withdrawal of Honorius from Mediolanum to Ravenna. This move signalled the preoccupation of the imperial government with the defence of Italy from the north-east and, most disastrously, led to a disengagement from events beyond the Alps, most importantly in Gaul and the Germanys, which had provided both the best sources of western military manpower and, along the Rhine, the forward defence line for Italy from the north-west, as well as for the other European provinces. If the court were to move, Arelate in the Rhône valley, the place to which the *praefectus praetorio Galliarum* withdrew his head-quarters from Treveri probably in 407, would have been strategically a better choice.[6] As it was, the consequences of the government's priorities were not slow to appear, the first almost immediately. In the light of the repeated unreliability of the barbarian allies, Stilicho was compelled urgently to strengthen the regular forces in north Italy. To this end he summoned units from the Rhine and Britain. Few, if any of them, seem to have been returned.

Three years later the Roman army was put to another test. In late 405 a

[5] Discussion of the evidence by Cameron, Alan, *Claudian* 180–8.   [6] Ferrill (1986) 95 and 115.

large force of barbarians, many of them Ostrogoths, under the leadership of Radagaisus, crossed the Alps from Pannonia. Since Stilicho's army, even reinforced by Alans, by Huns under Uldin, and by Goths under Sarus, was too small to risk in set battle, the invaders were allowed to overrun north Italy unopposed. The desperation of the Roman government is suggested by an edict inviting slaves to volunteer for military service, a rare breach of a long-standing Roman practice.[7] Fortunately, as often happened when a large force of invaders had to live off the country, they split into three groups, two of which disappear; presumably they left Italy. The third and largest, under Radagaisus himself, after failing to capture Florentia, was blockaded near to Faesulae and destroyed at leisure. Their leader was captured and executed at Rome.[8]

This success, though qualified by the devastation of north Italy, restored Stilicho's prestige, so that he was able to turn to a design which he had perhaps been planning before Radagaisus' invasion distracted him. He revived, or manufactured, a claim that the dying Theodosius I had ordered that the prefecture of Illyricum be attached to Honorius' part of the empire.[9] Until 379 this prefecture had been administered as part of the west, in which year it was handed by Gratian to the new eastern ruler, Theodosius himself. Although its status thereafter is not entirely clear, in 396 it appears divided, the western portion (the diocese of Pannonia) controlled by Honorius' government, the eastern part (the dioceses of Dacia and Macedonia) conceded to Arcadius by Stilicho's withdrawal at his command in 395. This was the situation in 405–6, by which time Stilicho had set aside his earlier aim of uniting the whole empire under his sway, and relations between the two emperors had broken down over the eastern government's ill-treatment of an embassy sent from the west to complain of the deposition of Chrysostom. Two considerations made control of all Illyricum by the west attractive and even imperative at this point: first, the prefecture offered an excellent source of Roman manpower for a government that was encountering increasing difficulty in raising the armies necessary to face the barbarian invaders; and second, the west would be able to deal with invasions of the prefecture, which posed a potential threat to Italy, without the interference from the east that had occurred in 395 and 397. The western claim to the whole of the prefecture was announced by the appointment of Jovius as *praefectus praetorio Illyrici* and the commissioning of Alaric to seize Epirus and await the arrival of Stilicho with Roman troops.

---

[7] *C.Th.* VII.13.16 (April 402). For the connection of this law, and the one following it in the Code, with the invasion of Radagaisus, see Bury, *LRE* I.167 n. 3. For the events, Heather, *Goths and Romans*.

[8] Bury's view (*LRE* I.160) that Radagaisus also led the Vandal attack upon Raetia and Noricum in winter 401–2 (see pp. 430–1 below) has been rejected by Baynes (1955) 338.

[9] For the view that control of Illyricum was claimed only about 405, and not from 395 as is sometimes stated, see Baynes (1955) 330, and Cameron, Alan, *Claudian* 59–62. The best discussion of the status of Illyricum at the period is still Grumel (1951); see also p. 164 n. 138 below.

At this juncture two developments in the northern provinces, both consequences of the western government's neglect of those regions, thwarted
Stilicho's plans. On the last day of 406, it is said, hordes of barbarians
crossed the now poorly defended Rhine. Asding and Siling Vandals, Alans
and Sueves had converged upon the river near to Mogontiacum. Rome's
Frankish federates attempted to block the advance and defeated the
Asdings, but were in turn defeated by the Alans. Thereafter, crossing the
river unopposed, the invaders sacked Mogontiacum, advanced into Belgica,
where Treveri, Remi and Ambianum amongst other cities fell to them, and
then turned south-west, leaving a path of destruction in Lugdunensis and
Aquitania until they reached the Pyrenees. At about the same time the
Burgundians and Alamanni, taking advantage of the collapse of the
Roman defences, crossed the upper Rhine into Upper Germany, capturing
Argentorate, Noviomagus and Borbetomagus.

Even before these invasions began, elements of the military and civilian
population in Britain, probably alarmed by the withdrawal of troops to
Italy and the consequent danger of isolation in the face of mounting
barbarian pressure, had broken into revolt. Beginning in 406 they raised
three usurpers in quick succession: Marcus, Gratian, Constantine. The last
– chosen, it is alleged, because of his name – gained control of the rebellion and in the spring of 407 crossed into Gaul with his army. Constantine's
aim was to challenge Honorius for the throne and, in pursuit of this objective, he seems to have made no attempt to attack the barbarian invaders. He
focused his efforts upon gaining control of the Roman forces and
administration in Gaul as he advanced up the Rhine towards the Alps,
securing the defences of the river as best he could.[10]

Faced with these two irruptions into Gaul, the reports of which must
have come close in time, Honorius' government could have had no doubt
which posed the most immediate threat to itself. Sarus, a Gothic federate
chieftain and a firm supporter of Stilicho, was given a Roman command
and Roman forces and sent against Constantine.[11] After a victory and a
brief siege of Valentia, Sarus was compelled to retreat to Italy. Stilicho,
meanwhile, having sent a substantial portion of his available manpower to
Gaul with Sarus, was unable to join Alaric, who had moved into Epirus and
was waiting for the promised reinforcements. At the end of the campaigning season Alaric, probably suffering from lack of supplies, withdrew north
into Noricum, from where during the winter of 408 he sent a demand for

[10] Fears of the Britons: Zos. VI.3.1. Constantine's accommodation with the barbarians: Oros.
VII.40.4, *saepe a barbaris incertis foederibus inlusus.* His attention to the Rhine defences: Zos. VI.3.3. (The
two citations from Zosimus are from a badly garbled passage.)

[11] Stilicho is sometimes criticized for ignoring the barbarian invasion of Gaul and treating
Constantine's usurpation as a priority. Given the timing of events and the line of Constantine's advance,
it is hard to see how he could have done otherwise.

compensation for his stay in Epirus. This Stilicho referred to the senate with the implication that the senate should foot the bill, putting war as the alternative. After a heated debate it was agreed that Alaric should receive four thousand pounds of gold. Stilicho's prestige and control of the government, already compromised by Sarus' failure to halt Constantine's advance to the Alps and not repaired by the marriage early in 408 of his second daughter, Thermantia, to Honorius in place of the deceased Maria, was seriously eroded by the payment to Alaric. Lampadius, a leading senator and one of Stilicho's most prominent supporters, openly dissented.[12] Other disagreements over policy now emerged. The designs on Illyricum having been abandoned, Stilicho wished to send Alaric and his followers together with Roman forces against Constantine, while others were more concerned with the threat that Alaric posed to Italy. This dissension spread to the army, where the mood of the Roman troops became mutinous. A palatine official, Olympius, began to orchestrate this disaffection and worked to widen the rift that had appeared between Honorius and Stilicho during the debate over Alaric's demand.

During the years from 405 to 408, while the west was troubled by invasion and usurpation, the east was entering a period of stability and reconstruction under the guidance of the *praefectus praetorio* Anthemius, who held office from 405 to 414. Eudoxia's governing clique, corrupt and ineffective in the face of the continued unrest caused by Chrysostom's supporters (Johannites), was by mid 405 replaced by a broader-based coalition. Its leader, Anthemius, was a man of considerable experience in government and had links both with the orthodox establishment and with educated pagan circles.[13] The early achievements of the new government were the ending of the Johannite disorders, which brought a measure of calm to Constantinople and its environs, and the establishment of enduring peaceful relations with Persia, which secured the eastern border, usually a major worry for the government. The first was achieved by a combination of firmness and moderation, assisted by the death of Chrysostom himself. The second was the fruit of good relations established earlier, perhaps in 399, by an embassy, or embassies, of Anthemius himself and Marutha, bishop of Martyropolis in Sophanene, to Yezdegerd I at the beginning of his reign. Stability thus established, Anthemius was able to begin strengthening the defences of the Balkans against both barbarian attacks and the plans of the western government. By forcing the postponement of the latter, the invasion of Radagaisus was crucial. When Alaric finally entered Epirus in 407, he achieved nothing.[14] Nevertheless, neither

---

[12] On the basis of Stilicho's support in the adherents of Theodosius I see Matthews, *Western Aristocracies* 258–64. On the significance of Lampadius' defection, *ibid.* 278f.

[13] On Anthemius' government see C. Zakrzewski (1928); Demougeot (1951) 338–51 and 499–519.

[14] Sozom. *HE* IX.4.4.

the government nor the ruling dynasty was so secure that, when Arcadius died on 1 May 408, a serious challenge to the succession of the infant Theodosius II could be ignored.

The most immediate effect of Arcadius' death was, however, felt in the west, where it spurred the opposition to action and forced into the open the disagreements between Honorius and Stilicho. When news of Arcadius' death was confirmed, Honorius' immediate wish was to travel to Constantinople to secure his nephew's throne. But in an interview at Bononia Stilicho prevailed upon the reluctant emperor to remain in Italy while he went to the east. At the moment when his primary objective, the reunification of the empire under his own guardianship, seemed within his grasp, Stilicho hesitated, and with good reason, since he had been warned that the Roman troops at Ticinum, whither Honorius was proceeding to see them off to Gaul, were in a dangerous mood. Olympius and his supporters were busy spreading the allegation that the purpose of Stilicho's journey to the east was to place his own son, Eucherius, on the throne. The allegation was widely believed, and on the fourth day of Honorius' visit the soldiers broke into a violent mutiny aimed at the high officials who were Stilicho's supporters. Many of them were massacred, and by the end of the day Stilicho's regime had been destroyed. The news of the revolt reached Stilicho while he was still at Bononia, followed by a second report that Honorius was safe. When he received the second report, Stilicho refused the demands of his barbarian troops that they be allowed to attack the mutineers. Having warned the cities of the region that the barbarians were angry and unpredictable, he set out for Ravenna to meet the emperor. At Ravenna, learning that Honorius had ordered his arrest, he took sanctuary in a church, but came out on a sworn promise that his life would be spared. When he came out, he was informed that the emperor had ordered his immediate execution. To this he submitted, refusing to permit his men to resist (22 August).

The half-Vandal, half-Roman who had guided the fortunes of the western Roman empire for over thirteen years died as he had lived, loyal to duly constituted authority and the house of Theodosius. His condemnation as a traitor by many of his contemporaries and as an incompetent by some moderns are slanders arising primarily out of his repeated failure to deal with Alaric.[15] His failures lay elsewhere. Insistence upon the unity of the imperial government, which was emphatically and consistently rejected in the east, proved divisive. Reliance upon barbarian federates and other allies both inhibited the rebuilding of the Roman army and in the end destroyed the governing consensus in the west that had been so carefully

---

[15] The most hostile judgement is that of Bury, *LRE* 1.172f. For a more favourable and reasonable estimate see Matthews, *Western Aristocracies* 282f. The emphasis on Stilicho's strategic failings is in Ferrill (1986) 101f.

cultivated. Finally, the identification of the defence of Italy (and the emperor at Ravenna) as the priority in the defence of the west reinforced a tendency already present to pay less attention to the security of the borders[16] and led directly to the loss of the northern provinces. These policies were a large part of the Theodosian legacy, so that in a very real sense the failure of Stilicho was the failure of Theodosius.

IV. ALARIC IN ITALY, 408–10

The new government at Ravenna, headed by Olympius, now *magister officiorum*, was strongly orthodox and stridently anti-German.[17] Its first and overriding concerns were to destroy Stilicho's remaining adherents and to gather evidence of his alleged treacherous intentions. Torture entirely failed to discover the latter. The Roman troops after the initial massacre of the high officials at Ticinum had turned upon the families of the barbarian allies. The slaughter that resulted drove the majority of the barbarians (said to number thirty thousand) to join Alaric; some loyalists first took Eucherius to temporary safety at Rome; Sarus and his followers remained aloof but ready to assist Honorius, if invited. Absorbed in eliminating the remnants of the previous regime, Olympius proved wholly ineffective in dealing with Alaric, who, since the planned invasion of Gaul had been abandoned, offered to withdraw into Pannonia in exchange for a small sum of gold and hostages. The government at Ravenna neither accepted this offer nor prepared to fight. As a result, having summoned his brother-in-law, the Ostrogoth Ataulf, to follow him from Upper Pannonia, Alaric marched straight upon Rome, where he arrived in late autumn 408, a few days after emissaries from Ravenna who came to seek out and kill Eucherius. As the Visigoths settled down to blockade the unprepared city, panic counselled both the murder of Serena, alleged to be an accomplice of Alaric, and the public performance of a pagan ritual to ward off the besieger. The former was done, the latter, because of the insistence of the bishop of Rome that it be kept private, was not. When famine and plague forced the senate to negotiate, Alaric agreed to lift the blockade in exchange for a heavy ransom (including five thousand pounds of gold and thirty thousand pounds of silver, as well as various costly commodities) and the promise of a treaty guaranteed by hostages. With the consent of the emperor the ransom was paid, and Alaric withdrew to Etruria in December. Honorius, however, despite the pleas of two senatorial embassies, failed to ratify the treaty or hand over the hostages. He did, however, attempt to throw a garrison into Rome. It was intercepted and destroyed on the way.

[16] See pp. 236 and 428 below.
[17] Demougeot (1951) 427–32; the best recent discussion of these events is in Heather, *Goths and Romans* 213ff., with Part IV, chapter 16, pp. 487–515 below.

At this juncture the government of Olympius fell. The immediate cause of his dismissal and flight to Dalmatia in early 409 appears to have been his failure to prevent Ataulf from reaching Rome. Although Olympius himself, leading a band of three hundred Huns, had inflicted a defeat upon Ataulf's force, which was not large, this success was not followed up. Bereft of manpower and almost bankrupt, Honorius was reduced to recognizing Constantine as Augustus, whereupon his new colleague offered assistance against the Visigoths.[18] That Olympius' fall was also brought about by a reaction to his extremism and intransigence is suggested by the background of the man who replaced him. Jovius, *praefectus praetorio Italiae* and now *patricius*, had been an adherent of Stilicho and a friend of Alaric, who in 406 had been named *praefectus praetorio Illyrici* as part of the plan to annex the whole of that prefecture to the west. Since the new government was prepared to negotiate, a conference was called at Ariminum at which Alaric demanded an annual income of gold and grain, and lands for his followers in Ventia, Noricum and Dalmatia. When reporting these terms to Honorius, Jovius suggested that Alaric also be appointed *magister utriusque militiae*, thinking thereby to persuade him to reduce his demands. This suggestion the emperor peremptorily rejected, and when Jovius read out this rejection to Alaric the latter broke off negotiations and threatened to march on Rome again. The government at Ravenna began to prepare for war, in support of which Honorius and Jovius swore never to negotiate with Alaric. Alaric, however, moderated his demands and through the bishops of the Italian cities made a new offer for a formal alliance: no office, no gold, land in Noricum, and only as much grain as the emperor thought reasonable. When Honorius, now committed to confrontation, rejected this offer, Alaric marched on Rome. When the Visigoths blockaded the food supplies at Portus, the senate, having briefly rejected a request from Alaric that it join him against Honorius, capitulated and agreed to form a government (late 409). The emperor chosen by Alaric was the *praefectus urbi* Priscus Attalus, an elderly pagan who, however, permitted himself to be baptized by an African bishop. While senators were appointed to civil offices, Alaric himself was made *magister utriusque militiae* and Ataulf *comes domesticorum equitum*. This unnatural alliance between Christian barbarians and Roman senators, many of whom were chauvinist and pagan, was inaugurated by Attalus in a speech before the senate which was both grandiloquent and unrealistic in its promise to restore Rome to its former greatness.

The immediate prospects of the new regime depended upon swiftly taking control of Africa, whose governor, Heraclian, remained loyal to Honorius. While Alaric offered to send a force of Goths against Heraclian,

---

[18] Honorius' purpose in recognizing Constantine was to attempt to save some relatives captured in Spain (Olympiodorus fr. 1.12 = 13.1 Blockley). Constantine was not recognized in the east.

Attalus, distrusting Alaric's intentions, probably wisely, opted to send a small Roman force. This force despatched, Alaric and Attalus marched on Ravenna. When Honorius in terror sent Jovius and others proposing to share the empire, Attalus in response offered Honorius the choice of place of exile. Jovius, expressing support for this, added the suggestion that Honorius be mutilated also, which Attalus rejected as non-traditional. Jovius, as he presumably had intended when he suggested mutilation of his own emperor, remained with Attalus, being named *patricius*.[19] At this point Honorius was ready to flee to Constantinople and was only persuaded to await events in Africa by the arrival of four thousand troops from the east. When news reached Alaric that Attalus' force had been destroyed by Heraclian, he again proposed, now supported by Jovius, that a force of Goths be sent. The senate and Attalus, who had now returned to Rome, continued to resist the proposal, though shortly afterwards, when lack of supplies from Africa had caused a severe famine, the senate came around. Attalus' intransigence decided Alaric, pressed by Jovius, to unmake his emperor. Having first secured from Honorius a promise of negotiations, Alaric summoned Attalus to Ariminum, where he ceremonially deposed him in summer 410. The promised peace conference was under way when Sarus, a sworn enemy of Ataulf, attacked the Goths. Alaric, suspecting treachery, broke off negotiations and marched again on Rome.

The third siege of the city was brief. On 24 August 410 the Visigoths entered by the Salarian Gate, opened, it was alleged, from within. For three days the Goths looted and burned. Then they marched south, taking with them amongst their prisoners Honorius' sister Galla Placidia. Alaric's goal was first Regium and from there Sicily and Africa. But when a storm wrecked the ships that they had collected, the Visigoths were forced to retreat north. At Consentia Alaric fell ill and died (late 410); it is said that those who buried him were put to death to preserve the secret of the location of his grave. Ataulf was chosen as Alaric's successor, and he began to lead his people on a slow journey north to the passes into Gaul.

As refugees spread the story of the sack of Rome throughout the Roman world, listeners reacted with shock and disbelief. Some recorded their horror. Jerome's cry, 'In one city the whole world perished' (*Comm. in Ezech.* 1 *praef.*), speaks for all. In contrast to individual reactions stood those of the governments. At Constantinople there was indifference, while for Ravenna the sack was one of a long list of reverses and humiliations,

---

[19] Jovius' manoeuvres earned from Bury the sobriquet 'the shifty patrician' (Bury, *LRE* 1.182). Matthews (*Western Aristocracies* 293f. and 297f.) implies that his manoeuvres were those of a politician attempting to obtain a settlement under rapidly changing circumstances. A complication for Jovius seems to have been that just before and after the fall of Stilicho Honorius began to assert himself in an unpredictable fashion (see the indirect evidence in Zos. v.30.4–5; 31.3–6; 48.4; vi.8.1 and 3). Jovius' behaviour, even after joining Attalus, is not inconsistent with a settled aim of achieving an agreement between Alaric and the western court.

endurable provided its own stronghold remained secure. Even for Alaric it was a final act of rage and despair, a confession of his failure to win a settlement and lands for his people.[20]

V. THE EARLY YEARS OF THEODOSIUS II, 408–14

At the death of Arcadius the government of the east expected a challenge to the throne of Theodosius II, who was only seven years of age, though Augustus since 402. The usual embassy was sent to the Persian court to announce the accession of the new emperor and, it seems, to persuade Yezdegerd to declare his support. Yezdegerd, having no interest in seeing the friendly Theodosian dynasty replaced, co-operated by sending a letter in which he recognized Theodosius and threatened war upon anyone who conspired against him. It is possible that Theodosius' supporters, eager to strengthen his position by all means, stretched the familial language of the letter, traditional in the formal correspondence between the emperor and shahanshah at the period, to suggest that Yezdegerd had agreed to act as testamentary executor in ensuring the fulfilment of Arcadius' will and the succession of his heir.[21] At all events, the government's hand was strengthened by the continuing good will of the Persian king, and the crisis passed. Furthermore, Marutha, already *persona grata* at the Persian court, persuaded Yezdegerd to permit the Christians in Persia to hold in 410 a synod at which their church was able to regulate itself through the adoption of various canons and the confirmation of Isaac, bishop of Seleucia-Ctesiphon, as its head (*catholicos*). This success must have redounded greatly to the credit of the government, Marutha's sponsors.

After the settlement of the succession crisis and the death of Stilicho, which led to an immediate improvement in relations between Ravenna and Constantinople, the most serious threat to the security of the east was offered by the Hunnic leader Uldin, who, having withdrawn from service with the western Roman army, in late 408 led a large force of Huns and allies across the Danube into Lower Moesia and Thrace. Roman diplomacy, aided probably by a shortage of supplies, broke up the invading force, so that the Roman army was able to compel Uldin to retreat with heavy losses. A year or so later the eastern government felt secure enough to send four thousand élite troops to help Honorius guard Ravenna (early 410).

The balance of Anthemius' prefecture was occupied with administrative

---

[20] Matthews, *Western Aristocracies* 301.

[21] The basic version in the Greek tradition is Procop. *BP* 1.2.1–10, which is not rejected by Agathias (IV.26.3–7), as is sometimes claimed. The Syriac tradition (e.g. in *Chron. ad a. MCCXXXIV* xxxviii (*CSCO Script. Syr.* III.14, pp. 136f.)) is in general agreement while adding details, notably that Marutha was the envoy. If this is correct then he must have travelled in 408 and again for the synod in 410. For legal limitations upon Yezdegerd's role, but the possibility of his acting as testamentary executor, see Pieler (1972) 411–15.

measures to improve the security of the empire, strengthen finances, eliminate abuses of various kinds, and ensure an adequate food supply for
Constantinople. Attention to the last was demanded by a severe famine and
consequent rioting in 408. By 413 the physical security of the rapidly
growing capital had been enhanced not only by continuing attention to the
defences of the Balkans (including the refurbishment of the Danube fleet),
but also by the completion of a new city wall, credited in an announcement
by Theodosius to the prefect himself (*C.Th.* xv.1.51), which gave protection on the landward side both to the city against barbarian invaders and to
the civil government and emperor against the ambitions of the military
forces in Europe.[22] Despite the expenditures which this and other projects
must have demanded, the finances of the state were sound enough in 414
to allow all fiscal arrears for the period 368 to 407 to be remitted in the prefecture of the East.

VI. BARBARIAN SETTLEMENTS IN THE WEST, 411–18

In Gaul, after the retreat of Sarus in late 407, Constantine garrisoned the
Alpine passes to Italy and established himself at Arelate. During 408 he
consolidated the Rhine defences and sent his son and Caesar, Constans,
together with the general Gerontius to take Spain, which they did,
Constans returning to Arelate with captive relatives of Honorius, who were
put to death. Constantine, having raised his son to Augustus, sent him back
to Spain. He himself entered Italy in early 410, purportedly to assist
Honorius against Alaric as he had promised. When, however, Honorius
had his *magister equitum* Allobich put to death on suspicion of plotting to
overthrow him, Constantine withdrew to Arelate. Whether this indicates
treacherous intent or whether Constantine simply declined to face Alaric,
who at the time was in north Italy, without co-operation from Ravenna, is
unclear.[23]

Constans, on his way back to Spain, learned that the troops to whom he
had entrusted the Pyrenees passes had admitted the Vandals, Sueves and
Alans into Spain (September or October 409) and that Gerontius, discover-
ing that he was to be superseded, had revolted and declared his own son
Maximus emperor. Worsted in battle, Constans fled back to Gaul. In 411
Gerontius, allied with some of the barbarian invaders, attacked and killed
Constans, who was holding Vienna, and then advanced against Constantine

---

[22] Holum, *Theodosian Empresses* 89.

[23] The time of Constantine's entry into north Italy is uncertain. The chronology adopted here would
have him in Liguria at the same time as Alaric was in the north, though I should not go so far as Stevens
(1957) 330f. in supposing that a defeat by Alaric caused his retreat. While all the sources say that
Allobich's death on suspicion of treachery led Constantine to withdraw, and Sozomen (*HE* ix.12.4)
says that Constantine planned to take Italy, none claims directly that Constantine and Allobich were in
collusion.

at Arelate. Meanwhile, however, a force under the generals Constantius and Ulfila was marching from Ravenna also against Constantine. At the approach of this army the majority of Gerontius' men went over to the forces of legitimacy, and Gerontius was compelled to retreat to Spain, where he soon perished in a revolt, Maximus fleeing to the barbarians. Constantius and Ulfila took up the siege of Arelate and, after they had crushed a relieving army, received the surrender of Constantine, who first put off the imperial regalia and had himself ordained priest. Neither ordination nor his captors' oaths were enough to save him and his surviving son Julian. On the way to Ravenna they were executed (September 411) at the command of Honorius in revenge for the deaths of his relatives two years before.

Gerontius' flight and the destruction of Constantine restored south-eastern Gaul to the control of Honorius and secured the approaches to Italy from that area. After their success Constantius and Ulfila returned to Italy, probably to watch Ataulf who was approaching the Alps, which he crossed early in 412. While Ataulf was passing into Gaul, another usurpation was under way, this time in Lower Germany where a Gallo-Roman noble, Jovinus, was declared emperor with the support not only of many of the regional nobility but also of Burgundians, Alans, Franks and Alamanni. The spectrum of support which Jovinus enjoyed both illustrates the role that the barbarian peoples were now taking in the politics of the west and suggests the unwillingness of many of the Gallo-Romans to accept the reimposition of Honorius' government.[24]

Advised by Attalus, Ataulf marched north to join Jovinus, who was embarrassed by this unwelcome ally. No doubt his disquiet was increased when Ataulf attacked and killed Sarus, who had deserted Honorius for the usurper. Ataulf appears to have been determined to impose himself upon affairs, and after his arrival nothing more is heard of the other barbarian supporters; indeed, the Burgundians may have begun to prepare an accommodation with Honorius, who recognized them as federates on the west bank of the Rhine immediately after the overthrow of Jovinus. Relations between Jovinus and Ataulf soon soured when, during the brief expansion of power into south-eastern Gaul, Jovinus named his brother Sebastianus emperor against Ataulf's wishes. Thereupon Ataulf proposed to Honorius that he destroy the usurpers and make a treaty with Ravenna. The Visigoths completed their part of the bargain without difficulty. Sebastianus' head was despatched to Honorius. Jovinus was sent off alive to Ravenna but was put to death on the way in autumn 413. The noble supporters of the usurpation were hunted down and killed.

[24] Olympiodorus fr. 1.17 (=18 Blockley); Greg. Tur. *HE* 11.9. The place of usurpation is unclear. Mogontiacum is often suggested, though this is not supported by Olympiodorus' text. Evidence in Matthews (*Western Aristocracies* 314f.) indicates that the revolt might have been a continuation of Constantine's, though Matthews himself does not bring this out.

In the negotiations that followed the destruction of Jovinus, Honorius agreed to furnish supplies to the Visigoths, which they badly needed, and perhaps granted them lands in Lower Aquitania. The Visigoths agreed to return Galla Placidia, the emperor's sister captured at Rome in 410 and still with them. Honorius was, however, prevented from fulfilling his part of the agreement when in early 413 Heraclian, whose loyalty in 409–10 had saved his throne, revolted in Africa, cut off the grain supplies, and invaded Italy. The attack, aimed perhaps not at Honorius but at Constantius, who since the defeat of Constantine had been in control of the government at Ravenna as *magister utriusque militiae*, was easily repelled.[25] Heraclian fled back to Africa and was dead before August 413. Honorius' failure to deliver the supplies, despite repeated promises to do so, gave Ataulf the excuse he desired to retain Placidia. By the time grain was again available the Visigoths had moved to Lower Aquitania and were in possession of Burdigala. By late 413 the agreement had clearly collapsed, and the Visigoths pushed into Narbonensis, occupying Tolosa and Narbo but failing to take Massilia.[26] The disagreement, which had now become a personal one between Ataulf and Constantius, centred not so much upon supplies as on Placidia, who had become the focus of the ambitions of both. Constantius desired her hand in order to enter the imperial family and consolidate his own position. Ataulf sought marriage with her in order to create a royal line that might bind the Romans and Visigoths together in a way no treaty could. It seems that Placidia's own ambitions, and perhaps personal affections, inclined towards Ataulf, and some at least of the Gallic notables, who were still not reconciled to government from Ravenna, offered encouragement. At Narbo on 1 January 414 the Visigothic king, dressed as a Roman, married the emperor's sister in a Roman ceremony; a son born of the marriage was named Theodosius. Constantius, his entry upon his first consulship on the same day soured by the resounding snub of Placidia's marriage to a barbarian, responded by coming in person to Arelate to direct a naval blockade of Narbo. Ataulf countered by setting up a rival emperor, Attalus, for the second time. This regime, without substance or real support from the outset, soon collapsed under the stress of the blockade, and by the end of 414 the Visigoths were compelled by hunger to move to Spain, abandoning Attalus to capture and transportation to Ravenna, where he was held for exhibition and mutilation at Rome in 416, followed by exile to Lipari.

The Visigoths established themselves at Barcelona, where Constantius

---

[25] See Oost (1968) 119. Constantius had Olympius beaten to death. Heraclian had personally decapitated Stilicho and thus might fear revenge.

[26] For this order of events see Oost (1968) 123f. That a treaty had been made seems clear from Olympiodorus fr. 1.20 (=22.1 Blockley). The more commonly accepted order of events, which places the attack on Massilia before the taking of Narbo, seems to imply no treaty.

maintained the blockade. In these circumstances the infant Theodosius died, and Ataulf himself was murdered (summer 415) as the result of a private feud and perhaps a conspiracy, since he was briefly succeeded as king by Sigeric, a brother of Sarus. After seven days Sigeric was killed in his turn and replaced by Wallia. The new king, hostile to the Romans, first attempted a crossing to Africa, but was thwarted when his transports were wrecked in a storm. Then the Visigoths, reduced to desperation by the blockade and exploited by the neighbouring barbarians,[27] offered to restore Placidia to Honorius in exchange for supplies and a treaty. This time the supplies were delivered, and the Visigoths were commissioned to attack the barbarians in Spain on behalf of Honorius. Placidia was returned to Ravenna and on 1 January 417, as he entered his second consulship, she was married to Constantius, much against her will.

The barbarians who entered Spain in autumn 409 had, after a two-year orgy of killing and destruction, begun to settle, though they continued to harass the provincials. The Siling Vandals occupied Baetica, the Alans Lusitania, the Asding Vandals and Sueves Gallaecia, while Carthaginiensis and Tarraconensis remained to a degree under Roman control. In their campaigns from 416 to 418 the Visigoths almost annihilated the Silings and crushed the Alans so thoroughly that the survivors fled to the Asdings, whose ruler henceforth was known as 'King of the Vandals and Alans'. At this point the Roman government, uneasy at the swift efficiency with which the Visigoths were clearing and taking control of Spain, decided to leave the Asdings and Sueves in Gallaecia (perhaps with federate status) and in late 418 summoned the Visigoths back to Gaul, where they were granted Lower Aquitania and parts of Novempopulana and Narbonensis, without, however, any access to the Mediterranean seaboard.[28] In the same year Wallia died and was succeeded by Theodoric I, said to be the grandson of Alaric.

At the end of 418 the western Roman government, while still in control of Italy and Africa and the western portion of the Illyrian prefecture (much of the latter held insecurely), retained only a part of the prefecture of the Gauls. In Spain Roman generals using Visigothic allies struggled with varying success to keep the Sueves and Vandals bottled up in Gallaecia. Most ominously in 421–2 the Vandals, after defeating a Roman force partly through the treachery of its Visigothic allies, occupied Baetica. The Britons, having defected from Constantine and having asked Honorius for aid, were in 410 authorized by the emperor to defend themselves. Thereafter they were in only the most tenuous contact with the mainland

---

[27] Exploitation by the Vandals: Olympiodorus fr. 1.29 (=29.1 Blockley).

[28] On the nature of the settlement see Goffart, *Barbarians and Romans*, esp. ch. 4, who challenges the conventional view that it was a land division based on the Roman rules of *hospitalitas* and argues that it involved primarily a redistribution of tax income.

as they struggled against increasing barbarian pressure. In Gaul itself imperial control of Narbonensis both shielded Italy and secured overland access to Spain. But the reduced perspective of the Roman government is clearly illustrated by an edict of April 418 in which Honorius makes provision for a provincial council to meet in the autumn of each year at Arelate to discuss matters of public importance with the *praefectus praetorio Galliae*. The representatives who were ordered to attend included governors of only seven of the seventeen provinces of Gaul, and even of these the governors of the 'more distantly situated' Novempopulana and Lower Aquitania were permitted to send deputies. At the end of the year in which the edict was issued, these two provinces were beginning to be settled by the Visigoths, and though legally the Roman citizens of these regions remained under the Roman authorities, it is unlikely that a Roman administration was long maintained there. The intent of the edict may well have been to focus the loyalties of the Gallo-Romans upon Arelate and thereby maintain their contact with the Roman empire, and in southern Gaul it succeeded, as the remarkable efflorescence of Gallo-Roman culture, centred upon Arelate and lasting well past the mid-point of the century, attests.[29] Nevertheless, the disruptions that engendered the edict prevailed elsewhere in Gaul, where the writ of the administration at Arelate ran very small. The Alamanni were across the upper Rhine, the Burgundians were settled under treaty around Borbetomagus, the Franks were beginning to expand in the north-east, and the north-west was chronically disturbed both by internal unrest and by immigrations, including waves of refugees from Britain. Maintenance here of a semblance of Roman authority and resistance both to barbarian settlers and marauders and to the ubiquitous Bagaudae (bandits) were left to local magnates.[30] The imperial government was able to offer only occasional help.

VII. THE ASCENDANCY OF PULCHERIA, 414–23

In 414 a change of government and policy took place at Constantinople. By May of that year Anthemius was out of office and probably dead. In July Pulcheria, Theodosius' fifteen-year-old sister and perhaps the most able of a series of remarkable princesses of the Theodosian dynasty, was proclaimed Augusta. By December Monaxius, Anthemius' successor as *praefectus praetorio*, had been replaced by Aurelian, the opponent of Gainas and now a very old man. During this year, or earlier, Pulcheria had dismissed Theodosius' childhood tutor and had herself assumed the oversight of her brother's education. To the enthusiasm for scholarship which Theodosius already possessed and maintained throughout his life,

[29] Matthews, *Western Aristocracies* 334–7.   [30] Van Dam, *Leadership and Community* 40–2.

Pulcheria added training in the appropriate imperial deportment and, most important, a pious, ascetic and strictly orthodox religious upbringing. Contemporaries remarked that under Pulcheria, who had dedicated herself to virginity in 413 and had later persuaded her sisters to do likewise, the imperial palace resembled a cloister thronged with bishops and holy men. When upon her proclamation as Augusta Pulcheria took up the regency for her brother, she also assumed a dominant role in government. Behind Aurelian's prefecture, itself perhaps a sop to traditionalists, the Augusta moved to replace Anthemius' broad-based and pragmatic regime with one that emphasized and enforced the virtues of orthodox Christian piety as the guarantors of the safety and prosperity of the state. The focus of this piety was the dynasty, the emperor and the capital, which began to accumulate prophylactic relics at an increasing rate.[31] The new direction was in harmony with the values of the age, which are exemplified in the career of Cyril, bishop of Alexandria, nephew of Chrysostom's adversary Theophilus, and an ambitious and ruthless man who encouraged and exploited the fanaticisms and social divisions of the time to increase his own and his church's power. Using as his agents bands of fanatical monks, Cyril waged open war upon Jews, pagans and the prefect of Egypt, Orestes, who attempted to restrain him. In 415 the brutal murder of the Neoplatonist teacher Hypatia, a friend of Orestes, by a band of fanatics compelled the government to hear the complaints of the authorities at Alexandria against Cyril's activities. The sanctions ordered were minimal: the *parabalani*, lay brethren who attended the sick and who were the most ferocious of Cyril's followers, were reduced in numbers, placed under the prefect's authority, and forbidden to appear in a body in public. The real attitude of the government, which was itself busy persecuting Jews and excluding pagans from imperial office, emerged sixteen months later when the *parabalani*, their numbers increased, were returned to Cyril.

Along with the new, aggressive, even crusading spirit in the government of the east went a deterioration in relations with Persia. Yezdegerd, tolerant of Christians for most of his reign, towards the end, infuriated by an attack by a Christian fanatic on a Zoroastrian fire temple, turned to persecution, both in Persia itself and in Persian-controlled Armenia. The Romans rejected Persian demands for the return of refugees from this persecution and prepared for war. After Yezdegerd's death in late 420 his successor, Varahram V, intensified the persecution and further provoked the Romans by harassing subjects of the empire in Persia on legitimate business. In 421, with both sides clearly set for war, the Romans struck into Armenia and against the stronghold of Nisibis in Mesopotamia. After initial success they became bogged down in Armenia and were driven from

---

[31] Holum, *Theodosian Empresses*, esp. 103–11.

Nisibis by Varahram himself. The failure of an attack upon Syria by Arab allies of Persia reduced the war to a stalemate. A Hunnic invasion of Thrace early in 422 inclined the Romans to peace, though it took a defeat in the same year to convince Varahram to settle. The losses on both sides had been severe; both sides claimed victory. Both sides also agreed not to persecute the adherents of the other's faith. To protect themselves further, the Christians in Persia at the synod of the *catholicos* Dadišo in 424 broke all official relations with the church in the Roman empire.

The unsatisfactory progress of the war led to a decline in Pulcheria's power, which was already under attack from traditionalists and others opposed to her intolerant religious policies. In June 421 Theodosius had married Athenais, the daughter of a pagan sophist, whose conversion to Christianity and new name, Eudoxia, erased neither her love of traditional learning nor her connections with the circles who cultivated it. Traditionalists began to appear again in high office, working to counteract the intolerance of the preceding years. Significantly, the commander of the army which in 422 defeated Varahram and brought him to terms was Procopius, the son-in-law of Anthemius. The elevation of Eudoxia to Augusta in January 423 signalled the emergence of a potent rival to Pulcheria in the palace, though by no means the end of her influence on affairs.[32]

VIII. THE LAST YEARS OF HONORIUS AND THE USURPATION OF JOHN, 419–25

The marriage of Placidia and Constantius, though not a happy experience for either, did produce an heir to the western throne, Valentinian, born in mid 419, a little over a year after his sister Honoria. In 421 Honorius – not entirely willingly, it is alleged – declared Constantius Augustus, Placidia Augusta and Valentinian Nobilissimus, which signalled for the infant the expectation of imperial office. The eastern court refused to recognize these titles, which caused Constantius to prepare for war. His death in September 421, seven months after elevation to an office which brought him only frustration, ended the hostilities. As after the death of Stilicho, the vacuum created by the removal of the dominant figure found candidates eager to fill it, prominent amongst them Castinus, the new *magister utriusque militiae.* Antagonism between Castinus and Bonifatius, a loyal supporter of Placidia, forced Bonifatius in 422 to flee to Africa, where his position was regularized somewhat later by his appointment as *comes Africae.*[33] Placidia

---

[32] Holum, *Theodosian Empresses* 112–28.

[33] Oost (1968) 173 n. 14, argues for 422. *PLRE* II 'Bonifatius' 3 suggests that he may have been appointed in 423–4 by Theodosius II, after Honorius' death; but Olympiodorus fr. 40 (= 38 Blockley) seems to indicate that he was governor at the time of Placidia's exile.

herself, determined to protect her position and that of her son, at first drew close to Honorius, but later relations between the two soured, and faction fighting erupted in the streets of Ravenna, in which Placidia's Gothic retainers played a prominent role. As a result Placidia was forced to withdraw with her children to Constantinople.

In August 423 Honorius died. The kindest thing that can be said about this most ineffective incumbent upon the imperial throne is that his long periods of inertia caused less damage than his bouts of relative activity just before and after the destruction of Stilicho.[34] At his death, Theodosius became sole ruler of the Roman empire and possibly planned to continue so.[35] However, at Rome a civilian official, the *primicerius notariorum* John, was declared emperor with the backing at Ravenna of Castinus and the now-rising Aetius. This challenge to the dynasty decided Theodosius to throw his support to Valentinian and his mother. Early in 424 he retroactively recognized the elevation of Placidia to Augusta (and Constantius to Augustus) and raised Valentinian to Caesar. An army commanded by the eastern generals Ardaburius and Aspar and by Placidia's own supporter, Candidianus, was concentrated at Salonae in Dalmatia. In 425 it advanced on Italy, part by land, part by sea. The commander of the seaborne force, Ardaburius, was captured and taken to Ravenna, where, given freedom of movement, he was able to suborn some of the officers, whose enthusiasm for John, perhaps never strong, was eroded both by the failure of the new regime to dislodge Bonifatius in Africa (thus weakening its support in Rome)[36] and by the successes of Aspar and Candidianus at Aquileia and other cities of north Italy. As a result Aspar was able to make an entrance into Ravenna and capture John, who was reserved for mutilation, public mockery and finally execution at Rome. Of John's prominent backers, Castinus was exiled, but Aetius, who arrived with a large force of Huns a short while after the capture of the usurper and engaged in fighting with the eastern army, was bought off with gold for his Huns and for himself the rank of *comes et magister militum per Gallias* with a commission to attack the Visigoths, who had sought to profit from the change of emperor by laying siege to Arelate.

On 23 October 425 at Rome, Valentinian III, now the betrothed of Licinia Eudoxia, the daughter of Theodosius II, was proclaimed Augustus by the *patricius et magister officiorum* Helion, acting for the ruler of the eastern Roman empire. As the historian Olympiodorus saw, this represented not only the restoration of the legitimate dynasty to the western Roman empire, but also the reinstitution of imperial unity under eastern primacy.[37]

[34] See p. 127 n. 19 above.   [35] Oost (1968) 178–80.

[36] The evidence that the Roman senate supported John is equivocal. Bury's citation of coin evidence to show that John was not supported at Rome is also indecisive (*LRE* 1.223 n. 1).

[37] Matthews, *Western Aristocracies* 382f.

This theme of eastern primacy, which entailed an obligation also to assist, remained powerful long after the political structure called the Roman empire had disappeared in the west.[38] But the restoration of the Theodosian dynasty failed to banish the ambitions and rivalries of the military commanders that had plagued the western court through the fourth century up to the present. Placidia was established as regent for her son, while Felix, who may have played some role in the manoeuvres after Honorius' death, was *magister utriusque militiae*. Those who were to be the principals in the next round of the struggle were as yet in the wings, Aetius in Gaul and Bonifatius in Africa. But the most potent players were far away, in Baetica at the straits which separated Spain from Africa and perhaps already raiding Mauretania.[39] Aided by the debilitating rivalries of those who sought power at the western court, the Vandals under their king Geiseric, probably the most adroit of all the German rulers of the period, were able to cross to Africa in 429, capture it all within a few years, and from Carthage deliver death blows to the Roman empire in the west.

---

[38] Cf. e.g., in addition to the obvious example of Justinian's reconquest, the embassies of the Roman senate and Nepos to Zeno in 476 (Malchus fr. 10=14 Blockley), and the appeals of the senate to Tiberius to aid Italy against the Lombards between 577 and 579 (Men.Prot. frr.49 and 62=22 and 24 Blockley).   [39] Hydat. *Chron. a.* 425.

CHAPTER 5

EMPERORS, GOVERNMENT AND BUREAUCRACY

CHRISTOPHER KELLY

I. INTRODUCTION

This chapter is about emperors and officials. Its primary concern is to understand how the later Roman empire was governed and how the power to rule was both conceived and justified. Imperial power is considered not only in terms of what emperors could do and how far their authority extended, but also in terms of how it was represented. Both are important. Comparisons with divinities (Christian and pagan), grand processions, long speeches and costly purple robes were as much a part of imperial rule and its enforcement as the capacity to issue decrees or command armies. This chapter also examines the consequences for emperors and their supporters of the increasing centralization of power and the continued growth of a sophisticated and well-organized bureaucracy. Centralization enhanced the position of emperors by making them the focus of all government activity; but in a large empire it also threatened to isolate them. Emperors risked being pavilioned in splendour within an inaccessible court. Similarly, the rise of bureaucracy held out certain clear and obvious administrative advantages. Above all, it enhanced the ability of imperial government systematically to enforce its policies and collect its revenues. Yet such a powerful and well-ordered institution also threatened to diminish the importance of emperors and the very centrality of their position. These conflicts dominate this account of later Roman government. Its chief purpose is to examine the tensions which resulted and the strategies deployed by emperors, courtiers and bureaucrats for the maintenance and improvement of their varying positions. A subtle and complex system emerges. It enables certain features – such as the sale of offices or the purchase of influence – to be seen in their proper perspective. These are not simply evidence of 'corruption' or 'moral decline'. Like other means of securing advantage or ensuring survival, they were part of a shifting set of tactical possibilities which marked out a difficult – and sometimes fatal – relationship between those who competed to rule the Roman empire.

138

II. THE EMPEROR IN THE LATER ROMAN WORLD

1. Perceptions of power

The emperor in the later Roman world was undoubtedly a powerful figure. 'He controlled foreign policy, making peace and war at will: he could raise what taxes he willed and spend the money at his pleasure: he personally appointed to all offices, civil and military: he had the power of life and death over all his subjects. He was moreover the sole fount of law and could make new rules or abrogate old at pleasure.'[1] The possible range and depth of emperors' concerns are quickly revealed in the law code promulgated by Theodosius II in 438. The Theodosian Code, which collated over two thousand five hundred imperial edicts issued since 312, contained legislation on such broad topics as taxation, property rights, contractual duties, judicial procedures and penalties, and the responsibilities, ranks and perquisites of civil and military officials, as well as laws regulating a widely diverse and varied set of specific matters including (for example) the demolition of tombs for building material, the construction of river patrol craft for the Danube, the price of bread in Rome's port town of Ostia and the care of horses no longer fit for chariot-racing.[2]

This extraordinary concentration of authority in the hands of one individual weighed heavily on the political imagination of contemporaries. For many, the extent and grandeur of imperial power could best be described by blurring the boundary between the earthly and the divine. The Gallic rhetorician Ausonius, elevated to the consulship in 379 by his former tutorial pupil the emperor Gratian, compared an imperial audience to standing before God; both inspired 'quiet dread and a reverent awe'.[3] For the court poet Claudian, celebrating Honorius' fourth consulship in 398, the emperor in his majesty could be likened to Jupiter, Mars, Apollo and Bacchus.[4] Honorius was a god; through marriage, his wife became the daughter of divinities.[5] Other fourth-century writers pictured emperors as standing 'in the first ranks of the gods';[6] in appearance they were like stars;[7]

---

[1] Jones, *LRE* 1.321; Demandt, *Spätantike* 214; Gaudemet (1967) 672; Piganiol, *Empire chrétien* 340–1 (cf. Firm. Mat. *Math.* 11.30.6). The most useful general accounts of later Roman emperors are to be found in: Demandt, *Spätantike* 212–31; Ensslin (1954), esp. 449–59; Gaudemet (1967) 667–75; Jones, *LRE* 1.321–9; Liebeschuetz, *Antioch* 105–10; Martin (1984b), esp. 126–9; Matthews, *Ammianus* 231–52; Piganiol, *Empire chrétien* 335–42.   [2] *C.Th.* IX.17.3; VII.17.1; XIV.19.1; XV.10.1.

[3] Auson, *Gratiarum Actio* 1.2: cf. Claudian, *De III Cos. Hon. pr.*

[4] Claudian, *De IV Cos. Hon.* 197–202, 523–6, 537–8, 602–10: Cameron, Alan, *Claudian* 193–9; MacCormack (1972) 737–9. For a good, brief introduction to Claudian's political poetry: Cameron, Alan (1974).

[5] *Ibid.* 136–7, 647–8: cf. *De III Cos. Hon. pr.* 15–16; *De VI Cos. Hon.* 35–8; *Pan. Lat.* XII.4.5.

[6] Firm. Mat. *Math.* 11.30.6.

[7] *Pan. Lat.* XI.2.3: cf. Amm. Marc. XXI.10.2, XXII.9.14; Claudian, *De III Cos. Hon.* 131–2, *De IV Cos. Hon.* 170–91; Symm. *Or.* 1.7 (*MHG, Auct. Ant.* VI.1.320): MacCormack, *Art and Ceremony* 45–50. For discussions of allusions to emperors' divinity in the *Pan. Lat.*: Béranger (1970), esp. 252–4; Burdeau (1964) 10–33; Nock (1947) 108–9; Rodgers (1986).

after death they took their rightful place in the heavens. In his panegyric delivered to celebrate Honorius' third consulship in 396, Claudian imagined the apotheosis of the recently deceased Theodosius I:

Heaven's fabric is loosened and of their own accord the shining portals open wide. Boötes makes ready the northern sky; swordgirt Orion unlocks the gates of the south. They welcome the new star, each uncertain as to which region he would seek out, what constellation he thought worthy of his presence, or in which quarter of the sky he would remain.[8]

More prosaically, away from the esoteric world of poets and rhetoricians, the well-tried language and rituals of the imperial cult continued to provide a traditional means for the empire's provincial citizenry both to parade its loyalty and to confirm its position in relation to a distant regime as seemingly far-off as the gods themselves. In the late fourth century, the townspeople of Lepcis Magna on the North African coast erected statues to the 'victorious and ever triumphant' emperors Arcadius and Honorius. In their dedicatory inscription the citizens declared publicly their devotion to the emperors' 'godhead and majesty'.[9]

The ambiguous position of an emperor, standing somewhere between divinity and humanity, was also accommodated within a rapidly developing Christian political theology.[10] At the beginning of the fourth century, Eusebius, bishop of Caesarea in Palestine, had stressed the close relationship between Christ and the emperor. In 336, in a speech given to celebrate the thirtieth anniversary of Constantine's accession, he described the emperor as 'the friend of the all-ruling God . . . arrayed, as he is, in the image of the kingdom of heaven, he pilots affairs here below, following – with an upward gaze – a course modelled on that ideal form'.[11] Subsequent fourth-century writers, while not so enthusiastically following Eusebius' view of the emperor as Christ's vicegerent, continued to exploit the idea that just government by earthly rulers was patterned – albeit imperfectly – on God's heavenly kingdom. For Athanasius, bishop of Alexandria, the emperor and God were both to be seen as rulers, each in his own sphere.[12] A more elaborate version of this privileged relationship was described, at the end of the fourth century, by the philosophically educated Synesius of

[8] Claudian, De III Cos. Hon. 169–74: cf. 106–10; Eunap. 28.6; Lib. Or. XVIII.304; MacCormack, Art and Ceremony, 121–50; Straub (1962).

[9] IRT 478, 479: Lepcitanti devoti | numini maiesta | tique eius no. 479 lines 6–8: Lepelley, Cités 1.357–69; Salzman, Roman Time, 131–46.

[10] The classic account remains Ensslin (1943), esp. 53–83; see too Dvornik, Political Philosophy II.672–705; Karayannopulos (1956), esp. 372–7; Taeger (1956), who rightly stresses the continuities with first- and second-century representations of emperors.

[11] Eus. Laud. Const. v.4, III.5 (GCS 7 (1902) : 204, 201): Barnes, CE 253–5; Farina (1966) 166–235; Setton (1941) 46–54; Straub (1939) 113–29.

[12] Athan. C. Gent. 38 (PG XXV.76A–77A) (perhaps written in the late 320s): cf. Or. II c. Arianos 79 (PG XXVI.316A–B), De Incarnat. 13, 55 (PG XXV.120A–B, 193B–D).

Cyrene, later bishop of Ptolemais in modern Libya. In a political treatise *On Kingship* Synesius argued that: 'God himself . . . desires things here [on earth] to be formed in imitation of the world above. Beloved then of the Great King is the one here who bears the same name, provided that he is worthy of that name.'[13] Non-Christian thought developed along similar lines, stressing the closeness and similarity of emperor and God, while underlining the superiority and supremacy of the latter.[14] The Greek-speaking orator Themistius, who across the second half of the fourth century delivered at least nineteen orations in praise of five emperors, repeatedly stressed that a good ruler in his just exercise of power was a reflection of the highest divinity.

According to philosophy, the king is the living law, a divine law which has come down into time from above, from the eternally benificent. The king is an emanation of that divine nature; he is providence nearer the earth; he looks towards Him from all directions, aiming at imitation of Him in every way.[15]

Despite such self-consciously subtle approaches, and sternly worded injunctions not to take parallels between heaven and earth too literally,[16] many authors – in their efforts to explain the nature of imperial or divine power – continued to rely on comparisons which frequently failed to distinguish clearly between this world and the next. Heaven remained a very Roman place. A fourth-century hexameter poem (preserved on papyrus fragments found in Upper Egypt) related the vision of Dorotheus, a Christian mystic who dreamt that he was transported to a heavenly palace, which in architecture and personnel was closely modelled on its earthly, imperial counterpart.[17] In the audience hall, guided by heaven's palace attendants, he saw the Father and the Son surrounded by their courtiers. After a series of tests, Dorotheus himself was promoted through the ranks of God's palace guard: 'I did not have simple clothing . . . but I was wearing a cloak made for me from two different sorts of linen. I stood with a kerchief around my neck and round my legs I wore long breeches and a multi-coloured belt.'[18] In the exegetical homilies of skilled ecclesiastical rhetoricians these crude comparisons became elaborate and sophisticated conceits. For John Chrysostom, bishop of Constantinople at the turn of the fourth century, the city of God was like an imperial palace, adorned

---

[13] Syn. *De Regno* VIII (for the date and circumstances surrounding the composition of this work: below n. 47): cf. *Pan. Lat.* XII.6.3–4; Auson. *Gratiarum Actio* V.21, VI.29, XVIII.79–80, 83.

[14] Lib. *Or.* XV.29–32, XVII.4–6.

[15] Them. *Or.* v.64b (to the emperor Jovian in 363/4): cf. 1.3a–b, VI.73b–74a, VII.89c–90a, XV.187b–189a, XVI.212d, XVIII.218b–219a, XIX.227b 228a: Dagron, 'Themistios' 121–46; Straub (1939) 160–74; Valdenburg (1924), esp. 568–70.

[16] Joh. Chrys. *De Incomp.* 3 (*SChrét.* 28: 188–90): Daniélou (1950) 178–87.

[17] *P.Bodm.* 29: Hurst, Reverdin and Rudhardt (1984) with corrections in Kessels and van der Horst (1987); Bremmer (1988); for the splendid uniforms worn by later Roman bureaucrats: below, nn. 162–6.

[18] *P.Bodm.* 29 lines 329–34.

with innumerable courts and buildings. 'Here angels stand, not before a mortal king, but before him who is immortal, the king of kings and lord of lords. They do not have a leather belt around their waists, but that glory which is unutterable.'[19] Christ in the splendour of his Second Coming could be compared to an emperor surrounded by his retinue processing in full ceremonial panoply before an awestruck crowd:

the men in golden apparel, and the pairs of white mules caparisoned with gold, and the chariots inlaid with precious stones, and the snow-white cushions . . . and dragons fashioned from silken cloth, and the shields with their golden bosses . . . and the horses with their golden trappings and gold bits. But when we see the emperor, we lose sight of these. For he alone draws our gaze: the purple robe, and the diadem, and the throne, and the clasp and the shoes – all the brilliance of his appearance.[20]

This inflated language, which associated the imperial with the divine and distanced both from the ordinary, was matched by the glittering reality of the magnificent ceremonial which attended emperors' public appearances. The imperial *adventus* (the arrival of an emperor in a city) was a carefully choreographed ritual which defined and expressed an ideal relationship between an emperor and his subjects.[21] In April 357, Constantius II made a triumphal entry into Rome to celebrate the twentieth anniversary of his accession as well as the defeat of the usurper Magnentius. The justly famous description by the contemporary historian Ammianus Marcellinus provides a vivid impression of that occasion.

The emperor sat alone in a golden chariot, shimmering in the glitter of various kinds of precious stones . . . he was surrounded by dragons, woven from purple thread and fastened to the gold and jewel-encrusted spear tips . . . on either side, there marched a double line of armed men, their shields and crests flashing with a dazzling light . . . [The emperor] did not move . . . and as if his neck were firmly clamped, he kept his gaze fixed straight ahead . . . and, as though he were the image of a man [*tamquam figmentum hominis*], neither did he sway, when jolted by the wheel of his chariot, nor was he ever seen to spit, or wipe or rub his face or nose, or to move his hands about.[22]

[19] Joh. Chrys. *Hom. in Ep. I ad Thess.* VI.4 (*PG* LXII.434): cf. *Hom. in Matth.* I.8 (*PG* LVII.23–4); Cyril of Jerusalem, *Procatech.* I (*PG* XXXIII.332A–33A).
[20] Joh. Chrys. *Hom. in Rom.* XIV.10 (*PG* LX.537): cf. *De Perf. Caritate* VI (*PG* LVI.286–7), *Hom. in Joh.* XII.I (*PG* LIX.82), *Hom. in Eph.* IX.I (*PG* LXII.70), *Hom. in Gen.* v.6 (*PG* LIII.54), *C. Anomoeos* XII.4 (*PG* XLVIII.809–10); further examples: *Synopsis Chrysostomi* v (*PG* LXIV.80); Dvornik, *Political Philosophy* II.692–9; Setton (1941) 187–95.
[21] Brown, *Power and Persuasion* 13–14; MacCormack (1972), esp. 721–3; Van Dam, *Leadership and Community* 20–4.
[22] Amm. Marc. XVI.10.6–10: on this important text: Charlesworth (1947) 36–8; MacCormack, *Art and Ceremony* 39–45; MacMullen (1964c) 438–9; Matthews, *Ammianus* 231–4; Warren Bonfante (1964) 414–16: more cautiously, Edbrooke (1976) and Klein (1979) both emphasize the specific political context of Constantius' entry into Rome. For the Hellenistic and early imperial antecedents to such ceremonies: Alföldi (1934) 88–118.

The focus of this splendid ceremonial set-piece, as in other descriptions of imperial *adventus*, was the relationship between the emperor and the multitude which pressed in on all sides.[23] The amazement at this extraordinary sight, and the shouts which greeted the imperial procession, established a bond between emperor and subject which, at the same time, emphasized the distance between them. The crowd in its enthusiasm was recognizably human. Young men scrabbled across roof-tops, or rushed ahead in the hope of getting a better view.[24] By contrast, the emperor, screened by his bodyguard, unmoved by plaudits, isolated, rigid and imperturbable, had no human characteristics. Constantius' individuality was effaced by the stiff formality of the occasion. To onlookers he became a godlike statue, a timeless icon of the dignity, remoteness and – for the majority – the unapproachability of imperial power.[25]

The distance separating emperor and subject, captured so forcibly in these ceremonial images, was reinforced by a repetitive insistence on the sanctity of all things imperial. In the Theodosian Code, the emperor's laws, bureaucratic offices, the palace, the court, the imperial wardrobe and even the imperial stables were described as 'sacred'.[26] Any questioning of the emperor's will amounted to 'sacrilege'.[27] Similar reverence was expected towards imperial images. Emperors' statues – like statuesque emperors – were important symbols of power. In the provinces, they were a focus for loyalty and a constant reminder of an ever-present, superior authority.[28] (The mutilated images of usurpers offered an equally salutary warning of the risks of revolt.)[29] Those approaching the emperor's statue were expected to adopt the same attitude and ceremony as if they stood before the emperor himself.[30] Equal respect was due to imperial edicts. According to John Chrysostom, imperial proclamations sent to the empire's cities were read out publicly, often in the theatre. They had a dramatic effect. A normally rowdy audience stood in awed silence, straining to hear the sacred commands, fearing what they might contain.[31]

[23] *Pan. Lat.* XI.6.3–5, XI.29.2, XII.37; Claudian, *De III Cos. Hon.* 126–30, *De IV Cos. Hon.* 564–85; Amm. Marc. XV.8.21, XXI.10.1, XXII.2.4–5.
[24] *Pan. Lat.* XII.37.3; Claudian, *De VI Cos. Hon.* 543–6. Naturally this became a *topos* in such descriptions.
[25] Cf. Amm. Marc. XXII.2.4; Claudian, *De IV Cos. Hon.* 570–4; for a matching image of the emperor in fourth-century art: Grabar (1936) 4–122; MacCormack, *Art and Ceremony* 43–5, 214–21.
[26] Laws: *C.Th.* I.15.8 (=*CJ* I.38.2), II.1.9, XIII.11.12: offices: I.10 (=*CJ* I.32), VI.26 (=*CJ* XII.19), VI.30 (=*CJ* XII.23): palace: VI.16 (=*CJ* XII.13), VI.35 (=*CJ* XII.28), XIII.3.12, XIII.3.16 (=*CJ* X.53.11): court: VI.23.4, XI.30.47: wardrobe: XI.18.1: stables: VI.13.1 (=*CJ* XII.11.1): Bréhier (1920) 49–50; Ensslin (1943) 50–3, 70–4. [27] *C.Th.* I.6.9 (=*CJ* IX.29.2).
[28] Alföldi (1934) 65–79, esp. 75–9; Bréhier (1920) 60–70; Dvornik, *Political Philosophy*, II.652–6; Ensslin (1943) 69–70; Hopkins (1978) 221–31, esp. 223–6; Kruse (1934), 23–50; Setton (1941) 196–211; Warren Bonfante (1964) 408–10; below, nn. 79–80. [29] Greg. Naz. *Or.* IV.96 (*SChrét.* 309. 240).
[30] Sev. Gabala, *in Sanct. Cruc.* in Joh. Damas. *Or.* III.385 (*PG* XCIV.1409A); Greg. Naz.*Or.* IV.80 (*SChrét.* 309. 202–4); Amb. *Ex. Ps. CXVIII* X.25 (*Amb. Op.* IX.426); *C.Th.* XV.4.1 (=*CJ* I.24.2).
[31] Joh. Chrys. *Hom. in Gen.* XIV.2 (*PG* LIII.112), XLIV.1 (*PG* LIV.406); *Hom. in Matth.* I.8 (*PG* LVII.24): cf. Lib. *Or.* I.157; Basil, *Ep.* 3.1.

Chrysostom's fleeting impression of a clamorous audience made silent, like Ammianus' description of an imperial *adventus*, emphasizes the extent to which these images of majesty set the emperor apart from the rest of humanity by stressing the extraordinary and the splendid. For fourth-century writers, that 'dramatic exaggeration'[32] was most strikingly evident in the emperor's regalia – the purple robe and jewelled diadem.[33] To be sure, these elements had always played an important role in the representation of Roman monarchy.[34] Yet, in a society which increasingly employed impressive uniforms and brightly coloured clothing as marks of status, the emperor's dress became a quintessential symbol of rule.[35] The imperial monopoly on the dyeing and weaving of purple cloth was jealously guarded.[36] Unauthorized possession was considered evidence of treason. In the mid 350s, a wealthy Gallic landowner was ruined following the disclosure that his tablecloths and couchcovers had broad purple borders and could be folded to resemble an imperial cloak.[37] Such seemingly harsh treatment underlines the symbolic significance of the purple in marking out an emperor and proclaiming his legitimacy. For Ammianus Marcellinus, the failure of Procopius' usurpation in 365 was presaged by his first public appearance wearing, like a second-rate stage-actor, a motley approximation of imperial dress and waving a small piece of purple cloth.[38] In contrast to Procopius' amateur performance, the emperor Julian's successful *coup d'état* in 360 was well ordered and carefully scripted. To the acclamation of his troops, he appeared (according to one account) wearing 'a cloak of sea purple and a jewel-studded diadem itself adorned with pearls taken from the sea'.[39] Similarly, in 367, to the shouts of soldiers and the clashing of arms, Valentinian appointed his son Gratian as co-emperor by presenting him with imperial robes and a diadem.[40] The dramatic exaggeration of such scenes – as with other images of emperors – was central to the representation of imperial power. In purple robes, wearing a jewelled diadem, surrounded by soldiers in shining armour and greeted by the rhythmic chanting of the crowd, an individual was transformed into an emperor by the sheer overwhelming 'brilliance of his appearance'.[41]

[32] MacMullen (1964c) 452.
[33] Avery (1940) 75–9; Delbrueck (1932), esp. 4–5; Demandt, *Spätantike*. 221–2; Reinhold (1970) 62–7; Treitinger (1938) 20–31; Warren Bonfante (1964) 410–12, and esp. Steigerwald (1990) 210–25.
[34] Alföldi (1935) 49–51, 145–50, with Avery (1940) 69–75; Löhken (1982) 48–53; Matthews, *Ammianus* 243–9.   [35] MacMullen (1964c) 445–52.
[36] *C.Th.* x.20.18 (=*CJ* xi.9.5); x.21 (=*CJ* xi.9).
[37] Amm. Marc. xvi.8.8: cf. xiv.7.20, 9.7–8, xvi.8.3–7, xxii.9.10–11, xxix.2.9–11.
[38] Amm. Marc. xxvi.6.15: cf. xv.5.16: Matthews, *Ammianus* 193–4; Seager (1986) 108–10.
[39] Lib. *Or.* xii.59, xiii.33: cf. Amm. Marc. xx.4.17–18; Julian, *Ep. ad Ath.* 284c–d: Bowersock, *Julian* 46–54; MacCormack, *Art and Ceremony* 192–6; Petit (1956b), 479–81.
[40] Amm. Marc. xxvii.6.10–11: cf. xv.8.4–17, xxv.5.5–6, xxvi.2.2–3, xxvi.4.3: de Bonfils (1986) 23–9; MacCormack, *Art and Ceremony* 196–202; for the military element involved in imperial ceremonial: Alföldi (1935) 43–68; Deér (1950) 51–64; Valensi (1957) 63–74.
[41] Joh. Chrys. *Hom. in Rom.* xiv.10 (*PG* lx.537): on the importance of clamorous acclamations on these occasions: Alföldi (1934) 79–88; MacMullen (1964c) 437–8; Roueché (1984) esp. 196–9.

Despite (for us) the often unpalatable degree of propagandistic exaggeration, hypocrisy or 'verbose and platitudinous vapouring'[42] which these inflated descriptions of later Roman emperors seem to involve, such rococo representations of power should be taken seriously.[43] An empire is held together not only by military force and efficient administration; it also requires an effective ideology to proclaim the rightness and authority of its government. Such a system can be as important (and as coercive for both rulers and the ruled) as more tangible expressions of power. From that point of view, the vast ceremoniousness of fourth-century society was a key element in helping to establish, and – through its unforgettable *tableaux* – to communicate, the legitimacy and dominance of an emperor and his regime. Pomp and power were inextricably linked. The deliberate and carefully exaggerated images of majesty not only elevated an emperor above the ordinary – they justified that distance by associating imperial rule with cosmic archetypes. The coalition of a political with a moral order reinforced the emperor's position as well as providing a way for those who rarely came in contact with the realities of imperial power to comprehend something of its extent and magnificence. Importantly too, ceremonial occasions permitted participants to glimpse something of a larger, transcendent order. Through elaborate rites, the 'permanent quasi-liturgical drama'[44] which dominated so much of late Roman public life enacted an exemplary model of society. Its focus was the emperor. Others could be located only in relation to a glittering imperial centre – a fixed, imperturbable point around which all else seemingly revolved. In that sense, too, ceremonies and the associated images of power were more than mere reflections of some external political reality. Rather, they were *in themselves* important elements in the formation and strengthening of an autocratic regime. Participation in familiar rituals enforced loyalty; loyalty enjoined participation – if only to chant in praise or gaze in wonder.

Splendid ceremonies (earthly or divine), grandiloquent language and flamboyant images naturally hold our attention. But it would be dangerously misleading to assume that they present a complete picture of imperial power. There were other, less dramatic ways of viewing later Roman emperors. Most importantly, the catalogue of imperial virtues (moderation, clemency, frugality, accessibility, willingness to obey laws) and vices

---

[42] Nixon (1987) 10.

[43] Burdeau (1964) 7–9; Hopkins (1978) 197–200; L'Huillier (1986) 529–31, (1992), esp. 132–9; MacCormack, *Art and Ceremony* 1–14; McCormick (1985); Treitinger (1938) 1–6; Van Dam, *Leadership and Community* 11: for a more sceptical approach: Cameron, Alan, *Claudian* 36–7; MacMullen (1964c) 437, *Corruption* 113; Straub (1939) 148–51. Contemporaries were, of course, well aware both of the brittle artificialities ceremonial occasions involved: Aug. *Conf.* VI.6.9 (*CCSL* XXVII.79–80); Auson. *Gratiarum Actio* 11.7; Jul. *Or.* 1.2b–c, 4b–c, 10b: and of the difference between those representations of power and the more sober formalities of history-writing: Amm. Marc. XXXI.16.9; Eutrop. X.18.3; MacCormack (1975) 152–4.   [44] MacCormack, *Art and Ceremony* 8.

(cruelty, capriciousness, unpredictability, inaccessibility), whose long tradition reached back to semi-philosophical treatises on kingship written in the third and second centuries B.C., continued to provide a grid on which contemporaries in the later empire could map their critiques of individual emperors.[45] In a stinging pamphlet, written in 398, Synesius of Cyrene accused the emperor Arcadius of haughtiness, luxurious self-indulgence and inaccessibility:

This majesty of yours, and the fear of being brought down to the level of mortals by becoming a familiar sight, causes you to be completely hidden away . . . rejoicing only in the pleasures of the flesh, and the most sensual of these, even as many as touch and taste provide; and so you live the life of a sea-borne jelly-fish.[46]

Such trenchant remarks are unlikely to have been made openly. At the time, Synesius, whose request for tax concessions for the cities of his province had been refused by the emperor, probably circulated his text privately in order to attract the attention and support of a powerful – and eventually successful – coterie in Constantinople opposed to Arcadius' senior court officials and their policies.[47] More public criticism of an emperor demanded greater subtlety. In 392, Ambrose, bishop of Milan, delivered a funeral oration on the unfortunate twenty-year-old emperor Valentinian II, who had ended an insecure reign over the western provinces by committing suicide. His death was followed by a serious revolt led by the Frankish general Arbogastes and his imperial nominee Eugenius. In a period of uncertainty, before the emperor Theodosius I, who retained control of the eastern empire, committed himself to suppressing the rebellion, Ambrose carefully avoided any direct reference to either side.[48] Instead (no doubt hoping the eventual winner would take notice) he presented Valentinian as a model emperor whose rule conformed to biblical *exempla* as well as to the traditional canon of Roman imperial virtues: modesty, frugality, abstinence and clemency.

And what more shall I say of one who considered that he should abstain even from the pastimes of youth? . . . At first, it was put about that he delighted in circus games. He distanced himself from this charge so that not even on official imperial birthdays, or for the sake of his own reputation as an emperor, did he think that circus games should be held. Some claimed that he spent his time at wild animal

---

[45] For a brief discussion of Roman imperial virtues in the early empire: Wallace-Hadrill (1981); for their use in the third century: de Blois (1986); Millar (1964) 78–82; Stertz (1979). The Hellenistic antecedents are explored in: Goodenough (1928); Schubart (1937).

[46] Syn. *De Regno* XIV; Demougeot (1946); cf. *Pan. Lat.* XII.21.3–4.

[47] Cameron and Long, *Barbarians and Politics*, esp. 91–142, followed here, also provide a detailed review and discussion of the long-running debate concerning Synesius' embassy, its date, and the meaning and purpose of his works written in Constantinople. For various alternative interpretations: Barnes (1986a), esp. 104–9; Dvornik, *Political Philosophy* II.699–705; Liebeschuetz, *Barbarians and Bishops* 104–45, 253–72; Setton (1941) 152–62.   [48] Matthews, *Western Aristocracies* 238–47.

fights and that he directed his attention away from affairs of state; immediately he ordered all the animals to be slaughtered.[49]

Traditional categories of virtue were also an important part of speeches delivered in the imperial presence.[50] Reflecting the long-standing practice of Graeco-Roman eulogistic oratory, a late-third- or early-fourth-century handbook on rhetoric ascribed to Menander instructed the prospective author of an address on kingship (*basilikos logos*) to present an emperor's achievements as illustrations of his virtue.

On every occasion divide the actions of those whom you are going to praise into the virtues (there are four virtues: courage, justice, moderation and wisdom) and see to what virtues the actions belong and whether some actions, in war or peace, are associated with one virtue – for example, with wisdom.[51]

Equally influential (and heading the *Panegyrici Latini* – a late-fourth-century collection of twelve speeches given before emperors) was the expanded version of a long address to the emperor Trajan delivered nearly three hundred years earlier by Pliny the Younger.[52] In that speech, Pliny was concerned to demonstrate the extent to which an ideal ruler conformed to a pattern of behaviour and morality sanctioned by the upper classes. Imperial virtues – clemency, friendship, frugality and accessibility – were presented as evidence of an emperor's preparedness to uphold and participate in the existing moral and social order. These were proofs of his *civilitas*, a word which evoked 'the behaviour of a ruler who is still a citizen in a society of citizens'.[53] Pliny's version of imperial power linked monarch and subject closely together; the actions of both could be judged on the same scale of values. A good king was also a good citizen; on that claim rested his authority: 'The emperor is one of us – and his superiority is greater and more conspicuous because he thinks of himself as one of us, and bears in mind that he is a man just as much as a ruler over men.'[54]

The image of the citizen-king retained some of its importance in the fourth century. An upper-class spokesman, Quintus Aurelius Symmachus, in two orations delivered in 369 and 370, stressed the importance of the Roman senate in the government of the empire by eulogizing the emperor Valentinian in terms strongly reminiscent of Pliny on Trajan.[55] In the early

---

[49] Amb. *De Ob. Val. Jun.* xv (*Amb. Op.* XVIII.172).

[50] Burdeau (1964) 25–9, 34–55; L'Huillier (1992) 325–60.

[51] Menander, *Rhetor* 373: for Menander's influence on fourth-century panegyrics: Gutzwiller (1942) 92–9; MacCormack (1975) 144–6; Straub (1939) 153–9; Struthers (1919) with Cameron, Alan, *Claudian* 253–60: specific borrowings from classical authors are traced for *Pan. Lat.* II–IX in Klotz (1911) 531–65.

[52] Gutzwiller (1942) 100–2; MacCormack (1975) 149–51. For a contrasting view, minimizing the influence of Pliny and Menander Rhetor: Vereecke (1975).

[53] Wallace-Hadrill (1982) 41–8, quoting 42. [54] Plin. *Paneg.* 11.4.

[55] Symm. *Or.* I.23, II.30 (*MHG, Auct. Ant.* VI.1.323, 329): MacCormack (1975) 174–7. For comprehensive treatments of Symmachus' views on monarchy: del Chicca (1984); Pabst (1989), esp. 171–301.

360s, Julian was similarly praised by those who approved of his attempts to present himself as a philosopher-king on the model of the second-century emperor Marcus Aurelius. In a series of speeches, the orator Libanius offered a virtuoso exposition of traditional virtues with appropriate classical parallels. Reaching a climax in his *Funeral Oration on Julian* (probably never publicly delivered), Libanius declaimed:

He was more self-controlled than Hippolytus, as just as Rhadamanthys, more intelligent than Themistocles, braver than Brasidas. He restored to health a world which had sickened. He hated wickedness, was kind to the just, hostile to the self-indulgent and a friend to all fair-minded men.[56]

Similar extravagant praise of Julian's moderation, justice, courage and foresight formed the unifying themes of a speech given before the senate of Constantinople by the consul Claudius Mamertinus on New Year's Day 362: 'Nor has he any need to acquire paintings, marble inlays, panelled ceilings decorated with solid gold, he who, for the greater part of the year, slept on the bare ground, sheltered only by the sky.'[57] The greater prominence of such rhetoric under Julian no doubt reflects something of that emperor's own – often idiosyncratic – views on the nature and presentation of imperial power.[58] Even so, for fourth-century emperors some conformity to the ideal of a citizen-king was an important demonstration of their fitness to rule. In Rome, following his splendid *adventus*, Constantius II addressed the senate and the people and went on an extensive, touristic walk-about through the city.[59] Similarly, also in Rome, even the emperor Theodosius I – perhaps more accustomed to the rhythmic chanting of the crowd – found time to exchange jokes with passers-by.[60]

This emphasis on the continuing importance of long-standing ways of coming to terms with imperial power should, in its turn, be matched by an equal stress on the ability of fourth-century orators to place these well-worn classical gems in startlingly new settings. In 389, the Gallic orator Latinus Pacatus Drepanius delivered a panegyric before the emperor Theodosius I in Rome. The use of familiar categories for the cataloguing of stock imperial virtues, placed Pacatus' oration firmly within a long-established rhetorical tradition.[61] The similarities with Pliny's speech in praise of Trajan are striking. So are the contrasts. In Pacatus' version, im-

[56] Lib. *Or.* XVIII.281: cf. XVIII.174–6, XVIII.184–5, XVIII.183–96, XII.92–6, XV.12–13, XVII.26–7: Liebeschuetz, *Antioch* 24–6; Petit (1956b) 486–8.

[57] *Pan. Lat.* XI.11.4: cf. XI.5.3–5, XI.12, XI.28–31: Blockley (1972); Pichon (1906) 114–36.

[58] Athanassiadi, *Julian* 161–91, esp. 174–81; Dvornik (1955); Dvornik, *Political Philosophy* II.659–72.

[59] Amm. Marc. XVI.10.13–17; the city of Rome was, unsurprisingly, a favoured site for displays of traditional imperial *civilitas*: Claudian, *De VI Cos. Hon.* 543–59, 587–94; *Pan. Lat.* XII.47.3: Cameron, Alan, *Claudian* 382–9; Straub (1939) 187–98.

[60] Claudian, *De VI Cos. Hon.* 60; cf. Amm. Marc. XVI.10.13.

[61] Lippold (1968); Pichon (1906) 136–50.

perial virtues were not presented as proofs of an emperor's willingness to conform to an aristocratic ideal of a citizen-king. Rather, they were divine qualities patterned on the heavens above. An emperor's virtues were further evidence of that vast distance which lay between citizen and king. Theodosius' concern for his friends did not reveal any desire for civic equality; rather – in Pacatus' elegant reworking of a well-worn motif – the emperor 'summoned Friendship not only to the palace, but clothed her in purple, wreathed her in gold and gems and placed her on the throne'.[62] Similarly, in his frugality, Theodosius did not seek to match any existing aristocratic ideal; rather, he set a model for others to follow.[63] Most telling is Pacatus' treatment of the emperor's accessibility. Theodosius – on the model of Trajan – did not remain 'shut away in a remote part of the palace', nor in his public appearances did he permit himself to be 'completely surrounded above and on all sides by a very dense screen of men and weapons'.[64] For Pliny, an emperor's visibility was a crucial demonstration of his *civilitas*. Trajan by making himself available to his people had bridged the gap between citizen and king.[65] But – for Pacatus – Theodosius' accessibility, like his displays of frugality and friendship, was yet another demonstration of the irreducibility of that distance. A virtuous emperor's willingness to be seen merely offered greater opportunity for awestruck crowds to gaze upon his divine countenance.[66]

Pacatus' speech before Theodosius I in 389 represents one possible perception of imperial power. Like Libanius, Ausonius, Themistius, Symmachus or Pliny, Pacatus arranged his carefully selected material into a pattern suitable for a specific occasion. That particularity is important. To plunder the sources in order to assemble an amalgam of qualities attributable to a late antique 'ideal prince' is to risk losing something of the delicate negotiation which any individual representation of imperial power inevitably involved.[67] In the later empire, a range of perspectives, laudatory and critical, was still available – even to court poets and orators. For the most part, despite a marked and steady rise in the importance of court and public ceremonial, and in closely associated images of majesty, the construction, presentation and perception of imperial power remained disputed territory. The fourth century, in particular, was marked by an unresolved tension between traditional moralizing views of imperial power, which stressed the close relationship between citizen and king, and other,

---

[62] *Pan. Lat.* XII.16.2; cf. XI.23.4.

[63] *Pan. Lat.* XII.14.4; cf. *Pan. Lat.* XI.10–12 where the emperor's frugality marks him off from the rest of society. [64] *Pan. Lat.* XII.21.3–4. [65] Plin. *Paneg.* XLVII.3–XLIX.

[66] *Pan. Lat.* XII.21.2 and 5. For another good example of new patterns formed from old material, see Dagron, 'Thémistios' 127–34; Valdenburg (1924) 570–80 for Themistius' reworking of traditional philosophical maxims on good kingship.

[67] MacCormack (1975) 159–66, *Art and Ceremony* 12–14: cf. Wallace-Hadrill (1981) 317–19: for a radically different approach to this material: Born (1934); Maguinness (1932).

more ceremonial versions which emphasized the distance between subject and ruler.[68] Only against that background is it safe to see such moments as the subtle reworking of traditional themes in Pacatus' speech, or Constantius II's *adventus* in Rome, or Chrysostom's close parallels between emperor and God, as edging towards a more settled image of a remote, divinely inspired monarchy. Although that perception of imperial power became increasingly significant in the later empire – and eventually prevailed – it is important not to pre-empt these more distant, Byzantine perspectives. In the fourth century, there was no one undisputed or clear-cut view. Standard categories of imperial virtue still sat uncomfortably alongside other, less traditional conceptions of power. Emperors, sometimes unavoidably, presented themselves (or were perceived) in a series of conflicting and contradictory images. The results – like Pacatus' version of Theodosius' 'accessibility' – were frequently confusing. When, in 362, the emperor Julian insisted on walking to the investiture of the consuls for that year, the historian Ammianus Marcellinus observed that this self-conscious rejection of accepted ceremonial protocol earned praise from some, but was regarded by others as 'cheap affectation'.[69] In his strong emphasis on tradition (and in the strong reactions he provoked) Julian was perhaps something of a maverick; but, for the onlooker, any final judgement on the actions, virtues or demerits of other fourth-century emperors remained similarly problematic. As Ammianus Marcellinus wryly remarked, Constantius II frequently asserted his *civilitas* – taking considerable pains to model himself on emperors like Trajan and Marcus Aurelius – while, at the same time, actively promoting elaborate court ceremonial and signing himself on (sacred) imperial documents: 'My Eternity' and 'Master of the Whole World'.[70]

2. Centralization

The splendid procession which heralded the arrival of the imperial court in a city was unquestionably focused on the glittering presence of the emperor himself.[71] Scarcely less eye-catching was the parade of the powerful which followed the imperial carriage. For John Chrysostom, these courtiers, in their closeness to the emperor, could be compared to a heavenly band surrounding the risen Christ: 'for we regard those as blessed who are near him and have a share in his speech and mind, and partake of the rest of his glory'.[72] The careful disposition of monarch, court and cheer-

---

[68] Dagron, 'Thémistios' 122–7; Demougeot (1946) 191–3.

[69] Amm. Marc. XXII.7.1: cf. XXII.7.31–4; Lib. *Or.* XVIII.155–6: Matthews, *Ammianus* 235–6.

[70] Amm. Marc. XV.1.3: on the representation of imperial power in Ammianus see too: de Bonfils (1986) 81–9; Tassi (1967) 164–8; Seager (1986) 18–36, 105–30.   [71] Above, nn. 21–5.

[72] Joh. Chrys. *Ad Theodorum Lapsum* 1.12 (*PG* XLVII.293).

ing crowd emphasized both the centrality of the emperor and – for those who desired power, wealth and position – the overwhelming importance of proximity to that imperial centre. (It is hardly surprising that, in the fourth century, high office-holders, military commanders and influential members of the imperial household were known collectively as *proximi*.)[73] More broadly, in bringing ruler and people face to face, the rituals of an imperial *adventus* underscored the determination of emperors to be able both to respond directly to the concerns of their subjects and to locate and suppress any possibly subversive activities. In practice, that determination was expressed by the 'fantastic degree' of centralization which character-ized later Roman government.[74] To be sure, this was, to some extent, an inevitable result of the rapid growth in the imperial bureaucracy at the beginning of the fourth century.[75] But centralization also protected an emperor's position. The concentration of power at court, and in the bureaucratic departments located near the imperial palace, helped emper-ors maintain a personal stake in the empire's expanding administration. Here, too, proximity mattered. It increased emperors' chances of success-fully asserting their will – sometimes violently – against the advice of their officials; it kept open the possibility of a personal, or even whimsical, response to embassies or petitions. Above all, centralization enforced the attendance of high-ranking officials at court. Their presence not only emphasized their dependence upon imperial good will for appointment and promotion; it also offered an emperor – aided by court intrigue or rival-ries – a better chance of policing or punishing the powerful who ruled the empire in his name.

An emperor's influence was most keenly felt in the world of the *potestates excelsae* – the 'lofty powers'[76] who surrounded the throne and offered advice in the debates and discussions of the *consistorium* (the imperial high council).[77] In formal terms, emperors emphasized their role in the selection of these senior administrative officials through the requirement that docu-ments authorizing their appointment bear the imperial signature[78] and – if possible – be presented by the emperor in person. The Missorium of Theodosius – an impressive silver plate, made to celebrate the tenth anni-versary of the emperor's accession in 388 – shows an impassive, statuesque Theodosius I enthroned between his junior colleagues Valentinian II and Arcadius; kneeling, a splendidly dressed official receives in carefully veiled

---

[73] Amm. Marc. XIV.11.1, XV.8.2, XXX.4.1.   [74] Jones, *LRE* 1.401–6, quoting 403.

[75] *Ibid.* 42–52, 100–4. For other brief descriptions of the administrative reforms of Diocletian and Constantine: *CAH* XII.389–96; Barnes, *NE* 195–225; Cameron, Averil, *LRE* 39–41, 53–4; Carney (1971) 1.89–102.   [76] Amm. Marc. XXVIII.6.9; Brown, *Power and Persuasion* 10.

[77] Jones, *LRE* 1.333–41; Demandt, *Spätantike* 231; de Bonfils (1981) 25–39; Kunkel (1968) 242–6; Weiss (1975) 6–38; Vogler (1979) 216–20.

[78] *C.Th.* VI.7.1 (=*CJ* XII.4.1), IX.27.1 (=*CJ* XII.1.12), XIII.11.11, XV.14.8: Jones, *LRE* III.81 n. 28; Noethlichs (1981) 21 n. 104.

hands a small case containing his letters of appointment.[79] Document cases (*codicilli*) consisted of two hinged ivory plaques (each about thirty centimetres long) decorated with gold trim; their outer face displayed a portrait bust of the emperor. They were an important part of a high-ranking official's *insignia*. Exhibited between burning tapers on a blue cloth-covered table, *codicilli* proclaimed both the legitimacy of an official's acts and his close dependence on the emperor for his position.[80]

In practice, emperors maintained the attraction of their persons and their court by ensuring that proximity brought success. The high-flying bureaucrat Anatolius owed a series of posts to his well-timed appearances. Having been proconsul of Constantinople in 354, he remained at court, pressing for preferment. He seems to have been offered the urban prefecture of Rome and to have turned it down. In 355, he returned on a brief visit to his estates in southern Asia Minor, but by spring of the following year he was back at court in Italy, lobbying for office, and was, in 357, appointed to the praetorian prefecture of Illyricum – one of the most senior posts in the empire.[81] In similar vein, the decidedly unmilitary senator and orator Quintus Aurelius Symmachus was granted the honorary rank of *comes* as a result of touring the empire's northern defences with the emperor Valentinian in 369.[82] More generally, emperors might favour their compatriots – a clique of Pannonians was particularly prominent under Valentinian – or grant promotion to the provincial associates of an already established official.[83] In the late 370s, the Gallic rhetorician Ausonius, former tutor to the emperor Gratian, obtained positions in the imperial administration for a wide group of his relatives and connections from his native Bordeaux. His immediate family enjoyed even greater success. Ausonius secured a praetorian prefecture and a consulship for himself, as well as prefectures for his son Hesperius and his octogenarian father Julius.[84]

Meteoric rises were matched by sudden falls. For those connected to a previous regime, or to an official fallen from grace, the consequences could be severe. The emperor Julian, on taking the throne, purged the leading advisers of his predecessor Constantius II. According to Ammianus Marcellinus, a show trial – which condemned both innocent and guilty

---

[79] MacCormack, *Art and Ceremony* 214–21.

[80] Berger (1981) 25–34, 175–83; Grigg (1979); Kruse (1934) 99–106; Lizzi (1988) 3–7; Verdickt (1968) 204–7. The *insignia* are known from the surviving medieval illustrations to the *Notitia Dignitatum* – the imperial register of office-holders: below, nn. 133–9.

[81] Lib. *Ep.* 311, 391.13–16, 423.3, 492: *PLRE*(1) 59–60 (Anatolius 3); Petit, *Libanius* 385–6; Seeck (1906), 60–4.   [82] Matthews, *Western Aristocracies* 32; *PLRE*(1) 865–70 at 866 (Symmachus 4).

[83] Matthews, *Western Aristocracies* 35–49; Matthews, *Ammianus* 271–3; Chastagnol (1963).

[84] *PLRE*(1) 140–1 (Ausonius 7), 427–8 (Hesperius 2), 139 (Ausonius 5), 1134–5 (Stemma 8); Hopkins (1961); Matthews, *Western Aristocracies* 69–76; Sivan (1993) 131–41. For further illustrations of the advantages of patronage and proximity: Matthews (1971).

alike – was followed by a general expulsion from the palace at Constantinople of all the emperor's attendants and household staff. Several who had hitherto enjoyed successful careers were burned alive.[85] For Christian writers, the perilous position of those who served the emperor inspired instructive homilies on the vicissitudes of human affairs. For his first sermon on the fall of the eunuch Eutropius – who from 395 to 399 had been a dominant influence at the court of Arcadius[86] – John Chrysostom took as his text Ecclesiastes 1.2.

Vanity of vanities, all is vanity . . . Where now are the splendid trappings of your consulship? . . . Where are the cheers which greeted you in the city, where the acclamations in the Hippodrome and the flatteries of the spectators? . . . These were all night-time dreams, dispelled at daybreak; they were spring flowers, all withered with the end of spring; they were a shadow which has passed, smoke which has dispersed, bubbles which have burst, cobwebs which have been swept away.[87]

Precipitous falls demanded high-flown rhetoric. But (less dramatically) high-ranking bureaucrats, even without incurring imperial displeasure, could not have expected to remain in office for long. In practice, senior administrative posts were held briefly and irregularly, and were only rarely renewed. On average, in the fourth century, praetorian prefects were replaced after three or four years;[88] urban prefects after only one or two.[89] Longer stints were exceptional. From an emperor's point of view – despite costs in efficiency and the accumulation of experience – a highly centralized system with a rapid turnover of personnel emphasized the importance of imperial favour in securing and holding office. Importantly too, it limited the opportunities within the administration for the formation of rival coalitions of interest opposed to imperial policy.

As far as they were able, emperors tried to replicate a similar level of personal control throughout the empire. In part, this was again achieved by the creation of an 'atmosphere of intimidation and violence'.[90] In Ammianus Marcellinus' history, the exercise of imperial power was inseparable from images of cruelty. Following the discovery of a plot against the emperor Valens, the accused were tortured to encourage them to confess:

The racks were tightened, the lead weights were made ready along with cords and whips. The whole place echoed with the terrifying cries of a cruel voice, as those who discharged their painful duty shouted amidst the noise of chains: 'Hold; clamp; tighten up; take him away.'[91]

[85] Amm. Marc. XXII.3–4: Matthews, *Ammianus* 92–3; Thompson (1947) 73–9 with Blockley (1972) 449–50; Vogler (1979) 147–8.   [86] Below, n. 195.   [87] Joh. Chrys. *In Eutrop.* 1 (*PG* LII.391)
[88] Jones, *LRE* 1.380.   [89] *Ibid.* 380, 690; Chastagnol, *Préfecture urbaine* 187–8; Dagron, *Naissance* 284.
[90] Matthews, *Ammianus* 256–62, quoting 256; MacMullen (1986a), esp. 156–62; for a less well-balanced analysis, but one which vividly conveys the terror imperial power could inspire: Alföldi (1952) 28–47.   [91] Amm. Marc. XXIX.1.23: cf. XIV.5.3, XIV.9.6, XV.3.10–11, XXI.12.20, XXVIII.1.54–7.

More memorably horrific are the accounts of the sheer terror which gripped the citizens of Antioch in 387 following a riot in which the statues of the emperor Theodosius I and his family were pulled down, pelted with filth and dragged through the streets.[92] Expecting, according to John Chrysostom, then a priest in the city, 'the wrath of emperor to come like fire from above', prominent Antiochenes fled into the desert. An ominous silence descended on the once busy public squares and porticoes.

For as a garden when the irrigation fails shows trees stripped of their foliage and bare of fruit, so now indeed is it with our city. For help from above having forsaken her she stands desolate, stripped of nearly all her inhabitants.[93]

The worst fears of the people seemed to be confirmed with the arrival of an imperial commission to investigate the unrest. According to Libanius, also an eyewitness, those suspected of involvement were arrested, condemned and punished – 'some fell by the sword, some lost their lives burnt at the stake, some were destroyed thrown to the jaws of wild animals'.[94] As the commissioners continued their grim deliberations, John Chrysostom delivered a (perhaps not altogether welcome) series of homilies which combined striking rhetorical images of a terrified populace with a strong apocalyptic theme. The fear in the city was a forewarning of the Last Judgement. The dread inspired by the imperial commission was a mere shadow of things to come:

Looking at these things, I cast in my mind that fearsome tribunal; and I said to myself: If now, when men are judges, neither mother, nor sister, nor father, nor anyone else (even though innocent of the acts committed) has the power to deliver the accused; who will stand by us when we are brought to trial at the dread tribunal of Christ? Who will dare speak out? Who will have the power to deliver those led away to unbearable punishments?[95]

In the end, the city was saved. Intercessions – in Antioch by monks who had come in from the desert to plead for the people, and at court by the city's bishop – secured the emperor's pardon. According to the early-fifth-century ecclesiastical historian Sozomen, the bishop, who had arranged that the emperor's choirboys should sing hymns from the Antiochene liturgy, so moved Theodosius that 'his anger subsided, and as he made his peace with the city, he shed tears into the cup he was holding'.[96] Such sudden benevolence, like random violence, both emphasized the dependence of all on the imperial will and underlined the risks taken by those

[92] For good accounts of the 'Riot of the Statues': Browning (1952); Downey, *Antioch* 426–33; Petit, *Libanius* 238–44; esp. van de Paverd (1991) 15–159.

[93] Joh. Chrys. *Hom. ad Pop. Ant.* II.1–3 (*PG* XLIX.35–8), III.6–7 (*PG* XLIX.55–8), XI.1–2 (*PG* XLIX.119–22), XIII.1–2 (*PG* XLIX.135–9), quoting II.1 (*PG* XLIX.35).   [94] Lib. *Or.* XIX.37.

[95] Joh. Chrys. *Hom. ad Pop. Ant.* VI.6 (*PG* XLIX.89), XIII.1–2 (*PG* XLIX.135–9), quoting XIII.2 (*PG* XLIX.138).   [96] Soz. *HE* VII.23.3 (*GCS* 50 (1960) 336–7).

who attempted to flout it.[97] These two dramatic acts – the threat of a massacre and the granting of clemency – brought the emperor close to his people. More importantly, the accounts of such actions endlessly retold (and, like all good stories, more terrifying at each retelling) made a lasting and uncomfortable impression on all who heard them. The chances of its happening again, perhaps somewhere else, could never be entirely dismissed. Imperial intervention remained an ever-present possibility. But, like lightning, it was impossible to predict where emperors might strike next.

Not all imperial interventions were terrifying. The threat of imperial retribution was matched by an ever-present chance of reward. Again, the centralization of imperial authority was a crucial tactic. It ensured that provincials continued to regard direct access to the emperor as the most effective method of solving their problems. The result was a never-ending flow of petitions and requests. In an attempt to stem the tide, in 382, the co-emperors Gratian, Valentinian II and Theodosius I moved to restrict the number of embassies travelling to the capital:

Just as we wish to allow the oppressed to lament their sufferings, so our provincials ·. . . shall know that they should convey to our sacred ears those matters which are most suitably litigated before emperors, and they should not assume that Our Everlastingness should be taken up with superfluous legal actions.[98]

But for those who could find a way through, access to the imperial centre might bring hope of immediate reward. In the late 250s, Lollianus, a teacher of rhetoric in the Egyptian town of Oxyrhynchus, petitioned the emperors Valerian and Gallienus.[99] Lollianus had been appointed as a public teacher by the town council and expected to receive his stipend at regular intervals. But the sums owing were only infrequently paid and then only – so Lollianus alleged – in sour wine and weevil-infested grain. He requested that the emperors should instruct the town council (which presumably had already rejected his proposal) to assign him, in lieu of further payments, an orchard within the town walls. Its rents would provide a satisfactory income. Lollianus' petition was a simple one; bringing it to the attention of the emperors was immeasurably more difficult. It needed connections – friends and friends of friends. First, he pressed into service a friend's brother, who was a minor official in the military bureaucracy, to take the petition and present it at court. Secondly, he wrote a letter to an apparently close associate, also at court, enclosing another copy of his petition. Lollianus pressed this friend to intervene on his behalf and secure him a

---

[97] Brown, *Power and Persuasion* 105–8.

[98] *C.Th.* XII.12.9.1: cf. 1.16.2, XII.1.9 (= *CJ* x.32.16), XII.12.3.

[99] Parsons (1976); for another good example, see the career of Flavius Abinnaeus: Barnes (1985); Bell *et al.* (1962), esp. 1–6; Jones, *LRE* 1.393, 637–9; Rémondon (1965), esp. 132–4; *PLRE* I.1–2.

hearing: 'For you will know the consuls, and generally give a lead in what is expedient, pursuing the matter on behalf of one who is a scholar and a friend and a suppliant.'[100] Regrettably, the outcome of Lollianus' action is unknown. All that survives are the draft letter and petitions. But at least this small-town teacher considered the effort of getting his case heard at court worthwhile. After all, he had friends at court (or so he thought), imperial policy (so he trusted) would favour public education and the emperors themselves (so he hoped) would take the opportunity to show that they cared about all the inhabitants of their empire. In extravagantly weighty phrases – given the subject matter of the petition – Lollianus addressed his wished-for benefactors:

Your heavenly magnanimity, which – like a sunrise – has enlightened your domains, which are the whole civilized world, and your fellowship with the Muses (for Education sits besides you on the throne) have given me the confidence to offer you a just and lawful petition.[101]

He also reminded his friend at court to secure an unambiguous imperial reply – one which the local authorities would be forced to accept even though they might attempt to reverse it (so Lollianus feared) 'through ill-will'.[102]

The petition of an insignificant man like Lollianus was an important token of the possible extent and range of imperial power and of the perceived ability of emperors to affect even small matters in a distant provincial market-town. It reinforced the impression that proximity to the imperial court was what really counted. Equally, the continual upward stream of petitions and requests provided opportunities for emperors to demonstrate their claim to universal authority and beneficence by cutting through obstacles imposed by those with more limited influence. The high level of centralization in later Roman government weakened local sites of authority, whose rulings might be cancelled or overturned without warning by those closer to the imperial centre. Of course, in practice, few provincials – especially those without friends in the right places – ever made contact with the imperial court or were able to air their grievances outside their own small communities. Fewer still joined the ranks of the *potestates excelsae*. But, as with Ausonius or Lollianus, such possibilities could never be entirely excluded. Possibilities – like threats – matter. Buttressed by the occasional well-advertised success or by the rapid advancement of those known to enjoy imperial favour, they ensured the continued irresistible pull of the court. The centralization of power held out an open-ended promise of success for anyone able to make contact. In the imagination of contemporaries, the emperor had the power to intervene to their advantage in any situation – if only he were told.

---

[100] Parsons (1976) 422 document B lines 35–6.   [101] *Ibid.* 420 document A lines 6–11.
[102] *Ibid.* 422 document B line 37.

3. The limits of rule

Later Roman emperors – despite their claims, and the hopes of provincials seeking redress – were not omnipotent. In an empire of fifty to sixty million people, which stretched from Hadrian's Wall in northern Britain to the river Euphrates in eastern Syria, there was a limit to the effective power emperors could possibly exercise. The empire's greatest tyranny was distance. Overland, Constantinople was a month's journey away from Antioch; Alexandria, at the Nile delta, was a further six weeks away. Journeys from cities in the Balkans to Rome took around seven weeks.[103] Communication by sea was comparatively quicker. A law issued by Constantine at Serdica (modern Sofia in Bulgaria) on the 4 December was posted in Cordoba in Spain three months later.[104] But 'standard times' are difficult to determine. Travel times – especially those by ship – varied markedly according to the seasons. A voyage from Rome to Africa which in the summer took thirty-one days might last eighty or more in the winter. Laws issued in Constantinople in the autumn were unlikely to reach Africa until the following spring or early summer.[105]

Administrative difficulties arising from the painful slowness of communications were compounded by the absence of any sophisticated methods of information storage or retrieval. Archives, at best, were haphazardly organized.[106] There was, for example, no official, consolidated collection of imperial edicts until the promulgation of the Theodosian Code in 438. The Code's compilers were instructed by the emperor Theodosius II to sort through 'that mass of imperial constitutions, which sunk in a thick fog, has, by a bank of obscurity, cut off knowledge of itself from human minds'.[107] Their task was made more difficult by the failure of central administrative departments systematically to record copies of laws they had themselves issued. The Code was patched together from a set of miscellaneous sources, including the archives of provincial governors who had received imperial edicts, and the private collections of academic or practising lawyers.[108]

The free flow of information to central government was further restricted by those who feared that their advice might be interpreted as hostile criticism of the emperor or his policies. The historian Ammianus Marcellinus regarded it as worthy of note that the high-ranking palace official Flavius Eupraxius was able to quell the emperor Valentinian's rages

[103] Jones, *LRE* III.91–3 n. 76.   [104] *C.Th.* IX.1.1 (= *CJ* III.24.1).
[105] Brown, *Power and Persuasion* 9–10; Duncan-Jones, *Structure and Scale* 7–29; Jones, *LRE* I.402–3.
[106] Kelly (1994) 161–6; Posner (1972) 205–23.   [107] Th. II, *Nov.* 1.1.
[108] Honoré (1986) 156–68; Jones, *LRE* I.473–6; Matthews (1993), esp. 31–41; Mommsen (1900), esp. 163–75; Seeck (1919) 1–18. For a contrasting view, arguing that the Code was compiled chiefly from copy-books (which recorded out-going legislation) in the imperial archives in Constantinople and Rome or Ravenna: Sirks (1993), esp. 49–56.

and persuade him to act with greater clemency.[109] Others were not always so successful. Perhaps in response to a report from Quintus Aurelius Symmachus which questioned the selection of officials in the urban prefecture of Rome and recommended revised criteria for future appointments, the emperor Valentinian II witheringly observed: 'There must be no questioning of the imperial judgement: it is a kind of sacrilege to doubt whether the person whom the emperor has selected is worthy.'[110] In the light of such a reaction, it comes as no surprise that, in the late 360s, the anonymous author of *De Rebus Bellicis* – a pamphlet which offered advice on a wide range of civil, fiscal and military affairs – should have advanced his case tentatively, observing the perfection of the emperors and their government, while, at the same time, nervously suggesting improvements.[111]

Inefficient communications, unreliable records and the risks involved in criticizing imperial policy allowed those sufficiently daring, or sufficiently far distant, to ignore imperial directives or knowingly supply the emperor with false or misleading information. In the 360s, Romanus, military commander in Africa, evaded any proper enquiry into his refusal to defend the city of Lepcis Magna against raids from desert tribes unless the townsmen supplied his troops with provisions and four thousand camels. He forestalled an embassy sent by the provincials to the emperor Valentinian by despatching a swift messenger to his relative Remigius – head of the palatine bureaucracy. Although the embassy presented its grievances to the emperor, Remigius was able to obfuscate the issue and delay any investigation. Meanwhile the raids continued. The emperor, learning of this, reopened the case, sending a court official (the *notarius* Palladius) to interview prominent local spokesmen in Lepcis Magna. They showed him the devastation the raids had caused and complained of the lack of proper military intervention. But Palladius too was suborned by Romanus. The evidence given by the provincial spokesmen was deliberately distorted and suppressed. Palladius (in Ammianus' words) 'through the wicked art of lying' convinced Valentinian that the provincials' complaints were groundless. The emperor – misinformed and misguided by his own (supposedly loyal) officials – in the belief that there was no irregularity, left Romanus, Remigius and Palladius unpunished. Instead, for supplying false information to an imperial official and attempting thereby to deceive the emperor, he ordered the provincial spokesmen's tongues torn out.[112]

In principle, the solution to such imperial difficulties was simply put. The

[109] Amm. Marc. XXVII.7.6, XXVIII.1.25.   [110] *C.Th.* 1.6.9 (=*CJ* IX.29.2); Symm. *Rel.* XVII: Vera (1981) 131–3, 156–7; Jones, *LRE* 1.391–2.

[111] Anon. *De Rebus Bell. pr.* 15–17: on the date: Cameron, Alan (1979).

[112] Amm. Marc. XXVIII.6.1–24, quoting 20: Matthews, *Ammianus* 383–7; Warmington (1956); for the disputed chronology of this affair: Demandt (1968). Further good examples of misinformation and false reporting are related by Ammianus: XV.5.3–16, XXX.5.8–10; see too: Blockley (1969).

orator Themistius, speaking before Constantius II in 350, advised the cultivation of friendships:

For the emperor who must hear many things, see many things, and at the same time pay attention to many things, his two ears and his two eyes and his body (which contains one soul) are very little indeed. But if he is rich in friends, he will see far and will hear things which are not close to him, and he will know what is far off – like the seers – and he will be present at the same time in many places – like a god.[113]

In practice, things were more difficult. Emperors attempted to secure a systematic flow of reliable information by entrusting special imperial missions to two groups within the palatine bureaucracy – the *notarii* (principally clerks and shorthand writers serving as an imperial secretariat)[114] and the *agentes in rebus* (principally imperial messengers and supervisors of the public post under the control of the *magister officiorum* – the head of the palatine administration).[115] In 359, Constantius II instructed the two *agentes* sent out to each province not to conceal 'anything which you see being done in the state'.[116] Similarly, *notarii*, sometimes working alongside *agentes*, acted as imperial representatives in a wide range of diplomatic, military, ecclesiastical and administrative matters.[117] The creation of a separate corps of officials, who could be employed as reporters, messengers or negotiators, allowed emperors to bypass normal channels of information and command. At the same time, *notarii* and *agentes* were also encouraged to inform on the activities of other administrative departments. Expanding the number of bureaucrats involved in cross-checking the conduct of their colleagues helped to reduce the likelihood of any one department or official being able to plan or conceal actions contrary to the imperial interest.

This broad remit, combining the conduct of sensitive and confidential missions with the surveillance of other departments' activities, made both *agentes* and *notarii* – like modern tax-inspectors or internal auditors – easy targets for those already highly critical of the growth of centralized bureaucracy. For Libanius, avowedly old-fashioned in his attitudes, *agentes* were the ubiquitous 'eyes of the emperor', interminable 'snoopers' ($\pi\epsilon\upsilon\theta\hat{\eta}\nu\epsilon\varsigma$) who, instead of seeking out genuine misconduct, terrorized innocent provincials.[118] *Notarii* – 'these Cerberuses, these many-headed monsters' – were vilified in similar textbook displays of traditional rhetorical terms of abuse:

It was impossible for anyone to live near them; no one who met them could speak to them without being robbed or plundered . . . they went about the common enemies of anyone who possessed anything worth having, whether horse, slave, fruit tree, field or garden.[119]

[113] Them. *Or.* 1.17c.
[114] Clauss (1980) 22–3; Jones, *LRE* 1.572–3; Teitler (1985) 21–6; Vogler (1979) 192–7.
[115] Boak (1924) 71–6; Clauss (1980) 23–32; Demandt, *Spätantike* 233–4; Jones, *LRE* 1.578–9; Vogler (1979) 197–210.   [116] *C.Th.* VI.29.4.   [117] Teitler (1985) 34–7.
[118] Lib. *Or.* XVIII.135–45, quoting 140, 143.   [119] *Ibid.* 134, 131.

For the most part, the reality was more prosaic. There were perhaps only about 1200 *agentes* in the administration, the great majority operating openly.[120] Given the size of the empire, the difficulty of communication and the volume of information involved, it is unlikely that these officials could ever have functioned as an all-pervasive, imperial 'secret police'.[121] Even so, as Libanius' lurid criticisms suggest, the very independence of such officials raised continual doubts as to their own trustworthiness. Emperors – acutely aware of the problem – tried to guard their guards by offering the attraction of rapid promotion within the administration and by carefully restricting their movements and activities in the provinces. In 416, the co-emperors Honorius and Theodosius II instructed Palladius, the praetorian prefect of Italy, that:

> If any person is to be sent on business [into the provinces] . . . he shall know that within the limit of a year he must draw up his accounts, return to his superior and prove to him his effectiveness . . . But if, after a year has passed, he should delay and be found to be a plunderer preying on the vitals of that region, then he shall be stripped of his belt of office and expelled from the imperial administration . . . If he fails to return, he shall be bound with iron fetters and put in the charge of the provincial office staff, and with a report of the case he shall be sent to the appropriate investigating authority.[122]

The uncertainties and doubts emperors faced in securing reliable reports on provincial affairs or the activities of their officials were increased dramatically in the pressurized atmosphere of a highly centralized court. For Ammianus Marcellinus, the endless rivalry and jockeying for position were reminiscent of the staged fights between gladiators and wild beasts in the amphitheatre.[123] Certainly, in a system where success demanded imperial favour, many were prepared to go to extremes in order to attract the emperor's attention. At the turn of the fourth century, Porphyry, bishop of Gaza in Palestine, secured the help of the empress Eudoxia in persuading her husband Arcadius to order the closure of pagan temples in Porphyry's see. Initial approaches were unsuccessful. Only after Eudoxia had given birth to a son did a suitable opportunity for cornering the emperor arise. On the day of the baptism, Porphyry was to be outside the church at the front of the crowd. As the imperial procession emerged, Porphyry rushed forward and presented a petition, listing his demands, to the courtier carrying the baby boy. That man (well briefed beforehand) put Porphyry's peti-

---

[120] *C.Th.* VI.27.23: Clauss (1980) 25.

[121] Clauss (1980) 72–5; Giardina (1977) 64–72; Jones, *LRE* 1.581–2; Purpura (1973) 231–42; Schuller (1975) 3–8; Teitler (1985) 236–7 n. 32; the opposing case is robustly put in Blum (1969), esp. 1–8; Sinnigen (1959); Vogler (1979) 184–92.

[122] *C.Th.* VIII.8.9 (=*CJ* XII.60.3): further examples in Delmaire (1989) 160–4; Monks (1957) 766–8.

[123] Amm. Marc. XV.5.23: cf. XXVIII.1.10, 12, XXIX.1.27: generally, on this imagery: Matthews, *Ammianus* 258–61; MacMullen (1964c) 441–5.

tion into the child's hands and declared that it had been approved. Arcadius had little option but to issue an edict for the closure of the temples in his own and his son's names.[124]

The delight of this tale lies in the duping of an emperor. The deceit is presented as harmless since the cause is just (although Arcadius may have taken a different view). Other stories of empresses' influence were more sinister. In 403 (and again in 404), Eudoxia's influence with her husband played a key role in securing the exile of the patriarch of Constantinople, John Chrysostom.[125] In the 350s, Constantius II, apparently 'won over most of all by the women' in the imperial household, supported Basil of Ancyra in a complex doctrinal dispute. Basil, on the strength of this support, illegally exiled his opponents' supporters. The emperor, learning of this by chance, was said – at least by the fifth-century ecclesiastical historian Philostorgius – to be 'amazed and struck with grief'.[126] Dark tales too were told of the improper influence exercised by eunuchs who waited on the emperor in private. It was widely rumoured that Constantius II's decision to execute his son and heir-apparent Gallus was the result of a whispering campaign by those who 'while performing duties of an intimate nature' knew how to play upon the emperor's fears.[127]

These images of gullible emperors at the mercy of their wives, courtiers and close associates form a sharp counterpoint to the impression of un-ruffled majesty conveyed by imperial ceremonial. But one should be wary of too strong a contrast. It is perhaps better to see imperial power, in its operation and representation, as a shifting set of tactical possibilities. The growth of a highly centralized system of rule – in part formed and rein-forced by splendid rituals – ensured that the court remained the glittering focal point of the late Roman political system. The concentration of power at court underscored emperors' determination to retain a personal stake in the government of empire. Above all, it kept emperors in close contact with officials whose own position was largely dependent on proximity to the throne. Yet, against these clear advantages, a high degree of centraliza-tion also restricted emperors' ability to gather a wide range of information; it exacerbated the problems of long distances and slow communications; it gave considerable authority to family, friends and officials at court.

[124] Marc. Diac. V. Porph 41–9: Holum, Theodosian Empresses 54–6; Jones, LRE 1.344–6. The authentic-ity of this saint's life, often doubted, is vigorously defended in a full discussion by Trombley, Hellenic Religion 1.246–82.
[125] Zos. v.23.2–3; Socr. HE vi.15–18 (PG LXVII.708B–721B); Soz. HE viii.16–22 (GCS 50 (1960) 370–9): Holum, Theodosian Empresses 69–78; Liebeschuetz, Barbarians and Bishops 195–222 showing Eudoxia as one element in a complex coalition of interests.
[126] Philostorg. iv.8, 10 (GCS (1981) 61–3).
[127] Amm. Marc. xiv.11.1–4, quoting 3: cf. Zos. 11.55; Jul. Ep. ad Ath. 272d; Philostorg. iv.1 (GCS (1981) 58): see too the alleged plots against Constantius' successor Julian: Amm. Marc. xvii.11.1–4; Jul. Ep. ad Ath. 274a–b, 282b–d; Dunlap (1924) 264–70; Vogler (1979) 211–16. For the traditional invective against eunuchs: below, n. 199.

Emperors countered. They relied on highly privileged officers to perform sensitive or secret missions and to report directly on affairs outside the palace. But, in so doing, they risked being misled even more seriously by those purporting to give 'accurate' reports. In response, emperors moved, as far as possible, to define and regulate the operation of their 'trusted' agents and to threaten transgressors with memorably horrific penalties. Of course, there were limits. Too many safeguards or double-checks could paralyse imperial rule. By turns, those who acted contrary to emperors' interests always chanced detection – and usually death. In an acutely imagined scene, Ammianus Marcellinus neatly summed up the difficulties which faced emperors attempting to police the activities of their courtiers. The emperor Valens, having declared his intention to act as a judge in private lawsuits, was dissuaded by the praetorian prefect Modestus, himself keen to prevent any imperial scrutiny of a lucrative market in the sale of verdicts.

Modestus, with a forced and deceptive demeanour, declared that the minutiae of private suits were far beneath the heights of imperial concern. Valens, thinking that the examination of myriads of cases was devised to degrade the loftiness of his power (as advised) completely gave up hearing such matters. By so doing, he opened the doors to robbery . . .[128]

This emperor was fooled; Modestus was a shrewd judge of risks – or perhaps just lucky. The *notarius* Palladius (the powerfully-backed, bare-faced liar in the Romanus affair) did not enjoy such sound judgement – or such good fortune. Following Romanus' fall from favour, amongst his papers was found a letter in which Palladius allegedly admitted that, in reporting to the emperor the situation in Africa and the grievances of the townspeople of Lepcis Magna, he had 'spoken to the sacred ears that which was not true'. He was immediately arrested. At one of the halting-stations on the way to the imperial court at Constantinople, while his guards were at prayer, Palladius – grimly recognizing the inevitable – hanged himself from a beam.[129]

III. BUREAUCRACY

1. Offices and officials

Later Roman emperors could not rule alone. As fourth-century commentators clearly saw, the effective governance of empire inevitably involved a close reliance on sometimes untrustworthy courtiers, relatives, officials and friends. The difficulty (for emperors) was neatly summed up by Synesius of Cyrene in his tract *On Kingship*:

---

[128] Amm. Marc. xxx.4.2.   [129] Amm. Marc. xxviii.6.26–7.

Now to seek to know each place, each man and each dispute would require a very thorough survey, and not even Dionysius, who established his rule over a single island – and not even the whole of that – would have been capable of performing this task.[130]

Emperors were trapped. Faced with a Mediterranean-wide dominion, they had little option but to depend on second-hand advice or information; no choice but to count on far-distant subordinates to carry out their commands. Delegation was an inescapable corollary of autocracy. But its benefits were obvious. Most importantly, it permitted the growth of a sophisticated state bureaucracy primarily dedicated to the establishment and maintenance of central government power through the collection of taxes and the administration of justice. Without this 'elaborate centralized machine' fourth-century emperors undoubtedly would have been less effective in exploiting the human and economic resources of empire.[131] It is difficult otherwise to see how emperors could have hoped (for example) to levy sufficient tax revenue, or to fund, supply and man the empire's armies, or to enforce the many detailed regulations collected in the Theodosian Code, or even to have received and processed the information which made the drafting of such directives possible. Crudely put, without a well-developed bureaucracy, imperial rule in the later Roman empire would have been considerably less pervasive, markedly less intrusive and significantly less effective.[132]

Information on the formal structure and organization of the imperial bureaucracy in the fourth century comes principally from the laws collected in the Theodosian Code (particularly books I and VI) and from a document known as the *Notitia Dignitatum*.[133] The *notitia omnium dignitatum et administrationum tam civilium quam militarium* is, as its full title declares, 'a list of all ranks and administrative positions both civil and military'.[134] Such a document was held by the *primicerius notariorum*, a high-ranking palatine official responsible for maintaining a list of all holders of senior posts and for issuing their codicils of appointment.[135] The copy of the *Notitia Dignitatum* on which the surviving manuscripts are ultimately based dates from after the political division of the empire following the death of Theodosius I in

[130] Syn. *De Regno* XXVII – see too Themistius: above, n. 113.

[131] Jones, *LRE* I.406; Matthews, *Ammianus* 253.

[132] For what it is worth, it has been estimated that there were about 35,000 salaried imperial officials in the later Roman bureaucracy, as opposed to well under a thousand during the Principate: MacMullen (1964a) 306–7; Jones, *LRE* III.341–2 n. 44 (for estimates of the numbers in the larger departments: Chastagnol, *Préfecture urbaine* 228; Stein (1922) 18–19). Whatever the accuracy of these figures, they emphasize that, compared to modern western states, the number of bureaucrats in the Roman empire – especially given its size and population – was tiny.

[133] There is a large and complex literature on the *Notitia Dignitatum*; older scholarship is usefully summarized in Clemente (1968) 11–24; Demougeot (1975) 1081–2. In English, the best introduction remains Jones, *LRE* III.347–80 and the articles in Goodburn and Bartholomew (1976); see further chapter 7, pp. 211–12 below. [134] *Not. Dig. Occ.* XVI.5, *Or.* XVIII.4.

[135] Clemente (1968) 360–7; Jones, *LRE* I.574; Demandt, *Spätantike* 241; Vogler (1979) 195–6.

January 395. The military and administrative establishments of the eastern and western governments are listed separately. The preservation of the document in the west, the cursory description of some eastern departments and the continued revision of the western sections down to the late 420s (compared to the eastern portion, which does not seem to have been much revised after 396) makes it likely that this version of the *Notitia* was put together by an official at the western court in Milan.[136] The bulk of the material in the eastern sections appears to date from before Theodosius' death. Indeed, on a close analysis of the military information, it has been argued that the basic eastern document was substantially compiled as early as 388 and subsequently amended to take account of developments down to 394.[137] It may be that a copy of the eastern *Notitia* was transferred to Milan after Theodosius' successful campaign against the western usurper Eugenius in late 394. It was perhaps to serve as a model for a reorganized western administration. The emperor's death forestalled any reunification; in the following decade, the west was ruled by Honorius (firmly under the control of the military magnate Stilicho) and the east by Arcadius (until 399, heavily influenced by the eunuch Eutropius). Only in May 408, with the death of Arcadius and the accession of Theodosius II, still in his minority, was the possibility of reunification once again canvassed by Honorius – now the senior emperor and Theodosius' guardian – who planned to send Stilicho to Constantinople to represent his interests. It may be at this point, somewhere in the western court, that a *Notitia* for both halves of the empire was compiled. The information on the eastern empire transmitted in late 394 was hastily updated and attached to the current working-copy of the western version. The re-edited document was never used. Stilicho's sudden death in August 408 ended any hope of reunification.[138] The *Notitia*

---

[136] Jones, *LRE* III.347.   [137] Hoffmann, *Bewegungsheer* I.25–53, 494–519.

[138] This reconstruction follows Seibt (1982), and Mann (1991), themselves refining the basic chronological framework proposed for the eastern sections by Jones, *LRE* III.349–51; Clemente (1968), esp. 378–80; Demougeot (1975), esp. 1133–4. One of the most significant deletions in the eastern material reflected the division of the prefecture of Illyricum, part of the eastern empire at the death of Theodosius I in January 395, but shared with the west in the following year: Cameron, Alan, *Claudian* 60–2; esp. Hoffmann, *Bewegungsheer* II.210–15; other possible explanations for the format of the *Notitia*'s sections on Illyricum are canvassed in Clemente (1968) 105–8; Demougeot (1975) 1083, 1104–12; Jones, *LRE* III.347; Ward (1974) 401. The extent of any updating of the eastern sections (the insertion of new material, as opposed to cuts) is also uncertain. Clemente (1968) 110–13; Demougeot (1975) 1088–9 suggested that a number of eastern provinces included in the *Notitia* – Macedonia Salutaris, Galatia Salutaris, Palestina III Salutaris, Syria II Salutaris and Phoenica Libanensis – were not created until after 395; but see Ward (1974) 402–3, 407–8; Jones, *LRE* III.350, 391 for earlier dates. Lastly, Demougeot (1975) 1134 proposed that the information on the eastern half of the empire was not transferred to the west until mid 408, when it was requested by Honorius. But the hasty nature of some of the corrections to the eastern material, and the severe truncation of the sections on finance (*Not. Dig. Or.* XIII–XIV), perhaps make it less likely that the western administration ever received an up-to-date copy of the eastern *Notitia*. It seems more probable that it hurriedly cobbled together a document incorporating a cut-down version of the eastern material transferred under Theodosius I in late 394, adding – somewhat haphazardly – whatever further information on the east was then to hand.

remained in the west and was periodically updated for another twenty years, chiefly recording military information. No further attempt was made to amend the eastern sections.[139]

The copy of the *Notitia Dignitatum* which survives therefore preserves – at least for the eastern half of the empire – a fairly comprehensive picture of the formal organization of imperial bureaucracy at the end of the fourth century.[140] At court, the detailed administration of empire and the regulation of imperial business, protocol and paperwork was dominated by six key high-ranking officials. The *praepositus sacri cubiculi* (PSC) ran the household with overall responsibility for the *castrenses* – the eunuchs who attended on the emperor's person – other palace staff (cooks, pages, attendants) and the imperial wardrobe.[141] The palatine administration was under the control of the *magister officiorum* (*mag. off.*) who supervised the *scrinia* (secretariats) dealing with a range of matters including petitions, reports, the requests of embassies – which might require translation – and the issuing of *probatoriae* (letters of appointment) to lower-ranking officials. The *magister* also had general – though not exclusive – responsibility for the organization and operation of the *cursus publicus* (the imperial postal system), the *scholae palatinae* (the palace guard), the *fabricae* (the imperial arms manufactories) and the *agentes in rebus*.[142] Two senior officials headed the imperial treasury – the *comes*

---

[139] Possible terminal dates for the western sections are discussed in Demougeot (1975) 1104–33; Jones, *LRE* III.351–5; Hoffmann, *Bewegungsheer* 1.55–60; Mann (1991) 218; Ward (1974) 421–33. The overwhelming military interest of these last sets of amendments makes it likely that the surviving copy of the *Notitia* came from the office of the *magister peditum* (commander of the field armies) in the west, rather than from the *primicerius*. Mann (1976) 31–5, Finally, it should also be noted that the high quality of the illustrations accompanying the text, and the clear invention of some of the military emblems depicted, have led the 'official' nature of the surviving manuscript copies to be doubted. Rather than in a working version of the *Notitia*, they perhaps have their origin in a *de luxe* production made for some wealthy patron: Alexander (1976) 18; Grigg (1983), esp. 140–1.

[140] The most useful formal accounts of later Roman bureaucracy are Demandt, *Spätantike* 231–55, with Karte II and the Schema following p. 504; Jones, *LRE* I chs XI, XII, XVI, XVIII; Piganiol, *Empire chrétien* 343–59. There are brief summaries in Gaudemet (1967) 675–84; Liebeschuetz (1987) 457–9; Noethlichs (1981) 37–48; Pedersen (1970) 205–9. Noethlichs (1991) provides a good survey of the structure and responsibilities of the palatine offices. Vogler (1979); Weiss (1975) 42–55 supply more detailed studies of the administration under Constantius II. On the various complex bureaucratic ranks and titles: Cosenza (1905) 95–105; Guilland (1967); Hirschfeld (1901), esp. 588–604; Koch (1903), esp. 10–73; and particularly the discussion of Löhken (1982) 69–111. Standard modern abbreviations for high-ranking officials are listed in *PLRE*(I) xx–xxi.

[141] *Not. Dig. Or.* x, *Occ.* xIV (these sections are substantially missing): Cosenza (1903) 51–4; Dunlap (1924) 178–223; Guyot (1980) 130–57; *RE Supp.* 8 (1956) *praepositus sacri cubiculi* cols. 556–67 (Ensslin). Costa (1972) argues that in the fourth century these functions were the responsibility of the *castrensis sacri palatii* (*Not. Dig. Or.* xVII, *Occ.* xV) demoted in favour of the PSC in the 380s.

[142] *Not. Dig. Or.* xI, *Occ.* IX: Clauss (1980), esp. 15–98 and the Schema at 131, largely superseding Boak (1924); Cosenza (1903) 55–64. See also, on the *scrinia* (*Not. Dig. Or.* XI.13–16, XIX, *Occ.* IX.10–13, xVII) Boak (1915) 91–112; Bury (1910); Harries (1988) 159–64; Vogler (1979) 169–83; *RE* 2A.2 (1923) *scrinium* cols. 893–904 (Seeck); below n. 171; on the *cursus publicus*, Holmberg (1933), esp. 59–150; *RE* 4 (1901) *cursus publicus* cols. 1846–63 (Seeck); on the *scholae palatinae*: Hoffman, *Bewegungsheer* 1.279–303; Frank (1969), esp. 99–126; on the *fabricae*: MacMullen (1960); Foss (1979); James (1988); *RE* 6.1 (1909) *fabricenses* cols. 1925–30 (Seeck); on the *agentes*, above n. 115.

sacrarum largitionum (CSL) and the *comes rei privatae* (CRP). The former super-vised the collection of indirect taxes, such as customs duties, and direct levies in precious metal used to fund the donatives periodically granted to the army. The CSL was also responsible for the administration of state mints, mines, quarries and textile factories. The CRP controlled imperial properties, their leasing, rents, sale and revenues. The money so raised was chiefly used in paying out disbursements or pensions granted at the emperor's discretion.[143] The judicial functions of the emperor were in the charge of the *quaestor sacri palatii* (QSP) responsible for the drafting of impe-rial legislation and from 429 to 438 for the compilation of the Theodosian Code.[144] Lastly, the corps of *notarii* – which acted as the imperial secretariat and functioned independently of the *magister officiorum* – was headed by the *primicerius notariorum*, who was also in charge of issuing codicils of appoint-ment for high-ranking officials and for drawing up the *Notitia Dignitatum*.[145]

Away from the court and its highly centralized bureaux, the basic unit of government throughout the empire remained the province; 114 are listed in the *Notitia*, each administered by a governor variously styled according to the seniority of the province.[146] Governors were responsible for local judicial, financial and administrative affairs; they supervised city govern-ments, oversaw public works, and carried out specific imperial directives.[147] The provinces (with the exception of Africa and Asia, whose governors had direct access to the emperor)[148] were grouped into fourteen dioceses, each under the control of a *vicarius* who had a general supervisory role and in some cases heard appeals from provincial courts.[149] Dioceses, in turn, were grouped into four prefectures – Gaul (which included Britan and Spain), Italy (which included Africa), Illyricum and the East – each in the charge of a praetorian prefect (PPO).[150] The eastern praetorian prefecture, the largest and most important in the empire, described an arc extending from the Balkans to modern Libya and was divided into five dioceses – Aegyptus (under the *praefectus Augustalis*), Oriens (under the *comes Orientis*),

---

[143] *Not. Dig. Or.* XIII–XIV, *Occ.* XI–XII: Delmaire (1989) provides a detailed and comprehensive treat-ment of both officials. See too for the CSL: Cosenza (1905) 71–9; Hendy, *Studies* 380–94; Karayannopulos (1958) 54–62; Kent (1961); King (1980b); for the CRP: Cosenza (1905) 80–9; Karayannopulos (1958) 62–72; Millar (1980); Monks (1957) 749–55.

[144] *Not. Dig. Or.* XII, *Occ.* X: de Bonfils (1981), esp 57–108; Harries (1988). See too Honoré (1986), esp. 144–56, 181–222 arguing for the proposed identification on stylistic grounds of various fourth-century QSP who drafted laws subsequently included in the Code.   [145] Above, n. 135.

[146] *Not. Dig. Or.* I.57–128, *Occ.* I.50–121: Jones, *LRE* III.381–91.

[147] Amongst more detailed studies, Liebeschuetz, *Antioch*, esp. 111–14, 119–66, 208–19 (on Syria); Fitz (1983), esp. 20–4 (on Pannonia); Nesselhauf (1938), esp. 79–101 (on Gaul); Lallemand (1964) (on Egypt); Bagnall, *Egypt* 62–7, capture particularly well something of the complex interaction between the various levels of imperial administration in the provinces.

[148] Jones, *LRE* III.80 n. 22. The status of Achaea is unclear. Like Africa and Asia its governor had the highest rank (*proconsul*) – *Not. Dig. Or.* I.27, XXI. But unlike these it appears in a list of provinces forming part of a praetorian prefecture – *Not. Dig. Or.* III.8. See Verdickt (1968), esp. 172–4.

[149] Arnheim (1970) 593–603.   [150] *Not. Dig. Or.* II–III, *Occ.* II–III.

Asiana, Pontica and Thrace.[151] Praetorian prefects were the most powerful
civil officials in later Roman government. They had overall responsibility
for the administration of the empire (they received the majority of laws
preserved in the Theodosian Code) and in judicial matters, along with the
emperor, they were the final judges of appeal. The praetorian prefects also
headed important financial departments, overseeing the levying of taxation
sufficient to finance imperial public works, the administration, the army
(both wages and *matériel*), and to ensure the supply and transport of grain
to the empire's capital cities.[152] Ranking equally with the praetorian prefects
– although, in practice, significantly less powerful – were the urban prefects
of Rome (PVR) and, from 359, of Constantinople (PVC). These prefects
controlled the administrative, financial and judicial affairs of their respective cities. In particular, they supervised officials in charge of the supply of
bread, oil, meat and wine, the maintenance of aqueducts, statues and public
buildings, and the organization of games and public entertainment.[153]

Provincial governors, *vicarii* and prefects each headed a permanent
administrative department. The *officium* of the eastern praetorian prefect
was divided into two branches – the administrative and judicial, and the
financial. The former was headed by the *princeps officii* (with overall supervision of the branch's activities as well as of the department as a whole) and
his deputy the *cornicularius*; beneath these officials, in descending order, were
the *primiscrinius* or *adiutor* (responsible for the enforcement of judgements
and court orders), the *commentariensis* (mainly concerned with criminal trials),
the *ab actis* (dealing with civil cases and judicial records), the *curae epistolarum*
(in charge of the paperwork associated with official reports and of correspondence with *vicarii* and provincial governors) and the *regendarius* (responsible for issuing warrants for the use of the imperial postal system). Each of
these officials – excepting the *princeps* – had three assistants (*adiutores*) who,
in turn, were assisted by *chartularii*. These were drawn from the *exceptores* – a
corps of junior officials, divided into fifteen groups (*scholae*), which formed
the basic administrative staff of the prefecture.[154] For the fourth century, the

[151] *Not. Dig. Or.* II.1–6, XXII–XXVI.
[152] *RE* 22.2 (1954) *praefectus praetorio* cols. 2426–78 (Ensslin); Cosenza (1905) 10–16; Vogler (1979)
110–44.
[153] PVR: *Not. Dig. Occ.* IV; Chastagnol, *Préfecture urbaine*, esp. 254–388 provides an excellent, detailed
account; in English, the best brief survey is Barrow (1973) 1–9. PVC: Dagron, *Naissance* 213–94.
[154] The details are disputed. The thumb-nail sketch here draws on Stein (1922) 31–77 with Jones
(1949) 48–9, *LRE* 1.586–90; see too Carney (1971) II.4–9; Teitler (1985) 73–80. The basic information
comes from *De Magistratibus*, a partly autobiographical account of the history of the eastern praetorian
prefecture written in the mid sixth century by John Lydus, a retired senior member of the prefect's staff;
for good introductions to this text: Caimi (1984), esp. chs I, III, V; Carney (1971) II.1–93; Maas (1992),
esp. 28–37, 83–96 with further bibliography in Kaster, *Guardians of Language* 306–9; *PLRE*(2) 612–15
(Ioannes 75). In making sense of the *officium* of the PPO as presented in *Not. Dig. Or.* II.59–71, III.20–32,
Occ. II.43–55, III.38–50 it was assumed by Stein (1922) 57–8 that the *subadiuvae* were synonymous with
the *adiutores*, but see Chastagnol, *Préfecture urbaine*, 233–4; Jones (1949) 48 n. 117. The *adiutores* listed by
the *Notitia* after the *exceptores* (e.g. *Not. Dig. Or.* II.70, III.31) are, it seems, a mistaken doublet, or perhaps

best evidence for the detailed organization of these lower grades in the *officium* of a high-ranking palatine official comes from a schedule attached to a law issued to the *comes sacrarum largitionum* by the emperor Theodosius I in 384. The 446 officials listed are grouped in eighteen divisions and graded in seven classes according to seniority. Eleven *scrinia* dealt with a range of administrative tasks: the receipt of gold bullion, the minting of gold, silver and bronze coinage, military uniforms, taxation and accounts.[155] A similar pattern of meticulous classification seems to have been observed at all levels of the later Roman administration. On the basic model of the praetorian prefectures, the *officium* of a provincial governor was also divided into a judicial and administrative, and a financial side. The former was headed by a *princeps officii* and, in descending order, a *cornicularius, commentariensis, adiutor, ab actis* and a *libellis* (probably responsible for receiving petitions), all drawing their clerical assistance from a corps of *exceptores*.[156]

The impression of detailed order and elaborate hierarchy conveyed by official documents such as the *Notitia Dignitatum* was underscored by the continued use of military terminology within the civilian administration.[157] All officials were technically soldiers: their service was known as *militia*;[158] they received rations (*annonae*) and a fodder allowance (*capitum*).[159] Bureaucrats in the *officium* of a praetorian prefect were enrolled in the fictive *legio I Adiutrix*[160] – even in the sixth century, the *princeps officii*, as part of his *insignia*, carried a centurion's swagger stick.[161] Above all, later Roman bureaucrats wore distinctive uniforms. An official was easily recognizable by his heavy, military-style cloak (*chlamys*), by his belt of office (*cingulum*) with its finely wrought and often highly decorated clasp, and by the brightly coloured patches (*segmenta*) sewn or embroidered on his tunic.[162] A mid- to late-fourth-century tomb painting from Durostorum (modern Silistra in Bulgaria) shows a provincial bureaucrat with attendant slaves carrying shoes, a tunic, a parti-coloured cloak and an impressively decorated *cingu-*

refer to the corps of junior officials comprising the basic staff on the lower-ranking financial side. The *officium* of the PVR (*Not. Dig. Occ.* IV.18–33) – in outline, similar to that of the PPO – is also known in some detail: Chastagnol, *Préfecture urbaine*, 218–43, superseding Sinnigen (1957).

[155] *CJ* XII.23.7 (=*C.Th.* VI.30.7): Delmaire (1989) 146–58; Jones, *LRE* 1.583–5; Karayannopulos (1958) 55–8; King (1980b) 142–6.

[156] *Not. Dig. Or.* XLIII–XLIV, *Occ.* XLIII–XLV (with some variations in the seniority of the *adiutor*): Jones (1949) 48–9, *LRE* 1.565–6, 593; Groag (1946) 80–1; Lallemand (1964) 72–5. All the civilian *officia* listed in the *Notitia* are usefully tabulated by Seeck on p. 335 of his edn of the text (Berlin, 1876).

[157] Jones (1949) 49, *LRE* 1.566.

[158] MacMullen (1963) 49–50; Noethlichs (1981) 20–34; Tomlin (1976) 191–2.

[159] Amm. Marc. XXII.4.9; *C.Th.* VII.4.35 (=*CJ* XII.37.15) of 423 instructing that these allowances were now compulsorily to be commuted to money payments.

[160] *CJ* XII.36.6, XII.52.3.2: Stein (1922) 15–16.   [161] Joh. Lydus, *Mag.* II.19.

[162] *C.Th.* VI.26.18, VI.27.17 (=*CJ* XII.20.2), VIII.I.11 (=*CJ* XII.49.3), XIV.10: Franchi de' Cavalieri (1928) 211–29; MacMullen (1964c), esp. 445–52; Chastagnol, *Préfecture urbaine* 221–2; Delbrueck (1932) 4–5. Some splendid belt buckles and other fittings formed part of a hoard found at Ténès on the coast of Algeria: Heurgon (1958) 31–6; for some British examples: Hawkes and Dunning (1961); Hawkes (1974).

lum.[163] Senior officials were even more splendidly uniformed. The eastern praetorian prefect wore a flame-coloured knee-length cloak striped with gold, a deep-purple tunic and an elaborately embellished crimson *cingulum.*[164] The urban prefect of Rome dressed in a toga decorated with broad purple bands; he wore red shoes with black straps crossed four times between ankle and knee, each intersection decorated with a small crescent in ivory.[165] Similarly dressed high-ranking palatine officials were depicted on the frescoed walls of an imperial audience hall built in the late third century within the fabric of the pharaonic temple of Ammon at Luxor in Egypt. All wore fine white tunics with exquisitely embroidered *segmenta*; some too had heavily jewelled belts. These officials formed part of a procession of soldiers and civilians which covered three walls of the hall; the fourth was dominated by a raised platform with a baldacchino (*ciborium*) over the emperor's throne itself.[166] In an imperial audience hall, in a province far distant from Constantinople, to all who saw them, these striking images of splendidly dressed dignitaries grouped around an imperial throne must have served as a permanent and forcible reminder of the power and magnificence of later Roman officialdom – the glittering uniforms an outward show of its meticulously graded hierarchies. In similar awe-inspiring splendour, in the sacred palace at the centre of the empire's capital, the serried ranks of sumptuously attired bureaucrats stood motionless in the emperor's presence, each carefully positioned – like exquisitely painted figurines – according to the strict order of precedence laid down in the *Notitia Dignitatum.*[167]

2. Emperors and bureaucrats

Formal descriptions are important. They rightly emphasize the complexity and sophistication of later Roman bureaucracy and the extent of its concerns. But one should not be too beguiled by an impression of unchanging order or of the clear-cut categorization of administrative duties. In its operation, and particularly in the allocation and re-allocation of responsibilities, later Roman bureaucracy reflected both the varying fortunes of high-ranking officials and their influence at court, and, more broadly, the insistent need of emperors to demonstrate their independence by asserting their own authority against the strictures of standard administrative procedure.[168] In 395, the emperor Arcadius stripped the eastern praetorian prefecture of

---

[163] Dimitrov (1962), esp. 38–9. [164] Joh. Lydus, *Mag.* II.13.

[165] Chastagnol, *Préfecture urbaine* 196–8.

[166] Kalavrezou-Maxeiner (1975), esp. 234–8, 242–3, 248–51; Monneret de Villard (1953), esp. 90–4.

[167] *C.Th.* VI.8.1 (= *CJ* XII.5.1).

[168] Kelly (1994) 167–8; Jones, *LRE* I.377; Boak (1924) 18–19; Carney (1971) I.92–3. Noethlichs (1981) 3–18, 34–7 has an instructive comparison between later Roman and modern western bureaucracies.

some of the jurisdiction over the *cursus publicus* (the public post), the *scholae palatinae* (the palace guard) and the *fabricae* (the imperial arms manufactories) which it had acquired under the influential prefect Rufinus, transferring these responsibilities to the *magister officiorum*.[169] The possibility of shifts in administrative competence was naturally attractive to aggrandizing officials (and, if carried too far, was potentially dangerous for emperors) but, in the main, the assignment of variable, indistinct or overlapping responsibilities helped ensure that no one department could become too independently powerful. Strategically sensitive areas were arbitrarily split. Supervision of both the *cursus publicus* and the *fabricae* was shared – with see-sawing shifts in specific responsibilities – between the praetorian prefects and the *magister officiorum*.[170] The organizing principles of irregularity, disruption and division were widely applied. Many comparatively minor functions were frequently distributed in a miscellaneous or patchwork fashion. The issuing of *probatoriae* (letters of appointment) to lower-ranking officials was divided in 'a quite arbitrary way' between the *scrinia* under the supervision of the *magister officiorum*. Alongside other varied duties, the *scrinium memoriae* dealt with the appointment of *agentes in rebus*, palatine officials of the financial departments and junior military commands; the *scrinium epistolarum* with the staff of praetorian and urban prefects, proconsuls and *vicarii*; and the *scrinium libellorum* with officials attached to senior military commanders.[171]

The overlapping of responsibility for various functions also increased the likelihood that departments – perhaps in the hope of enlarging their own sphere of operation – might monitor more closely the work of rivals. Cross-checking was an important factor in determining the distribution of administrative tasks and the allocation of personnel. The general principle of using *agentes in rebus* or *notarii* for a range of sensitive missions – cutting across the responsibilities of all other departments – was given particular force with the systematic secondment of senior *agentes* to the post of *princeps officii* (the senior-ranking official heading an administrative department) in the praetorian and urban prefectures, all dioceses and a number of important provinces.[172] Their position in these departments was ambiguous. On the one hand, along with the other – internally promoted – senior officials, such as the *cornicularius* or *primiscrinius*, the *princeps* worked closely with his superior (prefect, *vicarius* or governor), bearing a considerable part of the responsibility for the administrative activity of his new department. On the other hand, the *princeps* was also well placed to keep these men and

[169] Joh. Lydus, *Mag.* II.10=III.40; the accuracy of Lydus' statement (accepted here following Boak (1924) 36–7, 78–9; Clauss (1980) 50–1, 120–2; MacMullen (1960) 32) has frequently been doubted; for discussion: Giardina (1977) 16–18; Holmberg (1933) 125–30; Sinnigen (1962) 370–6; Stein (1920) 219–23.
[170] *cursus publicus*: Blum (1969) 49–78; Boak (1924) 80; Clauss (1980) 45–51; Holmberg (1933) 86–94; Stein (1922) 61–7; Vogler (1979) 176–7: *fabricae*: Clauss (1980) 51–4.
[171] *C.Th.* VIII.7.21 (=*CJ* XII.59.6), VIII.7.22–3; *CJ* XII.59.10.3–5: Clauss (1980) 16–18; Jones, *LRE* 1.368, quoting 576.   [172] Sinnigen (1964) 79; Clauss (1980) 37–8.

their affairs under surveillance and to report back to the *magister officiorum* to whom, as a serving *agens in rebus*, he remained ultimately responsible.[173] Reflecting on the history of the eastern praetorian prefecture in the late fourth century, John Lydus (himself an ex-*cornicularius*) had no doubt of the reason for this system of cross-departmental promotion: it was a deliberate restriction on the activities of the prefecture by an emperor who feared the autonomy of a powerful department.[174]

Similar tensions – and a repetitive insistence by emperors on the retention of some degree of independent action – were also played out in the selection, appointment and promotion of officials.[175] As in any administrative organization, seniority was a significant factor. In 331, Constantine affirmed this principle for the advancement of *exceptores* in the eastern praetorian prefecture: 'each shall succeed to a position according to his rank-order in the department and his merit, in so far as he would have deserved to obtain that position by length of service'.[176] In addition to recognizing the importance of promotion by seniority, imperial laws also entitled certain higher-ranking officials in the central administration to appoint on their retirement a son or brother to a junior post in the same department.[177] Alongside seniority and inheritance, merit and competence might also be represented as relevant criteria for securing advancement. In 393, Theodosius I, Arcadius and Honorius instructed the eastern praetorian prefect that promotions were to be made on the basis of proficiency: 'Enquiry shall be made to determine not who first entered the imperial service, but who has remained constant in the pursuit of his duty.'[178] In more extravagantly rhetorical terms, Constantius II praised the achievements and capabilities of Flavius Philippus, who in 351 had been stripped (perhaps mistakenly) of his praetorian prefecture after confusion over his relations with the usurper Magnentius. An imperial letter to the proconsul of Asia – subsequently inscribed and publicly displayed in Ephesus – proclaimed:

Innate virtue has this outstanding advantage for tested and faithful men, that when such a man is constantly alert in furthering the interests of his emperor and of the state, the glory of the endeavour compensates for the discomfort of the life itself, and besides, as regards fame, he is considered to have sought to obtain for himself this recognition: that by merit in the service of his employer he has succeeded as a result of hard work and long experience.[179]

[173] Clauss (1980) 32–9; the role and status of these so-called *principes agentium in rebus* has been much debated; for a range of views: Blum (1969) 9–27; Giardina (1977) 13–72 esp. 21–55; Jones, *LRE* III.168 n. 32; Holmberg (1933) 120–6; Purpura (1973) 242–7; Sinnigen (1957) 14–32, (1964); Stein (1920) 193 239; Vogler (1979) 207–9.   [174] Joh. Lydus, *Mag.* III.23.
[175] For good surveys of the diverse criteria involved in appointment and promotion: Pedersen (1970), esp. 175–205; Jones, *LRE* I.383–96, 602–4.
[176] *C.Th.* VIII.1.2: cf. VI.24.9, VI.27.7, VI.27.14 (=*CJ* XII.20.1), VI.27.19, VI.30.22, VI.32.1 (=*CJ* XII.25.1), VIII.7.1.   [177] *C.Th.* VI.27.8.2: cf. *CJ* II.7.23.2.   [178] *C.Th.* VII.3.1; cf. I.9.3, VI.24.6.
[179] Swift and Oliver (1962) 247 lines 2–6; for the background *PLRE*(I) 696–7 (Philippus 7).

Despite such fulsome imperial praise (for a safely dead official), the importance of proficiency or competence in ensuring selection should not be overstated. In many laws, *merita* seem merely to be synonymous with length of service.[180] Moreover, without entrance examinations or formal qualifications, any assessment of a candidate's ability was unavoidably dependent on personal recommendation. *Suffragium* – the influence exercised by family or friends (and their well-placed connections) – was frequently a key factor in ensuring a successful career.[181] Over a quarter of the nine hundred surviving letters of the fourth-century senator Quintus Aurelius Symmachus (urban prefect of Rome in 384) were directed to well-placed acquaintances, often themselves office-holders, who might be of help in finding posts for his protégés. Writing, perhaps somewhere in the 380s, to Virius Nicomachus Flavianus (in turn *quaestor sacri palatii*, praetorian prefect and consul),[182] Symmachus – with accustomed well-turned elegance – put his request:

Many people speak well of the merits of Sexio, who formerly governed Calabria. As a result of these, they have requested that I should recommend him to your patronage (*suffragium*). It is part of your customary good nature to regard as worthy of your affection those whom others have found agreeable. I ask you, then, that if nothing stands in the way of satisfying the wishes of those who make this request, you allow Sexio to profit from my words and the hopes of many.[183]

For those without access to grand patrons and their networks, recommendations for office (and often even the position itself) could sometimes be secured through the payment of money.[184] In 362, the emperor Julian legislated to prevent litigation for the recovery of monies paid out in exchange for recommendations.[185] In similar terms, in 394, Theodosius I affirmed that contracts to exchange gold, silver, movables and urban or rural property in return for a recommendation were enforceable in the courts.[186] As these legal provisions indicate, money transactions might be concluded openly and officially sanctioned. The acquisition of a post through purchased recommendation was no more clandestine or

---

[180] Pedersen (1970) 178, 189; Swift and Oliver (1962) 251; Schuller (1982) 205; *C.Th.* VI.14.2, VI.27.13, VI.27.14 (=*CJ* XX.20.1), VI.27.19, VI.29.4, VI.32.1(=*CJ* XII.25.1), VI.35.7, VIII.1.2 (quoted above), XII.6.4.

[181] de Ste. Croix (1954) 44–5; Frank (1967); Jones, *LRE* 1.392–3; Krause (1987) 50–8; Matthews, *Ammianus* 270–4; Pedersen (1970) 180.   [182] *PLRE* (I) 347–9 (Flavianus 15).

[183] Symm. *Ep.* 2.43: Matthews (1974), esp. 61–4; Roda (1986). For matching examples from the correspondence of the fourth-century Antiochene orator Libanius: Liebeschuetz, *Antioch* 192–8; Petit (1956a) 158–66, 183–8.

[184] For useful surveys of the evidence: Collot (1965) 190–211; Jones, *LRE* 1.393–6; Kolias (1939) 23–39; Krause (1987) 58–65; Liebs (1978) 170–83; Noethlichs (1981) 69–72; Vogler (1979) 247–52.

[185] *C.Th.* II.29.1 following Goffart (1970) with Barnes (1974); for a reading of this law as an attempt to ban or, at the very least, to discourage the purchase of *suffragium*: Andreotti (1975) 12–25; Collot (1965) 195–8; Jones, *LRE* 1.393; Liebs (1978) 174–82.

[186] *C.Th.* II.29.2 (=*CJ* IV.3.1): Andreotti (1975) 4–11; Liebs (1978) 182–3.

underhand than reliance on the support of friends or connections. Indeed, by the mid fourth century, *suffragium* was used, frequently without distinction, to refer to a candidate's influence – however obtained.[187]

This blurred spectrum of possibilities for appointment and promotion significantly reduced the independence and security of officials. Neither ability, nor seniority, nor inherited right, nor influence, nor the payment of money (nor some combination of these) was a sure guarantee of advancement. In such a system, emperors were more easily able to emphasize the importance of their own position – and the degree to which a successful career depended upon imperial favour – by encouraging or frustrating various tactics. A potentially threatening coalition might be weakened by the insistence on promotion by seniority or merit, rather than by the recommendation of senior officers or other influential persons; candidates not on existing networks might be brought into a department through the purchase of office. Conversely, a favoured individual might be allowed to strengthen his position by recommending the appointment of friends, family or associates. Taken together, imperial laws present a bewildering variety of tactics reflecting continual shifts in the criteria of appointment: the purchase of offices was not always sanctioned; seniority was not always preferred over merit.[188] More often than not, there was no attempt at setting out clear-cut or unambiguous provisions. Rather, imperial legislation revealed a series of kaleidoscopic combinations – inheritance, the payment of money, merit and seniority all jostled, overlapped and competed against each other:

The Emperors Theodosius II and Valentinian III to Nomus magister officiorum (26 February 444).

It is clear that it is utterly forbidden for any one, when he is later in the time of his appointment, to seek to gain the position of one ahead of him, unless perhaps it might be the case that there is a person who, held back by the time of his appointment, is superior in regard to his work... We also decree that this rule be observed, except by the sons of the heads of departments. And indeed we determine that it is possible for each head to give preference to one of his sons, who, as regards length of service, shall have the advantage [*suffragium*] that even if he is known to have paid little attention to the imperial administration, he shall be protected from those who are appointed subsequently with the merit of experience . . . Notwithstanding this, we order a person who has been granted a position in a department, to pay, in addition, 250 gold coins to the [retiring] head of department ... But if anyone ... in order not to pay the money, wishes to decline the position, freedom is granted to substitute the next candidate in order of appointment upon payment of the aforementioned sum of money, in such a way that it is clear that if

[187] de Ste. Croix (1954) 39 with MacMullen, *Corruption*, 265 n. 85.
[188] *C.Th.* VI.27.19, VI.29.4, VI.30.7, VI.38.1 (= *CJ* XII.32.1), VIII.1.1,VIII.1.13 (banning purchase of office); VI.24.6, VII.3.1 (merit over seniority).

the second, or even the third, or anyone of whatever number, should persist with the same wish to be excused, the same opportunity, as was given to the one above who refused it, may also be given to the next in order of appointment.[189]

In such an intricate (and often uncertain) system there were undoubtedly costs in administrative efficiency. But efficiency is only one way of judging success. Many of the complexities and confusions which characterize later Roman bureaucracy reflect a careful balance – delicately engineered by both officials and emperors – between the maintenance of an administration which enabled a greater degree of control to be exercised over empire, and the preservation of some measure of imperial autonomy. In 384, Quintus Aurelius Symmachus, then urban prefect of Rome, was required to adjudicate in a dispute over the appointment of one of the *archiatri* (state-funded doctors) in the city. In 370, Valentinian I had ruled that a new appointee should be selected by existing office-holders and be counted the most junior in order of precedence.[190] But in 384, when a vacancy arose, one John – a highly placed former bureaucrat in the central administration – presenting a special imperial grant of title, petitioned for the post and the second most senior rank. The doctors appealed to Symmachus, arguing that John's grant contravened previous legislation on appointment. In such a situation – faced with apparently contradictory imperial pronouncements – Symmachus refused to adjudicate. He referred the whole issue to Valentinian II. He closed his covering letter to the emperor by deferentially explaining his failure to decide the matter:

Therefore, disturbed by these uncertainties and neither venturing to quash the decree of your divine father nor to counter a particular imperial directive, I have left the final decision in this case to the divine judgement of your Godhead; I have appended the depositions of the parties involved and I await what your august counsels may decide.[191]

Symmachus' inability independently to resolve this difficulty was critical to the maintenance of imperial influence within later Roman bureaucracy. It drew attention to the central importance of emperors' decisions in determining rights or conferring legitimacy. By shifting responsibilities between departments or changing the criteria for appointment, emperors acted to prevent their exclusion from an administrative system more dependent for its successful day-to-day operation on predictable regulation than on the caprice of imperial will. For emperors, efficiency was not always an overriding consideration. The clear advantages of a more systematically organized bureaucracy had to be weighed against an equally pressing need to retain an effective level of imperial control over high-ranking officials and their departmental subordinates. The inevitable waste of resources caused

---

[189] *CJ* XII.19.7: Jones (1949) 50; Vera (1981) 198–202.

[190] *C.Th.* XIII.3.9 (= *CJ* X.53.10): Chastagnol, *Préfecture urbaine* 289–91.

[191] Symm. *Rel.* XXVII.4: cf. similar difficulties in *Rel.* XXII and XLIV.

by duplication, cross-checking, the transfer of personnel and the arbitrary division of tasks had to be balanced against an ever-present threat of further imperial isolation in the face of a more unified or streamlined administration. Later Roman emperors had no intention of becoming mere *rois fainéants*. There were limits to the order they sought to impose and to the degree of predictability they found desirable in government. In an increasingly bureaucratic world, the continued presence of doubt and ambiguity helped ensure that emperors – rather than their officials – stood the greater chance of remaining the final arbiters upon whom all depended.

3. Corruption

For some modern observers, the increased incidence of purchased office or influence in the later Roman empire has been a sure sign of administrative incompetence and moral decay – 'the will of a great empire dissolving in the uncontrolled impulses of private enterprise'.[192] Emperors' attempts to stamp out such practices have been seen as futile (if laudable) attempts to stem an inexorably rising tide of corruption and venality.[193] Some support for these views can be found in the fourth-century sources. In the late 390s, the military magnate Stilicho – who, after the death of Theodosius I in 395, had consolidated his influence over the young emperor Honorius and his court in Milan – commissioned the poet Claudian to write a set of invectives, exposing the faults of those highly placed officials in Constantinople who had strongly resisted Stilicho's attempts to extend his 'protection' to include the new eastern emperor Arcadius and his court. In his piece attacking Eutropius – Arcadius' *praepositus sacri cubiculi*[194] and consul in 399 – Claudian included (as part of a long catalogue of shameless abuses) the indiscriminate sale of offices:

All that lies between the river Tigris and Mount Haemus he puts up for sale ... A schedule affixed above the open doorway to his house lists provinces with their prices; so much for Galatia, Pontus goes for so much, such an amount buys Lydia. Should you wish to govern Lycia, then put down thousands; if Phrygia, add a little more.[195]

Less dramatically, a decade earlier, the famous orator and teacher Libanius had bitterly disapproved of the way in which purchased influence upset

---

[192] The most recent restatement of this case is strongly argued in MacMullen, *Corruption* esp. 148–97, quoting 197.

[193] Some examples: Collot (1965) 198; de Ste. Croix (1954) 39–40; Jones, *LRE* 1.496–7; MacMullen, *Corruption* 149–52; Monks (1957) 749, 758, 768; Schuller (1975), esp. 10–17.   [194] Above, n. 141.

[195] Claudian, *In Eutrop.* 1.190–221, quoting 196–7, 201–5: cf. 11.585–90. For the background to this piece: Cameron, Alan, *Claudian* 124–55; Dunlap (1924) 272–84; Liebeschuetz, *Barbarians and Bishops* 96–103; *PLRE*(2) 440–4 (Eutropius 1).

traditional relationships within the city of Antioch and its surrounding territory. In his oration *On Patronage*, Libanius complained that his traditional role as patron to tenants on his estates had been usurped by the local military commander, who had been presented with 'barley, corn, ducks and fodder' in return for his support in a court case.[196] This method of forming a business relationship – trading influence for payment like 'meat and vegetables'[197] – was in Libanius' view typical of the questionable behaviour of imperial bureaucrats. In his opinion such cavalier disregard for long-hallowed arrangements was only to be expected from officials like the *agentes in rebus* or *notarii* – these were snoopers and spies, low-born, ill-educated men whose fathers had been (at best) fullers, bath attendants and sausage-makers.[198]

Such trenchant moralizing must be put firmly in context. Claudian's accusations of administrative corruption against Eutropius were part of a carefully constructed and highly rhetorical picture of depravity and iniquity. Eutropius was a glutton, coward, ingrate, murderer, miser, perjurer, pander, pervert and – above all – a eunuch.[199] In some of 'the cruellest invective in all ancient literature',[200] Claudian mercilessly exploited long-standing prejudices against a group widely regarded as personifying every vice. Concentrating on the unnaturalness of a eunuch holding a consulship – the most prestigious honorary office in the empire – Claudian, in a witty parody of standard descriptions of the splendours of official ceremony, imagined Eutropius in his consular garb:

It was indeed a beautiful sight when Eutropius stretched his etiolated limbs burdened by his belt of office and the weight of his toga ... He was like an ape (that counterfeiter of the human countenance) which for a joke a boy has dressed up in costly eastern silks, leaving both back and buttocks bare to amuse the dinner-guests. Thus richly attired he walks upright and is more misshapen in his splendid dress.[201]

Given Claudian's aims and methods, one should be wary of singling out for approval his remarks on Eutropius' venality simply because they seem more closely to reflect modern, western attitudes to public morality. That

---

[196] Lib. *Or.* XLVII.4–18, quoting 13. For the background to this oration: Brown (1971) 85–7; Garnsey and Woolf (1989) 162–3; Liebeschuetz, *Antioch* 201–8; Harmand (1955), esp. 173–83; Pack (1935) 45–56; and particularly Carrié (1976), esp. 169–72, who stresses the importance of giving full weight to Libanius' rhetorical intentions, constructions and reuse of stock images and traditional topics.

[197] Lib. *Or.* 1.109.

[198] Lib. *Or.* XLII.24–5: and see above, nn. 118–21. Unsurprisingly, the accuracy of Libanius' remarks has been doubted: Pack (1935) 65–7; Teitler (1985) 64–8; Vogler (1979) 60–4.

[199] Some choice passages: Claudian, *In Eutrop.* 1.1–23, 110–37, 252–71, II *pr.* 21–32. For a catalogue of Claudian's categories of abuse: Christiansen (1969) 92–102, 120–4; Döpp (1980) 161–74. More generally, the position of eunuchs and the invective they provoked are discussed in Guyot (1980) 157–76; Hopkins (1963), esp. 64–9, 78–80; Jones, *LRE* 1.568–70; Liebs (1978) 183–6; Matthews, *Ammianus* 274–7.   [200] Cameron, Alan, *Claudian* 126.

[201] Claudian, *In Eutrop.* 1.299–307: cf. 24–31, 287–99, 317–70, II.24–94.

would be to privilege (in isolation) one particular element in a wide-ranging and consciously artificial critique. Accusations of corruption – like those of deformity, degeneracy, extravagance, excess and perversion – were part of a complex and highly charged rhetoric of execration. Claudian's abusive version of Eutropius was no more credible than his portrayal of Stilicho as the longed-for saviour of Rome – a general whose military prowess and popularity put him on a par with the gods and the great men of old.[202] In both his conquests and his temperament, Claudian's Stilicho was a second Scipio; an indomitable hero whose entry into Rome in 400 was the return of a victorious Mars from war.[203] These neatly contrasting caricatures of Stilicho's virtue and Eutropius' vice were skilfully and explicitly rhetorical. They were pieces produced to order, penned to please a powerful patron. Importantly, too, they were written as a partisan response to Stilicho's signal failure to advance his cause at court in Constantinople.

Loss of advantage was also central to Libanius' oration *On Patronage*. His reaction to being taken to court by his tenants and losing in public, in front of the governor, was predictably strong. He blamed his humiliation on his tenants' new-found supporter and the immorality of his methods.[204] There was a proper and time-honoured way of going about such things. Libanius presented a moralizing *tableau émouvant* in the finest classical tradition:[205]

For it is not proper for a slave who demands justice for wrongs he has suffered to look to one person and then to another, and to present himself before someone who is not his owner and ask his help, while ignoring his master . . . But suppose that those to whom they actually belong, by the will of god cease to be powerful. Then it is better that they should live their lives in their masters' weakness and put up with their fate rather than purchase such a power as this and show up their land-lords. Take the example of a woman: if she belonged to two men, she would be more powerful, but you would not be pleased at her having the one in marriage and the other in adultery . . .[206]

For Libanius – some of whose estates had been in the family for four generations[207] – an unchallenged, exclusive relationship with his tenants was self-evidently attractive and morally defensible. He dreamt of a cosy, comfortable world free of trouble and complaint; a world where the land-lord was firmly in control and alternatives could not be bought. His tenants (perhaps not surprisingly) assessed the situation differently. One should hesitate before condemning them as immoral and their supporters as corrupt, or before endorsing Libanius' complaints, his social pretensions, and his proposed, ethically correct solution. Like Claudian's invective

[202] Some choice passages: Claudian, *In Eutrop* II.501–15; *De Cos. Stil.* 1.24 35, 138–47, 291–313, II.1–5, 100–72, III.51–71: Döpp (1980) 175–98; Levy (1958). For a catalogue of Claudian's categories of virtue: Christiansen (1969) 16–26, 117–20.

[203] Claudian, *De Cos. Stil.* III pr. 21–4; II.367–70; *De Bello Getico* 138–44. [204] Lib. *Or.* XLVII.13–16.

[205] Carrié (1976) 162. [206] Lib. *Or.* XLVII.21–4, quoting 21 and 24. [207] Lib. *Or.* XLVII.13.

Against Eutropius or the praises of panegyrists before emperors, Libanius' moralizing, and his stress on traditional methods of initiating and maintaining a relationship, aptly suited his own position. It furthered and justified his own interests. Under such circumstances, it would be as pointless to disapprove of Libanius' arguments in favour of personal influence as it would be to approve of his stance against the payment of money.[208]

Not all contemporaries shared Libanius' or Claudian's moral preferences or found need of similar rhetorical condemnations. In some cases, payment for access to bureaucratic services was actively promoted, institutionalized and regulated. Central government issued 'price lists' which gave – often in considerable and complex detail – the fees for specific bureaucratic actions. One of the most comprehensive surviving examples (known as the *Ordo Salutationis*) was carved on a large limestone slab erected between 361 and 363 in the market-place of the North African town of Timgad – modern Thamugadi in Algeria. Issued by the provincial governor of Numidia, it laid down the cost of government services for those wishing to litigate in his court, and for the enforcement of judgements so obtained.

The payment which must be made to the head of the governor's *officium* [for enforcing a judgement]: within the town, five *modii* of wheat or the price thereof; within one mile of the town, seven *modii* of wheat or the price thereof; for every additional ten miles, two *modii* of wheat or the price thereof; if the official is required to travel overseas, then one hundred *modii* of wheat or the price thereof is required.[209]

The openness of these transactions is both striking and important. It underlines the importance of money in obtaining access to later Roman bureaucracy; it emphasizes that such payments were not necessarily grubby, under-the-counter dealings, always shameful for those involved. A similar frankness can also be seen in transactions aimed at securing influence or advancement. In a written contract dated 2 February 345, Aurelius Plas, a retired veteran and resident of Dionysias – a small garrison town in Middle Egypt – undertook to reimburse the camp commandant for any expenses incurred by him in securing the promotion of Aurelius' son to a junior command. The matter was straightforward; the agreement was concluded and signed openly; Aurelius Plas demonstrated his good faith by swearing 'before god'.[210] With an equal lack of embarrassment – and an equally shrewd judgement of advantage – Basil, bishop of Caesarea in Cappadocia (writing in 374

[208] For a different approach, arguing for a wider acceptance of Libanius' opinions: Harmand (1955) 106–10; MacMullen, *Corruption* 168–70, 196–7. A more moderate view is advanced in Liebeschuetz, *Antioch* 7–16.

[209] Chastagnol (1978) 76 lines 12–22; for other examples see Jones (1949) 51; MacMullen, *Corruption* 151–2; Noethlichs (1981) 195–9. One *modius* of wheat equals 7 kg.

[210] *P.Abinn.* 59, quoting line 14: Bell *et al.* (1962) 121–2; Liebs (1978) 173; Rémondon (1965) 140–1.

to his fellow bishop Amphilochius of Iconium – also in the southern hinterland of Asia Minor), offered to help seek an exemption from civic duties for an important member of his congregation. They, again with the assistance of the Almighty, had to decide tactics: 'so that we may set about asking this favour from each of our friends in power, either as a gift or for some moderate price, however the Lord may help us forward'.[211] A similar saintly combination of cash and connections was deployed in the early fifth century by Augustine, bishop of Hippo in North Africa. In April 418, after considerable lobbying at court in Ravenna, the emperor Honorius had been persuaded to condemn as heretical the beliefs of the monk Pelagius and his followers in Rome. However, the disputes following the death of the pope eight months later gave Pelagius' supporters an opportunity to reopen their case. Augustine, strongly convinced of the rightness of his cause, moved to block any such attempt. He relied on the good offices of Valerius – a high-ranking courtier and a close relation of a wealthy landowner in Hippo – to prevent any appeal.[212] In order to ensure widespread support amongst Valerius' military connections, Augustine sent his fellow bishop Alypius to court with – so the Pelagians later claimed – the promise that on the successful conclusion of the case he would ship to Italy eighty African stallions fattened on the estates of the church. For Augustine (or so it was alleged) horses were an acceptable price to pay for the maintenance of Christian orthodoxy.[213]

This wide variety of views on one particular method of forcing access to power should come as no surprise. It is a neat and not unexpected corollary to a system in which success demanded the skilful selection or combination of various, often conflicting, tactics. (Even Libanius, despite his strong views on the growth of fourth-century bureaucracy, was prepared, in his efforts to secure preferment for his former pupils, to write to well-placed officials – and, on occasion, even to *agentes in rebus*.)[214] For those whose primary advantage lay with their family, friends and connections, any other means of advancement constituted an unwelcome intrusion into a world tightly bound by the civilities of recommendation and the promotion of protégés and their causes. Those who remained unmoved by such long-hallowed ties were incontestably immoral. But for those without these advantages (or for those wishing to reduce the influence of any rival network) the payment of money offered an effective alternative method for securing a position or getting grievances heard. Set in this wider frame, what we call 'corruption' or 'venality' does not so unquestionably appear as a dubious practice whose very persistence stands as certain evidence of a deeply flawed administration on the

[211] Basil, *Ep.* 190.2 More generally, on Basil's advantageous use of powerful connections: Treucker (1981).   [212] *PLRE*(2) 1143–4 (Valerius 3).
[213] Aug. *Op. Imp.* 1.42 (*CSEL* LXXXV.1. 30–1): Brown, *Augustine* 361–2. For further examples of bishops using money to gain advantage: MacMullen (1986b) 339–41.
[214] Pack (1935) 20–1; Petit, *Libanius* 360–1.

brink of decline. Not all who sold recommendations for office or purchased preferment for themselves or their causes were immoral, undeserving or entirely self-seeking. Nor is there any particular reason to believe that men who had bought their positions were on the whole any less competent than those who had risen through the ranks or had been advanced by powerful friends. Some individuals were well-deserving; some causes worthwhile; others not. The same might be said of those who unashamedly relied on their contacts to help them get on in the world.

The payment of money – like the use of influential connections and the other various means of securing advancement – was integral to the workings of later Roman bureaucracy.[215] It was inseparably part of that shifting set of tactical possibilities which marked out the relationship between emperors, bureaucrats and those seeking access to the advantages they could offer. In the end, what really mattered – on all sides – was the ability to use, combine or block the various options which might lead to success (as well as to vil-ification by disappointed rivals, or to praise by admiring supporters). For Mark the Deacon, the biographer of Porphyry, bishop of Gaza, that holy man's ability to work through the intricacies of courtly politics (using and combining various tactics as he progressed) was itself worthy of note. The dramatic incident – in which the baptism of an infant prince provided the occasion for the successful presentation of a petition demanding the closure of pagan temples in Gaza[216] – was the result of long negotiation and con-tinual pressure. Arriving in Constantinople in 400, Porphyry had relied on the good offices of the patriarch John Chrysostom, who was himself friendly with Amantius, a high-ranking eunuch in the empress Eudoxia's entourage. Having used his powerful contacts and their connections to gain admission to the empress' presence, Porphyry persuaded her of the right-ness of his cause and – as a demonstration of his own high standing with a heavenly king – declared that the child she was carrying would be born alive and healthy. Eudoxia agreed to lend her support. She also presented Porphyry with money to defray the costs he had incurred in securing access to her presence. Suitably grateful – and to the evident admiration of his biog-rapher – the saintly Porphyry, in a shrewd combination of available tactics, left the imperial audience chamber blessing Eudoxia and scattering gold coins at the feet of her *decani* – the empress' doorkeepers.[217]

IV. CONCLUSIONS

The later Roman empire was before all things a monarchical state. The position of the emperor – so brilliantly emphasized by splendid courtly

---

[215] Schuller (1982) 206–8; and the thoughtful remarks of Veyne (1981), esp. 350–3.
[216] Above, n. 124.   [217] *V. Porph.* 36–40.

ceremony and its surrounding litany of praise – was central to its system of rule. Imperial intervention, at any time, at any place or on any pretext, could never be entirely excluded. Indeed, given the restrictions imposed by the vastness of empire, the slowness of communication and the technological limitations of a pre-industrial state, it might be argued that later Roman emperors were strikingly successful in imposing their will on the Mediterranean world. But such assertions should not be phrased too crudely. The exercise of imperial power in the later empire involved the continual and often delicate balancing of sometimes conflicting sets of interest and advantage. Emperors moved to strengthen and justify their own position by (for example) linking earthly monarchy with heavenly archetypes, by arrogating to themselves certain ceremonies, symbols and language and insisting on their exclusivity, and by ensuring that those close to the imperial person or loyal to imperial policy were well rewarded. Those who benefited – and those who sought or hoped to benefit – were keen to collude in the promotion of an image of imperial power whose continued efficacy guaranteed them further advancement. By contrast, those excluded or disadvantaged tended to portray emperors as vain fools or murderous despots.

Paradoxically, the same tactics which secured an emperor's position could also weaken it. The strong concentration of imperial power at the centre exacerbated its tendency to drain away at the edges of empire. Strong men in provinces far distant from Constantinople could frequently do as they pleased. Those who enjoyed influential connections were able to deflect unwelcome enquiries into their activities. In the imperial capital, the confinement of emperors within a court society difficult of access increased their dependence on family, followers and officials for information and advice. Emperors risked being trapped by the very concentration of power which made their court attractive. As far as they were able, emperors moved to counter these dual threats of ignorance and isolation. The continual rise and fall of favourites, the reliance on certain groups of well-tested officials who could be sent into the provinces on confidential missions, the brief tenure of most senior posts and the unpredictable shifts in imperial policy weakened the influence of opposition cliques. These tactics also ensured that the advantages of loyalty could be broadly distributed. New men might always hope for advancement, often by exposing the faults of those already in office. Importantly, too, emperors ensured that the penalties for flouting or misdirecting imperial power were severe and memorable. Just as the attractions of loyalty were both displayed and enhanced by the splendour of the emperor and his retinue, and by the ranks, titles and praise lavished – at least temporarily – on trusted officials, the consequences of disfavour were also loudly proclaimed. By widely advertising the beneficial or punitive consequences of imperial intervention, emperors sought to maintain the belief that similar actions could be repeated without warning anywhere in the empire. Threats and inducements, and the hope or fear they inspired, were vital to the maintenance of imperial authority. They helped bridge that perilous gap between the advantageous concentration of power around an emperor and his court, and the equally pressing need for a more certain degree of control over the empire as a whole.

A similar conflict of interest marked out an emperor's relationship with the bureaucracy. The development of an impressively organized and hierarchically structured administration was an important factor in the maintenance of imperial power. It improved the collection and collation of information from all parts of the empire; it permitted the more systematic enforcement of imperial regulations and (above all) the more efficient assessment and collection of taxes. But for emperors, the clear advantages of government by bureaucracy had to be balanced against the threat that, in the face of such an impressive administrative machine, the free exercise of imperial will might be greatly hampered – canalized in directions determined by the information or advice provided by officials, or simply dissipated in an endless, labyrinthine round of administrative regulation and appointment. In an attempt to minimize these risks, emperors moved to restrict the degree to which bureaucrats, carrying out their task or seeking preferment, could rely on predictable rules or routinized procedures. Administrative responsibilities were arbitrarily split or shifted; personnel were moved between departments; promotion was based on a set of often conflicting criteria – seniority, merit, money, inheritance, imperial favour. By preventing the formation of a self-regulating, rule-bound bureaucracy, emperors sacrificed administrative efficiency, preferring instead to ensure the continued importance of their own position and preferences.

For all involved – given both the extent of imperial power and its obvious limitations – loyalty or subversion, promotion or disgrace were always matters of advantage and risk. Most expected that government would 'give' if pressure were properly applied.[218] (Even emperors expected to be able to cut through their own administration and make contact directly with individuals in the provinces.) In that sense – taken together – centralization, the growth of bureaucracy and the set of tactical combinations deployed to limit their disadvantages offered benefits to emperors as well as to those who sought to channel imperial power for their own ends. This was a delicately balanced system of rule in which many chanced to gain. The wide distribution of benefits (some undoubtedly illegally or immorally acquired) was important both in maintaining a broad level of support for the system as a whole and in ensuring a continued willingness amongst participants to play – despite the risks – for the advantages to be

---

[218] Brown, *Power and Persuasion* 14.

won. Of course, there were successes and failures: emperors were some-times deceived, just causes were sometimes thwarted, dishonest officials were sometimes caught and killed. In a knife-edge game, results were inevitably uncertain. But emperors continually strove to tilt the balance of risk to their own advantage. In the face of competing and irreconcilable interests, their strength ultimately lay in ensuring that the chances of their succeeding (though not always certain) could never be entirely discounted. That likelihood – combined with the considerable advantages offered by centralization and the growth of bureaucratic government – was a crucial factor in securing their position and underpinning their importance. In an uncertain world, only emperors, as they repeatedly insisted, stood a chance of resolving what for the majority caught up in later Roman government remained a shifting set of tactical possibilities to be played (as far as they were able) to best advantage. From that point of view – as long as imper-ial intervention, for good or ill, was perceived as a real possibility – it was clearly in the interests of all jockeying for power, position or preferment to cheer loudly as the glittering procession of a godlike emperor passed them by.

CHAPTER 6

SENATORS AND SENATES

PETER HEATHER

At the start of the fourth century, the senatorial order was composed of the relatively few men – perhaps some six hundred or so – who were members of the senate of the city of Rome. Senatorial status was essentially inherited, although, since the beginnings of the empire, there had been a steady trickle of new elections to the order from the greatest provincial families across the empire, so that not all were of Roman, or indeed Italian, origin. In the fourth century, nevertheless, some still claimed more or less direct descent from old republican grandees such as the Gracchi and Scipios. All, whatever their origins, had the same formal status and the same attendant privileges. As a body, the senate had little real political power, and its true importance resided in the men of whom it was composed. Many belonged to the wealthiest stratum of landowners within the entire empire, and this wealth brought power, influence and ambition in its wake. It was the wealth of the individuals, indeed, and not the power of the institution which underlay the numerous senatorial candidates for imperial office in the political anarchy of the third century.[1]

By A.D. 400, much of this had changed. A second senate had been created in Constantinople, and the senatorial order itself had grown enormously in size. Senatorial status remained hereditary, but, in the course of the fourth century, it also became much easier for outsiders to acquire it, particularly by pursuing a career in the imperial bureaucracy. The order itself had been subdivided further into three grades, with varying rights and privileges for each grade. This total revolution in the nature of the imperial senatorial order sets the agenda for this chapter, which will consider the institutional changes put in place in the course of the century, the new career patterns which resulted, and the evolving political role of senators, both in central, imperial politics and in the governing of localities.

I. INSTITUTIONAL CHANGE

The most obvious institutional innovation of the fourth century was the creation of the senate of Constantinople. The new body did not spring

[1] On the development of the senate up to c. A.D. 300, Talbot (1984); Arnheim (1972), ch. 1; Jones, *LRE* 545 ff. Claims to ancient descent: e.g. Jerome *Epp.* 108.1–4; 77.2.

fully formed from the head of the emperor Constantine, however, having at least three marked phases of development. These phases each had their own political context, and subsequent developments were by no means a necessary consequence of Constantine's original act.

1. Constantine

Constantine's new senate was part and parcel of the new capital he founded to commemorate his great victory over Licinius. According to trustworthy report, its members were originally given a lower status than their counterparts of the senate of Rome: *clari* rather than *clarissimi*. It is evident, however, that Constantine meant his new body to grow, because, like its Roman counterpart, it was endowed with at least one praetorship. It was the giving of praetorian games which formally qualified a candidate for entry to the senate. Praetorships in Constantinople are first mentioned in a law of 340, but this is a *terminus ante quem*, and praetors were probably part of Constantine's original scheme. The emperor also provided houses and food rations as economic incentives to attract would-be senators.[2]

Constantine's motivation was no doubt in part ideological. According to a hostile pagan tradition, he was driven out of Rome and needed to set up home somewhere else. But Constantine's relations with Rome were in fact good; he built on a very substantial scale in the old capital, reincorporated its senators into political life after their exclusion under Diocletian, and made a special journey west in 326 to celebrate his twentieth anniversary there.[3] A more positive motivation for founding the Constantinopolitan senate is thus required and is not hard to find. Constantine may well have felt that the foundation of a second imperial senate was not megalomania but an entirely appropriate act for one who had reunited the Roman world for the first time in several generations (discounting, as did Constantine's propaganda, the tetrarchic period as one of fake unity). On one level, then, the new senate was designed to make a statement about the grandeur of the emperor's achievements.

At the same time, the new institution must also be set in its political context. Having defeated Licinius, Constantine faced a huge governmental problem. He had already ruled for the best part of twenty years, but only in the west; now he had taken over the east by force, where he knew nobody, where all senior appointees were Licinius' men, and where all local men of importance were used to operating through channels set up by

[2] Basic account: *Anon. Val.* vi.30. Secondary accounts: Jones, *LRE* 525 ff.; Dagron, *Naissance* chs 4–6; Chastagnol (1975) 341–56; Chastagnol (1982) 228–34. Praetors: *C.Th.* vi.4.5–6; cf. Chastagnol (1975) 346–7; contra Jones, *LRE* 132–3. Reference will be made to this secondary literature only on points of contention.
[3] Zos. ii.29–31 derived from Eunapius. Building: Krautheimer, *Rome* ch. 1. Visit: Barnes, *NE* 75–80.

Licinius. In essence, Constantine had to begin from scratch to establish the chain of relations which would make the east governable (this explains why Constantine made an eastern rather than a western city his capital after Licinius' defeat, and spent the vast majority of the rest of his reign in the Greek-speaking parts of the empire).[4]

The new eastern emperor took a series of measures to deal with this basic problem immediately after his victory. Taxes were reduced, those exiled by Licinius were recalled, and property confiscated by the previous regime was restored. Any individual who had also lost out under the previous regime was a potential supporter of the new emperor. Alongside this went a double-handed propaganda campaign, presenting Constantine as both 'triumphant' (*victor*) and most merciful (*clementissimus*). The message here seems clear; any supporter of Licinius who reacted positively to Constantine's victory could hope for a sympathetic reception from the new regime. The reality of his success was further driven home by a series of imperial visits to the main political centres of the east. *Adventus* coinages celebrated his visits to Nicomedia and Antioch, and we know that a further visit to Egypt (no doubt aimed particularly at Alexandria) was planned.[5]

At the same time, Constantine was giving away vast sums of money. The hostile pagan tradition in Zosimus (II.38.1) reports that the emperor 'wasted revenue by unnecessary gifts to . . . useless people'; this might be discounted, but a similar report couched in positive terms also appears in Eusebius' *Life of Constantine*. Giving a great deal away on acceding to a throne is part and parcel of making the relationships which, in the long run, will make for a successful reign. In 324, Constantine was actually starting his reign in the east, and inordinate generosity was very much to the point.[6]

The main point for present purposes is that Eusebius invites us to place the creation of the senate of Constantinople in precisely this context (*Life of Constantine* IV.1), reporting that 'the emperor devised new dignities that he might give tokens of his favour to a larger number of people'. Creating a new imperial senate in Constantinople thus assisted Constantine in his main political task after 324: generating from scratch a sufficient body of support to create a working governmental machine in the eastern Mediterranean. It gave him a new mark of status (with its own barrage of attendant privileges: see p. 206 below) with which to attract the landowning élites without whom he would have been unable to govern in the east.

[4] On regime-building, Matthews (1971). For one local group and their interrelations with central government, see Liebeschuetz, *Antioch*, esp. 41–51 and pts. 3–4.
[5] Eus. *V. Const.* II.24–42, 48–60; cf. Grünewald (1990) 134–41.
[6] *V. Const.* 1.9; 1.39; II.13; III.1; III.22; III.44; IV.1–4; IV.49; cf. Heather (1994b).

2. Constantius II

This first phase of revolution left the old senate of Rome more or less untouched. Its members retained in general a slightly grander status, as we have seen, and senators of Rome resident in the eastern Mediterranean were not required to re-register in Constantinople. In the later part of the reign of Constantine's son, Constantius II, however, two major initiatives were adopted with profound consequences for the older body as well as the new.

First, the emperor decided to split the senatorial order of the empire upon purely geographical grounds. Senators of Rome resident in the east now had to re-register with the senate of Constantinople; the correspondence of Libanius provides a pertinent example in Olympias, a Roman senator living in Antioch (*Ep.* 70). The importance of this move should not be missed. By this date at the latest, the collective formal status of the new senatorial body must have been raised to *clarissimus*, as henceforth the only distinction between the membership of the two institutions was geographical scope. This, of course, had important implications for the senate of Rome, which was now to serve not the empire as a whole, but only the western part of it, while the senate of Constantinople was to perform similar functions for the east.

At the same time, Constantius authorized a formal recruiting campaign to strengthen specifically the eastern body. The orator Themistius (himself adlected to the senate in 355) travelled round the cities of the eastern Mediterranean in 358–9 looking for likely candidates. A dozen or so of the new senators turn up in the correspondance of Libanius from this period, all of them from the curial classes of the cities. A law of 361 saw the culmination of the campaign, regulating various important matters and banning further recruitment.[7]

Constantius' measures also have an interesting context. The expansion of the eastern senate came at a moment when the emperor was running the whole empire and was himself in the west, hovering over his newly created Caesar Julian (Constantius returned to the east only in late 359). The year 359 also saw major treason trials, which made a considerable impact in the eastern provinces (Amm. Marc. XIX.12). Given the sequence of events

---

[7] Petit (1956a) 154–5; Petit (1957), esp. 349–54; Dagron, *Naissance* 132–4. Constantius' legislation: *C.Th.* 1.6.1; 1.28.1; VI.4.12–13; VII.8.1; XI.1.7; XI.15.1; XI.23.1; XIII.1.3; XII.1.48. There is some doubt over the size of the Constantinopolitan senate in the early 360s. In an oration of the 380s, Themistius says that in his time the senate grew from 300 to 2000, and some have taken it to mean that all this growth took place between 355 and 361: *Or.* XXXIV; cf. Chastagnol (1975) 350–1. This is possibly what Themistius meant posterity to understand, but the reigns of Valentinian and Valens saw many further extensions of senatorial status, and it seems unlikely that membership of the senate could have remained constant between 361 and the 380s. With Jones, therefore, I suspect that the growth in membership to which Themistius refers probably reflects development over thirty years; cf. Jones, *LRE* 144, 527.

which marked the brief rule of Constantius' previous Caesar Gallus, who was executed for showing too much independence, it is tempting to suggest that wooing important eastern curials with grants of senatorial status, while at the same time giving considerable publicity to treason trials, was a stick-and-carrot approach designed to keep the eastern empire in line, at a moment when Constantius had to be in the west.[8]

Possibly this is too bold a hypothesis; if so, a more straightforward one is available (and they are not mutually exclusive). The emperor's letter to the senate in 355, recommending the election of Themistius, lays down the qualities which should be combined in the ideal senator: movable wealth (cash), landed wealth, distinction acquired by office-holding, and the cultural distinction imparted by a first-rate education.[9] These criteria show that Constantius' extension of the senate was aimed directly at the old wealth of the Mediterranean world: the richer elements of the curial classes, and, to judge by the individuals mentioned by Libanius' letters of this period – as we have seen – it was precisely such men who were recruited. A general desire to widen his base of support among the powerful landowners of the eastern Mediterranean – perhaps given added point by a sense of fragility in the difficult circumstances of the later 350s – may well have underlain Constantius' expansion of the senate.

At the same time, Constantius' creation of two equal senates was probably also responding to a general increase in senatorial numbers which was under way across the Mediterranean. Already in his reign, there was a marked tendency for imperial bureaucrats to find their ultimate reward in a grant of senatorial status. Given that senatorial status remained hereditary (i.e. families could not easily lose it), this meant that numbers could only increase. The link between the bureaucracy and the senate was fully institutionalized in the reign of Valentinian I and Valens.

3. Valentinian, Valens and after

The Theodosian Code preserves several fragments from a crucial legislative sequence of the year 372 which marks a final evolution in the nature of the senatorial order under the late empire. These laws consolidated into one unitary system all the ranks and marks of distinction available at the time, whatever their origin. Instead of the full-time central bureaucracy (the *palatini*), the holders of occasional high governmental posts (*dignitates*), and the army all having entirely separate ladders to climb, these main strands (and other minor ones) were now brought together – at their upper end – by grants of a common senatorial status. This legislation was final

---

[8] On Constantius and his Caesars, Matthews, *Ammianus* 33–5, and ch. 6.
[9] W. Dindorf (ed.), *Themistii Orationes* (rpt. Hildesheim, 1961), 21–7.

Table 1. *The Imperial Bureaucracy in c. A.D. 400*

(a) Notaries:	520 in east in A.D. 381; all members had senatorial status by 381.[1]
(b) Sacra Scrinia:	130 in east in A.D. 470; senatorial rank upon retirement; waiting-list in fifth century.[2]
(c) Agentes in Rebus:	1174 in east in A.D. 430 (plus waiting-list); senior members have senatorial status.[3]
(d) Largitionales:	546 members in west in A.D. 399 (plus waiting-list); senior members first *perfectissimi*, then senators. 834 members in east in A.D. 399: 224 regular members, 610 supernumeraries.[4]
(e) Privatiani:	300 in west in A.D. 399.[5]
Total =	2700 approx. in each half of the empire (assuming similar numbers in east and west and ignoring waiting-lists).

[1] Jones, *LRE* 572–5; status: *C.Th.* VI.10.2–3; number: Libanius, *Or.* 11.58.
[2] Jones, *LRE* 575–8; numbers: *CJ* XII.19.10.
[3] Jones, *LRE* 578–82; numbers: *C.Th.* VI.27.23 (increased to 1248 under Leo: *CJ* XII.20.4).
[4] West: *C.Th.* VI.30.15; east: *C.Th.* VI.30.16. Cf. Jones, *LRE* 584–5.
[5] Jones, *LRE* 585–6; numbers: *C.Th.* VI.30.16.

confirmation of a trend whereby senatorial status ceased so much to designate a body of men marked out by particular biological descent (although this element never entirely disappeared, especially in Rome) as to become the ultimate distinction aimed for by all participating in the different career structures of the empire.[10]

The full significance of these laws emerges only when they are related to a transformation which had been working itself out within the upper levels of the imperial bureaucracy throughout the fourth century, especially (though not solely) among the palatine ministries. As Table 1 shows, by *c.* A.D. 400 there were five great central ministries. The number given for each department represents not the total of jobs available, but the number of very good jobs – very good jobs being defined as those which provided the holder with either top equestrian status (the perfectissimate) or, as was increasingly the case in the course of the fourth century, senatorial rank. In some departments, and this is again indicated, all jobs conferred high status immediately; in others, such advantages came only with the most senior positions. The standard pattern, however, was for the top men to retire each year and be succeeded by those next in order of precedence, so that, even in the less favoured departments, a bureaucratic career would bring high status by retirement.

[10] *C.Th.* VI.7.1; VI.9.1; VI.11.1; VI.14.1; VI.22.4: Jones, *LRE* 142–3.

By *c.* A.D. 400, then, there were something like 3000 jobs in each half of the empire leading more or less directly to senatorial status. This represents an extraordinary transformation. According to the most comprehensive study, there had only been something like 180 high-ranking bureaucrats in the whole of the empire in A.D. 249, none of whom were senators.[11] Top bureaucrats from the newly expanded offices of the fourth century had certainly been adlected *ad hominem* to the senate before 350; Constantius II's insistence on the importance of distinction via office-holding to the would-be senator (see above) hints that this may have happened regularly. Nevertheless, it was only with the legislation of Valentinian and Valens that the equation of high office and, increasingly, senatorial status became an absolute one. Senatorial status had become the ultimate prize for an increasingly large aristocracy of service.

The laws of Valentinian and Valens also institutionalized one other major change: distinctions of status within the senatorial order. This, no doubt, was a natural result of senatorial expansion. As numbers increased, the richer and more important were not content to be bracketed with parvenus. Already from the 350s, there is evidence for semi-official special titles, more important figures such as praetorian prefects being designated *clarissimi et illustres* rather than mere *clarissimi*. The legislation of 372, however, formalized such designations into a system of three separate senatorial grades: in ascending order, *clarissimi* (consular governors and some junior bureaucrats), *spectabiles* (proconsular governors, the four *comites consistoriani* and *duces*, high military officers), and *illustres* (praetorian prefects, urban prefects, consuls and *magistri militum*, top generals).[12]

Subsequent emperors, of course, continued to make changes to the senatorial order, and, although the run of legislation passes beyond the chronological boundary of this chapter, it is worth highlighting its two main trends. First, senatorial rather than top equestrian status was extended to most posts in imperial service. By the early fifth century, the equestrian order was largely moribund, and senatorial status had been extended to the lowest grade of provincial governor and all regimental commanders (tribunes).

At the same time, distinctions between the privileges accorded each grade of senator continued to grow. The fiscal and jurisdictional advantages of *illustres* increased, while those of *spectabiles* and *clarissimi* were whittled away. Indeed, effective membership of the senate had, by the middle of the fifth century, been confined to active, not honorary, *illustres*. This is signalled, above all, by a law of the emperor Marcian excusing *spectabiles* and *clarissimi* from the praetorship – i.e. from formal entry to the

---

[11] Pflaum (1950) ch. 2. Cf., e.g., Brunt (1983). This was much more a patronage machine than a regulated bureaucracy, and should be equated with the slow spread of senatorial status among provincials: Chastagnol (1975) 341 with refs.   [12] Jones, *LRE* 143–4, 528–9.

senate. The senate itself, therefore, became once again a more restricted body, but this did not mean that the changes of the fourth century had been reversed. The rank of *illustris* could be obtained only by an active bureaucratic career, and, while active senators were again relatively few, there remained many senatorial families, distinguished at least by the rank of *clarissimus*, whose individual members could, in the course of their lifetimes, seek to win the higher grades of distinction.[13] The fourth century thus saw the definitive creation of senatorial orders in each half of the empire which encompassed a much larger cross-section of the landowning élite, and also established a firm link between high status and imperial service.

II. SENATORIAL CAREERS

These fundamental changes in the nature of the senatorial order naturally affected the type of careers being followed by its members. With far more roads leading to senatorial status in the fourth century, the number of careers which might properly be called senatorial shows a corresponding increase. The century is marked, indeed, by a dual pattern. On the one hand, the traditional senatorial *cursus honorum* continued largely unabated. On the other, many newcomers followed quite separate paths to the senate through the imperial bureaucracy.

1. The traditional cursus

There is much western evidence for the enduring attraction of the traditional senatorial *cursus honorum* for established families of the senate of Rome. The writings of Symmachus and a host of Latin senatorial inscriptions have long established its basic patterns, and Symmachus himself provides a fine example of its classic progression.

Before the age of twenty, he had already held the three standard, now entirely honorary, senatorial magistracies: praetorship, quaestorship and suffect consulship. During the rest of his long career – he had fulfilled these early offices before A.D. 365 and seems to have died in about 402 – he held only three posts with administrative responsibilities. First came a governorship in Italy – Symmachus was *corrector* of Lucania in 365 – then a more prestigious proconsular governorship; Symmachus took his in North Africa in 373, but Greece was another possibility (*proconsul Achaiae*), held, for instance, by Symmachus' close friend Vettius Agorius Praetextatus. If the senator were prominent, then the urban prefecture of Rome marked the natural culmination of an administrative career, since the urban prefect, amongst other duties, acted as the head of the senate, responsible for all its

[13] Marcian: *CJ* XII.2.1 (450); cf., generally, Jones, *LRE* 528–30.

communications with the emperor (see below). Symmachus was urban prefect in 384–5.

None of Symmachus' periods in office lasted more than a year, and each tenure was punctuated by about a decade for recovery. The really prominent, like Symmachus himself in 391, might be further rewarded with the ultimate accolade of the consulship, but this was quite rare, and did not involve any actual administrative duties. Italian correctorship, proconsular governorship, and urban prefecture, with long periods out of office in between – such was the rhythm of the traditional western senatorial *cursus*. Such a progression also conveniently moved a senator up through the three grades of the senatorial order as established by Valentinian and Valens (see p. 188 above). Men less prominent or fortunate might go no further, of course, than the first step or two on the ladder.[14]

Once the senate of Constantinople had been fully established by the reforms of Constantius II, a similar *cursus* presumably existed in the east, although the evidence is not nearly so comprehensive. No letter collection survives from eastern senatorial circles, and late antique Greek commemorative inscriptions have a quite different nature. Instead of a careful and precise listing of offices held (the norm in Latin senatorial epigraphy), they tend to celebrate their subject in allusive (and hence elusive) Homeric verse.[15] The point here seems to have been to show that one was part of an educated élite, but it also makes career patterns harder to reconstruct. There is just enough evidence to suggest, however, that the lives of the eastern élite would have been recognizable to their western counterparts.

As we have seen, the praetorship existed as part of the Constantinopolitan senate from at the very latest A.D. 340, giving us reason to suppose that the full range of early, honorary administrative magistracies may well have existed. For the career patterns of older men, a different kind of insight is provided by the letters of Libanius. Libanius was not himself a senator, and many of his pupils were not of senatorial status. Of his former pupils appearing in the letters who later held high administrative posts, however, one-third (fourteen out of forty-two) only ever seem to have held a single provincial governorship. It may well be, therefore, that there was a substantial group among the élite of the eastern Mediterranean whose lives followed a pattern of occasional and brief tenures of high office, similar to those of Symmachus and his compatriots in the west.[16]

It is very easy to satirize the lifestyles associated with such career patterns. One contemporary, Ammianus Marcellinus, included in his history two

---

[14] Symmachus: *ILS* 2946; cf. *PLRE* 1.865ff. Praetextatus: *ILS* 1259; cf. *PLRE* 1.722ff. See generally, Matthews, *Western Aristocracies*, esp. 1–12; Chastagnol, *Préfecture urbaine*.

[15] Robert, *Hellenica* IV; cf. Rouéché, *Aphrodisias* XXI, 17–19.

[16] Petit (1956a) 166. Although – cf. Jones, *LRE* 554–5 – there were substantial differences in wealth between the two senates.

savage attacks upon the élite of Rome, and more modern commentators, particularly A. H. M. Jones in his magisterial survey of the later Roman empire, have been dismayed by the 'amateurism' of the empire's élite. Symmachus, indeed, often wrote consolatory letters to his peers when they were about to embark upon one of their rare periods in office (including Petronius Probus, on whom see below).[17] No doubt, much of such criticism is justified. There has never been a staggeringly wealthy élite which did not, a few notable exceptions aside, enjoy the fruits of that wealth to the utmost. There are a number of ways, however, in which the image of idle wealth which could be built up from the writings of Symmachus is substantially misleading.

To start with, a powerful ideology laid out an agenda for senators' extensive periods of leisure: *otium*. This was not to be devoted to dancing girls (although one of Ammianus' complaints was that, during a famine, foreign visitors were expelled from the city of Rome when 3000 dancing girls were not: xiv.6.19), but to the furtherance of classical literary studies. Again, one of Ammianus' complaints is that senators he knew took on nothing more exacting than the satires of Juvenal and the light biographies of Marius Maximus (xxviii.4.14), but some of Symmachus' friends were of rather different calibre. Praetextatus, for instance, translated Greek verse and prose, including Themistius' commentary on the *Analytics* of Aristotle; his love of philosophy and learning won even Ammianus' approval. And a totally different vision of the senatorial life parodied by Ammianus emerges from the *Saturnalia* of Macrobius, where a whole series of experts (including Symmachus and Praetextatus) is portrayed as gathering to engage in serious discussions of literature, religion and antiquarian lore. Moreover, this was not love of knowledge for its own sake. In the late-antique conception, the Graeco-Roman literary tradition lay at the heart of what it was to be civilized. By presenting the individual with countless examples of good and bad behaviour and of their consequences, this literature was considered to enable the individual to learn a higher morality, to subdue the shifting demands of the body by the stable power of the intellect. This, indeed, was the 'point' of the Roman empire; it protected and sustained a society where human beings could reach their full potential. A life devoted, in large measure, to literary studies was not self-indulgence, therefore, but serious business.[18]

On a second level, too, the image that might be fostered by a superficial reading of Symmachus' works is misleading, because they deliberately underestimate the involvement of the senatorial élite in imperial politics. For many of the senators who fulfilled the traditional *cursus* subsequently

---

[17] Amm. Marc. xiv.6; xxviii.4. Symmachus *Ep.* 1.58; cf. Matthews, *Western Aristocracies* 10–11. Jones, *LRE* 536; cf. 543–4.

[18] Praetextatus: *PLRE* i.723. See, generally, Chastagnol, *Préfecture urbaine* 435 (a dossier of the cultural activities of urban prefects); Matthews, *Western Aristocracies* 2–7, 370–2 (on Macrobius); Heather (1994a).

went on to hold important court or general administrative offices. A classic case in point is Petronius Probus. Although Symmachus consoled him on having to take office, an alternative picture is again provided by Ammianus who describes him as like a fish out of water when he had to endure periods of *otium*. Like Symmachus, he started gently enough with a traditional office (the proconsulship of Africa in 358), and paid more than lip-service to literature, dedicating a collection of his own and his grandfather's verses to the emperor Theodosius I. The bulk of his career, however, was passed in quite different circles. He held the most important general administrative position in the empire, the praetorian prefecture (there were three or four such officers with responsibility for different areas at any one time) on at least four separate occasions, including a mammoth seven-year tenure of office in Illyricum between 368 and 375 (the average tenure of the prefecture of the East, by comparison, was between eighteen months and three years: see p. 196 below). In the course of this long tenure, he ran Illyricum virtually as an independent fief, and became a prime mover in imperial politics. He was one of the major players in the crowning of Valentinian II after Valentinian I's death in 375, and a major pillar of the former's regime after the murder of his brother Gratian in 383.

Nor is Probus an isolated example. Vettius Agorius Praetextatus, Symmachus' great friend, went on from his proconsulship to become praetorian prefect of Italy, Africa and Illyricum in 384. Likewise Virius Nicomachus Flavianus, another of Symmachus' close friends, went on from traditional senatorial office to mainstream bureaucratic posts: vicar of Africa in 377, he was later imperial quaestor (chief law officer) in 389–90, and praetorian prefect in Italy for much of the early 390s. Love of literature and the senatorial *cursus* did not mean, therefore, that individuals necessarily avoided the great events and administrative offices of their day. Symmachus himself, indeed, was far from bypassed by great political currents. In the 380s, for instance, he gave a speech in praise of the western usurper Maximus, and, when Maximus was later defeated by Theodosius, was faced with the delicate task of apologizing, which he did successfully enough to be rewarded by Theodosius with the consulship. Moreover, much of Symmachus' life as a career-broker – recommending promising young men from the senatorial classes and the schools of Rome to the good and great at court – absolutely depended on his making and retaining multiple contacts in the mainstream of imperial political life. Hence his correspondents included leading bureaucrats such as Probus, top eastern generals such as Fl. Timasius, and even influential bishops such as Ambrose, little though he may have liked any of them.[19]

---

[19] Probus: *PLRE* 1.736–40; Praetextatus: *PLRE* 1.722–4. See generally, Matthews, *Western Aristocracies*, esp. 12–31; Matthews (1985), particularly on the way in which contentious issues were systematically avoided.

The career patterns of the traditional senatorial classes, therefore, are more complicated than a first glance might imply. They did represent a leisured élite of extraordinary wealth – in the east as much as the west. They were not, however, political amateurs, but, according no doubt to individual preference, wealth, and luck, combined traditional pursuits with a healthy interest and involvement, via a whole range of means, in contemporary affairs: from out-and-out office-holding to merely staying in touch. Their literature generates a deliberate smoke-screen, concentrating on the non-contentious in their lives, but, in reality, many within this élite were not the politically isolated figures – interested in dancing girls or books according to taste – they might appear to be. Nor could it have been otherwise, for at the imperial court crucial decisions were taken which dictated the pattern of their lives.

2. New senatorial careers

Alongside traditional senatorial career patterns, the institutional changes to the nature of the senatorial order created new senatorial careers. Once senatorial status – of whatever grade – came at the end of a bureaucratic career, then that bureaucratic career itself became senatorial. For the most part, these careers were not attractive to those who were already senators. They were *militia*, rather than *dignitates*, which meant that the occupants of such an office were required to serve a lengthy term, in many cases essentially a working lifetime (although lengths of service did tend to reduce: see below), rather than the normal year or so of a *dignitas* such as a provincial governorship. Nonetheless, these careers did create senators, and in that sense were certaintly senatorial.

We have now left the world of Symmachus, but the legal codes allow us to see how important a phenomenon the new senatorial bureaucratic career of the fourth century actually was. As we have seen, there were, by c. A.D. 400, some two thousand seven hundred bureaucrats among the eastern and western palatine ministries, many of whom would retire with at least the lowest grade of senatorial rank. Indeed, by this date virtually all public careers of any distinction whatsoever brought such a reward. The one hundred or so provincial governors, twelve vicars and three or four praetorian prefects all received senatorial rank upon appointment, if they did not already possess it, as did all military officers down to the rank of tribune (regimental commander). To envisage three thousand public officers in each half of the empire possessing or receiving senatorial rank at any one time, then, is no exaggeration.

Other features of service in the bureaucracy further increased the total number of such jobs *per generation*. First, as we have seen, many of the upper offices of state (for instance, governorships) were *dignitates* held only for short periods. Fifty proconsuls of Africa between 357 and 417 averaged little over a year in office each. Even a much more important job, such as the praetorian prefecture of the East, saw little greater continuity; between 337 and 369, the average was three years, and between 414 and 455 only eighteen months.[20] Second, in addition to their normal complement of staff (these numbers were regulated by imperial edict), the great central palatine ministries had large waiting-lists of supernumeraries (bureaux known to have had waiting-lists are indicated in Table 1, p. 189 above). In the east, for example, there were 224 *largitionales* in 399, but 610, nearly three times as many, supernumeraries (*C.Th.* VI.30.16). Limiting the discussion to established officers, then, will grossly underestimate total numbers. Letters of Libanius show children being enrolled in the *palatini*, so that 'putting the child down for Eton' may have been one function of the supernumerary list (*Epp.* 358–9, 362, 365–6, 875–6). Third, length of service was set by statute and tended to decrease. By 400, members of the *agentes in rebus* and *scrinia* served only for fifteen years, *privatiani* and *largitionales* for twenty (all had started at twenty-five years).[21] At least in the former departments, these were hardly jobs for life. The total number of people pursuing one of these new senatorial careers *per generation*, therefore, by the end of the fourth century must have been well over three thousand in each half of the empire, perhaps even double that number.

This is not huge compared, say, to the total population of the empire, current estimates of which vary between fifty and seventy millions. It represents a substantial redirection, however, of the energies of the empire's landowning élite, who numbered but a fraction of this, and from whom, it is quite clear, most of the new bureaucrats and senators were drawn. Admittedly, Libanius devoted one famous speech – Oration XLII – to showing that some very significant figures in the senate of Constantinople's brief past had had rather dubious origins. Three praetorian prefects of the 350s and early 360s, he reports – Domitianus, Helpidius and Taurus (the latter also consul in 361) – had fathers who engaged personally in manual labour, while a certain Dulcitius, proconsul of Asia from 361 to 363, was the son of a fuller, and the father of yet another praetorian prefect and consul, Philippus, made sausages.[22]

These men all represent, however, a particular group of Constantius II's appointees, and the bulk of evidence, even from his reign, suggests that senatorial expansion was aimed not at 'new men', but at mobilizing the loyalties of the already rich and powerful: the upper echelons of the curial classes who had long run the cities of the Mediterranean. As we have seen, the criteria Constantius laid down in his letter of recommendation for

[20] Jones, *LRE* 380–1.   [21] Vogler (1979) 163–9 with refs.
[22] *Or.* XLII.24–5; on these individuals, see *PLRE* I.262, 274, 414, 696–7, 879–80.

Themistius virtually excluded anyone else, and it was precisely such people that Themistius recruited (see p. 187 above). The expansion of the bureaucracy was sustained by recruitment from exactly the same groups. A lengthy run of imperial constitutions in the Theodosian Code, for instance, orders curials to return to their cities from imperial service. These are collected at *C.Th.* xii.1, and come thick and fast from the reign of Constantius II onwards. Libanius' letters, similarly, offer countless individual examples of curials entering imperial careers, and perhaps the most telling evidence is the fact that the *sine qua non* for entry into the bureaucracy was possession of the linguistic skills gained by full exposure to the literary education (whether in Latin or Greek) which was the norm for the late imperial élite. This involved at least ten years' private education, so that a family had to be well-off in the first place to be able to educate a child or children in this manner. The example of Augustine suggests that the cut-off line for this would have fallen broadly at the bottom end of the curial class; of poorer curial stock, Augustine had to delay for a year the later stages of his education while his family found the necessary money.[23]

Senatorial and bureaucratic recruitment thus drew on men who had previously tended to follow careers in the local politics of their home cities. Throughout the empire's history, there had been some tendency for the richest men in local society to gravitate towards imperial careers, but never on such a scale. The fourth-century transformation of the senatorial order thus represented a political revolution not only at the imperial centre, with the rise of a senatorial bureaucracy, but also in the localities, as a significant proportion of city landowning élites stretched their horizons beyond their local curias.

III. SENATORS AND EMPERORS

Individual senators and institutional bodies dominated by senators were deeply involved in a wide variety of ways in imperial politics: the formulation of policy and regimes. The most obvious senatorial bodies, the senates of Rome and Constantinople, had only limited formal roles in the running of the empire and virtually no political powers, but the senatorial orders were composed of rich and influential individuals, who were certainly of account both as landowners and increasingly as bureaucrats and politicians. It was mostly, therefore, as powerful individuals that senators had political importance, but, on certain specific issues, they could act much more as a body, and, especially from A.D. 400 onwards, a variety of institutional developments made it increasingly possible for two

---

[23] Libanius: Liebeschuetz, *Antioch* 175–180 and App. 3, with refs. Education: Kaster, *Guardians of Language* chs 1–2, esp. 27ff. on the Latin west, but his remarks are equally applicable to Greek grammarians of the east. Augustine: Brown, *Augustine* ch. 3.

regional groupings of western senators to act in concert over issues of common import.

For the formal role of the senate in the fourth century, our main source of information is again Symmachus. In particular, the urban prefect acted as intermediary between the emperor and the senate of Rome, and the *relationes*, official letters, Symmachus wrote in this capacity to the court of Valentinian II provide key insights into the relationship between emperor and senate. There is every reason to suppose that formal relations between eastern emperors and the senate of Constantinople functioned along similar lines. As the relationship emerges in Symmachus' letters, it seems to have consisted essentially in a mutual duty to keep one another informed. The senate as an institutional body had no constitutional rights to vote on, or even, as far as one see, to be consulted on imperial policy. Emperors seem to have made formal communications to the senate, the contents of which senators could vote formally to endorse, but there is no sign that they could put forward alternatives. In certain circumstances, the senate could take initiatives, by passing resolutions on particular issues which would then be passed on to the emperor. The classic example of this is the vote in favour of the altar of Victory which, as his famous third *relatio* makes clear, Symmachus had by law to communicate to the emperor. Minutes of all senatorial meetings, indeed, were passed on to the emperor by the urban prefect's office. The senate could thus use resolutions and votes to take some initiatives, but could not in the normal run of affairs interfere with what was already imperial policy.[24]

What is true of the senate as an institution, of course, is not necessarily true of its individual members. As has already emerged from senatorial career patterns, particular individuals who moved from the traditional *cursus* into imperial court circles could amass great power: none more so than Probus. Established senators from old families did not tend to put themselves forward as candidates for the throne in the fourth century – most emperors and imperial candidates not from existing imperial families were drawn from the upper reaches of the military or the bureaucracy – but many senators, as we have seen, were deeply implicated in different regimes. Perhaps more interesting in the present context, the senate, or, at least, the influential men of which it was composed, could on occasion act as one body, a political power bloc.

It is very important not to overestimate the prevalence of this phenomenon. A wide variety of evidence makes it clear that the senates of Rome and Constantinople were essentially composed of individuals, not parties, making it very difficult to reach anything approaching a common opinion or point of view. Libanius, for instance, put a considerable effort into mobi-

---

[24] *Relationes*, trans. Barrow; cf. Chastagnol, *Préfecture urbaine* ch. 3 and pt. 2 passim.

lizing support among Constantinopolitan senators for the election of his friend Thalassius, but the vote went against him. In the west, similarly, opinion was always likely to be divided over an issue such as the altar of Victory. Symmachus and his friends managed to engineer a vote in favour of their resolution, but Ambrose could claim that a majority of senators were Christian, and Symmachus, noticeably, nowhere claimed the opposite. Presumably, therefore, the vote had been carefully organized for a day on which the altar lobby felt it could achieve the necessary majority. Indeed, as the institutional changes of the fourth century worked their way through, the thousands of new bureaucratic senators must have made canvassing, lobbying, and the organizing of votes increasingly difficult, especially as many of the new men were not resident in Rome or Constantinople. A law of 383, presumably acknowledging a *fait accompli*, formally permitted senators to reside outside Rome and Constantinople (*C.Th.* VI.1.13), and Symmachus' correspondence suggests that, by 400, his senatorial colleagues were domiciled widely across the western empire. This certainly had its advantages when it came to procuring animals from far-off places for his son's praetorian games, but does underline that, in general, senators, even in just one half of the empire, could not function effectively as a single body of opinion.[25]

Over very specific issues, or in very specific circumstances, this norm was reversed. For instance, Symmachus, in a series of letters and speeches, claims to speak for the Roman senate as a whole when describing the collective relief felt at the death of the emperor Valentinian I in 375, and the subsequent fall from power of all his main henchmen. Here the notion of something approaching a common senatorial reaction, in Rome at least, is credible, because there was an obvious and substantial issue which might have generated it. Whether by design or accident, Valentinian's decision that magic should be treated as treason had meant that senators became liable to torture when facing the enquiries on this front of imperial officers such as Maximinus. This, understandably, outraged senatorial opinion in a general enough way to create a united front, and the regime of Gratian, Valentinian's son, which came to power on the latter's death, took carefully calculated steps to conciliate the offended senators.[26]

A particular recourse open to the senate, when some matter had generated consensus, and one that was utilized in the case of the magic-cum-treason trials, was the formally constituted senatorial embassy. The main

[25] Thalassius: Petit (1957) 350–1: there are twelve surviving letters from Libanius to senators from this campaign. Altar of Victory: Symmachus, *Rel.* III; Ambrose, *Epp.* 16–17; with the commentary of Matthews, *Western Aristocracies* 205–10. Games: Symmachus, *Epp.* 9, for example 12, 15–25, 132, 135, 137, etc.

[26] Symmachus esp. *Or.* IV–V, both delivered (in reverse order) to the senate; cf., generally, Matthews, *Western Aristocracies* 65–8.

advantage of this manoeuvre was that the emperor was duty-bound to receive such ambassadors, just as he had to take notice of formal written accounts of senatorial proceedings. Many senatorial embassies were routine, such as the one which brought Symmachus to Trier to congratulate Valentinian I on his *quinquennalia* (fifth anniversary) in 369. Special embassies could alert the emperor, however, to issues where imperial policy was significantly out of line with senatorial opinion. Thus an embassy composed of three senatorial big guns – Praetextatus, Venustus and Minervius – was sent to complain about the torturing of senators in the magic trials, and, when confronted by them, Valentinian backed down (Amm. Marc. XXVIII.1.24–5). This was only sensible; if a particular issue could unite such a diverse and faction-ridden body of rich, tax-paying landowners against imperial policy, then, unless the emperor was really seeking direct confrontation with them, it was much better to change the policy. Embassies, therefore, could signal when matters had got out of hand, and were clearly a general mechanism, bypassing normal channels, for communicating directly with the emperor in difficult times. A commemorative inscription of Memmius Vitrasius Orfitus, similarly, records the embassy he undertook as urban prefect for the senate *difficillimis temporibus*. This almost certainly refers to his role in achieving a reconciliation between the emperor Constantius II and Italian senators who had given their general support to the recently defeated usurper Magnentius.[27]

All the evidence discussed so far relates to the western half of the empire, and this emphasis very much follows the pattern of the evidence. Symmachus' writings, the nature of inscriptions and the particular historical interests of Ammianus Marcellinus all mean that we are much better informed about the west. Ammianus, for instance, devotes considerable space to Rome in general and to an almost continuous history of the city's urban prefecture in particular, while providing nothing comparable for Constantinople. There is plenty of evidence of a different kind, however, that the new eastern senate was important in similar ways. Again, there is no indication that it had formal, institutional powers of any great moment. There is also plenty of evidence that it was riven with political faction. The death of Theodosius I, for instance, was followed by virtually a decade of extraordinary political instability: a swift succession of regimes punctuated with exiles, treason trials and political murders.[28] As in the west, we can hardly talk of it as a united power bloc within the body politic of the eastern empire.

At the same time, panegyrics – formal speeches in praise of emperors given on public occasions – provide a different kind of evidence that the

---

[27] Symmachus and Valentinian: Symmachus *Or.* I–II; Matthews, *Western Aristocracies* 32ff. Orfitus: *ILS* 1243; cf. Chastagnol, *Fastes* 142. Other examples of senatorial embassies: Matthews (1992) 297 and n. 32.   [28] Most recently, Cameron and Long, *Barbarians and Politics*.

Constantinopolitan senate was an important forum for manipulating and testing opinion among the landowning élite of the east. As early as 362, for instance, in the course of thanking the emperor Julian for promoting him to the consulship, Claudius Mamertinus paid a series of graceful compliments to the senate before whom he was making the speech. Likewise, many of the political orations of Themistius, celebrating and justifying imperial policy, were given in front of the senate, whose spokesman he claimed to be. What is particularly striking about these speeches is the careful way in which senatorial opinion was prepared, in order that it might accept lines of policy which would not have been immediately attractive. Oration xv, for instance, of January 381 was already preparing opinion for the fact that the Gothic war could not be won outright (an event previously looked forward to in Oration xiv of 379), so that a group of at least semi-independent barbarians would have to be tolerated upon Roman soil. The actual peace treaty did not come until October 382. And throughout these political speeches, Themistius can be shown to have employed sophisticated propagandistic devices to make imperial policy into an unbroken chain of success. The fact that he bothered to work so hard is clear testimony to the importance placed by various eastern emperors, all Themistius' employers, in securing the good opinion and complaisance of the sample of the empire's richest landowners of whom the senate was composed.[29] Senators of Constantinople also used resolutions to attempt to influence imperial policy. When the city of Antioch was facing the threat of dire retribution after imperial statues had been overturned in the tax riot of 387, for instance, senators with Antiochene connections made sure that a petition was passed urging the emperor to be merciful (Lib. *Or.* xx.37; cf. xxii.33). A similar range of weapons, therefore, was available to eastern senators as to their Roman cousins, even if, like its western counterpart, their institution was mainly important as a touchstone of landowning opinion, rather than a political body which initiated policy.

At least in the west, changing circumstances led to some modification of this position from *c.* A.D. 400 onwards. Essentially, barbarian invasion, which really affected the west only after 405/6, and the responses of various imperial regimes combined to create two regional political forums, dominated by the relevant portion of the senatorial landowning élite. As a result, these institutions, if probably more by accident than design, allowed regionally based power blocs to be created, and gave them the institutional means of expressing themselves.

First, the intrusion of different barbarian groups into the empire led to a considerable loss of land and reduction in geographical scope for the

---

[29] Mamertinus, *Pan. Lat.* xi.2–3.1; 14.5–6; 24.5. Themistius: Heather and Matthews (1991) ch. 2; Heather, *Goths and Romans*, esp. 166–73 with refs. to those interpreting Themistius at face value.

senatorial landowning élite. Particularly important here seems to have been the loss of Africa to the Vandals in the 430s, for many Italian senatorial families also seem to have had holdings in Africa, the loss of which drove them back to Italy. Second, the effect of actually losing lands was magnified by the accompanying retreat of senators to safe areas. Rutilius Namatianus is famous for leaving Italy to return to Gaul, but his poem also mentions two Gallic landowners, Victorinus and Protadius, who took the opposite decision, leaving the partly Goth-occupied Gaul after 418 to move back to Italy (*De Red. Suo* 1.493ff., 542ff. respectively). In taking such a decision, these Gauls were matching the retreat of Roman administration in Gaul from its previous centre at Trier on the Rhine to Arles on the Mediterranean, a move taken in direct response to the barbarian invasion of 406. The end result of such manoevres was a 're-concentration' of senatorial families upon their estates in Italy. As a natural corollary, Italian senatorial families came to dominate to an unprecedented extent major offices within the remit of the imperial court which was now established at Ravenna.[30] Thus some of the circumstances which had prevented the Roman senate from acting as an effective political institution in the fourth century were incidentally overcome. Many conflicting interests remained among its members, and it formed no unified bloc against outsiders. None the less, most of its members now held most of their lands in Italy, and this, of course, gave them a much stronger common political interest.

Indeed, as lands were lost from central imperial control in Britain, northern Gaul, Africa and Spain, Italian landowners and their interests began to figure ever higher on the agenda of imperial regimes – that is, as potential rival interests were eliminated. Hence, once the assassination of Valentinian III ended dynastic continuity, Italian senators, such as Petronius Maximus and Libius Severus, once again became candidates for the imperial throne.[31]

At the same time, an institution with a similarly regional focus was emerging in southern Gaul. Some of the factors behind its creation paralleled those at work in Italy. Once the Goths had settled further west on the Atlantic coast around Bordeaux, Mediterranean Gaul, like Italy, became a relatively safe haven, a place of retreat for senatorial families who happened to have extensive holdings in the area. The key development, however, was an imperial initiative to revive the council of the seven Gallic provinces, which was put into action precisely in the years (416–18) that the Goths were being settled in Aquitaine. As many have argued, this can

---

[30] Africa: Matthews, *Western Aristocracies* 357–8. Move from Trier: Chastagnol (1973). Senators and offices: Sundwall (1915) 22; Matthews, *Western Aristocracies* 358–69.

[31] The literature on Italian senators and fifth-century imperial politics is extensive and polemical. See Stein, *Bas Empire* 1.337–8 with the replies of Twyman (1970) and Zecchini (1983) ch. 10. Note now the warning against oversimplification in Weber (1989) esp. 491–7.

hardly have been an accident. The remit of the council was that representatives of governors, city curial classes and *honorati* (by this date, ex-officials of largely senatorial status) should gather annually at Arles. Initially, no doubt, this was designed as a forum through which political consent could be constructed for the settlement of the Goths. In the longer term, however, it became a regional forum through which the Gallic aristocracy could express itself as a regional power bloc. As in Italy, offices in Gaul came to be dominated by Gallic aristocrats, and, like the Roman senate, the council became a real political centre. That, at least, is how it was operating by *c.* 450 when the writings of Sidonius Apollinaris begin. Thus, for instance, having launched his regime among the Goths, the second move of the emperor Avitus was to win the approval of his fellow Gallic landowners at a meeting of the council.

Again, it would be wrong to see the Gallic landowners as a single, united bloc. The revolutionary events of the fifth century produced many alternative and mutually contradictory responses from the Gallic senators of whom the council was composed. The writings of Sidonius, for instance, are full of references to their quarrels and disputes (such as the *coniuratio Marcelliana*, and the cases of Paeonius and Arvandus) as they tried to chart the best course in difficult times. *In extremis*, likewise, Sidonius was willing to sacrifice even the great city of Arles to the Goths so long as his native Clermont could remain part of the now rapidly diminishing Roman empire (*Ep.* 7.7). None the less, the council did provide an institution through which a second section of western senatorial landowning opinion was able to turn itself into a relatively unified pressure group. It was, however, emphatically an imperial institution which achieved this effect, and any idea that the council was a home for Gallic separatism is entirely misplaced. There is not the slightest evidence that senatorial landowners positively wanted to switch their political allegiance to incoming barbarian kings or to establish any kind of Gallic empire; political accommodations were made with the new powers in the later fifth century because the landowners had no choice.[32]

A delicate balance must thus be struck in any account of the involvement of senators in imperial politics. The senates of Rome and Constantinople had no important formal powers, and, as the fourth century progressed, their members were increasingly of diverse backgrounds, interests and opinions. As a result, emperors could for the most part deal with senators as important and potentially useful individuals, and no more. Just occasionally, particular issues or problems could unite

---

[32] Council: Matthews, *Western Aristocracies* 334–8. Office-holding: Sundwall (1915) 8–9, 21–22; cf. Matthews, *Western Aristocracies* 333–4, 346–8. A good introduction to the operation of upper-class politics, and the options facing the senatorial landowning élite, is now provided by Drinkwater and Elton (1992) esp. essays by Heather, Roberts, Harries, and Teitler. Arvandus and Paeonius: refs. as *PLRE* II.157–8, 817 respectively.

enough of them to create a real political power bloc composed of an important cross-section of the empire's richest men. And although even in these circumstances the senate could not have stood up to the emperor and his troops in open conflict, they were too important as taxpayers and as a force for order and the smooth extraction of revenue in the localities (on which see p. 208 below) to be ignored. Good political management, from an emperor's point of view, thus lay in making sure that such a consensus was not generated, in which case the Roman and Constantinopolitan senates could remain only passive political entities. As far as we can tell, this remained true of the senate of Constantinople into the fifth century. The sources for the internal politics of the eastern empire after 400 are pitiful, but there is no evidence that the senate as a unit was involved in any way in the construction of regimes. In the west, however, the loss of geographical diversity, as barbarian invasions reduced the empire to a more concentrated rump, combined with the side-effects of reviving the council of the seven provinces to create two more-consolidated regional power blocs of senatorial opinion. Anachronism must be avoided: these were not parliaments; they did, however, lead to a stronger senatorial influence on policymaking and on the construction of regimes.

IV. SENATORS AND LOCAL POLITICS

The institutional changes of the fourth century which greatly increased senatorial numbers also had a revolutionary effect upon local government, because, as we have seen, most of the new recruits to the senatorial order came from the curial landowning élite who had traditionally run the cities. Moreover, the three thousand plus jobs per generation in each half of the empire leading to senatorial status were only one way in which new 'imperial' careers impinged upon this élite. As Table 2 shows, there were at least another seventeen and a half thousand other new governmental jobs available empire-wide in the bureaux of praetorian prefects, vicars and provincial governors (known collectively as *cohortales*), which, under the early empire, had been filled by soldiers on secondment. At least some of these jobs were attractive to curials, perhaps the slightly less wealthy. Even so, one *cohortalis* was wealthy enough to commission an inscription honouring a governor of Caria in fifth-century Aphrodisias. Likewise, *cohortales* were a major source of recruitment for the legal profession, implying that their families were wealthy enough to afford the training involved (several extra years on top of a basic literary education), all of which is consonant with Egyptian evidence of *cohortales* as substantial landowners.[33] A full

[33] Roueché, *Aphrodisias* 73–5. To the list, we must add governor's legal advisers (*assessores*), smaller state bureaux, such as the *scrinium dispositionum*, and the legal profession, which again numbered several thousand; see further Heather (1994b) 21 with refs.

Table 2. *The Provincial Administration in c. A.D. 400*

(a) Praetorian Prefects' Staffs:	$3/4 \times 1000$ officers $= 4000$[1]
(b) Urban Prefects and Vicars' Staffs:	$12 \times$ c. 300 officers $= 3600$[2]
(c) Provincial Governors' Staffs:	$104 \times$ c. 100 officers $= 10,000$[3]

[1] Jones, *LRE* 586–92.
[2] Jones, *LRE* 592–3: numbers varied; the vicar of the Orient had a staff of 600, the vicar of Asia only 200.
[3] Jones, *LRE* 593–6.

catalogue of the new 'imperial' jobs attractive to curials can perhaps be put, therefore, as high as ten thousand per generation in each half of the empire.

The attraction of these jobs was increased by the fact that, at the same time, the central imperial authorities unleashed a severe crackdown upon the financial independence of the cities. From the mid third century onwards, the imperial government both levied higher rates of taxation upon the cities, and confiscated the bulk of their traditional revenues: income from local tolls and taxes (*vectigalia*) and the income derived from the cities' extensive holdings of public land. The quieter waters of the fourth century saw some relaxation, with Valentinian and Valens, following a trend established by Constantius II, returning up to one-third of these revenues, but much of the money which had previously provided the point of local political quarrels was now controlled from the centre. In migrating to 'imperial' careers, the curials were merely following the money, but this migration created a major structural problem within imperial administration. Senatorial (and even top equestrian) status, gained by imperial service, brought the holder immunity from curial duties, so that the pool of wealth available locally to fulfil governmental tasks shrank as the fourth century wore on.

In traditional historiography, these related phenomena are usually encountered as the 'decline of the curial classes' and considered an important factor contributing to imperial collapse, since the major motive ascribed to the curials who moved on is that they wanted to opt out of participation in the political life of the empire. Once it is realized, however, that they were responding to financial restructuring in the balance of power between central and local government by opting in in a different way, it becomes much less obvious that the overall effect was so negative. As the mass of imperial legislation trying to evict curials shows, imperial initiatives to expand the bureaucracy gained unexpected momentum from the response of local élites, who energetically seized the chance to graze in lush new meadows. The so-called 'decline of the curials' is as much a story of local élites coming to participate more fully in imperial structures, and hence a sign of success. Two further considerations help to sustain a less negative view of these phenomena.[34]

First, the evolving sequence of imperial legislation – attempting to close one loophole after the other – eventually seems to have achieved a compromise which dealt with the structural problem posed to local government. In the earlier part of the fourth century, emperors simply tried to ban curials from bureaucratic service and advancement to the senate. From the time of Valentinian and Valens, however, more of a compromise was adopted, whereby curials were allowed to advance, but only if they had already fulfilled their curial obligations, and in the case of senators, whose status was hereditary, left a son to fulfil them again in the next generation. By the mid fifth century, this had developed into a pattern whereby immunity from curial service was now allowed only to senators of the top grade (*illustres*), who tended anyway to be career bureaucrats (see p. 190 above). Others could obtain the lesser ranks, and even become honorary *illustres*, but did not lose their curial obligations.[35]

Second, it is far from clear that the main attraction of senatorial status was the negative one of escaping local service. Some of the new senators moved to the imperial capitals of east and west; many, however, had acquired their status either via honorary grants, which required no actual service at the centre, or via a year or so's tenure of a *dignitas*, which was again hardly a major commitment to life away from their locality. Likewise, as we have seen, the length of service required even in the palatine ministries tended to decrease over the century, and there are also references in the codes to government servants with extensive leaves of absence. These indications make it clear that a new 'imperial' career should not be seen as a complete alternative to the traditional pattern, where the majority of life had been spent in the locality where inherited familial estates lay. As we have seen, by 383 the imperial government was ready to acknowledge that many senators would be resident in the provinces rather than in Rome or Constantinople, and, indeed, made a virtue of necessity by giving a hugely important role to high-status former government servants – the so-called *honorati* – who had returned to the provinces (or never left them). The range of positive benefits enjoyed by these men, together with the roles in which they were employed, makes it clear that they had, by A.D. 400, become the new leaders of local society.

Honorati seem to have benefited, for instance, from deliberately low tax assessments on their holdings, and probably also enjoyed favourable commutation rates, when taxes in kind were to be converted into cash. Other aspects of the system also favoured them. Exemptions from extra-

---

[34] Constantius II: *C.Th.* IV.13.5; Valentinian and Valens: *C.Th.* IV.13.7. Attempts to evict: *C.Th.* XII.1. For a traditional commentary, see, e.g., Jones, *LRE* 732–4, 757–63. For an alternative view in more detail, Heather (1994b) 22ff., drawing on Roueché, *Aphrodisias* xxiv, 1–4; Crawford (1975); Durliat (1990) 14–30.   [35] Jones, *LRE* 528–9, 741–3 with refs.

ordinary taxes and *munera sordida* were granted such men, and the regular remissions of unpaid tax may also have worked to their advantage, since they in particular had sufficient influence to delay payment.[36]

More generally, their high status made *honorati* dominant in local society; they come above curials, for instance, in a ceremonial list from Numidia of the 360s detailing the order in which different groups were ceremonially to greet the governor every morning. That such matters were so carefully regulated is clear testimony to their practical importance. *Honorati* stood in a much stronger position, for instance, than other members of local society when it came to dealing with representatives of the imperial authorities, and must often have been of similar or higher status to the governors sent out to rule them. At least as important, however, was the relatively free access to the governor which high status gave these men, allowing them much greater opportunity to influence gubernatorial decision-making. The importance of this is signalled very clearly by a law of the emperor Gratian forbidding informal afternoon visits to governors (*C.Th.* 1.16.3: A.D. 377); these were notoriously the moments for underhand deals. All kinds of benefits flowed from access to the governor's ear. Libanius and all the Cappadocian fathers, for instance, considered it quite normal to write to governors in an attempt to influence their decisions in legal cases. *Honorati* even sat on the bench beside the governor during trials, acting as legal assessors. Similarly, a striking feature of fourth-century government was the new life breathed into annual provincial councils, which were very much precursors of the Gallic council, where central government met local government. At these meetings, the presence of *honorati* was demanded. Having to attend was no doubt a chore, but these councils were important social and political occasions where local opinion was tested and many a favour swapped. Much informal influence over local politics could flow from regular attendance.[37]

Their status thus afforded these men important powers of local patronage; informally, their privileged access to governors and the annual provincial councils naturally meant that they would be courted by their more modest fellow citizens.[38] This standing was also reflected in, and extended

---

[36] Tax assessments: *C.Th.* XI.20.6, reducing but not cancelling these benefits; cf. Jones, *LRE* 466. Delayed payments: Jones, *LRE* 466–7; cf. Basil *Ep.* 88. Gratian defined *munera sordida* as grinding corn and baking bread for troops, furnishing animals for the post and hospitality for officials, helping to pay for delegations to the emperor and for building and maintaining public works: Jones, *LRE* 452.

[37] Order of precedence: *FIRA* 1/2.64. *Honorati* and governors: Jones, *LRE* 502–3; cf. 490–1, on legislation (esp. *C.Th.* IX.1.13) which envisages that provincial governors might need assistance in dealing with senators. Legal matters: Jones, *LRE* 503–4; cf., e.g., Libanius *Epp.* 56, 105, 110, 1168–9, 1237–8, 1249, 1398; Basil *Epp.* 107, 109, 177–90; Greg. Nyss. *Ep.* 7; Greg. Naz. *Epp.* 22–4, 105, 146–8. Despite himself writing such letters, Libanius complains about whisperings in governors' ears during trials: *Or.* LII.4ff. Councils: Jones, *LRE* 763–6.

[38] Libanius wrote numerous letters to great men to procure favours for others: Liebeschuetz, *Antioch* 17–18. Though ecclesiastical rather than secular *honorati*, the Cappadocians worked in similar ways, esp. in letters to governors: Basil *Epp.* 3, 63, 84, 86, 137, 186–7; Greg. Naz. *Epp.* 10, 104–6, 125–6, 131, 140–1, 147, 154–6, 195, 198, 207.

by, some of the formal duties put upon them by central government. Amongst other things, *honorati* were responsible for conducting audits of their local curias, and, probably most important of all, for tax equalizations, when tax assessments were adjusted. The *de facto* power generated by the ability to influence one's neighbour's tax assessment can hardly be overstated. As Basil of Caesarea put it, control of the tax census gave a man the opportunity to benefit his friends, harm his enemies and generally make a lot of money (*Ep.* 299).[39]

The new political order thus offered considerable opportunities to those who could obtain imperial preferment. Apart from opening up a whole new world at court for those who wanted to operate in central politics, it also changed the rules by which local society operated, so that high imperial rank had considerable advantages even for those who just wanted to stay at home. And in practice, these two groups of new senators shaded into one. The right job meant that even a brief period of office-holding could be used to cement local standing. Out of eleven governors recorded as building in the city of Aphrodisias in late antiquity, five were local men and the father of a sixth had originated in the city; there is thus every reason to think that men often governed their own homelands.[40] Some of these men may well have been committed imperial careerists, but there must have been considerable ambiguity over whether others were serving central government in the localities, or using governmental office to enlarge their own local standing. Likewise, other aristocrats might have wished for a career at court, but returned to more local society when those ambitions were frustrated; the advantages obtained could be used interchangeably at either level.

The exploitation of ties between aristocrats in imperial government and aristocrats at home was also part of the system. The Cappadocian fathers exploited tame great men at court for help with a whole range of local issues – everything from alleviating the more unpleasant consequences of the subdivision of their province to adjusting tax assessments and validating wills. Gregory of Nazianzus, in particular, used his few years in Constantinople to build up a range of contacts which were assiduously maintained upon his return to Cappadocia.[41] Top equestrian or senatorial rank thus enabled great men either to find their way at court, or to play the game of local politics more effectively, or both. Salvian effectively, if nega-

---

[39] The Cappadocians correspondingly address many requests for favours to tax officials: Basil *Epp.* 83, 99, 104, 110, 142, 299, 309, 312–13; Greg. Naz. *Epp.* 67–9, 98, 211 (cf. 209–10).

[40] Roueché, *Aphrodisias* nos. 7, 24, 32, 38–40, 53–4, 55–8, 66 (a man honouring Aphrodisias as his father's homeland); cf. Basil *Epp.* 78 (cf. 63–4), 96, 137.

[41] Basil's main court contacts were natives of Caesarea: Sophronius *Mag. Off.* & *P.V.C.* (*Epp.* 32, 75, 96, 177, 192, 273) and Aburgius *P.P.O. Or.* (*Epp.* 33, 75, 147, 178, 196). Gregory of Nazianzus' wider range: e.g. *Epp.* 93–7 (shortly after his return to Cappadocia to friends in Constantinople), 128–30, 132–4, 136–7, 168–70. Basil *Ep.* 107 is good on the tact that had to be used when pestering great men.

tively, sums the matter up: 'an [imperial] office once held gives the privilege of a perpetual right of rapine' (*Gub. Dei* VII.92). A spell in imperial service had thus become part of establishing and extending a local political profile, and senators (originally top-grade equestrians and senators) were now the dominant force in the localities.

V. CONCLUSION

The essential problem in writing about senates and senators in the late imperial period should be clear. Many ancient senatorial traditions survived, and, particularly in the writings of Symmachus, receive rather full coverage in our sources. The emergence of a bureaucracy whose leading members were all rewarded with senatorial status by the end of the fourth century, however, meant that, in numerical terms at least, the traditional senatorial élite had been swamped by *arrivistes*. It is thus in the rise of the senatorial bureaucrat and the adaptation of the old aristocracy to new conditions that the real story of the fourth century lies. Likewise, the senates of Rome and Constantinople played no single, fixed institutional role. The extent to which their members, or some fraction of them, could act together as a political force – if at all – varied according to outside circumstance and the issues involved. Only rarely did senators use either senate as an active political forum, and it was only the very particular circumstances of the fifth century which breathed new life into senatorially dominated institutions.

More clearly in focus, if equally subject to infinite variation, depending on particular circumstance, is the role of the senator in localities across the empire. Here the decline of the curial classes consequent upon the shift of financial and political power towards the imperial centre, made curials-turned-senators into dominant figures within local society. It was now *de rigeur* for the local aristocrat to participate at least to some extent in imperial power structures.

To put these developments into broader perspective, we might consider the size of the Roman empire. In a world without telephones, telexes and faxes, much power had of necessity to be devolved to the localities. The main political problem, therefore, was how to manage devolution without generating fragmentation – political fragmentation, of course, having bedevilled the empire in the third century. The expansion of the senatorial order, and the new roles given its members, directly addressed this problem by giving dominant local landed élites everything to gain from the continued existence of the empire and their own participation in it. This extension of central state structures certainly impinged upon the autonomy of cities, but did so in ways which fostered political unity. Moreover, no form of social organization is ever perfect. There was plenty of scope for corruption in the new order, which handed enormous powers of local patronage to large landowners willing to invest in the imperial system. But corruption in the form of unfair competition is of the essence of all closed oligarchies, and this is what the old city curias had also been. The creation of new patronage networks, which tied local landowning élites more closely to the imperial centre, thus marks, contrary to more traditional views, no obvious decline in the socio-political organization of the later Roman empire.

CHAPTER 7

THE ARMY

A. D. LEE

The army was an institution of central importance throughout Roman imperial history. Its military effectiveness was obviously critical to the security of
the empire, but as the empire's largest employer and the biggest single item
on the imperial budget, it was also an organization whose impact on the
economy was wide-ranging, while the ever-present danger of its being turned
against a reigning emperor gave it a political dimension as well. In the late
Roman period, all these issues assumed heightened significance. The more
precarious strategic circumstances of the empire consequent upon the rise
of Sasanian Persia to the east and the emergence of the Frankish, Alamannic
and Gothic confederacies in the north meant that the army's military role was
even more vital. Whatever the precise magnitude of the increase, the
enlarged size of the fourth-century army had serious ramifications for the
empire's manpower and economic resources. And the alarming frequency of
military revolts during the mid third century must have left fourth-century
emperors even more conscious of their vulnerability from this direction.

Two sources, very different in character, are especially valuable for late
Roman military matters and deserve individual comment at the outset. The
administrative document known as the *Notitia Dignitatum* enables us to see
something of the formal organization of the empire's military forces – the
army on paper, as it were – while the *History* of Ammianus Marcellinus
allows us to observe the army in action, not only in its specifically military
capacity, but also in its wider political and social context.

The *Notitia* was a register kept by the senior notary (*primicerius notariorum*)
in which were listed the senior civil and military offices of the empire,
together with details of those under their authority. In the case of the military offices, this included not only immediate staff but also, very importantly, the names of the regiments under their command. Uncertainty
remains about the purpose of this register, but given that the *primicerius'*
duties included issuing commissions and keeping track of the size and disposition of army units, it was appropriate that he should be the official to
maintain it.[1] Since, from time to time, army units were relocated and

---

[1] Purpose: Mann and Hassall in Goodburn and Bartholomew (1976); *primicerius'* duties: Claudian,
Carmina minora xxv.82–91; Seeck (1924) 904; Clemente (1968) 361–3.

spheres of administrative responsibility were redefined, it was a document
subject to periodic revision, creating scope for the introduction of errors
over the years. For example, it still lists as being on active service certain
units known to have been destroyed in battle.[2] The fact that entries were
revised at different times makes dating the *Notitia* problematic. In its surviving form, it comprises two parts, one for the eastern half of the empire,
the other for the western, which implies a date after the division of the
empire between Theodosius' two sons in 395. However, since the eastern
portion contains virtually nothing datable after 395, the lists in this part
must largely reflect the situation prior to Theodosius' death, whereas
updating of the western portion continued, albeit inconsistently, into the
420s.[3]

The surviving (latter) half of Ammianus' *History* presents a narrative of
the empire's history between 353 and 378 in the classicizing mode – that is
to say, it sought to emulate classical models such as Tacitus in both subject
matter and style of presentation. Among other things, this meant a focus
on war, and since Ammianus had served as an officer in the army during
the 350s and 360s he had the practical experience to write authoritatively
about such matters, often from personal involvement in particular episodes. As a result his history is characterized by an attention to detail which,
combined with his generally even-handed assessment of individuals and
events, makes it an invaluable source for this subject.[4] He is, for example,
almost the only fourth-century writer who takes the trouble to include the
actual names of regiments,[5] and he offers detailed accounts of the army in
action, whether it be his descriptions of battle with the Alamanni at
Strasbourg in 357, of Roman forces under siege in the fortress of Amida
in 359, or of the army on campaign in Persia in 363. At the same time, he
shows a surprising readiness to offer comment critical of the military.[6] This
is not to say, however, that his work is without its difficulties. It is apparent,
for example, that loyalty to his general Ursicinus could sometimes result in
his misunderstanding imperial decisions,[7] while the literary canons to
which he adhered mean that his battle descriptions contain a certain
amount of rhetorical embellishment and that he generally avoids the use of
technical terminology, which would have been regarded as inappropriate in
a work with literary pretensions. These limitations must be kept in mind,
but they ought not to be allowed to obscure the fundamental value of

---

[2] Tomlin (1972) 255. Other anomalies: Jones, *LRE* 1420–1, 1426; Clemente (1968) 28–56; Grigg
(1983).

[3] Discussions of dating: Jones, *LRE* Appendix 11; Clemente (1968); Hoffmann, *Bewegungsheer*, chs.
1–3, 10; Mann (1991).

[4] For general appreciations, see Crump (1975); Austin (1979); Matthews, *Ammianus*, esp. ch. 13.

[5] 'As a retired officer, he may have respected their *esprit de corps*': Tomlin (1972) 255, with a complete
list of the units named in Appendix i.   [6] Demandt (1965) 28–44.

[7] Thompson (1947) ch. 3; Matthews (1986) 553–6.

Ammianus' history for understanding the Roman army of the mid fourth century.

I. ORGANIZATION AND DEPLOYMENT

The army inherited by the sons of Constantine was an institution which bore strongly the imprint of their father. But while Constantine himself was undoubtedly responsible for many of those organizational features which distinguished the army of the early fourth century from its second-century counterpart, he was in a number of respects also building on the initiatives of his predecessors, both immediate and more distant, even if the inadequacies of the surviving evidence from the third century make it difficult to discern little more than the bare outline of some developments. One of the most fundamental of these was the emergence of a two-tier system of organization whereby selected regiments formed a central field army, distinct from the remaining units stationed in the provinces. Certainly, the name by which field army troops of the fourth century were known – *comitatenses* – is first attested during Constantine's reign,[8] but the basic idea of the emperor retaining a significant body of troops for deployment wherever crises might require them can be seen to have precedents in the military arrangements of Gallienus in the 260s and, going back even further, in the dispositions of Septimius Severus.[9] Constantine's contribution was not to conceive the idea of a central field army as such, but rather, during the course of his campaigns against Maxentius and Licinius, to expand it significantly in size compared with the relatively modest forces retained by Gallienus and subsequent emperors, to create the new ranks of *magister peditum* and *magister equitum* (master of the infantry and of the cavalry) as field army commanders,[10] and to enhance the status of these élite troops with various privileges.[11]

This is not to underestimate the importance of these changes. They did represent a fundamental shift of emphasis away from the policy of Diocletian who, while maintaining a small field army, had sought to guarantee the empire's security by concentrating on reinforcement of the frontiers with both men and fortifications.[12] At the same time, Constantine's changes do not warrant Zosimus' polemical gibe that he removed *most* of the troops from the frontiers and left the empire fatally exposed to attack.[13] In order to expand his field army, Constantine naturally withdrew some units from the provinces, but many of the regiments which comprised his

---

[8] *C.Th.* VII.20.4 (325).   [9] Birley (1969).   [10] Demandt (1970) 560ff.
[11] As set out in *C.Th.* VII.20.4 (325).
[12] Mann (1979) 180–1. Further discussion and references to archaeological and epigraphic evidence of Diocletianic fortifications: Johnson (1983) 252–5 (Rhine to middle Danube), Isaac, *Limits of Empire* 163–71 (east).   [13] Zos. II.34.2.

comitatenses were new creations. Moreover, Constantine still acknowledged the value of the troops stationed in frontier regions – the *ripenses*, known later in the century as the *limitanei*, whose role was to remain vital – and he too was vigorous in the construction of military installations in frontier regions.[14] Indeed, Constantine completed a reform begun by Diocletian of direct relevance to local provincial troops – the separation of civil and military responsibilities and the creation of the office of *dux* with command over the military units in the frontier region of a province or group of provinces.[15]

Another distinctive feature of the army by the early fourth century was the proliferation of units and unit-types. The legions and *auxilia* of the principate were now only two out of a wider array of unit-types. The *comitatenses* comprised three types of regiment: cavalry squadrons (*vexillationes*) of perhaps 500 men, recruited predominantly from non-Roman peoples; infantry *legiones* of probably 1000 men, mostly drawn from inhabitants of the empire – some of these units were direct descendants of the legions of old; and a new type of infantry unit (500–800 men?) known as *auxilia*: they were first recruited by Maximian from Germanic peoples beyond the Rhine, and Constantine then increased their number and made them the backbone of his field army.[16] Troops stationed in the frontier regions included a more diverse mix of unit-types, comprising old-style legions, and *alae* and cohorts of the traditional *auxilia*, together with cavalry units of more recent origin designated *cunei* or simply *equites*. The early fourth century also saw the creation (possibly by Diocletian) of the *scholae*, a new imperial bodyguard which soon filled the role of the old Praetorian Guard once the latter body had been disbanded by Constantine. Although not formally a part of the field army – they came under the authority of a civilian official, the *magister officiorum* – they were nevertheless high-quality troops who, by virtue of having to be wherever the emperor was, took an active role in campaigning during the fourth century.[17]

Although considerable uncertainty surrounds the precise numerical size of all these units, it is clear both from literary sources and from the archaeological evidence of fort-sizes that units in the Constantinian army were significantly smaller in size than the traditional legion.[18] This development was part of a longer-term trend towards specialization of function or armament which can be seen occurring during the third century and which is reflected in the profusion of units bearing names such as *lanciarii*, *ballis-*

[14] Value of *ripenses*: *C.Th.* VII.20.4 (325) (the term *limitanei* is first attested in *C.Th.* XII.1.56 (363)). Archaeological and epigraphic evidence of Constantine's construction activities: Johnson (1983) 254–7 (Rhine to middle Danube); Brennan (1980) (lower Danube).   [15] Mann (1977) 12.

[16] Hoffmann, *Bewegungsheer*, ch. 6.

[17] Jones, *LRE* 613–14; Frank (1969); Hoffmann, *Bewegungsheer* I.279–303.

[18] For a useful tabulation of some of the archaeological data, see Duncan-Jones, *Structure and Scale* Appendix 4 (214–17).

tarii, clibanarii, cetrati and *funditores*.[19] Another consideration which encouraged the fragmentation of larger blocks of troops into smaller groupings lay in the area of logistical expenditure: 'in the scattering-about of soldiers in small clusters . . . there lay substantial savings in cost: for their distribution thereby conformed better with existing patterns of production and distribution'.[20]

The main theme in the organizational evolution of the field army after Constantine's death is regionalization. In the course of the final decade of his reign he gave regional responsibilities and the title of Caesar to his three sons and his nephew Dalmatius, which meant the creation of multiple field armies.[21] The murder of Dalmatius after Constantine's death, followed closely by the death of Constantine II in 340, soon reduced the number of successors to two, but it seems that even within their field armies there was already movement towards regionalization: Constantius II appears to have kept part of his field army in Syria and part in Thrace, while Constans divided his between Gaul and Illyricum. After Constantius became sole ruler in the early 350s, multiplicity remained the rule, which is hardly surprising given the size of the empire and the technological limitations on moving large bodies of men about quickly. In addition to the forces which always accompanied the emperor himself, substantial armies had to be kept in Syria and Gaul to cover the Persian frontier and the Rhine, with smaller ones in Thrace and Illyricum for the Danube; the latter two were commanded by officers titled *comes rei militaris*, a lesser rank than that of *magister*.[22]

The *Notitia* allows us to see how the field armies continued to evolve down to the end of the century. Although different patterns emerged in east and west, the overall trend in both was towards a larger number of smaller armies. A distinction developed among these forces between the so-called 'praesental' armies serving 'in the emperor's presence', and the remaining regional armies. The praesental armies acquired greater prestige by virtue of their proximity to the emperor, and regiments in them gained the epithet 'palatine' (from the Latin for 'palace') – a term first attested in a law of 365[23] – to distinguish them from the ordinary *comitatenses* of the regional field armies. Field army *auxilia* are found only in the praesental armies, emphasizing their élite status.[24]

The *Notitia* shows that by the end of the century there were five field armies in the eastern half of the empire, each under the command of a

---

[19] Brennan (1980) 553–4, with much fuller discussion in Brennan (1972).
[20] MacMullen (1984) 575; cf. Carrié, 'Esercito' 467. [21] Barnes, *CE* 250 3.
[22] Jones, *LRE* 124–5. [23] *C.Th.* VIII.1.10.
[24] Hoffmann, *Bewegungsheer* I.396–404. The *Notitia* listings obscure this distinction somewhat because of subsequent cross-postings of regiments between praesental and regional armies. Strictly speaking, the designation *comitatenses* for regional field armies is now anomalous since regiments in this category no longer 'accompanied' the emperor himself.

magister militum: they comprised two praesental armies based near Constantinople, and three regional armies of the East, Thrace and Illyricum.[25] For the western half of the empire, the *Notitia* reveals a rather different picture. On the one hand, the command structure is much more centralized, while on the other, there is a larger number of smaller regional armies. Thus there is one *magister peditum praesentalis* in overall command; the largest of the regional armies, in Gaul, was under a *magister equitum*, but the *Notitia* makes it clear that he was subordinate to the *magister praesentalis*, while the other armies, in Africa, Tingitania, Spain, Britain and Illyricum, were commanded by *comites*, also under the *magister praesentalis*.[26] It has been suggested that this arrangement, almost certainly the work of Stilicho, was a formalization of the measures forced on Julian and Valentinian in the 360s, when crises in Britain, for example, required the temporary despatch of detachments from the Gallic field army: 'given the scattered nature of the western provinces, particularly with long stretches of sea between the different areas, a larger number of small field armies was far more useful'.[27] Thus by the end of the century, in both east and west, the exigencies of space and time had resulted in the field armies being deployed in patterns which effectively represented a significant reformulation, if not a partial abandonment, of the original Constantinian model.

It is much less easy to trace developments in the deployment of what were to become the *limitanei* of the later fourth century, in spite of the fact that those chapters of the *Notitia* which list units of *limitanei* under their relevant *dux* also specify a geographical base for each unit. In the first place, it is not always possible to identify every ancient place name, while in the second, the *Notitia* does not reproduce the situation at one particular point in time. The *Notitia*'s distribution of troops for Britain and a number of the Danubian provinces, for example, still seems largely to represent Diocletianic arrangements which underwent little change during the fourth century, whereas that for the Gallic provinces reflects the turmoil of the early fifth century.[28] Various observations about the main frontier regions can nevertheless be made, proceeding clockwise from the north-west.

In northern Britain, where the Romans had to deal with the Picts, units were deployed along the Wall, but also in considerable numbers throughout the hinterland to the south, a distribution which has been seen as a classic example of 'defence-in-depth' in operation.[29] There is, however, a simpler explanation for this pattern: because of the large number of units relative to the shortness of the frontier, it was not feasible to post them all immediately adjacent to the frontier, and so some simply had to be placed to the rear.[30] Britain was also the location of the only major 'coastal fron-

---

[25] *Not. Dig. Or.* v–ix.　　[26] *Not. Dig. Occ.* v–vii.　　[27] Mann (1977) 14; cf. Mann (1979) 181–3.
[28] Jones, *LRE* 58, 610.　　[29] Jones (1979) 67.　　[30] Mann (1979) 180.

tier' in the empire, the so-called 'Saxon shore', whose series of forts along the Channel and lower North Sea coasts seems to have been intended to counter the threat of seaborne Saxon and Frankish raiders.[31]

Although the *Notitia* listings for the Rhine frontier are clearly incomplete, with a mere fifteen units between the three *duces* of Belgica, Moguntiacum and Sequanica – many limitanean units have been transferred into the western field armies as part of the response to the crisis of the early fifth century – it is likely that most *limitanei* were deployed adjacent to the Rhine during the fourth century. This is the implication of their earlier title of *ripenses*, and was certainly the pattern along the Danube frontier,[32] as well as being consistent with the numerous fourth-century military installations excavated along the Rhine, as along the Danube.[33] In this context it is worth drawing attention to the fact that by no means all of the military structures along the Rhine and Danube were narrowly defensive in purpose: a significant number of forts and fortified landing-places have been found on the opposite banks of both rivers,[34] at least part of whose purpose was to facilitate the launching of attacks against the Franks, Alamanni, Goths or other barbarian peoples. Ammianus describes a considerable number of such expeditions undertaken by Constantius II, Julian, Valentinian and Valens during the mid fourth century.[35] As his accounts make clear, however, a major weakness in such a strategy of forward defence was the difficulty of cornering the enemy and making them stand and fight: more often than not, they melted away into the forests and mountains, leaving the Romans to inflict what damage they could on their settlements and fields.

The deployment of Roman forces *vis-à-vis* Persia stands in sharp contrast to the essentially linear pattern along the Rhine–Danube frontiers. The *limitanei* of northern Mesopotamia were not stationed along a chain of forts and watch-towers, which would have posed few problems for the more sophisticated Persian army, but rather in a defensive network based on strongly fortified cities and towns such as Nisibis, Amida and Singara, whose effectiveness in preventing or at least hampering a speedy Persian advance into Syria was proved on a number of occasions during the mid fourth century.[36] To the south, the troops posted along the *Strata*

[31] Mann (1989). For late Roman naval forces more generally, see Demandt, *Spätantike* 260–1 with further references.

[32] See Wilkes (1989) 349–52; Mócsy (1962) 647–53; Fitz (1976); Aricescu (1980) ch. 3.

[33] See Johnson (1983) chs. 6–7 for a convenient summary of the evidence.

[34] Schönberger (1969) 180 (Deutz), 185 (Mannheim Neckerau, Engers), 186 (Whylen); Johnson (1983) 141 (Fig. 54), 255, 259; Mócsy (1974) 369–70. For late Roman structures deeper in *barbaricum*, about whose purpose(s) there is considerable uncertainty, see Pitts (1987); Lee (1993) 179–82.

[35] E.g. Amm. Marc. XVII.12, XVIII.2; XXVII.5, 10, XXIX.4, XXX.5 (cf. Brennan (1980) for Diocletian and Constantine). The troops involved in such expeditions will, of course, mainly have been *comitatenses* rather than *limitanei*. [36] Frézouls (1979) 209; Dillemann (1969) 212, 224.

Diocletiana, the fortified road stretching south-west from the Euphrates towards Damascus, were once again deployed in a linear configuration. The question here, however, and further south, concerns their purpose. The long-held assumption that it was to counter large-scale attacks by nomadic Arabs issuing from the Syrian desert has been challenged in recent years and the reality of the 'nomadic menace' called into question. A strong case has been made instead for seeing the function of these troops and associated installations in terms of the protection of travellers against small-scale Arab raids and brigandage.[37] In the adjacent region of Palestine, a number of units of *limitanei* are found deployed well away from the *Via Nova Traiana* and the eastern frontier, suggesting that their primary role was the maintenance of order in an area with a long history of resistance to Roman rule, whose terrain was also conducive to banditry.[38] Concerns about internal security would also appear to have been a factor in the distribution of units in Egypt, and similar considerations can be seen influencing the deployment of troops in North African Mauretania, where the main enemy was not some external threat from the south but rather the unruly tribesmen of the hills and mountains within the province.[39] It would be natural to place in this category the two regiments devoted to containing the endemic banditry of Isauria in south-eastern Anatolia, but it is unclear whether these troops should be classified as *limitanei*: certainly, they were under the command of the *dux Isauriae*, but the chapter heading in the *Notitia*[40] refers to the *comes per Isauriam*, and the units are not allocated the geographical bases which elsewhere in the *Notitia* are the distinctive mark of limitanean status.[41] Whatever the answer to this particular question, the cases of Palestine, Mauretania and Isauria are useful reminders that the army in its military role was not always directed against external enemies.

A final broader issue deserving comment in this context is whether it is realistic to think in terms of late Roman emperors co-ordinating the more general deployment of the empire's armed forces according to any sort of 'grand strategy', or whether it was rather a case of *ad hoc* responses to immediate problems – an issue of wider relevance, obviously, than the fourth century alone.[42] The idea of emperors being able to formulate strategy on an empire-wide scale has come in for sharp criticism, on the grounds that the prerequisites for the formulation of coherent policy at such a level – for example, accurate geographical knowledge, reliable sources of intelligence, even recognition of the very need for rational

---

[37] Graf (1989); Isaac, *Limits of Empire* ch. 4; for a response to these views, see Parker (1992).
[38] Isaac, *Limits of Empire* 208ff. Note particularly that the Samaritans revolted a number of times during late antiquity.   [39] Bagnall, *Egypt* 174–5; Matthews in Goodburn and Bartholomew (1976).
[40] *Not. Dig. Or.* XXIX.18.   [41] Cf. Mann (1977) 15 n. 18.
[42] Luttwak, *Grand Strategy*, in fact ends with Constantine.

decision-making – were limited, if not lacking, in the Roman context.[43] Observations of this sort are salutary reminders of the dangers of transposing modern concepts and assumptions into the ancient context, but there is a risk of carrying the critique too far. There are, for example, grounds for thinking that emperors in the late Roman period had access to more in the way of information and intelligence than has generally been recognized, especially concerning Persia and the eastern frontier.[44] And although the development of smaller field armies in the west can be seen as in one sense a response to various crises during the 360s, on the other hand the final pattern revealed by the *Notitia* at the end of the century is almost certainly the work of one man, albeit the commander-in-chief rather than the emperor himself.[45] While the notion of grand strategy on an empire-wide scale may therefore readily be abandoned, it is less certain that the same can be said for planning and strategy at the regional level. A more balanced and differentiated approach may be the way forward on this important question.

II. RESOURCES AND MANPOWER

The size of the empire's armed forces during this period is a matter of relevance not only to the army's ability to deal with foreign invaders, but also to its impact on the empire's economy, and as such requires careful consideration. Two sixth-century authors, John Lydus and Agathias, provide totals of 389,704 and 645,000 respectively. Although often taken as referring to the fourth century, the second figure is given only a very vague context by Agathias ('under the earlier emperors') and so is not in fact of much help, but the first is ascribed to the reign of Diocletian, and its very precision has made it more believable. Nevertheless, questions can be asked about the accuracy of the records John may have consulted – the problem of 'paper' strengths as against actual numbers – and of the subsequent transmission of his figure in the manuscript tradition.[46] There is also the possibility that, while accurate for Diocletian's reign, army numbers may have risen over the course of the fourth century. Another approach has been to make a calculation on the basis of the number of units listed in the *Notitia* and their estimated sizes. In principle, this has a greater claim to credibility, but different attempts over the years have produced quite a diversity of figures, ranging from around 500,000 to more than 700,000.[47] This diversity, the result of differences of opinion about the dating of the *Notitia* and about unit sizes, does not inspire confidence. Moreover, even

---

[43] Millar (1982); Isaac, *Limits of Europe* ch. 9. For a detailed response to these critiques, see Wheeler (1993).   [44] Lee (1993).   [45] Mann (1977) 14.

[46] John Lydus *De Mens*. 1.27, Agathias v.13.7, with Jones, *LRE* 679–80; MacMullen (1980) 455.

[47] For a useful summary of the different results, see Luttwak, *Grand Strategy* 188, 231 n. 222.

the lowest of these figures is difficult to accept in view of the small size of actual armies and units that appear in the narrative sources from the fourth century, such as Barbatio's army of 25,000 in 356, Julian's of 13,000 at Strasbourg, and the army of 65,000 for his Persian expedition, by far the largest Roman force of which we know from this period.[48] This suggests that calculations of half a million men or more, if approximately right, can nevertheless only represent 'paper' numbers, and that units were in practice significantly under strength – though by how much, we have no way of estimating.

From the point of view of feeding and paying the army, however, it was the paper figures which mattered. Even if one adopts the lowest of the calculated figures, about 500,000 men, one is still dealing with a significant increase in the nominal size of the army compared with the early third century (for which a more reliable estimate of 350,000–400,000 is available). This might have had very serious implications for the empire's tax burden, and in the light of bitter comments such as that of Ursulus on the ruins of Amida – 'see with what courage our cities are defended by men for whom the resources of the empire are denuded to supply them with pay!'[49] – there is a strong temptation to assume that this was in fact the case. Yet given that military expenditure was bound to be by far the largest item on the imperial budget,[50] it will have been natural to link complaints about taxation with criticisms of the army, irrespective of whether the actual level of military expenditure had changed for the worse. Heavier taxes need not have been the inexorable consequence of larger numbers, if the value of soldiers' income had declined relative to prices. Relevant data is scarce, but the best available, from Diocletian's reign, suggests that this was in fact the situation at the beginning of the fourth century,[51] and a continuation of this trend would help to explain the evident reluctance of individuals to serve in the army.[52]

Although fourth-century soldiers still received an annual *stipendium* paid in money, the inflation of the third century had rendered this all but worthless, and the main form of remuneration was payment in kind, principally food (*annona*) but also clothing. Indeed, one of the main points of Diocletian's new fiscal arrangements was the transfer of these material resources from taxpayers to the army. This process was supervised by the regional praetorian prefects, the most senior post in the civilian administration – an arrangement perhaps intended to discourage any inclination to revolt on the part of senior generals – and detailed regulations governed the collection, storage and issuing of the relevant

---

[48] Jones acknowledges this problem (*LRE* 684–5), without, in my view, providing a persuasive response.   [49] Amm. Marc. xx.11.5 (tr. Hamilton); cf. *De Rebus Bellicis* v.   [50] Hendy, *Studies* 157ff.
[51] Duncan-Jones, *Structure and Scale* ch. 7; cf. Whittaker (1980) 8–9; Bagnall, *Egypt* 172.
[52] See pp. 221–2 below.

foodstuffs (though as inflationary pressures eased during the fourth century there was an increasing tendency to commute the *annona* to money).[53] Specific campaigns entailed the provision of additional stores in the relevant region, and the ability of the Roman administration to make the necessary preparations is impressive, whether it be the three million *medimnoi* of grain stockpiled in Raetia in 360 in advance of Constantius II's projected riposte against Julian, or the complex operation co-ordinated by the praetorian prefect of the East Auxonius in 367 whereby supplies for Valens' expedition against the Goths were transported from eastern provinces via the Black Sea to the mouths of the Danube and thence upstream.[54] At the same time it is evident that these additional exactions did mean an increased, and much resented, tax burden on at least some of the empire's population.[55]

The army was of course also a consumer of human resources, and emperors of the period do seem to have had difficulties finding sufficient recruits. A sequence of laws throughout the century tried to tie sons of veterans to military service, but their very repetition betrays their ineffectiveness, while it is difficult to find more than two actual cases where individuals were inconvenienced by them.[56] Other evidence is more impressionistic – a report from Egypt in the 340s of an unsuccessful attempt to seize conscripts from a village, the surmise of a Cappadocian bishop in the 370s that an increase in applicants for the ministry was motivated in many cases by the desire to avoid conscription, the need to brand recruits, and the practice, apparently not uncommon in the fourth century, of chopping off a digit to disqualify oneself from military service.[57] As these examples suggest, the problem was not so much population decline as unwillingness to enlist.[58] This situation was exacerbated by significant losses of seasoned troops in battle at various points during the fourth century: Constantius' hard-fought defeat of the usurper Magnentius at Mursa (351), in which (according to a contemporary commentator) 'great resources were wasted, adequate for any number of foreign wars';[59] the siege of Amida (359), whose capture by the Persians meant the loss of seven legions (perhaps 7000 men); Julian's disastrous Persian expedition (363), involving at least 65,000 men, of whom a significant proportion must have perished in Mesopotamia; and above all,

---

[53] Jones, *LRE* 623–30; Isaac, *Limits of Empire* 285–91.

[54] Jul. *Ep. ad Ath.* 286b; Zos. IV.10.4; cf. Amm. Marc. XIV.10.2–5; XVIII.2.3–4. See also Lee (1989) with further references. [55] E.g. Zos. IV.16.1; Theod. *HE* V.19.1; cf. Hendy, *Studies* 221ff.

[56] *C.Th.* VII.22.4–10 (332–86); MacMullen (1964b), esp. 52 (citing *P.Abinn.* 19, Sulp. Sev. *V. Mart.* 11).

[57] *P.Abinn.* 35; Basil *Ep.* 54; *C.Th.* x.22.4 (398); VII.13.4 (367), 13.5 (368), 13.10 (381); Amm. Marc. XV.12.3.

[58] Another factor during the critical years after 395 was the obstructive tactics of senatorial landowners, when attempts were made to levy recruits from their estates: Matthews, *Western Aristocracies* 268–70, 276–8. [59] Eutr. *Brev.* x.12.

the Gothic victory at Adrianople (378), in which two-thirds of a field army was destroyed.[60]

Various steps were taken to try to compensate for these losses. Valentinian initiated vigorous measures in the mid 360s, which included the systematic hunting down of deserters and lowering of the minimum height requirement by 3 inches to 5 foot 7 inches.[61] These moves may also have been related to another development in the evolution of the empire's field armies – the emergence of paired units of *seniores* and *iuniores*. The lists in the *Notitia* and the evidence of Ammianus are consistent with the hypothesis that Valentinian's division of the empire with Valens in 364 included the splitting in two of about fifty élite regiments, while also providing a convenient explanation for the terms *seniores* and *iuniores*: the additional epithet *seniores* would be appropriate for those of the resulting units which accompanied the elder brother Valentinian westwards, *iuniores* for those which remained in the east with the younger brother Valens. But if this is what happened, then it must have involved more than simply splitting units. It has been suggested that 'Valentinian divided regiments into two cadres, not necessarily equal in numbers, age, or experience, which were then filled out with recruits who would mature more quickly side by side with old soldiers than if drafted into new regiments . . . By building from cadres, he could expand the field army rapidly, to compensate for Julian's losses in Mesopotamia.'[62] This interpretation makes good sense of much of the evidence, but it must nevertheless be acknowledged that some difficulties remain.[63]

Another approach to dealing with the manpower problem was the recruitment of barbarians. In the first instance, this meant drawing on peoples living in regions beyond the empire: defeated enemies might be required to provide men as part of the peace settlement; prisoners-of-war were sometimes placed into units; and individuals entered the empire on their own initiative seeking employment in the Roman army.[64] But recruitment of barbarians also meant making use of peoples whom emperors had settled within imperial territory, often in very large numbers. Indeed, some such settlers were admitted with this specific purpose in mind. The idea of

[60] Ammianus (XXXI.13.18) gives the proportion. Hoffmann (*Bewegungsheer* 1.444) argues for an army of 30,000–40,000, which would give casualties of 20,000–26,000; Heather (*Goths and Romans* 147) regards these figures as unrealistically high, and suggests losses of 10,000–12,000; cf. Austin (1972) 82–3.   [61] *C.Th.* VII.18.1 (365); 13.3 (367).

[62] Tomlin (1972) 264; cf. Hoffmann, *Bewegungsheer*, who reached similar conclusions independently and in much greater detail.

[63] Some aspects of the analyses of Tomlin and Hoffmann have been challenged on the basis of a new epitaph from Nakolea in Phrygia, dedicated to a soldier who had served in the *Io(vii/viani) Corn(uti) sen(iores)*, with a firm dating to 356 (Drew-Bear (1977)). This poses a problem for any exclusive association of the *seniores/iuniores* division with 364 and for crediting Valentinian with originating the idea, but it does not rule out the possibility that it was employed on a large scale in 364.

[64] Hoffmann, *Bewegungsheer* 1.141–5.

incorporating barbarians in the army was by no means novel. Nevertheless, the scale on which there was recourse to it during the fourth century was unprecedented. One indication of this is the number of individuals of barbarian extraction, especially Germans, who rose to high rank in the army during the period.[65] Another is the fact that the élite cavalry *vexillationes* and infantry *auxilia* of the field armies drew heavily on barbarians, again particularly those of Germanic origin. Those Germans who reached high office can only have been a fraction of the total number who served: since the number who did reach high office was considerable,[66] the total number in lower ranks must have been very great indeed.[67] It was these developments which prompted Fustel de Coulanges' wry observation that, for many Germans, the Roman empire was not an enemy, but a career.[68]

The battle of Adrianople and its aftermath resulted in a significant increase in the use of barbarian troops. First, one of the ways in which Theodosius sought to make good the men lost at Adrianople itself was by a recruiting drive north of the Danube.[69] Secondly, the compromise settlement which he finally reached with the Goths in 382 placed them under a general obligation to do military service for the empire, but mostly in the form of contributing units of allied status (*foederati*) for specific campaigns rather than supplying men for long-term service in the regular army.[70] The crucial difference here was that these federate units consisted exclusively of Goths under Gothic command, thereby introducing a significant degree of independence compared with the regular army, where barbarians were under the command of others and tended to serve in mixed units. This change was one of the factors which contributed to the Gothic problem which emerged after Theodosius' death, the eventual outcome of which was the settlement of the Goths in southern Gaul.[71]

The term 'barbarization' has often been used to sum up this nexus of developments across the fourth century. In so far as barbarians made up a steadily larger proportion of the army's numbers and were increasingly prominent at the highest levels of command, use of the term may be justified. The problem is that it has come inevitably to carry with it an unwarranted bundle of pejorative connotations, especially concerning the loyalties and effectiveness of the army – prompting some scholars to talk, instead, of the 'un-Romanization' of the army and the 'demilitarization' of the empire.[72] The pejorative connotations are unwarranted because, first,

---

[65] Waas (1965); Stroheker (1975); Demandt (1970); Hoffmann (1978); MacMullen, *Corruption*, Appendix A; Liebeschuetz, *Barbarians and Bishops* ch. 1.

[66] 'The fact that German officers often Latinized their names means that we are more likely to underestimate than to exaggerate their numbers': Liebeschuetz, *Barbarians and Bishops* 8.

[67] Hoffmann, *Bewegungsheer* 1.145.   [68] Cited in Whittaker (1983) 117.   [69] Zos. IV.30.1.

[70] Heather, *Goths and Romans* 160–4.

[71] Liebeschuetz, *Barbarians and Bishops* chs. 4–5; Heather, *Goths and Romans* chs. 5–6.

[72] MacMullen (1964c) 446; Liebeschuetz, *Barbarians and Bishops* 1–2.

there is very little evidence to suggest that barbarians in Roman employ were disloyal, or wavered in the heat of battle when fighting other barbarians – in talking about 'the Franks' or 'the Alamanni' (let alone 'Germans'), it is easy to gain a misleading impression of the degree of ethnic self-consciousness that existed in what were, after all, still loose confederations of smaller tribes between whom co-operation was by no means guaranteed; and secondly, the fact that the barbarian presence was particularly concentrated in the *vexillationes* and *auxilia*, élite units in the field armies, should give the lie to the idea that greater numbers of barbarians in the army were responsible for any decline in its effectiveness.[73]

III. THE ARMY, POLITICS AND SOCIETY

From the advent of monarchy under Augustus, maintenance of a good relationship with the army was always one of the most important political priorities of emperors.[74] The spate of army revolts and usurpations during the mid third century can only have served to re-emphasize to emperors of the fourth century, if they needed reminding, the fundamental necessity of retaining the allegiance of the soldiery. On numerous occasions Ammianus presents emperors addressing troops, often in politically charged circumstances, and such speeches are invariably couched in terms of the language of comradeship – the troops are the emperor's *commilitones* (fellow soldiers) or *socii* (comrades) – and of deference to their wishes ('if I have your consent' and the like).[75] Such speeches need to be treated with caution, given that they were part of the literary stock-in-trade of the Graeco-Roman historiographical tradition – not to mention the practical problems of an emperor or general making himself heard by more than a small proportion of his army.[76] At the same time, they ought not to be dismissed out of hand. For one thing, non-literary records of imperial communications with troops which survive from this period show that emperors really did use the language of comradeship.[77] Nor, importantly, was this mere rhetoric, in so far as most emperors of the fourth century involved themselves actively in campaigning and the rigours of military life.[78] The language of deference cannot be documented in the same way as that of comradeship, but by portraying emperors as flattering troops about their importance in imperial decisions, Ammianus was reminding his audience of a basic truth: in the final analy-

---

[73] On which see pp. 232–7 below.   [74] Campbell (1984) Part I.

[75] E.g. XIV.10.13–15; XVI.12.30–1; XXI.5.2–5; XXVII.6.6–12; cf. Symm. *Or.* 1.19.

[76] Cf. Hansen (1993).

[77] *C.Th.* VII.20.2 (Constantine greets troops as *conveterani*); Honorius' letter to Spanish soldiers, whom he addresses twice as *commilitones nostri* (Sivan (1985)).

[78] Cf. Zos. II.44.3 (Constans); Amm. Marc. XVI.5.3 (Julian); XXIX.4.5, XXX.9.4 (Valentinian).

sis the troops *were* in a strong position to act as 'arbiters of imperial power'.[79]

Other factors capable of influencing military loyalties are suggested by an account of the way in which Constantius II apparently won back mutinous troops from the usurper Vetranio in 350: 'throughout his speech he reminded the soldiers of his father's liberality to them and of the oaths they had sworn to remain loyal to his children'.[80] The ability to claim blood-relationship with a former emperor clearly carried weight with soldiers, as indeed more generally – this was one of Procopius' strongest cards in his attempt to overthrow Valens,[81] and Nepotianus, one of those who tried to seize power in 350, could also claim descent from Constantine's family.[82] Lack of such a connection was not, however, an insurmountable obstacle to winning military support for a *coup*, as demonstrated by the cases of Magnentius, Magnus Maximus and Eugenius, among others. A more important determinant of loyalties, as Constantius acknowledged in 350 by his reference to Constantine's liberality, was the prospect of material gain. Vetranio, for example, had originally won the support of the troops for his usurpation by means of 'rich presents'; it was the 'hope of great rewards' which was said to have induced soldiers to back Procopius in 365; and there were units in the Gallic army of the 350s 'whose loyalty was apt to waver and who could be influenced in any direction by a handsome bribe'.[83] Emperors attempted to insure themselves against this sort of danger by means of regular donatives to the troops. Such payments were made several times annually, on the birthday and on the accession-anniversary of the reigning emperor(s), and represented a substantial financial supplement to the basic military pay.[84] And just in case the soldiery missed the point, their distribution could be accompanied by exhortations to loyalty.[85]

It will already be apparent, however, that even regular donatives were not necessarily sufficient to guarantee loyalty – a determined usurper with adequate resources could always offer more money. What is not so easy to explain is the lopsided geographical distribution of usurpations between 337 and 425: with the exception of Procopius' attempt, they all occurred in the western provinces, but scholars have had little success in accounting satisfactorily for this pattern.[86] Troops in the west undoubtedly had a reputation for political unreliability, as Ammianus explicitly acknowledges in describing the tense days which followed the death of Valentinian in 375: 'anxious fears were felt about the attitude of the units serving in Gaul, who were not always loyal to the legitimate emperors and regarded themselves

---

[79] Amm. Marc. xxx.10.1; cf. xiv.10.15; xxvii.6.12.   [80] Zos. ii.44.3 (tr. Ridley).
[81] Amm. Marc. xxvi.6.18; 7.16.   [82] Zos. ii.43.2.
[83] Zos. ii.44.4; Amm. Marc. xxvi.6.13; xv.5.30 (tr. Hamilton); cf. xiv.11.19.
[84] Jones, *LRE* 623–4.   [85] Amm. Marc. xv.6.3.   [86] Cf. Jones, *LRE* 1033–4; Wardman (1984).

as arbiters of the imperial power'.[87] Nevertheless, it is by no means clear why troops in the west should have been particularly prone to this. One thing which certainly will not have helped to ameliorate this situation, however, is the practice, apparently common in the fourth century, of not disbanding units involved in an unsuccessful usurpation – they were, quite simply, too valuable, and adopting a severe line would only have served to discourage precious potential recruits.[88]

A subject of possible relevance to the issues of usurpation and revolt is that of the religious loyalties of the army. But while a certain amount is known about the changing pattern of religious affiliation amongst senior commanders over the course of the fourth century,[89] the attitudes of the rank-and-file are more difficult to chart. Certainly, in spite of the presence of some Christians in the ranks at the start of the century,[90] it seems a reasonable assumption that the majority of Constantine's soldiers were pagan in sympathy, on the basis that the army's major recruiting grounds comprised the relatively un-Christianized rural inhabitants of Illyricum and Gaul, and non-Christian barbarians.[91] How rapidly did this situation change under Christian emperors?

A number of Christianizing measures were introduced on imperial initiative, particularly by Constantine. Some form of Christian symbol was displayed on his soldiers' shields during the battle against Maxentius in 312,[92] thereafter becoming a regular feature.[93] Constantine also introduced the *labarum*, a special imperial standard modelled on the cross, though probably not until the mid 320s;[94] it too became an established part of the army's symbolic regalia, except for the brief period during which Julian predictably did away with it. Constantine is further credited with granting leave on Sundays to those troops wishing to attend church, while those who did not were required to parade and recite a monotheistic prayer.[95] The claim by one fifth-century church historian that he appointed the first military chaplains seems, however, to be mistaken, since there is no independent attestation of clergy in attendance on troops before the mid fifth

---

[87] XXX.10.1.

[88] Hoffmann, *Bewegungsheer* 1.30, 398–9, II.11 n. 41 (to which add Constantius' incorporation of Vetranio's troops into the forces he led against Magnentius in 351: Zos. II.45.2). Note, however, the uncertain case of the *Divitenses-Tungrecani iuniores*: their absence from the *Notitia* has been taken as indicative of their having been disbanded by Valens following their support of Procopius (Tomlin (1972) 258), though Hoffmann argues otherwise (*Bewegungsheer* 1.398).

[89] von Haehling (1978) 238–83, 453–83.   [90] Helgeland (1979).

[91] Jones (1963) 23–4; Gabba (1974) 97–104; MacMullen, *Christianizing* 44–5.

[92] Lact. *De Mort. Pers.* 44.5–6, with discussion and references in Creed (1984) 119.

[93] MacMullen, *Christianizing* 140 n. 23 (for references to subsequent iconographic evidence).

[94] Eus. *V. Const.* 1.28–31, written at the end of Constantine's reign, places it in 312, but the earliest representations of the *labarum* appear on coins datable to 326: Bruun (1962) 27.

[95] Eus. *V. Const.* IV.18–20.

century;[96] the same author also says that Constantine used a portable prayer-tent and provided one for each legion, but if so the practice apparently fell out of use during the remainder of the fourth century at least, for Constantius II and Theodosius I resorted to nearby chapels before the battles of Mursa and the Frigidus.[97] There is no doubt, however, that a revised version of the military oath came into use at some point during the fourth or early fifth century, whereby soldiers swore obedience in the name of the Trinity.[98]

It is difficult to assess the impact on soldiers of these measures. They certainly do not amount to the direct imposition of Christianity on soldiers, though before dismissing them out of hand as merely superficial gestures, it is worth remembering that legionary standards had long been the focus of religious cult in the army, in the light of which Constantine's introduction of the *labarum* acquires more profound significance; and the swearing of the military oath (*sacramentum*) was, as its name implies, a ritual act likewise imbued with religious meaning. Nevertheless, it is likely that their influence on the ethos of the army was only very gradual and indirect. In 361 Julian, *en route* to the east, was able to report that 'we worshipped the gods openly, and most of the army which accompanies me reveres them'.[99] His troops at this stage were of course drawn mostly from the under-Christianized west, and it is western units whom Ammianus later singles out when censuring the over-indulgence of soldiers during sacrifices in Antioch in 363.[100] There is, moreover, archaeological and epigraphic evidence that pagan shrines in military contexts remained in use along the Rhine and Danube until late in the fourth century.[101] Julian had to work harder to win back to the old gods the troops stationed in the more Christianized east,[102] some of whom had, for example, already assisted in the destruction of pagan shrines during the reign of Constantius II.[103]

---

[96] Soz. *HE* I.8, with Jones (1953). I am less confident than Woods (1991) 42 that the πρεσβύτερον τῶν σχολῶν referred to by Palladius *c.* 404 (*V. Joh. Chrys.* xx) was a priest to the *scholae palatinae*: σχολή can mean 'catechumens or newly baptized persons' (Lampe, s.v. σχολή, 6b), and later in the same chapter Palladius is careful to describe a soldier in the *scholae palatinae* as a στρατιώτης τῶν περὶ τὸν βασιλέα σχολῶν.

[97] Woods (1991) 43, citing Sulp. Sev. *Hist. Sac.* II.38, Theod. *HE* v.24; for Constantine (the precedent), cf. Eus. *V. Const.* II.12, 14.

[98] Veg. *Epit. Rei Militaris* II.5. A firm date for Vegetius would help to define the parameters for the introduction of the new version: Milner (1993) xxv–xxix has recently presented a cogent argument for Theodosius I being the dedicatee of the work, and it would be consistent with the tenor of his reign for Theodosius to have introduced a Christianized form of the oath.   [99] Julian *Ep.* 26 Bidez.

[100] Amm. Marc. XXII.12.6 (Petulantes and Celtae).   [101] References in Bowder (1978) 95, 205.

[102] Cf. Lib. *Or.* XVIII.167–8.

[103] Fowden (1978) 59. The best-known individual soldier from this period and part of the empire, Abinnaeus, long thought to have been a pagan, was probably in fact a Christian, while arguments for continuing paganism among his troops based on the cult-statue found in his Egyptian camp are insecurely founded: Barnes (1985) 373–4.

Some soldiers refused to burn incense when receiving donatives from Julian,[104] but there is no indication that his return to paganism prompted widespread dissatisfaction in the army, and embarrassed Christian apologists had to resort to explanations couched in terms of the simple nature of soldiers and of their being inured to obedience to the imperial will.[105] On the other hand, there are no obvious signs of discontent in the army when the imperial office was resumed by avowed Christians after Julian's death – and this in an age when soldiers were certainly willing to revolt over other issues.[106] Soldiers supporting the usurper Procopius in 365 may have sworn by the name of Jupiter 'in the usual military way',[107] but Procopius is shown winning the support of units by alluding not to Valens' Christianity, but to the fact that he was an upstart from Pannonia;[108] and although Eugenius numbered some prominent pagans among the supporters of his usurpation in the 390s, it would be unwise to make deductions about the religious sensibilities of his troops from the pagan symbols reported to have been present on the battlefield at the Frigidus.[109]

The overall impression from the fourth century, then, is one of acquiescence or indifference on the part of soldiers with respect to the religious affiliation of emperors, and of emperors treading with caution in any religious requirements made of their troops. After all, they could hardly afford to alienate this fundamental element of their power-base. Whether pagans were formally banned from service in the army in the early fifth century (as Jews certainly were) remains unclear,[110] but if so, recruitment problems must in practice have dictated the same sort of pragmatic approach which had operated at the level of senior commanders during the fourth century,[111] and which clearly continued to operate in their case well into the fifth century.[112] Certainly religious loyalties cannot be shown to have exercised a significant influence on the stance adopted by soldiers in any of the usurpations or attempted usurpations of the fourth or early fifth century.

As already observed, the personal involvement of emperors with their troops on campaign was an important factor in retaining their loyalty.

---

[104] Soz. *HE* v.17.   [105] Greg. Naz. *Or.* iv.64.   [106] Cf. Nock (1952) 227.
[107] Emphasized by MacMullen, *Christianizing* 46.   [108] Amm. Marc. xxvi.7.16–17.
[109] Szidat (1979) 504–5. For what it is worth, the collection of late-fourth-century military epitaphs from Concordia in northern Italy, which *may* commemorate soldiers associated with the conflict in 394 (for other possibilities, see Tomlin (1972) 269–72), includes three men who advertise their Christianity (Hoffmann (1963) nos. 11, 14, 35), while the remaining tombstones provide no explicit indications of paganism.
[110] *C.Th.* xvi.10.21 (416) has been so interpreted (Clauss (1986) 1108; Woods (1991) 43), but *militia* can refer to the civilian administration in the late Roman context, whereas the ban on Jews (*C.Th.* xvi.8.24 (418)) refers explicitly to the *militia armata*. The story of Generidus, of potential relevance, presents many difficulties: see Paschoud's commentary on Zos. v.46.
[111] E.g. in contrast to his policy in senior civilian posts, Julian left experienced Christians in important commands: von Haehling (1978) 537–47.
[112] E.g. the *magister* Litorius consulted haruspices before battle in 439, while Marcellinus, *magister* in the 460s, was an avowed pagan (see *PLRE* ii, *s.v.* Litorius, Marcellinus 6).

However, the death of Theodosius in 395 precipitated a very significant change in this respect, the unavoidable consequence of the youth and inexperience, first, of Theodosius' two sons Arcadius and Honorius, and then of Theodosius II and Valentinian III, their effective successors in east and west until the mid fifth century. Non-participation in campaigning served to distance these emperors from the soldiery, and facilitated the emergence of army commanders as highly influential figures in political life, particularly in the west. This development had in fact been presaged by the one-sided relationship of the *magister* Arbogast and the young Valentinian II prior to 395; thereafter western affairs were dominated by a succession of powerful figures, of whom the most prominent were Stilicho and Aetius.[113] The east had its fair share of ambitious generals, too – the most serious challenge came from the *magister* Gainas in 400 – but here the emperor, or at least his civilian officials and advisers, managed by and large to maintain control.[114]

A formal division between military and civil spheres of responsibility was of course a distinctive feature of office-holding during the fourth century. Moreover, there are various indications from the period of antagonism between the two arms of government. During the reign of Constantius II, a praetorian prefect was 'exposed to extreme danger' at the hands of soldiers who were hungry but also, says Ammianus, 'naturally inclined to be hostile and harsh towards those holding civil positions'. Another of Constantius' civil officials, the *comes sacrarum largitionum* Ursulus, likewise brought down the wrath of the military on his head through his rash remark about the ruins of Amida.[115] It has rightly been observed that the military had some justification for resentment against the civil officials of Constantius' court, for it was a group of them who had conspired against the *magister* Silvanus and brought about his downfall a few years before.[116] At the same time, however, one should beware of assuming that relations between the two groups were consistently characterized by enmity. 'Within the setting of the imperial court, military officers and members of the administrative bureaucracy were not part of separate groups, but moved in the same circles and shared many interests',[117] and there are undoubtedly a number of instances where military figures can be seen co-operating with civilian officials, whether in political intrigues or the choice of an emperor.[118]

There is also another, less formal sense in which one can talk about 'military–civilian relations', removed from the sphere of high politics – interaction between soldiers and civilians in the broadest sense, in ordinary,

---

[113] Cameron, Alan, *Claudian*; Demandt (1970); Matthews, *Western Aristocracies* ch. 10.
[114] Liebeschuetz, *Barbarians and Bishops*, Part 2; Cameron and Long, *Barbarians and Politics* 323–36.
[115] XIV.10.4; XX.11.5, XXII.3.7–8.   [116] Tomlin (1976) 192–3.
[117] Matthews, *Western Aristocracies* 120.   [118] Tomlin (1976) 193–4.

everyday contexts. The most intimate and exacting form this could take was having to accommodate soldiers within one's own home, a practice sometimes given the euphemistic label *hospitalitas*. The soldiers in question would be troops of the field armies, who were usually billeted in cities and towns when not actually on campaign. Subject to certain privileged exceptions, the householder was obliged to surrender without recompense one-third of his home for occupation by the military. Theoretically, this was supposed to involve nothing more than the relevant room or rooms, but it is apparent that in practice these unwanted guests could be very demanding, even threatening violence if their hosts did not supply additional items such as mattresses, oil and wood.[119]

Even in the case of the *limitanei*, who had their own camps or forts in which to live, there remained plenty of scope for contact with the local population. The dossier of documents from the Fayum in Egypt known as the Abinnaeus archive provides particularly valuable insights into this aspect of military life. Flavius Abinnaeus was commander of a unit stationed at Dionysias during the 340s, and the surviving letters and petitions addressed to him reveal the involvement of his men with the local population through policing, and assisting the civilian authorities in the collection of taxes.[120] In fact, of course, a large part of soldiers' time must have been taken up with these and other peace-time activities, such as supervision of cross-frontier travellers, collection of customs tolls, and construction work of various sorts.[121]

Abinnaeus' papers also show him receiving complaints from local communities and individuals about the violent or criminal behaviour of some of his troops, ranging from the protest by the headman of a village about the way a detachment had looted a house and driven off cattle, to the accusation that some soldiers had literally fleeced a man by shearing his sheep under cover of darkness.[122] Though by no means a phenomenon unique to the late Roman period, this sort of behaviour was an unfortunate and all too common feature of military–civilian relations during the fourth century, attested by a wide range of sources. The humorous *Testamentum porcelli*, chanted by unruly schoolboys of this period, appears to have been in origin a clever piece of pointed satire directed against the 'licentious and destructive soldiery' of the fourth century.[123] Most contemporary commentators, however, found little cause for amusement. A bishop in Asia Minor alluded in a matter-of-fact manner to 'the violence and injuries which the soldiery by reason of their arrogance are accustomed to inflict on the peasantry'; a pagan rhetor in a large eastern city regarded as typical

---

[119] *C.Th.* VII.9, with Jones, *LRE* 631–2; Goffart, *Barbarians and Romans* 41–7; Isaac, *Limits of Empire* 297–301.   [120] *P.Abinn.* 3 and 9.
[121] MacMullen (1963) ch. 3; Carrié, 'Esercito' 460; Demandt, *Spätantike* 265.
[122] *P. Abinn.* 18, 49; cf. 28.   [123] Champlin (1987).

the way in which 'a soldier provokes a market trader, employing abuse and verbal insult: he lays hands on him, manhandles and ill-treats him'; a spokesman from North Africa argued before an audience in Constantinople that 'the troops should be ordered to show consideration for those dwelling in the cities and countryside, and not cause them trouble, being mindful of the exertions which they undertake for their sake'; even a commander in Gaul pleaded with his men – 'see that none of you is carried away by the heat of the moment into inflicting harm on private persons'.[124]

There were, however, other sides to this picture. First, there is the general point that soldiers brought economic benefits to civilians. Although the concentration of too many troops in one place for an extended period could cause severe economic dislocation, such as Antioch experienced during the preparations for Julian's Persian expedition, the presence of troops was usually more benign in so far as they constituted a substantial market with a steady income. Northern Italy, for example, appears to have experienced a period of prosperity during the late 380s and early 390s, a development which has been linked with the presence in the region during those years of the imperial court and field army, while the military units permanently stationed in the Syrian hinterland have been seen as partly responsible for the prosperity enjoyed by the region during the fourth century.[125]

Secondly, there were situations in which military muscle was flexed on behalf of civilians, or at least certain groups within civilian society. Such patronage could take traditional forms, arising naturally from the position of authority and power which military officers understandably held within the local community. The petitions directed to Abinnaeus illustrate this – requests that he use his influence to resolve petty problems of various sorts, sometimes accompanied by material inducements, in one case comprising 'two jars of quails, one pot of fish paste and a flagon of grape syrup'.[126] The latter half of the fourth century also witnessed the development of a new species of patronage. Powerful men – in some cases, military officers – began to offer protection to peasants, even whole villages, against the demands of landlords and local government. In Syria, tenants started using the influence of generals to win court cases against their landlords, while peasants invoked their help to shield them from tax-collectors. In return for their services, the military received, at the very least, gifts of produce or money, and perhaps in some cases virtual possession of the village and its lands. Similar developments, involving officers even as high

---

[124] Greg. Nyss. *Or. in XL Martyres* (11) (*PG* XLVI.784); Lib. *Or.* XLVII.33 (tr. Norman); Syn. *De Regno* 18; Amm. Marc. XXI.5.8 (tr. Hamilton).
[125] Ruggini, *Economia e società* Part 1; Liebeschuetz, *Antioch* 80; more generally MacMullen (1963) 89–95.   [126] *P.Abinn.* 31.

as the *dux* himself, are apparent in Egypt.[127] Although military involvement is not explicitly attested in other parts of the empire where the general phenomenon is also in evidence (e.g. Gaul), there is no obvious reason why it should have been confined to the two eastern regions already noted.[128]

IV. MILITARY EFFECTIVENESS

Did developments of this kind adversely affect the performance of the army's military duties? Was there a deterioration in the army's military effectiveness during the fourth and early fifth centuries? Definitive answers to these questions are impossible, but a number of observations can be made which go some way towards providing answers. First, there is the question of soldiers' armour. One contemporary source claimed that until the reign of Gratian troops continued to be well equipped with armour and helmets, but thereafter they became lazy, abandoned drill and training, and gave up wearing protective armour because of its weight, with disastrous consequences in battle.[129] Although the strongly moralizing character of this claim should prompt caution, it continues to find unquestioning acceptance in some quarters.[130] Indolence and abandonment of armour by soldiers were something of a literary *topos* and it is possible that Vegetius was generalizing from a particular incident,[131] while other evidence, particularly iconographic, supports the conclusion that armour remained in widespread use well beyond the early 380s.[132] Furthermore, one implication of the inclusion in the *Notitia* of the state-run arms factories (*fabricae*) is that their products – which included not only weapons but also protective armour – continued in use after the time of Gratian.[133]

As for discipline in battle, the detailed evidence of Ammianus provides no support for the conclusion that this had undergone serious deterioration in the field armies down to the battle of Adrianople. At the battle of Strasbourg (357), it was certainly the case that cavalry units on the Roman right wing panicked and broke ranks when the commander was wounded, but this incident cannot be used to support a more generalized thesis of a decline of discipline in the fourth century: panic by individual units was hardly a phenomenon without precedent in Roman history, and the potentially disastrous consequences on this occasion were forestalled by the discipline of adjacent infantry regiments which held steady in spite of the danger of their being trampled underfoot by the retreating

---

[127] Lib. *Or.* XLVII; *C.Th.* XI.24; Liebeschuetz, *Antioch* 192–208; Garnsey and Woolf (1989) 162–6. Note also the cautionary remarks of Bagnall (1992).   [128] Whittaker (1993).

[129] Veg. *Epit. Rei Militaris* 1.20.

[130] E.g. Piganiol, *Empire chrétien* 369; MacMullen, *Corruption* 175, 274 n. 15; Liebeschuetz, *Barbarians and Bishops* 25.

[131] As observed by Milner (1993) 18 nn. 2 and 6 (citing Tac. *Ann.* XIII.35.1, Fronto *Princ. Hist.* 11–12).

[132] Coulston (1990).   [133] For full discussion of the *fabricae*, see James (1988).

cavalry.[134] Moreover, although Ammianus' detailed account of this battle fails to explain precisely why, after a long and hard-fought contest, the Romans finally achieved such a decisive victory, the outcome seems to have hinged on the simple inability of the Alamanni to break the Roman centre, in spite of being superior in numbers.[135]

But what about the great military disasters of the fourth century – Julian's Persian expedition, and Adrianople? The outcome of the former was not in fact determined by a major set-piece battle, since the Persians preferred to wage a very effective campaign of attrition and harassment. The débâcle is explicable in terms not of poor battlefield discipline, but rather of planning and execution – such as the non-appearance of the second Roman army, and the failure of the Romans to anticipate the willingness of the Persians to hamper the Roman advance through the destruction of irrigation canals and dykes.[136] As for Adrianople, the Roman line did eventually break, but only, according to Ammianus, under the pressure of overwhelming numbers and after the Roman front-line troops had fought ferociously in utter disregard of their personal safety.[137] Errors of judgement on the part of the emperor Valens provide a more persuasive explanation for this defeat than deficiencies in discipline or courage.[138]

The termination of Ammianus' history with this battle makes it much more difficult to gauge the quality of field army troops subsequently. Detailed accounts of the Roman field armies in action after 378 are lacking, while other evidence is far from satisfactory. Much has sometimes been made of Libanius' claim in a speech of 380/1 that 'all the enemy needs to do in action is to set up a yell, and they are off and away, and any who stays, stays to be beaten'.[139] Yet less than two years earlier, in a speech from 379, he is full of praise for the quality of Roman soldiers – 'let there be no talk of cowardice, weakness or lack of training!'[140] Such inconsistency, no doubt due to the underlying argument in each speech requiring a different emphasis, must cast doubt on the value of any of Libanius' statements about military efficiency, whether positive or negative.

The performance of the army during the decades after 378 was by no means an unmitigated disaster. The main western field units under Stilicho managed to hold Alaric twice in 402, at Pollentia and Verona, and defeat

---

[134] Amm. Marc. XVI.12.37–8.   [135] Matthews, *Ammianus* 298.

[136] Cf. *ibid.* 139, 159–60. This is not to deny individual cases of cowardice or lack of discipline during the course of the expedition (e.g. Amm. Marc. XXIV.3.1–2), but such incidents cannot be regarded as having had any serious influence on the overall outcome of the campaign.

[137] XXXI.13.5–7. When the *Batavi*, held in reserve, were called on to join the battle, none of them were to be found (13.9): it is possible that they had deserted, but it may equally have been that they had already 'become helplessly involved in [the battle]' (Matthews, *Ammianus* 298).

[138] Cf. Crump (1975) 94–6.

[139] *Or.* 11.38 (tr. Norman): see e.g. MacMullen, *Corruption* 175, 274 n. 15.

[140] *Or.* XXIV.5 (tr. Norman).

Radagaisus at Faesulae in 406 (albeit with the aid of Gothic, Hun and Alan cavalry units in this last instance), while the *magister* Constantius was able to dictate terms to the Goths in southern Gaul during the next decade. Matters cannot therefore have deteriorated irretrievably even by that stage. On the other hand, the *magister* Aetius, who dominated western affairs from the 430s onwards, clearly had to rely heavily on the troops of barbarian allies – a development which can plausibly be linked with the casualties suffered during the various civil wars of the early fifth century, and the decline in revenues consequent upon the loss of Britain, Gaul and Spain.[141] In the east, Theodosius certainly proved unable to expel the Goths from Thrace during 379–82, but this was of course the period when the losses at Adrianople were still being made good. A few years later, in 386, the *magister* Promotus managed to defeat another invading force of Goths. The record of the eastern field armies after Theodosius' death remains problematic because of the inadequacies of the sources. The apparent inability of the eastern government to employ a military solution to the revolt of Gainas in 400 has been seen as indicative of the inadequacies of the eastern field armies at this time,[142] but this is by no means the only possible interpretation of this complex episode.[143] The eastern armies did achieve success against the Huns in 398,[144] and although unable to win a decisive victory against the Persians in 421–2, they seem to have acquitted themselves adequately in that campaign.[145]

The starting-point in assessing the effectiveness of the *limitanei* must be the question of whether they were in origin a peasant militia, given land to farm while they performed military service. The implication of this definition is that they were only part-time soldiers, in which case there might be reason to query their military utility. Careful analysis of the relevant texts shows that there are in fact no grounds for describing the *limitanei* as a peasant militia. In particular, too much credence has been given to a passage from one of the most unreliable 'Lives' in the *Historia Augusta*.[146] The fact that units of *limitanei* were sometimes transferred into the field army further supports this conclusion, as does the way in which *limitanei*, like field army troops, received part of their pay in kind – surely an unnecessary step if they were farming land to support themselves. Moreover, the practice of granting land allotments to soldiers upon retirement presupposes that the *limitanei* did not already possess land to farm.[147]

---

[141] Cf. p. 535 below; Liebeschuetz in Rich and Shipley (1993).
[142] Liebeschuetz, *Barbarians and Bishops*, Part 2.
[143] Cf. Jones, *LRE* 202; Cameron and Long, *Barbarians and Politics* 223–32.
[144] Liebeschuetz, *Barbarians and Bishops* 99–100.
[145] Cf. p. 435 below. Holum (1977) 167–9 presents a more sceptical assessment, a divergence which reflects the problems of the sources.
[146] Isaac (1988) 139–46, reiterating and strengthening the conclusions of Jones, *LRE* 649–54.
[147] Jones, *LRE* 650–1.

This is not to deny the existence of statements in contemporary sources critical of the efficiency of the *limitanei*. The rhetor Themistius described the condition of the troops in the most easterly sector of the lower Danube frontier before Valens' reign in the following terms:[148]

Until now, on account of the neglected state of our defences, the enemy used to think that peace and war depended utterly on them. They saw our soldiers not only without arms but even in many cases without adequate clothing, dejected in spirit and squalid in body. They saw our officers and centurions were more like traders and slave-dealers: their one concern was to buy and sell as much as possible. The number of soldiers dwindled, while these officers drew the pay for soldiers who did not exist, as profit for themselves. Our fortresses were falling into ruin, destitute of both arms and men. Seeing all this, they naturally considered themselves superior when it came to fighting.

These are damning criticisms, but it is worth recalling their context – a speech addressed to the emperor Valens in 370 following his campaigns against the Goths in 367 and 369. These campaigns had not produced any victories in the field, and Valens had finally had to force the Goths to parley by means of a trade embargo, so there was no great military triumph to eulogize. Instead, Themistius had to praise the emperor for his clemency in granting peace to the enemy, and for his restoration of the frontier. It was clearly in Themistius' (and Valens') interests that the poor state of the troops and defences prior to Valens' campaigns be exaggerated in order to magnify the extent of the emperor's achievements. No doubt there were some abuses on the part of officers and some lack of discipline on the part of soldiers, but these were hardly phenomena unknown before the fourth century,[149] and while epigraphic testimony confirms that Valens had some *new* defensive structures built,[150] archaeological investigations have revealed no evidence of forts in the region undergoing repairs in the years immediately following 369.[151] Moreover, Ammianus has the following to say concerning the state of the Danube frontier in the early 360s:

Julian did not neglect military matters . . . He strengthened all the cities of Thrace as well as frontier fortifications, and took particular care that the troops posted along the Danube, of whose watchfulness and energy in the face of barbarian attacks he heard such good reports, should not lack either arms or clothing or pay or food.[152]

Granted that imperial attention during the mid 360s was of necessity directed elsewhere, it remains difficult to believe that the condition of the

---

[148] *Or.* x.136B.

[149] Cf. Tac. *Ann.* 1.17; XIII.35; *Hist.* 1.46; Pliny, *Ep.* VII.31.2; *P.Mich.* 468 ll.38–41 (early second century); *PSI* 446 (130s).   [150] *ILS* 770.

[151] Neither of the two most recent and detailed studies of the archaeology of Scythia (Aricescu (1980); Scorpan (1980)) refers to evidence of rebuilding or repairs on any site in the early 370s.

[152] XXII.7.7.

lower Danube frontier had deteriorated to the extent portrayed by Themistius in so short a space of time.[153] In the light of all this, it would be unwise to take Themistius' description at face value, let alone generalize from it about the condition of *limitanei* throughout the empire.

Similar difficulties arise with respect to Synesius' portrayal of the *limitanei* in early-fifth-century Cyrenaica. He paints a dismal picture of the fighting qualities of the troops who were supposed to defend Cyrenaica from the raids of the nomadic Austuriani, with inhabitants of the region largely forced to fall back on their own devices. Yet while, compared with the statements of Themistius, this picture emerges in a more circumstantial manner from Synesius' correspondence,[154] it is apparent that he also had his own axes to grind. The local *dux* may well have had to abandon rural areas (including, significantly, Synesius' own estate) to the raiders temporarily, but the archaeological evidence indicates vigorous measures to defend the cities and the eventual re-establishment of wider control through the construction of fortified block-houses which were garrisoned into the sixth century.[155]

As for other parts of the empire, the frontiers were undoubtedly breached at various times during the fourth and early fifth centuries, but it is worth recalling that in many instances this happened only after the defences had been weakened by the withdrawal of units for other purposes: the Alamannic invasion of the early 350s was greatly facilitated by the usurper Magnentius having stripped the Rhine of troops for his confrontation with Constantius; and Stilicho permanently removed units from the Rhine to help deal with Alaric in 402, thereby fatally weakening the remaining forces which had to confront the Vandals, Alans and Sueves at the end of 406. As for the eastern frontier, *legio I Parthica Nisibena* must have contributed substantially to the successful defence of Nisibis on the three occasions it was besieged between 337 and 350,[156] and although Amida was captured by the Persians in 359, Ammianus' detailed eye-witness account shows that it was only after a lengthy siege in which the Roman troops involved acquitted themselves with vigour and courage.[157] Moreover, the *dux Osrhoenae* is mentioned as participating in Julian's Persian expedition, which implies that the *limitanei* under his command cannot have been considered significantly inferior to field army regiments[158] – a conclusion given more general validity by the frequency with which limitanean units were transferred into field armies (they are designated *pseudocomitatenses* in the

[153] Although *C.Th.* xv.1.13 (365) has Valentinian instructing the *dux* of Dacia Ripensis to construct towers along the frontier, the additional command to repair towers carries the important qualification 'if any, by chance, are in need of restoration'. [154] References in Tomlin (1979).
[155] Goodchild (1976) chs. 15 and 19. [156] Lightfoot (1988) 108–9.
[157] The defenders were not, however, exclusively *limitanei*, since units of *comitatenses* were also present (Amm. Marc. xviii.9.3–4). [158] Amm. Marc. xxiv.1.2.

Notitia).

On the other hand, it is less easy to avoid the conclusion that the *limitanei* had undergone some deterioration by the mid fifth century even in the more stable east. It is apparent from an imperial law of 443, clearly concerned with *limitanei* throughout the eastern empire, that officers had been indulging in corrupt practices, troop numbers had been allowed to fall, and daily drill had been neglected.[159] The problem here is to know just how widespread these problems were, how long it had taken for them to come to the attention of the central government,[160] and how effective the proposed remedies proved to be, but this was certainly not the end of the eastern *limitanei*. It is unclear whether their western counterparts were already beyond redemption by this stage. Our final glimpse of them is in Noricum in the years prior to 476. Troops here continued endeavouring to fulfil their duties in spite of shortages of arms and of pay, and it was only when it became clear that no more resources could be expected from the government in Italy that the regiments in the region finally dispersed for good.[161]

[159] Theodosius II *Novel* 24.
[160] Was the law perhaps a reaction to the performance of units during the wars with Persia and/or the Huns in the early years of the 440s?   [161] Eugippius, *V. Severini* 4, 20.

CHAPTER 8

THE CHURCH AS A PUBLIC INSTITUTION

DAVID HUNT

I. INTRODUCTION: BISHOPS AT COURT

To the experienced and observant eye of Ammianus Marcellinus, composing his history at Rome in the 380s, the Christian church and its institutions were an unremarkable component of his contemporary world. Christian buildings had come to share the urban landscape with the rest of the public architecture of the age, and Christian leaders were recognizably prominent in the affairs of their communities and of the empire at large. In an often quoted observation on the hectic ecclesiastical politics of the reign of Constantius II, Ammianus (xxi.16.18) noted the strains to which the *cursus publicus* was subjected in having to provide for bishops summoned to a succession of church councils at the emperor's bidding. Despite its element of satirical exaggeration – most of Constantius' councils (save the 'universal' gatherings at Sardica and, jointly, at Rimini and Seleucia) were modest affairs, and the travelling bishops must have been outnumbered many times on the road by secular officials going about the emperor's business – the historian's comment none the less captures a vivid snapshot of Christian bishops now participating in the public life of the Roman empire, and sharing the privileges and precedence accorded to the emperor's own subordinates. For the 170 or so bishops who came to Sardica in 343 this public profile itself contributed to the political division between east and west which paralysed the council. The easterners complained of wasted journeys which diverted the attention of state officials required to look to the needs of the bishops and, in a foretaste of Ammianus' later criticism, exhausted the resources of the *cursus*;[1] while western bishops took issue with the prevailing tendency for ecclesiastical matters to have become the public business of the empire. They urged Constantius to restrain his provincial governors from entering into judgement on clerical cases;[2] and endorsed decisions to uphold the autonomy of ecclesiastical procedures and provide for recourse not to the secular hierarchy of the empire, but to St Peter's

---

[1] See ch. 25 of their synodical letter: *CSEL* lxv.64. [2] *CSEL* lxv.181–2.

successor in Rome.[3] Led by their doyen Ossius of Cordova these western bishops castigated those of their fellows who habitually frequented the imperial court from motives of worldly ambition, and not a proper Christian concern for the poor and underprivileged (Can. 8); and they aimed to regulate such episcopal approaches to the government by having them channelled through provincial metropolitan bishops, even authorizing bishops travelling to the court to be interrogated *en route* about the reasons for their journey (Can. 11).[4]

That Ossius and his colleagues at Sardica should lay claim to ecclesiastical autonomy and seek to distance the church and its concerns from the secular government was less a matter of principle than a fact of current church politics: the supporters of Athanasius consistently accused his detractors of sheltering behind the apparatus of the state to subvert the church's own procedures, and it was in such a context that bishop Julius of Rome first invoked the tradition of his authority as the successor of Peter.[5] But in the post-Constantinian empire, 'church' and 'state' were inseparable categories, and neither camp at Sardica was in any position to evade the legacy of Constantine's imperial takeover of Christian institutions – not least the management of church councils: both west and east assembled on the instructions of the emperors, and both travelled with access to the facilities of the imperial *cursus* – none could be under any illusion that the gathering was other than an instrument of imperial policy with the object of forging ecclesiastical unity, especially in the presence of a senior *comes* and palace official from Constantius' court.[6] There is some irony in the fact that Ossius should take the leading role in affecting to separate church from emperor, when it was he who, at Nicaea, had been actively involved in the Constantinian revolution which had irrevocably united them. The Christian church in the Roman empire had been transformed from an object of (at best) official indifference and (at worst, and most recently) active hostility into the recipient of favour, privilege and protection. The *beneficia* which the Roman emperor traditionally bestowed on his most honoured subjects were now the preserve of the Christians, as churches acquired new buildings and prosperity, and their leaders recognition and status in the world at large. For an emperor increasingly convinced of his own special responsibility as a servant of his new-found God there was never a question that he – even though an unbaptized layman – was intervening in matters beyond his sphere; indeed the church's own bishops,

---

[3] On these 'appeal canons', nos. 3c, 4, 7 (Latin), see Hess (1958) 109–27, with summary by Barnes, *Athanasius* 78–80.   [4] Hess (1958) 128–36 (I follow his numbering of the Latin canons).

[5] In writing to Athanasius' opponents in the east: see Athan. *Apol. c. Ar.* xxxv.

[6] The *comes* Strategius Musonianus (future praetorian prefect of the East) and *castrensis* Hesychius: Athan. *Apol. c. Ar.* xxxvi, *Hist. Ar.* xv. A former prefect of Egypt, Philagrius, was also close at hand: *Festal Index*, 15. On the political context of the council, Barnes, *Athanasius* 71ff.

encouraged by their unaccustomed recognition, were only too ready to 'appeal to Caesar' and invoke the emperor as arbiter of their differences. Their access to the court made them a new breed of *amici Caesaris*, 'fellow servants' of Constantine in their Christian duty, and receiving from him hospitality and generosity on an imperial scale: one of their number, Constantine's panegyrist Eusebius of Caesarea, in a moment of exuberant fancy imagined the emperor surrounded by bishops in his palace as an image of God's kingdom in heaven.[7]

Of many Constantinian occasions which might serve to illustrate this convergence of state and church the most pervasively influential was the council of Nicaea in the summer of 325 (actually the context of Eusebius' foretaste of the kingdom). With the aid of bishop Ossius, Constantine had turned the church's internal conciliar mechanism into an instrument of his own grand design for ecclesiastical harmony, and the bishops who attended in his presence into something resembling imperial agents and courtiers. It was a process reminiscent of the transformation of the Roman senate under Augustus and his successors, accompanied by the same exaggerated expressions of deference and respect on the part of the emperor, and the same acquiescence among bishops eyeing the opportunities of the moment. Nicaea even revealed no lack of willingness to accept the implications of the 'secular' enforcement of the council's conclusions – that dissenting bishops would incur the emperor's punishments. Bishops ordered from their sees by imperial command (a catalogue which begins with the aftermath of Nicaea) were to become as revealing an indication of the church's 'public' status as were those who shared the emperor's table. Some two years after the council of Nicaea, a gathering of bishops at Antioch issued canons which show the first signs of reaction against the emperor's role in the resolution of ecclesiastical disputes; yet that did not prevent the bishops whom this council deposed from office (including the bishop of Antioch) from being sent into exile on the emperor's orders.[8]

II. ORGANIZATION AND HIERARCHY

Besides reflecting the political absorption of the church's leaders into the machinery of imperial rewards and punishments, the council of Nicaea had also given formal recognition to an ecclesiastical organization based on that of the Roman state.[9] However varied and irregular the advance of

[7] *V. Const.* III.15.2. For Constantine's self-portrayal as the 'fellow servant' of bishops, see (e.g.) *V. Const.* III.17.2.

[8] For the exiled bishops, see Barnes, *CE* 227–8. *Conc. Antioch.* Can. 12 (Jonkers, *Acta* 52) expresses reservations about 'troubling the ears of the emperor' (these canons were wrongly attributed in the tradition to the 341 council at Antioch).

[9] For what follows in this section, see generally Gaudemet (1958) 322–30, 378–407; Jones, *LRE* 874–94.

Christianity in different areas of the empire, it had adopted structures which stemmed from the surrounding 'secular' framework. In the early fourth century this process of structural assimilation was far more advanced in the eastern empire (whence almost all of the bishops at Nicaea originated), where not only was Christianity more deeply entrenched, but the civic focus of secular administration had the longest history. For the bishops assembled at Nicaea, the fundamental unit of ecclesiastical organization as of secular government was the city and its surrounding territory, each with its own autonomous bishop and dependent clergy who had the care of the congregation within their boundaries. Even before Nicaea it had become a tenet of church discipline – to be reiterated by subsequent synods – that no bishop, priest or deacon should transfer from the city in which he was ordained – although no ecclesiastical canon, any more than imperial laws striving to enforce immobility, could contain the ambitions and careers of individual clerics, especially bishops who gained political advantage from moving to more influential sees (among the notable prelates of Constantius' reign, for example, Eusebius of Nicomedia, Valens of Mursa and Eudoxius of Antioch all defied the rules against episcopal translations).[10] Yet the identification of bishop and clergy with the basic unit of secular government remained a cardinal reflection of the church's acknowledged place in the workings of the empire. Each bishop should have his civic status. Thus the western half of the council at Sardica in 343 accepted that it was inappropriate to consecrate a bishop for a 'village or small city, for which one presbyter alone is adequate ... if a city is discovered to have a congregation sufficiently numerous to be thought worthy of a bishopric, it shall have one'.[11] The bishops were perhaps reflecting the less urbanized government of the western provinces which they represented, as also their less advanced state of Christianization; but they share the sense of the bishop's local importance dictated by his identification with his city. Constantine had earlier provided an example of precisely what the Sardica bishops envisaged, when in according city status to Maiuma, the port of Gaza, he had provided its predominantly Christian population with their own bishop and clergy – who survived even after Julian reincorporated Maiuma into the city territory of Gaza (Sozom. HE v.3.6ff.).

The number of bishoprics was constantly on the increase, though with much regional variation in their distribution. Even into the fifth century the remote Black Sea province of Scythia had only a single bishop, at Tomi (Sozom. HE vi.21.3), while at the other extreme the North African provinces could count their sees in hundreds; here the pattern of

---

[10] For the prohibition on moving to another city, see *Conc. Arelat.* Can. 2, 21 (Jonkers, *Acta* 24, 28); *Conc. Nicaen.* Can 15 (Jonkers, 44); *Conc. Antioch.* Can. 21 (Jonkers, 54). Socr. *HE* vii.36 provides a list of bishops who changed sees. [11] Can. 6 Latin (Hess (1958), 100–3).

correspondence with the secular administration breaks down, for the rivalry of Catholics and Donatists led not only to the proliferation of bishoprics competing for the same towns, but to each side accusing the other of creating sees on estates and in the countryside as well as in the cities.[12] Behind such accusations, however, still lurked the view represented by the council of Sardica that a bishop's status required that he should have a city to his name. The same conclusion is to be drawn from the fact that in areas of the empire where 'rural bishops' (*chorepiscopi*) were a recognized institution, as for example in the extensive region of central Asia Minor attached to Cappadocian Caesarea, their authority was officially circumscribed and subordinate to the bishop of the city in whose territory they lay: having no separate cities of their own, they were not bishops in their own right.[13]

Bishoprics based in the city territories of secular administration fell naturally within the boundaries of the Roman province to which they belonged. Christian organization again took its institutional lead from existing structures, and once more it was the council of Nicaea which formally regulated what was already the practice of the evolving church in the eastern empire. To resolve disputes between bishops, or between bishops and their clergy or laity, Nicaea (Can. 5) prescribed councils of bishops to be held twice a year in each province, in spring and autumn – times which were further specified by the bishops who met at Antioch in 327 (Can. 20) as 'in the fourth week of Pentecost' (i.e. the season after Easter) and the Ides of October. These arrangements provided prominence and authority to the bishop of the chief city in each province, or 'metropolitan', who had responsibility for summoning the provincial synod and charge of its proceedings, and whose consent was required for any agreed action, as for any intervention by an individual bishop outside the bounds of his own see. He was also accorded a formal veto over the appointment of bishops in his province.[14] Where the city autonomy of local churches was represented by the single bishop, the autonomy of each province thus focused on its metropolitan. The bishops at Antioch (Can. 9) found very practical reasons why this should be so: 'the bishop in the metropolis undertakes responsibility for the whole province because it is in the metropolis that all those with business to settle assemble from everywhere'. The basis of the ecclesiastical hierarchy which elevated the metropolitan bishop in each province was simply that his was the most important city, centre of communications and

[12] See the proceedings of the first session of the conference at Carthage in 411 (ed. Lancel, *SChrét.* 194), 181–2; on the number of African sees derived from documents of this conference, see Lancel's introduction, 107–90. For African bishoprics, see further Eck (1983), Lancel (1990).

[13] So *Conc. Ancyr.* Can. 13 (Jonkers, *Acta* 32), *Conc. Antioch.* Can. 10 (51), *Conc. Laodic.* Can. 57 (95). For instances of *chorepiscopi*, see refs. at Jones, *LRE* III. 295 n. 14.

[14] *Conc. Nicaen.* Can. 4, 6 (Jonkers, *Acta* 40–1); see further, Gaudemet (1958) 380–9.

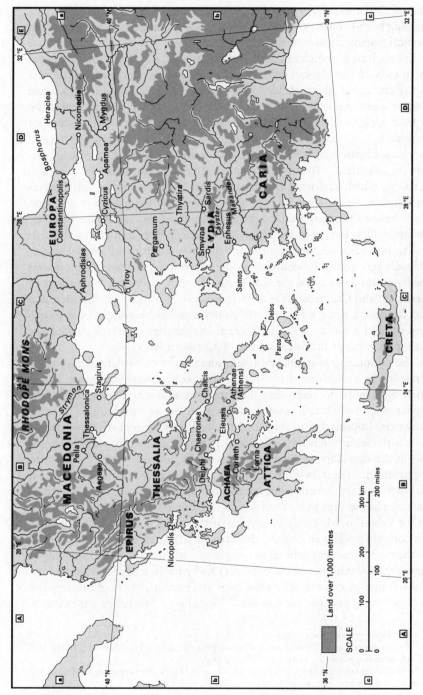

Map 5 Greece and Asia Minor

seat of the provincial government: with the principal city of the province housing both Roman governor and metropolitan bishop, secular and ecclesiastical organization converged.

Yet such neat coincidence, which might appear logical and practical to the minds of synods seeking to order and regulate church discipline, was not always so readily workable 'on the ground'. The bishops at Nicaea had already identified one local instance where the secular arrangements did not sit well with ecclesiastical claims of precedence. The bishop of Jerusalem, cradle of the faith and prime see of Christendom, was a reluctant subordinate of his metropolitan superior at the provincial headquarters of Caesarea.[15] To this the council offered a judgement of Solomon (Can. 7), which endorsed the 'custom and ancient tradition' giving preeminence to Jerusalem, while at the same time according its bishop second place below the metropolitan, even emphasizing the secular basis of the hierarchy by referring to Jerusalem by its official Roman name of Aelia. It was to be over a century before the primacy of the see of Jerusalem was officially recognized by church canons, but in the intervening generations the issue was a source of running political conflict between the bishops of Jersualem and Caesarea.[16] The prerogatives and status of the metropolitan had become a prize reflecting the church's public standing in the fourth century, and it was a matter of resentment that they should be denied to a bishopric with the historical stature of Christian Jerusalem.

The continuing reorganization and subdivision of provinces might also threaten the synchronism of secular and ecclesiastical structures. It was open to bishops to claim that metropolitan authority sanctioned by the higher verdict of church councils was not subject to the whims of redrawn provincial boundaries: in the words of bishop Innocent of Rome in the early fifth century, 'it is not right that the church of God should be changed to suit the flexibility of worldly requirements, nor should it be subject to the promotions and divisions which the emperor may presume to make for his own reasons'.[17] Similar arguments had doubtless encouraged Basil of Caesarea in the 370s in his feud with the bishop of Tyana over responsibility for Valens' newly created province of Cappadocia Secunda.[18] The same tensions are evident among the churches of southern Gaul around the end of the century, as they aspired to a degree of organization and hierarchy to match that which the eastern provinces had already attained by the time of Constantine. A council across the Alps at Turin in 398 sought to regulate disputes over episcopal precedence.[19] Proculus of Marseilles, for example,

---

[15] See Walker (1990) passim, esp. 52–7.

[16] For the recognition of a 'patriarchate' of Jerusalem by the council of Chalcedon in 451, see ACO (ed. Schwartz) II.1, 364–6.   [17] Ep. 24.2 (PL xx.548–9).

[18] On this 'war between bishops', see Greg. Naz. Or. xLIII.58 (PG xxxvI.571), with Van Dam (1986) 62–8.   [19] See Mathisen (1989) 22–6.

although his see belonged to the province of Viennensis, was acting as metropolitan and consecrating bishops over the border in the recently formed province of Narbonensis Secunda; while within Viennensis itself, in a situation reminiscent of that which prevailed in Palestine, the metropolitan claims of the administrative centre of Vienne were being challenged by the ancient and grander bishopric of Arles – which advertised apostolic connections through the tradition of its foundation by St Trophimus, despatched from Rome by no less than St Peter himself. The Turin council sat magnificently on several fences: upholding the principle of observing provincial boundaries, yet endorsing the extra-provincial prerogatives of Proculus as a personal privilege for his own lifetime; and recognizing that the province of Viennensis should have a single metropolitan, yet decreeing in the interim that the two disputants should divide its territory between them.[20] The ecclesiastical ambitions of Arles, it would soon emerge, would not rest content with such diplomatic fudging.

The Nicaea principle of an ecclesiastical hierarchy mirroring the institutions of civil government thus found itself in competition with the political rivalries and inherited traditions of certain bishops and sees, which did not always conform easily to the contemporary map of the Roman empire. The very principle of identifying the structures of church and state was in itself an invitation to bishops to display the worldliness and ambition of public figures at large. Nicaea had already had to acknowledge the wider remit of certain sees whose authority transcended even provincial boundaries, endorsing (Can. 6) the 'ancient custom' which granted the bishop of Alexandria prerogatives over 'Egypt, Libya and Pentapolis'. Alexandria was thus confirmed in its exercise of metropolitan rights over the whole of pre-Diocletianic Egypt, regardless of the new smaller provinces into which the area was now divided – ecclesiastically, it remained the single preserve of the bishop of Alexandria, whose control over the rest of the bishops, not least authority over their appointment, was what gave Athanasius and his successors their formidable power-base in the wider political controversies of the day. The neighbouring province of Pentapolis (Cyrenaica), although never part of Roman Egypt, also fell within Alexandria's empire: when Synesius became bishop of Ptolemais in 411(?), although formally metropolitan of the province, he owed his consecration to Theophilus of Alexandria, and he continued to recognize Theophilus as his superior when it came to the internal ordering and discipline of the churches in Pentapolis.[21]

---

[20] For text of the council's decisions, see Gaudemet (ed.), *Conciles Gaulois du IV* *siècle* (*SChrét.* 241) 136–40.

[21] See Liebeschuetz, *Barbarians and Bishops* 233. For the disputed date of Synesius' consecration, see Liebeschuetz (1986) 180–3, and now Cameron and Long, *Barbarians and Politics* 409–11. Barnes (1986b) argued for 407.

The special authority accorded to the bishop of Alexandria at Nicaea had been justified on the grounds that such a position was already customary for his counterpart in Rome and, the same canon proceeds, 'privileges are to be preserved for the churches in Antioch and in other provinces'. In the case of Rome, the bishop's metropolitan arena was the group of provinces in the south of the peninsula which made up Italia Suburbicaria: as with Alexandria and the rest of Egypt, the prerogatives of Rome defied the new borders of Diocletian's provincialization of Italy, and extended over all the local bishops in the region.[22] The formal extent of Antioch's primacy is less apparent. The city's importance in the east, and especially its credentials as a place of Christian origins – which were second only to those of Jerusalem – naturally gave it a special rank in ecclesiastical precedence, and the elections of its bishops were occasions important enough to draw representatives from all round the eastern Mediterranean;[23] but Antioch did not lay claim to metropolitan authority beyond its own province of Syria, and the rest of the provinces of the east retained their own metropolitans in their principal cities as envisaged by the council of Nicaea. Antioch's position in the region appears similar to that of Carthage in North Africa, where again the prestige of city and bishopric gave it a primacy by no means confined to its immediate province: the Donatist controversy would not have arisen but for the interest of the Numidian bishops in the appointment of a bishop of Carthage satisfactory to them.

These questions of precedence again commanded the attention of the council of bishops which Theodosius summoned to Constantinople in 381, provoked once more by the ambitions of the see of Alexandria – the previous year the Alexandrian bishop had briefly intruded his own nominee Maximus (the 'Cynic') as bishop of the Catholic congregation in Constantinople.[24] This was a political intervention well beyond the formal bounds of his authority in Egypt, and the bishops at Constantinople proceeded to define the extent of Alexandria's prerogatives no longer (as at Nicaea) in terms of privileged custom, but now in conformity with the territorial limits of the secular diocese of Egypt (which had been separated from the diocese of the East in the reign of Valens).[25] In invoking the five dioceses of the eastern empire – Egypt, Oriens, Asiana, Pontica and Thrace – the Constantinople council was extending the identification of ecclesiastical and secular structures to the administrative level above that of the province (where it had rested at Nicaea), and providing for a layer of church jurisdiction to correspond to that of the diocese, although still

---

[22] Including, it appears, the island of Sicily, but not Sardinia: Jones, *LRE* 884.

[23] As at the gathering *c.* 328 which elected Euphronius as bishop: Euseb. *V. Const.* III.62.1.

[24] An episode narrated from a hostile standpoint by Greg. Naz. *De Vita Sua*, 728–1112 (ed. Jungck); for summary, Dagron, *Naissance* 450 n. 2.

[25] *Conc. Constant.* Can. 2 (Jonkers, *Acta* 107). For discussion, Ritter (1965) 85–96.

explicitly preserving the autonomy of the metropolitan and his provincial synod in each province. Where disputes could not be resolved in the province, the bishops at Constantinople expected that neighbouring provinces within the diocese might be called upon to provide a wider 'court of appeal'.[26] But the dioseses were also envisaged as the boundaries of the bishops' affairs, beyond which they were not to trespass; more particularly, the traditional primacies of Alexandria and Antioch (the only two sees specifically identified in the canon) were limited to their respective dioceses of Egypt and Oriens. The reason for the restrictive emphasis – besides the specific occasion of Maximus' intrusion – is not far to seek: Alexandria and Antioch now faced competition for supremacy among the churches of the eastern empire from the awakening pretensions of the see of Constantinople. The 381 council identified a new 'seniority of honour' for the bishop of Constantinople, 'next after the bishop of Rome because Constantinople is new Rome' (Can. 3).[27] Such was the secular status of Constantinople as the eastern capital and equal of Rome that by 381 its Christian bishop could not be left behind. The bishops gave no precise definition or scope to his authority, but implied a general superiority over all the churches of the east.

Like Nicaea before it, the council of Constantinople was occupied in regulating discipline and precedence for a church which was now insepa-rable from the political and administrative organization of the Roman empire. Brought together under the emperor's patronage, the bishops agreed canons which were essentially an exercise in providing a cover of ecclesiastical order and dignity for a church structure which at every level from city to imperial capital reproduced its secular surroundings. The rise of the see of Constantinople is the most striking instance: its challenge to the inherited ecclesiastical standing of Antioch and (especially) Alexandria was dictated entirely by its imperial status. Even before emperors took up permanent residence in the city, careerist bishops like Eusebius of Nicomedia (in 337) and Eudoxius of Antioch (in 360) had seen the polit-ical advantages of a transfer to Constantinople and proximity to the court; with the advent of Theodosius and his dynasty, and a continuous imperial presence in Constantinople, its bishops were at the centre of government, and could expect imperial endorsement of their authority – as when, in 421, Theodosius II instructed the prefect of Illyricum to observe 'the ancient canons of the church' (i.e. canon 3 of the council of Constantinople) which gave to the see of Constantinople 'the prerogatives of old Rome'.[28]

---

[26] The possibility that a metropolitan bishop might summon arbiters from a neighbouring province had already been envisaged by the Antioch council of 327, Can. 14 (Jonkers, *Acta* 52).

[27] On the emergence of the 'patriarchate' of Constantinople, see Dagron, *Naissance* 454ff.

[28] *C.Th.* XVI.2.45. For the context, the intervention of the Roman see in the affairs of Illyricum, see p. 249 below.

Although the bishops of Alexandria continued to strive against this inbuilt precedence – and Theophilus' prominent contribution to the downfall of John Chrysostom indicates a measure of success – they now confronted a rival with all the advantages of a position established at the heart of the empire.[29] As in the provinces the metropolitan bishop in the chief city was at the centre of communications and the natural focus for church affairs in his area, so Constantinople was the metropolitan 'writ large': local church leaders from around the eastern provinces, like their secular counterparts, gravitated towards the hub of the imperial city – and it became established practice for the bishops of Constantinople to reinforce their authority by assembling regular synods of those bishops who found themselves in the capital (σύνοδος ἐνδημοῦσα).[30] When it came to the settling of disputes or receiving appeals, Constantinople had no formal authority like that speci-fied for Alexandria in Egypt or Antioch in Oriens, but its 'seniority of honour' could be invoked to justify intervention, especially in the three neighbouring dioceses of Asiana, Pontica and Thrace, where the council of Constantinople had identified no sees with special status. In 402 John Chrysostom used the occasion of an invitation to settle the disputed affairs of the bishopric of Ephesus to show his hand in the Asian diocese, depos-ing a number of bishops and installing his own protégés in their stead, and replacing the bishop of Nicomedia (in the diocese of Pontica).[31] Such actions in practice owed more to Constantinople's prestige as the capital city than to the vague affirmations of ecclesiastical canons.

The progress of the bishop of 'new Rome', disputing dominance of the eastern church with Alexandria or Antioch, was also a matter of no small interest to the occupant of the see of old Rome on the Tiber. Over and above its formally defined rights as the metropolitan bishopric of Italia Suburbicaria, Rome of course had appropriated a more universal primacy as the only apostolic see in the western empire, its bishops the successors of St Peter. The bishops at Sardica in 343 began to formulate the appellate jurisdiction of the Roman bishop ostensibly, as we have seen, as a reaction against the rush to involve the imperial power as a court of last resort for settling church issues. But it would be misleading to suppose that the early growth of the papacy was itself a development untainted by the pervasive overlap of sacred and secular institutions. The roots of its bishop's supremacy lay in Rome's unique status as the real 'metropolis' of the empire: as early as the second century, arguments for the authority of the Roman see had been based on the city's cosmopolitan and universal char-acter; and when Constantius in 355 sought to bolster the condemnation of

---

[29] On the rivalry between Alexandria and Constantinople, see the classic treatment by Baynes (1955) 97–115.   [30] An instance at Pall. *Dial. de Vita S. Ioh. Chrys.* XIII.150–9 (ed. Malingrey, *SChrét.* 341).

[31] Sozom. *HE* VIII.6; for the Ephesus episode, Pall. *Dial.* XIII.147ff. Cf. Liebeschuetz, *Barbarians and Bishops* 214–15.

Athanasius with the endorsement of the 'higher authority of the bishop of the eternal city' (Amm. Marc. xv.7.10), he was deferring as much to the universal symbolism of *urbs Roma* as to any ecclesiastical primacy on the part of bishop Liberius. Liberius' successor Damasus, at a Roman council in 382, solemnly proclaimed the Petrine basis of his authority in answer to the novel pretensions of Constantinople endorsed by the eastern bishops only the previous year;[32] yet a few years earlier, in 378, Damasus and fellow bishops had not been averse to invoking the support of the emperor Gratian and secular officials to enforce his papal jurisdiction.[33] Even before this, the dispute over Athanasius and his allies had already drawn Julius and Liberius into the empire's political divisions. The bishop of Rome was thus no more immune than other church leaders from absorption into the contemporary Roman state.

It was a tendency only accelerated by the ecclesiastical rivalry with 'new Rome', and the political separation of western and eastern empires. Precisely in the years after 395, when the lordship of the Roman world was divided between the sons of Theodosius, and the secular dioceses of eastern Illyricum – Macedonia and Dacia – became part of the eastern territory of Arcadius, the successors of Damasus on the *cathedra Petri* were extending their ecclesiastical empire over this region through the institution of the 'vicariate' exercised in their name by the bishop of Thessalonica.[34] Popes from Siricius onwards delegated to successive bishops of Thessalonica a primacy in eastern Illyricum, and authority to represent the *sedes apostolica* in an area which now fell within the territory of the eastern government at Constantinople. This outpost of the Roman bishop not only challenged the 'upstart' claims of Constantinople, but also embroiled him in political confrontations between the two emperors: in 421, for example, when pope Boniface's involvement in a dispute over the bishopric of Corinth led to an exchange between Honorius and Theodosius II over the respective ecclesiastical rights of Rome and Constantinople,[35] and this at a time when there was already serious friction – even threats of war – between west and east (the eastern government had refused to recognize Honorius' elevation of Constantius III as Augustus in February 421).

The fortunes of other western sees also illustrate the close conjunction of secular importance and aspirations to ecclesiastical pre-eminence. In the last quarter of the fourth century the combination of influential bishop

[32] *Eccl. Mon. Occ. Iur. Ant.* (ed. Turner) 1.2, 156. 'sancta tamen Romana ecclesia nullis synodicis constitutis ceteris ecclesiis praelata est sed evangelica voce Domini et salvatoris nostri primatum obtinuit'. For this council, see Piétri, *Roma Christiana* 866–72.

[33] *Coll. Avell.* (*CSEL* xxxv) xiii.11–14 (rescript of Gratian to Aquilinus, *vic. Rom.*); cf. Piétri, *Roma Christiana* 741–8.   [34] See Piétri, *Roma Christiana* ii, ch. 14.

[35] For the imperial letters, see *PL* xx.769–71; cf. *C.Th.* xvi.2.45.

(Ambrose) and frequent residence of emperors turned Milan into a see which was a match for Damasus' Rome, wielding an influence felt beyond northern Italy as far afield as the Balkans, and across the Alps in Gaul.[36] In Gaul itself the leadership pretensions of the see of Arles, already on display at the Turin council of 398, were substantially strengthened when the city became the seat of Roman government in the region (in place of Trier) in the early years of the fifth century. Political demands and episcopal ambition coincided in the role exercised by bishop Patroclus, who owed his possession of the see of Arles to the victory of Honorius' general Constantius over the rebel Constantine III in 411; it was in the interests of the re-establishment of legitimate government in Gaul for the authority of Patroclus to be advanced at the expense of his rival Proculus of Marseilles (who had been linked to the regime of Constantine) – and the bishop of Rome was a willing ally in the process.[37] After his election in March 417 the new pope Zosimus lost no time in advising bishops in Gaul of the special merits of Patroclus of Arles, and of his see's cherished association with Rome through the tradition of St Trophimus: Patroclus alone was empowered to issue letters of recommendation to bishops travelling to Rome or elsewhere from Gaul, and was specifically accorded the right of metropolitan to consecrate bishops, not only in his own province of Viennensis, but in the two Narbonensis provinces as well.[38] It was an encroachment on their territorial authority which neither Proculus of Marseilles nor the bishop of Narbonne, Hilary, would be content to accept, and Patroclus' primacy was surrounded by controversy. Yet he continued to be seen as a useful ally by the government; when order was restored, and church privileges renewed, after the overthrow of Johannes' usurpation in 425, it was still Patroclus who would be singled out as the representative of authority among the Gallic episcopate.[39]

III. A CHRISTIAN ENVIRONMENT

The formalities of ecclesiastical organization and the prominence asserted by some leading bishoprics, reflected a church increasingly identified with the public structures and political life of the late Roman empire. Its new place in the contemporary world was no less apparent in the physical evidence provided by its programme of new building and its expanding resources. In the generations after Constantine, following the example set by the first Christian emperor, church building replaced temples, baths and other secular works as the principal source of outlay for public and private munificence, and the civic landscape took on an increasingly Christian

---

[36] On Ambrose's appointment of a bishop for Sirmium, chief city of Pannonia, see Paulin. *V. Ambros.* xi; and for his presiding over a synod of Gallic bishops in Milan (390), Ambr. *Ep.* 51.6. For his role in northern Italy, Lizzi (1990), esp. 157–61.   [37] See Mathisen (1989) 44–68.
[38] Zosim. *Ep.* 1 (*PL* xx.642–5); cf. also *Epp.* 5–7 (665–9), 10–11 (673–5).   [39] *Const. Sirm.* 6.

character – reflected not only in places of worship, but in a variety of charitable establishments (hospitals and hostels) and monastic communities.[40] Nor were such Christian buildings any longer confined to the peripheral locations which had been occupied by the first martyr shrines, as churches now began to encroach upon the heart of the city, alongside the rest of the public buildings and residential quarters which comprised the urban centre. This transformation of city topography was nowhere more apparent than in Rome, where the Constantinian foundations on the burial-grounds and imperial estates of the perimeter were supplemented not only by more such extramural churches (most notably the new basilica at St Paul's tomb on the Ostian way, to this day designated as S. Paolo *fuori le Mura*), but also by a succession of church buildings within the walls to replace the 'house churches' of an earlier era.[41] Bishop Julius in the 340s built a basilica 'close to the Forum of the divine Trajan', and another 'across the Tiber' (the ancestor of S. Maria in Trastevere); his successor Liberius added 'the basilica which bears his name close to the market of Livia'; while later Roman bishops in their turn contributed to this proliferation of urban churches. More new ecclesiastical building in Rome was owed to the generosity of wealthy laymen, like the pious senator and friend of Jerome, Pammachius, whose church foundations included SS. Giovanni e Paolo in a residential quarter on the Caelian Hill, or the rich widow Vestina, among whose bequests was the basilica in honour of the Milanese saints Gervasius and Protasius, dedicated by pope Innocent in the early years of the fifth century (the present S. Vitale).[42] By the middle of the century most of Rome's administrative *regiones* – and its residential areas – would each embrace one or more of these congregational basilicas (to say nothing of baptisteries and other attendant buildings), enough to provide clear confirmation of the public standing and centrality of Roman Christianity, even if not to accommodate all of the city's burgeoning Christian congregation.[43]

The other major cities of the empire have left less documentation of the extent of their church buildings, but the same growing urban prominence was clearly widespread. Athanasius' Alexandria was a city of numerous churches, dominated by a new 'great church' built in the 350s on the site of a temple of the imperial cult.[44] Meanwhile Antioch's monumental

[40] 'The urban tissue of the classical town was already weakening in many places': Markus, *End of Ancient Christianity* 150 (with bibliography at n. 34). Cf. esp. for Italy, Ward-Perkins, *Public Building* 51–84. For the main themes of this urban transformation, see Dagron (1977).

[41] On the post-Constantinian ecclesiastical topography of Rome, see Krautheimer, *Rome* 33ff. and (1983) 93–121.

[42] The principal source is the catalogue preserved in the *Liber Pontificalis* (ed. Duchesne, vol. 1), 36ff For Pammachius' foundation, see De Rossi, *ICUR* 11, 150 no. 20.

[43] A point stressed by Krautheimer (1983) 102–3.

[44] The subject of accusations that Athanasius had conducted services there before the building was formally consecrated: Athan. *Apol. ad Const.* xiv–xviii. On churches in Alexandria, see Martin (1984a); the main source is Epiphan. *Pan.* 69.1–2 (*GCS* xxxvii.152–4).

buildings were enhanced by the new golden-domed cathedral dedicated in Constantius' presence in 341, to which bishop Meletius was later to add a church to house the remains of the local martyr-saint Babylas.[45] At Constantinople the tally of church buildings increased steadily in the generations after Constantine (in the 380s Egeria found there 'churches, apostles' shrines and very many *martyria*' in which to offer her prayers: *It. Eg.* 23.9), while in the time of bishop Macedonius, under Constantius II, the eastern capital also began to witness the emergence of a network of monasteries and charitable establishments (which would be further developed during the episcopate of John Chrysostom).[46] Among western cities Carthage in the late fourth century could boast at least a dozen churches (including three shrines of its principal saint, Cyprian);[47] while Milan in Ambrose's day already had both 'old' and 'new' cathedrals within the city walls, as well as several extramural basilicas, to which Ambrose himself added a further three to accommodate the newly acquired remains of saints.[48] Away from the limelight of imperial cities, bishop Augustine at Hippo occupied what has been described as a 'Christian quarter' in the midst of the town's wealthy residential suburbs, with his bishop's house alongside the main church and its baptistery; elsewhere in Hippo in his day, besides the rival church of the Donatists, were at least two other basilicas as well as local *martyria* and monasteries.[49] In the territory of Cappadocian Caesarea, bishop Basil's celebrated building-complex of hospitals, hostels and other charitable institutions was so extensive that it amounted to a 'new city' in itself.[50]

This proliferation of church buildings around, and increasingly within, the cities of the empire represented more than an obvious transformation of the physical landscape – it testified also to a sea-change in the rhythm of civic life. The cycle of communal festivals and religious ceremonial once the preserve of the old gods and their temples was being eroded by the new prominence of Christianity, and the feasts of the church began to displace pagan celebrations at the heart of public experience.[51] It was a lengthy and uneven process in different regions of the empire, and one which would not be complete for several generations, but it was the second half of the fourth century which saw the greatest impetus for change. The Roman

[45] See Downey, *Antioch* 342–69, 415–16.

[46] On monastic foundations in Constantinople, see Dagron (1970) 246ff., and Dagron, *Naissance* 439, 510ff.   [47] Saxer (1980) 182–7, 189ff.

[48] The ecclesiastical topography of fourth-century Milan is a controversial minefield, reflected in Krautheimer (1983) 68–92.

[49] On Hippo and its churches, Van der Meer (1961) 16–25; cf. Brown, *Augustine* 190. Marec's archaeological reconstruction is queried by Saxer (1980) 173–82.

[50] Greg. Naz. *Or.* XLIII.63 (*PG* XXXVI.577); cf. Sozom. *HE* VI.34.9.

[51] For Christianized perceptions of the passage of time, see Markus, *End of Ancient Christianity*, pt. II.

Calendar of 354, for example, while recording an official almanac which remained that of the traditional festivals associated with the pagan gods, also bears witness to a growing list of ceremonies and commemorations which marked the Christian year in the capital.[52] With the passage of time redefined from a Christian perspective, Roman chronology would depend as much on computations of the date of Easter and catalogues of bishops and martyrs as on lists of consuls and prefects. Around the winter solstice, the festival of *Sol Invictus* made way for the celebration of the birth of Christ, and a clutch of spring pagan festivals falling in March and April came to be overshadowed by the Christian Good Friday and Easter: an 'ecclesiastical year' was beginning to shape the civic calendar, with its proto-type in the pattern of annual liturgy established around the places marking Christ's earthly life in the Holy Land – and transmitted far afield by return-ing pilgrims.[53] In the face of this recurring cycle of Christian worship, enacted in newly prominent church buildings, the festivals of the old gods ceased to define the framework of urban public life.

The framework was constructed not only out of the universal cere-monies of the church's year, but also increasingly out of the commemora-tion of local saints and martyrs whose feasts crowded into the emerging Christian calendar. In every sense, the sacred dead moved to the centre of the urban stage.[54] Towns and cities which had previously traced their origins to pagan heroes or had revered protecting deities from the old pan-theon now enthusiastically embraced Christian patron saints. At Rome bishop Damasus, through new buildings and grandiose inscriptions, pub-licized the martyrs whose tombs ringed the walls as the new champions of the city's prestige – and none more so than saints Peter and Paul, now set to displace Romulus and Remus in the role of Rome's founding fathers.[55] The martyr poems of Prudentius evince a similar parade of civic pride in the identification with local saints among the cities of Spain;[56] while in Africa the memory of Cyprian was so central to the Christian identity of Carthage that among its fourth-century churches the city boasted no fewer than three separate shrines in honour of the martyred bishop.[57] Even small communities like Nola in Campania, by promoting the glories of its local martyr Felix, redirected civic loyalties towards Christian saints. In terms of

[52] Salzman, *Roman Time.*
[53] On the influential Jerusalem liturgy, see Hunt, *Holy Land Pilgrimage,* ch. 5; Baldovin (1987) 45–104; Smith (1987) 91–5 (esp. 92, on the movement from private worship 'to an overwhelmingly public and civic one of parade and procession').
[54] I take my cue from Brown, *Cults of the Saints* 4ff., and Markus, *End of Ancient Christianity,* esp. 145ff.
[55] Piétri, *Roma Christiana* 529–46; Huskinson (1982). On Damasus, see further Piétri (1986), esp. 51ff.
[56] See Matthews, *Western Aristocracies* 148, 'a Christian alternative to the civic patriotism of the pagan empire'; Palmer (1989) 95–6; Roberts (1993) 19–37, on martyrs and community. Note esp. *Peristeph.* IV.53ff., on the benefits to Saragossa, in contrast to other cities, because of its numerical superiority of martyrs. [57] See p. 252 above, n. 47.

the physical environment, this meant the appearance of new church buildings to house the treasured remains and the congregations who assembled
to honour them – Nola, thanks to the munificence of the aristocratic landowner Paulinus, gained a whole new urban complex around the cemetery
site of Felix's tomb[58] – as well as a new centre of gravity for public festivals and ceremonial. Cities were turned inside out as Christian bishop and
clergy led their people away from the old urban centre, heartland of now
discarded pagan gods, to the martyr shrines which encircled the outskirts.
Paulinus regularly exulted in the crowds which flocked around Felix's buildings at Nola for the annual commemoration;[59] while Jerome (*Ep.* 107.1)
would portray the whole city of Rome 'uprooted from its foundations' as
the people deserted pagan temples for their new Christian patron saints.
Another Roman visitor, Prudentius, pictured the crowds assembled for the
joint celebration of Peter and Paul (29 June), and the swirling movement
of the *plebs Romula* making its way through the city between the two shrines
on the Vatican hill and on the *Via Ostiense* – enveloping Rome in an active
public demonstration of its people's new-found Christian heritage.[60]

The saints themselves were increasingly abandoning their extramural
tombs to be ceremoniously reinterred in new city basilicas. In 362, for
example, Antioch's Christian population asserted their defiance of Julian's
pagan revival by triumphantly escorting the body of their martyr Babylas
to his resting-place within the walls (where he would later be honoured with
a new basilica by bishop Meletius);[61] while at Milan, amid much popular
acclaim, bishop Ambrose presided over the 'translation' of martyrs'
remains to august new basilicas around the city.[62] In the same year (386) as
the most celebrated of these transfers, that of Gervasius and Protasius, an
eastern law of Theodosius vainly tried to confine the martyrs to their burial
places beyond city walls.[63] The traditional prohibition of tomb violation
was assuming a new urgency, as communities sought to enhance their
Christian credentials by importing into their midst the remains of saints
and martyrs which had hitherto lain in peripheral cemeteries. There were
widespread transfers of relics, and on a scale which far transcended local
reinterments.[64] Already in the 350s Constantinople was fast accumulating a
Christian pedigree by means of the importation of apostles' remains from
elsewhere in the east, and by the end of the century, as far away as northern Gaul, bishop Victricius of Rouen was hailing the advent of a diverse
collection of martyrs' relics which would provide new heavenly patrons for
his city.[65]

The most prized source of such sanctified credentials was the Holy Land

---

[58] Testini (1985).   [59] E.g. *Carm.* XIV.82–5, XXVII.379–81.   [60] Prudent. *Peristeph.* XII.57–8.
[61] Sozom. *HE* V.19.18–19, with Lieu (1989) 46–54.   [62] Dassmann (1975).
[63] *C.Th.* IX.17.7 'humatum corpus nemo ad alterum locum transferat'.   [64] Hunt (1981).
[65] *De Laude Sanct.* I; on Constantinople, cf. ch. 1, pp. 38–9 above.

itself – the reception of relics associated with the actual holy places of Christ would naturally serve to bolster the public prestige of local churches and their leaders not otherwise so blessed by Christian history. The most conveniently portable item was the *lignum crucis* – so much so that by the middle of the fourth century numerous congregations around the Mediterranean world were already claiming possession of fragments of the cross originating from Jerusalem.[66] The possibilities were further enlarged when the 'Holy Land connection' and the enthusiasm for martyr-cult combined in the instance of St Stephen, the first Christian to die for his faith, whose tomb was remarkably 'discovered' near Jerusalem in December 415.[67] Through the agency of Augustine's protégé Orosius, Stephen's remains were transported to North Africa and elsewhere in the west, where they were to achieve wide circulation.[68] Given both his pre-eminence in the galaxy of saints and his Holy Land origins, Stephen brought confidence and esteem – to say nothing of his heavenly advocacy – to those communities which claimed a share of his relics, and his very mobility across the empire was symptomatic of the church's public prominence and internationalism (precisely at a time when the western Roman world was becoming fragmented and isolated by the onset of barbarian occupation).

This movement of relics was facilitated by the travels of pilgrims returning from the shrines and celebrations of the saints: sermons preached in honour of martyrs commonly lay stress on the crowds of pilgrims who gathered for the commemoration.[69] Although primarily, as we have seen, advertisements of local Christian identity and community, many cults – like those of the Roman martyrs – were sufficiently famed to attract a wider circle of worshippers. Prudentius portrays the Roman congregation at Hippolytus' tomb on the *Via Tiburtina* swollen by the convergence of the faithful from other Italian towns;[70] and similarly diverse gatherings marked Felix's annual celebration at Nola, when Paulinus imagined the Appian Way 'disappearing' under the swarm of pilgrims approaching the shrine.[71] Paulinus himself was one of the many from central Italy and further afield who made the annual journey to Rome in June for the festival of Peter and Paul, the Christian 'birthday' of the city at the traditional heart of the Roman empire. But the most extensive Christian journeying in the post-Constantinian era was directed towards Jerusalem and the holy places of Palestine. While each locality was acquiring a new Christian topography and identity constructed around its churches and martyr shrines, the map of the Roman empire at large was being redrawn to focus on the Holy Land at its

[66] Hunt, *Holy Land Pilgrimage* 128ff.   [67] Hunt, *Holy Land Pilgrimage* 211–20.
[68] For the impact of their arrival on the island of Minorca, see Hunt (1982).
[69] See examples from Basil of Caesarea and Gregory of Nyssa cited by Delehaye (1933) 44–5.
[70] *Peristeph.* XI.195–212; on Roman pilgrimages, see further, Bardy (1949).
[71] *Carm.* XIV.49–81, esp. 70 'confertis longe latet Appia turbis'.

centre.[72] Already as early as 333 an anonymous traveller from Bordeaux on the Atlantic seaboard of Gaul set out on a distant pilgrimage to Jerusalem, intent only on the objective of the holy places of the Bible: the city of Rome was no more than a staging-post on the return journey, and even the newly founded Constantinople claimed no special attention.[73] By the time Egeria and her companions were in Jerusalem some fifty years later (381–4), its Christian festivals and holy places were the focus for assemblies of well-travelled devotees from east and west alike.[74] At the same period, as exemplified by the westerners Jerome and Rufinus and their respective entourages, the region had begun to play host to an international concentration of pious endeavour and monastic settlement which would place it at the hub of the Christian Roman empire – a standing which would soon receive further confirmation in the arrival at the holy places of a stream of refugees uprooted from their environment by barbarian incursions in the west.[75]

The practical response to this upsurge of mobility, whether localized or long-distance, was the emergence of a network of hostels (*xenodochia*) administered by churches and monasteries to provide for the needs of the 'private' Christian traveller plying the routes of the empire (to be distinguished from those Christian bishops journeying to councils at imperial invitation, who were granted privileged access to the *cursus publicus*), and in the vicinity of pilgrim shrines and holy places.[76] The fourth century saw the main thoroughfare across Asia Minor linking Constantinople with the eastern Mediterranean (the route followed by both the Bordeaux pilgrim and Egeria) begin to assume the characteristics of an organized 'pilgrims' road' – the institutions of Christian hospitality in the region were sufficiently in place by 362 to provoke envious observations from Julian on the charity of the 'Galilaeans'[77] – while holy places and saints' tombs acquired conveniently adjacent *xenodochia*. Cyprian's shrine on the waterfront at Carthage could provide Augustine's mother with lodging on the night when he set sail for Italy (*Conf.* v.8.15); the younger Melania on arriving in Jerusalem in 417 was able to reside in close proximity to the Holy Sepulchre, in the buildings surrounding Constantine's church (*V. Mel.* 35). Paulinus' Nola, too, had its pilgrim hostel, sufficiently close for its occupants to gaze into Felix's shrine itself.[78] Unlike the Bordeaux pilgrim of 333, whose journey was still conducted against a background of 'secular' facil-

---

[72] See Hunt, *Holy Land Pilgrimage*; Maraval (1985); Ousterhout (1990); Wilken (1992) 101–25.

[73] For text of the *Itinerarium Burdigalense*, see the edition of P. Geyer and O. Cuntz, *CCSL* 175 (1965).

[74] *It. Eg.* is most recently edited by P. Maraval, *SChrét.* 296 (1982); Engl. trans. Wilkinson (1981). For Jerusalem's cosmopolitan worship, see *It. Eg.* 47.3–4 (the trilingual liturgy), and 49.1 (pilgrims at the Dedication festival 'de *omnibus* provinciis').   [75] See Hunt, *Holy Land Pilgrimage* chs. 7–9.

[76] Hunt, *Holy Land Pilgrimage* 62–6; Maraval (1985) 167–9.   [77] Jul. *Ep.* 84.430b–d Bidez.

[78] Paul. Nol. *Carm.* XXVII.400–2. Roman travellers would have the benefit of the Christian hostel at Portus founded by Pammachius: Jer. *Ep.* 66.11, 77.10.

ities for the traveller, without benefit of ecclesiastical provision, later pilgrims might expect to travel in an identifiably Christian environment, as the
institutional organization of the church extended beyond urban centres
and along the highways of the Roman empire.

IV. WEALTH

The provision of hospitality was only one of the manifold charitable
commitments undertaken by a now institutionalized church mindful of the
Gospel injunction to cater for the poor and needy. The selective generosity of wealthy individuals which had characterized the secular tradition of
munificence gradually gave way to organized and universal Christian
charity administered by bishops and their clergy.[79] This called for extensive
building-schemes to provide the necessary facilities for the sick, poor and
displaced – Basil's 'new city' at Caesarea was the most famous example –
and the administration of formal registers of those in need: Antioch offers
the clearest evidence, where towards the end of the fourth century the
church was providing each day for 3000 widows and virgins, as well as an
unspecified number of other recipients, and attending to those in prison,
hospital or on the move through the city.[80] Generations earlier, in the mid
third century, the church of Rome was already supporting 'over 1500
widows along with others in distress', in addition to the growing numbers
of its own clergy (Eus. *HE* VI.43.11). These statistics imply an availability
of wealth and resources which the churches could command even before
Constantine, and which naturally expanded in the more favourable circumstances of the fourth century.[81] Christian congregations had been formally recognized as owners of buildings and property (chiefly burial
grounds) at least from the time of Gallienus, and in the aftermath of persecution Constantine had restored to them the corporate possession of
assets which had been confiscated or had fallen into other private hands.
The emperor himself redirected the great tradition of imperial public
works into Christian building, instructing his subordinates in the provinces
to provide resources and manpower, and transferring the ownership of
imperial properties to endow church foundations; as a more tangible
advertisement of the emperor's generosity, churches were presented with
donations of precious plate and possessions from the palace coffers.[82]
Constantine's successors followed his precedent. In Rome, for example,

[79] For economic background, see Patlagean, *Pauvreté* 181–96; and on charitable enterprises, Herrin
(1990).
[80] Joh. Chrys. *Hom. in Matt.* LXVI.3 (*PG* LVIII.630). For similar provision by the church in Gaza, cf.
Marc. Diac. *V. Porph.* 94.
[81] On the church's wealth, see generally Gaudemet (1958) 288–315, Jones, *LRE* 894–910.
[82] See, above all, the Roman list preserved under the name of bishop Silvester in *Lib. Pont.* 34 (ed.
Duchesne, vol. I. 172ff.).

scene of many of Constantine's ecclesiastical benefactions, Constantius
added his own contribution to the completion of St Peter's basilica, and in
the 380s Valentinian II and Theodosius in turn embarked on the new and
enlarged St Paul's on the Ostian Way.[83] In Jerusalem, another principal
target of Constantinian patronage, churches at the holy places received
further gifts from his sons, and were later to benefit from the pious
generosity of Theodosius II and his imperial relatives.[84] Also in the Holy
Land, Arcadius' empress Eudoxia is credited with the endowment of a
church in Gaza on the site of the destroyed temple of Marnas, as well as a
hostel for travellers to the city (*V. Porph.* 53). It is hard to imagine many
local church leaders having the will to follow the austere example of bishop
Martin at Tours, who reportedly refused gifts offered by Valentinian I;[85] for
Rome's Christian rulers it was the church which now provided the
appropriate arena for traditional displays of virtuous imperial giving.

The emperor's wealthier subjects had similar notions, deriving both
from a continuing history of aristocratic munificence, now redirected into
ecclesiastical patronage, and (in some) from a new-found conversion to
ascetic piety which disdained the possession of secular wealth: the Gallic
senator Meropius Pontius Paulinus, to take one well-documented example,
deserted a secular career for ordination to the priesthood, and devoted his
very considerable resources to the glory of St Felix at Nola – to the
incomprehension of his more worldly compatriot Ausonius.[86] In the
western provinces in the early years of the fifth century this impetus
towards pious donations was accelerated by the disruption of barbarian
incursions threatening the stability of landed estates. Such was the background to the liquidation of the widespread properties belonging to the
refugee heiress Melania (the younger) and her senatorial husband Valerius
Pinianus, a landholding said to have once yielded an annual revenue of
120,000 *solidi*: of the proceeds given away, the lion's share went to the
benefit of the church, from occasional gifts of vestments and plate to substantial monastic foundations (notably on the Mount of Olives in
Jerusalem).[87] In her lavish donations Melania was following the precedent
of other well-to-do *grandes dames* who had exchanged their affluence for a
life of ascetic renunciation, such as her grandmother and namesake
Melania the elder, or Jerome's pious patroness Paula, whose wealth supported his monastic establishment in Bethlehem.[88] Before they arrived in

---

[83] Krautheimer (1983) 104, with *Coll. Avell.* III (the imperial rescript initiating the work); for St Peter's, Krautheimer (1987).

[84] See Holum, *Theodosian Empresses* 103; for sons of Constantine, Hunt, *Holy Land Pilgrimage* 142.

[85] See Sulp. Sev. *Dial.* II.5.10.

[86] See Matthews, *Western Aristocracies* 151–3. For evidence that Paulinus and other senatorial ascetics were not as careless of family fortunes as is sometimes supposed, see Harries (1984).

[87] See *V. Mel.* 15ff. (ed. Gorce, *SChrét.* 90); Pall. *Hist. Laus.* 61, with Clark (1984) 92ff., and Giardina (1986).   [88] On foundations in the Holy Land, cf. Hunt, *Holy Land Pilgrimage* 137ff.

the Holy Land, Melania and Pinianus had been among those senatorial landowners who fled to North Africa before the onslaught of Alaric. There they took up residence for seven years on their extensive estates in the neighbourhood of Thagaste, which were the source of gifts for the church and generosity lavish enough, it is said, to endow the foundation of two monasteries.[89] Not surprisingly, they were local celebrities. When they visited Hippo, Augustine's congregation were on the verge of a riot in their enthusiasm to detain them and secure the services of Pinianus as a priest – despite Augustine's attempts to argue otherwise, it is hard to resist the conclusion that they were attracted less by the visitors' pious credentials than by the prospect of a share of their wealthy patronage.[90] Comparable to Melania's donations were those of the well-connected widow-turned-deaconess Olympias, who lavished riches on the church of Constantinople during John Chrysostom's bishopric. The 'great church' in the capital benefited not only to the tune of revenues from Olympias' estates in surrounding provinces, but also from a number of urban properties transferred to its ownership; Olympias was also the foundress of a monastery attached to the great church in which she installed her aristocratic relations and dependents.[91]

Such financial support for the church was not confined to the living – it might also be expected from beyond the grave. Damasus' Roman clergy, for example, earned a reputation as the new 'legacy-hunters' of their day, attaching themselves to the households of aristocratic widows in expectation of rich pickings – and provoking the condemnation of the emperor Valentinian in 370 (as well as an expression of outrage from the pen of Jerome).[92] But such conduct was only an extreme form of what Constantine's general emancipation of Christianity had made possible, by recognizing the church as a legitimate beneficiary for legacies (*C.Th.* XVI.2.4) – and thus placing it in competition with the survival of family fortunes.[93] The wills of well-to-do members of the congregation became a regular source of income for the churches to supplement the more spectacular and occasional windfalls from the living. The sensitive handling of such legacies ranked among the more demanding aspects of Augustine's episcopal concerns at Hippo: recognizing the need to balance the interests of surviving descendants against the charitable commitments of the church, he argued that 'Christ' (i.e. the church) should be regarded as an addition to existing heirs to an estate, and not as the exclusive beneficiary.[94]

[89] *V. Mel.* 20–2 (ed. Gorce). According to the Latin version of the *Vita*, the church at Thagaste received an estate larger than the town itself.

[90] For Augustine's arguments, see his *Ep.* 126.7ff. On the whole episode, Van der Meer (1961) 143–8.

[91] *Vita Olymp.* 5–6 (ed. Malingrey, *SChrét.* 13*bis*), with Dagron, *Naissance*, 501–6.

[92] Jer. *Ep.* 52.6, with *C.Th.* XVI.2.20.

[93] For this issue in relation to Roman senatorial estates, see Harries (1984).

[94] Aug. *Serm.* 355.3; cf. Possid. *V. Aug.* XXIII–XXIV.

Besides benefiting from individual acts of munificence on the part of the emperors, the church also enjoyed more 'institutional' generosity from the state. Government revenues and resources were tapped, not only to build churches, but to provide assistance for the poor, for the maintenance of widows and virgins, the care of the sick and all the other good works which fell within the remit of Christian charity.[95] This was the context in which his political opponents could accuse Athanasius of misappropriating grants of corn which he had received for the benefit of widows.[96] The apostate Julian, observing the effective way in which the church's charity was furthered by this 'state aid', sought to foster the pagan revival by making official provisions available for distribution by the provincial priesthood to 'strangers and beggars'.[97] With public grants went tax privileges and immunities: bishop Basil, for instance, expected the hostels for the poor founded at his instigation in the territory of Caesarea to be granted financial concessions by the imperial authorities.[98] The bishops assembled on Constantius' orders at Rimini in 359 took time off from their deliberations about doctrine to press the emperor for a ruling on the exemption of church lands from tax demands: Constantius in response drew a distinction between the corporate estates of churches – which were exempt – and the personal landholdings of the clergy, which remained liable to taxation.[99] The same recognition of the corporate status of churches extended to their protection from demands for the wide range of supplies and services which the late Roman government might extract from its subjects in the name of *munera sordida*. Even when, by 423, this protection no longer extended to the obligation to contribute to the repair of roads and bridges, the church was still keeping privileged company – for the emperor did not even exclude his own estates from this particular liability.[100]

Accumulating assets from imperial benefactions, individual donations and legacies, and exempted from tax demands and sundry *munera*, the churches acquired undoubted wealth – and, at least to some, presented an appearance of handsome riches. Ammianus' acute observations of the social scene in Rome conjure up an image of the extravagant lifestyle of its bishops: 'enriched by the gifts of matrons, they ride in carriages, dress splendidly, and outdo kings in the lavishness of their table' (xxvii.3.14). The portrait owes a good deal to satirical exaggeration, but gains at least some anecdotal support from the well-known story of the pagan senator Praetextatus' mock-enthusiasm to swap places with bishop Damasus.[101] Another reputedly scandalous exemplar of ecclesiastical extravagance was

[95] Theod. *HE* i.11.2–3: such grants were suspended during Julian's rule.
[96] Athan. *Apol. c. Ar.* xviii; Socr. *HE* ii.17.   [97] Jul. *Ep.* 84.430c Bidez; cf. pp. 68–9 above.
[98] Basil, *Epp.* 142–3; Giet (1941) 377–80.   [99] *C.Th.* xvi.2.15, with Elliott (1978) 332–3.
[100] *C.Th.* xv.3.6; for comprehensive exemption, see e.g. xi.16.15 (382).
[101] Recorded by Jerome, *C. Ioh. Hier.* viii.

the bishop of Jerusalem, who could be accused by Jerome of exploiting for his own pleasure the wealth of his church, which was owed to the 'faith of the whole world' (*C. Ioh. Hier.* xiv) – an allusion to the flow of pious offerings sent to the Holy Land and the donations of wealthy pilgrims. But in a different context Jerome was ready to acknowledge that the Jerusalem churches needed all their resources to expend on charitable purposes, and to meet the imperative of coping with the crowds of the faithful who flooded the holy places.[102] Although pilgrims like Egeria might voice their amazement at the sight of new church buildings and opulent decorations (*It. Eg.* 25.8–9), it is unlikely that the churches in the Holy Land enjoyed any surplus revenue; more probably, the requirements of pilgrim hospitality placed them under financial strain, if there is any truth in the charge levelled against bishop Cyril of Jerusalem by his opponents that he had sold off church treasures to raise funds for poor relief in a time of famine (similar charges were to be included in the indictment aganst John Chrysostom).[103] The truth is likely to be that the wealth of the churches was easily consumed by their increasing charitable functions. Even Ammianus acknowledged that the affluence of the Roman church was exceptional by comparison with the run of more modest provincial sees; yet much of this appearance of wealth was superficial finery, the precious adornments which attracted attention – the actual revenue, on the other hand, from its Constantinian endowments amounted to *c.* 400 pounds of gold (as calculated from the data surviving in the *Liber Pontificalis*), and thus less than a quarter of the income attributed to the properties of the younger Melania, and a mere tenth of the sum which the wealthiest of Rome's senators are said to have commanded.[104] In Antioch towards the end of the fourth century the church was having to meet its range of charitable commitments on an income which, according to John Chrysostom, matched that of one of the city's wealthier – but not wealthiest – residents.[105] On becoming bishop in Constantinople John would encounter perhaps more substantial ecclesiastical riches, for in the eastern capital he took responsibility for a church which already by 380 had impressed Gregory of Nazianzus with its much-vaunted wealth, and which was to benefit further from the lavish gifts of pious donors like Olympias.[106] In provincial North Africa, Augustine's world was far less affluent than that of the grandees of Rome, Antioch or Constantinople: although he claimed that his family fortune at Thagaste amounted to barely a twentieth of the

---

[102] Hunt, *Holy Land Pilgrimage*, 145–7.

[103] For the accusations against Cyril, see Sozom. *HE* iv.25.3–4, Theod. *HE* ii.27.1–2. On John Chrysostom, see pp. 262–3 below.   [104] The *locus classicus* is Olympiod. fr. 41.2 (Blockley).

[105] *Hom. in Matt.* lxvi.3 (*PG* lviii.630). On the church's need of resources for charity, cf. *Hom. in Ep. I ad Corinth.* xxi.6–7 (*PG* lxi.178–80).

[106] For Chrysostom's financial regime at Constantinople, see Dagron, *Naissance* 498ff., Liebeschuetz, *Barbarians and Bishops* 209–10; cf. Greg. Naz. *De Vita Sua* (ed. Jungck), 1475–8, and below, p. 262.

church resources which it fell to him to administer as bishop of Hippo, he could still describe African churchmen as 'poor' (*Ep.* 126.7). It is not then so surprising that far-flung British bishops who were called to undertake the long journey to Rimini for the council in 359 could apparently only afford to travel with the aid of the public purse.[107] To seek to generalize about the wealth of churches in the generations after Constantine would clearly be misleading: local circumstances and commitments differed, and impressions of affluence varied with the vantage-point adopted. But there is no denying the broad conclusion that, in a period when civic resources were under increasing strain, ecclesiastical wealth across the cities of the empire was conspicuously on the increase.

V. THE CHURCH AS A CAREER

The management of these expanding assets of the church rested principally with the local bishop and his clergy. In recalling pastoral leaders to their duty of charity and almsgiving, John Chrysostom preaching at Antioch saw the bishops of his day turned into estate managers and financial overlords, their responsibilities directed towards land and property, even animals and transport vehicles: they were daily preoccupied more as merchants and shopkeepers than as the guardians of men's souls and protectors of the poor which they ought to be.[108] It was a concern about priorities heeded by the likes of bishop Augustine, whose biographer acclaims his humanitarian management of the church revenues of which he had charge in Hippo: the day-to-day administration was delegated to experienced members of his clergy, who reported annually to the bishop on their stewardship of the finances (*V. Aug.* XXIII–XXIV). Yet that did not free Augustine himself, as we have observed, from facing difficult decisions over the disposal of legacies. Bishop Basil of Caesarea, it emerges, could be seen traversing the routes of his far-flung diocese in the course of administering revenues due to the church; elsewhere we have evidence of such tasks entrusted to deacons who gathered the rents from eccleasiastical properties.[109] When Chrysostom became bishop of Constantinople he did not forget the strictures which he had levelled at the worldliness of financial administration: unlike his predecessor Gregory of Nazianzus, he is said to have kept close scrutiny on the management of church resources and, among other things, to have transferred expenditure away from aggrandizing the episcopal residence into the building of a hospital.[110] Like Basil of Caesarea, Chrysostom presided over a regime of founding hostels and other charitable institutions around Constantinople, and was an easy

---

[107] Sulp. Sev. *Chron.* II.41.3.   [108] *Hom. in Matt.* LXXXV.3–4 (*PG* LVIII.761–2).
[109] Marc. Diac. *V. Porph.* 22; for Basil, see Greg. Naz. *Or.* XLIII.58 (*PG* XXXVI.572).
[110] Pall. *Dial.* V.128–39 (ed. Malingrey, *SChrét.* 341).

target for his opponents' accusations that to raise funds he sold off treasures belonging to the church.[111]

As custodians managing wealth and property, and by the same token now the main purveyors of poor-relief in their cities, bishops could not escape assimilation into the role of those local magnates who had traditionally monopolized civic patronage.[112] However much by their Christian preaching and ascetic lifestyle an Augustine or a Chrysostom might claim a gulf between themselves and the 'world', and endeavour to keep secularity at a distance, they failed to dispel the perception of bishops and the church establishment as a focus of power and influence in the surrounding community. Bishops presided over an institution which not only increasingly vied for a pre-eminence of wealth and prestige, but which also comprised a visible hierarchy more extensive and widespread than any other on the local scene. Only cities which were major centres of government, housing the bureaucracy of senior imperial functionaries, will have had anything equivalent to the ecclesiastical establishment of bishop and grades of clergy which went with every episcopal see. As early as the middle of the third century, the Roman bishop could lay claim to 154 clergy, including forty-six priests and seven deacons;[113] by the sixth century (*Nov.* III.1, 535) Justinian was ordering the manpower of Haghia Sophia alone in Constantinople to be *reduced* to a total of 485 (including sixty priests and a hundred deacons). At the time of the council of Chalcedon the bishop of Edessa claimed his clergy to number 'more than 200', while also in the fifth century the tally of clergy at Carthage was reported as over 500.[114] Constantine and his successors had vainly attempted (in the interests of maintaining local *curiae*) to restrain the rush to ordination, but such figures – comparable to the staffs of major officials in the empire – point to the conclusion that the numbers of its clergy easily kept pace with the church's growth in stature and privilege.[115] The lower grades of this recruitment were naturally of humble social background – entry into the clergy did not, for instance, protect them from liability to torture in court (*C.Th.* XI.39.10, 386) – who might well continue their previous craft or trade after ordination; as clergy they were freed of the burden of the business tax, the *collatio lustralis*, in the expectation (according to the laws) that they would now devote the profits from their trade to the charitable relief of the poor.[116] In one of his letters (*Ep.* 198) bishop Basil characterizes the majority of his clergy as men who continued to gain their livelihood from practising a

---

[111] Among the charges at the Synod of the Oak: Photius, *Bibl.* LIX.19–22, 39–40 (ed. Malingrey, *SChrét.* 342).   [112] See Brown, *Power and Persuasion* 89–103.

[113] Bishop Cornelius, cited by Eus. *HE* VI.43.11.   [114] Vict. Vit. III.34; for Edessa, *ACO* II.1, 386.

[115] For numbers serving in *officia*, see Jones, *LRE* ch. 16 and see ch. 5, pp. 165–6 above. Restrictions on curial access to clergy: (e.g.) *C.Th.* XVI.2.3, 6 (both dated by Seeck (1919) to 329).

[116] *C.Th.* XVI.2.10, 14. On clergy exemption from *collatio lustralis*, see refs. at Jones, *LRE* ch. 13 n. 52, with Dupont (1967) 739–52, Elliott (1978) 330–2.

domestic craft – but who refrained from wider commercial enterprises which would have required them to travel away from their churches.

If the prospect of evading the trade tax was some inducement to entering the lower ranks of the clergy, then the privilege of curial immunity was an obvious spur to the more senior levels of deacon and priest.[117] The literate classes in the cities were offered career possibilities which may have seemed to many more attractive than local office or imperial service. In the case of the church, financial privilege and public prestige were not tied to the uncertainties of a secular career, and the impermanence of the positions which came with it, but to lifelong clerical status with responsibilities in the community which extended far beyond the confines of the church building, and allowed for the exercise of traditional social habits of leadership and patronage. The proliferation of laws from Constantine onwards aiming to deter those of curial eligibility from entering the clergy clearly suggests that the educated urban élite was the principal reservoir of clerical recruitment: by 361 (C.Th. XII.1.49) it was being stipulated that those who fled the *curia* for the clergy should at least be required to surrender a proportion of their property, or substitute a relative to undertake their obligations. Despite this and subsequent attempts to protect the city councils from ecclesiastical competition, it was the curial class which continued to furnish the bulk of the church's senior manpower. The emperors' efforts to stem the tide met with resistance from bishops: Ambrose, for example (*Ep.* 40.29), conveyed to Theodosius in 388 the complaints of bishops in Italy that long-serving priests were being ordered back to curial duties. The petition met with some success, to judge from a Theodosian law of 390 issued in Milan (*C.Th.* XII.1.121) which concedes to curial ordinands of more than two years' standing the right to retain their property. For bishop Innocent of Rome, too, the constant threat of recall to the *curia* was a 'source of tribulation' to the churches, and a reason for bishops to be wary of too many curial ordinations.[118]

Besides such practical problems associated with ordaining those of curial standing, Innocent also voiced a more theological concern about conflicts between the calling of the Christian priesthood and the functions of *curiales*: those who held civic positions and whose task it was to satisfy the people with games and theatrical performances were not best fitted to be ordained into the clergy.[119] Yet papal disapproval, no less than the frequency of imperial legislation, only reinforces the point that, for many, an ecclesiastical career was now an option competing with the opportunities of the secular world: the church, too, offered a *militia* of public service – and its accompanying rewards. In the disciplinary language of papal letters

---

[117] On the curial background of clergy recruitment, see Dupont (1967), Noethlichs (1972), Elliott (1978), and (for Gaul) Rousselle (1977).   [118] *Ep.* 37.5 (*PL* xx.604); cf. *Ep.* 2.14 (477–8).

[119] Innoc. *Epp.* 2.14; 3.7, 9 (*PL* xx.490–2).

there was an incompatibility between the demands of the *militia saecularis* and the service of the church, and those who had held worldly office were deemed unworthy for ordination;[120] but this perception is unlikely to have been shared by civic leaders observing the prosperity and prospects of the ecclesiastical establishment – here was a natural (and attractive) alternative to secular public office. Many indeed who rose to be bishops belonged to families which also provided officials of the empire (John Chrysostom, to take one instance, came from a line of functionaries serving the *dux* of Syria), or had themselves held high office before turning to a career in the church:[121] among bishops of known pedigree we can number former court officials – Eleusius, the future bishop of Cyzicus, who had 'served with distinction in the palace' (Sozom. *HE* IV.20.2), or the *notarius* Theodorus who was later bishop of Mutina in Italy (Paulin. *V. Ambr.* xxxv) – and provincial governors like Evagrius, the one-time *curialis* of Antioch and friend of Jerome who became one of the rival contenders for the bishopric of his city.[122] The fact is that the cultural and social milieu which nurtured the urban upper classes of late antiquity did not distinguish future bishops from future bureaucrats; and any perceived incompatibility of the respective *militiae* existed more in the niceties of ecclesiastical regulations than in the real world.

Yet there was at least one species of *militia* less capable of absorption into a career in the church: there are few recorded instances of soldiers or army officers opting for the clerical alternative. Even so, Gaul provides the notable exceptions of bishops Martin of Tours and Victricius of Rouen, both former soldiers[123] – and there is evidence to indicate that the lower reaches of the clergy were a recognized escape route for those seeking to evade military conscription.[124] None the less, as St Martin discovered, the prospect of deciding between army and church posed a sharply defined conflict of alternatives, and one less easily resolved than that which faced those in civilian positions.

Most of those who emerged as bishops had served the apprenticeship of a clerical career. But it was already being envisaged in 343, by the western bishops gathered at Sardica, that prominent laymen ('a wealthy man, advocate or civil official': Can. 13 (Lat.)) might be in demand as bishops; it was

[120] Innocent was repeating what had already been affirmed by bishop Siricius, e.g. *Epp.* 5.2 (Can. 3: *PL* XIII.1158–9), 6.3 (1165), 10.7 (1186), that the requirements of public office were incompatible with a clerical career.
[121] On John Chrysostom, see Pall. *Dial.* v.2–3 (with Malingrey *ad loc.*). For the origins of bishops, see Eck (1978).
[122] *PLRE* I.285–6 'Evagrius 6'. Note also Augustine's fellow townsman Evodius, future bishop of Uzalis, who had served as an *agens in rebus* (*Conf.* IX.8.17).
[123] For Martin's military career, Sulp. Sev. *V. Mart.* II–IV; for Victricius, Paul. Nol. *Ep.* 18.7.
[124] *C.Th.* VII.20.12 (400); cf. the concern of Basil, *Ep.* 54, about the unsuitability of such would-be ordinands.

stipulated that such candidates first had to pass through the clerical orders of reader, deacon and priest. This insistence against directly consecrating laymen as bishops was to become a familiar piece of church discipline, and reiterated in future papal pronouncements;[125] but in reality it could do little to conceal the prevalent perception of the bishop in terms of worldly stature and credentials – the bishops at Sardica were perhaps more revealing on the subject of the social standing of some of their peers when they agreed (Can. 15) that time should be allowed for bishops to travel away from their sees in order to attend to their personal property elsewhere. Gregory of Nyssa surely had contemporary realities in mind when he advised the presbyters of the church of Nicomedia against turning worldly leaders into bishops: the apostles, he reminded them (*Ep.* 17.10ff.), had been humble private citizens and not 'consuls, generals and prefects, or distinguished in rhetoric and philosophy'. It was a warning delivered in a context which meant, for some at least, an easy transition from high office in the world to the equivalent in the church. The most celebrated example was the son of a former praetorian prefect of Gaul who enjoyed aristocratic Roman patronage to become a provincial governor in northern Italy: in that capacity Ambrose was chosen as their bishop in 374 by the Catholic congregation in Milan (and notoriously rushed through the requisite holy orders).[126] In 381 a lay senator of Constantinople and sometime urban praetor, Nectarius, was named bishop of the eastern capital by Theodosius.[127] Later in Constantinople Chrysanthus, who had been vicar in far-off Britain and hoped to crown his career with the city prefecture, found himself instead made bishop of the Novatian congregation.[128]

Leading laymen claimed for bishoprics in such circumstances customarily displayed reluctance at the prospect. Synesius, *curialis* of Cyrene, sought to avoid consecration as the local bishop, and imagined death a preferable fate.[129] Ambrose's biographer (*V. Ambros.* VIII–IX) has him twice fleeing from Milan in the face of the popular (and divine) will demanding him as bishop. Appropriate demonstrations of *recusatio* notwithstanding, there is no reason to disbelieve that the occupants of positions of secular influence and authority might at first recoil at seeing themselves turned into prelates of the church; yet the very fact that these transitions occurred – with a large measure of popular endorsement – is some indication that the role of the bishop in his community was seen as one analogous to that of other public figures, and one for which the experience and credentials of worldly power

[125] As in Siricius' concerns about suitable ordinations: *Ep.* 10.15 (*PL* XIII.1192).
[126] *PLRE* 1.52 'Ambrosius 3' (retaining the traditional date for his consecration), with Matthews, *Western Aristocracies* 183ff., on social and political context, and Lizzi (1989) 28–36 on Ambrose's aristocratic milieu.   [127] *PLRE* 1.621 'Nectarius 2'.   [128] For his career, Socr. *HE* VII.12.
[129] Liebeschuetz (1986) 183–6; on Synesius' intellectual objections, Bregman (1982) 155–63, with Cameron and Long, *Barbarians and Politics* 19–18. For episcopal reluctance – analogous to the traditional refusal of secular rulers – see Lizzi (1987) 33–55.

were deemed appropriate qualifications. By the same token, a bishopric was deemed incompatible with the ideals of the monastery, and hagiographic sources applaud the unwillingness of monks to be pressed into becoming bishops: from the perspective of those whose chosen course was ascetic withdrawal, the office of a bishop might easily appear too contaminated by preoccupations at odds with the unworldly demands of a monastic life.[130]

The expectations which assimilated the bishop's position to that of a public official are evident in the popular interest, and often disorder, which attended episcopal elections.[131] Ecclesiastical discipline dictated that the choice of a new bishop rested with the clergy and congregation, subject to the endorsement of the other bishops in the province, and of the metropolitan bishop in particular. But orderly church procedure often fell victim to factional in-fighting within the churches, and the wider politicization of episcopal appointments. In the major cities of the empire the bishopric inherited something of the political rivalries and popular fervour which had by the fourth century all but disappeared from 'elections' to the civil magistracies; these positions were now dependent upon curial nomination or imperial appointment, whereas the choice of bishop, by contrast, might well assume the characteristics of a real electoral contest. When controversy surrounded an episcopal succession – as, for example, when the legitimacy of Athanasius' election at Alexandria was challenged by his political opponents – it was important to invoke the claim of universal popular support.[132] Church councils warned against the appointment of bishops falling into the disorderly hands of a mob;[133] but such rulings had no power to prevent some notorious episodes of communal *stasis* over rival claimants to a bishopric. One such riot in Constantinople in 342 (between supporters of bishops Paul and Macedonius) claimed the life of Constantius' *magister equitum* Hermogenes;[134] while the disputed succession to Liberius of Rome in 366 saw the partisans of Damasus and Ursinus locked in violent strife over the possession of churches in the city – one day's death toll in Liberius' own basilica may have been as high as 160.[135] In Rome again, around Easter 419, the churches were once more at the mercy of rival episcopal factions, on this occasion the supporters of Eulalius and Boniface, who both claimed the succession to pope Zosimus.[136] These Roman incidents constituted

---

[130] Famous examples include the Egyptian hermit Ammonius (Pall. *Hist. Laus.* 11) who cut off his ear rather than accept a bishopric, and Martin of Tours (Sulp. Sev. *V. Mart.* IX) who had to be inveigled out of his monastery.

[131] See, generally, Gaudemet (1958) 330–41; Jones, *LRE* 915–20; and the useful collections of material by Gryson (1979), (1980).

[132] Athan *Apol. c. Ar.* VI.5 6; for the opposition case, see Philostorg. II.11 (ed. Bidez/Winkelmann, 22–3), with Arnold (1991) 25–62.   [133] So Laodicea Can. 13 (Jonkers, *Acta* 88).

[134] For refs. see *PLRE* 1.422–3 'Hermogenes 1'.

[135] According to the partisan version in *Coll. Avell.* 1.7; Amm. Marc. XXVII.3.13 has '137 corpses'. On the whole episode, Piétri, *Roma Christiana* 408–18.

[136] See documents assembled in *Coll. Avell.* XIVff., with Piétri, *Roma Christiana* 452–60.

major breakdowns of public order requiring the intervention of a succession of city prefects, who in turn involved the emperors in settling the disputed elections: Damasus and Boniface were to occupy the see of Rome with the endorsement respectively of Valentinian and Honorius.

When the peace of the *urbs aeterna* was under threat – symbol of the emperor's historic role – it is perhaps not so surprising that an imperial fiat should accompany the appointment of the city's bishop. Yet the legacy of Constantine's appropriation of the church's internal machinery meant that the emperor's interest in the outcome of episcopal elections was by no means confined to Rome. Constantine himself had sent an imperial *comes* to investigate public differences over the election of a new bishop in Antioch, and presumed to write to the congregation with advice about their choice (although imperial intervention, it has to be said, failed to prevent the possession of the see of Antioch from being a matter of dispute for most of the fourth century).[137] Athanasius, it is alleged, lost no time in communicating to the emperor the news of his election at Alexandria.[138] Ambrose, too, is reported to have abandoned resistance to the moves to make him bishop of Milan on hearing of the emperor Valentinian's confirmation of the people's choice (*V. Ambr.* VIII). Above all, the occupancy of the see of Constantinople – in every sense an imperial creation – was in practice in the gift of the emperor. It was Constantius, newly Augustus in the east, who (in defiance of the ecclesiastical rules forbidding translation) contrived the transfer there of the loyal Eusebius of Nicomedia (Socr. *HE* II.7); and it was Theodosius who, almost immediately on his arrival in the city in November 380, involved the imperial power in the possession of the bishopric – deposing the Arian Demophilus, and himself escorting Gregory of Nazianzus to succeed him, then the next year imposing his choice of the senator Nectarius.[139] On Nectarius' death in 397 it was again the imperial court – a coterie of officials led by the all-powerful chamberlain Eutropius – which managed the episcopal succession at Constantinople, summoning the presbyter John Chrysostom from Antioch.[140] There were also occasions, in the context of ecclesiastical disputes, when the emperor's secular arm might need to be invoked to ensure that newly consecrated bishops were actually able to take up their appointments: it was the constant charge of Athanasius and his supporters that bishops sent to 'replace' him in Alexandria needed the escort of no less than the prefect of Egypt and troops of soldiers to secure entry to the city.[141]

---

[137] Eus. *V. Const.* III.59ff.   [138] So Philostorg. II.11 (disputing the legitimacy of his accession).

[139] For narrative, see Matthews, *Western Aristocracies* 121–7.

[140] Liebeschuetz, *Barbarians and Bishops* 166. Pall. *Dial.* v.53ff. (ed. Malingrey, *SChrét.* 341) mentions the involvement, besides Eutropius, of the *comes Orientis*, a eunuch and a 'soldier of the *mag. offic.*' (i.e. an *agens in rebus*?).

[141] As, for example, the 'intrusion' of bishop Gregory in 339: *Festal Index*, 11; *Ep. Encycl.* 2–5; *Apol. c. Ar.* XXX.1 (the first mention of soldiers). See further, Barnes, *Athanasius* 47–50.

VI. BISHOPS AND THE COMMUNITY

That the appointment of a bishop might be fought over in the streets and require the deployment of soldiers to restore order is some confirmation that he was in practice no ordinary private citizen, but had come to be regarded – both by his fellows and by the imperial authorities – as a figure of authority in the local community. As leader of an organization now central to the life of the city and its surroundings, the bishop had entered the ranks (if his earlier career had not already placed him there) of those few powerful *patroni* who were expected to look after the weaker majority confronting the harsh world of late Roman officialdom.[142] We learn from a letter of Synesius how the people of Palaebisca in the west of Cyrenaica had been dissatisfied with the lack of protection afforded by the elderly and feeble bishop of Erythrum, who had charge of their village, and so had succeeded in acquiring a bishop of their own: their choice, revealingly, fell upon a former court official of the emperor Valens who chanced to be visiting them on business connected with his estates, a man of experience in the ways of the world 'who could harm his enemies and help his friends' (*Ep.* 67: *PG* LXVI.1413C). Synesius himself carried over into his eventual occupancy of the bishopric of Cyrene many of the functions which had been required of him as a secular *curialis* and civic leader. As bishop he was the spokesman for his people, writing letters of recommendation and petitioning the Roman authorities on their behalf; his approaches went beyond the local provincial governor in Cyrene to the centre of government in Constantinople, where he continued to exploit the influential connections he had established on his earlier mission as a provincial envoy in the capital.[143] As bishop, too, Synesius found himself at the forefront of the opposition to the oppressive governor Andronicus, adding the ecclesiastical weapon of excommunication to the existing armoury of local defiance against an unpopular official: the governor was isolated, and before long dismissed from his position – only then to find himself in need of the intervention of the bishop to save him from prosecution.[144] As he had been before his consecration as bishop, Synesius remained at the heart of the local politics of Cyrene. He was also called upon to resume his role in the defence of his community against the hostile incursions of desert nomads. As a lay landlord Synesius had organized the resistance on his estates, a task which he shared with the clergy of villages in the countryside. Such clerical involvement in facing up to military emergencies was to come closer to home when he was bishop: one of our last glimpses of bishop Synesius

---

[142] For bishops as patrons, see Brown, *Power and Persuasion*, esp. ch. 3.
[143] Bregman (1982) 174–6; Liebeschuetz (1986) 186–93; Lizzi (1987) 57–84; Brown, *Power and Persuasion* 136–9.   [144] Lizzi (1987) 85–111.

(*c.* 412) catches him doing guard duty on the walls of Cyrene, his sleep interrupted by the bugles calling him to his post (*PG* LXVI.1572C). In other parts of the empire caught in greater military crisis, it is not unfamiliar to find the Christian bishop rallying local opposition to invasion and attack, be it (for example) against Persians in the frontier strongholds of Mesopotamia, or against Goths in the cities of northern Italy.[145] If circumstances should demand negotiation with an enemy at the gates, the task of diplomacy to save the lives of the citizens might well fall upon the bishop or one of his clergy: during the Persian offensive of 360, a celebrated example, it was the bishop of the Tigris fort of Bezabde who pleaded – unsuccessfully – with king Sapor to lift the siege and spare his people.[146]

No less delicate might be the episcopal diplomacy called upon at the court of the Roman emperor. The crowds in Antioch in 387 protesting against the government's extra tax demands had looked first of all to bishop Flavian to win them concessions: then, as the citizens confronted the prospect of fearful imperial reprisals against their rioting, it was the elderly bishop who hastened to the court in Constantinople to intercede for his people before a receptive Theodosius.[147] Bishop Basil of Caesarea was another vocal advocate for his community, using his influential position of local leadership to plead for concessions and benefits in a wide correspondence with friends and officials.[148] In 371 Basil wrote several letters to friends in high places (*Epp.* 74–6) bemoaning the reduced circumstances of Caesarea resulting from the new administrative division of the province of Cappadocia, and appealing for relief; elsewhere he was ready to seek a helping hand against tax burdens – both for his clergy and for other suppliants – from no less a luminary than the eastern praetorian prefect Modestus, though carefully articulating his consciousness of the privilege inherent in access to so eminent a functionary.[149] Approaching a governor of Cappadocia on another matter of financial relief, on this occasion an individual's claim to curial exemption, Basil sought – again with the appropriate protocol of deference – to excuse the impression that he was always interceding for benefits: just as 'a shadow always pursues those who walk in the sun', wrote the bishop, so magistrates had to expect their correspondence to contain pleas of help for the afflicted (*Ep.* 84). Basil was obviously no stranger to the diplomatic niceties of winning favours from government officials.

[145] For illuminating comparison of the resistance activity of Synesius with that of his contemporary, bishop Maximus of Turin, see Tomlin (1979).
[146] Amm. Marc. xx.7.7–9. For bishops and clergy as emissaries, see the summary of Matthews (1976a) 673–4.
[147] Brown, *Power and Persuasion* 105–7, 'a fully public mobilization of the persuasive powers of both the bishop and the civic notables'; cf. Ruggini (1986).
[148] Gain (1985) 291–322; Van Dam (1986); Mitchell (1993) II.76–81.
[149] *Ep.* 104, on tax exemptions for the clergy. For other requests to Modestus, *Epp.* 110–11, 279–81.

Church leaders thus had to be capable of displaying a wide variety of representative public faces to the world beyond their own cities, be it facing down the local provincial governor, appealing to higher officials and emperors, even acting as ambassadors before the kings and chieftains of threatening enemies. Such tasks put to the test all the rhetorical skills with which their education and social position had equipped them. Within his own community, however, the assimilation of the bishop into the civic establishment meant – in addition to his command of charitable resources – a new and readily accessible avenue of settling disputes, more immediate and perhaps less awesome than the court of a Roman judge. Even before Constantine, the role of arbiter and reconciler had been an acknowledged aspect of the episcopal function within the church, and bishops were exhorted in manuals of church order to give time and care to a fair hearing for both sides of the case;[150] but with their wider recognition in the public life of the empire, bishops came to devote more and more of the time not spent on specifically ecclesiastical functions to the business of being a judge. For Augustine at Hippo it was the capacity in which he was in most demand, for a large part of the day beset by crowds of litigants – by no means all from his own flock – whose attentions were a constant distraction from more spiritual occupations.[151] Although Augustine saw his judicial role as an opportunity to apply Christian principles beyond the confines of his congregation – advising the disputants as a religious pastor and giving judgement in the tradition of the scriptures – most of those who sought a settlement in the episcopal court were probably attracted less by any religious distinctiveness than by the prospect of an effective and reasonably swift outcome. As against what might seem the arbitrary unpredictability – and remoteness – of secular justice, the bishop was a permanent figure of authority close at hand, an arbiter who could be approached free from the intimidating need to navigate the channels of influence and favour which customarily surrounded secular Roman officials. Not that the bishop's court was necessarily immune from patronage or partisanship, especially if the *causa religionis* was at issue: Libanius, for one, objected to the favouritism shown by the bishop of Antioch – the same Flavian who effectively pleaded his city's cause before the emperor Theodosius – towards the monks who were the subject of complaints by landowners at their looting of pagan shrines in the countryside.[152] Yet behind Libanius' criticism there lurks the recognition even on the part of those who resented the monks' behaviour that the Christian bishop was not to

---

[150] So *Didascalia Apostolorum* (ed. Funk), 11.47ff.

[151] Possid. *V. Aug.* xix; Aug. *Enarr. in Ps.* 46.5; *Enarr. in Ps.* 118, 24.3–4; with Brown, *Augustine* 195–6.

[152] Lib. *Or.* xxx.11, 15. On bishops perceived to favour the wealthy, cf. Aug. *Enarr. in Ps.* 25, 2.13.

be ignored as a focus of local power in Antioch and a ready source of judicial settlements.[153]

VII. BISHOPS AND THE LAW

Although the bishop's role of judge and arbitrator for his fellow citizens had a history in earlier church procedure, and was enhanced by the increased public profile of the church in the fourth century, it was also given an institutional footing by the endorsement of imperial decrees.[154] As early as 318 a pronouncement of Constantine upheld the 'sacred' inviolability of episcopal judgements, evidently at a time when the possibility of transferring civil litigation to a hearing before a bishop was already recognized procedure;[155] and in 333, in a famous rescript addressed to the eastern praetorian prefect Ablabius, Constantine gave extravagant and unqualified authority to the 'sententiae episcoporum' (*Const. Sirm.* 1). Episcopal verdicts, according to this law, might be unilaterally invoked at any stage in the legal proceedings and by either party to the dispute (regardless of the wishes of the other): freed from the 'ensnaring bonds of legal technicality', the bishop's judgement was necessarily incorruptible, final and overriding, enabling 'wretched men' to escape from the 'long and almost endless toils of litigation' by an early settlement. Although such a wholesale right of reference to *episcopalis audientia* was subsequently modified, and the consent of both parties came to be required for the transfer of a case to the bishop's tribunal (on the analogy of the appointment of a private arbitrator), later laws continue to maintain the superiority of episcopal judgement. In 408 it was held up as deserving the same respect as that accorded, no less, to the verdicts of the praetorian prefects: from both bishop and prefect there was no appeal (*C.Th.* 1.27.2). By implication it was a comparison very flattering to the status of bishops, since the reason that praetorian prefects could not be appealed against was precisely that their judgements alone shared in the sacred authority of the emperor himself (*C.Th.* XI.30.16).

The judicial activities of the local bishop – so consuming to the time and energy of Augustine at Hippo – were thus not merely the product of his *de facto* standing in the eyes of his community, but also carried the *de iure* affirmation of the Roman emperor. Through imperial legislation the church establishment was being formally deputed to undertake functions which had been the preserve of secular magistrates, and bishops were caught up in the time-honoured Roman practice of involving local élites in the tasks of government. Just as they acted as petitioners and emissaries to

---

[153] Cf. Liebeschuetz, *Antioch* 239–42.

[154] On *episcopalis audientia* and its development, consult Steinwenter (1950); Gaudemet (1958) 229–52; Selb (1967); Hunt (1993) 152–4.

[155] *C.Th.* 1.27.1 'pro sanctis habeatur quidquid ab his fuerit iudicatum'.

the emperor and his officials, so they were in turn recognized and adopted as the allies of a Christian Roman government, with many of their activities enshrined not only in theological treatises on the duties of bishops, but in Roman laws.[156] One of the earliest instances, along with the institution of *episcopalis audientia*, had been the extension to bishops of the right to preside over the manumission of slaves in their churches: for the beneficiary to be in legal possession of Roman citizenship, the transaction had to have taken place 'under the eyes of the bishops'.[157] Later on, by the early fifth century, bishops and clergy had a recognized place in certain administrative procedures: in a constitution of 409 they were named alongside the rest of the local oligarchy ('honorati, possessores, curiales') in the list of those enjoined to make the choice of *defensores civitatis*, to ensure that their candidates were 'imbued with the sacred mysteries of orthodox religion' (*CJ* 1.55.8). Besides enrolling church leaders in this way in official functions, the law in its turn came to encompass more of the church's own tasks and bring them within the purview of the Roman state. Matters of ecclesiastical discipline, such as the suitability of candidates for ordination or a bishop's control of monks in his diocese, were brought into the realms of legislation.[158] On the provision of sanctuary in church precincts – a matter in which the state had perhaps a more obvious concern – the law acknowledged a space of refuge in and around the church building, and gave specific voice to the charitable responsibility of bishops and clergy to tend to prisoners and intercede for the innocent, but it also expected bishops to come to the aid of the government in countering abuses of the privilege – the church was not to harbour debtors, and bishops were to play their part in disarming fugitives who took refuge in their buildings.[159] The imperial law is shown to have had a common interest both in those whom the bishops enrolled in the privileged ranks of the clergy (and thus removed from the roll of the *curia*) and in those whom they chose to shelter on church premises.

The Christian government's crusade against paganism and heresy was naturally an area which saw the church and its leaders marshalled alongside the coercive power of the state, although in the case of the suppression of the pagan cults, the laws were in fact slow to recognize the involvement of bishops – their own 'private' campaigns against the temples, aided by their monks and other actively pious parishioners, had been wreaking their destruction long before the process came to be institutionalized in imperial pronouncements.[160] So it was in 407 that Honorius formalized the right of

---

[156] See Noethlichs (1973); Hunt (1993) 151ff.   [157] *C.Th.* IV.7.1 (321); cf. *CJ* 1.13.1 (316).

[158] See Gaudemet (1986), on fragments of a large law addressed to the eastern prefect Eutychianus in 398.   [159] *C.Th.* IX.45.4 (431); for debtors, IX.45.1 (392).

[160] E.g. Fowden (1978), Trombley, *Hellenic Religion* 1.108–47, for the east; Lizzi (1989) 59–96, and (1990) 167ff., for north Italy; Stancliffe (1983) 328–40, for Gaul.

bishops and their 'ecclesiastica manus' to prohibit the practice of pagan funeral rights, in the same breath as acknowledging the authority of *agentes in rebus* to enforce laws against heretics and pagans (*Const. Sirm.* 12 = *C.Th.* XVI.10.19) – a striking juxtaposition of ecclesiastical and secular power in collaboration. Two years later another law of Honorius enrolled the church in the procedures for suppressing astrology: the burning of the books of the *mathematici* was to take place 'beneath the eyes of the bishops' (*C.Th.* IX.16.9).

But it was principally in the enforcement of Catholic orthodoxy and the outlawing of heretical congregations, which gained its impetus from the Theodosian establishment of 380 onwards, that the church hierarchy was cast in the role of servant of the imperial government. The very fact that 'right belief' had entered the realms of Roman law – Theodosius' formative pronouncements of 380–1 establishing Catholic orthodoxy actually included credal statements in their text – is itself clear testimony to the incorporation of bishops into the mechanism of imperial law-making; for it was the faith as determined by them (either as, in the case of Damasus of Rome and Peter of Alexandria, purveyors of the 'apostolica disciplina', or through their conciliar decisions at Nicaea and Constantinople) which was now issuing in edicts and rescripts from the mouth of the Roman emperor.[161] Moreover, when it came to the enforcement of these and subsequent imperial orders against dissident Christian groups, it will have been the local Catholic bishops who stood in the front line. The laws themselves, to be sure, are generally silent about the role expected of the church and its leaders in the suppression of heresy, and place the responsibility of enforcement on the shoulders of secular officials;[162] but the bishops were far better placed than transient and remote functionaries – and had greater cause to be concerned – to identify and isolate rival congregations and clergy. In the best-documented situation, the coercion of the Donatists in Augustine's Africa, the evidence from local communities points to the Catholic bishop as the figure most identified with state 'persecution': only with his active participation could the laws take effect.[163]

The church's expanding role alongside and in collaboration with the imperial government was matched by its favoured standing in the eyes of the state. In the official language of the laws it was a matter of privilege that bishops were left to judge their own, and that issues of ecclesiastical discipline involving the clergy were no concern of the secular courts: bishops were not, in the words of a law of 399, to be 'troubled' (*agitare*) by extraneous cases.[164] It was in the context of reasserting church privileges after the overthrow of Johannes' usurpation in 425 that the independence of clerical matters was once more affirmed: 'it is not right that ministers of God's

---

[161] *C.Th.* XVI.1.2, 3, 5.6; with Hunt (1993) 146–50. Cf. still Ensslin (1953), Ritter (1965), esp. 221–39.
[162] E.g. *C.Th.* XVI.5.30, 45, 46, for penalties against officials who fail to enforce the laws.
[163] See Brown, *Religion and Society*, esp. 321ff.   [164] *C.Th.* XVI.11.1, with Hunt (1993) 153–4.

service should be subject to the judgement of the powers of this world' (*temporalium potestatum: Const. Sirm.* 6 = *C.Th.* XVI.2.47). In thus reserving clerical concerns to be settled by bishops, the laws were adding a gloss of privileged independence to the functioning of *episcopalis audientia* and church councils: whether as individual judges or collectively deciding issues of discipline and doctrine, bishops were formally recognized as masters in their own house, and the independence of their deliberations endorsed and deferred to in imperial pronouncements. Whatever the realities of the bishops' assimilation by 'the powers of this world', the laws still marked them out for honour and privilege. A fragment of the minutes of a meeting of Theodosius' consistory in 381 preserves the emperor's view that it dishonoured the priestly dignity of a bishop for him to be called to give evidence in court (*C.Th.* XI.39.8); while a few years later (XI.39.10, 386) it was affirmed that priests, 'sub nomine superioris loci', were exempt from torture in the courts (although, in confirmation of their humble station, the favour was not extended to the lower echelons of the clergy). Above all, from the earliest months of Constantine's profession of Christianity, the laws blessed Christian clergy with personal tax exemptions and immunity from curial and other obligations demanded by the state. For all the subsequent official efforts at stemming the tide of curial evasions, or to oblige would-be clergy to surrender at least some of their property to the service of the council, these fiscal privileges remained in the eyes of the laws the hallmark of a favoured institution, one charged with the responsibility of conducting the empire's religion. The legal rhetoric of justification for freeing the clergy from taxes and civic duties was that they should be able to devote their time and resources to their religious and charitable functions, which sustained the well-being of the state: 'let them rejoice forever protected by our generosity', proclaimed Honorius in 412, 'as we rejoice in their devotion to the worship of eternal piety' (*Const. Sirm.* 11). Earlier, in 361, Constantius II had grandly announced to the people of Antioch that the virtuous practice of the *lex Christiana* should entail privileged exemptions 'since we know that our state is sustained more by religious observances than by official duties and the labour and sweat of the body' (*C.Th.* XVI.2.16).

Behind such accolades of the church's honoured place as a partner in the Roman state lay the practical realities of law-making at the late Roman court, and the now regular presence there of leading churchmen among influential voices seeking the ear of the emperor and his officials. Many of the laws which dispensed clerical favours and benefits are likely to have stemmed from the interceding of those bishops who now habitually came and went in the imperial palace – to the concern of Ossius and his western colleagues at the council of Sardica.[165] Such episcopal lobbying is seldom

[165] See pp. 238–9 above.

explicit in the texts themselves, save perhaps for the 'petition of the most reverend Asclepiades bishop of the city of Chersonesus' which secured (in 419) the sparing of some of his fellow citizens accused of collaboration with enemies (*C.Th.* ix.40.24); but no assessment of the status and privilege enshrined in laws can ultimately avoid concentrating on the host of individual churchmen pursuing their public concerns – ecclesiastical or otherwise – from local communities to provincial *officia* and to the audience halls of the imperial palace. To glimpse the realities of the church as an institution in the Roman empire of Constantine's Christian successors we need only return to Ammianus' observation of a *cursus publicus* overstretched by the demands of travelling bishops.

CHAPTER 9

RURAL LIFE IN THE LATER ROMAN EMPIRE

C. R. WHITTAKER AND PETER GARNSEY

It should go without saying that in the pre-industrialized society of the later Roman empire the major source of private wealth and public revenue was the land. Although we do not know precisely how or when the *annona militaris* became a state tax – since it originated in the late second century as a levy or requisition of corn for the use of the army – by the fourth century it was the principal instrument by which the state raised revenue.[1] It had perhaps become so in the third century as a means of raising quick funds from the countryside by various claimants to the empire at a time when paying off the armies was their main avenue to legitimacy. By the fourth century, however, it was neither a special requisition, nor particularly burdensome, nor necessarily paid in kind. But the name underlines the important fact that taxation was, as ever in the Roman economy, largely devoted to army pay and that it came for the most part from the profits of the land.

I. RURAL PRODUCTION

Rural production, therefore, was a central concern of the state, and it is for this reason that we cannot rule out the possibility that most of the fiscal legislation was aimed in that direction. Taxation, however, is a delicate fiscal instrument which can either stimulate production or kill off the goose that lays the golden egg. While there is some evidence to suggest that land may have suffered from heavy-handed bureaucratic exploitation, we are now less inclined to believe that over-taxation was a general problem in the later empire.[2] For instance, even though Diocletian imposed a land tax on Italy for the first time since the second century B.C., Aurelius Victor, who was a contemporary senator and our sole source, makes no complaint about its effect, despite the fact that some marginal land probably went out of use.[3]

The first thing, therefore, which must be studied in any discussion of the countryside in late antiquity is whether production on the land had

---

[1] Van Berchem (1937); Carrié, 'Economia e finanze'.
[2] Whittaker (1980); Carrié, 'Economia e finanze' 767, cites Egyptian records to contradict the exaggerations of Lactantius, *De Mort. Pers.* VII.3.
[3] Aur. Vict. *Caes.* XXXIX.32; Giardina (1986) 24–5; Hannestad (1962).

declined. There are some reasons why it might have done so: war damage, particularly in frontier regions; loss of land (with its revenue) to barbarian settlements; over-taxation in certain parts; shortage of manpower; bad management, particularly as a result of absentee landlords or imperial ownership. But we must look also at the positive evidence: whether there was better management and technological improvement; and whether new land was being brought into production and new labour resources made available. It hardly needs repeating that all such evidence is impressionistic and has little statistical validity.

1. War damage

The second half of the third century had been a period which had hit parts of the empire hard, particularly as a result of invasions and the breakdown of frontiers. Almost all the provinces in the western empire show a drop in rural occupation levels, although interestingly enough not Britain or southern Spain, which confirms the evidence of literary sources. In the frontier region of Trier, for instance, one study estimates there were as much as 40 per cent fewer habitations, although this seems too high.[4] The loss of the taxes from the Agri Decumates in Upper Germany and the abandonment of the provinces of Dacia must have reduced the net income of the Roman state but by how much we cannot tell.

The same must have been true of the partial withdrawal from Mauretania Tingitana, although recent studies have shown that this again was not as extensive as was once thought.[5] The development of fortified farms (*gsur*) and nucleated sites in Libya was perhaps a reaction in the third century against desert raiders, and there is evidence in all the rich North African provinces of war, plagues, a decline in monumental urban inscriptions and some disruption in the monetary system. But it is impossible to say that there was really an agrarian crisis, since oil and other produce continued to be exported and land was not extensively abandoned.[6] Our sources say that the Gothic sea raids on Asia and the Aegean islands in the mid third century were devastating, and this may have had a long-term effect on the population, although the early-fourth-century census lists are not complete enough for us to be sure.[7] The provinces of Syria, too, suffered both from Persian invasions and from internal wars which ended up with the destruction of Palmyra and its trade network.[8]

---

[4] Lewit (1991) 27; Keay, *Roman Spain* 176; Wightman (1985) 244; but see Ossel (1992) 70.
[5] Euzennat (1989).
[6] Rebuffat (1989) 60–1; Lepelley (1989) 21, with the comments of N. Duval, 31–3.
[7] Jones, *LRE* 818.
[8] Isaac, *Limits of Empire* ch. 5; Kennedy and Riley (1990) 32–3; the sources are conveniently collected and translated in Dodgeon and Lieu, *Eastern Frontier*.

The real question, however, is whether the effects of the third century were serious enough to have lasted into the fourth century and whether further frontier pressures seriously damaged agriculture. We cannot assume that land which had been raided did not recover quite rapidly once the frontiers were stabilized. After the accord with the Goths following the battle of Adrianople, for instance, Themistius says the population returned to the land. Recent studies reject *Katastrophentheorie* in the Balkans, since not a single major city fell to Goths or Huns in the fourth and fifth centuries.[9] Some of the frontier regions, to be sure, were exposed to attacks and must have suffered. Julian in Gaul may have exaggerated but he did not totally invent when he claimed that forty-five towns had been damaged by the Alaman invasions of A.D. 355 and that the countryside bordering the frontier was unsafe to a distance of a hundred miles.[10] The rebellion of Magnus Maximus was probably responsible for permanent damage in the north and central Rhineland–Luxemburg region in the mid fourth century.

But recent archaeological work in Belgium, northern France and the Rhineland demonstrates that there is far more fourth-century material and a much higher survival rate than was once thought. On some sites, such as Famechon in Picardy, one of the few villas to have been excavated, the main *villa urbana* was abandoned *c.* 270 without signs of violence but the *pars rustica* continued. Surface surveys in the same region on known villa sites show that, although late Roman ware is less common than earlier, it is almost always present.[11] Only in the north-west of Gallia Belgica and the northern part of Germania Inferior does there seem to have been serious depopulation in the fourth century; though this was perhaps aggravated by the rise in sea-level known as the Dunkerque II Transgression, it was almost certainly the result of continuing attacks by Saxon and Frankish sea raiders. The general picture of northern frontier regions in the fourth century, apart from this, is of prosperity up to the middle of the century and a low scale of abandoned sites before Valentinian's death, but former villas were progressively occupied by squatters.[12] On the other frontiers of the empire in the east and in Africa there is no sign of land abandoned because of war in the fourth century.

2. Barbarian settlements

There are numerous literary and legal references to large groups of peoples from beyond the frontiers who, either voluntarily or as prisoners-of-war, were settled by the Romans within the provinces of the empire

---

[9] Them. *Or.* xxxiv.62; Wolfram, *Goths* 128ff.; Velkov (1977) 59.   [10] Jul. *Ep. ad Ath.* 279a.
[11] Ossel (1992), esp. 63–81; a survey of the region of Picardy around Amiens by a group from Amiens–Cambridge–Oxford, directed by G. Woolf, is still in progress.
[12] Ossel (1992) 172–83; Lewit (1991) 29.

throughout the late third and fourth centuries. Although this was not a new policy of the later empire, the frequency of the references and the numbers cited, sometimes in their thousands, make it fairly certain that the movement was significant.[13] These people, variously called *laeti, dediticii* and *tributarii*, were settled mainly, as far as we can see, in western provinces and usually, but not always, near the frontiers. We have references to them in cities quite far south in Gaul and in northern Italy. In A.D. 370, for instance, Alamannic prisoners were sent on the emperor's orders to Italy, 'where they received fertile districts (*pagi*) and now cultivate around the Po as *tributarii*'.[14] Their importance from the point of view of rural production is that they worked the land on which taxes were paid, as the term *tributarii* implies. They also served in the army, thereby releasing other labour to work the fields. Their status was not always the same. One well-known example is that of the Sciri, a Hunnish group defeated in 409, who were offered to landowners 'to supply their fields' in conditions of near slavery.[15]

All efforts to identify such people archaeologically have been questioned, since they were either indistinguishable from federated military settlers, who also used German-looking artefacts, or they were integrated into Roman peasant society. But it is reasonable to suppose that some of them were settled on the lands of the villas of Belgica and Germany abandoned in the third century, since we know from the Gallic panegyrist of Autun that Gallic cities saw them as a valuable means of maintaining cultivation. At Lixhe and Harff in Belgium, for instance, German-style wooden buildings were put up on former villa sites but no German objects were found.[16] One particularly interesting example of a large-scale intrusion occurred under Julian in Gaul, when a group of Franks asked his permission to take over the region of Toxandria in north-western Belgica and lower Germany. Julian agreed, but only on condition that they accepted the status of *dediticii* – that is, they became taxpayers. Doubly interesting is the fact that this area west of the road from Amiens to Cologne coincides with the archaeological blank noted earlier where Roman artefacts do not appear much in the fourth century, demonstrating that one cannot thereby assume that the region was a rural desert.[17]

After the battle of Adrianople in 378 the emperor Theodosius I began a new policy, for which orators like Themistius gave him much credit, of settling federated (allied) Goth soldiers and their families within the empire in self-governing enclaves. We know little about the places or the extent of

[13] Typical of such references is *SHA, Claud.* IX.4–5 – 'The Goths were turned into settlers on the barbarian frontier.' Most references are collected by de Ste. Croix, *Class Struggle* Appendix A; cf. Whittaker (1982).   [14] Italy – Amm. Marc. XXVIII.5.15; cf. *C.Th.* XIII.11.10. Gaul – James (1988) 39.
[15] *C.Th.* V.6.3.
[16] Autun – *Pan. Lat.* VIII(IV).21.1; Belgium – Ossel (1983). See G. Halsall in Drinkwater and Elton (1992) ch. 17, for a recent survey of so-called laetic graves.
[17] Amm. Marc. XVII.8.1–4; cf. Mertens (1986).

such settlements, but there is some evidence to show that it began on the middle Danube frontier and then spread to the provinces, especially, though not exclusively, of the west.[18] The terms of the settlements did not include the payment of taxes, since the federates gave their military service instead. Presumably this meant that the state saved in military pay what it lost in revenue. But the effect on the countryside was to populate frontier regions, while removing them from central state control, which led in the fifth century to the growth of local warlords and independent states such as the kingdom of Aquitania in A.D. 418. The same effect must have been created by rebellions such as that of the Bagaudae in Gaul or the circumcellions in Africa. In the fifth century, Salvian tells of the poor preferring barbarians to Roman tax-collectors, a tendency which increased the fragmentation of central state control and the growth of powerful patrons, whether Roman or German.[19]

3. Taxation and agri deserti

There is a substantial body of law in the codes dealing with 'deserted lands', which has encouraged many scholars in the past to believe that this was a major cause of the decline of the later empire, although most admit that the concern of the laws was fiscal, not economic.[20] The impression one gets from the laws is that the administration fought a constant battle to compel people to take on abandoned land through emphyteutic (or quasi-permanent) leases, in return for which temporary immunity from tax was offered as a inducement – but in vain, since in the end the burden of taxation was too great. Typical is a law of 386 which tried to check the abuse of extra taxation on the land once it had become productive and to reassure the new owner that 'apart from the rent to the imperial chest' (*salvo patrimoniali canone*) no further charge would be permitted.[21] One favoured method of keeping up the revenue was to impose the tax for the deserted land on neighbouring owners or communities, although a law of 365 notes that it would have been equally possible to sell the land by auction, a fact which tells against the notion that the land was undesirable.[22]

The codes are not the only evidence of deserted lands. A celebrated case was recorded when the emperor Julian made a donation to Antioch of 3000 lots (*kleroi*) of uncultivated land which had been formerly civic public land. Much to his anger, the land was given to the rich, not the poor, and still

[18] Them. *Or.* CLXVL.211a. Pannonia – Mócsy (1974) 341ff.; Wolfram, *Goths* 133.

[19] Salvian, *Gub. Dei* v.21; discussed below, p. 293.

[20] Most prominently Jones, *LRE* 812ff. Rostovtzeff (1922) 13–14 argued that this was a serious problem in Egypt already in the second century. Other authors cited in Whittaker (1976)=*Land* ch. 3.

[21] *C.Th.* v.14.30; the laws are collected by Jones, *LRE* ch. 20, n. 101.   [22] *C.Th.* v.11.9.

remained untaxed or unused.[23] In Syria, Libanius talks about villages becoming deserted through the pressure of the tax-agents and marauding monks.[24] Another well-known case concerns the Gallic city of Autun, which pleaded before the emperor Constantine for a reduction in its tax assessment on the grounds that the inhabitants did not have the right kind of land or labour to meet state demands.[25]

It would be foolish to deny that land sometimes went out of cultivation or that the state taxation sometimes contributed to this condition, particularly in the case of land where profits were only marginal. There is a long history from the early empire to the Byzantine period of the use of *epibole* or *adiectio sterilium* as a fiscal instrument, particularly in Egypt, to counter the abandonment of land.[26] Since Italy was first taxed by Diocletian, it would not have been surprising if some land had become no longer worth cultivating. 'If there is land which cannot meet its taxes', says the Gallic panegyrist cited above, 'it is necessarily deserted.' But Italy was a special case. The real problem is to know how widespread the desertion was and what its effect was on production generally. Marginal land is only marginal to total production. Diocletian's taxes do not appear to have been as excessive as Lactantius' biased opinion would have us believe and would not have driven large areas out of production.[27]

Decline in production in the later empire has often been attributed also to manpower shortages. But evidence that there was an empire-wide decline in population is inevitably either anecdotal – references to losses in war, plague and famine which lack any scientific value[28] – or inferential, involving legislation about tied tenants and deserted lands, which, it is argued, must have been issued to counter shortages of manpower. But legislation which bound *coloni* to the land (examined at p. 287 below) is at best ambiguous and is more plausibly explained as a fiscal device. There is as much anecdotal evidence for the replacement of manpower as there is for its shortage – such as the *receptio* of foreign settlers, the return of Roman prisoners-of-war, new land developments and so on.

There are good reasons, also, for hesitating to accept the theory that deserted land was a major problem for the later empire, not least because of the unreliability of the sources.[29] Neither rich nor poor were on oath when they claimed excuses for tax remissions. We can hardly take Symmachus seriously when he says that his land, from which he drew huge rentals, was not paying.[30] Taxation can stimulate production by the poor,

[23] Jul. *Misop.* 370d.   [24] Lib. *Or.* xi.32; Liebeschuetz, *Antioch* 71,164.
[25] *Pan. Lat.* v(viii).6 – but, note, it was not a claim that the manpower did not exist; Galletier, *loc. cit.*, thinks it was a demand for *laeti* workers.   [26] Johnson (1936) 65–71.
[27] See note 2 above; even Jones, *LRE* 68, mistrusts Lactantius.
[28] Boak (1955); reviewed by Finley (1958).
[29] Whittaker (1976) (=*Land* ch. 3) and (1980) (=*Land* ch. 10).   [30] Symm. *Ep.*1.5.

since the labour capacity of peasants is rarely taken up fully. Good land was still sought after and even poor land had its prestige value. Church fathers like Ambrose constantly drew images of the greedy rich man 'forever extending the boundaries of his villas and driving out his neighbours'. But Ambrose adds that the rich man's land could become so extensive that 'his *tributa* became greater than his *fructus*'.[31] That serves as a reminder that the very wealthy may not have cared if some of their land was not fully productive, since prestige derived from ownership as much as from income. In the time of Theodoric we hear of a rich noble, Olybrias of Ravenna, who put his own *famuli* to work a piece of his own land which had lain unworked and which was made profitable in ten years.[32] The case of Antioch's land was far from an isolated example, showing that the real problem of land was correctly identified by the state as fiscal.

There are particular difficulties about the legal evidence. Legislation about land taxes, which fills the codes, is not by itself sufficient evidence to prove agricultural decline, since emperors were always anxious to increase revenue. It seems fairly certain that the laws about *emphyteusis*, which concerned the renting out of property on long (and therefore advantageous) terms, were not primarily targeting land that had degraded through neglect – although that was certainly true of some cases – but imperial properties which had become too extensive to be properly managed. Emphyteutic contracts, for instance, are commonly found in Africa, which was exceptionally prosperous in the later empire and also renowned for massive imperial estates. The land was sometimes desirable, since we hear of bidding.[33]

Emphyteusis, in fact, appears to have become general throughout the empire and to have replaced the older *locatio–conductio* short-term contract with a longer-term (*possessio ad tempus locata*) or even a permanent leasehold, provided the rental terms were respected (*vel iure perpetuo vel titulo conductionis*).[34] Although such contracts were usually only feasible for rich *conductores*, who became almost like owners, subletting to poorer *coloni* tenants, we do hear of some cases when *coloni* themselves took on the contracts. But it looks as if most of the legislation was designed to help large proprietors against the poorer tenants, and its effect was certainly to increase their property holdings.[35]

Whether the legislation actually increased production is a matter of judgement to be set against the general economic condition of the empire. In Africa, where evidence of *conductores* is most abundant, the rural economy was booming in the fourth century. This makes it all the more

---

[31] Ambr. *Exp. Ps. cxviii* VI.32, VII.5 = *PL* XV.1278, 1285.
[32] *V. S. Hilarii, AASS Maii III*, 15 May, pp. 471–6; Ruggini, *Economia e società* 338.
[33] Vera (1986), (1988b).   [34] *CJ* XI.71.5.6–7 (429), XI.66.3 (377).
[35] Contracts to *coloni* – *C.Th.* XI.19.1 (321); checks against *coloni* – *CJ* XI.63.1 (319).

paradoxical that one of the pieces of evidence most frequently cited to prove deserted land is a law of A.D. 422 granting tax-exemption on huge tracts of imperial land in the provinces of Africa and Byzacena – about 3000 square miles in each – for whose desertion local rebellions are sometimes held partly responsible. But a better explanation is that this figure reflects the amount of uncultivable, rather than deserted, land and that the exemption was a recognition of this reality, perhaps for reasons of political favour.[36]

Emphyteutic leases on imperial land underline the difficulty of administering the vast property which had been acquired by the emperor over the centuries. We know of many complaints from tenants in the earlier empire about their exploitation by *conductores* or imperial agents, with threats to leave the land if they could not get justice. It was this which led Rostovtzeff to his negative view of state socialism, and to attribute to these abuses a decline in productivity on the land.[37] A similarly negative conclusion has been drawn from remarks made by aristocratic writers, such as those by Symmachus concerning the maladministration of his distant estates by dishonest managers, 'as only happens when the owner is absent'.[38] Absentee ownership, taken together with the undoubted growth in the numbers of properties held by the rich in the later empire, is, therefore, thought to have lowered the productivity of the land. The so-called Catonian villa system of the earlier empire, it is argued, disintegrated through the concentration of properties, the growth of administrative costs and the general 'inelasticity' of its slave labour organization.[39]

Although imperial property did greatly increase, it was precisely in response to consequential managerial difficulties that the shift was made towards the leasing of land to *conductores*. Some *conductores* now lived on the land among the *coloni* and were closely associated with their daily lives, as Augustine's letters from Africa show.[40] From what Symmachus says, we can see that the collection of dues was difficult not only because of the absenteeism of the owner but also because of protection offered to tenants by landowners or state officials, because of brigandage or because of the burden of debt on tenants.[41] Some of these are problems familiar from Pliny and writers of the earlier empire.

It is not clear whether dishonest managers necessarily caused a fall in productivity, or whether it simply meant that a diminished revenue came to rich proprietors. Nor is there any good reason to think that the change

---

[36] *C.Th.* xi.28.13; Jones, *LRE* 816, countered by Lepelley (1967).

[37] This view was attacked by Mickwitz (1932); cf. Mazzarino, *Aspetti sociali* 14.

[38] Symm. *Ep.* 1.64, 7.6.6, 9.6, 9.130, etc. Cf. Vera (1988b).   [39] Capogrossi Colognesi (1986).

[40] In a protest against an unpopular bishop, the *conductor* led the *coloni*; Aug. *Ep.* 20*; see Lancel (1983) 276.

[41] Protection – Symm. *Ep.* 7.56; brigandage – Symm. *Ep.* 2.22; debt – Symm. *Ep.* 5.8.7; problems discussed by Roda (1981) 293.

altered the basic farming units on many imperial or private estates. If there was a move away from the centrally organized slave villa towards the use of *coloni*, as seems likely in Italy at least, it can be regarded as a move towards a more efficient system of labour for far-flung properties.[42] A survey of the territory of Cherchel (Caesarea) in Mauretania shows that, while many urban aristocrats abandoned their rural villas, there is no sign of decline in agriculture on the land which formerly fell within the villa networks.[43]

4. Technology and development

There is much positive evidence of rural development and prosperity in the later empire to balance adverse reports. The redress has principally come from archaeological surveys like that of Caesarea just mentioned. The employment of the Gallic reaper, which is described by Palladius, and the increasing use of water-mills in the later empire, have sometimes been cited as examples of technological inventions to compensate for manpower shortage, although they could just as easily be arguments in favour of increased production. Both, however, were inventions of the earlier empire, when there is no question of manpower difficulties, and neither seems to have been extensively used in the later empire.[44] There is no evidence to show any technical improvement of the plough before the eleventh century. But there is some archaeological proof in Britain that the technology of crop-growing improved in the later empire.[45] Interestingly, Britain became a major exporter of corn to the Rhine army in the fourth century, perhaps to compensate for the fall in production in northern Gaul and Germany.

It is, above all, the archaeological evidence of continuity or growth in agriculture which is the most telling argument against any overall decline of production. Africa has already been referred to a number of times. A coastal survey in the region east of Zaghouan in Tunisia shows a very obvious increase of mainly villa sites in the third and fourth centuries, with no decline until the fifth and sixth centuries. The same is true of the survey in southern Tunisia around Kasserine, where a new form of group habitation dominated by a single farm developed, reflecting perhaps the *conductor–coloni* relationship described in the laws. The southern regions of Libya show a similar development, where in the third and fourth centuries there was evident prosperity of villages and settlements around a central fortified *gsur*, which a site like Ghirza has demonstrated vividly through its carved scenes of agriculture. The domination of the markets in east and

---

[42] Giardina (1986) 2; Capogrossi Colognesi (1986) 358–9.   [43] Leveau (1989) 46 and 51.
[44] Pallad. *De Agr.* vii.2; White (1984) 60–1, 65–6.
[45] Cavallo and Giardina (1993) 334; Jones (1982).

west throughout the fourth and fifth centuries by Tunisian oil, garum, fine polished ware and lamps is testimony to this growth.[46]

Africa was perhaps exceptional. But the story is not so very different on the chalk massifs of north Syria or on the plains around Antioch and Chalcis, as indeed all over Syria, including the Hauran. There was not, as once thought, a monoculture of olives in north Syria managed by veteran settlements, but polyculture with signs of the natural demographic growth of a quite prosperous peasantry.[47]

Any attempt to summarize developments throughout the whole empire, however, suffers from enormous gaps, since even archaeological surveys are highly selective. Nevertheless, one recent assessment of the overall rural scene in the western provinces from the evidence of two hundred sites comes to the conclusion that there was a net expansion throughout most of the fourth century (although a decline in northern Gaul and Germany) both of overall numbers and of individual sites, with a surprising increase in the number of medium-size farms against a decline in small farms. The latter could be the result of the method of surface prospection and the archaeological invisibility of the very poor; but a recent study of 'small agglomerations' in France, Luxemburg and Germany shows a definite rebirth, if not a net increase, of village-type settlements in the later empire, which may account for the disappearance of single small sites.[48] In the Danube provinces the information is less easy to summarize, but the fourth century once again looks like a period of growth rather than decline.[49]

It is no easier to draw up a balance sheet for Italy than for the provinces. Almost certainly the countryside underwent quite considerable changes in site occupation. In south and central Etruria, for example, more than fifty per cent of settlements which had been occupied in the earlier empire had been abandoned by A.D. 400, and some excavated villas show radical alterations in land use and labour organization. A similar situation appears to hold true in Sabina. But there was also what one recent study calls 'renewed investment' in south Etruria in the late empire.[50] Despite this, however, most commentators would probably accept that there was at least some overall decline in production in Etruria, where legislation includes it within an area of mounted shepherds and banditry.[51]

As for the rest of Italy, a number of studies have appeared in recent years which are at least making the situation clearer, even if the final judgement

---

[46] Segermes valley (Zaghouan) – Carlsen and Tvarno (1990); Kasserine – Hitchner (1990); Libya – Rebuffat (1988) 63–5; Mattingly (1989); pottery – Panella (1989).

[47] N. Syria – Tchalenko, *Villages*, modified by Tate (1989); Hauran – Dentzer (1985–6).

[48] Lewit (1991), Petit (1994).   [49] Lewit (1991) 47–9 provides a summary of recent studies.

[50] Potter (1979), modified by Potter (1991); Carandini (1985) 183–5 presents the most pessimistic picture.   [51] *C.Th.* ix.30.

remains ambiguous.[52] Despite a clear decline in the number of sites in a survey of northern Campania, all our sources indicate that huge incomes were still made by senatorial families with property in Campania, which was called by the *Expositio totius mundi* 'the storeroom of Rome' (*cellarium regnanti Romae*). The most recent study of Sicily, where many of Rome's rich also had estates, finds a period of prosperity in the fourth century and many new villages. Even in inland north and central Etruria a number of new villas have been discovered, although they may have been less productive than their predecessors.[53] But north Italy and the Po valley – the region called *Italia annonaria* in the late empire – were producing supplies for the imperial court and army. Overall, there seems to have been a decline in small sites in Italy but a growth in large farms and villages.[54]

II. LABOUR AND PROPERTY OWNERS

Assessment of the productivity of the land must include some discussion about the forces of production and the ownership of land. Slaves and *coloni*, peasants and landlords – these are probably the most debated and disputed subjects of any in the later empire. Did slaves, who had been such a distinctive form of labour in Italian rural society, even if not in every province, disappear in the later empire? The fate of slaves is bound up closely with the question of the status of *coloni* – that is, of tenants whose labour supplemented and often replaced that of slaves. Those who take the most pessimistic view of the economy of the later empire have characterized it as an age when there was a spectacular growth in tenancy, a sharp decline in the rights of tenants as freely contracting parties, a corresponding assimilation of the status of *coloni* with that of slaves and the disappearance of independent peasants or medium farmers, who were swallowed up by rich landowners. How true is all this?

When we examine the ancient texts, the most striking thing about them is that they contain no systematic description of *coloni*, no single law of 'the colonate' defining their status or rights, no single category of *coloni*. We do not even know from when to date the appearance of *coloni* as a class of labour different from the tenants of the earlier empire. What we have in fact is a haphazard number of references, mostly in the law codes but not organized under headings, which simply take for granted from their first appearance in the fourth century that everyone knew what a *colonus* was.

[52] E.g. Barker and Lloyd (1991). Contrasting optimistic and pessimistic assessments are made by C. R. Whittaker and by A. Carandini in C. Nicolet (ed.), *L'Italie d'Auguste à Dioclétien* – Coll. EFR (Rome, 1994).

[53] *Expositio* LIV; cf. Cassiod. *Var.* XII.22 (*urbis regiae cella panaria*); Campania – Arthur (1991); Sicily – Wilson (1990) 225–33; Etruria – Ciampoltrini (1990).

[54] E.g. Patterson (1988) and (1991) for Molise, Samnium and the *ager Falernus*; Franzoni (1987) for the Veneto.

Obviously they were the successors of the *coloni* farmers of the late republic and early empire who held legally enforceable contracts of tenancy (*locatio–conductio*). But now in the fourth century they appear to have lost status, although still legally free, and often to be in a near-servile condition, even if the laws are always careful to maintain the distinction between *coloni* and slaves. They appear, too, under different names – *inquilini, originarii, originales, adscripticii* – some of which terms seem to be interchangeable and some to refer to different status categories. Many of the laws deal with *coloni* who ran away from the estates on which they worked. Many are concerned with the tax liability of the owners on whose land the *coloni* were registered.

The first reference to what might be called 'servile' *coloni* is in the *Sentences* of Paul in the third century, but this is often thought to be an interpolation, though mainly because there are still references to *coloni* who made legally enforceable contracts in the time of Diocletian.[55] The first references to *coloni* in the Theodosian Code appear quite early in Constantine's reign, and show that they were by then regarded as tied in some way to rich landowners and of low status.[56] The first reference in the code to *coloni* being tied to the land is in a law of Constantine of 332 (*C.Th.* v.17.1) which says:

Any person in whose possession a *colonus* that belongs to another is found not only shall restore the aforesaid *colonus* to his *origo* but shall also assume the capitation tax for this man and for the time he was with him . . . [Then the law goes on] *Coloni* who meditate flight must be bound with chains and reduced to a servile condition, so that by virtue of the condemnation to slavery, they shall be compelled to fulfil the duties that befit free men.

The first reference to a general colonate status (*ius colonatus*) is in 342 (*C.Th.* xII.1.23) in a law which stressed the privileges those *coloni* had whose *origo* was on imperial estates. By 393 (*CJ* xI.52.1) *coloni* were referred to as 'slaves of the land'. The context of the reference is after the abolition of the capitation tax in Thrace, when tenants were told that they must not think they could move freely, for 'although they appear free in status, they are still slaves of the land'.[57] In 396 (*CJ* xI.50.2) *coloni* were described as *quadam dediti servitute* – that is, almost as though they were prisoners-of-war, which may be significant. By 530 a rescript of Justinian (*CJ* xI.48.21) went so far as to ask whether there was a difference now between a slave and an *adscripticius* in relation to property ownership. What these laws show is that, although sometimes the term 'slave' was used in a metaphorical and limited sense, there was almost certainly a progressive degrading of the condition of

---

[55] E.g. *CJ* IV.65.27 (294), IV.10.11 (294).

[56] E.g. *C.Th.* xI.7.2 (319) – a decurion was responsible for the debts of his *colonus* or *tributarius*; *C.Th.* xI.21.2 (321) – *coloni* in the same category for punishments ass *conductores, actores, incolae.*

[57] *Licet condicionis videantur ingenui, servi tamen terrae ipsius, cui nati sunt existimentur* (*nati* is emended to *dati* by Piganiol).

some *coloni* throughout the fourth century. But at the same time the laws were always underlining the difference between slaves and *coloni*.[58]

That is the legal evidence in bare outline. There is little doubt that the main motive behind the legislation was a simple desire, which carried on through the fourth century, to improve the collection of taxes. The idea was probably initiated by Diocletian's reforms, which required that each tenant should be registered (*adscriptus*) for purposes of the *capitatio* tax, which then restricted his movement to prevent tax evasion.[59] But that is where simplicity ends. Taxation is not enough to explain why, even after the abolition of the capitation tax in some provinces such as Thrace, the movement of *coloni* was still prevented. In 371 a law concerning Illyricum (*CJ* XI.53.1) specifically said that *coloni* were not tied to the land by the tax (*tributario nexu*) but just because they were *coloni* (*sed nomine et titulo colonorum*). Nor does taxation explain why there was a series of laws from the mid fourth century which deprived *coloni* of various freedoms, such as the ability to dispose of their own property or to marry as they wished.[60]

In short, the state was intervening regularly and progressively to reduce the labour rights and mobility of *coloni* in favour of landowners or *conductores*. The question is, why? And how seriously did it alter the face of the countryside in the later empire? Shortage of labour and an attempt to stimulate production is, as we have seen, an unsatisfactory answer to the question. On the contrary, in Italy the availability of manpower would have been increasing since the early empire, if the population had been stable, since fewer and fewer Italians served in the Roman army. Tenancy was already in Pliny's day becoming a preferred form of labour, while marginal land was probably being worked less in the later empire than before – thereby increasing the poverty and debt of poor peasants.[61] In the later empire, parallel efforts were taking place in other spheres of life to freeze labour and establish a caste system, particularly among public employees, such as mint workers or minor urban functionaries (*collegiati*). But, as far as one can judge, this development had more to do with management than manpower.[62]

Here we may have one clue to government thinking. If the desire to collect revenue from imperial estates was the main reason for the change from the old short-term *locatio–conductio* to emphyteutic leases, the prospective emphyteutic owner could only be induced to take on such long leases if the terms were attractive. That included a guaranteed and stable labour

---

[58] Johne *et al.* (1983) 1. Marcone (1993) 827 thinks (correctly, in our view) that the law of 332 (quoted above) means that fugitive *coloni* were literally reduced to slavery.

[59] Note *C.Th.* XI.24.1 (360), where runaway *coloni* in Egypt sought the protection of high officials to avoid tax.

[60] Property – e.g. *C.Th.* V.19.1 (365); marriage – e.g. *CJ* XI.68.4 (367). Diocletian – Jones, *LRE* 796. Restrictions – Johne *et al.* (1983) 18–19, Carrié, 'Economia e finanze' 309–10, 761.

[61] De Neeve (1984), esp. 119–20, Whittaker (1987).   [62] Jones, *Economy* ch. 21.

force. Preventing the movement of tenants, therefore, and diminishing their rights was a way of rendering them more pliable to the wishes of the new owner. With that in mind, it is interesting to see how many of the early laws about tenancy were specially aimed at the imperial *res privata* – restricting movement of imperial tenants (*coloni patrimoniales*) and slaves, preventing their recruitment for military service or preventing them being taxed by governors, since they were engaged on 'essential work for the emperor' (*principales necessitates*).[63]

Not all the laws were restrictive. Some also offered incentives to imperial *coloni* not to run away. Imperial *coloni* had tax privileges when they traded, and they were excused the minor public duties normally required of citizens (*munera sordida*). So advantaged were they that a law of 342 says that some people were avoiding curial duties by claiming the 'privileges of the imperial estates . . . by the right of the colonate' (*privilegia rei privatae . . . colonatus iure*). Other laws protected the *conductores*. One of the earliest laws in 319 forbade *coloni* to usurp the water rights of the *emphyteuticarii* on imperial land in Africa.[64] So, although the needs of imperial estates will not serve as a complete explanation for the legislation, some of the laws may have become generalized after being aimed at *coloni* on the imperial estates.

Another factor which could have influenced the legislation was the large numbers of prisoners-of-war or voluntary immigrants (*laeti, dediticii, tributarii*, etc.) who were settled on the land as a condition of their admission to Roman territory. The land in question often belonged to private owners and the state was concerned to see that they did not dissipate or over-exploit this labour force. This was apparently a danger in 409 when the state invited landowners to make use of Sciri prisoners as *coloni* on their private land but insisted that they could not be reduced to slavery or moved. The term *tributarii* seems to have been used indifferently for *coloni* or for such settlers, showing how similar their conditions were. A law of 368 talks about servile labour within which the categories of *tributarii* and *inquilini* were included, and in 465 we hear of *laeti* who joined with *coloni* and slaves to form a *collegium*.[65]

The use of colonate status as a punishment for vagrancy or for dissidents had a similar effect, fusing the rights of state and private tenants. A law of 382 instructed the urban prefect to put beggars as *coloni* on the land of those who informed against them 'for ever'. In the later fifth century, Catholic bishops of Africa were exiled from the cities by the Vandal king

[63] Movement – *CJ* xi.68.1–3 (325–6); military service – *C.Th.* vii.13.2 (370); tax by governors – *C.Th.* xi.7.11 (365). In general, see Rosafio (1991).
[64] Trade – *C.Th.* xiii.1.10 (374); *munera sordida* – *C.Th.* xi.16.5 (343); *colonatus iure* – *C.Th.* xii.1.33 (342); water rights – *CJ* xi.63.1 (319).
[65] Foreign settlers – e.g. Amm. Marc. xix.11.16, xxviii.5.15, xxxi.9.4; Sciri – *C.Th.* v.6.3 (409); *coloni-tributarii* – *C.Th.* x.12.2.2 (368); cf. *C.Th.* xi.7.2 (319); *laeti* – *NSev.*2.1 (465).

Hunerich, 'but in exile you shall receive land to cultivate under the *ius colonatus*'. [66]

Whatever its origin, the tied colonate suited the richer landowners well. Growing accumulation of scattered properties, which inevitably meant more absentee owners and more estate management through agents, had encouraged the use of tenants in place of centrally organized farms since the early empire, while at the same time it had become more difficult to keep an eye on the turnover of short-term contracts. In the early second century Pliny found that he was constantly troubled by the problems of debt-ridden tenants and their leases. A labour force bound to the same land and with limited contractual rights benefited the rich enormously and no doubt encouraged them to support the emperor in his legislation. But there was perhaps another problem, again linked to the change in the tax system introduced by Diocletian. It is evident from many of the laws that very rich proprietors were often harbouring fugitive *coloni* on their estates without declaring them, thereby either robbing other landowners of the labour for whose capitation tax they were liable or depriving the state of the tax, if the tenants paid their own taxes directly. The legislation was a direct attempt to control the excessive power of the rich. [67]

How much the status of *coloni* was in reality degraded is difficult to judge. Already in the second century a distinction was made in law between the punishments given to *honestiores* and *humiliores*, which perhaps reflected the incapacity of the poor in any circumstances to oppose the rich, whether they had legal rights or not. *Coloni* on the imperial estates in second-century Africa did not appeal to any law of contract for redress when they were exploited by the *conductor*. Instead they appealed directly to the emperor. [68] We know too little about the state of the majority of peasants and workers on the land in the provinces to be sure whether they were worse or better off in the later empire. Both Fustel de Coulanges and, later, Finley believed in the essential continuity of the conditions of peasants in the Roman provinces, and argued that the laws concerning *coloni* and the disappearance of *locatio–conductio* contracts in the later empire were only *de iure* recognition of a long-standing reality. [69] We may be too much influenced by the history of Italy in making judgements about the status of rural labour in the provinces. In Italy slavery and the spoils of empire had combined to produce a free, politicized peasantry in the republic and a tradition of legal rights. But, as the governing class of Rome was infiltrated by more and more large landowners from the provinces, the newcomers may, more than

---

[66] Beggars – *C.Th.* XIV.18.1 (382); bishops – Vict. Vit. *Hist. Persecut. Afr.* III.20.

[67] Senators were exempt from liability for the unpaid taxes of their *coloni*, but only provided they harboured no fugitives themselves: *C.Th.* XI.1.7 (361).   [68] Garnsey (1970); Johne *et al.* (1983) 422.

[69] Fustel de Coulanges (1885) 15–24, Finley (1980) 142–4; cf. Whittaker (1980). The historiography of the colonate has been traced by Marcone, *Colonato*.

we realize, have influenced the state's attitude to labour rights by means of their own traditional practices, which were unmodified by Italian political history.

The important point, however, is not to exaggerate the slave-like condition of *coloni* or the changes that took place. It is a myth that all laws of tenancy disappeared in the later empire. Not only do we hear of poorer *coloni* profiting from emphyteutic contracts, sometimes acting in syndicates, but even the old *locatio– conductio* contract on land apparently continued in vulgar law (that is, in practice) and it was still in general use for certain specific types of property as late as the age of Justinian.[70] It also seems that private contractual arrangements continued to be made (presumably without any legal validity). A law of 371, for instance, refers to fugitive *coloni* going off and making private contracts 'as though they were their own masters and free'.[71]

This last reference not only proves that some tenants were entering into contracts for their land but also that there existed a recognized category of 'free' *coloni*, even if, according to this law, some tied tenants were usurping the status. A number of laws refer to the provision that, if a tenant stayed on a property for thirty years, then he was tied forever. This implies that some movement was permitted to certain tenants. It is equally clear from the laws that there were various categories of *coloni*, some of whom paid their own taxes and others who were on the tax roll for which the owner or *conductor* was responsible.[72] It was presumably the former who were 'free' to move, provided that they met the requirements of the tax register.

The various terms applied to *coloni* – such as *originarii, inquilini, adscripticii* – probably reflect differing statuses with historical and regional variations. As plausible as any explanation of these confusing names is the theory that in the fourth century all *coloni* were registered for tax in their place of origin. Hence all were *censibus adscripti* and *originarii* (or *originales*). The name *inquilinus* seems always to have referred to a more lowly class of *colonus*, who in earlier periods was only allowed to cultivate marginal land of the estate. But towards the end of the fourth century there was a modification in the capitation-tax system, making it necessary to define those who had the right to move. Then, in the fifth century, the unstable conditions and the relative absence of central control in the west led gradually to the emergence of *clientes* or free bondsmen, who were distinguished from tenants tied to the land. They were the ancestors, perhaps, of the medieval

[70] Levy (1951) 62; de Martino (1993) 883. See the title in *CJ* IV.65, *de locatione et conductione*, which includes contracts on some types of property, such as *domi, ergasteria* and *loca*.

[71] *CJ* XI.48.8 (371) – *quasi sui arbitrii ac liberi apud aliquem se collocaverunt . . . nam manifestum est privatum iam esse contractum*.

[72] Thirty-year rule – *NVal* 31.1 (451); tax-paying *coloni* – *C.Th.* XI.1.14 (371) names two categories of *coloni*: *originales* whose *domini* must ensure that they fulfil the obligations of the *annona* tax and others who 'are registered on their own plots under their own names in the tax list'; cf. Cerati (1975) 66–7.

'hommes de corps' – men bound, that is, not to the land but to the service of their patron and apparently of higher status. The Gallic aristocrat Sidonius Apollinaris, for instance, discussed with a friend how an *inquilinus originalis* could be upgraded to *cliens* and therefore have a 'plebeian' rather than a 'colonary persona'. In the east, meanwhile, the law made a sharper distinction between a free *colonus*, who paid taxes while being allowed to own property, and an *adscripticius*, who was little more than a slave with a *peculium*.[73]

What we cannot tell is how common any one of these categories was compared to another, nor how important the differences were. Tenants are often referred to in non-legal texts, almost always as oppressed by the rich. But it is not easy to distinguish between free and tied categories nor, indeed, between tenants in general and wage-labourers. Zeno, bishop of Verona, attacked the rich for 'adding tenancy to tenancy', while Ambrose of Milan wrote of the burdens of compulsory state transport laid upon the wage-labourers without payment. In theory the law offered protection, since it was in the state's interest to keep tenants out of debt, so that they could keep up tax payments. But churchmen, such as John Chrysostom of Antioch, regularly accused landlords of illegal loan contracts which removed up to 50 per cent of the harvest, 'alike whether the land produces or does not produce'. The most savage and celebrated attack is that by Salvian of Marseilles in the fifth century, as law and order were breaking down in the west, when he accused the rich of forcing the free peasant to sell his property birthright and become a tenant. A man, he says, 'gives himself to the upper class in return for care and protection . . . and passes over into their jurisdiction and dependence'. Yet even then 'when they have lost their property they bear the taxes for the things they have lost'.[74]

But the story is not all one of oppression. The mobility of *coloni* appears much greater in actual examples than one might infer from the legislation. In Numidia the *coloni* of one estate threatened to leave their land, if the *domina possessionis* (the proprietor) permitted the return of a bishop they detested, and it is evident from the letters of Augustine, who recounts this incident, that there were many aspects of the law which were not understood. It is equally clear from the legislation quoted earlier that rich landowners were quite prepared to ignore the laws and accept fugitive *coloni* into their protection. This became a means by which poor tenants could avoid the oppression of state taxation and rich landowners could increase their

---

[73] For the best discussion of the categories, see Rosafio (1991); cf. Whittaker (1987). For Sidonius Apollinaris, see *Ep.* 5.19.1. For the east, see the law of Anastasius *CJ* xi.48.18 – *alii quidem sunt adscripticii et eorum peculia dominis competunt; alii vero tempore annorum triginta coloni fiunt liberi manentes cum rebus suis.*

[74] Zeno=*PL* xi.328; Ambr. *Ep.* 2.30–1; laws – *CJ* ii.50.1 (325), xi.48.5 (366?), etc.; John Chrys. *Hom. in Matth.* lxi.3; Salvian, *De Gub. Dei* v.9 – whether Salvian means literally 'slaves' when he speaks of those who come to the farms of the rich as *servi* is discussed by Whittaker (1987).

power. The solidarity which *coloni* often showed with their *domini* is an indication that they knew where their interests lay. The tight control exercised by masters over the lives of the *coloni*, which extended to religious beliefs as well as to economic relations, was usually enough to ensure their subservience. But obedience need not be interpreted as devotion.[75]

1. Slaves and peasants

The apparent domination of the rural scene in the later empire by tenants has led in recent years to a debate about the extent to which slavery had declined as a consequence.[76] But it is important to keep in mind that, apart from Italy and some of the older Roman territories of southern Gaul, Spain and parts of Africa or the Greek cities, there never had been a great use of slave labour on farms, not even in the earlier empire. Conversely, there are plenty of references to slaves on the land in the later empire, although the law codes give no idea of the normality or otherwise of their presence. The most quoted example is that of a noble lady, Melania, and her husband, Pinarius, who in an act of piety freed 8000 slaves, which represented only a part of the total number they held on estates in Italy and in the provinces of Sicily, Spain, Africa, Numidia, Mauretania and Britain.

Not all slaves were employed as labourers in the fields, since we know that many overseers and managers of the rich continued to be slaves as before; and there were still many domestic, urban slaves. But the letters of Symmachus are full of his fears about a slave revolt in the countryside of Italy, which implies that they were numerous and not in responsible positions.[77] So many are the references, not only to slaves in general but also to the trade in slaves on the frontiers, slaves taken as prisoners or slaves owned by quite poor people, that it is difficult to believe that there had been a significant decline, if any, in total numbers. For what it is worth, direct or indirect references to slavery in the Edict of Theodoric, one of the first known barbarian codes in the west, appear in about one-third of the 154 articles.[78]

[75] Africa – Aug. *Ep.* 20*; Lepelley (1983a); Lancel (1983). Giardina (1986) 29 cites in support of social control by *domini* the occasion in sixth-century Italy when *coloni* and slaves supported their masters against Totila (Procop. *BG* VII.22). But Procopius says that they deserted the Roman cause when promised the property of their owners. *C.Th.* XVI.5.52.4 (412); 5.54.8 (414) say that *coloni* and slaves were liable to flogging or loss of their *peculium*, if they supported Donatism; Aug. *Ep.* 58.1 gives an example. For dissident pagan *coloni*, see Cavallo and Giardina (1993) 326–7.

[76] The case for decline is set out by de Ste. Croix, *Class Struggle* and Westermann (1955); the opposite by MacMullen (1987) and Whittaker (1987).

[77] Melania – Pall. *Laus. Hist.* 61.5 but *V. Mel* (Latin) 10 proves some were domestic; discussed by Giardina (1986) 31–6. Symmachus – e.g. *Ep.* 2.22 – *pericula ruris*.

[78] Frontiers – Symm. *Ep.* 2.78; kidnapping – Aug. *Ep.* 10*; slaves owned by poor – Lib. *Or.* XXXI.11. Even in Egypt, which had always been a land of poor peasants and tenants, slavery was still important in the later empire; Bradley (1984) 103–4. Theodoric's code – *FIRA* II.694–710; for other references to barbarian codes, see Whittaker (1987) 103.

The real debate, however, is not so much over whether there were fewer slaves, about which no statistical certainty is possible, but whether slaves were still employed in the same way on farms as they had been in the great days of the Italian villa – that is, in gangs under a bailiff and herded into confined barracks. Most scholars believe that, by the fourth century, slaves were regularly employed like tenants (*quasi-coloni*), and often permitted to live with their families on separate plots of land, for which they paid rent. The arguments and examples in favour of the latter case are quite strong. For instance, we are told that some of Melania's estates in Italy contained 400 slaves in sixty-two *villulae*. This (though ambiguous, since it might mean there were 400 slaves on each of the sixty-two farms) is thought to indicate that there were six or seven slaves per farm – and, therefore, too few to run a centralized villa, but possible if they were *quasi-coloni*.[79] Palladius, the fourth-century author of a treatise on agriculture, is strangely reticent about the farm workers, thereby showing – or so it is argued – that he was indifferent to the status of the labourers because they were all employed in the same way as tenants. There are some references, too, in the codes and on inscriptions to *casarii* or *casati* (cottagers) on estates, as opposed to *coloni* – terms which almost certainly refer to slaves with their own domicile, who are believed to have worked their own plots of land.[80]

On the other hand, it is difficult to be sure that all use of slaves on central domanial systems had disappeared. It is far from true, in any case, that all centrally organized villas in the earlier empire had employed large numbers of slaves. There is surprisingly little explicit mention of slaves as tenants in the later empire, given the frequency of general references to slaves. Domanial farming was not extinct. For instance, we hear of a nobleman, Olybrias of Ravenna, who put his own *famuli*, probably including slaves, to work a deserted estate in north Italy in the fifth century. When the priest Barnabas in Augustine's diocese of Hippo could not find tenants for his small estate, he too ran it himself with direct labour, although in Africa slaves were relatively rare on the land. Some of the Greek islands, however, seem to record estates still worked by gangs of slaves.[81] At least the examples show that many different modes of organizing production on the land were prevalent.

[79] See Vera (1986) 417 against Finley (1980) 123. The main argument to refute Finley's high total (62×400=24,800) is that Melania only manumitted 8000. But the life tells us that many of the slaves refused manumission (see refs. above). In support of Vera is a reference by Gregory the Great, *Ep.* 9.233, to a farm in Sicily of about 48 *iugera*, on which were employed three *pueri*, five slaves and which contained forty sheep, three yoke of oxen, ten horses, ten cows and vines; but this is a sixth-century example and may not be typical.

[80] Palladius – Giardina (1986) 33; *casarii* – e.g. *C.Th.* XI.42.7 requires that inventories of confiscated property shall record 'how many slaves, urban or rustic . . . how many *casarii* and *coloni*'. In the sixth century, Gregory the Great instructed a Jew at Luni to manumit his slaves and to leave them as *coloni* on the land 'they have been accustomed to cultivate' (Greg. Mag. *Ep.* 6.21).

[81] Olybrias – see above, n. 32; Barnabas – Aug. *Serm.* 356; Greek islands – Jones, *LRE* 793.

This could mean that Palladius' vagueness about what type of labour to employ was deliberate. He explicitly said, 'There cannot be one way of organizing the work when there are so many different types of land.' Archaeological evidence for the disappearance of large villa accommodation for slaves may only be an indication that in the later empire more and more slaves were home-born and for that reason lived away from the villa in their own groups of houses with their families. In the ante-bellum United States slaves who lived apart like this with families still sometimes served central farms. Sicily, which had run huge slave estates in the earlier empire, shows no perceptible change in labour regime, according to the most recent archaeological study.[82] These are, however, mostly negative arguments, and we must accept that the weight of the evidence in Italy, at least, points to a general shift from the old slave-villa economies of domanial farming to small tenant plots, whether held by *coloni* or by slaves.

It would be reasonable to assume from this conclusion alone that the distance between slaves and free-born tenants had narrowed in the later empire. By the end of the fourth century, when all *coloni* appear to have been finally tied to the land of their origin and after many cases when fugitive *coloni* had been returned as slaves to their owners, the difference between many of them and slave tenants must have been small. But, as we saw, it was not until the fifth century that the condition of one class of *coloni* had become so like that of slaves that Justinian could demand in A.D. 530, 'What then is understood to be the difference between the two?' The same law, however, was at pains to point out that such slave-like status only applied to *adscripticii*, who appear to have been a diminishing number, and not to free *coloni*.[83]

In the fourth century, by contrast, there was a constant insistence in the laws on the differences between a free-born tenant and a slave, the main one being that *coloni* were liable to military service.[84] It may well be that the large injection of foreign and federate soldiers into the army in the later fourth century influenced the debasement of the rights of *coloni*, whose military services could then be dispensed with. Although it may appear reasonable to think that the condition of slaves improved as they became virtual tenants living in their own houses, the many references to slave rebellions and inhumane treatment of slaves proves that they did not enter a new golden age. The fact that some slaves preferred servitude to freedom, as we know from several examples, including that of Melania's household,

---

[82] Pall. *Agric.* 1.6.3. Villa to village in Sicily – Wilson (1990) 215, 230–3; cf. Whittaker (1987) 91. Labour regimes – Wilson (1990) 234, but disputed by Vera (1988b), who believes that a slave revolt in the mid third century (*SHA Gall.*4.9) radically altered the desire for slave labour.
[83] *CJ* xi.48.21 – the *colonus adscripticius* is in this law finally described as being *in domini sui potestate*.
[84] *C.Th.* vii.13.5 (368/373), vii.13.6 (370).

may only show that the debt-ridden rural tenant was even less secure than the domestic slave.[85]

2. Middle and peasant landowners

We sometimes forget that between the very rich and the tenants, about whom we are quite well informed, there existed a class of free farmers – that is, anyone from a medium-size owner of land (such as a small town *curialis*) to a peasant living just above subsistence. About them we have all too little information. Yet Salvian's evidence of such smallholders, who had to sell up to the rich in the fifth century, shows that many had continued to survive until then. The pressure came, according to Salvian, 'when either they lose their homes and fields to the invaders or they flee as fugitives from the tax-collector'. Such statements have stimulated speculation that in northern Gaul, at least, many of the quite prosperous farmers of Picardy and the Ardennes, where hundreds of Roman villas have been plotted from the air, abandoned their homes and fled south in the fourth century. Recent research, however, proves a much greater degree of continuity in the northern frontier regions during the fourth and fifth centuries and far less nucleation on large surviving villas than was once thought. While habitations of the fourth century often appear poorer, and villas frequently show signs of occupation changes, most survived in some form until the end of the fourth century and many continued into the fifth or later.[86]

A similar sort of picture seems to be true of Britain, where what is described as 'squatter occupation' of villas has been observed in the later fourth century. This does not necessarily signify a population decline, even if in many cases the villas appear to have been abandoned and the number of villages to have grown in the course of the fourth century. Unfortunately archaeology cannot tell us about the status of the small farmers who inhabited these sites, although the evidence shows that in some places, when a group of poor farmers took over a villa, one of them was richer than the others.[87] In general, there is a net expansion in numbers of recorded medium-size, archaeological sites all over the western provinces, apart from in southern Spain, and a steady decrease in numbers of small sites. But this information cannot tell us whether it was tenants or owner-occupiers who farmed the land. A study of villages and 'small agglomerations' recently shows that in most of the west there was a 'renaissance' of such sites in the

---

[85] Melania – *V. Mel.* (Lat.) 10; John Chrysostom advised the poor to prefer servitude to freedom (*PG* LIV.606).

[86] Salv. *De Gub. Dei* v.8; Drinkwater (1992). Recent research – Ossel (1992) 177, 182, etc., challenging Wightman (1985). [87] Cleary (1989) 134–6; Higham (1992) 61.

fourth century. But the inhabitants could have been dependants of rich proprietors.[88]

Away from the west, there is considerable evidence of the growth of smaller proprietors in Syria without much sign of domination by rich estate-owners, although again it is impossible to guess their precise tenurial status. Many were the inhabitants of the large villages which were a distinctive mark of this region from the mid fourth century. Libanius writes about some of them as being free rather than *coloni* on estates, even if this did not prevent them from falling under the patronage control of the rich. If, however, they were small, independent farmers settled on the land by imperial direction, as many archaeologists think, then we may be seeing here what the system of emphyteutic long leases produced on the ground.[89]

That certainly seems to be true in fourth-century Africa, although, unlike in Syria, the small farms of the Kasserine survey carried out in southern Tunisia appear to have been dominated by a single estate centre for the production of olive oil. In northern Tunisia an inscription from a farm called the *fundus Aufidianus*, dating from the later empire, documents one such *conductor* who benefited from a long-term contract to restore to prosperity the land on which he lived. These middle-ranking farmers may not have been strictly owner-occupiers, but long-lease contracts were viewed in law as making them *domini possessores* – in other words, virtual owners in perpetuity.[90]

While leasing of imperial property was an area of growth, the constant erosion of the property rights of poorer farmers or even of lesser decurions in the city hierarchies is a theme of the literary sources. Theodoret, bishop of Cyrrhus in Syria, speaks of the severity of the taxation in the fifth century which caused most of the landowners to flee. The Roman tax regime was always regressive. But in addition it was often applied by state officials more rigorously against the poor than the rich, since the resistance of the rich to the tax-collector was endemic in the later empire. In Gaul Julian refused to declare a tax amnesty for late payment, because, he said, 'As is well known, it is the poor who are forced to pay in full without any relaxation at the beginning of an indiction.' The effect was to aggravate the

[88] Lewit (1991) 31–3. See Petit (1994) for a colloquium held in 1992 on *Les agglomérations secondaires de Gaule Belgique et des Germanies*.

[89] Tchalenko, *Villages* 414–15; Tate (1989) 73–4, modifies Tchalenko's vision of monoculture of olives but agrees about imperial direction. Free villages – Lib. *Or.* xi.230; Liebeschuetz, *Antioch* 67 interprets Lib. *Or.* xlvii.4 – 'there are great villages each belonging to many masters' – as evidence of free peasants because Libanius goes on to say they paid direct tax. This may be correct but, as we saw, *coloni* also could pay direct tax.

[90] Hitchner (1990); an excellent pictorial summary of the survey has been produced by Hitchner and Mattingly (1991). *fundus Aufidianus* – Peyras (1975), who dates the inscription hesitantly to the later third century. *domini* – Vera (1986) 284–8 gives references.

tax burden on the poor, causing unevenness in its application, an iniquity about which Ammianus often complains. But Libanius and the law codes prove that the system was sometimes further manipulated by the *principales* within the decurion class to bring bankruptcy to their lesser colleagues.[91]

Apart from the injustice of taxes, church fathers such as Basil in the east or Ambrose in the west regularly delivered homilies about how the rich oppressed the poor with debt and terror to gain their property. 'The rich', Ambrose complained, 'invade the fields and drive off their neighbours . . . The poor man burdened by his debt pledge migrates with his poor belongings.' Basil's message is remarkably similar. The rich, he said, made false accusations to get their neighbour's property, while the poor were reduced to slavery.[92] The close similarity of the examples does not mean they were invented. But a sermon was not the considered conclusion of economic research.

3. The rich

It is inevitably about the rich landowners that we hear most, since they occupied positions of prominence in the literary sources and were the most likely group to be targets of the law. The two most important questions concerning their ownership of land are, first, whether the overall numbers of large property owners increased in the later empire or whether land simply became more concentrated in the hands of fewer, richer rich. The second is whether, as a consequence of the change, the rich became more liable to live on their estates, or less.

As far as concentration of wealth is concerned, the overwhelming weight of the evidence goes to show that the gap between the rich and the poor widened, although this does not necessarily mean there were fewer large landowners than before. The archaeological record in the west, for instance, which was always by repute the territory of large country estates, shows that in numbers of large rural sites there was no great change in their size from the early empire to the fifth century. But that may not be much of a guide, since a land register from Volcei (Lucania) in Italy, dating from A.D. 323, shows that the rich family of the Turcii possessed no fewer than seventy farms scattered in several different districts. Exactly as in earlier periods, concentration of estates into large single sites was not a favoured land strategy of the rich. Ausonius, the wealthy Gallic senator and poet, who became Gratian's close adviser and courtier, talks about his 'little

[91] Theod. *Ep.* 42. Julian – Amm. Marc. XVI.5.15. Ammianus – Frank (1971). *principales* – Lib. *Or.* XLVIII.40; *C.Th.* XI.16.4 (328), XII.1.4 (359) are attempts to check the practice, but by 371 the *principales* were in control – cf. the commentary by A. F. Norman, *Libanius, Select Letters*, Loeb trans., vol. II, 412–14.
[92] Ambr. *De Nabothe* 1; Basil, *Homil. in Divites* 57a=*PG* XXXI.293. Cf. Jones, *LRE* 774–8 for many other citations.

ancestral plot' (*herediolus*) near Bordeaux; but it was only one small part of his property, which included estates in the Poitou, the Saintonge and the Gironde.[93] Nevertheless the *cupido iungendi* of the rich, was, as we have seen, a constant theme of moral discourse. A stream of legislation was issued from the imperial chancery against violent usurpation of property; but protection of the *coloni* or the lesser landowners against the rich was clearly a losing battle. The men who usurped the public lands of Antioch were the richer decurions. Fictitious sales to rich patrons in order to protect the poor against tax tended to turn into permanent loss of ownership.[94]

The dilemma for the state was that, while it wished to encourage the rich to invest in emphyteutic leases to raise revenue, too much land in the hands of the rich gave them uncontrollable power. Our sources are clear about the immense property holdings of the richest families; the younger Melania's annual income from rents from all over the western provinces was 12,000 *solidi* (about 1700 pounds of gold), apart from the value of her movable goods 'which were so great they could not be reckoned'. The annual income of 'many senators', according to the fifth-century historian Olympiodorus, was valued at over 5000 pounds of gold and even medium-rich senators received incomes of 10,000–15,000 pounds of gold. Melania's cousin Petronius Probus 'possessed domains in almost every part of the Roman world', as did the prefect Flavius Rufinus.[95] Ten or twenty properties of 1000–2000 hectares was not unusual for a Gallic senator. Some of the figures for property ownership are staggering, running into several thousand hectares.[96] Like the imperial estates, they were let out to *conductores*, though apparently on short leases, or they were directly managed by *vilici* or *actores*. The recently excavated villa at Nador in Algeria shows such a property refounded in the later third century. It contains inscriptions which name the owner, who was a decurion of a nearby city, but the accommodation is too modest to be his residence and was probably, therefore, the home of his *vilicus*. The same appears to be true of the villa at Castagna in Sicily.[97]

There can be little doubt, therefore, that the rich grew richer. The luxury of the villas in Sicily, such as that at Piazza Armerina or at Patti Marina, point in that direction. Location of villages, markets and fairs on the estates, which had been closely controlled and restricted in the earlier

---

[93] Western sites – Lewit (1991) 31. Volcei – *CIL* x.407; Champlin (1980).

[94] The whole title *unde vim* of *C.Th.* iv.22 is devoted to cases over a century of violent usurpation of private and fiscal property. For usurpation of *ager publicus*, see n. 23. Usurpation through patronage – Zulueta (1909) 23–7.

[95] *V. Mel.* (Greek) 15, (Latin) 1.15; Olympiod. fr. 41.2 (Blockley). Probus – Amm. Marc. xxvii.11.1. Rufinus – Claud. *In Ruf.* 1.187–95; cf. *C.Th.* ix.42.14 (396).

[96] Jullian (1920–6) viii.137 (=(1993) 11.462); Jones, *LRE* 781–8.

[97] Management – Jones, *LRE* 788–92; Nador – Anselmino *et al.* (1989) 230; Castagna – Wilson (1990) 196.

empire, probably became commonplace.[98] Did the rich also become fewer? The records of a sector of Hermopolis in Egypt in the fourth century show that about 3 per cent of the landowners owned half the land; another incomplete list of the fourth century from Maeander in Asia Minor list 7.5 per cent owning half the land (although it is probably incomplete). But it is almost impossible to compare these figures with those from the earlier empire.[99] All we can really say is that, while unequal landholding was an inherent characteristic of all periods of Roman history, it is probable on *a priori* grounds that over the course of centuries, without any mechanism for the redistribution of wealth and without any gross increase in production, the riches of the Roman world became progressively more unequally divided.

There were two massive landowners in the later empire about whose increase in property holding we need have no doubts – the emperor and the church. The steady accumulation of property by the emperor through confiscation, inheritance, intestacy, takeover of city public land and so on is too well known in earlier imperial history to need repeating here. The size of the final result in the fourth century can only be guessed at. But the figures in Africa quoted earlier suggest that between one-seventh and one-sixth of the province was in imperial possession. Much of this, of course, was successfully returned to quasi-private exploitation through emphyteusis. The church began its steady accumulation with the huge donations of Constantine, recorded in the *Liber Pontificalis*, which in Rome alone brought rents of 400 pounds of gold, quite apart from further active gifts and transfers of property by pious donors all over the empire. By the time of Gregory the Great, whose correspondence does much to explain the workings of the massive *patrimonium Petri*, the church vied with the state as the Roman world's greatest landlord. In fifth-century Gaul, bishop Patiens of Lyons was able to bring such massive famine assistance from church estates to the damaged cities of the south that the roads were said to have been jammed with grain traffic and the two rivers of the Rhône and Saône filled with his ships.[100]

The other important question is about the place of rural property in the life of a noble – whether, that is, great owners in the later empire were only interested in rents at the expense of proper management of their rural estates or whether, conversely, they became more attached to their country villas at the expense of their urban duties. The conventional answer is that

[98] Sicily – Wilson (1990) 215, 225. Markets – de Ligt (1993), ch. 5, collects the evidence, but notes that estates' markets were rarely immune from tax. Giardina (1986) 27–8 refers to Olympiod. fr. 41.1 (Blockley), describing the vast self-contained houses of the great, which Giardina (followed by others) uses as evidence of the separation of country-folk from the town; in fact, it is a description of city houses in Rome.   [99] See Duncan-Jones (1976) for a prudent summary of the data.
[100] Africa – see above, note 36. Donations of Constantine – *Lib. Pont.* 34; Jones, *LRE* 89–90. Patiens – Sid. Apoll. *Ep.* 6.12; cf. Whittaker (1983) (=*Land* xiii) 168.

in the east the towns continued to hold the enthusiasm of the rich but in the west, where city life had never been as highly developed, the rich disappeared into their rural retreats and neglected the cities. But this is not a satisfactory account and if we look at the example of a senator such as Symmachus, we see that no such simple response is possible. As far as management is concerned, inevitably, if the rich grew richer and possessors of more and more scattered properties, they must have visited and, therefore, resided in each property less often. That applies to both east and west. Symmachus, who only ranked as a medium-wealthy landowner, owned property entirely in the west – twelve country estates in Italy alone, apart from others in Sicily, Africa and Mauretania. Only in the last of these did he complain of bad management due to his absence. The many letters he wrote about the returns from his estates in Italy demonstrate the close interest he took, and he made sure he was present in the countryside on occasions such as the harvest. But neither was Symmachus only concerned about city life, despite his duties in Rome. In Italy, at least, it is difficult to see that he was any more or less attentive to his estates than Pliny was in the second century or that he represents a new mercenary attitude by the rich to the land.[101]

Away from Italy there is indeed evidence in some regions of the west, such as in Spanish Tarraconensis or Lusitania, of a move by the rich from the towns to their enormous villas in the countryside. The large luxurious quarters attached to working villas, such as that at Foz de Lumbier (near Pompaelo) with its complex of 135 rooms, leaves little doubt that the owner was in residence. In southern Gaul, too, some massive estate buildings appeared in the later empire, such as that praised by Sidonius Apollinaris belonging to the Pontii Leontii on the Gironde. Ausonius and Sidonius give descriptions of the life in their own or their friends' country villas which is a testimony to the importance of these homes, where the rich nobility retired when not engaged in affairs of state. But it does not necessarily mean that Gallic nobles deserted the towns. 'You grumble at my staying in the country', Sidonius writes to a friend, 'when I really ought to be complaining about you being detained in town.'[102] In the north of Gaul and in Britain, as we have seen, the opposite seems to have been true; many villas were abandoned by their owners in the course of the fourth century. Often cited in support of the notion of urban decay is an imperial edict to the prefect of Gaul in A.D. 400 about the desertion of the towns by *collegiati*,

---

[101] Symm. *Ep.* 9.6 – '*actores* of absentee masters who are entrusted with distant business, live as though they were free from the law'; cf. *Ep.* 5.87, 6.81. *Ep.* 9.130 was probably written to his land agent about the problem of rents. *Ep.* 3.23 describes Symmachus' visit to his estate in Campania for the wine and olive pressing. De Martino (1993) 807 attacks the view that owners were separated from their estates; contra Vera (1983).

[102] Spain – Keay, *Roman Spain* 191–7; Gaul – Auson. *Ep.* 25, 28, 35, etc.; Sid. Apoll. *Carm.* xxii, *Ep.* 2.2. For life in late Gallic villas, see Stevens (1933) 68–74.

who 'are following the country life by taking themselves off to secret and remote regions'. But it must be doubtful whether this is any more significant than legislation about *coloni* who deserted one master for another. We do not know of a single case in history where a member of the urban élite in Gaul avoided his urban responsibilities, or where the governor was forced to step in to nominate urban magistrates.[103]

In Africa the magnificent mosaics of rural sporting life, such as that of 'Seigneur Julius', are often cited as proof of a rural drift of the later empire. But it turns out that almost all come from urban sites, such as Carthage and Utica. The archaeological evidence from Cherchel in Caesariensis shows the same abandonment of peri-urban villas as in Britain and the growth of villages. By contrast, in Tunisia and in Libya rural olive-oil production centres appear to have flourished in the later empire, although, as at Nador, these central farms were probably managed by agents. But we must not forget that it was in North Africa, too, that the rebellions of Firmus and Gildo broke out in the later fourth century, and they relied upon the *plebs*, *servi* and *satellites* belonging to the massive estates held by the Mauri lords in the Kabylie mountains, who were almost certainly resident.[104] There is, in short, no consistent evidence of desertion of the towns by the rich in the west.

How different from all this was rural life in the east? We know a fair amount about Libanius and his rich friends in Antioch. Libanius himself spent time on his family estate when a boy and in later life took an interest in the revenues or production of his scattered properties, which were run by agents, although he never mentions visiting them personally. His ex-soldier great-uncle, however, did apparently run a small estate personally with eleven slaves, and we hear of a high official, Leotius, spending a year on his estate in Euphratensis. But the real attractions for the rich of Antioch were the luxury villas in the suburbs of Daphne, where excavations confirm that many had houses. The letters of Basil, who came from a rich landowning family in Cappadocia, describe his boyhood on his estates in Pontus and speak of his foster-brother, perhaps an agent, who ran one of the estates with slaves when Basil renounced his wordly goods. The portrait that Basil presents of the world of a rich family like his own is one of hunting, shepherds, baths in country villas and households which included farmers.[105]

In short, the general picture that emerges from these texts contains

[103] *C.Th.* XII.19.1 (400). Goudineau *et al.* (1980) 384.
[104] African mosaics – Dunbabin (1978) 46–64. Caesariensis – Leveau (1989) 51; see n. 43 above. Firmus and Gildo – Amm. Marc. XXIX.5.36, 39, *C.Th.* VII.8.7 (400), IX.42.19 (405); cf. Camps (1985).
[105] Libanius as a boy – *Or.* 1.4–5; great-uncle – *Or.* XLVII; Leotius – *Ep.* 1175, 1190, etc; villas at Daphne – *Ep.* 660, Liebeschuetz, *Antioch* 51. Basil – *Ep.* 3, 36, 37; *Hom. in Divites*, 53c–54a=*PG* XXXI.284–5.

nothing like the harsh contrast between east and west which is often painted. We must remember that the church in the west was no different from that in the east in being largely an urban-based organization, lending life to the cities and there absorbing large sums of money and support from the rich. Nevertheless, although the differences may be less stark than sometimes described, it is true that on the whole the attractions of rural life in the east seem to have been less than those in the west.

III. THE ORGANIZATION OF THE COUNTRYSIDE

A good deal has already been said about the way property was distributed and about how methods of farming changed in the later empire. There was in the later Roman world a veritable 'explosion' of documentation and pictorial representation of rural life that paved the way to the medieval world by illustrating the ruralization of the lives of even urban inhabitants. In the fifth and sixth centuries it was perhaps a sign of the adaptation of the Roman world to the lifestyles of the German invaders.[106]

1. Units of production

There is no reason to believe that in the later empire the configuration of farming units had changed greatly from that of earlier periods. The enormous imperial and private estates were divided up between *conductores*, often on emphyteutic leases, or placed under the management of *procuratores*, *actores* and *vilici*. But thereafter they were subdivided between *coloni* or slaves. So that even if estates grew more extensive, the size of the units of production did not expand and may even have contracted. The *fundus Aufidianus* in Africa, which is one of the best-known on the ground and is calculated to have covered about 1600 hectares, appears to have consisted of a central residential farm and a number of lots of about four hectares on the estate proper worked by resident tenants. If we can extrapolate from the terminology of second-century African inscriptions, these tenants would have been the *coloni intra fundum*, while the marginal lands on the edges of the estate were probably occupied by *coloni extra fundum*, who in the second century, at least, were the *inquilini*.[107]

Calculation of the size of the church estates in Sicily from the rents listed in Constantine's donations indicate that there was no standard size, since revenue varied from 115 *solidi* to 1000 *solidi* (corresponding, maybe, to something like between 90 and 800 hectares); and, although we know of the existence of some very large *massae* in Sicily in the sixth century and of

[106] Cavallo and Giardina (1993).
[107] Peyras (1975). The well-known second-century African estate inscriptions, *CIL* VIII.25902, etc., easily fit into the ground survey of the *fundus Aufidianus*.

four hundred *conductores*, there is no reason to think the units were cultivated any differently. One of these farms of about twelve hectares, paying fourteen *solidi* in rent, was cultivated by five slaves and three 'boys', although we do not know how they divided up the work. The same applies to the farms of Melania, each of which employed perhaps about seven slaves alongside an unknown number of *coloni*. The holdings listed on one of the rent rolls of the Ravenna church in the sixth century were very small, with the majority of tenants paying three or four *solidi* – perhaps, therefore, no more than two or three hectares each.[108]

What this means is that economies of scale, whether through central estate management or through reducing the number of estate buildings by amalgamating adjoining estates (something which Pliny discussed in the second century), did not attract the rich. This may have been partly the result of the accident of inheritance and partly due to the belief that natural disasters could be avoided if not all one's property was in the same region. But it also shows that maximizing profits was not the sole aim of the aristocracy.

2. Estate management

As we have already seen, there was no single regime or mode of organizing labour. Management of the estates was inevitably carried out through a network of managerial intermediaries, although this did not necessarily mean that the owner was absent. Although the wealthy Nicomachi family had an estate at Erice in Sicily run by an *epitropos* (*procurator*), we happen to know that the younger Nicomachus Flavianus spent time on his estate at Enna when he was revising the text of Livy.[109] Some managers or *conductores* were less than scrupulous about their accounts or about the excesses they squeezed out of the *coloni*, despite attempts by the state to prevent the abuse on imperial land. They probably relied upon this source of income for their profits. The council of Carthage forbade clergy from serving as *procuratores* because of their unpopularity, and John Chrysostom preached about *epitropoi* who tormented the labourers, dragging them about and putting them in prison.[110]

---

[108] Sicily – Wilson (1990) 220. Jones, *LRE* 790, 805, cites papyri (*P.Ital.* 1 and 3) which give details of how estate business was conducted for the church in Ravenna. Farm – Greg. *Ep.* 233. Vera (1988a) thinks that the units became smaller in the later empire, but offers no direct evidence. Melania – see above, n. 79.

[109] See above for Symmachus' estates, and Symm. *Ep.* 1.5, 2.3, 3.23, 5.78, etc. Sicily – *IG* xiv.283–4, Wilson (1990) 217.

[110] Abuses – e.g. Valentinian's rescript of 370/1, found on an inscription at Ephesus concerning former municipal land, which demands that *actores* cease drawing *super statutum canonem* and selling the surplus for themselves; *Inschr. v. Ephesos* 1a, n. 42. Carthage – *C. Carth.* 1, can. 6. The letters of Gregory in the sixth century are full of the ways in which *conductores* cheated and exploited the *coloni*. John Chrys. *Hom. in Math.* LXI.3.

Probably the most complete and yet the most disputed text we possess about estate management is that written by Palladius, who discussed the management of the estate by a *praesul* or *procurator*. The main buildings of the estate that he describes were devoted entirely to servicing the estate with presses, barns, gardens, haystacks, cattle ponds and so on. But there is no reference to a *pars urbana* for a resident owner, and it is generally believed that the central *praetorium* he refers to was no more than a kind of estate office. This has prompted speculation that Palladius' villa was typical of late Italian estates. But the letters of Symmachus do not really support this conclusion, since he regularly stayed on his country estates. Furthermore, the excavated villa at S. Giovanni di Ruoti in Basilicata, which seems to have been reconstructed in the late fourth or fifth century and to have corresponded in form and style quite closely to the *praetorium* recommended by Palladius, is thought to have been luxurious enough to have served as the residence of a rich owner. This was certainly true of other late villas in Spain and elsewhere. On the other hand, the farming complexes around Kasserine in Tunisia look more like Palladius' model, with a central working farm managed by an agent surrounded by smallholdings. Even Palladius, however, recognized that some villas might be the domicile of the owner when he said, 'The presence of the master advances the land.'[111]

Unfortunately Palladius gives us no hint of the way the workforce of the estate was organized. The facilities of the central buildings argue for something rather more than a mere estate office for the mobilizing of tenants. He notes, for instance, that for the vineyards there had to be a *custos* (a foreman, perhaps) to supervise the work, which must surely indicate that they were not just individual plots.[112] It is this ambiguity which has prompted the debate about whether all estates throughout the empire were run by tenant smallholders or whether sometimes there was a large 'home' farm on which the tenants had to provide corvée labour services (*operae*) in a proto-medieval fashion.

The evidence for such domanial organization is scanty, the best, ironically, dating back to the inscriptions of second-century Africa, where the tenants had to provide six days work for the farmer general or imperial manager per year. In sixth-century Italy the rent rolls of the church at Ravenna also required some labour from the smaller tenants. But between these two dates there is no single clear reference to *operae* in all the many laws and literary texts about exploitation of the poor. We must, therefore, assume that the practice was rare. But this does not preclude the possibility that slaves or *coloni* were still sometimes used for direct domanial farming, as some of the evidence cited earlier suggests. Some Spanish

---

[111] S. Giovanni – Small (1986), 112; Kasserine – see above, n. 46. Pall. *Op. Agr.* 1.8 (describes the *praetorium*), 1.6.1 – *praesentia domini provectus est agri.*   [112] Pall. *Op. Agr.* 11.10.4.

villas, which included as many as forty small rooms in rows attached to the villa, look very much as though they were provided for either hired hands or slaves for use on the domain.[113]

The tenants paid in either cash or kind. It is unclear sometimes which was the norm but there were apparently different 'customs on estates' (*consuetudines praedii*). The massive gold incomes of senators, about which we hear so much, do not prove that tenants paid in cash, since the *conductores* or agents could have collected the rents in kind and then sold the produce, as some sources confirm. It is now believed that the monetization of the later empire had penetrated the countryside far more than was once thought, partly owing to the enormous finds of small coins as change. On the other hand, there was a large sector that remained in the natural economy. Olympiodorus, who informs us about the incomes of senators, says that a quarter of it was provided in kind. 'Gifts' in kind had always been a practice in the countryside, and these we find written into rent agreements in the Ravenna rolls. But it was also common for great landlords, starting with the emperor and the church, to collect part of the produce from their estates for the use of their large households or for exchange of gifts with friends. So much so that this constituted a sizeable proportion of the exchange transactions in the later empire.[114]

3. The ruralization of the later empire

Nothing said so far really gives us much impression of what the country-side looked like in the later empire or how much it had changed from earlier periods. The great majority of the population still lived in the rural territo-ries around the urban centres, and the main crops were still probably more or less the same as those they grew before. Although in Italy there was some shift from intensive vineyards to extensive cornfields in certain regions, such as Etruria, during the earlier empire, the main quality wines of Italy continued to be produced. In the later empire some parts of south and central Italy, as we can see at S. Giovanni di Ruoti, became more wooded and adapted to the raising of pigs, stimulated probably by state legislation that was almost obsessive about making the supply of pork to the people of Rome a compulsory burden on the land.[115] Cattle thieving and a conse-quent state restriction on the use of horses in southern and central Italy is perhaps another sign of the increase in open grazing land.[116]

[113] Jones, *LRE* 805–6 collects the evidence. Spain – Keay, *Roman Spain* 192.

[114] Customs – *CJ* xi.48.5 (365). Basil – 'Corn is turned into gold for you; wine is transmitted into gold; wool is made into precious metal; every sort of sale, every sort of idea brings you gold': *PG* xxxi.269; cf. Vera, 'Forme e funzioni'. Monetization – Carrié, 'Economia e finanze' 759. Ravenna – Jones, *LRE* 804. Gift exchange – Whittaker, 'Trade and traders'.

[115] Wine – Tchernia (1986) ch. 5. Pigs – Barnish (1987); Cavallo and Giardina (1993) 340; *C.Th.* xiv.4.

[116] *C.Th.* ix.30.

Rural banditry was probably becoming a greater problem all over the empire, as the authority of the state grew weaker. But we should not exaggerate the difference, since robbers were an endemic problem throughout all periods of the empire. Banditry was often a term applied by the state to religious or political dissidents, such as the Bagaudae in Gaul or the Manichees. But extremes of poverty, frontier raids, increasing desertion from the army and the growth of private militias must have combined to make the countryside more insecure for the poor and, correspondingly, to make the need for protection by the rich more essential. Since shepherds were identified as more prone to banditry than others, they were forbidden to rear other people's children, as was the practice in the countryside. In rural areas of Syria Libanius tells how robbers ran protection rackets, and were suspected of being in league with innkeepers. Ammianus reports that the Maratocupreni, an entire village of bandits near Apamea, used to attack towns, often posing as traders or state officials.[117]

Whether this contributed to a greater isolation of the town from the countryside is more debatable. There are some who argue that such segregation is evident in Palladius' advice that a rural estate should retain its own craftsmen, 'in order that a reason for seeking the city [sc. to buy the produce of craftsmen] should not divert countrymen from their usual work'. But we must remember that even in the first century A.D. Varro gave similar advice about discouraging rural workers from going too much to urban markets. It does, however, appear true that the establishment of rural markets and country fairs on the great estates, although carefully controlled by the government in the earlier empire, became more common in the later empire, and that would have encouraged such segregation. Estate markets also increased the prestige and control of the rich. In Sicily places marked on the Antonine Itinerary with names like Calvisiana, Philosophiana, etc., were probably local village markets which derived their names from the villa owners on whose estates they were located.[118]

The fact that the term pagani, meaning inhabitants of the rural pagi, became synonymous with non-Christians illustrates the extent to which the culture of the city, where the church had established itself, was diverging from that of the countryside, despite the effort of church and state. The life of Martin of Tours tells how he converted Gaul in the later fourth century by going out from the city and overthrowing the country shrines of rural communities, who appear to have been untouched by influential, earlier bishops of Gaul, such as Hilary of Poitiers. But Martin was obviously not as successful as his hagiographer would have us believe, since his

[117] Van Dam, Leadership and Community 49–58, 81; Shaw (1993), esp. 321. For legislation identifying banditry among shepherds, see C.Th. IX.31.1 (409). Syria – Lib. Ep. 27.4, 33.40, Amm. Marc. XXVIII.2.13.
[118] Pall. Op. Agr. 1.6.2; Varro, RR 1.16.5; Giardina (1986) 31–6. Prestige – De Ligt (1993) 176–85. Sicily – Wilson (1990) 215, 223.

disciple Martin of Brive is reputed to have done exactly the same thing as his master – and to have suffered execution for his pains. The state held the religion of rural tenants to be the responsibility of landowners, who could be punished for allowing Donatism (which became a heresy in the fifth century) to flourish. John Chrysostom urged the rich to found churches on their estates and Melania provided on her African estates both Catholic and Donatist churches, before the latter was declared heretical. In the country-side around Antioch, however, Christian inscriptions are few and the general interest of city dwellers in the rural villages was low.[119]

Villages have been mentioned several times, and it has often been thought that in the later empire they grew at the expense of the towns. One reason for this may have been the temptation for traders to remove their activities to the villages and to estate markets in order to avoid the hated city trade tax.[120] In Sicily many of the villages became virtual agro-towns, some of quite sizeable settlements. In Italy the codes and an inscription from Trinitapoli near Foggia provide evidence that rural districts (*pagi*) in some parts of Italy were playing an administrative role, under their own *praepositi*, in the tax regime. But in the north-western provinces the number of small settlements declined somewhat from the high empire. In the Franche-Comté and Burgundy, for example, about one-third did not survive the third century into the later period. Some, however, took on new life and became like fortified towns, a development which supports the picture of greater nucleation due to rural insecurity. In Britain, smaller establishments disappeared but differentiation increased among large agglomerations. In the east, although villages flourished, increasing in both size and numbers, they never took on the aspect of small towns, as happened in the west.[121]

4. Patronage in the countryside

The countryside in the later empire was dominated by the growing inde-pendence of the rich landowners, whose power of patronage and protec-tion was a constant subject of legislation. The dilemma began with taxes, since the rich, often in collusion with provincial and state magistrates, evaded or were slow to pay their full tax liability. The additional burden thereby thrown onto those *coloni* and free owner-occupiers who paid their own taxes encouraged them in turn to seek the protection of the rich as a

[119] Landowners and heresy – *C.Th.* xvi.6.4.1 (404). Melania – *V. Mel.* (Lat) 21.16ff.; cf. Aug. *Ep.* 58.1 for the example of Pammachius, who drove Donatists off his estate. Antioch – Liebeschuetz, *Antioch* 121.

[120] *NVal* 24 (447) attempted to legislate against traders operating *declinatis urbibus per vicos portusque quamplures possessionesque diversas*; cf. Giardina (1981). Estate owners with the privilege of holding markets on their land were not supposed to levy tax on goods; *CJ* iv.60.1 (370).

[121] Sicily – Wilson (1990) 230–2. Codes and Trinitapoli – Giardina and Grelle (1983). North-western provinces – Petit (1994). East – Tate (1989).

means of survival. The Trinitapoli inscription records the effort of
Valentinian I to place governors between the *possessores* and the poor in the
pagi as safeguards against the injustice of the state tax officials or the *curiales* in the cities. But the effect was often to increase the influence of the
great landowners, who doubled as provincial governors.[122]

What the farmers paid in return for protection we do not always know.
Extensive patronage and the prestige it brought to the rich were features
deeply embedded in Roman society from the very earliest period of the
republic, and it is evident that one reason why the high aristocracy of the
later empire continued to seek high office was more for the rights of
patronage it bestowed than for any direct power. In the Veneto, around
Histria, Aquileia and Verona, an inscription records the Veneti and Histri
people as the *peculiares* of the great praetorian prefect Petronius Probus;
from Capua, another inscription names him as *originalis patronus*. Both
terms indicate extreme dependence and widespread influence.[123] But
patronage worked to the detriment of the state when the rich used their
power to prevent the state from collecting its essential revenues. A series of
edicts from 360 onwards makes it clear that this was what was happening,
since patrons were not only protecting farmers from the fulfilment of their
tax duties but also, as the law puts it, 'They have begun to possess landholdings under the title of protection.' The land, in other words, was
passing into the name of the patron, and peasant farmers were becoming
his dependent *coloni*.[124] That, as we saw earlier, was the practice against
which Salvian inveighed in fifth-century Gaul.

The consequences of such appropriation through patronage were many
and varied but almost all were injurious to the state. Libanius composed a
speech *Concerning Patronage* which was principally an attack on military and
state officials who were undermining the traditional, inherited patronage of
landlords. They were making it impossible, he says, to collect taxes and were
creating brigandage in the countryside, as villagers raided their neighbours
with impunity, thereby destroying the natural order of the curial class.
Richer landowners were, therefore, poaching both free farmers and *coloni*,
making themselves too powerful in the countryside to be approached by
tax officials and using their position in towns to offload their responsibility
for tax-collection onto their poorer colleagues. The effect in Antioch,
according to Libanius, was ruinous to the middle-ranking property
owners.[125]

---

[122] For the Trinitapoli inscription, see the previous note.

[123] For a recent general discussion of patronage, see Garnsey and Woolf (1989). Inscriptions of
Petronius Probus and the related Anicii family influence – *ILS* 1266, *AE* 1972, 75–6; cf. Giardina (1986)
27.   [124] *C.Th.* XI.24 is a full title under the heading *de patrociniis vicorum*.

[125] Zulueta (1909) is a good guide to Libanius and the legislation on patronage. For Libanius' speech,
see the commentaries by Harmand (1955) and Carrié (1976).

This adds particular interest to a phenomenon which developed in the west earlier than in the east: the growth of private armies, many of which were recruited from *coloni* and slaves of the estates or from fugitive soldiers and dissident farmers who sought refuge on the country estates of the rich. In Spain, where a regime of huge residential villas had developed, there is a striking example of such a private army recruited in 408–9 from the estate workers of the noble family of Verenianus and his brothers, who were related to the emperor Honorius, in order to resist the usurper Constantine. The example is similar to that of the armies belonging to the rich estate-owners of the Kabylie mountains in North Africa or to the armed bands raised by a bishop in southern France in A.D. 445. The phenomenon of 'warlordism' was the natural consequence of the weakness of central government and the growth of patronage by the rich in the countryside.[126] Landlords who ceased to owe loyalty to the central state ushered in the Middle Age.

[126] Spain – *PLRE* II, s.v. 'Verenianus'; bishop – *NVal* 17.1 (445). Warlordism – Whittaker, *Frontiers* ch. 7.

CHAPTER 10

TRADE, INDUSTRY AND THE URBAN ECONOMY

PETER GARNSEY AND C. R. WHITTAKER

I. INTRODUCTION

Most of the inhabitants of the Roman empire were farmers who consumed food that they had themselves grown. Production, harvest performance and storage were of primary significance; distribution was correspondingly less crucial.

Distribution was important none the less, and also problematic. Most inhabitants of cities lacked direct control over the products of the land and depended for their survival on food grown by others. In the early Roman empire perhaps 15–20 per cent of the population were city dwellers – in Italy around 30 per cent, because of the huge size of the city of Rome. In the fourth and early fifth centuries, the balance is normally supposed to have swung further in favour of the countryside. Yet there continued to exist in the late empire an urban plebs that was significant in numbers and dependent for its survival on other individuals and agencies, including, crucially, traders and transporters. Further, non-producing consumers had an importance disproportionate to their numbers by virtue of the fact that they were concentrated in the city, the power centre of the ancient world. This was a group which, if its own essential requirements were not met, was capable of showing restlessness and resentment which sometimes spilled over into violence:

I was sitting at home working [wrote Libanius of Antioch] when a roar went up from a mob apparently out of control. I raised my hands to my eyes to see what was happening. Just then my nephew ran in gasping for breath with the news that the archon was dead, his corpse torn apart and mocked by his killers. Euboulos and his son meanwhile had escaped a stoning, fled and sought refuge in the mountain tops. The rioters, having missed out on their bodies, were now releasing their anger on their house. Smoke, the harbinger of fire, was filling the air, and was only too obvious to the eye.

They set fire to Symmachus' beautiful house in the Transtiberine district [wrote Ammianus Marcellinus], spurred on by the fact that a common fellow among the plebeians had alleged, without any informant or witness, that the prefect had said that he would rather use his own wine for quenching lime-kilns than sell it at the price which the people hoped for.[1]

---

[1] Lib. *Or.* 1.103, of the grain shortage of A.D. 354 (cf. Amm. Marc. XIV.7.2); Amm. Marc. XXVII.3.4, under A.D. 364–5. See Kohns (1961) for hunger riots in Rome.

If the lives of the mass of ordinary people were dependent on suppliers and distributors of staple foods (by far the most significant item of production and distribution), the propertied classes looked to traders and transporters to bring them the wide range of luxuries and exotic goods that their lifestyles demanded. The houses of the Milanese élite in the time of St Ambrose were well-stocked with silks, carpets, curtains, jewellery, foreign wines, perfumes, unguents, rare marbles and slaves.[2] In addition, relatively cheap, mass-produced manufactures continued to have a role to play in the economy. Clothing, metals and building materials were especially important. But how does the volume of commodities produced and distributed compare with that of earlier periods? Did industry and trade decline in the period under survey, and if so, how far, and why?

An initial argument for decline has already been hinted at. Cities are often held to have been depleted of residents at all levels, including at the top, as the élite progressively withdrew from an urban base to luxurious country villas, transforming them into oases of prosperous self-sufficiency. The retirement of the élite to the countryside could only have substantially reduced the level of economic activity in the city, especially if, as is commonly supposed, they took the artisan class with them to service their needs. It was traditionally in the cities that the élite spent most of the surplus wealth that issued from their rural estates, generating in the process employment for artisans, merchants and unskilled labourers.

Other arguments commonly employed for a decline of market activity in the late empire take us into the realm of central government policy. The supposed developments include:

1. The establishment or expansion from the time of Diocletian of state factories producing arms and equipment for the military.
2. The hereditary attachment of workers' associations (*collegia*) to public service from the time of Constantine, with a view to ensuring that important public functions were performed and essential supplies furnished.
3. An increase in taxes in kind, and an ever-growing tax burden.
4. A progressive demonetization of the economy.[3]

---

[2] Ruggini, *Economia e società* 91.

[3] On this issue (which we do not treat in detail) we are in general agreement with the account of Carrié, 'Economia e finanze'. The state, as before, issued coinage primarily for its own purposes rather than for individual use. But this was compatible with the use of money in commercial transactions, nor did the manner in which this policy was followed in our period bring about a demonetization of the private economy and a diminution of monetary exchange. Money produced by the state to meet its own expenses circulated through, and was absorbed by, the wider economy. In particular, the quantity of copper coinage available in our period (see the perhaps unexpected findings of Reece (1973) for Britain (especially), southern France and Italy) points to vigorous, everyday, market activity. The state received back as taxes gold that it had issued, but for this to be possible taxpayers had to be able to exchange goods for gold.

Whether these factors existed in reality and what effect they had are two questions that have to be assessed in the context of a general discussion of the character and health of the non-agricultural sectors of the late Roman economy. Such an account can draw on a whole range of sources, all of which, literary and non-literary, familiar and less well-known, have something to offer. Rather than produce an inventory of sources here, we will restrict ourselves to a few critical evaluations of some of them, in the process raising some of the historical issues that will concern us. Literature is of course an indispensable resource – and not merely canonical texts, for profitable use can be made even, for example, of obscure hagiographical material.[4] Yet the limitations of such evidence, though they are or should be familiar enough, are worth recalling briefly: literary texts are often tendentious and they are usually isolated. Some are, literally, fragments, relics of lost works, preserved without their context. Of such a kind is a passage from the *History* of Olympiodorus on which all accounts of senatorial wealth in the late empire are based.[5] The legal material is of central importance, but is frequently more informative concerning the mentality and preoccupations of legislators and their advisers, or, at best, contemporary conditions in the region at which a law is directed, than concerning broad historical processes.

While literary or documentary sources will sometimes be qualitatively significant, we cannot look to them for quantitative data. There is a total absence of detailed records of production, trade or taxes, for this as for all other periods of antiquity. Attempts to circumvent this problem have been uniformly unsuccessful. An example is Jones's suggestion that trade contributed 5 per cent of the imperial revenues and the overall wealth of the empire. This figure was arrived at by a comparison of the contributions made in the late fifth century by the city of Edessa in western Mesopotamia to the *collatio lustralis*, commonly referred to as the 'trade tax' (an invention of the reign of Constantine), with sixth-century returns in the land tax from two Egyptian towns.[6] However, the 'trade tax' was by no means charged against all trading activities, since tolls, sales taxes and, above all, customs duties did not come within its range, but were collected separately. In any case, there is ample evidence for tax-evasion by powerful men and by their clients. More fundamentally, to infer the relative importance to the economy of trade and industry from their contribution to tax revenue requires that rates of taxation and the extent of state ownership and hence the scope of a taxable private sector were equal in the agricultural and non-agricultural sections of the economy. But we know neither whether the so-called 'traders' of Mesopotamia and the peasants of Egypt paid taxes at a

---

[4] Patlagean, *Pauvreté*, makes good use of these sources.
[5] Olympiod. fr. 44. It is worth asking how reliable the testimony of Olympiodorus is, how he arrived at his figures.   [6] Jones, *LRE* 465; cf. Garnsey and Saller (1987) 46–7; Pleket (1984).

comparable rate, nor the extent of state ownership in each area of the economy. That commerce and industry were much less significant than agriculture as wealth-creators and revenue-earners for the state is unproblematic, but cannot be established by this methodology.

An argument from shipwrecks for decline in the trading sector provides a further example of the dangers of pseudo-quantification.[7] The graph of shipwrecks shows a distribution across time of over a thousand wrecks, with a progressive decline from a high point between c. 150 B.C. and c. A.D. 150 to the mid seventh century A.D. However, the evidence is unbalanced: it strongly favours the coastline of the Mediterranean from Genoa to Narbonne, and reflects the zeal of underwater archaeologists of France and Italy rather than the pattern of Mediterranean sea traffic overall.

Another kind of archaeological evidence for trade, available in quantity, is provided by the millions of pottery sherds that have been found on sites all over the Roman world. Without this evidence, we would have little knowledge of the movement of objects of trade.[8] It reveals, for example, the changing patterns of provincial exports in food (especially oil, wine and fish-sauce) to Rome, the emergence of North Africa as the epicentre of Mediterranean trade from about the early third century, and, more generally, the persistence of long-distance commodity movement in considerable quantity in late antiquity. This was an age thought by some to have been unfavourable to trade because of a decline of Roman naval power in the Mediterranean following barbarian invasions.[9]

The pottery evidence has clear limitations. It is selective, offering information (and that mainly by proxy) about the movement of some foods and manufactures and not of others. Notoriously, nothing is disclosed about the most important staple of all, wheat, except indirectly, in so far as fine tableware travelled pick-a-back on cargoes of cereals.

In addition, archaeology cannot reveal the nature of the transactions that took place when commodities were moved and exchanged, a prime concern of the economic historian. Not all commodity movement is trade. Trade is essentially free market exchange, and is to be distinguished from transference of goods taking place outside the market, through, in the language of Polanyi, 'reciprocity' (gift exchange) and 'administered trade' (or 'redistribution'); by the latter we are to understand the movement of goods outside the market under the direction of governments, large institutions (the church) or wealthy private landowners.[10] This matter is germane to the issue of decline. Suppose it is suggested (as it will be below) that only some cities declined, in some parts of the empire, and that the loss in individual

---

[7] Parker (1980) with Hopkins (1980); Parker (1989), (1992). Critiques by MacMullen, *Corruption* 8–10; Whittaker (1989).

[8] Pottery evidence is surveyed in Giardina, *Società romana* III. See review by Wickham (1988).

[9] See Rubin (1986), discussing Rougé (1966).   [10] Polanyi *et al* (1957).

cases and regions was to some degree offset by gains elsewhere: it would
not follow that the 'non-agricultural sector' in aggregate remained at its
earlier level. The volume of transactions might have remained more or less
constant while the share of non-market transference increased.

There is a final preliminary point. The significance of the issue of the
decline of trade and industry in late antiquity is commensurate with the significance of those sectors themselves in relation to agriculture. Those
scholars who place stress on the non-market character of much commodity movement, and the importance of the household as an autarchic unit,
also tend to rank trade and industry low – in all periods of antiquity. The
issue cannot be skirted (though it would be barren to build our discussion
around it). The comparison alluded to earlier between the revenues from
the 'trade tax' and the rather more substantial receipts from the land tax is
a specifically late antique contribution to this debate. The question also
arises in connection with the 'consumer city' model, according to which
ancient cities were typically units of 'consumption' rather than 'production', living parasitically off the countryside rather than paying their own
way through exchange with the outside world of goods manufactured
within their boundaries. An implication of this theory is that a significant
proportion of the economic transactions between city and country is to be
placed in the non-market category, and that city-based commercial and
industrial activities were quantitatively insignificant.[11]

These are some of the issues confronting the economic historian of late
antiquity. The discussion that follows will focus on possible large-scale
structural developments affecting the non-agricultural economy, on the
assumption that there is more profit to be gained from this approach than
from, on the one hand, attempting quantification and, on the other, illustrating economic life over a broad spectrum of activities by means of isolated anecdotes and references.

II. STATE INTERVENTION AND ITS LIMITS

State ownership and control in the spheres of industry and trade appear to
have expanded considerably in the late empire. From the time of
Diocletian, state direction of the 'defence industry' increased, state-run
factories grew in size and number, and more artisans were locked into the
industry. In so far as the state factories took care of most of the requirements of the army in the matter of weapons and equipment, private producers lost an important customer. In addition, the use of taxes in kind and
levies for other supplies for the military, as well as for the court and bureau-

[11] For the 'consumer city' see Finley (1981) 3–23; Hopkins (1978); Whittaker (1990). For general discussion of the significance of trade, see Finley (1985); Whittaker, 'Trade and traders'; Vera (1983);
Carandini (1986); Jongman (1988) 28–55; Wickham (1988).

cracy, limited the sphere of activities of private traders and cut into their profits.

This is all relatively uncontroversial, though proof is possible only up to a certain point, the evidence for industry, whether state-directed or not, being thin. However, there are at least three reasons for steering away from an extreme position on the extent and range of state control, the stifling of private enterprise, and the declining volume of trade.

First, the scope of state interest in the manufacturing sector was limited. Basic military equipment without which the army would have been useless is a special case; the government had no comparable interest in other man-made products designed for civilian consumers. The same applies in relation to other supplies: once the court, the administration, the military and the citizens of the two capital cities had received their due, the involvement of the government had approached its limit. The impression conveyed by the legal sources is that the interests of the state were primarily fiscal, that it was more concerned to ensure that workers organized into *collegia* performed the various compulsory public services (liturgies, corvées, *munera sordida*) than to control their professional activities.

A second qualification is that the levy and tax system did not deprive the private trader of a role altogether. Landowners might have had to purchase the goods in question sometimes, or regularly. Further, as levies were progressively commuted for gold, from the late fourth century onwards, soldiers and other government employees would have had increasing recourse to the private trade sector.[12]

Third, there is an argument against the occurrence of radical change in relevant institutions and practices. The army of the principate, from the time it became a stationary frontier force (around the second half of the first century A.D.), was already in part catering for its own needs in on-site establishments under its control. Private producers would have made a contribution, though not necessarily in a free market: weaponry, armour, ammunition and other such equipment were too crucial to be left entirely to the operation of market forces. Requisitioning of such goods from independent producers was standard practice. Meanwhile, the exaction of food and other basic supplies as taxes in kind, supplemented by levies, was common in the military provinces of the Roman empire already in the early empire.

It has been argued that the imposition of money taxes in the period of the principate forced farmers to sell their produce to raise cash to pay money taxes (and money rents), thus stimulating trade. Under a system of tax in kind, such as is commonly thought to have operated in the late

---

[12] *Adaeratio* was not imposed before Theodosius I. See Kolb (1980); Carrié, 'Economia e finanze' 763–5.

empire, one might predict a decline in trade. Farmers no longer had to sell their produce to raise cash for tax purposes. Trading activity that had been centred on these transactions was thereby reduced in scope. There was less for middlemen to do in the way of transforming natural produce into saleable processed goods, transporting them, and disposing of them in a market.

There are problems with the argument and its extension from principate to late empire. In the first place, taxes in kind were significant under the principate (as already suggested), and money taxes were significant under the late empire. Furthermore, *adaeratio* (or the substitution of cash payments for payments in kind) was introduced from the time of Theodosius I. The tax–trade relation is difficult to gauge for any period; the problem of deciding whether it changed significantly from early to late empire is quite intractable.[13]

A second issue – the status of artisans and tradesmen – is related. Craftsmen and traders were less free than previously, it is often supposed, to engage in a commodity market. For example, the workers in the imperial factories (*fabricenses*) were members of workers' corporations (*collegia*) who had been tied to their occupation by the government. Waltzing in his classic study of *collegia* stopped short of claiming that the government achieved the objective of compulsory 'unionism'. Membership of a *collegium* was not in fact necessary for the practice of a craft, either in theory or in practice. But Waltzing did hold that all workers' associations were hereditarily attached to some public service from the time of Constantine – the aim being to ensure that vital public functions were performed and essential supplies furnished.[14]

A crucial question is, how far was the imperial government capable of controlling the activities of *collegiati*, or interested in doing so? The public bakers – that is, those who baked bread for the state distribution system in the capital cities – were one group that was subjected to a high degree of physical control. It appears that they were virtual prisoners and slaves throughout their working lives. A colourful (and perhaps unbelievable) story from the fifth-century ecclesiastical historian Socrates represents the Christian emperor Theodosius I as putting a stop to one method of recruiting the bakers, on moral grounds, but without querying their status and working conditions.

During the short stay of the emperor Theodosius in Italy, he conferred the greatest benefit on the city of Rome, by grants on the one hand, and by abrogations on the other. His largesses were very munificent, and he removed two most infamous

---

[13] Hopkins (1980); Duncan-Jones, *Structure and Scale* 30–47, 187–98; cf. Garnsey and Saller (1987) 83–106. An additional, related problem is how far taxes increased in the late empire. See Jones, *Economy* 82–9; *contra*, Carrié, 'Economia e finanze' 767–8.   [14] Waltzing (1896); Mickwitz (1936).

abuses which existed in that mighty city. There were buildings of immense magnitude, erected in former times, in which bread was made for distribution among the people. Those who had the charge of these edifices, whom the Romans in their language term *mancipes*, in the process of time converted them into receptacles for thieves. Now the bakehouses in these structures being placed underneath, they built taverns at the side of each, where prostitutes were kept; by which means they entrapped many of those who went thither either for the sake of refreshment or to gratify their lusts. For by a certain mechanical contrivance, they precipitated them from the tavern into the bakehouse below. This was practised chiefly upon strangers; and such as were in this way caught, were compelled to work in the bakehouses, where they were immured until old age, their friends concluding that they were dead. It happened, that one of the soldiers of the emperor Theodosius fell into this snare; who, being shut up in the bakehouse and hindered from going out, drew a dagger which he wore and killed those who stood in his way; the rest being terrified allowed him to escape. When the emperor was made acquainted with the circumstance, he punished the *mancipes*, and ordered these haunts of lawless and abandoned characters to be pulled down.[15]

Public bakers were an exceptional case. The distribution of bread in the capitals, whether free (*panis gradilis*) or cut-price (*panis fiscalis*), was of both nutritional and political importance. It was a vital protection against hunger (for in antiquity cereals constituted the bulk of the diet of everyone, especially the lower classes), and at the same time a symbol of the generosity of the ruler and his special relationship with a privileged sector of the populace.[16]

It is difficult to find other workers who were confined and degraded in the way that public bakers were. The treatment of miners and some *fabricenses* may provide parallels of a kind. But, for example, the shippers tied to the *annona*, the government supply system of the capital cities, although they too were doing an essential job, could not be controlled as bakers were (see below).

In general, the concerns of the government were narrow, and amounted to a great deal less than the sum total of trading and industrial activity of the late empire.

There are other qualifications to be made to the notion of the regimentation of *collegia*.

First, owners and managers did not share the status of the rank-and-file workers. The owners of Rome's baking establishments were invariably landowners and might indeed border on senatorial rank.[17] Their financial interests will have extended far beyond breadmaking, and their personal freedom was not confined by their trade in any way. In contrast, as we saw, the bakers they employed were tantamount to slaves. Shipowners

[15] Socr. *HE* v.18.
[16] For wheat as food, see Foxhall and Forbes (1981); as an instrument of politics, see e.g. Sirks (1990).
[17] e.g. *C.Th.* xiv.3.4, 364.

(*navicularii*) were inevitably landowners, and some, it seems, were substantial landed magnates and men of power and influence. They were on the fringe of the senatorial class, are described in laws as *potentiores*, and might be recruited from former administrators.[18]

Second, involvement in a commercial or industrial activity over which the state tried to maintain close supervision and control did not prevent its leading members from pursuing private profit. In Constantinople, according to the *Notitia Dignitatum*, there were about six times as many private as public bakeries. In Rome, the large number of public bakeries (274, or more than ten times as many as in Constantinople) probably means that there was less scope for private enterprise. But the demand for bread in Rome was not exhausted by the provision of free and cheap bread (no more than it had been by the distributions of the early empire). There was a free market in cereals, and the public bakeries, together with an unknown number of private establishments, not to mention private landowners, may be expected to have cashed in on this.[19] The *annona* shippers were guaranteed, in addition to immunity (from civic burdens, guardianship and so on), a profit on the grain that they carried for the state of a little less than half (five-twelfths) of that allowed in Diocletian's Price Edict. But they indulged in profit-making on the side, through the sale of private merchandise and of state-owned goods:

We learn that shipmasters are converting into profits in business the produce which they have received and thereby are abusing the indulgence granted them in the law of Constantine, which permitted them to deliver the receipts for such produce at the end of two years from the day when they received it.[20]

Annona shippers, we learn from other laws, were apt to plead shipwrecks to account for non-delivered cargoes and to retreat into and tarry in 'remote recesses of the islands'.[21] They also sought protection from powerful patrons. Money changed hands, and the corruption had penetrated as far as the offices of the urban prefect and the prefect of the corn supply themselves.[22] A law of A.D. 364 implies that traders 'attached to Our Household' did private business on the side: they are threatened with the trade tax. Many more escaped government service altogether through their own influence or the patronage of the influential.[23]

[18] e.g. *C.Th.* XIII.9.4, 391; XIII.5.20, 392.

[19] Jones, *LRE* 699–701; Herz (1988) 268–73; Sirks, *Food* 307–60 (bakers); Chastagnol, *Préfecture urbaine* 301 (free market).

[20] *C.Th.* XIII.5.26, 396 (to PPO Italiae). On *navicularii* in general, see Jones, *LRE* 827–9; Herz (1988) 234–62; Sirks, *Food*. For their immunity and privileges, see *C.Th.* XIII.5.7, 334.

[21] Manfredini (1986) on shipwrecks; *C.Th.* XIII.5.32, 409 (islands).

[22] *C.Th.* XIII.5.34, 410; 36.1, 412 (Africa); XIII.7.1, 399 (Egypt); 2, 406 (Italy).

[23] *C.Th.* XIII.1.5, 364 = *CJ* IV.63.1, with 1.4.1; Whittaker, 'Trade and traders' 166; *C.Th.* XIII.7.1, 399 (Egypt); 2, 406.

The state authorities, then, exercised only a limited control over the activities of their own shippers. And there were in addition plenty of ship-owning *privati*, some of them hiding behind the *annona* shippers and free-loading on their privileges.[24] In theory they could be called upon by the state; in practice, the government at times had problems keeping the numbers of the fleet up to a satisfactory level (let alone securing satisfactory performance from present members). In a rescript Honorius and Theodosius complain that the association of shipmasters throughout the provinces of the orient 'was tottering because of a shortage of ships'.[25] It was not unusual for wealthy men who were predominantly landowners, from cities such as Antioch, to own ships which were not enrolled in state service.[26] A landowner who did not own land that was tied to the *functio navicularia* could avoid serving the *annona* on a regular basis; he could similarly evade the 'trade tax' (*collatio lustralis*) by claiming that his commercial activity was limited to shipping his goods to the market.[27]

In the case of other products distributed in the capital cities free or at a subsidized price (pork, oil, wine), there was similarly scope for profit-taking by those involved in transport and distribution.[28] But in addition a free market existed outside the state supply system where landowners could sell their surplus when price-levels were sufficiently attractive. Senators and other men of pre-eminent wealth no doubt made the most of such opportunities for speculative profit.[29]

Emperors actually granted monopolies to certain groups of *corporati* engaged in the food trade in the capital cities; later emperors revoked them, because they were held to be abused. In a constitution that can be dated to A.D. 483,[30] Zeno addresses to the prefect of the city of Constantinople an order against monopolistic practices and price-fixing within the basic trades, especially those responsible for provisioning the capital. The preface begins as follows:

We command that no one engaged in trading any article of clothing whatsoever, or fish, shellfish or sea-urchin, or any other kind of object or material which is food or has other uses, should dare to exercise a monopoly on his own authority or that of a sacred rescript past or future, or pragmatic sanction or sacred annotation of our piety.

The law comes a little later to the construction industry:

Building artisans and men undertaking such work . . . must likewise be prevented from making agreements among themselves which are intended to restrain anyone from completing a piece of work entrusted to another man . . . and every man shall

---

[24] See e.g. *C.Th.* XIV.22.1, 364 (Rome); XIII.5.16.2, 380. [25] *C.Th.* XIII.5.32, 409.
[26] Liebeschuetz, *Antioch* 45–6. [27] See *C.Th.* XIII.1.13, 384.
[28] Chastagnol (1953); *Préfecture urbaine* 325; Jones, *LRE* 701–5; Herz (1988) 325–8.
[29] See below, pp. 333–5. [30] *CJ* IV.59.2, cf. IV.59.1, A.D. 473.

have the right to complete without fear or injury of any kind a piece of work begun by another when abandoned by him.

Organized intimidation of workers who were not members of the *collegium* of the builders of Constantinople, and who were abandoning a project unfinished while pocketing their wages, is attacked by the same emperor in a second, undated, constitution.[31] In the final clause of the law of 483 Zeno restates his opposition to monopolies and threatens with heavy fines the leaders (*primates*) of the several essential trades if they conspire to raise prices above accepted or acceptable levels.

How did these developments come about? Mickwitz argued that the imperial government was unable to impose obligations on the corporations without at the same time awarding privileges – in the first instance immunity, subsequently, at least in some cases, monopoly rights. This, coupled with a labour shortage associated with a decline in slavery, created a new syndicalist spirit. While this hypothesis cannot be accepted in all its aspects (manpower shortage and decline of slavery are controversial), the central contention is plausible. Ruggini's more recent formulation is along the same lines.[32] State control served to strengthen the internal organization of corporations and increase their sense of indispensability and their readiness to extort further advantages. In addition to the paradoxical freedom exercised by *collegia* employed in supplying the capital cities, Ruggini highlights the public profile of *fabricenses*, imperial factory workers, in certain cities of the eastern empire, where (typically) bishops engaging in religious disputes found it useful to harness their active support. Whether she is right to contrast the aggressiveness (*riottosità*) of eastern *corporati* with the abject submission or flight of their western counterparts is another matter. The behaviour of city-based artisans in the west deserves reassessment (see below). But we may agree with her general conclusion that the extent to which *collegia* were regimented and controlled has been exaggerated. And we have thus far been concerned exclusively with those activities in which the state authorities had the closest interest. The professional activities of other tradesmen and workers must have been relatively unregulated.

III. EXPANDING ESTATES, DECLINING CITIES

1. Expanding estates

Throughout the period of the Roman empire there was a steady, inexorable increase in the size of estates and the land-derived incomes of rich landlords – that is, the *res privata* (imperial properties), the church and private individuals. We have explored in the previous chapter some of the

---

[31] *CJ* VIII.10.12.9.   [32] Mickwitz (1936); Ruggini (1976a); (1976b) 466ff.; cf. de Robertis (1955).

implications of this development for landholding and land-use by wealthy proprietors and institutions. In this section we are interested in the consequences for trade in our period. To the extent that large estates were increasingly independent of the market, producing for their own domestic consumption and exchanging surplus goods outside the market, then the sphere of private trade would have been correspondingly reduced. But, as with state intervention in the economy, the problem is how to assess the scale of the development. Enumeration of anecdotes illustrating, on the one hand, gifts and exchanges between friends, patrons and clients and domanial estates, and, on the other, buying and selling in the market, will not settle the issue. Nor in this case does qualitative evidence fill the gap left by the absence of quantitative data. For example, Olympiodorus fails us at this point. He claims that the produce of the estates of Roman senators (grain, wine and so on) was worth approximately a third of the gold revenues, 'in the event of sale'. But he does not estimate (or guess) how much of the crop was actually sent to the market, and how much was disposed of in domestic consumption or redistribution through the social network (a category which in any case is missing from his analysis).[33] Nor can we. We can at best set rough limits to the process of encroachment on private trade and industry which is to be envisaged.

Meanwhile there are crucial preliminary questions to be addressed, principally two: Where are the large landowners of late antiquity to be located? Were the cities of late antiquity in economic decline? The two questions are interconnected. If the landed élite, who had always been the life-blood of the cities, abandoned their traditional base, then the consequences for the commercial life of the empire would have been serious. The landowners in question are the secular aristocracy, the traditional ruling class of the cities of the Graeco-Roman world, not the hierarchy of the Christian church,[34] for the latter established and maintained a strong presence in the cities – an important point, to which we will return.

Here we can repeat the conclusion arrived at in the previous chapter – that there was in our period nothing that can be called a general and large-scale abandonment of the cities for the countryside by the landed élite in west or east. Moreover, this applies not only to the very rich members of the *rentier* class of the cities, but also to the middle and lower echelons of this class, the rank-and-file *curiales*. The unauthorized disappearance of *curiales* is amply attested.[35] On the other hand, it must be asked whether their escape (in so far as it was successful or common) boosted the villa economy at the expense of that of the cities. The code headed 'If a decurion should desert his municipality and prefer to live in the country' includes precisely

---

[33] Olympiod. fr. 44; Vera (1983) 489–91; Vera, 'Forme e funzioni'.
[34] But bishops were frequently recruited from the traditional, landowning élite.
[35] *C.Th.* XII.1 *passim.*

two laws, out of the two hundred or so designed to bind decurions to their civic obligations.[36] The more attractive escape-routes were those leading into other more promising or less burdensome occupations (senate, church, civil service, army). The rest of the disappearing decurions were downwardly mobile, and in no position to set up a powerful, semi-autarchic rural establishment. And the cream of the urban élite appears to have maintained an urban base. They were, for example, the 'chief decurions' (*primates ordinis*) who are enjoined in a law of A.D. 400 addressed to Vincentius, the praetorian prefect of the Gauls (whose 'province' included Britain and Spain as well as Gaul), 'not to allow a fugitive from a municipal council or trade association to wander abroad, to the disadvantage of the public'.[37]

In this law *collegiati* are mentioned as fugitives alongside *curiales*. Disappearing *collegiati* attract a small cluster of laws addressed to western officials around the turn of the fourth century and a handful of laws from the east, far fewer than the *curiales*-recalling constitutions, which cover the whole period and much of the empire. The laws for the most part try to control the mobility upward of *collegiati*: they are banned from the civil service, the army and the clergy.[38] The other laws say very little about the whereabouts of the missing men. When a rural location is alluded to, the fugitives have apparently joined the *agricultural* workforce[39] rather than expanded the stock of artisans. Artisanal activity certainly took place in late Roman villas, and Palladius recommended that landowners keep a stable team of tradesmen on their estates, but there was no novelty in this.[40] Some of the missing *collegiati*, in any case, had little to offer to the rural economy – the 'jugglers, fortune-tellers, standard bearers and banner carriers' of one law.[41] In the urban context such people could be called upon for the performance of corvées. A law of A.D. 369 ruled that alongside *collegiati*, petty retailers and people in the 'hospitality trade' were to be leant on for such services, rather than peasants:

Your Sincerity shall command that the provincials shall cease furnishing services which have heretofore been unlawfully required of them. Moreover, when animals arrive for which escort is due, if the members of the *collegia* should appear to be insufficient for the number of animals, you shall not allow freedom from this service to any person who acquires personal gain from an inn, a drinkshop, or a tavern. For it is better that such services should be the task of persons of leisure rather than that even the cities also should be ruined by the unhappy withdrawal of the rustics.[42]

---

[36]   *C.Th.* XII.18.1, 367 (Egypt); 2,396 (Illyricum).
[37]   *C.Th.* XII 19.3; cf. Norman (1958); Liebeschuetz, *Antioch* 171–4 (*protoi* of Antioch); *C.Th.* XII.1.75, 371; 77, 372 (*principales*).
[38]   *C.Th.* VII.21.3, 396; XII.1.156, 397; I.12.6.2, 398; VI.30.16, 399; VI.30.17, 399; VII.20.12.3, 400; NVal XXXV.3, 452; NMaj. VII.7.7, 458.
[39]   e.g. *C.Th.* XIV.7.1, 397 (interpretation) (Campania; marriage with *colona*); X.22.5, 404.
[40]   See Whittaker 'Trade and traders' 171, with refs.; Palladius 1.6.2.   [41] *C.Th.* XIV.7.2, 409.
[42]   *C.Th.* XI.10.1, 369.

This law implies that the *collegiati* might be insufficient for the task in hand, the escort of animals ('si collegiati numero inpares videbuntur'). However, a similar law addressed to the vicar of Italy fills in the background: there, it is a matter of conscripting 'very many men' to cope with the 'unexpected' arrival of 'an unusually large number of animals'.[43] It is not a natural inference from the law that there was an absolute shortage of *collegiati* in the cities which it covers – those of Gaul, Britain, Spain and Italy.

Of course, the presence of a number of privileged tradesmen freed from all compulsory public services by a law of Constantine of A.D. 337 must have considerably reduced the numbers of those liable to such services, supposing their immunity was retained. No fewer than thirty-five trades are cited, from panellers to purple-dyers, workers in ivory, plumbers and furriers.[44] When the laws mention the occupations of fleeing workers, they are *fabricenses* (weavers, minters or armourers) or miners; neither of these groups was central to the *city* economy.[45]

Geographical mobility among urban craftsmen and traders was surely not a new phenomenon. The interest of the authorities, local and central, in controlling it goes back into the principate and is connected with the policy of drawing on the plebian population for the performance of compulsory public liturgies, and the tendency to increase such services and devolve their organization on to the corporations of tradesmen. In the late empire the marshalling of the workforce through the corporations became more systematic, but the only genuine innovation was the introduction of the *collatio lustralis* or 'trade tax' by Constantine. All in all, the pressure on *collegiati* increased, but there is no evidence to justify the common assumption that they abandoned the cities *en masse*, and even less support for a corresponding expansion of the industrial base of the villa economy. Some depletion of numbers, in some periods and in some areas, is a reasonable assumption, though one should not succumb to the temptation of tying one's reconstruction to texts which reflect the mentality of their authors as much as broad historical processes. Other texts suggest the continued presence of tradesmen in the cities, ranging from those excused from civic duties and evading the trade tax through the aid of patrons to those who could escape neither liturgies nor tax. Of course, the existence of a tax raised essentially from urban commerce and industry presupposes the presence of tradesmen. There is no suggestion in the sources or in the secondary literature that the revenues from this tax went into steep decline in our period because of an outmigration of the workforce.

---

[43] *C.Th.* XI.10.2, 370.   [44] *C.Th.* XIII.4.2, 337.
[45] *C.Th.* X.19.5, 369; 6, 369; 7, 370; 9, 378; 15, 424 (miners); X.20.1, 317 (minters); X.20.2, 357; 6, 372; 7, 372; 8, 374; 9, 380 (weavers); X.22.5, 404 (armourers).

2. Declining cities

The hypothesis that city populations were not heavily depleted in the fourth and early fifth centuries by the loss of either élite or workforce can be checked with reference to evidence bearing on the fate of the cities in general. To this end, we can now bring into the reckoning archaeological evidence which has tended to be neglected in the older accounts of decline. Such accounts[46] are heavily influenced by the legal texts and the gloomy picture painted of civic life by literary sources such as Libanius. Once archaeological evidence is brought into play, it becomes easier to distinguish between the (declining) fortunes and administrative role of the *curiales* and the traditional civic institutions that they manned, and the (often healthy, even buoyant) economic condition of cities.[47]

It must be emphasized that, although the archaeological evidence is considerable – and growing – no global view of the condition of the cities of the empire is as yet possible. In any case, variation both within and between regions and over time is a necessary, preliminary assumption.

Recent discussions, drawing on archaeology, contrast east and west, the former characterized by the survival or even vigour and growth of urban life, and the latter by ruin, under the twin scourges of barbarian invasion and government exaction. The archaeological reports from the eastern part of the empire create an impression of urban continuity and prosperity. Sardis may serve as an example. The Harvard excavations have revealed expansion and prosperity in the western part of the city. The area was completely transformed in late antiquity. Once desolate, it was now covered with colonnaded streets, public buildings (of which the bath and gymnasium complex stand out), commercial buildings, houses and luxury villas. An inscription of A.D. 459 shows that Sardis was home to an ebullient association of construction workers, who indulged in various kinds of profitable malpractices, capitalizing on the fact that business was good and skilled workers in short supply, as they always were in antiquity.[48]

It may be that large cities – regional centres like Sardis (and Ephesus, Antioch and Nicaea, among others) – increased in size and prosperity at the expense of the very numerous small communities. Yet, to judge from, for example, the *Synekdemos* of Hierocles, large numbers of small cities were able to survive into the sixth century, many of them doubtless small communities, hardly distinguishable from large villages. Korykos in Cilicia is one, its commercial life exposed by a rich store of inscriptions covering the period from the fifth to the seventh century. In the east, the turning-point

---

[46] The best of these accounts is by Jones, *LRE* ch. 19, at 757–63.

[47] See Whittow (1990) for a critique of Jones and others. General treatments in Barnish (1989); Liebeschuetz (1992).   [48] Foss (1976); Garnsey (1985); in general, Claude (1969).

in the fortunes of the cities appears to have been the mid sixth century or even later.[49]

What of the west and north of the empire? In the North African provinces even modest cities witnessed growth: in fact, there was hardly an African city which did not visibly expand in the late empire.[50] Thrace, Macedonia, Gaul and Italy apparently saw less urban prosperity than North Africa (or Asia Minor). The evidence is patchy and problematic. Literary texts, which are isolated, often highly rhetorical, and cumulatively of mixed import, have to be interpreted with circumspection. The archaeological evidence, similarly, is ambiguous, in particular the archaeology of city walls. The existence, dimensions and history of walls are an uncertain guide to the condition of cities. In general, regional variation over space and time must be acknowledged. Barbarian invasion and insecurity had an uneven impact in the third century and later, and even in the more exposed areas the story is not one of permanent abandonment. According to the more recent and authoritative analyses, there was no general decline or transformation of classical cities in the west until the sixth and seventh centuries.[51]

The church made a significant contribution to urban survival, as witnessed in the steady development of complexes of ecclesiastical buildings, and the public benefactions (euergetism) and charitable activities of wealthy clergy and laity. But then the secular or lay aristocracy had not severed their connection with the cities (nor did their future lie entirely in the provision of members of the ecclesiastical hierarchy). Ausonius the professor of Bordeaux and, in a later age, Sidonius Apollinaris the bishop of Clermont-Ferrand form a pair in the way they divided their lives between civic and imperial duties and retreat in the countryside.[52]

To sum up: at the end of our period as at the beginning, a landowning aristocracy resided in the cities of the empire as absentee landlords, or divided their time and attention between city and countryside. There was some loss of numbers, some change of personnel. The élite had been reconstituted. It was less egalitarian than before, for the widening of the gap between rich and poor had made inroads into the middle and lower ranks of the decurions. The secular aristocracy was swelled, at least in the major cities, by retired functionaries (honorati). In addition, there now existed a second force, the clergy, who were men of property in their own right (in so far as they were descended from local, prosperous families) and who administered extensive church properties. Together these groups dominated urban society.

---

[49] See Barnish (1989); Whittow (1990); Brandes (1989); Haldon (1985), (1990) 92–124; Patlagean, *Pauvreté* 158–70 (Korykos); for cities in the period A.D. 425–c. 600 see also Liebeschuetz in *CAH* xiv (forthcoming).   [50] Lepelley, *Cités* (A.D. 361–95 as the main period of growth); Lepelley (1992).
[51] Février (1974), (1980), (1981); Ward-Perkins, *Public Building*; MacMullen, *Corruption* 15–35. See further *CAH* xiv.   [52] Février (1980) 470–2; see also Harries (1992).

The 'villa economy' became more powerful and independent in some areas, especially where it was already well-entrenched. This development, however, did not proceed *pari passu* with the expansion of the properties of the rich (a ubiquitous phenomenon, not confined to areas where a villa economy was prominent), because a significant proportion of wealthy landowners was still resident at least part-time in the cities. To this extent they continued to play a vital role in the city economy. This role and the nature of the economic life of the city in general require closer definition.

IV. THE CITY ECONOMY

Given that goods had to be introduced on a large scale into the cities in order to satisfy the needs of both the few and the many, by what mechanisms were they brought in and distributed?

1. The command economy and its limits

The supply and distribution systems of Rome and Constantinople have already been described (see p. 320 above), and a brief summary will suffice here. Grain with the status of tax in kind (exacted from provincials) or rent in kind (from estates owned by the *res privata*) was conveyed to the capital cities by the association of shippers, *navicularii*, who were bound by the imperial government to this service in return for tax concessions and exemption from civic burdens, and in return for a payment raised from landowners. The grain was transformed into bread in state bakeries, and handed out gratis to numerous Romans and Constantinopolitans. Few figures are available for the number of recipients, which is unlikely to have remained constant, but in any case always amounted to fewer than the total population. For Rome, the often-quoted figure of 120,000 is actually for meat-recipients. Moreover, it comes from a law of A.D. 419 and thus falls within a decade of the Visigothic sack of Rome. The city might still have been in the process of recovering from short-term population loss. There were 80,000 recipients of free bread at the inauguration of the dole in Constantinople on 18 May 332, but this was before the city reached its apogee. We know of one small increment thereafter in a law of Theodosius. A supplementary distribution scheme is attested for both capitals, which rewarded houseowners with the so-called *panis aedium*.[53] The government imported into the capital cities more tax grain than was handed out free; additional stocks were made available at reduced rates.[54]

---

[53] *CJ* XI.25.2, 392, cf. *C.Th.* XIV.17.14, 402; XVI.2, 416; Herz (1988) 314–18 (*panis aedium*).
[54] To judge from *SHA Sept. Sev.* 23 and *Just. Ed.* XIII.8 (neither, however, referring to the period under discussion), the state may have imported through the *navicularii* five to six times as much grain as was needed for the distribution.

Not all of this grain was made available to the general public – for example, the rations paid to the government officials in lieu of cash salaries were presumably drawn from this stock. In addition, free pork and oil and cheap wine were furnished to the recipients of bread in Rome and Constantinople.

Outside the two imperial capitals permanent supply and distribution schemes were rare.[55] A few individual cities were singled out for special attention by emperors because of their role in supplying the capitals. Thus a durable distribution scheme can be identified at Alexandria, and, on a rather smaller scale, at the Campanian cities of Puteoli and Tarracina. Antioch and Carthage have been thought by some to fall in the same category of beneficiaries of state grain, but the evidence is thin for our period.[56] Alexandria shared with Rome and Constantinople the bread-for-householders scheme. Alexandria was also allowed to keep a portion of the *annona* shipment to feed widows (and perhaps the poor), and its administration was apparently entrusted to the church. Athanasius was accused of selling the grain for his personal gain.[57] This may have been part of a wider scheme inaugurated by Constantine for the support of clergy and the care of virgins and widows.

The rest of the cities of the empire were left to their own devices, with the exception of those specially patronized by emperors and their households, notably Jerusalem, and major provincial cities when they became bases for emperors or Caesars. The food supply of Antioch, as an important regional capital and the launching pad for military expeditions against the Persians, received imperial attention from time to time, more than once with unhappy consequences. Gallus Caesar in A.D. 354 brought the wrath of the mob down on the heads of the provincial governor of Syria, Theophilus, and of leading Antiochenes by blaming them publicly, and repeatedly, for the dearth. Theophilus' counterpart in Carthage was better placed to relieve food shortages in his city, having ample stocks of tax grain at hand *en route* to Rome, and, presumably, imperial permission to dip into them in emergencies. Julian, arriving in Antioch eight years after Gallus' débâcle, intervened more positively in a food shortage by fixing grain prices, but was easily outsmarted by the speculators. The crisis was finally resolved only by better harvests and the departure of the emperor, his entourage and a large army, who had aggravated the shortage by their presence and the need to be fed in the present and supplied for the future.[58]

---

[55] Our analysis differs from that of Durliat (1990), who presents a picture of large-scale state interference in the food supply of cities. The capitals are further considered in chapter 12 below, pp. 371–410. [56] Herz (1988) 330–7; Liebeschutz, *Antioch* 127–9; Ruggini (1969).

[57] Athan., *Apol. c. Ar.* xviii; Socr. *HE* ii.17; Soz. *HE* iii.9, cf. Hollerich (1982), at 191; Theod. *HE* i.11.2–3.

[58] Amm. Marc. xiv.7.5–6; Lib. *Or.* xix.47–9, cf. xi.153ff. etc. (Gallus); Lib. *Or.* i.126, xv.8ff.; Amm. Marc. xxii.14.1–2; Jul. *Misop.* e.g. 368c (Julian) (all Antioch); Amm. Marc. xxviii.1.17ff. (Carthage).

Without a *deus ex machina*, however incompetent, the mass of the cities of the empire had to fall back on themselves and their own resources.

2. *Élite redistribution – liturgies, euergetism and patronage*

Traditionally, the solution to the supply problems of the ordinary cities of the Mediterranean world, and to their economic feasibility in general, lay with their leading citizens rather than with any formal and permanent institutional structures. The essential fact is that the cities' financial assets were meagre. These were further reduced in the later empire when the cities lost all or most of the revenues from civic lands and taxes.[59] Public poverty coexisted with private affluence. The measure of the prosperity of a city was its success in tapping the resources of its resident élite.

In the past, wealthy individuals had contributed their services, and their surplus wealth, in three main areas.

First, they undertook magistracies and other public services (liturgies) judged vital to the proper functioning of the life of the city in its various dimensions – political, economic, social, cultural and religious. A modest financial outlay was usually enjoined on holders of these posts in virtue of their office.

Second, they furnished from their ranks individual benefactors (*euerge-tai*) who made voluntary expenditures, either connected with the holding of office (in which case those expenditures were over and above those legally required) or in a private capacity. Euergetism, as traditionally prac-tised, might take the form of the construction of public buildings, the pro-vision of public pleasures, the entertainment of the populace in circus or arena, or the provision of food in times of dearth – food which repre-sented part of the surplus harvested from their own properties.[60]

Third, they exercised patronage.[61] Patrons – at least in principle – were prepared, where necessary, to feed their clientele and provide legal and financial assistance and other such services. Patronage is not the same as euergetism. Every local rich man, it can be safely assumed, was already a private patron, with a circle of clients and dependents to whom he made available, when he chose, material goods (including food from his store) and other benefits. He was a patron, but not necessarily a euergetist. The generosity of the benefactor was displayed for the benefit of the citizenry at large, not for his personal clients, nor for that matter for any other portion of the citizenry or of the residents of the city, such as 'the poor'. Poor people did benefit from his activities, in so far as they were citizens,

[59] Jones, *LRE* 732 and 1301–2, nn. 43–7.   [60] Veyne (1976); rev. Garnsey, *JRS* 81 (1991) 164–8.
[61] On patronage, see Gellner and Waterbury (1977); Saller (1982); Garnsey and Woolf (1989).

but the poor as a whole were not targeted. Citizenship, not poverty, was the main qualification for receipt of benefits. In particular, the free poor tended to slip through the patronage net, essentially because they had no reciprocal benefits to bestow, and patronage was a relationship of reciprocity. In these circumstances, slaves might actually do better than the free poor. They were fed by their masters, often amply, in order to maintain their fitness for work and to preserve their market value. The absence of relief for the poor in pagan society is striking. Already in the period of the principate a new form of giving, which did target the poor, was emerging in Christian circles. This system became public and institutionalized in the post-Constantinian period (see below).[62]

The hallmark of the traditional systems of giving was their more or less voluntary nature. Office-holding was not compulsory, and the obligation to undertake liturgies was moral rather than legal. Of course, the hold of the ruling classes on their cities was conditional on their preparedness as a group to carry out the 'parish-pump jobs' vital to the proper functioning of the city, to maintain and improve the physical fabric and amenities of the city, and to respond with generosity in times of need. Beyond this, the system of euergetism gave opportunities to more wealthy and ambitious individuals to steal a march on their peers in the competitive struggle for honour and prestige that characterized all oligarchies; and oligarchy was the characteristic form of government in the cities of antiquity.

The wealthy were not invariably public-spirited; in fact, there were probably few public benefactors, and those few were two-faced, unable to resist the temptation to profit from their possession of stocks of cereals or other foodstuffs when prices were high. Public benefactors included those of the wealthy prepared to reduce the scale of their speculative activities in times of inflated food prices; very few abandoned them altogether.

Gradually in the course of the principate the atmosphere of local government changed in response to interference from outside. The wealthier citizens were progressively forced as individuals and as a collective – through their membership of the local council, as *curiales* – to operate and finance the political machinery and cultural institutions of their cities, and to undertake in addition a mounting load of burdens imposed on them by the central government, especially in the realm of taxation. The late empire witnessed both the culmination of this system and the crisis of the *curiales*, now a hereditary class, but diminished in numbers, wealth and patriotic zeal. Euergetism did not disappear, but from about the middle of the third century it is associated with governors[63] and other imperial officials (and ex-officials) and the upper echelon of the *curiales*, who had been able to

[62] Patlagean, *Pauvreté* 81–96; Février (1981) 200ff; Lepelley, *Cités* 376–85.
[63] Robert, *Hellenica* IV 127–9.

protect and indeed strengthen their position as rank-and-file *curiales* were squeezed.

Two more striking and characteristically late antique developments are a consequence of the gradual emergence of the Christian church as the dominant influence in late Roman urban society. The first is that rich men tended to give in a religious context. Spending on the traditional civic monuments, amenities and services was reduced; spending on ecclesiastical buildings and their decoration and periodic renovation and refurbishment was greatly increased. This was a species of euergetism rather than a substitute for it, in so far as jobs were created for the unemployed (and underemployed), and ecclesiastical buildings came to be used and valued by a population that was progressively becoming Christian. The second development is charitable almsgiving, as practised by the institutional church under the supervision of the higher clergy. Bishops in virtue of their office came to control resources and distribute them among the poor, widows and orphans (of whom a list was maintained, at least in major cities like Rome and Jerusalem). Bishops thus became patrons automatically and *ex officio*. Almsgiving was enjoined on rich and, for that matter, ordinary laymen. Jews and Christians had always been obliged to give alms to the poor, but almsgiving could not become a conspicuous, structural feature of society until the society became Christian. Charitable almsgiving was not a latter-day form of euergetism, but filled a gap that euergetism had always left. When the church gave cash, clothes and food to the abject poor (*ptochoi*), estimated by John Chrysostom at 10 per cent of the population of Antioch, it was targeting a class that had been systematically neglected by the political authorities and the social élite in the pre-Christian era.[64]

3. Cities as markets

For who is so insensitive and so devoid of human feeling that he cannot know, or rather has not perceived, that in the commerce carried on in the markets and conducted in the daily life of cities immoderate prices are so widespread that the uncurbed passion for gain is lessened neither by abundant supplies nor by fruitful years.

So Diocletian prepares the ground for his fixing of maximum prices (and wages) in the Edict of 301. In the process, he identifies cities as a seat of commerce, the arena of the profiteering of which (he complains) his soldiers fall victim.[65] Not the only arena, however. Diocletian's soldiers were fleeced wherever they went, 'not in villages or towns only, but on every road'. Commerce was not an exclusively urban concern. Nor was manu-

---

[64] John Chrys. *Hom. in Ep. ad Cor.* xv (*PG* LXI.179); cf. *Hom. in Matt.* LXVI (*PG* LVII.658); and see n. 62.
[65] Frank (1933–40) vol. I, 310ff.

facture. Village and villa artisanal activity was standard practice and is well-attested especially in the north-western provinces.[66] This was a feature of the Mediterranean world in all periods of classical antiquity, not just the late empire. Jones writes, of the decentralization of trading activity:

The area which each city served was small, since a peasant would normally prefer to walk in with his donkey, do his business, and walk back within a day. Where cities were closely set, they were no doubt the sole markets of the country. But in many districts territories were large, and here the cities served only their immediate neighbourhood, and in outlying areas the peasants frequented small market towns or seasonal fairs.[67]

Only one adjustment needs to be made to this nice summary. Cities, including those with large territories, because they attracted a wider range of commodities, played a positive role in distributing both foods and manufactures to lower-order markets that were located in villages or in a rural environment. This dimension is also missing in a misleading passage of Libanius, which is often taken as casting the villages of the territory of Antioch as independent of the city:

There are large and well-populated villages, populous no less than many cities, and with crafts such as are in towns, exchanging with each other their goods through panegyrics, each playing host in turn and being invited and stimulated and delighted and enriched by them through giving of its surplus; or filling its needs, setting out some things for sale, buying others in circumstances far happier than the merchants at sea. In the place of the latter's waves and swells they transact their business to laughter and handclapping, and have little need of the city because of their exchange among themselves.

This issues from a rhetorician, not an economic historian, and he is praising Antioch *through* its villages. Libanius refers elsewhere to peasants visiting the city because they 'needed' it, and having their pack-animals requisitioned by the authorities.[68]

To be sure, the urban economy revolved not so much around peasant demand for goods as around the income of landowners from their estates. It follows that the scale of urban markets is related to the extent of élite participation in commercial activity. What can be said on that score?

All classes of society apart from the utterly destitute made use of the market, not excluding the landowning élite. Let us consider first the supply side. Diocletian towards the end of his preface notes that itinerant traders ('buyers and sellers who customarily visit ports and foreign provinces') will

[66] For industry in the countryside, see de Ligt (1991) 33–42; cf. Whittaker, 'Trade and traders' 171 (villas).

[67] Jones, *Greek City* 260. For periodic markets, see de Ligt and de Neeve (1988); de Ligt (1991) 51–8; de Ligt (1993); Shaw (1981).

[68] Lib. *Or.* XI.231; cf. *Or.* L.29; with de Ligt (1990) 30–3; (1991) 48–9, against Finley (1985) 21; de Ste Croix, *Class Struggle* 541 n. 16.

be restrained by his Edict. But those he charges with avarice are the very wealthy: 'men who individually abound in great riches which could completely satisfy whole nations try to capture smaller fortunes and strive after ruinous percentages'. In antiquity the very wealthy were invariably landowners. Ambrose directs unambiguously at landowners (without mentioning anyone by name) his powerful indictment of those who seize the opportunities provided by crop failure to 'amass wealth from the misery of all, calling it industry and diligence, when it is merely cunning shrewdness and an adroit trick of the trade'.[69]

The propertied classes throughout the Roman world counted on marketing a proportion of their surplus, from the senators of Rome, the wealthiest men in the world, down to the *curiales* of the ordinary cities in the empire. No doubt they chose moments when they could do so most profitably. The elder Symmachus (from a senatorial family of only middling wealth, according to Olympiodorus) was suspected of withholding a desirable product in a time of shortage (wine), and lost a beautiful house to fire in consequence. His son on a later occasion, in a time of shortage, shifted grain from Apulia to Campania, and thence presumably to Rome.[70] One wonders what Ambrose would have made of the behaviour of the two Symmachi: it was easier to attack avarice in general than to indict individuals. Ammianus was not disposed to condemn the elder Symmachus. Even if he had not admired Symmachus as a person and an official, class solidarity would probably have prevented him from taking the high moral ground.

Members of the élite of Antioch indulged in profiteering in staple foodstuffs. This is unproblematic, essentially because we have not only the accusations of an emperor (Julian), and of a Caesar (Gallus), but also the reluctant admissions of Libanius. In his attempt to repair the damaged relations between Julian and his city, Libanius conceded that men of his class were involved in aggravating the food crisis. He did, however, plead adverse weather conditions as the root cause of the shortage: 'the earth did not support his edict'.[71] Libanius' ideological position is laid bare in a letter to Rufinus, count of the east. While applauding the official for some unspecified intervention 'worthy of Rome' (as he had earlier complimented Julian for the purity of his motives), Libanius enunciates a preference for 'the free market' (*ten agoran automaton*).[72] He was here speaking for the propertied class of the whole Graeco-Roman world, not just of Antioch.

The participation of the landowning élite in the market on the supply side is neither surprising nor novel. But one development can be suggested. The polarization of wealth that was a feature of late antique society may well have had the consequence that the pool of potential suppliers steadily

[69] Ambr. *De Off.* III. 41.   [70] Symm. *Ep.* 6.12.5; Amm. Marc. xxvii.3.4; Chastagnol (1960).
[71] Lib. *Or.* xv.21.   [72] Lib. *Ep.* 379.

diminished while the surpluses at their disposal grew correspondingly larger. Some scholars talk of a senatorial 'monopoly' in the market for staples.[73] This is almost justified in the case of Rome (though 'oligopoly' would be more appropriate), in view of the extraordinary wealth of Roman senators. The economic power of senators was displayed most conspicuously in shortages, when small distributors, who were plentiful in normal conditions, ran out of supplies and the people were thrown back on the 'mercy' of big men like the Symmachi. Other cities would have experienced a similar phenomenon, in so far as they witnessed a widening of the gap between rich and poor.

So much for the supply side. The rich also purchased in the market, both by necessity and by choice. Even the largest landowners could not satisfy all their needs and desires from the produce of their own properties and those of their friends. Nor would they have wanted to. Ambrose had in mind city-based *rentier* landlords, presumably those of Milan in the first instance, when he wrote:

If someone has in mind throwing a feast, he sends off to a tradesman to order a cask of wormwood wine; he heads for a tavern to enquire after Picene or Tyriac wine, to a butcher for a sow's matrix . . .[74]

But the owner-occupiers of grand villas – those of Aquitanian or Belgic Gaul, for example – are unlikely to have thought differently. Few villa-residing aristocrats would have sacrificed the practice of conspicuous consumption for the ideal of self-sufficiency. The pursuit of autarchy and the consumption of expensive imports are two faces of the snobbery of the landed élite.

V. CONCLUSION

The argument of this chapter has revolved around urban demand for commodities, both staples and luxury goods. This is because it was in the cities that the mass of non-producing consumers and most of the wealthy were concentrated. Goods changed hands in other settings, but the city remained the central place where rural production converged and exchange took place.

Demand was continuous and remained high, for two main reasons. First, though traditional civic institutions did decline, the cities on the whole survived as economic units (though not all at the same level of activity). Second, their economic life was still dominated by a landed élite. This élite, though somewhat reordered, was still made up essentially of *rentier*-landlords, who drew wealth into the city in the form of rents and

[73] Vera (1983); Carandini (1986) 13–15.   [74] Ambr. *De Tob.* 17.

interest-payments from tenants and dependent small farmers, together with a proportion of the surplus harvested from those of their estates that were directly managed. This surplus wealth was consumed in their large households, redistributed among clients and dependants (and occasionally among the urban residents at large), and sold in the market.

The movement of goods over medium or long distances did not dry up in the late empire,[75] as the finds of pottery (above all) amply demonstrate. Cities looked in the first instance to their dependent territories, but self-sufficiency within the city/territory unit was unobtainable, even if it had been the goal. Some cities were very large and had outgrown their rural hinterlands. Rome, Constantinople, Alexandria, Carthage, Antioch and Ephesus, among others, had populations of 100,000 or rather more. Some of their inhabitants would have starved but for the activity of importers. Even those very numerous communities whose rural territories could in principle feed them had to bring in goods from outside when local harvests were poor. In addition to the inevitability of harvest fluctuations, social and political conditions (man-made shortages) and regional variation in resource-distribution ensured that the scale of medium-range movement of staple foodstuffs would be substantial. Equally certainly, the rich were not satisfied, either in principle or in practice, with the economic output of city-plus-territory, and sought out regional specialities, both foodstuffs and more durable consumer items. A papyrus of A.D. 325 shows that the councillors of Oxyrhynchus, by order of the governor of Egypt, purchased 150 *paragaudia* – gold-embroidered silk chitons – each one costing 65,000 *denarii*.[76]

The city authorities did not develop a network of institutions to administer long-term exchange or trade relationships in late antiquity or in any earlier period. The capital cities apart, no permanent system of supply and distribution of food was instituted by governments, because no city had the resources to run such a system.

Elsewhere, state intervention in the market was rare and ineffectual. The Price Edict of Diocletian was a one-off measure and a complete flop.[77] Julian's tampering with the grain market in Antioch in a shortage also failed. As Libanius wrote: 'when excessive profits were curtailed, the bottom fell out of the market'.[78] No wonder that bishops emerge as relievers of food crisis and controllers of granaries.

Government regulation of trade and industry was more visible than in earlier periods and made an impact on the economy, though it was less pronounced than has sometimes been thought. Private commerce and industry continued to operate even in the capital cities, where most supervision

[75] For trade across the frontiers, see, recently, Callu (1993).
[76] *P.Oxy.* 3758, with Pleket (1988) 36 n. 55.   [77] Lact. *De Mort. Pers.* VII.6.7.   [78] Lib. *Or.* XV.21.

was exercised, and among the tradesmen who supplied them and the artisans who serviced them. Some workers' associations were able to exploit their clients by price-fixing and other malpractices. On the other side, it seems likely that a larger number of transporters and traders (artisans likewise) worked for the state and with considerably less freedom in the late empire than previously. Again, the trade tax (which was new) and the imposition of civic liturgies (not new, but now more systematically organized) would have squeezed the more vulnerable traders and artisans.

Large landowners, private or institutional, had a certain number of commercial agents and dependent craftsmen in tow, who serviced their needs; to this extent the opportunity for free, entrepreneurial activity was circumscribed. But this was not an exclusively late antique phenomenon. The problem is how to decide whether, and how far, the size of this group expanded in the late empire, and if the volume of entrepreneurial trading activity decreased in consequence. Few if any of the wealthy would have been 'self-sufficient' in traders and artisans; it is still less probable that every itinerant trader, shopkeeper and craftsman was bound to a patron and served him in the first instance, or exclusively. Even if there was some shrinking of the pool of free traders, the significance of such a development is not clear. Traders whose major employer or patron was a large landowner are unlikely to have been as dependent as agricultural workers became in our period. The descent from free tenancy into tied colonate is not an appropriate model for the non-agricultural sector: traders were harder to control than peasants.

Within the cities, an issue is whether redistribution (through patronage, euergetism and charity) increased at the expense of market exchange. The spread and institutionalization of Christianity, ushering in a new agent of redistribution, and, in particular, a new mode in the form of charitable almsgiving, changed the face of redistribution without necessarily forcing a contraction of market-transactions. Nor is it clear that the concentration of wealth into fewer hands and the widening of the gap between rich and poor – that is, the emergence of fewer, richer patrons with wider networks of dependency – would necessarily entail a larger aggregate volume of non-market exchange. In any case, excessive extra-market redistribution, no less than the erosion of profit margins in consequence of state policies, was incompatible with the ideal of the 'free market' which the élite espoused. The class that redistributed a portion of its surplus also had goods it wanted to sell and cash it wanted to spend. It was above all the participation of the propertied classes in the urban economy which guaranteed a certain level of independent economic activity, a certain volume of market exchange.

CHAPTER 11

LATE ROMAN SOCIAL RELATIONS

ARNALDO MARCONE

I. INTRODUCTION

The most obvious characteristic of Roman society, its verticality, became more accentuated in late antiquity. The impression we receive is of a marked hierarchization which conditioned modes of thought as well as every other aspect of social relations. However, it would be wrong to derive from this the mechanical concept of a 'caste system', implying a rigidly bound society that did not permit any form of internal social mobility.[1] It is understandable that the state, once reorganized after the disastrous period of crisis in the third century, acquired a crucial importance, and would retain it, in so far as politics and the economy were geared to serve, at any price, the primary needs of military deference and the maintenance of a constantly growing administrative apparatus. We thus witness the unprecedented phenomenon of the state seeking to tie to their occupations increasingly broad categories of people, and their children. Not even the class of town councillors, the *decuriones* or *curiales*, escape the fetters of the state. Having presided, at the local level, over the most prosperous era of the empire, they now found themselves compelled to manage the economic crisis.

This phenomenon has sometimes led historians to stress the coercive element in the state organization, which certainly existed, and the adjunct of which would have been a closed and immobile society.[2] In reality, we note that a very characteristic phenomenon of late antiquity is the parallel opening-up of new channels of social mobility, which permitted unexpected opportunities for advancement. It seems too optimistic to assert that later antiquity saw a greater degree of social mobility than existed in preceding centuries. But it is important to recognize that social mobility was a reality, that it existed alongside a policy of coercion on the part of the state, and that routes to social advancement were different from those that operated in the past.

---

* I should like to thank my friend Peter Garnsey for his help and advice while I was writing this contribution.
[1] Jones, *Economy* 396–418.   [2] Heuss (1986).

Among the major changes produced by the reforms of the state apparatus was the effective destruction of the equestrian order, which had attained the peak of its success in the preceding century. By the second half of the fourth century, however, it is no longer practical to speak of an equestrian order.[3] It was not suppressed by any act of legislation; rather, it was absorbed *de facto* by the senatorial class. The different composition of the ruling class of the empire necessitated a new internal hierarchy, which became fixed from the reign of Valentinian I onwards.

It is also worth noting that, in contrast to the privileged classes – to designate whom different terminology is used – the mass of individuals without power were and remained plebs. The demarcation line which formerly ran between the equestrians and the rest of the free population (not to mention the fundamental distinction between the free-born and slaves) now marked off, with equal precision, the new enlarged senatorial order (and at the local level the *curiales*) from all those who did not belong to it. This latter category, comprising as it does those without any property at all, as well as artisans, independent smallholders and tied tenant farmers, is too broad and insufficiently homogeneous for us to be able to use the term class.[4] In order to define this lower class as a 'class' in the Marxist sense, we need evidence of conflict with the upper class over the means of production; such evidence is lacking.

The changing social hierarchy corresponded to an altered power structure. This was reflected, for example, in unequal treatment before the law; thus, punishments varied according to social rank. The political hierarchy, however, did not precisely mirror the hierarchy of wealth. In particular, while it is problematic to speak of the *curiales* as a 'middle class' in an economic sense, it does seem justified to see the *curiales* as the representatives of a socially and politically intermediate class.

II. THE SOURCES

Compared with that of the preceding epochs, the history of social relations in late antiquity certainly benefits from being illuminated by sources notable for their quantity and quality. This said, there are limitations in our documentation which need to be mentioned. The sources issue, as always in antiquity, from the upper classes of society, and the silence of the lower classes is almost total. The great works of historiography, most notably that of Ammianus Marcellinus, are imbued with the aristocratic ethos – this is all the more striking if we consider the Syrian and possibly curial origins of the author – in a programmatic revival of the classic works of the genre, above all those of Tacitus.[5] The historian rejects with disgust the very idea of taking

---

[3] Lepelley in Giardina, *Società romana* I (1986) 227–44.   [4] Alföldy (1975) 165–77.
[5] Matthews, *Ammianus*.

an interest in the concerns of the *plebs imae sortis et paupertinae*.[6] Important information about the Roman senatorial aristocracy is provided by the collection of letters of one of its leaders, Quintus Aurelius Symmachus, the urban prefect of 384 and consul of 391. His letters, less important as sources for political history, are a true monument to the spirit of cohesion of a class, in which the effort to protect its privileges coexisted with the assiduous defence of its own social identity.[7] A valuable document of an administrative character is the so-called *Notitia Dignitatum* (or, more fully, List of All the Offices, both Civil and Military), a sort of manual for the use of the state administration which goes back, at least in its basic core, to the end of the fourth century. It is interesting because it indicates the position in the hierarchy of every office-holder within the basic division of the empire between east and west.[8] A particularly important source for late antiquity is the *Codex Theodosianus*, a collection of laws assembled under the emperor Theodosius II and published in 438.[9] The laws have an authentic ring about them, even after undergoing editing at the hands of the compilers. Still, they do offer problems of interpretation. It is sometimes difficult for us to understand the true significance of laws which are in some cases repeated at short intervals of time with small variations. One sometimes has the impression of dealing with a grandiose monument to the incapacity of the emperor to render his own legislation effective. Nevertheless, the abuses which the laws were intended to redress were historical facts, and the justifications which often precede the regulations are of considerable importance for our understanding of social relations. The Codex opens up before our eyes an entire world of administrative and fiscal problems, of civilians and soldiers, and also, by this time, of clerics and laity. The copious ecclesiastical literature occupies a distinct position of its own. The letters and, in many cases, the homilies rival in value the great histories of Eusebius, Socrates and Sozomen. The letters of Ambrose and of Augustine, like those of Basil and Gregory, are sometimes addressed to officials and local or imperial magistrates, and are an interesting reflection of social tensions. The same applies in more general terms, beyond narrowly theological matters, to the homilies.

III. A SOCIETY IN TRANSITION

1. Between philanthropy and Christian charity: the poor

In the society of late antiquity there is a striking contradiction between the coercive structures bequeathed by the reforms of Diocletian as a response

[6] Amm. Marc. xiv.6.25.
[7] Paschoud (1986); commentaries by S. Roda (Book ix); D. Vera (*Relationes*); A. Marcone (Books vi and iv), Pisa 1981, 1983 and 1987.   [8] Clemente (1968); Goodburn and Bartholomew (1976).
[9] Archi (1976).

to the convulsions of the third century and the considerable change actually produced by that crisis. At the beginning of the age of Constantine,
political, like military and administrative, power was in the hands of
persons for the most part of low extraction, and the state created by
Diocletian's reforms presupposed a reformed ruling class in which a new
class of officials had a prominent position alongside the aristocracy of
birth. The Code of Theodosius is a unique document of the ideology of
the restored state, which animated this ruling class and inspired legislation
from the time of Diocletian. Nevertheless, it was precisely this ideology
(which aimed at creating a static social system based on compulsion to
follow a particular profession and the hereditary nature of the professions)
that obscured the dynamics of the new power relations which were being
established progressively in the different parts of the empire. Society, faced
with the instruments of oppression by which legislators set out to control
it, responded with its own mechanisms of self-defence which, in the long
term, constituted a factor in the disintegration of the state.

It is difficult to overestimate the role which Christianity, in its very varied
forms, played in this process. It is enough to think of that characteristic
polarity between 'office-holders and religious leaders' which was so often
visible from the time of Constantine. However, Christianity itself transmitted important elements of continuity, within the new system of values
which it helped to create. This happened in one of its most crucial areas of
intervention, namely charity and poor-relief, which tended to assume
increasing importance in the social relations of late antiquity.

The ecclesiastical economy, even in the third century, was based essentially on the donations of the faithful and was directed by the bishop, who
provided ordinary social welfare, besides intervening in emergencies – to
ransom prisoners-of-war or to provide assistance during epidemics. It was
his responsibility, assisted by the deacons, to organize this work in support
of the poor, while every individual Christian was obliged to co-operate
according to his own personal means.[10] The donations of believers, collected in a fund, were distributed by the bishop through his assistants to the
poor in the form of alms. It is clear that, in this way, the bishop had the
capacity to intervene in areas where no public intervention was to be
expected, and developed a 'democratic' function which the state economy
did not succeed in fulfilling.[11]

Christian charity undoubtedly represented a significant departure from
the typical forms of munificence of the pagan empire, precisely because of
the universalistic ideology which directed it towards groups which were
normally neglected (widows, the sick, prisoners, foreigners). Christian
charity also had no connection with the political use of personal wealth

[10] Piétri, *Roma Christiana* I, 129ff.   [11] Mazzarino (1973) II, 467–9.

which lay behind the interventions of the well-to-do classes in the cities. The construction or restoration of public buildings, with *ob dedicationem* ceremonials, games in the circus, and distributions of food or money, were aimed at acquiring prestige and popularity with one's fellow citizens and were often used as a springboard for obtaining posts in the imperial administration. Otherwise, it was the magistrate in office who did not hesitate to encumber his own estate in providing gifts, if this was necessary in order to preserve popular favour. However, an even more important difference was that traditionally the beneficiaries of philanthropy were not classified according to their material needs; the distribution took place in the context of the city, and, in fact, membership of the civic body gave access to the goods doled out.[12] The same philanthropy, when exercised by the state, was aimed at citizens as such: at Rome the plebs received food from the emperor and attended the games he provided because they were citizens, not because they were poor. We see how selective such munificence was when some famine or natural calamity struck. Foreigners then ran the risk of being expelled from the city and sometimes actually were. The very words used are a significant indicator. The terms which designate almshouses, orphanages and hospitals are not attested in classical Greek or Latin and only appear in the Christian era: brand-new names correspond to brand-new institutions.[13]

The situation changes with Constantine and the recognition and protection of the church's social functions by the state. If giving assistance to marginal groups previously excluded from any humanitarian consideration remained highly valued as a motive, then in the cities a significant harmony of aims was realized between classical and Christian acts of philanthropy. A similar outlook persisted, even if it was within a different framework of ideological references. This had particular importance for the financing of religious buildings: the members of the local élites, who formerly would have presented their fellow citizens with baths or a theatre, now financed the construction of a church or chapel. The argument holds good both for laity and for bishops, who were often deliberately selected from the members of the well-to-do classes. We can see in the munificence of a recently elected bishop an act resembling that of a patron whose gift is a response to the community's election of him as leader so that he can offer them assistance and protection. The bishop therefore took upon himself the traditional responsibilities of the magistrates and prominent citizens, in addition to his *ex officio* duties.[14]

Two examples provide a model of euergetism in a Christian setting. From a letter of Paulinus of Nola we learn that Pammachius, who had just lost his wife, had made distributions to the poor in St Peter's: so great was

---

[12] Patlagean, *Pauvreté* 182–3.   [13] Veyne (1976) 65–6.   [14] Bowersock (1986).

the appeal of this act of generosity that the poor literally invaded the basil-ica, the atrium and all the surrounding area.[15] A similar gesture, but done in a different spirit and with a different intention (although in the same place), was performed by the future praetorian prefect Lampadius. Like the insolent and vain man that he showed himself to be during his prefecture, he gathered the poor in the Vatican and handed out gifts, in order to show at the same time his own generosity and the contempt in which he held the masses.[16] It is not surprising that the preaching of the church fathers some-times includes censure of the vanity (John Chrysostom devotes a treatise specifically to this topic) displayed in the search for social prestige and advancement in public life which was deeply rooted in pagan society. Augustine, for example, takes care to stress that his own wealth is 'non-wealth', in the sense that what he disposes of as an administrator is not his own personal property, but that of his church. He is often careful to account to his flock for the qualities of his priests and for their poverty.[17] We learn from his biographer Possidius what types of intervention were needed to assuage popular envy of religious men.[18]

On the other hand, the manifestations of philanthropy connected with the construction of monuments (one of the more ostentatious forms of public munificence in antiquity) could represent a dangerous form of seduction, with ambiguous implications for the Christian donors them-selves, lay and ecclesiastical. If the construction of a basilica or an oratory represents an act of piety, as so many dedicatory inscriptions testify, this is not the end of the matter; otherwise, the ecclesiastical and, in the majority of cases, civil titles which appear on these monuments are inexplicable. An epigraphic dossier such as that of Rusticus of Narbonne shows the bonds of power joining together the bishop and the richer classes of the city.[19] The fathers did not fail to call upon believers to avoid those same forms of 'conspicuous consumption' which the rich pagans championed. Thus Ambrose maintains that the good priest, and the Christian in general, must not undertake 'superfluous building', because such extravagance does not become the perfect Christian.[20] A passage of Palladius can serve as confirmation of how justified such apprehensions could be. A pious and rich widow of Alexandria had scruples about making donations to the local church, because these could support the pharaonic lithomania (passion for building) of the bishop Theophilus (though Paulinus of Nola was affected by the same disease). For this reason, the lady hoped that Theophilus would not find out about her bequests.[21] In a context of this kind the expectations of the citizen populations concerning prospective bishops were under-standable: one sought to bind a possible candidate to one's own city by

[15] Paul. Nol., *Ep.* 13.11.   [16] Amm. Marc. XXVII.3.5.   [17] Aug. *Serm.* 355 and 356.
[18] Possid. *V. Aug.* XXIII.2.   [19] Marrou (1970).   [20] *De Off. Ministr.* II.109–110.
[21] Pallad. *V. Joh. Chrys.* VI.

means of an opportune ordination as priest, or even an election to the post of bishop.

One episode, with which we are acquainted through two letters of Augustine, illustrates well the social dynamics which came into play in the urban society of late antiquity.[22] As a result of the sack of Rome by Alaric in 410, a family of rich aristocrats moved to Africa Septentrionalis. At Thagaste, as guests of the local bishop Alypius, they marked their stay with rich donations to the local community. Pinianus then moved with his wife to Hippo, out of a desire to meet Augustine. During a religious ceremony there, the faithful tried to have Pinianus proclaimed a priest. Not succeeding in getting his consent, they abandoned themselves to a full-scale riot, going so far as to threaten the innocent Pinianus with physical violence. He saved himself by promising that he would continue to live at Hippo as a lay person and would not accept a priesthood elsewhere. He was thought of in the same way as an estate, and Alipius was suspected of wanting to kidnap him to benefit Thagaste. Augustine was embarrassed by what can be considered a genuine rivalry between the cities. An episode like this can be seen as symbolic of how a phenomenon typically linked to the philanthropy of the classical world – envy – persisted in a Christianized society.[23]

2. Women

In the context of the success of Christianity and the consideration newly given to some categories of persons, women experienced in the fourth century an unprecedented importance from the point of view of social relations. Among the groups of marginalized people to which Christian thought, right from the outset, granted particular respect were poor widows; they came to constitute a particular category entrusted to the protection of the church. Next to this group were placed the virgins, who, like the widows, were bound to remain chaste and to pursue charitable practices. These two categories represent the chief route by which women came into their own in the Christian community. They were still excluded from officiating in the liturgy; the association of women with men in sacramental acts was a characteristic of heretical sects.[24]

Nevertheless, the participation of women in the life of the church represented a considerable break with the traditional customs of the pagan world. Tertullian has left us a vivid picture of the domestic tensions which were generated in a household in which the husband could not tolerate his wife's escaping his control by spending nights far from home during the Easter vigils, or by entering the hovels of the poor to distribute alms.[25] On the other side, Christian moralists themselves did not remain indifferent in

---

[22] *Ep.* 125–6.   [23] Cf. Cecconi (1988).   [24] Witherington (1988).   [25] *Ad Uxorem* II.8.

the face of this problem. Augustine records the disturbances that he saw while participating in the celebrations of the liturgy, and Jerome urges Christian mothers to keep their daughters close to them during the vigils, which he saw as dangerous to family solidarity.[26]

In the second half of the fourth century, a further way of advancement opened up for Christian women in the form of an ascetic lifestyle. This was inconceivable within traditionalist pagan circles, where females were caught in a relationship of subordination: Symmachus, in a letter to his daughter, who appears regularly in the sixth book of his correspondence but without being named, extols the figure of the *matrona lanifica*.[27] Ambrose, therefore, is probably not exaggerating when he lauds the freedom established for virgins by Christian asceticism. Moreover, to be able to boast a female relative who had given proof of her sanctity could even serve to enhance the reputation of those resolutely engaged in a polit-ical career, especially in a Christianized court like that of Milan. There was thus created a sort of genealogy parallel to the traditional one, where women had their own autonomous role in that they were capable of estab-lishing a *vera nobilitas* additional to that of blood:[28] it is enough to imagine the appeal which the *velatio* – taking the veil – must have had for virgins of every social class when undergone by Demetrias, a member of the dis-tinguished *gens Anicia*.[29] This is an important factor if we consider how much the aristocratic origin of female correspondents was respected and emphasized by the males who wrote to them, even if a Jerome and an Augustine had different ends in view in the creation of ascetic female models.

In the west great care was given to the foundation of monasteries for women and to the criteria by which they ought to be run, as we see with Caesarius of Arles.[30] But the most important episodes were those involv-ing rich women who became superiors of the monasteries whose construc-tion they had financed. This is the situation of Olympias, who founded at Constantinople probably the first female monastery in the city, or of Paula at Bethlehem and of Melania the Elder, who set up monasteries for both sexes on the Mount of Olives. Of course, such activity had important polit-ical implications, at least as far as ecclesiastical politics were concerned. The rivalry existing between the monastic community of Bethlehem, which was dependent on Jerome, and that of the Mount of Olives, sustained by Rufinus, is important for the history of the Christianity of the end of the fourth century.[31] Whereas the first, the *villula Christi*, seems to have con-sisted of a group of persons tightly bound by intimate ties of loyalty and personal devotion to the founders, the second is clearly caught up in the

[26] Aug. *Conf.* III.3.5; Jer. *Ep.* 107.9; *Contra Vigilantium* 9.   [27] Symm. *Ep.* 6.67.   [28] Jer. *Ep.* 39.4.
[29] Aug. *Ep.* 150; Jer. *Ep.* 130.3. Cf. Patrucco (1989).
[30] Caesar. Arelat. *Regula ad virgines*; Clark, *Ascetic Piety* 51–2.   [31] Hunt, *Holy Land Pilgrimage* 175–6.

high politics of the court of Theodosius. The importance of these monasteries was linked to two factors, one of a contingent nature, the other more properly connected with the change of social values. The first factor can be traced back to the critical times of the barbarian invasions, in particular to the destructive intrusion of the Goths under Alaric into Italy and Gallia Meridionalis at the beginning of the fifth century; the second factor can be ascribed to the phenemenon of pilgrimage to the Holy Places; this was another new element introduced by Christianity into the society of late antiquity and it became enormously popular towards the end of the fourth century. This development was given a strong impetus by the journey of Helena, the mother of Constantine, and the legend which arose from it concerning her discovery of the cross. The pilgrim arrived in Palestine at the end of a complicated and difficult journey, which could take several months and which culminated in the visit to Jerusalem, the city richest in important memories for the devout visitor: it is enough to cite the so-called *Itinerarium Burdigalense*, which lists the localities passed through by an unknown pilgrim from Bordeaux to the Holy City, or the account given to her sisters by a nun coming from Gallia Meridionalis or Spain. The travellers, once arrived, wanted accommodation and, above all, an escort of monks to take them around the holy places. This pious yearning to 'see' with one's own eyes is perhaps derived ultimately from the 'historia' of the Herodotean tradition. But the frame of reference is completely changed: *Roma aeterna*, if it is not actually *praeterita*, is simply one stage in a long itinerary. The long journeys undertaken by Christian women for ascetic purposes are typical: the devotional purpose of the pilgrimage made the two sexes equal *de facto*, so that female fragility acquired an aura of 'virility'. And the women pilgrims were greeted and welcomed with full honours at every stage of their journey by monks and, more usually, bishops.[32]

The foundation of monasteries represents, of course, an outstanding act of munificence, and the fact that this was done by women is another sign of the changing times. This form of munificence, which originated from an aristocratic class with strong political as well as propertied interests, and which was sometimes displayed in a radical way, nevertheless needs to be assessed in the light of the peculiarities of late antique society. The classic case is that of Melania the Younger, and is known to us in detail through a biography which is one of the first lives of holy women in the Christian tradition. Melania belongs to the second generation of Roman aristocrats converted to Christianity. She was born in 385, the daughter of Valerius Publicola, who was in his turn the son of Melania the Elder (whose fame was so great that literally 'volumes' would have been written about her),[33] and married at the age of thirteen her cousin Pinianus, who was a little

younger than she. Although Melania intended to devote herself from first
to last to the ascetic life and wished that her husband supported her in this,
she let the matter lie until the birth of two sons, who would have been heirs
to her patrimony. Although they died prematurely, only on the death of
their father was the chosen ascetic life realized in its complete form. An
interesting section of the *Vita* is devoted to the difficulties which the young
couple encountered in attempting to free themselves from their own property. Charitable zeal seems to clash with the objective constraints set by economic necessity and social considerations: the couple did not succeed in
persuading Serena, the daughter of Theodosius and wife of Stilicho, to buy
their villa on the Caelian hill, and their parents became involved in the
attempt to buy back their various properties or to prevent the manumission
en masse of their slaves.[34] It is characteristic that such 'extravagant beneficence' not only conflicted with secular values, but also encountered resistance on account of its aim. Jerome, indeed, does not seem to have viewed
the total dispersion of one's patrimony as the beginning and foundation of
an ascetic life; when Melania and Pinianus arrived in Africa, the bishops, in
the face of their want of 'restraint' in donating their possessions to
immediate charitable ends, warned them that the gift made to the
monasteries was not enough unless, in addition to their houses, they also
awarded them their private incomes, for the money obtained from the sale
of their estates was quickly dispersed.[35]

An interested observer such as the emperor Julian did not fail to notice
the increasing role played by women in the diffusion of Christianity
(though their function in reality went far beyond charity and munificence).[36] In particular Julian was struck by their zeal in helping the needy
and their capacity to condition the religious attitude of their husbands.
Mixed marriages were without doubt one of the means by which
Christianity penetrated not only Antioch but also the traditional stronghold
of paganism, the Roman senatorial aristocracy. It will suffice to recall that
the daughters of two of its well-known representatives, Caeionius Rufius
Albinus and Caeionius Caecina Albinus (who were certainly still militant
pagans in the last quarter of the fourth century), Albina and Leta respectively, were Christians, while their grandchildren Melania the Younger and
Paula were quite dominant personalities in the advance of Christianity. St
Jerome, who spoke of these things in a way at once ironical and self-
congratulatory, acknowledged the force that resided in these aristocratic
women and saw the point of surrounding himself with them.[37] The biography of Melania the Younger reveals, in particular, her strong rejection of
the role of passive instrument of family continuity. In a social context

[34] Giardina (1988).   [35] Geront. *V. Mel.* 20; Clark, *Ascetic Piety* 61–94.
[36] *Misop.* 363; Kabiersch (1960).   [37] Jer. *Ep.* 107.1; Brown (1961).

where considerations of convenience or interest made marriages between young girls and mature men frequent, premature widowhood was bound to be relatively common. Among aristocratic women, widows had an important position: the renunciation of a second marriage was the price a woman had to pay who wanted to keep herself on the social level of her own family.[38] According to the dogmatic assertion of Jerome, a *matrona nobilis* could not be inferior to those Teutonic women prisoners who preferred suicide to concubinage.[39]

3. The new face of social mediation: the holy man, the bishop, the eunuch

The transformations which took place in the world of late antiquity crystallized around figures which acquired greater value then they had possessed in the past. The conditions for their emergence depended on heterogeneous factors but, with the exception of the eunuchs, they can be traced to the particular developments set in motion, in an increasingly complex social reality, by the great religious revolution of the fourth century. Holy men, together with bishops and women, found themselves working as agents of new possibilities in a context of profound change, which reached beyond mere regional differences. The milieu which is taken for granted in the speeches of Libanius is the same as that of the *Religious History* of Theodoret. The inhabitants of the villages of the Limestone Massif where, as in general in Syria, the holy man is very clearly the leading figure, needed a mediator, someone who was in a position to aid them in their needs and was at the same time capable of putting them in contact with the outside world.[40] For this the holy man, who along with the monk accomplished the great task of bringing the countryside close to Christianity, became a variant, an alternative possibility, to that power which the peasants were used to seeking in the military or in other local potentates. The miracles which he performed were the external mark of this power. One of the duties of the good patron, according to Libanius, was that of acting as arbiter in the disputes of his own tenant farmers.[41] The holy man assumed by himself this traditional function of the patron who grows rich through his own charisma and out-of-the-ordinary capacities. The exorcist and the thaumaturge are, in the final analysis, merely new forces in an ancient relationship which has been rebuilt on a new basis. The need for authority and for new certainties which is typical of late antiquity, by contributing rapidly to the breakdown of social relations in their classical form, was an important driving-force in the dissemination of Christianity.

The bishop was the equivalent, at the institutional level, of the holy man.

---

[38] Consolino (1986).   [39] Jer. *Ep.* 123.7.   [40] Brown (1971) 80–1.   [41] *Or.* XLVII.19 and 22.

Despite all the differences, we find in the bishops a relatively traditional form of late Roman political behaviour, a continuation and a revival, following clearly intelligible models, of the aristocratic ethos. It is quite clear that the process that produced the movement of these representatives of an elevated social class into the lofty hierarchies of an institution like the church which stood outside the state belongs to that category of complex political (and also social and cultural) phenomena which determine the character of an historical epoch.

Moreover, many episcopal ordinations from this period reveal an analogy of form no less than of substance between ecclesiastical hierarchies and political hierarchies in respect of the assumption of responsibilities. One need only think of the ordination of Augustine himself, which is presented to us by his biographer as taking place in stages which have already become ritualized: the nomination by the people, the reluctance to accept office, the retirement for reflection and study before the final accession.[42] In this significant ritualization we have an indication of the tensions which were generated in a social context in which the revived aristocracy of rich Christians contributed to the promotion of the new episcopal élite through a process of osmosis in which the traditional relation of patronage comes into play in its characteristically late antique form. At Rome itself, the Christian church seems to have grown by virtue of a constant increase of well-endowed lay patrons. The cult of the saints played a quite individual role in this matter, in that wealthy families were involved in its development through their acquisition of the remains of the martyrs, while at the same time it was manipulated by the bishops. The classic example is that of St Ambrose at Milan, who in 385 transferred the mortal remains of the saints Gervasius and Protasius to the new basilica, with the double purpose of removing them from the ambiguities of private celebrations and institutionalizing their cult for the benefit of the community.[43]

Moreover, the unquestionably political element inherent in the office of bishop, given the growing importance which this was assuming within the community, was not ignored by contemporary Christian thought. Here, too, it is easy to see that the debate between monks and bishops was rooted in the classic contrast of *agrum colere et in urbe lucere*, between *otium* and *negotium*, the point of contemporary reference being the public offices, to which the correspondence of Symmachus again gives us important testimony.[44] The freedom of the desert is for the monk, the hell of the city for the bishop. Jerome, the great champion of the monastic vocation, in a letter to Paulinus of 395, tells him that if he wants to perform the functions of a priest or even of a bishop – burden or honour! – then he should live in a city and try to profit his own soul from the salvation of others.[45] It is well

---

[42] Possid. *V. Aug.* viii.   [43] Brown, *Cult of the Saints* 36–7.   [44] Roda (1985).   [45] Jer. *Ep.* 58.4–5.

known how pleasant life in the country was for the rich aristocrats, who enjoyed retiring there in the company of a chosen band of friends. In this same brief period of time Ausonius suggested to Paulinus of Nola that he abandon the bustle of Bordeaux so as to return to his true self.[46] And there is much that is traditional in the way in which Paulinus thinks of his own special relationship at Nola with St Felix, *amicus et patronus*.[47]

Also conspicuous are the economic considerations which made the religious orders attractive. But, as always, complex phenomena presuppose complex causes. The ecclesiastical career was bound to appeal to many young men as a genuine ideal. The case of John Chrysostom is typical: trained to become an advocate and to undertake a career at court like his father, he chose the religious life out of a profound disaffection with the world. It is, however, clear that the changes initiated by Constantine in 312 conditioned perceptibly all subsequent developments: starting from that moment every bishop was destined to receive special consideration, for the very reason that he was bishop, from the emperor, who in his turn actually considered himself a bishop, though 'of those who stand outside'.[48] One must begin from this premise if one is to understand the self-affirmation, in the west, of that extraordinary *Kirchenpolitiker* who was the bishop of Milan and a former *consularis Aemiliae*, Ambrose.[49] The history of a good part of the last quarter of the fourth century is dominated by his relations with the Milanese court and with Theodosius. His interventions in imperial affairs must not make us forget his own indefatigable activity as organizer of the ecclesiastical hierarchies and strenuous defender of Catholic orthodoxy. From his writings it is clear how interchangeable the episcopal and imperial attributes were from his perspective, the former involving an accumulation of civil and political functions which increasingly made the bishop a rival to the emperor. In the rapid disintegration of the western empire, it is easy to recognize in this line of action the prefiguration of the role developed, some decades later, at Clermont-Ferrand by Sidonius and many other bishops in Gallia Meridionalis: the aristocratic landowner-become-bishop rises to lead his own local community, in a final re-enactment of the relations of civic patronage.[50] On his canonization, the bishop's remains were preserved and a basilica built over them as a tangible mark of the ties which bound him to that city.

The considerable power acquired by the eunuchs in the course of the fourth century – one of the many pecularities of the *pars orientis* – is to be explained by the complex power relations that arose within the court of Constantinople.[51] Their power is inversely proportional to the social regard which they enjoyed: for many of them there seems to have been no alter-

---

[46] Auson. *Ep.* 6 (*Opusc.* 18, 6). Fontaine (1980) 241–65.   [47] Brown, *Cult of the Saints* 53–7.
[48] Eus. *V. Const.* IV.24; Straub (1972) 119–33.   [49] Von Campenhausen (1929).
[50] Van Dam, *Leadership and Community* 141–56.   [51] Hopkins (1987) 172–96.

native between a prominent role and an ignominious end (we have a good example in the text of the decree preserved in the Code of Theodosius which sanctions the punishment of Eutropius in 399).[52] This state of affairs is confirmed by the position of the *primicerius sacri cubiculi*, the great court chamberlain, eunuch and ex-slave, in the order of precedence of the eastern empire, where he appears in the fourth place and is preceded only by the praetorian prefects, the urban prefect and the *magistri militum*.[53] The rise of the eunuch, however, can also be seen as an expression of the need for mediation in the society of late antiquity: the fact that his power depended exclusively on the emperor made him into an obligatory route, as it were, for reaching the sovereign, whom the court ceremonial had increasingly isolated.

IV. THE REGIONAL REALITY

The immense extent of the empire had always implied varying degrees of difference between the various regions. Nevertheless, as long as the unitary centralized state was kept alive, these divergences were only of minor significance. The change came with the reforms of Diocletian, which removed the emperor and the effective government of the empire from Rome, creating four capitals in place of the single former capital. The political failure of the tetrarchy did not change things substantially. In the east the foundation of Constantinople made a great administrative centre of the new capital: although its prestige could not compete with that of Rome, it was quite obvious that all the Greek-speaking world found its focal point there.[54] In the west events are more complicated. Certainly, the ephemeral success of Trier under Valentinian I, before the seat of the empire was transferred to Milan, is indicative of how important the emperor's place of residence was.

Within the general weakness of the empire, its two parts were already markedly different from each other before their final partition by Theodosius I in 395 made this difference even more apparent. However paradoxical it may seem, the eastern half benefited from the absence of a powerful aristocracy like that of the west, who, drawing strength from their social standing and the extent of their possessions, tended to share out among themselves and monopolize any offices by which they could better defend their interests. The east was bound to be relatively more homogeneous than the west, and the inequalities of wealth were less profound. While in the west the prosperity of most cities apart from Rome and Milan seems to decline, in the east we are struck by the vitality of Antioch, for example, towards which gravitated the flourishing region of northern Syria, a society

---

[52] *C.Th.* IX.40.17.   [53] *Not. Dig. Or.* I, Index.   [54] Dagron, *Naissance*.

of small, reasonably well-off, free farmers.[55] In general the productive capacities of the region seem to remain stable until the era of Justinian. Nor should we underestimate the greater extension of Christianity, which, despite the intensification of theological disputes and the wide prevalence of the phenomenon of monasticism, helped to enliven urban life in the east.

V. THE EMPEROR

The increased verticalization of the society of late antiquity is most apparent in the emphasis on the figure of the emperor (or emperors).[56] To a large extent the constraints (of a formal or less formal nature) which conditioned the action of the *princeps* became fewer. The immediate consequence of the removal of the seat of government from Rome was the alteration of the basis of the emperor's dialogue with the senatorial class. The power of the emperor was almost absolute in every field – military, administrative, judicial and fiscal – and he was himself the source of law: *quod principi placuit legis habet vigorem*. But in addition the imperial power was renewed in its ideological base, laden with charismatic and providential forces, in the face of which failure to respect an order of the emperor was no longer a simple crime, but sacrilege. Holiness is the proper sphere of the sovereign, not an emperor-God but an emperor by divine grace:[57] the terms *sacer* and *sacrum* become synonymous with 'imperial'. This applies in general for the emperor. The Christian monarch in the political theology of Eusebius of Caesarea is elevated to the level of a vicar of Christ on earth, whose work he extends in this sphere.[58] For Augustine the good emperor is the man who places his power at the service of God. The religious functions of the *pontifex maximus* are therefore significantly enlarged. The absolutist and autocratic ideology of the new monarchy has a ceremonial to match, the ultimate expression of which is the *adoratio* of the purple, which stresses the inaccessibility of the person of the emperor.

However, not even the monarch of late antiquity reigned alone. He also needed an increased number of collaborators precisely because the exigencies of the civil administration and government of the provinces were greater in number and scale. The blurring of the distinction between senatorial and equestrian orders caused a change in the criteria for the selection of officials. In the east, the senate of Constantinople was formed of necessity from men who did not derive prestige from their own 'pedigree' and set itself up as an assembly of functionaries.[59] In the west, on the contrary, there was still a group which claimed privileged access to some

---

[55] Liebeschuetz, *Antioch.*   [56] Alföldi (1970).   [57] Ensslin (1943).   [58] Farina (1966).
[59] Vogler (1979).

traditional magistracies, like the prefecture and some governorships, and whose relations with the bureaucracy of the court were not always easy. In this context, the emperor represents the centre and the driving-force of the system. It is precisely the proximity to the centre of power which becomes the determining factor within the organization of the new ruling centre.[60] The *comes* of the emperor, the man who enjoys his friendship and respect, is his 'companion', therefore his confidant, above all his minister, not to mention the fact that he developed senatorial and equestrian functions. The formalization of this criterion is translated into the *comitiva*, the government formed of the *comites* – those, that is, who are 'close' to the emperor: it is no accident that the imperial court was mostly called *comitatus* (more rarely *aula*), precisely to remind people that it 'accompanied' the emperor. It was Constantine who realized the implications of this principle: in addition to extending the application of the term, he made of it a full-blown title. Moreover, *comes* might be an integral part of the official titulature of a certain number of other civil and military office-holders (e.g. *comes sacrarum largitionum* and *comes rei militaris*). The system underwent a further development in so far as *comes* could be conferred simply as an honorific title without any implication of a function carried out close to the emperor. The honorary *comitiva* is characterized by its division into three classes, *ordinis primi, secundi* and *tertii*.[61] It is worth mentioning that, at least in some cases, a proper 'career' ought to have been possible within these classes of honorary *comites*. This development would have important consequences for the evolution of the late imperial bureaucracy. Compared with the past, the new system gives evidence of a greater rationalization. The emperor was no longer required to concern himself, even if only formally, in his own person with all that was directed to his attention: the head of the court bureaucracy, the *magister officiorum*, had the official duty of laying business before the sovereign. The vagueness of his title is indicative of the variety of his competences.[62] A second guiding principle, related to the first, was that monarchs conferred rank on the basis of 'merit'; here, 'merit' clearly means punctual and precise fulfilment of one's tasks for the good of the emperor and the state. An example is provided by the case of the praetorian prefect Flavius Philippus, a person of low birth, who pursued his career under Constantius II. An inscription at Ephesus which reproduces the contents of an imperial letter is particularly important evidence for such an ideology.[63] The praise of Philippus, called *parentem et amicum nostrum eximium*, expresses the gratitude of Constantius to a loyal servant who has worked without affectation for his own good and that of the state. These are the *inlustria merita* which deserve to be recorded, because these are the men in whom the sovereign delights. This ideology

[60] Löhken (1982).   [61] Eus. *V. Const.* IV.I.   [62] Clauss (1981).   [63] Swift and Oliver (1962).

of 'merit' is a corollary of the greater freedom which the emperor possessed in choosing his own collaborators. It was in his interest to have at his disposal the broadest possible base of recruitment; this was a system which permitted him to promote those who were most agreeable to him, and which could offer even the person of modest station the hope that his merits would open up a good career for him. In this context the case of Stilicho, the Vandal general who held supreme power in the west at the end of the fourth and the beginning of the fifth century, can be considered paradigmatic. An inscription mentions how he managed to arrive *ad columen gloriae* by passing through the stages of the military career, and by having been *comes* of Theodosius in all his wars.[64] In the inscriptions frequent allusion is made to the *merita* of personages who had obtained the highest distinctions from the various emperors.

VI. THE UPPER CLASSES

The subdivisions within the upper classes came to be more marked in the west than in the east. As we have already had occasion to mention briefly, in the west there was a social gap between the senatorial aristocracy, who were powerful because of their property and nobility of birth, and the functional aristocracy, who could boast a rank acquired only for good services at the court and who were considered a sort of 'noblesse d'empire'.

In the preceding section we have seen the advantages that had accrued to the emperor from putting distance between himself and Rome. There were benefits too for the senate, within its newly defined though limited sphere of influence. The senate certainly could not claim to be a centre of decision-making, but it was not merely a 'town council' either. If senators did not normally have access to the great central offices, the military commands and the bureaucracy, their internal cohesion was promoted precisely by the specialization of the careers that could be pursued and their secure hold on a few posts:[65] this is proved by the different fate of the senate of Constantinople, a direct emanation of the imperial court, by which it was smothered. The offices held by senators of Rome consisted of the government of the regions where the greater part of their landed properties were concentrated – Italia Meridionalis and Africa, in addition to Greece – and of the urban prefecture, which was the most sensitive of all the offices.[66] The short duration of these magistracies – one year or a little longer – is characteristic, and typical of the oligarchic egalitarianism of the senate. Precisely in the sphere of its competence, the importance of which was directly proportionate to the apparent limits set on it, the senatorial *nobili-*

[64] *ILS* 1277.   [65] Chastagnol (1970).   [66] Chastagnol, *Préfecture urbaine; id., Fastes.*

tas became what it had never been before – namely, an hereditary class of government with a certain degree of freedom of action.

We are well informed concerning the mentality of this class by the surviving works of one of its leaders, Quintus Aurelius Symmachus.[67] An aristocrat by birth, he was also aristocratic both by conviction and by 'trade'. Symmachus was indefatigable in forging links with the high-ranking representatives of the imperial court, including bishop Ambrose himself, with whom he was able to work in a civilized way.[68] The organization of the games provides a typical example of the duties of a senator. A fragment of Olympiodorus confirms that payments made for the *ludi* could represent a sort of standard of wealth against which to measure the more immense properties.[69] In the Constantinian reorganization the *sumptus* was rigorously fixed and there was no means of avoiding something which was tantamount to a tax. The dangers inherent in the psychology of a 'well-to-do class' such as the traditional senatorial aristocracy are manifest: the *foeda iactatio*, 'conspicuous consumption', could, if the competitive spirit was carried to excess, lead to financial ruin. It is interesting to see how Symmachus, who as urban prefect had advocated moderation, changed his tune when it fell to his son Memmius to organize the games.[70] Symmachus was aware of the popularity that accrued to the organizer of the games and how integral a part they were of the political system.[71] The quest for popularity, *laus plebeia*, is not an end in itself but represents a full-scale 'status bloodbath'.[72] The zeal of Symmachus in seeking the collaboration of the imperial power for the success of the games given by his son is very instructive. His good relations with Stilicho, who around 400 was *de facto* ruler of the west, advanced his purpose. But the message is clear: the greater the magnificence of the games, the greater the credit attaching to the *editor* and to his imperial supporter. We are faced with a sensitive aspect of the production of consent in the society of late antiquity. The imperial power (whoever represented it) was aware of the expectations in Rome. The games were presented by a magistrate, often in the age-group thirteen–sixteen, who engaged the resources of his family in the endeavour, and at the same time acted as a sort of proxy for the absent emperor. The games remained a fundamental aspect of the life of the city. The plebs expected to be entertained no less than appeased. The regular supply of food was likewise important, but the implications are the same: if the senators were in the front line, in the sense that the Roman *nobiles* were the first to endure the consequences of the anger of the hungry plebs, the imperial authority was no less exposed. One of the typical roles of the senatorial aristocracy actually consisted of

---

[67] See n. 7, p. 340 above.   [68] Patrucco (1976).   [69] Olympiod. fr. 44; Cameron (1984).
[70] Symm. *Rel.* VIII.   [71] Marcone (1981).   [72] Hopkins (1983) 9.

mediation, on the one hand with the court, on the other with the local aristocracies.[73]

In consequence of the unprecedented expansion of the senatorial order, the title *clarissimus*, which previously applied to all senators, became the title of least prestige, and was surpassed by *spectabilis* and *illustris*. Within the *illustres*, the *nobiles* were the members of those families whose importance had endured over generations.[74] On them fell the greater responsibilities in respect of relations between the imperial authority and the urban plebs. On close examination, the same principle of differentiation is at work, on a local level, in the town councils, where, within the order of decurions, one can discern a restricted group of persons who were in effective control of the government of the city, the so-called *principales*.

This hierarchization within the ruling class is confirmed in the texts of laws: in the provincial assemblies, for example, the *honorati* – that is, all those who had held a state office (or an honorary codicil) – came before the *principales*, who are in their turn distinguished from the rest of the decurions. In the east the aristocracy was composed of two levels: the first is represented by the senate of Constantinople, which had been organized on the model of that of Rome, in large measure by Constantius II; the second is formed of the members of the senatorial order who had held a particular office or who had received honours. The senate of Constantinople in terms of social status was substantially homogeneous with the town councils, but carried higher political prestige and fiscal advantages in as much as entry into the senate freed its members from curial burdens.[75] Libanius' criticism of low-born personages or those equipped with merely technical knowledge who reached the senate is a reflection of this situation, and also reveals something of the tension that existed between the cities of the east and the new capital.[76] The discomfiture of the old ruling class of a city of the economic and political rank of Antioch is apparent: in a famous speech in support of the co-optation of a rich Antiochene arms-manufacturer, Libanius did not hesitate to review the not-very-honourable professions of the fathers of many of those senators who were now putting obstacles in the way of his candidate.[77]

VII. THE LOWER CLASSES

Whereas the upper stratum of society had developed a more elaborate hierarchization, the lower classes, in spite of their size, were relatively homogeneous. This does not mean that there were no perceptible differences, of which the most obvious is that between urban plebs and rural

[73] Matthews, *Western Aristocracies.*   [74] Barnes (1974).   [75] Dagron, *Naissance* 147–90.
[76] Petit (1957).   [77] Lib. *Or.* XLII.

plebs. Nevertheless, the juridical weakness of the lower classes, and their subjection to obligations of a personal and patrimonial nature, are recurrent and typical elements. On a strictly economic level, in the society which was restructured after the crisis of the third century, the difference between rich and poor was accentuated more and more, particularly in the west.

The traditional basis of Roman wealth – landed property – was, even more than it had been in the past, the foundation of great wealth concentrated in the hands of a few proprietors, who passed on to the population in their service the increasingly great burdens imposed by the state. In the countryside, the fundamental and traditional distinction between free men and slaves became more formal than substantial, almost a legal relic with little correspondence to reality. The question of how far slaves declined in number in the fourth and fifth centuries is complex and cannot be answered easily.[78] To speak of a general decline of slavery is overbold, even if it is true that the sources of supply were effectively reduced. It is certain that the complex and in some respects controversial legislation on the *coloni*, starting with the notorious law of Constantine of 332, rendered the condition of this peasant farmer, who was nominally free, very close to that of the slave.[79]

The language of the law, which became increasingly brutal, must incline one to caution, but the important fact is that it is clearly stated that *coloni* suspected of planning to run away ought to be put in chains like slaves (*in servilem condicionem*), so as to be compelled to carry out, while being punished like a slave (*merito servilis condemnationis*), those functions which were suited to free men. The tying of the agricultural population to the land, perhaps the most striking aspect of the condition of the *coloni*, was not introduced simultaneously for all *coloni* in the empire, but progressively in the different regions: certainly in 371 in Illyricum,[80] in 386 in Palestine[81] and in Egypt not before the fifth century.[82] At the same time, the legislation records a regular loss of rights on the part of the *coloni* (whose condition in the meantime became hereditary), such as the possibility of selling their property without authorization on the part of the master or of prosecuting him. The degradation of their status proceeded steadily until the age of Justinian, when the position of the *adscripticius* was very hard to distinguish from that of an agricultural slave.[83] The *colonus* was as a rule considered *pauper*, meaning by this that he disposed of modest resources, but not necessarily that he was indigent.[84]

The precariousness of the condition of the *coloni* lay essentially in the uncertainties of agricultural management, in as much as one or more

---

[78] See pp. 294–7 above.
[79] *C.Th.* v.9.1. Cf. Rosafio (1991). For the colonate of late antiquity in the historiographical debate, cf. Marcone, *Colonato.*   [80] *CJ* xi.53.   [81] *CJ* xi.51.   [82] Jones, *Economy* 293–307.
[83] Johne (1988).   [84] Aug. *En. in Ps.* 93.7; *Ep.* 247.1 and 4; cf. Krause (1987) 108.

harvests could be enough to compel a *colonus* to sell his sons into slavery. Masters, whose position was favoured by the legislation, sometimes made things worse with oppressive and dishonest treatment. The gloomy picture which we obtain from many homiletic passages is not encouraging. John Chrysostom writes in one of his sermons on the Gospel of St Matthew: 'Who could be more oppressive than a landowner? If one looks at the manner in which they treat their poor tenants, they appear fiercer than barbarians. They continually impose intolerable taxes on men who are weakened by hunger and suffering and exact from them the labours of burdensome drudgery, using their bodies as if they were those of asses or mules.'[85] Continual additional requests for rent could create the occasion for further forms of malversation. St Ambrose recalls having seen a man compelled to pay an amount he was not able to afford and dragged into prison because the table of some rich man lacked wine.[86]

If social relations in the country indubitably deteriorated at the expense of the lower classes, it does not follow that life in the cities followed a parallel course. Our information is confined to the great metropolises of the empire – Rome, Antioch, Constantinople – and is to a large extent of a moralistic and satirical nature. The position of the *plebs urbana* of these cities could not have been typical of all the other cities of the late empire. Nevertheless, it is not clear that it had changed much from an earlier era.[87] The care which the imperial power took in appointing the prefect of Rome is indicative of the importance which the plebs had in the complex game of political balances. The scorn which pervades the literature and also the legislation for the 'plebeian scum and meanness', for the 'idle and indolent plebs',[88] betrays the hatred of a class which despises but also fears the strength of an inferior social category whose consent, however, they must win. The unfortunate experience of Julian at Antioch is revealing: the religious conflict plays a secondary role in that failure compared with his unsympathetic attitude towards all that Antiochenes held dear, including the games.[89] The riot was the only effective instrument of pressure which remained to the lower classes after they had been deprived of their political rights, and to this they had recourse periodically to obtain the satisfaction of their primary needs, 'bread and circuses'. The importance of games in the society of late antiquity consists in their being a moment of political confrontation between the mass of the population and the ruling class (or even the emperor, if present). For the urban magistrates the danger was also physical: it was not uncommon for the members of the more influential families to leave the city in moments of crisis. Ammianus Marcellinus has left us an account of a dramatic scene in which the prefect of Rome of 357,

[85] Joh. Chrys. *Hom. in Matt.* LXI.3.   [86] Ambr. *De Nab.* v.21.   [87] Seyfarth (1969) 7–18.
[88] *C.Th.* IX.42.5; Amm. Marc. XXVIII.4.28.   [89] Bowersock, *Julian* 94–105.

Tertullus, managed to placate the mob, which blamed him for the delay in the provision of food, by presenting to them his sons and inviting them to wreak their vengeance on them too.[90] The main characteristic of the plebs, their indigence (*egestas*), was felt as something repugnant. A law of Gratian and Valentinian II of 382 addressed to the prefect of Rome is perhaps indicative of a plan to remove from the city some of the most socially maladjusted elements: the mendicants who were healthy and capable of working ought to be assigned as (perpetual) *coloni* to whoever denounced them.[91]

VIII. OTHER SOCIAL DISTINCTIONS

As the gap between rich and poor widened in late antiquity, so the position of the latter in relation to the former worsened in every sector of civil life, but in particular in the law. Already under the old empire there was, at least in the field of penal law, recognition of the division of society into two groups, the *honestiores* and the *humiliores*,[92] the differential treatment of whom at law sanctioned the social pre-eminence of persons whose position or function conferred on them particular prestige. All those who were separated from the mass of the plebs by virtue of their membership of the senatorial or equestrian order or of a town council (and under certain circumstances army veterans also) were *honestiores*. They enjoyed the privilege of milder punishments than those inflicted for the same crimes on *humiliores*: for example, in place of the death penalty they could expect exile or deportation. It is essentially a matter of a legal distinction which was strongly anchored in the objective social placing of persons. This type of privilege was maintained in the late imperial period: in the *Acta* of the trial of Felix of Abthungi of 313–14, the testimony of the duumvir Alphius Caecilianus was accepted by the proconsul without his needing to furnish supplementary proofs, precisely in consideration of the office he held in his own city.[93] In the course of the same trial, the scribe Ingentius escaped torture on the basis of his declaration that he was a decurion. It was standard practice to establish at the beginning of a hearing the condition and social status of a person. The grammarian Victor, when brought before the governor of Numidia, Zenophilus, for interrogation, replied that his *condicio* was that of professor of Latin letters and that his *dignitas* was that of the son of a decurion and grandson of a soldier. The sum of these elements of *condicio* and *dignitas* sufficed to place Victor in a relatively elevated social position with its connected legal privileges.[94]

---

[90] Amm. Marc. XIX.10.   [91] *C.Th.* XIV.18.1 = *CJ* XI.26.1.   [92] Garnsey (1970).

[93] *Acta Purgationis Felicis* (*CSEL* 26) 197–206. A more general late imperial development, reflecting both the growing severity of penalties and the social divisions within the privileged classes themselves, was the vulnerability of lower-ranking *honestiores*, especially *curiales*, to harsher punishments.

[94] *Gesta apud Zenophilum* (*CSEL* 26) 185ff.

Honestiores in late antiquity include, apart from the categories mentioned before, all those who practise prestigious professions, such as architects, doctors and professors, priests, officials and soldiers. But even here the more complex hierarchization of the upper classes makes itself felt with time. An important confirmation of this is the law against the Donatists of 412, where the various social classes are listed in descending order of dignity.[95] Each level of rank is threatened with an appropriate monetary fine. From the holders of the highest imperial offices one passes to the senatorial aristocracy and thence to the municipal aristocracy (with further, perceptible differentiations within it). Below them are placed the *humiliores*: it is interesting that the first to be designated, the *negotiatores* and then the *plebeii* (small artisans), pay the same amount as the lower level of the *curiales*, that is five pounds of gold. Next come *circumcelliones* (agricultural workers), who pay a fine of ten pounds of silver. Corporal punishment is reserved for the even lower categories of the *coloni* and slaves.

This is still, then, a legal system of social classification based on relatively objective criteria, but there is a new reality in the society of late antiquity, represented by the emergence of the *potentiores*. The legal texts do not give a satisfactory definition of this group.[96] It is clear that we are dealing with an extrajuridical term denoting a social and economic category which is stigmatized in the law codes for abuse of power. Large estates provide the basis of their *potentia*, which can be turned to every kind of malversation and perversion of justice. *Potentior*, then, becomes a synonym for large landowner. In this the testimony of the church fathers is in agreement with that of the laws: for example, an edict of Theodosius I of 384, regarding the requisition of natural produce in the provinces, clearly identifies *potentiores* and landowners:[97] here it is clearly stated that the injunction to provide produce concerns only the houses of *possessores*, while the *inferiores vel plebeii* are excluded. The *potentiores* do not necessarily coincide with the *honestiores*, of whom they represent, at the most, a small part. *Potentiores* are those who are engaged in making use of their *potentia* and seeking to increase it by practising every kind of abuse and interference through the exercise of some political office: opposed to them is the great mass of the defenceless, the *tenuiores* (the term is used by the sources generally as a synonym of *humiliores*), whose weakness of status, which is sanctioned and at the same time guaranteed on the juridical level, is now further aggravated.

The position of the *curiales* as men invested with political office but possessing only modest wealth was problematic, in that they were exposed to the blackmail of the rich. A decree of 386 of Theodosius I, which makes the sale of curial property subject to the confirmation of the provincial

[95] *C.Th.* XVI.5.52. MacMullen, *Changes* 256–7.   [96] Wacke (1980).
[97] *C.Th.* XV.2. MacMullen, *Corruption* 96.

governors, suggests that they had to be protected from the corrupt practices of the *potentiores*.[98] This is attested in more explicit terms by a law of
410 of Theodosius II in which, in order to assist the less rich members of
the senate, it is laid down that tax assessments did not have validity until
they were registered at the offices of the governors.[99]

The threat presented by the *potentiores* affected more than the poorer *curiales*; it undermined the state apparatus itself. We are talking here of a factor
of dislocation bequeathed by the crisis of the third century, which the
reforms of Diocletian and Constantine did not succeed in overcoming.
Already in 293 Diocletian had issued a universal law against the *patrocinia
potentiorum* in the legal system, pointing out that this was a re-enactment of
an earlier law of Claudius Gothicus.[100] There are later imperial interventions (no fewer than eight laws of Constantine concern this problem),
emphasizing the concern of the state and the weakness of its response.
The institution of the *defensores plebis* by Valentinian in 368 had precisely the
aim of protecting the weak from the abuses of the *potentes*, above all in the
fiscal area.[101] It too achieved little.

IX. FROM PATRONAGE TO *PATROCINIUM*

In late antiquity there is a continuation of the traditional relation of patronage, as characterized by the exchange of favours between the patron and
his clients and by the inequality of status of the parties in question; presumably the more important the social position of the former, the better
guaranteed were the interests of the latter. It is clear that those best placed
to develop a patronal role were members of the imperial court and of the
senatorial aristocracy. Patronage can of course imply different kinds of
behaviour; it can consist in protecting one's own clients if they find themselves in difficulty, or, at a higher level, in intervention in favour of persons
who need help to further their careers. It is this latter behaviour which we
see so often in Symmachus: his correspondence is to a large extent a monument to his activity as a patron with regard to friends, acquaintances or
mere dependants whom he recommends to those who can be of use to
them.[102]

The society of late antiquity displays a vital need for mediators and
champions, on the individual as much as on the collective level. It is no surprise that patronage of the citizen community continues to be well attested,
but with one significant difference compared with the past: even in
Italian towns, members of the municipal upper classes gave way as munic
ipal patrons to provincial governors or, less commonly, other imperial

---

[98] *C.Th.* XII.3.1. [99] *CJ* x.22.1. [100] *CJ* II.13.1. [101] Jones, *LRE* 726–7.
[102] Cf. Roda (1976).

dignitaries. They disappear almost completely as private patrons, to be replaced, characteristically, by senators who hold some imperial office. The inscriptions show what was expected by the cities of their patrons: the patrons are praised for the realization of important building projects, more often involving the restoration of public works than the construction of new ones.[103]

It seems clear that the communities wanted long-term relationships with those who governed them; hence inscriptions often mention their equity as judges. The patron, in exchange for the social prestige which he derived from this title, was supposed to serve the city which had honoured him as a spokesman for its interests with the ministers of the court. We see this behaviour realized in the interventions of Symmachus on behalf of some townspeople of Campania.[104] Even if his official position as patron is not attested explicitly by the epigraphic sources, his interventions allow us to presume it or, at any rate, constitute an equivalent of it; it is known that he had a villa at Formiae. There is an interesting counterpart, peculiar to Campania, in the relations with this region of the powerful family of the Anicii, who were native to Praeneste. Anicius Auchenius Bassus, governor of Campania between 379 and 382–3, was recognized as *patronus originalis* by many cities, like Anicius Paulinus, who had preceded him in the office.[105] Nevertheless the relationship between a patron and a community was not an exclusive one, as is proved by the fact that often more than one representative of the senatorial aristocracy is found as patron of the same city.

Up to this point we have dealt with traditional forms of patronage, which continued, with important modifications, until late antiquity. A completely new phenomenon, however, emerges in country districts and goes under the name of *patrocinium*; in this term the idea of protection, which was a function of old-style patrons, assumes the full meaning of 'defence'. This particular type of social relation can be reduced to two fundamental aspects: the first is protection afforded to those escaping their condition; they might be slaves or *coloni*, fleeing from one master or landlord to another, or else decurions, artisans or tradesmen seeking to place themselves under the protection of a great landowner. The second aspect of *patrocinium*, which is more important from the economic point of view, concerns countrymen and is known by the name of *patrocinium vicorum*. We are informed of it in particular by an important speech of Libanius (*Or.* XLVII), some chapters of the *De Gubernatione Dei* of Salvianus (v.35–46) and some laws: both the code of Theodosius and that of Justinian devote a separate heading to it.[106] The testimony of Libanius is particularly vivid.[107]

---

[103] Krause (1987) 68–72.
[104] Symm. *Ep.* 9.58 for Formiae; 9.138–9 for Suessa; *Rel.* XL (as urban prefect) for Pozzuoli and Terracina. Cf. Ruggini (1969).   [105] Cf. Vera (1981) 213.   [106] *C.Th.* XI.24.1–6.
[107] Cf. Carrié (1976).

The background of the speech lies in a case he lost against Jewish *coloni* who, in return for the support offered them by certain military elements, had refused to perform some agricultural tasks. Libanius requests the intervention of the emperor to restore the situation which seemed to him the best – the one, that is, whereby the landlord was responsible for every form of assistance to his peasants, including their relationship with the outside world. Libanius attacks the intervention of 'strong men' from outside – here, military men – which prevented officials of the town from performing their traditional roles, among them, tax-collection.[108]

The laws offer precious confirmation of the credibility of this speech. From a regulation of Constantius of 360 concerning Egypt, it is clear that the relations of *patrocinium* established between *coloni* and high dignitaries, among them *duces*, aimed at protecting them from the tax-collectors of the treasury in exchange for a form of tax which was payable to the patron.[109] Subsequent laws, which are of more general significance and impose more serious punishments, suggest that the *patrocinium* relationship was extensively practised. An edict promulgated for Egypt in 415 in effect gives it some sort of recognition in law.[110]

One can deduce from the legal sources that patronage was practised by the most diverse categories of people (one law speaks of *ex quocumque hominum ordine* or *cuiuslibet dignitatis*),[111] even if it was the patronage practised by civilian officials and by the *curiales* themselves (besides that practised by the military) which particularly troubled the authorities. The status of one Mixidemus, apparently a civilian patron who is alleged by Libanius to have sought to extend his control over entire villages, is not clear.[112]

Even if the laws issue from emperors of the eastern empire and concern Egypt especially though not exclusively, illegal forms of patronage certainly existed in the west too. Salvianus attests that, at least towards the middle of the fifth century when he was writing, fiscal pressure had driven many peasants to place themselves under the *patrocinium* of *potentes*, to whom alone they could look for help against the agents of the treasury. It may be too early to look for proto-feudalism in the countryside.[113] All the same, it is plain that the spread and consolidation of *patrocinium* are a further indication of the weakening of the central power in face of the emergence of disintegrating tendencies of various kinds.

X. SOCIAL MOBILITY

The effort expended by the state in tying the greater part of the population to its role and place of residence for economic and fiscal reasons seems

---

[108] Garnsey and Woolf (1989) 162–6.   [109] *C.Th.* XI.24.1.   [110] *C.Th.* XI.24.6.
[111] *C.Th.* XI.24.3 and 24.4.   [112] Lib. *Or.* XLI.   [113] Percival (1969).

paradoxically to have produced the contrary result: a greater social mobility than had existed in the past. Nevertheless, in the absence of statistics and comparative data some caution is necessary. A part of the mobility that characterized late antique society was an induced or reflex mobility which was a reaction to the coercive pressure of the state. A discussion of social mobility in late antiquity should distinguish carefully between this kind of (horizontal) mobility which was nothing but a flight from one's obligations, and another kind of mobility whereby one's condition was improved, not without the connivance of the state authorities, whose main effort might seem to have been directed to petrifying society. The state offered two basic routes for advancement, namely, administration and the army. First, the administration. The empire created by the reforms of Diocletian needed an increased number of qualified functionaries, if only because of the doubling of the number of provinces and the new organization which caused more provinces to be regrouped in dioceses and more dioceses in prefectures. All this meant an expansion of the bureaucracy and its specialization, at least in embryo form. Another factor was the promotion of new men by emperors who did not themselves come from established families and tended to favour men like themselves and of similar origins. New categories and new social classes might then come into the reckoning, especially in the east. A large part of the legislation of Constantine II turned on the creation of the senate of Constantinople, while also in the east (a related development) the civil service emerged as an important motor of social ascent.[114]

This reality also explains the singular importance assumed by university life and by education and culture in general in late antiquity. A good preparation was an indispensable entrée to service in the palace, in particular. These necessary preconditions are reflected in an edict of the Code of Theodosius addressed by Valentinian to the prefect of Rome in 370 and concerning the organization of the higher studies of the capital.[115] The emperor wanted to examine the matriculation lists and to learn from them 'the merits and the degree of preparation of the individual students and to judge if these could ever be useful to him'. The imperial administration consciously monitored the channels of recruitment, while at the same time asserting the hereditary principle as regards the professions.

The second major route of social mobility was the military career. Here too there was a basic necessity to fill additional posts. In late antiquity the type of the official of 'good' social extraction is a great deal less common than in the past. The chief characteristic of the army of Constantine is that the possibilities of entry and promotion were not linked to membership of a particular social order, but rather to personal ability and the favour of the

---

[114] Petit, *Libanius* 362.   [115] *C.Th.* XIV.9.1.

emperor. This, together with the growing barbarization of the army, explains the good prospects of advancement enjoyed by assimilated Germans, who were preferred as professional soldiers to members of the traditional classes, and could aspire to the highest military offices.[116]

In addition to the two types of career offered by the state as a vehicle of social mobility, there was a *de facto* third one in competition with them, the church. In the course of the fourth century the church was very successful in attracting to itself men of the first rank, from Ambrose and Jerome in the west to Gregory of Nazianzus and Basil of Caesarea in the east. The singlemindedness with which such great representatives of the upper classes abandoned their traditional roles and pursuits to undertake an ecclesiastical career is one of the socially more significant phenomena of late antiquity. The famous witticism of one of the leaders of the dying paganism, Vettius Agorius Praetextatus – 'Make me bishop of Rome and I will immediately become a Christian' – may be symptomatic of the attitude of the senatorial aristocracy to the new positions of power offered by the church.[117] The adherence of such substantial numbers to an ecclesiastical career has complex motivations but, at least for the members of the town councils, it is explained by the opportunity that the church offered of escaping from the heavy burdens of the *municipia*. It is relevant in this connection that Constantine quite quickly reversed his decision to free churchmen from the obligation to serve as decurions. This circumstance helps to explain the substantial homogeneity which was realized between the representatives of the ecclesiastical and civil hierarchies.

However, these undeniable conditions of mobility and social ascent must not blind us to the fundamental fact that, in a world in which the small farmer was preponderant, mobility, even in the sense of the simple geographical movement of persons, could only be a relatively minor phenomenon. We have seen the importance of education in late antiquity when, in addition to constituting one of the more important features of status, it became one of the principal requisites of a good career. The prosopographical data in our possession suggest that very few lower-class students attended the classes of the grammarian and even fewer those of the rhetorician. One example of this is the career of Aurelius Victor, who, although an African of modest origin, thanks to his abilities and his education was able to become a senator: he was already governor of a province in 361 and even attained the urban prefecture in 389.[118] The brilliant and fortunate case of Augustine, 'a poor man born of poor parents', who only possessed 'a few fields inherited from his father', and who succeeded in entering upon higher education thanks to the intervention of a rich friend who supplemented the relatively limited means of the family, ranks as one

---

[116] Demandt (1980).   [117] Jer. *C. Joh. Hier.* VIII.   [118] Cf. Bird (1984) 5–15.

of those situations which made social relations in late antiquity so singular.[119] The second book of the *Confessions* in particular is an extremely interesting document for the phenomenon of social advancement – in which, obviously, the prospect of a brilliant marriage played a part – through higher education. Then, in the sixth book, Augustine recounts how, consumed by ambition, he used his own office of public orator to form valuable contacts which were to lead to an office in the imperial administration.[120] His success is in some ways similar to that of Eunomius, bishop of Cyzicus between 360 and 364, who, it was alleged, had learnt to read and write from his own father, a Cappadocian peasant.[121]

On the other hand, the case of Ausonius is usually regarded as having singular features. His rise from professor to praetorian prefect, and the domination by members of his family, around 380, of the highest magistracies of the west, are truly extraordinary.[122] The fact that he came, at least on the maternal side, from good provincial Gallic stock was less crucial than the circumstance of his invitation to the court on the part of Valentinian to be the tutor of his son Gratian. But it is precisely the subsequent fortunes of his family that illustrate how precarious social advancement could often be. His nephew Paulinus of Pella, whose class and education promised a brilliant career, ended his days by himself, miserably cultivating a small plot of land near Marseilles, the only property that remained to him after all those that belonged to his family had been lost.[123] Even this is only one example of how religious and military conflicts, fiscal pressure and other things besides could cause a loss of dignity and rank and serve as conditions of negative mobility.

XI. SOCIAL MARGINALIZATION

In the complex and fluid social reality of late antiquity there existed a world with its own characteristics whose main actors were different from those to whom we normally give attention. In any form of state organization, even the best-organized one, there are persons or groups of persons who cannot be integrated. The countryside in the ancient world was traditionally the meeting-place of stragglers and rebels of every kind. Banditry was endemic. In the late empire, however, the activity of dissidents and outcasts appears to have been on the increase in the rural areas.[124] Firstly, the countryside was full of people on the run. Peasants fled in the face of fiscal pressure and maltreatment, heretics fled to escape religious coercion by the

---

[119] Aug. *Conf.* 11.3.5; *Serm.* 356. Cf. Kaster, *Guardians of Language.* The 'poverty' of Augustine is to be interpreted as a moderate degree of comfort.   [120] Cf. Lepelley (1987) 229–46.
[121] Greg. Nyss. *Contra Eunomium* 1.9.   [122] Hopkins (1961).
[123] Paul. Pell. *Euchar.* 522–34. Cf. Marcone (1992).   [124] Shaw (1984); MacMullen (1966).

orthodox, soldiers who did not want to fight any longer deserted. For the author of the small treatise *De Rebus Bellicis* it was the economic revolution of Constantine that created conditions of life which were unbearable for the defenceless poor (the *afflicta paupertas*) and led them into crime.[125] In some cases social hardship assumed decidedly subversive characteristics, which compelled the imperial power to react with measures of a military kind. The most serious movements of revolt are those which assailed Gaul and Africa Septentrionalis.

Gaul began to experience towards the end of the third century a movement of revolt associated with the activity of so-called Bagaudae. The information provided by our sources for these events is not very secure. The terms used to designate the Bagaudae ('rustics', 'farmworkers', 'shepherds', 'bandits') are too general to enable us to pin them down to a geographical location.[126] However, the local origin of the name, together with the fact that it comes from the Celtic term for war, suggests that underlying the revolt might have been not so much a desire for revolution as a felt need to re-established the protective bonds of a society that the receding tide of Roman power had undermined. This supposition receives support from the absence of any mention of Bagaudic movements in the fourth century and their reappearance at the beginning of the fifth, when the imperial court had abandoned Trier for Arles. That the presence of leaders with strong personal qualities was required in Gaul is indicated also by the career of Martin, who as a bishop brought to Tours an ideology appropriate to a former soldier of Pannonian origin. The work of Christianization and the re-establishment of Roman authority over the countryside were for him parallel activities. It is easy to see in the difficulties encountered by Martin a manifestation of the attachment of the rural population to their own pagan traditions and of their open opposition to Roman civilization.[127]

The ambiguous relationship with the Roman government in Gaul – its authority supported when efficient but rejected when felt to be unnecessarily oppressive – emerges also in the *Querolus*, an anonymous comedy which is clearly traditionalist in ideology, in which the protagonist speaks of desiring power but without holding any office. The ideal society that is depicted beside the river Loire, where a company of outlaws inhabit 'free' woods on the basis of no other law but the law of nature, seems to project, in a world outside time, a mood of regret at the passing of ancient values belonging to a time when the social order was guaranteed.[128] There are not incompatible statements in other contemporary works, one of Orosius and

[125] Anon. *De Rebus Bell.* II.5–6.
[126] Cf. *Pan. Lat.* II(10).4.3; Eutr. IX.20.3; Aur. Vict. *Caes.* XXXIX.7; cf. Van Dam, *Leadership and Community* 28–34.
[127] On the evocations of bandit and martyr cult raised by these incidents, and their interrelation, see Giardina (1983).   [128] Mazzarino (1974) 281–98.

another of Salvian. Orosius laments the preference of certain Romans for 'a miserable liberty among barbarians' over the 'anguish' induced by the Roman fiscal system, while Salvian recalls how many 'seek among the barbarians the humanity of the Romans, because they cannot bear the barbarous inhumanity of the Romans'.[129]

In Africa Septentrionalis religious dissent characterizes in a more precise way the forms of violent protest against the established power. Here the main actors are the so-called *circumcelliones*, the most radical group of Donatists. These were, in essence, seasonal workers who gathered in bands and attacked the estates of the Catholics with the cry *Dei laudes*. Their acts of terrorism, which hit the rich Catholics hard, and which are alleged to have consisted in freeing slaves, cancelling debts and preventing creditors from recovering their debts, were represented as manifestations of a will to social revolution.[130] We can properly take the religious motivation as primary without diminishing the social weakness of the *circumcelliones* as compared with the Catholics. Their origin might have had some significance for the least Romanized part of the population, the Berbers, for whom forms of resistance and reaction towards the Roman social organization will perhaps have found expression in religious *jacquerie*. Our sources (all firmly on the opposite side) do not allow us to untie the knot of the problem, which lies in the connection between social and religious transformations. It is certain that at Hippo, at the time of the episcopacy of St Augustine, the *circumcelliones* seemed like a brotherhood of pious fanatics, ready to use force to defend the Donatist church.[131]

In addition to the various kinds of rebellion that took place in a rural context, traditional banditry infested entire regions to the point of rendering them impassable (Cilicia, Isauria).[132] Even in Italy the situation must have been serious. A decree of Valentinian I of 364, which was aimed at putting a stop to the robberies and thefts of livestock committed in Apulia, placed strict limits on the use of the horse, in order to deprive the bandits of the indispensable means for bringing their undertakings to a successful conclusion, and to ensure the prevalence of the forces of order over the outlaws.[133] It is significant that for the legislator of late antiquity terms like *rusticani, agrestes, rustici, agricolae, aratores, pastores, latrones* were equivalents: *latro* is a direct synonym of *tyrannus*, usurper. The relation between city and country became increasingly problematic, the country serving with greater frequency as a place of refuge from the cities.

The city of late antiquity has a new main actor: the poor man, the free citizen deprived of the means of self-defence and subsistence, is a leading candidate for the role of outcast from the city and rebel of the

[129] Oros. VII.41.7; Salv. *De Gub. Dei* v.21.3.   [130] Frend (1969).   [131] Cf. Lepelley (1983b).
[132] Isaac (1984).   [133] *C.Th.* IX.30.3; De Robertis (1974).

countryside.[134] At Rome, as we have seen, the privileged relationship of the plebs with the aristocracy and the emperor remained. The case of Constantinople, the new capital, was peculiar: here ambitious provincials who hoped to make a career as officials at the imperial court gathered *en masse*. Here too, however, immigrants swarmed in from the whole of Anatolia, so that poverty soon became one of the determining factors of the life of the city. Material assistance to the needy became an absolute necessity and it is no surprise that the church took the leading role. In Constantinople, unlike Rome, rich widows were unable to dispose freely of their own patrimony. Olympias, granddaughter of a politician of the first rank at the court of Constantinople, was left a widow when she was little more than twenty years of age. To enable her to use her inherited wealth, she was made deaconess at the age of thirty (though the legal age was sixty), with the obligation to expend her patrimony to the advantage of the church. Her palace, next to the Hippodrome at Constantinople, was one of the most important centres of poor relief.[135]

XII. CONCLUSION

If there is one thing that can be claimed with certainty about the society of late antiquity, it is that it was in rapid transformation. The new empire of the fourth century was characterized by the confrontation between an increasingly demanding state and a society that resisted its claims. The ruling class, the aristocracy, was to a large extent renewed: equestrians were absorbed into the senatorial order, and new hierarchies, connected with the holding of the more important civil and military offices, articulated the top echelons of the empire. A law such as that of Valentinian I of 372[136] or, at the provincial level, the so-called *ordo salutationis* of the *consularis Numidiae*,[137] with its analytical definition of ranks and precedences, are important expressions of new equilibria and of different power relations. Late antiquity experienced considerable social fluidity, and personages of modest condition, especially in the east, obtained positions of importance. This was in contradiction to the coercive image of the state which is evoked in numerous laws contained in the Code of Theodosius. In fact, all that is radically new in the world of late antiquity seems to escape the repressive intentions of the legislator. The church and the barbarians – the latter assimilated because it was impossible to combat them adequately – are decisive factors in political and social relations. At Rome during the papal election of 366 there were more than a hundred deaths.[138] At Constantinople between the fourth and the fifth century the arbiters of the

---

[134] Patlagean, *Pauvreté*.   [135] Brown, *Body and Society* 282–4.
[136] *C.Th.* VI.7.1; 9.1; 11.1; 14.1; 22.4.   [137] *FIRA* I, n. 64; Chastagnol (1978) 75–88.
[138] Amm. Marc. XXVII.3.11–13.

political struggle are the barbarians in the army and the bishops.[139] The question whether in the late empire there was a lesser or greater degree of social mobility must therefore be answered with circumspection. The channels of social ascent are various and one can hence understand the irritation of traditionalists like Libanius who, by emphasizing some cases, seem to exaggerate the frequency of the phenomenon. In the social relations of late antiquity, gradations and distinctions multiply at the bottom of the social scale as at the top: the classification of the various types of *coloni* in the codices corresponds to the various levels to which their status was reduced, turning the ancient, free peasant almost into a slave. The cleavage within society between those who are guaranteed a position of power and the great mass of those who are excluded, the *tenuiores* (where the idea of legal weakness prevails over that of economic poverty), becomes ever more dramatic. Inequality is the foundation of civil life. The relations between individuals are conditioned by their status. Gregory of Nazianzus asks himself in a letter why Helladius of Caesarea was hostile towards him. Even if Helladius did not take account of his (Gregory's) priestly dignity, he would have lacked any justification for insulting him, since he was not superior in respect of either birth or rank.[140] The praise of inequality – that it issues from the design of Providence – which Gregory the Great would produce in a famous missive of 595, arguing that the community could not exist in any way if the global order of inequality did not preserve it,[141] is only the recognition and sanction by the church of the end result of a long process.

---

[139] Liebeschuetz, *Barbarians and Bishops*.
[140] Greg. Naz. *Ep.* 249 (=Greg. Nyss. *Ep.* 1); Kopeck (1973).   [141] *Ep.* 54.

CHAPTER 12

THE CITIES

BRYAN WARD-PERKINS

I. WHAT IS A *CIVITAS* AND WHAT IS A CITY?

Large settlements are difficult to define and describe in a few words.[1]
Working in the English language, we use two distinct but interlocking
words, 'town' and 'city', to denote them, and we tend to seek definition in
terms of the very vague criterion of relative size (towns are larger than villages, and cities are larger than towns), but at the same time we maintain in
our usage confusing and contradictory terminology denoting administrative status. Cambridge, for instance, is the 'county town' of Cambridge-
shire, but the much smaller settlement of Ely is the local 'cathedral city'. In
scholarly prose some of us even attempt to introduce criteria of economic
function ('towns' should be involved in 'non-rural' activities). Our definitions of 'town' and 'city' overlap, and our definitions of 'town' shade off at
the lower end into the category 'large village', without any hard and fast
dividing lines being possible.

The Romans, however, had an immediate and precise understanding of
the term *civitas*.[2] The empire was made up of a patchwork of hundreds of
civitates (or *poleis* in Greek): territories each ruled from a local capital-town
by an aristocratic council (the *curia* or *boulē*). For various geographical and
historical reasons, the size of these *civitas*-territories varied greatly from
region to region – in Gaul, for instance, they were tiny in the south-east and
very large in the north.[3] The nature and size of the capitals of the *civitates*
also varied greatly. Some, particularly in the east, were famous and ancient
centres, already equipped before the Roman conquest with a long history
and splendid buildings (like Athens, Antioch and Pergamum). Others were
Roman settlements, like the towns in the Po plain or those of Roman

---

[1] I would like to thank the people who have read and commented on a first draft of this chapter,
saving me from errors and suggesting new directions and changes of emphasis. Averil Cameron, Peter
Heather, Wolf Liebeschuetz and Simon Loseby all provided particularly helpful advice. Within a broad
thematic chapter of this kind I have allowed myself on occasion to step outside the chronological
boundaries of the volume (337–425). This is particularly the case in the section on the Christianization
of the city, where the events of Constantine's reign form the necessary beginning.
[2] When I have used an English term for this I have used 'city' or 'city and city territory'.
[3] A useful distribution map of most of the cities of the empire appears as Map v in Jones, *LRE*.

371

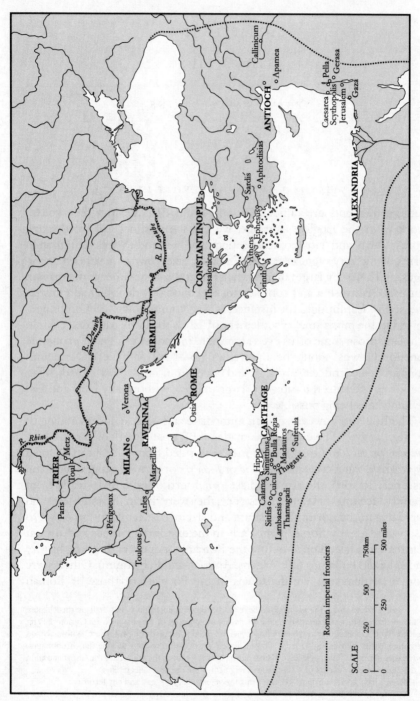

Fig. 1. The principal cities discussed in chapter 12

Britain. In size they varied between cities like Antioch, Alexandria and Carthage, covering areas substantially over 100 hectares and with populations that may have been of well over 100,000, to tiny centres with populations perhaps even as low as a hundredth of that size (see Fig. 2).[4] Small cities were particularly common in agriculturally poor areas, such as Apennine Italy, or in areas where there was a dense network of cities each with a very small *civitas*-territory, as in much of North Africa. However, all these cities, great and small, were readily identifiable as *civitates* through their role as the capitals of administrative units each with a *curia* or *boulē*. The only confusion present in Roman texts is whether the terms *civitas* and *polis* are being used to refer to the administrative capital alone or to the city and its surrounding dependent territory.

Occasionally, late antique commentators did remark on an anomaly caused by the definition of a *civitas*-city using administrative criteria alone, so as to exclude other settlements which in size and splendour looked like *civitates*, and relegate them instead to some humble category, such as *vicus* or *kōmē* (a village), or *locus* or *chōrion* (a 'place'). For instance, there is a famous passage in Gregory of Tours' *Histories* (III.19), composed at the end of the sixth century, in which he expresses surprise that a settlement as impressive as Dijon is a mere *castrum* and not a *civitas*.

But, in general, contemporaries were used to the distinction between *civitates* (however small) and other settlements (however large). They were indeed happy to play with the occasional ironies that this created, as when Theodosius threatened to degrade the great but rebellious *polis* of Antioch to the status of a mere *kōmē* after the Riot of the Statues in 387, or as when Justinian turned the tiny agricultural *chōrion* of Caputvada in Africa into a *polis* to celebrate the fact that his army had landed there during the Vandal campaign.[5] At Caputvada, by imperial decree alone, and by the institution of a *boulē* and some public buildings, rather than through any economic logic, a tiny *chōrion* had become a *polis*.

II. THE DECLINE OF THE *CURIAE* AND THE 'END OF THE CLASSICAL CITY'

The fourth and early fifth centuries did not see any major change in the administrative role of the *civitates*.[6] Rather, they remained the basic local units of administration, except in a very few massively disrupted regions

---

[4] Some literary evidence suggests an Antiochene population of well over 100,000. see Downey (1958). However, a recent reassessment of the archaeological and comparative evidence for Carthage suggests a maximum population of 70,000–100,000: Hurst (1993).

[5] For Antioch, Ruggini (1986) 271–5; for Caputvada, Procop. *Aed.* VI.6.8–16.

[6] For this entire section I have been heavily dependent on the excellent surveys in Jones, *LRE* 712–66 and Liebeschuetz (1992). See also Liebeschuetz in *CAH* XIV, ch. 8.

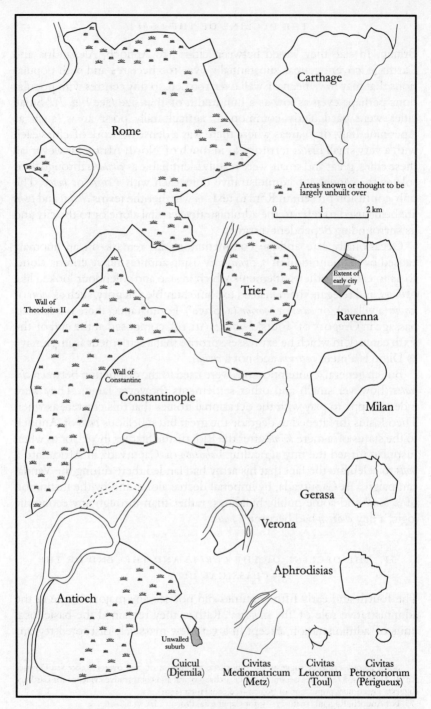

Rome

Carthage

Areas known or thought to be
largely unbuilt over

0   1   2 km

Trier

Extent of
early city

Ravenna

Wall of
Theodosius II

Wall of
Constantine

Constantinople

Milan

Gerasa

Verona

Aphrodisias

Antioch

Unwalled
suburb

Cuicul
(Djemila)

Civitas
Mediomatricum
(Metz)

Civitas
Leucorum
(Toul)

Civitas
Petrocoriorum
(Périgueux)

Fig. 2. The comparative size of fourteen walled towns and cities in the Roman empire,
c. A.D. 350–450

like Britain, where government in the fifth century clearly devolved on to a non-urban tribal basis. In most of the empire or former empire the essential elements of administration (that is, the raising of armies and tax, and the maintenance of internal order) remained based on a network of cities with their dependent territories, right into the sixth century and even beyond.

The administrative role of the city was even enhanced in the fourth century by the increasing demands of imperial taxation. However, for the very same reason, the political position and status of the local aristocrats who ran the cities and who constituted the *curiae* (the *curiales* or decurions) was considerably eroded. In particular, the pre-eminent local position of the *curiales* was threatened in two different ways by a growth in central government.

Firstly, after the third century, the central imperial service took from the *civitates* a far greater proportion of local wealth than it had done under the early empire. This redirection of funds came about in part through the direct confiscation of much civic revenue which was taken from the *curiae* for the benefit of the imperial service. For instance, in the early fourth century all civic revenue and civic lands were confiscated by the emperors, though later, under Julian and under Valentinian and Valens, some restitution was made.[7] On top of direct confiscation, the emperors also removed a higher proportion of local weath by their demands for a greatly increased land-tax (raised in order to fund the enlarged army).

Secondly, and partly in order to facilitate the smooth gathering of imperial taxes and dues, the emperors of the third and early fourth centuries set up over the network of *civitates* a considerably enlarged and enhanced network of imperial power. Many more (smaller) provinces were created, and their imperially appointed governors exercised much stricter control over their constituent *civitates* and *curiae* than had provincial governors under the early empire. Furthermore, above these provinces and their governors was set a superstructure in which provinces were grouped into dioceses (under *vicarii*), and dioceses grouped into prefectures (under praetorian prefects). This new power structure, of imperial provinces, dioceses and prefectures, was where authority really lay in the fourth century and where it was perceived to lie by contemporaries.[8]

Like all ancient government, the late imperial system looks tighter and more efficient on paper than it was in practice. Despite the changes, there was, almost certainly, still considerable room for local manoeuvre, and for the use and misuse of local curial power. Our clearest and most vivid picture of a direct clash between declining local aristocratic power and the

[7] Jones *LRE* 732; Heather (1994) 23–4, with further references.
[8] For fourth-century debates on the nature of imperial power, see Dagron, 'Thémistios' 83–146.

newly dominant position of imperial appointees derives from Antioch, where, thanks to the writings of Libanius in the later fourth century, we can follow this change in some detail.[9] However, Antioch was not typical of the cities of the empire. It was in the fourth century a major capital of the imperial civil and military services (the seat of a provincial governor, the seat of a *comes* over the diocese of Oriens, and the seat of a military *magister* responsible for the vital Persian frontier), and it was often the residence of the emperor himself. It was, therefore, a city where the presence of imperial power was strongly and directly felt. In lesser cities the local *curiae* were probably left much more to their own devices. Indeed, even within Antioch, local power was not entirely eclipsed by the rise of the imperial service. Libanius complains about the excessive influence within the Antiochene *boulē* of a small élite group which evidently still felt that the use and abuse of local power was well worth its while.[10]

Although the change can perhaps be exaggerated and certainly cannot be quantified, it is none the less certain that, in comparison with their predecessors of earlier centuries, fourth-century *curiales* had lost much of their power and status. Furthermore, their imperial duties were in one important and unpleasant way considerably extended – the *curiales* remained responsible for raising the imperial land-tax from each *civitas*, and the amounts demanded for this tax were much increased.[11] If *curiales* failed to meet imperial demands, consequences that were both brutal and humiliating could follow, such as public beating with lashes whose cutting power might even be enhanced with lead weights.[12] The late Roman state was not a benign institution: it needed money badly, and it was backed by the force of the army; the *curiales* had the misfortune to be essential to the raising of that money.

As a result, civic office became much less popular in late antiquity than it had been in the early empire, when local aristocrats had competed fiercely and spent heavily in order to hold local office and to gain a place on the *curia*. By contrast, in late antiquity many aristocrats attempted to get out of curial service, particularly through the holding of honorary or real offices within the imperial service – offices which both granted immunity from curial service and give real status and real influence within the altered power-structure of the late empire.

This flow of power and status, away from local office and towards imperial positions, is well-documented in a number of fourth-century sources. In particular, imperial laws sought to restrict immunity and to enforce curial office and duties on reluctant local landholders.[13] Others too noted the

[9] Liebeschuetz, *Antioch*.   [10] Liebeschuetz, *Antioch* 171–86.
[11] These changes are explored in Jones, *LRE* 737–57, and in Liebeschuetz, *Antioch* 167–219.
[12] C.Th. XII.1.126; Jones, *LRE* 750; Liebeschuetz, *Antioch* 166; Brown, *Power and Persuasion* 53–7.
[13] C.Th. XII.1, 'De decurionibus'. Of the 192 laws under this title, the large majority are concerned to prevent decurions evading their curial duties. For the growth of immunities, see Millar, 'Empire and city'.

change; in particular the Antiochene Libanius bewailed both the decline of the local *curia* and the rising power of the imperial servants:

I am no councillor: I have immunity because of my concern with rhetoric, but I can still be upset at the poverty of the councillors and the wealth amassed by those in the governors' service. Some of these, only recently sellers of meat, bread or vegetables, have grown great on the property of the councillors and enjoy just as much respect as they, so great is the wealth they possess. Others, just by the size of their houses, are a nuisance to their neighbours, for they do not allow them the enjoyment of full clear daylight.[14]

That the change was widespread and real, and not just a localized obsession of Libanius or of central government, is amply proved by the evidence of inscriptions. During the third and fourth centuries the earlier tradition, whereby local aristocrats had proudly recorded on inscriptions their local offices and their local munificence, virtually disappeared. It was replaced in the eastern provinces by a new style of verse inscriptions which generally record only imperial titles.[15]

At first sight this shift away from local autonomy and towards more central control might not seem particularly interesting or important: it could be depicted as merely an adjustment in the forms of local government. But, in the context of the ancient world, it was a vitally important change, with wide-ranging consequences for aristocratic culture and for the style of city life. The Romans had inherited from the Greek world a tradition of 'politics' and 'civilization' which was profoundly tied up with the urban life of the *polis* and the *civitas*, and even in out-of-the-way provinces like Britain the local landed aristocracy were encouraged to participate fully, through membership of the *curia*, in the life of their local *civitas*.

Such involvement created the distinctively 'classical city', be it Greek or early Roman, filled it with public monuments erected through local aristocratic munificence, and paid for expensive amenities and entertainments, in order to create a suitable backdrop to 'civilized' life and to gain for the donors the applause of their fellow citizens. These are the amenities and monuments – *fora*, theatres, temples, baths, paved streets, etc. – that particularly impress us when we visit an excavated Roman city, be it Wroxeter, Ostia or Ephesus. That such voluntary spending was universal in the early empire is shown by a vast number of inscriptions from all provinces, testifying to the outpouring of huge quantities of aristocratic money on entertainments and buildings designed to impress fellow citizens and to enhance the amenities and appearance of a local town. These inscriptions show beyond dispute that in the early empire sentiments of civic pride and

---

[14] Lib. *Or.* 11.54–5 (based on the Loeb translation).
[15] Robert, *Hellenica* IV; Roueché, *Aphrodisias* XXI.

the desire to gain local status were strong enough to reach where it counts, deep into aristocratic pockets.

However, in the late empire the decline of the real power and, in particular, the perceived status of the *curiales* had a marked impact on this particular type of aristocratic spending. Aristocrats began to see little gain in spending on traditional civic amenities, when real power and real status (whether at home or within the empire at large) now lay in imperial service.

Although the broad pattern of aristocratic disillusionment with civic life, coupled with a decline in aristocratic civic spending, was everywhere the same, the pace and scale of the change were very different in different parts of the empire. In Italy, and probably in most of the northern provinces, aristocratic munificence almost completely disappeared at an early date. In the first and second centuries Italian cities had been full of local aristocrats competing for local prestige and local office, and in the process providing their cities with a plethora of fine buildings and lavish entertainments. However, by the end of the fourth century this tradition had died in most of the peninsula. The only private patrons still paying for entertainments and still building and repairing civic monuments were members of the extremely wealthy and historically-minded senatorial aristocracy of Rome. They alone continued to finance shows and continued to pay for the occasional building in Rome itself and in the central and southern provinces where they held estates.[16]

In other parts of the empire the old traditions of spending persisted for longer. In some of the great cities of the east some private patronage of urban amenities can be documented throughout the fourth century and into the fifth. At Ephesus, for example, a rich aristocrat, Scholasticia, renewed a bath building at the cost of 'a great quantity of gold' and was rewarded with the traditional honour of a statue; her munificence cannot be dated precisely, but was certainly late antique, since the inscription that records it opens with the sign of the cross.[17] We lack inscriptions of this period from Syrian Antioch, but we learn from the written evidence of Libanius of a series of public buildings paid for by private individuals in the fourth century, and, from the evidence of John Chrysostom, of the great expense shouldered by aristocrats in the late fourth century in the provision of games and shows.[18] At least in cities of this importance, some private munificence clearly persisted, though it is interesting to note that the main patrons of Antioch whom Libanius recorded were now above all former imperial dignitaries.

The richest group of inscriptions from a city of the eastern provinces

---

[16] Ward-Perkins, *Public Building* 14–37.

[17] *Jahresheft des österreichischen archäologischen Institutes in Wien* 43 (1955), Beiblatt, cols. 22–6.

[18] The evidence from Libanius is collected and discussed by Petit, *Libanius* 319–20; John Chrysostom, *Sur la vaine gloire et l'éducation des enfants* (ed. A.-M. Malingrey, *SChrét.* 188), 80–2.

presently known comes from Aphrodisias in Caria. This shows some continuity of private munificence into late antiquity, with a very few private gifts to the city documented in the fourth century (alongside the more extensive activity of the provincial governor) and rather more from the later fifth and early sixth centuries. However, the evidence from Aphrodisias also allows us to put this late antique survival of munificence into some sort of comparative context. In comparison to the vast number of earlier imperial inscriptions and to the scale of earlier building and munificence, these late antique examples are very small beer.[19]

One region of the empire that has been studied in depth, with the particular problem of the survival or decay of older civic values in mind, is North Africa.[20] Here it is clear that, in contrast to Italy, a tradition of munificence persisted up to the Vandal invasion, even in towns of only local importance. For example, at Lambaesis a local man, holding the civic office of *curator rei publicae*, restored at his own expense in the period 379–83 both the *curia* building ('rightly called by our ancestors the temple of the curial order') and the aqueduct, and recorded his work in a long inscription dedicated to the 'Golden Times' of Gratian, Valentinian and Theodosius.[21] From all over the central provinces of Roman North Africa there is good epigraphic evidence of continued munificence of this kind. Much of it dates from the reign of Valentinian I, and this must reflect the successful impact of an imperial policy of 374, which returned some revenue to the cities in the hope of reviving something of the ancient traditions of civic life.

However, none of this tradition survived the Vandal invasion, and even in the most golden years of the fourth century the situation was not as it had been under the early empire, when local munificence had continuously added larger and more lavish buildings to the townscapes. Despite the considerable prosperity of late antique Africa, in the fourth century it is predominantly repairs to the secular monuments that are recorded, often to important buildings which, if we are to believe the rhetoric of the inscriptions, had already been allowed to fall into serious decay. At Lambaesis, for instance, before the repairs of 379–83, the aqueduct was not working at all and the *curia* building was 'collapsed, defaced and despised through age or rather through the unconcern of our elders'. Another sign of the times on this inscription is the naming of the imperial provincial governor in a position of greater honour than the local curial benefactor who had actually paid for the work. Even where private munificence persisted, it was now tightly controlled and encouraged by imperial officials.

The survival of civic pride and civic munificence seems to have been

[19] Roueché, *Aphrodisias* xix–xxvii.   [20] Lepelley, *Cités*.
[21] Lepelley, *Cités* ii.420–1; and Lepelley (1992) 58 (with English translation of the inscription).

closely connected with a sense of well-being and of confidence in the ancient institutions, which was easier for aristocrats to feel in some regions of the late empire than in others. Africa's enduring tradition of munificence in the fourth century must be connected firstly with the region's happy isolation from the troubles and horrors of the third century, and secondly with its exceptional prosperity in the third and fourth centuries, which we shall examine later in this chapter. With the Vandal conquest of 429–39, all trace of civic munificence in Africa disappears, just as all trace of senatorial patronage in the *civitates* of south–central Italy ends abruptly with the sack of Rome in 410 and Alaric's subsequent harrying of the south (the last dated inscription is of 408). In both regions the invasions did not wipe out overnight a rich landed aristocracy, but they certainly destroyed its will to spend on traditional civic munificence. In the later fifth century the only provinces to produce evidence of continued private munificence are those of the east Mediterranean, then enjoying a period of exceptional tranquillity and prosperity.

The gradual ending of aristocratic spending on local entertainments and monuments certainly had a remarkable effect on the cities of the empire, even though we cannot document the process of decline in any detail. The literary references to amenities (whether functioning or abandoned) are very scattered, and only recently and in a very few cases has archaeological excavation of public buildings, such as baths and theatres, been sufficiently meticulous to provide reliable dates of abandonment or of adaptation to new uses.

Presumably the pattern of abandonment and survival of amenities varied, like that of munificence, between different parts of the empire and between different cities within each region. Where private munificence persisted, traditional amenities might still be found in even small local towns. For example, in Africa Proconsularis in around 400 Augustine could still be outraged at the existence of a flourishing tradition of secular entertainment in the small town of Bulla Regia, though he also records that in neighbouring Hippo and Simitthus entertainments were no longer a regular feature of life.[22]

In cities where voluntary aristocratic spending had disappeared, the imperial government attempted to fill the gap by trying to enforce curial office and duties (which included some spending on civic amenities) on all born to curial families.[23] But there is so far little evidence to show whether these attempts at enforcement had much effect. Where the imperial government was undoubtedly much more successful in maintaining buildings and amenities was in those cities favoured as capitals by its own administrators, as we shall see in the next section of this chapter.

---

[22] Aug. *Sermo Denis* XVII.7–9 [=*Miscellanea Agostiniana* i, Rome 1930].   [23] See n. 13, p. 376 above.

In less favoured regions and cities, the decay of the classical townscape probably set in early, creating a gulf that had not existed in the earlier empire between privileged capitals and lesser cities. Already in 333 a governor of Campania took pride in the fact, as though it were already exceptional, that he paved streets 'with blocks cut from the mountains, not taken from ruined monuments'.[24]

Although the gradual decay of the civic monuments is an important change and one that strikes a profound chord in any visitor to a classical city, it is important to put it in perspective. This change did not necessarily damage the Roman city as a centre of population and as a centre of economic activity, nor even necessarily as a centre of aristocratic life and of aristocratic pride and competition for local status. What had changed was how that status and pride were expressed – no longer through civic office and the provision of civic amenities, but through the holding of imperial titles which carried with them none of the traditions of civic spending.

Aristocrats, in most provinces at least, certainly continued to live in cities. Archaeology even shows that they continued to build on a grand scale, which in part they must have done in order to gain status. But the buildings they now paid for were not the civic amenities of bygone days. In the fourth and fifth centuries they built, as ever, sumptuous private houses (of which late antique examples have been excavated all over the empire); and now, increasingly, they built churches which had the great advantage of providing opportunities for both conspicuous public expenditure and eternal private gain.[25]

Late Romans continued to see themselves not only as citizens of Rome, and hence of a single unified empire, but also very much as citizens of their own native *civitas*. Ausonius, writing in the later fourth century, opens his 'Order of Famous Cities' with Rome, but closes it with praise for his native Bordeaux. He ends the poem with an account of the complementary feelings he has for the city of his birth and for Rome, the traditional and emotional heart of empire (although in reality Ausonius' political career was lived out in the new frontier-capital of Trier):

Bordeaux is my homeland [*patria*]: but Rome stands over all homelands.
I love Bordeaux, and cherish Rome; I am citizen in one,
Consul in both; here my cradle, there my chair of office.

In the fourth and fifth century and into the sixth, Romans were able to add to traditional love of *patria* a new focus for local loyalty: their pride in their native cities' saints and churches.[26]

But the decline of the early imperial civic ideal did mean the slow death of the 'classical city' as a particular townscape and as a particular style of

---

[24] *CIL* x.1199=*ILS* 5510.   [25] Ward-Perkins, *Public Building* 65–84.
[26] See, for Gaul, Harries (1992); and, for the cult of the saints in general, Brown, *Cult of the Saints*.

urban life provided by local aristocratic munificence and enjoyed by all citizens. That this was a remarkable change, though one which was not necessarily inimical to all urban life, is nowhere better seen than in the history of the great open porticoed streets that were a prominent feature of many towns of the eastern Mediterranean. These great public spaces were never as clear and neat as we see them today, cleaned up by the passage of time, but were in antiquity filled with a clutter of temporary booths and stalls, which city councils, governors and emperors periodically attempted to tidy up. But, at some point between the fourth and eighth centuries, control over these public spaces gradually lapsed, allowing temporary booths and stalls to become permanent and solid shops and adjuncts to houses, and leaving only narrow alleyways between private buildings where once there had been twenty-metre-wide concourses flanked by publicly protected and maintained marble colonnades (Fig. 3). Where this happened, the town as a centre of population and economic activity was clearly thriving, but equally clearly the classical city as a townscape and way of life was being slowly allowed to die.[27]

III. THE NEW STRUCTURES OF POWER AND LOYALTY

The decline of the *curiae* is rightly seen as a major change in city life. It is also generally depicted in an entirely negative light, as the end of a tradition of local oligarchic rule which reached back through the centuries to the Greek city-states. This perspective is understandable, given the vehemence with which some contemporaries decried the change and given our standpoint in the modern liberal tradition with its deep respect for Greek political culture. It would indeed be difficult to be enthusiastic about the decline of classical city culture, and about the erosion of local government by a harsh and centralizing empire.

However, it is important to realize that some cities gained under the new system and that many individuals also did well, or at least adjusted satisfactorily to the new dispensation. Libanius of Antioch is the most vociferous critic of the decline of the *curiales* in the fourth century, and yet his own actions provide some of the best examples of an influential figure playing the new system to full advantage. Although bewailing the decline of the Antiochene *curia*, Libanius was happy to write letters on behalf of friends trying to gain themselves honorary or real posts within the

[27] The 'privatization' of the colonnaded streets is a fascinating and much studied phenomenon. However, the archaeological evidence has seldom been good enough to provide clear dates for the process, from which we could reconstruct a detailed chronology and explore diversity between different regions, different types of town and, indeed, between the fate of different streets within a single city. On the history of the colonnaded street in late antiquity: Sauvaget (1949); Claude (1969) 44–59; Liebeschuetz, *Antioch* 55–6; Patlagean, *Pauvreté* 59–61; Kennedy (1985).

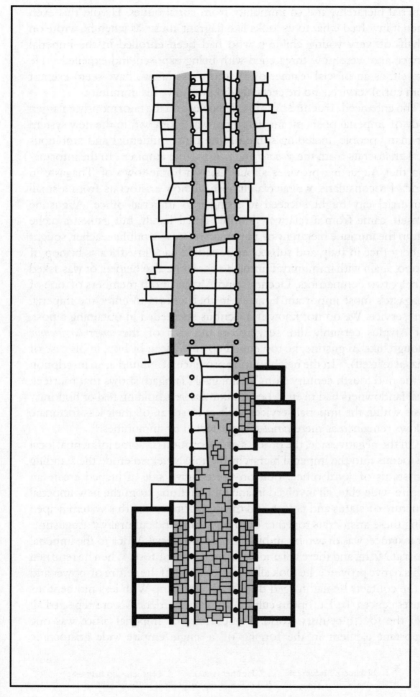

Fig. 3: From colonnaded street to souk: Sauvaget's famous hypothesis of how the transformation came about. The figure has to be read chronologically from left (the late antique street) to right (the fully developed souk)

imperial hierarchy, and so immunity from curial duties. He did this even when it involved what to us looks like flagrant abuse, as when he wrote on behalf of very young children who had been enrolled in the imperial service and were now threatened with being exposed and expelled.[28] He himself, as an official teacher of rhetoric, was (as we have seen) exempt from curial service, and he certainly did not waive his immunity.

The enhanced structure of imperial power and the enormously enlarged body of imperial posts meant that there was room within the new system for many people, including some of the most influential and ambitious local aristocrats from the *civitates* and *poleis* of the empire.[29] In the informa-tion that Augustine provides about his own home-town of Thagaste in Africa Proconsularis, we have a glimpse of how aristocrats from a small provincial city might succeed in rising into imperial office. Augustine himself came from a relatively humble curial family, but gained a niche within the immune hierarchy of imperial service as a public teacher, sought higher office in Italy, and subsequently settled back in Africa as bishop of Hippo, again with immunity. During his career he also helped, or was asked to help, two compatriots, Licentius and Alypius, both members of one of Thagaste's most important families, in their efforts to enter the imperial civil service. We do not know if Licentius succeeded in obtaining a post, but Alypius certainly did, serving on the staff of the *comes largitionum* (though, like Augustine, he too ended up an African bishop, in his case of Thagaste itself).[30] In the neighbouring province of Numidia, an inscription of the mid fourth century from Thamugadi (Timgad) shows that fourteen local landowners had risen to be immune *honorati*, holding real or honorary posts within the imperial service, while at least 126 of their less fortunate fellows remained as mere *curiales*, unprotected by immunities.[31]

On the negative side, the process of absorption of some influential local aristocrats into the imperial hierarchy obviously helped erode the standing and status of local office. But, on the positive side, it helped create an empire-wide élite, all involved in and all benefiting from the new imperial structure of status and power, and their participation in this system helped bring these aristocrats together both physically and culturally.[32] Augustine, for instance, was drawn by ambition from provincial Africa to the imperial court at Milan, and there fell under the spell of Ambrose. When he returned to his native province, he took all his experiences at the centre of power and all the contacts he had forged there back with him. With less momentous consequences for European culture, similar experiences were repeated all over the fourth-century world. The exercise of imperial office was one important element in the forging of a single empire-wide aristocratic

[28] Liebeschuetz, *Antioch* 178.   [29] Heather (1994).   [30] Lepelley, *Cités* ii.177–82.
[31] Lepelley, *Cités* ii.459–70.   [32] I owe this important point to Peter Heather.

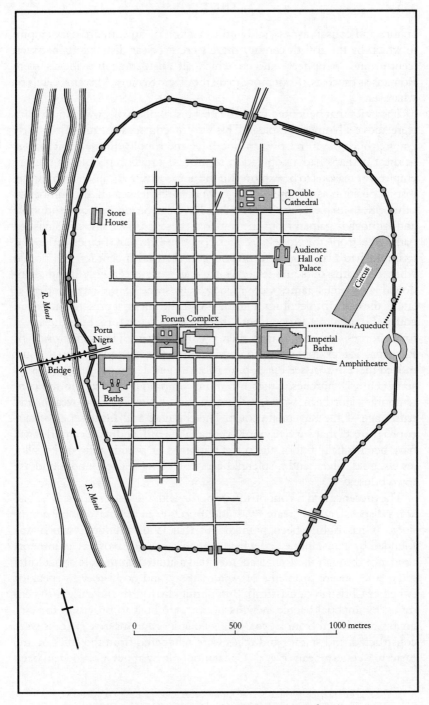

Store
House

Double
Cathedral

Audience
Hall of
Palace

Circus

R. Mosel

Forum Complex

Aqueduct

Porta
Nigra

Imperial
Baths

Bridge

Amphitheatre

Baths

R. Mosel

0   500   1000 metres

Fig. 4. Late antique Trier (based on Wightman (1970), fig. 12)

culture and consciousness, and in the creation of an extraordinary empire in which by the fourth century there were no clear distinctions between 'centre' and 'periphery' and in which all aristocratic provincials were Romans as much as, if not more than, they were Syrians, Africans, Gauls or whatever.

The cities that benefited from the new distribution of power and wealth were above all imperial capitals. This was, of course, also true of the early empire, but only in relation to one huge metropolis, Rome, which at its greatest perhaps had a population of around a million people. In the late empire, for reasons to be explored in the next section of this chapter, Rome lost its position as the pre-eminent imperial residence, while a number of other cities – in particular Trier, Milan, Ravenna, Sirmium, Constantinople and Antioch – gained from the imperial presence. The emperor lavished patronage from the imperial coffers on these favoured cities. Trier, for example, had two huge bath buildings in the fourth century, at a period when the baths of some lesser Gallic towns were certainly being abandoned, and circus-games were requested by some of the city's leaders as late as the early fifth century (Fig. 4).[33] Also, the imperial presence attracted court officials and aristocrats into these cities, who, in turn, built their own town houses and indulged in their own patronage. The minor *civitas* of Ravenna, for example, tripled in size after the western imperial court moved there in 402 (see Fig. 2, p. 374 above), and a host of fifth- and early-sixth-century churches, larger and more sumptuous than any in the contemporary northern world, still testify to the exceptional wealth and patronage of the Ravennate court. The churches and a fine series of sarcophagi are all that survive, but Ravenna in the fifth and sixth centuries will have been equally full of the other trappings of wealth and power: silks, jewels, gold, silver, and a splendid array of public palaces and grandiose town houses.[34]

The presence and favour of the emperor, with the huge resources he had at his disposal, could create a vast metropolis even in unfavourable conditions. It has rightly been pointed out that Constantinople, which was founded by Constantine and which gradually gained favour as an imperial residence through the fourth century, had a limited immediate agricultural hinterland, severe problems of water-supply, and no history to speak of (whether Christian or classical). But, during the fourth and early fifth centuries, by imperial decree, new harbours were built to provision the city, grain was shipped from Egypt, a long aqueduct and massive cisterns were constructed, and statues and relics were plundered from the cities of the eastern Mediterranean (Fig. 5). Constantinople by about A.D. 400 had been

---

[33] For Trier, see Wightman, *Trier*; for the circus games, Salv. *De Gub. Dei* VI.85.
[34] For Ravenna, see Deichmann (1958).

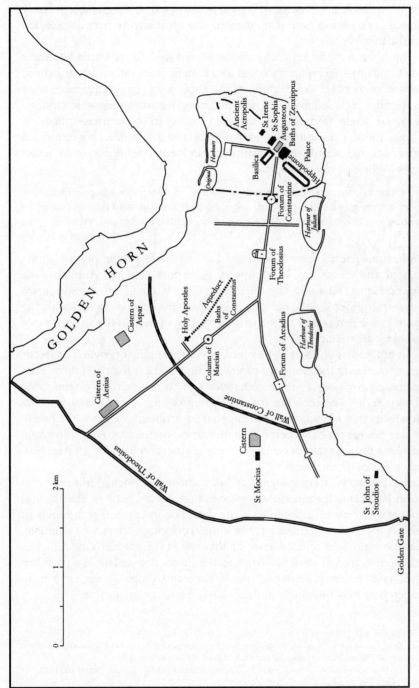

Fig. 5. Constantinople in the later fifth century (based on Mango (1985), plans I and II)

GOLDEN HORN

Ancient Acropolis
St Irene
St Sophia
Augusteon
Baths of Zeuxippus
Basilica
Hippodrome
Palace
Original Harbour
Forum of Constantine
Harbour of Julian
Forum of Theodosius
Harbour of Theodosius
Holy Apostles
Aqueduct of Constantius
Baths of Constantius
Cistern of Aspar
Column of Marcian
Cistern of Aetius
Forum of Arcadius
Wall of Constantine
Cistern
St Mocius
Wall of Theodosius
St John of Stoudios
Golden Gate

2 km
0   1   2

given a suitable appearance of venerable antiquity and a suitable array of Christian protectors, and had emerged as a great city of perhaps 400,000 inhabitants.[35]

But it was not just imperial capitals that did well. Cities within but lower down the imperial hierarchy could also benefit from the greatly enhanced flow of power and wealth through the imperial system, at the expense of those cities excluded from it. The same imperial government which robbed cities of their statues and relics in order to concentrate them in Constantinople issued laws to curb an abuse whereby governors of provinces transferred embellishments and entertainments from lesser cities to their provincial capitals:

We forbid any further presumptuous behaviour of governors who, to the ruin of lesser towns, pretend that they are adorning their metropolitan or finest cities, by seeking to transfer, from the one to the other, statues, marble and columns.

(C.Th. xv.1.14 of A.D. 365)

We have also heard the complaints of Libanius at the presumptuous behaviour of the servants of the imperial governors based in Antioch. One problem that Libanius identified was their building of massive town houses: in other words, the wealth of these imperial servants was being spent inside Antioch to the benefit of the city, even if to the annoyance of the older aristocracy.

In the greater cities of the empire, governors in their provincial capitals and emperors in their imperial capitals maintained a regular and sometimes splendid provision of those amenities that were gradually disappearing elsewhere. For example, in the east, the financing of games and shows slowly became a function of the imperial government, so that in the fourth century shows probably persisted in the capitals of each province, and even as late as the sixth and seventh centuries persisted in the very greatest provincial cities of the empire.[36]

Equally, some archaeological and documentary evidence from the east confirms that at least in some great cities substantial parts of the classical townscape were maintained to a late date. For instance, the chronicle of Joshua the Stylite at Edessa records the work of governors to maintain, decorate and light the porticoes of that city in the years around A.D. 500, and archaeological evidence from Sardis shows that as late as 616 (when they were violently destroyed) the portico and shops of the city's main street were fully functional in their classical monumental form.[37]

[35] Mango (1985).
[36] Rouché (1993) 5–11, 25–30, 76–9, 143–56. At Ephesus two inscriptions of the factions date from the reign of Phocas (602–10) and one from the reign of Heraclius (610–41).
[37] Ps. Joshua the Stylite, *Chronicle* (trans. W. Wright, Cambridge 1882), chs. xxix, xxxii and xliii. For Sardis, Crawford (1990).

IV. MILITARY NEEDS

The early empire was a period unparalleled in the history of European towns until the modern age, in that the cities of the interior of the Roman world were often unwalled, because it was felt that the army at the frontiers provided sufficient security to defend them. The crisis of the third century, which saw almost all the provinces of the empire overrun, or at least severely threatened, dramatically altered this perception and led to the repair of decayed walled circuits or to the building of new defences.[38] Only a few exceptionally secure areas, in particular central North Africa, were spared serious threat in the third century and hence did not acquire town walls until later.

However, although city walls are amongst the most impressive and long-lasting physical remains of late antiquity, it would be a mistake to exaggerate their influence on fourth-century urban life. Peace, as in the early empire shaken only by occasional civil war, was restored to most provinces by the emperors of the late third and early fourth centuries. In the fourth century, urban defences were only essential to security in the frontier zones, as they had been in the early empire. In other regions, though this is impossible to prove, recently-built circuits may even have been allowed to fall again into disrepair, and certainly they did not necessarily define the limits of settlement. In the east many areas were, after the third century, spared invasion until as late as the sixth and seventh centuries, when new walls were constructed, presumably to replace those allowed to fall into decay during the preceding peaceful centuries of late antiquity.[39] Even in the west it was only the extreme crisis of the early fifth century that brought the continuous insecure conditions in which the town walls became the constant and essential feature of urban life that they remained in most of Europe until high explosives finally rendered them obsolete in the nineteenth century.

The comparative security of the whole Roman world up to the end of the fourth century and of the east throughout late antiquity was only achieved by the presence of a very large army. This was based permanently along the most threatened frontiers, which ran from Mesopotamia up through Armenia to the Black Sea, and then along the Danube to its headwaters, and from there along the Rhine to the North Sea. The threat to these frontiers and the resulting presence there of the army had a decisive effect on the geography of power in the late empire, and consequently on the siting of large imperial capitals.

Emperors had to remain near the frontiers, partly because of the threat

[38] There is no overall survey of late Roman defences. Johnson (1983) covers the northern provinces; Lewin (1991) 9–98 (unillustrated) surveys the evidence for the eastern ones.
[39] As at Ephesus: Foss (1979) 103–15.

posed by the enemy without, but mainly for fear of a potential enemy within: they could not afford to leave their own armies in case of attempted military usurpation. Consequently, emperors of the fourth and early fifth century always resided within reach of the frontier armies. They never, or almost never, visited the greater part of their empire. Britain, Gaul west of Paris and Arles, the whole of Spain, the whole of Africa and Egypt, the southern provinces of the Near East, western Asia Minor, and southern Greece all lay outside the broad frontier zone where the emperors resided. As a result, most of the empire, and some of the empire's wealthiest, largest and most historic cities (such as Carthage, Alexandria, Ephesus and Corinth) never saw the emperor at all and did not regularly receive imperial largesse.

Even Rome itself, a popular imperial residence until Maxentius' death in 312, received only very rare imperial visits.[40] For obvious reasons, however, Rome never lost its position as the ideological heart of the empire, and continued to enjoy into the fifth century and beyond a degree of imperial patronage quite out of keeping with its real political importance. In particular, the massive food-grants of earlier centuries were maintained, and emperors still graced the city with new monuments. Constantine built new baths, Constantius II brought Egypt's largest obelisk to the Circus Maximus, Valentinian, Theodosius and Arcadius built the vast new basilica of S. Paolo, and Honorius very substantially enlarged the walls and gates of the city.[41]

Rome remained prominent in the political ideology and sentiment of the late empire, but, because emperors now had to live within easy access of the frontiers, it was within the broad frontier belt that they chose to locate their capitals and lavish their greatest largesse. These capitals were either close to a particular frontier, such as Trier for the Rhine, Sirmium for the Danube, and Antioch for the Persian frontier in Mesopotamia, or were strategically placed to provide ready, if more distant, access to more than one frontier at a time. Milan, a favoured residence in the west, was admirably sited for access to the armies of either the Rhine or the upper Danube, and Constantinople, on the Bosphorus crossing from Europe into Asia, was well-placed for access to either the lower Danube or the Persian frontier to the east.

The presence of the emperor, as we have seen, attracted an immense amount of money and a large number of followers to these favoured cities, which therefore flourished within the frontier zone. At one level the privileging of frontier cities is a sign of the increased insecurity of the fourth century; because of the barbarians and Persians, and because of the army,

---

[40] Such as the visit by Constantius II in 357, described by Ammianus Marcellinus (XVI.10.13–17); see ch. 5, pp. 142–3 above.   [41] Ward-Perkins, *Public Building*, ch. 2.

the emperors now had to live at Trier or Antioch rather than Rome, and what had once been peripheral zones had become the new centres of empire. But the presence of the emperors in these towns is also a sign of the very security of those frontiers and of imperial self-confidence in the face of the barbarians. Emperors in the fourth century could happily live right up on the frontiers, in towns like Trier and Sirmium, chosen for convenience rather than for their natural defensive strengths.

It was only in the early years of the fifth century in the west and in the Balkans, and much later in the east, that this situation changed and emperors were forced to scuttle back from the frontiers to cities which were safer and which were often chosen primarily because of their defensive strength. In 402, in the face of Alaric's invasion of the Po plain, the western emperor abandoned Milan (for good, as it turned out), and holed up in the insalubrious but secure marshland town of Ravenna; and increasingly during the fifth, sixth and seventh centuries Constantinople became the established imperial residence of the east, at least in part because it was so easily provisioned and defended.

The renewed barbarian threat of the years around 400 affected not only the fourth-century frontier capitals, but also Roman cities deep in the interior of the empire: in 376 the Goths crossed the Danube into the northern Balkans, in 378 they defeated and killed the emperor Valens outside Adrianople, and in 402 they crossed the Alps into Italy; the Vandals and others crossed the Rhine into Gaul in 406, reaching Spain in 409; and the Vandals went on to cross the Straits of Gibraltar into North Africa in 429. These fresh threats led to a renewed spate of defensive building, often exceeding in scale even the considerable efforts of the third century. The walls of Rome were strengthened in the early years of the fifth century in the face of the Gothic threat, and vast new towers were added to defend the gates; at Constantinople in 413, by which time it had become clear that full security was unlikely to return to the Balkan provinces, a huge new double land-wall was begun to replace the earlier walls of Constantine; and Carthage, which had so far remained unwalled, was provided, in the face of the Vandal threat, with an imposing circuit over nine kilometres long and enclosing an area of some 320 hectares.[42]

The walls at Rome and Carthage failed to keep the barbarians out: Rome was sacked by the Goths in 410 and by the Vandals in 455, and Carthage fell to the Vandals in 439, with disastrous results for the western empire, since this meant the loss of its richest province and its only secure one. But the walls of Constantinople were perhaps the most successful and influential town walls ever built – they allowed the city and its emperors to survive

---

[42] For Rome, Richmond (1930); for Constantinople, Krischen *et al.* (1938–43); for Carthage, Lepelley, *Cités* II.17, and Hurst (1993).

and thrive for more than a millennium, against all strategic logic, on the edge of the extremely unstable and dangerous world of the post-Roman Balkans.

V. THE IMPACT OF CHRISTIANITY

After Christianity became the usual religion of the emperors from 312 onwards, it spread more rapidly than before through the cities of the empire, and a gradual process began whereby the traditional pagan cults were starved of patronage by the civic and imperial authorities. Throughout the empire this change affected urban populations first, long before the new religion made any significant inroads into the countryside. The conversion of the towns was indeed the one essential step needed for the eventual spread of Christianity throughout society, since the conversion of the countryside was to be achieved partly through the influence of landowners and their building of estate-churches; most of these landowners probably acquired their new religion through exposure to it during sojourns in the cities.

The demise of paganism and the spread of Christianity were by no means uniform processes, and even neighbouring *civitates* might have very different religious histories in the fourth century. For example, in Palestine the city of Gaza remained a pagan stronghold, and its great temple of Marnas was only closed and destroyed by violence in 402; but the neighbouring settlement of Maiuma was already sufficiently Christian at the beginning of the century for Constantine to remove it from the authority of Gaza and give it independent *civitas* status.[43] Similarly, we learn from the writings of Augustine that the provincial town of Bulla Regia in Africa Proconsularis was Christian by around 400; whereas in nearby Calama, perhaps as late as 407, the pagans burned down the church and killed a priest.[44]

In Antioch a strong pagan element existed amongst its cultured aristocracy until at least the end of the fourth century, exemplified by the traditionalist Libanius. But already by 362, when the pagan emperor Julian came to Antioch in the hope of finding a flourishing pagan city, much of the population was Christian (particularly amongst the broad body of the citizens, the *dēmos*) and the traditional cults had apparently lost most of their appeal. In a well-known passage, that probably contains a substantial dose of gloomy hyperbole, Julian complained to the Antiochenes of how, on a feast of Apollo, he hastened to the god's temple at Daphne:

[43] Jones, *LRE* 91. The pagan Julian, of course, reversed this ruling: see p. 542 below.
[44] Bulla Regia: Lepelley, *Cités* I.377–8 and II.87. Calama: *ibid.*, II.97–101.

Thinking that at Daphne, if anywhere, I should enjoy the sight of your wealth and public spirit . . . I imagined in my own mind the sort of procession it would be . . . beasts for sacrifice, libations, choruses in honour of the god, incense, and the youths of your city there surrounding the shrine, their souls adorned with all holiness and themselves attired in white and splendid raiment. But when I entered the shrine I found there neither incense, nor a cake, nor a single beast for sacrifice . . . When I began to enquire what sacrifice the city intended to offer to celebrate the annual festival of the god, the priest answered, 'I have brought with me from my home a goose as an offering to the god, but the city this time has made no preparations.'[45]

It might, however, be a mistake to place too much historical weight on the scrawny shoulders of this unfortunate goose. The incident must indeed reflect a decline of the traditional public festivals – but perhaps as much through the decline of curial status and curial spending, which we have investigated above, as through the death of pagan sentiment. To survive in all their splendour, the great civic festivals and sacrifices needed both belief in the pagan gods and funding for the traditional ceremonies of the *polis*. At Antioch and elsewhere, a more 'private' paganism may have been stronger; Ammianus recounts how Julian, as he entered the city for the first time on 18 July 362, was greeted by the ill-omened wailing of those marking the feast of the death of Adonis.[46]

In Antioch, as in many other cities of the empire (particularly in the east), it was not the case for most of the fourth century that there were but two religions on offer. The Christians were already deeply divided between various groups, each claiming to follow the legitimate bishop, and there was also a strong Jewish element in the city, which John Chrysostom felt was threatening enough to the Christian position to merit his golden-mouthed attention.[47]

For much of the time, different religious groups coexisted in peace within the cities, a peace which was in most periods carefully protected by the state, and which was fostered by the needs of communities divided by religion but united by many social and economic bonds.[48] John Chrysostom's anxiety about the Jews in Antioch, for instance, was not caused by the threat of Jewish–Christian antagonism (which indeed he hoped to stir up), but by the close religious ties between the two communities, which Chrysostom felt to be threatening the Christians' distinctive identity. Respectful coexistence may even on occasion have led to some curious syncretistic beliefs. The emperor Julian was shown round the sights of ancient Troy by a certain Pegasius who was the Christian bishop and who none the less supported the worship of the heroes Achilles and

[45] Jul. *Misop.* 362a–b (based on the Loeb translation). And *Misop.* 357d for the religion of Antioch's *dēmos.*   [46] Amm. Marc. XXII.9.15.   [47] Wilken, *John Chrysostom and the Jews.*
[48] See pp. 632–64 below.

Hector as entirely natural, 'just as we worship the martyrs' (Jul. *Ep.* 19). This position did not entirely satisfy Julian and it certainly would not have satisfied a Chrysostom, but it was evidently a comfortable one for Pegasius.

Archaeological evidence can also point to harmonious coexistence between different religious groups. At Sardis in Lydia, for example, a substantial synagogue was built in the fourth century within one of the city's great monumental complexes, the baths and gymnasium, presumably with curial support. The building is eighty-five metres long (including its forecourt) and is as elaborate and impressive as any contemporary Christian church. As far as we can tell from the archaeological evidence, this synagogue stood undisturbed throughout late antiquity, and was only destroyed by external enemies in the seventh century.[49]

However, it is also true that religious difference could and did lead to violence, particularly when local extremists sensed that the governor or the emperor would turn a blind eye to acts against public order carried out in the name of a greater religious good. On the accession of the pagan Julian in 361, the pagans of Alexandria, trusting (rightly) that the new emperor would secretly applaud their crime, lynched their overbearing Christian bishop George. In the 380s and 390s, the boot was on the other foot, and, as local Christians realized they could increasingly rely on the tacit, and sometimes even the active, support of Christian governors and the Christian emperor, there was a spate of violence against pagan temples in the eastern provinces, culminating in the destruction of the temple of Serapis in Alexandria in about 391 and of the temple of Marnas in Gaza in 402.[50]

The Jews and their synagogues could also suffer in this climate. In 386, Ambrose in Milan prevented the emperor Theodosius from enforcing an order on the bishop of Callinicum in Mesopotamia, commanding him to rebuild at his church's expense a synagogue burnt down by the local Christians. Ambrose successfully argued that, whatever the requirements of secular law and order, the building of a new Jewish shrine with Christian money was, in the eyes of God, an absolute incontrovertible wrong.[51]

Christians did not deploy their violence exclusively to browbeat those of other religions; they were quite capable of fighting bloody civil wars amongst themselves. Ammianus Marcellinus tells of a battle for the bishopric of Rome between rival candidates, which in a single day left 137 dead in one church (xxvii.3.11–13).

But while the religious debates of the fourth century were sometimes conducted on the streets, they took place for the most part in peoples' minds. The different fortunes of the various religions and sects were slowly reflected in the changing religious topography of the empire's cities.

[49] Seager and Kraabel (1983).   [50] Fowden (1978).   [51] Ambr. *Ep.* 40–1.

Towards the end of our period, in all cities of the empire, the temples were required by law to be closed, and during the fourth and early fifth centuries many were demolished or adapted to new purposes; but, unsurprisingly, the stages whereby this change was achieved varied from region to region and from city to city, according to circumstance.

As we have seen, in the case of some of the great temples of the east the destruction was both sudden and violent. However, in the western provinces they seem rather to have been allowed to rot away, to be reused for other purposes or to be despoiled for their building materials only when they had already ceased functioning.[52] Augustine, writing in the 390s to the decurions of Madauros in Africa Proconsularis, suggests that, although cult-statues were deliberately destroyed, the temples themselves were much more gradually transformed or allowed to decay: 'You have, of course, seen how some temples of the idols have collapsed for lack of repair, some are ruinous, some closed, and some adapted for other uses. The idols them-selves have either been broken up, or burnt, or locked away, or otherwise destroyed.'[53] This process had begun before the imperial ban on pagan worship in 391, since an inscription of 379/83 from the same city of Madauros refers to a temple of Fortune that was already being used for another purpose, probably as a market building.[54]

In one special case, Rome, many of the temple buildings were inextric-ably entwined with Roman pride and the Romans' sense of their own past. The temple of Jupiter Capitolinus, protected by Juno's sacred geese against the Gauls in 390 B.C. and the culmination of every republican and imperial triumph until Constantine, or the temple of Castor and Pollux in the Forum, where the heavenly twins appeared after the Roman victory at Lake Regillus, could hardly be wilfully destroyed, even when their divine pro-tectors were no longer needed. As late as Ostrogothic times, in 510/11, efforts were made to protect the temple buildings of Rome alongside its other classical monuments; according to an anecdote recorded by Procopius, the temple of Janus in the Forum was still standing in 537 with its valuable bronze doors and, even more surprising, its bronze cult-statue still in place. Lesser temples were almost certainly allowed to be destroyed, but the great historic temples of Rome's past survived and must have pre-sented an extraordinary sight in their solitude. 'The gilded Capitol is covered in filth, and all the temples of Rome are coated in dust and spiders' webs' – for Jerome this was a triumphant statement of the power of Christianity, but we can enjoy a moment of romantic regret at the power-ful image of decaying grandeur that his words conjure up.[55]

While the temples decayed, or were violently destroyed, churches were

---

[52] For Italy, see Ward-Perkins, *Public Building* ch. 5.   [53] Aug. *Ep.* 232.3.
[54] Lepelley, *Cités* II.130–1.   [55] Cassiod., *Var.* III.31; Procop. *BG* 1.25.18–25; Jer. *Ep.* 107.1.

slowly being built in the cities of the empire. Again the pace of change must have varied greatly according to circumstance, and, unfortunately, only very seldom can we accurately date the building of the first substantial churches. It is likely that in most cities the organization and funds for such a major enterprise did not exist until the late fourth century or into the fifth. At Gerasa (Jerash), in modern Jordan, it is possible that the undated first church of the cathedral complex may be of the late fourth century. But, of the remaining fourteen churches now known from the site, none of the twelve that are datable was built before the year 464. In Gerasa the main effort of church-building was undoubtedly in the later fifth century and the sixth century.[56] At the other end of the empire, in Roman Britain, archaeologists have so far discovered remarkably little evidence of urban church-building, and the absence of churches must in part reflect the slow pace of Christian building, which was here overtaken, even before it was substantially under way, by the disasters of the early fifth century.[57]

In a few privileged cities, however, the impact of Christian building was more sudden and impressive. Imperial patronage, in particular, could bring about substantial and swift changes to a city's religious topography. In Rome, after he captured the city in 312, Constantine set about honouring his God and the great martyrs with whom the capital was associated (Fig. 6). He built two vast churches, each five aisles wide and some hundred metres long, one at the Lateran, and one on the Vatican hill over the grave of St Peter; and he and his family built further large churches at S. Croce, S. Agnese, S. Lorenzo and SS. Marcellino e Pietro. With Constantine, Rome retained its old secular and pagan monuments, but it also became a great Christian city, with a distinctive and obvious Christian monumentality. Before Constantine's building-efforts, Christians had met in houses indistinguishable from other domestic buildings; thereafter they met in huge and elaborately decorated churches.[58]

The remarkable impact that the emperor's Christian patronage had on Rome is best seen in the case of St Peter's. Here Constantine wished to place the high altar directly over the place sanctified by tradition as the grave of the apostle. Before his work, this spot was marked only by a small aedicula in the middle of a busy necropolis of substantial family tombs. It must have been entirely unknown to all but the devout. As a result of Constantine's work, the foot-slopes of the Vatican hill were levelled to form a great raised platform some hundred metres long (or some two hundred metres long, if, as seems probable, the atrium was his); the necropolis was closed down and covered over; and a great five-aisled basilica was constructed, with its high altar directly over St Peter's resting-place.[59] This

---

[56] Karaeling (1938) 171–264; Zayadine (1986) 16–18.   [57] Thomas (1981) 166–80.
[58] Constantine's churches in Rome are discussed in Krautheimer, *Rome* 3–31.
[59] Toynbee and Ward-Perkins (1956) ch. 7.

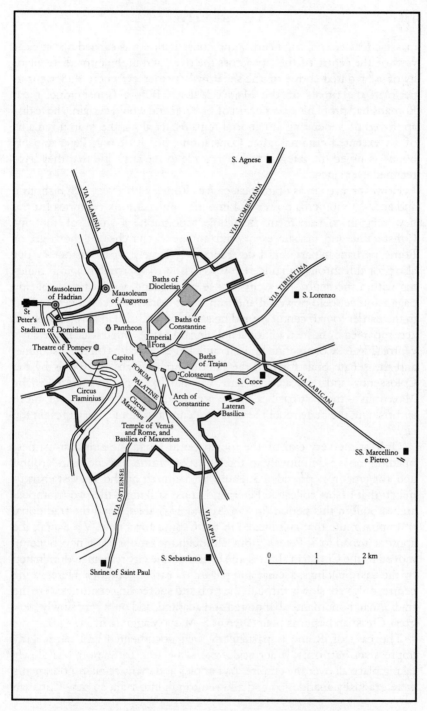

Fig. 6. Rome at the death of Constantine, A.D. 337 (based on Krautheimer (1980), fig. 1)

massive feat of civil engineering and construction was carried out in clear view of the centre of the city across the river, and in the immediate vicinity of a favoured shrine of the senatorial aristocracy, where they went to perform the rituals of the Magna Mater.[60] Before Constantine, most Romans had probably never heard of St Peter and would certainly have disapproved of venerating any mortal remains, let alone the mortal remains of an executed criminal; after Constantine, like it or not, Peter and his bones assumed the integral and major role in the city's life that they have retained ever since.

However, even in as dramatic a case as Rome, with a very rich bishopric and access to imperial power and imperial funds, it took centuries for the new religion to transform the whole topographical shape of the city. Constantine and his successors did not build churches in the heart of Rome, perhaps in part out of deference to its largely pagan aristocracy, but also probably through an uncertainty as to how to approach religious building within the centre of a city whose monuments were often explicitly pagan and yet held powerful and important historical resonances. Indeed in the earlier fourth century, building at the new Christian shrines was still accompanied by more traditional building on a substantial scale in the city's centre (Fig. 6). Constantine himself built large new baths on the Esquiline; and the senate built for him the famous arch which still stands by the Colosseum, and dedicated to him two massive projects undertaken by Maxentius – the vast basilica to the north-east of the Forum, and, more surprisingly, the huge rebuilt temple of Venus and Rome, the largest in the city.[61]

Only at the very end of the fourth century had the emphasis in new building moved definitively to the Christian shrines. In the years around 400, the emperors provided St Paul with a church on the Via Ostiensis to match that of his colleague Peter; and, most strikingly, the two triumphal arches built in this period (in 379/83 and 405) abandoned the traditional triumphal route that culminated in the Capitol for a new 'Via Sacra', the approach-road to St Peter's.[62] But, although the emphasis of new building moved to the Christian shrines, the centre of the city remained dominated by the vast buildings, secular and pagan, of earlier centuries. Here, in the centre, only very slowly through the fifth and succeeding centuries were the traditional monuments abandoned and adapted, and only very slowly were great Christian basilicas built (such as S. Maria Maggiore in 432/40).

The case of Rome is particularly well documented and particularly impressive, but, on a lesser scale, the same transformation was slowly taking place all over the empire. As temples and many secular monuments were gradually abandoned and allowed to fall into ruin, so new Christian

[60] *Ibid.* 6.   [61] Aur. Vict. *Caes.* XL.26.   [62] Ward-Perkins, *Public Building* 80.

buildings emerged – in particular, the great church of each city's bishop and the shrines in the extramural cemeteries, built over the graves of the martyrs.

The change in the cities from paganism to Christianity was played out not only in shifting monumental topography, but also in the organization of time, with a slow change in the calendar away from the celebration of the feasts of one religion and towards the feasts of another. This move was neither easy nor rapid, nor indeed ever fully completed, because the traditional feast-days, like 1 January, and the traditional rhythms of the year had such a profound hold. The survival of ancient feast-days was unacceptable to many churchmen, in part because of their enduring pagan associations, even if stripped of overt pagan practices (such as sacrifice), and in part because they were times for spectacles in the theatre, amphitheatre and circus, of which the more austere Christian teachers did not approve. Christian writers and teachers, like Chrysostom, Augustine and Salvian, attempted to make clear to their flocks that they should eschew these pleasures.[63] but, unsurprisingly, ordinary Christian men and women continued to enjoy the traditional entertainments for as long as there were patrons prepared to provide them.

The legislation of Christian emperors attempted to steer a middle path between the more ascetic teachings of the church, and the dictates of tradition and desires of the people. For instance, in 399 Honorius wrote to the governor of Africa Proconsularis:

When through a salutary law we abolished profane rites, we did not wish to abolish the festive assembly of citizens and the common pleasure of all. Therefore we decree that entertainments should be provided for the people, in accordance with ancient custom, but without any sacrifice or damnable superstition.

(*C.Th.* XVI.10.17)

The celebrations of the major Christian festivals, both empire-wide (as in the case of Easter and Christmas) and locally (as in the case of the feast of a local patron saint), were, of course, very different in style from the days of sacrifices, shows and spectacles characteristic of antiquity. But, like the feasts of the past, when patricians and plebs had met together (in suitably differentiated seats) in theatre, amphitheatre and circus, the Christian feasts gradually came to serve as moments of reunion, suitable for the reaffirmation of both civic unity and of the correct ordering of society. In each *civitas* the Christian aristocracy were expected to come into town from their estates for the major feasts of the Christian year, which the whole community celebrated together in the great church. In this way the cities retained their central ritual and social function within the very different context of a new religion.

---

[63] Liebeschuetz, *Antioch* 228–32; Markus, *End of Ancient Christianity* 107–23.

More fundamentally, the cities also retained their importance because the structure of the new church, as established before and during the fourth century, not surprisingly followed quite closely the city-based pattern of the secular imperial administration. Although there were exceptions to this rule, in general each *civitas* or *polis* acquired a bishop based in the capital city of that *civitas*. Subscriptions to early church councils, such as that at Arles in 314, show that many *civitates* already had bishops by the early fourth century; but in some regions, such as northern Gaul and Britain, it was perhaps only by about 400 that a full network of bishoprics had been set up.[64] The bishop and his church were central to the Christian lives of his whole flock, both rural and urban. He appointed and could dismiss all priests within his *civitas*, and he controlled all church finance. The only baptistery within a *civitas* was normally that attached to the bishop's church, and dwellers in the rural areas had to come into town for baptism, as well as to celebrate the major feasts of the Christian year.

In a further reflection of the secular administrative hierarchy, a bishop whose city was the capital of an imperial province had special status, being termed a 'metropolitan' (later an 'archbishop'), with some authority over all the other *civitates* and bishops of the province. The powers of these metropolitans were not well defined in the fourth century, but from the time of the council of Nicaea (325) they did include, at least in theory, the all-important right and duty to confirm all episcopal elections within their province (Nicaea canon 4).

Above these metropolitans were a handful of bishops, sometimes called patriarchs, in the great traditional centres of empire – Alexandria, Carthage, Antioch and Rome.[65] The patriarchates, however, never evolved into a coherent scheme covering with identical authority all the provinces of the empire, and so at this level the church no longer neatly mirrored the all-embracing secular structure of dioceses and prefectures. Nor was the arrangement of patriarchates static. Not surprisingly, powerful bishops periodically attempted to create for their sees wider jurisdictions, and in the late empire they were likely to have some success if their see was one of the rising cities within the secular administration. Thus Ambrose in fourth-century Milan temporarily asserted his authority in the church as far afield as Sirmium and Dacia; and inevitably, as Constantinople emerged as a major and favoured imperial residence, here too there developed the problem of the status of its bishop.

The church of Constantinople (or rather of Byzantium, as the small town on this site was called before Constantine) had no historic rights within the Christian community and indeed had no good biblical or early

---

[64] Wightman (1985) 286–91; Esmonde Cleary (1989) 121–4.
[65] Jones, *LRE* 883–94; see pp. 245–7 above.

Christian claims to fame. In this respect it started a very long way behind Rome, which possessed the bodies of both Peter and Paul (not to mention a host of famous local martyrs), but also behind other Aegean and eastern cities with well-known early Christian histories and martyrs, such as Ephesus or Corinth. Constantinople could only manage two highly obscure local martyrs, Mocius and Acacius, though Constantine did his best for them by building a vast basilica over Mocius' tomb.[66]

However, although the bishop of Constantinople did not formally lay claim to the rights of a patriarch until the council of Chalcedon in 451, already in the fourth century bishops and emperors were working to adjust Christian and sacred geography to fit the reality of Constantinople's growing political importance. In 381 the bishop of Constantinople was accorded an undefined but highly prestigious status immediately beneath the bishop of Rome, on the grounds that Constantinople was the New Rome.[67] And at the end of his reign Constantius II (337–61) moved to the city the bodies of three illustrious saints, Timothy, Luke and Andrew.[68] This is the very first recorded instance of the movement of relics away from their traditional homes, and it is not surprising that this important precedent was set in the interests of providing a popular imperial residence with better-quality saints and protectors. Like Constantine, who had been prepared to use his imperial power to despoil the cities of the east of classical statuary in order to enhance the aura of his new city, so Constantius was prepared to despoil cities of their saints in order to create a more imposing sacred environment within Constantinople.

In fourth-century Milan, Ambrose attempted something rather similar. The city, although a favoured imperial residence, like Constantinople lacked a really good local saint. Ambrose did what he could to rectify this position by 'discovering' further relics to build up the number of local martyrs, by building new and large churches over the sacred graves, and by bringing in relics from outside (though these were contact-relics rather than the whole bodies which were moved to Constantinople). Nevertheless, when he built the Basilica Ambrosiana, with space for his tomb under the high altar, he also perhaps accurately predicted that his greatest gift to the Milanese church would be his own sainthood and his own body.[69]

As the church grew in numbers through the fourth and early fifth centuries, so it grew in endowment and in its capacity to spend and to play a major role in urban life. As so often, the pace of change is rarely well-documented and must have been very different in different cities. The Roman see was wealthy from an early date, and in the mid third century already supported 154 clergy and over 1500 widows and poor people; it was

---

[66] Mango (1985) 35–6.   [67] Jones, *LRE* 886.   [68] Dagron, *Naissance* 459.
[69] For Ambrose's churches, Krautheimer (1983) 77–81, with further references. For Ambrose and relics, see Brown, *Cult of the Saints*.

further enormously enriched by Constantine, who provided gifts worth over 400 pounds of gold a year. It is therefore no surprise that the luxurious lifestyle of Rome's fourth-century bishops came in for severe censure from Ammianus.[70]

However, the wealth of the Roman see was very exceptional, and many churches remained poorly endowed into the fifth century and beyond. For instance, the fortunes of the needy North African bishopric of Thagaste were transformed in the early fifth century by a single windfall, the pious gifts of two visiting aristocrats, Melania and Pinianus; but Thagaste had to protect its benefactors carefully against the attempts of other jealous sees to milk them.[71] Even in a great city like Antioch, likely to attract imperial patronage, the church (if we are to believe John Chrysostom) was in the second half of the fourth century still not as well-endowed as some individual Antiochene families.

However, though there were yet wealthier landowners, the scale of operations that the Antiochene church was able to maintain shows beyond doubt that it had a very considerable income at its disposal and was spending it not only on its clergy but also on extensive poor-relief. In Chrysostom's time it was apparently helping to support 3000 widows and virgins, as well as other members of the poor.[72] On a smaller scale, such charitable giving had clearly become the norm in the cities of the empire by the mid fourth century, since the pagan Julian paid Christianity the compliment of attempting to set up a rival pagan system of poor-relief (Jul. *Ep.* 22).

As the churches of the empire very gradually became established in power, status and wealth, so they increasingly attracted men of rank into the episcopate. When in 374 Ambrose, the son of a praetorian prefect and himself the governor of the province of Aemilia and Liguria, was selected as bishop of Milan, this was still an unusual development; but in the late fourth century and through the fifth, similar career patterns (from the high-ranking secular aristocracy straight into the episcopate) became increasingly common in east and west alike.

Gradually, too, as his flock and endowments grew and as emperors came to see their role increasingly in Christian terms, the power and influence of the bishop increased, and he became accepted as the defender and representative of his community. When in 387 the people of Antioch faced the possibility of dreadful retribution, following a riot and the destruction of the imperial statues, it was the bishop and the monks, rather than the local *curiales*, who were most effective in obtaining imperial clemency.[73]

By about 400 we are beginning to see a world that will be familiar to

[70] The wealth of Rome and other sees, with full references, is discussed by Jones, *LRE* 904–6.
[71] Lepelley, *Cités* 1.385–8.   [72] Downey (1958) 89.
[73] Brown, *Power and Persuasion* 105–8; Ruggini (1986); see pp. 154–5 above.

historians for the whole Middle Ages (and indeed beyond), a world in which the cathedral and the local saints were an established and central part of city life, and in which aristocratic bishops were either the most powerful and wealthy citizens, or were at least amongst the very top members of urban society. The creation of this new structure within the cities of the fourth century was to prove not only durable, but also, as it happens, fundamental to the very survival of towns in the difficult centuries ahead. For, as many of the structures of Roman power and Roman society disappeared between the fifth century and the seventh in a period of great political and economic upheaval, so the church remained remarkably resilient as an institution. It kept much of its wealth and it kept its urban roots; consequently, when other elements of society that helped sustain town life were either disappearing or were greatly attenuated, the urban church and the urban bishop often remained as solid foundations to the continuity of city life.

VI. THE SIZE AND WEALTH OF CITIES

Any discussion of the cities of the late Roman world must end with some assessment of a difficult and somewhat controversial issue. Were cities in general in this period flourishing, or were they in decline?[74]

Our main source of information on urban size and prosperity is now archaeology, which can, in theory, provide many answers – revealing areas of dense new housing or areas of abandonment, and uncovering evidence of a rich material culture or evidence of impoverishment. However, at present, it remains in practice difficult to generalize about late Roman urban demographic and economic fortunes from the archaeological evidence. This is so for a number of reasons, the most straightforward and basic being that until recently there was little archaeological interest in ancient cities other than as repositories of 'great' art and architecture. Consequently, few efforts were made to record the humbler details of city life or to bother about centuries, like those of late antiquity, that did not normally produce high cultural artefacts. Most sites were simply cleared down to some impressive structures, and, particularly in the west, these tended to be early Roman.

Even today, particularly in the Mediterranean region, few excavations (and even fewer that are published) meticulously document the changing face of a variety of types of urban area. Much excavation is still glorified clearance in the interests of art history and tourism, and most of it is still aimed at smart housing and monumental buildings. Consequently, the

[74] I am particularly grateful, in this section, for the comments made by Simon Loseby and Peter Heather on a first draft.

present archaeological record is much richer for those structures that have always interested archaeologists, namely monumental buildings and aristocratic houses, than it is for the humbler details of urban life, such as artisan dwellings and workshops; and, unless there are datable inscriptions, our dating of buildings still depends all too often on shifting and loose chronologies based on the style of mosaics and architectural fittings, rather than on the evidence of coins and datable pottery reliably recorded in association with different structural phases.

Dating is a particular problem when the period prescribed for discussion is, as in this volume, less than a century long. For example, the fifteen churches excavated at Gerasa (Jerash) are good evidence of continued urban life and prosperity within the broad period 'late antiquity'; but, as we have seen, not one of them is unequivocally datable before 464. Can the evidence they present be projected back into the fourth century, or did Gerasa flourish particularly from the fifth century onwards?

Even when the dating evidence is abundant and good, it tends to relate only to a handful of public buildings (supplemented, perhaps, by a few loosely-dated aristocratic houses), and it is hard to generalize with confidence about the fate of an entire town from these. But it is particularly difficult to do this in the fourth and fifth centuries, since, as we have seen, this was a period of revolutionary change in both religious and secular public building, with a formal classical townscape of regular streets, temples, *fora* and bath buildings beginning to give way to a far less organized townscape, dotted with churches, but with few surviving traditional secular monuments. This change reflects a marked transformation in the internal arrangement of the city, but, as the souks of Aleppo and Damascus show (see Fig. 3, p. 383 above), it need not reflect overall decline in economic and demographic well-being.

Nevertheless, although the problems with the archaeological evidence are manifold and serious, it would be defeatist not to attempt an overview of the state of towns in the late empire. By standng back far enough from the many detailed problems of each individual site, a broad picture does perhaps emerge, possibly even a picture that commands fairly wide scholarly support. As it appears at present, this picture shows a fourth-century urban history of the northern provinces which is markedly different from that of the south and east, with perhaps a 'middle zone', comprising Italy, southern Gaul and Spain, lying both geographically and in experience somewhere in-between the two extremes.[75]

In much of the southern half of the empire – the central provinces of North Africa, the Near East, and Aegean Greece and Asia Minor – there

---

[75] I am here going much further than Garnsey and Whittaker in ch. 10 (p. 326 above), who are cautious about the possibility of regional difference in fourth-century urban history.

is no sign that towns were in decline in size and prosperity in late anti-quity.

The evidence from central North Africa (the provinces of Proconsularis, Byzacena and Numidia) is perhaps particularly clear and useful. Here the recent UNESCO project has investigated the region's prin-cipal city, Carthage, on a number of sites which include carefully excavated areas of housing. The excavations of Carthage show, beyond reasonable doubt, that the city reached its greatest extent in the fourth and early fifth centuries, shortly before it was walled in the face of the Vandal threat; and that this great size was matched by great wealth, reflected in large churches and richly decorated houses. Carthage in the early fifth century was a city of some 320 hectares, an inhabited area perhaps about twice that of fourth-century Trier, despite the fact that the latter was an imperial capital (see Fig. 2, p. 374 above).[76]

Alongside the work on Carthage, there has also been extensive excava-tion, though generally of a much more old-fashioned kind, in a number of towns of the interior, including many which were never important in the administrative hierarchy (such as Cuicul, Sufetula and Thamugadi). The dating evidence from these excavations tends to be very vague, and con-fined to churches and aristocratic mosaics, but the current conviction amongst scholars is that, as at Carthage, the fourth century was, through-out central North Africa, a high point of both population and prosperity.[77]

In the Near East and Aegean, evidence of urban prosperity precisely datable to the fourth century seems less abundant than it is in Africa. This may well be the result of a genuine difference, with urban prosperity coming to the east a little later than it did to Africa (which would mirror the evidence of rural settlement, as we shall see below). But our perception may also be slightly distorted, since Africa has produced far less evidence of later-fifth- and sixth-century prosperity than has the east, so that the fourth-century African evidence stands out with particular clarity.

There is also a problem with the eastern evidence, that in the Aegean region the excavations that have produced the best evidence of late antique urban life are all, with the exception of Athens, late Roman imperial, regional or provincial capitals – Corinth, Thessalonica, Constantinople, Ephesus, Sardis and Aphrodisias. As we have seen above, there is good reason to believe that cities such as these benefited considerably from their administrative status, perhaps even at the expense of their less well-docu-mented neighbours. However, in the provinces of the Near East the evi-dence is better distributed, since excavation has included both late antique capitals (such as Antioch, Apamea, Scythopolis, Caesarea and the new

[76] The evidence from Carthage is well summarized, with full further references, in Hurst (1993).
[77] Février (1964); Duval (1982); Thébert (1983); Lepelley, *Cités*.

religious 'capital' of Jerusalem), and lesser towns, like Gerasa and Pella, which were mere *poleis* and never served as provincial capitals.[78]

In all these eastern regions there is no doubt of the existence of flourishing urban life in the late Roman period. The precise nature of the evidence varies from city to city: in some we have evidence of public monuments that were maintained and rebuilt (such as the porticoes of Apamea, Antioch, Ephesus and Sardis), in others of the rich aristocratic houses that were embellished and added to (such as those excavated at Apamea, at Antioch's suburb of Daphne, at Ephesus, and at Athens), and from almost all we have evidence of the building of large numbers of new churches, sometimes on a grand scale. In summary, a substantial number of sites have produced no clear evidence of late antique urban decline, and plenty of evidence of urban prosperity.

The picture is very different in the provinces along the northern fringe of the empire: in the north Balkans and along the Danube, in northern Gaul, and in Britain.[79] In Britain, for example, there is much debate about the precise fate of towns in the fourth century, but the parameters of the debate are set between mild decay and total collapse, and all scholars agree that there was some decline. In northern Gaul, except in the frontier region, where the army and imperial service may have sustained urban life at an exceptionally high level, the fortifications built around cities in this period enclosed only very small areas, often of fifteen hectares or less (Fig. 2, p. 374 above).[80] In the fourth century and later, houses are recorded in some cases outside the walls of these tiny circuits, so that the walled area cannot be taken as a straightforward index of urban size; but, even so, building was certainly on nothing like the scale so readily documented in the cities of the southern and eastern Mediterranean. In these northern regions the only two towns that are definitely known to have been flourishing in the fourth century were both imperial capitals, Trier and Sirmium, supported by the vast wealth and manpower of the imperial government.

Between the northern provinces, on the one hand, and Africa and the east Mediterranean on the other, lies a large central area, including Spain, southern Gaul and Italy, where the broad picture of fourth-century town life is less clear.[81] There is in these regions less evidence of decline than we find further north; for example, the tiny walled circuits characteristic of northern Gaul are here much rarer. There is also some good evidence of

---

[78] For Asia Minor and the Near East, with full further references, Whittow (1990). For Thessalonica, Spieser (1984); for Athens, Frantz (1988); for Corinth, Scranton (1957).

[79] There are good regional surveys for the whole of Gaul, in Février (1980); for Britain, in Esmonde Cleary (1989) 64–85; and for the northern Balkans, in Poulter (1992).

[80] Randsborg, *First Millennium* 90–5.

[81] For southern Gaul, see Février (1980). There are no good overall surveys for Spain and Italy; but see Keay, *Roman Spain* ch. 8 for the patchy and so far ambiguous Spanish evidence, and Ward-Perkins, *Public Building,* for some of the Italian evidence.

urban prosperity, particularly in the building during the fourth and fifth centuries of large numbers of imposing urban churches; and there are even some towns, like fourth-century Toulouse and fifth-century Marseilles, which seem to have grown in size during this period, despite remaining of limited importance within the administrative hierarchy.[82]

However, although this admittedly is an impressionistic, rather than a strictly quantifiable statement, the evidence of extensive new building in late antiquity (whether of churches or of rich houses) in the towns of Spain, southern Gaul and Italy is much less obvious and widespread than that so readily documentable in Africa and the east. The few cities in the north-west Mediterranean which have produced excellent evidence of large late antique populations, combined with large numbers of impressive late Roman buildings, are all important capitals – Rome, Ravenna and Milan – where (as at Trier or Sirmium) an impressive scale of city life was 'artificially' sustained by the spending of emperors and of the most powerful and wealthy aristocrats and bishops of the west. Probably, it is safest at present to see the broad urban history of this 'middle zone' as lying somewhere in-between the decline of the north and the prosperity of Africa and the east.

At first glance, the distribution of urban prosperity which we have been examining seems to anticipate the clear pattern of the later fifth century and the early sixth, in which the east is far more urbanized than the west. However, on closer examination, the fourth-century pattern is neither so simple nor so clear. The contrast in the fourth century is less between west and east than between north and south, with one of the most (if not the most) urbanized and prosperous regions, Africa, falling within the area of the western empire, and one of the least urbanized, the northern Balkans, within the eastern. It is also important to remember the precise chronological focus of the present volume. While few would disagree with the proposition that by the end of the fifth century a significant gap had opened between the urban histories of, say, Italy and Syria, it is at present impossible to decide whether that gap was a significant one by the end of the fourth century. In looking at the broad patterns of fourth-century urban life, it is important to bear in mind both the north–south (rather than east–west) divide and the current uncertainties about what exactly was happening in the fourth century, because otherwise it becomes easy to slip into the assumption that the west was already widely deurbanized and 'medieval', and only waiting for the barbarians to walk all over it.

Why the size and prosperity of towns in the fourth century should be different in different regions of the empire is not yet clear. We can, however, confidently reject one possible explanation – that in some regions cities lost their administrative role. As we have seen, the evidence is quite clear that

---

[82] For Toulouse, Auson. *Ordo Nob. Urb.* XVIII; for Marseilles, Loseby (1992).

this did not happen until the fifth century, and then only in a few marginal areas; rather, the new institutions of the church everywhere added a novel and important administrative role, and more potential wealth, to the *civitas*-capitals. At a local level, different cities played administrative roles of very different importance, and benefited or lost out accordingly; but these differences are local ones, between individual towns in a single region, and will not explain the overall regional differences that we have outlined above.

Another possible explanation, explored and I believe rightly played down in chapter 10 (p. 323 above), is that many provinces saw a wholesale flight to the countryside by aristocrats and craftsmen alike, so that towns lost their earlier role as centres of aristocratic life and as centres of artisan and trading activity. It is possible that during the fourth century such a thing happened on a limited scale in some of the northern provinces of the empire. In fourth-century Britain, for example, both the rural *villae* of the aristocracy and some small market-settlements seem to have been flourishing, in the very period that the *civitates* were shrinking in both density of population and prosperity.[83]

However, in most provinces the limited documentary evidence and the more extensive archaeological evidence (of sumptuous town houses and splendid churches) strongly suggest that late Roman aristocrats retained earlier habits of urban life. Where those aristocrats were, there artisans, with their keen eye for a market, are likely to have remained, even though archaeologists have seldom bothered to look for them.[84]

A simpler explanation for the difference between the regional histories of late Roman towns would assume a more or less continuous role for towns within society and the economy, absorbing in all periods a similar proportion of the local population and of local wealth; but with different areas of the empire enjoying changing levels of overall prosperity and population. In this model, fluctuations in the fortunes of towns would closely mirror broader regional fluctuations in prosperity.

There are, I believe, good reasons for adopting this explanation. In particular, there does seem to be a close correlation between areas of the empire where towns were flourishing in late antiquity and areas where rural life in this same period was doing well.[85] In particular, the third and fourth centuries would seem to be the high points of rural settlement in the central provinces of North Africa, with evidence of both extensive and profitable settlement, and exactly the same is true of a slightly later period, the fourth to sixth centuries, in the Near East and Greece. It should be no surprise

[83] Esmonde Cleary (1989) ch. 3.

[84] An honourable exception is the excavation and publication of the shops at Sardis: Crawford (1990).

[85] Rural evidence is usefully summarized in Randsborg, *First Millennium* 40–81 and in MacMullen, *Corruption* 15–35.

that, in these same areas in these same periods, towns flourished. Equally, areas where towns do not seem to have done so well in the fourth century, like Italy, appear to be the same areas where rural settlement too was either static or in decline.

This congruence of rural and urban fortunes strongly suggests that towns played substantially the same role in all parts of the empire, but within regional economies which were more or less successful in different provinces. A few great cities, like Trier, stood outside the overall urban and economic history of their region, because of massive injections of imperial funds; but, for the most part, towns, whether serving as the home of aristocratic landholders or as the home for artisans and traders servicing a rural market, obviously depended for their survival and prosperity on the general health of their own regional economy. For some reason, which is not yet at all clear to scholars, regional economies in this period seem to have flourished better in the southern half of the empire than in the north.

VII. CONCLUSION

The Roman empire of the fourth and early fifth centuries remained, as it had always been, city-based, with political, religious and aristocratic life revolving around the *civitates* and around major capitals. Only at the very end of our period did this situation change at all, and then only in an exceptional area, Britain, which had slipped out of imperial control.

However, although their importance remained unchanged, the cities of the late empire differed in several obvious ways from the cities of the earlier Roman world. First, the reorganization of the empire in the third and early fourth centuries and the increase in state demands of service and taxation tied cities much more closely into an empire-wide network of rewards and duties. This change helped erode a centuries-old ideology of local political life and service, while at the same time creating in the frontier zone a number of great imperial capitals. Secondly, the collapse of internal and external security in the crises of the third and fifth centuries provided many cities with walls and with a potential military role which only the towns of the frontier had exercised in earlier centuries. Thirdly, through the fourth century and into the fifth, the Christian church and the Christian bishop gradually became powerful forces within the cities of the empire. Fourthly and finally, broader economic trends created differences, along a roughly north–south divide, between areas of the empire where towns were in overall decline in the fourth and fifth centuries, and areas where they were flourishing.

This fourth change (in the overall economic context of urban life) is perhaps controversial, and certainly needs testing and refining on the ground. But the first three changes (in the political, military and religious role of the cities) are all very familiar to scholarship, and there is no doubt that they had a marked effect on the politics of city life and on the way that the aristocracy played out its role within the cities. The fourth to sixth centuries saw the decline of the centuries-old ideal of the classical city governing the patterns of local political life and spending. But these centuries also saw the gradual emergence of a 'new' city, playing an important part within the overall administrative, financial and military structures of church and state, and increasingly focused on a Christian ideology of saints and their churches.

None of these changes has been easy to describe. A chapter like this requires a delicate balancing act between the need to achieve clarity, by simplifying and generalizing, and the need to allow for many variations in type of city and in the pace of change. The empire of the later fourth century included cities as diverse as Bulla Regia, a small and prosperous agricultural centre in North Africa, secure enough to be unwalled and already solidly Christian; Trier, a powerfully fortified and imposing showpiece of imperial power behind the northern frontier; and Gaza, a bustling commercial port and a bastion of paganism. The historian has somehow to allow for such diversity, while identifying broad empire-wide changes which had already affected each of these cities, though in different ways and to different degrees, and which, by 425, would go on to destroy both Trier's proud invincibility and Gaza's temple of Marnas. Describing the cities of the empire is like describing a moving target made up of different parts, all travelling in roughly the same direction, but at very different speeds and with different individual trajectories.

CHAPTER 13

WARFARE AND DIPLOMACY

R. C. BLOCKLEY

I. WAR, DIPLOMACY AND THE ROMAN STATE

To the Romans, as to most people of antiquity, war was the primary means by which the state defined and maintained itself against outsiders. In the Roman historical tradition military prowess and success in war had guaranteed the survival and then the expansion of the state. From the foundation of the Roman polity to the end of the republic the possession of military skills, demonstrated by success in war, underwrote the preeminence of the aristocracy and the rise to prominence and authority of individuals within this élite. Augustus, in establishing a hereditary principate, cut the aristocracy at large off from the most powerful office then available and thus both consummated and altered the role of military success in the political process. But he in no way diminished the importance of war in Rome's relations with its neighbours. Rome of the principate, like Rome of the late republic, was a conquest state in which success in war retained its prestige. As a result, even though the emperor might contrive to rest his claim to his position on factors other than success in war – dynastic, or, later, theocratic – he was careful to retain at the very least the symbolic status of a great warrior through the insistence that all wars were fought under his auspices and through the appropriation as triumphal titles of the names of the peoples defeated by his generals.

In late antiquity this tradition remained alive. Alexander and Trajan were the paradigms against which emperors were judged, and it was no accident that the winged Victory was the last of the pagan personifications to survive on the Roman coinage well into the fifth century. When the poet Claudian declared (*IV Cons. Hon.* 619–33) that the emperor Honorius had in his first consulship (A.D. 386), at the age of two years, been the author of a defeat of the Greuthingi, his claim was not ridiculous since the very existence of the emperor and his presence on the battlefield, even if only in portraits, were held to be major factors in military success. The physical presence of the emperor in the war area was even more potent, and until the death of Theodosius I in 395 and the succession of his palace-bound sons, the movements of the emperors and even the appointments of fellow Augusti and Caesars were to a great extent dictated by the need to have an imperial presence near to the main theatres of war.

The continued expansion of the Roman empire under Augustus and his immediate successors was driven both by traditional respect for military success (and hence the emperor's need for it) and the desire for resources acquired by conquest. The instrument of this expansion was the versatile army, based upon though not limited by the legions, which was well-suited for conquest in that, with its multiplicity of engineering, manufacturing and organizational skills – all of wide application – it carried its own basic infrastructure for control and administration forward as it advanced. Setbacks occurred, of course, such as the Illyrian revolt of A.D. 6–9, the massacre of Varus' army in A.D. 9, and the revolt of Julius Civilis in A.D. 69–70. Moreover, some peoples outside the empire, especially the Parthians and Dacians, were strong enough to mount threats. Since, however, these peoples lacked the organizational sophistication of the Romans, their attacks were generally uncoordinated, unsustained and relatively easily contained or beaten back. Under these circumstances the Romans were able to assemble relatively large armies for foreign (or civil) wars from the forces stationed in the border provinces at an acceptable level of risk for the denuded areas.

In the fourth century both the nature of the Roman army and the circumstances which it faced were much changed. The army itself consisted broadly of two components: units which were stationed in the border regions under the command of *duces*, whose roles were primarily those of garrison troops and local police controlling the movements of people; and units of the *comitatus* under the command of *magistri militum* (the term varies) or *comites*, whose role was mainly to engage in open-field battle. Although these roles were to a degree interchangeable, a large measure of specialization is suggested by, for instance, a passage of Ammianus (XIX.5.2–3), which describes the uselessness and frustration of Gallic troops, trained for open-field battle, when shut up in Amida during the siege of 359. Conversely, garrison troops do not seem to have adapted readily to open-field warfare. Specialized cavalry forces, fighting with a variety of weaponry, were also present in far greater numbers in the fourth-century army than they had been in the army of the principate. Although their prestige seems to have been high, their effectiveness, especially in the west, appears to have been limited. The major battles of the period, including the battle of Adrianople in 378 (often represented as a cavalry victory), were conflicts decided by foot-soldiers.

While the army of the principate had made use of foreign soldiers, the army of the fourth century came to employ large and growing numbers of non-Romans of various origins – Germans, Sarmatians, Alans, Armenians, Arabs, even Persians, and later Huns. They served not only as individuals in auxiliary units under Roman or Roman-appointed officers (the practice under the principate), but also in homogeneous groups under their own leaders. The officer corps, too, which by the fourth century had been reorganized, contained a large number of career soldiers of non-Roman origin, even at the highest level. By the end of the century it appears that the majority of the units of the Roman army fit for battlefield duty were manned by barbarians.

The army of the period was maintained primarily for defence. Advances beyond the borders were usually for the purpose of retaliation or to forestall an anticipated attack. Large-scale incursions, such as Julian's invasion of Persia in 363, were rare and demanded a major effort, drawing upon units from both parts of the empire. The preservation of manpower was an important objective of strategy, and the avoidance of war on more than one front at the same time became a concern of diplomacy.

The enemies of the empire differed greatly in their resources and technology of war. The Persians were the equals of the Romans in siege warfare – one of the main forms of fighting in Mesopotamia and Syria, where fortresses controlled the major routes – and were their superiors in cavalry. Their infantry was, however, weak, and because of their very decentralized political and economic system they had difficulty in keeping large armies in the field for long periods. As a result, in the fourth century, wars between the Romans and the Persians tended to be either a series of sieges or fast-moving incursions of limited range and duration. Set battles were rare and usually indecisive. Significant territorial gains came only as 'windfalls', as when Julian's army was trapped in Persia in 363 and had to buy its way to safety with the cession of territory. The swift-moving incursion was also the form of warfare favoured by the Arabs to the south, who during the period were regarded by the Romans and the Persians as useful allies, but not as a serious threat.

In Europe the enemies of the Romans were on the whole technologically and organizationally their inferiors, although by the end of the fourth century access to Roman weaponry and training might have helped some peoples to narrow the gap. As in the east, major set battles were rare – indeed, most set battles during the period were fought when Roman army met Roman army in civil war. Instead, groups of barbarians raided when and where they could. If caught by a Roman force they were often destroyed as they fought, undisciplined and without defensive armour. For the Romans the threat lay in the large and increasing number of such groups raiding over the long Rhine–Danube border.

In the Roman tradition diplomacy – that is, 'direct communication state to-state'[1] – was viewed mainly as an adjunct or epilogue to war, as when a victorious general negotiated the surrender of a defeated enemy, or an

---

[1] The definition is from Harmon (1971) 13.

alliance was struck for a military goal, or a truce was agreed to forestall an attack or bury the dead. While these and related kinds of diplomatic activity continued during late antiquity, towards the end of the fourth century another kind of diplomacy, which sought to replace war in regulating inter-state relations, began to emerge first in dealings between the Romans and the Persians, who attempted to stabilize their own relations the better to deal with threats to their borders elsewhere. This diplomacy, which made some advance towards treating international relations as an ongoing process (although it never developed permanent representation), laid the ground for the emergence during the fifth century of the instruments and protocols which in turn made possible the mature diplomacy of the Byzantine period. Its importance, however, should not be overestimated: its effectiveness in conflict resolution was limited, and war remained by far the most important determinant of international relations.[2]

II. SOURCES

In the fourth century, the composition of large-scale contemporary, or near-contemporary, history in the classical manner revived. Writing in this tradition, with its emphasis upon events of military and political significance, Ammianus Marcellinus, a Syrian Greek and an army officer, produced towards the end of the fourth century a history, written in Latin, of the period from the death of the emperor Nerva to the battle of Adrianople and the death of Valens (96–378). The surviving part of the work, books 14 to 31, covers the years 354 to 378 in detail, and it constitutes the best single source for the military and political history of late antiquity before the regin of Justinian. The rest of our period is nowhere near as well served. A pagan, Zosimus, writing in Greek probably during the reign of Anastasius (491–518), produced a very biased and uneven account, which covers the whole of the fourth century, terminating abruptly in 408. The value of Zosimus' New History (as it is called) lies in the contemporary sources which he used for the period – mainly two: first, Eunapius of Sardis, a Greek pagan who wrote a large-scale but very partial history from the death of Claudius II (270) to the year 404, and then another Greek, Olympiodorus, who wrote a much more informed and interesting commentary on events down to 425. What Zosimus preserves from these works is supplemented by passages of Eunapius incorporated in a number of Byzantine collections of excerpts, and by a summary of Olympiodorus in the Bibliotheca of the patriarch Photius. While Zosimus wrote a work which was hostile to Christians, on the Christian side the

[2] For a discussion of the develoment of international diplomacy in the east through the fourth and fifth centuries, see Blockley, Foreign Policy.

Adversus Paganos of Paulus Orosius covers in its seventh and last book the history of the Roman empire to 417. In addition to these histories, a large number of chronicles written in Latin and Greek (but none, with the exception of Eusebius–Jerome, contemporary with the fourth century) provide a chronological framework and accounts of various events in varying detail and of varying reliability. Contemporary epitomes, by Festus, Aurelius Victor, Eutropius and the anonymous author of the *Epitome de Caesaribus*, offer sketchy but fairly authoritative material. And the ecclesiastical histories written in the fifth century make some mention of secular events.

In addition to the historical writings, there survive a number of commentaries on contemporary events, usually cast in the form of public speeches to an emperor or a powerful official. Encomiastic in form and intent, the surviving examples from the period are, with the important exception of those by Claudian, in prose. In Greek such speeches survive by Themistius, Libanius and the emperor Julian, while in Latin there are eleven of the twelve speeches in the collection *Panegyrici Latini* and works by Ausonius and Ambrose. For the period of the ascendancy of Stilicho in the west (395–408) the political poems of Claudian are of capital importance; they are mainly panegyrical, although two are attacks on eastern politicians (Rufinus and Eutropius). Finally, there are other political statements by Julian (especially his attack on the emperor Constantius II in his Letter to the Athenians) and two speeches by Gregory of Nazianzus against Julian. All of these works are, of course, extremely partial and their commentary tendentious, so that the details which they offer have to be approached with care.

A few writings of a more technical nature are also relevant. First there are the law codes, the *Codex Theodosianus* and the *Codex Iustinianus*, compiled at the command of Theodosius II and Justinian, which preserve many ordinances concerning the military and a few that offer information on diplomacy. The organization of the late Roman administration, including that of the military, is set out fairly completely in the *Notitia Dignitatum*, which appears to reflect the situation in the east in about 394 and in the west *c.* 420. A handbook by Vegetius offers commentary on military practices of the period, and an anonymous tract, *De Rebus Bellicis*, written apparently in the third quarter of the fourth century, offers a rather idiosyncratic discussion of deficiencies in the military posture of the period and rather wild suggestions for improvement.

Information from the works noted above, supplemented by details offered in other writings and contextualized by the enormous amount of data now available from archaeology, makes it possible to construct a fairly ample account of the warfare of the period. In contrast, the peripheral position of diplomacy in the fourth century is demonstrated by the almost complete lack of interest shown in it by the Greek and Latin sources, which have to be trawled for the scraps of information which they offer almost incidentally. Indeed, it is writings in other languages which show us more clearly that at the end of the fourth century the Romans and the Persians, at least, were communicating by other means in addition to fighting. Most useful are works in Armenian, especially the writings by Faustus of Byzanta and Moses Khorenats'i, which trace the violent history of the Armenians (supplementing and in some cases correcting the military and political accounts in the Roman sources), and a number of chronicles in Syriac, usually anonymous, which indicate a considerable level of diplomatic activity at the end of the fourth and the beginning of the fifth centuries. The Greek and Latin sources begin to show a greater interest in diplomatic activity only during the later part of the reign of Theodosius II. Thereafter a fuller, though still not satisfactory, account of Roman diplomacy can be attempted.

III. THE DEFENCE OF THE EMPIRE TO CONSTANTINE

By the reign of Hadrian a non-expansionist military posture had evolved, with the legions and auxiliaries in the north and west strung out in a cordon along a heavily guarded border (but still ready to counter-strike against an enemy threat), while those in the east guarded the main invasion routes and backed up and ensured the loyalty of the client rulers of the kingdoms and cities of Mesopotamia and the Arabian and Armenian marches. By the reign of Marcus Aurelius, however, the Romans were on the defensive against a new threat which was developing along the Rhine and especially the Danube border: large-scale movements of peoples over an extended area that could flood and overrun the Roman perimeter defence at various points, a situation that the Roman defensive profile was not designed to meet. Furthermore, Roman military planners were posed new tactical problems by the appearance of new peoples with new military technologies and skills, such as the Sarmatians with their armoured lancers and mass cavalry charge.

The onset through much of the third century of various tribes along the Rhine and Danube and from the region north of the Black Sea, as well as the rapid consolidation of Sassanid power in Persia and the aggression of its two warrior-kings, Ardashir I (?224–40) and Shapur I (240–c. 272), placed such great pressure on the Roman defences that they collapsed. A series of major invasions, the most spectacular of which were the Persian attacks on Syria in 256 and 259–60 (the second culminating in the capture of the emperor Valerian), together with recurring bouts of civil war and natural disasters, brought the empire to the verge of disintegration, from which it was saved by the efforts of soldier-emperors such as Aurelian.

Militarily, the most significant developments of this period were the fortification of towns even far into the interior of the empire, an indication of and defence against ever-deeper enemy penetration, and the development of efficient and highly mobile cavalry forces (traditionally the weaker part of the Roman army) to intercept quick-moving, often mounted, bands of raiders. While the first of these developments made use of traditional Roman skills in military architecture, the latter entailed the enlistment of large numbers of non-Roman, mainly Gothic and Sarmatian, mercenaries in the Roman armies.

Diocletian and Constantine completed the work of the third-century soldier-emperors in saving the Roman empire from its external enemies. In the process, they radically reshaped the Roman state. Well before the end of Constantine's reign the borders of the empire had been restored (with some adjustments) and strengthened through the systematic repair of fortifications or the building of new ones, and the improvement of military communications behind the forward lines. The ideally impermeable perimeter cordon of the second-century defences was not restored. Instead, a frontier zone was created, dotted with fortified farmhouses, refuges and storehouses, as well as the forts and walled towns in which the regular border troops were posted. This forward defence-in-depth, which was manned by second-rate regulars and barbarian settlers, was similar to the system that had long existed on the eastern frontier, though there the forts and walled towns were more clearly aligned along the axes of the few main invasion routes. Behind this forward defence was a mobile élite field army (the *comitatus*), perhaps one-third cavalry, the nucleus of which had been formed early in Constantine's reign at the latest. The functions of this field army, which was dispersed amongst the towns behind the forward lines to be collected comparatively speedily for service where necessary, were to intercept raiders as they forced their way through the frontier zone and to form the core of a strike force should the Romans decide to carry the war into enemy territory.[3]

The restoration of the empire and the creation of the system of defence that ensured its survival were achieved at high cost to its inhabitants. Behind the defences a state of siege was created through the mobilization and militarization of all parts of society, whose resources were devoted to

[3] The above paragraph summarizes the traditional view, still tenable in my opinion, although Luttwak, *Grand Strategy*, goes too far when he presents this and earlier configurations as results of the integrated planning of a 'scientific' frontier. A comprehensive rejection of Luttwak's position has been set out by Isaac, *Limits of Empire*, who argues that systematic defence was never a factor in the installation of a Roman frontier, but that administrative concerns, especially the control of people, were paramount. While Isaac convincingly demolishes the overly systematic and simplistic models of the political scientist, nevertheless, in discussing late antiquity he undervalues well-attested defensive concerns and other factors (such as control of trade). To Ammianus Marcellinus, for instance, *limes* seems to have meant an area (not a line) that had a defensive capacity.

the maintenance of the army and the greatly increased, and also militarized, bureaucracy that oversaw the collection and allocation of these resources. The enlarged army of the restored empire was no less strong than that of the first or second centuries A.D. Indeed, for much of the fourth century it might have been stronger in resources and manpower, professional skills (especially in its upper command) and flexibility (with better cavalry and siege weaponry). But the situation that it faced was far more threatening: in the east a still-aggressive Persia, led for much of the fourth century by one of its greatest rulers, Shapur II (309–79); along the Rhine and Danube a number of developing confederacies of German and Sarmatian tribes, which were centralizing under kings, which had developed an ability to co-ordinate their actions over a wide area, and whose armament and tactics might have been somewhat improved by contact with the Romans (this is not clear); and behind these, pressing upon or supplanting them, new peoples with new skills, such as Ostrogothic or Alan cavalrymen on the lower Danube or Saxon sailors in the North Sea, who posed new problems for the Romans.

In the face of these threats the restored Roman empire enjoyed considerable success until past the middle of the fourth century. By 293 the tetrarchic system devised by Diocletian was in place, and the empire was ruled by two Augusti and two Caesars, the latter mainly of military competence. Each ruler had an army, and aggressive campaigns were carried out almost every year. The greatest triumph of Roman arms, and one which avenged the capture of Valerian, was achieved in 298, when the Persian king Nerseh (293–302), who in the two previous years had beaten the Romans and overrun much of Armenia and Roman Mesopotamia, was defeated by Galerius, losing his treasury and some of his close family to the victor. For the return of his family Nerseh was compelled in 299 to agree to a peace treaty under which the Romans acquired eastern Mesopotamia and its key fortress Nisibis, some Armenian principalities along the upper Euphrates and Tigris, and suzerainty over Armenia and Iberia.[4] As a result the Romans were able to shorten and strengthen their eastern border and cut the Persians off from access to the Black Sea, thus assuring the security of Asia Minor and Syria.

The abdication of Diocletian and Maximian in 305 was followed by twenty years of internal conflict and instability. Nevertheless, when Constantine defeated and deposed Licinius in 324 he ruled an empire that was militarily strong. During the period of instability there had been barbarian unrest along both the Rhine and the middle and lower Danube, but the raiders had been thrown back. Most important, the Persians kept the peace during the reigns of Nerseh and Hormizd II (302–9) and during

---

[4] For the dating of the treaty to 299 rather than the usual 298 see Barnes (1976) 182–6.

the long minority of Shapur II, who was crowned in 309 while still an infant. As a consequence, Constantine, both before and after he became sole emperor, was free to pursue a policy of aggression against the enemies across the Rhine and Danube, invading their lands, dictating terms and deporting large numbers of them into Roman territory. A measure of Roman confidence at this period is the rebuilding in 328 of Trajan's old stone bridge across the Danube into Sarmatia.[5] While, on the one hand, Constantine sought to terrorize the barbarian enemies of Rome, on the other, he made careers in the Roman army readily available to non-Romans, especially to Franks and Alamanni, some of whom rose to high command under his sons and one of whom, Nevitta, reached the consulship in 362.

IV. FROM CONSTANTINE'S DEATH TO THE TREATY OF 363

By Constantine's death in 337 Roman–Persian relations had deteriorated to the point of war. As early as *c.* 326 Shapur in person had campaigned successfully in the Arabian peninsula, advancing right up to the Roman zone of influence south of the province of Arabia. Some time afterwards there is evidence of Christian missionary work and Roman diplomatic activity in south Arabia and Ethiopia, and perhaps even a Roman-inspired attack by the Ethiopians on south Arabia, all of which might have served to counter Persian activity further north and to protect Roman access through the strait of Aden. In the last years of Constantine's reign a proxy war had erupted between the Arab allies of Rome and Persia, and by *c.* 334 relations were so bad that the emperor sent his second son, Constantius, to oversee the eastern defences and to prepare for the possibility of war; Constantius' foundation of Amida (Dyarbekir) and fortification of Constantia (Tella de-Mauzelat) date from this period.[6] Moreover, in Armenia after the death of Tiridates IV in 330 there was turmoil as an anti-Christian, Persian-supported claimant attempted to seize the throne and Constantine retaliated by invading the country and proclaiming his nephew Hannibalianus king.[7] In 336 a Persian embassy arrived at Constantinople, apparently demanding a renegotiation of the treaty of 299, to which Constantine replied that he would attack Persia and conquer it for Christianity. His death in the next year, however, and the manoeuvres amongst his sons that followed the elimination of other family members and supporters, including Hannibalianus, caused the invasion to be postponed. Shapur, meanwhile, seized the initiative and attacked Nisibis,

[5] *Chron. Pasch.* (Bonn edn) p. 527; Aur. Vict. *Caes.* XLI.18; Anon. *De Caes.* XLI.14.

[6] For the events in the Arabian peninsula during the last decade of Constantine's reign see Shahîd (1984b) 29–66.

[7] For events in Armenia from 330 to 339 see the radical revision of the traditional order by Hewsen (1978–9).

though the Persians were forced to withdraw. In 338 Constantius II, whose
share of the empire was the east and Thrace, was able to restore the new
king of Armenia, Arsak III, who had been briefly driven out, and crowned
him in 339. Although Armenia was thus returned to the Roman sphere,
Shapur continued to attempt to win over Arsak by diplomacy.

The Roman empire at Constantine's death appeared to be militarily
strong and able to act aggressively towards its enemies. After the elimination of Constantine II in 340 the western part, reunited under Constans
and controlling the major recruiting-ground of Illyricum, seemed the more
powerful of the two. Constans, with a stronger army, was able to continue
his father's policy of carrying the war to the hostile tribes along the Rhine
and Danube – with success, according to the very scanty sources for the
period. In 338 he is attested fighting the Sarmatians on the Danube; in 341
and 342 fighting and defeating the Franks on the lower Rhine, whom he
installed as subject-allies in Toxandria; in 343 he crossed to Britain to repel
an invasion of the provinces there.[8] According to Ammianus (xxx.7.5) the
Alamanni were in terror of him.

In the east Constantius was apparently considered by some not to have
done well in the division of the empire and its military resources.[9] Faced at
the beginning of his reign by unrest in his army and then the civil war
between his brothers, he abandoned his father's planned invasion of Persia
and developed a rather more complex policy that formed the basis for most
of Rome's subsequent dealings with her eastern neighbour. Its aim was not
the acquisition of more territory but the defence of the Tigris border and
the maintenance of the Roman position in Armenia. The policy had three
components: first, the holding of a strong forward defensive line in eastern
Mesopotamia based on well-manned and well-stocked fortresses covering
the major invasion routes from southern Mesopotamia to the Euphrates,
perhaps backed by subsidiary defences along the Euphrates itself; second,
raids across the Tigris to tie down local Persian forces and, by destroying
crops, to prevent them from amassing supplies for a prolonged invasion of
Roman territory; third, diplomatic efforts to ensure the continued loyalty
of the king of Armenia and, both in south Arabia and amongst the Arabs
of the desert, to cause problems for the Persians in their south-west and to
protect Roman sea routes through and beyond the Red Sea. This policy,
which, if successful, would restrict conflicts to the border areas and regions
beyond the Roman border, made sense from Constantius' position, since
the military resources available to him were much smaller than those of his
father. But there was a danger that in abandoning the threat of large-scale
and sustained aggression, for which the Romans at the period were usually

[8] The sources for the movements of Constans are collected by Barnes (1980) 164–6.
[9] Jul. *Or.* 1.18c–20a.

better organized than the Persians, he would concede the initiative to the Persians who would themselves become the raiders, while the Roman troops, a large part of whom became garrisons for the fortresses, would cease to be an effective battlefield force. Although the panegyrists of Constantius speak of many raids on Persia, and in 343 the emperor celebrated a triumph, probably for a successful raid across the Tigris,[10] in the second half of the 340s the Persians do seem to have seized the initiative, and the fighting appears to have moved to Roman territory. Roman response to Persian attacks was vigorous, and it seems that between 342 (or possibly 344) and 348 at least four set battles were fought, without, however, any significant Roman success. In the last of these battles, the famous 'night-battle' near to Singara on the south-eastern border of Roman Mesopotamia, Constantius appears to have planned a major confrontation in which he hoped to destroy the Persian army led by Shapur himself and one of his sons, Nerseh. The importance and magnitude of this battle are demonstrated by the presence of the emperor himself, presumably with the full praesental field army. At the beginning of the conflict the Romans were successful, routing the Persian attack. But the indiscipline of some of their troops drew the Romans into an ambush with the result that the fighting ended in a bloody draw.

The usurpation of Magnentius and the death of Constans in 350 had serious repercussions for both the western and eastern parts of the empire. Constantius, refusing to accept a non-dynastic co-emperor, placed the east in a state of passive defence that relied on the strength of the border fortresses to resist the Persians, while he, leaving behind his cousin Gallus to represent imperial authority as Caesar, marched west to face his brother's destroyer. This state of passive defence, which Libanius (*Or.* xviii.205–7) claims was the consistent policy throughout Constantius' reign, was, in fact, a temporary expedient while the larger part of the eastern field army was away with the emperor in the west. There is every indication that Constantius intended at the conclusion of the civil war to return to the east with the united resources of the empire to face the Persians in battle. Fortune joined with the fortresses to protect the east for almost a decade since Shapur, after a determined, very costly and unsuccessful attack on Nisibis in 350, was distracted by nomad incursions against Persian territory in the north-east, where he was tied down until 356–7, leaving his local commanders to mount what were merely nuisance raids on the Romans.

Magnentius, who advanced to face Constantius in the Balkans, must have withdrawn troops from the Rhine defences. Constantius, in order to tie him down, is said to have commissioned the Alamanni to attack him,

---

[10] For Roman raids see Jul. *Or.* 1.22b–c; Lib. *Or.* LIX.100. For Constantius' triumph see Cedren. (Bonn edn), I, p. 522.

which they chose to interpret as permission to take whatever territory they could.[11] Vetranio, the commander of the Illyrian army, after a brief, and possibly staged, usurpation, handed it to Constantius. Thus, significant elements of all three armies – Rhine, Danube and eastern – must have been involved, and destroyed, in the costly battle of Mursa where Constantius defeated Magnentius in 351. The consequent weakening of the Rhine and Danube defences encouraged the Franks, Alamanni, Sarmatians and other peoples to press into Roman territory, which they did with devastating effect. Constantius himself, after the final defeat and death of Magnentius in 353, confronted the Alamanni and compelled them to withdraw temporarily in 354. But the revolt and speedy death of the *magister peditum* Silvanus at Colonia Agrippinensis in 355 led to the complete collapse of the Rhine defences. Constantius' response at the end of that year was to appoint his cousin Julian as Caesar with responsibility for the defence of Gaul, while he himself oversaw the defence of the Danube. Once they were reorganized, the Romans began a vigorous counter-offensive against their barbarian invaders in which, despite Ammianus' efforts to obscure the fact, Constantius played his part to the full. The first phase was aimed at the Alamanni, who in 356 were attacked by Julian in Upper Germany and by Constantius from Raetia. In the next year, while Constantius beat off Suevian attacks on Raetia, Julian crushed, but did not eliminate, the Alamannic threat with a spectacular victory near to Argentorate. The defences of these regions at least temporarily restored, in 358 Julian moved down the Rhine to carry the war to the Franks and Chamavi, and Constantius fought the Quadi and Sarmatians on the Danube and Theiss. Both Augustus and Caesar were successful, though in 359 a revolt by the Limigantes, a people subject to the Sarmatians, detained Constantius from his intended return to the eastern frontier, while Julian delivered a harsh lesson to the still-restless southern Alamanni, invading and devastating their lands across the Rhine. The traditional Roman response to barbarian invasions, counterattack and a dictated peace guaranteed by hostages, had proven highly and quickly effective, a lesson learned by Julian that had disastrous results later.

While Constantius was detained on the Danube, the defence of the east, after the elimination of the Caesar Gallus in 354, was in the hands of the *pro magistro militum per Orientem* Prosper (replaced by the returning *magister* Ursicinus in 357), the *dux Mesopotamiae* Cassianus, and the senior civilian official, the *praefectus praetorio per Orientem* Musonianus. Hostilities with the Persians had remained at a low level since the end of 350, and in early 357 Musonianus, probably buoyed by reports of Roman successes in the west, attempted a diplomatic approach to the Persians. He suggested unofficially

[11] Lib. *Or.* XVIII.33 and 107; Amm. Marc. XVI.12.5; XXI.3.4; Zos. II.53.3.

to the Persian area commander (*marzban*), Tamsapor, that the time was ripe to negotiate a formal end to hostilities. Tamsapor, relying on his own source of information that led him to conclude that the Romans were in difficulties in the west, reported the approach to his king, who had recently brought his war with the nomads in the north-east to a successful conclusion. Shapur, who was now free to bring against the Romans his full army reinforced by his new nomad allies, sent an embassy to Constantius, probably in early summer 358, threatening war if the Romans did not cede to him Armenia and Mesopotamia, by which he apparently meant the lands taken in 299. Constantius rejected Shapur's demand, and thus Musonianus' attempt at diplomacy failed in its primary objective. But the emperor was now alerted to the Persian position and intentions, and, since he wished to secure the Danube frontier before war with Persia flared up, he quickly sent an embassy, which was followed by a second in late 358 or early 359 with instructions to learn the details of Shapur's intentions. Probably shortly before this, Constantius, in order to confirm the loyalty of the Armenian king Arsak, took the step, unusual for the period, of marrying to this foreigner a Roman noblewoman, Olympias, who had once been the betrothed of Constans. When Shapur launched his promised invasion in 359, one of the members of the second embassy, which had been detained in Persia, smuggled back a message that led the Roman generals, Ursicinus and Sabinianus, to conclude that the Persians intended to strike straight across the Euphrates into Syria. They shaped their strategy accordingly, but Shapur, marching north instead of west as expected, surprised and destroyed Amida, an important fortress and artillery depot, capturing its garrison of around 7000 men. Constantius, who had himself planned to campaign in the east in 359 but had been detained by a revolt of the Limigantes on the middle Danube, determined to face the Persians in the next year and demanded troops from Julian for the war, Julian's revolt in early 360 and his recall of those detachments which had already set out for the east did not halt Constantius' preparations, since he was also recruiting Gothic mercenaries. But the preparations were set back, so that before the Roman army reached Mesopotamia, the Persians had broken through again, capturing Singara and Bezabde, the latter of which they garrisoned. The damage to the Roman defences was real but limited as long as Nisibis held firm, and when in 361 Constantius was finally ready, for the first time since 348, to meet the Persians in set battle, Shapur declined, and abandoned his invasion for that year. What would have happened next can only be guessed at since Constantius, marching to meet Julian who was advancing on Thrace, fell sick and died in Cilicia. Shapur did not attack in 362 and sent an embassy to Julian offering to negotiate. Whatever Julian's propagandists might claim, the offer was probably encouraged by Constantius' preparations for war.

Julian's reign as sole Augustus ended attempts at diplomacy in the east. As Caesar in Gaul, employing the traditional tactics of battlefield confrontation and devastating counter-strike into enemy territory, Julian had from 356 enjoyed such success that when he led off a large part of the Gallic field army to face Constantius in 361, the border was not violated. His success in the west had convinced him that he could deal with the Persians in the same manner, and, having rejected the Persian offer to negotiate, in 363 he invaded southern Mesopotamia, striking straight at Ctesiphon. Although Hormizd, Shapur's brother who had fled to the Romans in 324, accompanied him, Julian is unlikely to have had any serious expectation of placing him on Shapur's throne. He seems to have planned to spend only the present campaigning season in Persia, and his intention probably was, like Carus and other emperors before him, to devastate what was the richest part of Shapur's kingdom to compel the Persians to accept disadvantageous terms, as he had done with the Germans.

Even some of Julian's supporters opposed the invasion as ill-advised, and their fears proved well-founded. The Roman attack lost momentum before the walls of Ctesiphon, and the army was retreating and in difficulties even before Julian was killed. Jovian, his successor, in order to extricate the starving and demoralized army, was compelled to agree to a thirty-year treaty under which the Persians took control of eastern Mesopotamia (including Nisibis) and the easternmost of the Armenian principalities that had been ceded to the Romans in 299, and the Romans agreed not to help Arsak, the king of Armenia, leaving him to face the Persians alone. Many Christian writers, elated over Julian's death, defended the settlement, while the people of Syria were angered by the loss of their forward defences, especially Nisibis. Ammianus, marshalling some notably weak special pleading to turn the blame from Julian to Constantine as the originator of the war (xxv.4.23–7), cannot obscure the fact that Julian's strike deep into Persia was a disastrous failure. The lesson was well learned by the Romans: it was not until 581 that Maurice attempted the next march on Ctesiphon, which also failed, though not disastrously as in 363. The Persians for their part, having secured their defences of Adiabene and southern Mesopotamia, did not use their advantage to attack Syria, even when fighting with the Romans flared up in Armenia in 371.

V. THE PANNONIAN EMPERORS

After the death of Julian the western part of the empire faced attacks in many regions. Ammianus (xxvi.4.5) lists the invaders: Alamanni and Saxons in Gaul, Sarmatians and Quadi in Pannonia, Picts, Scots, Saxons and Attacotti in Britain, Moors in Africa. The new western emperor, Valentinian I, responded vigorously and in the traditional manner: meet the enemy, crush them, devastate their lands and force them to beg for peace. Valentinian and his generals were successful and praised for it, and the emperor was linked with Trajan as Rome's great soldier-ruler. Valentinian was also the last great builder and repairer of fortifications, especially along the Rhine; and here, too, his aggressive spirit is demonstrated by his readiness, remarked by Ammianus (XXVIII.2.5–7; cf. XXX.7.6), to build even outside Roman territory.

In the east Valens, in dealing with Rome's enemies as in many other matters, followed his brother's lead. At the beginning of his reign the Gothic tribes along the lower Danube were raiding Roman territory. They also sent troops to aid the usurper Procopius. These the Romans captured and refused to send back, so that war broke out in 367. Through a series of raids across the Danube, in combination with a trade-embargo, Valens brought the Goths to terms by 369. He also took a strong, if cautious, line against Persian attacks on Armenia, which began soon after the death of Jovian with the objects of removing Arsak and bringing the country under Persian control. Once freed from his war with the Goths, Valens, probably in 369, permitted the return to Armenia of Arsak's son Pap to replace his father, who had been captured by the Persians in the previous year. In probably 370 Pap was crowned king and given Roman military assistance. Despite Persian protests that this contravened the treaty of 363, the Romans took an active part in ejecting the Persians; a Roman force also reinstated the Roman-sponsored king of Iberia in half of that country, leaving the other half in the hands of the Persian nominee who had earlier replaced him. Although Pap ruled Armenia as a Roman nominee, he attempted to assert independence of his masters, which led to his murder by the commander of the Roman forces there in 375 and the succession of Varazdat. At the news of Pap's death Shapur proposed to Valens that the Romans either evacuate Iberia or alternatively agree to abolish the Armenian crown, which would have resulted in the division of the country between the Romans and the Persians. Valens rejected the proposal and sent Shapur an ultimatum to leave Armenia alone or face war. Shapur accepted the challenge, and Valens began to prepare for an invasion of Persia in 377.

One of the measures which Valens took to build up his army for the Persian war was to admit to Roman territory Visigothic refugees from the Hunnic onslaught in *c.* 375–6. Yet it was the revolt of these very refugees, joined by others including Ostrogoths and some Alans who were fleeing the Huns, that compelled Valens to settle with Shapur, perhaps on the understanding that the Persians restrict their activity in Armenia to the central province, Ayrarat, and the east and south of the country. The Roman forces in Armenia were withdrawn to help oppose the barbarians who were devastating Thrace. The outcome of the campaign in Thrace, the death of Valens and the destruction of a large part of his army at Adrianople in 378, was a result of the same readiness for confrontation that had brought some success against the Persians and, earlier, the Goths on the lower Danube. At Adrianople, however, Valens' overeagerness for set battle led him to abandon the successful hit-and-run tactics that the general Sebastianus had been using, to refuse to await reinforcements which were on the way from the west, and to commit fatal tactical blunders on the day of the battle itself.

VI. THEODOSIUS I: THE AFTERMATH OF ADRIANOPLE

The disaster of Adrianople marked a watershed for Roman policy both along the Danube and on the eastern frontier. In the east, Persian intentions would be unknown, and they might be expected to seize the initiative when news of the disaster arrived. Gratian, even before making Theodosius the eastern Augustus, had appointed a Persian, Sapores, as *magister militum per Orientem* (378–81), presumably to keep an expert watching-brief on his country of origin. In fact, the Roman border remained undisturbed, and although the Persians, at the invitation of the territorial princes of Armenia (*nakharars*) who had ejected the Roman-supported Varazdat in 377–8, established themselves briefly in that country, the Armenians unaided appear to have driven them out and to have maintained their independence for a number of years. Persian inaction was probably the result of the death of Shapur II in 379 and the disturbed conditions under the weak kings who succeeded him. That, for his part, Theodosius desired good relations with the Persians is shown by the friendly reception afforded the envoys who came in 384 to announce the accession of Shapur III. Around the same time or shortly thereafter civil war erupted in Armenia between the Roman-supported Arsak IV and a Persian nominee, Khusro III, who had been sent at the request of some of the *nakharars*. After a brief threat of Roman–Persian hostilities the two powers agreed, probably in 387, to divide Armenia into Roman and Persian spheres of influence, not at this point delimited by a fixed border and each under its king, to whom the *nakharars* gave their allegiance. This arrangement, which led to the abolition of the Arsacid crown in both sectors by 428 and the emergence of a border at about the same time, greatly eased, though it did not eliminate, Roman–Persian tensions in the region.[12]

During the first part of his reign Theodosius, free from pressure on his eastern border, was able to concentrate his main efforts in the Balkans, where the defences of the lower Danube had collapsed and groups of Visigoths, Ostrogoths and others were overrunning the area. The details of

[12] For this interpretation of the Armenian settlement during Theodosius' reign see Blockley (1987).

the campaigns of the years 379–82 are lost, but the broad developments are clear. Operating from Thessalonica with a rebuilt army that probably already included many Goths, Theodosius and his general Modares pushed the enemy out of Thrace into Lower Moesia in 379. In the next year, however, with Theodosius recovering from a serious illness and the Romans apparently disorganized (a good illustration of the importance of the imperial presence), the Visigoths broke into Macedonia, while the Ostrogoths, Alans and others attacked Pannonia and Upper Moesia. Gratian himself led an army against the invaders of Pannonia and despatched reinforcements to Theodosius, who was able to push the Visigoths back north by the end of the year. In perhaps 381 Gratian terminated the fighting in the north-west by settling the Ostrogoths and others in part of Pannonia as *foederati*, while in the next year (3 October 382) the Visigoths made peace in exchange for land in Lower Moesia and the status of *foederati*. It is sometimes suggested by both ancient and modern authorities that Visigothic readiness for peace was enhanced by the magnificent reception and then funeral which had been given at Constantinople in early 381 to their old leader (*iudex*) Athanaric, who had declined to flee to imperial territory in 376.[13]

These settlements differed significantly and, it turned out, disastrously from early ones, which had usually been established by the Romans from a position of strength and had consisted of barbarian settlers (often deportees or prisoners) who were either scattered amongst the indigenous population or gathered together under Roman prefects and subject to Roman jurisdiction. In contrast, it appears that the new settlements were the result of Roman weakness or loss of nerve. For many of the *foederati* were given lands upon which they lived as homogenous communities under their own elected chiefs and governed by their own customs; often they were also paid subsidies in return for their commitment to supply troops on request. While this gave the empire a reservoir of good-quality troops at a time when it might have been experiencing difficulty in finding enough suitable manpower for the armies, the extent to which it accelerated the 'barbarization' of the army and the ultimate collapse of its organization in the west is unclear. But the regular subsidies, nominally in return for military aid, tied the empire more closely than before to inherently unstable groups in a relationship of growing mutual dependence: that is, the Romans came to depend upon the manpower of the barbarians, who in turn came to depend on Roman resources. The autonomous and homogenous nature of the settlements, the population of which often behaved differently from, encroached upon and clashed with the

---

[13] Doubts about this connection have been most recently expressed by Liebeschuetz, *Barbarians and Bishops* 28 n. 24.

indigenous inhabitants of the area, must have posed serious problems of control, which in turn are reflected in complaints of indiscipline and even disloyalty in the Roman army, where the federates both served in separate formations under their own leaders and enrolled in large numbers as individual mercenaries in Roman units officered by Romans or barbarians.[14] Theodosius himself dealt with the problems of control by abandoning the aloofness of a Diocletian or Constantius II and forming ties of friendship and personal loyalty with the band chiefs, some of whom received high rank in the Roman army or even Roman wives. This policy, which was condemned by some Roman 'nationalists' as weak and dangerous,[15] did prove to be so under those emperors who were either unable to maintain the loyalty of the chiefs or, if they were able to do so, failed to keep it subordinate to broader imperial policy. Then even 'loyalists' like Arbogast were out of the emperor's control, and chiefs like Alaric were able to act wholly independently while destroying the empire from within.

This change in policy towards the northern barbarians had important consequences for Roman military strategy. The vigorous counterattack into enemy territory, the almost invariable reaction to raids from Constantine on, was abandoned along the Danube and later along the Rhine. Invaders were still at times confronted and pushed back; in late 386 the *magister militum* Promotus destroyed a force of Goths that was trying to cross the lower Danube. Other groups, however, were received into the empire on favourable terms. Once these federate groups were settled behind the defences of the border provinces, while the main border fortresses were still held, the full *limes* system could hardly be maintained. Early in Honorius' reign the defences of Pannonia were gone; indeed, after Valentinian I there was very little building of new fortifications anywhere, merely repair. Furthermore, the civil wars between Theodosius and Maximus and Eugenius stripped much of the manpower from the border defences, a process that was continued by Stilicho and Constantine III with disastrous results for Roman Gaul, Spain and Britain. In the Balkans the zone of defence-in-depth became progressively deeper as more people under continued pressure from the Huns pushed into the empire, until finally the whole region, including Thrace and Greece, became a battleground. After the death of Theodosius and the rupturing of the ties of personal friendship that he had formed with the band chiefs, the new settlers proved less willing to submit to Roman control. The mixture of fighting and diplomacy which had been evolving in relations with the Persians began now to be used in dealings with the northern barbarians, who, however, lacked the state structure that would have enabled them to

---

[14] Liebeschuetz, *Barbarians and Bishops* chs. 3 and 4.
[15] Eunap. frr. 55 and 60 (in *FHG* IV pp. 38f., 41f.=frr. 48.2 and 59 (Blockley)); Zos. IV.33.2–4; 56.

respond to it with any consistency. On the Roman side, diplomacy was usually the reactive diplomacy of appeasement, a substitute for fighting and a confession of weakness. Its only consistently effective element was the regular payment of subsidies, a long-standing Roman practice but one which was now transformed from a payment for services rendered or expected, made from strength, into a rental of good behaviour, paid out of weakness.

The dangers latent in the federate settlements became clear soon after the death of Theodosius and the division of the empire between his ineffective sons, Arcadius and Honorius. These were under the control of 'strongmen', usually soldiers in the west, and the consequent intrigues, as individuals sought to advance their own or their clique's interests, not only weakened the governments of the two parts of the empire, but also accelerated the tendency of the east and west to drift apart. The squabble over the control of eastern Illyricum, which Stilicho alleged had been returned to the western empire by Theodosius before his death; eastern intrigues with Gildo in Africa; western support for John Chrysostom in his disputes with the court at Constantinople – these and other matters, in a situation in which there was no mechanism for regular contact and consultation, undermined the ability and willingness of the two parts to co-operate against external enemies. In these circumstances of division and increasing disorganization, especially in the west, the barbarian chiefs such as Alaric frequently performed two roles – that of agents in the Roman political process, at times with the rank of military *magister*, and that of leaders in the settlement and territorial aggrandizement of their own followers; and the latter role usually took precedence. Yet at this time, when co-operation against such dangers from the barbarians on the inside became more necessary, the governments of the eastern and western parts of the empire became less capable of it.

VII. THE REIGNS OF ARCADIUS AND HONORIUS

After the death of Thedosius I the eastern part of the empire seemed to be in the most difficult circumstances. While Rufinus and Eutropius, and then Gainas and others, competed for control of the government, the Visigoths who had been settled in Lower Moesia revolted under the leadership of Alaric and from 395 to 398 devastated Thrace, Macedonia and Greece before settling in Epirus under a treaty which gave Alaric the rank of *magister militum per Illyricum* and thus access to the Roman arsenals of the region. Moreover, in 395–6 a force of Huns (who had pressed not only to the north of the Black Sea but also to the south-east) broke through the Caucasus Mountains and ravaged Armenia, Asia Minor and Syria. While the eastern government after initial failure was able to beat off the Huns, it made no attempt to oppose the Visigoths and forbade Stilicho to continue a campaign which he had undertaken against them.[16] The recovery from this period of turmoil and weakness in the east began in 400 with the destruction of Gainas and his German supporters. Germans were by no means eliminated from the eastern army, as some had demanded, though after the death of the *magister militum per Orientem* Fravitta in 401 no German appears amongst the senior generals until 419 when Plintha, a Goth, was *magister militum in praesenti*. Most importantly, however, the civilian administration, usually represented by the *praefectus praetorio* or the *magister officiorum*, regained and maintained a large measure of control over the state and the military officials, which it achieved partly through a deliberate policy of keeping the army small and relying upon negotiation to deal with threats. Furthermore, as in the difficult years at the beginning of the reign of Theodosius I, the recovery was assisted by peace on the eastern frontier. Although at the accession of Yezdegerd I in 399 there was a brief war scare, the new Persian king was not bent on hostilities and perhaps, at this time, as an earnest of his friendly intentions, permitted the Roman captives whom the Huns had taken in 395–6 and the Persians had rescued to return home.[17] The security of the eastern empire was placed on a firmer footing by Anthemius, praetorian prefect and virtual ruler of the east from 404 to 414, under whose government the defences were strengthened, good relations with the Persians were confirmed by regular embassies, and the internal equilibrium of the state was restored. During the same period in the west this equilibrium was being irretrievably lost.[18]

In the year 400 the western part of the Roman empire appeared to be in a comparatively healthy condition. Although the emperor Honorius was a feeble nonentity, the government was firmly in the hands of the *magister utriusque militiae* Stilicho, an able soldier and administrator who was allied by marriage to the imperial house. The Rhine border was quiet; attacks by Scots, Picts and Saxons on Britain had been severely punished, according to the rather dubious testimony of Claudian (*De Cons. Stil.* 11.250–5; *In Eutrop.* 1.391–2); Alaric had been twice cornered, though not destroyed; and the revolt of Gildo in Africa in 399 had been crushed. But in 401 the deluge began that within a few years had swept away or irreparably undermined Roman rule in much of western Europe. In late summer of that year Alaric entered northern Italy. During the winter of 401–2 Stilicho was occupied with Vandal and Alan raids in Noricum and Raetia. In order to raise enough troops to meet the Visigoths, Stilicho recruited auxiliaries amongst those Vandals and Alans whom he had been fighting. With his army thus strengthened Stilicho was able to face Alaric, who was advanc-

---

[16] A second expedition by Stilicho against Alaric in 397 was also aborted.

[17] *Chron. ad a. DCCXXIV (CSCO Script. Syr.* 111.4) p. 106.

[18] Detailed discussion of these developments in Liebeschuetz, *Barbarians and Bishops* 89–131.

ing westwards towards Gaul, at Pollentia in April 402. Although the battle was drawn, Alaric was compelled to retreat eastwards. When, however, he turned north and attempted to make for the Alpine passes, he was defeated twice, at Hasta and Verona, and then permitted to withdraw into western Illyricum. In 405 a large force of Ostrogoths, Vandals, Alans and Quadi led by Radagaisus crossed the Alps into Italy. The greater part of this force was blockaded and destroyed at Faesulae, but only after it had ravaged northern Italy for six months.[19]

The motives of Stilicho in permitting Alaric to escape in 402 (as well as in 395 and 397) have been much discussed, especially in relation to Stilicho's designs on eastern Illyricum or on control of the eastern government. But the events of the years 401 to 405 also illustrate, as they must have helped to shape, the western government's attitude towards the defence of the state. The Alpine defences of Italy, the Julian sector of which had been abandoned by its garrisons during the civil war between Theodosius I and Eugenius,[20] were clearly inadequate; by 407 the Roman military presence was so weak that the general Sarus, returning with an imperial force from Gaul to Italy, had to surrender part of his booty to the Bagaudae to ensure safe passage through the Alpine passes.[21] Under these circumstances, and especially under the threat of Alaric from the east, the impulse of the western Roman government was to act like a government of Italy. Abandoning the clear and consistently held view of all of its predecessors that the safety of Italy was guaranteed by the security of the northern and western provinces, it gave up a large part of the defences of the upper Danube and withdrew from the Rhine and Britain troops whom it never returned. This preoccupation with the defence of Italy, whether justified or not under the circumstances, led directly from the federate settlements under Gratian and Theodosius I to the ruin of the western provinces. Furthermore, even the army in Italy at this juncture was dangerously dependent upon federate troops.[22]

The blow fell on the last day of 406, it is said.[23] On that day a host of Vandals, Alans and Sueves, having crushed the Frankish federates who attempted to fend them off, crossed the now undefended Rhine near to Mainz and began a three-year rampage through northern and western Gaul. At about the same time, Burgundians and Alamanni, apparently also unopposed, poured into Upper Germany. While the Roman forces in Gaul were unable to halt the invaders, Britain, turning to self-help in the face of the Italian government's inactivity, raised three usurpers in quick succession, the last of whom, Constantine, crossed to Gaul in 407, rallied

---

[19] For a more detailed account of these events see ch. 4, pp. 118–21 above.
[20] Oros. *Adv. Pag.* VII.35.3.   [21] Zos. VI.2.5.
[22] See Liebeschuetz, *Barbarians and Bishops*, esp. 35–43.
[23] *Cons. Ital. a.* 406 (*MGH., Auct. Ant.* IX p. 299); Prosper Tiro, *Epit. Chron. a.* 406 (*ibid.*, p. 465).

whatever remained of the Gallic forces and, according to an eastern writer, secured the Rhine border more firmly than at any time since Julian.[24] Whatever Constantine's immediate achievements might have been, he was able neither to refortify the Rhine nor expel the invaders of 406–7. His ambition, it seems, was not to be a second Postumus preserving the Gauls for Rome, but to supersede Honorius as emperor of all the west. In this he failed, while squabbling amongst his own supporters let the Vandals, Alans and Sueves into Spain, and Britain, abandoned to its own devices by the emperor whom its army had created, renounced its allegiance to him and defended itelf as best it could against increasing Saxon attacks. In Italy, meanwhile, the imperial government was faring no better. In 408 Stilicho, his prestige sapped by his failure to deal with Alaric and his position undermined by anti-German plotters at court, was killed in a military revolt. Those who controlled the government after him were incompetent and divided, and Alaric, strengthened by the adherence of the Roman auxiliary troops, whose families had been slaughtered at Stilicho's death, marched into Italy and captured Rome itself in 410.

The year 411 provides a measure of the disintegration that had occurred in the western empire over the previous decade. Constantine's general Gerontius, who had revolted and proclaimed his son Maximus emperor in eastern Spain, advanced on Arelate, where he besieged Constantine, only himself to be driven off by an army from Italy which captured Constantine, who was later executed; Gerontius retreated to Spain, where he was killed in a revolt of the Spanish troops; another usurpation, backed by Burgundians and other barbarians, was under preparation in Lower Germany. While the Roman armies were fighting one another, Britain had been told by Honorius to look to its own defence; north-western Gaul was effectively independent; most of Spain except for Tarraconensis and part of Carthaginiensis was occupied by Vandals, Alans and Sueves; the Burgundians and Alamanni were consolidating and expanding their holdings west of the Rhine; and the Visigoths, now led by Ataulf, were marching through Italy on their way to Gaul. That same year saw the emergence as *magister utriusque militiae* of Flavius Constantius, whose military and diplomatic efforts until his death in 421 brought a measure of order to the barbarian settlements, especially in Gaul. However, neither he nor later Flavius Aetius (*magister utriusque militiae* 433–54) could do more than postpone the inevitable.

Given the weakness and disorganization of the Roman government of these years and the dissipation of resources in internal conflicts, it is hardly surprising that the Roman army ceased to exist as anything more than a series of discrete and diminishing units. The surviving border fortifications

[24] Zos. VI.3.3.

were now abandoned unless they served purely local purposes, and the defence of Roman territory outside Italy, south-east Gaul and (for another twenty years or so) Africa was left to local officials and warlords operating from the fortified towns, who might be able to exert a temproary regional authority through forces levied locally or alliances with bands of barbarians. Hereafter, 'Roman' armies in the west appear to have included only a small and diminishing number of Roman troops beside a large and increasing component of barbarian allies of unreliable temper. As a consequence, whatever military successes were achieved in Gaul and Spain during the remainder of Honorius' reign were achieved by barbarian allies in the name of Rome. For the Roman government and regional authorities the most important resources that remained were organizational and diplomatic – still important assets in dealing with the fractious barbarian groups, many of whom continued to view the Roman emperor as the source of legitimacy. But these resources were inadequate to revive the disintegrating empire in the west or halt the consolidation of the emerging Germanic states.

VIII. THEODOSIUS II: THE EMERGENCE OF DIPLOMACY

In 408 the eastern emperor Arcadius died, and during the long reign of his son and successor Theodosius II, the recovery of the eastern empire was consolidated. The death of Stilicho in the same year made possible more normal relations with the west, while the prefecture of Anthemius continued to strengthen internal stability. In the year of Theodosius' accession a Hunnic king, Uldin, led a mixed force against Lower Moesia and Thrace, but he was forced to retreat by a combination of Roman resistance and diplomacy that detached many of his followers. Thereafter until war with Persia in 421–2 the eastern empire was troubled only by raids of desert tribes on Cyrenaica and Upper Egypt and Isaurian depredations in Asia Minor. As a result the Romans were able to repair their Balkan defences and improve the Danube fleet.

Relations with Persian continued to be good during the reign of Yezdegerd I (399–420), who signed or reaffirmed a peace treaty with the Romans, permitted regular commercial relations and, until the final year of his reign, showed himself tolerant towards Christians in Persia. In the oriental sources this earned for him the sobriquet of 'The Sinner' (which probably reflected Zoroastrian rage at his control of the activity of their clergy as much as his toleration of Christians), while the paradigmatic anecdote in the Greek sources is the claim that when Arcadius in his will named Yezdegerd the guardian of the infant Theodosius, the Persian king accepted the legacy, sent a tutor for Theodosius and wrote to the senate threatening that he would make war on anyone who conspired against his ward. The story as it stands might be a fiction, but it might also reflect a willingness on Yezdegerd's part to co-operate in protecting the infant's throne.[25]

Underlying tensions continued to exist between Rome and Persia, two being of particular and long-term importance. The passes in the Caucasus Mountains gave access by which raiders from the north, like the Huns of 395–6, could penetrate into both Roman and Persian territory. After 363 the Persians were usually in control of the region and expended considerable resources building and maintaining defences there. They sought Roman aid on the ground that the defences protected the territory of both powers, an argument that the Romans rejected, saying that the defence of Persian-controlled territory was solely a Persian problem. During the reign of Yezdegerd the matter was not pressed and it did not become a serious issue until towards the middle of the fifth century.

The second point of tension was the position of Christians in Persia and Persian-controlled Armenia and Iberia. Ever since Constantine had established Christianity within the Roman empire, the Persian authorities had, with some justification, regarded Christians, who were mainly Syrian, many of them descended from the captives deported from Roman territory by Shapur I in the third century, as a potential fifth column for Roman interests. There was, however, no close correlation between attacks on Christians and Roman–Persian hostilities. The sporadic persecutions that were mounted, the worst under Shapur II, usually occurred when the Zoroastrian clergy had influence over the king and turned him against what they regarded as a danger to their church, or when fanatical Christians courted royal wrath either by overenthusiastic proselytization of native Persians (who were forbidden by law to convert to Christianity) or by attacks on Zoroastrian fire-temples. It was the destruction of a fire-temple that led Yezdegerd, towards the end of his reign, to review his policy of toleration; and the subsequent Roman refusal to return those who had fled persecution was one of the main causes of war at the beginning of the reign of his successor, Varahram V.

During the reign of Yezdegerd the Romans and the Persians controlled these and other points of tension through a deliberate effort. Anthemius himself might have been part of the congratulatory embassy to Yezdegerd in 399,[26] and from then onwards the sources indicate that there were frequent missions from one side to the other. Often present on these missions were Christian clergy with medical skills and almost always of Syrian origin from Roman- or Persian-controlled Mesopotamia. They seem to have been *personae gratae* to the other side, could move freely between the two states,

---

[25] For a more detailed discussion see ch. 4, p. 128 above.

[26] Theod. *Hist. Rel.* xviii (*PG* lxxxii.1369) mentions his return from an embassy to the Persians.

and possessed the necessary linguistic skills. One of the earliest and most effective of these diplomatists was Marutha, the bishop of Martyropolis (Mayafarquin) in the Armenian principality of Sophanene. He made a number of visits to the Persian court and he might have been the envoy who announced the accession of Theodosius II in 408. He used his healing skills to ingratiate himself with the king and he achieved such a degree of influence that he is alleged to have been instrumental in the elections of the Persian *catholicoi* Isaac (399–400) and Ahai (411), and he certainly persuaded Yezdegerd to permit the Persian church to hold a council at Seleucia in 410, at which he was present.[27] After his death Acacius, bishop of Amida, appears to have played a similar role.[28]

Roman–Persian relations, which deteriorated in the last year or so of Yezdegerd's reign, turned to hostility at the beginning of the reign of Varahram V, who not only intensified the persecution of Christians in Persia, but also, perhaps in retaliation for the Romans' refusal to surrender Persian refugees, declined to return goldminers who had been hired from the Romans and permitted Roman merchants to be plundered. The Romans opened the war in 421 by invading Arzanene, driving the Persian army to Nisibis, where it was besieged. The Romans were, however, forced to retreat by the arrival of the Persian king, who invaded Roman Mesopotamia and invested Theodosiopolis (Resaina) for a month. The Persians lifted this siege, probably because of the failure of an allied Arab attack on Syria. At this point negotiations began, perhaps at the initiative of the Romans, since the Huns had seized the opportunity to attack Thrace. Varahram, perhaps to strengthen his position, tried a surprise attack on the Romans that was roundly defeated. A peace was then made under which the Persians agreed to end the persecution of the Christians, and both sides undertook not to receive the Arab allies of the other. The losses on both sides seem to have been heavy, but the Roman army was judged to have performed well, and the success of the generals Areobindus and Ardaburius in the war rehabilitated Germans in the Roman high command.

The period thus ended on a high note for the eastern Romans. The Persians had been defeated and relations with the Arabs regulated;[29] the Danube defences had been rebuilt; the government was stable and civilian-dominated. In 423 Honorius died, appropriately enough of dropsy. In 425 John, who had seized power at Ravenna, was deposed by an eastern army

---

[27] On Marutha see Socr. *HE* vii.8, Theoph. *Chron. a.m.* 5900 and 5906; *Chron. Seert.* i.lxvi (*PO* v p. 317) and lxix (p. 411); *Synodicon Orientale* (tr. J. B. Chabot, Paris 1902) pp. 254–8 and 293; *Chron. ad a. MCCXXXIV* (*CSCO Script. Syr.* iii.14) pp. 137f.

[28] On Acacius see *Syn. Or.* pp. 276f. and 283; *Chron. Seert.* i.lxxi (pp. 326f.).

[29] For relations between the Romans and their Arab allies during the reign of Theodosius II, see Shahîd (1989), esp. 22–54.

led by Ardaburius, one of the heroes of the Persian war, and his son Aspar. In the same year at Rome the young Valentinian III was crowned emperor of the west by the eastern *magister officiorum* Helion. But signs of a gathering storm were present. The Hunnic breakthrough into Thrace in 422 indicated the weakness of the eastern Roman armies when forced to fight on two fronts, and in 425 a force of Huns brought by Aetius to help the usurper John had to be paid off. The storm broke in the next decade, when the Vandals established themselves in Africa and the Huns began systematically to ravage the Balkans. The dilemma of the eastern Romans, at perhaps the nadir of their fortunes in 448, is well, if unsympathetically, put by Priscus of Panium (fr. 6 = fr. 10 Blockley):

[The Romans] were not only wary of starting a war with Attila but they were afraid also of the Parthians [i.e. Persians] who were preparing hostilities, the Vandals who were harrying the coastal regions, the Isaurians whose banditry was reviving, the Saracens who were ravaging the eastern part of their dominions, and the Ethiopian tribes who were coming together. Therefore, having been humbled by Attila, they paid him court while they tried to organize themselves to face other peoples by collecting their forces and appointing generals.

The measured application of military and economic resources and diplomatic skills here implied, which is characteristic of the early Byzantine state, reflects the lessons learned and the strengths developed during the previous 150 years. They enabled the eastern Roman empire to weather the storm. They were unable to save the west.

CHAPTER 14

THE EASTERN FRONTIER

BENJAMIN ISAAC

I. ROME AND PERSIA

Any description of the eastern frontier must start with a discussion of the relationship between Rome and Persia. The current period is marked by several clearly distinct stages: tension and intermittent warfare from 337 till 363, Julian's major campaign into Mesopotamia in 363 with the subsequent peace settlement, and, finally, the brief war of 421–2. The immediate cause of the chronic strain between the two empires in the fourth century must originate in the territorial gains achieved by Rome in the settlement of 298–9.[1] As a result of this Roman victory, her sovereignty now extended beyond the Tigris and thus reached farther eastward than the empire ever achieved at any other time.[2] Persia also recognized Roman sovereignty in Armenia and Iberia (modern Georgia). Rome gained control over all the important cities in north-eastern Mesopotamia: Amida, Nisibis, Singara and Bezabde. However, the Parthian and, later, Persian kingdom never accepted a permanent Roman presence in Mesopotamia east of the Euphrates. This, then, naturally led to renewed warfare, although it took several decades for hostilities to be resumed.

When Shapur II (309–79) became king of Persia he repudiated the settlement of 298, sending an embassy (probably in 334) to demand frontier changes.[3] Following Constantine's refusal, Shapur abducted Diran, king of Armenia, violating the agreement. Constantine reacted by nominating his nephew Hannibalianus as the new king.[4] In 336 Hannibalianus drove the Persians out of Armenia, and at least one source mentions Persian incursions launched into Roman territory. Hannibalianus was killed in 336 and succeeded, in 338, by a Roman vassal, Arsak (Arsaces), of doubtful loyalty. Constantine was preparing for a major campaign when he died in

---

[1] Barnes (1976); Blockley (1984); Winter (1988). The main source: Petr. Patr. fr. 14, Müller, *FHG* IV.189, trans.: Dodgeon and Lieu, *Eastern Frontier* 133.
[2] Fest. *Brev.* XIV; XXV; Pet. Patr. fr. 14, *FHG* IV.188f. The precise status of the territory east of the Tigris is not clear from these sources. On these and other passages in Festus, see the historical commentary in Eadie (1967).   [3] Lib. *Or.* LIX.71–2.   [4] Hewsen (1978–9); ch. 1, p. 3 above.

437

May 337.[5] This was clearly planned as a large-scale expedition into Persia, similar to many in the second and third centuries.[6] However, on this campaign the emperor had decided to take bishops with him (Eus. *V. Const.* IV.56).[7] This innovation introduced an element of ecclesiastical involvement into warfare. Constantine was also the first Roman emperor who intervened against the Persian king on behalf of his Christian subjects.[8]

The ancient sources do not make explicit the cause of the war between Rome and Persia in the period which followed the death of Constantine in 337, nor are we informed of the aims of either party. Julian, in his panegyric in honour of Constantius, merely says that the enemy had broken the peace and was aggressive, so Constantius had to fight (*Or.* 1.18b). It is, however, quite likely that the momentum created by Constantine's plans made the hostilities which followed inevitable, even if Constantius did not pursue his predecessor's ambitious military plans.[9] According to Festus, nine major battles between Persians and Romans were fought during the reign of Constantius. At least five of these were Persian sieges of cities held by the Romans in northern Mesopotamia: he lists three unsuccessful sieges of Nisibis (337–8, 346 and 350), the fall of Amida (359) and Singara (360).[10] The defence of Nisibis was organized by the local bishops, a novel feature at the time.[11] Serious fighting in 359–360[12] had been preceded by negotiations.[13] Shapur II had written to Constantius that he could have demanded all his ancestral territory as far as the river Strymon and the boundary of Macedonia, but in fact he was offering peace, in exchange for Armenia and Mesopotamia (Amm. Marc. XVII.5.5–6). Constantius in reply insisted on the preservation of the *status quo* in Armenia and Mesopotamia (XVII.14.1–2), and it was on this condition that the Romans offered peace (XVII.14–19). These negotiations show some characteristics of earlier and later diplomacy between the two empires: political rhetoric is combined with straightforward references to the essence of the conflict: sovereignty over the region east of the Euphrates and control, direct or indirect, over Armenia. Two elements missing here, but usually present between the fifth and seventh centuries, are religious conflict and disagreement about the payment of

---

[5] Fest. *Brev.* XXVI; Eutr. X.8.2; *Anon. Vales.* VI.35; Oros. *Adv. Pag.* VII.28.31; *Chron. Pasch.* p. 533.

[6] Fest. *Brev.* XXVI; 'cunctis agminibus' i.e. 'with all the units (at his disposal)'; Barnes (1985).

[7] Constantine appears in Syriac sources as self-appointed liberator of the Christians of Persia: Barnes (1985).

[8] Letter of Constantine to Shapur II, cited by Eus. *V. Const.* IV.8–13; trans.: Dodgeon and Lieu, *Eastern Frontier* 150–2.

[9] There were expectations that he would: see the *Itinerarium Alexandri*, cited by Barnes (1985) 135.

[10] Eadie, commentary on Festus, *ad loc.*; Warmington (1977).

[11] Jacob of Nisibis in 337/8: Jer. *Chron.* 234, 24–5; Theod. *HE* II.30; *Hist. Rel.* I.11–12; Syriac sources, translated by Dodgeon and Lieu, *Eastern Frontier* 168–71; for the sieges of 346 and 350: 191f.; 193–7; add: P. Kawerau (trans.), *Die Chronik von Arbela* (Leuven 1985), 74f.

[12] Sources listed by Eadie (1967) 151.

[13] Sources: Dodgeon and Lieu, *Eastern Frontier* 211f.; comments: Isaac, *Limits of Empire* 21–3.

subsidies. The nature of the warfare which followed between Constantius and Shapur II was, in a sense, a prelude to what was to occur in the sixth century over an even longer period: a sporadic and exhausting struggle for control of the cities of northern Mesopotamia, which rarely led to major shifts in the balance of power. When Shapur disbanded his army in 361, the net result of twenty years of intermittent warfare was that Rome still held the Tigris, except at Bezabde, and that Armenia was still a Roman ally. It is unclear whether Rome still controlled any regions east of the Tigris.

The war of 363 was entirely different from the struggles in the pre-ceding period. Julian fought this war along the lines of those planned by earlier generals, from the first half of the first century B.C. onwards, who had hoped to emulate Alexander. It took the shape of a massive Roman invasion of Mesopotamia, making for the Persian capital.[14] This is the best-documented of all the Roman campaigns into Mesopotamia, yet our sources do not agree about the number of Roman soldiers involved,[15] nor are they clear about the crucial question of Julian's war aims in political terms. According to Ammianus, Julian went to war against Persia for three reasons: to punish the Persians for the previous war,[16] because he was tired of idleness, and because 'he was burning to add the title "Parthicus" to the ornaments of his glorious victories' (Amm. Marc. XXII.12.2). The anonymous *Epitome de Caesaribus* XLIII merely says that 'Julian, being excessively eager for fame, set out against the Persians.' Those are impressions written down after Julian's death and failure. At the time of the campaign, Libanius, staying at Antioch, expressed the hope 'that the emperor would come leading (in captivity) the present ruler and handing over the (Persian) government to the fugitive (i.e. Hormisdas, Shapur's brother, who had joined the Romans)'.[17] It is possible, but not certain, that the lack of precision in these sources reflects a similar vagueness on the part of the emperor. It is clear, however, that he went to war, like so many others, with the image of Alexander of Macedon in mind.[18] Many modern commentators suggest that Julian had the modest and realistic expectation that he would merely change the balance of power, but there is no trace of such calculations in the contemporary sources. Like many rulers before him he may genuinely have thought that he was going to conquer the rival empire.

There is no uncertainty, however, about the results of the war, which can

[14] The main source; Amm. Marc. XXIII.2–XXV.3; also important is Zos. III, based on Eunapius; other sources, listed and partly translated: Dodgeon and Lieu, *Eastern Frontier* ch. IX, 231–74; for the historical geography of Babylonia and relevant Talmudic sources: Oppenheimer (1983).
[15] 65,000 men according to Zos. III.13.1, with discussion by Paschoud, Budé edn, II¹, 110f.
[16] Punishment of the Persians is emphasized also by Lib. *Ep.* 1402.1–3; *Or.* XVII.19–21.
[17] *Ep.* 1402.3 (to Aristophanes), trans. Dodgeon in Dodgeon and Lieu, *Eastern Frontier* 258.
[18] Jul. *Caes.* 333a; Amm. Marc. XVI.5.4–5. In the *Itinerarium Alexandri*, written c. 340, (above, n. 9) Constantius was expected to follow in the footsteps of Alexander and Trajan.

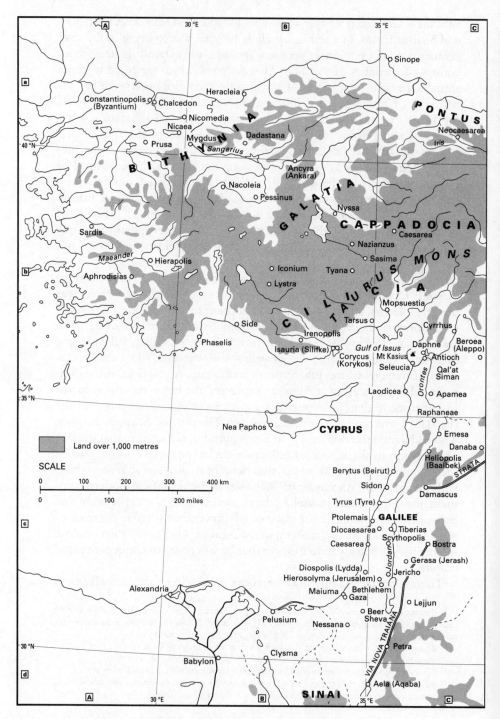

Map 6 Asia Minor and the eastern provinces

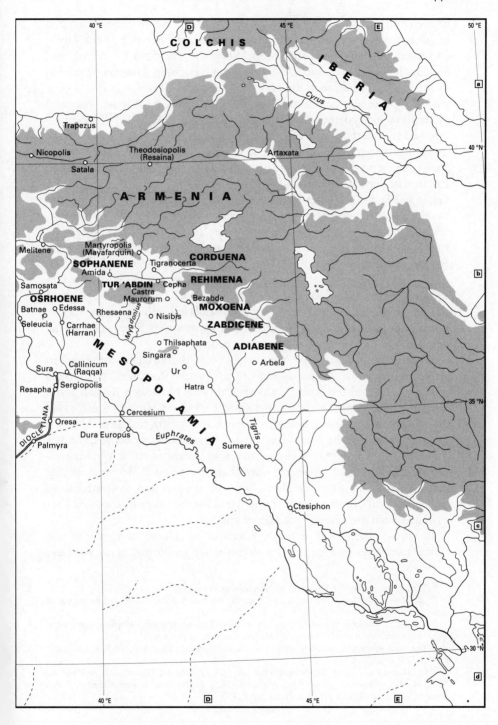

COLCHIS

IBERIA

Cyrus

Trapezus

Nicopolis

Theodosiopolis
(Resaina)

Artaxata

Satala

A R M E N I A

Melitene

Martyropolis
(Mayafarquin)

CORDUENA

SOPHANENE

Tigranocerta

Amida

REHIMENA

Samosata

TUR 'ABDIN

Cepha

Castra
Maurorum

Bezabde

OSRHOENE

Batnae

Edessa

Rhesaena

MOXOENA

Seleucia

Nisibis

Carrhae
(Harran)

ZABDICENE

M E S O P O T A M I A

Thilsaphata

ADIABENE

Singara

Ur

Arbela

Callinicum
(Raqqa)

Sura

Resapha

Sergiopolis

Hatra

Cercesium

DIOCLETIANA

Oresa

Tigris

Dura Europus

Euphrates

Sumere

Palmyra

Ctesiphon

40 °E

45 °E

50 °E

40 °N

35 °N

30 °N

be seen in the unfavourable terms of the thirty-year peace treaty negotiated by Julian's successor Jovian.[19] Rome gave up all territory east of the Tigris, and north-eastern Mesopotamia, including the key cities of Nisibis and Singara. It also gave up support for its client Arsaces in Armenia, which led to the loss of influence in the eastern part of the kingdom. It is less clear whether Jovian also committed Rome to participate in the maintenance of a garrison which guarded the Darial Pass across the Caucasus.[20] Contemporary and later authors consider the withdrawal in Mesopotamia one of the major disasters suffered by the Roman empire. Augustine (*De Civ. Dei* IV.29) gives the perspective of the early fifth century: in the distant past Rome had had to withdraw in the reign of Tarquinius, and had suffered defeat by the Gauls and Hannibal. Later Hadrian had given up 'three noble provinces to the rule of the Persians' – and then Augustine mentions Jovian's withdrawal. 'The boundaries were established where they are still today. The loss of territory was not so great as that caused by Hadrian's concessions, but the new frontier was fixed in the middle by a compromise.'[21] While he disapproves of Hadrian's concessions and Julian's rashness, Augustine concedes that Jovian had no choice. Seen from another perspective, however, the peace of 363 may have contributed decisively to the political stability of the region. Julian's campaign remained the last major expedition of either side into the heartland of the enemy till the late sixth century.

During the decades after the war of 363, the struggle continued in Armenia and Iberia (see p. 425 above).[22] In 369 the Roman vassal in Iberia was deposed, and the country was then divided between a Roman and a Persian vassal (Amm. Marc. XXVII.12.4, 16f.). In 387 Armenia was divided into two parts, four-fifths going to Persia and one-fifth to Rome. Thus the Roman position in the north-east was also significantly weakened, another development which, paradoxically, may have enhanced stability in the relationship of the two empires rather than impairing it. In view of the increased pressure from the Huns, however, it was a loss of control in an area which had become far more important for the safety of the Near East than had been the case in previous centuries.

In 395–7 there was a major invasion by Huns from across the Caucasus.[23] They crossed the Darial Pass while the Roman army was busy

---

[19] The sources are listed in Dodgeon and Lieu, *Eastern Frontier* 237.

[20] John Lydus, *De Mag.* 52, ed. Bandy, 213. This may not have become an issue before the war of 441–2.

[21] '. . . nisi . . . illic imperii fines constituerentur, ubi hodieque persistunt, non quidem tanto detrimento quantum concesserat Hadrianus, sed media tamen compositione fixi'.

[22] The main sources: Amm. Marc. XXVII.12; XXIX.1.1–4; XXX.1f.; Faustus IV (*FHG* V 2 s. 232ff.); Procop. *BP* I.5.10–40.

[23] Ch. 16, pp. 502–5 below; Maenchen-Helfen, *Huns* 51–9. Ammianus' digression on the Huns and Alans: Matthews, *Ammianus* 332–42, bibliography: p. 528, n. 47. The main sources: Claudian, *In Ruf.* II.26–35; Jer. *Ep.* 60.16; Socr. *HE* VI.1; Philostorg. XI.8.

in Italy. Armenia, Cappadocia, Syria and the Persian part of Mesopotamia were affected. The invaders came as far as Edessa and Antioch. A letter written by Jerome vividly describes the anxiety felt all over the Near East at the time. This was a major threat which the two empires would have to face for a long time to come and it would strongly influence their mutual relations.

During most of the reign of Yezdegerd I (399–420) and in the first years of Theodosius II (408–50), relations between Rome and Persia were marked by a policy of mutual tolerance (see p. 433 above). Trade was regulated, for a Roman law of 408–9 prescribes that merchants may hold markets only at the places agreed upon, namely at Nisibis, Callinicum and Artaxata (*CJ* IV.63.4). The reason given for the restriction is the prevention of spying, but it is clear that this sort of agreement also represents a form of mutual accommodation. There was also tolerance on both sides in the sphere of religion. This ended with the ascendancy of Theodosius' sister Pulcheria at the eastern court, while provocations by Christians in Persia (Theod. *HE* v.41) led in 420 to renewed persecution there. Two Arab allies played an interesting role at the time: Aspebetus, an ally of the Persians who went over to Rome (see below) and Mundhir I of al-Hira who had great influence on Yezdegerd's successor, his son Vahram V. The persecution of Christians was continued and even intensified by Vahram (*Chron. Min.* II.74f.). Finally, Theodosius II, probably under the influence of Pulcheria, decided to embark again on a full-scale war (A.D. 421–2).[24] The Romans besieged Nisibis, following which the Persians penetrated Roman territory and besieged Theodosiopolis (probably Resaina in Mesopotamia). Both enterprises were unsuccessful. In 422 an agreement was reached which restored the *status quo*, including religious freedom in both empires.[25] The accord probably stipulated that Rome was to contribute towards the costs of defending the Caucasus passes.

The war of 421–2, then, was the first time in history when one state went to war with another for the sake of Christianity. Constantius' campaign had also been remarkable for several features which first appeared at that time and became common afterwards. Constantius made no attempt at long-distance moves into Syria or Mesopotamia: the fighting concentrated on efforts to besiege cities in the frontier zone in northern Mesopotamia. The stamina of the local population played a key role, as we see from a law of 420 (*CJ* VIII.10.10) which exhorted property-owners in provinces exposed to Persian attack to protect their estates with private fortifications. The list of provinces mentioned in the text includes virtually the entire diocese of

---

[24] The main source: Socr. *HE* VII.18.9–25, 20 (*PG* LXVII. 776); cf. Holum (1977); Schrier (1992); ch. 13, p. 435 above.

[25] *Chron. Min.* II.75; Sozom. *HE* IX.4; Socr. *HE* VII.20; *Chronicle of Arbela* 16 (ed. P. Kawerau, *CSCO* 467, *Scriptores Syri* 199), trans. p. 91.

Oriens, but significantly excludes the provinces of Palestine, Arabia and First Syria, which were apparently considered safe. It is clear that this was not an exceptional measure, for more than a century afterwards, in the sixth century, the law was incorporated into Justinian's Code. We should note, too, that the siege of Theodosiopolis was organized by bishop Eunomios (Theod. *HE* v.39). Thus we can see both the extent to which the central authorities had to rely on local initiative. and the key role which the bishops played in this process, a role which, in the third century, would still have been played by the civic authorities.[26]

II. ARABS AND DESERT PEOPLES

In the fourth century the Arab nomad forces – 'Saracens', as they are called in the contemporary literature – became an important factor in the warfare between Rome and Persia to an extent previously unknown. The Arabs are occasionally mentioned in the sources during the first three centuries A.D., but from the fourth century onwards every author who discusses wars in the east refers to the Saracens as a significant element. There is indeed evidence of a new social and political development whereby larger and more cohesive Arab tribal federations form links with the governments of the two empires. A notable illustration of this is the well-known inscription of 328 from Namara, north-east of the Jebel Druz in southern Syria, which refers to a *mlk*, a 'lord' or 'king' of the 'Arabs'. It is one of the oldest documents in classical Arabic; it is written in Nabataean characters and has a problematic text.[27] Imru'l-qais, who had become phylarch for the Romans, is described as conqueror of tribes living in a wide range of territories extending to the borders of the Yemen. The contents of the text and its find-spot Namara, a settlement in the province of Arabia, leave no doubt that Imru'l-qais was an ally of the Romans. He also appears in Arabic sources and was apparently related to the newly established Lakhmid dynasty of al-Hira in south-western Babylonia, who were allies of the Persians. Even if we have little information about the social organization implied in the inscription, and the real measure of political control suggested by the term *mlk* (king or lord) of the Arabs, both clearly represent a tangible consolidation of the military and political power of the Arab peoples at the fringes of the empires.

Ammianus, discussing the early stages of the eastern war in the year 356, says that the Persians applied a new technique: instead of the usual set battles, they now practised raids and guerrilla warfare (Amm. Marc.

---

[26] Cf. Isaac, *Limits of Empire* 252–60.
[27] Cf. *CAH* xii[2], ch. 21; A. Beeston, *BSOAS* 42 (1979) 1–6. A recent, revised reading: Bellamy (1985); discussion: Sartre (1982) 136–9; Bowersock (1983) 138–42; Shahid (1984b), 31–53.

XVI.9.1).[28] This means that the Persians allowed their Saracen allies to do what they were good at, carrying off property and cattle in quick raids. The Saracen nomads did not engage in siege warfare; against towns or in set battles they were totally ineffective, as was observed in well-known statements by Ammianus (xxv.6.8), Procopius (*BP* II.19.12) and commentators of other periods. Thus, while the pre-Islamic nomads refrained from attacking settlements, they turned on anything of value outside the fortified quarters, destroying water systems, crops, palm groves and fruit trees. This, then was a form of harassment initiated by the Persians, which was intended to cause economic and social havoc in the frontier regions. Ammianus, however, had his doubts as to the effectiveness of the new use of Saracens as a means of achieving the war aims of either party. He found the Saracens 'desirable neither as allies nor as enemies' (XIV.4.1), a judgement echoed in the sixth century by the Syriac chronicler Joshua the Stylite: 'to the Arabs on both sides this was a source of much profit and they wrought their will on both kingdoms'.[29] We cannot judge the real impact of this new phenomenon on the course of the wars, but, whatever it was, participation of tribesmen in the fighting continued whenever the two powers fought each other, from the fourth century till the Islamic conquests. While this is a reality to be reckoned with, it does not mean that the Roman empire faced constant pressure on the frontier from nomad groups originating in the Arabian peninsula. It is often taken for granted that the Roman imperial army was continually threatened with imminent invasion and conquest by nomads from the desert, which it succeeded in preventing up to the seventh century. However, there is little support for such views in the ancient sources. It is true that wherever settled regions adjoined the desert the Romans faced the phenomena of nomadic pastoralism and transhumance – the seasonal migrations of pastoral peoples who lived in marginal climatic conditions – but it does not necessarily follow that these formed a major threat to the stability of the settled regions. Whenever there is evidence of large-scale hostilities between Rome and the Arabs from the desert, this is usually part of the wars between Rome and Persia.

Saracens are mentioned several times in connection with Julian's Persian campaign in 363, when the desert population acted as allies of both sides. We have the name of the Persian ally 'Malechus [the King] son of [or named] Podosaces, phylarch of the Assanitic Saracens, an infamous bandit, who had long raided our border districts with great violence'.[30] 'Malechus'

[28] Also: XIV.3.2; XXIII.3.8; XXXI.16.5. For Ammianus and the Saracens: Matthews, *Ammianus* 342–53; Shahîd (1984b) 82–6; 107–24. For the Persian allies, Bosworth, *Camb. Hist. Iran* III.2 (1983) 593–612.

[29] *The Chronicle, composed in Syriac, AD 507*, text and trans. W. Wright (1882), 79.

[30] Amm. Marc. XXIV.2–4: 'Malechus Podosacis nomine, phylarchus Saracenorum Assanitarum, famosi nominis latro, omni saevitia per nostros limites diu grassatus'. Cf. Sartre (1982) 139f.; Shahîd (1984b) 119–121.

clearly derives from the Semitic title *mlk* which we saw above in connection with Imru'l-qais. As in the Namara inscription, here too this title is combined with the Greek term phylarch, the traditional rank of a tribal chief recognized by the Roman authorities as an ally. The term 'bandit' (*latro*), which Ammianus applies to Malechus, has been used through the ages to disqualify the moral and legal standing of enemies. More specifically, the Romans used it for any enemy who was not a recognized head of state. In the present case 'bandit' or 'robber' is a term used to denote an ally of the enemy, who practised irregular warfare. Malechus had long harassed the Roman frontier districts, according to Ammianus, which implies that, in times of peace, his people carried out raids against Roman territory, while sparing that of the Persians.

The best-known long-term allies of Persia in this period were the Lakhmids, who lived at Hira on the lower Euphrates (near An Najaf and al Kūfah).[31] The allies of the Romans were at first the Tanūkh, in the desert west of the Euphrates.[32] Towards the end of the fourth century these were superseded by the Salih, who lived in the Syrian and Mesopotamian deserts. The latter were supplanted by the Ghassanids towards the end of the fifth century. It is possible that Malechus, whom we have seen described as the 'phylarchus Saracenorum Assanitarum', was an ancestor of the Ghassanid rulers, since Assan may well stand for Ghassan.

Participation in full-scale campaigns was only one of the tasks of the phylarchs, although the nature of our sources is such that they are most visible to us in that capacity. Their permanent role is clear from occasional scraps of evidence, many of them relating to the fifth and sixth centuries. Thus we have evidence that they carried out raids against the rural population in the territory of the rival empire. They also defended the friendly civilian population against similar raids by the other empire's allies, and protected the settled population against nomad raids, both by refraining from raiding themselves and keeping other tribes from doing so. In case of need, they could assist the Roman army in internal police duties. Eventually the phylarchs became a regular part of the Byzantine provincial organization. This is clear from a legal stipulation of 443, which warns the *duces* that they have no right to remove and seize any part of the subsistence allowance granted to the Saracen allies and other peoples.[33] Such allies apparently received an allowance, like the regular *limitanei*, but, unlike the latter, they were not supposed to contribute part of their allowance to the Roman officers, although the very fact that there is legislation on the subject shows that there were irregularities in the fifth and sixth centuries.

---

[31] Bosworth, *loc. cit.*, esp. 597–609.   [32] Sartre (1982) 134–6.

[33] Theodosius, *Nov.* XXIVI.2 of 443, 12 Sept. (*CJ* 1.46.4.2): 'De Saracenorum vero foederatorum aliarumque gentium annonariis alimentis nullam penitus eos decarpendi aliquid vel auferendi licentiam habere concedimus.'

It is impossible to say exactly when these relationships developed. We learn of them through incidental or random events recorded in the literary sources and inscriptions. Two early references are found in Ammianus, both in connection with Julian's campaign of 363. Ammianus (xxv.6.10) records that Julian's army found the Saracens east of the Tigris hostile because Julian had vetoed their subsidies and the many presents they had been used to in the past. The implication is clear: when Roman sovereignty extended east of the Tigris there were arrangements with Arab tribes in those parts, which entailed financial support in return for various services of the kind described above. Payment for services as an instrument of empire is less glorious than the exaction of tribute or the exertion of power, and many of our literary authorities tend therefore to look askance at the practice. When it is mentioned, it is usually because the payments themselves were a source of conflict. Julian was the first of several emperors who caused serious problems because he refused to pay subsidies, although he needed the support of the very allies whom he refused to pay.[34]

It should be noted that it was a different group of Saracens which approached Julian at Callinicum on the Euphrates, also in 363, presenting him with a crown and offering their services (Amm. Marc. xxiii.3.8). These were accepted because this sort of fighter was 'good at covert tactics' ('ut ad furta bellorum appositi'). The difference between the attitudes to and relationships with the two groups of Saracens mentioned above may be explained by the respective geography: those east of the Tigris were living on the periphery of the empire, beyond the reach of the standing army in peacetime, while those who assembled at Callinicum, even if they were nomads, lived in a region where they were dependent on relationships with towns and settlements under firm Roman control.

So far we have only heard of Arab allies active in the struggle between Rome and Persia in northern Syria and Mesopotamia. The first time when Saracens are known to have caused serious trouble independent of hostilities between Rome and Persia was fifteen years after Julian's expedition, shortly before the battle of Adrianople in 378. Mavia (or Maouia), queen of the Saracens, broke an existing agreement with Rome and carried out raids in the border regions of Palestine, Phoenice and Egypt after the death of her husband. We are not told why she did this.[35] After various military successes by the Saracens, an agreement was reached between Rome and the queen. Peace was made on condition that a Saracen monk named Moses be ordained as bishop, in order to convert the Saracens to Christianity. Mavia's daughter was married to a Roman general named Victor.

---

[34] Isaac (1995).
[35] The main sources: Rufin. *HE* xi (ii). 6 (*GCS* ix.2, 1010–12); Socr. *HE* iv.36; Sozom. *HE* vi.38; Theod. *HE* iv.20. Cf. Sartre (1982) 140–4.

Our sources on the Mavia affair are all ecclesiastical, so that their interest focuses exclusively on the religious aspects of the episode. The history of Mavia has been discussed frequently in the modern literature, and some scepticism expressed as to the reliability of these sources. However, even a minimalist interpretation allows several conclusions. We have here another instance in the fourth century of a federation or grouping of tribes, with apparently a strong leader, Mavia's unnamed husband, about whom we know nothing. He was succeeded by the queen, herself semi-legendary, who maintained power and started hostilities. These tribes were based somewhere in the general area of Palestine, Arabia and Sinai and had made a treaty with the Romans. This is clear from Sozomen's statement that agreements were broken when Mavia attacked in 378. The scale of the warfare is impossible to judge from the available sources and may have been far more localized than they imply. It is certain, however, that these events coincided with the revolt of the Visigoths, which forced the emperor Valens to leave Antioch, withdraw his troops from Armenia and campaign in Thrace. Following Saracen successes, the Romans agreed to negotiate, and a new agreement was reached, presumably advantageous to the Saracens. The treaty comprised a dynastic marriage and the giving of a bishop. Rome undoubtedly promised subsidies, although these are not mentioned by the church historians. The Saracens must also have accepted military obligations: this is the sole element of the entire affair to be mentioned indirectly by Ammianus (xxxi.16.5–6).

After the Roman defeat at Adrianople (378), a Saracen detachment helped to save Constantinople from the Goths – the curious details are often repeated in the literature – and it is quite likely that these were soldiers sent by Mavia, for Socrates (*HE* v.1) and Sozomen (*HE* vii.2) both report that she sent Saracens to Constantinople. It remains to be observed that it was the shocking behaviour of one of the Saracens, rather than their fighting skills, which gave them the upper hand. Ammianus emphasizes that such troops are better at covert raiding expeditions than at pitched battles.[36] Yet the tactics of other Saracens, with their speed and manoeuvrability, were also effective on another occasion earlier in the same year (Zos. iv.22).

A few years after Adrianople, some time before 389, a treaty was broken by Saracens (Pacatus, *Pan. Lat.* ii(xii).22.3), but it is not at all certain that these were Mavia's subjects: as already indicated, Mavia had her base somewhere in the region of Palestine and Arabia, but the Romans also had relationships with various groups of Saracens living further north, in northern Syria and Mesopotamia. It is equally uncertain that the Mavia who is recorded on an inscription of 425 had any connection with the queen. The

---

[36] xxxi.16.5: 'ad furta magis expeditionalium rerum, quam ad concursatorias habilis pugnas . . .' Cf. xxiii.3.8; 'ad furta bellorum appositi' (above).

inscription was found in southern Syria, and records that a woman named Mavia had been responsible for the construction of a martyrium of St Thomas (*AE* (1947) 193). The find-spot may suggest a connection, but the name Mavia (Māwiyya) was not unique.

Sozomen tells the history of Zokomos immediately following his account of Mavia. Zokomos was a Saracen phylarch of Rome who was baptized with his tribe and then fought the Persians and other Saracens. This must have taken place in the last quarter of the fourth century.[37] As with Mavia, we have no precise geographical information, but evidently similar arrangements between Rome and these nomads were involved and Christianization was part of them.

A form of coexistence at another level may be observed in the same period in Sinai. In the early 380s, the nun Egeria made a pilgrimage to the Holy Land, including a journey from Jerusalem to Mount Sinai and back, via Clysma (Suez), Pelusium and the Sinai desert coastal road.[38] While travelling in the Sinai desert, she was escorted by native camel-riders centred at Pharan (*It. Eg.* VI.2(46)): there was no Roman military presence there. However, when she entered Egypt at the important harbour city of Clysma, she found a functioning chain of road-stations and bases for soldiers. These soldiers escorted the travellers along the trade route from the Gulf of Suez to the Mediterranean. Thereafter, along the coast road from the Thebaid to Gaza, there was no need for a military escort (IX.3(49)). The relationship between the walled town of Pharan in Sinai and the nomads was not regulated by the Roman state. It was regulated by local agreements which entailed the payment of protection money by the local authorities.[39] Without such arrangements there could be trouble. In 373 Saracens attacked hermits living near the traditional site of the burning bush in Sinai (Nilus, *Narratio* IV, *PG* LXXIX.625 ff.). This site was only fortified in the reign of Justinian. Mount Sinai was an extremely remote and isolated spot, but there were also problems with banditry quite near more settled lands. In the first half of the fourth century Hilarion withdrew to an area about seven miles south of Gaza-Maioumas. This region, at the edge of the desert, was infested by bandits, according to his biographer Jerome (*V. Hil.* 3, *PL* XXIII.31; 12; 33). The same author, in his Life of Malchus, describes the main road from Beroea (Aleppo) to Edessa in north Syria as unsafe for merchants because of the presence of Saracen robbers: 'The desert is near the road. There Saracens without permanent homes wander everywhere.'[40]

---

[37] Sozom. *HE* VI.38; cf. Sartre (1982) 143–6.

[38] *It. Eg.* I–X (*CCSL* CLXXV.37–51); Petrus Diaconus, *Liber de Locis Sanctis* Y (*CCSL* CLXXV.100–3); cf. Hunt, *Holy Land Pilgrimage* 58–60; ch. 8, pp. 256 and 261 above.

[39] Nilus, *Narrationes, PG* LXXIX.661, written *c.* 400; cf. Isaac, *Limits of Empire* 247.

[40] Jer. *V. Malchi* IV (*PL* XXIII.55): 'vicina est publico itineri solitudo, per quam Saraceni incertis sedibus huc atque illuc vagantur'; Segal (1955) 127f.; 133.

In the early fifth century the activities of Honorius and Stilicho in North Africa caused migrations of Berbers from the Macae, and Austurians from Cyrene eastwards. In 411 Jerome describes alarming incursions into the frontier districts of Egypt, Palestine, Phoenice and Syria (*Ep.* 126.2).[41] The episode is instructive: scholars used to consider the events described by Jerome a classic case of pressure on the empire engendered by migrations from the outside. It is quite possible, however, that this movement of peoples in the frontier provinces was caused at least partly by military activities of the Roman army.[42]

As we have already noted in connection with the war of 421–2, two Arab allies of the Persians played an important role at this time: Mundhir I of al-Hira, and Aspebetos, whose name derives from the Persian title *spahbadh*. Migrations of nomad clans are not often mentioned in the literary sources, and even when they are, they cannot usually be traced with any accuracy. However, in the period covered by this volume, there is at least one recorded instance of significant movement between the Persian and Roman empires. In about 420 Aspebetos, chief of an Arab tribe or group of tribes, was ordered to prevent converts to Christianity from fleeing from Persia to Roman territory. However, Aspebetos himself went over with his people from the Persian sphere of influence to the Roman empire.[43] With the permission of the Roman authorities he settled in Palestine, near the monastery of Euthymius, between Jerusalem and Jericho.[44] He was accepted as an ally and made 'phylarch of the Roman federates in Arabia', a title of higher rank than that granted to previous phylarchs. Aspebetos and his son Terebon were then baptized by Euthymius. He assumed the name Petros and was consecrated as bishop of the camp-dwellers (τῶν παρεμβολῶν ἐπίσκοπος). His duties were the same as those of other phylarchs: to protect the settled population against harassment by nomads, from his own and other tribes. This was particularly relevant for the area between Jerusalem and Jericho (where Aspebetos and his nomads settled). In the early fourth century Jerome records the presence of highwaymen on the Jerusalem–Jericho road.[45] In case of need Aspebetos would also have to support Rome in its wars with Persia. The information is relayed by Cyril of Scythopolis, who got it directly from Aspebetos' great-grandson Terebon II in the middle of the fifth century. A Petros, bishop of 'those in the encampment' was present at the council of Ephesus in 431, which may serve as indirect confirmation of the story. The descendants of Aspebetos'

---

[41] '... sic Aegypti limitem, Palaestinae, Phoenices, Syriae percurrit ad instar torrentis cuncta secum trahens, ut vix manus eorum misericordia Christi potuerimus evadere'. The other key source is John Cassian, *Collationes* I (*SChrét.* 42), 117f.   [42] Roques (1983); Graf (1989) 349f.

[43] Cyril of Scythopolis, *V. Euthymii* x, ed. Schwartz, 18–25; also: Socr. *HE* VII.18. Cf. Sartre (1982) 149–53; Rubin (1986) 680f.; Isaac, *Limits of Empire* 246f.   [44] Hirschfeld (1992).

[45] See Jerome's translation of Eusebius, *Onomastikon* (ed. Klostermann), XXV.10–14; Jer. *Ep.* 108.12.

followers were attacked by nomads, and their settlement was then transferred to a place closer to Jerusalem, where, however, it was attacked again.[46]

Three points are noteworthy in the story of Aspebetos: first, the political importance of the conversion of an Arab chief and his followers to Christianity, which we also saw in the cases of Mavia and Zokomos. Secondly, it is clear that the escape of Saracen Christians to Roman territory greatly angered the Persians and, as noted above (p. 443), religious conflict ultimately led to the war of 421–2 (Socr. *HE* VII.18, *PG* LXVII.773). One of the fifth-century treaties between Rome and Persia included a provision that neither party would accept rebellious Saracen allies of the other state (Malchus, fr. 1, *FHG* IV.112f.) and this is repeated in the treaty of A.D. 562 (Menander Protector, fr. 11, *FHG* IV.208 ff.=fr. 6.1 Blockley). The relationship between the two empires and their respective Saracen allies remained an important issue till the seventh century. Finally, nomads who became sedentary appear to have lost the qualities which made them useful in controlling other nomads, for the descendants of Aspebetos' followers could not defend themselves adequately against attack by other nomads.

In order to interpret correctly all this information about pre-Islamic Arabs in the two empires, we must never lose sight of the perspective of our sources. The urbanized élite who produced the Roman literary sources had no interest in the lifestyle of nomads or transhumants. They did not attempt to understand the relationship between the settled inhabitants of the marginal areas and the nomads of the steppe, and the picture we can obtain from them is necessarily incomplete. Thus it would be wrong to claim that there was no symbiotic relationship between settlers and nomads because the Roman historians did not notice that it existed. Patristic literature does occasionally give the perspective of isolated individuals or communities living at the periphery of the settled lands. Thus, biographies of saints may testify to the presence of bandits along desert roads or nomad attacks on monasteries. However, this kind of information is not of the same order as reports of major tribal movements into the settled areas of the empire. Only the latter were usually of interest to the urban upper class. None the less, even when our sources report nomad attacks, it has to be kept in mind that such reports may contain some rhetorical exaggeration. In the fourth century, then, the Saracens began to play a role in the wars between Rome and Persia which they did not have before. Indeed, the reports we have about Mavia may indicate a consolidation of military power and a willingness to act which were unheard of in the third century. The Saracen phylarchs became an integral part of the apparatus of imperial control in the eastern frontier zone. Yet all this should be clearly

---

[46] Cyril of Scythopolis, *V. Euthymii* (ed. Schwartz), 67f.

distinguished from large-scale and independent military activity or heavy pressure from nomads on settled regions. From the fourth till the seventh century, the Arabs never seriously endangered the stability of the provinces and they never engendered pressures comparable to those caused by peoples from the north, such as the Huns and the Goths.

III. REGIONAL AND LOCAL UNREST

1. *Isauria*

The Isaurians inhabited the mountainous hinterland of the coast of southern Asia Minor, from Side in the west to Seleucia (Silifke) in the east.[47] 'The region is mountainous, difficult of access, and affords an unstable economy. Although it is in the middle of the empire, it is surrounded by an unusual kind of guard posts, as if it were a frontier district, for it is defended not by men, but by the nature of the country.'[48] Consequently, for most of the time, the inhabitants were only partially controlled by the imperial authorities. The fourth century, however, marked a gradual change from endemic banditry to periodic full-scale guerrilla war and wide-ranging raids into several provinces. In the period under discussion, various sources record four or five outbreaks of aggression, in the years 353, 359,[49] 367–8, 376–7[50] and around 404–7.[51] The first three are recorded by Ammianus, but only the first of these is described extensively (XIV.2). The last is mentioned by Jerome and Zosimus among others, and appears to have been the most dangerous of all: the Isaurians ravaged Phoenice and Galilee and caused panic in Palestine. The walls of Jerusalem were strengthened.[52] At this time a law in the Theodosian Code provided that Isaurian bandits could be tortured during Lent and on Easter Day (*C.Th.* IX.35.7 of 408). All these episodes ended inconclusively: the Romans were unable to engage the Isaurians in set battles and the Isaurians, like the Saracens, could not force sieges. From the second half of the fourth century onwards, the governor of Isauria had special military powers. He was a *comes rei militaris*, rather than a regular *dux*, and probably also *praeses*.[53] This means that the civil and military government was combined. The governor was provided with a strong

---

[47] Rougé (1966); Hopwood (1986); Hellenkemper (1986); Syme (1987); Matthews, *Ammianus* 355–67 with map.

[48] *SHA, Trig. Tyr.* XXVI; 'in medio Romani nominis solo regio eorum novo genere custodiarum quasi limes includitur, locis defensa, non hominibus'.   [49] Amm. Marc. XIX.13.1.

[50] Zos. IV.20.1–2. Paschoud, Budé edn, II².371f. suggests that the disorders described in the context of 376/7 by Zosimus are in fact those described by Ammianus for 367/8 (XXVII 9.6–7).

[51] Zos. V.25, with Paschoud, III¹, n. 52 on pp. 188–91; Jer. *Ep.* 114.1.

[52] Jer. *Ep.* 114.1: 'Isaurorum repentina eruptio: Phoenicis Galilaeaeque vastitas: terror Palaestinae, praecipue urbs Hierosolymae: et nequaquam librorum sed murorum extructio.'

[53] *Not. Dig. Or.* XXIX.6; cf. Isaac, *Limits of Empire* 75.

garrison, in the words of Ammianus, 'based in many neighbouring towns and forts'.[54] In other words, the Roman troops did not occupy the heartland of Isauria itself, but rather the towns at the fringes of the area and various sensitive points which controlled access. Thus Isauria furnished a steady flow of recruits for the imperial army, and one of their generals eventually became the emperor Zeno (474–91). His death was followed by outbreaks of violence. In the reign of Zeno's successor Anastasius (491–518) the Isaurians appointed a tyrant for themselves and erupted into the neighbouring provinces before being defeated (Zachariah of Mitylene, *Chronicle* VII.2).

2. Palestine

References to a revolt in Palestine in 351–2 have been variously interpreted.[55] Aurelius Victor (*Caes.* XLII.11) reports briefly: 'And meanwhile a revolt of the Jews, who impiously raised Patricius to royalty, was suppressed.'[56] Jerome also mentions these events: 'The Jews rebelled and murdered the soldiers during the night and took their arms, but Gallus thereafter suppressed their rebellion and burned their cities: Diocaesarea, Tiberias and Diospolis, and many villages.'[57] Theophanes (ed. C. de Boor 1.40) adds that the revolt was directed against 'Hellenes' (i.e. pagans) and Samaritans. Several Talmudic passages have been cited in connection with these events.[58] There is disagreement about the historical significance of information from the Talmudic sources, for they derive from material which is not historiographical in nature and they contain no explicit reference to a revolt. On one point, however, they are unanimous – namely, that Ursicinus visited several places in Palestine at this time, among them Diocaesarea. Ursicinus was the senior commander in the army of the Orient.[59] If he was present in small towns in Palestine, not long after a large-scale campaign by Shapur II in northern Mesopotamia, there must have been a real military need for him to go there. The *magister equitum Orientis* would not have interfered in a mere local police action. The *dux Palaestinae*, who had a considerable force at his disposal (see below), could have suppressed limited disturbances.

Brief mention must be made here of other significant events concerning the Jews in Palestine, beginning with Julian's abortive restoration of the Jewish Temple at Jerusalem. The history of Ammianus (XXIII.1.2–3)

[54] XIV.2.5: '... milites per municipia plurima, quae isdem conterminant, dispositos et castella ...'
[55] Lieberman (1945/6) 337–40; Geiger (1979–80); Stemberger (1987) 132–50; Mor (1989). Sources and older literature listed in Stern (1974–84) II.501.
[56] 'Et interea Judaeorum seditio, qui Patricium nefarie in regni specie[m] sustulerant, oppressa.'
[57] Jer. *Chron.* 282, ed. Helm, 1.238. Cf. Socr. *HE* II.33; Sozom. *HE* IV.7.5.
[58] Stern (1974–84) II, 501.   [59] *PLRE* I.985f. s.v. 'Ursicinus 2'.

mentions it, as do many patristic sources; it is also referred to in a letter from Julian to the Jews, but totally ignored in the Talmudic literature.[60] This failed attempt probably coincided with the preparations for the Persian campaign, and was clearly connected with the emperor's anti-Christian policy, a connection ignored by Ammianus. The work was started, but a natural disaster, presumably an earthquake, prevented completion of the project.

The Jews in Palestine and the Diaspora had enjoyed a considerable degree of autonomy under Roman rule from the second century onward. At the pinnacle of the Jewish leadership stood the patriarch (*nasi*), who possessed considerable political and judicial powers and received dues from Jews in Palestine and abroad.[61] Under the Christian emperors, the legal position of the Jews gradually worsened, a development which is expressed most clearly in four laws: (1) *C.Th.* II.1.10 (*CJ* 1.9.8) of 398, restricting the judicial powers of the Jewish authorities;[62] (2) *C.Th.* XVI.8.14 of 399, a prohibition on the collecting of tax by the patriarch, which, however, was revoked by *C.Th.* XVI.8.17 of 404; (3) *C.Th.* XVI.8.22 (*CJ* 1.9.15) of 415, demoting the patriarch Gamaliel VI from the rank of illustrious honorary praetorian prefect and restricting his authority and powers; (4) *C.Th.* XVI.8.29 (*CJ* 1.9.15) of 429, transferring to the treasury the crown tax which the Jews used to pay to the patriarch and his household. This text refers to the patriarchate as having been extinct for some time (*post excessum patriarcharum*). Since the position was hereditary, it is possible that it was abolished by default and not by imperial interference. The Jews in Palestine were left with only the leadership of the rabbinical authorities, who formed two *synhedria* in the provinces of Palaestina I and II.

Finally, we should note here the editorial activity in Tiberias (and perhaps partly in Caesarea) which gave the Palestinian Talmud its final written form. The Palestinian Talmud reflects the interpretative activities of Jewish sages in the third and fourth centuries, with the latest events and persons referred to belonging to the middle of the fourth century. It is therefore plausible to assign the editorial process to the last part of the fourth century and perhaps to the beginning of the fifth. Unlike its Babylonian counterpart, edited in the fifth century, the Palestinian Talmud is incomplete. We do not know why the Palestinian Talmud was edited at this period in history, but it is quite possible that the deteriorating position of Judaism in the Christian Roman empire accelerated the process.

---

[60] Comments on Ammianus and references to patristic sources: Stern (1974–84) II.608f. Julian's letter to the Jewish community: no. 204, pp. 396d–398 (Bidez and Cumont, 1922); Stern, no. 486a, pp. 559f., comments on pp. 508–11; 561–8. A supposed letter of Cyril of Jerusalem and discussion of other sources: Brock (1977).   [61] Juster (1914), I.391–400.

[62] Comments on this and related laws: Linder (1987).

IV. MILITARY ORGANIZATION

Military organization in the period under consideration can only be discussed profitably in connection with a number of related developments. First of all, as we have noted above, Roman military and political expansion in the east reached its farthest limits in the last years of the third century. These boundaries were maintained until the settlement of 363, which entailed a withdrawal that still kept the frontier far beyond that established in the reign of Hadrian. Warfare in the fourth century and afterwards tended to focus on the fortified cities on either side of the border.

Secondly, from the fourth to the seventh centuries the population of the Near East was denser than at any other time before the twentieth century. Many cities expanded (Apamea, Aleppo, Sergiopolis, Zenobia, Caesarea on the Sea, Jerusalem), although others declined (Cyrrhus, Emesa). Yet the cities apparently did not drain the prosperity of the rural areas. Villages grew in size, and farmhouses or small settlements are found on virtually every hill-top over wide areas. Settlements which had no city-status often had three or four churches. Even the marginal zone at the edge of the steppe was populated. This can be seen, for example, in southern Syria in the Hawran, or in northern Mesopotamia in the Tūr Abdin,[63] and in many parts of Palestine. Whatever the reasons for this demographic expansion, it is not a local phenomenon, since the same has been observed in other parts of Mesopotamia, notably in Babylonia, which belonged to the Sasanian empire.

Thirdly, it was in this period that the Saracens became an important factor in the relationships between the two empires, and in the exercise of control over marginal areas and trade routes.

Any attempt to understand Roman military organization in the Near East at this period must consider all these factors, both separately and together. As we shall see, the army moved into the marginal areas on an unprecedented scale, maintaining a strong presence along the main routes, and garrisoning some of the important cities in the area of confrontation with Persia. The combination of all these elements gives the military organization in the Near East a character distinct from that in other parts of the Empire.

A general discussion of army organization at this period may be found in chap. 7 above, pp. 211–37. Here we shall note briefly that part of the field army which served under the command of the *magister militum per Orientem*, who was based at Antioch (*Not. Dig. Or.* vii). The centrality of Antioch throughout the later Roman period must be emphasized. The city was the residence of both the *consularis* of Syria and the *comes Orientis* (whose

---

[63] Tate (1989b), esp. 107: 'les campagnes'; Sodini *et al.* (1980).

functions are a matter of debate), and of their staffs. It was also the site of one of the fifteen arms factories (*fabricae*) maintained by the state in the east (*Not. Dig. Or.* XI.18–39), the other arms factories in the diocese of Oriens being at Damascus, Edessa and Irenopolis in Cilicia. Above all, Antioch was an imperial residence for extended periods, especially during the campaigns against Persia. This is true for most of the years between 338 and 378.[64] The presence of expeditionary forces in and near Antioch regularly caused stress or even famine in the city.[65] Here as elsewhere, we have no clear impression of where the units of the field army were stationed in peacetime, nor do we know enough about their numerical strength to reach any reliable calculation of the total force involved.

While we have little information about the eastern field army, we know much more about the troops serving under the regional military commanders, the so-called *limitanei*. This is a term often misunderstood in the modern literature, like its complement *limes*.[66] *Limes* is not a term used to designate military structures or physical army organization. From the fourth century onward it is the formal term used to designate a frontier district under the command of a *dux*: it denotes a concept of military administration and never refers to a defended border. The *limitanei* were units under the command of a *dux limitis* and the term is used to distinguish such troops from the *comitatenses*, the field army. The term does not designate farmer–soldiers or members of a peasant militia, as has been assumed by some scholars.

The troops under the command of the *duces* are listed, together with the locations of their bases, in the *Notitia Dignitatum*. This material can be partly verified or augmented through comparison with inscriptions and some other literary sources. For instance, fourteen of the twenty-nine garrisons listed for Palaestina are found in other sources, nine of these in Eusebius' *Onomasticon* of biblical place-names, and five in other documents, such as the Theodosian Code, the fragments of decrees found at Beer Sheva, and the Colt Papyri from Nessana. Eusebius lists one garrison not attested (or identified) elsewhere,[67] and one which is not mentioned in the *Notitia* but attested elsewhere.[68] Thus we have more textual evidence of the distribution of garrisons at this period than at any other period in antiquity.

Archaeological research has identified many of these sites, and some have been excavated. The material remains of other installations have been explored, but not identified with locations mentioned in the texts. All the information thus made available allows extensive description, but it is less easy to reach a clear idea of the function of the system. In the case of individual installations, it is a mistake to assume that we can always easily

---

[64] Isaac, *Limits of Empire*, Appendix II, 436–8.　　[65] Downey, *Antioch* 354, 365, 383.
[66] Isaac (1988).　　[67] Theman (*On.* 96.20).　　[68] Carcaria (116.18).

understand the motives for chosing a particular site as a fort, or the probable tasks of the men on the spot. Where the regional organization of the army is concerned, we need explicit statements if we want to have a real insight into the original aims of those who planned it. Ancient literature does not contain much explicit information of this kind. We must therefore consider various possibilities, such as the maintenance of security on the roads, and internal and local police functions. Any hypothesis should take into account settlement patterns. Military garrisons in or near settlements must have had functions relating to the civilian inhabitants in the region, while soldiers stationed along a desert road are likely to have provided road security. Units stationed in settlements on nodal points of the road-network may have had a combination of such tasks.

During the late third and early fourth centuries, in the reigns of the tetrarchs and of Constantine, a major reorganization is known to have taken place. There are scattered references in literary sources to the reforms in the Near East. Ammianus says that Diocletian fortified Cercesium on the Euphrates when he organized the 'inner *limites*' – i.e. the frontier regions further inland – as a response to the Persian raids into Syria (XXIII.5.1–2). Malalas, a less dependable author, relates that Diocletian built forts in the frontier districts from Egypt to the Persian frontier (*Chron.* p. 308 Bonn). they were manned by border troops on guard duty under the command of *duces*. *Stelae* were set up in honour of the emperor and Caesar. According to Zosimus (II.34.1), Diocletian made the empire impenetrable to barbarians by stationing troops in cities, *castella* and towers in the frontier zones. Constantine, however, abolished this system by withdrawing the troops from the frontier to cities in the interior which, Zosimus says, did not need them.

These statements do not get us very far, particularly when we recall that the term *limes*, which recurs in many sources of this period, means no more than the regional command of a duke, or, vaguer still, a 'frontier district'. Even so, there is clearly an idea that there was a chain of military installations from Egypt to the Euphrates. This can indeed be identified with the aid of the *Notitia* and the results of exploration in the field.[69] The *stelae* mentioned by Malalas may be recognized as the milestones marking the *Strata Diocletiana*, a road from north-east Arabia and Damascus to Palmyra and the Euphrates. Apart from Lejjun in southern Arabia/Palaestina Tertia, legionary bases are found along the major roads. Many of them were located in towns, as was usual in the Near East, unlike the western parts of the empire. At the southern end of the line we find Aela on the site of modern Aqaba.[70] Moving to the north we should note Udruh (not mentioned in the *Notitia*), Bostra, Danaba (probably on the road from

[69] Van Berchem (1952).   [70] Isaac, *Limits of Empire*; Kennedy and Riley (1990), ch. 9.

Damascus to Sura), Palmyra, Oresa, Sura on the Euphrates, and finally Cercesium, 150 km down the river. The two legions in the old province of Judaea and the one at Raphaneae near the Syrian coast were withdrawn at unknown dates before the fourth century. Similarly, the legions along the Euphrates, at Samosata and Zeugma, were also transferred once the river had ceased to be the border in northern Syria. Two of these bases have been extensively excavated: Lejjun and Palmyra.[71]

We know less about the distribution of troops in Mesopotamia, but it is clear that one legion was still based at Singara, and perhaps another at Bezabde. After the loss of eastern Mesopotamia, these were withdrawn to Cepha and Constantina. Further north, the old stations of Melitene, Satala and Trapezus on the Black Sea shore were legionary bases. While Melitene and Satala had been legionary bases before Diocletian, the key site of Trapezus was new as a legionary establishment. It should be kept in mind that a fourth-century legion of perhaps 1500 men was a much smaller unit that the legion of the principate with its full complement of around 6000 soldiers. The largest unit of the later Roman empire, then, was perhaps only a quarter of the size of the second-century unit. However, it is quite possible that many old units had long since been split up into permanent detachments. It is clear that the most important units were stationed on the strategic north–south routes from the Black Sea to the Red Sea, and between Damascus and the Euphrates. Many of these were based at nodal points in the road-system. Auxiliary units, also reduced in size, were stationed along the routes closer to, or within, the arid zone east of the *Via Traiana*, in the Aravah north of Aela, along the *Strata Diocletiana*, and elsewhere. An inscription from Azraq in Arabia also suggests that there was a link between Bostra and Dumata (Jawf), 500 km away in the northern Hijaz.[72] Finally, we should note that there are many smaller structures along the roads in the desert and steppe. They look like small military outposts or police-stations and many of them go back to the fourth century, but they rarely bear inscriptions designating their function or the identity of their occupants.[73]

This brief outline cannot form the basis for a discussion of the nature and purpose of the system. However, it is essential to note that even considerations based on the fullest possible description still end with fundamental queries. Attempts have been made to describe the organization as a 'system of defence in depth'. However, such notions are copied from modern parallels and do not reflect what is known about ancient military organization.

A few observations can be made. First of all, the connection between

[71] Parker (1987); Gawlikowski (1984).   [72] Most recently: MacAdam (1989).
[73] Kennedy and Riley (1990) ch. 10.

the road-system and the choice of sites is obvious. This is true not only for the many small posts which presumably may be described as police-stations, but also for the largest units. Topography, logistics and the existing road-system determined the location of military establishments. This is not a matter of course, for at this period there were many military systems in which the roads were constructed specifically to connect their bases – in other words, systems in which the roads were a secondary element, developed to serve the military structure. In this connection it is of interest that most or all of the *Strata Diocletiana* in Syria already existed as a road in the Flavian period. It is now clear that Resapha, a site on this road, which was a military base in the fourth century (*Not. Dig. Or.* XXXIII.27), was already occupied in the Flavian period.[74] All this fits John Mann's observation that the keynote of Diocletian's army reforms was consolidation rather than innovation.

Secondly, there was some expansion of the Roman presence in the steppe and a corresponding reduction of troops in the interior of Palestine and the coastal area of Syria. This may be connected with the expansion of settlement in the marginal areas during the Byzantine period. A third point worth repeating here is that in this period the Saracens became a significant factor in the exercise of control over the marginal areas and the trade routes. This was particularly important in the southern part of the region. In the north-eastern part, the relationship with Persia was the factor which determined military organization, but here too the Saracens achieved a role which they had not played in previous centuries. However, in the wars between the later Roman empire and Persia, the primary issue was the fortified cities of northern Mesopotamia. These were the focus of the fighting; they played a key role in the wars of the period in that they were responsible for the maintenance and manning of roads, bridges and road stations.[75] The citizens often had to defend themselves without effective support from the regular army. This is well described by Ammianus in the extreme case of Singara, which was taken by the Persians in 360, when there were not enough troops and local people to hold it:

even in earlier times, no one had ever been able to bring help to Singara when it was in danger, because all the surrounding country was dried up from lack of water. The place had been fortified in days of old as a convenient outpost to obtain advance information of any sudden enemy movement, but in fact it had proved a liability to Rome, because it was taken on several occasions with the loss of its garrison.[76]

Singara was chosen as the easternmost legionary base after the annexation of the region by Septimius Severus, and lost to Persia in 363, together with

---

[74] M. Konrad, *Damaszener Mitteilungen* 6 (1992) 313–402.
[75] Joh. Chrys. *Ad Stag.* II.189f. (*PG* LX.457). Also: Segal (1955) 114f.
[76] Amm. Marc. XX.6.9, trans. Walter Hamilton, Penguin.

Nisibis and Bezabde. These cities, while Rome held them, and other fortified cities in the east fulfilled various functions. They were refuges for the
army, staging-posts for campaigns, armouries, customs posts, bases for
troops and refuges for the population during major wars. At such times no
effort was made to protect the countryside. Ammianus impressively
describes the Roman preparations for the Persian invasion of 359: the peasants were compelled to move to fortified places, Carrhae was abandoned
as being indefensible, and the plain was set on fire (Amm. Marc.
XVII.7.3–4). The loss of such cities was considered a major change in the
balance of power. Throughout the later Roman empire, wars in
Mesopotamia were fought for cities, not for territory or lines of defence.

V. CONCLUSION

The period covered in this volume is marked by elements characteristic both
of the previous period and of the following centuries. Thus we have seen
that Constantine was the first to introduce religion as a serious factor in the
conflict between the two empires, using it as a tool for the justification of
war. Shortly afterwards Julian was the last of a long line of Roman emperors to organize a major campaign into Babylonia. The failure of Julian's campaign and the subsequent settlement, which was unfavourable to Rome,
paradoxically stabilized the relationship between the two powers to some
extent. The invasion of the Huns in 395–7 was the first confrontation in the
east with a potentially dangerous enemy from north of the Caucasus. More
important, however, is the fact that pre-Islamic Arabs, 'Saracens', became a
significant factor in the warfare between Rome and Persia as allies of both
sides and as agents maintaining control over marginal areas between the
settled lands and the desert. Here too religion played a political role, although
it is difficult to trace. It is clear, however, that conversion was part of the
process whereby Saracen nomads accepted the role of Byzantine allies or
federates. Within the empire the status of the Jews deteriorated as the result
of various measures taken by the Christian emperors. On the other hand, the
Isaurians achieved a semi-independent status in their own region and, for
some time, influence in the army through the troops and officers they supplied. Finally, the military organization of the second half of the fourth
century had more in common with that of the sixth than with that of the
third. This period witnessed the institution of territorial commands (*limites*)
held by *duces* as distinct from the field army. A further separation was that of
the military and civilian hierarchy and, in emergencies, a marked dependence
on the resilience and self-reliance of the fortified cities in the east.

CHAPTER 15

THE GERMANIC PEOPLES

MALCOLM TODD

I. INTRODUCTION

In the reign of Constantine I, the peoples of northern Europe were contained by frontiers that were recognizably derived from those of the early empire. A century later, those frontiers had effectively disappeared. Germans and other barbarians were settled in Gaul, Britain, the provinces on the Rhine and Danube, in the Balkans, Italy, Spain and North Africa. The period covered by this volume thus saw a radical transformation in the relations between the Germanic peoples and the Roman empire, bringing to a culmination changes that had begun in the previous hundred years.[1] Since the conflicts of the later second century, there had followed a century of tumultuous change in the tribal geography of the lands between the Rhine and the western steppes. Large confederacies of peoples had emerged by the middle of the third century, now strong enough to pose a serious military challenge to the Roman frontiers. Many of the small tribes known to Tacitus and Ptolemy had vanished, presumably absorbed in greater, though still loose, political organisms. It is not possible in the literary record to detect the first moves towards the formation of primitive states.[2] If they were made at so early a date as the fourth and early fifth centuries (a point on which there must be serious doubt), they were not recorded by the writers of the late empire. Interest in the detailed workings of barbarian society was no higher than it had been in the first and second centuries and was in any case only expressed within a Roman frame of reference which was not equipped to reflect the realities of preliterate societies. What we read in the ancient sources, therefore, gives little indication of the nature and variety of political and social organization likely to have existed over the vast area of northern and central Europe occupied by the Germanic peoples. The archaeological evidence reveals something of the variety of barbarian organization, but does not go far towards outlining political structures. It can be more helpful in the matter of social relations, in so far as these can be revealed by settlements and artefacts alone, and it is on these that this chapter focuses.

---

[1] Todd (1992). [2] Demandt (1980).

461

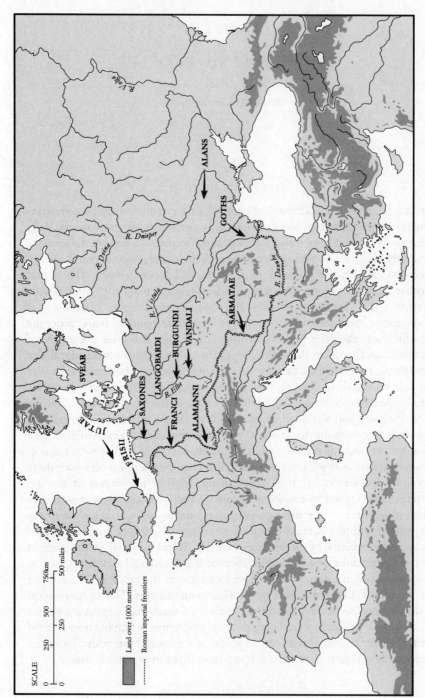

Fig. 7 Major barbarian peoples and Roman frontiers: late fourth–fifth centuries

As in earlier periods of the Germanic Iron Age, much more is known about the settlement pattern, settlement types and the social units housed in them in northern Germania than in any other region.[3] Slow processes of change are in evidence from the second century onward, some perhaps stimulated by contacts with the Roman provinces, others more certainly resulting from developments within Germanic society which owed little or nothing to external factors. Roman written sources suggest little change within the social order of the Germanic peoples from the first contacts to the migrations.[4] The archaeological record has a different story to tell. The impact of environmental change in the later Roman Iron Age must also be allowed for, in certain areas at least, most notably in the northern coastlands. A major phase of marine flooding has long been attested for the fourth century in the regions from the Rhine mouth to the Jutland peninsula, with severe effects for local settlement. While study of individual settlements has made great progress in the past forty years, especially in Holland, Denmark and northern Germany, in relatively few parts of the Germanic territories have detailed regional surveys been undertaken; these alone can reveal the settlement pattern of the later Roman Iron Age and the early Migration Period. Thus far, the evidence for the distribution of settlement presents a very varied picture, and it would be mistaken to look for the working of similar processes over so vast a tract of northern and central Europe. For much of central Europe, in any case, the settlement record is poor, while for the critically important area between the lower Danube and the Black Sea hinterland it is virtually non-existent.

One of the most important advances of recent decades has been the recognition in archaeology of Germanic settlers within the Roman provinces in the fourth and early fifth centuries.[5] In some cases, these were associated with the provincial population or with the defenders of particular frontiers, as on the upper Rhine and middle Danube. In others, barbarian groups seem to have maintained a more or less independent existence. The circumstances under which barbarians entered the Roman empire had always been various, ranging from relatively peaceful resettlement through military service to forced intrusion. It must be kept in mind that archaeological evidence will rarely be sufficient on its own to clarify how barbarians were established on Roman soil, revealing though it might be on where and when this was done.

Barbarian settlements within the empire, even when considerable numbers of people were involved, remain notoriously difficult to identify and study before the middle of the fifth century. The movement of Goths and others into the northern Balkans in the 370s can scarcely be traced in the archaeological record. The invasions of Italy by Alaric's forces in the

---

[3] Todd (1987) 79–99.   [4] Thompson (1965) 29–71.   [5] Böhme (1974).

first decade of the fifth century are likewise all but invisible in material remains, a single eastern Germanic brooch from Rome or its vicinity and possibly the burial of the great silver treasure on the Esquiline[6] being all that can be tentatively linked with the Gothic presence in the Urbs. These invasions were, in archaeological terms, brief episodes and they cannot be expected to leave much behind them. More strikingly, the settlement of the Visigoths in Aquitaine after 418 is barely attested, either in the archaeology of the region or in the toponymy.[7] Even Germanic metalwork, that staple of Migration Period studies, is very scarce in south-western Gaul in the fifth century.[8] The customs of burial remained overwhelmingly Roman provincial. The dead were laid to rest in clothing but rarely with accompanying grave-goods. Wealthier graves reveal a preference for sarcophagi of late Roman style. A search for a typically 'Germanic' burial of the fifth century yields only a single example, at Valentines. Recognizably Visigothic material is equally elusive in urban and rural settlements. Much the same can be said of the Burgundian settlement in eastern Gaul. Both these barbarian peoples brought relatively little of their cultural paraphernalia into their new homes; once established here, they took over the dress, material equipment and customs of the provincial population among whom they were lodged. Thereafter, their ethnic identity found no expression in material terms and in any case was probably much diluted by contact with the other resident populations of Gaul.

II. GAUL, THE GERMANYS AND RAETIA

The earliest clear indications of the establishment of Germans on provincial land are to be seen in an impressive series of cemeteries between the Rhine and the Loire.[9] These contain distinctively furnished graves whose occupants were, in the majority of cases, German warriors in the service of Rome, and their adherents. Although they are generally similar to the fourth-century Gallo-Roman burials, the male burials frequently contain weapons (occasionally swords, more often spears and axes) and the fittings of military belts, and the female graves ornaments which were normally current in the northern coastlands; this puts it beyond reasonable doubt that these were incomers from east of the Rhine. Among the most distinctive of the metal ornaments is the so-called tutulus-brooch – a conical brooch, often in silver, worn in a pair on the shoulders – and the brooch with expanded foot, which formed a prototype of the equal-armed brooch frequently associated with the early Anglo-Saxons. The area in which these

---

[6] Shelton (1981) 53–5, suggesting a burial-date for this great silver hoard in the late fourth or early fifth century.   [7] Rouche (1979).

[8] Excluded from consideration is the miscellaneous collection of material claimed to have been found at Herpes (Charente-Maritime).   [9] Böhme (1974).

brooches originated lies between and about the lower Weser and Elbe in Lower Saxony. In that same area, it is striking that late Roman military fittings occur in graves at exactly this time, probably representing warriors who had returned to their homeland after service in the Roman world. The date of this series of graves may be set between 370 and 450 at the latest, with a strong bias towards the late fourth and early fifth centuries. They occur in the very region – the basins of the Meuse, Seine and Somme, and westward to the Loire – where the *Notitia Dignitatum* locates *praefecti laetorum* at towns and other strongholds about this date. It is not proven that the warrior burials are specifically those of *laeti*, whose settlement of parts of Gaul had begun in the reign of Probus.[10] More probably they are the graves of a much wider range of German recruits. Several of the burials were furnished in some style and are presumably those of high-ranking officers. The cemetery at Vermand contained more than eighty graves (out of a total of 429) with Germanic associations, several of them richly furnished. One grave stands out from the rest, with its silver-gilt spear-fittings and belt-mounts, as that of a chieftainly commander.[11] This and other richly furnished graves in Gaul are suggestive of the presence of aristocratic Franks and Saxons and their retinues in the decades on either side of 400. Interestingly, there was no segregation of Germans from provincials within the cemetery at Vermand.

Vermand and a number of other cemeteries continued without break into the sixth century, perhaps indicating that the early settlements of German warriors had provided the nuclei for stable and enduring communities. In their mixed population, the Germanic element may have played an increasingly significant part. After the middle of the fifth century, several such enclaves took on much greater importance. At Tournai, Metz, Trier and Cologne they may have formed the core of the earliest petty kingdoms.

Rich burials of a different type reveal wider cultural, and possibly political, connections in fifth-century Gaul.[12] The grave of a woman found in 1876 at Airan (Calvados) contained two large round-headed brooches in silver covered with gold foil and encrusted with coloured stones *en cabochon*, along with other personal ornaments in gold. The brooches indicate a date of about A.D. 400 for this burial and provide a secure link with the middle Danube workshops of that time. Such material could have reached Gaul early in the fifth century in the great westward sweep which brought the Vandals, Suevi and Alans across the Rhine at the end of 406. But there are other possible explanations for the Airan jewellery, notably high-level contacts such as marriage alliances between early Germanic settlers in Gaul

---

[10] Roosens (1967).　[11] Böhme (1974) 174; Périn and Feffer (1987) 61–9.
[12] Kazanski (1982); Périn and Feffer (1987) 116–17.

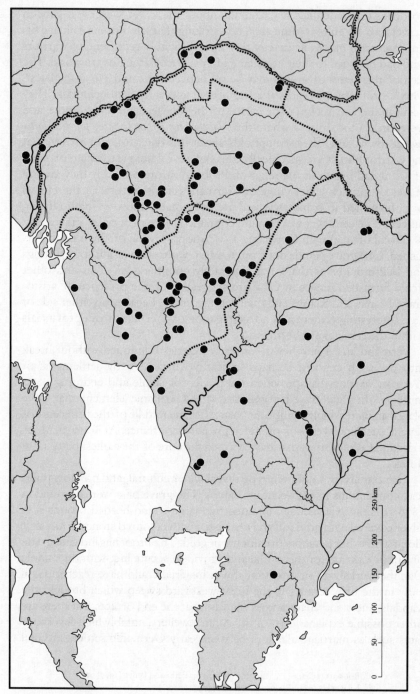

Fig. 8. Warrior burials in northern Gaul and the German provinces: late fourth–early fifth centuries

and the powerful peoples massing on the Danube who were mounting an increasing threat to Italy and the Balkan provinces.

Connections with the Danube lands are pointed to by graves of a later date. A warrior burial found at Pouan (Aube) in 1842 contained two swords, the hilts and scabbards of which were decorated with garnets, a belt with similarly adorned fittings, a gold torque and other jewellery. This ensemble finds its nearest analogues in Pannonia after the middle of the fifth century, probably between 460 and 475. Its owner was thus a contemporary of Childeric, the first barbarian ruler of Gaul whose material surroundings are illuminated by archaeology. The discovery of his grave at Tournai in 1653 marks the foundation of the archaeology of the Migration Period and it still provides a fixed point – 481 – in the chronology of early Frankish Gaul.[13] Here, too, were represented the rich and glowing garnet cloisonné work on the sword-hilt and scabbard, the weighty gold fittings of a cere-monial belt and, in addition, a massive gold crossbow brooch of a type earlier worn by both Roman officers and barbarian allies. The grave-goods of Childeric are recognizably those of a ruler living at a time when alliance with Rome, and what it had stood for, were not yet entirely forgotten.

The more mundane archaeology of the early Franks in the Rhineland and northern Gaul is notoriously difficult to define. The literary sources tell us that the Franks were in possession of sizeable areas by 450 and yet the archaeological record in its sum shows little that can be labelled 'Frankish' or even 'Germanic' at that date or for some decades later. Thus, Cologne was first a target for Frankish assaults and then a base of local Frankish power. Extensive excavations within the walls of Cologne since 1945 have produced little that can be linked with Frankish occupation in the fourth and fifth centuries, while, outside the walls of the city, known Frankish cemeteries do not begin before 480 at the earliest. Trier and the valley of the Moselle were even more of a target for attack, the city being sacked on at least three occasions in the first half of the fifth century. The cultured Frankish leader Arbogast, a descendant of the late-fourth-century com-mander of the same name, is described as a *comes* and what we know of his tastes and connections gives colour to the idea that he supported Roman authority on the Moselle.[14] But of his Frankish entourage there is scarcely a trace. As in the Cologne area, it is not until the later fifth century that the earliest Frankish cemeteries appear around Trier, and the record of them remains thin until after 500.[15] None of this suggests any marked degree of continuity in the areas increasingly dominated by the Rhineland Franks. Few rural sites have yet revealed undoubted traces of occupation in the fifth century, though it must be admitted that not many have been exam-ined with the necessary sensitivity. The large villa at Echternach in

---

[13] Chiflet (1655).   [14] Sidonius Apollinaris, *Ep.* 4.17.   [15] Böhner (1958).

Luxemburg continued to be occupied, though its proximity to a fortified stronghold may have given it a special advantage.[16] The defended village at Bitburg also provided a refuge for a small population in the fifth century, but there is no indication that any of them were Franks. Most of the earliest Frankish cemeteries occur on sites that were entirely new or were established alongside a Roman settlement, usually a villa, perhaps indicating that the estate had been divided between the incomers and the surviving provincials. The majority of villas, however, had been abandoned by 450 and many of them long before that date. By the sixth century, Frankish settlements normally occupied new sites, well clear of late Roman villas and other settlements. By then, it is plain, a new social order had emerged.

By far the most informative of the few cemeteries which do show clear continuity from the fourth century into the Migration Period, and beyond, are those associated with the site of the Roman fort and *vicus* at Gelduba (Krefeld-Gellep) on the lower Rhine.[17] More than six hundred graves here can be dated to the fourth century, but the total number of interments of that date can be increased by an unknown proportion of the inhumations which were unaccompanied by datable grave-goods. From the later fourth century, the number of grave-goods shows a decrease and their character changes. Parts of belts, knives and occasionally weapons are to the fore, suggesting change in the composition of the community at Gelduba by about A.D. 400. These burials in turn give way to a series in which distinctively Germanic components are present, so that it may be inferred that settlers from east of the Rhine had arrived here by that date or somewhat before, presumably on military service in the first instance. This cemetery continued in use until well into the fifth century. The Gelduba community, whatever its composition, thus remained in being into the period when Frankish settlement on the lower Rhine was consolidating. Exceptionally, or so it would seem, the site became a focus for aristocratic settlement in the sixth century, as is revealed by a remarkable series of *Fürstengräber*, of men and of women. On the face of it, it is strange that this sequence is not clearly in evidence elsewhere in the Rhineland and northern Gaul. The prevailing picture is of discontinuity of settlement after 400, the pattern of Frankish control not emerging in the archaeological record until the later decades of the fifth century.

From some areas of northern Gaul, however, there have come clear signs of German settlement dating from the late fourth and early fifth centuries. Two instances, differing in character, are worth examination. In the middle valley of the Meuse lie a number of hill-top strongholds fortified in the late Roman period. One of these, at Vireux-Molhain, suffered severely in the disturbances of the mid fourth century.[18] Reoccupied late in

---

[16] Metzler *et al.* (1981).   [17] Pirling (1966–74), (1979).   [18] Lemant *et al.* (1985).

that century, the stronghold received a small garrison, perhaps twenty-five strong. The military character of this occupation is clearly demonstrated by its cemetery. Of more than fifty graves, an overwhelmingly large number are those of men accompanied by weapons and military accoutrements. That these include burials of barbarians from east of the Rhine is put beyond reasonable doubt by the presence of throwing-axes and other non-Roman equipment. In the small number of women's graves, two contain brooches of German manufacture. Unusually for barbarian graves of this date, a number contained coins, and these enable the main period of use to be fixed in the early years of the fifth century. The latest piece, a *solidus* of Honorius in mint condition found in a cremation (another pointer to non-Roman usage), suggests an end to this phase at Vireux-Molhain about 430–5. This is the clearest case yet defined of a garrison including or consisting of barbarians well inside the frontiers.[19] It is interesting that occupation of the site ended at about the time when Roman control of this part of Gaul was coming to an end and that it was not continued by incoming Franks.

Contemporary with Vireux-Molhain and also situated in the valley of the Meuse is the site of Neerharen-Rekem, seven kilometres north of Maastricht.[20] Here, on a site close to a small Roman villa destroyed and abandoned in the third century, a German community established itself, or was established, in the later fourth century. The village (for this was no mere farmstead) was composed mainly of *Grubenhäuser*, though at least two large rectangular halls also existed. The entire site would not look out of place east of the Rhine or on the north German coast. It came into existence about or shortly after 350 and ended not long after 400. Not far away, at Donk, another German settlement existed in the fourth century, thus raising the possibility that Franks settled in the Meuse valley in greater numbers before 400 than has so far been considered likely. More detailed study of settlements will certainly enlarge the modest total of information at present available. In the case of the lower Meuse, and of the Rhine, sites of this and earlier periods are likely to lie deeply buried beneath alluvium deposited by those rivers, so that their discovery is usually a matter of chance.

What was taking place on the lower Rhine was the emergence of a frontier society, its roots deep in Roman–German relations over the previous century and a half. At the upper end of the social scale were Germans who took service in the Roman armies at the highest level. Their names and deeds are frequent visitors to the pages of Ammianus Marcellinus. Below the ranks of Silvanus and Merobaudes, there were untold numbers of other

---

[19] Furfooz is another case: see J. A. E. Nenquin, *La Nécropole de Furfooz* (Bruges, 1953).
[20] G. de Boë in Otte and Willems (1986) 101–10.

lesser warriors who made up the military units on the frontiers or were settled on the land. It is now clear that other barbarians were entering the Rhine provinces about the end of the fourth century, not necessarily under any officially sanctioned scheme of settlement. This is what the German settlement at Neerharen-Rekem seems to represent, as do the earliest graves at Krefeld-Gellep. A mingling of Roman provincial and barbarian populations is obviously indicated, and this is not something revealed by the literary record. The formation of a distinct frontier society, neither wholly provincial nor wholly barbarian, would scarcely be surprising to either side of a frontier which had brought Roman and German together over four centuries.

The military deployment of Alamannic groups by Roman commanders is to be expected and is attested for several parts of the western provinces. It is also revealed on the Roman frontier which faced the Alamanni themselves, most clearly in a fourth-century cemetery at Neuburg on the Danube.[21] Here, over 130 graves, predominantly military in character, included a significant number which contained Germanic material. Three main chronological divisions have been identified within the cemetery. The first, dating from 330–60, is to be related to a mixed garrison which included Germanic troops, attached to a small fortification, perhaps established in the Constantinian reorganization of the frontier and brought to an end in the Alamannic invasion of 357. The next phase, from 360 to about 390, is marked by Elbe-German connections and may represent a mixed provincial and German force, eventually dispersed after the defeat of Magnus Maximus in 388. The third group of burials, of the end of the fourth century, betrays no link with the middle Danube lands but rather points further east, to the barbarian groups on the lower Danube and in the northern Balkans. A number of these settlers might have entered Roman employment there or moved westward to be later lodged in Raetia Secunda. The successive phases of the Neuburg cemetery thus exemplify the volatility of frontier dispositions over this period and illustrate well the range of expedients to which Roman commanders had recourse. Other upper Danube forts and towns have produced evidence that they were settled by Germans in the fourth century. At Günzburg the garrison included elements from the upper Elbe basin before 350, and this is also hinted at in a string of forts north of Lake Constance and on the upper Rhine.

Alamannic settlements which had no connection with the needs of Roman frontier defence are poorly recorded for the fourth century. The archaeological record consists largely of small groups of graves or single burials, suggesting a scattered population with no focus upon one particular area.[22] Most of the early Alamannic graves seem to be unrelated to the

---

[21] Keller (1979).   [22] Veeck (1931); Franken (1944); Roeren (1960); Christlein (1978) 22–6.

earlier Roman settlement pattern north of the Danube. Some Roman sites, however, including a few villas, did attract attention from the incoming Germans. At Holheim, the Roman villa buildings were partly restored by the new settlers, while the Praunheim villa, near the Roman town of Heddernheim, was also crudely refurbished by its barbarian inhabitants. At Baldingen, a remarkable series of *solidi* (otherwise rare on villa sites) and a later Roman military brooch may indicate either a local estate garrison or a settlement of Germans who had returned from service in the Roman provinces. In its sum, this evidence does not point to a major influx of Alamanni into the old *agri decumates* after the abandonment of the *limes*. That does not seem to have occurred until later in the fourth century at the earliest.

That some Alamannic settlements might be enclosed is revealed by the site at Sontheim in the Stubental, a palisaded enclosure with a stout timber gatehouse protecting a number of rectangular buildings.[23] This fortified residence or small village was established before 300 and continued through the fourth century. Other complexes of more modest timber buildings have been identified, mainly of *Grubenhäuser* associated with no more elaborate structures, as at Wittislingen, where the Germanic settlement may have immediately followed one of Roman provincials. None of these seems likely to have been the residence of an Alamannic *regalis* or *regulus*. That social level is more convincingly represented by a number of hill-top strongholds now well established in the archaeology of the region. The most fully examined is the fortified site on the Runder Berg at Urach.[24] Here, a massive timber rampart was constructed around an ovoid space up to seventy metres long and fifty metres across, in the late third or early fourth century. Within lay timber buildings of various dates, mainly later fourth and fifth century, and other structures occupied the lower slopes of the hill. The latter may have housed dependent craftsmen. Chieftainly residences may have occupied other hill-tops in the fourth century. The Gelbe Burg near Dittenheim probably belongs here, though its defences are at present dated to the fifth century. Other such strongholds may be expected to emerge with further research. The overall pattern of Alamannic settlement, however, is inadequately recorded and may remain irrecoverable. Many of the earliest occupation sites will have given rise to flourishing communities in the sixth and seventh centuries and now lie inaccessibly buried beneath medieval and modern villages. Centres of power, aside from local strongholds like the Runder Berg, are not to be looked for before the later fifth century, when at last Alamannic leaders began to aim at centralized control of their entire territory.

---

[23] Christlein (1978) 40–1.
[24] Christlein (1979). The main report on the excavation is unpublished.

III. THE NORTHERN COASTLANDS AND HOLLAND

The peoples of the northern German coastlands who posed an increasing threat to the security of the frontier on the lower Rhine and to the coasts of northern Gaul and Britain in the fourth century were lumped together by Roman sources as 'Saxons', though that name embraced wide ethnic variety. The area usually designated the heartland of the Saxons lay about the lower courses of the Elbe and Weser, but sea-raiders from the north might also come from Friesland to the west and the Jutland peninsula to the east. The fourth-century Saxons were ambitious in their attacks on the Roman provinces. Their ability to mount long-distance raids far from their homelands put the lower Rhine frontier in jeopardy about the middle of the fourth century, and Saxons were just as likely as Franks to seek settlement in the provincial areas they had entered. Like the Franks, they also might take service with the armies of Rome. Roman military belt-sets and other equipment are found in some quantity in the Elbe–Weser region, some of them booty perhaps, but a proportion at least probably taken there by warriors returning from Roman employment.[25] Roman gold coinage, found east of the Rhine in quantity in the second half of the fourth century, may also have been linked with military service and not merely with successful raiding.

The archaeological cultures of the northern coastlands are very complicated, and increased attention to them has not led to simplification. A nexus of relatively small cultural groups extended from the lower Ems to the base of the Jutland peninsula in the fourth century. Connections existed between these groups, without amounting to wholesale unity. The coastlands were not by any means a closed world in the fourth century. Influences were felt from the middle basin of the Elbe, and there were connections eastward with the lands between Rhine and Weser occupied by Franks. There have been many-sided studies of the settlements in the coastal margins over the past three decades, with a consequent increase in the appreciation of demographic change in this region, as well as of settlement history and social structure. It is now abundantly clear that a considerable increase in population was registered during the late Roman Iron Age, a peak possibly being reached during the fourth century. The evidence of cemeteries such as Westerwanna, Mahndorf, Issendorf and Liebenau[26] has long pointed to this conclusion, a marked increase in the number of burials from the later third century onward being recorded. This increase in population, and the consequent pressure on economic resources which it presumably entailed, is a fact to which full weight must be given when the origins of the migrations of the fifth century are under consideration.

[25] Böhme (1974).   [26] Grohne (1953); Röhrer-Ertl (1971); Janssen (1972); Hassler (1983).

The great cemeteries of the Saxon lands long dominated research and provided the bulk of our information about their inhabitants. These were cremation cemeteries, often containing thousands of urn-graves and in use over several centuries. Inhumations first began to appear in the fourth century, as at Liebenau, but they remained scarce for another hundred years. Settlement and environmental evidence of outstanding quality has been provided by the programmes of work at Tofting, Flögeln and, above all, the marshland settlement at Feddersen Wierde near the estuary of the Elbe.[27] This mound settlement had grown steadily from modest origins in the first century B.C., until in the fourth century it comprised about thirty main steadings, each with its own long-house, radiating from a central space. On the south-western side, an enclosure marked off a space within which craftsmen were at work, evidently under the control of a chieftain or local headman whose residence also lay within the enclosing fence. The fourth century saw this settlement reach its greatest extent. Early in the fifth century came decline, and the place was wholly deserted by 450. This is also true for several settlements in the vicinity of the lower Elbe, and there is little doubt that this is a result of migration westward, for some perhaps towards the lower Rhine and northern Gaul, for others, however, into eastern Britain, where Germanic pottery of the earlier fifth century closely matches that from the final phases of Feddersen Wierde.[28]

The flat lands north of the lower Rhine in what is now Holland had long sustained communities which enjoyed close contacts with the Roman world. Some of these communities were remarkably stable and grew considerably in size during the later Roman Iron Age, as is well demonstrated by the settlement at Wijster.[29] From the third century onward, this comprised a large agglomeration of long-houses and their ancillary buildings in a regular layout of streets and palisaded enclosures. The population of Wijster at its fourth-century peak may have numbered fifty or sixty families, two hundred or more people. The territory which supplied this community must have been considerable in its extent, and the intensification of agriculture and crafts in evidence goes far beyond what was demanded by a merely self-sufficient unit. A sizeable surplus in agricultural products seems reasonably certain, and a ready market for such a surplus lay only a hundred kilometres to the south, in the Roman garrisons and towns on the lower Rhine. Roman mass-produced goods acquired in exchange are well represented among the material from Wijster.

Wijster did not stand alone as a barbarian settlement which enjoyed prosperous relations with the adjacent Roman frontier land. At Bennekom, in Gelderland, no more than forty kilometres from the Rhine, a settlement

---

[27] Haarnagel (1979).
[28] E.g. at Mucking, Essex (Hamerow (1993)); West Stow (Suffolk) (West (1985)); and Caister-by-Norwich, Norfolk (Myres and Green (1973)).   [29] Van Es (1965).

grew steadily from the second century to the late fourth.[30] This was much smaller than Wijster, at its peak probably no more than four substantial farmsteads with their associated buildings, and less regularly planned. But in other respects, Bennekom had much in common with the larger settlement. Like Wijster, its most prosperous period was the later third and fourth centuries, tailing off markedly after 400. The progressive weakening of the economic system of the frontier provinces in the fourth century offered considerable opportunities to barbarian communities like Wijster and Bennekom. They could provide food, commodities such as leather, and manpower to an increasingly hard-pressed provincial administration. Co-operative barbarians were not unfamiliar beings to Roman commanders and administrators. In the fourth century on the lower Rhine, they will have been more welcome and more necessary than ever before.

The abandonment of settlements early in the fifth century, in some cases probably abruptly, has been noted in several areas of Holland close to the Roman frontier. In some cases, at least, settlement continued on a new site nearby; in others, wholesale abandonment occurred. Sites like Bennekom and Wijster are likely to have been directly affected by the final collapse of Roman authority on the lower Rhine. But the phenomenon seems to have been so widespread that this will not serve as a general explanation. Several of the coastal *terpen* (settlement mounds) were also given up about or shortly after 400, as were settlements in the lower Elbe–Weser region. Significant changes in the coastal environment were being wrought at this time by a general rise in sea-level, rendering considerable tracts of land less productive or, at worst, uninhabitable. A still more fundamental agent of change in the settlement pattern was an increasingly mobile population in search of land and a better livelihood within the Roman provinces. The decline of Roman power in the north-western provinces opened up to those prepared to move inviting paths to the relatively rich lands of northern Gaul and Britain, hitherto accessible only to raiders or recruits to the armies of Rome. Although not every barbarian peasant was prepared or able to migrate in search of land, many will have been impelled to do so, by the ambition of their masters if not by their own. Those left behind, or those arriving from the east and north, may have taken the opportunity to reorganize their landholdings and settlements to take full advantage of a fluid situation, thus stimulating major shifts in local settlement.

IV. BRITAIN

The archaeology of the earliest Germanic settlements in Britain has been considerably enlarged in the past thirty years. We are no longer dependent

---

[30] Van Es *et al.* (1985).

upon detailed (and to a large extent subjective) study of brooch-types and pottery for our knowledge of the beginnings of Anglo-Saxon England. Excavation of settlement sites now offers some impression of the early communities as a whole. More importantly, the Germanic migration into south-eastern Britain can be more clearly seen within its fuller north-west European context.[31]

The contents of certain graves in southern Britain indicate an involvement by warrior groups in early settlement which is similar to that evidenced in northern Gaul. Among the earliest of the burials are those of men equipped with belts and other military accoutrements which are closely akin to those of the warrior burials in northern Gaul and the Rhine provinces of the period 370–420. The British graves occur in small groups in and south of the Thames valley – for example, at Dorchester-on-Thames, Mucking (Essex), Croydon and Milton (Kent). The men were buried with weapons, the women with late Romano-British ornaments and occasionally brooches from the north German coastlands. The connections with the north Gaulish burials is obvious, and there can be little doubt that these are the graves of barbarians, probably including both Franks and Saxons, who had died in late Roman service. But the British burials are much less likely than those in Gaul to represent men recruited into the army of Britain in the late fourth and early fifth centuries. That was the very time when the army in the island was being seriously depleted. More probably, they were brought in by the leaders of *civitates* and local magnates (who might be identical) to protect their lands. That is in accord with the distribution of the graves, which is exclusively south-eastern and distant from the main military forces of the north and the Saxon Shore. Other paramilitary equipment found on villas and other rural sites may suggest that the employment of private forces was widespread in the late fourth century.

In East Anglia and the south Midlands there occur other graves which contain brooches of types normally current in the lower Elbe–Weser region and which thus suggest direct links across the North Sea. The equal-armed brooch and its progenitors are the leading types. These are not easy to date with any precision, but the decades immediately following 400 should contain most of them. Further north, in the east Midlands and in Yorkshire, there are occasional signs of contemporary Germanic metalwork. A tutulus-brooch found at Kirmington in north Lincolnshire, supporting-arm brooches from Hibaldstow and Elsham in the same area, and a stud-brooch found in east Yorkshire should date around 400 or only shortly afterwards. The evidence of pottery in the early cremation cemeteries is broadly in agreement with a Germanic settlement early in the fifth century. Urns of that date have been reported from several sites in East

---

[31] In general, Myres (1969); (1986); Campbell (1982); Böhme (1986).

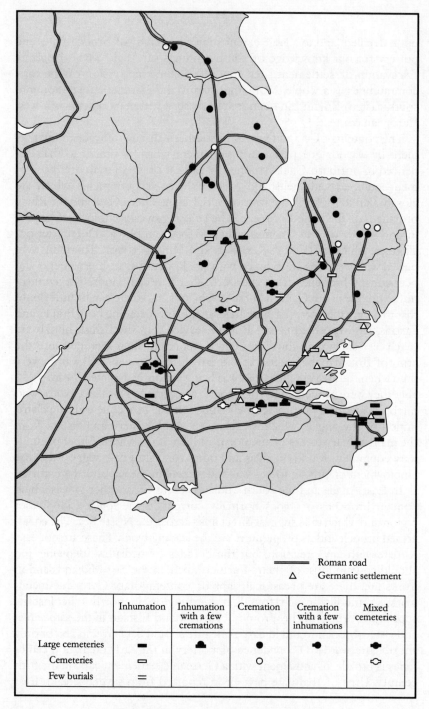

	Inhumation	Inhumation with a few cremations	Cremation	Cremation with a few inhumations	Mixed cemeteries
Large cemeteries	▬	▲	●	◖	◕
Cemeteries	▱		○		◁
Few burials	=				

Roman road
△ Germanic settlement

Fig. 9. Fifth-century Germanic burials in Britain

Anglia and the eastern Midlands, most notably from cemeteries in the vicinity of Roman towns and cities, as though the Germanic settlers had entered a region where a recognizably Romano-British order had not entirely vanished and to which they could be deliberately introduced. The Germans at Caister-by-Norwich seem to have been relatively numerous.[32] Many of their cremation urns are to be assigned to the first half of the fifth century, though Myres has argued that some are as early as the fourth century, on insecure typological grounds. Not surprisingly, Kent also reveals early-fifth-century material, though not yet a major cemetery of that date. The coastal forts of Reculver, Richborough and Dover might seem to offer possible points of entry for German immigrants, but as yet little evidence for them is to hand.

One of the most significant advances of the past quarter of a century in Britain has been the recovery of settlement sites, the earliest phases of which are dated to the fifth century. One of the earliest and most extensively excavated is that at Mucking (Essex) on the northern shore of the Thames estuary near Thurrock.[33] This large agglomeration of *Grubenhäuser* and larger hall-like structures had begun its existence before the middle of the fifth century, possibly as early as 420. What was this community of Germans doing there, only twenty miles from Londinium? There were military burials in the cemetery at Mucking, carrying more than a hint of official control early in the century, but any such control is unlikely to have been effective for long after 420. The early Germanic pottery at Mucking is closely matched by material in the north German coastlands, especially in the late phases at Feddersen Wierde, and a direct overseas connection seems virtually certain. That would suggest that settlers from northern Germany could, without let or hindrance, make their way to Britain by 425 at the latest and establish themselves close to what had been the premier city of Britannia. Other Germanic settlements were in existence in the first half of the fifth century in East Anglia. At West Stow in Suffolk migrants from the Elbe–Weser area had arrived and established themselves by 450 and probably before, on ground which had long been cultivated by Romano-British farmers.[34] Such barbarian enclaves were small about 450, but over the next half-century the influence of their inhabitants grew steadily. What relationships existed with a remnant Romano-British population is obscure, but the occurrence of early-fifth-century Germanic cremation burials close to such Romano-British towns and cities as Caister-by-Norwich, Cambridge, Leicester and Ancaster plainly implies a mingling of Germanic and British populations, on whatever terms. But there were other cities which seem on present evidence to have remained free of Germanic intruders before 500. These include London, Verulamium,

[32] Myres and Green (1973).   [33] Hamerow (1993).   [34] West (1985).

Silchester and Lincoln. At Winchester and Canterbury, the evidence is suggestive of complication. Canterbury, at the heart of a territory open to
influence from northern Gaul, cannot have remained long unnoticed by
barbarian incomers. Germanic houses and pottery are indeed recorded
within the city at several points, but not before the late fifth century. A few
German burials occur in cemeteries close to the walls in the fifth century,
but no concentration is known which is comparable with that at Caister-
by-Norwich. That some measure of orderly urban life was maintained, at
however modest a level, must be inferred to explain the survival of two
Roman churches into the sixth century – that which Augustine took over
as his cathedral in 597 and the church of St Martin which the Kentish queen
Bertha had earlier used.[35]

Winchester presents a range of evidence that is more reminiscent of
northern Gaul than southern Britain. In the extramural cemetery at
Lankhills, a number of burials of the late fourth century contain material
which has its closest analogies on the upper Danube.[36] The associations are
clearly military and can be best explained in terms of a military unit drawn
from Raetia or possibly upper Germany. This could have contained
German troops (or even consisted of Germans, as in the case of the
numerus Alamannorum known to have been serving in Britain in the 370s),
but its composition is likely to have been mixed. The men buried at
Lankhills may have included Germans in their number, but their presence
at Winchester probably had to do with the latest Roman garrisoning of
Britain, not with any solely barbarian enterprise.

Although the beginnings of Germanic settlement can now be distinguished in south-eastern Britain early in the fifth century, barbarian
immigrants before 425 can scarcely have been numerous. There is still no
warrant for suggesting a major phase of land-taking by Anglo-Saxons
before mid century at the earliest. Even in many parts of the south-east,
the provincial population probably saw few, if any, Germans for decades
after the end of Roman administration.

V. SCANDINAVIA AND THE WESTERN BALTIC

The settlements of southern Jutland reveal the process of shifting settlement over many centuries of the pre-Roman and Roman Iron Age.[37] At
Hodde, an orderly community settlement was maintained throughout the
Roman period. In the later phases, large component long-houses were built,
each serving as the focus of a substantial family group pursuing a variety of
economic activities. A rather similar development is evident at Vorbasse.[38]

[35] Brooks (1984).   [36] Clarke (1979).   [37] Jensen (1982) 214–22.   [38] Hvass (1978).

A settlement here reached its peak in the fourth century, at which time some twenty long-houses existed, each situated within its own fenced enclosure and accompanied by ancillary structures such as store-buildings. The population of Vorbasse in the fourth century must have reached two hundred at least, probably more, and there is an obvious degree of planning in the settlement which argues for a well-structured social unit. Secondary functions such as metalworking and quern-production are suggestive indications of internal organization. The shifting focus of settlement is clearly in evidence at Hodde, Vorbasse and elsewhere in Jutland. At Drengsted, for instance, a small area saw a mobile pattern of settlement over five or six centuries, as communities moved within more or less closely defined territories. Later, secondary crafts gained in importance, and the settlements tended to grow in size and economic complexity. It is possible that the resource-territories within which these settlements lay were centres of localized power, and the steady growth in settlement size is an important witness to the enhanced authority of local chieftains. In such circumstances, competition for the finite resources of land and its products was inevitable. The growth in population demonstrated in these settlements is a fact to be noted when considering the reasons for increased mobility and eventual migration from these regions. Landlessness and the restrictions which follow from it will have provided a powerful incentive to look elsewhere, especially to the south and west.

One of the most fully recorded of Scandinavian settlements is Vallhagar on the island of Gotland.[39] this comprised five or six farm units set within a complex of walled fields and closes, each farm consisting of a single large dwelling and associated buildings. The social unit represented at Vallhagar was probably a group of interrelated families, each centred upon its own dwelling, but joining with its neighbours for certain social and economic purposes. The main period of occupation of the site was from about A.D. 400 to the mid sixth century, though the presence of earlier steadings beneath and beside the Migration Period settlement indicates the kind of shifting focus also seen in Denmark at this time (see p. 463 above). The economy of Vallhagar and the other Gotland farms was based on mixed agriculture, though with stock-rearing predominating over cereal-growing. Cattle and sheep were to the fore, with pigs and domestic fowl also present. Semi-wild russ horses were exploited, probably after round-ups once or twice a year. Cattle were stalled over the winter in the long-houses, implying winter feeding from the meadows which are evident in the pollen record. The cultivated crops grown by the community were varied and included *Einkorn*, emmer wheat, barley, rye and spelt. Wild seeds were also collected and consumed. Flax was cultivated, probably for its oil-bearing

[39] Stenberger (1955).

seeds. The Vallhagar settlement was by no means isolated. The trade-network brought to it pottery and metalwork from other areas of the western Baltic, and glass vessels from the Rhineland, presumably in exchange for agricultural products.

Considerable numbers of farms like Vallhagar have been identified in the Gotland landscape, and it is obvious that the small family groups that were responsible for them were major components of the Baltic social order. But there are indications of greater nucleation and concentration of resources. One of the distinctive features of the present landscape of Gotland, Öland and southern Sweden is the large number of walled strong-holds, most of them sited on hill-tops and high ground. Hundreds of these strong points are known but few have been adequately investigated. Finds from them indicate a general period of occupation at some time between the late Roman Iron Age and the high Middle Ages. Some had a brief life, confined to a generation or two. Others were intermittently occupied over centuries. The best-excavated of the strongholds lie on the island of Öland: Gråborg, Ismanstorpborg and Eketorpsborg.[40] The largest is Gråborg, an irregular fortification more than two hundred metres across and with a perimeter wall still standing to a height of five metres. Occupation may have begun in the fifth century, but it certainly continued, with intermissions, for several centuries after that. This was a roughly circular fort, about 125 metres in diameter, its wall pierced by no less than nine gate-openings. In the interior lay a carefully planned series of rectilinear buildings, many radially arranged against the back of the rampart, others occupying the central space. The most fully studied of the Öland forts is Eketorp.[41] This began as a small circular fort of the late Roman period, its internal stone buildings abutting the back of the rampart. This was later replaced by a more densely occupied fort surrounded by a stout stone wall containing three gates. The interior was largely occupied by well-planned rectangular buildings. The community here in the Migration Period was both sizeable and subject to a central direction which aimed at a high degree of order. The remarkably regular planning of Eketorp has led some to seek its inspiration in circular Byzantine strongholds of the fifth and sixth centuries, but the matter is as yet beyond proof.

The import of coinage, especially gold *solidi*, into the Baltic lands as the fourth century advanced is increasingly attested, both by hoards and by single finds.[42] Fourth-century gold reached Denmark in appreciable quantity, the island of Fyn receiving a high proportion of it. The area of Gudme provides particularly compelling evidence.[43] Here, in an area some five kilometres from the eastern coast of the island, a huge settlement complex has

[40] Stenberger (1933) 235.   [41] Borg *et al.* (1976).   [42] Fagerlie (1967); Hansen (1987) 229–31.
[43] Thrane (1987) 1; Randsborg (1990).

been identified, originating in the third century A.D. and extending down to at least the sixth. Since the nineteenth century this settlement area has yielded an astounding quantity of gold and silver objects, including several hoards. Imports from the Roman and later from the Frankish world are to the fore, indicating a major centre of trade, a precursor of the great Baltic emporia of Carolingian and Viking date. The probable entry point for this trade was a port at Lundeborg on the east coast of Fyn, where another large hoard of gold has been recorded, the second-largest gold hoard of the Migration period yet found in Denmark. Fyn and Zealand had earlier been the focus of high-level trade with the Roman empire, but Gudme represents a markedly changed world, in which imported luxuries were channelled to a limited number of sites. The concentration of wealth which this implies is evident in certain other elements of the archaeological record, including both graves and settlements. There is no need to argue that what was happening on Fyn was the beginning of early state formation, but it did mark an important preliminary stage in that development. The main stream of gold from the fifth century onward was directed at the islands of Öland and Gotland. Byzantine *solidi*, mainly of late-fifth- and sixth-century emperors, were transported to the Baltic in immense quantity, some to be turned into the magnificent collars and other ornaments of leading families, others to be stored in hoards which would not be recovered. Precisely how this mass of gold reached the north is unknown. Direct payments by east Roman rulers to barbarian warriors based so far to the north seem implausible. It is easier to see it as a result of high-level exchanges between northern chieftains and barbarians in south-eastern Europe, with whom Byzantium was in close contact in this period.

Votive deposits were still being made in peat-bogs and pools in the fourth century, in several instances in the same places as in the previous two centuries. Both Vimose and Thorsbjerg received offerings of weapons and weapon-parts in the late fourth century. But the most productive of the late votive finds is that at Nydam, near Østersottrup.[44] Here, in an area measuring about a thousand square metres, was found a mass of war-equipment, including about 100 swords, 550 spears and javelins, 40 bows and 170 arrowheads, along with belts, brooches, pottery and other vessels. The bulk of this deposit was consigned to the peat after the middle of the fourth century, presumably after some local conflict. Also in the peat-bog were three sizeable ships, one of which was recovered entire, another later destroyed and a third left in the ground. The surviving Nydam ship provides us with our only complete Germanic vessel of this date. It was an oared ship, large enough to carry thirty men, clinker built and some twenty metres long. It was clearly best suited to service as a conveyance for

---

[44] Engelhardt (1863). Excavations by the National Museum of Denmark resumed here in 1989.

warriors, there being very little space for a cargo. The absence of a sail further suggests that it was intended for use in the inlets of the tideless western Baltic and not usually in the open sea. It is unlikely to have been a safe craft for crossings of the North Sea and the English Channel by migrating northerners.

The best-known of the large deposits were excavated by Conrad Engelhardt in the mid nineteenth century. More recent work has provided important detail on the nature and date of other deposits, notably at Ejsbøl and Illerup. The deposits in the Ejsbøl bog are broadly contemporary with the main offering at Nydam and also consist mainly of spoils of war.[45] The larger of two offerings, some five hundred objects in all, seems to represent the equipment of about two hundred warriors, sixty of whom had carried swords and nine possessed horses. A late-fourth-century deposit at Illerup shows striking similarities with Ejsbøl, having produced over sixty swords, the same number of knives and spearheads, and over ninety lance-heads.[46] Both these deposits thus seem to contain the equipment of about sixty well-armed warriors. Deposits of rather more varied character occur elsewhere in the western Baltic. At Skedemosse on Öland, a long series of offerings was made from the third to the sixth centuries.[47] In the late fourth and early fifth, a particularly rich series of objects was deposited, including seven gold snake-headed rings. The remainder of the offerings were weapons and other military equiment, including quantities of horse gear. A large quantity of animal bones points to contemporary sacrifice, the horse being the most common victim. Human remains also occurred at Skedemosse, again in such quantity as to suggest sacrifice, perhaps of war prisoners.

VI. THE EASTERN TERRITORIES AND THE DANUBE LANDS

In the eastern Germanic territories, two broad cultural complexes were dominant in the late Roman Iron Age. The Przeworsk culture was distributed over a large part of central and southern Poland, extending southward towards the middle Danube.[48] Its bearers were earlier identified as the Vandals, but it is certain that several major peoples lie behind the archaeological grouping. The Przeworsk culture is known largely from cemeteries, mainly of cremation burials. Grave-goods were commonly broken or damaged before being placed in the ground. Warrior-graves are fairly commonly encountered, a high proportion of them containing horse gear and spurs. Very richly furnished graves occur sporadically in the late third and fourth centuries, the best-known being those at Zakrzow (Sakrau)

---

[45] Ørsnes (1963).   [46] Ilkjaer and Lønstrup (1983).   [47] Hagberg (1967).
[48] Godlowski (1970); Kenk (1977).

in Silesia. During the third century, the forms of Przeworsk culture began to spread southwards towards the Carpathians and east to the upper Dniestr valley. This has been linked by some scholars to a migration towards the fertile Ukraine by groups following in the wake of the Goths. Although not entirely implausible, this is supported by no other evidence. The Przeworsk culture flourished throughout the fourth century and into the fifth, being eventually swept away in the complex movements of population from the steppes after A.D. 400.

Further to the south-east, in the Ukraine and on the Black Sea shore, the large grouping known as the Černjachov culture, after a large cemetery site excavated near Kiev, had developed since the later second century.[49] Černjachov plainly has mixed origins, but contribution to it by Gothic settlers seems certain. There has been vigorous debate about the possible contribution of other peoples, not least the forerunners of the Slavs and nomads such as the Alans and Sarmatians. That debate will continue, but the area covered by the Černjachov culture closely corresponds with that which the Goths are known to have occupied in the fourth century. It would be perverse to deny them a primary role in the maintenance of the cultural record of the region.

The archaeology of the peoples beyond the middle Danube, long in close diplomatic and commercial contact with the provinces of Pannonia and Noricum,[50] is extremely complex and not yet convincingly related to the historical record. Influences from the eastern Germanic peoples are in evidence, as are connections with the Sarmatians, Alans and other nomad groups from the Black Sea hinterland. Increased mobility among the peoples of the upper Elbe and Oder regions led to intensified barbarian settlement close to the middle Danube from the early fourth century and brought other cultural influences into play. Identification of the tribes involved in what was clearly a complicated nexus of population groups is hazardous. The southward advance of the Lombards along the Elbe valley was only one factor, albeit an important one, in the movement towards the Danube. A loose association of peoples about the confluence of the Elbe and the Saale, to which the name Thuringi was later attached, also contributed, while other peoples including the Rugi, Marcomanni, Quadi and Burgundians are variously mentioned as enemies and allies of Rome on or close to this sector of the frontier. The westward thrust of the Huns after 370 brought further confusion, both to the population of the region and to our inadequate sources for it. Gothic groups are reported in the area of the Danube bend in the late fourth century, though they are invisible in the archaeological material. After Adrianople, it is also reported that a mixed band of Goths, Huns and Alans was settled as *foederati* under their leaders

[49] Diaconu (1965); Horedt (1967); Scukin (1975).   [50] Klose (1934); Pitts (1989).

Alatheus and Saphrac on the middle Danube, probably in the province of
Valeria south of Aquincum.[51]

Barbarian material is relatively abundant in the towns, forts and watch-
towers of the middle Danube frontier in the later fourth and early fifth centuries and it seems reasonably clear that Germanic groups were being
settled on provincial land with some frequency. In certain areas, it is far
from easy to distinguish provincial elements from barbarian in the material
of the late fourth century, or even to be clear about which side of the
Danube individual artefacts were produced on. Craftsmen were working
for a mixed clientele and may themselves have been of mixed origin. One
of their commonest products was a range of pottery vessels in burnished
ware, displaying a general similarity with the pottery of the Černjachov
culture north of the Danube. This material is found in great quantity in
many of the watch-towers and forts on the Pannonian frontier, along with
hand-made pottery of evident barbarian origin.[52] Although not specifically
referable to barbarians, the burnished pottery appeared at a time, after 370,
when barbarian settlement greatly increased on both sides of the Danube,
and it may have owed its wide currency to the new settlers, including the
followers of Alatheus and Saphrac. Little is yet known about the character
of individual barbarian settlements on either side of the river frontier
before the late fifth century. They appear to have been scattered and relatively small, befitting a mixed population which had arrived in the region at
different times and often in confused circumstances.

The widespread connections of the eastern Germans – with
Scandinavia, the Black Sea hinterland and the steppes, and with the eastern
Roman world – led to advances in craftsmanship which were to have the
widest repercussions throughout the Germanic world in the fifth century
and later. Major developments in fine metalworking, especially in gold, and
in the design of jewellery which incorporated ornamental stones are
evident from the late fourth century onward, and these were to provide the
basis for the outstanding achievements of Germanic craftsmen in these
media over the following centuries. The supply of gold to the barbarian
world appreciably increased after 350, as can be seen in the finds of *solidi*
and gold medallions beyond the Roman frontiers. Gold in the form of
plate or even bars of bullion could have been transferred to leading warriors or kings. After 400, the immense sums of gold paid in various forms
to barbarians are reflected in the numerous hoards of *solidi* found in the
Baltic islands and southern Scandinavia, and also in objects of astonishing
richness which were deposited in the graves of leading barbarians, most
notably in the lands about the lower Danube. The greatly increased availability of gold and the rising ambitions of leaders to put their wealth and

---

[51] Soproni (1978); Soproni (1985) 86–92.   [52] Soproni (1985) 27–52.

status on display acted as a considerable stimulus to Germanic craftsmen to develop new ornamental styles in order to satisfy an increasingly flamboyant clientele.

Earlier, these advances in the working of gold and decorative stones were attributed to the impact of Gothic craftsmen who moved westward from the Black Sea hinterland in the disturbed conditions which followed upon the irruption of the Huns in the 370s. The 'Gothic cultural stream' was assigned a primary role in the dissemination of Germanic designs and metalworking techniques over most of Europe and in the formation of Germanic taste at a time when the political influence of barbarian kings was in the ascendant. A specifically Gothic origin for these developments has been viewed with scepticism for some time. Recent finds of fine metalwork on the lower Danube and in the Carpathians have added much to the earlier record, and it is now evident that some of the most innovative craftsmen were working in a relatively restricted area on and just north of the lower Danube after 400. The splendidly furnished grave at Apahida, near Cluj, found in the nineteenth century, now has a companion burial close by.[53] Both date about or shortly after the middle of the fifth century. Not far away, at Cluj-Someseni, a hoard of gold objects, including a magnificent pectoral and the gold fittings of a belt, relates to the same world and possibly came from the same workshops.[54] This region has also yielded the most outstanding hoard of the fifth century yet discovered, the treasure of Pietroasa, found in 1837.[55] This contained such a stunning range of gold and silver objects (eighteen kilograms of gold alone) that earlier opinion was inclined to link it with one of the great episodes of Gothic history, the overthrow of Gothic power by the Huns after 370. That date can now be seen as too early. Most would now accept that the Pietroasa hoard was accumulated in the late fourth and early fifth centuries and finally buried about 450. The treasure contains some of the most idiosyncratic products of the period. The most dazzling is a sacrificial dish of solid gold, twenty-five centimetres in diameter, its interior adorned by a frieze of divinities and other figures in high relief. In the centre is set a figurine of a female on a circular throne, holding a goblet in her cupped hands. The frieze of figures displays an extraordinary gathering of divinities, few of whom can be identified with complete confidence. Although some are presented in classical garb and posture, others are more readily assignable to the Germanic world. Thus, a powerfully built male figure holding a club and a cornucopia may seem at first sight modelled on Hercules, but the fact that he is seated on a throne in the form of a horse's head suggest that he is more convincingly identified as Donar. A group of three goddesses is

---

[53] Horedt (1982); Horedt and Protase (1972).   [54] Horedt and Protase (1970).
[55] Odobescu (1889–1900); Dunareanu-Vulpe (1967).

clearly referable to the world of natural fertility over which the Germanic *matres* or *matronae* presided, while a heroic warrior-figure in full armour and with hair worn in three knots is obviously a barbarian – a deity or a king, or a conflation of the two. The seated goddess in the centre of the dish is also not easy to place within the late classical pantheon. Her protective attitude and her central position mark her out as a presiding force, perhaps a Persian *mater deorum*. A plain gold platter and a jug are products of late Roman workshops and, apart from the mass of gold they represent (the platter alone weighs seven kilograms), are not remarkable. But the two polygonal bowls of gold cagework, originally encrusted with precious stones, and with twin handles in the form of springing panthers, are unique objects, bearing the impress of Persian or Pontic workmanship. Four immense brooches in the form of birds of prey also belong to a non-Roman tradition. Finally, there were several torques, one of which bears an inscription in runes, the meaning of which has spurred controversy for over a century. *Gutani o wi hailag* is the most widely accepted reading. The meaning of the runes, however, has not been resolved with complete certainty. *Gutani* probably refers to the protective deity of the Goths, or possibly to the Gothic king, rather than to the Gothic people. *Hailag* is related to *heilig* in the sense of 'pure' or 'inviolate' as well as 'holy'. The inscription may thus be a dedication of the torque, if not of the entire treasure, to 'the god who protects the Goths, most holy and inviolate'.

Great advances in the working of gold (and to a lesser extent of silver) are also evident in other parts of the Germanic world from the late fourth century onward, most spectacularly in southern Scandinavia. Among the objects which mark the opening of this phase of high craftsmanship are the most extraordinary of all in design and motifs, the two great golden horns from Gallehus in southern Denmark, now lost and known only from engravings and copies.[56] The astonishing range of deities and mythological creatures depicted on the horns offers a brief glimpse of a cultic world of which little other trace has been recorded. The gold of which the horns were made probably came from the eastern Roman provinces; the motifs belong firmly to the Germanic north. The wide contacts that existed at the highest level in the Germanic world at this time, contacts that might link the lower Danube, Gaul and Scandinavia, can thus be traced out in the work of craftsmen in the most enduring of metals. By the early fifth century, whether in Gaul, the Danube lands or Scandinavia, Germanic leaders could express a growing confidence that their place in a changed world was assured as never before.

[56] Oxenstierna (1956); Härtner (1969).

CHAPTER 16

GOTHS AND HUNS, *c.* 320–425

PETER HEATHER

For half a century, from *c.* 320 to *c.* 370, Germanic Gothic tribes were the dominant foreign power north of the Roman empire's lower Danube frontier. Relations between the two were often strained, if always close. Between *c.* 370 and 425, however, the non-Germanic and originally nomadic Huns pushed a series of Gothic (and other) groups across the Roman frontier, and at the same time began to consolidate their own power north of the Danube. By the end of this period, the Roman state had thus had to accommodate itself to two separate if linked developments: the existence of large bodies of autonomous Goths within its own borders, and the rise of the Hunnic empire in central Europe.

I. SOURCES

The physical culture of the Gothic world before the arrival of the Huns has been illuminated by numerous excavations in the Ukraine, Moldavia and Romania, which have identified the period of Gothic domination of these lands with the so-called Sîntana de Mureş-Černjachov culture (henceforth Černjachov culture). The documentary evidence for the Goths before *c.* 370, while limited in absolute terms, is also richer than that available for any of the Roman empire's other European neighbours. Historical narratives are provided by the *Anonymus Valesianus*, Eunapius of Sardis and, above all, Ammianus Marcellinus. A further dimension is added to these narratives by a series of speeches made before the emperor Valens and the senate of Constantinople by the orator Themistius. In addition, Ulfilas created a Gothic alphabet to translate the Bible in the middle of the fourth century. The Bible is itself an important source, and can be taken together with a body of material about Ulfilas' life, works and beliefs, and a number of texts generated by persecutions of Gothic Christians: in particular, the *Passion of St Saba*.

After the arrival of the Huns, archaeological evidence becomes less helpful. That the Gothic world was overturned emerges clearly enough, but the chronology of the artefacts, settlements and cemeteries is not well enough established to provide a detailed picture of the Huns' impact. The literary evidence is only a little better. Ammianus provides a striking, if brief, account of events up to 376, but from that point until the 430s, when the work of Priscus begins, information is sparse.

Inside the empire, the main outlines of the history of those Goths forced across the frontier can be reconstructed. Ammianus furnishes a detailed account of events from the crossing of the Danube in 376 to the battle of Adrianople in 378. From 378 to 395, material from the history of Eunapius provides the only narrative. It is not as detailed as that provided by Ammianus, but not so deficient as is sometimes portrayed, and, up to the mid 380s, is again supplemented by speeches of Themistius. From c. 395 to 405, no narrative source survives, but much can be gleaned from the works of Claudian and Synesius of Cyrene. If the full text of the history of Olympiodorus of Thebes had survived, the final part of our period, from 405 to 425, would have been illuminated by a narrative of precision and detail. Unfortunately, the original text is not preserved, and we have to make do with extracts and partial summaries via intermediaries such as Zosimus, Sozomen, Philostorgius and the Byzantine bibliophile Photius.

II. THE GOTHS TO c. 370

1. The Goths and the Černjachov culture

The geographical area dominated by the Goths before the arrival of the Huns is broadly defined by the extent of the Černjachov culture. As Fig. 10 shows, it extended over many thousands of square kilometres in the north-eastern hinterland of the Black Sea. In the past, the association of this culture with the Goths was highly contentious, but important methodological advances have made it irresistible. The ability to date clustered archaeological finds – regularly occurring associations of pottery, tools, jewellery, etc. – has demonstrated that the culture came into existence in the third century at precisely the moment when Goths started to spread their power towards the Black Sea. The latest finds have also been dated no later than the early fifth century – the moment when Gothic domination of the region was overthrown by the Huns.[1]

Precisely how should the Goths be associated with this culture? It used to be thought that the boundaries of physical cultures corresponded closely to political boundaries, each 'people' leaving behind its own distinctive material remains. But anthropological studies have shown that boundaries in material culture reflect zones of social or economic interaction rather than political frontiers. People with the same material culture

[1] Introductory accounts: Heather and Matthews (1991) ch. 3; Kazanski (1991) 39ff.; Ščukin (1975). Major publications of finds: Mitrea and Preda (1966); Palade (1986); *Materialy i Issledovniya po Arkheologii SSSr* (1960a); (1960b); (1964); (1967).

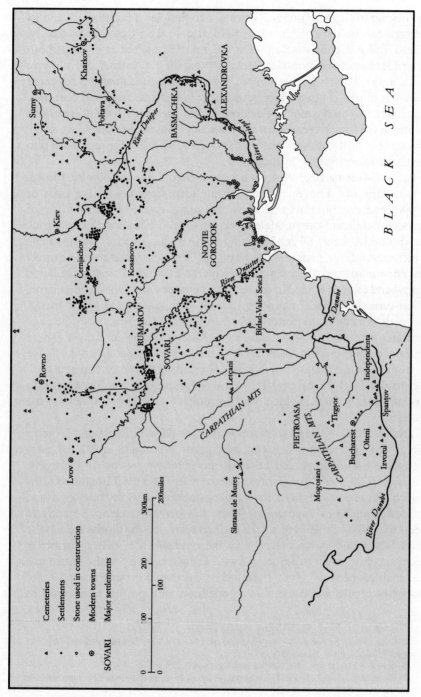

Fig. 10. Settlements and cemeteries of the Černjachov culture

Cemeteries
Settlements
Stone used in construction
Modern towns
SOVARI   Major settlements

0   100   200   300km
0   100   200miles

B L A C K   S E A

Sumy
Kharkov
Poltava
Kiev
BASMACHKA
ALEXANDROVKA
River Dnieper
River Donetz
Černjachov
Kosanovo
NOVIE
GORODOK
River Dniester
Rumarov
SOVARI
Rovno
Bîrlad-Valea Seacă
Lvov
Leţcani
CARPATHIAN MTS
R. Danube
Independenţa
PIETROASA
Tîrgşor
Bucharest
Spanţov
Mogoşani
CARPATHIAN MTS
Olteni
Izvorul
Sîntana de Mureş
River Danube

can belong to separate political entities, and people with different material cultures can be part of the same poliical unit. The Černjachov culture, indeed, did not consist solely of immigrant Goths, but comprised both other Germanic and non-Germanic groups. Of the former, Heruli were active in the Black Sea region in the third century, and, although not mentioned in fourth-century sources, reappear in the fifth and sixth centuries. It is likely that they were somewhere within the area of the Černjachov culture in the fourth century (perhaps under Gothic hegemony: see below). The same is probably also true of the Gepids, whose close relationship to the Goths is stressed by Jordanes.[2]

For non-Germanic groups, we have to turn to the archaeological record. It is notoriously difficult to make ethnic identifications on the basis of physical remains, but the Černjachov culture was created from a number of strands of different origin. Metalwork, personal ornaments and, above all, the distinctive habit of mixing inhumation and cremation within single cemeteries indicate that, in some ways, the Černjachov culture was a direct descendant of the Germanic Wielbark culture which had dominated central and eastern Poland in the first two centuries A.D. On the other hand, wheel-turned Černjachov pottery, in both technique and range of forms, descends directly from pottery in use around the Carpathians in the early centuries A.D., and is not dissimilar to Roman provincial wares.[3] These separate strands quickly coalesced to create an homogeneous whole. Grave 36 from Letçani contained an individual buried with large amounts of non-Germanic wheel-turned pottery, but one of these pots was inscribed with Gothic runes.[4] The individual was presumably Gothic, then, despite the pottery.

This throws up a crucially important but difficult question. To what extent did distinctions between immigrant Germanic and local non-Germanic populations, and between the different groups of Germanic immigrants, survive through the fourth century? Did the immigrant Goths absorb a large proportion of the indigenous population, or were social and political boundaries maintained? There has been a tendency recently to stress the multi-ethnic basis of the realms created by the Goths around the Black Sea: a necessary corrective to the outdated idea that a distinctive material culture must be associated with a single people.[5] At the same time, the establishment of Gothic and other Germanic groups north of the Black Sea involved considerable competition with powers indigenous to

---

[2] Heruli: Zos. 1.42; Procop. *BG* VI.14–15. Gepids: Jordanes, *Get.* XVII.94–5.

[3] Wielbark culture: Ščukin (1989) 292–301; Kazanski (1991) 18–28. Černjachov pottery: Häusler (1979) 40–1; Palade (1980); Kazanski (1991) 39 ff.

[4] Illustrated in Bloşiu (1975) 267; Heather and Matthews (1991) 86.

[5] E.g. Wolfram, *Goths* 85ff.; Kazanski (1991) 39ff.; essays by Diaconu and Ionita in Constantinescu *et al.* (1975).

the region. The immigrants did not create multi-ethnic confederations by negotiation, but intruded themselves by force, and it is quite clear that Dacian Carpi and nomadic Sarmatians, amongst others, were the losers in the process. The original pattern of units created, therefore, was probably a mixture of dominant Germanic, especially Gothic, groups and subordinate locals. Consonant with this is the fact that, viewed from across the frontier, Germanic immigrants were the obviously dominant force in this region; fourth-century Graeco-Roman sources mention only Goths north of the Danube. Likewise, the Gothic language of Ulfilas' Bible is Germanic. A mixed population, then, but not an equal one, and this lack of equality is likely to have hindered absorption, since dominant groups had every interest in maintaining their superiority. A parallel might be the Hunnic Empire of Attila, similarly established by force, where certain individuals were absorbed, but where larger subordinate groups maintained their own identity over several generations.[6]

2. Gothic subdivisions

It is traditional to conceive of the Goths as being divided in the fourth century into Visigoths and Ostrogoths. This is based on the testimony of the sixth-century *Getica* of Jordanes (v.42; xiv.82). Jordanes also reports that the fourth-century king of the Ostrogoths, Ermenaric, belonged to the ancient ruling Amal dynasty and controlled a vast multinational empire between the Black Sea and the Baltic (xxiii.116–20). But Jordanes' testimony cannot be accepted at face value.

Ammianus calls the Gothic groups of his day not 'Visigoth' and 'Ostrogoth' but Tervingi and Greuthungi, and one approach has been to take the two sets of terms to designate the same political entities. This, however, is illegitimate. If we use 'Visigoth' to mean that Gothic group which settled in south-western Gaul in 418, it was not the direct descendant of the fourth-century Tervingi. As we shall see, three previously separate Gothic groups (Tervingi *and* Greuthungi, together with the followers of Radagaisus) made more or less equal contributions to what was a quite new Gothic political unit. This new grouping was also headed by a new royal dynasty (a similar process of development lay behind the emergence of the Ostrogoths, but this story lies beyond our compass). Visigoths and Ostrogoths must not be imported anachronistically, therefore, into the fourth century.[7]

[6] Generally: Heather *Goths and Romans* 89–97. Third-century rivalries: Pet. Patr. fr. 8 (*FHG* iv.490–1). Hunnic empire: compare Priscus frr. 11.2 (pp. 266ff.) and 49.

[7] Wolfram, *Goths* 5–12, 24–7, 164ff., 168ff., 248ff. (after Wenskus (1961) 471ff.). Taken further by Heather, *Goths and Romans* ch. 1; cf. Liebeschuetz, *Barbarians and Bishops* 48–85 on Alaric and the Visigoths.

Jordanes' description of the empire of Ermenaric is similarly problematic, because it is a carefully constructed expansion of the account of Ermenaric that can still be read in Ammianus. Rather thin narratives of supposed victories, together with a list of Gothic equivalents for names common to classical ethnography and some biblical references have been used to fill out Ammianus' account of a 'most warlike monarch' who ruled 'extensive and wide dominions' (XXXI.3.1–2). Although obviously an important figure in Ammianus, Ermenaric becomes a much grander one in the *Getica*, deliberately recast as a Gothic precursor of Attila: the ruler of 'all the Scythian and German nations'. The point of this reworking emerges from the *Getica's* Amal family tree where Ermenaric links together the ancestral line of Theoderic the Ostrogoth with that of Eutharic, his adopted heir and son-in-law. Both the kind of material used in the reworking and its manipulative genealogical point (substantiating a claim that Theoderic and his adopted heir anyway belonged to the same family – Theoderic having failed to produce a son) suggest that the *Getica's* expanded version rests solely on its author's imagination. The size of Ermenaric's kingdom thus becomes very much an open question.[8]

From Ammianus it is clear that he was a substantial figure, but it is not at all certain that he ruled all Goths other than the Tervingi. The latter seem to have spread as far east as the Dniester,[9] leaving most of the Černjachov area (cf. Fig. 10 above) unaccounted for. Ammianus' account reads as though all of Ermenaric's people made their way across the Danube in 376 (XXXI.3.3ff.), but in fact they were followed, during the next hundred years, by four more large Gothic groups, together with at least four smaller ones. Either a far-reaching process of fragmentation followed Ermenaric's death, therefore, which the normally careful Ammianus did not mention, or several Gothic groups already existed north of the Danube before the arrival of the Huns.

Though views differ, the latter seems the likelier alternative. A king who ruled every Goth other than the Tervingi would actually have ruled by far the greatest number of Goths (the Tervingi account for only one out of five major Gothic groups known from the period after *c.* 370). Such a realm would have been much more powerful than that of the Tervingi and ought to have been the major focus of Roman policy. Yet Greuthungi barely intrude into the story of fourth-century Gotho–Roman relations. It is difficult to believe that a much bigger Gothic political unit could have existed just behind the Tervingi and left no real trace in the historical record. If this is correct, we must envisage perhaps half a dozen or more independent Gothic units within the bounds of the Černjachov culture.[10]

---

[8] Heather (1989) 110–16.

[9] Amm. Marc. XXXI.3.3: Tervingi advance to the Dniester to meet retreating Greuthungi.

[10] Jordanes' account of Ermenaric is usually accepted without question: Wolfram, *Goths* 86ff.; or Kazanski (1991) 33ff. Further discussion, Heather, *Goths and Romans* 84–9, cf. 13–14.

3. Social and economic organization

The nature of the economy practised within the confines of the Černjachov culture seems clear enough. As is apparent from Fig. 10, the settlement pattern consisted of villages clustered close to water in the major river valleys of the region. Some of these villages were substantial, although they did vary in size. The largest settlement of all, Budeşty, covered an area of thirty-five hectares, and several others were around twenty hectares (e.g. Zagajkany, Kobuska and Veke), although, at the other end of the scale, Petrikany was only two hectares, and Komrat four and a half. The evidence clearly indicates that the population of these villages derived its subsistence from mixed farming. Quite a high priority was given to the production of cereals. To judge from deposits in storage pits, the most important crops were wheat, barley and millet; rye, oats, peas, acorns and hemp were also harvested. Considerable effort was also put into animal husbandry. Cattle bones are the most common among domestic animals; sheep and goats were also kept, along with pigs and some horses. In the foothills of the Carpathians, the countryside was most suitable for sheep and goats; in the Ukraine proper, pigs took second place behind cattle, and it was only out on the steppe that horses seem to have played a prominent role. Hunting seems to have been no more than a very subsidiary part of the economy.

Any talk of industry would be misleading. It seems, for instance, that every major settlement had its own potter and kiln, suggesting that there was no organized pottery industry as such. There is, however, some interesting evidence for craft specialization. The village of Bîrlad-Valea Seacă had, at the last count, produced some sixteen huts containing bone combs in various stages of production. Glass was also produced for the first time beyond the Roman frontier within the Černjachov area; one centre of production was the village of Komarov in the north-eastern foothills of the Carpathians. Iron too was extracted and worked.

A variety of evidence indicates that different kinds of exchange had considerable importance. Internally, for instance, the combs and glass produced at the craft centres circulated freely by some mechanism among the population. There was also considerable trade with the Roman world. As we shall see, trade regulations always formed part of diplomatic agreements, and trade was never cut off even when relations were far from good (see p. 496 below). From literary sources, we know that a considerable slave trade operated out of Gothic territory, and archaeological evidence illuminates some of the goods which flowed into Gothic territories in return. Černjachov sites and burials have turned up Roman (probably wine) amphorae in considerable quantities, and huge numbers of Roman coins.[11]

---

[11] See generally Heather and Matthews (1991) ch. 3; Häusler (1979); on the glass, see Rau (1972).

If a simple outline of the economy is thus fairly easy to sketch, much more difficult is the nature of the social order it maintained. There was some social stratification and some specialization of labour. The literary sources refer to nobles who kept retainers and used them to enforce their rulings. The *Passion of St Saba* names two such leaders – Atharid and his father Rothesteos, called 'prince' (βασιλίσκος) – and a Gothic document from the same persecution names Winguric as a third. The *Passion* also describes the way in which Atharid used his retainers to enforce the persecution in a Gothic village.[12] The events of 376 and after provide us with other nobles of the Tervingi such as Alavivus and Fritigern. Less is known of the Greuthungi, but a powerful noble class had probably established itself throughout Gothic society by the fourth century. Certain prominent non-royal Greuthungi are named (Alatheus, Saphrac and Farnobius: Amm. Marc. XXXI.3.3; 4.12), and a class of such men is a constant feature of Gothic groups met in the fifth and sixth centuries.

Leaders such as Atharid must have been in receipt of tribute – not least, food renders – to support their non-producing retainers. Consonant with this is archaeological evidence for 'central places': sites with unusually extensive storage facilities suggestive of leaders taxing a dependent agricultural population (these are marked on Fig. 10). In similar vein, there is little sign among the fourth-century Goths of formally democratic – or, at least, egalitarian – institutions such as the gathering of all adult male tribesmen which Tacitus describes among Germani of the first century.[13]

The *Passion of St Saba* warns us not to overestimate the degree of control that this noble class exercised. In the face of orders to persecute Christians, villagers were prepared to protect Christians in their midst by swearing false oaths and by eating meat that they had only pretended to offer to idols. An arresting picture of both the vertical and horizontal bonds of society emerges. The primary social unit was the village (as the archaeological pattern might indicate), but numbers of villages were clustered under the control of individual nobles, the same villages presumably providing for the upkeep of retainers. How many villages a given noble might have controlled is unknowable. The higher authorities met in the *Passion of St Saba* do not seem to have been well acquainted with the village, since it was only Saba's refusal to co-operate which undermined the attempted deceptions. Correspondingly, village authorities in the *Passion* exercise considerable authority. When Saba's refusal to co-operate threatened the safety of other villagers, the elders expelled him for a time. The village authorities are likely to have had similar control over many aspects

---

[12] *Passion* trans. in Heather and Matthews (1991) 111–17. Wingurich: Menologium of Basil II: *PG* CXVII.368, trans. in Heather and Matthews (1991) 126–7.

[13] Central places: refs. in Heather and Matthews (1991) 57. Social institutions: Thompson, *Visigoths* 43–55. A good introduction to social stratification in Germanic society is Hedeager (1988).

of daily life (such as grazing and water rights, tribute collection and religious ceremonial).

Whenever we meet Greuthungi, they are led by kings (Amm. Marc. xxxi.3.1–3), but leaders of the Tervingi in the better sources are called 'judge'. The particularity of this title has occasioned considerable scholarly debate, and the judge of the Tervingi has generally come to be characterized as a temporary figure who was given special powers only when the Tervingi faced specific dangers. At other times, the nobles are held to have exercised autonomous control over their villages. The fourth-century Goths used 'king' (*reiks*) of these men, in fact, with the general meaning of 'leader of men' or 'distinguished' rather than 'monarch' or 'overall ruler' (hence Ambrose correctly styles the judge as 'judge of kings').[14]

It has been shown, however, that the office of judge among the Tervingi descended through three generations of the same family, adding weight to references of Zosimus (following Eunapius) to a Gothic 'royal clan' (iv.25.2; 34.3).[15] This need not mean that the judge was a permanent monarchical figure, and two arguments have been put forward to suggest that he was not. The first is that we hear of no confederation or judge in peacetime. But our sources never in fact refer to the Tervingi in normal times of peace; Romans were only interested in Goths when they caused difficulties. The first argument is very much from silence, therefore, and can actually be reversed. We hear of the Tervingi on essentially three occasions before the arrival of the Huns: in the 330s (when they made peace with Constantine), the 340s (the expulsion of Ulfilas) and the 360s (the war between Athanaric and the emperor Valens). On each occasion, they had an overall leader (whether styled judge or king) and we have no indication that a judge had not been continuously in office in between.

The second argument is based on two occasions when sources record 'king*s* of the Goths' (meaning Tervingi) taking action, with no mention of a judge. Both, however, occur in passing references to Gothic activity (Amm. Marc. xxvi.10.3; Lib. *Or.* lix.89–90), rather than in detailed reports. And in a fuller account of the same incident – the sending of Gothic help to the usurper Procopius – elsewhere in his history, Ammianus specifically blames it on the judge of the Tervingi (xxxi.3.4). Given that overall leaders often act with the counsel of their great men, there seems no need to build a complicated hypothesis on the back of two passing remarks. Indeed, a whole array of contemporary sources found the judge of the Tervingi eminently confusable with the kind of king more familiar to us (*rex* = 'monarch', rather than Gothic *reiks* = 'distinguished'). Themistius described Athanaric, judge in the 360s and 370s, as 'lord' or 'ruler'

---

[14] See e.g. Thompson, *Visigoths* 43–55; Wolfram, *Goths*, esp. 94–100; Wolfram (1975).
[15] Wolfram, *Goths* 62ff.

(δυνάστης: ed. Downey, *Or.* XI p. 221. 9, XV p. 276. 5), the *Anonymus Valesianus* distinguished between two levels of leadership among the Tervingi in the 330s – a *rex* Ariaricus (VI.31) versus the *regalis* Alica (v.27) – and Eunapius (and, following him, Zosimus) consistently referred to the 'king' of the Goths. These sources are impressive collective testimony that the ruler of the Tervingi looked to the Roman world very much like a monarch.[16]

We must probably include, then, a permanent overall ruler, deriving from different generations of the one family, in our picture of the fourth-century Tervingi. A strong noble class had also established itself, and no doubt overall leaders could not afford to ignore its members' demands. And as we shall see, when the Hunnic invasions undermined the hold on power of established leaders, the noble class threw up many pretenders to take their places. None of this denies, however, that the judge of the Tervingi was a permanent leader. When and how this dynasty established itself is a question our sources do not answer.

4. Gotho–Roman relations to c. 370

On four occasions, Gothic contingents, perhaps three thousand strong, served in Roman wars, and on three of them went all the way to Persia. In their third-century raids the Goths had also taken large numbers of Roman prisoners, whose descendants remained a recognizable group in the fourth-century Gothic society. This was the background of Ulfilas, whose family remained conscious of its Cappadocian origins, and it was no doubt central to Ulfilas' expertise in Greek, Latin and Gothic. Such permanent and temporary exchanges of population were matched by a series of individual contacts. From the 330s to the 360s trade was allowed at any point along the frontier. Roman products, particularly amphorae, have turned up in Černjachov finds, and the export of slaves from Gothic territories was common. Individual Goths, and large groups, were also recruited into the Roman army.[17]

The huge fortifications of the Lower Danube frontier did not prevent, therefore, a whole range of contacts – from the commercial to the ideological (such as the spread of Christianity; on this, see p. 499 below). Even after the treaty of 369 re-established a stricter division between Roman and Goth, two centres for cross-border trade remained open, and during the persecution of the 370s, Gothic Christians moved easily back and forth.[18]

[16] In more detail with full refs.: Heather, *Goths and Romans* 97–103.

[17] Gothic contingents: 348 (Lib. *Or.* LIX.89), 360 (Amm. Marc. XX.8.1), 363 (*ibid.* XXIII.2.7), 365 (*ibid.* XXVI.10.3). Ulfilas: Heather and Matthews (1991) chs. 5–6 for texts in translation and discussion. Trade: Thompson, *Visigoths* 34ff. Slaving: Wolfram, *Goths* 97–8. Recruits: Amm. Marc. XXXI.6.

[18] Trade: Them. *Or.* X ed. Downey, p. 206. 7–8 (trans. in Heather and Matthews (1991) ch. 2). Christians: *Passion of St Saba* in Heather and Matthews (1991) 114, 117.

But the empire had also to deal more formally with the Gothic kingdoms of the region, and here the fortified frontier played a substantial role. How matters were arranged with Goths east of the Dniester is unclear; much more is known about the evolution of relations with the Tervingi.

This group of Goths would seem to have established itself on the frontier only from the 310s, pushing into the power vacuum left by the tetrarchs' forced resettlement of Carpi inside the Roman empire. In the 320s, Gothic forces intervened on the side of Licinius against Constantine (*Anon. Val.* v.27), and from that point the Tervingi became the focus of Roman policy north of the lower Danube. In the 330s, partly in response to the help they had sent Licinius, Constantine undertook a general pacification of the Tervingi and, indeed, of the entire Danube frontier. By 335, the Goths of the lower Danube together with Sarmatians of the middle Danube had been forced to acknowledge Roman power. With the Tervingi, Constantine made a treaty which brought Roman and Goth into unprecedentedly close contact. Coins were issued with the legend *Gothia*, a form implying that, in some way, Goths had been made part of the Roman empire. The entire length of the Gothic frontier was also opened for trade, when normal Roman policy was to control cross-border trade through a small number of designated outlets. The son of the then judge of the Tervingi came to Constantinople as a hostage (where a statue was erected to him behind the senate house), and the Tervingi henceforth provided troops for Roman campaigns. The Goths were entitled in return to 'gifts' and 'presents' – money and clothing – which may well have been presented annually. It was in the aftermath of the treaty, too, that Ulfilas was consecrated bishop and sent back to his homeland, seemingly with imperial backing. He was consecrated by a leading bishop, Eusebius of Nicomedia, and, when expelled after eight years, was greeted personally by the emperor Constantius II.

Apart from a disturbance in the late 340s, resolved by negotiation and the expulsion of Ulfilas, the treaty endured down to the 360s. A three-year war (367–9) with the emperor Valens was then followed by a treaty reestablishing a much greater distance between the formerly intimate partners. Roman gifts ceased; trade was allowed only at two designated points. The Tervingi also launched a persecution of Christians in their lands, which, the sources tell us, was done to spite the Christian Roman emperors. Roman propaganda likewise stressed the importance of an impregnable frontier opposite the Goths, and the obligation to furnish military assistance lapsed. Constantine's activity was thus followed by thirty years of close relations before another war ushered in a reseparation.[19] Whose will

---

[19] This much is now broadly agreed. Thompson, *Visigoths* 9ff., argued that the Goths reversed the defeat suffered under Constantine in the 340s, considering that a Roman victory would not have led to 'gifts' and such a trading regime. See, amongst others, Chrysos (1972) ch. 2; Wolfram, *Goths* 57ff.

did these treaties primarily reflect? Did the Romans or the Goths prefer the close relations which prevailed in the middle of the century?

The current orthodoxy is that it was the Goths who preferred relations to be close, and that their nobility, in particular, desired the annual gifts which came their way. This is based on a speech of Themistius from 370 in which he declared the war of 367–9 to have been a Roman victory since it brought these payments to an end. But Themistius' task was to present imperial deeds in the best possible light. Victory was the prime imperial virtue, and no emperor could ever admit to having been dictated to by mere 'barbarians'. In other words, whatever had happened, Themistius would have found some way of presenting it as an imperial success. The actual course of events suggests on the contrary that, while the war was not a Roman defeat, Valens did fail to maintain the level of domination over the Goths achieved by Constantine.[20]

While Constantine's intervention north of the Danube had led unambiguously to a Gothic surrender, Valens enjoyed only mixed success. In 367, the Roman army destroyed many Gothic villages, but the bulk of the population escaped to the Carpathian mountains. In 368 an unusually high spring flood made it impossible for the main Roman force to cross over the river, and in 369, although Valens' troops ranged widely, Athanaric, the judge of the Tervingi, was never defeated in a pitched battle (Amm. Marc. xxvii.5; the point was conceded by Themistius Or. x). The peace of 369 was negotiated on a ship in the middle of the river, acknowledging that Athanaric still controlled the territory beyond it.

It is of a piece with this evidence that the Goths were actually the aggressors in the 360s – i.e. they were the ones wanting to modify Constantine's arrangements. In 362, before Julian's campaign left for Persia, a Gothic embassy came to him requesting a change in the terms of their treaty (Lib. Or. xii.78); it was dismissed. The Goths then seized the opportunity presented by Julian's defeat to cause further trouble. In response, Valens sent troops to the Danubian region, but they were suborned by Julian's uncle Procopius to start his usurpation. This presented the Goths with a further opportunity. Instead of confronting the empire head-on, they responded to a request for aid by sending Procopius some three thousand troops (Amm. Marc. xxvi.6.11–12; 10.3). No doubt the Goths hoped that a grateful usurper would grant them the modifications they desired without recourse to battle. As it turned out, Procopius was defeated and Valens mounted his punitive campaign, but by the 360s the Goths were clearly anxious to change their treaty, and trying every means to do so. Valens' campaign failed to reimpose the Constantinian relationship, and the peace

---

[20] Orthodoxy: (e.g.) Thompson, *Visigoths* ch. 1; Chrysos (1972) 97ff.; Wolfram, *Goths* 66–7. Them. *Or.* x trans. with commentary in Heather and Matthews (1991) ch. 2.

of 369 was a compromise which reflected the wishes of the Tervingi leadership more than had the peace of the 330s. Themistius' emphasis on gifts was no more than a smokescreen. Annual gifts had been part of Roman frontier policy for centuries, but, by concentrating attention on this side issue and misrepresenting gifts as 'tribute', Themistius could present a setback as success.[21]

This has important implications for our understanding of the Goths. The current orthodoxy presents them as interested primarily in a steady flow of Roman gifts, and happy to accept the partial subjection of the Constantinian regime so long as the flow was maintained. They can now be seen as a much more independent-minded group, who preferred independence to Roman blandishments (though, no doubt, they would have preferred both, if possible). They had enough self-consciousness to seek to overturn Roman domination, resenting its practical intrusions into their affairs. One source of resentment was perhaps the obligation to provide troops (it was after 382; see below); another was the intrusion of Christianity, perceived as an alien Roman religion. The leadership of the Tervingi attempted to halt the spread of Christianity in two periods of persecution: one in the 340s, associated with the expulsion of Ulfilas, the second immediately after the peace of 369. To judge by the *Passion of St Saba*, this second persecution was not totally successful, but it is the fact that a persecution was mounted at all which is really significant. It represents a deliberate attempt to spite the Romans by enforcing a contrary ideological uniformity among the Goths, and broadly confirms the picture which has emerged from the discussion of diplomatic relations.[22] By the fourth century, Gothic society had thrown up substantial political entities which wanted to hold their own, politically and ideologically, against the Roman state.

III. GOTHS AND HUNS BEYOND THE ROMAN FRONTIER,
c. 370–425

The established political order beyond the Danube was completely overturned in the last quarter of the fourth century by the intrusion of a mysterious third party: the Huns. Of their origins, Ammianus reports that they came from the north, near the 'ice-bound ocean' (XXXI.2.1). Arguments have long raged as to whether this should be taken literally – in which case the Huns might have had Finno-Ugrian roots, like the later Magyars – or whether they were the first known group of Turkic nomads to disturb the frontiers of Europe.[23]

---

[21] Fuller argumentation and refs.: Heather, *Goths and Romans* 108–21.

[22] See Thompson, *Visigoths* 94–103; Wolfram, *Goths* 75 ff.

[23] Maenchen-Helfen, *Huns* chs. 8–9 is in the end inconclusive; see also Thompson, *Attila* 15 ff.

Ammianus' famous digression on their customs and manners portrays them as a nomadic group of tribes without a single overall ruler (XXXI.2.2–11). There is no reason to disbelieve this basic characterization, even if Ammianus' understanding of nomadism was limited. Nomadism is a specialized form of animal husbandry designed to exploit marginal grazing areas by moving flocks between designated blocks of summer and winter pasture. Characteristically, movements are neither vast in distance, nor random; grazing rights have to be carefully defined and jealously guarded if the somewhat hazardous exploitation of margins is to be successful. That the Huns were steppe nomads in no way explains, therefore, their sudden impact upon the fringes of Europe. Their movement into these new areas was a deliberate decision for which there must have been specific motivation. What that may have been is unclear. It is a fair guess that some economic motive was involved, whether positive, such as a growth in population, or negative, such as a decline in the productivity of the steppe region.[24] But there are other possibilities. The Arab conquests show that nomad expansion can also be the result of socio-political revolution.

Somewhat clearer is the impact of the Huns upon the Goths. As Ammianus records, the Huns first subdued the Goths' Alanic neighbours east of the Don (the Alans were Iranian nomads), and then attacked the Goths themselves. After the death of two kings, Ermenaric and Vithimer, a group of Greuthungi controlled by two generals, Alatheus and Saphrac, in the name of Vithimer's son Vitheric, retreated west to the Dniester (cf. Fig. 11). There they halted while Athanaric, ruler of the Tervingi, advanced east to the same point. Further Hunnic attacks undermined Athanaric's attempts both to hold the Dniester and to construct a fortification further west. The bulk of Athanaric's followers then decided, under the leadership of Alavivus and Fritigern, to seek a new home in Roman territory. The retreating Greuthungi decided to do likewise, and sometime in 376, two Gothic groups arrived on the Danube requesting asylum (XXXI.2.12; 3.1ff.). The Huns thus set in motion a domino effect which posed entirely new problems for the Roman state.

Some features of Ammianus' account require further discussion. It is usually thought that, in 376, the Goths were retreating before a solid mass of Huns who had suddenly overturned the hold of the Goths on lands north of the Black Sea, and who immediately advanced in large numbers right up to the Danube, capturing any Goths who had not retreated before them. This seems mistaken. Ammianus' account implies that Hunnic pressure built up over a not inconsiderable period. Ermenaric resisted 'for a

[24] A 'warm period' in Europe in the fourth century is now well documented, and might have led to droughts on the steppes.

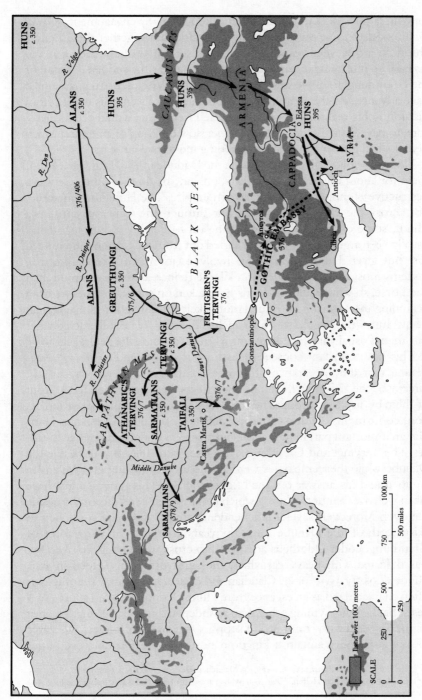

Fig. 11. The arrival of the Huns c. A.D. 370–95

long time' (diu: XXXI.3.1), and Vithimer fought many engagements (multas clades: XXXI.3.2). Neither indication is specific, but together they imply a chronology of several years. Likewise, what set in motion the events of 376 was not so much an increase in Hunnic pressure as the sudden decision of the Greuthungi to move west after the death of Vithimer (Athanaric must have advanced to the Dniester at least in part to prevent this retreat from disrupting his realm). The retreat of the Greuthungi would seem, therefore, to have been a sudden reaction to a slow build-up of pressure, which perhaps had grown up over the preceding ten to twenty years.[25]

Nor did a solid wall of Huns reach the Danube in 376. Little is heard of them for about the next twenty years; only in 395 do the sources report a destructive Hunnic raid on the eastern empire. The Huns then attacked, not across the Danube, however, but through the Caucasus into Asia Minor, some of the raiders even going on to Persia (cf. Fig. 11). It has usually been argued that the Huns started out from the Danube and moved east, but, given that this would have involved a journey of 1100 kilometres, it seems most unlikely. Every extra kilometre increased the strain on man and horse, so why would the Huns have taken on such a trek before even beginning their attack? The much more likely interpretation is that a great many Huns – those, at least, who launched the raid – were still much further east than is usually imagined, making a Caucasus route the natural choice.[26]

This has important consequences for our understanding of 376, suggesting that the appearance of Goths on the Danube was caused not directly by the arrival of the Huns but reflects the chaos generated in front of them by displaced groups and small raiding parties. A number of indications confirm this picture – not least, details reported by Ammianus. Huns play an important part in the action, but always as raiders rather than invaders. The Tervingi and Greuthungi, likewise, were able to wait beside the Danube while their embassies went all the way to the emperor Valens in Antioch and his answer returned (XXXI.4.1, 12). This process must have taken well over a month, during which no Huns harassed the Goths beside the river. Moreover, several independent groups of Goths continued to exist north of the Danube for many years after 376. In 386 a force of Greuthungi under Odotheus attempted to cross south over the river, but was defeated with heavy casualties, the survivors being settled in Asia Minor (Zos. IV.35.1; 38–9; Claudian IV Cons. Hon. 626ff.). Odotheus is often characterized as an escapee from Hunnic control, but no source suggests that he was anything other than an independent Gothic king. The rest of the Tervingi who continued to support Athanaric in 376 were also able to establish and maintain a kingdom north of the Danube, even after

---

[25] Heather, Goths and Romans 135–6; contra, e.g. Maenchen-Helfen, Huns 26–7; Thompson, Attila 20ff.
[26] Contra e.g. Maenchen-Helfen, Huns 52–9 (whose account of the raid is much superior to that of Thompson, Attila 26ff.).

Athanaric himself was ousted in winter 380–1 (Amm. Marc. xxxi.4.13). Likewise, the kingdom of a certain Arimer existed beyond the Roman frontier at some point between 383 and 392, and, even as late as 405–6, another Gothic king, Radagaisus, broke through the Roman frontier, this time invading Italy.[27] Again, modern commentators consider that Radagaisus had thrown off Hunnic dominion, but there is not a word of this in the sources. If the idea that the Huns had arrived *en masse* in 376 is abandoned, there is no reason not to accept him too as a Gothic king independent of Hunnic control.

The arrival of Goths on the Danube in 376 was thus only the first stage in a lengthy process. Its nature seems clear enough. On the one hand, the Huns themselves moved west from the fringes of Europe to its heart; Attila's empire of the 440s and 450s seems to have been centred on the Great Hungarian Plain of the middle Danube, west of the Carpathians (cf. Fig. 12). At the same time, the Huns established dominion over a wide variety of subject peoples. Already in the 370s, some Alans were under Hunnic control (Amm. Marc. xxxi.3.1), and Attila's empire was built upon the subjection of many different peoples – separate groups of Goths as well as numerous others.[28] So much is uncontentious, but the chronology of the process must be revised. Hunnic domination of the Danubian region was not established at a stroke in the 370s, and independent Gothic kingdoms survived as late as the 400s.

All the different stages by which the process was advanced are impossible to recover. The departure of numerous Goths in 376 obviously represents one phase, so too the appearance of other refugees in subsequent years. Likewise, we should note the first Hunnic kingdom directly on the lower Danube frontier: that of Uldin in the first decade of the fifth century. The story of the individual conquests by which Hunnic power was carried forward cannot be told, however, and events probably did not move entirely in the one direction; as late as the 420s, the Romans detached one Gothic group from Hunnic rule. At least three other separate groups of Goths eventually formed part of Attila's empire: those of Valamer, of Bigelis and of a mixed Hunnic–Gothic force defeated in the 460s. All of these emerged separately from the Hunnic empire in the era of its collapse; their original incorporation was probably equally separate.[29]

Though many details are thus lost, the first decade of the fifth century may well have marked a particularly significant moment of Hunnic

[27] Arimer and Radagaisus: Wolfram, *Goths* 133, 168 70.

[28] After the collapse of Hunnic dominion in the 450s, Jordanes, *Get.* L.259ff. records competition between many of its former subjects, including Gepids, Herules, Sciri, Suevi and Sarmatians.

[29] Uldin: Maenchen-Helfen, *Huns* 59ff.: Uldin was clearly a relatively minor figure compared to Attila; Thompson, *Attila* 60 (to be preferred to Maenchen-Helfen, *Huns* 71). 420s: Croke (1977) 358ff. On the Goths under Attila: Heather, *Goths and Romans* 229–30, 240–2.

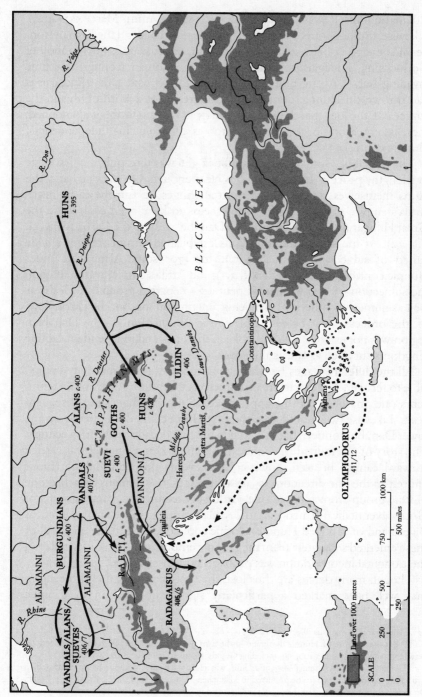

Fig. 12. The crisis of A.D. 405–8 and Huns west of the Carpathian mountains

expansion. The crisis of 376, as we have seen, undermined, if largely indirectly, the established political order east of the Carpathians. In 405–6, the sources report an even larger influx of peoples into the Roman empire. The Gothic king Radagaisus invaded Italy in 405, and on 31 December 406 there occurred the famous Rhine crossing involving a whole host of peoples: particularly Vandals, Alans and Sueves. No source describes the events which led up to this incursion, and Hunnic involvement in them has been doubted.

Radagaisus' invasion and the Rhine crossing together represent, however, a large exodus from areas west of the Carpathians (cf. Fig. 12). That Radagaisus invaded Italy rather than Thrace suggests this origin for his force. Suevi is probably a collective name for the older tribes of the middle Danube, and, while we have no information on the Alans, Vandals were to be found in precisely this region in 402 (Claud. *Bell. Get.* 363ff.). For some reason, therefore, a huge outpouring of peoples from the middle Danube occurred in 405–6. Given that Hunnic power in Europe built up only slowly, it becomes more likely that the model observed in 376 again applied – namely, that Hunnic pressure (whether direct or indirect) underlay this second revolution affecting areas west of the Carpathians. Moreover, while the invasions of 305–6 caused a crisis inside the western empire, they were not taking advantage of any obvious weakness, and many of the invaders met a sticky end. Radagaisus was executed outside Florence in the summer of 406 after a defeat which led to many of his followers being sold into slavery *before* the Rhine crossing was effected (Oros. VII.37.13ff.), and the Vandals and Alans were later savaged in Spain (see below). And while the first unequivocal evidence for Huns in the middle Danube region comes from the 420s (their famous alliance with Aetius), we have some indications that they had been there since *c.* 410. In 409, the western imperial authorities negotiated the assistance of a large Hunnic force (Zos. V.50.1). Help had previously been obtained from the Hunnic king Uldin, but he had just suffered a major defeat, so that these arrangements were probably made with some other Hunnic group, and the middle Danube would have been a convenient region for the authorities in Ravenna to look to for assistance.[30] In 412, similarly, Olympiodorus went on an embassy to the Huns, leaving Constantinople by ship. After a severe storm, his ship put in at Athens, suggesting that it was travelling west through the Aegean, presumably before heading up the Adriatic (cf. Fig. 12), not east to the Black Sea. If so, the Hunnic chiefs he visited were established in the middle Danube region, not east of the Carpathians (Olympiod. frr. 19; 28 Blockley). The argument is not conclusive, but does make it reasonably likely that a first revolution east of the Carpathians in

---

[30] Refs. as note 29.

the 370s was followed by a similar convulsion west of them some thirty years later.

The Hunnic empire of Attila lies beyond the compass of this volume, but it is worth considering the social and economic structure of the Huns and its transformation in our period. The Huns were steppe nomads, and their social structure reflected the demands of this way of life. Ammianus reports that they had no overall leader in the 370s (xxxi.2.7), and in 412 Olympiodorus encountered a series of Hunnic leaders (ῥηγῶν: fr. 19), one of whom was known as 'first among the kings of the Huns'. Priscus reports a similar pattern of seemingly largely independent chiefs with, neverthe-less, a developed internal ranking system among another contemporary nomadic tribe, the Akatziri (fr. 11.2, p. 258 Blockley), and such systems may well have been standard, reflecting the basic fact that, in order not to exhaust grazing, nomads had to operate in fairly small, largely autonomous social units.[31] Indeed, it is highly likely that the Huns were originally sub-divided into families (the primary stock-rearing group), clusters of families forming marriage groups, and a third set of groups, perhaps those headed by chiefs, whose function might be termed political: securing and pro-tecting grazing rights.

The westward movement of the Huns and the establishment of an empire generated substantial changes in this pattern. By the time that Priscus visited Attila, there is no sign of the ranked chiefs reported by Olympiodorus. A decentralized power structure had been replaced by a much more authoritarian system. The economic basis of Hunnic society had also changed. Certain nomadic features are likely to have survived, but the Huns were no longer simple steppe nomads. They exploited the agri-cultural surpluses of conquered subjects (Priscus fr. 49 Blockley), and the military component of their lifestyles had increased dramatically. Raiding, especially stock rustling, had probably always been a useful source of extra income, but proximity to the rich Roman empire and the war machine created by drafting in the manpower of their conquered subjects made warfare a much more valuable form of activity.

From *c.* 400 onwards, we find a succession of Hunnic groups employed by the Roman state (both its eastern and western halves) in a military capac-ity – in particular to help control the Germanic invaders whom the arrival of the Huns had pushed across the imperial frontier. Uldin was used in this way by Stilicho in the first decade of the fifth century, and other groups were an essential aid to Fl. Constantius in the 410s, and to Fl. Aetius from the 420s. By the 430s, Hunnic power had increased dramatically, and war

---

[31] Maenchen-Helfen, *Huns* 12–13 discounts Ammianus, claiming that someone must have co-ordinated the sudden attack which destroyed Ermenaric's empire. But that empire was a figment of later imaginations (see p. 492 above), and the fourth-century Hunnic leader Balamber of Jordanes' *Getica* is a confused reminiscence of the Gothic king Valamer: Heather (1989) 116ff.

was now waged independently of and indeed against the Roman state. Warfare none the less retained its economic function; the demands and treaties of the Huns in the period of Attila indicate that plunder was its main purpose. I would not go so far as one recent study in supposing that by this date the Huns no longer had horses, but whether, after the establishment of the empire, much effort went into tending flocks must be doubtful. The middle Danube region offers only restricted room for grazing, and this may well have combined with the increased attractiveness of warfare as an economic option to lead Huns to favour the breeding of horses – the animal of war in nomadic society – over the maintainance of the other herds which had previously formed the backbone of their economy.[32] A full enquiry is hamstrung by the lack of evidence, and this chapter must anyway not stray too far beyond its date limits, but these developments must already have been under way by 425.

IV. GOTHS AND ROMANS, c. 376–425

Our sources are quite unanimous that the emperor Valens was overjoyed to receive the Goths who turned up on the Danube in 376, seeing this as an opportunity to recruit many of them into his army. But, as we have seen, imperial ideology made it impossible for an emperor ever to admit that policy towards 'barbarians' had been dictated by events beyond his control, and the detailed account of Ammianus makes it clear that Valens was actually highly suspicious of his supposedly welcome recruits, admitting only one of the two groups gathered on the river bank. The Tervingi under Alavivus and Fritigern were ferried across, under an agreement which probably included the stipulation that the Goths would accept the emperor Valens' non-Nicene Christianity.[33] All available troops were posted, however, to keep the Greuthungi of Alatheus and Saphrac north of the river. Moreover, the local commander Lupicinus then attempted to disrupt the coherence even of the admitted Tervingi. Inviting many of their leaders to dinner in Marcianople, he sprang a trap; Fritigern escaped only with difficulty, Alavivus is never heard of again. The kidnap attempt, not surprisingly, sparked off a general revolt (XXXI.4–5).

Ammianus implies that the trap was Lupicinus' initiative but this does not ring true. A senior local commander (who referred back to Valens before admitting the Tervingi) is hardly likely to have attacked those whom

---

[32] The argument of Sinor (1977) ch. 1 is very suggestive. Lindner (1981) argued that the Huns had given up horses, but his argument incorporates the misconception that Attila's army was composed entirely of Huns, when we know that their Germanic subjects also fought (mainly on foot). By Lindner's calculations, there would be enough grazing for horses for at least 10,000–15,000 Huns in the middle Danube; I would not expect the Hunnic core of the empire to have been much larger.

[33] Heather (1986).

he knew to be his emperor's welcome allies. Hijacking important tribal leaders was anyway a standard feature of Roman frontier policy. The key to this apparent contradiction between Valens' reported happiness and Roman action is provided by events on the eastern frontier. As the Goths approached the Danube, Valens was confronting Persia over Armenia. Most of Valens' troops were committed to this theatre, and it took two years to disentangle them for war in the Balkans. Policy towards the Goths was thus actually dictated by the non-availability of reinforcements for the Balkans. The Roman empire had previously resettled many immigrants within its borders, but only on its own terms, subduing them thoroughly first and breaking them up into small groups which were spread widely over the map. In 376, the empire was in no position to enforce such policies, and may well have had just enough troops in the Balkans to attempt to keep one of the two groups out. The Tervingi were admitted only because Valens had no other available option.[34]

This perspective is vitally important because much of the subsequent dynamic of Gotho–Roman affairs would be lost if it were thought that the Romans had entered into the relationship voluntarily. The Goths too were hesitant. They reached the decision to seek asylum inside the Roman empire only after lengthy consultation (*diuque deliberans*, as Ammianus puts it: XXXI.3.8), and remained suspicious of Roman motives and policy. Even after the Tervingi had been admitted, their leaders remained in contact with the excluded Greuthungi. Alavivus and Fritigern advanced only slowly from the Danube because they knew that the Greuthungi had forced a crossing and wanted to give them time to catch up (XXXI.5.3–4). The Goths were thus seeking to establish a united front against the Roman state.[35]

Immediately after the revolt, the Romans could do little because of the shortage of troops. Lupicinus was defeated, and Gothic raiding parties from probably both the Greuthungi and the Tervingi ranged far and wide in search of food and plunder. In 377, Valens managed to detach some troops from the east, and these in combination with some western forces drove the raiders north of the Haemus mountains. A head-on confrontation (probably near Ad Salices in the Dobrudja) ended in a bloody draw, and an attempt to hold the line of the Haemus in autumn 377 failed when the Goths negotiated the assistance of some Huns and Alans. By 378, Valens had extricated himself from the east, and entered the Balkans with the majority of his mobile troops. His nephew and co-emperor Gratian

[34] Heather, *Goths and Romans* 128–35 against the prevailing consensus which takes the sources at face value. Valens and Persia: Amm. Marc. XXVI.4.6; XXVII.12; XXIX.1; XXX.2. Hijacking tribal leaders: Amm. Marc. XXI.4.1–5; XXVII.10.3; XXIX.4.2ff.; 6.5; XXX.1.18–21 (though note XXIX.6.5 for an authorized attack). Valens' delight may reflect a lost speech of Themistius: Heather, *Goths and Romans* 134.

[35] According to Eunapius (fr. 59 Blockley), the Goths may have sworn an oath never to let any Roman blandishment divert them from overthrowing the empire. Much was made of this by Thompson (1963), but it is impossible to be certain of its veracity: Heather, *Goths and Romans* 139–40.

was in the meantime bringing a large force from the west. Between them, they no doubt hoped to drive the Goths beyond the Danube and/or enforce a more usual mode of settlements on any Goths left south of the river. But Gratian was delayed by problems on the Rhine, and Valens, moved by jealousy of his nephew's successes there, refused to wait. A mistaken report that he was facing only half the Goths led him to commit his forces to battle just outside the city of Adrianople on 9 August 378. All the Goths were present, however, and the fighting started before the Romans were fully deployed. Valens and two-thirds of his army (probably 10,000–15,000 men) were killed; the triumphant Goths swarmed over the Balkans, even contemplating a siege of Constantinople (Amm. Marc. XXXI.6–16).[36]

Gratian seems to have made no further moves against the Goths in 378, and it was only in January 379 that Theodosius, replacing Valens as eastern emperor, was given command of the Gothic war. Establishing himself in Thessalonica, he was mainly concerned in 379 to rebuild the eastern army. Deserters were rounded up, new recruits (Roman and barbarian) drafted, and veteran regiments transferred from the east. The Goths moved west from Thrace, where they were probably running short of food, to Dacia and Upper Moesia in Illyricum. In 380, again perhaps driven by hunger, the Goths divided. The Greuthungi of Alatheus and Saphrac moved north-west into Pannonia, while Fritigern moved south-west towards Theodosius. The fate of the Greuthungi is unclear; they may have been checked by Gratian. Further south, Theodosius' new army fell apart in battle and, ceding control of operations to Gratian, he moved on to Constantinople. In 381, Gratian's troops drove Fritigern's Goths east from Illyricum, and a lengthy process of negotiation culminated in an agreement formalized on 3 October 382.[37]

The terms of the peace reflected the rough military balance established in six years of warfare. The Romans had been unable to defeat the Goths in all-out battle; the Goths had, however, suffered heavy casualties and been forced to curb any ambitions for an independent kingdom. The Roman state granted the Goths land for farming, and allowed them to maintain their own laws. To this extent, the agreement broke with tradition and gave the Goths considerable autonomy within the imperial frontier. In return, the Goths owed military service, and the Roman state refused to recognize any leading individual as overall leader of the Goths. Fritigern had clearly

[36] The extent of Roman losses at Adrianople and the precise moment when the Tervingi and Greuthungi united in revolt are the only major issues. For discussion and refs.: Heather, *Goths and Romans* 146–7.

[37] The main source is Zos. IV.24–34 (after Eunapius): a better account than is usually thought: Heather, *Goths and Romans* 147–56; Appendix B. It is also generally held that Gratian made a separate peace with the Greuthungi, but the reconsideration of Zosimus undermines this view.

had such ambitions, asking Valens before Adrianople to recognize him as *rex socius et amicus* (Amm. Marc. XXXI.12.9): the traditional title accorded fully recognized allied kings. Fritigern's exact fate is unclear, but he is not mentioned after 380 (nor, indeed, are Alatheus and Saphrac), and it seems pretty clear that, even if he were still alive, the Romans would not have been ready, in 382, to grant honours to the victor of Adrianople.

Face had been saved, then, to a certain extent, but public opinion required reassurance, and Themistius again attempted to make the best of the situation. A series of orations between 381 and 383 gradually built up the case that it was better to conquer the Goths by friendship than by violence, and his oration on the actual peace agreement stated that Theodosius could have utterly defeated the Goths if he had wanted to. This should not be believed, but shows how carefully policy had to be presented to fit the expectations of its audience. Themistius also looked forward to the time when the Goths would be totally absorbed into Roman provincial society.[38]

The treaty of 382 held more or less until the death of Theodosius in 395. In one incident, a crowd lynched a Goth in Constantinople (Lib. *Or.* XIX.22); in another, a regular garrison unit on the Danube seems to have attacked a force of Goths; the commander of the regular unit was disciplined, presumably to forestall a general Gothic uprising (Zos. IV.40). The emperor also invited Gothic leaders regularly to dine with him (Eunap. fr. 59 Blockley): a channel of communication through which the difficulties of coexistence could be eased away. This period of reasonable calm was first punctuated and then brought to an end, however, by major revolts associated with the two occasions on which Theodosius obtained military service from the Goths. In 387, he waged war on the usurper Maximus, mobilizing the Goths *en masse*. Some rebelled before the campaign started (suborned, it is said, by Maximus), but a much larger revolt followed the Goths' return to the Balkans after Theodosius' victory. This was eventually solved by negotiation, but a campaign in 392–3 against a second usurper, Eugenius, suggests its root cause. In 393, the Goths found themselves in the front line at the battle of the Frigidus and suffered heavy casualties in fierce fighting (the sources say 10,000). Orosius commented that the battle saw two victories for Theodosius: first, a usurper had been defeated, and, second, Gothic numbers had been heavily eroded (VII.35.19). Where such attitudes prevailed, the Goths had every reason to be suspicious of Roman motives, and it seems likely that already on the Maximus campaign they had realized that casualties incurred in Roman civil wars threatened their continued independence. The Roman state tolerated Gothic autonomy only

---

[38] Them. *Or.* XIV–XVI; on the peace more generally, Heather, *Goths and Romans* ch. 5; Wolfram, *Goths* 131ff.; Chrysos (1972) ch. 4.

because it had no choice; should Gothic manpower be whittled away, that necessity would disappear.[39]

Soon after the Eugenius campaign, therefore, this time under the leadership of Alaric, the Goths again revolted, Theodosius' death in early 395 presenting them with the perfect opportunity. Alaric is a somewhat mysterious figure. He had played some role in the revolt which followed the Maximus campaign, but it has been doubted that in 395 he led a general revolt of the Goths. His demands in 395 – that he wanted to 'command an army' rather than just barbarians (Zos. v.5.4) – better fits, it has been suggested, a man wanting a career in the Roman army (a path followed by Gothic nobles such as Fravitta and Modares) than a traditional tribal leader of the Goths. But, as we have seen, the Frigidus provided the Goths with every reason to revolt, and, from 399 at least, Romans were seeing Alaric's enterprise as a general Gothic revolt; Alaric had also had sufficient followers to stand up to Stilicho, ruler of the western empire, in both 395 and 397. As to the military command, Alaric was to demand a Roman generalship at intervals throughout the next fifteen years, even after 408 when he certainly commanded a large force of Goths. Such a command cannot have been incompatible with kingship of the Goths, therefore, and was probably designed to strengthen Alaric's hold over his followers. From 405, when we have more details, a generalship for Alaric was always associated with a large annual payment in gold for his followers (notionally, perhaps, their pay). A generalship also implied Roman acceptance of Alaric as the overall ruler of the Goths – something Theodosius had been able to deny Fritigern or Alatheus and Saphrac in 382.[40]

By 395, therefore, Alaric was the Goths' most powerful leader, and probably controlled most of the Tervingi and Greuthungi settled under the treaty of 382. Only Ammianus, of our sources, makes the distinction between these originally separate groups, and writers of the 390s and 400s talk as if there had only ever been one group of Goths. This is indicative of an important transformation; Tervingi and Greuthungi had become one. As early as the Adrianople campaign, they had co-operated in the face of Roman power. Another facilitating factor was the eclipse of established dynasties. The Huns had undermined one set of leaders before the Goths reached the Danube (Athanaric, Ermenaric and Vithimer), and the Romans another by 382 (Fritigern, Alatheus and Saphrac). The dynastic interests which might have kept the groups apart were thus swept away, leaving the

---

[39] The connection between military service and both revolts is established by Heather, *Goths and Romans* 183–8. Other accounts: Liebeschuetz, *Barbarians and Bishops* 51ff.; Wolfram, *Goths* 136ff.

[40] Revisionary view of Alaric: Liebeschuetz *Barbarians and Bishops* 51ff. More detailed counter-argument: Heather, *Goths and Romans* 193ff. Claud. *Bell. Get.* 166ff.; 610ff., dating from 402, and Synesius, *De Regno* ed. Terzaghi 19–21, in 399, both characterize Alaric as the leader of a general revolt of the treaty Goths. See further Heather (1988).

way open for a new overall leader to control the newly united Goths. Alaric's part in the revolt after the Maximus campaign was probably an important factor in his rise to power. It was also furthered in 392 by a struggle between two other leaders, Eriulph and Fravitta, ending in the former's death and the latter's enforced flight to escape the workings of feud. Two potential rivals thus disappeared in one fell swoop.[41]

The next fifteen years saw Alaric attempt to renegotiate with a succession of imperial regimes the terms agreed in 382. Between 395 and 400, manoeuvres were assisted by Roman disunity. Theodosius' sons were minors at his death: Honorius in the west, ruled by Stilicho, Arcadius in the east, ruled by first Rufinus and then Eutropius. Stilicho had designs on the whole empire, and, in both 395 and 397, intervened in the east ostensibly against Alaric's Goths, but with the real aim of securing power in Constantinople. In 397, Eutropius (still dealing with the Hunnic raid through the Caucasus: see p. 502 above) preferred to negotiate with Alaric rather than submit to Stilicho. The full terms of the peace are unknown, but Alaric did get his coveted generalship, and this no doubt included other, particularly financial, benefits for his followers.

The treaty left Eutropius open, however, to accusations of having pandered to 'barbarians'. This was one of the prime charges made against him by Stilicho, a line strongly echoed in the east by Synesius' *De Regno*, a political pamphlet probably issued on behalf of Aurelian, one of Eutropius' rivals. In the summer of 399, Eutropius' regime fell, and after two years when power oscillated among a number of figures, Aurelian's brother Caesarius finally secured his position in summer 401. Almost immediately Alaric moved his followers to Italy, seeking a deal from Stilicho. That Alaric should have abandoned the Balkans and the eastern political establishment with which he had enjoyed some success suggests that Caesarius' regime took a similar line on Gothic policy to that advocated in the *De Regno*, and was refusing further negotiations.[42] Alaric's first invasion of Italy was no more successful. Crossing the Dinaric Alps in autumn 401, he fought two battles against Stilicho in the following year: Verona and Pollentia. Both were draws, but they were enough to check Alaric's designs; Stilicho seems to have parried the Goths until logistic problems forced their withdrawal. By 403, Alaric was back in the Balkans, an outlaw rejected by both halves of the empire.

[41] Eunap. fr. 59 Blockley; Zos. IV.55.3–56.1 (on the date, Wolfram, *Goths* 147). Significance: Heather, *Goths and Romans* 186–7, 190, 196–9. The incident is also discussed by Thompson (1963).
[42] Fundamental is Cameron, Alan, *Claudian* chs. 4, 6, 474–7; cf. Heather, *Goths and Romans* 199–208; Heather (1988). 399 also saw a revolt under Tribigild of followers of Odotheus settled in Asia Minor (see p. 502 above). They were eventually incorporated into the power-base of the Gothic general Gainas. Gainas has been seen by Liebeschuetz, *Barbarians and Bishops* 100ff. as potentially an alternative Alaric, but he should rather be seen as a would-be Stilicho: more interested in becoming imperial regent than outright Gothic leader: see the translation and commentary on Synesius *De Providentia* by Cameron and Long, *Barbarians and Politics*.

He was rescued from this precarious position by a further bout of imperial rivalry, when Stilicho fell out with Caesarius' successor Anthemius, and sought to wrest eastern Illyricum from his control. To this end, he negotiated a joint campaign with Alaric, agreeing that Alaric should receive in return the coveted generalship and granting his followers a large annual payment. The campaign was delayed, however, first by Radagaisus' invasion of Italy in 405–6, and then by the Rhine crossing of 406, which also provoked a series of usurpations. By 408, the usurper Constantine III had spread his power to the Alps and Pyrenees, and broken Stilicho's hold on Honorius. There followed a *coup* in which Stilicho and his son were arrested and killed.[43] These events furthered Alaric's position in two ways. First, the collapse of political unity in the west allowed him to move safely into Italy. Second, after Stilicho's death, Alaric received substantial reinforcements. On defeating Radagaisus, Stilicho had drafted a large number of his followers (probably over 10,000 men) into his army. In the *coup*, their families, quartered in Italian cities, were subject to pogrom, causing the menfolk to join Alaric. At a stroke, he increased his forces by perhaps as much as fifty per cent.[44]

For the next eighteen months, to August 410, events followed a set pattern. Alaric sat outside Rome and threatened to sack it unless the imperial authorities in Ravenna negotiated; his demands are well documented. At most, he offered a military alliance, wanting in return a generalship for himself, a large annual payment in gold, substantial corn supplies, and his troops to be settled in the Venetias and Raetia, where they could control Ravenna and routes over the Alps (Zos. v.48.3). The level of ambition here is remarkable. When these demands were rejected, and despite the fact that the Roman position was no stronger, he then offered an alliance in return for just a land settlement in Noricum (well away from the political heart of the empire), and some corn each year (v.50.3). Even contemporaries found this surprising, but it suggests that Alaric expected the weakness of the western empire to be merely a passing phenomenon.[45]

None the less, no agreement followed. Honorius was willing to sacrifice Rome rather than negotiate, and, in disgust, Alaric finally sacked the city on 24 August 410. Indeed, Alaric failed to achieve any agreement before his death from disease shortly afterwards; the next year, his brother-in-law and successor Athaulf led the Goths, now short of food, to Gaul. There Athaulf tried a mixture of force and persuasion to obtain advantageous terms. He first suppressed one usurper, Jovinus, then set up another of his own: the Roman senator Attalus (Alaric had earlier done the same outside

---

[43] Cameron, Alan, *Claudian* ch. 7; Matthews, *Western Aristocracies* ch. 10.
[44] Zos. v.35.5–6; cf. Heather, *Goths and Romans* 213–14.
[45] See further Matthews, *Western Aristocracies* ch. 11.

Rome). His last move was to marry Honorius' sister Galla Placidia, who had been captured in Rome. The marriage was celebrated in Roman splendour in a villa at Narbonne, and when they had a son, they named him Theodosius (Olympiod. 18; 22; 24; 26 Blockley). Honorius had no children, and the new Theodosius was grandson to one emperor by that name and first cousin to another (Arcadius had been succeeded by Theodosius II in 408). Athaulf clearly had it in mind to become the power behind the imperial throne. This was also the tenor of his famous remark that he had first thought to replace the Roman empire – Romania – with Gothia, but then decided to use Gothic arms to uphold Roman rule (Oros. VII.43.2–3).[46]

But Honorius' general Fl. Constantius had other ideas. He first defeated various usurpers to reunite the western army under central control, and then turned on the Goths, subduing them by blockade and starvation. This aroused latent Gothic discontent towards Athaulf. After he himself had been mortally wounded, one Sergeric mounted a *coup*, killing Athaulf's brother and children. Sergeric himself lasted only seven days, before another *coup* replaced him with Vallia, no known relation of the previous kings. Under Roman pressure, instability thus returned to Gothic politics. Alaric had gathered under his rule elements from three previously separate Gothic groups: the Tervingi and Greuthungi of 376, together with many of Radagaisus' followers. His command of this new Gothic group rested on his own ability; there was no established dynastic tradition to exploit. In such a situation, there were many potential heirs for Alaric's position. Vallia was succeeded in turn by Theoderic I in 417–18, and it was only thanks to his longevity and fertility that a ruling dynasty finally established itself. A huge revolution in Gothic society, started some fifty years earlier by the Huns, had finally come to fruition in the creation of the Visigoths.[47]

Theoderic I also established a new order in Gotho–Roman relations. The efforts of Fl. Constantius constrained Vallia to make an initial agreement in 416, which seems to have been confirmed by Theoderic in 418. Its terms are nowhere fully recorded, but the Goths were settled in the Garonne valley between Toulouse and Bordeaux. No payments in gold are mentioned, and neither Vallia nor Theoderic received a generalship. The limited evidence suggests that their economic well-being was guaranteed by grants of land, rather than tax revenue. With the Goths clinging to the Atlantic seaboard far away from Ravenna, the agreement seems to have been closer to Alaric's minimum demands (see p. 513 above).

Compared to the limited advantages they gained under the treaty of 382, however, the concessions the Goths had extracted were considerable. The

---

[46] Matthews, *Western Aristocracies* chs. 12–13.
[47] The process: Heather, *Goths and Romans* 28–33; 220–1. Subsequent dynastic events: Wolfram, *Goths* 173ff.

empire had been forced to recognize their king's leadership, and even sent hostages to his court after 418. Nor is there any sign after 418 that hopes of snuffing out Gothic independence lingered in imperial minds. The new social unit created by Alaric and sustained by his successors was much larger than anything that had gone before, and was hence that much more difficult to defeat. In addition, after the Rhine crossing of 406, the Goths were no longer the only tribal group established on Roman territory, and the Romans preferred to negotiate with them rather than with the newer arrivals. Goths and Romans thus co-operated in Spain, destroying one out of two Vandal groups, and savaging various groups of Alans. For the Romans, the Goths had become a lesser evil, and, with that in mind, they were willing to countenance their autonomous settlement within the Roman frontier and sanction it with a formal alliance. The evolution of that settlement into an independent kingdom is a story for another volume.[48]

[48] See generally Heather, *Goths and Romans* 221–4; Liebeschuetz, *Barbarians and Bishops* 71ff., esp. on the economics of the settlement against Goffart, *Barbarians and Romans*, esp. 103ff. followed by Wolfram, *Goths* 222ff. (Wolfram discusses other aspects of the treaty at 170ff.). Another line of argument has concentrated on the reasons for picking Aquitaine: Thompson, *Romans and Barbarians* 251–5 v. Wallace-Hadrill (1961); neither really considers the fact that the Goths had to be put somewhere.

CHAPTER 17

THE BARBARIAN INVASIONS AND FIRST SETTLEMENTS

I. N. WOOD

In the mid fourth century the barbarians who inhabited the territories beyond the Rhine and the Danube frontiers presented no great threat to the survival of the Roman empire. That is not to say that they were peaceful neighbours; the Franks and the Saxons on the lower Rhine mounted numerous raids into Germania, Belgica and along the coasts of Gaul; and there was intermittent fighting against Goths settled north of the Danube. Nevertheless, these peoples could be held in check by a mixture of military force and diplomacy; military reprisals were directed against the Franks and Saxons, and the Burgundians were persuaded to take Rome's side against the Alamans.

To a large extent these policies worked because they dealt with settled peoples. Although the names of the tribes were not names which would have been familiar to the early empire, and although the tribes themselves were not static units but rather confederations which expanded and contracted according to the prestige of individual leaders, they were not nomadic. The Burgundians were said to be so-called because they lived in *burgi*[1] – almost certainly a false etymology, but one which is revealing of their way of life. They were also said to be brothers of the Romans,[2] but this origin legend probably has more to do with fourth-century politics than any real ethnogenesis. For the Gothic Tervingi, the fourth-century *Passion of St Saba* reveals a world of peasant villages dominated by a pagan aristocratic élite.

The social hierarchies of the Tervingi which are known from the *Passion of St Saba* are an important antidote to the notion that the early Germans were egalitarian peoples. Such a notion could equally be challenged by archaeological finds, which provide evidence of distinctions in wealth and social status. There were also political hierarchies, culminating in the office of judge, which seems to have been held, in the middle of the fourth century at least, by the members of one family: the best known of the judges is Athanaric.[3] Although there were barbarian groups who lacked

---

[1] Oros. VII.32.12.   [2] Amm. Marc. XXVIII.5.11.

[3] Amm. Marc. XXVII.5.6. For an interpretation of Tervingian judgeship see Heather, *Goths and Romans* 97–107, and ch. 16 above.

royal leadership, most notably the Saxons, in many respects Athanaric's judgeship does appear to have been monarchical. Nevertheless it probably differed from the kingship which was subsequently created amongst the Goths, once they were inside the empire. Here the military and economic needs caused by migration, and the pressures of imperial politics, created what was in many respects a new type of ruler. Similar transformations can be assumed even for those peoples, like the Franks and the Burgundians, who already had kings before they crossed on to Roman soil.

The life of the settled Tervingian community was changed dramatically by the arrival of the Huns, a nomadic, Asiatic people, in 376. They had already overthrown the Gothic empire of Ermenaric, to the north of the Black Sea, and now they destroyed the Tervingian state which was guided by Athanaric. The majority of the Tervingi decided to abandon their home-lands, and under the leadership of Alavivus and Fritigern petitioned to cross the Danube and enter the Roman empire. With this crossing, and the officially approved settlement of the Tervingian Goths in the Balkans in 376, the narrative of the barbarian invasions and settlements can be said to have begun.

This period of invasion can usefully be distinguished within the larger history of barbarian migration and assimilation into the Roman world. Study of the migrations properly involves not just the relatively well evi-denced entry of the barbarians into the empire and subsequent movement within it, but also the legendary origins of the Germanic peoples in Scandinavia and their journeys through eastern Europe as recorded by Jordanes and later, for the Lombards, by Paul the Deaon. The reality behind these accounts is difficult to fathom: the origin legends which Jordanes recounts are likely to have been influenced by fifth- and sixth-century pol-itics, and also by the requirements of narrative history, although they may still contain kernels of information relating to particular leading families and stages of tribal development. As a result, an understanding of migra-tion history involves the political and cultural history of the post-Roman period as well as the archaeology of the Roman Iron Age in northern and eastern Europe. The history of the assimilation of the barbarians, by con-trast, includes the earlier history of the empire, which had long settled barbarian groups within its borders, sometimes for military reasons, and often with social repercussions in its frontier zones. The barbarian inva-sions were only one element in these larger histories.

The entry of the Tervingi into the empire was followed in 377 by an uprising of the settlers and, a year later, by the defeat and death of the emperor Valens at the battle of Adrianople. As a result, the western emperor Gratian despatched Theodosius to deal with the problems in the east, and within a year some semblance of order had been restored. Apparently in 382 a treaty was concluded, whereby the Visigoths were resettled in the north of the provinces of Thrace and Dacia. The death of Theodosius in 395, however, rendered the treaty void. It also left the empire divided between his sons Arcadius and Honorius, with their respective courts. In the ensuing years the Visigoths took advantage of political in-fighting to leave the lands to which they had been assigned, and to move south, under the leadership of Alaric I. In 397 a new treaty was made with Theodosius' elder son, the eastern emperor Arcadius, who granted the Goths territory and Alaric, perhaps, high military command. Four years later Alaric and his people set out once again, this time for the western empire, and from 401 until 412 they presented a problem to the govern-ment of Italy, most notably in 410, when they captured and sacked Rome. Nor were they the only invaders of Italy in this period; in 405–6, another group of Goths, led by Radagaisus, entered the peninsula, but it was largely destroyed by Stilicho at the battle of Fiesole.

Meanwhile, supposedly on the last day of December 406, groups of Vandals, Alans and Sueves crossed the frozen Rhine. The pre-migration histories of these peoples are more obscure than those of either the Visigoths or the Burgundians. They neither attracted a Jordanes to write up their origin legends, nor did they impose themselves firmly enough on the consciousness of the Romans to have their ethnogenesis recorded in passing by one of the Latin or Greek historians. Their social structure is illuminated by no equivalent to the *Passion of St Saba*, although the Alans appear to have differed from the others in being nomadic pastoralists. The cause of their migration, however, is likely to have been the same as that which pushed the Tervingi across the Danube: pressure from the Huns. Something of their itinerary, beginning in eastern Europe to the north of Pannonia and Moesia, can be reconstructed from passing references in contemporary sources, but it is only at the end of 406 that they enter the limelight.

After they had crossed the Rhine they plundered the provinces of Germany and Gaul for some two years. The devastation which they caused is well known in general terms from the rhetorical outbursts of Gallic writers lamenting the smoking ruins of the north-east. In 409, however, they moved on to Spain, and around the year 411 they established terri-torial bases for themselves – the Alans in Lusitania and Carthaginiensis, the Siling Vandals in Baetica, and the Hasding Vandals with the Sueves in Galicia. Settled in Spain, they became the focus for attacks launched by the successors of Alaric and his followers, now known to history as Visigoths. Between 416 and 418 the Silings were destroyed, as were the Alans, at the hands of the Visigothic king Wallia. In order to understand the role of the Visigoths in all this, it is necessary to return to their movements after their departure from Italy in 412.

Having entered Gaul, they took over much of Aquitaine, from the

Mediterranean to Bordeaux, and by 414 their king Athaulf had set himself up in Narbonne, where he married the emperor's sister Galla Placidia, who had fallen into Visigothic hands at the time of the sack of Rome. Within the next year Athaulf and the Visigoths were driven out of Gaul, and moved to Barcelona, where Athaulf was murdered. His successor but one, Wallia, then made a treaty with Honorius, and it was as his agent that Wallia embarked on the destruction of the Alans and Vandals, before being called back, with his people, by the Roman general Constantius, to be settled in Aquitaine, in the region around Toulouse.

This withdrawal of the Goths left the Vandals and the Sueves of Galicia as the only substantial barbarian groups in Spain, and within a year the former attempted to annihilate the latter, only to be prevented by the intervention of the *comes Hispaniarum* Asterius. Two years later, apparently in 422, the *magister militum* Castinus attempted to destroy the Vandals, but was himself defeated and killed. Subsequently the Vandals moved south, reaching Seville, Cartagena and even the Balearics around 425. They nevertheless continued their wars against the Sueves right up until their departure for Africa, possibly in 427, but probably 429. Thereafter, having crossed the Straits of Gibraltar, under the leadership of the king of the Hasding Vandals Gaiseric, they headed eastwards for the Proconsular province, reaching Hippo in the summer of 430, shortly before the death of Augustine. Five years later, following the failure of imperial attempts to defeat them, a treaty was signed, granting territory, which seems largely to have been in the northern part of the province of Numidia, for the Vandals to settle. In the event, this did not content Gaiseric, who besieged Carthage in 439. His actions prompted the intervention of the eastern emperor Theodosius II, who sent a fleet in 441, only to recall it the following year, leaving Gaiseric to negotiate a new division in 442, which left him with all of Africa Proconsularis and Byzacena, and much of Numidia and Tripolitana.

These two treaties with the Vandals coincide with the dominance within the western empire of the general Aetius, who was also responsible for a number of other barbarian settlements in about the year 440. They include two grants of land in Gaul to the Alans, the first of *agri deserti* belonging to the city of Valence, and the second of territory in an area defined as Gallia ulterior, presumably to the north of the Loire. It is possible that some concession was made to the Saxons in Britain in the same period. More certain is the settlement of the Burgundians in a region called Sapaudia, seemingly to the north of Geneva.[4] This move apparently marks a change in the policy of Aetius towards the Burgundians, whom he had earlier defeated and almost destroyed with the aid of the Huns. His new policy

[4] Duparc (1958).

can be compared with the settlement of the Visigoths in Aquitaine, but at the same time it effectively marks the end of the deliberate settlement of barbarians on the Roman soil of the western empire. Henceforth, concessions to the barbarians would be much closer in spirit to the treaties made with the Vandals – that is, they were little more than official recognitions of barbarian expansion and conquest.

While such a general outline of the barbarian settlements is not difficult to establish, any attempt to provide greater detail or to offer a fuller interpretation of the events runs into considerable problems. This is true even at the basic level of chronology, for although some events can be dated with certainty, particularly where a number of overlapping sources are in agreement over the information which they contain, other events are variously dated by different sources, while some are only recorded in one source whose chronology is known from elsewhere to be suspect. Nor are problems of this sort confined to the evidence for minor events. For instance, the settlement of the Visigoths in Aquitaine is dated in three chronicle sources, but each source assigns the event to a different date. Prosper of Aquitaine, who might reasonably be thought to have been best placed to provide an accurate date, puts the grant of Aquitaine to Wallia into the consulship of Monaxius and Plinta – that is, 419. Historians have, however, preferred to follow Hydatius, writing in the far north-west of Spain, who uses regnal and Olympiad dates to identify the year of the grant as 418. The *Chronicle of 452*, which is at least in part a compilation of the 450s, probably made in southern Gaul, differs radically by recording a transfer of Aquitaine to the Visigoths, admittedly not necessarily the same transfer, under the year 414, according to a regnal and Olympiad system of dating identical to that used by Hydatius.

The oddities of the *Chronicle of 452* are somewhat more alarming when it comes to events for which it provides the only evidence, as in the case of the series of grants and settlements made by Aetius around the year 440. Here, moreover, there is the added complication that at this stage in the chronicle the regnal and Olympiad dates are out of kilter, since an extra Olympiad was erroneously added at the end of the reign of Honorius. Thus the cession of Valence to the Alans is dated by the chronicler both to 440 and to 444; the fall of Britain to the Saxons to 441/2 and 445/6; the submission of Gallia ulterior to the Alans to 442 and 446; the grant of Sapaudia to the Burgundians to 443 and 447; and the capture of Carthage by the Vandals to 444 and 448.[5] Of these events, only those relating to Britain and Carthage are attested elsewhere. The first of them is placed in 440 in the *Chronicle of 511*, while both Prosper and Cassiodorus assign the second to 439. It is possible that the chronicler has confused the capture of

[5] Wood (1987); Jones and Casey (1988) 393–6.

Carthage with the official ratification of its transfer to Vandalic hands, but even the date of that event, 442, does not coincide with either of the chronologies in the *Chronicle of 452*. Clearly it would be unwise to place much faith in the dates given to events which are attested nowhere else.

Chronology, however, is only the simplest of the problems relating to the barbarian invasions and settlements. More important are questions relating to their scale. For the Tervingi and their successors in the Balkans, figures of between 10,000 and 20,000 fighting men may well have been the norm, with Alaric perhaps commanding 30,000 men in Italy.[6] The size of most other groups is more difficult to assess. Jerome estimated the numbers of the Burgundians at 80,000 during the reign of Valentinian I – that is, before the disasters inflicted on them by Aetius and his Hunnic allies.[7] Orosius follows Jerome, but provides the additional piece of information that this was the number of their fighting men.[8] Unfortunately, there is no way of testing the accuracy of Jerome's figure, or of Orosius' gloss. Even more questionable is the number of Vandals said to have crossed to Africa with Gaiseric. Alarmingly, Victor of Vita records this as being, once again, 80,000,[9] which is a number also given by Procopius.[10] It might be thought that Procopius was here following Victor, who might, equally, have taken the figure from Jerome or Orosius. There are, however, crucial differences between the accounts of Victor and of Procopius, which render their figures suspect from another point of view. According to Procopius, Gaiseric appointed eighty chiliarchs, each of whom was supposed to command a thousand men. This apparently marked an increase in the numbers of Vandals and Alans, who had previously amounted to only 50,000. Victor's account provides a different solution to the increase in Vandal numbers, for he explains that Gaiseric achieved this figure of 80,000 by counting everyone, including slaves, and he did this in order to make his following sound more frightening than it was. Numbers, in other words, could be part of a propaganda exercise. Elsewhere there is even less to go on, although in the case of the Anglo-Saxon invaders of Britain the logistics of sea-crossings, especially in barbarian ships, can scarcely have allowed large numbers to cross at any one time. In short, any attempt to compute the real size of an invading force, or to estimate the ratio of fighting men to others, can be nothing but guesswork.

There is a further difficulty in assessing the scale of the invasions, and that is the fluidity in the composition of any barbarian tribe. Procopius' figure of 80,000 is of Vandals and Alans. The latter had probably joined the Hasdings after they had been defeated by Wallia. Later, too, Gelimer claimed to rule over both peoples.[11] Probably the remnants of the Silings

---

[6] Heather, *Goths and Romans 332–489*, 213–14. [7] Jer. *Chron.* 2389. [8] Oros. VII.32.11.
[9] Vict: Vit. 1.1.2; Goffart, *Barbarians and Romans* 231–4. [10] Procop. *BV* 1.5.18.
[11] Procop. *BV* 1.24.3.

had also joined Gaiseric. In addition, there are said to have been Goths in his army.[12] Such confederations, under a successful war-leader, are likely to have been the norm. Nor would free barbarians have been the only people to join a victorious army; Zosimus claims that the numbers of Visigoths who withdrew from the siege of Rome in 408 were inflated to 40,000 by the presence of runaway slaves, some of whom may have been the enslaved survivors of Radagaisus' army.[13] Equally, after a major defeat, a barbarian group could dissolve, as happened to the Alans and the Silings in Spain. Thus, although the sources appear to record the movements, victories and defeats of clearly labelled units, in reality the composition of a tribe was constantly changing.

Not only are the composition and size of a Germanic tribe open to question, so too is the nature of the barbarian settlements. Traditionally they have been interpreted in the light of two clauses from fifth- and sixth-century law codes. The first of these, which is contained in the Code of Euric, dating to the period between 466 and 485, speaks about a Roman *tertia*, implying that the Goths held two such *tertiae* for every one held by the Romans.[14] The second comes from the *Liber Constitutionum* issued by the Burgundian king Sigismund in 517, although the law in question is probably earlier.[15] It too refers to a partition into thirds, but is more specific, speaking of the Burgundians (*populus noster*) as having two-thirds of the land and one-third of the slaves. It also refers to an equal division of woodland into halves. Between them these laws have led historians to assume that in 418 the Goths and in 443 the Burgundians were given two-thirds of the lands, one-third of the slaves and a half of the woodlands in the areas in which they were settled. Unfortunately everything about this interpretation, including the chronology, is questionable. There is nothing in earlier sources to suggest that these clauses represent the first stage of settlement, and there is good reason to believe that the type of settlement changed over time. This is certainly the case for the Burgundians, since the clause of the *Liber Constitutionum* in question, 54, itself makes it quite clear that there had been prior allocations of land made by the king and his predecessors to their followers, and that the grant of *tertiae* was only to those who had not benefited from this earlier largesse. This grant was, therefore, not part of the original settlement of the Burgundians, nor was it even made in the reigns of the first Gibichung kings to be established on Roman soil. Further, an edict appended to the *Liber Constitutionum* reveals a subsequent set of allocations, probably made in the 520s, in which land was divided equally between Romans and barbarians.[16] In short, the laws refer to at least four allotments made to the Burgundians, none of which need be the same

[12] Possid. *V. Aug.* XXVIII.4.   [13] Zos. v.42. Heather, *Goths and Romans* 332–489, 214.
[14] *Codex Eurici* 277.   [15] *Liber Constitutionum* 54; Wood (1986) 10.
[16] *Liber Constitutionum constitutio extravagans* 21, 12.

as that recorded in the *Chronicle of 452* or that recorded under the year 456 by Marius of Avenches. In the light of all this, it is clearly unwise to assume that evidence from the late fifth and early sixth centuries provides an accurate account of arrangements made in the first half of the fifth century.

Early information on the first settlements, therefore, is very slight. The chief material which can be said with certainty to relate to the allocation of lands to the Vandals, Alans, Sueves, Visigoths and Burgundians is to be found in the chronicles of Prosper and Hydatius and in the *Chronicle of 452*. Interestingly, each of these sources employs a different vocabulary. Prosper tends to refer to territory being handed over for habitation (*data ei*; *eis ad habitandum*).[17] A similar phrase is used once by Hydatius, who also refers to the acceptance and occupation of land (*occupant; acceperunt*), as well as the allocation of provinces (*sortiuntur*).[18] The *Chronicle of 452* talks about areas being handed over for partition (*partienda traduntur; dividendae . . . traditae fuerant; datur . . . dividenda*), and appears to make a distinction between such partition and possession, since the Alans in Gallia ulterior took possession of land by force after an initial division.[19] That all three sources sometimes use different vocabulary to describe the same event suggests that their terminology cannot be entirely technical – indeed, that none of it may be. Nevertheless, the use of the verb *sortiri* and of the noun *sors* by Hydatius could be an exception, since the second of these words is used in the later law codes with reference to barbarian settlement.

In the Burgundian *Liber Constitutionum* the word *sors* seems to refer to land held under a particular title, the *ius sortis* – that is, to the two-thirds allotment held by barbarian settlers,[20] and this is certainly a meaning of the term in the Code of Euric.[21] Although it is difficult to see a *sors* as anything other than a special kind of real estate in these two law codes, it is, nevertheless, possible that the word once had slightly different connotations, relating to an allocation of tax revenue due from an estate rather than to the land itself.[22] The Greek term *kleros* is thought to have the same meaning in the context of Vandalic landholding in Africa. There is, therefore, the possibility that at least a part of the original allotments to the barbarians was made up of a proportion of tax revenues rather than land. This interpretation has considerable attractions; redistribution of fiscal income would have been well within the competence of Roman tax officials; under such a system the barbarians would have been no drain on private resources, and would, therefore, not have alienated the provincials; moreover, although the imperial government would have been faced with a decline in revenue, the availability of Germanic troops to fight in support of the emperor would have been a compensation. Further, the revenues in

---

[17] Prosper, *Chron.* 1271, 1321.   [18] Hydat. *Chron.* s.a. 411, 418.   [19] *Chronicle of 452 s.a.* 440–3.
[20] *Liber Constitutionum* 14, 5.   [21] *Codex Eurici* 277.
[22] Goffart, *Barbarians and Romans, passim;* Durliat (1988), 40.

question are likely to have been in kind, obviating the need for coin to pay barbarian soldiers: a point of considerable significance, given the decline of coinage in the western empire during the fifth century.

Hydatius, however, only uses the verb *sortiri* in the context of the Alan settlements in Lusitania and Carthaginiensis and the Siling settlements in Baetica, neither of which was organized or ratified by the imperial government. To this list the *Chronicle of 511* adds the settlements of the Vandals and Sueves in Galicia.[23] But, despite this addition, the *Chronicle of 511* appears to be following Hydatius in the entry in question, and other chronicles do not use the verb *sortiri*. Moreover, neither Hydatius nor the chronicler of 511 uses this vocabulary to describe other settlements. If the precise words used by Hydatius are important, then the allocation of fiscal income rather than land, even if it did take place, need not have been a widespread technique of accommodating the barbarians.

Commenting on other settlements, the chroniclers seem to imply that there was an allotment of land. This is true for the Visigoths in Aquitaine, the Alans in Valence and Gallia ulterior and the Burgundians in Sapaudia. For the first of these instances, the Byzantine historian Philostorgius provides additional information, referring specifically to the allocation of rations and land.[24] What such allocation might have entailed, however, is by no means certain. For instance, the barbarians may have been installed as tenants rather than as owners of estates; this at least is implied by the forcible seizure of possession from the landlords of Gallia ulterior by the Alans, subsequent to their original allocation. At the same time, as tenants or landlords, the barbarians are likely to have left the agricultural labour to the peasantry who were already established on the estates – in which case, they would have been little more than recipients of renders, which would explain the lack of Visigothic place-names in Aquitaine. Yet accommodation for the barbarians must also have been a significant factor in the allocation of estates, since it is unlikely that any barbarian group was small enough to be accommodated in military barracks, which in areas like Spain and Aquitaine, away from the empire's frontiers, were few and far between.

One other solution to the problem of accommodation which was unquestionably used was billeting. Paulinus of Pella in his poem the *Eucharisticon* comments that barbarian 'guests' could play an important role in protecting a 'host's' property.[25] Moreover, in the second half of the fifth century Sidonius Apollinaris lamented the presence of Burgundians who had been billeted on him.[26] The practice of quartering troops is also well known from the Roman period, and there is legislation to regulate it. There is even a reference to soldiers being apportioned one-third, or a half, of a

---

[23] *Chronicle of 511 s.a.* 413.   [24] Philostorg. *HE* xii.4.   [25] Paul. Pell. *Euchar.* ll. 282–90.
[26] Sid. Apoll. *Carm.* xii.

house, which has been thought to provide a precedent for the *tertiae* of the barbarians.[27] Further, among the words used to describe the obligation to provide imperial officials with accommodation is one which is also familiar from the Burgundian *Liber Constitutionum*: *hospitalitas*. In the Burgundian case, however, the word is used both in the context of accommodating officials in transit and to describe the allotment of land to a barbarian.[28] Indeed *ius hospitalitatis* and *ius sortis* are synonymous. Thus, just as the word *sors* seems to imply more in the context of the barbarian settlements than it might have done in that of the imperial fiscal system, so too the word *hospitalitas* encompasses much more with regard to barbarian settlement in the late fifth and early sixth centuries than it had over the quartering of imperial troops. The Roman practice of billeting, therefore, provided a model which could be developed for the settlement of the barbarians, but there is no evidence to show that, in its original form, it was one of the major methods employed to accommodate them, and while *hospitalitas* was crucial to land-allotment in the late fifth and early sixth centuries, it was a practice much extended from its Roman origins.

Although the scarcity of evidence may encourage the historian to attempt to reconstruct a single unified policy from what little there is to work on, it is likely that a considerable variety of policies were utilized in the accommodation and settlement of the barbarians. The possibilities seem to have ranged from simple billeting and diversion of fiscal revenue, through allocation of proportions of estates, to wholesale confiscation, as happened in Africa under Gaiseric. The policy employed is likely to have depended on such factors as the relative strengths in the positions of invaders, imperial officials and provincials at the precise moment of negotiation, as well as such factors as the availability of *agri deserti*, as attested at Valence. It is also probable that the earliest beneficiaries were the closest followers of the barbarian king involved: the actual distribution of Roman revenue or land would have been determined by the social structures of the barbarian groups, which were highly stratified. This is implied by the Burgundian evidence, where it is also clear that there could be more than one moment of distribution in the history of the settlement of a single tribe. Moreover, it is likely that the techniques of accommodation were being continuously developed over the period, and that this development was a crucial aspect of the settlement of barbarians. Thus, combining information from different regions, and from different moments in the development of the settlement, may well be a misleading method of embarking on the interpretation of the process.

In general, the evidence is not well suited to answering precise questions relating to the chronology, scale and nature of the barbarian settlements;

[27] *C.Th.* VII.8.5; Goffart, *Barbarians and Romans* 162–75.   [28] *Liber Constitutionum* 38; 55, 2.

such issues seem not to have interested contemporary writers. Nevertheless, there is much to be learnt from a consideration of what information was thought worthy of record, and how that information was used. A considerable quantity of information relating to the activities of the Germanic peoples in the western empire in the opening decades of the fifth century is recorded in theological or moralizing works. Even the *Histories* of Orosius are best seen in their theological context, as a response to the pagan reaction to the disasters which were afflicting the empire, although the final chapters are perhaps rather more forthcoming about the horrors of the period than the intended scheme of the work allowed. It was left to Augustine to provide a full response to the pagans in the *De Civitate Dei*. In the anonymous *Carmen de Providentia Dei*, and the works of Orientius and Salvian, the theological and moral intentions of the writers are rather more in evidence, and the barbarians are used as one element in the battery of arguments put forward. How far these arguments actually involve a distortion of the facts is beyond investigation, and it is, therefore, dangerous to plunder such texts for detailed pieces of information.

One particularly problematic area is that of the Christianization of the barbarian peoples. It appears that Fritigern and his followers accepted Christianity as a condition for entering the empire in 376. In addition, a letter of Auxentius, relating to the Gothic bishop Ulfilas, throws some light on missionary work among the Visigoths. Inevitably they were converted to the orthodoxy of the mid fourth century, to which the emperor Valens subscribed, but which was subsequently condemned as Arianism.[29] The Visigoths may have been responsible for the initial process of evangelization among other Germanic peoples, who as a result became Arian and were therefore attacked by later church writers. Apart from the Visigoths, however, Orosius appears not to have recognized the early converts among the barbarians as being heretical. Indeed, he singles out the Christianity of the Huns, Sueves, Vandals and Burgundians as a mark of God's mercy.[30] This optimistic interpretation of the Christianization of these peoples is shown to be hollow by a cursory glance at Gaiseric's anti-Catholic policy in Africa, and the whole passage can be attributed to Orosius' determination to emphasize the glories of the Christian era. Yet there may be more to Orosius' claim than meets the eye; the Sueves in Galicia did have Catholic kings in the fifth century, and the Burgundian royal family included a number of orthodox Christians in the same period. Indeed, it is possible that Gregory of Tours' later condemnation of the Burgundians as Arian is as misleadingly simplistic as Orosius' propagandist statement about the Christianity of the barbarians.[31]

Because of the distortions and omissions of fifth- and sixth-century

---

[29] Heather (1986), and ch. 16 above.   [30] Oros. VII.41.8.   [31] Wood (1990) 58–61.

sources, the history of the barbarian settlements has to be considered in a broader context than that implied by a single-minded pursuit of the narrative of the invasions. Such an approach may help explain the extraordinary impact of the barbarians on the west in the early fifth century, by revealing the priorities and, therefore, the misjudgements of the emperors and their officials. Thus, the evidence relating to the Visigoths under the leadership of Alaric I survives very largely in fragments of fifth-century Greek historians, preserved, although not always accurately, in later historical works. In these Greek fragments, Gothic activity in the Balkans is set within the context of court politics. Eunapius claims that the ravaging of Greece by Alaric in the mid 390s was prompted by Rufinus, who was attempting to force Arcadius to make him co-emperor.[32] Similarly, the presence of the Visigoths in Illyricum in 408 is revealed as being part of Stilicho's policy to hold the province for Honorius against Arcadius and his advisers.[33] As for the sack of Rome, Olympiodorus ascribes it to Alaric's anger at the execution of Stilicho, and the failure of Honorius to implement promises he had made.[34]

For the last years of the fourth century and the first of the fifth, some of the most revealing information to have survived from the west comes from the poet Claudian, and the general picture he presents is one that is entirely compatible with that of the Greek historians. To a great extent Claudian's poems are propaganda works, written in support of Stilicho, and as such they illuminate the political in-fighting of the period, both that between east and west, and that at the western court. Stilicho's inability to deal with Alaric, which may well have stemmed from his fear of relying on an already barbarized Roman army against the Goths, is glossed over; in the light of the picture presented by the Greek sources and, retrospectively, in the light of the fall of Stilicho and the murder of his wife, it is likely that Claudian's treatment of events was intended to deflect criticism and comment in Ravena.

Ravenna, however, was not the only focus for discontent with Stilicho's regime. Apparently in 406, before the Vandals, Alans and Sueves crossed the frozen Rhine, the army in Britain had supported at least two usurpations, first by Marcus and then by Gratian, who is described by Orosius as a civilian (*municeps eiusdem insulae*).[35] Gratian was subsequently deposed in favour of the soldier Constantine, who proceeded to establish himself in Gaul and Spain. Although it is likely that Constantine III was acclaimed emperor because of the barbarian influx into Gaul, the sources do no more than hint at any successes he had against the invaders. Instead they emphasize his attempts to establish his own power, in opposition both to Honorius and his family, and to his one-time supporter Gerontius, who

---

[32] Eunap. fr. 64 Blockley.   [33] Olympiod. fr. 6 Blockley.   [34] Olympiod. fr. 6 Blockley.
[35] Oros. VII.40.4.

subsequently proclaimed his own son Maximus as emperor. Against these imperial rivalries, the question of dealing with the Vandals, Alans and Sueves seems to have taken second place. Certainly, according to Orosius, Honorius realized that he could do nothing against the barbarians until he had dealt with the usurpers.[36] It is even possible that Orosius overestimated the emperor's awareness of the barbarian problem, but his identification of the order of priorities at the imperial court is telling.

One indication of imperial priorities can be found in the so-called *Ravenna Annals*. Although these only survive on a single parchment leaf of the eleventh century, there can be little doubt that the surviving manuscript fragment provides an accurate transcript of the text and illustrations of a fifth-century annalistic work from the imperial circle in Ravenna.[37] The fragments cover the years 411–13, 421–3, 427–9, 434–7, 440–3 and 452–4, and for these years the chronicler records emperors, consuls, usurpers, the patriciate and the death of Aetius, together with the death of Boethius, and natural disasters. There is, however, no mention of the barbarians or their settlement within the empire. It was possible, therefore, for someone associated with or close to the imperial court in the fifth century to compile a set of annals which were concerned with nothing other than emperors, legitimate or otherwise, leading officials and earthquakes. The absence of any reference to the barbarians, although unfortunate, is a striking indication of the way in which matters of seemingly great importance could be ignored in particular circumstances. As such, it is a reminder that, however much the historian may lament lacunae in the evidence, those lacunae may themselves provide material for an interpretation of the contexts in which specific events took place.

Almost all the narrative sources dealing with the western empire in the opening decade of the fifth century concentrate more on the usurpers than on the barbarians. As a result it is not easy to provide a narrative account of the movements of the various barbarian groups with any certainty from 407 to 409, despite the catalogue of destruction which can be drawn up for the towns of Germania, Belgica and northern Gaul. Apparently Constantine III was successful in breaking up the invading forces, and it may be that some provided useful troops for the contenders to the imperial throne. Constantine's son Constans is said to have led a force of barbarians to Spain,[38] and Constantine himself sent his general Edobich to recruit Franks and Alamans from across the Rhine. In addition, Gerontius gathered a barbarian following, and he had an Alan slave with him at the time of his death.[39] According to the Greek historians, the fall of Constantine was a significant moment for the Vandals, Alans and Sueves, who are said

---

[36] Oros. VII.42.1.   [37] Bischoff and Koehler (1939).   [38] Oros. VII.40.7.
[39] Olympiod. fr. 17, 1–2 Blockley.

to have taken advantage of the collapse of his authority, apparently in 411, to seize strongholds in Spain and Gaul, as well as capturing his supporters.[40]

The execution of Constantine, however, did not mark the end of the usurpation of imperial power. Already Alaric had seen the advantage of having a puppet emperor in his control. He had proclaimed Priscus Attalus as emperor at the time of the sack of Rome. Although Alaric subsequently deposed him, Alaric's successor Athaulf also elevated Attalus as emperor for a short period of time. Meanwhile, the Alan chieftain Goar and the Burgundian leader Guntiarius raised Jovinus to the purple in Germania Secunda, and Attalus persuaded Athaulf to join forces with them, which he did for a while. But when Jovinus appointed his brother Sebastian as co-emperor, Athaulf put himself at the service of Honorius, and secured the overthrow of both usurpers. Their deaths are recorded in the *Ravenna Annals*, which also include an illustration of their heads stuck on poles.

Of all the usurpers from this period, only Constantine III attracts much attention from modern historians, and then because of his importance in removing troops from Roman Britain. The others tend to be overshadowed by preoccupation with the barbarians. Nevertheless, the emphasis placed by the court at Ravenna, and by the sources, on the destruction of the usurpers is worth some attention, for although retrospectively the Vandals, Alans, Sueves and Visigoths can be seen to be more significant, this was not perceived at the time. Moreover even the barbarians recognized the importance of usurpers and usurpation. Both Alaric and Athaulf deliberately involved themselves in the making and unmaking of emperors. This involvement raises an important issue: the relationship between the barbarians and the empire. Many aspects of this are touched on in the famous anecdote which Orosius claims to have heard from a certain Narbonensian.[41] According to this, Athaulf had originally intended to wipe out Rome, substituting Gothia in place of Romania, but because the Goths would not obey the law, he decided to restore Rome with Gothic arms. There are some undoubted problems with the detail of Orosius' account, which turns on a definition of the *respublica* which Augustine would have understood, but which is unlikely to have been on the tip of Athaulf's tongue. Nevertheless, the central point of the story may be authentic. And in any case there can be no question about the general respect which Athaulf showed for the traditions of the empire, which Alaric had revered before him. Both wanted recognition from Honorius; both appointed puppet emperors to wring concessions from him; and both were prepared to depose their puppets when *rapprochement* with Ravenna seemed possible. Athaulf also married an imperial princess, Honorius'

---

[40] Olympiod. fr. 13, 2 Blockley.   [41] Oros. VII.43.4–6.

sister Galla Placidia, and had Priscus Attalus deliver an epithalamium at the wedding. It is possible – indeed probable – that this respect for Rome was more widespread amongst the barbarian leadership than amongst the rank and file.[42] It may even be that it exacerbated class antagonisms, although to link the murder of Athaulf with such conflicts, as has been done, is unnecessary, since his assassin is said to have been pursuing a blood-feud.[43]

With the death of Athaulf a different set of issues comes into prominence. It is not that the sources pay any more attention to the barbarians; if anything, the reverse is true. They do, however, reveal a shift in the political climate. The emergence after 410 of the general Constantius marked a temporary end to the series of usurpations which had threatened the empire, and also saw the beginnings of a genuine attempt to deal with the barbarian problem, involving, first, the use of the Visigoths against the Vandals and Alans, and, second, their settlement in Aquitaine. Quite apart from the insoluble problem of how the Goths were settled, there is a further question as to why they were settled in Aquitaine. It is a question which has been much debated, and which has prompted many different answers, which have variously stressed the wealth of Aquitaine and its strategic position with regard to routes from the north-west of Gaul to Provence and the Mediterranean, as well as the presence of dissident groups to the north of the Loire.[44] Some or all of these factors may have impinged on the consciousness of Constantius and Wallia as they negotiated the settlement, but none of them can be said to be interpretations required by the evidence, which is terse in the extreme.

Constantius' dominance over affairs may be said to begin with Athaulf's murder at Barcelona. After the reign of Singeric, which lasted a matter of days, Wallia was acclaimed king. From the start, he was inclined to follow Athaulf's advice and return the dead king's widow to her brother Honorius. Olympiodorus appears to have ascribed the pliancy of the Goths to hunger, and he states that 600,000 measures of grain were sent to the Visigoths in exchange for Galla Placidia.[45] His reference to the Vandals selling corn to them 'at one *solidus* per *trula*' is usually taken to illustrate their hapless state at the time of Wallia's accession.[46] It is even possible that Constantius had deliberately tried to starve the Visigoths into submission. According to Orosius, after Constantius had forced Athaulf and his followers to move from Narbonne into Spain, he cut maritime links and trade.[47]

Whether this amounted to a full-scale blockade – indeed, whether a blockade of Spain was feasible – is open to doubt. The threat of famine, however, can never have been far from the barbarians during their migra-

[42] Thompson, *Romans and Barbarians* 43–50.   [43] Olympiod. fr. 26, 1 Blockley.
[44] Thompson, *Romans and Barbarians* 23–37, 251–5; Wallace-Hadrill (1962).
[45] Olympiod. fr. 30 Blockley.   [46] Olympiod. fr. 29, 1 Blockley.   [47] Oros. VII.43.1.

tions. Most of them were not used to the nomadic life, but without lands to cultivate they had to rely on others to provide grain. For a short period they might have been able to extort food from the indigenous populations, but those same populations can rarely have had the necessary surplus, and they too will have been forced to the brink of famine. In this context, the various attempts to reach Africa, by the Visigoths under Alaric and his successors, as well as by the Vandals under Gaiseric, may well indicate that the corn-supplies of the southern Mediterranean were the barbarian equivalent of El Dorado. Equally, it is not surprising that the provision of food played a significant role in relations between the Romans and the Germans, and that the failure of such provision was a cause for rebellion, as with the Visigoths in 377,[48] and, apparently, with the Saxons in Britain in the mid fifth century.[49]

Orosius, however, does not attribute Athaulf's willingness to make peace to Constantius' blockade, but rather to the remembrance of a storm, which had destroyed a band of Visigoths who were intent on crossing to Africa in the previous year.[50] The peace to which Wallia agreed may not have represented an absolute victory for the Romans. Nor do the Gothic campaigns against the Vandals and Alans necessarily mean that the Visigoths had been reduced to being agents of Constantius and nothing more. Their removal from Spain, and subsequent settlement in Aquitaine, need not, therefore, represent a policy forced on them by the Romans without their having had any say in the matter. If the settlement does reflect Visigothic as well as imperial interests, it may be significant that Athaulf had established himself in the region between Bordeaux and Narbonne before Constantius had driven the Visigoths into Spain. Wallia and his followers were returning to a region which they had left not long before.

The settlement in Aquitaine may also have been influenced by recent developments within the provinces of Gaul. Some indication of these is to be found in Rutilius Namatianus' poem *De Reditu Suo*, which records the poet's return from Rome to Gaul in the year 417.[51] Among his friends he lists Exsuperantius, who had just re-established order in Armorica. The problem to which Exsuperantius had addressed himself was probably that of the Bagaudae, dissident groups which are sometimes seen as being made up of rebellious slaves or peasants.[52] This definition of the Bagaudae, however, is unquestionably too narrow. From Salvian's account of them, it is clear that they included men who had suffered under the imperial regime at the hands of tax-gatherers and other officials, and who had been driven out of their estates.[53] A curious fourth-century comedy, the *Querolus*, which may even have been dedicated to Rutilius Namatianus, confirms this

[48] Amm. Marc. xxxi.5.1.   [49] Gildas, *De Excidio Britanniae* 23, 5.   [50] Oros. vii.43.11.
[51] Rut. Namat. 1.215–16.   [52] Thompson (1952a).   [53] Salvian *Gub. Dei* v.24–8.

impression by suggesting that a dispossessed landowner could join the society of free men who lived by the Loire. This picture is given a further nuance by the identification of a later leader of the Bagaudae as a doctor.[54] That this group presented a threat to the ruling establishment is very likely; that the threat was essentially lower-class is not an interpretation supported by the sources.[55]

It is possible, although not proven, that there was a relationship between Exsuperantius' military activities and the settlement of the Visigoths. Certainly any attempt to make a direct link between the two is undermined by the difficulty of dating the second event with any certainty. Leaving aside the eccentric date of 414 provided by the *Chronicle of 452*, there is still the problem of weighing Hydatius' 418 against Prosper's 419. Rather than looking for a very precise explanation for the settlement, it is perhaps better to look at the general context. Here Rutilius' return to Gaul is suggestive. That an aristocrat who was well established in Rome should want to return, at an unseasonable time of year, to his Gallic estates suggests that something of significance was about to take place. Rutilius may have been warned about the imminence of the Visigothic settlement; he is almost certain to have been aware of the proposed reconstruction of the council of the Gauls, which took place in 418.[56] In all probability the council was involved in the settlement, or at least in its repercussions.

What does seem significant is the cluster of events in Gaul during the period from 417 to 419, and this remains true whatever the date of the Visigothic settlement. Taken together, all these developments can be seen as aspects of the re-establishment of order, under Constantius and his allies, in the provinces of Gaul. From an imperial point of view, however, the forces of disorder were not simply, or even primarily, the barbarians, but the usurpers and their followers. In this context the Visigothic settlement in Aquitaine may have been intended to keep a check on the Bagaudae, but the Bagaudae may have been at least in part the remnants of the supporters of Constantine and Gerontius. Equally, Constantius may have had a more general concern to secure the loyalty of Aquitaine, and to stifle the possibility of further usurpations. In other words, by placing the Visigoths in an area which they had once occupied, he may well have hoped to gain their support in the process of establishing his own authority, alongside that of Honorius, in an area which had lately been outside the control of the court of Ravenna.

A background of imperial politics is as important for the history of the Vandalic seizure of Africa as it is for that of the Visigothic settlement in Aquitaine. This was already recognized in the sixth century, when the Byzantine historians Procopius and Jordanes accused Boniface, the count

---

[54] *Chronicle of 452 s.a.* 448.   [55] Wood (1984) 2–5.   [56] Matthews, *Western Aristocracies* 325–8.

of Africa, of inviting the Vandals into the province.[57] The context of these accusations is provided by Prosper, who records two expeditions sent against Boniface by the *magister militum* Felix in 427, the year to which he assigns the Vandal invasion of Africa. Subsequently Aetius overthrew Felix, but inherited his hostility to Boniface, who crossed from Carthage in 432 and defeated him, only to die shortly after in suspicious circumstances. Hydatius and the *Chronicle of 452* provide the additional information that Boniface was called to Italy by Galla Placidia.[58] It is difficult to see how a Vandal invasion in the late 420s could be anything other than deleterious to Boniface, who was already faced with enemies in Ravenna. By contrast, it is easy to see how Felix and Aetius might have hoped to blacken the count of Africa by accusing him of collusion. The suggestion that he had called in the Vandals probably belongs to court propaganda surrounding the attempts by rival factions to get control over the young Valentinian III. That Aetius was adept at such dirty tricks was recognized by John of Antioch, who records one of Aetius' attempts to discredit Boniface in the eyes of Galla Placidia.[59] Whatever the truth of such allegations, it is scarcely questionable that the rivalries of the Roman generals played into Gaiseric's hands. Once again, the progress of the barbarian invasions was aided by the failure of the western generals to set their own ambitions on one side, and to concentrate instead of the threat posed by the invaders.

With the death of Boniface, Aetius was in a position analogous, in certain respects, to that of Constantius after the fall of Jovinus and Sebastian. For the first time in a decade there was a single military leader, without a rival; as for the emperor, there had been no significant attempt at usurpation since Valentinian III had been established in Ravenna in 425. A more aggressive policy against the barbarians was, therefore, a possibility, and Aetius did indeed launch campaigns against the Visigoths in Gaul and the Burgundians on the Rhine, as well as against lesser peoples called the Iuthungi and the Nori.[60] Nevertheless, he still made concessions to the barbarians, notably to the Vandals in Africa, but also to the Alans and the Burgundians in Gaul. These last two grants, in particular, are reminiscent of Constantius' policies. The allocation of Sapaudia to the Burgundians has been compared to that of Aquitaine to the Visigoths, although the context of the settlement of the Burgundians is completely obscure. The settlement of Alans in Gallia ulterior, however, does appear to be related to events and policies which stretch back to the time of Constantius.

The evidence for this depends almost entirely on the *Chronicle of 452*, but since, in certain crucial respects, this information can be dovetailed with material from elsewhere, there seems to be no reason to reject the basic

[57] Procop. *BV* 1.3.22–6; Jordanes, *Get.* XXXIII.167.
[58] Hydat. *Chron. s.a.* 432; *Chronicle of 452 s.a.* 432.   [59] Jo. Ant. fr. 196.
[60] Hydat. *Chron. s.a.* 430–1; *Chronicle of 452 s.a.* 430–1.

outline of events. According to the *Chronicle*, Aetius handed the lands of Gallia ulterior over to the Alans, who were to divide them with the local population (*cum incolis*). However, there was resistance to this, so the barbarians took possession of the region by force, and drove the landlords out. These events can be related to earlier annals in the same chronicle, which deal with Gallia ulterior. For instance, in the year variously dated 435 and 439, the chronicler records the rebellion of Tibatto, and the consequent Bagaudic conspiracy; two annals later, the capture of Tibatto and the suppression of the Bagaudae is related. A moment in between these two events is described by Constantius of Lyons, who recounts a meeting between Germanus, bishop of Auxerre, and the rebels, as well as the bishop's subsequent attempt to prevent the use of Goar and the Alans to suppress the uprising.[61] Constantius makes it clear that the Alans were involved in the destruction of the Bagaudae, whilst the chronicler's information suggests that Aetius subsequently gave the Alans a share in the region where the Bagaudae had been established, and that the barbarians took control of the area by force, because of local opposition. In short, the problem of the Bagaudae, which had apparently occupied Exsuperantius, and which may have been a factor in the placing of the Visigoths in Aquitaine, was certainly central to the allocation of lands in Gallia ulterior to the Alans.

The use of the Alans against the Bagaudae is also significant in that it draws attention to the dependence of Aetius on barbarian allies when dealing with rebellious groups within the Roman empire. This reliance on barbarians can be documented from the first major appearance of Aetius on the political stage, when he recruited an army of Huns, supposedly 60,000 strong, to support the usurper John.[62] After his defeat by Boniface, he seems to have determined on flight to the Huns, and he later used them unsuccessfully against the Visigoths, and with devastating effect against the Burgundians. Barbarian federates and mercenaries had long been used by the Romans; what is striking about the campaigns of Aetius, however, is the almost complete silence relating to any Roman troops. Even in 451, when his relations with the Huns failed and Attila turned on the western empire, there is little to suggest that Aetius had access to a substantial Roman army. Indeed, Jordanes, who provides the most detailed account of the battle of the Catalaunian Plains – though this was admittedly written in Constantinople in the mid sixth century – describes what is essentially an army of barbarian allies, although he does refer to the Olybriones as 'having once been Roman soldiers'.[63] Given Aetius' previous dependence on the Huns and his hostility to the Visigoths, it is surprising that he

---

[61] Constantius, *Vita Germani* 28; Wood (1984) 15–16.   [62] Olympiod. fr. 43, 2 Blockley.
[63] Jordanes, *Get.* XXXVI.191.

managed to gather together so sizeable a confederacy. Much of the credit should doubtless go to Avitus, who was held in high regard by the Visigoths, who later made him emperor.

The apparent insignificance of Roman troops at the battle of the Catalaunian Plains raises the problem of the chronology of the decline of the Roman army. This is not a problem that is easily solved. The narrative sources are rarely specific about the constitution of any campaigning force, and from the 420s onwards, where they do provide detail, it is of barbarian troops, almost without exception. The one non-narrative source which ought to be relevant is the *Notitia Dignitatum*. Unfortunately, although this document may have been compiled as late as the 420s,[64] the information it contains is highly suspect. No narrative source for the period after 406 confirms the accuracy of any part of it, and some sections, like those relating to the provinces of Britain, Belgica and Germania, are unquestionably anachronistic.[65] In all probability the work as it stands is a nostalgic statement of what had once been available to the emperor, and as such it is as optimistic a creation as the bizarre military manual, the *De Rebus Bellicis*, which survives alongside it.

If the narrative sources are trustworthy over this matter, it appears that a crucial shift in the constitution of military forces available to the emperor or his generals took place in the first three decades of the fifth century. At the time of the usurpation of Constantine III, there was still a sizeable Roman army in existence. By the 430s Aetius was clearly dependent on barbarian troops. The factors most likely to have contributed to the decline of the army in the intervening period are the civil wars between the usurpers and the court of Ravenna. Significant losses and the disbanding of rebellious units may well have weakened the army greatly, while the presence of rebels and barbarians in Britain, Gaul and Spain is likely to have meant a decline in Honorius' tax revenues, and consequent difficulties in paying those troops who were loyal. Were this to have been the case, two points of importance for the barbarian settlements would follow: first, after 406 the army would have been less capable of dealing with the invading forces than it had been at the start of Honorius' reign; second, the empire would have been desirious of harnessing the manpower of the barbarian forces, however sizeable they were.

This particular concern of the emperors and their advisers is easily overshadowed by the history of settlement, and yet there are indications that, for all the problems presented by the barbarians, it is one area where Constantius and Aetius achieved remarkable success. There were failures as well. Prosper records Visigothic attacks on Arles in 425 and Narbonne in 436, as well as fighting which lasted until 439. Further, despite the treaty

---

[64] Salway (1981) 476 n. 2; chs. 5 and 7, pp. 163–5 and 211–12 above. [65] Wightman (1985) 300.

of 435, Gaiseric continued to harass Roman Africa until 442. Nevertheless, the Visigoths kept the peace made with Constantius for over a decade, during which time they campaigned against the Vandals and the Alans on behalf of the empire, and having come to terms with Aetius in 439 they again served the emperor, fighting on the Roman side at the Catalaunian Plains. Moreover, the chronology of their breaking the first of these treaties, although it could suggest opportunism following the usurpation of John, could also suggest that once they had made a treaty, the Visigoths were prepared to observe it during the lifetime of the emperor with whom they had come to terms. There is a similar ambiguity about the sack of Rome by Gaiseric which followed soon after the death of Valentinian III in 455. The Vandals may have taken advantage of the chaos which followed the emperor's murder, but the Greek historian Priscus states directly that Gaiseric reckoned that the treaty he had made with the empire was dissolved with the death of those with whom he had negotiated.[66] The seizure of part of Gaul by the Burgundians and the division of that land with the senators, dated by Marius of Avenches to 456, might imply that they too regarded themselves as bound only to Valentinian III. That treaties were broken after the demise of an emperor could be said to show the limitations of the good faith of the barbarians, but it could also be said to reveal considerable loyalty within those limitations. Although Aetius is sometimes held to have been responsible for the survival of the western empire into the second half of the fifth century, if the Roman army was in significant decline, as it seems to have been, after the civil wars of the first decade of the century, then Aetius' achievement depended on the acquiescence of the barbarians. A similar conclusion might be drawn from the speed with which the empire collapsed in the twenty years after Valentinian's death.

The relationship between the murders of Aetius and Valentinian and renewed aggression on the part of the barbarians highlights once more the interaction of imperial politics and barbarian migration and settlement, and reinforces the importance of treating the settlements in a broad context. The success of the Visigoths in the first two decades of the fifth century was closely related to the preoccupations of the emperor and his generals with usurpation. By the time the internal threats to Honorius had been dealt with, the Visigoths were already too well established within the empire to make their destruction or removal an easy matter. Besides, it is by no means clear that Constantius or any later general had sufficient military resources to reassert imperial authority in much of Gaul without relying on Visigothic manpower. The later rivalries of Boniface, Felix and Aetius provided the Vandals with the opportunity to seize the great corn-producing lands of Africa, and thereby to destroy the political and eco-

---

[66] Priscus fr. 30 Blockley; John of Antioch fr. 201.

nomic unity of the western Mediterranean. Once again, the military leaders of the empire were too preoccupied with their own positions to deal with the barbarian threat, even if there was a Roman army capable of withstanding the invasion.

The barbarians themselves, however, although prepared to take advantage of these political divisions, were also ready to come to terms with the emperor and his agents in order to negotiate a place for themselves within the empire. Alaric and Athaulf were both intent on receiving some form of recognition from Rome, and once Wallia had gained that recognition, he and his successor were prepared to serve Honorius. The Alans also acted as servants of the state, and even Gaiseric, who was less constrained by the terms he secured from Valentinian, seems to have regarded himself as particularly bound to that one emperor. This willingness to fit into the structure of the empire ensured the preservation of Roman society, culture and provincial administration within the early barbarian kingdoms. It also obscured the extent of the collapse of imperial power in the first half of the fifth century. Because the empire of Valentinian III was shored up by the barbarians, it was possible to think that little had changed since the days of Theodosius I. When the Visigoths did decide to assert their independence in the second half of the century, some Gallic aristocrats, like Sidonius Apollinaris, were shattered by the change, but in fact most of the transfer of power had taken place surreptitiously over the previous half-century.

CHAPTER 18

POLYTHEIST RELIGION AND PHILOSOPHY

GARTH FOWDEN

At Constantine's death, and for decades to come, polytheism could still be represented as Rome's natural religion, its 'lawful cult' (Lib. *Or.* xxx.6; cf. Porph. *ap.* Eus. *HE* VI.19.7). The gods who had protected and nourished one's ancestors and parents might still show themselves publicly, as did Athena on the walls of Athens in 395/6, to save her city from Alaric. When in 408 Alaric appeared at the gates of Rome itself, there were demands for the restoration of polytheist rites, and bishop Innocent – so it was claimed – was disposed to permit them, in private.[1] Rome fell anyway. The Christians remained unabashed, for they deemed punishment of sin as much God's prerogative as the protection of the Earthly City. But it was undeniably a part of polytheism to secure such protection.[2] So close, indeed, was the relationship between the old cults and the state that, in the opinion of some, 'the ceremonies were not ritually accomplished if the state did not pay for them' (Zos. IV.59.3, V.41.3). Taking its cue, then, from the vocal polytheist élite of Rome, whose vested interest it was to maintain the public cults, modern scholarship has held that 'in the fourth century paganism appears as a kind of living corpse, which begins to collapse from the moment when the supporting hand of the State is withdrawn from it'.[3] But the Roman senate's view of polytheism is too political, too formalist, to serve as a comprehensive gauge of the old gods' performance and popularity in the fourth century. The pages that follow will indeed have much to say about the hand of the state and about its role, whether active or passive, in the foundering of public polytheism. But interwoven with that will be countless threads of uninterrupted communal and personal polytheism, not lacking in nostalgia, but among those, from peasant to philosopher, who were anyway used to doing without the supporting hand of the state, not without conviction either.

---

[1] Zos. V.41.2.
[2] See Maximin Daia's rescript against the Christians, *ap.* Eus. *HE* IX.7.7–8; Lib. *Or.* xxx.33; Zos. IV.3.3, 59; Fowden, *Egyptian Hermes* 13.   [3] Dodds (1965) 132; echoed by Frend (1984) 554.

I. REPRESSION AND COMPROMISE, 337–61

The reign of Constantius is peculiarly elusive for the historian of religion. Unlike his predecessor and successor, Constantius neither chose nor rejected Christianity, so that his personal spiritual history lacks a dramatic turning-point. He took a strong theological interest in the religion that was his birthright, but the church itself was still struggling to come to terms with Constantine's revolution, and was plagued by problems of self-definition. The same was true of polytheism. The modern scholar is hampered by his sense that he knows what he means when he talks about 'Christianity' or 'polytheism', 'orthodoxy' or 'heresy'. In the mid fourth century only a few individuals made so bold; and they – one thinks of such as Athanasius or Julian – were not pure scholars, but also men of action whose success depended on nerve and certainty.

The physical state and psychology of polytheism under Constantius are ill documented. Firmicus Maternus' tract *On the Error of Profane Religions*, addressed to Constantius and Constans, alternately crows over the fallen gods and demands a crack-down on their followers – an eloquent confusion. A crack-down there was, on paper. Constantine's ban on divination and sacrifice, no more than a gesture in the direction he would have liked to take, had been patchily enforced. It was reiterated in 341; and in 356 the closure of all temples was commanded.[4] Julian was to observe that Constantine neglected and robbed the temples, while his sons overthrew them.[5] Libanius too alleged that temples were destroyed in Constantius' reign, and that it was dangerous to frequent them.[6] Optatus of Milevis (*fl.* 370) implies that polytheists were prevented from sacrificing under Constantius,[7] a view supported by Eunapius, who thought it daring that the praetorian prefect Anatolius had offered sacrifice at Athens in the late 350s, and considered that under Constantius the tide finally turned against the worshippers of the old gods.[8] What we know about Julian's attempts to restore the temple cults (see p. 546 below) supports this picture of neglect and attrition under Constantius. Apart from Optatus', though, the general remarks just quoted are from sources polytheist and ill disposed. In practice, the attrition was opportunistic and haphazard. Systematic destruction of temples, let alone with explicit imperial approval, was unknown before the end of the century; but an impetuous local bishop who saw his chance might well take it.[9] As for public worship, it is abundantly attested under Julian's successors. Although the same emperors reiterated Constantius' anti-polytheist legislation (e.g. *C.Th.* XVI.2.18, of 370; Lib. *Or.* XXX.7), it was possible to interpret these laws as permitting sacrifice 'for the purpose of

---

[4] *C.Th.* XVI.10.2, 4.   [5] Jul. *Or.* VII.228bc.   [6] Lib. *Or.* I.27, XVIII.114–15, LXII.8.
[7] Opt. Mil. *Parm.* II.15.   [8] Eunap. *V. Soph.* x.6.3, 8.   [9] Barnes (1989) 325–9.

propitiating the deity, [but] not of trying to reach a higher station by [one's] investigations' (Amm. Marc. XIX.12.12). Admittedly, one could not always rely on observance of this fine distinction, either by the authorities at the time or by hostile or confused historians later.

Under Constantius it was possible, even at the highest levels, for there to be a wide gap between public declarations of policy and what was actually done at a particular time and place. At Delphi, an unpublished inscription put up between 342 and 344 preserves a letter addressed collectively by all three of the praetorian prefects to Flavius Felicianus, the priest of Apollo. Felicianus had in some way, possibly by Christians, been hindered in the performance of his duties; and now, soon after the ban on sacrifices issued in 341, we find Constantius' immediate subordinates going out of their way to guarantee Apollo's servant against further molestation.[10] Constantius himself, when he visited Rome in 357, removed the altar of Victory from the senate house, but was otherwise conciliatory towards the traditional cults, so that some thirty years later Symmachus could hold him up as (almost) a model for Valentinian II. 'Though he himself followed other rites, he preserved established rites for the empire' (Rel. III.7, tr. Barrow). Nor was such moderation reserved for obvious polytheist strongholds. In the 340s a young philosopher called Themistius began to teach in Constantine's new capital. Themistius was a polytheist, but not a Platonist enthusiast – he preferred to be thought of as a follower of Aristotle. Instructed no doubt by the experiences of Iamblichus' pupil Sopater, who had attained intimacy with Constantine only to be brought low by an all-too-plausible charge of practising magic, Themistius trimmed to the prevailing winds, and by 358–9 had become proconsul of Constantinople, with duties that included supervising recruitment to the city's new senate. For the next thirty years he was the confidant of emperors, the Christian capital's most prominent representative, and a tireless advocate of moderation, not least in religious affairs.

These 'inconsistencies' were not imperial whim, but inherent both in the transitional character of the age and, more profoundly, in the fact that the cities were infinitely better placed than the emperor to bring about cultic change.[11] The situation may be illustrated from the neighbouring and closely related regions of Cilicia and Syria. Though Christianity had a long history in these parts, it was still, in the earlier fourth century, a mainly urban religion, weaker in the villages and virtually non-existent in the mountains which cover Rough Cilicia, north-west Syria and Lebanon. Constantine, appreciating the region's strategic, economic and cultural importance, had attacked three of its major polytheist sanctuaries, those of Asclepius at Aegeae on the Gulf of Issus, and of Aphrodite at Aphaca and

[10] Vatin (1965) 258–64.   [11] Dagron, 'Thémistios' 181–2; Van Dam (1985) 13–17.

Heliopolis (Baalbek) in Lebanon,[12] each of which combined local influence with wider reputation. But all these shrines outlived the first Christian emperor. Aegeae, it is true, was reduced to a sorry state, and Julian apparently failed to make the local bishop restore the columns he had carted off to build a church. Yet people were still going there even in the 380s, in the hope that Asclepius might yet have the power to cure them – after all, Aegeae lay on the vital sea-route along the Cilician coast, and its clientele had been thoroughly international.[13] As for Aphacan Aphrodite, it is unlikely that Constantine did her cult serious damage, at least in its popular, local aspect. Aphrodite's power to sustain a polytheist community well into the fifth century is known from Carian Aphrodisias;[14] for a sixth-century Antiochene Christian, 'Aphrodite' and 'paganism' were virtually synonymous;[15] and at Aphaca itself the goddess continued to be honoured, under a thin Christian/Muslim veil, into the twentieth century.[16] Heliopolis too remained an active centre of polytheism well into the sixth century.[17]

Just north of Heliopolis rises the Orontes river, which flows past Emesa, praised by Julian for its loyalty to his cause,[18] and Apamea, renowned for its devotion to Zeus-Belus 'even when one could be punished for honouring the gods' (Lib. *Ep.* 1351.3, of 363), and for a tradition of Pythagorean and Platonist philosophy most recently represented by the theurgist Iamblichus. In general, the Christianization of the more southerly parts of Syria seems to have lagged fifty to a hundred or more years behind that of the north-west.[19] In the hinterland of Antioch it was already making substantial progress in the reign of Constantine; and soon this region was to become one of the forcing-houses of Christian asceticism. The metropolis itself harboured an ancient, and by Julian's day numerically dominant, Christian community. The fabric of public and private life, education and so on remained impregnated with Hellenic values; but the Christian community was already turning its hand to the destruction of temples, though some remained, in a neglected state, for Julian to sacrifice in.[20] Addressing the Antiochenes in his *Misopogon*, Julian pointedly praised the inhabitants of certain neighbouring cities for their devotion to the old ways, and during his subsequent journey eastwards he was able to experience at first hand the diverse and often ambiguous religious situation in the cities through which he passed.[21] At Beroea the city council was collectively unmoved by a characteristically Julianic lecture 'on piety', though some individuals

---

[12] Eus. *V. Const.* III.55–8.   [13] Robert (1969–90) 7.225–75, esp. 252–7.
[14] Roueché, *Aphrodisias* 85–96, 153–5   [15] *V. Sym. Styl. iun.*, 141.
[16] Kriss and Kriss-Heinrich (1960–2) 1.262–3.   [17] Hajjar (1985) 379–83; *SEG* 7.195.
[18] Jul. *Or.* XII.357C.
[19] Liebeschuetz (1990) VIII; on the widely varying rates of Christianization in adjacent regions see also Mitchell (1993) II.57–64.
[20] Lib. *Or.* XV.53; Jul. *Or.* XII.346bc, 357, 361b–363c; Wilken, *John Chrysostom and the Jews* 16–33.
[21] Jul. *Or.* XII.357c, 360d–361a; *Ep.* 98.

sympathized; while at Batnae even Julian saw through the marathon round of sacrifices that happened to be in progress when he arrived. Edessa, which already had a long Christian tradition, the emperor disliked and avoided; but at polytheist Harran nearby he lingered and sacrificed.[22] The two cities felt an intense neighbourly antipathy for each other,[23] like polytheist Gaza in Palestine and its Christian port Maiumas, which Constantine made an independent *polis* and renamed Constantia, and which Julian vengefully demoted.[24] It was perhaps understood that a degree of cultic specialization among neighbours helped dampen the prospects for communal violence.

Not that one necessarily chose either Christianity or polytheism. In 348

a mighty earthquake hit Beirut in Phoenicia, and the larger part of the town col-lapsed, with the result that a crowd of pagans came into the church and professed Christianity just like us. But some of them then introduced innovations and left, stripping off as it were the conventions of the Church. Dedicating a place of prayer, they there received the crowd, and in all things imitated the Church, resem-bling us just as closely as the sect of the Samaritans does the Jews, but living like pagans. (*Ar. Hist.* 23; ed. Bidez and Winkelmann, *Philostorgius*[3], Berlin, 1981)

But most of our evidence concerns individuals rather than groups or whole communities. In 354 Pegasius, bishop of Troy, was visited by the young and officially Christian prince Julian, who recorded (*Ep.* 79) how the bishop showed him altars of the old gods still alight and statues polished, and eventually turned out to be a crypto-polytheist who had never done any harm to the temples beyond removing a few stones for appearances' sake. Pegasius' was an unusual and thoroughly personal choice; but situations could and did arise, both at this time and later in the fourth century, in which participation in both religions was imposed. A polytheist sophist might find himself declaiming in praise of the dedication of a Christian church, or even in favour of toleration of Nicene Christians by an Arian emperor;[25] Christians held traditional civic priesthoods;[26] and the so-called *Calendar of 354*, a compendium of information designed for use by a high official at Rome, contains calendars of both polytheist and Christian festi-vals along with imagery whose essentially polytheist character is softened in order not to offend Christian sentiment.[27]

One's reaction to this fluid situation depended on both circumstance and character. Soldiers and others in public life, encouraged to be polytheists by Julian but discouraged under Jovian and his successors,[28] had no need to feel guilty; but a sophist like Hecebolius, a Christian under Constantius, a

---

[22] Jul. *Ep.* 115; Amm. Marc. xxiii.3.1–2.   [23] Ephr. Syr. *Carm. Nisib.* xxxiii, xxxiv.
[24] Glucker (1987) 43–6.   [25] Lib. *Or.* 1.39; Dagron, 'Thémistios' 186–91.   [26] *C.Th.* xii.1.112.
[27] Salzman, *On Roman Time* 33–4, 115.
[28] Jul., Bidez and Cumont (1922) no. 50; Them. *Or.* v.67b–68c; Socr. *HE* iii.22.

polytheist under his pupil Julian, and a Christian again once Julian was dead, could reasonably be accused of brazen hypocrisy. Another sophist who moved in high places, Themistius, remained a worshipper of the old gods while showing broad-mindedness and tolerance; but Julian was impelled, in similar circumstances, to focus and deepen his Hellenic identity. Libanius claims that this was a common reaction – that the sight of the gods' 'temples in ruins, their ritual banned, their altars overturned, their sacrifices suppressed, their priests sent packing and their property divided up between a crew of rascals' brought 'to the lips of every man of sense the prayer that the young man [Julian] should become the ruler of the empire' (*Or.* XVIII.23, 21, tr. Norman).

Yet this was the *post eventum* view of an encomiast; and Julian's actual accession to the throne evoked uneven support from his co-religionists, presumably because their experiences under Constantius had been so far from uniformly negative. More representative, perhaps, of the attitude of intellectuals was the deliberate silence on sensitive subjects such as theurgy maintained by some of Iamblichus' followers.[29] Their tendency was towards discretion rather than revolt; nor did the structures of the old religion offer the means by which revolt might be raised or sustained, or an equivalent of the monkish militias whose terrorism Libanius and Eunapius decry. As for the uneducated, their self-awareness was anyway less clear-cut. Rather than belonging to a category of polytheists, distinct from 'Christians', they saw themselves as devotees of certain specific, local gods, who might appear more or less worthy of worship according to their capacity to defend themselves and their friends. In this situation, it was easy for an aggressive new god to gain footholds in polytheist territory, but difficult to conquer it definitively and possess it, in the manner implied by traditional accounts of the 'conflict of paganism and Christianity'.

II. JULIAN, PHILOSOPHER AND REFORMER OF POLYTHEISM

Julian had spent the three years (351–4) before his summons to Constantius' court at Milan (and his incidental visit to Troy) as a student of philosophy at Pergamum and Ephesus. He had gone to Pergamum for the sake of Aedesius, Iamblichus' pupil and main successor; and through Eunapius' account of the Pergamum circle as it was in Julian's day, it is possible for us to discern certain significant tensions in the Iamblichan tradition.

Aedesius taught at Pergamum from (perhaps) the late 330s until his death in the early or mid 350s.[30] Like Iamblichus, he covered in his philosophical teaching the whole conventional curriculum; and his higher

---

[29] Eunap. *V. Soph.* VI.1.5, 10.7–10; VIII.1.1–2; Lib. *Or.* XIII.11.   [30] Penella (1990) 64.

doctrine seems to have had a strongly religious colouring.[31] Yet he was accounted inferior to Iamblichus in 'divine inspiration' (*theiasmos*: Eunap. *V. Soph.* VI.1.4), and was conscious of the dangers of indiscreet polytheism. His pupils ranged from Eusebius of Myndus, by inclination a logician, through Chrysanthius of Sardis, whose mixture of religious enthusiasm and common sense was perhaps closest to that of Aedesius himself, to Maximus of Ephesus, whom Eusebius opposed in his lessons because of his absorption in 'the impostures of witchcraft and magic that cheat the senses' (Eunap. *V. Soph.* VII.2.3) – theurgy, in other words. Julian was drawn to Maximus, who by the early 350s had established himself at Ephesus; and the notoriety that accrued on Julian's account to both Maximus and Chrysanthius, who also moved to Ephesus at this time, has caused them to be seen as Platonism's main representatives in the third quarter of the century – along, of course, with Julian himself. Since our sources are almost wholly concerned with Julian and his background, we have few means of controlling this picture. But we know that there were 'heretics', like Theodore of Asine, a pupil primarily of Porphyry but possibly also of Iamblichus, though he esteemed neither theurgy nor even the authority of Plato enough for Iamblichan taste, and contributed to the perpetuation of a Porphyrian current frequently deprecated by Julian.[32] And though we are ill informed about Athenian philosophical life at this period, the signs are that Iamblichanism was making rather slow progress there. Athens was admittedly noted for its conservatism, but there is even less evidence for theurgical Platonism in fourth-century Alexandria. In the west, Iamblichus never displaced the influence of Plotinus and Porphyry, who had lived there, and parts of whose works were translated into Latin.[33]

The Iamblichans should not, then, be allowed to hold the whole stage. They did not even enjoy a monopoly of the Platonist tradition. And although Platonism, variously defined, was the dominant philosophical current, there were still adherents of other schools – Cynics, for example, much derided by Julian, and even the occasional Aristotelian like Themistius, who resisted the Platonists' annexation of Plato's most famous pupil, admired Plato the politician rather than Plato the metaphysician, and strongly criticized what he saw as the Iamblichans' obscurantism.[34] It should also be borne in mind that any philosophical idea, once it ceased to be the preserve of professional philosophers and entered wider circulation, was likely to lose the distinctive colouring of the school traditions. We can see this in the *Expositio Totius Mundi*, a description of the Roman world written in Latin under Constantius by a person of very average intelligence and education, though well travelled. Probably he was a merchant.

[31] Eunap. *V. Soph.* VII.1.9–2.13, XXIII.1.5–2.2; Lib. *Or.* XVIII.18.   [32] Deuse (1973).
[33] On the geographical spread of Iamblichanism see Fowden (1982) 38–48.
[34] Blumenthal (1990); Fowden (1982) 56.

Certainly he was a polytheist who believed firmly in individual gods who inhabited particular parts of the earth: Venus of Heliopolis (Baalbek), for example, or the many gods 'of whom we know that they inhabited and still inhabit' Egypt (*Expositio* 30, 34). But he also makes reference to a creator god who is omniscient and responsible for the whole universe (*Expositio* 19, *Descriptio* 68) – a reflection, clearly, of the philosophical ideas in circulation at this time, but simplified and certainly not enough to make its author, even in his own estimation, the adherent of any particular 'school'.[35]

We recognize the same lack of philosophical sophistication in the historian Sextus Aurelius Victor, author of a treatise *On the Caesars*. When he met Victor at Sirmium in 361, Julian made him governor of Pannonia Secunda; yet this very traditional polytheist, who exalted Rome while refusing even to pronounce the name of Constantinople, was not the most obvious collaborator for an emperor who never visited Rome, snubbed the Etruscan seers during his Persian campaign, and surrounded himself with the intellectual progeny of Iamblichus. Victor and his like were the sort of constituency to which Julian needed to appeal; but how could the emperor harness the sophisticated sacramental theology of the Iamblichans in such a way as to galvanize the inchoate religion of his forefathers? Or was this itself too ambitious a policy? Granted that both Constantine and Constantius had practised a *de facto* toleration of polytheism, Julian could probably have secured wide support had he confined himself to the revocation of hostile legislation, especially since this was accompanied by a renunciation of imperial involvement in questions of Christian dogma.[36] Instead, as a Christian once himself, Julian aspired to create a polytheist church militant which would destroy Christianity. Through his writings one can still come into contact with that most unnerving but potent of political animals, the enthusiast for an idea. But since the idea was not realized, the broad historical significance of Julian's reign is limited to the provocation of a body of polemical writing without which our knowledge of late polytheism, and of Christian insecurities, would be immeasurably poorer.

Julian's fundamental philosophical conviction was that by self-knowledge we may become like the gods (*Or.* VII.225d, IX.183a). By its 'atheistic' denial of the gods, Christianity prevented its adherents from attaining this goal, and could not therefore be assimilated (*Or.* VIII.180ab). But polytheism had imperfections too. Its philosophers were discordant and at times in error, so had to be corrected and harmonized (*Or.* VIII.162cd, IX.184c); its myths, to which Julian attached great importance, were obscure and at times rebarbative, and had to be explained in such a way that the uninitiated might through them reach a closer understanding of the divine world (*Or.* VII.216b–217d), perceiving for example in Attis' self-castration the arrest

[35] See Rougé's edition, 53–5.   [36] Amm. Marc. XXII.5.3.

of our tendency away from the One towards infinitude (*Or.* VIII.169d). Julian believed that the gods had sent him to save the empire and initiate the ignorant (*Or.* VII.227c–234c, VIII.179d–180c), so he did not hesitate to expound tradition in an original and authoritative manner, as he thought best in the light of Christianity's challenge (*Or.* VII.220ab; VIII.160a, 161c, 174b, 178d–179a). In his discourses *To the Mother of the Gods* (*Or.* VIII) and (especially) *To King Helios* (*Or.* XI, esp. 131c, 138b, 151ab), he beats out before our eyes an original theology of monotheistic tendency, an amalgam of the old polytheistic myths and the new theurgical philosophy, of the still popular cult of Sol[37] and of the mystery-theology of Julian's own personal patron Mithras, who was widely identified with Sol. Likewise in his polemical treatise against Christianity (*Against the Galilaeans*), Julian underlines the firm bonds that unite the different races of men with their national gods; but over them all he places 'the creator . . . the common father and king of all peoples' (*c. Gal.* fr. 21.115d Masaracchia; cf. Iambl. *Myst.* v.25).

In the little book *On the Gods and the World* written by Julian's close friend and adviser Saturninius Secundus Salutius, we see an attempt to distil the emperor's impassioned but not always easily comprehensible (*Or.* VIII.172d–173a) doctrine into guidelines for the priests and teachers who were to propagate the restoration. But the difficulties remain obvious. Salutius resumes Julian's exposition of the problematic Attis story, but avoids the Egyptian myths, recognizing in them a too easy target for Christian attempts to dye all the manifold strands of 'paganism' in the lurid colours that were deserved only by a few (IV). Salutius accepts the doctrines of theurgy, and perceives the potential of a sacramental polytheism for bringing men into closer communion with the divine (XV); but he seems only half committed, failing to escape from the philosophical élite's conviction that it alone can be truly pious (I, XIII), and showing lordly indifference to the spread of Christianity, on the grounds that it cannot touch the gods themselves (XVIII).

Julian himself, though, hoped to move the common man, in the first place by restoring the gods' traditional public rites. 'By plain and formal decrees he ordered the temples to be opened, victims brought to the altars and the worship of the gods restored' (Amm. Marc. XXII.5.2, tr. Rolfe). 'Some temples he built, others he restored, while he furnished others with statues. People who had built houses for themselves from the stones of the temples began to contribute money. You might have seen pillars carried by boat or by waggon for our plundered gods' (Lib. *Or.* XVIII.126, tr. Norman). The temples' lost incomes were restored along with their priests' privileges and immunities, while abuses in their administration and liturgy were corrected.[38] In a series of pastoral letters addressed to provincial high priests

---

[37] Salzman, *On Roman Time* 127, 149–153.   [38] *C.Th.* v.13.3, x.1.8; Sozom. *HE* v.3.1–2.

(esp. *Ep.* 84, 89), Julian expounded his vision of a church endowed with local infrastructures, an independent and professional hierarchy capable of teaching and setting personal example to the ordinary faithful, a regular liturgy to refresh the soul, and a sensitivity to the material and bodily needs of the poor. To a limited extent, these ideas may even have been translated into practice: Augustine alludes to philosophical interpretations of the old myths being 'read to people gathered in the temples yesterday and the day before yesterday' (*Ep.* 91.5, cf. 8). But the establishment of a polytheist church, as Julian clearly understood, presupposed the reversal of the impoverishment and subordination to central control that had undermined the cities, their councils, learned men and gods, since the high point of their fortunes in the second and early third centuries. It also required a break with the old-fashioned politically involved and socially élite priesthoods of the Graeco-Roman *poleis*.

Julian could call on a number of personal collaborators, philosophers like himself, to assist in the central formulation and local propagation of his cultural revolution. Some, such as Chrysanthius, he appointed local high priests, with authority to appoint other priests and supervise all matters of cult. Others he kept beside him, such as Maximus, who quite probably played a leading part in formulating the edict of 362 by which Christians were banned from teaching what they did not believe in – Homer and Hesiod, for example, with their host of gods. Reaction to this edict was sharply negative, and points to a certain lack of common sense or at least common touch that was one of the reasons for Julian's failure.

When Julian died, the army's first reaction was to offer the succession to another polytheist, the praetorian prefect Saturninius Secundus Salutius. Officialdom in general still at this time and for decades to come contained a polytheist element,[39] so there was nothing intrinsically shocking in the idea of an emperor with such beliefs, especially one who belonged, as Julian did, to the house of Constantine and who had already been a highly visible and successful Caesar. What *was* shocking about Julian was his zealously ideological approach to his faith (part perhaps of his Christian heritage),[40] along with his indiscretion, both personal and political. There was, for example, nothing in principle strange about inviting intellectuals to court; but Julian made a point of behaving to them with complete familiarity, and Maximus, for one, had no idea how to deal with that: he soon made enemies by his pomposity and showy way of dressing. Even Julian's warm admirer Eunapius observes of Maximus and another of Aedesius' pupils, Priscus, that 'they had their share of wisdom, but very little experience of politics

[39] Lib. *Or.* xxx.53; Prudent. *C. Symm.* 1.161–21. The size of this element is disputed. Barnes (1989) 311–21 produces figures for the period 317–61 that show already a clear majority of Christians over polytheists, but neglects the significance of the numerous indeterminates.

[40] O'Donnell (1979), esp. 52–3.

and public affairs' (*Hist.* fr. 19 Müller-Dindorf = 25.4 Blockley) – almost the same words he attributes to the empress Eusebia when she recommended Julian himself to Constantius, with 'arrière-pensée machiavélique', for the job of Caesar (*ap.* Zos. III.1.3; cf. Paschoud's n. *ad loc.*). As for Julian's zealotry, it led him in his last months into unreason and even impiety, as he defied his own gods' warnings against the Persian expedition. This arrogance he had learned from Maximus; their embryonic church had no means by which to restrain its all-powerful head; and the objections of the Etruscan diviners were easily overruled.[41] Julian failed to realize that the private individual's habit of speaking in tones of intimacy or even reproof to his gods[42] could only with extreme circumspection be replicated on the public stage. But these – and the brief eighteen months for which he reigned – are relatively superficial reasons for the collapse of Julian's plans. Far more significant was the cities' lack of interest and initiative – their indifference, laziness and vulgarity that Julian saw as the besetting sins of polytheists in his generation (*C. Galil.* fr. 3.43b, 58.238b Masaracchia). Julian was perfectly aware of the problem with the cities (see pp. 541–2 above; cf. p. 550 below). In his enthusiasm, though, he may not have noticed how incompatible his own cultic *dirigisme* was with the *polis*-centred character of traditional religion. A number of city councils simply refused to take any notice of the emperor's wish that the temples and their cults be restored,[43] confirming what Julian's own pastoral letters both imply by their imitation of the church's example, and explicitly accept (e.g. *Ep.* 84.429d–430a) – namely, that the initiative in religious matters had finally passed to Christianity, even in those social milieux whose vested interest in the survival of the old religion, its cults and priesthoods and festivals, was the strongest.

III. JOVIAN TO THEODOSIUS II: THE ATTRITION OF POLYTHEISM

Though there was some anti-polytheist reaction immediately after Julian's death, his successor Jovian (363–4) espoused a 'Constantinian' policy of broad toleration which permitted, according to Themistius (*Or.* v.70b), 'legal [i.e. non-magical] sacrifices'.[44] In practice Valens (emperor in the east, 364–78) and his brother Valentinian (emperor in the west, 364–75) likewise tolerated public cult of the gods, though they took back the properties Julian had returned to the temples,[45] and by a lost law of unknown

[41] Amm. Marc. XXIII.5.10–11, XXV.2.7–8; Eunap. *V. Soph.* VII.3.9–13 (on Maximus).
[42] To Veyne (1986) 261–2, add Iambl. *Myst.* VI.5–7.
[43] E.g. Jul., Bidez and Cumont (1922) nos. 91 (Nisibis), 125 (Caesarea of Cappadocia). Kotula (1994) points out that not a few cities put up inscriptions lauding Julian's restoration – but they may have been as insincere as the people of Batnae (above, p. 542).   [44] Dagron, 'Thémistios' 164–75.
[45] Amm. Marc. XXX.9.5; above, n. 38.

date banned animal sacrifices and permitted only the burning of incense.[46] Nocturnal sacrifices were also forbidden, primarily in order to discourage divinatory magic.[47] Divination had always been feared by those in power, and Ammianus chillingly recounts Constantius' and Valens' efforts to suppress it. But magic was indiscriminate in its exploitation of the gods, and therefore confessionally neutral. Those accused of its practice might be polytheists, Christians or 'heretics',[48] and the trials Ammianus describes, though they involved prominent adherents of the old religion like Maximus of Ephesus, did not aim to eliminate polytheists as such, though they may at times have been manipulated to that end. Some such manipulation was evidently feared in Greece, where the proconsul of Achaea, Vettius Agorius Praetextatus, obtained exemption from the ban on nocturnal sacrifices for the sake of the mystery-cults to which the Greeks attached such significance.[49] This period of phoney war, due partly to the shock people still felt at the surprise Julian had sprung, and partly to distraction caused by internal ecclesiastical feuding, continued into the 380s, while Theodosius I fought to re-establish the Nicene position against the Arians Valens had favoured. Significantly, five constitutions from the period 381–91 deal with the problem of apostates from Christianity.[50] But Theodosius felt free to move decisively against polytheism, the lesser threat, only at the end of his reign.[51] A glance round the empire during the 360s to 380s reveals wide variation in the condition of polytheism, depending on geographical and political factors and the disposition of local governors and bishops. The only generalization that can be offered is that there was no systematic persecution.

In his *Oration* xxx, *For the Temples*, the Antiochene rhetor Libanius succinctly describes official policy during the 380s. Theodosius has confirmed the ban on animal sacrifice issued by Valens and Valentinian; but, Libanius continues, addressing the emperor,

You have neither ordered the closure of temples nor banned entrance to them. From the temples and altars you have banished neither fire nor incense nor the offerings of other perfumes. (*Or.* xxx.8, tr. Norman; cf 52–3 and Zos. IV.29.2)

Theodosius himself conceded, at much the same time as Libanius was writing, that public polytheism, the 'templa et templorum sollemnia', still

---

[46] Lib. *Or.* xxx.7.   [47] *C.Th.* IX.16.7–8.
[48] See respectively Marc. Diac. *V. Porph.* 71 (a source to be used with reserve, though its core is probably genuine: Nau (1929–30); Peeters (1941), esp. 97; Trombley, *Hellenic Religion* 1.246–82); Jer. *V. Hil.* XI.12, XXIII.5; *C.Th.* XVI.5.34. The *C.Th.* carefully distinguishes laws 'de maleficis et mathematicis' (IX.16) from those 'de paganis, sacrificiis et templis' (XVI.10). That Themistius partially admits the vulgar Christian equation of magic with polytheism (*Or.* v.70b) perhaps reflects his antipathy towards theurgical Platonism. Brown, *Religion and Society* 128 (and cf. 126), rightly holds that the magic trials reflect social tensions rather than fear of polytheism.   [49] Zos. IV.3.2–3.   [50] *C.Th.* XVI.7.1–5.
[51] A neglected exception is *CJ* XI.66.4 of 383, confiscating all temple estates; cf. *PLRE* I, 'Nebridius 2', and *C.Th.* XVI.10.20.1.

existed (*C.Th.* XII.1.112, dated 386). This was especially true in rural areas: the relatively thorough archaeological investigation of the Trier region, for example, has shown how some village sanctuaries succumbed in the later third and fourth centuries to barbarian incursion and Christian hostility, while others continued to function even into the fifth century. In the sixth century there were still plenty of Treveran polytheists for St Vulfolaic the Lombard to convert.[52] Of course, what Theodosius had mainly in mind was the cities, and in particular those major centres whose polytheist élites he had not yet dared alienate. Among these, Rome and Alexandria most conspicuously maintained their public rites.[53] But the feasts of the old gods were no longer observed officially;[54] Gratian became the first emperor to repudiate the title Pontifex Maximus, with the result that vacant official priesthoods could no longer be filled; and he also withdrew state subsidies and immunities from the polytheist cults, even those of Rome itself.[55] Such imperial indifference dampened both civic and – inevitably, if less directly – private devotion.

In many cases the public cults, whether official or unofficial, were, if not defunct, then at least moribund. In Syria, for example, where the limestone massif that rises just north of Apamea and reaches as far as Beroea to the north-east and Antioch to the north-west provides a virtually unique example of a late antique rural landscape only recently reoccupied, the remains are overwhelmingly Christian. They include such rarities as dated churches from the fourth century, while surviving temples hardly ever postdate the second century and are few in number, the rest having been destroyed by the roaming monkish bands denounced by Libanius, *For the Temples*.[56] Eunapius describes his native Sardis as having become a virtually Christian city.[57] Though Julian's teacher Chrysanthius had been its high priest during his pupil's reign, and continued thereafter to play an honoured role in its life, he had avoided provoking the Christians and done little to stop the ruin of its sanctuaries. Eunapius mentions a senior imperial official of polytheist sympathies who, probably in the reign of Theodosius I, restored some of Sardis' temples, built improvised altars and even sacrificed publicly for puposes of divination, apparently without encountering serious opposition. Likewise in Numidia, two successive governors under Valentinian actively encouraged the cult of the old gods to an extent that had not been seen in Africa since Diocletian; while firm official moves against the African temples were postponed until 399, when Honorius sent the counts Gaudentius and Jovius to close officially the temples of Carthage.[58] But if polytheist governors could act outside the law and delay

---

[52] Heinen (1985) 343–4, 364–5, 419–20; Greg. Tur. *HE* VIII.15.   [53] Lib. *Or.* XXX.33, 35.
[54] *C.Th.* 11.8 ('de feriis').   [55] Noethlichs (1986) 1159–60.
[56] Tchalenko, *Villages* I.13–16; II, pl. VII, XXXIV–XXXV, CLIII; III.34–6; Peña *et al.* (1987) 7.
[57] Eunap. *V. Soph.* XXIII.2.7–8, 4, confirmed by excavation: Foss (1976) 28, 37–8, 48.
[58] Lepelley, *Cités* I.348–9, 353.

application of what was clearly the drift, if not yet the letter, of imperial policy, an especially zealous Christian official could do the opposite. The praetorian prefect of the East from 384 to 388, Maternus Cynegius, used his position to sponsor illegal attacks on polytheists and their temples 'from the Nile to the Bosphorus' (Lib. *Or.* XLIX.3), quite possibly with Theodosius' tacit support.[59] Bishops and monks were even more effective enemies of the temples, as they knew better the local situation, could act 'spontaneously', and would hardly be punished for actions which offended only the letter of the law.[60] About the year 386, for example, we find bishop Marcellus of Apamea encompassing, in that famous centre of polytheist religion and philosophy, the destruction of the temple of Zeus. The local bishop, Theophilus, also took the initiative in the assault on the Alexandrian temple of Serapis in (probably) 391. This was a world-famous holy place, and its destruction made a deep impression. The polytheists of Alexandria had mobilized and run to the defence of their gods; and the secular arm had quelled the uprising by force. The cult-statues and offerings were destroyed, and a church was built on the site of the temple – a method of neutralizing the divine powers inherent in polytheist holy places that was to become increasingly common.

As for Rome, the polytheist party in the senate, led by such as Vettius Agorius Praetextatus, Quintus Aurelius Symmachus and Virius Nicomachus Flavianus, contrived until the 380s not only to retain, in all probability, a majority,[61] but also to maintain public sacrifices and, at public expense, to restore and embellish temples, so that the Eternal City came to seem a rallying-point for beleaguered polytheists even in the Greek east.[62] It was not unusual elsewhere in the empire for the vested interests of the curial élites to act as a dyke that kept the public face of polytheism from complete submersion by Christianity's incoming tide – as much in the country, thanks to the tenant's fear of his landlord, as in the city.[63] But the Roman senator possessed a unique combination of wealth and proximity to power – indeed, in the emperor's absence from the old capital, the senate incarnated Rome, while its polytheist members stood firm before the altars of the Capitoline gods, and proclaimed that theirs was still the religion of the state. In the New Rome, polytheism had no such place.

The polytheists of Old Rome were careful to underline their attachment to the whole of their tradition, Roman, Greek and Oriental. Praetextatus' tomb proclaims him

[59] Fowden (1978) 62–6.
[60] Fowden (1978), esp. 64–7 (Marcellus of Apamea), 69–71 (Alexandrian Serapeum; see also Baldini (1985)).   [61] Wytzes (1977) 296–300.
[62] Lib. *Or.* XXX.33; Ward-Perkins, *Public Building* 85–91; Dagron, '*Thémistios*' 191–5, 197–8.
[63] E.g. Fowden (1978) 71; Lepelley, *Cités* I.326, 361.

augur, priest of Vesta, priest of Sol, *quindecemvir*, *curialis* of Hercules, consecrated
to Liber and in the Eleusinian [mysteries], hierophant [of Hecate at Aegina], *neo-
corus* [i.e. priest of Serapis], initiate of the taurobolium [of Cybele], Father of
Fathers [i.e. initiate of Mithras]

(*ILS* 1259)

while his wife, Fabia Aconia Paulina, was

consecrated at Eleusis to the god Iacchus, Ceres and Cora, consecrated at Lerna
to the god Liber, Ceres and Cora, consecrated to the goddesses at Aegina, initiate
of the taurobolium [of Cybele] and of Isis, hierophant of the goddess Hecate and
consecrated to the Greek goddess Ceres [i.e. Demeter].

(*ILS* 1260)

Here too the Romans of Rome had their provincial analogues: at Lepcis
Magna, probably under Constantine, we find a local dignitary, T. Flavius
Vibianus, who was *flamen perpetuus, pontifex* and *praefectus omnium sacrorum* in
the civic cults, Punic and Graeco-Roman, and priest of the province of
Tripolitania, but also held priesthoods of the Mother of the Gods and of
the Lavinian Laurentes, a purely Roman cult.[64] The reason for this
accumulation of diverse priesthoods, so characteristic of the fourth
century, is to be found in the demise of the emperor cult, or rather its transformation into a cult in which Christians too could participate and even
hold priesthoods.[65] Now that the emperor was a Christian, somebody else
had to stand for the potential unity of the old religion. That role might be
assumed by the social élite, especially in that city which had always seen
itself by right of conquest, and was now insistently proclaimed by polytheists locked in combat with the enemy within, as the 'templum mundi totius'
(Amm. Marc. XVII.4.13); or by a holy man such as was Proclus in fifth-
century Athens, 'hierophant of the whole world in common' (Marin. *V.
Procl.* 19). Here, as in Julian's writings, we see at work a certain tendency
towards a more universalist, coherent view of polytheism. But these tendencies did not galvanize the inchoate old religion into becoming a force
that could withstand Christianity. The centre of the world had moved to the
Bosphorus; the polytheism of late-fourth-century Rome was *vitesse acquise*,
not (as is often claimed) a revival; and its high points were not initiatives but
reactions, as when Symmachus eloquently but ineffectively deplored
Gratian's disestablishment of the old gods and removal of the altar of
Victory from the senate house,[66] or Nicomachus Flavianus achieved
concessions, mainly financial, for Rome's now outlawed polytheist cults
from the usurper Eugenius (392–4), not himself one of their adepts.[67]

---

[64] *IRT* 567–8; Lepelley, *Cités* II.347–8, and cf. I.349.
[65] See Fowden (1993) 48–9, and in general ch. 2 on universalist tendencies in late polytheism.
[66] Symm. *Rel.* III.
[67] Szidat (1979), rejecting the traditional view of Eugenius' reign as a polytheist 'revival'.

In 391 Theodosius gave up the pretence that subordinates' (even Cynegius') energies, or his own calls for the universal adoption of catholic Christianity,[68] would ensure the demise of ancient pieties. 'No person', he ordered, 'shall be granted the right to perform sacrifices; no person shall go around the temples; no person shall revere the shrines' (*C.Th.* XVI.10.11). Of the three anti-polytheist constitutions (*C.Th.* XVI.10.10–12) issued in 391–2, the first is addressed to Ceionius Rufius Albinus, the learned polytheist prefect of the city of Rome, and the second to the authorities at Alexandria. The two cities thus singled out were potent symbols, both of catholic Christian dogma[69] and, embarrassingly, of surviving polytheism. But the constitutions were also intended for universal application. And they were much more thorough than earlier ones – in particular, all manner of sacrifice was now banned, by night or day, in temple, house or field, and whether or not for purposes of divination. As for 'more secret wickedness', the less accessible of the myriad springs of *dynamis*,

no person ... shall venerate his *lar* with fire, his *penates* with fragrant odours; he shall not burn lights to them, place incense before them, or suspend wreaths for them ... If any person should venerate, by placing incense before them, images made by the work of mortals ... and if, in a ridiculous manner, he should suddenly fear the effigies which he himself has formed, or should bind a tree with fillets, or should erect an altar of turf that he has dug up, or should attempt to honour vain images with the offering of a gift ... such person, as one guilty of the violation of religion, shall be punished by the forfeiture of that house or landholding in which it is proved that he served a pagan superstition.

(*C.Th.* XVI.10.12)

In cataloguing these sources of power in order to suppress them, this text describes better than any other the personal piety of the late fourth century. To it we may add Rufinus' report[70] of how, after the destruction of the Serapeum, the busts of Serapis that protected the walls, doorways and windows of every house in Alexandria were chipped off and replaced by crosses, painted to begin with, but soon to be carved, as one can still see in the abandoned villages of northern Syria.

Theodosius I's constitutions of 391–2 were part of the necessary legal substructures of the fully fledged Christian state, and caused him to be regarded as a second Constantine – for good by ecclesiastical historians such as Rufinus, for ill by polytheists like Zosimus. To begin with, it is true, the destruction of temples was not explicitly enjoined, partly because it was happening anyway,[71] and partly out of a feeling that, in the cities, temples ought to be preserved as 'ornaments of public works' (*C.Th.* XVI.10.15 and cf. 18, both dated 399). But countryside shrines were deemed less decorative, and peasants less easy to keep an eye on:

---

[68] *C.Th.* XVI.1.2 (380).   [69] *Ibid.*   [70] Rufin, *HE* 11.29.   [71] *C.Th.* XV.1.36.

If there should be any temples in the country districts, they shall be torn down without disturbance or tumult. For when they are torn down and removed, the material basis for all superstition will be destroyed.

(*C.Th.* XVI.10.16, also dated 399)

Eventually, the indiscriminate destruction of temples was commanded (*C.Th.* XVI.10.25, of 435). This constitution is the last of no less than thirteen issued between the death of Theodosius I and the end of the period covered by the Theodosian Code, and grouped in the section entitled 'On pagans, sacrifices and temples'.[72] Those just quoted prove official awareness that polytheism could still need subtle handling, according to local circumstance. Of this, more will be said in the next section. The other constitutions tend to repeat or extend legislation already in place, and rail against those who fail to execute it. New, so far as we are aware, is the grant to bishops of authority to enforce such legislation (*C.Th.* XVI.10.19, of 407/8; see also IX.16.12, of 409), the exclusion of polytheists from imperial service (XVI.10.21, of 415/16 – but see already XVI.5.42, of 408), and the imposition of exile on those caught sacrificing (XVI.10.23, of 423). Theodosius I's measures had been no panacea; but Theodosius II ruled an empire that was wholly intolerable for 'pagans' to live in – at least on paper.

IV. POLYTHEIST RESISTANCES

The constitutions of 391–2 coincided with a major polytheist–Christian crisis in Alexandria and a more generally difficult period at Rome, and helped to focus pressure already building up on the old religion in other cities too. At Gaza, bishop Porphyry tried for some years to get the emperor Arcadius to apply his own laws to the city's patron, Zeus Marnas. Arcadius feared to offend Gaza's powerful polytheist community, and prevaricated until 402, when he finally sent a high official and a force of soldiers to demolish the temple and build a church on its site.[73] Meanwhile, in 399 Honorius closed Carthage's temple of Caelestis, which a few years later was turned into a church. But then a prophet foretold that the building would soon return to its rightful owner, and the authorities were panicked into demolishing it (421).[74] Behind this remarkable story one senses a considerable and powerful polytheist remnant. In other cities that remnant's resistance was far more durable. At Heliopolis (Baalbek) in Lebanon, the wealthy and influential polytheist section of the community could still in the later sixth century make life difficult for the Christians, who were 'few and destitute' (Joh. Eph. *HE* III.3.27). At Mesopotamian Harran (Carrhae), the old order continued as if nothing had happened. The Harranians are a unique instance of a polytheist community that main-

---

[72] See also *C.Th.* XVI.5.43, 46, 63.   [73] Marc. Diac. *V. Porph.*   [74] Lepelley, *Cités* I.353, II.42–4.

tained its cultural tradition intact, along with temples and priesthood, well into the Islamic period.[75] Explanations for this are to be found in the proximity of an ultrasensitive frontier, and the benevolence Iran showed towards a minority community right on Byzantium's threshold;[76] and in the fact that the Harranians were an urban group with a clear-cut self-image and a highly educated élite. Paradoxically, the intense Christianity of neighbouring Edessa will have helped too, enabling the Harranians to be seen as a harmless curiosity rather than a regional power. The polytheists of Gaza also had advantages: strategic position, money and a strong Christian community at neighbouring Maiumas.[77] What made the difference was the impetus Porphyry gave to the previously quiescent local Christians. Otherwise the emperor would no more have intervened at Gaza than he did at Harran.

Besides the usually short-term resistance to Christianity mounted by groups more or less representative of a city, even if a minority within it, and focused on the preservation of public places of worship, there were longer-term resistances offered by educated élites concerned with the preservation of something less tangible, a tradition of thought and personal conduct as well as of cult.[78] But the resistance of the intellectuals occurred at widely varying intensities. Society continued to esteem learning, while insisting that its context be Christian. The compromises or accommodations that resulted puzzle those who think in terms of conflict or of dramatic conversion. In that perspective, a Firmicus Maternus may seem straightforward enough: he wrote on astrology as a polytheist (*Mathesis, c.* 335–7), and violently against polytheism as a Christian (*On the Error of Profane Religions, c.* 346). But for all we know, he may have been a lukewarm polytheist and a Christian of convenience. At least Firmicus conveys some sense of having made a transition, unlike the fifth-century Egyptian poet Nonnus, who wrote a verse paraphrase of St John's Gospel as well as an epic on Dionysus, yet leaves us unsure whether he became or was born a Christian. And then there was the Cyrenaican landowner Synesius, who became bishop of Ptolemais only after being exempted from subscribing to doctrines incompatible with his Platonist education.[79] Synesius was unusual only for his explicit acknowledgement of the conflict, which was and remained familiar to Christians who wished to expound their faith in the light of philosophy. Origen, Arius, Evagrius Ponticus, Nemesius of Emesa, John of Apamea and John Philoponus are just a few examples of Christian intellectuals who, even when not actually condemned by the church, have been marginalized within the patristic canon or forced to accept the reattribution of their works to more respectable authors.

[75] Rochow (1978) 233–6.   [76] Procop. *BP* 11.13.7.   [77] Glucker (1987) 12–13, 43–6, 86–94.
[78] For the background of this and the following paragraphs see Fowden (1982), and relevant entries in *PLRE*.   [79] Syn. *Ep.* 105.

As for the pure 'succession' (*diadochē*) of uncompromising polytheist Platonists, it lacked in the aftermath of Julian's death the topographic focus that Rome, Apamea or Pergamum had once afforded, not to mention the institutional focus provided by the synagogue or the church. Inevitably it drifted to society's margins; and that is the note on which Eunapius concludes his collection of philosophical biographies, without allusion to the state of philosophical teaching in Alexandria or Athens at the time he was writing. Yet both of these cities played a significant part in the preservation of polytheist Platonism through the fifth century.

At Alexandria, the murder of Hypatia in 415 by a Christian mob was a signal to the city's philosophers quite as unambiguous as that sent to the polytheist community at large by the destruction of the Serapeum. Hypatia does not at first seem the sort of person to have posed a serious threat to the powerful Alexandrian church.[80] Like her father Theon, she was absorbed in the study of mathematics and astronomy. Her circle included many Christians, notable among whom was the future bishop Synesius. Although Synesius was well acquainted with the *Chaldaean Oracles*, neither he nor Hypatia seems to have had any special commitment to theurgy or the teachings of Iamblichus. Synesius' *Dion* proclaims the studied moderation of a circle acutely sensitive to criticism from enthusiasts both polytheist and Christian, Platonist and monastic, who doubted the usefulness of the cultivated gentleman's wide *paideia* and, like Icarus, believed that with one leap they might reach heaven and obtain knowledge of God (*Dion* 10–11). But Hypatia's teaching was popular among the Alexandrian élite; and those influential elements within the church who were opposed to compromise clearly saw a real threat in those who occupied with conviction rather than by default the area between hard-line polytheism and hard-line Christianity. Their terror tactics were successful. Synesius' contemporary Hierocles taught philosophy at Alexandria and stood firmly in the Iamblichan tradition.[81] But he too suffered violence for his doctrines; and the fact that his successors' voluminous literary production consists largely of commentaries on Aristotle suggests that they knew how to counter threat with tact.

At Athens too, Christianity was in the ascendant, but the Platonists occupied a strong position within the élite of this provincial city, whose atmosphere was so different from that of metropolitan and unruly Alexandria. It was during the lifetime of Hierocles' teacher, the Athenian Plutarch (*c.* 350–*c.* 432), that Iamblichanism at last established itself in this conservative milieu, which now became a refuge for those who saw philosophy as indissociable from the (at least surreptitious) practice of polytheist cult.

---

[80] On Hypatia and Synesius see Cameron and Long, *Barbarians and Politics* 39–62.
[81] O'Meara (1989) 109–18.

Plutarch was the offspring of one of the local learned dynasties. Conventionally enough, he wrote commentaries on Plato and Aristotle; but he also passed on much theurgical lore from his grandfather, the hierophant Nestorius, to his own daughter Asclepigenia. Apart from Hierocles, Plutarch's best-known pupils were Syrianus and, at the very end of his life, Proclus, who was to become late Athenian Platonism's brightest star. As we learn from his biography by Marinus, Proclus was able to study Aristotle and Plato with Syrianus, but also to make a start on the Orphic and Chaldaean writings; while Asclepigenia initiated him into the arcane rituals of theurgy. Both Syrianus and Proclus had a firm commitment to collecting and synthesizing the doctrines of the Greeks and, in Proclus' case, of the barbarians too. Proclus inherited the house that Syrianus and Plutarch had lived in; and one could hardly want clearer proof that here, at last, an Iamblichan *diadochē* had re-established itself in an appropriate physical milieu.

It can, then, be readily understood that the date 425 has no significance in the context of the very gradual and uneven fading away of the polytheist world during the fifth century. To describe this process, 'conversion' is no less unfortunate a term than 'conflict'. In communities but recently thrown into disarray by attacks on their sanctuaries, and in individuals too, conversion might be a purely external conformity, an either more or less selfconscious crypto-polytheism from which stress easily provoked return to the old, well-tried gods.[82] To assume that the tearing down of temples would destroy 'the material basis for all superstitition' (*C.Th.* xvi.10.16) had been naïve; but anyway there were still plenty of temples to be seen in the fifth century, such as Apollo-Sarpedonius' oracle near Seleucia on the Cilician coast, whose continuing hold on its clientele was in the 440s a living reality for the author of the *Miracles* of its industrious competitor, St Thecla.[83] This fifth-century survival of polytheism[84] was a provincial phenomenon, the product – for example, at Athens and in part at Harran too – of isolation from power-centres. Even more specifically, the survival of polytheism was a rural phenomenon. The big early-fifth-century mopping-up operations against polytheism were in the countryside – those of John Chrysostom, bishop of Constantinople, and his bands of monks in Phoenicia, and Hypatius, abbot of a monastery near Chalcedon, in Bithynia.[85] In the Tripolitanian predesert, the Libyo-Punic polytheists of Ghirza, safely remote from the Christianized coast, were still building temples in the fourth century, and maintained their cults into the sixth, perhaps indeed much longer.[86] The same applies to other Saharan oases

---

[82] *C.Th.* xvi.7 ('de apostatis'); Eunap. *V. Soph.* vii.6.11; Mathisen (1986) 126–7. On crypto-polytheism (a little-researched subject) see e.g. Lib. *Or.* xxx.28; Eunap. fr. 48.2 Blockley; Dagron (1978) 92–3. [83] Dagron (1978), esp. 80–94. [84] Much material is assembled by Kaegi (1982) v. [85] Fowden (1978) 75–6. [86] Brogan and Smith (1984), esp. 36, 230–2.

such as Ghadamès and Augila;[87] while the most famous of all polytheist survivals along Rome's southern frontier, the great temple of Isis at Philae on the Nile, owed its fortune to diplomacy as much as remoteness, since it was a useful means by which to maintain contact with and influence over the unruly tribes of Nubia.[88]

The full extent of polytheism's resilience only became clear when Justinian launched a new wave of measures against it. Indeed, Justinian was the first emperor since the end of the fourth century to recognize the essentially local, non-universal character of polytheism by taking a series of measures against specific areas and even individual cult-centres, rather than promulgating general laws for empire-wide application. He commanded a massive campaign of forcible conversion in the countryside of western Asia Minor,[89] put an end to the frontier polytheism of Ghadames, Augila and perhaps Ghirza, and of the Tzani in Iberia,[90] and closed the temple of Isis at Philae; while Theodora converted the Nubians beyond the frontier to Monophysite Christianity.[91] And by banning in 529 all teaching conducted by polytheists, the emperor made a start on the urban resistances too.[92] The year 529, far from being, as traditionally held, the last date in the history of polytheism, simply marked the first official recognition of what apologists and bishops had been proclaiming for generations: that polytheism was a force within, a state of mind as much as a physical context or a ritual. *Contra idola facilius templa quam corda clauduntur* (Aug. *Ep.* 232.).

V. POLYTHEISM AND CHRISTIANITY

As a form of local and especially rural religion, polytheism showed remarkable powers of resistance. As a state of mind, whether the peasant's perception of the world around him, or the philosopher's doctrine, it could survive within Christianity. But polytheism had also been a public cult susceptible of formal allegiance; and it is this primarily urban religion that we have principally in mind when we talk about the Roman empire's transition from polytheism to Christianity. From the vantage-point of the fifth century, it is possible at last to generalize about this transition.

Although there is an obvious connection between the triumph of Christianity and the demise of polytheism, these were two distinct processes with independent timetables. The church had grown rapidly in the third century, and the emperor Constantine had espoused its cause. That rendered the Christianization of the empire very probable, but did not

---

[87] Procop. *Aed.* VI.2.14–20; 3.9–10.   [88] Procop. *BP* I.19.27–37.
[89] Joh. Eph. *Lives of the Eastern Saints* 40, 43, 47; *HE* III.2.44, 3.36–7.   [90] Procop. *Aed.* III.6.1–13.
[91] Joh. Eph. *HE* III.4.6–7.
[92] *CJ* I.11.10; Joh. Mal. XVIII.451 Bonn (on Athens in particular; and cf. 449, 491, on Justinian's general pursuit of polytheists among the urban élites).

accomplish the process, because polytheism continued to exist. Constantine, aware that the two religions had coexisted for centuries, never treated them as mutually exclusive, despite his increasing commitment to Christianity's claims. It is true that Constantius used harder language, which Julian duly echoed, polarizing the situation and splitting cities, households and even individual consciences along confessional lines.[93] But Constantius' preoccupation was Christian heresy; and even after Julian, Christians did not consider the destruction of polytheism to be as necessary to their survival as the purification of the church's dogma. The concerted moves that were eventually made against polytheism, in the 390s, were part of the selfconsciously orthodox Theodosian state's drive to eliminate nonconformity, not a sign of serious concern with polytheism as an independent threat. Diocletian's persecution had endangered the church's survival more than Julian's, but even it had benefited Christianity in the long run, by helping to precipitate the Constantinian revolution. And the ineffectiveness of the polytheist state's attacks on Christianity was certainly construed by its opponents as a symptom of the inner weakness of polytheism itself − its gods had been shown to be less potent than the Christian God. What then were the causes of this inner weakness?

Part of the problem lay in the old religion's highly local character and its lack of oecumenical structures or, indeed, teachings. The drawbacks of this situation had become apparent long before Constantine, and are discussed in *CAH* vol. XII. What became much clearer during the fourth century was polytheism's inability to compete with Christianity as a context for daily life and piety − and that, after all, was the old religion's essence. Indeed, polytheism was so bound up with the life-cycle, the crops and all else that mattered, that it was in some respects simply self-evident, and could just as well survive within Christianity. So thoroughly immanentist a religion could not easily be conceptualized or, therefore, defended. An inarticulate religion was forced to fight a world-view − a Gospel proclaimed and a case argued, for the Transcendent that had also, in Christ, become immanent, and remained so through the church. Intellectuals like Julian and Salutius tried hard to respond by systematizing and propagating a polytheism that included the Transcendent; but they did not move the masses, whereas Christian thinkers succeeded in turning arguments into slogans. We should entertain no illusions about how often conversion to Christianity came about unthinkingly or under duress − and increasingly one was born Christian. But still there were not a few who were forced, by the religious flux of their time, to a small moment of reflection as the water of baptism closed over them. There were good reasons for choosing Christianity, not unlike those for which some polytheists chose philosophy. It offered not

[93] Greg. Naz. *Or.* IV.75.

just a mythology, but the prospect of progress towards goals which were at once personal, and encouraged by the church community. Its gospels were accessible, not arcane as the writings of the philosophers. And it offered an understanding of God, as One, that had long beguiled polytheists far beyond the philosophical schools. Some of these had, for that reason, tried Judaism; but Judaism fatally compromised the unity of God by denying the unity of his creation, mankind, and treating truth as the preserve of one nation among many. Finally, Christianity's leaders were brilliant, unscrupulous, and not conservative. They possessed spiritual power, and knew how to transmute it into political and social power – as when, during the altar of Victory debate, Ambrose's eloquence served simply as a vehicle of logic and conviction, while Symmachus' fine language adorned wheedling and defensiveness. Handling divine power, the gods, had been polytheism's central concern; but Christianity's spiritual leaders, by accepting without demur the transcendence of God, freed themselves to become the channel and expression of divine power rather than its manipulators, and to play on this world's stage a part more autonomous and more impressive even than that of the almost but not quite divine Roman state.

CHAPTER 19

ORTHODOXY AND HERESY FROM THE DEATH OF CONSTANTINE TO THE EVE OF THE FIRST COUNCIL OF EPHESUS

HENRY CHADWICK

'Heresy' is derived from a transliteration of the ordinary Greek word for choice, *hairesis*. The word came to mean a 'school of thought', a philosophical tendency. But already in some New Testament texts it acquired a pejorative overtone for a sect or faction (e.g. Acts 5.17; 24.5; 24.15; 26.5; 1 Cor. 11.19). The term, especially after Justin in the mid second century,[1] could indicate both a deviationist doctrine and the group asserting it. From the beginning there was a considerable degree of diversity among different Christian congregations. Debate became warm when deviation from affirmations regarded by the main body as the norm appeared to threaten the possibility of salvation or to deny the goodness and power of the Creator manifest in the visible creation. The community felt threatened in essential matters of belief if one denied either the need or the possibility of redemption for humanity, or if one denied either the full humanity of the Redeemer or the full presence in him of the supreme divine power. In the fourth and fifth centuries many controversies turned on one or other of these issues.

Before Constantine's time ecclesiastical writers had come to see that some affirmations were more central than others; that there are areas where dissent can be without prejudice to these central affirmations; moreover, that one must distinguish between a heresy and a mistake. Strictly, no one

---

* Guides to the editions of early Christian authors are by E. Dekkers, *Clavis Patrum Latinorum* (3rd edn, 1995) and by M. Geerard, *Clavis Patrum Graecorum*, 5 vols. (1983–7).
   Bibliographies of the secondary literature are in B. Altaner, *Patrologie* (Freiburg, Herder), and J. Quasten, *Patrology* (with supplement by A. di Berardino). Christian authors are included in the annual bibliographies of *L'Année Philologique*, *Revue d'histoire ecclésiastique*, and *Bibliographia Patristica*. For early Latin Christianity everything of importance is noticed in *Revue des études Augustiniennes* (Paris).
   For general reference consult *Encyclopedia of the Early Church*, edited by Angelo di Berardino (English translation, Cambridge, James Clarke, 1992); *Theologische Realenzyclopaedie* (de Gruyter, Berlin – not yet complete).
   Many of the principal Christian sources are well edited in the French series *Sources Chrétiennes* with translation and notes. The main texts for the councils of Nicaea and Serdica are edited by C. H. Turner, *Ecclesiae Occidentalis Monumenta Iuris Antiquissima* (Oxford, 1899–1939). Turner also printed many supporting articles in the *Journal of Theological Studies* until his death in 1930.
   [1] Justin composed a (lost) work entitled *A Treatise against All the Heresies* (mentioned in *Apol.* 1.26.8).

could properly be deemed a heretic unless he or she was a baptized believer. The original sense of the word *hairesis* came through in the recognition that a heretic was someone deliberately, indeed obstinately, setting aside affirmations felt to be of high importance to the community. A bishop censured for heresy could ordinarily save his position and standing by submitting to the authority deciding against his views, whether council or primate speaking on behalf of a council.

Heresy is to be distinguished from schism, which is a separation and suspension of ecclesiastical communion and eucharistic sharing without this entailing deviation from accepted central affirmations of the community or from the forms of ministry through which continuity was preserved. The obvious fourth-century instance is Donatism. Although Augustine's polemic against the Donatists could sometimes plead that their separation from the *ecclesia catholica* had left them open to heretical infiltration, he nevertheless argued in the opposite direction to the effect that Donatist sacraments (especially baptism and ordination) were wholly valid, a proposition which seemed novel and went against the normal view (as held, for example, by pope Innocent I)[2] that only lay communion could be offered to former schismatics.

Since the third-century debates about the terms of readmission to be offered to those who compromised their faith in persecution, it was agreed that, in cases where scripture could be quoted on both sides in a debate, a council of bishops could rely on divine guidance to reach agreement so that the church was not torn apart by dissension. There remained some lack of clarity about the power and authority residing in a metropolitan (i.e. bishop of the metropolis of a province) or the bishops of such great cities as Rome, Alexandria and Antioch – to which the fourth century added Constantinople and the fifth century added Jerusalem. At Nicaea in 325 it was recognized that provincial metropolitans should have a veto in the election of bishops in their province, and that was an implicit recognition of a wider teaching authority. But an episcopal council or synod (in antiquity these terms, Latin and Greek respectively, are synonyms, not yet distinguished in any way) was the ordinary organ for the determining of disagreements, whether in customs, or in the discipline of clergy and laity, or in matters of doctrine. The classical form of doctrinal affirmation rested in the trinitarian baptismal profession. By Constantine's time in both east and west, the baptismal creed had been shaped to give affirmations which were simultaneously denials of gnostic heresy. This controversial pressure on the wording of the creed is strikingly apparent in the absence, in the creeds of Nicaea and Constantinople, of a clause

---

[2] *PL* xx.532A. Innocent reluctantly accepted an exception to the rule, but reaffirmed that in future the normal rule must be kept.

about the eucharist, this not being a subject of general debate in the early church.

Differences between east and west were brought into the open as a result of the doctrinal controversies. To western theologians it seemed instinctive to think of God as one and then to explain how as Father, Son and Holy Spirit he is also three. To eastern theologians the intuition was to begin by affirming Father, Son and Holy Spirit, and then to explain that, although three, they are also an undifferentiated unity. Latent here were complex questions about identity and difference. There were also differences between east and west about authority. For the west it was increasingly natural to look to St Peter's see at Rome for a final court of appeal in both teaching and jurisdiction, but without diminishing respect for episcopal synods, which were respectful to Rome but not subservient. In the Greek east an episcopal council, at which metropolitans would give a lead, was a normal organ for decisions. Greek synods expected the west to confirm, but not to constitute a court of appeal. A censured Greek bishop with no synod to appeal to and with hope for no assistance at the emperor's court (such as John Chrysostom at Constantinople in 403–4, or Theodoret of Cyrrhus in 449) would appeal to Rome for a review of his case,[3] but no rapid or immediate result could be achieved. In the majority of instances the emperor upheld a synod's decision, and (as at Nicaea in 325) imposed exile on bishops who refused to submit to the verdict of his episcopal colleagues, such being necessary to avert threats to public order from squabbles between the deposed bishop and his successor. In any event bishops expected a Christian emperor not only to suppress violent disorders but also to uphold divine truth. All the ancient oecumenical councils were called on the initiative of emperors,[4] whose ratification of the decisions was of material importance in establishing the authority of those assemblies.

It was not a new thing that with the coming of Constantine the church was troubled by conflicts between bishops and theologians to establish what was and what was not the authentic apostolic tradition. But the penetration of the church to the emperor's court and many of the ruling officials gave such conflicts a new social and political dimension. Bishops censured by synods quickly began to treat the emperor as a higher court to

---

[3] John Chrysostom appealed not only to Rome, but also to Milan and Aquileia. He had the highest estimate of St Peter's place among the twelve apostles, but never spoke of the Roman see as entrusted with a unique and universal jurisdiction. Pope Innocent I understood himself to have such a responsibility and power by virtue of his Petrine office. In practice, Rome's jurisdiction was effective only in the western provinces, which during the fourth century included Illyricum; and in the ancient church the pope did not nominate bishops outside the suburbicarian region attached to Rome.

[4] Hence the permission given for bishops to travel to synods by means of the *cursus publicus*, which obstructed secular business.

which they were entitled to appeal.[5] Those dissatisfied with an emperor's verdicts in ecclesiastical disagreements might then denounce him as a heretic.[6] On the other side, there were always to be those for whom the ultimate power of decision was located in the emperor and who were content to follow the direction laid down by the secular power. 'Secular' is here an unsympathetic epithet, since the emperor's office was understood as a divine commission to protect the church from error and schism, with the corollary that toleration of such defects in the church would bring the danger of calamity to the empire.

The impression that the Christians of this age did little but harass one another is of course illusory. The ascetics withdrawn in their monastic communities were not much sucked into the theological controversies before the fifth century. Many texts attest other activities such as the exposition of holy scripture, preaching, prayer and liturgy, and social action for the poor and wretched. But debates about the nature of orthodoxy loom large in the principal sources. As is normal in such cases, the winners wrote most of the history, but not all of it, and a surprising amount of good evidence survives to tell us about the beliefs and affirmations of those who finally lost and were marginalized. The revisionists are not entirely silent for us.

Constantine the Great, convinced that his military victories over successive colleagues were granted by the 'God of the Christians', nursed high aspirations that the church would not only support him loyally but also be a source of unity and reconciliation within and beyond the frontiers of the empire. It was a body with a tightly knit episcopal structure, yet with a mission of universality and influential writers who believed in a providential destiny for the empire and for a believing emperor. Such language was congenial to a strong man convinced that heaven was using him for a grand design to unite not only an empire racked by civil wars but also nations beyond the frontier in one faith and Roman ethic. Shocks soon came. In 313 his agreement on religious toleration with his pagan colleague Licinius at once met a painful split in the North African churches caused by the Donatist schism. Elimination of Licinius in 324 brought Constantine to the east with hopes that here, with churches focused on the Holy Land, he might find unity and could offer himself for baptism in the Jordan. He found the Greek churches riven with controversy about an Alexandrian presbyter, Arius, excommunicated by his bishop Alexander for denying Christ to be fully divine. Arius was understood to teach that, just as a human

---

[5] Greek canon law of the fourth century deplored this. Jerome, however, could take it for granted that an imperial rescript could reverse the decision of the episcopal synod (*Apol. contra Rufinum* III.18).

[6] The zealot anti-Arian Lucifer of Calaris (Cagliari) could say to Constantius: 'Do not take it as an insult if I call you precursor of Antichrist' (*De non parcendo in Deum delinquentibus* 25, *CSEL* XIV.262.28). Athan. *Hist. Ar.* LXXVII.

son is later in time than his father and obedient to him, so also the Son of God is posterior and subordinate to the Father, having his origin in the Father's will so that he might mediate between the transcendent Absolute and this created world; so the Father is 'true God', while the Son has the divine title by grace, almost by courtesy, in virtue of his participation in divine substance (*ousia*). In principle the Son could have erred, but by determination of his will he never did so. The Son grew in wisdom, suffered temptation, wept, did not know the time of the End, experienced dereliction on the cross. Therefore the difference between Father and Son is as important a truth as their affinity. One must sharply distinguish the divine Triad, distinct from one another in their essential being.

Bishop Alexander of Alexandria was disliked by Eusebius, bishop of Nicomedia, the principal residence of the eastern Augustus. Eusebius supported Arius. Constantine had a conflagration on his hands.

Arius and Eusebius of Nicomedia scorned the notion that the Son could be said to be 'identical in essence' (*homoousios*) with the Father. Thereby they offered their opponents the word needed to crush them. At the large council of Nicaea in 325 Constantine achieved an astonishing success in winning the signatures of almost all the 220 bishops present[7] to the conciliar creed and canons. Even Eusebius of Nicomedia signed. Two Libyan bishops refused and were exiled: the sixth canon subjected them to the jurisdiction of Alexandria. The creed affirmed that the Son is identical in *ousia* with the Father, derived from the Father's *ousia*. The appended anathema condemned propositions attributed to Arius, viz. that the Son belongs to the creaturely order, is created out of nothing and morally mutable, and is of a distinct '*hypostasis* or *ousia*'.

This last phrase caused a little difficulty to learned bishops like Eusebius of Caesarea, the church historian and biblical scholar, who had learnt from Origen that, to avert the doctrine of Sabellius that Father, Son and Spirit are no more than three human names for God in whom there is no differentiation, it is necessary to say that the divine Triad is 'three *hypostaseis*'. The Nicene creed and anathema were more naturally interpreted to mean that the Triad is one *ousia* and a single *hypostasis*. The Roman legates sent to Nicaea by pope Silvester would have understood the Triad to be, in Tertullian's language, 'three *personae* in a single *substantia*', and *substantia* would be the equivalent of *hypostasis*.

Within the spectrum of theological doctrine represented at Nicaea, Eusebius of Caesarea and his friends needed to gloss the creed as allowing for Origen's language of three *hypostaseis*. But among the Greek bishops there were important figures highly critical of Origen's doctrinal legacy, in

---

[7] Concern to magnify the authority of the council led to claims for a larger number, at first 300, from which it was easy to produce 318, a sacred number symbolizing the 'Cross of Jesus' (Epistle of Barnabas 9.8), and the number of Abraham's servants in Gen. 14.

particular Eustathius, bishop of Antioch-on-the-Orontes, and Marcellus, bishop of Ancyra (Ankara), who were both ill content that Eusebius of Caesarea and his friends should find it possible to sign the creed and the attached anathema.

Constantine regarded the creed of Nicaea as the sufficient criterion of orthodox faith for the church in his empire, and was displeased with bishops who urged that it had defects or inadequacies. Eustathius of Antioch unwisely complained of the emperor's policy of comprehensiveness, allowed himself to utter critical comment on the emperor's mother Helena on her pilgrimage to the Holy Land, and was soon deposed from his see to go into exile.[8] He left behind him at Antioch a small congregation of faithful upholders of the Nicene creed who would not hold communion with his successors. Marcellus of Ancyra addressed to the emperor a polemical attack on Eusebius of Caesarea, Eusebius of Nicomedia and other members of the party soon to be nicknamed 'the Eusebians', accusing some of them of being tritheists. Marcellus hated talk of three *hypostaseis* whose unity might be located in harmony of will, and accused Origen of excessive Platonism. His own theology, however, appeared vulnerable to attack because he wished to suggest that the coming forth of the divine Triad was necessary in relation to creation and redemption; at the last, Christ would deliver up his kingdom to the Father (1 Cor. 15.28), and the Triad would once more be an undifferentiated unity. Marcellus disavowed Sabellianism, but to his critics that disavowal seemed unimpressive. In 336 he refused to soil his conscience by joining the Eusebians at the dedication of the church of the Holy Sepulchre[9] at Jerusalem which was also a climax in the celebration of the thirtieth anniversary of Constantine's accession. The slight to the emperor enabled a synod of Marcellus' opponents to secure his deposition and exile.

In 328 bishop Alexander of Alexandria died, and was succeeded by the young zealot Athanasius, who had been Alexander's attendant deacon at the council of Nicaea. Athanasius stood in intransigent opposition to any request that, once Arius had put his signature to the Nicene creed, he might be readmitted to communion at Alexandria. A similarly tough stand against Egyptian schismatics, adherents of Meletius of Lycopolis, gave a handle to Athanasius' opponents. Methods used against them by Athanasius involved physical coercion, and complaint was made. At a council at Tyre in 335 Athanasius was declared deposed on the ground of violence unfitting in a bishop.[10] His appeal from the council to Constantine failed, and

[8] Spanneut (1948) gathers the fragments of his works; Cavallera (1905). Marcellus' fragments: ed. E. Klostermann, *Eusebius Werke* IV, 3rd edn by G. C. Hansen (Berlin, 1991).
[9] In antiquity called the Anastasis (Resurrection). See Coüasnon (1974).
[10] That there was truth in the charge of violence seems certain from the evidence of the letters of a Meletian priest, published by Bell (1924), speaking of imprisonment and scourgings.

he was exiled to Trier. There was no doctrinal accusation against Athanasius.

Constantine's death brought amnesty; exiled bishops could return, but since they had been replaced, rival factions produced disorders. Both Athanasius and Marcellus retreated to Rome, where pope Julius accepted them to communion – Marcellus on his profession of the old Roman creed (ancestor of the 'Apostles" creed).[11] Athanasius convinced Julius that his accusers were Arian heretics. Julius' action precipitated a crisis between east and west. Eusebius of Caesarea had written two works to establish the dangerous, heretical nature of Marcellus' theology. The Greek bishops were sure that Marcellus was unacceptable, and felt offended by Julius' assumption that he had the right to sit in judgement on the decisions of Greek synods without consulting them.

In the year 341 a large council of Greek bishops gathered, with the emperor Constantius presiding, for the dedication of the great church at Antioch-on-the-Orontes in Syria.[12] They rejected Marcellus' ideas as heresy: did not scripture (Luke 1.33) say expressly that Christ's kingdom would have no end? The western accusation that the Greeks were Arians was sharply rejected as offensive, and the rebuttal was reinforced by a creed with clauses vigorously rejecting propositions associated with Arius, similar to the Nicene anathema. On one crucial point the Greek bishops were firm: one must distinguish three *hypostases*, and see their unity in agreement of will. But Arian ideas about the difference between Father and Son were expressly set aside: the Son is called 'the indistinguishable image' of the Father. In reply to pope Julius, the council refused to concede that Rome could hear appeals from eastern synods. Each side felt the letters from the other side to be insulting.

Of Constantine's three sons, Constantine II was eliminated in civil war with Constans in 340, so that Constans in the west could put under pressure his brother Constantius II in the east. The emperors could not tolerate Greek east and Latin west excommunicating each other, and called both sides to meet at Serdica (Sofia) in the autumn of 342.

The eastern bishops, almost eighty strong, did not want to come to Serdica, and their antipathy turned to horror when on arrival they found Athanasius, Marcellus and other bishops deposed on disciplinary charges by Greek synods, already received to communion by the western bishops. They met separately to issue an incendiary statement about the outrageous behaviour of the western bishops, particularly denying any authority in canon law for Rome to be judge of eastern councils.[13]

---

[11] Marcellus' letter to Julius (fr. 129=Epiphan. *Pan*. 72.2–3).

[12] Athan. *De Syn*. xxii–xxv; Socr. *HE* ii.10.

[13] The letter of the eastern bishops survives in a Latin version, printed in *CSEL* lxv.48–78, from the ninth-century Paris codex, Arsenal 483. Pope Julius in 340 (cited by Athan. *Apol. c. Ar.* xxii) claimed that the council of Nicaea gave authority for the decisions of a council to be reviewed by another council.

Despite their anger, the eastern bishops produced a surprisingly conciliatory creed, dropping the three *hypostaseis* and expressly rejecting Arian
propositions, but insisting (against Marcellus) on the unending kingdom of
Christ. On that they would make no concessions.

The western bishops were no less angry than their eastern colleagues.
They enacted a canon affirming the right of the Roman see to hear
appeals.[14] They approved a theological statement, perhaps drafted by
Marcellus himself, insisting on the one *hypostasis* of the Trinity, attacking
those who located the unity of the Trinity in a harmony of will, and dis-
avowing the eastern accusation that for the west the distinctions between
Father, Son and Spirit are no more than nominal. The statement is not cast
in the form of a baptismal creed, and was not intended to replace the
Nicene formula. The bishops issued a fiery encyclical denouncing the
Greek bishops, declaring Athanasius the victim of scurrilous defamation
and justifying their acceptance of Marcellus and others.

The emperor's hopes for peace were crushed. They had on their hands
not a trivial quarrel but a bitter schism. Constans told Constantius that he
must bring his bishops to be co-operative, or there would be civil war.[15] It
is a measure of what seemed to matter most to the Greeks that they could
endure the reinstatement of Athanasius of Alexandria but not that of
Marcellus at Ancyra. Marcellus' deacon Photinus had been advanced to
become bishop of Sirmium (Mitrovica, Serbia) in Illyricum, where there
were bishops of Arian sympathy for him to combat, notably Valens of
Mursa (Osijek) and Ursacius of Singidunum (Belgrade). This promotion
confirmed the deep anxieties of the eastern bishops. In 346 Athanasius
returned to Alexandria on the authority of Constantius, not of any synodical hearing of his case. At Ancyra Marcellus had been replaced by a very
moderate bishop, Basil, not in the least sympathetic to Arianism, but also
convinced that the Nicene formula could not be deemed adequate if the
creed provided cover for Marcellus. Marcellus could not be reinstated in his
see, but was allowed to return to the vicinity and to minister to a small
group of adherents.

Rome and the western bishops silently dropped support for Marcellus,
and at a council in Milan (345) even agreed to censure Photinus of
Sirmium.[16] Until 351, however, nothing was done to remove him from his
see. Meanwhile in 347 the Illyrian bishops Valens and Ursacius had to
submit to pope Julius and to assent to the legitimacy of Athanasius' tenure
of Alexandria. Theologically that cost them nothing. The ascendancy of

---

[14] Since the western bishops were justifying the authority of Rome to sit in judgement on the decisions of Greek synods, it is evident that the canon was intended to hold good beyond the provinces of
the Latin west.
[15] Socr. *HE* II.23; Lucif. *De S. Athan.* 1.29 (*CSEL* XIV.116); Athan. *Apol. ad Const* II–III.
[16] *CSEL* LXV.142.18.

Valens of Mursa shot into prominence in 351 when at Mursa Constantius defeated the army of Magnentius – at huge cost in slaughter on both sides – and during the battle was at prayer with Valens in a nearby shrine.[17] Thereafter Valens was an influential figure at Constantius' court. Photinus of Sirmium was immediately deposed from his bishopric by a synod which approved a series of anathemas.[18] Significantly this synod avoided the sensitive terms *ousia* and *hypostasis*, terms which had hitherto been indispensable to the controversy. The silence at this point was the first indication of what was shortly to come.

Though at Tyre in 335 and later, no charge of heresy was brought against Athanasius of Alexandria, from 338–9 onwards he was defending himself with the plea that his accusers were disqualified by virtue of their sympathy with the condemned Arius – a sympathy which the synod at Antioch (341) sharply disavowed. But it was not until the 350s that the identification of Athanasius' cause with that of Nicene orthodoxy became a fortissimo in his eloquent pamphlets. In 350–1 Constantius' political challenger in the west, Magnentius, sought Athanasius' support. So after Magnentius' fall (353) Constantius had ground for thinking Athanasius tainted by treason. Even the vehemently anti-Arian Lucifer of Calaris thought Athanasius had made mistakes which he hoped Constantius would forgive.[19] Late in 352 a synod at Antioch of thirty bishops reaffirmed Athanasius' deposition and replaced him by an anti-Nicene successor, George, a Cappadocian without Egyptian associations.[20] With implicit criticism of Constantius it was observed that Athanasius had resumed his see in 346 merely on the say-so of Constantius, without synodical action. The synod's action could not, however, be implemented without the secular arm.

Meanwhile Constantius required western bishops in Gaul and Italy to assent to Athanasius' removal from office. The few who resisted (Hilary of Poitiers, Dionysius of Milan, Eusebius of Vercelli, Lucifer of Calaris, and at first pope Liberius, warned by eighty Egyptian bishops that he must not accept the Antioch synod)[21] suffered exile. Liberius tried unsuccessfully to treat the Egyptian synod's intervention as an appeal probably under the terms of the third canon of the western council of Serdica.

Athanasius' claim that the reason for the mounting attack on him was hostility to the Nicene creed was astonishingly vindicated in 357. In this year three events coincided to provide confirmation. At Sirmium Valens of Mursa and Ursacius of Singidunum were able to get the nonagenarian Ossius of Cordoba to sign a manifesto affirming to be self-evident the

---

[17] Sulp. Sev. *Chron.* II.38. (*CSEL* I.91f.).   [18] Athan. *De Syn.* XXVII.

[19] Lucif. *De S. Athan.* II.19. Athanasius' disavowal of treachery is in *Apol. ad Const.* VI–IX.

[20] Sozom. *HE* IV.8.3ff.

[21] Liberius' exile letters are printed in *CSEL* LXV.155–73. Those of Eusebius of Vercelli are in *CCSL* IX, ed. V. Bulhart.

Son's subordination to the Father (John 14.28) and deploring any use of *ousia, substantia, homoousion* or *homoiousion* (like in essence): 'they upset people, are not in scripture, and make assertions beyond human knowledge'.[22] This manifesto moved Gallic bishops to protest. To Hilary it was the 'Blasphemy of Sirmium'. But at Antioch in Syria it was welcomed by an ambitious new bishop, Eudoxius (translated to Constantinople in 360), and by a radical group hostile to the Nicene formula, led by Aetius and Eunomius. One of this group was George, consecrated to be bishop of Alexandria in rivalry to Athanasius. For this group the difference or unlikeness of Father and Son was primary. They were soon to be labelled by opponents the Dissimilarians or Anomoeans.

The capture of major sees by sympathizers with the questions associated with Arius caused profound alarm, especially among the moderate Greek bishops, who preferred to say 'like in essence' rather than the Nicene 'of one essence' and whose leader was Marcellus' successor at Ancyra, Basil. Basil and his friends communicated their consternation to the emperor who was, for a time, impressed. Perhaps Basil's formula could even gain the support of Athanasius, who was willing to gloss the Nicene term as meaning 'like in every respect'. Athanasius held out an olive branch of reconciliation: could not Basil and his party accept the Nicene creed, ratified by the great emperor Constantine? In effect this plea was to accept a formula acceptable to the unacceptable Marcellus. Constantius soon found Basil intolerant and unable to deliver a consensus. The emperor rightly judged that dogma in a universal church cannot be regional or partisan.

Advised by Valens of Mursa, Constantius came to adopt a liberal policy which sought consensus by a formula on which no one could disagree, namely that the Son is 'like the Father as the scriptures teach'. A plan was formed for a general council where Constantius, with the concord of east and west, would achieve unity much as his father had done at Nicaea (325). Earthquake and travel costs combined to make it convenient to gather western bishops at Ariminum (Rimini), eastern bishops at Seleucia in Isauria (Silifke). A steering committee agreed beforehand that *ousia* should be avoided as unscriptural: it was enough to affirm 'likeness in every respect in accord with the scriptures'. Constantius had been convinced by Basil of Ancyra that the Dissimilarians led by Aetius were heretics and hypocrites – hypocrites because even Aetius could accept 'likeness' as long as it was not a likeness of *ousia* or substance. Basil of Ancyra's party was attached to *homoiousios* – like in essence – because it excluded Aetius and the radicals. Aetius and Eunomius could accept 'like, as scripture teaches'. The western bishops at Ariminum accepted the vague formula, 'like', on an assurance that the eastern bishops at Seleucia had already agreed on it, and therefore

---

[22] Athan. *De Syn.* XXVIII.

they were agreeing to a universal faith. The Greek bishops at Seleucia were assured the western bishops had assented to it. Protests from Basil of Ancyra resulted in the crushing defeat of his party and the expulsion of many from their bishoprics. At a synod in Constantinople, gathered for the enthronement of Eudoxius and the dedication of the first church of Holy Wisdom, the Son was declared to be 'like the Father as the scriptures teach'.

Basil of Ancyra's defeat shattered the reconciliation proposed by Athanasius in 359. Basil and his party had been destroyed, perhaps because Athanasius' irenic proposal was a kiss of death, and they no longer existed to respond to advances from the pro-Nicene side. Nevertheless, a reconciliation was to occur, so that in 364 Athanasius could boldly assure Julian's short-lived successor Jovian that the Nicene creed now commanded general assent among all orthodox persons.[23] The assertion contained some circularity in that acceptance of the creed was Athanasius' definition of orthodoxy. But it was not nonsense. A growing number of bishops who in 360 had been content to accept Constantius' formula were as alarmed by Aetius and Eunomius as Basil of Ancyra had been. *Rapprochement* would come not so much between the Nicene and the homoiousian party now defunct as between Athanasius and Greek bishops who had signed the vague 'like' formula (and therefore were labelled by him 'Arians') but who held Aetius and Eunomius in horror.

Constantius' formula, ratified by general councils of east and west, was nevertheless hard to shift. Some remained unconvinced that the Nicene *homoousios* was correct; even Hilary of Poitiers conceded that unorthodox persons could accept it.[24] The emperor Valens (364–78) maintained the 'likeness' formula as normative in the Greek east. In the west Valentinian I refused to interfere in ecclesiastical affairs, and bishops who wanted to stand by the council of Ariminum were secure.

Reconciliation, however, was delayed by the divisions in the church at Antioch-on-the-Orontes. In this great Syrian city, the old Nicene congregation loyal to the memory of Eustathius of Antioch was under the care of a presbyter called Paulinus. He held communion with Marcellus of Ancyra, stood firmly on the western Serdican statement that the Trinity is a single *hypostasis*, and refused to share communion with other Christians in the city. In 360 Eudoxius, on his move to Constantinople, was replaced by Meletius, who had been a bishop in Roman Armenia and was now asked to hold Constantius' comprehensive policy in a city where the rancorous Christian divisions made the pagans mock. Meletius was ejected from the see after only a month in office,[25] and replaced by an old Alexandrian friend of Arius

---

[23] Athan. *Ep. ad Jov. PG* XXVI.813f. [24] *De Syn.* 67f., *PL* X.525.

[25] Complaints were laid against him that he had treated some clergy in a manner contrary to canon law; there were also anxieties that he thought the term *homoousios* could be acceptable. He was exiled by Constantius. See *RE* XV (1932) 500–2. Hostile notice in Jer. *Chron. s.a.*

named Euzoius. A congregation faithful to Meletius also formed, and their bishop fully shared the alarm felt by many when radicals like Aetius and Eunomius could accept the 'like' formula without mental reservations. Meletius thought 'like' compatible with the Nicene creed. The two dissenting congregations, though both able to accept the Nicene *homoousios*, could not unite. Meletius spoke of three *hypostaseis* in the Trinity, which Paulinus heard to mean three independent divine beings, graded at different levels and quite distinct from each other. The claim that this could be brought into line with the true meaning of the Nicene creed seemed to him hypocrisy. And as for the vague word 'like', he pertinently observed that 'the kingdom of God is like a grain of mustard seed, but not much'.[26]

Paulinus' position at Antioch was strengthened early in 362 when the returning exile Lucifer of Calaris (Cagliari) went to Antioch and consecrated Paulinus to be orthodox bishop,[27] in antithesis not only to the official bishop Euzoius but also to Meletius. Since it was axiomatic that there could be only one bishop of the true church in each city, Paulinus' elevation made reconciliation with bishop Meletius inherently problematic on largely non-theological grounds. However, Paulinus' congregation had its own internal disagreements: some among them were in close contact with Apollinaris, the vehemently anti-Arian bishop of the Nicene congregation in Laodicea on the Syrian coast. Apollinaris was critical not only of Arians but of upholders of the Nicene creed who talked as if the Son of God and the Son of Man were virtually distinct persons. Such talk was found among the Eustathian or old Nicene group at Antioch, and Apollinaris thought it disastrous. He was not reassured by the theology of an Antiochene presbyter of Nicene sympathies, Diodore, who was associated with Meletius and by his influence became bishop of Tarsus about 378. Diodore thought that to answer the Arian argument from the frailties of Christ's humanity it was essential to stress the full and natural humanity of his soul, distinct in nature from the divine Word united with that soul.

Apollinaris possessed an acute mind and a pungent pen. To make any separation between the divine and human in Christ seemed to him a lethal threat to the salvation of the human race, which depended on the total unity in one *hypostasis*, indeed 'one nature' (*physis*). In the eucharist the faithful receive the life-giving body of the Lord; nothing is said about Christ's human soul. The body of Christ is life-giving because it was made a single *hypostasis* and *physis* with the divine Word. Therefore the conclusion may be boldly drawn, that the divine Word replaced the human mind and soul as the source of reason and life in Christ, and therefore that there could be no conflict of wills in the God–Man, in the human mind of Christ no struggle with 'filthy thoughts', but a single person (*prosopon*). There is 'one

---

[26] *PG* xxviii.85.   [27] Jer. *Chron. s.a.* 362 (ed. Helm-Treu, 242): two other bishops assisted.

nature incarnate of the divine Word', a phrase which became a winged word encapsulating the essential affirmation of theologians alarmed by the dualistic terms of Diodore and his successors, who seemed to teach 'Two Sons', the son of Mary being distinct from the eternal Son. Apollinaris' denial that Christ possessed a human soul and mind caused uproar among the Nicene congregation at Antioch, and his supporters, led by a disciple named Vitalis, soon became an independent group for worship with Vitalis as their own bishop.

The split at Antioch among the old Nicene adherents of Paulinus entailed a breach between the Apollinarians and the bishops supporting Paulinus. Hence the surprising fact that the earliest synodical condemnation of Apollinaris' doctrines came not in the east but from pope Damasus at Rome in 377, followed in the next two years by synods first at Alexandria and then at Antioch under Meletius and at Constantinople in 381. Apollinaris himself seems to have survived until about 390. His enthusiastic followers in the east solved the problem of the condemnation of his writings by simply circulating them under the names of others such as Julius of Rome and Athanasius himself. In consequence, a number of Apollinarian texts came to influence orthodox writers unaware of their origin.[28]

A divisive terminological factor remained the question whether one should speak of the divine Triad as a single *hypostasis* or as three *hypostaseis*.

The language of Plotinus and his Neoplatonic successors played a part at this point. Plotinus in the third century had written of the three supreme entities in his metaphysical system – the One, Intellect (*nous*), and the World-Soul – under the title of 'the three primary *hypostaseis*' (*Enneads* v.1, a text intimately studied by Basil of Caesarea). Plotinus explained that between them there is no distinction except that they happen to be different (v.1.3.22). Together they are 'god' and a plurality (v.1.5.1), and the relation is one of 'likeness as light is from the sun' (v.1.7.4). The epithet *homoousios* was an ordinary term in Plotinus' vocabulary, especially for the affinity of the human soul with the world-soul. Porphyry, editor and biographer of Plotinus, summed up Platonic teaching as saying that 'the *ousia* of the divine extends to three *hypostaseis*: the supreme god, the creator, the world-soul'.[29]

Plotinus and Porphyry contributed a vocabulary, therefore, and a framework of ideas. On the other hand, the Neoplatonic metaphysic as a whole was for Porphyry and his successors an alternative scheme exclusive of a Christian interpretation; for the Christian thinkers the dogmatic definitions of the church depended for their authority on scripture and the interpretation of the community of faith, and made a philosophical

---

[28] Lietzmann (1904). [29] *PG* xxxix.760B.

metaphysic subordinate. They used philosophical terms but not much of the framework.

The Latin Neoplatonist Marius Victorinus, an African teaching in Rome who was dramatically converted to Christianity in the 350s, composed a treatise against Arianism about 360–1. He there mentioned the notion that the one divine *ousia* is manifested in three *hypostaseis*. Victorinus was much influenced by Porphyry, who is therefore a highly probable source for this way of distinguishing *ousia* and *hypostasis*. Perhaps a Greek theologian had anticipated Victorinus in using the distinction. The formula offered a golden possibility of harmonizing the two rival theological traditions which had been in unhappy juxtaposition in the eastern churches since the council of Nicaea.

After Constantius' death (November 361), Julian's amnesty enabled Athanasius to return to Alexandria, at least for six or seven months, during which he gathered a council of bishops there.[30] The programme was to try to reconcile the factions at Antioch who could all accept the Nicene creed but were in disagreement on other matters, such as whether those who said 'one *hypostasis*' were Sabellian and whether those who said 'three *hypostaseis*' were tritheists or Arians; and whether the Christological problems raised by Apollinaris could be solved by a simple agreement that Christ was 'not mindless or soulless'. More capable of ready consensus was the sharp rejection of the thesis advanced by some bishops (notably Macedonius of Constantinople, extruded from his see in 360)[31] that while the Son had the same *ousia* as the Father, the Holy Spirit did not. Since the third article of the Nicene creed laconically declared only for belief 'in the Holy Spirit', without further qualification, the council of Alexandria was led by Athanasius to affirm the sufficiency of the Nicene creed to repel heresies, subject to the expansion of the third article to mean a rejection of the doctrine that the Holy Spirit belongs to the created order. The critics of Apollinaris denied teaching two Sons.

Shortly before the council of Alexandria, Athanasius, while still in hiding in the desert, had learnt from his suffragan Serapion, bishop of Thmuis, the news that among those wholly opposed to Arianism there were some who were saying that the Holy Spirit is created and a kind of archangel. He replied by appealing to the triadic baptismal formula: the Triad is one God. Argument which proves the Son to be no creature holds good for the Spirit also. So 'the Spirit proceeds from the Father and belongs to the Son', who bestows the Spirit on the disciples (John 20.22).[32]

---

[30] *Tomas ad Antiochenos*, PG xxvi.796–810.

[31] Socr. *HE* ii.42. His fall was engineered by the anti-Nicene faction on disciplinary charges. He accepted the Nicene creed. His name was associated with the group which did not wish to affirm either that the Holy Spirit is fully divine or that the Spirit belongs to the created order.

[32] *Epistolae ad Serapionem*, PG xxvi.525–676; see the annotated translation by C. R. B. Shapland (1951).

The two disputes, concerning the full divinity of the Holy Spirit and concerning Apollinaris' theses in Christology, continued to be debated among the adherents of the Nicene creed throughout the 360s and 370s. During the twenty years from Constantius' death to the advent of Theodosius to the east, the Greek churches continued to be dominated by an emperor, Valens, who wished to continue with the imprecise and comprehensive formula that the Son is 'like' the Father. The leading bishops of this party under Constantius had played a prominent role in the dismantling of polytheistic temples, and under Julian suffered an emperor's revenge. Adherents of the party wrote heroic accounts of the martyrdoms (all of which resulted from provocative anti-pagan actions) and lurid descriptions of the fate of apostates.[33] But the growing support for the Nicene *homoousios*, and the final victory of this cause under Theodosius, made Valens and his bishops unpopular with the Nicene party in Syria and Asia Minor. The catastrophic defeat of Valens at Adrianople (378) brought upon him the dislike of the pagan historian Ammianus, while his failure to be convinced of the unifying power of the Nicene creed bequeathed a legacy of hostility in the orthodox church tradition.

The retrospective judgement of fifth-century writers cannot be thought fair and just to Valens.[34] Confidence in the Nicene creed as the flag under which all those hostile to radical Arianism should rally was relatively slowly achieved. Until 374 Marcellus of Ancyra was still living, and the communion with him maintained by Paulinus of Antioch did not encourage other bishops in Syria and Asia Minor to follow the lead of Athanasius and pope Damasus (366–84) in recognizing Paulinus as the orthodox bishop of Antioch. From 372 Antioch became Valens' principal residence. The presence of the emperor strengthened the position of the bishop Euzoius, whose antipathy to the Nicene *homoousios* was considerable. Paulinus' sole source of strength was his recognition at Alexandria and Rome. But the body of moderate Greek bishops rallying to the Nicene formula had confidence in Meletius, and regarded both Euzoius and Paulinus as ultimately divisive. When Eudoxius, bishop of Constantinople, died in 370, a group of pro-Nicene clergy and laity in the capital attempted to push their candidate into the see, and suffered for it when the emperor nominated the soundly comprehensive Demophilus, translated from Beroea in Thrace.[35]

A more successful *coup* by the pro-Nicene party in Asia Minor in 370 was the installation at Caesarea (Cappadocia) of Basil as bishop and

---

[33] *Chron. Pasch.*, PG XCII.740–5, using a contemporary source; Eng. tr. Whitby and Whitby (1989) 36–41.

[34] Julian's successor Jovian supported the Nicene party. His sudden and premature death may well have seemed a sign of celestial displeasure for his ecclesiastical policy and justified Valens in looking elsewhere. To Augustine (*De Civ. Dei* v.25) the death of Jovian, like that of Gratian, was a mystery by which providence may teach us not to overvalue temporal prosperity. Augustine well knew that under Valens orthodox Christians in the east suffered.   [35] Socr. *HE* IV.1–16.

metropolitan. Basil possessed valuable assets such as high social rank and culture. He had made a name for himself in the church about 364 by writing a powerful refutation of Eunomius' version of Arianism, arguing that Eunomius' thesis of the vast difference between 'unbegotten' and 'begotten' fails to establish a difference of substance (*ousia*) between Father and Son: all human talk about the transcendent God is no more than relative, a groping after a profound mystery, and Eunomius' assertion of the total adequacy of human language and reason for embracing even the being of God is arrogant absurdity. Basil's onslaught on intellectual Arianism helped forward his high standing with strongly pro-Nicene groups in Asia Minor. After a hesitant start in his church career Basil soon began to look towards theologians of Nicene sympathy, as is proved by the extant correspondence which he had as a young man with Apollinaris of Laodicea – a correspondence with which critics and opponents tried later to embarrass him.[36]

As metropolitan of Cappadocia Basil could influence episcopal appointments in neighbouring sees. He sought to ensure that new elections were of men sympathetic to Nicene theology, not to the official formula of 'likeness' approved by the emperor Valens. The political situation required Basil to proceed more cautiously than strictly Nicene theologians wished. In 371 Valens visited Caesarea, and the zealots longed for a dramatic confrontation with Basil. Basil disappointed them and admitted the emperor to communion.[37] Moreover, in the controversy about Apollinaris' doctrines Basil was deeply reluctant to move to a verdict, and in the debate about the place of the Holy Spirit in the divine Triad Basil made no public stand before 375. If the Nicene creed was sufficient, no addition was required, and that would help to keep a united front among the pro-Nicene groups.

In 375 Basil's friend and colleague Amphilochius bishop of Iconium (Konya) persuaded him to stand up and be counted. After Athanasius' death in May 373, pro-Nicene Christians in Alexandria and Egypt were being persecuted; it seemed no time for silence. So Basil came to write his treatise *On the Holy Spirit*. As in Athanasius' *Letters to Serapion*, the central argument is that the trinitarian baptismal formula (Matt. 28.19) presupposes one God who is Father, Son and Spirit, not Father, Son and some kind of super-archangel. A delicate point which affected liturgical practice was the form of the Gloria: should one say 'Glory be to the Father with (*meta*) the Son with (*syn*) the Holy Spirit' or '. . . through (*dia*) the Son *in* the Holy Spirit'? This was sensitive not only because it upset people at worship to hear different formulas, but also because radical Arians argued from the difference of prepositions to a difference of *ousiai* in the Triad. Basil and

---

[36] Basil, *Epp.* 361–4, examined by Prestige (1956).

[37] Greg. Naz. *Or.* XLIII.52 (*PG* XXXVI.564A) describes Basil's embarrassment. On Valens' religious policy, *RE* VIIA, 2132–5 (1948).

the ascetics of Caesarea used the twofold 'with'. He defended this proposition with an anthology of texts from authoritative Christian writers of earlier times – Irenaeus, Clement of Rome, Gregory the Wonderworker and apostle of Pontus, and learned theologians (even if not invariably sound) such as Origen, Dionysius of Alexandria, and Eusebius of Caesarea. Basil's florilegium is the earliest example of this kind of appeal to tradition – a genre which during the next three centuries was developed on a large scale in the Christological controversy. Among his authorities Basil brings in Meletius of Antioch. He was never to give support to Paulinus, the bishop of Antioch recognized by Rome and Alexandria.

To Basil, as to his friend Gregory of Nazianzus and his younger brother Gregory whom he put into the see of Nyssa (pursuing his policy of keeping out the wrong sort of bishop), it was evident that the neo-Nicene movement gathering strength in Syria and Asia Minor could never find reconciliation and unity if Paulinus of Antioch were put forward as the rallying figure. Meletius and Basil saw that 'three *hypostaseis*' must be accepted, and that the Nicene anathema had to be interpreted to allow *ousia* to be a generic term, *hypostasis* particular. The one *ousia* of the Godhead has three manifestations, distinct in their mutual relations in that the Father is the ultimate source, the Son is 'begotten', the Spirit 'proceeds' (John 15.26). But in activity the Triad is one and undivided, as also in will and knowledge.

Basil's programmatic restatement of trinitarian doctrine was filled out in the writings of his brother, Gregory of Nyssa, notably in his long and able refutation of Eunomius. Critics of Basil, Gregory of Nyssa and Gregory of Nazianzus concentrated on their difficulty in explaining how their doctrine of the Trinity escaped the charge of tritheism. Gregory of Nazianzus bluntly affirmed that 'the Godhead exists in separate beings undivided, like three mutually connected suns giving a single light'.[38] Both Basil and Gregory of Nazianzus defended the enlargement of the creed on the subject of the Holy Spirit by resorting to the concept of reserve in communicating truth to those not yet ready to receive it. Not all fundamental doctrine is explicit in holy scripture, and the tradition of the community is that which gives coherence to the isolated texts found in the Bible. Gregory suggested that the Nicene doctrine of the consubstantiality of the Son had first to be received before minds were ready to make a similar affirmation of the Spirit.

Basil corresponded with pope Damasus in a vain attempt to persuade him that Meletius should be recognized as true bishop of Antioch. Meletius was able to hold a synod at Antioch in 379 which went out of its way to approve of every document from Rome which it could lay hands on, and may have been responsible for drafting a creed, 'Nicene' in the

[38] *Or.* XXXI (theol. 5).12 (*PG* XXXVI.149A).

sense that it incorporated the *homoousios* and some phrases from the formula of 325, but also using phrases from the old Roman creed and above all having an expanded third article on the Holy Spirit, expressly affirming that the Spirit is the source, not the receiver, of life, and is equal with the Father and the Son in the doxology.

Meanwhile Damasus at Rome held a council which reached major decisions on reports about the conflicting opinions in the east, evidently supplied to him by Paulinus of Antioch. Anathema was pronounced on denial that the Spirit is of the same power and substance as the Father and the Son; on those who speak of two Sons; on those who say the divine Word replaced the rational soul in Christ, or who say that, while in the flesh on earth, the Son was not also with the Father in heaven; on those who are orthodox about the Father and the Son but not about the Spirit. This western intervention in the debates of the pro-Nicene groups in the east had a catalytic effect, particularly in strengthening the hand of those, like the Cappadocian theologians, who saw that the Nicene creed must be supplemented in its third article. Damasus included an ominous censure of the common eastern practice of bishops moving from see to see in a *cursus honorum*.[39]

Popes and councils could censure and deplore, but tended to be less than effective unless the decisions were supported by imperial authority. Pope Damasus (see below) could protest but only powerlessly against the anti-Nicene bishop of Milan Auxentius (d. 374).

The death of Valens at the battle of Adrianople in August 378 brought Theodosius from the west to control the east. Theodosius made it certain that the pro-Nicene party in the Greek churches would dominate the future. Initially Theodosius decreed that communion with pope Damasus and bishop Peter of Alexandria would be a criterion of recognition, a formula which entailed the acknowledgement of Paulinus of Antioch. He arrived at Constantinople late in November 380. Within two days the Arians had to hold their worship outside the walls in the open air. Theodosius soon learnt that the Nicene groups could never trust Paulinus as a criterion of orthodox communion but would rally to Meletius.

To achieve order and unity among the back-biting pro-Nicene groups a great council was called for May 381. Demophilus, the bishop of Constantinople favoured by Valens, quietly vacated his throne, so that the succession for New Rome had to be decided. The first Nicene consecration was that of an eminently unsuitable character, a Cynic philosopher named Maximus; he was soon told to go. Next was Gregory of Nazianzus, who had emerged from retirement in 379 to become pastor to the pro-Nicene people in Constantinople. His discourses there were heard by

---

[39] *Tomus Damasi*, in *Eccl. Occ. Mon. Iur. Ant.* 1.281–94.

Jerome. Gregory was a splendid orator and no mean theologian, strongly negative to Apollinarianism and to those who denied the divine equality of the Holy Spirit; but he was no natural leader of an incoherent council badly in need of firm leadership. The presidency was entrusted by the emperor to Meletius, but Meletius died during the sessions. Gregory could not persuade the council that this death gave the bishops the opportunity to ensure peace with the west by recognizing Paulinus. His authority was weakened. The recent death (14 February 381) of Peter of Alexandria meant that his successor Timothy arrived late. The pope sent no legates from Rome at all, but the bishop of Thessalonica[40] came and together with Timothy of Alexandria expressed disapproval of Gregory's translation to the capital. Gregory resigned the see, and retired to Cappadocia. There in 382 he composed two 'letters' (101, 102) with a powerful critique of Apollinaris based on the old axiom (found in Irenaeus and Origen) that what Christ did not assume is not saved. He also composed in verse a disillusioned autobiography. He could think of no good that ever came of synods.[41]

For the succession at Constantinople the choice fell on a high lay bureaucrat named Nectarius. For Antioch, recognition of Paulinus being judged impracticable, the choice fell on an Antiochene presbyter named Flavian. Both appointments angered Damasus, Ambrose of Milan, and the west. Further displeasure to the west and to Alexandria was caused by the conciliar canons, one of which declared the see of Constantinople to rank second after old Rome 'because it is New Rome'. The creed, however, was moulded with phrases that would be congenial to the west, and in its expanded third article on the Holy Spirit owed something to Damasus' Roman council. Admittedly, Gregory of Nazianzus regarded the creed (and the general church policy of Theodosius) as excessively conciliatory to those who affirmed the original Nicene formula of 325 but had not yet become convinced about the Holy Spirit. The creed did not exclude either them or the Apollinarians. There was no anathema. Theodosius longed for the maximum of consensus, subject to the condition that the creed with the *homoousios* was accepted. On the other hand, the emperor also disturbed Gregory by enforcing the council's decisions with legal enactments, as if orthodoxy could be compelled by edict.[42]

On 30 July 381 Theodosius issued an edict naming the bishops in each civil diocese with whom it was necessary to hold communion; they included Nectarius of Constantinople, Timothy of Alexandria, Diodore of Tarsus, Amphilochius of Iconium and Gregory of Nyssa.

Among those who gathered at Constantinople during the council of 381 were wandering ascetics from Mesopotamia, called by their critics

---

[40] Bishop Acholius of Thessalonica was a westerner; he baptized Theodosius, and may have been entitled to claim a mandate to speak for pope Damasus.   [41] *Ep.* 130.

[42] *Carm. Hist.* XI.1282ff. (*PG* XXXVII.1110f.).

'Messalians' from the Syriac word for 'people of prayer'.[43] They alarmed some bishops by their belief that baptism and the eucharist have not the power to expel the indwelling devil, latent deep in the heart of every individual, who can be conquered only by prayer of extreme intensity. The most zealous among them were indifferent to the ordered life and sacramental worship of the church, and held manual work to be a distraction from prayer. Their meetings were marked by charismatic excitements, dancing, ecstatic visions of demons and angels, special exorcisms. Flavian of Antioch was to have considerable difficulty in controlling these ascetics. But at Constantinople Gregory of Nyssa found himself impressed by their devotion, preached a sermon of welcome for them, and later adapted a discourse on Christian perfection by a Messalian leader so as to make it safe for orthodox Catholic readers. In Mesopotamia, Syria and Asia Minor, Messalian influence among the monks long remained potent. The stress on prayer and on visions was congenial to quietists (hesychasts). In episcopal vocabulary, however, 'Messalian' was a label for most forms of extreme religious excitement, and the indifference to order could often bring with it possibilities for social disturbance and disruption.

Nevertheless the principal Messalian texts, edited in the tenth century under the name of the 'Homilies of Macarius', enjoyed an immense future as spiritual reading in Greek and Russian Orthodox monasteries.

The policy of imposing the Nicene creed as the official norm of orthodoxy, which Theodosius was able to carry through at Constantinople in 381–2, was an example followed in the west by Theodosius' imperial colleague Gratian. Arianism in the sense of an aversion to the Nicene formula had come to have supporters after the council of Ariminum even in Italy (e.g. at Centumcellae (Civita Vecchia), Naples, Puteoli and Parma). At Milan Auxentius, appointed in 355, remained bishop to his death in 374, despite demands from pope Damasus that he must go. In Illyricum several bishops upheld the Likeness formula of Ariminum, and both Valens and Ursacius stayed in office to their death in the 370s. Auxentius' death brought sharp faction at Milan, and the provincial governor Ambrose came to restore order in a turbulent situation. He found himself the people's choice for the see, probably because he came of an aristocratic family and was not identified with either pro- or anti-Nicene factions. The election was approved by Petronius Probus the prefect, and Valentinian I.

Ambrose had no confrontations with the supporters of Auxentius.[44] He accepted the clergy ordained by Auxentius, whose sacraments were invalid in the eyes of ultra pro-Nicenes. Moreover, the immigration of many out of Illyricum under the impact of Gothic invasion moved the emperor

---

[43] Bibliography in Stewart (1991).

[44] Ambrose's tract on duties (*De Off.* 1.7.23) invokes Psalm 38 (39) as authority for avoiding quarrels by saying nothing. His silence clearly attracted criticism.

Gratian to allocate a basilica in Milan for the worship of those who were not of the Nicene persuasion. Among the immigrants to Milan was Justina, widow of Valentinian I and before him of Magnentius; she was no supporter of the Nicene theology. Tension began to develop between her and Ambrose, who was becoming explicitly hostile to the Likeness formula. To assure Gratian that Nicene orthodoxy would bring victory against the invading Goths, Ambrose wrote first a defence of the creed against its critics (mainly based on Hilary of Poitiers, Athanasius and Didymus of Alexandria, but caricaturing his opponents as indistinguishable from Eunomius and the Dissimilarians), then an argument for the equality of the Spirit in the divine Triad (with many debts to Didymus and Basil of Caesarea). The citadel of opposition to him lay in Illyricum. Two 'Arian' bishops, Secundianus of Singidunum and Palladius of Ratiaria (Dacia), persuaded Gratian to call a general council at which their Greek friends would support them. Ambrose turned it into a mainly north Italian assembly at Aquileia, without eastern representation, and fixed the deposition of the two Arians.[45]

The strength of Illyrian Arianism lay in the Goths, converted by bishop Ulfilas who laboured as missionary in Moesia for over forty years, translating the Bible into Gothic. He had been consecrated by Eusebius of Nicomedia, from whom he could have acquired no favourable impression of the Nicene creed and its supporters. He was present at the Constantinople synod (360) which declared the Son to be 'like the Father as the scriptures teach', and was to die in 383. A bitter critic of Ambrose preserved Ulfilas' creed: 'I believe there is one God the Father, alone unbegotten and invisible, and in his only-begotten Son, for us Lord and God, Creator and maker of the entire Creation, having none like him . . . and in one Holy Spirit, illuminating and sanctifying power . . . who is not God or even God for us but Christ's servant, subordinate and obedient to the Son in all things.'[46] Ulfilas and the Gothic churches were adamant that their trinitarian doctrine was scriptural as the Nicene *homoousios* was not, and therefore they had as many hesitations about the validity of Ambrose's sacraments as he had about theirs. The outcome of Ambrose's tough policy at the council of Aquileia was the creation of rival hierarchies until, a century or more later, few towns in Italy had not two competing bishops. In Milan a bishop Auxentius of Durostorum (Moesia) arrived to provide pastoral care for the non-Nicenes. The basilica once granted by Gratian had been handed back to Ambrose; but now Justina (mother of the child emperor Valentinian II and effectively regent) in 386 enacted freedom of assembly for upholders of the creed of Ariminum, leading to

[45] Acts of Aquileia: *CSEL* LXXXII.3.315–68.
[46] Gryson (1980) 250; Heather and Matthews (1991) 153.

confrontation with Ambrose, who mobilized his people, including Augustine's mother Monica, to resist her. Politically Justina's agitation was risky, since the charge of fostering heresy provided Magnus Maximus in Gaul with a plausible ground for representing an attack on north Italy as a religious crusade for the Nicene cause. The civil war between Maximus and Theodosius in 388 was bad news for the western upholders of the creed of Ariminum, whichever emperor won the battle.

The western provinces were more troubled by Manichee missionaries than by Arians who, apart from Gothic soldiers, were relatively few. Mani's pessimistic dualism[47] solved the agonizing problem of evil not by pantheistic solutions or by relativizing the goodness of God, but by concluding that the good Creator has only limited power to contain, not to eliminate it. Mani's cosmic dualism was pictured in a rich and partly erotic mythology. Missionaries successfully planted Manichee cells, despite hostile government legislation confiscating their places of assembly. Under Theodosius Manichees were deprived of the power to make valid wills. About 374 they acquired their most famous Latin recruit: the young Augustine was converted to the sect and for nine years became a formidable controversialist against Catholic orthodoxy, feared by bishops in North Africa with modest intellectual equipment. After his conversion to Neoplatonism and then to orthodox Christianity at Milan in 386–7, he composed a series of anti-Manichee tracts, culminating in the autobiographical *Confessions* of 397–400, written after he had become bishop of Hippo (Annaba).

To the imperial government, since the time of Diocletian at the end of the third century, the Manichees were an occult foreign importation from Persia, rotting the morale of the empire, with which Persia was at war. Banned by imperial edict, they had the perennial attraction of a secret society with a network of influence and patronage which could penetrate high strata in the social hierarchy, and with a promise to reveal grand cosmic mysteries to their members. Manichees were divided into the Elect, a small minority committed to celibacy, vegetarianism and teetotalism, and the Hearers, who were allowed wives or concubines but were expected to avert procreation, which imprisoned more divine souls in soggy matter.

The Manichees were widely diffused, and Hearers were fairly numerous.[48] The ascetic movement in the Catholic church during the fourth century was frequently attacked as a disguised Manichee infiltration. In the case of the ascetic revival led by Priscillian of Avila in Spain and southern Gaul, there is good reason to think Priscillian was to some extent influenced by Manichee apocrypha and other texts. When Orosius from Spain

---

[47] Bibliography in Lieu, *Manichaeism*.
[48] Augustine (*De Mor.* 11.19.70; *C. Faust.* xxx.6) attests numbers.

asked Augustine to combat the followers of Priscillian, the short work that resulted was composed on the assumption that Priscillianism was a form of Manicheism.[49] The Priscillianist controversy provided a context for a Latin translation, made in North Africa, of the second-century work *Adversus Haereses* by Irenaeus of Lyons.

A far graver problem for the empire and for the churches in North Africa was presented by the Donatist schism. The Donatists were not heretics but schismatics. There was virtually no difference from Catholicism in their doctrines of the Trinity, the Person of Christ, the sacraments and the Last Things. They and the Catholics regarded each other with profound rancour, but used the same lectionary and psalm-cycle. The source of passionate disagreement was the identity of the authentic church. The Donatists asserted that the principal consecrator of Caecilian to be bishop of Carthage, perhaps in 307 after the great persecution, had compromised his faith to the point of apostasy by surrendering the scriptures to the authorities. From that they deduced that all bishops in communion with Caecilian in Africa or elsewhere were polluted: they were 'traitors' (*traditores*). Caecilian and the bishops in communion with him replied that there was no reliable evidence to support the accusation against the principal consecrator, and at no stage an accusation against Caecilian himself; moreover, they were in communion with Rome, Jerusalem and the universal or Catholic church. Donatism assumed that the true church survived only in Africa. The issue therefore turned in part on whether in defining the church holiness is prior to unity or unity to holiness. Augustine would argue that since holiness is nothing without charity there can be no choice between these two marks of the church. Optatus of Milev, writing about 365–85, contended against the Donatists but in a conciliatory way: they were schismatics but not heretics, and in any event the second and third generations of the sect could not be held responsible for the actions of their forefathers. In his anti-Donatist writings Augustine would suggest that a schism, persisted in, passes over into heresy (an argument that could bring Donatists under the penalties of Theodosius I's edicts against heresy). He was sure that 'anyone separated from the church would end by saying false things', and that 'a characteristic of heretical sects is to be incapable of seeing what is obvious to everyone else'.[50]

When Constantine failed to heal the Donatist schism, he 'left them to the judgement of God' – a decision Augustine would regard as ignominious.[51] In 336 a Donatist council of 270 bishops mustered a spectacular show of support and strength, especially in Numidia and Mauretania

---

[49] Aug. *Ad Orosium contra Priscillianistas et Origenistas*, ed. K.-D. Daur, *CCSL* LXIX (1985) 165–78; *PL* XLII.669–78. See Chadwick (1976). [50] Aug. *Enarr. in Ps.* 57.6; *C. Ep. Parmeniani* II.5.
[51] Aug. *Post Coll.* XXX.56. Frend, *Donatist Church*, gives a general history of the sect; cf. Maier (1987–9).

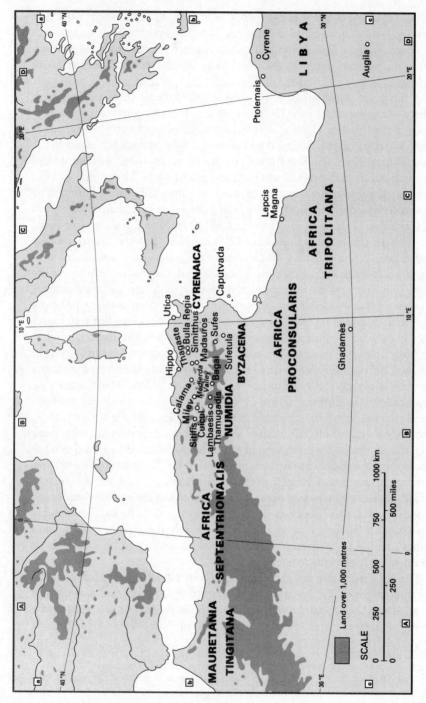

Map 7 North Africa

Sitifensis. The regional character of Donatism was its weakness. Outside Africa it hardly existed at all. Under Constans in 346–7 imperial agents, Paul and Macarius, attempted repression, which was counter-productive. Donatists gloried in the honour of the martyrs, and now they themselves could directly share in that. Julian's accession brought them toleration, and the Donatist bishop of Carthage 362–92, Parmenian, led what was the majority body in the African provinces as a whole. Knowledge of Latin was relatively slender in Numidia,[52] and there is reason to think that Donatism could be for some an expression of Punic regionalism against the Latin culture dominant in the other provinces, especially in Proconsularis. On Parmenian's death the Donatists suffered the common fate of separated bodies: they confronted splinter groups in their own ranks, especially between Numidian hard-liners and the more moderate voices of Proconsularis. Parmenian had even excommunicated their best theologian Tyconius for dangerously affirming that the true church could only be universal and not confined to Africa, and for suggesting that Antichrist was at work not only in the Catholic church but also in his community. Jerusalem and Babylon coexist everywhere, he thought.[53] The main Donatist body was confident of purity from the pollution that in their view had overwhelmed all other churches in the Roman world, and of a holiness in their own sacraments assured to them by an untainted episcopal succession. Harassments by the imperial government only vindicated their conviction that persecuting Catholics in league with the secular power could not be the authentic church of Jesus Christ. Protests against state pressure led fanatics to throw themselves over precipices, and the suicides added much fuel to Donatist hatred of the Catholics.

The Donatists' cause was supported, however, by violence of their own making. Wandering groups of ascetics, called Militants (Agonistici) by Donatists and Circumcellions by Catholics,[54] enthusiastically celebrated their martyrs, and specialized in making devastating, unstoppable charges which destroyed the bands playing music at pagan festivals.[55] They soon turned these onslaughts against Catholic clergy and their church buildings. Circumcellions also attacked defenceless landowners, some of whom were forced to walk before their own cart while their slaves occupied the driving seat.[56] Circumcellion zeal to change the social order (if that is what it was) was not generally shared by Donatist bishops, who disowned strong-arm methods. But there was some apocalyptic millennialism.

A bloody attack on a Catholic bishop at Bagai in southern Numidia came

---

[52] So Augustine, *Ep.* 84, contrasting Numidia with Mauretania where Latin was more general. Latin inscriptions of Numidia in *CIL* VIII.1 are, however, fairly numerous.
[53] Tyconius, *Regulae*, ed. Burkitt p. 75, 5 and p. 50 (Burkitt's edition is reissued with English translation by W. S. Babcock (Atlanta, 1989)). [54] Aug. *Enarr in Ps.* 132. 2.
[55] Aug. *Ep.* 185.12 and elsewhere. [56] Optatus, III.3.

to the emperor's notice at Ravenna, and so became the catalyst for serious repression. In May 411 a vast conference of Donatist and Catholic bishops gathered at Carthage under the presidency of an imperial commissioner, Marcellinus.[57] Inevitably, his verdict said the Catholics had won, and was intended to justify a renewed repression: Donatists with money had to meet fines, peasants endured floggings. After initial hesitations Augustine discovered that these moves were bringing over to the Catholics believers more devout and virtuous than many of his own flock.[58] Fears of insincere conversions proved largely unfounded.

Augustine provided a theory of remedial punishment to justify the coercion which, he insisted, was loving correction to give Donatists a chance of getting to heaven such as their uncharitable schism barred to them. Internal assent comes with time. Schoolboys need to be beaten into learning their lesson, but are afterwards grateful for what they have learned. The master in the parable said 'Compel them to come in', and the cleansing of the temple shows that even Christ did not always limit himself to gentle persuasion. When Augustine wrote 'Love and do as you like',[59] his context was both a justification of coercion and an insistence that its mode must be limited to a paternal loving correction, never vindictive. To Donatists the floggings did not seem too loving.

Augustine had some difficulty in opposing the Donatist understanding of church and sacraments, because his opponents stood by Cyprian, the hero-martyr of the African churches whose annual commemoration was marked by all-night dancing in the streets of Carthage. Augustine felt sure that Cyprian was humble enough to learn as well as powerful to teach. So great a saint would have come round to see that the validity of baptism depends not on the holiness of the minister but on Christ whose sacrament is being given. Donatists rigorously followed Cyprian's doctrine of the church, the walled garden of the Beloved in the Song of Songs, and denied validity to all Catholic sacraments. In their eyes Augustine was a schismatic layman. Augustine's ecumenism astonished many Catholic colleagues by affirming the validity of all Donatist sacraments including ordination (so that converting Donatist clergy should not be reordained), with the qualification that the proper efficacy of their sacraments was found only when they joined the Catholic communion.

Most of what Augustine knew about eastern heretics he derived from his reading of Epiphanius of Salamis in Cyprus.[60] In the prologue to his own work on the heresies, he commented that a universally valid definition of

---

[57] See the richly annotated edition of the Acts of this conference by S. Lancel (1972–91).
[58] Aug. *De Bapt.* IV.10.14; *Ep.* 93.16f.   [59] Aug. *In Ep. Joh.* VII.8.
[60] In 375 Epiphanius published his *Panarion* or *Medicine Chest for the Cure of all Heresies*. He dealt in detail with eighty, corresponding in number to the concubines of Solomon.

heresy is impossible. In his understanding, orthodoxy was as much a matter of will and intention as of mental assent to propositions in the apostolic role of faith. On obscure points outside the credenda (especially incarnation and resurrection), ignorance and error are compatible with orthodoxy; theological mistakes are not to be classified as heresies. Augustine knew many Christians who shared the intellectual difficulties felt by thoughtful pagans who found it hard to believe in Christ's wonderful birth and resurrection. But puzzled believers were a very different matter from heretics who reformulated Christian beliefs in ways unacceptable to the community and who refused correction.

In North Africa, Arianism was known about but was a marginal issue. Augustine encountered immigrant 'Arians', followers of the doctrines of Palladius of Ratiaria; and near the end of his life Gothic soldiers were billeted in Hippo (c. 427) accompanied by their bishop Maximin, with whom Augustine engaged in public disputation. Augustine was much aware that unsophisticated laity, without training in philosophical or theological questions, could easily suppose that the Father precedes the Son in time, and that the Johannine text 'The Father is greater than I' clinches the debate in a non-Nicene sense. So it was necessary for him to show that to say the Word of God is 'begotten' of the Father is not to think there is any change in God, a birth in the least like physical human birth; and above all it is not an event in time. Augustine's big book on the Trinity (a work of which he himself was severely critical but which must certainly rank among his greater achievements) was not a formal or direct attack on Arianism, but rather an attempt to make the doctrine of the Trinity more accessible to educated pagans who thought it unintelligible gobbledegook and to state the doctrine in a way that was invulnerable to the Arian flank attack which claimed that orthodoxy itself used arguments which conceded the subordination of the Son.

To make sure of averting the Arian contention that the Holy Spirit is at the summit of the created order, not on an equality with the Father and the Son in total unity, Augustine diffidently suggested that on the basis of John 15.26 and 20.22 the Spirit may be said to be sent forth by the Father and the Son together.[61] There is a single *principium*. But to speak of the Spirit as proceeding from the Father, and not to affirm that the Son is united with the Father in this, seemed to Augustine to leave the orthodox doctrine of the Trinity insecure before acute Arian onslaughts. But, he conceded, 'it is a rare soul that when speaking of the Trinity knows the meaning of the words he is using'. Indeed, the more confident the claim to understand everything in this matter, the more sure one can be that the claimant has not the light of truth (*Conf.* XIII.11.12 and *Ep.* 242.5).

---

[61] Among the Greek theologians similar language appears in Epiphanius and Cyril of Alexandria. Controversy between east and west on this issue first appears in the mid seventh century.

The troubles of a monk from Gaul named Leporius brought the Christological problem to Augustine's attention. Leporius upset the bishop of Marseilles by so stressing the distinction of the divine and human natures that he forgot to safeguard the union. Under Augustine's guidance he formulated a statement of his penitence to the Gallic bishops, regretting that he had denied that Mary's child was the Son of God. He averted Sabellianism by declaring that the *persona* of the Son of God, not the *natura* of the divine Trinity, was united with the flesh. Christ is, he said, both *totus Deus* and *totus homo* (*PL* XXXI.1225).

For Augustine it was essential for the salvation of humanity that the mediator be both God and man, not merely (as he himself had once believed) a man of superior wisdom. The humanity of Christ is 'the milk of babes', who advance to acknowledge the presence of God in him. By the incarnation humanity was drawn into the divine, not the divine stripped away. Neither the divine nor the human natures are changed from what they are. Even the ascended and glorified humanity of Christ is not coeternal with God. Yet he is one Christ, 'a single *person* constituted from two substances', his human soul being the mediator between the divine Word and the body. Were Christ no more than a wise man, he would give us an example but no more. It was the error of the British monk Pelagius to suppose that an example could suffice.

The dispute with Pelagius turned on issues of extreme intricacy but of an apparent simplicity. Is salvation a free gift of divine grace which no human being can merit? Or is there an element of reward for a life of virtuous and charitable actions and sentiments? The second question could be restated as asking if there is moral value before God in goodness of life, so that even if salvation is not something to which anyone has a claim and right, it is nevertheless appropriate to think that heaven is where the wicked will not be at home and the good will be (or may become so). The first question may presuppose that the inherent sinfulness in human nature is so deeply ingrained that only a sovereign act of divine omnipotence can redeem, and that 'the only thing of one's own that one can contribute to one's salvation is the sin from which one needs to be saved'.[62]

Pelagius feared Manicheism with its dualism and determinism. In Rome he heard a bishop[63] condoning the unregenerate sexual lives of professing Christians in the city by quoting from Augustine's *Confessions* (X.40): 'You command continence; grant what you command, and command what you will.' Such a doctrine of human impotence seemed to Pelagius morally enervating and a fatal encouragement to the evasion of responsibility. Pelagius did not for a moment deny that human wills are weak and need the help of grace, or that in baptism there is a free remission of all sins

[62] *Tract. in Joh.* v.1; XLIX.8, and often elsewhere.   [63] Aug. *De Dono Perseverantiae* 53.

which is in no sense merited; but he was also sure that in scripture, in the example of Christ and of righteous persons, God's help takes the form of ethical instruction and demand. To make the grace of God entirely responsible for any good action or thought and to deny any degree of need for human co-operation seemed to him the way to catastrophe.

Augustine first began to take notice of the argument in 411–12. The Gothic invasion of Italy and sack of Rome in 410 created many refugees; pope Innocent I himself left Rome for Ravenna,[64] and Pelagius with a disciple Celestius (a well-to-do lawyer who had embraced the ascetic life) went initially to Sicily and then to North Africa. At the time of the great Catholic/Donatist conference at Carthage in May 411, Augustine and Pelagius saw one another but without having conversation, and Pelagius went on to the Holy Land, leaving Celestius in North Africa. Celestius precipitated dissension. He was credited with denying that physical death is a punishment for sin; that Adam's fall injured anyone but himself; that newborn infants have any sin to be remitted in their baptism; that the moral law is less important than the gospel of forgiveness in gaining entry to heaven; and that before Christ's coming there were no saints of spotless life. An accusation of heresy was brought before Aurelius, bishop of Carthage, at which, despite his eloquent protests that he was not denying the need for infants to be baptized, Celestius was declared excommunicate. He left for Ephesus.

Augustine was moved to write by the sympathy which Celestius' theses evoked in Africa. He composed first a refutation of an extant tract by Rufinus the Syrian (On the Faith) to which Pelagius' sympathizers were appealing.[65] Rufinus there contended that physical death is a natural human condition, not a penalty for Adam's sin, and that infant baptism is not the remission of an inherited flaw, though from birth infants are open to contracting sins and are in need of redemption. A potent argument on the Pelagian side was that God cannot be thought to give commands which it is impossible to carry out. Augustine's willingness to say that the roots of human sinfulness lie in carnal begetting was difficult to clear of the accusations that this was Manichee. He affirmed that the human will is of divine gift, but this must be understood as a cold capacity for choice rather than an actual desire to do the right and the good. A person experiencing temptation does not feel the scales to be equally weighted between right and wrong. Moreover, that the flaw in fallen humanity is linked with sexual reproduction seemed to Augustine demonstrable from an observation adumbrated in Cicero's *Hortensius*[66] – namely, that the sexual impulse in human beings is not controlled by the rational will, and its effects engender shame.

---

[64] Innoc. *Ep.* 16, *PL* xx.519; Oros. vii.39.
[65] Rufin. *De Fide*, in *PL* xxi.1123–54. Augustine replied with his *De Peccatorum Meritis*.
[66] Fr. 84 Grilli=Aug. *C. Jul.* iv.14.72 (*PL* xliv.774); also echoed in *De Civ. Dei* xiv.16.

Augustine dedicated his discussion of these questions to Marcellinus, tribune and *notarius*, who had been the government's representative presiding over the Donatist/Catholic conference of May 411. His remarks troubled Marcellinus, to whom it seemed paradoxical to say that while a sinless life is possible, no one except Christ has been known to achieve it. Marcellinus' puzzlement evoked from Augustine his best-thought-out tract in the Pelagian controversy, entitled *On the Spirit and the Letter*. He feared that Pelagius might be taken to be saying that anyone can do what is right by mere effort of will without the internal help of grace, whereas St Paul is clear that we are justified by grace, which is not to say that our will plays no part in our justification. What grace gives, therefore, is the *desire* to do what is right and good. To say that human nature is endowed with the power to choose what is good and right is of merely academic interest if the urgent longing to achieve it is absent. The inward motivation is the crux. And for Augustine the moral value of an action is immediately dependent on the intention with which it is done. Therefore, the letter which kills is the moral command which tells the conscience what to do and confers no impetus to do it.

Pelagius in the Holy Land found Greek supporters and friends, but crossed swords with Jerome, living in his monastery at Bethlehem, and with Orosius, the Spanish priest who fled from the barbarians invading Spain to join Augustine at Hippo and then travelled on to the holy places.

The debate in its next stage increasingly concentrated on the flaw in human nature which Augustine called 'original sin' and which, in his view, allowed sinlessness to be affirmed only of Christ and perhaps (Augustine neither asserted nor denied it) of Mary his mother, the model for women ascetics.[67] In the Holy Land Orosius, soon to be supported by two Gallic bishops expelled from Arles and Aix, accused Pelagius before the bishop of Jerusalem and his synod. The question was whether Pelagius taught the possibility of avoiding sin. Pelagius agreed that he did so teach, but not that it was possible without the help of God, and not that there was a concrete instance of a human being living wholly without sin. At a provincial synod at Diospolis (Lydda) in December 415 Pelagius was acquitted of heresy. He stood by his position that a sin is a freely chosen act for which the doer is responsible and that, with God's help, it is possible to avoid sin. When Augustine was able to study the record of the synod, he felt that Pelagius had not made clear what he meant by God's help. For Pelagius, was this no more than the prescription of a moral code? Or did he agree with Augustine that the necessary help must include an interior grace working within the soul to impart delight in the doing of the good and the right?

The vindication of Pelagius in the Holy Land moved Augustine to take

---

[67] Aug. *De Natura et Gratia* XXXVI.42; *C. Julianum opus imperf.* IV.122.

political steps in support of his theological campaign. He was already disturbed to discover how much support at Rome Pelagius was receiving from some Roman clergy and from the powerful house of the Anicii.[68] In 416 Augustine arranged for a grand riposte to the synod of Diospolis. Two African councils, at Carthage and at Milev, censured Pelagius as a heretic denying both prayer and infant baptism, and asked pope Innocent I for his confirmation of their judgement. Innocent concurred that unless Pelagius repudiated such opinions he must be held excommunicate.[69] He was pleased that the African bishops (often minded to assert some independence of Roman authority) had appealed to Rome for a final verdict. Augustine triumphantly declared that a decision given by two councils and confirmed by the Roman see had put an end to the controversy: *Causa finita est.*[70] In actuality the theological debate was still in its early stages, and the political situation vastly changed on the death of Innocent I on 12 March 417. He was succeeded by Zosimus,[71] a Greek who owed his election to the support of influential persons sympathetic to Pelagius. Zosimus' declaration that Pelagius was not a heretic caused consternation to Augustine and his African supporters. It seemed unimaginable to him that the apostolic see of Peter should reach a decision at variance with what he confidently believed to be the general mind of the universal church. There remained only one court of appeal to which he could turn in hope of obtaining a reversal of the Roman decision in Pelagius' favour – namely, the secular power.

The plea was put to the imperial court that at the city of Rome the Pelagian issue was becoming socially divisive. The populace was becoming excited about the debate, and there was a threat of considerable public disorder. Riots occurred in Rome which the Pelagians believed to be instigated by Augustine's supporters. Moreover, in the Holy Land Jerome's role in the controversy had made him sufficiently unpopular to be the target of an attack on his monastery. The rising tension made it simple to deploy persuasive arts upon high officials at Ravenna. Augustine was helped by his old friend Alypius, bishop of Thagaste, who was a trained lawyer and was more expert in dealing with bureaucrats. Alypius' activity was able to gain support at the emperor's court in Ravenna (there were allegations of vast bribery) and to obtain a crushing edict (30 April 418) expelling all Pelagians from Rome as a threat to public order.[72] Faction had been developing at Rome, as is evident from the divided papal election following Zosimus' death in 419, which pro-

---

[68] Aug. *De Gestis Pelagii* 46 (Pelagius highly respected in Rome).

[69] Aug. *C. Jul.* 1.13 ('Innocent had no alternative but to ratify what the African councils and the Roman church, with the others, had always held').

[70] Aug. *Serm.* 131 (23 September 417). He also used the same phrase after the verdict against Donatism at the Carthage conference of 411 (e.g. *C. Gaudentium* 11.14).   [71] *RE* xA (1972) 841–4.

[72] Aug. *C. Jul.* 1.42; III.35 (Alypius bribed the court at Ravenna with eighty horses). Edict: *PL* LVI.490.

duced two rival bishops. Zosimus bowed to the emperor's will and demanded
the signatures of all Italian bishops to a profession of faith to the effect that
baptism communicates remission of sins to all, including infants, who are
thereby liberated from the guilt attaching to the sin inherited from Adam.[73]
That demand evoked protest from a learned bishop in south Italy, Julian of
Eclanum. But by the edict Pelagians were treated as common criminals.

Augustine's invocation of first the pope and then the emperor hugely
raised the stakes in the Pelagian controversy, and made an intricate theological issue a grand question of authority. Innocent and Zosimus were both
ignored by the court, and Zosimus correctly saw that the standing of his
see left him no option but to submit to the emperor's policy of supporting
the African bishops. He could not leave the imperial edict without the reinforcement of his episcopal ruling, for that would have made his humiliation even greater.

The Pelagians expelled from Italy and Africa found support in the Greek
east, but their attempts to win recognition in the west failed. The last decade
of Augustine's life, however, became dominated by the need to defend
himself against the powerful attack of Julian of Eclanum. The two overriding issues in this stage of the debate were the goodness of sexuality and
marriage and the correct understanding of divine predestination. For Julian
sexuality was part of the order of creation, and it was intolerable that
Augustine should disparage it as a corrupt instrument for the transmission
of original sin from Adam. Augustine replied that in paradise the sexual relation between Adam and Eve was flawless, rational and a source of supreme
pleasure to them; but the Fall brought the penalty that the sexual impulse was
no longer under the control of reason (an idea Augustine had found in
Porphyry,[74] reinforcing the influence of Cicero's *Hortensius*), often aroused
when not wanted, and failing to be aroused when the partners wished for it.[75]

The supreme argument for the sovereignty of divine grace was the doctrine that the elect souls who are saved are predestined by the inscrutable
judgement of God. The Greek theologians believed God's judgement to
be based on his foreknowledge of the choices made by the individual.
Augustine came to fear that this must imply salvation on the ground of
merit rather than of grace. Elect human souls, he believed, were the
number required to replace the fallen angels who lapsed with Satan.[76] They
were a substantial minority (*magna massa*) of the human race.[77] That grace
to save was not imparted to the majority enabled divine justice to be
manifested. Yet his justice is always merciful.[78]

---

[73] *PL* xx.693–5. Only fragments survive.   [74] Porph. *Sententiae* XL.5.

[75] Aug. *De Nuptiis et Concupiscentia* II.59.

[76] *Enchiridion* 29; cf. 61–2. He rejected, however, the opinion of Apuleius (*De Deo Socratis* 15; *De Civ.
Dei* IX.11) that at death souls become *daemones*.   [77] *De Correptione et Gratia* 28; *Serm.* 111.1.

[78] *Enarr. in Ps.* 39.19. Election may depend on hidden merit (*Div. Qu.* 83, 68).

By 420 Augustine was beginning to attract criticism not only from Julian but from others, in Africa and then in southern Gaul, who thought his doctrine of grace was failing to preserve responsibility and the reality of free choice. Augustine replied that only the elect had the freedom not to sin, and this reply was hard to distinguish from the doctrine of Manicheism. Augustine remained unmoved by the charge. His statements became increasingly uncompromising. As early as the *Confessions*, written soon after he became bishop of Hippo, he was declaring that 'in crowning our merits God rewards his own gifts'.[79] The heightened awareness of the Pelagian controversy made everyone sensitive to the implications of such a declaration. A pagan intellectual whom he sought to convert to Christianity blandly replied that divine grace had not yet granted him the will and that he would wait until that occurred.[80]

Augustine moved to the sombre view that, just as the saved are predestined to receive grace, so the majority of souls, created to vindicate divine justice, receive what they deserve, which is condemnation. In short, divine predestination is more than a passive foreknowledge; it is causal.[81] God's election is not grounded in any quality of piety in the elect individual which divine foreknowledge has foreseen. No human mind can know what reason moved God to save one and not another, but there can be no complaint of injustice. God's saints become holy because they are predestinate, not predestinate because they become holy.

The louder the cries of outrage greeting his language, the more uncompromising the old Augustine became, but at the same time the more apparent became the weaknesses in his position. He allowed that a sign of being among the elect is to persevere in faith and grace to the end of life. As long as life lasts, it is uncertain whether the elect are truly elect, and Christians pray for perseverance. The fact of their praying shows that perseverance is itself a gift of grace. Admittedly perseverance must be prayed for, but prayer is not in itself a meritorious act. So when the question is put, Why do some who have worshipped long years in good faith, fail to persevere while others do so, Augustine can only say he does not know.

A further awkward question is whether predestination should be preached. Augustine's answer is that it should be mentioned but not frequently or prominently; 'it is to be preached inoffensively, but not in such a way as to be self-evidently wrong',[82] and therefore a congregation should not be told that some of them are predestinate, some reprobate. The third person, not the second, should be employed.

The western church did not accept Augustine's predestinarianism as authentic Catholic doctrine. It was always open to the lethal charge of *curiositas*, claiming to know matters which God has not thought fit to reveal.

---

[79] *Conf.* IX.13.34. The epigrammatic statement occurs about a dozen times in Augustine's writings.
[80] Aug. *Ep.* 2.7 Divjak (*CSEL* LXXXVIII).   [81] *De Dono Perseverantiae* 41.
[82] *De Dono Perseverantiae* 57.

In the background of the Pelagian controversy the texts on either side make periodic references to Origen, whose polemic against Gnosticism in the third century laid stress on freedom as an indestructible possession of the rational being (angelic or human) and on the subordination of divine justice to divine goodness. A controversial figure in his lifetime, Origen became a contentious name after a vehement attack on his orthodoxy by Epiphanius of Salamis (Cyprus), published in 375.[83]

Jerome's work as a biblical commentator depended to a far-reaching degree on the Greek commentaries of Origen, and initially he had been an avowed admirer. Epiphanius of Salamis, with whom he travelled to Rome in 382 to take part in discussions with pope Damasus about the western response to the council of Constantinople (381), convinced Jerome that Origen was dangerous, the father of Arianism, sponsor of hazardous and unorthodox speculations about the salvability of the devil and universal salvation for all souls. Epiphanius vehemently attacked Origen for teaching the pre-existence of souls, imprisoned in material bodies because of the Fall but destined to return in the resurrection to ethereal vehicles.

At Bethlehem and Jerusalem Jerome fell into sharp controversy with his old friend Rufinus of Aquileia, who shared his enthusiasm for the monastic life and remained an admirer of Origen after Jerome's respect had been eroded by Epiphanius. The Origenist controversy had at its centre the question whether, subject to acceptance of the apostolic rule of faith, the theologian and exegete is thereafter free to speculate, asking legitimate questions, but content to know that answers are not vouch-safed by revelation. In the monasteries of sixth-century Palestine there were admirers of Origen who urged that his speculations fell into the area of *adiaphora*, matters on which orthodox believers could legitimately disagree, provided that there was no questioning of the basic credenda.[84]

Fuel was added to the all too personal squabble between Rufinus and Jerome by the spiritual teaching of an impassioned Origenist and ascetic in the Egyptian desert, Evagrius from Pontus (d. 399).[85] Evagrius combined rigorous discipline in the ordering of the life of prayer with exciting, often obscure and mysterious speculations inspired by Origen. In Alexandria the blind teacher Didymus also held Origen in high regard. But in Egypt there were monks who distrusted these Origenist teachers, especially when they began to teach that authentic prayer is achieved by a negative subtraction from the mind of all physical images of God, or of Christ. The monks forced their archbishop at Alexandria, Theophilus, into censuring the

---

[83] *Panarion* 64.

[84] Cyril of Scythopolis, *Life of St Cyriacus* 12 (ed. E. Schwartz, TU 49, 2 (1939) 229, 26); Eng. tr. by R. M. Price (1991) p. 253.   [85] Guillaumont (1962) with bibliography.

Origenist ascetics.[86] Four of the ascetics travelled to Constantinople and were welcomed there by the recently appointed successor to Nectarius, John – later known as Chrysostom – golden-mouthed – because of his spell-binding oratory in the pulpit. The move precipitated an angry quarrel between Theophilus of Alexandria and John, ending in John's defeat and death in exile. The controversy about Origen's orthodoxy became acute again in the time of Justinian who, by decree, condemned Origen, Evagrius and Didymus.[87] But before the sixth century it did not become a grand issue in church and state.

The Arian controversy had apparently been a continuation of third-century debates about the mutual relations of Father and Son in the eternal Trinity who is one God, and about the proposition implicit in the writing of Justin Martyr (c. 150) that 'Father' is a name for God transcendent, 'Son' for God immanent. Soon after Justin, Athenagoras had already proposed the distinction 'begotten not made';[88] and in the third century Origen persuasively contended that the generation of the divine Son could not be a temporal event but must be an eternal timeless fact.[89] Before 360 much of the debate revolved round questions, and employed terminology, that belonged to the previous century. But underlying the fourth-century controversy lay the Christological problem. Whether one followed Arius at one extreme or Marcellus of Ancyra at the other, the incarnation was the doctrine that held the key. This truth was clearly seen by Apollinaris of Laodicea, whose relations to Athanasius were close; and both in his third *Oration against the Arians* and in a major *Letter* to Epictetus, bishop of Corinth, written in the 360s, Athanasius directly grappled with some of the issues. The letter to Epictetus enjoyed high authority in the fifth century as an Alexandrian statement of orthodox Christology.

In Arian Christology the Son is inferior and less than fully divine because he suffers: the Logos is the moving mind in the body, which is the seat of the 'passions' (i.e. all experiences in which the mind is not the active agent). The reaction of Eustathius of Antioch, Marcellus of Ancyra and his pupil Photinus of Sirmium was to stress that Jesus, though united to the Word, was fully, spontaneously human. In the west, Hilary of Poitiers vigorously affirmed the completeness of the humanity of Christ, but added that because of the union with the divine Word this humanity could suffer as and when the Word so willed and not otherwise.[90]

Athanasius did not make it a charge against his 'Arian' opponents that they allowed no place for a human soul in Christ. His way of reconciling

---

[86] Socr. *HE* vi.7f. On the quarrel between John and Theophilus see Liebeschuetz, *Barbarians and Bishops*, biography of John by Baur (1929–30), translated by M. Gonzaga (1959); J. N. D. Kelly (1996).
[87] This censure was confirmed by the fifth ecumenical council at Constantinople (553), the Acts of which survive in a Latin version.   [88] Athenagoras, *Legatio* x (ed. Schwartz, p. 11. 8).
[89] Origen, *De Principiis* i.2.9.   [90] *De Trinitate* x.20–1.

divine immutability and transcendence with the frailties and sufferings of mortal humanity was to attribute everything to the body rather than to the soul which, though not denied, played no significant part in his thinking about salvation. For him the crux was that the incarnate Lord must be God; one who is himself part of the world, involved in our human transience, ignorance and weakness of will, cannot be the Saviour of the world.

The Alexandrian 'Logos-Flesh Christology' naturally stands in contrast with a Logos-Man Christology often associated (but loosely) with Antioch. The latter was expounded with power and verve by Theodore, bishop of Mopsuestia (near Adana) in Cilicia.

Theodore understood sin to have been conquered by the acts of Christ's human free will united to the Holy Spirit. Accordingly the rational soul of the redeemer is essential to the very possibility of salvation, and cannot be – must not be – obliterated by absorption in the engulfing greatness of the divine Word. Therefore one must carefully distinguish between the two natures, even though they were intimately united and bonded to form one *prosopon* and a single *hypostasis*. Theodore was falsely criticized for teaching two *hypostases* in the one Christ. He believed the worshipper adores Christ in one undivided adoration. He affirmed Mary to be 'Mother of God' (Theotokos). He did not wish to speak, as Gregory of Nazianzus had spoken, of a 'mixing' of the two natures.

Nestorius, a disciple of Theodore but altogether less tactful and careful in his language when excited in the pulpit, became famous as a preacher at Antioch. He was carried off by force to be patriarch of Constantinople in 428. He had a particular dread of subtle infiltration on the part of Apollinarian theologians, and offended pious ears in the monasteries by deploring a veneration of Mary which went 'over the top' and treated her as a goddess.[91] Moreover, the title Theotokos, well established since the first half of the third century, and not rejected out of hand by Nestorius as unacceptable, seemed to him to be used to encourage the confusion of the divine and human natures. She was mother of Christ's humanity and on that ground to be honoured. But to invoke her intercession as 'Mother of God' left him feeling ill at ease. It might prejudice her solidarity with humanity.

In 412 Theophilus of Alexandria died, his most famous achievements being the destruction of the Alexandrian temple of Serapis and of John Chrysostom at Constantinople. He was succeeded by his nephew Cyril, whose prejudices in regard to Constantinople were similar. In 428 some malcontents disciplined by Cyril travelled from Alexandria to Constantinople to appeal to the emperor Theodosius II. The emperor naturally referred their case to the patriarch Nestorius, lately installed and enthroned.

---

[91] Cyril of Alexandria, *Adv. Nestorium* 1.9 (VI p. 90 Pusey).

Cyril took umbrage at this new patriarch of an upstart see sitting in judgement on his rectitude and justice. Cyril was not by nature a man who found toleration easy, and he had a profound dread of a Christology which divided Christ. Theodore of Mopsuestia used language which alarmed him, and in a large commentary on St John's Gospel written before Nestorius arrived in Constantinople Cyril had taken frequent occasion to proclaim the unity of Christ. He disliked those who split up the words and sayings of Christ, allocating miracles to the divine nature, weaknesses to the human. Primary for Cyril is the 'sharing of the properties' (*communicatio idiomatum*), and therefore paradox is inevitable. None of the frailties and limitations of human nature is applicable to the divine nature; none of the divine characteristics (omniscience, omnipotence, omnipresence, pre-existence) can be asserted of humble human flesh; so if it is agreed that Arianism is to be rejected, and that the Word is as fully divine as the Father, high tension results. Devotional language may want to say 'God died on the Cross', but the theologian in his study has to draw distinctions, for suffering is not to be predicated of the transcendent God.

But for Cyril nothing is worse than to assert the distinctions in such a way as to leave the believer with two Sons, two *prosopa* – namely, the pre-existent Son of God and the inspired man who was son of Mary, these being only rather loosely connected. That Cyril understood to be a divorce between the Christ of faith and the Jesus of history. Nestorius' slighting remarks about the Theotokos title offended Cyril deeply. To prove that Nestorius was deviating from the classical tradition of Catholic orthodoxy, Cyril sought to compile an anthology or florilegium of texts from orthodox authorities to support his case. Several, current under the name of Athanasius or pope Julius, were Apollinarian work. Apollinaris had spoken of Christ as one nature and one *hypostasis*. For him, to assert two natures meant to assert a psychological duality. Terminology fluctuated in this area. One anti-Apollinarian tract, published under Athanasius' name probably about 390–400, attacked as inherently impossible a union constituting one *hypostasis*, but asserted the correctness of saying that the union in Christ produced one *physis*.[92] At some points in the argument of both Apollinaris and Cyril, it is explicit that the reception of the divine body of Christ in the eucharist is central to the Alexandrian comprehension of religion. The communicant worships one Christ, not a duality.

Cyril wrote an irate letter to Nestorius accusing him of heresy which therefore disqualified him from judging. When Nestorius secured some support in the imperial palace, Cyril resorted to a stronger letter with twelve anathemas denouncing the notion that Jesus was an inspired man distinct from the divine Word, and requiring Nestorius to assent to the 'hypostatic

[92] *PG* XXVI.1113B.

union' of the Word with the flesh of Christ. Irritation which Nestorius caused to pope Celestine by being hospitable to Pelagian refugees from the west made it easy for Cyril to win Roman support; in the summer of 430 pope Celestine held a Roman council which condemned Nestorius' doctrines, as supplied to Rome by Cyril, and remitted to Cyril the task of implementing this censure.

So on the eve of the council of Ephesus in June 431 the stage was set for a major conflagration. The council of Ephesus inaugurated a series of ecumenical councils, and numerous colloquia and lesser councils, to try to reach agreement between the two main groups. The party of 'one nature', called by their opponents 'Monophysites', regarded the party of 'two natures' as holding Jesus to be no more than an inspired man. The party of 'two natures' regarded the opposition as losing the humanity of Christ altogether.

In the 370s Basil of Caesarea described the controversies in the church as a night battle in fog during which those who were on the same side were unable to distinguish friend from foe.[93] In the 430s Firmus of Caesarea wrote of the endeavour to heal the breach at and after the council of Ephesus as resembling the tragic struggles of Sisyphus in Hades, for ever fated to push a boulder up a steep hill only to find it escaping his grasp just as he reached the top.[94]

Often the issues revolved round slogans, and the phenomenon soon appeared in which people could oppose their own theology if expressed in terms with which they were unfamiliar. Yet the issues in the controversies were important and real. In a Christian doctrine of redemption it was necessary to have no doubt that the redeemer is divine – from the divine side of the gulf between Creator and dependent creation made out of nothing at his will – since (as the Alexandrians repeatedly said) one who is part of the world cannot be its redeemer. It was no less necessary that the redeemer be in solidarity with humanity, and therefore should unambiguously be man, conquering sin and death by fidelity to his vocation and obedience to the divine will. The estimate of human nature was likewise an underlying issue. The Pelagian doctrine of human capacity to keep the commandments of God seemed to make redemption by grace a matter of modest assistance but perhaps not utterly necessary. The Manichee doctrine seemed to put ordinary mortals so sunk in the mud of matter and sex that they are irretrievably lost and beyond the (limited) power of divine rescue.

Beyond these permanent questions within Christian thought there also lay a problem in effect arising from the opening words of St John's Gospel that the Word of God is both 'with God' and 'God'. The Arian controversy required some answer to the question how Christ can be both identical with

---

[93] *De Spiritu Sancto* 76.   [94] Firmus, *Ep.* 38 (*SChrét.* 350, 1989).

the object of worship and at the same time a mediator towards the object of worship. Athanasius judged that Christ could be the second only if he were also the first: it was an axiom inherited from Irenaeus that 'through God alone can God be known'.[95] The Arian controversy therefore turned on the concept of Mediator: is he, as it were, half-way between Creator and creature? or is he both Creator and creature, and, if so, how can the unity of his person be intelligibly asserted?

It will have been clear that the question of redemption lies at the heart of the fourth- and fifth-century controversies. Even in Donatism this question is acute, because the two sides in the debate both claimed to be the unique and exclusive ark outside which there is no salvation. To Athanasius, Arius' desire to see in Christ the supreme figure in the created order, the apex of the communion of saints, lost sight of the need for a fully divine redeemer to bridge the gulf between the Creator and the finite created order made out of nothing and morally unstable in consequence. To Cyril of Alexandria, Nestorius' language had many of the same defects, because the unity of the person of Christ was threatened by strong assertions about the two natures. In Augustine's eyes Pelagius offered believers an external moral code and a noble example in Jesus, but less than the pouring of the love of God into the inner being of the believer without which the moral life is not achieved.

The social and political effect of the controversies in the church was considerable. In North Africa the rancour of the dissension between Catholic and Donatist made many peasants revert to their old polytheistic rites.[96] Augustine knew pagan intellectuals who pointed to the easy tolerance characteristic of paganism in matters of belief, and contrasted it with the passionate intolerance of Christian controversy.[97] Ammianus Marcellinus – often, for a pagan, surprisingly sympathetic to Christianity – comments on Julian's antipathy to the animal savagery that Christians could show to one another, and on the ferocious faction at episcopal elections in great cities, that at Rome in 366 resulting in 137 dead in the basilica.[98] The incident was not typical, but some degree of partisanship at elections was very common.[99] The Roman empire had concentrated power at the top, and steadily eroded that of local councils. People were not accustomed to a popular movement in which everyone was understood to be an active participant. The consent of the plebs was indispensable to an episcopal election, and in that they were commonly led by the magistrates and well-to-do citizens. The church was a democracy in the sense that the consent of the

[95] Irenaeus, *Adv. Haereses* IV.6.4.   [96] Aug. *Ep.* 20.20 (368) Divjak, *CSEL* LXXXVIII.

[97] *De Utilitate Ieiunii* 9; *Serm.* 47.28. *Ep.* 118. 21 (debates between philosophical schools are now replaced by theological controversy).   [98] Amm. Marc. XXVII.3.12–13.

[99] Joh. Chrys. *De Sacerdotio* III.10. On elections in the fourth century see Gryson (1973); (1979), with bibliography.

faithful as a whole possessed authority. Bishops often found their congregations critical of their sermons or of their administration of the church chest. Nevertheless the power-base of a bishop in his city rested on the degree of his mass following among the people. For the Roman empire that was an uncomfortable development, and one which the secular authorities did not know how to cope with.

CHAPTER 20

ASCETICISM: PAGAN AND CHRISTIAN

PETER BROWN

In A.D. 360, Julian, then Caesar in Gaul and already a convinced polytheist, scanned the roads leading into Besançon in the hope of catching a glimpse of a figure wearing the unmistakable dark cloak of a philosopher – his mentor, Maximus of Ephesus (Jul. *Ep.* 8). Only a few years before, immediately after the death in Egypt of the great Christian hermit in 356, the *Life of Antony* had appeared in Greek. It enjoyed instant success throughout the Roman world. By 370, a Latin translation existed, and was soon available in Gaul, being read by a group of ascetics settled in a cottage outside Trier (Aug. *Conf.* VII.6.15). Henceforth in Gaul, as elsewhere, the roads would never lack their share of Christian monks – austere, instantly recognizable figures. Later in the century, when passing through the Touraine, the horses of an imperial coach shied at the sight of a traveller striding alongside them 'in a shaggy tunic, with his black cloak flapping' – St Martin of Tours visiting the country churches of his diocese (Sulp. Sev. *Dial.* II.3).

In many provinces, Christian and non-Christian ascetics eyed each other with curiosity and, frequently, with unconcealed disapprobation. When, in the 340s, a party of monks arrived at Panopolis to found a monastery outside the city, the local philosophers came out to warn them that they were bringing 'olives to Panopolis', coals to Newcastle: Panopolis already boasted possessors of an austere and ancient wisdom (*Vita Pachomii Graeca* 82).

Later in the century, as Christian monks came to play a prominent role in the destruction of their temples, polytheists committed themselves to memorable denunciations. Eunapius of Sardis, writing his *History* around 400, believed that the barbarous Visigoths had made use of Christian monks in their dealings with the empire. He was not surprised. In these sad times, he wrote,

It was sufficient to trail along grey cloaks and tunics, to be a ne'er do well and to have the reputation for being one. The barbarians used these devices to deceive the Romans, since they shrewdly observed that such persons were respected among them.

(Eunap. *Hist.* fr. 48.2)

Yet, at the turn of the fifth century, Christian ascetics were not invariably viewed in such alarmist terms by all bearers of the traditional culture. Synesius of Cyrene, for instance, though probably born a Christian, had been trained in philosophy by none other than the non-Christian Hypatia. Defending his own distinctive brand of spiritual training in studiously non-confessional terms, he invoked the names both of St Antony and of Zoroaster (Syn. *Dion* 10, ed. N. Terzaghi. Rome, 1944 259). Both could now be spoken of as remote 'culture heroes', as the representatives of a venerable Alien Wisdom.

Egyptian papyri connected with the regions of Oxyrhynchus and Antinooupolis enable us to glimpse, through the eyes of their admirers, both a Christian and a polytheist exponent of the ascetic life. The Christian hermit Paphnutius was approached by the lady Valeria in around A.D. 340: 'I believe that I receive healing on account of your prayers, for the revelations of the ascetics and worshippers [of God] are clear' (*P. London* 1926). Paphnutius received letters from clients and potential pupils:

because of your most holy and well-reputed way of life, and because you renounce the pretensions of the world and hate the arrogance of the vainglorious. We then rejoice in the report that you make manifest the most noble struggle.

(*P. London* 1927, tr. in Wimbush, 1990, 460–1)

Not far away, the philosopher Sarapion received a somewhat similar letter.

Our friend, Callinicus, was testifying to the utmost about the way of life you follow . . . especially in your not abandoning the *askēsis* [of your life] . . . Courage! Carry through what remains like a man! Let not wealth distract you, nor beauty, nor anything of the same kind: for there is no good in them, if virtue does not join her presence, no, they are vanishing and worthless.

(*P. Oxy.* 3069)

Sarapion was the reclusive hero of a group of gentleman-scholars. Rather than receiving from his correspondent a request for his prayers, he was asked to send a puppy to Soteris, a lady living in retirement on her country estate.

For worshippers of the ancient gods, there was nothing new about asceticism. *Askēsis* was long expected of a philosopher. A fourth-century papyrus from Panopolis contains a list of Greek thinkers and their schools from the time of the Pre-Socratics. The philosophers who went out to meet the monks evidently preserved the memory of the masters of Greek thought (W. H. Willis, *Illinois Classical Studies* III (1978) 140–51). Nothing less than a thousand years of intellectual and moral endeavour tended to fall into line, in their imagination, as a single chain, or series of chains, of great thinkers, who were also thought of as spiritual guides. Each one of them, if in very different and hotly contested ways, was believed to have developed his philosophy as a form of spiritual exercise, capable of transforming the personality of those who practised it. The claim to truth of any one 'philosophy' – or, we might say, way of life – was indissolubly linked to the claim that its adherents could achieve, through it, a measure of transformation.[1]

Thus, centuries of existential seriousness weighed on the figure of any thinker in late classical times. To live a life different from the thoughtless majority of one's fellows had long been *de rigueur*. What was specific to the late Roman period was the frequency and the urgency with which such rival claims to truth were made, in a manner that required constant, dramatic validation. Writing in 381 to justify his failure as bishop of Constantinople, Gregory of Nazianzus presented himself and the teachings of his own party with inimitable, classical fastidiousness. Faced, in his view, with intellectual *parvenus*, with 'pushers' of instant truth unrooted in a lifetime of spiritual growth, Gregory urged his readers to look, instead, to leaders whose claims to other-worldly authority were stamped on their very bodies: doctrines such as theirs bore 'the noble seal of a flesh worn down by prayer and countless hardships' (Greg. Naz. *Poemata de se ipso* XII.586, *PG* XXXVII.1208). In this brilliant travesty, we see the ancient mystique of the philosopher, as a figure whose teachings were guaranteed by his *askēsis*, invoked, this time, in the intensely competitive arena of the Christian church.

What is truly striking, in the ascetic literature of both polytheists and Christians, is the warm conviction, persistently, at times stridently, maintained, that through ascetic discipline – a discipline most usually initiated in response to a divine calling and brought to perfection by divine aid – profound transformations of the human person were possible. These transformations, known to have been successfully realized in men and women of flesh and blood, served to teach others about the essential structures and potentialities of the human person, about the relation between individual and society and, above all, about the relations of God or the gods to this world. Seldom had the potential for spiritual achievement in human beings, of either sex and of all classes, been debated with such vigour and with such lasting consequences as in this short period.

The outburst of creativity associated with the rise of asceticism in the later empire will always remain mysterious. We should remember, however, that the primary meaning of *askēsis*, as the intelligent and unremitting 'training' of mind and body, had long been associated with the supreme aristocratic refinement of the gymnasium. It summed up a sense that the human person was refinable. A craft of the self could be applied to the individual. Human beings were expected to respond, in a manner that far exceeded normal expectations, to the skilful application of a discipline.

[1] See esp. Hadot (1981) 13–58 with Hahn (1989).

This was held to be the case even by those religious thinkers, of which Augustine of Hippo was the most notable example, who tended to delegate that skill to God alone, as he worked upon the soul with the supreme skill of a master-goldsmith (Aug. *Serm.* 15.5). A sentence in the Syriac version of the *Life of Antony* makes this explicit: the great hermit made his début as an ascetic by becoming 'a perfect craftsman', a craftsman skilled 'in matters appertaining to the fear of God'.[2] *Idiopragmosynē*, careful application to the self, combined with constant prayer, was the hallmark of the ascetic and of any would-be imitator of ascetics (Pall. *Hist. Laus.* Praef. 7).

Altogether, a remarkable degree of confidence that it was possible to create new and exceptional persons characterized much of late Roman upper-class society, even outside the narrow circles discussed in this chapter. The public presentation of the self was an urgent matter. Conflicting groups competed for deference on the basis of distinctive life-styles, often shown even by clearly distinguished dress codes. The dark *tribônion* of the philosopher and now the studiously commonplace, rough robe of the Christian monk – the *schēma* – were but examples among many of the styles of clothing adopted to make plain the status and the chosen career of their wearers. Frank asymmetries of power were 'naturalized' by being presented as springing from intrinsic personal excellence, polished to perfection by long years of patient labour on the self. The star rhetoricians of the age claimed that their own skills were also the fruit of *askēsis*, of a lifelong, painful discipline of words.[3] The works of art produced by the upper classes – such as poetry and the study of occult lore – claimed superior authority through having emerged, not from the bustle of everyday life, but from minds healed by the deep therapy of leisure, associated with the aristocratic ideal of *otium* (Firm. Mat. *Math.* ix.proem.3). Whole classes claimed superiority on the basis of adherence to exacting codes of deportment. In the words of an ascetic writer:

Acquaint yourself with the way in which the daughters of the nobles of this world conduct themselves, with the manner of life they usually show and with the exercise with which they usually train themselves . . . [They] apply themselves to the creation of a different nature [from their fellows] by their conduct.

(*De Virginitate* 14, *PL* xxx.178A, tr. B. R. Rees, *The Letters of Pelagius and His Followers.* Woodbridge, 1991, 84)

In an analogy such as this, we can sense the adrenalin of aspirations – to excellence and to personal transformation – that ran in the veins of many late Roman persons. We should always bear in mind this wider background to the prestige of asceticism in the later Roman period. It was not a new phenomenon – not even in Christian circles. Nor can the motives that led

---

[2] *Vita Antonii Syriace* 7, tr. R. Draguet, *CSCO* ccccxviii, *Script. Syr.* 184. Louvain, 1980 13.2; on this text, see Barnes (1986).   [3] Kaster, *Guardians of Language* 16–17.

men and women to the ascetic life be treated under the single rubric of hatred of the flesh and flight from a declining world.[4] In a tense and ambitious age, asceticism was one possible form of achievement among many.

But asceticism was also a statement. Through an ascetic discipline that touched (with various degrees of severity) on primary bodily needs – food, sleep, shelter and clothing – and that even threatened, in certain circles, to undo indispensable links in the chain by which normal society reproduced itself – marriage, wealth and culture – ascetics could carry in their own bodies a whole alternative world-view – a view of the human person and an imagined model of society that flatly contradicted or at least challenged and rendered problematic the assumptions of the unthinking majority. Most important of all, late Roman asceticism would not have been so exuberantly creative if the 'statements' made by differing ascetic traditions and 'read' by those around them had not varied dramatically.

It is important to stress this diversity. At first glance, it is the common features of asceticism, as practised by Christians and non-Christians alike, that are striking. This is not only because the human person is only capable of a limited range of privations, so that fasting, sexual renunciation, indifference to wealth and studied disregard of social status tend to recur in roughly similar forms and with similar intensity among widely differing groups: to a modern reader all late antique ascetic practices can appear equal, because all seem to be equally a departure from what we have been accustomed to regard as the less ascetic, more world-affirming tone of the classical period. This chapter, by contrast, will concentrate on the differences in meaning, attached by differing groups, to what were often commonplace ascetic practices. In so doing, it will leave aside other issues. The origins and the social background of Christian monasticism, and the eventual role in late Roman and early Byzantine society of the holy persons pushed to the fore by the ascetic movement, will be dealt with in other chapters in this and in a subsequent volume. For what characterizes the fourth and early fifth centuries, as a clearly defined and crucial period in the history of the ancient world, is not so much the rise of those forms of Christian asceticism associated with the growth of monasticism; for this was a development whose roots lay in far earlier periods, and whose definitive establishment took place later, in the fifth and sixth centuries. Rather, it was the elaboration, in both Christian and non-Christian circles, of an unprecedented range of interpretations, assuming widely different views of the human person and of society, that clustered around the common pool of ascetic attitudes and patterns of behaviour.

In approaching asceticism in this manner, we are faced by a paradoxical situation. Because held to be grounded in human reason, *askēsis* had always

---

[4] On this issue, Brown, *Body and Society, passim*, parts company with Dodds (1965) 1–36.

been considered to be a universal art of the soul, potentially available to all human beings. The Christian church carried yet further the strong universalizing tendencies that had already existed in the philosophical tradition. When Augustine wrote his *Confessions*, he implied in no uncertain terms that he wished to speak for all mankind, just as Evagrius of Pontus wrote for all awakened souls. By the end of our period, indeed, the monastic culture of Egypt claimed to have achieved a synthesis of the experiences of the past century. A tradition of desert wisdom, 'a royal road ... made smooth by the footsteps of the saints' (Cassian, *Institutiones* Pr. 4), could be confidently presented to Christians, from Gaul to the Euphrates, as a *koinē* of Christian asceticism. The sources to which scholars turn most frequently to study the 'origins' of Christian asceticism – most notably, the *Apophthegmata Patrum* (written down around 440), the *Lausiac History* of Palladius (of 420) and the *Institutes* and *Collationes* (*Conferences*) of John Cassian (of 426–8) – were written so as to mark the end of an epoch.[5] They imposed their hindsight and uniformity of vision on what had been an age of great diversity. Their success is a remarkable testimony to the homogeneity of a Mediterranean-wide Christian culture, whose conductivity was at its highest on matters of ascetic thought and organization. As a result of this rapid spread of a single *koinē*, the intense fragmentation and localism of much of fourth-century Christian asceticism can now be recaptured only with the greatest difficulty. In a not dissimilar manner, the vivid portraits of men and women philosophers, collected by Eunapius of Sardis in his *Lives of the Sophists* of around 399, were intended to present the experiences of what was, in fact, a limited circle of persons in a specific region of Asia Minor as paradigmatic for the achievement of sanctity among all true worshippers of the ancient gods.[6]

In reality, profound differences of world-view, summed up by ascetic gestures, coexisted within seemingly united religious communities – such as the Christian church – while, at the same time, the subtle constraints of class and of a shared moral culture (factors which we should never underestimate in the later empire) brought together Christians and non-Christians in shared patterns of behaviour and in common ascetic techniques, in a manner that blurred their evident religious differences. Indeed, no small part of the excitement of the abundant spiritual literature of the period is the manner in which a number of truly creative minds, many of whom came from the same culture, had read each other's books and had watched each other's behaviour, followed the thread of ascetic endeavour into the passages of a labyrinth of possible notions on human nature and society, whole galleries of which had never been explored before by ancient persons.

[5] Guy (1962), Rousseau, *Ascetics*, de Vogüé (1991) and Burton-Christie (1992) are model treatments; Chitty (1966) remains the classic account of monasticism in Egypt and Palestine.

[6] Fowden (1982) 41–3 and Penella (1990).

It is well to begin with the different forms of asceticism that developed in specific milieux. Nowhere are the social determinants of the meaning of ascetic practices more plain than in those groups that claimed, with good reason, to represent the traditions of the classical past – the polytheist philosophers of the fourth century, as we meet them in the works of Eunapius of Sardis. These quiet figures sum up the moral potentialities of a whole class. Not surprisingly, they tend to be overshadowed by the more dramatic forms of asceticism that had recently developed in the very different social worlds of Egypt and Syria among Christians, most of whom would have been perceived, by contrast to the educated élites of the Aegean, as *agroikoi*, even *barbaroi*, lower-class, rural and largely untouched by Greek culture.[7] As a result, it is easy to misread the asceticism current in polytheist circles – to fail to appreciate the weight of meaning attached by philosophers to some gestures of renunciation, and their relative indifference to other gestures that bulked large in the minds of contemporary Christians, who came from very different social backgrounds and regions of the empire.

Seen from the outside, in terms of their social position and style of life, Eunapius' philosophers seem an exceedingly decorous collection of persons. Their sheltered lives pale in comparison with the vibrant ascetic Odyssey presented in the Christian *Life of Antony*. Their numbers were insignificant compared with the thousands believed to have settled, as Christian monks, in the Egyptian desert. The philosophers of Ephesus, Sardis and Pergamum (and, we may assume, figures like Sarapion, the Egyptian philosopher, and many others all over the empire) came from well-to-do backgrounds. They contributed to the life of their cities. Some of them were content to act as teachers of rhetoric, passing on to the well-born young a thoroughly this-worldly and pedestrian traditional culture. Many owned well-appointed country houses and paid attention to their estates. These activities formed the solid ground-course of their lives, barely perceptible beneath the towering spires of their inner life.

Aedesius, for instance, saw his vocation in terms of a characteristically ambiguous oracle: either he would retire to his ranch in Cappadocia to 'be, one day, the associate of the blessed gods', or he would choose 'the cities and towns of men . . . shepherding the god-given impulse of youth'. In around 335 (when Antony had already been installed for over a decade in a lunar landscape, close to the Red Sea), Aedesius left his estates to take up a post as a teacher at Pergamon and lived there for the rest of his life (Eunap. *V. Soph.* 464). In such families, only the women could escape entirely from the gravitational field of the city, around which the men continued to

---

[7] On the social background of Christian asceticism in Egypt, see Rousseau, *Pachomius* 1–35 and Brown, *Body and Society* 213–24 with the excavations of H. Buschhausen now reported from Abu Fana: Buschhausen (1992) 22–3; for Syria, see Brown (1971) 82–91 and Adshead and Adshead (1991).

maintain their ancient orbit. Sosipatra grew up on a farm in the Cayster valley. She was believed to have gained her entire spiritual culture from mysterious strangers, who had worked as migrant labourers on the family's vines. As an older woman, she acted as a spiritual guide, residing in a country house outside Pergamon (Eunap. *V. Soph.* 467–71). A generation later, a Christian, Macrina, the elder sister of Basil of Caesarea, lived out her life in a similar manner in Pontus, in a farmhouse set beneath wooded hills in the smiling landscape of the valley of the Iris. Far from such quiet, her brothers battled, now as Christian bishops, with the art of words and with the affairs of their cities.[8]

Yet within the narrow horizons of the possible experienced by the gentry of Asia Minor, vast differences existed between Christians and non-Christians as to the nature of the human person that was expressed by such roughly similar styles of life. It is easy to forget that the heroes of Eunapius were gods incarnate. Their vibrant souls had been sent down from heaven to earth, to administer, for the short duration of their allotted lifespan, an evanescent constellation of matter called their 'body'. The huge energy of such souls was instantly apparent in the piercing glance of their eyes. It suffused their bodies with apparently effortless ease (Eunap. *V. Soph.* 460 and 473). Conscious self-mortification – such as courting acute discomfort and undergoing heroic fasts – is barely mentioned in polytheist sources. The austere and punctilious tenor of the philosopher's life had a mainly declaratory purpose. It made plain to others the pre-existing, immovable harmony of a superior soul.

By contrast, vegetarianism was a highly charged issue. The intake of meat condensed, in a grippingly concrete manner, all that the embodied soul must avoid in its relation to matter. Dead flesh added to the lethal inertia that opposed the soul's return to the realm of spirit. Worse still, bloody substances positively activated negative powers, thought of as endowed with intensely specific, 'demonic' energy. These energies added momentum to the dread entropy of matter, to the sullen urge to formlessness, by which the body threatened to entrap the soul (Porph. *Abst.* 1.56–7; 11.31 and 46).

We should never forget that the 'austere detached tolerance'[9] which appears to modern readers to be such an attractive feature of polytheistic mysticism, as opposed to the more blatant ascetic mortifications of many Christians, was based on a view of the human person seen from a dizzy height. The body appeared always as if through the diminishing end of a telescope. It was not the true self. The joining of body and soul generated, for a time, a perilous lower level of consciousness: the soul had to divert its attention to the need for food; and, more mysteriously, the lower

---

[8] Brown, *Body and Society* 277–9 and 301–3.   [9] Armstrong (1967) 229.

soul was plagued by an unconscious urge to replicate the primal joining of body and soul, through further embraces and through further acts of creation in the world of matter – that is, through sexuality (Plotinus, *Enn*. III.5.1). The existence of this lower consciousness was regrettable; but it was not very significant. For souls on whose highest reaches the sun of God's illumination shone for ever, such experiences were as insubstantial and as transient as mist trapped in the bottom of a valley. In weakened souls, they did, indeed, exercise a dire, barely intelligible fascination, akin to the mesmerizing power of a love-spell. But spells, for the philosopher, were trivial things, mere will-o'-the-wisps, the aimless stirrings of a lower realm. They were there to be broken. When Sosipatra felt herself falling in love with her cousin Philometor – noticing a stab of regret whenever he left the room – Maximus of Ephesus simply diagnosed a love-spell and countered it successfully. 'And for the future, Sosipatra beheld Philometor with pure and changed eyes, though she continued to admire him for so greatly admiring her' (Eunap. *V. Soph*. 470). For a polytheist such as Eunapius, the delicious inconsequentiality of this anecdote was a firm reminder of a hierarchy of significance, in which the body and its forms of consciousness were dwarfed by the Himalayan majesty of the soul.

It was not only the body which was dwarfed in such an image of the person. Society itself seemed strangely evanescent. Many of its central institutions did not elicit, in polytheist ascetics, the symbolic fury that was expended upon them in Christian circles. Marriage, for instance, was a matter of relative indifference. The city needed children. Learned dynasties recruited their students and passed on their traditions largely through the links created by kinship and intermarriage, very much as among the rabbis in Judaism. It might be part of the destiny of a superior soul to meet these needs. Trivial though married intercourse might be, *sub specie aeternitatis*, the continuance of the human race was one small part of the seamless web of an eternal universe, whose very perfection included the fateful leap of souls into matter. It was not for a philosopher, and certainly not for a woman, to tear abruptly at those ancient threads. Sosipatra agreed to marry Eustathius, a fellow philosopher; but not before she had prophesied to him that she would bear him three children and that he would die within five years, thereby enabling his true self, his soul, to regain 'with blessed and easy motion' its appointed place above the moon (Eunap. *V. Soph*. 469). In a universe that 'pulsed with the vigour of eternity' (*Consultationes Zacchaei et Apollonii* 1.1, ed. G. Morin. Bonn, 1935, 8), existence in a body, even marriage, childbirth and care for the ancient things of the city, were infinitesimal moments in the vast trajectory of a superior soul. Nothing was lost to Sosipatra by accepting them, with a god's quiet sense of possessing infinite time.

The Christian, Macrina, as we have seen, lived in much the same rural setting as did Sosipatra. The city's need for children (and her own family's need for allies) almost claimed her, as it had claimed Sosipatra. Only the unexpected death of her fiancé gave Macrina the opportunity, that she might otherwise not have had, to assert her own wish to remain a perpetual virgin. We see her through the eyes of her brother, Gregory of Nyssa, a man who moved in a 'Platonic universe of ideas' very similar to that of Eunapius. Yet, in the case of Macrina, the renunciation of marriage was the central statement of her life. It was a statement about time and society. She did not live in a timeless universe: majestic though it might be, the material world was a created thing, 'time-bound and of brief duration' (*Consultationes Zacchaei et Apollonii* 1.1). The coming of Christ would bring it to an end. The human race stood at the end of time. Time as we know it, indeed, came into existence because of the human race. It was a social creation, characterized by deep human anxiety in the face of death. It was measured by the passing of the generations. For marriage and childbirth were the devices by which a fallen humanity consoled itself, through the prospect of a long future guaranteed by children, for the loss of an original, timeless, because ecstatic, immortality. As the human race reached its fullness, the anxious tick of the clock of human time – measured off by marriage, childbirth and death – would fall silent. The next event would be the coming of Christ. Macrina always carried the ring of her deceased fiancé, who had died abroad, together with an iron cross; she would await Christ, her true promised love (Greg. Nyss. *V. Macr.* 5 and 30), surrounded by a group of virgins and widows, in whom the tragic sense of time, that demanded their bodies for childbirth, had faded away. Unlike Sosipatra, Macrina's peace of mind came not from a sense of timelessness, in the embrace of a godlike universe, but from a narrower, more urgent viewing point. She made time stand still by snapping a fundamental link in the chain of human society.[10]

We should look elsewhere for the symbolically charged renunciation that inspired most admiration in philosophical circles. The philosopher was admired, in a centuries-old tradition, for being utterly uncompromised by the dark taint of power. He drew from his *askēsis* a physical and moral courage that enabled him to demonstrate, in the face of domineering authority, the precious virtues of *parrēsia*, the ability to speak the truth without fear or favour, and *karteria*, the capacity to face the great with unfailing poise, unshaken by browbeating and by physical threats.[11] It was a quality which Eunapius relished in his own teacher, Chrysanthius. Here was a man who treated visiting governors with the same noble absent-mindedness as he treated his own body.

---

[10] Brown, *Body and Society* 296–301.   [11] Brown, *Power and Persuasion* 61–70.

In his intercourse with those in authority, if he seemed to use excessive freedom of manner, this was not due to arrogance or pride, but must rather be regarded as the perfect simplicity of one who was totally ignorant of the nature of authority.

(Eunap. *V. Soph.* 501)

In an authoritarian age, physical and moral courage had a rarity value that we should not underestimate. Ruined by extortion, the provincial gentry of Epirus sent a philosopher to the court of Valentinian I: only 'a man renowned for his strength of soul' could be trusted to speak out in front of the studiously ferocious emperor (Amm. Marc. xxx.5.9–10). Dressed in the dark robe of a philosopher, Themistius of Constantinople was able to bring petitions before Valentinian's morose and suspicious brother, Valens (Them. *Or.* xxxiv.14). He was of use even to Christians, for he persuaded Valens to withdraw the death penalty that had threatened leaders of the Nicene cause (Sozom. *HE* vi.36). A figure widely deemed to be unstained by power and unmotivated by political calculation, the philosopher was permitted at least a 'walk-on part' in the ceremonious drama that attended the emperors' exercise of their supreme prerogative of mercy.

We should not exaggerate the practical effectiveness of these interventions. Given the frosty climate of a Christian empire, overtly polytheist philosophers found that alienation from power was, alas, a virtue forced upon them.[12] But it remained the virtue that gave meaning to their other social renunciations. Philosophers remained tied to their cities. They evinced little interest in shifting those primary building-blocks of their society, on which Christians concentrated much of their attention. What they avoided, rather, was the dark heart of public life – the violence, favouritism and obsequious self-serving that characterized so much of an imperial system, from the court down to the micro-politics of their home towns. They treated wealth much as they treated their own bodies. Like married intercourse, it could be greatly attenuated, but it did not need to be abruptly abandoned in its entirety. Installed comfortably on their farms (where life, in any case, was cheaper than in the city), they saw to it that their wealth was not so great as to get them involved too deeply in local politics (Eunap. *V. Soph.* 501; cf. Pall. *Hist. Laus.* 66). It was essential that it should not be increased by violence, extortion and the spoils of office – the dense red meat that nourished social power in the later empire.

Their renunciations were all the more authoritative for having come from persons of high birth, wealth and culture, whose families had always played a role in the life of their cities and regions. So firm were the expectations of the philosopher, in this respect, that even a woman could live up to them in a fully public manner. Unmarried, praised by admirers as a 'stainless star of Wisdom's discipline' (Palladas, *AP* ix.400), the middle-aged

---

[12] Fowden (1982) 51–4 and Sacks (1986).

Hypatia acted, in Alexandria, much as Themistius claimed to have done in the imperial court. In the words of an admiring Christian source, her 'self-possession and freedom of speech' came from her high culture (Socr. *HE* VII.15). Her brutal murder in 415 was a testimony to the threat that an ancient discipline of public courage could still pose to the rising power of the Christian patriarchs of Alexandria.[13]

It was on the issue of the philosopher's relation to power that ascetic ideas passed virtually unnoticed along an unbroken continuum that linked Christians and non-Christians of the upper classes. In its handling of the leaders of the church throughout the fourth century, the political establishment of the empire showed itself to have changed very little since the days of the martyrs: it had merely learned greater finesse in its combination of browbeating and cajolery. It frequently attempted to intimidate any bishop who opposed its religious policies. Hence the very real relevance to Christians of an ancient style of 'political' asceticism. Old-fashioned methods of government were met by thoroughly old-fashioned virtues. Some bishops had to 'hang tough'. The ascetic life was presented as a discipline calculated to 'harden' a bishop for the discomforts of exile – a potentially lethal fate, to which many elderly men were subjected in this period (Ambr. *Ep.* 64.71). Threats from courtiers were met by Basil of Caesarea with the same unruffled wit as was displayed by Chrysanthius (Theod. *HE* IV.16). When it came to his dealings with the emperors, Ambrose felt himself at his most secure when his occasional resort to a confrontational style could be seen in terms of ancient paradigms. Thus, when he confronted the imperial court at Milan on the issue of the basilicas in 386, the sermons that he preached on that occasion show a man adept at presenting himself in such a manner that ancient traditions lent a density, a third dimension, to Christian notions: the 'philosophical' courage of the Maccabaean martyrs was made to stand out against an image of the immobile sage, derived from the *Enneads* of Plotinus.[14]

On a less spectacular level, many Christians, who felt alienated from the politics of their church and region, fell back on this ancient image of low-profiled integrity. They retired to their estates. Paulinus of Nola wrote of his first spell of *otium* in Spain (in 386 – a time of acute political and religious uncertainty) as if his 'way of life already bordered' on a full, monastic conversion (Paul. Nol. *Ep.* 5.4). For persons facing difficult choices, there was nothing alien about non-Christian ethical treatises. They simply condensed the moral common sense of the age. Thus, the austere 'consciousness-raising' maxims contained in the *Sentences* of a Pythagorean philosopher, Sextus (confidently ascribed to a third-century pope!), were

[13] Brown, *Power and Persuasion* 115–16 and Cameron and Long, *Barbarians and Politics* 59–62.
[14] Nauroy (1974).

presented by Rufinus, in Latin translation, to the senator Apronianus and his wife, friends of Paulinus, who lived in continence on their estates in Campania. A work of *askēsis* of the old school, the *Sentences* were entirely appropriate as a quasi-monastic rule for a sober Christian household.[15]

The huge literary prestige later enjoyed by these few representatives of the high aristocracy of the western empire should not make us forget the prevalence of such solutions, on almost every social level and in every region during the fourth century. The ecclesiastical landscape was dotted with Little Giddings – *ecclesiolae* set up in pious households. Relatively humble countryfolk, settled on their farms in Egypt, and pious women living with their lady-companions in rented rooms, as we see from papyri in Oxyrhynchus, were frequently the best representatives of Christian piety in their region (*P. Oxy.* 3203). Furthermore, the rapidly expanding ranks of the clergy made room for the occasional unreconstructed philosopher. Maximus, a Cynic philosopher, complete with long hair, was chosen by the rivals of Gregory of Nazianzus to replace him as bishop of Constantinople. Far from being a freak, Maximus had made a name for himself, in the Cynic tradition, as an outspoken defender of Nicene orthodoxy at a time of official disapproval (Gre. Naz. *Poemata de se ipso* XII.750–72; Sozom. *HE* VII.9). Augustine, converted Manichee and now upholder of Catholicism, must have seemed not very different to his predecessor as bishop of Hippo, Valerius, when Valerius snatched him, by forcibly ordaining him as a member of the clergy in 391. The bishop of Tomi retained his shaggy locks and long cloak, becoming known to the neighbouring Huns as 'the god of the Romans' (Sozom. *HE* VII.26). Synesius of Cyrene, pupil of Hypatia and later (somewhat reluctantly) bishop of Ptolemais, though the best-known of such philosopher-bishops, was by no means a unique figure.[16]

It is, however, important to note that only in Christian circles do we catch hints of what must have been a vigorous 'philosophical' sub-culture, occupied by unassuming recluses and hardy characters, endowed with intelligence and the courage of their own eccentricity. We may be dealing here simply with a blind spot in our evidence: such persons may well have existed (like Sarapion the philosopher in Egypt) in many areas, and especially in the eastern provinces. A fragment from a later source, Damascius' *Life of Isidore*, gives us a tantalizing glimpse of what such persons might have been. Probably connected with the great, half-emptied temple, Akamatios of Baalbek, a diviner, was by the high standards current in Athens and Sardis totally uneducated. An amiable eccentric, the locals were vastly proud of him: they could not be brought to call him anything but

[15] Chadwick (1959), with Carlini (1985).
[16] Brown, *Power and Persuasion* 136–9 and Cameron and Long, *Barbarians and Politics* 13–69.

'The Philosopher' (Dam. *V. Isid.* fr. 34–5, ed. C. Zintzen. Hildesheim, 1967, 279).

Even if they existed, polytheist literature had little or no place for uncultivated practitioners of *askēsis* and, apparently, few heroes other than philosophers. This fact alone points to a decisive parting of the ways between Christians and non-Christians in this period. For the renunciations valued by Christians were that much more drastic, in part, because they could be made by a far wider spectrum of persons. They touched on the basic essentials of social living as these affected both men and women, and almost all classes. Only truly upper class men, from families with political traditions in their city, could be admired for having skirted with heroic *insouciance* the volcanic crater of power. But everyone, on a wide social spectrum, from owners of empire-wide estates to 'comfortable' farmers such as Antony, could follow the words of the Gospel, 'Go, sell all that you have and give to the poor.' All but the indigent had families and kinsfolk that they could leave; and everyone had sexual urges that they could renounce. All classes could mingle at the feet of acclaimed ascetics, who protected them all equally by their prayers. In an empire-wide religious community, on which ever greater differences in wealth and culture, and increasingly sharp distinctions in organizational structure, had begun to leave their mark, asceticism, for Christians, was the great equalizer.

By the time that the *Life of Antony* appeared, in 357, this constellation of renunciations had come together in a single organizing myth – the myth of the desert.[17] The *Life* made it plain that it was possible to narrate the life of Antony in strictly topographical terms. As a young man, around 270, he had moved from having lived a reclusive life in his farmhouse out to the edge of the village – a place 'preserved from the tread of human feet' (*V. Ant. Syr.* 3, Draguet 16.16). By 285, he was in a deserted fortress across the Nile. After 315, he had made his way by tracks travelled only by Arab nomads (whose language, as a Copt of Egypt, he would not have understood) to the edge of the Red Sea. There he lived until his death in 356, 'in full magnificence, like a king in his palace' (*V. Ant. Syr.* 50, Draguet 50.23). In this way, the ascetic trajectory of a heroic soul was made palpable by being laid out in stages, across immense wastes of dead earth. Those who became monks, the *Life of Antony* insisted, had 'made the desert a city' (*V. Ant. Syr.* 14). They had created a world outside the world.

By the fourth century, the desert was already a landscape of the mind, created by the interplay of powerful antitheses and associated even then with ancient legends. In the vast hush of the desert of Sinai, the people of Israel had lived for forty years in the presence of God, in a state of suspended animation, it was believed, not unlike that ascribed to the great

---

[17] Brown, *Body and Society* 213–22; Guillaumont (1975).

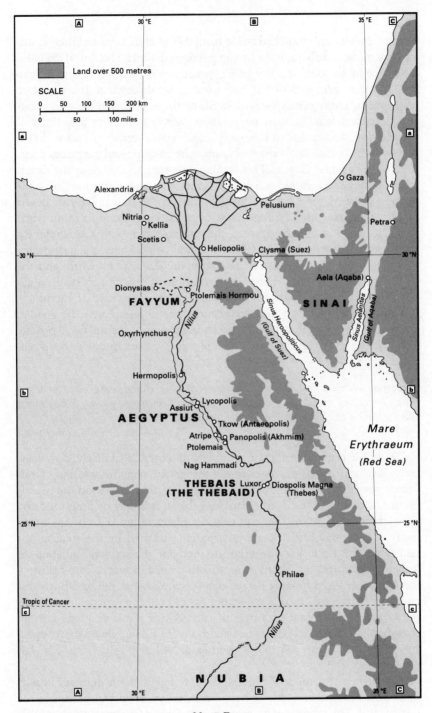

Map 8 Egypt

ascetics: their sparse food had come from the hand of God and their clothing was miraculously unworn by the passing of time. The desert was also
the home of the demons. For an Egyptian, it was the place where human
love and the warm gifts of the Nile came to an abrupt end. It was a place
of the dead, whose eerie spaces of sterile earth, inhabited by the wild beasts
and defended from human penetration by the punishing afflictions of
dehydration, sunstroke and sensory deprivation, spoke of those lower
powers, whose chill self-sufficiency, uncanny cunning and perpetual anger
were pitted against God and his human worshippers. To enter the desert
and to emerge victorious, as Antony had done, was to claim for Christ the
furthest edge of the Christian imagination. In the fourth century, desert
monks, *erēmētikoi*, men of the *erēmos*, hermits, were 'good to think with'.
Human beings in inhuman places, they represented, with a concreteness
and a precision on which the Christian mind could linger, the past drama
of Christ's own heroic descent to defeat the demons on earth, and the
future – as yet far from definitive – triumph of the church over an all-
pervasive polytheism that still ruled much of the green land of Egypt.

Relocated in this way, Christian asceticism made a statement designed to
challenge the social imagination of contemporaries. Julian the Apostate
knew of the Christian myth of the desert and reacted to it with deep religious anger.

Some men there are who, though man is a social and civilized being, seek out desert
places instead of cities. For they have been given over to the power of evil spirits
and are led by them into hatred of their own kind.

(Julian, *Letter to a Priest* 288b)

We should not underestimate the ability of a myth, that received its clearest expression in Egypt, to charge with instant religious meaning landscapes very different from the dead margins of the Nile. Soon the islands
of the Adriatic and the Tyrrhenian Sea – bleak splinters of limestone and
karst, thrown off by the Ligurian tectonic plate, within sight of the green
fields of the mainland – even escarpments washed by the treacherous
eddies of the Loire became little 'deserts' for their ascetic inhabitants.
Touching attempts by distant groups to share in a monastic folk-culture –
the Christian Egyptomania of the age – ensured that the well-born disciples of Martin of Tours, for instance, would reject garments made from
the local wool in favour of authentic camel's hair – just as a later hermit,
outside Nice, would rely on its busy harbour for his supply of the 'correct'
Egyptian herbs (Sulp. Sev. *V. Mart.* x; Paul. Nol. *Ep.* 29.1; Greg. Tur. *HF*
vi.6).

The effect of the myth of the desert was to heighten the dramatic impact
of renunciations that had long been practised by devout Christians in the
settled land. The monk was no more than the good Christian writ large. We

should never forget that the average Christian community in the post-Constantinian church still wished to be seen as a gathering of exceptionally sober persons. In an age before the final emergence of monasticism, asceticism was not an achievement attached to a specific group within the Christian community. The moral common sense of the age was against such specialization: even when, in fact, restricted to a limited number, *askēsis* was regarded as a potentially universal therapy of the soul. Christians, in particular, were committed to standing out, as a group, through a shared moral excellence. In many Christian circles, indeed, the *succès d'estime et de scandale* of the new monks was regarded with deep suspicion – not, in any way, because their ascetic practices were seen as excessive, but because unthinking admiration for monastic achievements seemed to imply that prayer, austerity and attention to scripture-reading were not to be expected, as a matter of course, from every baptized Christian (e.g. John. Chrys. *Hom. in Matt.* 11.10 and VII.8, *PG* LVIII.29 and 81).

Nēphômen, 'let us live soberly', was the *leitmotif* of most pre-baptismal homilies in this period.[18] The life of the Christian group was punctuated by extended periods of heavy, penitential fasting and by frequent spells of sexual abstinence: by the fifth century, the married laity of Egypt found that only Monday, Tuesday and Thursday remained to them for the duties and pleasures of the bed (*The Answers of Apa Cyril*, ed. W. E. Crum. Strasbourg, 1915, 103). These periods of abstinence were accompanied by intense prayers, vigils and restless nights spent sleeping on the hard ground (Epiphanius of Salamis, *Expositio Fidei Catholicae* XXI, *PG* XLII.824). The accounts of the sufferings of the martyrs brought the triumphant pain of Christ close to successive generations. The tale of these sufferings was assumed to have a sobering effect on those who heard of them in later times.

And I, Julius [the town-clerk], by reason of the pains which I saw the saints suffering, will never again drink wine or anoint my body with oil, till the day of my death.

(*Martyrdom of S. Shenoute*, tr. E. A. E. Reymond and J. W. B. Barns, *Four Martyrdoms*. Oxford, 1973, 222)

The myth of the desert simply touched humdrum and uncomfortable practices, that were widespread in the Christian churches, with the stillness of eternity. It was good to think that, somewhere to one side of settled society, a few Christians lived in this way, at every moment and for all their lives. But despite their crucial personal encounters with the ascetic movement, Basil, John Chrysostom and Augustine would have preached as austerely as they did even if Antony and the desert had never existed.

[18] E.g. Joh. Chrys. *Cath. Bapt.* IV.26 and V.28, ed. A. Wenger, *SChrét.* 50 bis. Paris, 1970, 196 and 214.

For this reason it would be misleading to see, in the ethical codes presented to lay Christians in this period, the sudden and irrevocable victory
of an ascetic rigorism, upheld only by a vociferous élite of monks and
clergy of 'monastic' background.[19] At this time, the principal division
within the Christian community was less between a clearly defined 'ascetic
movement' and all other Christians, than between those who had decided
to undergo the drastic rite of baptism, so as to become members of the
'faithful' in the full sense, subject to stringent moral codes, and the increasing numbers of those who held back and were content to remain catechumens for much of their lives. In some churches, this development had the
effect of rendering the new-style ascetics even more unpopular: they were
held to have contributed to a further fragmentation of a Christian community that was already divided between the baptized and a large body of
half-participants.[20] In other environments, baptized lay persons and monks
were driven closer together. Both groups stood out from their fellows as
bearers of a 'true' Christianity in their neighbourhood. Baptism itself came
to be regarded, especially by late-adolescent and adult initiates, as leading
almost inevitably to a further, ascetic vocation. The moral upheaval of
Augustine's renunciation of future marriage was the prelude to his decision
to be baptized. His friend Verecundus refused baptism simply on the
grounds that he was married (Aug. *Conf.* IX.3.5). In Alexandria, a young
man could grow up in a climate of opinion that identified conversion to
Christianity as in itself an ascetic renunciation: in the 320s, a seventeen-
year-old could pray that

If the Lord leads me on the way that I may become a Christian, then I will also
become a monk, and will keep my body without stain until the day when the Lord
will come for me.

He served for some years in a local church.

He met with no woman at all . . . When he read the lessons in church, he would
strive not to let his eyes rove over the people.
(*Vita Pachomii Bohairica* 89, ed. T.-L. Lefort, *CSCO* LXXXIX. Louvain, 1925, 102. tr.
A. Veilleux, *Pachomian Koinonia*. Kalamazoo, Mich., 1980, 117)

His final retirement to the desert proper, by joining a Pachomian
monastery, came as a relief to him. His trajectory illustrates what many
contemporaries feared – that it was difficult for the baptized Christian to
live a life of full commitment within an urban Christian congregation.

The myth of the desert had one immediate effect: it made all renunciations equal, because equally drastic. *Anachôrêsis* came to be treated as the
central act of the ascetic life. *Anachôrêsis* implied the crossing of a boundary imagined to be as clear-cut and as charged with drastic significance as

---

[19] Brown, *Body and Society* 250–8.   [20] Markus, *End of Ancient Christianity* 18–83, for the west.

the ecological divide between green land and the shimmering sands of a desert. It was a symbolic 'death' to the world. At a slightly later time, Egyptian monks consciously designed their cells to resemble tomb-houses. In this living 'valley of the dead', there could be no such thing as a privileged renunciation.[21] Sexual abstinence, separation from kin, absence of property and a life of unending vigilance, characterized by considerable physical hardship, were thought to have come together. Any differences in their relative significance were flattened in the single, drastic act of social death associated with *anachôrēsis*.

This, in itself, marked a significant shift in the Christian ascetic sensibility. In many regions of the Christian world – most notably, but not exclusively, in Syria – the suffocating demonic energy of the 'world' had long been thought to be summed up in the sexual drive. Those who renounced marriage, or who lived in chastity as married couples, were held to have freed themselves definitively from the power of the world. It was not that these continent persons were not subject to severe, supplementary abnegations. But the 'statement' that counted most for those around them was that the demonic power-lines of sexual joining no longer hummed through their lives. Their social world was not greatly dislocated by this one, essential renunciation. There was no need to seek out an alternative world in the awesome stillness of the desert. In Syria, the continent had formed the core of the settled church, in towns and villages. Living in their own houses, they would troop to church. Often as a choir group, they would represent the 'true' church of Christ – a reassuring presence, among the faithful, of 'separated', 'single' persons, in whom the ache of male and female had been stilled by the Holy Spirit. They made of each church, and especially through the chaste sweetness of their mingled voices, a little Ark of Noah, bobbing in wide waters. It was an apposite image for congregations placed in cities and villages that stood at the cross-roads of Asia and the Mediterranean.[22]

With Ephraim the Syrian (306–73), in Nisibis and, later, for a decade in Edessa, contemporaries recognized an ascetic poet of towering stature. His hymns (as much the audible quintessence of a distinctive religious tradition as the *Kirchenkantaten* of Johann Sebastian Bach) retained their beauty even in Greek translation. Leading the choirs of continent men and women, the 'sons and daughters of the Covenant', in the oldest and most spacious cathedral in the eastern provinces, in the crucial frontier city of Nisibis, Ephraim was no St Antony. He was a 'single one' in an ancient tradition, a Christian sheathed in the glorious robe of continence. Yet fifth-century biographies of Ephraim, by presenting him as a 'monk' and by making him pass long spells of his life in the desert, travestied the life of this busy, town-centred man – an active clergyman as much engaged in the affairs of

---

[21] Torp (1981).   [22] Brown, *Body and Society* 81–102.

his city as were any of the heroes of Eunapius. It is an indication of the rapidity with which, in the later fifth century and the sixth century, a *koinē* of asceticism, that looked to Egypt, came between early Byzantines and the astonishing diversity of 'readings' of the ascetic life current at an earlier time.[23]

In a characteristically late Roman manner, the *koinē* associated with the Egyptian desert was put forward, in part, to bring order and a Mediterranean-wide unity to a potential anarchy of conflicting asceticisms.[24] It did not exhaust the diversity of ascetic lifestyles current in this period. We have already seen the proliferation of forms of 'philosophical' seclusion in Christian circles in almost every region. Such seclusion owed little to the myth of the desert. More important still, half of the Christian community, as women, could only be fitted with difficulty into the crisp outlines of the myth of the desert. Seclusion, and not the wilderness, was the woman's lot. Ancient forms of seclusion kept all but the most exceptional woman close to the settled land, and indeed to her own family. This had been the case with Macrina, as with so many others.[25] As a result, ascetic values were often mediated to the urban laity by pious women rather than by men. Holy men were supposed to avoid cities. Only in Antioch, a city dominated by Mount Silpius, whose slopes were settled by Syrian hermits less touched by Egyptian notions of the total separateness of the desert, could John Chrysostom advocate a Sunday afternoon's walk to a hermit, as a sovereign remedy for post-pubertal stirrings in the young (Joh. Chrys. *De Inani Gloria* 78). In fact, we know that, even in Antioch, a network of ascetic women, frequented by pious Christian mothers, played a decisive role in Christianizing the young. It was pious women, also, who played a large part in deciding to which holy man the laity should turn (Theod. *HE* III.10; *Hist. Rel.* IX.6–7).

Only through pilgrimage could women create for themselves an equivalent of the desert. They lingered in neighbouring sanctuaries and, in the case of women of the western aristocracy, they moved as impressive 'strangers' up and down the Nile to visit the holy men of Egypt, or they settled around the Holy Places in Palestine. Distant holy places, and not the desert, provided many devout women with a refuge from the moral torpor of their local churches.[26]

Though it did not by any means cover all the phenomena of asceticism at this time, the new *koinē* was welcomed in many regions as a bulwark against more disturbingly radical traditions. We should never take its victory for granted in this period, or underestimate the symbolic power,

[23] Griffith (1989–90).   [24] Judge (1977) 78–80.

[25] Brown, *Body and Society* 256–84; see esp. Elm (1991); (1994) *passim*, with Clark, *Ascetic Piety*.

[26] Hunt, *Holy Land Pilgrimage, passim*. Pilgrimage was by no means restricted to upper-class women: Brown, *Body and Society* 271–2 and 328.

and the implications, of other forms of the ascetic life. The enormously prestigious holy men of Syria, for instance, owed little to the Egyptian model. In northern Syria and in eastern Asia Minor, the highly compart-mentalized imaginative landscape that gave such meaning to the ascetic 'labour' of the Egyptian monk carried less symbolic weight. The ascetics of Syria were figures whose bodies were 'clothed' with the Holy Spirit. They had become living emblems of the vast freedom of the angels, beings of fire, fed by the very rays of the divine presence. It was a matter of little importance, for such vivid vehicles of the Spirit, that the monk should stand out, as a human being, in sharp contrast to an inhuman landscape. Nor was it of interest that the monk should carry with him into the wild-erness tokens of humanity, as this was defined in the settled land of Egypt – dependence on human food, bought through human labour, so that bas-ketwork and the little piles of village-baked loaves play such an essential role in Egyptian anecdotes. 'Angels' could dispense with such cares. Syrian hermits are rarely shown working for their living.[27]

In any case, ever since the tale of Gilgamesh and Enkiddu, the Mesopotamian steppe land and its surrounding mountains had stood for a land of liberty, where human beings, their bodies free from the normal associations of settled life (thought of in terms of the heavy scent of women and the sweat of labour at the plough) moved with ease among the fleet-footed deer and the mountain eagles.[28] They fed as did the beasts, becoming known as *boskoi*, as human 'grazers', living on what were, in fact, the surprisingly nutritious herbs of the steppe and mountainside.[29]

If the boundary between desert and settled land was no longer seen as a primary antithesis, then other boundaries might also be breached. In the late fourth century, bishops in western Syria and Asia Minor readily believed that women mingled with the wandering bands of Messalian, 'praying', monks. For the Messalians believed that their perpetual 'angelic' prayer, unbroken by human time and by a human need to work, could fill ascetics of both sexes with so great a measure of the Holy Spirit as to make them indifferent to normal codes of sexual avoidance.[30] Worse still, if the desert was not a distinct zone, but only one locus, among many, for the exercise of an 'angelic' freedom, then even the cities would lie open to such disturbing persons.

In the fourth century, the most direct challenge of a free-ranging ascet-icism came from the Manichean elect. The Manichees were disturbing mutant figures from a recognizable Syrian tradition. They were filled with

---

[27] The point is made in a well-known Egyptian anecdote: *Apophthegmata Patrum*. John Colobos 2, *PG* LXV.204D; see Brown, *Body and Society* 218–22 (for Egypt) and 330–4 (for Syria) with Harvey (1988) 378–86. [28] Cassin (1973).

[29] Sozom. *HE* III.33; see Hirschfeld (1990), an important contribution, to set beside Rousselle (1983) 105–226, on Egyptian ascetic diet, based largely on agrarian products. [30] Gribomont (1972).

the energies of the Kingdom of Light, and the whole material world was their 'desert'. They were as free as a fine gas to waft wherever they wished, following the busy trade routes of the Mediterranean and Asia, from Carthage to the Punjab, and later as far as China.[31] The unearthly pallor and the total continence of the Elect impressed both Christians and non-Christians (among them, Augustine's friend Alypius) more than did their metaphysics (Aug. *Conf.* VI.7.12, cf. *Ep.* 258.3 and Lib. *Ep.* 1253). Their attitude to food, in particular, made shockingly present an alternative view of the universe. The Elect were totally cut off from the production and preparation of food. The Hearers gained spiritual merit from housing them and from providing their meals.[32] The hideous spread of matter had been brought to a halt, in their bodies, by rigid abstinence. They had become a door into the Kingdom of Light. For even their digestive processes reversed the normal course of human food: when eaten by the Elect at their solemn meals, the sweet spirits of light that lay trapped beneath the shining surfaces of chosen fruits would float softly back to heaven.[33] Seldom since the days of Pythagoras and Gautama Buddha had an ancient society derived so many sharply contrasted views of the world from the relatively limited cluster of renunciations of which a human body is capable.

These vivid ascetic 'statements' greatly preoccupied contemporaries and have rightly fascinated scholars. Their diversity is a tribute to the communities that surrounded the ascetics: differing groups and regional traditions each saw a different world in the ascetic practice of their heroes and heroines. But asceticism was also a spiritual struggle, a form of hard labour on the self. For this aspect of the ascetic movement, the evidence from this short period is unequalled in its diversity and high intellectual quality. We have the Neoplatonic tradition in polytheism, the ascetic *Rules* of Basil of Caesarea (*c.* 330–77), the spiritual manuals of Evagrius of Pontus (346–99), the *Confessions* of Augustine (written around 397–400) and the Egyptian traditions of desert wisdom, summed up in the *Apophthegmata Patrum* and brought to the Latin world by John Cassian in the late 420s in his *Institutes* and *Collationes*. Reading through these texts, we can sense nothing less than the outlines of a revolution in the ancient notion of the self.

For the ascetic in the philosophical tradition of polytheism, the greatest pain lay in the mind. The disruptive consequences of embodiment were neutralized by the physical renunciations we have described. These renunciations left the philosopher's true self free to engage, with as little distraction as possible from the adventitious body, in the unremitting labour required to awaken the dormant energies of the mind. Contemplation of the order of

---

[31] Lieu, *Manichaeism* 60–133 with Metzler (1989), and a further bilingual Coptic–Syriac text discovered at Ismant el-Kharab in the Dakleh Oasis (Egypt): see Gardner and Lieu (1996).
[32] See the fragments of a Manichean document regulating relations with the Elect: *PL Suppl.* II.1378–80.   [33] See esp. Drijvers (1984).

the universe; analysis of the principles of human knowledge; heartfelt and prolonged engagement in the practice of the Platonic dialectic; often, the slow and subtle labour of scholarship and exegesis: these activities were frankly intellectual and assumed continued dependence on a learned tradition in its fullness – libraries full of books and an intense study-circle of well-born disciples. But they were activities engaged in with deep religious reverence. They were solemn rites of the mind, performed so as to arouse to action the great god that *was* the philosopher's self.[34]

No more than with any other ritual was there room, in the closely knit universe of the Neoplatonists, for short-cuts.[35] Self-mortification and anti-intellectual techniques of meditation were not enough. Defending his own idiosyncratic combination of a literary and philosophical way of life in his *Dio* (of 401), Synesius of Cyrene appealed to this deep-seated belief. His critics (who may have included Christian ascetics) had suggested that it was possible to dispense with the elegant first stages of the Platonic ascent. Synesius would have none of this.

> For their procedure is like a Bacchic frenzy – like the leap of a madman . . . a passing beyond reason without the previous exercise of reason . . . It seems dangerously near to impiety to suggest that the Divinity will dwell in any other part of us than in the mind, since that is God's own temple.
>
> (Syn. *Dion* 8 and 9, ed. Terzaghi, 254 and 256)

The esoteric theurgic rituals justified by Iamblichus in his *De Mysteriis* appealed, at this time, to a select circle. They condensed, in effect, a more optimistic view of the relation between spirit and matter than those current among thinkers committed to labour in the mind alone. Given the tightly interwoven structure of a Platonic universe, by which each lower level 'touched' that above it, embodiment, far from being a sad accident, might prove to be an opportunity. A great soul might live in the body like a god ruling its own small universe. This did not necessitate a withdrawal from matter. Far from it: correctly mobilized through sacramental actions (of which we, unfortunately, know nothing), matter itself might reverse its own disorder. Every level of the material person, and not only the mind, would become a dwelling-place for the divine.[36] Even the material imagination, usually dismissed as a distorting mirror, filled with disintegrating sense-images and with the chaos of dreams, would come to move in perfect step with the divine, responding to invisible presences, who existed on the level of pure spirit, with their exact material equivalents. The philosopher's mind would receive truthful dreams and light-filled visions that would be every bit as filled with divine certainty as were his higher mental processes (Syn. *De Insomniis* 4, ed. Terzaghi, 151).

---

[34] Fowden (1982) 33–8 with Saffrey (1976).   [35] Fowden, *Egyptian Hermes* 116–53, esp. 128.
[36] Shaw (1985).

The seance performed by Maximus of Ephesus in the temple of Hecate at Pergamon in around 352, and vividly described to the young Julian the Apostate, was not a theurgic ritual in the strict sense. It had been undertaken as a mere demonstration of magical power. The narrator Eusebius, and Eunapius himself, sincerely disapproved of such theatrical and competitive gestures. But the seance showed to non-initiates, in a strikingly visual manner, the capacity of the human soul to become, in this life, a fully prepared dwelling-place of the gods. In the darkened temple at Pergamon, a smile had crept over the face of a statue of Hecate and the torches in her hands flared with unearthly light, as the goddess came to dwell in her material vehicle. If the divine presence could suffuse with life the dull marble of a statue, how much more would it suffuse the 'living statue' of a wise person? (Eunap. *V. Soph.* 475)

For all the dogged self-mortifications associated with the preliminary stages of Christian asceticism, many Christians believed that body and soul could be suffused with divine energy with similar, palpable results.

They said of Apa Pambo that he was like Moses, who received the image of the glory of Adam, when his face shone. His face shone like lightning, and he was like a king sitting on his throne. It was the same with Apa Silvanus and with Apa Sisoes. (*Apophthegmata Patrum* Pambo 12, *PG* LXV.372A)

Wrenched apart by the first sin of Adam, its tragic wilfulness made plain by the disorder of death, the body could be brought back to the soul by unremitting discipline. The body also could share in the beauty of the image of God, 'just as gleaming iron is drawn to the magnet' (Greg. Naz. *Poemata de se ipso* 1.465, *PG* XXXVII.1004–5). After a lifetime in the desert, a few great ascetics would recover a palpable measure of the ancient glory of the undivided person and so would provide for others a foretaste of the glory of the spiritual body that the faithful would receive at the Resurrection.[37]

Equally prepared to look for transformed persons, the two traditions differed radically, however, on the viewing point from which this transformation was to be traced. In this century, many of the 'fixed components'[38] of ancient views of the person underwent a sea-change in the hands of Christian writers on the ascetic life. Christian ascetic literature remained close, on a 'cognitive' level, to previous traditions. The axiomatic opposition of body and soul came easily to Christian pens. There was no other way with which to assert a hierarchy of aims in the ascetic life. The untransformed body was best treated, for all practical purposes, as the enemy of the soul or, at best, as an untrustworthy and ever rebellious subordinate. But these writings betray a subtle shift in 'affective' tone through

---

[37] Brown, *Body and Society* 222–4.   [38] The term of Nock (1926) xxxix.

the choice of subjects on which spiritual guides chose to write most exhaustively and the phenomena that they regarded as significant.[39] Put very briefly: compared with the distinctly *de haut en bas* view of the body current in the philosophical tradition, even compared with the somewhat ethereal and ceremonious attention to matter evinced in theurgic circles, Christian writers tended to linger by preference on the body and on what a Platonist would have called the lower levels of consciousness. They wrote of physical mortification in such a way as to suggest, in the very rhythm of their language, the notion that body and soul formed a single field of force, in which what happened in the one had subtle and lasting effects on the other. It was not enough simply to neutralize the body, to think it away by mental exercises, even to charm it into quiescence by esoteric rituals. Somehow, the body itself was the companion of the soul in its effort to recover the 'image of God'. It could act as a diagnostic mirror, even, indeed, as the discreet mentor of the soul.

This last function of the body is made particularly clear in the *Rules* of Basil of Caesarea. A searching analysis of the force of habit underlies Basil's ascetic writings. A *diathesis* of the soul would be built up in the true Christian through the almost imperceptible accretion of the physical details of everyday life.[40] Hence his emphasis on the shared rhythms of work imposed on members of his 'brotherhoods' through the very fact of having abandoned their property (Basil, *Regula Fusius Tractata* 27.1, *PG* XXXI.1009A). Physical labour at tasks assigned by others, the stark uniformity of a single coarse robe, close attention to the physical details of gait, facial expression and tone of voice (Basil, *Reg. Fus. Tract.* 10.2; 13; 945C; 949B. *Asceticum* II, *PG* CXXI.502–4): these were supposed to impose humility on proud souls and to contribute decisively to the dismantling of the social and mental habits of the past (Basil, *Reg. Fus. Tract.* 5.2; 921A).

The ascetic writings of Basil take us into a very different social world from the absent-minded enjoyment of wealth current in philosophical circles. Their consequential 'behaviourism' was based on previous Stoic traditions: a Christian Stoic of an earlier age, such as Clement of Alexandria, would have relished the classical precision of Basil's *Rules*. The manner in which he presented a life lived 'according to the exactitude of the Gospels' (Basil, *Reg. Fus. Tract.* Prol. 1; 892B) was a triumph of pedagogic skill. But it was a pedagogy that already began with the body. The starting-point for the transformation of the soul was not to be the Platonic dialectic. Only when the body itself was fully mobilized, through the deep, subliminal force of new habits, would the deep-seated love of God – a love as overwhelming and as natural for Basil (a warm soul, for all his harsh

---

[39] I owe this distinction to the discussion of Buddhism in Gombrich (1971) 9.
[40] Bamberger (1968).

precision) as was the first joy of a child at the mother's breast – well forth like an unblocked fountain (Basil, *Reg. Fus. Tract.* 2.2; 912C).

A generation later, we find, in Evagrius of Pontus (a former protégé of Basil's friend Gregory of Nazianzus), a further shift of attention. Here was a man who inherited from Origen an exceptionally austere, Platonic cast of thought. He directed his ascetic endeavours to the flowering of the unriven soul, to the fullness of a person dematerialized as pure spirit, because filled with the raging fire of God's love. Transformation, for Evagrius, was as much a taking-over of the soul by a divine energy as it was for any of the heroes of Eunapius.[41] Yet in plotting the stages of this transformation, Evagrius looked to what, in the Platonic view of the person, were the lower levels of consciousness, where soul and matter joined. It was through these tenacious lower layers of the mind that the ascetic must pass before standing before God in a state of clear, imageless prayer. Shifts in sexual fantasies, the quality of dreams, the complex interweaving of the thought-flow – phenomena, that is, which tended to be regarded as evanescent eddies of the nether soul, the trivia of consciousness, with which mere magicians would play in their love-spells – were treated as sure diagnostic pointers to processes that went on in the deepest reaches of the person. These phenomena formed the subject matter of spiritual notebooks of absorbing interest, written by Evagrius in the late 380s and 390s from his desert cell at Kellia, near the Nile Delta, the most notable of which were the *Antirrheticus*,[42] the *Praktikos*[43] – on the *Praktikē*, the *Herzwerk* of the monk – and the *Kephalaia Gnostika*.[44] These insights were taken up, if in a less awesomely introspective and transformative manner, by John Cassian, a former visitor to the Great Old Men of Egypt. His *Collationes*, that took the form of interviews with leading Egyptian hermits, were written at Marseilles in the 420s.[45] The emergence of views formed through the experiences of the Egyptian desert marks a parting of the ways between Christian and non-Christian notions of the spiritual struggle.

Evagrius deliberately claimed experiential knowledge. His insights derived from placing his own heart in the hands of the Great Old Men of Egypt. These were the *praktikoi*, wise persons 'practised' in the art of souls.[46] They knew nothing of books or of the Platonic dialectic. In the silence of the desert, they lived as if on a different planet from that of their near-contemporary, the philosopher-bishop Synesius. Evagrius himself provided such services to others. Every Saturday evening, monks would gather in his cell.

---

[41] Guillaumont (1962) with Bunge (1986) and Elm (1991) 106–11.

[42] Ed. Frankenberg (1912), partly translated by M. W. O'Laughlin in Wimbush (1990) 243–62.

[43] Ed. Guillaumont and Guillaumont (1971).

[44] Ed. Guillaumont (1958) partly trans. D. Bundy in Wimbush (1990) 175–86.

[45] Ed. E. Pichéry, *SChrét.* 42, 54 and 64. Paris, 1953, 1958 and 1959.   [46] Bunge (1988).

They would spend with him the whole night, speaking about their thoughts, then listening to his powerful words until they left at sunrise. They would leave full of joy ... for truly his discipline was gentle.[47]

In his writings, Evagrius offered to his fellow *praktikoi* a glimpse of the soul tested to breaking-point in the new laboratory of the desert. He had no doubt as to the terrors of the self. The unguided soul was a place of peril as savage as was the desert.

Let one of you come, and I will shut him into a dark cell. Let him pass only three days there, without drinking, without sleeping, without seeing anyone, without reciting the Psalms, without prayer, without so much as the memory of God – and he will see what the passions of his soul will do to him.

(Evagrius, *Kephalaia Gnostika* iv.76, *PO* xxviii.188)

Nor did he doubt the ability of the *praktikos* to see through the most devastating experiences. For each temptation contributed to the diagnosis of a perpetually changing soul: it was a battle that revealed a specific aspect of the self, caught at a specific stage in its development.

If there is a monk who wishes to take the measure of some of the most fierce demons ... let him keep careful watch over his thoughts. Let him observe their intensity, their periods of decline, and follow them through as they rise and fall ... Then let him ask of Christ the explanation of what he has observed.

(Evagrius, *Praktikos* 50)

A follower of Origen, in this as in so much else, Evagrius saw each soul as surrounded by invisible helpers and invisible enemies, as encouraged by loving angels and beleaguered by the chill cunning of the demons. It was to the demons that the *praktikos* must pay the most alert attention.[48] These were invisible beings, separate from the self, yet mysteriously continuous with it: for they could adapt themselves with uncanny flexibility to its moods and moral temper. The demons ringed the person with a zone of agonizing ambiguity. They were the lords of illusion. Their promptings to despair or to heightened ascetic endeavour could easily be mistaken for the voices of angels. Much of the thought-flow of the monk betrayed their guileful presence: recurrent inappropriate images, obsessive trains of thought, tenacious sexual fantasies and inexplicable changes of mood showed the demons at work, manipulating the lower levels of consciousness. As a result, these lower levels – and especially the forms of the imagination associated with sexual feeling – were of great interest to Evagrius and his followers. They were treated as diagnostic 'sensors' that registered the activity of demons along the unconscious edges of the soul. Small phenomena in themselves, they warned the *praktikos* of the tread of

---

[47] The Coptic additions to Pall. *Hist. Laus.* 38, in Amélineau (1887) 114, tr. O'Laughlin (1987) 70.
[48] Brown, *Body and Society* 166–7 and 227–31 with Foucault (1982).

heavier beasts – of anger, wilfulness and remembrance of past ills – who stalked those desert regions of a soul that had not yet yielded to the sweetness of Christ. Through them, the ascetic gained knowledge of the deepest reaches of the self (Cassian, *Collationes* 1.22).

As a result of this concern to trace, in the thought-flow itself, symptoms of the activity of angels and of demons upon the soul, the mind ceased to be an object of clear self-recollection, the locus of mental exercises that were intended to develop its autonomy over and against the blurred world of matter. The mind itself was perched on the brink of the unknown. It was swayed by forces outside or beneath itself. The experienced monk stood guard like a sentry, asking of each thought and of every motivation, 'Friend or foe?' (*Anon. Apophthegmata* 99, ed. F. Nau, *Revue de l'Orient chrétien* XII (1907) 402) – peering into the darkness, straining to make out the faceless presence of the beneficent or deceiving powers, traces of whose movements on the very edge of consciousness were signs of the otherwise unfathomable vicissitudes of the soul.

By a strange historical coincidence, Rufinus of Aquileia, himself once a visitor to Egypt and for many years the colleague at Jerusalem of Melania the Elder, the one-time guide and admired correspondent of Evagrius, finished his Latin translation of that part of Origen's *On First Principles* that dealt with the spiritual struggle (the theoretical ground-plan of Evagrius' own art of the soul) in the same year (398) as Augustine may have written the tenth book of his *Confessions*. As he told his Roman patron, with a touch of pride, in his preface to the translation of Origen's third book – here, at last, was the book which had 'finally laid bare the secrets of the demons . . . all the unconscious, hidden ways by which they creep into the human heart' (Rufin. *Praef. in Origenis de principiis* III, ed. M. Simonetti, *CCSL* xx.248).

Though soon accepted as a classic study of the human heart, Augustine's *Confessions* was a book strikingly different from any work that came out of the experiences of the Egyptian desert.[49] While he had been converted to continence ten years earlier by the story of Antony, Augustine knew little of the Egyptian tradition and may well have deliberately kept his distance from the cosmic speculations of Origen, if he knew them at all at that time. Angels and demons are notably absent in the *Confessions*, as is the wish to diagnose the slow, impalpable growth of the soul, that had used angels and demons as necessary categories of analysis. Paradoxically, Augustine, the founder of so much of western introspective piety, had been touched by a spiritual tradition of a more austere and frankly non-Christian nature than any of his eastern contemporaries. Whatever Platonic books he had read in Milan, they did not offer him a Platonism mulled over, for a century or

---

[49] Now admirably translated by Henry Chadwick, Oxford 1991, and provided with an exhaustive commentary by J. J. O'Donnell, Oxford, 1992.

more, by great Christian minds – such as Evagrius had received, possibly from Gregory of Nazianzus. In 386, Augustine's mind had been indelibly 'imprinted' (through Plotinus and, one suspects, Porphyry) by a sharply introspective and intellectualist version of the Platonic *askēsis* of the mind. God and the lonely soul, and not the soul ringed by loving and hostile powers, were the focus of his concern. Later, his powers of introspection came to bear most intensely on the will. As a result, Augustine tended to take for granted, even to ignore, the vast cosmic setting that was essential to Evagrius and his school. He did not think in terms of the long journey of the soul, subtly wooed and heartened by innumerable invisible companions, across periods of time that seemed as limitless as the desert sands. Augustine, rather, was a man in a hurry. The Neoplatonic discipline of contemplation, to which he had given himself so wholeheartedly at the time of his conversion, had brought him more than once to a fleeting taste of the sweetness of God. But these had been tragically transient experiences. He now could see only a sad dislocation of the will that held him back from the timeless joy of which he had been granted a foretaste.

Only the hand of God himself could heal the will. And this healing was not accessible to the human mind: apart from moments of joyful deliverance from bondage, there were no clearly marked staging-posts to the Promised Land, by which the believer could sense the growing warmth of Christ within the soul. An alert if suspicious sentry for Evagrius, self-knowledge is invoked by Augustine throughout the tenth book of the *Confessions* only so as to highlight its radical insufficiency. Seldom had the traditions of non-Christian spiritual exercises, which Augustine knew far better than the new ascetic literature of the east, been undermined with such supreme literary artistry. Those passions which a writer such as Porphyry had been accustomed to conjure up, in vivid colours, as part of a mental 'aversion therapy', designed to break the mesmeric spell of matter on the mind – the excitements of the hippodrome, the rippling bodies of dancers and wrestlers, the sight of beautiful women, the thrill of music and the languorous seduction of perfumes (Porph. *Abst.* 1.33–4) – now sink to microscopic proportions. The baleful glare of material beauty has become no more than a passing sadness, a realization on Augustine's part that he tends to become depressed when deprived of sunlight, 'the Queen of all Colours', whose 'gentle subtlety' had imperceptibly lulled his soul when out-of-doors. The pomp and cruelty of the arena have become a moment of abstraction, when Augustine abandons his train of thought to watch a spider grappling in its web with a fly – a tiny gladiatorial combat played out on the edge of the bishop's writing-desk (Aug. *Conf.* x.34.51 and 35.57).

These infinitesimal distractions hint at a deep inertia of the self, all the more tenacious because betrayed in all human experience, right down to such small, seemingly innocuous details. They do not show, as they would have done to Evagrius, the brushing of invisible powers against his soul. Rather, they remind Augustine of the extent to which the wings of the mind will always remain slowed down by the fine, adhesive birdlime of disordered love, until wiped clean by the hand of God (Aug. *Conf.* x.30.42). The rest he cannot know: 'there is in man an area which even the *spirit of man* knows nothing of' (Aug. *Conf.* x.5.7, cf. x.32.48).

Modern students of the notion of the self have long appreciated the implications of this mood of uncertainty, based on a sense of self wider than the conscious mind, that crept into western thought through such outstanding exponents of ascetic discipline as Augustine and John Cassian. For a late Roman person, however, the most immediate significance of the change would have lain elsewhere. A self, shaded in this way by profound ambiguity, could no longer rely upon itself. It had to subject itself to an outside authority – to persons and to a group who would carry for it some of the burden of so great a mystery.

The non-Christian philosophers we have described were persons whose spiritual lives assumed, on many levels, a fierce autonomy. *Sub specie aeternitatis*, the vibrant soul that was the true self must always think of itself as free from the irrelevance of matter. As a temporarily embodied creature, the philosopher in his home town must be equally free from the irrelevant world of power: he must owe nothing to any man and was joined to society in a severely attenuated fashion. What he could depend on – and he often did so with poignant reverence – was a learned tradition that seemed to stretch through successions of revered teachers to the very origins of human knowledge. Apart from his teacher, a majestic chain of tradition summed up in ancient books, and a devoted group of disciples (who, none the less, went their separate ways after his death), the philosopher was reluctant to place his heart in any man's hands. Vastly respectful of tradition, he did not depend in any very obvious way on a contemporary religious community, nor did he seek to found one.[50]

For all his fierce introspection, Evagrius depended on the *praktikoi*, the Great Old Men of Egypt. He brought to perfection a spiritual system that was impossible without dependence on others. Above all, his emphasis on a bookless, experiential wisdom of the desert, though somewhat of a pose, given his own great sophistication as a writer and an exegete, had the immediate effect of undermining any other learned tradition than one based strictly on the Christian scriptures and on the authority of those Fathers who had made their own the message of the scriptures. Cassian found it easy to move one step further towards a notion of group-authority.[51] The monk was to examine his thoughts like an alert money-changer. He must be constantly on the look-out for debased coin. He was

---

[50] Clearly seen by Fowden, *Egyptian Hermes* 159.   [51] See esp. Rousseau, *Ascetics*, 181–2.

only to trust those thoughts and ideas that were consonant with the traditions of the elders and the teachings of the Catholic church, 'as if officially
issued from an imperial mint' (Cassian, *Collationes* 1.20). To a later Roman
reader, the overtones of imperial authority implied in that analogy would
have spoken volumes.

With Augustine the process is complete. Only through Christ and the
Catholic church had the tragic gap between the world of unchanging truth
and the world of time – the central awareness taught to him by his reading
of Platonic manuals – been bridged.[52] It was the consolation in which he
took his rest at the end of the tenth book of the *Confessions*. Tied now to
the church of Hippo as its Catholic bishop and consoled by the presence
of Christ within that church, Augustine did not need to flee to the desert
(Aug. *Conf.* x.42.67–43.70). His slow healing depended on the grace of
Christ, aided by the prayers of a Mediterranean-wide religious institution.

The message carried clearly. Two centuries later, another Latin writer, as
agonized as Augustine had been at the ease with which the soul slipped
from the presence of God into a heaving sea of worldly cares, pope
Gregory I, would find his consolation, even more explicitly than had
Augustine, in the Catholic mass, 'by which the heavens open at the priest's
calling'. The solemn ritual that brought an invisible community of angels
and departed souls together with a community of worshippers on earth,
and not the austere and lonely labour of the mind upon the mind associated with the ancient tradition of *askēsis*, was the one plank that could bring
the Christian believer, lay person and monk alike, across the ocean that
separated man from God.[53] In the next centuries, the history of asceticism,
especially in the west, would increasingly coincide with the history of the
Christian church. By decisively modifying the notion of the person, and by
doing this in such a way as to heighten dependence on a rapidly growing
religious community, Christian asceticism helped to bring about the end of
a very ancient world, in a manner more irrevocable than Julian the Apostate
or Eunapius of Sardis had even dared to fear.[54]

---

[52] Madec (1989).   [53] Gregory, *Dialogi* ix.60.3 with de Vogüé (1986).
[54] On Egyptian and Syrian monasticism of the fourth century, the following two articles add a
further dimension: Rubenson (1995) and Griffith (1995).

CHAPTER 21

CHRISTIANIZATION AND RELIGIOUS CONFLICT

PETER BROWN

At some time in the fourth century, Annianus, son of Matutina, aggrieved at the theft of a purse of six silver coins, placed a leaden curse tablet in the sacred spring of Sulis Minerva at Bath. The traditional list of antithetical categories that was held to constitute an exhaustive description of all possible suspects – 'whether man or woman, whether boy or girl, whether slave or free' – begins with a new antithesis: *seu gentilis seu christianus quaecumque*, 'whether a gentile or a Christian, whosoever'. It is a sign of the times that the practitioner who prepared this tablet should have included a further division of the human race according to purely religious criteria, 'Christian' and 'gentile' – a dichotomy whose awesome generality could only have originated among Christians. Yet it is equally revealing that, at the temple of Sulis Minerva, an entirely new way of compartmentalizing Roman society should serve to emphasize the power of the local deity: 'Christian' and 'gentile' alike remained subject to the vengeful scrutiny of the 'lady goddess'.[1]

In the period from the death of Constantine in 337 to the accession of Valentinian III at Ravenna in 425, a considerable section of the population of the Roman empire, at all social levels, remained largely unaffected by the claims of the Christian church. They were impenitently polytheistic, in that the religious common sense of their age, as of all previous centuries, led them to assume a spiritual landscape rustling with invisible presences – with countless divine beings and their ethereal ministers. Exclusive loyalty to the One God of the Christians, the dismissal of all ancient gods as maleficent (if not ineffectual) demons, and a redrawing of the map of Roman society in such a way as to see the world in terms of a single, all-embracing dichotomy between Christians and non-Christians; these views were already asserted, at this time, by some Christians; they would enjoy a long future in Byzantium and the medieval west; but in the year 425, they were not yet the views of the 'cognitive majority' of the Roman world.

Wherever spiritual presences were thought to be available, Christian and non-Christian powers jostled each other for recognition. To take one

[1] Tomlin (1988) 232–4.

example among many: the great Christian pilgrimage shrine of St Thekla was a relative newcomer in a landscape of magical tranquillity, surrounded by a grove of cypresses, on a hill overlooking the Mediterranean outside Seleucia in Cilicia. In around 430 the sophist Isocasius retired to the shrine, at a difficult moment of his career, much as Gregory of Nazianzus had done fifty years previously, after his exhausting fiasco as bishop of Sasima. Christians claimed that Isocasius had received his cure from St Thecla; but he remained a polytheist, despite the saint's rebuke. The rhetor Aristarchus of Seleucia declared that he had been healed, not by Thecla, but by the semi-divine hero Sarpedon, whose tomb was visible on the seashore, though now flanked by a Christian monastery. Aba, a leading lady of Seleucia, though a polytheist, 'felt no aversion to Jews nor to Christians'. Her broken leg claimed the attention, first, of Jewish magical healers, then of Sarpedon, and only eventually of St Thecla (*Miracula Sanctae Theclae* 18 and 39–40, ed. G. Dagron, *Vie et Miracles de Sainte Thècle*. Brussels, 1978).

What has to be explained in this chapter is the process by which these hints of the infinitely diverse religious climate that prevailed in much of the Roman empire in the fourth and fifth centuries have remained what they are for any modern reader – tantalizing fragments of a complex religious world, glimpsed through the chinks in a body of evidence which claims to tell a very different story. The notion that this one short period of time (of under a century) witnessed the 'death of paganism'; the concomitant notion that the end of polytheism was the 'natural' consequence of a long-prepared 'triumph of monotheism' in the Roman world; the presentation of the political and religious history of the period as fraught with high drama, as a succession of Christian emperors, from Constantine to Theodosius II, played out their God-given role in abolishing the entire 'error of the Greeks', despite moments of dramatic but hopeless resistance by the devotees of the old gods; and the view that the definitive humiliation of the Jews throughout the Roman world was a further, logical corollary of these momentous events: all this amounts to a 'representation' of the religious history of the age, constructed by a brilliant generation of Christian writers, polemicists and preachers in the last decade of our period.

A Christian 'representation' of the history of the fourth century has survived, in thinly laicized form, in the majority of modern narratives of the period. From Gibbon and Burckhardt to the present day, it has been assumed that the end of paganism was inevitable, once confronted by the resolute intolerance of Christianity; that the interventions of the Christian emperors in its suppression were decisive; and that much of the tragic interest of the period for a modern scholar consists in the examination of the few, forlorn 'pagan revivals' that are held to have occurred towards the end of the fourth century, or in the tracing of those few 'pagan survivals' that somehow escaped destruction at this time. For this reason it is important to capture the original meaning of the Christian representation of their age for those who first propounded it.[2] In the first place, it was a representation that imposed a firm narrative closure on the events of what had been, in reality, a 'wavering century'.[3] Between Constantine and Theodosius II, a mighty conflict had taken place, and the Christian church had emerged as the victor.

The pagan faith, made dominant for so many years, by such pains, such expenditure of wealth, such feats of arms, has vanished from the earth.

(Isidore of Pelusium, *Ep.* 1.270, *PG* LXXVIII.344A)

We tend to forget how much of this conflict was considered by late Roman Christians to have been fought out in heaven rather than on earth. In the Christian representation of their own history, the end of polytheism had occurred with the coming of Christ to earth. It was when he was raised on the cross and not, as we more pedestrian moderns tend to suppose, in the reign of Theodosius I, that heaven and earth rang with the crash of falling temples.[4] The alliance of emperor and church to rid the world of polytheism, that took place after the conversion of Constantine, was simply a last, peremptory 'mopping-up' operation. It made manifest, on earth, a victory already won centuries before, by Christ, over the shadowy empire of the demons.

It is important to stress one aspect of this attitude. A dramatic acceleration of historical time was a striking feature of almost all Christian accounts of the high points of the end of polytheism. Not only was the triumph of the church preordained; it was thought to be instantaneous. As a result, its immediate human consequences were taken for granted. The gods passed away from whole regions, much as in the Christian rite of exorcism the demon was believed to have passed out of the body of the possessed, ideally in a single, dramatic spasm, enabling the sufferer to return immediately to normal health of mind and body. Narratives of the destruction and desecration of major shrines – that of Zeus in Apamea, in Syria, in 386, and of the Serapeum of Alexandria, in around 392 – took place according to an analogous, brisk rhythm. It was enough that Serapis should be seen to have been driven from the temple that he had 'possessed' for so many centuries, by the power of Christ made present in the successful violence of his servants. It was simply assumed that Alexandria had been 'healed' of ancient error by the abrupt passing of its greatest god.

We should not dismiss out of hand such a drastic stylization of reality. We are dealing with more than a tendentious account, of which the historian must beware. For contemporaries, such accounts served as facilitating

[2] See Thélamon (1981), *passim.*   [3] Chuvin, *Chronicle*, ch. 3.
[4] Jacob of Sarug, *On the Fall of the Idols* 180, tr. Landersdorfer (1913).

narratives. They even helped non-Christians to live with a brutal *fait accompli*. The ecclesiastical authorities used the account to claim instant, supernatural victory. The bishop Theophilus was portrayed, in an illustrated chronicle of the fifth century, surrounded by palms of victory, standing upon the ruined Serapeum. But even the devotees of Serapis came to terms with defeat, by offering their own, equally supernatural version of the story. They declared that, in a manner characteristic of the gods of Egypt, Serapis had withdrawn to heaven, saddened that such blasphemy should have occurred in his beloved city. Many of his priests became Christians. They brought with them prophecies in which Serapis had foretold his own departure, the desecration of his shrine and, even, the victory of the sign of the cross. Years later, Christians as far away from Alexandria as Carthage were impressed by the power of the gods to foretell their own defeat, as demonstrated by the prophecies concerning the Serapeum (Aug. *De Divinatione Daemonum* 1.1). Seen with Egyptian eyes, the spectacular end of polytheism in Alexandria had been a retreat according to plan. For both sides, an austerely supernatural interpretation of the event served to defuse recrimination. What had happened at Alexandria, brutal though it was, merely reflected on earth a conflict of mighty invisible beings. The acclaimed triumph of the one and the lordly retreat of the other had to be accepted by mere mortals. No further questions needed to be asked, and life could resume as usual.

We are dealing with a representation of their own times calculated to shield the majority of Christians from the perilous complexities of real life in an empire in which long-established alternatives to Christianity had by no means disappeared. A sense of the victorious logic of events, persistently conveyed in compact narrative sequences, constituted the *strepitus mundi*, the reassuring 'roar' of a world believed by Christians to be rushing swiftly towards final absorption into the church. When a group of polytheists entered the Christian basilica in the small city of Boseth in the Medjerda valley, possibly in 404, they had taken the opportunity presented by the visit to their city of the famous bishop and orator, Augustine of Hippo, to make their peace, in as dignified a manner as possible, with the local bishop. It was high time, Augustine told them, to wake up and listen to that 'roar'.[5]

The 'roar' of a Christian narrative has made it exceptionally difficult to recapture the mentalities of the fourth and fifth centuries. Hence a paradoxical situation. The late antique period witnessed several experiments in the imposition, upon a wider society, of religious norms upheld by a determined and articulate group. The period is characterized by the successful imposition of a rabbinic interpretation of Judaism among the

Jewish communities in Palestine, Mesopotamia and elsewhere, and by the formalization and propagation of Zoroastrianism throughout the Sasanian empire. Both are remarkable events of which we know singularly little, compared with the process that we call the 'Christianization of the Roman empire'.[6] Yet in our evidence, this process is not simply misrepresented by our Christian sources: it is rendered largely invisible to us by the implicit narrative structures that we have described.

It is difficult to get behind the deceptive trenchancy of such narrative structures and the view of what constituted the process of 'Christianization' that they implied. In order to recapture the horizons of the possible, within which late Roman persons actually experienced the changes associated with the post-Constantinian empire, we must attempt to do this – to evoke the more elusive, but enduring mental structures which the majority of Christians shared with their contemporaries. Seen with the hindsight afforded by the eventual triumph of the church in the next centuries, the ambiguities and hesitations that characterized the actions even of those who would have considered themselves undoubted Christians in the fourth century (let alone the less well-documented attitudes of non-Christians) seem opaque and puzzling to us. Yet, what often appears to modern eyes as inconsequential and inconsistent in their attitudes reveals the silent working-out of a complex 'logic of the possible' that was specific to the period.

We often forget how alien to a modern mentality (even, indeed, to the mentality of Christians of the immediately succeeding centuries) many of these mental structures were. Nowhere is this more plain than in the attitudes of many believers to the invisible powers that were thought to surround late Roman persons. Christian assertions of the unique power of their God and of his servants coexisted, among most Christians, with a collective representation of the universe shared, if in differing ways and to differing degrees, by all religious persons in late antiquity. It was a collective representation that tended to stress, in practice, the supernatural compartmentalizing of the universe at the expense of its notional unity. The highest powers inhabited the shining upper reaches of the *mundus*, of a vast universe. They lived far beyond the solid brilliance of the stars. To human beings, placed on an earth that lay *in sentina mundi*, 'in the sump-hole of the universe', they communicated their benevolence through hosts of lower spirits, who brushed the earth with their ministrations, ever open to human requests for aid and comfort, and redoubtable when slighted. An imaginative structure of such majesty and self-evident truth endured almost unchanged and unchallenged in the minds of the majority of Christians. In the words of Augustine:

---

[6] MacMullen, *Christianizing* puts together much of the relevant evidence.

There are those who say: 'God is good, He is great, supreme, eternal and invio-
lable. It is He Who will give us eternal life and that incorruption which He
promised at the resurrection. But these things of the physical world and of our
present times – *ista vero saecularia et temporalia* – belong to *daemones* and to the invisible Powers.' . . . They leave aside God, as if these things did not belong to Him;
and by sacrifices, by all kinds of healing devices, and by the persuasive advice of
their fellows . . . they seek out ways to cope with what concerns this present life.

(Aug. *Enn. I in Ps. 34* 7)

It was further assumed that the favoured servants of the One High God
were those best informed, also, about the turbulent lower reaches of the
mundus, as these affected health and happiness in this world. When, in the
420s, Shenoute of Atripe observed that a provincial governor, 'a man who
had the reputation of being wise', wore a jackal's claw tied to his toe, the
governor informed him that he did this on the recommendation of a 'Great
Monk'. A leading Christian ascetic had validated what appeared to
Shenoute to be a palpably non-Christian occult remedy.

Faced by the thoughtful governor, Shenoute did not deny the collective
representation of a universe filled with serried ranks of invisible powers.
He provided, rather, an exaltation of the victorious power of the name of
Christ, of the one being who was uniquely able to bridge the fissure that
ran across the universe, separating its highest from its lowest reaches. Christ
was able to touch all aspects of daily life in the material world:

Try to attain to the full measure of this Name, and you will find it on your mouth
and on the mouths of your children. When you make high festival and when you
rejoice, cry Jesus. When anxious and in pain, cry Jesus. When little boys and girls
are laughing, let them cry Jesus. And those who flee before barbarians, cry Jesus.
And those who go down to the Nile, cry Jesus. And those who see wild beasts and
sights of terror, cry Jesus. Those who are taken off to prison, cry Jesus. And those
whose trial has been corrupted and who receive injustice, cry the Name of Jesus.

(Shenoute, *Contra Origenistas* 821, ed. T. Orlandi. Rome, 1985, 62–3)

In the same way, Ephraim the Syrian warned the Christian women of
Nisibis to look only to the church. Priests carrying the gospels must be the
only religious practitioners to enter their homes, and not diviners and
magical healers. God alone could heal the shame of infertility:

His will is a key,
that alone opens and shuts the womb.

(Ephraim, *Memre on Nicomedia* XI.517, *PO* XXXVII.257)

For men such as Ephraim, Augustine and Shenoute, confronted with
so widespread and deeply rooted a view of the spiritual world,
'Christianization' meant nothing less than staking a claim to a monopoly. For them, monotheism meant the exclusion of all other sources of
spiritual power. Outside the church, the power of the gods was declared

bankrupt; Judaism was said to have forfeited the protection of the One God; and within the church itself, the lordship of Christ over all other invisible powers was asserted in such a way as to support a structure of religious observance largely exercised and defined by the clergy. Compelling though such a claim might seem, because presented to other Christians as the only consistent interpretation of their monotheistic creed, it was not an assertion that carried instant conviction at the time. Throughout this period, it was effectively held in check by an ancient, more compartmentalized model of the universe. This model had remained firmly lodged in the back of the minds of Christians of all levels of culture and of religious background. It did not do so only out of mindless inertia. Far from it. It summed up a view of the world that provided contemporaries with an array of mental tools with which to think through a wide range of problems. It gave the average Christian freedom of manoeuvre in a society where the stability of the Roman order still rested, at this time, on a tolerance of ambiguity that flouted the single vision of men such as Augustine, Shenoute and Ephraim.

We can see this most clearly in the exalted, but well-documented, level of the public life of the empire. If there is one trait that characterized this particular period in the long history of the Roman empire, it was the spasm of imperial self-assertion that left no aspect of late Roman society untouched. The fourth century was the Age of Authority *par excellence*. With the exception of the unnerving but mercifully brief reign of Julian, this authority supported the Christian church. A law of Theodosius II, in 438, speaks, without exaggeration, of the 'thousand terrors of the laws' that defended the *insatiabilis honor*, the 'boundless claim to honour', of the Catholic church (*Nov. Theod. II* III.10). By 425, the laws against polytheists, Jews and heretics had congealed into a system which, for the first time in the history of Rome, presented correct religious adherence as a requirement for the full enjoyment of the benefits of Roman society.[7]

In a manner entirely characteristic of the period, the laws were frankly intended to terrorize the emperor's subjects on matters of religion. Their language was uniformly vehement. The penalties they proposed were frequently horrifying. They included capital punishment for the performance of sacrifices. To take only one, chilling example: the threat of flogging with leaden whips (a punishment known to be almost certainly lethal) was decreed against a minor heretical leader, Jovinian, at Rome, prior to his exile (*C.Th.* XVI.5.3; Aug. *Ep.* 10*.4.3, ed. J. Divjak, *CSEL* LXXXVIII. Vienna, 1981, 48). Yet fear of these penalties was not the sole agent in the conversion of the mass of Roman subjects to the Christian church. The local authorities, whose resources were already strained to the limit by other,

---

[7] Gaudemet (1990) provides a useful summary, as do other articles in the same volume.

more urgent efforts to make good the assertion of imperial authority, such as the collection of taxes, were notoriously lax in imposing them. Christian bishops frequently obstructed their application: they insisted on their right to intercede for a remission of threatened punishments, seeing in this right a valuable source of local prestige and authority.[8]

The cumulative effect of the laws was to set in place a religious ordering of society that would henceforth prove an inseparable adjunct of imperial rule, in the empire itself and, later, in the sub-imperial states of the west. The laws offered, as it were, an official map of Roman society, increasingly drawn according to Christian categories. It is revealing that, as early as 370, the imperial chancery should have adopted the term *pagani*, 'pagans', as the official term with which to describe polytheists (*C.Th.* XVI.2.18; cf. XVI.5.46). *Paganus* was a term circulated by Christians as a 'lump word' for all who were not heretics or Jews. It took the term as it had been used by non-Christians to describe various forms of non-participants: the *pagani* or *paganoi* were non-combatants as opposed to professional soldiers, the rank and file of the administrator's staff as opposed to high officials. In an etymology made explicit by Orosius in his *History against the Pagans* of 416, and followed ever since in the Latin world, polytheists, as 'pagans', were further identified with men of the *pagus*, peasants, *paysans*, as opposed to sophisticated urban dwellers.[9] By A.D. 425 few could be unaware of what had become a fourfold categorization of Roman society. There was the Catholic church. Along its fringes lay 'all heresies, all perfidies and schisms' – in effect, all forms of religious teaching among Christians that Catholic bishops might persuade an emperor to denounce as 'errors' hostile to the true faith. Then there were the two great outsiders: 'the madness of the Jewish impiety' and 'the error and insanity of stupid paganism' (*C.Th.* XV.5.5 and XVI.5.63).

Many of the laws collected in the Theodosian Code were rescripts. They were answers to enquiries by local governors or to petitions by local interest-groups. As a result, we can follow in the laws the emergence of a language of intolerance shared by the Christian court and by vocal elements in provincial society. It was a language that ran parallel to the repeated efforts of learned Christians – apologists such as Augustine of Hippo and Theodoret of Cyrrhus, and heresiologists such as Epiphanius of Salamis – to reduce the infinite variety of unorthodox beliefs – heretical, Jewish and polytheist – to a single common denominator of demonically inspired 'error'. In the words of a sermon of Augustine, preached at a time of heightened imperial legislation: 'heretics, Jews and pagans: they have formed a unity over against our Unity' (Aug. *Serm.* 62.18).

---

[8] Brown (1963).   [9] O'Donnell (1977).

It is important to define precisely in what manner the imperial legislation was intended to impinge on contemporaries. It has been assumed, on the strength of an articulate body of Christian opinion, that the iron logic of intolerance demanded that, once they possessed such formidable power, Christians should use it to convert as many non-Christians as possible – by threats and disabilities, if not by the direct use of force. But the horizons of the possible in a given society follow their own logic. It took a further century of social and religious changes before Justinian could envisage the compulsory baptism of remaining polytheists, and a further century yet until Heraclius and the Visigothic kings of Spain attempted to baptize the Jews. In the fourth century, not only were such ambitious schemes a physical impossibility, given the large numbers of non-Christians in every region: the horizons of the possible, that enabled such ventures to be contemplated, did not exist. They were blocked by an alternative narrative of success. The most potent social and religious drama in the fourth-century Roman empire was not conversion – it was triumph. Christianity must defeat, and be seen to defeat, its enemies, not to convert them. Christian writers and imperial legislators alike drew on a rhetoric of incessant conquest and reconquest that affected every facet of upper-class society. The triumphal ending of civil wars, the instantaneous *damnatio memoriae* of fallen usurpers, the eternal victory that accompanied the emperors in their wars against the barbarians, even smaller rituals of power, as when the servants went around the palace of a great man at the end of the evening, extinguishing the lamps to a chant of 'May we conquer' (Amm. Marc. XVI.8.9): these experiences provided by far the weightiest imaginative components in any contemporary reading of the progress of the church.

Thus, the physical limitations imposed on the coercive powers of the imperial government were tacitly justified by a widespread mentality. Most Christians were content with a 'minimalist' definition of the triumph of their church. It was important that the triumph of the church should have happened, and that it should be seen to have happened. As for non-believers, it was sufficient that they should be humbled, rather than that they should be converted. The one might follow from the other, but this consequence was treated as merely a by-product. It was not the principal aim in the setting in place of a social order that declared the God-given dominance of Christianity and the defeat of its enemies. On the other hand, any attempt to weaken that structure of dominance provoked vociferous protest. In 423, an edict was issued at Constantinople to the effect that a bishop who had confiscated a Jewish synagogue should compensate the local Jewish community as a way of making amends for an illegal recourse to violence, long forbidden by the laws. The edict was not well received by the Christians of Syria:

And the edict of the king and the command of the prefect in regard to this was promulgated in many cities and was read to everyone. Then there was great grief among all Christians, especially because they saw the Jews and heathen clothed in white and appearing glad and merry.

(*V. Sym. Styl.* 636, tr. F. Lent, *JAOS* xxxv (1915) 195)

Such breaches in the fixity of a Christian order were supposed to be rare. The incident shows an intense local sense of honour, an insistence that the church should not be shamed by concessions to its enemies. It does not show a determination to use the laws to convert unbelievers. It was sufficient that non-Christians should keep a low profile. In this period, at least, the *quid pro quo* of Christian dominance was inexplicit but firm. In many areas, polytheists were not molested as long as they kept their beliefs to themselves in front of Christians; and, apart from a few ugly incidents of local violence, the Jewish communities enjoyed a century of stable, even privileged existence. Both non-Christian groups enjoyed a tolerance based on contempt. In the words of a law that was repeated in the *Code* of Justinian:

We especially command those persons who are truly Christians, or who are said to be so, that they should not abuse the authority of religion and dare to lay violent hands on Jews and pagans, who are living quietly and attempting nothing disorderly or contrary to law.

(*C.Th.* XVI.5.60; *CJ* 1.11.6)

Having, in 423, been declared by the emperor Theodosius II not to exist, large bodies of polytheists, all over the Roman empire, simply slipped out of history. They continued to enjoy, for many generations, the relatively peaceable, if cramped, existence which, only two centuries after the reign of Theodosius II, would fall to the lot of Christians themselves in another great Near Eastern empire, raised up in the name of one God – that of Islam.

As a result, the religious landscape of the Mediterranean continued to be characterized by a patchwork of religious communities. Regions that boasted a triumphant, long-established Christianity were often flanked by equally tenacious settlements of polytheists. Polytheism itself evolved, often by adopting aspects of the new religion. The Euphemitai of Phoenicia emerged as a new cult in the mountains of Lebanon. Their gatherings, from which blood sacrifice was pointedly absent, were marked by hymn-singing and by blazing lights in buildings that could be mistaken for Christian basilicas.[10] Rather than becoming uniformly 'Christianized', the Roman empire remained a land of religious contrasts. In Ephesus, for instance, the name of Artemis was chiselled from the inscriptions on the

---

[10] Epiphan. *Pan.* 80.2.1, *PG* XLII.757; for other such evolutions, see Bowersock, *Hellenism* 41–53.

Harbour Baths and from the portico that ran in front of the Prytaneion. The statue of Artemis in the centre of the city was torn down and replaced by the sign of the cross. It was a civic magistrate, Demeas, who claimed the honour of declaring the city officially Christian: 'He honoured God Who drives away idols, and the Cross, the victorious, immortal symbol of Christ' (H. Grégoire, *Inscriptions d'Asie Mineure*, no. 104. Paris, 1922, 34). Yet in the hinterland of Ephesus, in the small towns and mountain villages of Lydia, Phrygia and Caria, so many polytheists remained that over a century later, in 542, John, the Monophysite roving bishop of Ephesus, could claim to have baptized 23,000 converts, to have destroyed 2000 idols, and to have established 96 new churches.[11]

Religious coercion on a large scale was mainly practised by Christians on other Christians. From 405 onwards, the extensive writings of Augustine justified a suppression of the Donatist church that amounted to a forcible 'transfer of populations' from the Donatist to the Catholic church.[12] But Africa was the exception. Elsewhere, throughout the Mediterranean, the rule seems to have been the *convivencia* of a triumphant Christianity with a tenacious, if discreet, polytheism, and with confident Jewish communities. Not for the last time in the history of the Near East, it was agreed that strong fences made good neighbours.

Nothing, indeed, illustrates this situation more clearly than does the status of the Jews. In the legislation of the period, rhetorical humiliation of Judaism as a religion coexisted with extensive corporate privileges for Jewish leaders and for Jewish synagogues.[13] Although Judaism was repeatedly branded as a 'mad impiety' (*C.Th.* xv.5.5), the leaders of the Jewish community – a succession of patriarchs in Palestine, and other groups of representatives in other provinces – received from all Christian emperors repeated reassurance that Judaism, unlike polytheism and many forms of heretical Christianity, was 'not a sect prohibited by the laws' (*C.Th.* xvi.8.9). Jewish synagogues enjoyed the exemptions associated with 'holy places' (*C.Th.* vii.8.2). The personnel of the synagogues enjoyed the same privileges as did the Christian clergy: for they also were persons 'truly devoted to the service of God' (*C.Th.* xii.1.99).

Such laws, of course, needed to be reiterated. The few violent clashes between Christians and Jews of which we know show only too clearly how easily the legal protection afforded to synagogues could be pushed aside. From Callinicum (Raqqa) on the Euphrates to Mahon in Minorca, the triumph of the church expressed itself spasmodically in the destruction or appropriation of synagogues: at least five such incidents occurred in one

---

[11] Joh. Eph. *HE* III.3.36–7, tr. E. W. Brooks, *CSCO*: Script. Syr. ser. 3.3. Louvain, 1936, 124–5; *Lives of the Eastern Saints* 47, *PO* xviii.681; Michael the Syrian, *Chron.* ix.33, tr. J. B. Chabot. Paris, 1901, 270–1: but note that the numbers vary in each source.   [12] Brown (1964).
[13] The relevant laws are collected, translated and commented by Linder (1987).

generation, after 388. However, these incidents should be seen in proportion. They do not in themselves amount to evidence for a generalized, and inevitable, trend toward the victimization of Jews in the post-Constantinian empire. The evidence from Palestine, for instance, points to the flowering, in full-blooded, Jewish form, of yet another of those sturdy provincial élites who profited from the *pax Byzantina* in the eastern provinces. In other areas, also, Judaism retained its ancient prestige, to the annoyance of Christian preachers such as John Chrysostom at Antioch.[14]

Despite this distinctive combination of prudent inertia with mental structures that made it difficult even for zealous Christians to imagine a world without enemies, even if these were humbled enemies, the imperial declaration of the triumph of the church posed the issue of coexistence with non-Christians in an acute form. Religious toleration was, at best, a fragile notion. It contributed little to the working-out of codes of coexistence between the adherents of different religions.[15] We should not read modern associations into those few texts in which it was invoked. When canvassed with sincerity, it derived its conviction not from a widespread consensus, but from principles that characterized small groups of intellectuals who had always been treated as marginal to Roman society. Many mystical philosophers, both polytheist and Christian, believed that God was so distant from mankind that his nature escaped the narrow certainties of all sects. God might even play hide-and-seek with the many groups of his worshippers. In the words of Themistius, speaking in 376, in the reign of the ill-tempered and intolerant emperor Valens:

It might possibly be pleasing to God not to be so easily known, and to be subject to divergence of opinion, so that each sect might fear Him the rather, since an accurate knowledge of Him is so unattainable.

(Sozom. *HE* vi.36)

A philosopher, who was careful to wear his dark *tribônion* on all state occasions, Themistius was licensed to utter such Utopian sentiments. When invoked by rival Christian groups, claims to freedom of conscience did not ring so true. They were too often brought forward with transparent opportunism. The historian Socrates, himself a member of the sturdy minority of Novatians in Constantinople, remarked drily of the rhetoric used by the defeated Arians in 382:

They say now *Many are called and few are chosen* – an expression which they never used when on account of fear and terror the majority of people were on their side.

(Socr. *HE* v.10)

The search for examples of religious toleration may lead us to look in the wrong direction for the forces that moderated religious conflict in this

---

[14] Stemberger (1987) and Wilken, *John Chrysostom and the Jews.*   [15] Garnsey (1984).

period. Most people agreed that authority, fear, even the direct use of force, might be mobilized to impose truth and to banish error. But they subjected to sharp scrutiny the manner in which this authority was asserted. Precisely because correct religion was the glory of the empire, it had to be imposed in a manner that reflected the overwhelming dignity of the imperial power. Power was associated with serenity and persuasive force. It was by showing these that the emperor was believed to elicit the loyalty of his upper-class subjects, and they, in turn, were expected to adopt a tone of quiet certainty when commanding their inferiors. A note of unhurried, because unquestioned, superiority, and not violent threats and the imposition of savage punishments, was held by a large section of upper-class opinion, even by Christians, to set the style for the implementation of the imperial laws on religion. The modern issue of toleration was swallowed up in a specifically late Roman insistence on civility.

Thus, under Julian, Libanius wrote to the governor of Syria, Alexander, a fellow polytheist, on how best to handle Eusebius, a potentially recalcitrant Christian town-councillor of Apamea. Though commendably zealous for the gods, Alexander must learn to play the game by the rules: 'Consider this – whether it is better to show gentleness and get the job done, or to show yourself a hard man and make matters hard for yourself.' As for Eusebius, Alexander had little cause to worry: though a Christian, he was a typical member of the urban upper classes; he could be counted on to give way. 'He is not the sort of man to be unaware of the prevailing climate of the regime, and is guided by calculation rather than by courage' (Lib. *Ep.* 1411). The humane tolerance for which Libanius has been justly praised by modern scholars was based, not on any clear notion of toleration, but on a solid bedrock of political good sense. The eventual conformity of the upper classes to any strongly maintained imperial policy could be taken for granted. But, precisely for that reason, it was better that it should appear not to have been extorted by force. It was difficult enough, in truly urgent issues such as the collection of taxes, to strike the right balance between browbeating and cajoling the local notables, without this delicate equilibrium being upset by the righteous anger of a true believer.

It is, perhaps, the overwhelming emphasis on the orderly assertion of authority and on conformity that explains a certain collusion by all parties in accepting the dramatic and other-worldly Christian narrative of their own success. In that narrative, it was first and foremost the gods who were defeated, not their worshippers. Constantine's vehement break with the 'contagious supersititon' of blood sacrifice, and the consequent harsh laws against it, reflected a one-sided, Christian reading of polytheism. The ban was shocking to many polytheists. In the fourth century, it was often evaded by special pleading; and it was later flouted, whenever possible, by clandestine sacrifice.[16] To Christians, the prohibition of sacrifice represented the ultimate act of violence against the gods. No longer could the demonic hosts hover around the smoking altar, deriving sustenance from the polluted stench of burnt meat. The fact that the gods did not avenge this abrupt disconnection of their imagined life-support system further proved their impotence. But polytheists had been accustomed to offering prayers to the gods in innumerable ways – at the healing springs of Britain, Spain and Gaul, in caves cluttered with late Roman lamps, as in Attica, and with lights and with heavy clouds of incense all over Syria.[17] Though essential to the Christian representation of the end of polytheism, and deeply resented, laws against sacrifice may have been less disruptive to traditional piety than we might suppose.

In practice, the ban on sacrifice was a mercifully delimited measure. It meant that Christians and polytheists of the upper classes were able to mingle freely in public space without the risk of encountering a smoking sacrificial altar, a certain source of demonic pollution for Christians, and a truly divisive symbol of the old order. One suspects that most fourth-century Christians remained more concerned to avoid the 'pollution' associated with direct contact with sacrificial rituals than they were with suppressing all forms of polytheistic worship. Thus, when serving under Julian, the future emperor Valentinian I was believed to have drawn his sword and pointedly hacked off that part of his cloak on which a few drops of lustral water had fallen, sprinkled by a priest at the entrance of a Gallic temple (Sozom. *HE* vi.6). Yet Valentinian I, whose horror of sorcery and apostasy was well known, could be praised by Ammianus Marcellinus as the one Christian ruler who 'took his stand in the middle of a diversity of faiths' (Amm. Marc. xxx.9.5). An ancient Christian model of reality gave a politician such as Valentinian I room to manoeuvre. He could allow polytheistic rituals to continue as long as he distanced himself and his entourage from the contagion of sacrifice.

One thing which we will never know for certain is how many Christians in high places were not simply content to avoid sacrifice. The model of the universe that so many carried in the back of their minds permitted them, in their domestic life, to approach the lower powers for material favours. It is possible that they also viewed the public rituals of the old religion as not invariably polluting and maleficent, but as addressed, rather, to those lower powers of the material order, the 'angelic' servants of the One High God, from whose care the mighty fabric of the empire and its cities could not conceivably be disjoined. Later legends ascribed immunity to earthquake at Constantinople and Antioch to talismans prepared through sacred rites by

---

[16] Harl (1990).
[17] Rousselle (1990) 31–41 and 65–75 (for Gaul); Fowden (1988) 48–9 (Attica); Lib. *Or.* xxx.8 and 18 (Syria).

the wise Apollonius of Tyana. Many Christians seem to have accepted that such talismans exercised an uncanny power derived from the spirits of the lower air (Anastasius Sinaita, *Quaestiones* 20, *PG* LXXXIX.524–5).

Altogether, the most striking feature of the fourth century was the ability of the upper classes to muffle religious conflict. We are dealing with a class in the grip of a 'lifeboat mentality'. They stood at the head of a social system that faced far more pressing dangers than those associated with religious error. They tended, instinctively, to emphasize what they had in common – a common upper-class culture and a common loyalty to the emperor. The warm tone of the correspondence between Libanius and the Jewish patriarch Gamaliel; the manner in which the prudent administration of friendship by letter-writers such as Symmachus and Libanius embraced persons of all religions; the difficulty experienced by modern scholars in establishing the religious affiliations of most members of the governing élites, and the even greater difficulty they have experienced in discovering how the public behaviour and political fortunes of those members were determined by such affiliations: these all point to a huge reticence.[18] Christians and non-Christians alike drew on well-established notions of civility, that expressed their overriding sense of a shared upper-class identity, so as to contain the conflicts implicit in the rise of Christianity.

In the late fourth and early fifth centuries, the issue was whether the implicit consensus of the upper classes would continue to contain the violence associated with the religious movements of the time. This, in turn, depended on the extent to which the leaders of the Christian communities – the bishops, clergy and monks – were prepared to challenge that consensus. The pace and final upshot of this dialogue between consensus and violence varied greatly from region to region and from generation to generation.

In the eastern empire, for instance, the decade of violence that saw Cynegius' destruction of temples throughout Syria in 386, the burning of the synagogue at Callinicum in 388, and the spectacular end of the Serapeum of Aleandria in around 392 marked a high moment of religious conflict. Harassed by civil wars and his authority challenged by two major urban riots in four years (the Riot of the Statues at Antioch in 387, and the riot that led to the massacre of Thessalonica in 391), Theodosius I abandoned, for a time, the more distant, less brutally confrontational style associated with earlier rulers. He allowed the vehemence of local power-groups, the Christian bishops and the monks, to have a free hand, with occasional spectacular results that were remembered as decisive in later Christian sources.

---

[18] Wilken, *John Chrysostom and the Jews* 58–60; Matthews (1974); Frezza (1989) (Libanius); von Haehling (1978).

Yet all contemporaries did not see this chain of events in the same light. We know so much about Cynegius' activities in Syria and about the fate of the synagogue at Callinicum largely because articulate and well-placed persons still felt free to present the incidents as flagrant departures from the norm. The fact that their opinion was overruled on these particular occasions does not mean that their views did not continue to be held at a later time. We can be misled by the dramatic nature of our sources. In these, for instance, the zeal of the monks was thrown into high relief. Eunapius of Sardis wrote of their *tyrranikē exousia*, of their violently usurped authority (Eunap. *V. Soph.* 472). Libanius left a memorable characterization of their actions at this time:

This black-robed tribe who eat more than elephants . . . sweep across the countryside like a river in spate . . . and, by ravaging the temples, they ravage the estates.

(Lib. *Or.* xxx.9)

Yet it would be wrong to conclude from these statements alone that the monks had emerged as the undisputed leaders of an intolerant 'grass-roots' Christianity, and that they would henceforth be allowed by all Christian authorities to destroy temples, burn synagogues, and terrorize Jews and polytheists with impunity. Far from it. Monks were often referred to in our sources because they constituted a form of 'deniable' violence. They were not protected by the official privileges of the clergy. They were technically laymen, and, being often persons of low social status, they might be punished with exemplary brutality. They were the one segment of the Christian church who could be convincingly accused by non-Christians of *latrocinium*, of the use of force unsanctioned by the Roman state. Far from being treated by all Christians as the unquestioned leaders of Christian 'activism', many zealous monks were told to mind their own business. When, in 434–5, the prefect of Constantinople, Leontius, proposed to hold Olympic games at Chalcedon, the abbot Hypatius marched into town at the head of twenty monks. The bishop Eulalius refused to have anything to do with his protest.

Are you determined to die, even if no one wishes to make a martyr of you? As you are a monk, go and sit in your cell and keep quiet. This is my affair.

(Callinicus, *Vita Hypatii* 33)

Throughout the empire, bishops and laymen alike remained determined that if Christianity were to triumph through their authority, they alone should have the monopoly of the use of force. They showed little enthusiasm for the destructive exploits that bulked so large in Christian sources and, consequently, in most modern accounts of the period.

Any attempt to draw a scale of religious violence in this period must place the violence of Christians towards each other at the top. Graphic

accounts of physical violence at the hands of other Christians formed part
of a litany of mutual accusation that continued, without a break, throughout this period. Ammianus Marcellinus understandably concluded that
Christian groups behaved toward each other 'like wild beasts' (Amm. Marc.
XXII.5.4). What gave distinctive flavour to Christian violence was the fact
that they often fought for the control of crowded urban assembly-halls,
with the occasional, predictable and terrible consequences. In 366, a clash
between bishop Damasus and his rivals at Rome left at least 137 corpses in
a major basilica (Amm. Marc. XXVII.3.12). In the 420s, seventy persons were
trampled to death in a schismatic Novatian church on the southern outskirts of Constantinople, as a result of a 'demonic' panic triggered by the
rumour that the rival Novatian bishop and his clergy were marching on the
building (Socr. *HE* VII.5).

With the exception of the patriarch Cyril's attack on the Jewish community in Alexandria in 415, Christian violence against Jews was less bloodthirsty than was Christian violence against rival Christians. But it was no
less overbearing. What was most often at stake was the destruction or the
appropriation of the local synagogues. Such incidents were usually spas-
modic. But the fear remained that when carefully publicized by the bishops
of the affected cities, they might trigger off an empire-wide movement.
This happened after the discovery of the relics of St Stephen in 415.
Bishop John of Jerusalem used the discovery to assert his authority over
Judaeo-Christian groups in the city; and in the same year bishop Rabbula
of Edessa petitioned the emperor for the right to convert a synagogue into
a church dedicated to St Stephen.

Two years later, in 417, Severus, bishop of Mahon in Minorca, seized on
the occasion provided by the arrival of the relics of Stephen to destroy the
local synagogue. He faced a hitherto influential and respected Jewish community with the alternative of exile or conversion. We know in detail of this
incident from the *Letter* of Severus which was written to convince other
bishops of the eminent correctness of his actions.[19] It is a chilling document. It takes us uncomfortably close to the combination of ceremonious
bullying and calculated disregard for its human consequences which, rather
than outright bloodshed, characterized the triumph of Christianity in so
many areas. The capital of an isolated island, Mahon may have been a miniature of Antioch, a city where we know from the sermons of John
Chrysostom that Jews and Christians had come to live together in a manner
too close for the comfort of the bishop and clergy. The heads of the Jewish
community enjoyed imperial privileges and held high municipal office.
Christians were aware of how much they shared with their neighbours:
both groups had in common the chanting of the Psalms and were in the

[19] Seguí Vidal (1937); see esp. Ginzburg (1992).

habit of telling each other their dreams. The arrival of the relics of St Stephen, doubtless accompanied by news of events in Jerusalem and elsewhere, gave Severus the opportunity to reaffirm boundaries that had become blurred. Jews and Christians suddenly ceased to greet each other in the street. The bishop summoned a reinforcement of Christians from a neighbouring town that did not have a Jewish community. For the first time, the Jews of Mahon could be seen as a minority on a Christian island. Sensing his advantage, Severus displayed a high-handed economy in his use of direct force. The Jewish leaders were summoned to a religious debate in the bishop's basilica. They refused to come, claiming that they had been summoned on the Sabbath. They further questioned the sincerity of Severus' oath that he intended no violence against them. Their preparations to defend the synagogue were deemed to constitute an act of *latrocinium*, an illegal resort to force. Severus proceeded to the synagogue at the head of a crowd. He burnt out the interior, having first set aside the Torah to 'protect from desecration', at the hands of the Jews, the holy books of the Old Testament, to the possession of which Christians claimed they were alone entitled. The silver ornaments and ex-votos, however, were punctiliously handed back to the personnel of the synagogue, lest the Christians be accused of looting (*Ep. Severi* 9–10).

Next day, the leader of the Jewish community was shouted down in a debate that took place in the burnt-out shell of the synagogue. Others fled to the bare hillside. Faced with the alternative of conversion or exile and the loss of their lands, the leaders of the Jewish community gradually made their peace with the bishop. Some made clear that they had acted under duress. Others, more opportunistic or more sanguine, hoped to preserve intact their positions in the previous social hierarchy. One convert claimed that the head of the synagogue would still sit above his fellow Jews, if now as a Christian, at the right hand of the Catholic bishop (*Ep. Severi* 11–14). Less subject to public considerations of status, the wives of the Jewish notables held out longest (*Ep. Severi* 18). As for the rank and file, they barely received a mention. Whenever a welcome rainstorm passed over the city, the Christians would joke: 'It is raining today; a Jew must have converted' (*Ep. Severi* 17.4).

Compared with a dramatic account such as the *Letter* of Severus, the surviving evidence allows us barely to glimpse the sufferings of polytheists. They seem to have followed a different rhythm, governed by different imaginative patterns. Polytheists feared more for their gods than for themselves. Violent clashes occurred when outraged communities avenged the desecration of holy statues and temples. Bloodthirsty incidents were usually followed by sullen withdrawal. Whole villages regrouped themselves. After 306 of their idols had been smashed by bishop Macarius of Tkow, the inhabitants of a Nile-side village carefully 'hid the remainder of their gods in the depths of their cisterns': 'as for those who fled, the Christians dwelt in their houses.'[20]

As in the Protestant Reformation, iconoclasm was 'the argument to end all arguments'.[21] In one violent gesture, it both removed objects of devotion and proved the impotence of the gods. While the archaeological evidence for the extent of iconoclasm is inconclusive – not all collapsed temples and shattered statuary need be ascribed to Christian agency – the nature of the iconoclasm itself is clear. All over the empire, calculated acts of desecration were committed, designed to rob the gods of their power. Hands and feet were broken; heads and genitals were mutilated; sacred precincts were purged with fire.[22]

Though studiously vindictive – and perhaps for that reason – Christian iconoclasm was not indiscriminate. Nothing illustrates more clearly the determination of the upper classes to conduct the Christianization of the cities on their own terms than does the fate of statues of the gods at this time. So many were preserved. The mentalities we have described made it easy to effect a 'laicization' of the urban landscape. Temples and statues often survived intact as 'ornaments' of the city. Once detached from the 'contagion' of sacrifice, the shining marble of classical statues was held to have regained a pristine innocence (Prudent. *C. Symm.* 1.501–5). The idols became what they still are – works of art. It was a situation whose humour was not lost on that wry polytheist Palladas of Alexandria as he viewed the splendid art-gallery set up in the palace of the Christian lady Marina:

The inhabitants of Olympus, having become Christian, live here undisturbed: for here at least they will escape the cauldron that melts them down for small change.
(Palladas, *AP* IX.528)

It is typical that we should know of one of the most bloody clashes in North Africa, in which sixty Christians were killed when they overturned a statue of Hercules at Sufes, only through a letter of Augustine. The bishop had been provoked to write a rebuke to the city because the town-council, with a stolid sense of its own rights, had insisted that the Christians should bear the cost of regilding the beard of the statue – the city's proudest monument (Aug. *Ep.* 50).

Elsewhere, caches of carefully preserved images tell their own tale. Augustine realized that many polytheists converted so that their gods should remain safe.[23] In the words of Shenoute of Atripe, such persons now stood in the Christian basilicas, shouting Christian prayers, swaying and raising their arms in Christian gestures of worship. They cared as little

[20] *A Panegyric on Macarius, Bishop of Tkow attributed to Dioscorus of Alexandria* v. 11, tr. D. W. Johnson, *CSCO* 416: Script. Copt. 42. Louvain, 1980, 29–30.   [21] Aston (1988) 215.
[22] On the dilapidation of temples in Gaul, see Rouselle (1990) 45–6; for a particularly revealing example of iconoclasm at Palmyra, with commentary, see Gassowska (1982).
[23] Dolbeau (1991) 48.

for what they were told as did the ornamental peacocks who strutted and squawked in the sunlit courtyard outside.[24]

Altogether, we are dealing with a period characterized by acute disjunctions. The issue is how these disjunctions should be viewed. For many scholars, they require little explanation. They are treated as no more than merciful suspensions (due largely to prudence or inertia) of the remorseless logic of Christian expansion – as so many sandcastles on the wide beach of ancient culture that have not yet crumbled before the advancing tide. Much of the best recent work on Christianization has implicitly accepted this model: evidence for a Christian 'presence' in various regions and in various aspects of late Roman life – the evidence of ecclesiastical organization, of church buildings, of the spread of Christian nomenclature, the adoption of Christian religious terms or of a Christian ordering of time, and the appearance of Christian symbols on articles of daily use – has been used to measure the level and the speed of that incoming tide.[25] With a few notable exceptions, what has received less attention is the manner in which late Roman society itself changed, and the Christian communities within it, in such a way that what constituted 'Christianization' for certain generations and regions – a Christianization seen, above all, in terms of a dramatic narrative of supernatural triumph over the gods – came to appear insufficient to vocal groups of Christians in other times and places.[26] But this chapter offers a guiding thread to the period that can, at least, claim the advantage of remaining close to what the majority of contemporaries regarded as the limits of the possible in their own time.

One fact is indisputable. The late Roman revolution in government, which had placed the authority of the emperors at the service of the church, had, at the same time, created a governing class whose culture owed little or nothing to Christianity. Even though this governing class might contain increasing numbers of Christians, it owed its cohesion first and foremost to traditions and to rituals that were taken directly from the non-Christian past. The array of symbolic forms by which the *potentes* of the later empire expressed their dominance was impressive. Hauntingly post-classical mythological mosaics adorned their villas. Exuberant new urban rituals celebrated their power. An elaboration of ceremonial characterized the imperial court. Poetry, letter-writing and panegyric flourished in styles that expressed the solidarity of the governing classes and acted as emblems

---

[24] Shenoute, *Ep.* 18, tr. H. Wiessmann, *CSCO* 96: Script. Copt. 8. Louvain, 1953, 22.

[25] Selected regional studies illustrate a wide range of approaches and conclusions: see Thomas (1981) with Watts (1991); Gauthier (1980); Lizzi (1990) (Northern Italy); Kennedy and Liebeschuetz (1988) (Syria); Wipszycka (1988) (Egypt); on Christian names in Egypt as an index of rapid and extensive Christianization, see Bagnall (1982), with the reservations of Wipszycka (1986); on time, Piétri (1984); on Christian imagery on ceramics, see Salomonson (1979).

[26] Markus, *End of Ancient Christianity* 1–17, is an exemplary discussion, to which I am indebted for what follows.

of their authority.[27] The drastic rearrangement of so many classical traditions to create a new heraldry of power was one of the greatest achievements of the period. It would be profoundly misleading, even trivial, to claim that changes in this large area of social life reflected, in any way, a process of 'Christianization'. What matters is, perhaps, the exact opposite. We are witnessing the flowering of a vigorous public culture that polytheists, Jews and Christians alike could share.

This culture could only be said to have become 'Christian' in a narrow sense. Blood sacrifice was allowed to play no part in it – although, even there, visual and literary memories of the sacrificial act survived. But it remained a profoundly religious culture. Late Roman rituals of power maintained a high seriousness that had lost none of its numinous overtones. To take one example: the imperial images now found themselves without rivals as the focus of heady expressions of loyalty. Incense continued to be burnt in front of them. They were placed on altar-like tables in the audience halls of all governors. Their presence, on state occasions, released an adrenalin of worship which pious Christian emperors only very occasionally attempted to curtail.[28] But this worship remained majestically opaque. It was singularly resistant to one-sided 'confessional' interpretations. What shocked Christians about the public ceremonies of the reign of Julian was that Julian added to his own portraits figures of the gods bestowing on him the symbols of imperial rule. As good late Romans, Christians had plainly thought nothing of prostrating themselves wholeheartedly before such images, if the emperors alone were represented on them (Greg. Naz. *Or.* IV.80–1).

In the great cities, the annual high festivals associated with the Kalends of January and the magical 'good cheer', the *laetitia*, associated with the theatre, circus and hippodrome were still thought to bring heaven close to earth. In all major cities, these ceremonies remained impressive. They projected the upper-class sense of the stability of the imperial system. They derived majesty from the collective representation of the universe that we have described. Beneath a distant high God, they celebrated the resilience of the material world, a world touched, at times, by the eternal energy that pulsed in the stars and that manifested itself in the triumphant renewal of the seasons. In a manner that did not lend itself to precise confessional analysis, the imperial order was still widely believed to merge, with ease, into the serene backdrop of an eternal universe.

The sheer success of the post-Constantinian state ensured that the edges of potential conflict were blurred in the golden glow of a God-given order.

---

[27] The implications of this change are best discussed in Schneider (1983); Meslin (1970); Salzman, *Roman Time*; MacCormack, *Art and Ceremony* and Cameron, Averil, *Rhetoric of Empire.*

[28] *C.Th.* XV.4; cf. *Consultationes Zacchaei et Apollonii* 1.28, ed. G. Morin. Bonn, 1935; see J.-L. Feiertag, *Les Consultationes Zacchaei et Apollonii.* Fribourg, 1990, 68–97.

The *potentes* were left in little doubt that it was through an emperor who claimed privileged protection from the Christian God, and from no other deity, that they themselves enjoyed, for a few generations, a situation of unusual stability. The Christogram, the *labarum*, and, later, beautifully carved crosses came to be placed on almost any significant and prestigious object – on milestones, on mosaic pavements, on sets of luxury cutlery, eventually on the gates of all cities, even on the iron collar fastened round the neck of a slave, with the inscription, 'Arrest me, for I have run away, and bring me back to the Mons Caelius, to the palace of Elpidius, *vir clarissimus*' (*ILS* 8730). These signs made the supernatural power, under whose aegis the emperor had made the world a comfortable place for the powerful, formidably familiar, much as the scenes of emperors sacrificing had done in earlier centuries, placed as they had been on innumerable small objects – on coins, terracottas and cake-moulds.[29]

Yet we would be wrong to look for further signs of 'Christianization' at this time, if by this we mean a deliberate attempt to replace the public rituals and codes of behaviour that governed the life of the ruling élites with others that were deemed preferable because they were more unambiguously Christian. Rather, a studied ambiguity prevailed. For this reason, it is impossible to speak of a 'Christan empire' as existing in A.D. 425 in the same unambiguous manner as it did in the early Byzantine empire of Justinian and his successors.

The strength of the Christian community, at this time, lay in an ability to profit from the stability of a public order that most Christians had neither the means nor the ambition to change. Against the grandiose background of world-wide victory over the gods, a fierce sense of the life of the local church as a community of believers provided Christians with basically unpretentious modules for change. Christianization, for them, was a local matter.

Christians were expected to go to church regularly.

He who cometh out of the church after he hath heard all the lessons [thereby avoiding the sermon] and sitteth at the door of the church, such a man is only half a believer . . . He who cometh out of the church before receiving the 'Peace', none of the help of God shall be his.[30]

The regular assembly of Christians, to listen to readings of their sacred texts and to a subsequent sermon, was essential to every Christian community in this period. Such gatherings constituted a decisive novelty in the religious and moral life of the time, whose social and cultural consequences have yet to be measured fully.[31]

All the same, we should not be misled by the vast number of sermons.

[29] Brandenburg (1969).   [30] Budge (1915), 1204.
[31] But see the reservations of MacMullen (1989).

These survive because they were appreciated by later Christians. At the time, the local Christian community was not held together only by the preaching of its bishops and clergy. Important though preaching might be, the morale and momentum of the local church depended to a large extent on the presence of what a sociologist would call its 'primary groups'[32] – on small groups of devout Christians, men and women of all classes, lay and clerical alike. The activities of these primary groups are largely lost to us. They followed the lines of local networks. They made use of client–patron relationships, and of ties of kinship and marriage; above all, they worked through the intense friendships between men and men, and women and women, in which all late Roman persons gloried. We can only occasionally glimpse (more often, significantly, in the case of women than of men) a Christian community held together by slender filaments of friendship and admiration. The son of a polytheist priest in Antioch was brought regularly by his mother to visit a saintly Christian woman. One lady in Seleucia passed on a copy of the gospels to an acquaintance who, to her surprise, found that she could read the text. Two women in Constantinople were buried side by side, 'for the two ladies were knit together by the most warm friendship and had been of one mind on all doctrinal and religious subjects'.[33]

The notion of sanctity was crucial in the formation of many such networks. The Christian community, as a whole, thought of itself as an assembly of the saints; but it helped to meet occasionally, in a man or a woman, the genuine article. When St Matrona settled in the hills outside Beirut, the ladies of the city would take their daughters out to visit her: 'Come, let us go and look at the Christian.'[34] Sanctity, indeed, often proved decisive in sealing the alliance between the church and influential lay patrons. The activities of St Martin in Gaul would not have come to be treated as exemplary – even, indeed, as desirable – if it had not been for the loyalty he inspired in a circle of great landowners.

As a result, every community generated its own group of exemplary Christians. The affairs of a whole neighbourhood might end by passing through their hands. Basil, bishop of Ancyra, had to warn dedicated Christian virgins not to take part in matchmaking negotiations. In Egypt, priests were forbidden to act as brokers in divorce proceedings.[35] Behind the growing public privileges and status-consciousness of the Christian clergy, there lies the constant pressure of each local Christian community to maintain, in the persons of its clergy, a 'primary group' of persons who

---

[32] Shils (1975) 349–54.
[33] Theodoret, *HE* III.10; *Miracula Sanctae Theclae* 45.8; Sozom. *HE* IX.2 – respectively.
[34] *Vita Sanctae Matronae* 22 (*Acta Sanctorum: Nov. III*. Brussels, 1910, 801B).
[35] Basil of Ancyra, *De Virginitate Tuenda* 21, PG XXX.712C; *Canons of Athanasius* 46, ed. W. Reidel and W. E. Crum. London, 1904, 35.

could be relied upon to make Christian values real in an untidy world. A priest must be careful to leave part of his field and vineyards unharvested, so as to provide gleanings for the poor. His behaviour was carefully watched by the average layman: 'so shalt thou be for him as a Scripture of God, wherein a man will read the ordinances of God' (*Canons of Athanasius* 70, ed. Reidel and Crum 47).

The ability of Christians to give reality to the notion of a 'community of believers' through intense religious networks affected all levels of society, from the well-known stories of the zeal of Christian wives for their sons and husbands, through innumerable less insistent encounters, to the impressive aristocratic circles gathered around a Martin, a Jerome and a John Chrysostom. Such networks brought influence to bear on individual officials and landowners in the interest of the self-consciously 'activist' Christianity that characterized the late fourth and early fifth centuries in many regions.

The strength of the Christian primary groups was decisively amplified, in the course of the fourth century, by the development of monasticism and by an empire-wide expansion in the numbers and social composition of the Christian clergy. The clergy was recruited on a wide basis – and often with frank opportunism – from a pool of talented lay persons: Ambrose, Augustine, Olympias (all three forcibly ordained as bishop, priest and deaconess respectively) are only a few well-known examples of a process by which the Christian churches harnessed the religious energies of their locality. This ambitious recruiting-drive included the ordination of men previously associated with learning and with supernatural expertise – philosophers, doctors, astrologers, even recently converted polytheist priests were to be found among the clergy. The carefully graded ranks of the clergy, from bishop down to humble lay-readers and door-keepers, constituted a city in miniature. The clergy, therefore, offered avenues of promotion for the talented few, Christian counsel for the many and, it was hoped, examples of Christian conduct for the world at large.

But the rise to prominence of the monks and clergy reflected an essentially inward-looking mentality. The principal imaginative effort expended by fourth-century Christians was not directed towards the goals which modern scholars might expect. The Christianization of Roman society, if imagined at all, took second place to a dramatic concentration on the 'hyper-Christianization', within the Christian church itself, of increasingly visible 'primary groups' within the Christian community.

Confident that they remained in contact with true believers – that they could count on the prayers, the visionary powers, the advice and ritual services of local, admired figures, whether these were members of the clergy or lay persons with a reputation for sanctity – the majority of Christians discreetly backed away from the rigours of exemplary behaviour. They tended to deal with their own dilemmas at one remove, in the persons of their leaders. To take one example: military service and judicial activity that involved the imposition of the death penalty were issues that continued to trouble the consciences of Christians. But only prospective members of the clergy had to bear the full weight of the laity's scruples on this score. To have been a soldier or a judge still constituted a formidable stigma for anyone who aspired to join the clergy. When Ambrose was acclaimed against his will as bishop of Milan while acting as governor of Liguria, he could be convincingly presented as having sought to debar himself from further consideration as a bishop by ordering the application of torture in his courtroom (Paulin. *V. Ambr.* vii). Anomalies with which the average Christian had learned to live were instantly noted and condemned when perceived in monks and clergymen. Protests were raised when a bishop lapsed from the studied simplicity of a style modelled on the gospels into unintelligible Attic phrases, or when a clergyman was seen to dine off silver-ware covered with mythological scenes.[36] When a south Italian bishop slept with his wife before celebrating the Sunday Eucharist, his delinquency was promptly denounced to the pope by none other than a retired *agens in rebus*, a layman and former member of the imperial secret police who apparently still occupied his pious leisure spying on others (Innoc. *Ep.* 38, *PL* xx.605b).

These statements emerge from a debate that affected a group of persons who performed on the brightly lit stage of late Roman Christian opinion. This does not mean that members of the laity did not struggle, in their way, to create for themselves codes of Christian conduct that they sincerely hoped would be recognizable as such to the outside world. But the degree of the Christianization of the majority of adherents of the Christian church in the later empire should not be measured according to standards which contemporary Christians were usually content to apply only to a small and highly visible élite of clergymen and ascetics.

We should look elsewhere for evidence of the slow formation and diffu-sion of specific Christian traits among the silent majority of fourth-century Christians. In the great Christian cemeteries of Rome, Sicily and Carthage, for instance, Christian 'epigraphic habits' emerge clearly by the fifth century. Many of these show significant changes, if only in the manner in which Christian families wished to be seen by their fellow believers. Previous tendencies to concentrate on the nuclear family were heightened in Christian tombstones, and greater attention was paid than among non-Christians to the deaths of young children.[37] What is striking in these developments is the near-total absence of evidence for clerical guidance

[36] Photius, *Bibl.* LIX.19a – it was charged against John Chrysostom that he mentioned the 'Erinnyes'; Jer. *Ep.* 27.2.   [37] Shaw (1991).

from above. We are dealing with the self-regulation of a community of believers. Lay persons created for themselves, and not only at the behest of their preachers, strong notions of Christian propriety that seem to have been effective even in areas where ecclesiastical structures were weak and monasticism non-existent.

On issues more public and more contentious than the grave, however, Christian propriety worked in a distinctly piecemeal fashion. Even within the Christian community, there was no agreement on who could be expected to practise the austere codes associated with Christian behaviour. For, though defined by firm boundaries against non-believers, the Christian community was fissured by the central importance, within it, of the rite of baptism. Only the baptized Christian, the *fidelis*, was a real Christian. Only the baptized could be certain of salvation and would receive a Christian burial, in the form of a triumphant procession to the chanting of Psalms, from which all traces of mourning were excluded. Presented, therefore, as the celebration of an *adventus*, of a joyous entry into heaven, such a burial was remarkable group-testimony to the uniqueness of the baptized Christian. The unbaptized members of the community, even though enrolled as catechumens, could not be buried in this manner with the *fideles*.[38]

The fourth century was an age of spectacular mass-baptisms. A thousand persons might be initiated every year at Easter in any large city. Riding at dawn, after the Easter festival in the parade ground outside Constantinople in 404, the emperor Arcadius saw the crowds of newly baptized in their white robes, looking like a field of flowers (Pall. *V. Joh. Chrys.* IX, *PG* XLVII.34B).

But the very majesty of the rite gave others the opportunity to hold back. Adult baptism was common in many areas. It appealed particularly, one suspects, to the upper classes. It gave them a chance to pace themselves according to the limits of the possible, in their approach to unambiguous adhesion to Christianity. Stark choices were softened by being seen in chronological terms, as spaced out according to the natural rhythms of the life-cycle. Full initiation as a Christian took second place to the orderly unfolding of a public career. Even stringent Christians postponed baptism until they had gained what they needed from the non-Christian world. Gregory of Nazianzus, for instance, was baptized only after he had returned from Athens to Cappadocia in his late twenties, formed by the classical culture he had absorbed in the same class of students as Julian the Apostate. The tedious *sic et non* on the relevance of classical literature to Christians that was put on display by some Christian writers was declared a non-problem by the majority of upper-class believers. They were careful to complete their education before they became *fideles*.

[38] See the recently discovered sermon of Augustine: Dolbeau (1991).

Not all were as sincere, perhaps, as was Gregory. In around 428, Firmus, a notable of Carthage, wrote to Augustine that he was not yet ready for baptism. By our own loose meaning of the term, Firmus was a representative of a largely 'Christianized' élite. He was married to a baptized wife. He was far better read in Christian literature than she. He had made his way through the first ten books of the *City of God*, and had listened, for three afternoons on end, to public readings of its eighteenth book. But, in an age where a transforming ritual, and not anything as frail as a mere change of mind, was held to mark the true moment of conversion, Firmus appealed to ritual in its strongest sense so as to remain not fully a Christian:

The burden of such a great weight cannot be borne by the weak ... For he gives assurance of reverence for the faith who, to attain the august secrets of the sacred majesty, approaches its inmost reaches with due hesitancy.

(Aug. *Ep.* 2*.4.6, ed. Divjak)

It was on the basis of an implicit acceptance of two clearly distinguished levels of Christian observance within the church itself that many Christians made their peace with the world. They remained perpetual catechumens. At Bulla Regia, in 411, the whole Christian population of the city turned out to watch spectacles that made their town the equal of Carthage. Augustine's rebuke left them unconvinced. They were good Christians. As catechumens, they had received the sign of the cross on their foreheads. They were safe from the taint of idolatry. But they were not *fideles*, even less were they *clerici*: 'It is good for you to stay away. You are bishops, you are clergymen. You are not lay folk like us' (Aug. *Serm. Den.* 17.8).

Divided in this way between a core of *fideles* and a large body of members who, although they might be proud to be Christians, did not consider themselves held to the same standards as were the baptized, the impact of the Christian church on the *mores* of any given local society was subject to perpetual shortfall.

To take one pertinent example: Constantine's recognition of the *episcopalis audientia*, the bishop's court of arbitration, encouraged the Christians' tendency to look after their own affairs. Given the state of our evidence, the workings of the bishop's court remains the dark side of the moon in all studies of the fourth-century church.[39] Its influence could have been considerable. We know that well-to-do persons converted to Christianity so as to avail themselves of the cheap and expeditious services provided by the court. Yet the overall impression of the *episcopalis audientia* is that it owed its success to the inward-looking quality of the Christian community. Its judgements were binding only on those who agreed beforehand to accept

---

[39] Selb (1967), and the new letters of Augustine, *Epp.* 8* and 24*, discussed in *Les lettres de Saint Augustin découvertes par J. Divjak.* Paris, 1983; see also Langenfeld (1977).

the bishop as arbiter. Roman legal principles governed its settlements; and these settlements depended for their effectiveness on the persuasive power of the bishop and clergy. Altogether, it was an institution that was only as effective as local Christian opinion allowed it to be.

The bishop's court settled the affairs of Christians in such a way as to circumvent the need to alter the existing structures of Roman law in the direction of Christian teaching. Nothing is more impressively ambiguous than is the legislation on social *mores*, and on marriage and the family, issued by the Christian emperors in this period. The more closely it is studied, the less it seems to betray direct Christian influence.[40]

The local Christian community, of course, could bring considerable pressure to bear on individuals. But this was usually done to maintain the boundaries of the group against outsiders. Apostates, for instance, were marked men: they would be pointed out in the street. 'as if they were horses with bells on their bridles' (Asterius of Amaseia, *Hom.* III.10.3, ed. C. Datema. Leiden, 1970, 34). But when the clergy attempted to mobilize similar public indignation against mere adulterers, blasphemers and circusgoers, the laity refused to act. People who were prepared to brave the disapproval of the clergy could avail themselves of laws that had changed little since before the reign of Constantine. In fifth-century Oxyrhynchus, for instance, Aurelia Attiaena, though urged by the local clergy to stay with her ne'er-do-well husband, finally presented him with a bill of repudiation 'according to the Imperial laws' (*P.Oxy.* 3581). At Rome, the aristocratic Fabiola had done the same a generation earlier. She only came to do penance for her action when, many years later, in her old age, she decided to move closer to a Christian 'primary group', by seeking a place among the official 'widows of the church' (Jer. *Ep.* 77.3–4). Otherwise, her thoroughly Roman way of dealing with her marriage would have gone unnoticed.

Up to around the year 400, lay persons and, one suspects, many clergymen had tended to define what constituted acceptable Christian behaviour on their own terms and in a largely informal manner. They accepted with relative indifference the public rituals that enlivened their cities. They shared many of the mental structures that went with these. As long as it was not unambiguously tainted with polytheism, much of the public life of the empire seemed innocuous to them.

Rather than attempting to replace public rituals by more 'Christianized' forms of urban ceremonial, the Christian communities were content to develop a festive life parallel to that of the cities. The feasts of the martyrs, in particular, were recurrent high points in the Christian year. On these occasions, the Christian community as a whole, baptized and unbaptized alike, could view itself in a more resonant manner than in the somewhat

[40] Bagnall (1987) and Evans-Grubbs (1989) are model studies; see also Beaucamp (1990).

austere, regular assemblies associated with Christian preaching. Celebrating as they did the heroes of the Christian triumph over the gods, the martyrs' feasts were unambiguously Christian. Yet their very ebullience drew on a universal, late antique religiosity of festival.[41] Their high good cheer – which included drinking and even, on occasions, dancing – carried deep religious overtones. They expressed a sense of participation in the world-renewing triumph of Christ and of his servants that amplified, in Christian terms, traits common to the church and to the rituals of the city. The frequent echoes of circus imagery in Christian art and preaching betray something far more than isolated 'borrowings' from an alien institution. As places of triumph and of mystical participation in a greater, more exuberant order, church and circus were joined through common imaginative structures. A team of circus horses, framed by palms of victory, appears on the mosaics of a Christian church in North Africa.[42] When incessant rain threatened the crops around Constantinople, the Christians moved with ease from crowded vigils at the shrines of the martyrs to the solemn excitement of the hippodrome, much to the annoyance of John Chrysostom (Joh. Chrys. *De Spectaculis*, *PG* LXVI.263–70). For both actions addressed, if in different idioms, the same need at a time of crisis to seek reassurance by recalling, through festival, the triumph of the good.

The cult of the martyrs brought heaven closer to earth through an ancient moment of euphoria. Good weather, fertility, safe childbirth and escape from enemies, private and public, were associated with martyrs' festivals (Prudent. *Peristeph.* 1.118; Paul. Nol. *Carm.* XXI.25–36). They brought down the blessing of a distant God on ordinary things. As a young man, Paulinus of Nola, when governor of Campania, made the solemn offering of the first shaving of his beard at the shrine of St Felix (Paul. Nol. *Carm.* XXI.377–8). When he himself became bishop at Nola, he would describe the peasants of the hill-towns trudging to the shrine with their prize pig, so as to slaughter it with the blessing of the saint (Paul. Nol. *Carm.* XX.62–92).

In an analogous manner, the Christian kin who gathered at the graves of their deceased could still believe that their actions had an effect upon the invisible world. Their solemn, slightly tipsy mood participated in the respite of God's paradise; and, in turn, the dead participated in the comfortable glow of their wine. All over the Mediterranean, Christian burials implied just such a view. They betray a deeply rooted consensus that Christian propriety might include a belief that the Christian kin-group was able to play an active role, through ancient physical gestures such as feasting, in ensuring the eternal rest of the departed soul.[43]

From the late fourth century onwards, the self-regulatory powers of the

[41] Saxer (1980); Harl (1981); Lepelley (1987).   [42] Dunbabin (1978) 103.
[43] Février (1977); (1984).

Christian community came to be challenged with ever greater insistence, in many areas, by a 'primary group' of self-styled *districtiores Christiani*, 'more stringent Christians' (*Consultationes Zacchaei et Apollonii* 1.28), most of whom were members of the clergy. Practices that had appeared to be traditional within the Christian communities were condemned. In their place, the clergy proposed rituals which were both less exuberantly physical and, at the same time, undercut the active role of the kin in furthering the comfort of the deceased. In the 380s, Ambrose of Milan condemned feasting at the graves of the martyrs and at family tombs, as resembling too closely the *parentalia* of Roman polytheistic practice (Aug. *Conf.* vi.ii.2; Gaudentius of Brescia, *Tractatus* iv.14–15). In the 390s, Augustine followed his example in North Africa: wine and dancing were to vanish from the *laetitiae*, the 'good cheer', that had characterized the feasts of the martyrs. Feasting at family gatherings at the tombs of kinsfolk was severely curtailed (Aug. *Ep.* 22.6). Over a century later, Jacob of Sarug told the women of Syria that they keened in vain among the tombs:

Call not on the dead at the grave ... Seek them rather in the House of Mercy ... Around the sweet perfume of Life, that rises from the Eucharist, all souls hover, to draw in sustenance.

(Jacob of Sarug, *On the Offering for the Dead* 90, tr. Landersdorfer 305)

We are dealing with the claims of an austere, transcendent monotheism, put forward by the clergy in the name of their own monopoly of access to the divine. Ultimately, only the Eucharist celebrated by a priest at the altar of a Christian church could bridge the gulf between heaven and earth. Christian prayers associated with the Eucharist and Christian almsgiving alone could help the departed soul – not wine and the warmth of a feast.

These criticisms increasingly took cognizance of civic rituals that occurred outside the Christian community.[44] The civic rejoicings of the post-Constantinian age were 'de-mystified' by preachers such as Augustine and John Chrysostom. Though untouched by sacrifice, they none the less were held to attract the demons to them. They did not have to be crassly immoral or cruel to be condemned. What mattered was the enthusiasm they inspired in Christians. They emphasized a civic consensus that veiled the triumph of the church even from its own members. They must be boycotted by Christians, so that Jews and polytheists would be left to celebrate them alone. Uncushioned by the solemn ambiguities of public ritual, the great cities of the empire could then be seen as clearly divided between Christians and non-Christians, with the Christians, now, in the majority (Aug. *Serm.* 62.7.11). Voices were even raised, criticizing the cult of the imperial images as betraying an excessive, un-Christian adulation of the great.

[44] Markus, *End of Ancient Christianity* 107–23.

There is a considerable element of wishful thinking in these protests. The evidence from Christian cemeteries, the continued development of the imperial ceremonial and the huge importance of the hippodrome throughout the eastern empire and in major western cities show that the wishes of the clergy were seldom implemented. What matters more is that by protesting in this manner, a generation of articulate clergymen created the notion of Christianization with which we still live. In the early fifth century, Christian critics conjured up a 'representation' of their own times that was the sombre counterpoint to the triumphant image with which we began this chapter. A myth of the decline of the church, accompanied by an idealization of the pre-Constantinian period, came to be accepted by many Christians.[45] In this myth, the decline of the church was presented as being intimately linked to the nature of its triumph. The original zeal of Christians had 'cooled'. Furthermore, the church was not only corrupted by the heavier sins of avarice and ambition among its leaders, nor was its peace disrupted only by the demonic incitement of ever-new heresies. Now even Christian worship itself was held to have been tainted by the sheer weight of new members. Rituals of which a group of devout Christians, largely of ascetic temperament, came to disapprove were confidently ascribed to habits that had been brought into the church by recent converts from polytheism. The church had defeated the gods; it had not defeated in their former worshippers the towering force of religious habits taken directly from the non-Christian past.

When, in 392, Augustine was faced, as a priest at Hippo, by a delegation of old-fashioned Catholics who regarded their funerary customs and their cult of the martyrs – and with good reason – as wholly Christian traditions, he gave them an historical explanation of the situation that they found themselves in. After the conversion of Constantine, he said, 'crowds of the heathen' wished to enter the church. They could not bear to give up the 'revelling and drunkenness with which they had been accustomed to celebrate the feasts of the idols'. A soft-hearted clergy had let them in. Hence the practice. Hence Augustine's decision to abolish it (Aug. *Ep.* 29.8–9).

From this time onwards, such a view has been taken for granted, as a common-sense glimpse of the obvious. Untouched today by the sense of tragedy that stirred those who first propounded it, we tend to agree with Augustine's diagnosis. It is natural to assume that Christianity, which had been prepared to embrace a myth of instant triumph, must sooner or later have had to face up to the superficiality of its own conquests. Yet what was at stake was less clear than Augustine made it appear to be. It was very much an issue of authority. Augustine and his clerical colleagues claimed to be

---

[45] See esp. Cassian, *Collationes* XVIII.5.23, with Markus, *End of Ancient Christianity* 166–7; but also Sulp. Sev. *Chron.* II.32; Jer. *V. Malchi* 1; Isidore of Pelusium, *Epp.* II.54 and 246. *PG* LXXVIII.460D–461A and 685BC.

able to tell long-established Christian congregations exactly what polytheism had been and how much of it survived within the church itself in the form of habits that must be avoided by all Christians, whether baptized or unbaptized. This claim involved a subtle 'historicization' of polytheism. The idea of the triumph of Christ over the demons and the horror of sacrifice as a demonic activity remained, but they were joined by another theme. Polytheistic worship was not an exclusively supernatural matter. The power of the demons was more insidious because less clearly focused. It showed itself in centuries of misdirected habit that had affected all aspects of life. Any custom, therefore, that did not win the approval of an austere group of critics might be deemed a 'habit of the heathen'. Polytheism could be anywhere. It was not reassuringly circumscribed in the cult of the gods. As a result, while polytheism might be abolished, the past itself remained a pagan place. It was not enough to cast off the 'contagion' of sacrifice and to destroy the idols. Those who entered the church brought with them the shadow of an untranscended ancient way of life. *Antiquitas*, 'antiquity, the mother of all evils', was the last enemy of all true Christians (*Sermo de Saltatoribus. PL Suppl.* iv.974). The world itself would have to change beyond recognition for that *antiquitas* to lose its grip upon the weaker members of the Christian community.

Within such a perspective, the Christian believer was no longer presented, in largely supernatural terms, as poised between sin and salvation, between the pollution of idols and a new freedom from demonic assault, gained through the unique power of Christ. The believer was poised, also, between two cultures – even, indeed, between two historical epochs – between the growing Christian culture of the Catholic church and a profane world whose roots were clearly seen to reach back into the rich soil of a past once ruled by the *dei buggiardi* (the lying gods). It was a past whose darkened majesty was conjured up with memorable circumstantiality in the pages of Augustine's *City of God*.

These views were forcibly stated by a generation of western writers. They were amplified by the severe crisis of the Constantinian empire that occurred in the western provinces at the time of the barbarian invasions. The past of Rome itself became problematic. Pre-Christian institutions and social practices were no longer veiled by the magnificent opacity of a more confident generation that had allowed the religious and the profane to blossom side by side. But this anxious questioning of the past was by no means universal. What came to be stressed in the eastern empire, by contrast, was almost the exact opposite. Greek writers of the fifth century lingered by preference on the excitements of a great *metabolē*. They celebrated a mighty transmutation, by which the non-Christian past flowed into a triumphant Christian present. It was a declaration of total victory that left much of the past untouched. Even the statues of Augustus and Livia would continue to stand outside the Prytaneion of Ephesus. With the sign of the cross neatly carved on their foreheads, they gazed down serenely on the prelates summoned by their orthodox successor, Theodosius II, to the great council of 431.

By A.D. 425, as we have seen, the Roman empire was by no means Christianized. Pockets of intensely self-confident Christianity had merely declared the Christian religion to have been victorious. It was a glorious victory. But much of it had taken place on an invisible plane, leaving what could be seen on earth still veiled in a merciful ambiguity, such as often favours the forcible establishment of dominant faiths.

Yet in the western parts of the empire, at least, the basic narrative of Christianization, with which we moderns are most familiar, had been created. This was not the narrative that counted most at the time. This is, in itself, a measure of our distance from late Roman persons. Christianization has ceased to mean, for us, what it still meant for the majority of Christians of the fourth and fifth centuries: the story of a stunning, supernatural victory over the gods. The alternative story offered by the critics of the age lends itself more readily to a modern historian's sense of the possible. We take it for granted that Christianization must have been a slow, heroic struggle on earth against the unyielding protean weight of an unconverted ancient world. By A.D. 425, this unredeemed past had taken on recognizable features. Thanks largely to the writings of the generation of Augustine, a charged memory of the Roman past would linger in the imagination of all future westerners as a potent fragment of 'encapsulated history'. *Antiquitas*, an ancient past that dogged the Christian present, lay close to the heart of medieval Christendom, as close as did the challenging strangeness of the world of the Old Testament. It was an inescapable and fascinating companion, all the more disquieting because not limited to a precise period of history, but suffused with associations that endowed it with the weight and the resilience of the human condition itself, lived out in the shadow of Adam's fall. It is precisely for this reason that the reader of modern accounts of Christianization in the Roman empire must struggle so hard to glimpse, behind the reassuring familiarity of a story retold continuously in western Europe from this time onwards, the outlines of a world profoundly unlike our own, in which the decisive changes of this 'wavering' century took place.

CHAPTER 22

EDUCATION AND LITERARY CULTURE

AVERIL CAMERON

I. INTRODUCTION

In the period covered by this volume, state support and protection for Christianity transformed what had previously been a minor element in Roman culture into a highly disturbing factor. Already in the third century, and under the influence of Origen in particular, Christian learning had developed alongside the institutional organization of the church itself. But the pious court of Theodosius II in fifth-century Constantinople was different in atmosphere from the courts of Constantine or Constantius II, enthusiasts though both these emperors had been. The change did not come about straightforwardly or without tension. Even without the intervention of a highly vocal and state-supported religion, the fourth century saw a consolidation of late Roman society sufficient to elicit a range of cultural responses. By the end of the period, moreover, the empire was split between east and west, and in many areas of the west the issue of the acculturation of Romans and barbarians had already become a burning question. The fourth and early fifth centuries are thus characterized by rapid and varied cultural change, a change that is clearly illustrated in the variety and the vigour of literary, artistic and other forms of creativity.

The nearest thing to a shared cultural system in the fourth century (though one available only to the wealthier classes) was that provided by the traditional educational system, with its overwhelming emphasis on rhetorical skill. Educated Christians in this period received the same training as pagans; their responses to classical culture ranged, not surprisingly, from appropriation to outright hostility. By a semantic development which

* This contribution has benefited from the criticism of several colleagues, among whom I particularly wish to thank J. H. W. G. Liebeschuetz. For a recent detailed survey and guide to the Latin literature of this period see Herzog (1989) (for discussion see Barnes (1991) and Vessey (1991)), and more briefly Browning (1982); for the Greek literature see Christ-Schmid-Stählin, 6th edn 1924. Generally, also Dihle (1989) 442–618. The Christian works of the period are well covered by reference works: Altaner and Stuiber (1980); Quasten (1950). There is a convenient introduction to the Greek texts in Young (1983); for the Latin see Rusch (1977). The literary history of this period is also covered in part in the standard reference works to Byzantine literature, in particular Hunger (1978); Beck (1959); Winkelmann and Brandes (1990).

took place early in our period the Greek terms 'Hellenic' and 'Hellenism' came to be used by Christians to mean simply 'pagan' and 'paganism', a development about which one scholar has written: 'since paganism and Greek culture are patently not the same thing, the consequences of their being designated by the same word were obviously momentous. This was particularly true for those Christians who were busy writing and praying in Greek.'[1] This notion of a culture of the 'other', as in the concept of worldly culture and the constructed images of 'pagans', heretics and Jews, provided a device which many Christian writers of this period used to great advantage.[2] The fourth and early fifth centuries are rightly considered as the 'golden' age of Christian literature, characterized by the writings of major Fathers of the church – in Greek, Athanasius, the Cappadocians (Basil, Gregory of Nyssa and Gregory of Nazianzus) and John Chrysostom, in Latin, Ambrose, Jerome and Augustine. Traditionally, such writers have been studied under the heading of 'patristics', separately from secular culture or general history. Such a division is questionable.[3] Historians of the period can no longer ignore 'patristic' sources, least of all cultural historians. In turn, theologians have become more interested in literary issues, the act and manner of writing.

This period also saw changes in the balance and interaction of 'Greek' and 'Roman' elements. Cultured upper-class Romans had long since been open to Greek intellectual currents, especially in philosophy; but by the turn of the fourth century the situation had changed. While some were still deeply influenced by Greek philosophy, most now relied in the main on translations. Many of the Christian works written in Greek during the fourth century were soon translated into Latin for western use. In turn, the Greek culture of the eastern half of the empire had been influenced and subtly transformed by several centuries of Roman rule. Yet here again the situation now changed. Constantine's interest in Jerusalem, together with the rapid growth of pilgrimage to the Holy Land in the fourth century and the development of Constantinople as the Christian capital of the eastern empire, brought a growing focus on the east. In cultural as well as economic and political terms, the eastern empire flourished, while at the same time its Greek-speaking citizens were made increasingly aware of other eastern languages and literatures – Coptic, Syriac, Armenian, Georgian. The interrelation, which involved translation into and from these languages, was to increase on a striking scale until the Arab conquest and after.[4]

The equation of the terms 'Hellene' and 'Hellenic' with 'pagan' in fourth-century and later Greek texts misleadingly assumes an entity which can be labelled 'paganism' as surely as it begs the question of the reference

[1] Bowersock, *Hellenism* 10.   [2] See Cameron, Averil, *Rhetoric of Empire* 7.
[3] See Vessey (1991); Roberts (1989) 122–4.   [4] Fowden (1993); Peeters (1950).

of 'Hellenic'. In contrast to contemporary Christians, modern scholars tend to emphasize the elusive and plural nature of ancient paganism and the variety of its manifestations, a disadvantage *vis-à-vis* Christianity that was ruefully recognized by the emperor Julian and a few others.[5] On occasion there was out-and-out aggression by Christians, especially in the years following the anti-pagan legislation of Theodosius I at the end of the fourth century, and often a degree of less overt unease; however, there was also a large area of cultural consensus. The eventual dominance of Christianity was by no means certain in the fourth century, however much fifth-century Christian writers may have tried to imply the opposite, and 'Christianization' proceeded as much by ambiguity and cultural appropriation as by direct confrontation.[6] This chapter will concentrate on literary culture and on the cognitive aspects of cultural systems. But it is also necessary to consider the circumstances in which literature was produced, the kind of education available, the various types of writing that emerged during the period, and the other means by which ideas were transmitted. The nature of the audience is also an important factor. Moreover, the same period saw the emergence of an overtly Christian visual environment, displaying similar ambiguities and ambivalences, and, like Christian literature, at once drawing on and transforming the existing repertoire of images.[7]

II. CHRISTIANITY AND TRADITIONAL EDUCATION

The traditional rhetorical education continued to be valued throughout this period; it was indeed the only kind of education generally available, except in special fields like philosophy and law. Surprisingly, perhaps, and despite the Christian intellectual traditions of a few centres such as Alexandria, Caesarea and, in the east, Edessa and Nisibis, for the vast majority, Christian training remained largely informal. The beginnings of a concept of monastic education can be seen in the writings of Basil of Caesarea. But Basil himself, like his brother Gregory of Nyssa and their friend and contemporary Gregory of Nazianzus, had received the standard rhetorical education of the well-to-do, and only put his concern for Christian education into practice during his later life as a bishop. Since in the traditional curriculum the authors studied and the content of their works were exclusively classical, the great majority of Christian writers had themselves been educated in this way; thus they had to come to terms somehow with

[5] Thus the preference for the term 'polytheism', for which see Fowden, ch. 18 above, on late paganism see also Trombley, *Hellenic Religion*.

[6] This is the argument of Cameron, Averil, *Rhetoric of Empire*; the aggressiveness of some Christians is not however to be denied: see Brown, *Power and Persuasion*.

[7] See Elsner, ch. 24 below; Mathews (1993) discusses a wide and less commonly cited range of visual evidence, while challenging many existing assumptions about the nature of Christian art in the fourth and fifth centuries.

classical rhetoric, just as they did with other 'worldly' matters such as wealth and family. Jerome famously dreamt that he would be accused of being a Ciceronian instead of a Christian;[8] Basil, about whose education at Athens we learn in detail from the brilliant funeral oration composed by Gregory of Nazianzus,[9] advocated a judicious reading of classical works by young Christians, in an atticizing treatise that was itself modelled on Plato, Demosthenes and Xenophon.[10] Augustine had been a teacher of rhetoric, and Sallust, Livy, Cicero and Virgil continue to play a major role in his great work, the *City of God (De Civitate Dei)*, written between 413 and 426. Gregory of Nazianzus put the matter clearly: 'we must not then dishonour education, because some men are pleased to do so, but rather suppose such men to be boorish and uneducated'.[11] None the less, there was room for much ambivalence: Gregory of Nyssa, Basil's brother, claims that their sister Macrina, who had been educated at home in the scriptures, converted Basil, the wonder-pupil, to asceticism, the 'true philosophy',[12] in contrast to the worldly teaching of Athens. 'Scorning the fame which came to him from eloquence, he "deserted"', says Gregory, 'to this hard life of manual labour, preparing for himself a life with no impediments to virtue.' But while Basil also wrote of giving up rhetoric for religion, he continued to advocate the reading of suitable classical authors, and his encomiast, Gregory of Nazianzus, specially commended him for his Christian eloquence. Gregory Nazianzen himself was one of the most accomplished Greek orators and rhetoricians of any period; his speech on Basil follows the standard rules for a classical encomium laid down by Menander Rhetor, and here as elsewhere, for instance in his *Apologeticus*, in which he explains his feelings of unworthiness at the thought of ordination, he adapted scriptural allusions perfectly to classical models. He passionately defended the right of Christians to have access through teaching to the classical heritage in the face of Julian's law seeking to forbid them, yet he sometimes felt overburdened by his own reputation and claimed to want only a life 'dead to the world and hidden in Christ'.[13] The contribution of Basil's brother, Gregory of Nyssa, was more philosophical than rhetorical, but his own debt to Plato was just as great, as is revealed in the Platonic framework of his *Life* of his sister Macrina, and in his conception of *paideia*.[14] With due and conventional modesty, Gregory of Nyssa himself claimed that he had received his education from his brother Basil,[15] but he became a rhetor when he gave up his bishopric,[16] and he could hardly have composed *encomia*, homilies and lives had he not had a thorough grounding in rhetoric. Finally, John Chrysostom, one of the greatest Christian preachers of any period, had been a pupil of the pagan rhetor Libanius, and a contemporary

---

[8] *Ep.* 22.30.   [9] *Or.* XLIII.   [10] Wilson (1975).   [11] *PG* XXXVI.509A, tr. Laistner.
[12] *V. Macr.* 6.   [13] *Or.* IV.100f.; XIX.1f.   [14] Jaeger (1962) ch. 7.   [15] *Ep.* XIII, to Libanius.
[16] Greg. Naz. *Ep.* 11.

of Theodore of Mopsuestia.[17] The leading teacher of his day, Libanius had both Christians and pagans among his pupils, though he had no high opinion of the former himself; all of them, however, necessarily came from among the better-off.[18]

Whatever they may have claimed on occasion, the three great Cappadocian bishops felt no real hesitation in using their rhetorical skills to maximum advantage. Other Christian writers were more uneasy about it. They were conscious that Jesus and his disciples had themselves been unlettered, and thought of Christian literature as having had equally lowly origins. Its style, termed the 'language of fishermen' (*sermo piscatorius*), had to be defended and justified; moreover, there had long been a tendency in Christian writing to contrast worldly learning and the 'tricks' of rhetoric with the 'true simplicity' of the faith.[19] The fourth- and early-fifth-century Fathers justified or explained this situation in various ways, satirically contrasting Horace, Virgil and Cicero with the Psalms and the scriptures, like Jerome,[20] or facing the problem directly, as Augustine does in the *De Doctrina Christiana*, where he argues for the value of secular learning even while attempting to give proper weight to Pauline texts such as 1 Cor. 1.17–31 (cf. 27: 'God has chosen the foolish things of the world to confound the wise'). But 'simplicity' could also be an advantage, as Augustine well knew, in enabling churchmen to reach out to every member of their congregation. It had a powerful attraction for the conventionally educated. The *Life of Antony* attributed to Athanasius, generally regarded as the first Christian saint's life and one of the most influential literary productions of the fourth century, depicts Antony (d. A.D. 356) as having come from a family well enough off to send him to school; however, his ascetic renunciation implied the rejection of education and rhetoric along with rich food and other luxuries.[21] The theme recurs as a standard component in the Greek monastic literature which begins to develop in the late fourth century, where the Egyptian monks and hermits are depicted either as illiterate peasants themselves, or else as men who have turned their backs on education along with other emblems of worldly attachment. Yet the Egyptian desert also attracted intellectuals like Evagrius Ponticus, and, once translated into Latin, the *Life of Antony* exercised a deep fascination on aristocratic Christian ladies in Rome and on the young professionals in Augustine's circle at Milan. Jerome, an enthusiastic proponent of the Latin version of the *Life*, composed his own supposedly artless lives of hermits (Paul, Malchus and Hilarion) in emulation of it; coming from such an

[17] Socr. *HE* vi.3. [18] Brown, *Power and Persuasion* ch. 2.
[19] Auerbach (1965) ch. 1; for Augustine, see Gillian Clark (1993) 70–82. The most accomplished Christian writers were adept at exploiting its advantages to the full: see Cameron, Averil, *Rhetoric of Empire*: e.g. 95, 112, and on literary style in Christian writing, cf. Roberts (1989) 124–47.
[20] *Ep.* 22.29. [21] *V. Ant.* 1, 80, 81.

author, they are of course highly sophisticated in their simplicity. The same Jerome wrote of the advantage to be gained by combining secular eloquence with careful study of the scriptures.[22] On closer inspection, the *Life of Antony* itself is very far from being either 'popular' or simple.[23] It reflects a conception of the soul's search for God and a concern for Christian *gnosis* redolent of Origen, and its preoccupation with the ideological contrast between worldliness and simplicity is both artful and disingenuous. Antony, the allegedly simple hero who had rejected worldly culture, is represented as disputing with pagan philosophers, replying to imperial letters and delivering well-structured discourses. It was not an easy matter to balance the competing claims of traditional rhetoric and Christian communication. Sulpicius Severus, author of the late-fourth-century *Life of Martin*, felt it necessary to remind his readers that the kingdom of God rested on faith, not on rhetoric. But learning was also important: while the Roman ladies encouraged in the ascetic life by Jerome buried themselves in their houses and dressed in sackcloth, their conception of Christian simplicity also embraced a form of Christian literary patronage; they commissioned the copying of texts, and took Christian scholarship to the length of learning Hebrew themselves.[24] Even Jerome complained at the demands which Marcella placed on him for texts and for explanations of difficult passages.[25]

The appeal of Christianity to the lower classes had been one of the taunts traditionally made against it by pagans; however, in this period of increasing confidence for the church, Christian 'simplicity' emerged as a useful rhetorical tool. Moreover, the catechetical aim demanded that all classes be considered, and many late-fourth-century bishops were adept communicators. Augustine was to the fore in addressing the issue overtly, and discussing the problems of the preacher in reaching an audience composed of confused masses, 'the straw of the Lord's threshing floor'.[26] John Chrysostom's homilies were preached in the very different urban setting of Constantinople and naturally address themselves to the vices of the rich city-dwellers there; yet even they show that he had all levels of the populace in mind.[27] Even though at this period bishops would normally be drawn from among the better-off (and Paulinus of Nola and Ambrose of Milan came from the élite), they were also acutely aware of the need to evangelize the uneducated, as is shown by Ambrose's concern for the evangelization of the countryside by his fellow bishops in north Italy. In their evangelizing, apologetic and didactic aims, willingness to combine modes of direct communication with the full apparatus of classical

[22] *Ep.* 58.11, to Paulinus.   [23] Rubenson (1990) 126–32.
[24] Pall. *Hist. Laus.* 55; for Marcella's knowledge of Hebrew and zeal for Bible study see Kelly, *Jerome* 94f., and further below.   [25] *Ep.* 29.1, cf. 28.1. Paula's Hebrew: Kelly, *Jerome* 97.
[26] *De Rud. Catech.* VII.11.   [27] *Contra*, MacMullen (1989).

rhetoric gave Christians a distinct advantage, pursued with vigour in the favourable climate of imperial support. Not surprisingly, therefore, the fourth and early fifth centuries are marked by energetic experimentation with new forms, as well as with the adaptation of existing rhetorical techniques, not least in literary invective against Jews, pagans and their own religious opponents. John Chrysostom learned the technique of rhetorical *psogos* from Libanius, who used it against the theatre claque at Antioch, monks, imperial bureaucrats and his own rivals; Chrysostom in turn employed it to devastating effect in his homilies against Judaizers and in his attacks on the loose Christian discipline of his congregation.[28] As for heretics, Epiphanius of Salamis' catalogue of heresies, the so-called *Panarion* or 'Medicine-Chest', which belongs to the 370s, was to provide an unforgettable model for later writers in the genre.[29] To modern eyes it is a curious document, based as it is explicitly on classical treatises on poisons and bites and their antidotes, while drawing many of its formal details from the typology of the biblical Song of Songs. Yet this work too illustrates the experimentation and the vigour of some Christian writing in this period, as well as the adaptation of classical rhetoric to Christian uses.

Unlike their pagan counterparts, Christian writers had to engage with the Bible, thus owing a dual debt to their scriptural base and to their rhetorical training which occasionally led to curious results, such as the effort made by the two Apollinarii, father and son, to recast the scriptures into classical literary forms – epic, tragedy or Platonic dialogues.[30] In certain of the works of Eusebius of Caesarea, a great biblical scholar and Christian apologist, one can see how even someone who was himself steeped in scriptural models would present his Christian thinking in rhetorical dress; thus the preface to the *Life of Constantine* is couched in flowery language full of familiar rhetorical *topoi*, and Eusebius goes to some trouble in his presentation of his analogy between Constantine and Moses not to disturb the surface of what at least starts out as a conventional imperial encomium.[31] Many Christian works, however, incorporated large numbers of scriptural citations and vocabulary. But while Greek-speaking Christians could cite the Septuagint (Hellenized Jews generally preferring the version of Aquila), the Latin translation of the Bible in use throughout the fourth century was highly unsatisfactory, until Jerome translated the entire Old Testament afresh direct from the Hebrew after intensive preliminary study; his translation (subsequently known together with the Latin New Testament as the Vulgate), which entailed rejecting the apocryphal books included in the Septuagint, was not finished until A.D. 405–6. Already in the 380s, however,

---

[28] See Wilken, *John Chrysostom and the Jews* ch. 4; for the genre, Parkes (1934); Williams (1935).
[29] See ch. 19 above.   [30] For biblical epic see Roberts (1985).
[31] *V. Const.* I.12, 20, 38; II.11–12; further below.

Jerome had revised the Old Latin (*Vetus Latina*) translation of the Gospels, also in a very confused state, by collating it against the Greek text. Typically, he defended the procedures he adopted in his Old Testament translation by hitting out vigorously at his critics, and with success, for despite various defects his version soon became standard. He conspicuously refrained from attempting to produce a translation in elegant literary Latin, justifying his procedure of keeping as close as possible to the original with the claim that the majority of Christians, being themselves uneducated and uncouth, needed a simple unadorned language. Thus, in one modern judgement, Jerome the stylist 'raised the vulgar Latinity of Christians to the heights of great literature'.[32]

Vulgar or not, the linguistic and other influences which the Bible exerted on Christian writers were profound. Their works were studded with verbatim or near-verbatim quotations and allusions to scriptural passages; Augustine's *Confessions* is just such a mosaic, contrived with the utmost art and sophistication. One biblical text, the Song of Songs, exerted an enormous impact in this way, as can be seen through the many fourth-century allusions to it and commentaries on it; ironically, in spite of the developing controversies surrounding Origen, the example set by his third-century commentary on the Song of Songs effectively provided the key elements in the language and imagery of fourth-century ascetic writing. Biblical exegesis was a central feature of Christian literary activity – not only was it practised by all the leading writers but it also formed the basis of oral preaching. Here again, the habit of typology and the long tradition of allegorical interpretation gave to later Christian writing a distinctive and enhanced dependence on imagery and metaphor.[33] It would be difficult to overestimate the depth of this influence. It is true that we are still a long way here from a scripture-based culture founded on private reading and ready access to the Bible by individuals – all books, not just the scriptures, were far beyond the reach of any except the rich. But scriptural influence was also exercised indirectly, through preaching, liturgical recitation and teaching, and later through pictures; in so far as a Christian consciousness came into being, it was moulded by scriptural patterns, both inside and outside the Christian élite. It is worth asking, then, which models the scriptures most often provided in late antiquity – that is, which parts were most often used, and to what ends. They tended, very naturally, to be those which most closely engaged with contemporary concerns – the exemplary models of Moses and Job, or the book of Genesis for its cosmology, its support for divine providence over determinism and its relevance to issues such as those of

---

[32] Kelly, *Jerome* 162. This period also saw the emergence of the Gothic Bible, attributed to Ulfilas under Constantius II: Socr. *HE* vi.37; Philostorg. ii.5, above, ch. 16, pp. 487, 497.

[33] Song of Songs: Cameron, Averil, *Rhetoric of Empire*: 174–6, with bibliography; figurality and metaphor in Christian writing: *ibid.* ch. 5.

the creation of man in the image of God, the relation between the sexes, the origin of sin and the nature of Paradise. Less evident in this period are many of the themes for which later generations were to draw on the Bible – divine retribution, the last judgement, political liberty and civil disobedience, and the downfall of tyrants.

III. LITERARY EDUCATION AS A PATH TO ADVANCEMENT

The educational system itself remained extremely conservative. Prowess in traditional rhetoric was the pathway to advancement in late Roman society, as is exemplified most conspicuously by the career of Ausonius of Bordeaux. From being a provincial rhetor, Ausonius was summoned in the 350s to the court of Trier as tutor to the young Gratian, and rose under Gratian's father Valentinian to be quaestor; when the latter died and Gratian succeeded in A.D. 375, Ausonius was well placed to become praetorian prefect and consul, and to bestow his patronage on family and friends. As consul in 379 he turned his provincial background into a virtue by boasting of 'a city which is no mean one, a family which is nothing to be ashamed of, a home that is blameless';[34] however, disingenuous though his description may be, he also wrote frequently in his poems about Bordeaux, its countryside and its academic advantages (it was a considerable intellectual centre, many of whose teachers Ausonius praises in his collection of poems on the rhetors and *grammatici* of Bordeaux).[35] The poet Claudian is another example of provincial *litteratus* made good. Claudian came from Alexandria, where he received his early training within a predominantly Greek culture; yet his skill in Latin verse was such that he became a *tribunus et notarius* with the rank of *clarissimus*, the court poet of the powerful general Stilicho, and the author, in the interests of the western government, of a series of long and important political poems in polished Latin hexameters (see further below). A traditional education was a *sine qua non* for any public position above the lowest level. It consisted theoretically of three stages – learning to read and write, going to the grammarian for a thorough grounding in correct language and the works of the poets, and finally to the rhetor in order to study the orators and historians, and to learn how to compose in the appropriate style and language. In practice, however, the distinctions were often blurred, even though Diocletian's Edict on Maximum Prices (A.D. 301) laid down differential rates of pay for the teachers of the three grades.[36] By modern standards the curriculum was extremely limited at all stages: though arithmetic and other subjects were taught to some degree, education (*paideia*) was defined narrowly in terms of literary culture, taught in such a way as to inculcate the rules of rhetoric

[34] *Grat. Act.* xxxvi.   [35] On which see Green (1991) 328ff.; Sivan (1993).   [36] vii.66–71.

expounded in surviving rhetorical treatises. The effect was to produce pupils who would be distinguished from the rest of mankind by their superior, if narrow, skills.

The *grammaticus* or 'grammarian' was the backbone of this system;[37] fifteen such teachers are named by Ausonius, who had taught grammar himself, in his poem on the teachers of Bordeaux, and a grammarian is among the dramatic personages in the early-fifth-century *Saturnalia* of Macrobius. The *grammaticus*' role was to inculcate close acquaintance with a canon of classical literature, and in so doing to impart to his students competence in an archaic literary language very different from the spoken one. The study of grammar in the narrower and technical sense was essential to this aim. Jerome was sent to Rome by his father from Stridon in Dalmatia to be taught by Donatus, author of an *Ars Grammatica* as well as commentaries on Terence and Virgil (the latter destined to be used as the basis of Servius' own Virgil commentary in the fifth century). Jerome absorbed the lessons well, gaining a love of grammatical detail and often referring in later life to his early training. Terence, Cicero, Sallust and Virgil were staples, but Jerome also knew Plautus, Lucretius, Horace, Persius and Lucan, as well as Ovid, Seneca, Martial and Quintilian. Greek was taught up to a point in the west, but Jerome's own knowledge of Greek owed much to later study, and he did not acquire the same detailed knowledge of Greek as of Latin classical authors. But Ausonius prescribes Homer and Menander as reading for a grandson who is about to start learning with the *grammaticus*,[38] and we have some indication of the bilingual exercises that were used in the schools of Gaul from a later manuscript. A poem by Ausonius tells us about school life.[39] Drill and rote-learning were evidently the norm. Beating had always been common in ancient schools, and the dominance of the grammarian and his syllabus, which had changed little if at all since the early empire, sanctified certain classical authors of the past as models for imitation, and ensured the continued centrality of traditional literary culture among the élite of both parts of the empire throughout the period.

The training of the advanced pupil in what may be termed 'higher' education began with exercises known as *progymnasmata* in which he (for the pupils were overwhelmingly male) learnt to imitate examples of rhetorical tropes found in the classical authors,[40] and proceeded to declamation, the composition and performance of speeches on imaginary themes. The surviving treatises are hard to date, but the handbook on *progymnasmata* by Aphthonius is generally put in the late fourth century, the similar treatise attributed to Hermogenes apparently being somewhat earlier. The treatise

---

[37] Kaster, *Guardians of Language*. [38] *Protr. ad Nep.* 45 f. [39] Aus. *Ephemeris*; see Dionisotti (1982).
[40] For the repertoire of examples, see Hock and O'Neill (1986).

on declamation by Sopatros may belong to the late fourth or more probably to the fifth century, while those on epideictic by Menander Rhetor have been attributed to the late third or early fourth century. Again, the sheer continuity of theory and practice is striking, as is the universality of this type of educational training. Public life now more than ever required the high-level rhetorical skills so painfully acquired by means of this long and expensive training, essential for every recruit to the enlarged late Roman bureaucracy or for the legal profession; even quite trivial late Roman documents are remarkable for the extravagance of their rhetoric. The system amounted to a form of recruitment to official or public careers based not so much on birth as on a form of education accessible to anyone with the requisite wealth or background. Within these limits, it encouraged social mobility, and laid no bar on anyone except that of the necessary degree of educational achievement. At the same time, it imposed a considerable degree of cultural conformity, and laid stress on that rather than on originality. Like the Chinese civil service under the Manchu emperors, entry to which was by competitive examination based on calligraphy, rhetoric and the study of set topics from Chinese classics, the late Roman official class found difficulty in adjusting its mentality in order to deal with 'barbarian' incomers. The empire-wide system of a thorough grounding in a small canon of classical texts, which pupils studied line by line, made for uniformity of outlook and even uniformity of language, while catering for the need for a constant supply of office-holders; since these posts were extremely desirable for financial and social reasons, and there was always, by the later fourth century, a large number of supernumeraries waiting for their turn, rhetorical training became even more desirable as time went on. The system affected everyone, Christians included. The more public forms of Christian oratory inevitably followed the same patterns as secular rhetoric – for instance, funeral orations such as that by Ambrose on the emperor Theodosius I – and the rules for encomium prescribed in the rhetorical handbooks exercised a profound influence on the development of Christian hagiography. Christians inherited the sense of importance attached to oratorical performance, as much in their homilies as in the public speeches of great bishops, with the result that the fourth century became a great age of revived eloquence, and the norms of classical rhetoric passed almost unnoticed into much of later Christian literature. But as we have seen, Christian writers were also uneasy about their debt to classical literary culture, and some kinds of Christian writing deliberately subverted it.

A modern observer cannot help but be struck by the absence from the curriculum of most of the subjects normally taught today. History and geography appear only incidentally, in relation to the subject matter of the classical texts studied, while the academic disciplines of arithmetic (aside from basic counting, taught at the earliest stage), geometry and astronomy featured only in the context of philosophical studies. We have already mentioned the schools of Gaul, where Greek had for long been well established alongside Latin. At the 'University of Constantople' (a modern and misleading term), founded in A.D. 425 by Theodosius II, there were three rhetors and ten grammarians for Latin, five rhetors and ten grammarians for Greek, one professor of philosophy and two of law.[41] Other major centres were Rome, where chairs of Greek and Latin rhetoric had been established by Vespasian in the first century A.D., Athens, where there were also rhetors, as well as considerably more philosophers, Alexandria, Antioch and Beirut, the home of legal education until the city was hit by a major earthquake in A.D. 551. The 'professors' received salaries, as apparently also did those grammarians and rhetors who were maintained by cities all over the empire, from Gaul to the east. In addition, since the time of Augustus such teachers had been exempted from municipal *munera*, a practice repeatedly confirmed in our period (by Constantine, Valentinian and Theodosius II).[42] There had thus been a long tradition of emperors concerning themselves with the provision of higher education; by the fourth century they were as interventionist here as in other matters, and might even nominate individual teachers. Eventually all prospective local teachers had to be approved by the municipal council (the *curia*) and confirmed by the emperor; thus when Julian also restricted Christians from teaching,[43] thereby causing the famous convert Marius Victorinus to leave his post in Rome, he was, despite Ammianus' disapproval, in a sense merely extending an existing tendency. Christians were indignant at the measure, not only because it barred them from occupying these posts themselves, but also because access to the schools was so essential for public success that they were afraid for the prospects of their children: according to Ammianus, Julian showed equal lack of tact in lawsuits, when he was prone to ask at inappropriate moments what religion each of the parties professed.

This did not, of course, amount to a state-run system as we now know it, and despite this high-level attention to education, access to the system on the pupils' side was limited for the most part to those with above-average means. As grammarians, no less than rhetors, were based in towns, few opportunities presented themselves to the rural population. In the minds of ascetic Christians, education stood for travel as well as the other worldly snares of civilization, and indeed it was often necessary for a boy ambitious for higher education to go further afield than merely to the nearest large town.[44] Augustine complained of the unruliness of student

[41] *C.Th.* xiv.9.3; *CJ* xi.19.1.   [42] *C.Th.* xiii.3.1–3; x.16–18.
[43] *C.Th.* xiii.3.5; Amm. Marc. xxii.10.   [44] For an explicit statement see *V. Ant.* 20.

life at Carthage, and hoped to find things better in Rome,[45] but Libanius suggests that students at Athens could be rowdy too, and student life in Rome had to be regulated by a law of 370. The social origins of Libanius' pupils show the privileged status of those who were lucky enough to move on to higher education.[46] Teachers had to be paid, and even for *curiales* or landowners, this was often no easy matter, as is shown in the case of Augustine, who did not himself come from the wealthy ranks of his own little city. In these circumstances much of the population remained illiterate, or nearly so. To judge from the evidence of papyri, frequent use was made by ordinary people of professional scribes for both legal transactions and letter-writing, and there are many references to illiterates in other sources. While it has been argued that the level of literacy actually declined from what it had been in the early empire, perhaps under the influence of the disruption of the third century,[47] it is more probable that the level of literacy, however defined, had never been other than very low for the vast majority of the population in the empire.[48] But even in fourth-century Egypt, the province from which we have by far the most evidence, the actual extent of literacy is difficult to establish, and was probably higher than is usually imagined.[49] The question remains open; at least we can say, however, that the overall decline in the number of inscriptions in our period as compared with earlier ones is more likely to relate to changes in commemoration and in the relation of town and country than to any general decline in literacy or education,[50] especially in view of the voluminous quantity of official documents generated by the bureaucracy and the fact that Greek verse inscriptions proliferate, especially from the late fourth century onwards (see p. 694 below).

Whether Christianity acted as an incentive to literacy, as has often been supposed, is difficult to demonstrate directly, for much Christian teaching was propagated orally or through pictures like the figural mosaics which begin to adorn the interiors of churches from the end of the fourth century. Christianity certainly did call forth certain kinds of book production, like the fifty copies of the scriptures which Constantine commissioned from Eusebius for the new city of Constantinople (*V. Const.* IV.36), and inspired a new kind of scholarship among some of its well-to-do adherents. Christians initiated the copying of religious texts, though they were also among the patrons of secular learning who edited and copied classical texts in late-fourth-century Rome (see p. 695 below). What is more

[45] *Conf.* v.7.14.   [46] Petit, *Libanius*.   [47] E.g. MacMullen (1976) 58ff.

[48] So Kaster, *Guardians of Language* 35–47; the chronological terms within which decline is posited by Harris, *Ancient Literacy* 285, are extremely wide (third to seventh centuries), and include the period of the main barbarian invasions and break-up of the western empire.

[49] See Bagnall, *Egypt* ch. 7; Wipszycka (1984).

[50] As assumed by Harris, *Ancient Literacy* 287–8.

striking, perhaps, in relation to Christianity in our period is the use it made of a combination of oral and written dissemination; Christians heard hymns, psalms, homilies and readings on a regular basis, and were in addition exhorted to study the scriptures at home.[51] Their use of books did not so much affect the level of literacy as change the uses to which it was put. They were, for example, eager to exploit the new Christian oratory, using stenographers to record sermons as they were delivered, a technique also extended to other kinds of Christian public utterances. While it is indeed difficult to demonstrate the proposition that Christianity was spread to any great extent by the written word during the first three centuries,[52] the volume of Christian writing greatly increased during our period, as the official favour now shown to the church allowed Christians access to a greatly enlarged audience, together with the opportunity to develop literary forms hitherto the preserve of pagans.

Public oratory, for which rhetorical skills were essential, was another field entered by Christians during the fourth century. Eusebius delivered speeches on the dedication of the new church at Tyre and more than one on the Holy Sepulchre in Jerusalem in A.D. 335;[53] but he also delivered in the presence of the emperor at Constantinople an encomium on the thirtieth anniversary of Constantine's accession (335–6), setting out his conception of worldly empire as the microcosm of God's rule. Bishops were favoured by Constantine and his son Constantius II, so long, of course, as their views were acceptable. Nor did Constantine hesitate to pronounce discourses which amounted to virtual sermons.[54] Julian, another imperial orator, after having had to deliver an embarrassing encomium on the hated Constantius II, turned to more congenial subjects after he had become emperor himself. Ammianus depicts Valentinian introducing the young Gratian to the army and then speaking to Gratian himself in suitably high-minded orations,[55] But Christian emperors also employed pagan orators such as Themistius, who served Constantius II and later emperors. Every imperial occasion required skilled orators, particularly for encomia and congratulatory speeches, and it was not surprising that men with the requisite training found themselves preferred; funerary orations, of which Ambrose's speech on the death of Theodosius I is a famous example, again brought bishops into this domain. Similar requirements held good at the local levels of urban life, with its continued public occasions and emphasis on civic values. Themistius, himself a pagan, though writing for Christian

---

[51] K. Hopkins, commenting on Harris's book, in Humphrey (1991) 73f.

[52] Harris, *Ancient Literacy* 299.

[53] Among several others delivered on that occasion: *V. Const.* IV.45; cf. IV.33 for Constantine's flattering reaction.

[54] *Ibid.* IV.29; the surviving *Oration to the Saints* is one such discourse, cf. IV.32.

[55] Amm. Marc. XXVII.6.

emperors, shared the civic mentality of Julian, Libanius and Ammianus, emphasizing the traditional values of the curial class, while the many orations of Libanius, composed throughout a teaching career in Antioch and Constantinople, put the precepts of the schools to practical purpose on a wide range of contemporary topics. Despite the complaints in the literary sources about the state of cities during the fourth century, these cities still provided the training and the opportunity for the exercise of oratory. In the case of the so-called 'affair of the statues' at Antioch in 387, we have a rare chance to compare Christian and pagan speeches directly, since we have surviving examples from both John Chrysostom and Libanius; though they naturally use different repertoires of *exempla*, at a deeper level they are strikingly similar. Bishops such as Gregory of Nazianzus and others in the east or Ambrose in the west gave a new life to public speaking. They did so in the context of a lively environment of which they were themselves also the products.

But classical rhetoric did not account for the entirety of the higher education that was on offer in the period. On the fringes of the empire in the east, the deacon Ephrem, the greatest writer in Syriac of the fourth century, left Nisibis for Edessa when the former was ceded to the Sasanians by Jovian in 363 and spent the last ten years of his life there, where he is traditionally associated with the 'School of the Persians'. The theological and catechetical School of Edessa flourished until its connection with Nestorianism and the latter's condemnation in the fifth century led to its closure. This period was also important for the steady development of the Jerusalem or Palestinian Talmud, and for the Jewish academies in Palestine, principally at Sepphoris and Tiberias. This was not necessarily the internalized and defensive reaction it has often seemed. Moreover, while the many different elements which form the Talmud were recorded in Hebrew and Aramaic, Jerome, for example, became familiar with rabbinic scholarship through the medium of Greek during his own stay in the Holy Land. Even though imperial policy towards Jews hardened in the late fourth century, and the Jewish patriarchate was abolished (A.D. 438), the Jews in Palestine enjoyed a period of distinct material prosperity, during which rabbinic and scholarly traditions continued alongside strong Hellenizing influences. Outside Palestine, in the substantial Diaspora communities in cities such as Antioch, Apamea, Sardis and elsewhere, Greek is the main attested language, and the language in which Jews will have communicated with their neighbours. The Septuagint translation gave way in popularity in these communities during this period to that of Aquila, and both were in use even in the Holy Land, especially, no doubt, in the more Hellenized cities like Caesarea.[56]

---

[56] The relation between the rabbinic learning of Palestine and the Jews of the Diaspora in our period is hard to establish: Millar (1992) 110; for the school in Palestine see also ch. 14 above, p. 454.

IV. NEOPLATONISM

Christians and pagans alike were deeply influenced by Neoplatonism, and especially by certain key texts. Julian was introduced under Aedesius at Pergamum to Iamblichan Neoplatonism, with its emphasis on mysticism and the ritual of theurgy,[57] and imbibed a deep respect for the so-called *Chaldaean Oracles* (on which both Porphyry and Iamblichus wrote commentaries) from Maximus of Ephesus; by the second half of the fourth century, however, translation into Latin was of central importance for the diffusion of Neoplatonic writings in the west. Marius Victorinus, converted to Christianity in old age, translated Plotinus and Porphyry into Latin. In the 380s Augustine obtained and read these and other Platonist books, as Ambrose had done before him; while the 'Platonic books' did not contain all that he was looking for, they led him, he says, in the direction of God,[58] and he remained Neoplatonist in his anthropology and epistemology. Jerome knew Plato's *Timaeus*, possibly in the original, or more likely in the Latin translation by Cicero, while Macrobius made much use of the Neoplatonist commentary on the *Timaeus* by Porphyry; yet another commentary on the *Timaeus* was composed by Chalcidius in the fourth century. Certain of Plato's other works also lent themselves well to Christian use, especially the *Phaedrus*, on the soul, a basic model for Gregory of Nyssa's *Life of Macrina* and probably also for Gregory of Nazianzus' *Apologeticus*. Many other works, like Synesius' *De Regno* and *De Providentia*,[59] show the extent of the general debt to Plato among cultured writers. The boundary between philosophy and rhetoric was thus apt to be blurred. The thought of Themistius, for instance, orator and spokesman for emperors, who himself taught philosophy at Constantinople, came with strong Platonic overtones,[60] as had the Christian political theory of Eusebius, formed around the Logos theology of Origen and the Platonized kingship theory of Dio Chrysostom.[61] Around 400, Eunapius of Sardis (died *c.* 414), a pupil at Athens of the Christian Prohaeresius, composed a set of *Lives of the Sophists* in which 'sophists', or rhetors, are seen more as idealized philosophers than as teachers of rhetoric.

Thus quite apart from the more specialized Neoplatonic schools, such as the school of Aedesius at Pergamum, or the Academy at Athens, re-established by the end of the fourth century, a general acquaintance with Platonism (though far less often real technical knowledge) was part of the intellectual background of many, perhaps even most, cultured persons. This was even more the case in view of the mobility of both students and

---

[57] For the importance of Iamblichus, see Athanassiadi (1992), (1993); Chaldaean Oracles: Lewy (1978).   [58] *Conf.* VII.26–7; cf. IX.13, 16.
[59] Cameron and Long, *Barbarians and Politics*, with earlier bibliography.   [60] Dagron, 'Thémistios'.
[61] Farina (1966); Calderone (1985).

teachers. Eunapius' collection of biographical notices illustrates the easy slide from rhetoric to philosophy and thence to religion; like Themistius and Eunapius himself (also the author of a lost but strongly pagan history – see p. 700 below), many of his subjects are pagan. The diffusion of Neoplatonic, and pagan, ideas, and indeed their interrelation with Christian themes, is demonstrated by splendid fourth-century mosaics from Apamea in Syria, where Iamblichus had taught in the early fourth century, which depict the Seven Sages with Socrates and the myth of Cassiopeia. The latter is also paralleled at New Paphos in Cyprus, where six mosaic panels show, as well as Cassiopeia, scenes from the story of Dionysus, among them the baby Dionysus seated on the lap of Hermes, evidence, perhaps of a Christianizing of pagan mythology.[62] Further discoveries at Apamea show the seven liberal arts under the guise of handmaidens (*therapainides*), whom Odysseus leaves as he returns to Philosophy, represented by Penelope.[63]

Neoplatonist educational theory also exerted lasting influence. The idea of a regular progress of studies leading to a certain goal is found in Porphyry's *Life of Pythagoras*, and again Iamblichus seems to have been an influential figure in the development of a Neoplatonist educational system.[64] The appearance of a sevenfold system of 'liberal arts' in Augustine's *De Ordine* has recently been traced to Neoplatonic sources, rather than originating in the Hellenistic period as previously supposed,[65] and Augustine himself went so far as to embark on a series of treatises on each of the seven sciences (completing only grammar and music). Educational theory and development feature among Augustine's manifold interests, both in his accounts of babies and young children in the *Confessions*, and in more theoretical guise in the *De Magistro*. However, the *De Ordine*, already mentioned, belongs to a period soon after his conversion, when he was still deeply influenced by Neoplatonism; in his later work on Christian education, the *De Doctrina Christiana*, where his focus was that of a bishop rather than that of a philosopher, a wider range of ancillary disciplines is recommended, not for themselves, but strictly as aids towards the interpretation of the scriptures. But Martianus Capella, in his *De Nuptiis* (*Marriage of Mercury and Philology*, c. A.D. 400), also took up the idea of the seven liberal arts, in an elaborate and artificial work which also praises theurgy and divination. This is the realm of learned theory rather than practice. In such indirect ways as these, Neoplatonist educational ideas gradually penetrated late antique theory, and prepared the way for the medieval curriculum. In Alexandria, during the same period as Augustine and Martianus Capella, Hypatia (killed by a Christian crowd, A.D. 415) was teaching Neoplatonist philosophy and writing treatises on

[62] For discussion, see Bowersock, *Hellenism* 49f.   [63] Balty (1992); see also Sorabji (1990) 9–10.
[64] See O'Meara (1989).   [65] Hadot (1984) 101–36; Martianus Capella: *ibid.* 137–55.

mathematics,[66] while her pupil Synesius advocated in the *Dion* a Neoplatonist conception of education as consisting of 'lower' subjects, such as rhetoric and poetry, which are propaideutic to the highest educational aim, which is the contemplation of reality.[67]

Those who studied philosophy as such generally did so as a more specialized continuation of a rhetorical training. The latter came in many forms, depending on location and on the contacts and purse of parents. The great revival of the Academy at Athens as the centre of late Neoplatonism is mainly associated with Proclus (d. A.D. 485). In the fourth century, the most notable figures at Athens were Prohairesius and Himerius, both rhetoricians, or 'sophists', and famous orators. But while Himerius' speeches survive in quantity, the volume of his work is nothing to that of Libanius, who taught at Constantinople and Nicomedia, but who is best known for his dominant influence at Antioch between 354 and his death in the 390s. Libanius was not a philosopher but an epideictic orator in the classical manner, whose speeches range from pieces composed for particular occasions to others dealing with more political or civic issues. His many surviving declamations, set-pieces serving as models for the instruction of his numerous pupils, tend to be on traditional mythological or historical themes. As in modern times, therefore, individual centres of education took their particular colour from the influence of individual teachers, and the experience of the students varied accordingly – with the difference, however, that as there was of course no registration or examination structure, it was possible and common for the students to go from place to place in order to be taught by a particularly famous teacher.

V. LEGAL AND OTHER STUDIES

The main alternative to rhetoric in late Roman higher education was law, which occupied an important place in the bureaucratic system.[68] By the fourth century the collections of Papinian, Paulus, Ulpian and Modestinus were in place as the authoritative sources for private law (Valentinian added Gaius in 426),[69] and imperial legislation proliferated, though there was no official attempt at codification until the *Codex Theodosianus* (A.D. 438): the two Diocletianic collections, the *Codex Gregorianus* and the *Codex Hermogenianus* (in its earlier versions) were unofficial and made by individuals. The lack of copies made when constitutions were promulgated, and the inadequacy of their publication, must have made for an extraordinary degree of confusion, and was doubtless a factor in the development of professionalization. The legal profession itself was rigidly organized, but

---

[66] Beretta (1993); Cameron and Long, *Barbarians and Politics* 39–46.   [67] *Dion* 8.2–7.
[68] See ch. 5 above, pp. 162–9, and on the Code, Harries and Wood (1993).   [69] *C.Th.* 1.4.3.

could be lucrative, especially at the higher levels; more important, it might give the entrée to rank and dignity, and, by the fifth century at least, it counted as a branch of the bureaucracy, with the attendant benefits which that entailed. Legal training as such was not yet essential in the fourth century, though professional training was on offer, and there were chairs at Rome and Constantinople, and a law school at Berytus. Libanius complains that young men were going straight to their legal studies without having had a proper education in rhetoric.[70] Thus our period seems to be marked by a gradual development towards specialization, which reached its culmination in the sixth century, when detailed regulations existed for the legal training provided at Berytus; even at this date, Latin was essential for lawyers in the eastern empire as well as in the west. But the fourth-century constitutions included in the *Codex Theodosianus* give ample evidence of the rhetorical training which their drafters will have received; verbose, moralizing and pretentious, they must have purveyed a sense of the imperial majesty, though to us they often succeed only in being obscure. As well as rhetoric, philosophy and law, medicine was taught – as at Alexandria; more commonly, it was taught by the doctors themselves, who were maintained by cities or by the court; they had a similar status to that of teachers, and some (especially the court doctors) reached the rank of *comes* or higher. Public posts were few, but there were also private doctors just as there were private teachers. However, medicine could equally be combined with philosophical interests, as it was for example in the case of Nemesius of Emesa. The emperors also concerned themselves about the supply and privileges of architects or what we might term engineers, but for these too a liberal education was expected.

The reasons for the vigour of both Christian and pagan literary activity during the fourth century must be sought in general social conditions rather than in any development within the educational system. Increased competition for advancement in the late Roman bureaucratic system, or for prestige within the élite, and the tensions and adjustments caused by the move of Christianity into the public sphere provided powerful incentives for spending time and money on the traditional training offered by grammarians and rhetors. The possibility of patronage and the opportunity for advancement were important stimulants to secular letters; thus a Latin literary centre was created in Gaul by the presence of the court and the development of schools there. Christian writing, on the other hand, was stimulated by internal controversy and by the Christian propaganda offensive, and was multi-centred, from Cappadocia to the Egyptian desert, and from Carthage to Milan. It was a period of unprecedented literary energy, and the rhetorical education thus revived was to continue long

---

[70] *Or.* 11.43–4.

afterwards, not only beyond the establishment of the Germanic kingdoms in the west, but also into the Byzantine period, where it formed the basis of education for many centuries to come.

VI. HISTORY-WRITING AND ITS CONTEXT

By no means all fourth-century literature was clearly distinguishable as 'classical' or Christian. The issue was simply unimportant in the case of some genres – for instance, didactic or practical works. Moreover, the very term 'literature' needs to be taken in a broad sense. The place of history-writing, for instance, had always stood high in the ranks of classical literature, though in our period Christian historians, epitomators and chroniclers approached it pragmatically and with didactic purpose (see p. 688 below). As Momigliano argued, the brief Latin epitomes of men like Aurelius Victor, Eutropius and Festus, themselves imperial officials in the generation after Constantine, filled a need felt by the new governing class of the fourth century, in particular the men promoted by Valentinian and Valens and their sons. Aurelius Victor caught the attention of Julian, with whom Eutropius also served, and the latter, having been *magister epistularum* under Constantius, was, like Festus, *magister memoriae* to Valens, to whom he dedicated his work, and went on to become prefect of Illyricum under Theodosius I (380–1); Eutropius was among the correspondents of Symmachus, and attained the honour of being appointed consul in the same year as the emperor Valentinian II (387).[71] The short and workmanlike productions of these writers have no particular religious axe to grind; they are more interested in imperial character, the role of the senate and (in the case of Festus and Eutropius) the eastern frontier, serving imperial interests by promoting the idea of a more aggressive foreign policy against Persia. Except that Festus' work is briefer, there is not much to choose between them, though Eutropius' *Breviarium* achieved the distinction of being translated into Greek; all belong to a larger group of similar or related works, including the so-called *Origo Gentis Romanae*, the *De Viris Illustribus*, covering between them legendary times to the fall of the republic, and the *Epitome de Caesaribus*, brief imperial biographies from Augustus to Theodosius. A shared source was the lost chronicle of the second and third centuries composed under Diocletian or Constantine and known as Enmann's *Kaisergeschichte* after E. Enmann, who first posited its existence.[72] Another of these brief and anonymous works, first edited by Henri de Valois (1636), is the *Origo Constantini*,[73] probably written under Constantius

---

[71] *PLRE* I, s.v.; see Momigliano, *Conflict.*

[72] Enmann (1884); Schmidt accepts its use by Aurelius Victor, Eutropius, Festus, the *SHA* and the *Epitome de Caesaribus* (see Herzog (1989) no. 536).

[73] König (1987) argues for a date post A.D. 380; see however Barnes (1989).

II, which preserves details about Constantine not found elsewhere and for the most part presents him from a pagan or religiously neutral standpoint, despite subsequent interpolations from the early-fifth-century Christian historian Orosius. The existence of early accounts more hostile to Constantine and the Christian empire can be deduced from later Byzantine chronicles, and the pagan history of Eunapius, followed closely by Zosimus, took a line similar to the scornful picture of Constantine drawn in Julian's *Caesares*; but Ammianus, independent as usual, seems to have kept his religious criticism muted.[74] Also from the late fourth century came the lost *Annales* by the leading pagan senator Virius Nicomachus Flavianus, whose son of the same name was the editor of Livy. The work is indicated in two inscriptions, in one of which Flavianus is termed *historicus disertissimus*.[75] But tempting as it has been to many to see the *Annales* as a pagan manifesto, in view of Flavianus' attachment to the cause of the usurper Eugenius, on whose defeat in 394 he committed suicide, we have no actual information even about the period which the work may have covered.

The relationship between this and other pagan historical works remains highly contentious, with the result that their importance has been much exaggerated. Ammianus Marcellinus is famously scathing about the reading-habits and general tastes of the Roman aristocracy in the 370s and 380s, depicting them as interested only in sensational biography, and in writers like Juvenal and Marius Maximus.[76] Indeed, one of the most scabrous of the potted biographies was being put together while he was living in Rome himself and completing his own history there in the early 390s. Probably most scholars would now agree that the *Historia Augusta*, a set of imperial biographies running from A.D. 96 to the accession of Diocletian, is the work of one author of the late fourth century rather than of the six outlandishly named 'Constantinian' authors claimed in the work itself. There is also less of a tendency nowadays to read it as yet another work of pagan propaganda against Christians. Ronald Syme indeed argued that the work was intended as a playful literary fiction, to suit exactly the reading public described so memorably by Ammianus. But the date and sources of the *Historia Augusta* remain a vexed question, and the controversy is not yet likely to die down. There is very little to go on; one should also remember that the Roman senatorial class itself was by no means homogeneous, so that generalizations about its tastes or affiliations can be as misleading as Ammianus' blanket condemnation. Two military treatises perhaps also belong with this group – the anonymous *De Rebus Bellicis*, an intriguing pamphlet apparently addressed to Valentinian and Valens in the

---

[74] Matthews, *Ammianus* 447–50; the so-called 'Leoquelle': Bleckmann (1991). Eunapius: Blockley (1981–3); and Ammianus: Matthews, *Ammianus* 164–75.

[75] *ILS* 2947.

[76] Amm. Marc. xxviii.4; cf. xiv.6.

late 360s, and proposing a series of ingenious inventions whereby to restore the success of the Roman armies, yet showing clear links with the pagan historiographical tradition,[77] and a Christian, though not a sectarian, work, Vegetius' *Epitoma Rei Militaris*, a conservative military handbook probably dedicated to Theodosius I and consisting of a mixture of rhetorical display and practical information. Vegetius' short preface, in which he links his own with earlier works of rhetoric dedicated to emperors, and his Virgilian quotations demonstrate the effects of a standard rhetorical education; the author, who is likely also to have composed a surviving treatise on horse and cattle ailments, writes his technical work in the traditional mode directed at laymen.[78]

Against such a background the *Res Gestae* of Ammianus, a 'lonely historian' in many senses, stands out all the more.[79] His is (so far as we know) the only history in Latin on the grand scale after Tacitus, with whose work it deserves to be compared. For energy, vividness and sustained power of writing it can hardly be matched in any period of classical literature, and certain subjects, especially the military narratives of Julian in Gaul as Caesar and in the east as emperor, will always be seen through Ammianus' eyes. Ammianus was a pagan, but his relation to the remaining pagan aristocrats in Rome and to Roman literary circles remains one of the many mysteries which still surround the man and his work. The surviving portion ends in book XXXI with the disaster of Adrianople in 378 but begins only at book XIV, taking up the narrative in 354 with Constantius II; thus what we have covers a period of only twenty-five years out of the whole. Since Ammianus tells us in his famous concluding remarks that he had begun at the accession of Nerva in A.D. 96,[80] the earlier part (257 years), or most of it, must have been covered far more briefly. In the same passage he refers to himself as *miles quondam et Graecus*, a phrase which expresses, by contemporary standards, a twofold paradox. Not many ex-soldiers would have been likely to compose a work of such power and range, and the *Res Gestae* does indeed bear many traces of Greek as a language and of Greek styles of historiography. Ammianus combines a deep reverence for Rome and a passionate advocacy of Roman virtues such as *moderatio* with a late antique love of curious information and long digressions.[81] We still do not know how he came to compose his history in Rome, in Latin, or under what patrons, if any. But Ammianus no longer appears the herald of decline that earlier critics saw in him. He expresses his approval of the traditional Roman virtues of moderation, caution and restraint in language which verges on the extravagant; his pages are full of unforgettable phrases. In the course of his account of the Persian siege of Amida in 359, in which

---

[77] See Hassall and Ireland (1979).
[78] Some argue for Valentinian III (425–455) as dedicatee; see Milner (1993) xxv f.
[79] See Momigliano (1974).   [80] XXXI.16.   [81] Matthews, *Ammianus* 462f.

he took part himself, he describes the frustration of Ursicinus, unable to implement his plan of diverting the attackers: 'all his helpful schemes could effect nothing. He was like a lion of huge size and grim aspect which does not dare to go to the rescue of its trapped whelps because it has lost its claws and teeth.'[82] Ammianus was acutely aware of colour and of visual effects, whether in his famous account of Constantius II's entry into Rome in 357,[83] or in details such as his observation of how carefully the senators in Rome showed off their fringed and decorated tunics.[84] Nor did the unsavoury tactics of Christian pressure groups escape his attention,[85] any more than the vices of the Roman aristocrats, which he satirizes scathingly and memorably.[86] The surviving books offer an exciting panorama of military history and a sympathetic, though detached, portrayal of the career of the admired Julian; but later, Rome became Ammianus' theme, and in the last books the scope narrows. In this part of the work the moral and political behaviour of the upper classes absorbed him, just as it had his predecessor Tacitus. Such is the stature of Ammianus' work that it does not need to be explained in terms of literary models; yet while the differences are many, he is fully Tacitus' equal in literary genius and moral seriousness.

In what sense is Ammianus a late antique writer? His importance was amply recognized by Gibbon in the reliance which he placed on the work of 'the philosophic soldier', while he has been read by Auerbach as reflecting that breakdown of classical styles which the latter took as heralding the Middle Ages, and by others – for example, R. MacMullen – as providing vivid insights into the social *mores* of the period, as well as evidence of its alleged decline and corruption.[87] He is a major historian on any count, and one whose range and geographical scope are far greater than had previously been seen among Roman historians. He belongs to his age in many ways, not least in the fact that he writes as a member of a bureaucracy whose officials were liable to find themselves in any part of the empire, and who were in close contact with numerous others like themselves, both civilian and military. It is Ammianus who gives us our best information both about the late Roman army in action and about the extraordinary juxtapositions of life in imperial and senatorial circles. Finally, it is Ammianus the writer who, once read, is never forgotten.

Eunapius of Sardis covered some of the same events as Ammianus and had access to good information about Julian's Persian campaign; though comparison is hindered by the facts that his work is preserved only indirectly through its use by the pagan historian Zosimus in the late fifth or early sixth century, and the dates of the successive editions are

---

[82] XIX.3.   [83] XVI.10.   [84] XIV.6.9.
[85] XXVII.3.5, the election of Pope Damasus; however, while Ammianus himself was clearly not a Christian, Petronius Probus' Christianity is not included in the impressive list of the latter's faults at XXVII.11.   [86] XXVIII.4.   [87] Auerbach (1953) ch. 3; MacMullen (1964), *Corruption*.

controversial, Matthews argues that Ammianus did use it for details of Julian's Persian campaign. Ammianus' work has resemblances of scope and style to the Greek classicizing tradition of which Eunapius was a main representative, and is written with the same aspirations to high style and traditional form. But the *Res Gestae* differs fundamentally in its 'moral and dramatic intention';[88] in other words, it is simply better and more serious history. It is also distinct in its general lack of religious bias, unlike the notoriously anti-Christian stance of Eunapius, which also comes through strongly in Zosimus. Ammianus is no pagan propagandist – while he is outspoken in his criticism of Christians when they break the bounds of moderation, he is no more so in their case than in that of other groups. Julian's edict directed at Christian teachers, which we might have expected Ammianus to approve, is one of the few points singled out for criticism in his obituary of the emperor,[89] and religion in general receives little prominence in the history. Not all fourth-century writers were obsessed with religion, it seems. On the other hand, the consequent degree of distortion of recent history entailed by the selectivity and omissions of religious matters in Ammianus' account is also something to bear in mind.[90] But there are other omissions in his work too, notably in relation to the reasons for the failure of Julian's Persian expedition, and the defeat of Valens at Adrianople; nor does he venture easily into topics which might be construed as criticism of Theodosius I, who was on the throne when he finished his history.

Eunapius was to be followed by an impressive list of Greek secular historians, from Olympiodorus in the fifth century to Procopius, writing under Justinian, and finally to Theophylact Simocatta, writing under Heraclius. But history was also a key area where religious divisions might be expected to show themselves. The first in the field of church history had been Eusebius' *Ecclesiastical History*, to which the final revisions were made after Constantine's defeat of Licinius in 324 and before the council of Nicaea in the following year. After Eusebius, historiography diverged into church history on the one side and secular classicizing history on the other. They differed in a number of obvious ways: in scope and content (the history of the church as against the traditional subject matter of wars, politics and court affairs), treatment (secular historians aimed at high style, which precluded them from citing the documents which are such a feature of Eusebius' work), ideology (church history located itself within a temporal frame dictated by the sense of God's purpose for the world, from the creation to the second coming), and finally, presumably, audience (those who read church histories only sometimes coincided with the educated élite

[88] Matthews, *Ammianus* 164–75; see also 445–6.   [89] xxv.4 (see above).
[90] Barnes, *Athanasius* 166–7.

and pagan officials who formed the audience for the secular works). The writers of ecclesiastical history tended to be bishops, like Eusebius, though Socrates and Sozomen, the authors of two such works written in Constantinople in the 440s, were both lawyers. Eusebius' history was not continued until the now lost work of Gelasius of Caesarea late in the fourth century and the Latin version by Rufinus of Aquileia. The major surviving Greek church histories following Eusebius all belong to the mid fifth century, with a Eunomian church history by Philostorgius, the works of Socrates and Sozomen, and the church history of Theodoret of Cyrrhus in northern Syria.[91] Nevertheless, the differences between ecclesiastical and secular history can be exaggerated. Secular historians did not exclude Christian material altogether, while ecclesiastical historians, beginning with Eusebius, necessarily also included secular matter. Ammianus did not exclude mention of Christians from the *Res Gestae*, even though he was not particularly impressed by what he saw of them. The two types could show similarity even in their presentation of historical causation and their admission of the miraculous.[92] Nor did Christian controversialists make historiography their main arena, preferring polemical or apologetic treatises, letters and works of exegesis (see pp. 696–704 below). The religious divisions of the post-Constantinian period, not to mention Eusebius' own tendency towards Arianism, also made the idea of a continuation of Eusebius' work highly sensitive.[93] But the fact that church history as a genre developed within the context of the church itself helped to maintain a degree of separation.

It is easy to underestimate the uniqueness and variety of Eusebius' own contribution. Biblical scholar, protagonist in contemporary church politics, and prolific writer, Eusebius was also a propagandist of Constantine; not only did he establish the twin genres of church history and Christian chronicle; he also laid down, in his later works, the *Tricennalian Oration* (A.D. 336) and the *Life of Constantine* (*Vita Constantini*),[94] the essentials of a political philosophy for a Christian empire. Of these late works, the *Life of Constantine*, nowadays agreed to have been written by Eusebius, is particularly curious; it was little read in the fourth century, if at all, though it was used by the fifth-century church historians, and it is in literary terms an awkward mixture of panegyric and narrative.[95] In the elaborately self-justifying preface Eusebius draws on the conventions of the *basilikos logos* as prescribed by Menander Rhetor, even to the extent of including the

[91] The works by Gelasius of Caesarea and Philostorgius survive only in fragments; for bibliography see Winkelmann in Winkelmann and Brandes (1990) 202–12; Philostorgius' dependence on an 'Arian history' of the 360s: Bidez and Winkelmann (1991) 208–9, with Brennecke (1988) 92–5; 114–57.

[92] See Ruggini (1977), (1981).   [93] Clark (1992) 181–2.

[94] The *V. Const.* recounts the death of Constantine, A.D. 337; chapter headings were added after Eusebius' own death, which followed soon afterwards, perhaps A.D. 339.

[95] Barnes (1989), building on Pasquali (1910); see however Cameron, Averil (1997b).

prescribed comparison of Constantine with the great kings Cyrus and Alexander. But the main body of the work, at least in the narrative up to the final defeat of Licinius, adopts a Christian typology and casts the emperor in the role of Moses and likens the ending of the persecutions to the deliverance of the Israelites from Egypt. Christian hagiography had not yet taken shape when Eusebius wrote (Antony did not die until 356), yet the *Life* seems to foreshadow its future development: Constantine's selection by God, Eusebius claims, was manifested by signs, the greatest of which is the emperor's vision before the battle of the Milvian Bridge, inserted here into an account taken closely from the much earlier narrative of the same events in the author's own *Ecclesiastical History*, but here adapted and subtly enhanced.[96] Eusebius' tendentiousness in the *Vita Constantini* has occupied modern scholars since Burckhardt, particularly in relation to the many documents included on the model of the documents quoted in and appended to the *Ecclesiastical History*. But the *Life* also attempted to present a Christian emperor in the guise of a holy man; thus it was an answer, in literary terms, to the *Lives* of pagan holy men by Eusebius' *bête noire* Porphyry and others,[97] and a demonstration of how he saw the role of Constantine in the Christian providential scheme of history. The latter view, already inherent in the closing section of the *Ecclesiastical History*, a work conceived without that end in view,[98] found deeper expression in the group of later works as Eusebius pondered the implications of what it would mean to have a Christian state. If the *Life of Constantine* was indeed an experiment in Christian hagiography, this was a sensationally bold stroke on Eusebius' part.

In several other ways, too, Eusebius was ahead of his time. His *Chronicle* drew together several existing chronological systems into a continuous synthesis of world history from creation to the present day and beyond it to the expected second coming. It was to be copied and emulated countless times, both in the medieval west and in Byzantium, but the Greek version is lost, though an early Armenian one survives, and Jerome translated the work into Latin and continued it. The *Chronicle* imposed the conception of Christian time; it was built on the idea of a narrative, what the Christians called the 'economy' of salvation, whereby God's plan for the world was demonstrated in the movement of history, and specifically in the history of the Roman empire. The assumptions on which it rested found expression in other works by Eusebius, notably his *Preparation for the Gospel*,

---

[96] *V. Const.* 1.28f.; cf. *HE* IX.9.9; for the technique, and the relation of *HE* and *V. Const.*, see Hall (1993).

[97] That Eusebius was fully aware of the tradition of pagan 'lives' may also be seen, if it is actually by Eusebius, from the *Contra Hieroclem*, an answer to the anti-Christian arguments which Hierocles had based on Philostratus' *Life of Apollonius of Tyana*; for pagan *Lives* see further below.

[98] For the date and successive editions see Barnes (1980); Louth (1990).

Demonstration of the Gospel and *Theophany* (the latter surviving only in Syriac).[99] Time, creation and the creation narratives in Genesis were all to become central themes in fourth-century theological writing. However, the questions about providence and the history of the Roman empire which had been raised by Eusebius were addressed most directly and with the most sophisticated arguments only in Augustine's *City of God* (A.D. 413–26). Whereas Eusebius had written in a mood of understandable euphoria, Augustine had to explain why God's providence had allowed the Christian empire to experience such an event as the sack of Rome by Alaric in 410. Against Eusebius, he held that Christians could not expect happiness on earth, for the present was still a time of trial; nor was the Roman empire essentially different from other empires. Whereas Eusebius had written as an eastern churchman steeped in the thought of Origen, the *City of God* is the work of an extraordinary individual in the western, Latin tradition, a former rhetor converted to philosophy, thence to be cast in the mould of a bishop. It takes the form of a sustained historical argument about the nature of Roman civilization and the Roman past, and of a confrontation between the classic works of Latin literature and Christian culture. The themes of historical time, classical versus Christian culture, political theory and the nature of Christian providence intertwine through the twenty-two books, in comparison with which Orosius' *Historia Adversus Paganos* (A.D. 417–18), composed to answer essentially the same question, pales into insignificance.[100]

VII. HIGH LITERARY CULTURE

The fourth century was a time of vivid juxtapositions. The urban culture which supported rhetorical education and now gave a place to Christian oratory also provided the stimulus, especially from the later fourth century onwards, for a revival of composition in verse. L. Robert drew attention to the amazingly rich collection of Greek verse epigrams inscribed from the fourth to the sixth centuries in honour of officials or civic occasions, which show a technical expertise and a vocabulary indicative of the widespread existence of training and patronage.[101] But the phenomenon was not confined to Greek – pope Damasus (366–84) was only one of the many who composed Latin epigrams. Again, subjects, styles and types of verse composition ranged from the most classical to the most Christian. Almost all took as their starting-point the aim of *imitatio*, adopting, and in the

[99] The earlier part of Eusebius' very large output as scholar and apologist, including the *Ecclesiastical History*, falls before the period covered by this volume; Barnes, *CE*, chs. 6–10, provides a comprehensive discussion.
[100] Brown, *Augustine* is still the starting-point for the study of Augustine; that of Chadwick (1986) stands out among recent short introductions. [101] Robert, *Hellenica* IV.

process also adapting, earlier models. Among the Latin poets of the late fourth and early fifth centuries, Ausonius and Claudian dominate the field in the sheer volume and technical accomplishment of their verse. The former produced over a long career an extraordinarily large and varied output, ranging from poems dealing with events or people in his personal life, longer descriptive poems on themes such as the river Moselle, the subject of his famous *Mosella*, and *jeux d'esprit* or, perhaps rather, technical exercises, which tackle such unpromising material as the names of Roman emperors or the signs of the zodiac, and put it into difficult forms; the so-called *Technopaegnion* consists of sets of hexameters in which every line ends with a monosyllable. Decoration and technical display were highly valued in late Latin poetry; poets demonstrated their skill in vivid description and in the *variatio* with which they treated familiar subjects and rhetorical tropes.[102] Some of Ausonius' epigrams incorporate Greek words and phrases or are versions of Greek originals, while his *Cento Nuptialis* is an epithalamium in the form of a compilation of Virgilian lines and half-lines; the prose preface explains its origin in the fact that the emperor Valentinian had engaged in just such a *tour de force* and then invited competition. The poem ends with a graphic description of sexual intercourse ingeniously put together from Virgilian phrases whose original application was totally different. Fifty years before, Porfyrius Optatianus had composed Christian poems in acrostics, addressed to Constantine. Such bravura displays were highly valued in some fourth-century circles; modern readers less attuned to their like may feel more drawn to Ausonius' poems about his family or those in various different metres about his fellow rhetors and *grammatici* from Bordeaux (see pp. 673–4 above). These have something of the ring of personal feeling, and are full of fascinating information about individuals and about the social and educational context of the region. Their personal, and even domestic, tone is unusual in contemporary learned literature, though we can also find it in Gregory of Nazianzus' epigrams about his mother, or in the autobiographical parts of Augustine's *Confessions*.

The poems of Claudian, long hexameter compositions on political themes, mostly written from a strongly partisan viewpoint,[103] are also highly formal and accomplished, using all the devices of rhetoric and most of the paraphernalia of classical Latin epic. Claudian seems also to have been the author of a short Christian poem *De Salvatore*, but if so, his Christianity is kept firmly to one side in his public poems, which are full of pagan gods, goddesses and personifications. Claudian was a master of invective as well as of praise: the explicitness of his attacks on the eastern

---

[102] Roberts (1989) ch. 2; Roberts attempts to link literary technique with the techniques of contemporary visual art, *ibid.*, ch. 3; see also Mathews (1993) ch. 6, with *Corippus, In laudem Iustini*, ed. Cameron, Averil, London, 1976: 119, 141 (processional and axial schemes).

[103] Cameron, Alan, *Claudian*.

ministers Rufinus and Eutropius would shock a modern critic, though their satirical bite is equalled by Jerome. But if Claudian's skill lies less in innovation than in his mastery of rhetorical technique and versification, other Latin poets were more willing to experiment. Prudentius' *Peristephanon* is a collection of Latin poems in lyric metres about Roman and Spanish martyrs (he was himself a Spaniard), with their gruesome ordeals described in loving detail. Building on classical models, Prudentius attempted to carve out a new form, in both subject matter and treatment. His verse preface records the preferment he received from the emperor Theodosius I, who was also from Spain.[104] But he uses his art to dwell lingeringly on the burning of the virgin martyr Eulalia and similarly prurient topics. Prudentius was a prolific and varied poet, in whom we can see a sustained effort to apply the diction and metres of Latin poetry to Christian subject matter: he also wrote a book of daily prayers and hymns in lyric metres (*Cathemerinon*), two long hexameter poems with iambic prefaces on doctrinal matters (the *Apotheosis*, against heresy, and the *Hamartigena*, on the origins of sin), an allegorical epic (the *Psychomachia*) and the *Contra Symmachum*, two books of hexameters in which he dramatized the conflict which had taken place nearly two decades previously, in 384, over the imperial removal of the altar of Victory from the senate house. Elaborate and allusive, the poem praises the victory of Stilicho and Honorius over Alaric and the Visigoths at Pollentia (A.D. 402), and rebuts the pagan claim that Roman military defeats were the result of abandoning the gods. The argument, cast in the form of a confrontation between the pagan Symmachus and Arcadius and Honorius, the sons of Theodosius I, is followed by a long and emotional speech addressed to the emperors by the personified Rome: 'Do not, I beg, be swayed by the voice of the great orator [Symmachus], who . . . bemoans the death of his rites and with the weapons of his intellect and the powers of his eloquence dares, alas, to attack our faith.'[105] But Christian Latin poetry was not confined to heroic compositions like these. There were also more practical needs, including pastoral ones: Ambrose, a fine poet himself, is said to have introduced hymn-singing at Milan in the 380s, and Prudentius' hymns may also have been written with performance in mind. Like Damasus, Ambrose composed epigrams to be inscribed in churches; and Paulinus of Nola, a former pupil of Ausonius at Bordeaux and later governor of Campania, experimented with the combination of scriptural, Virgilian and Horatian elements in a series of poems ranging from occasional poetry based on classical types such as the *consolatio*, the *propemptikon* or the epithalamium to a set of poems celebrating the feastday of Felix of Nola, in whose honour Paulinus and his wife Therasia

---

[104] *Peristeph.*, *praef.* 16–21; see Palmer (1989) 24–8.
[105] *C. Symm.* II.761–4; the allusiveness of the poem itself makes the historicity of the alleged embassy by Symmachus controversial: see e.g. Cameron, Alan, *Claudian* 240–1; Barnes (1976).

erected an elaborate and ambitious complex of buildings.[106] To some extent, as in the case of the Christian letters of this period (a large collection of Paulinus' letters survives), the writing of Christian poetry in Latin was linked with patronage and *amicitia*, and with the demands of court or upper-class life. But it might also reflect the growing needs of cult or liturgy, and here its development paralleled that of Christian art and, even more important, church-building.

The phenomenon of verse composition itself was in fact empire-wide, and very varied. The learned empress Eudocia composed an epic on her husband Theodosius II's Persian wars (she later wrote biblical paraphrases in Greek verse, and rather bad verses on a set of baths which she restored in the Holy Land). Gregory of Nazianzus adapted the Greek epigram for Christian purposes with a series of long and interesting poems in which he wrote about his mother Nonna and about his own life; and the caustic pagan epigrams by the fourth-century poet Palladas of Alexandria were already anthologized and known in the west.[107] Dedicatory inscriptions in Greek verse are a striking feature of eastern cities in the fourth to sixth centuries, and suitable inscriptions were also needed to fulfil the growing requirements of church-building and Christian patronage. A stylized vocabulary soon developed both for honorific inscriptions on officials and for Christian dedications; but some at least of these hired poets also had literary pretensions. They wrote, in any case, in the context of as vigorous a background of verse composition as existed in the Latin west. 'Wandering poets', especially from Egypt, who lived on their literary skill to travel and gain advancement, are a phenomenon of the fifth-century east,[108] but there were already poet-grammarians or poet-rhetors from Egypt in the fourth century, such as Harpocration, who became a teacher in Antioch, apparently with Libanius, and was then invited to Constantinople by Themistius as a sophist; his fellow Egyptian, Eudaimon, followed a similar path at least as far as Antioch, and there was also a probably different Harpocration who is named in a papyrus as a panegyrist from Panopolis in the fourth century.[109] Greek acrostics revealing the name Magnus may be the work of a doctor, Magnus of Nisibis, who practised in Alexandria and is the subject of an epitaph by Palladas.[110] Eunapius' remark that Egyptians were mad on poetry[111] seems to have been justified. There was also a strong connection between Greek poetry and late paganism. The poets Helladius and Ammonius of Alexandria, both pagan priests, prudently left Alexandria for Constantinople at the time of the destruction of the Serapeum there in 391, setting up schools in the capital.

---

[106] Paulinus' poetry: Roberts (1989) 133–8.   [107] See Cameron, Alan (1993) 80f., 90f.

[108] Cameron, Alan (1965); the library at Panopolis: *Egypt* 103–4.

[109] For their careers, and for a prosopography of late antique grammarians and others, see Kaster, *Guardians of Language*, Part II, with nos. 210 and 226.   [110] West (1982).   [111] *V. Soph.* 493.

Earlier, the emperor Julian had composed Greek hymns to Helios and Cybele,[112] just as he had shown interest while on his Persian expedition in the eastern towns that were still centres of paganism – Beroea, Batnae, Hierapolis and Harran (Carrhae), home of the cult of the moon.[113] Behind much of this exoticism lay the *Chaldaean Oracles*, which were much in vogue in Julian's Neoplatonic circles (see p. 680 above) and were a strong influence on the Christian but platonizing hymns of Synesius and, later, one of the two favourite books of Proclus.[114] Allusive and learned, imbued with the vocabulary of the *Chaldaean Oracles*, Synesius' hymns have led several scholars into the trap of taking them as a guide to 'pagan' and 'Christian' phases in his life – yet another example of the danger of reading off the character of the author from a literary composition. They represent rather, as so often, the interconnectedness of the various cultural strands in the period. The so-called Orphic hymns were a further important source for pagans, and in the fourth and fifth centuries Neoplatonists, like Christians, made use of prayers and hymns, as their philosophy acquired all the hallmarks of a religious system. Hymns were not the unique preserve either of Christians or of pagans.

Both this material and its authors clearly belong in a learned context. The Egyptian poets are frequently also grammarians, and amateurs like the empress Eudocia liked to pride themselves on their erudition. As for Latin literary culture, Macrobius' *Saturnalia*, with its *Dream of Scipio* consciously evoking Cicero's *De Republica*, and Servius' great commentary on Virgil belong to the early fifth century, but in the last decades of the fourth century, too, members of the senatorial élite in Rome showed their concern for traditional literary culture, in recopying texts of classical authors (and appending *subscriptiones* to record what had been done and by whom), reviving the works of neglected Silver Latin writers such as Juvenal, and translating Greek works (though they tended to choose abstruse works of limited interest). It is striking to find Christians as much involved in this activity as pagans.[115] Even overtly anti-pagan literary works by Christians, such as Prudentius' *Contra Symmachum*, the *Carmen ad Senatorem*, or the mysterious *Carmen contra Paganos*, presented Christianity in Virgilian guise, and even as its members were becoming Christian, the educated élite belied Ammianus' scathing jibes[116] by making its love and knowledge of the classics an important element in its self-identity. A rare contender in the category of pagan propaganda against Christians may have been the translation

[112] The cult of the latter, which could be given a cosmic interpretation, was a favourite in late Greek paganism, and achieved a fashionable following also among Roman pagans: consequently it also occupied a central place in Christian polemic.
[113] *Ep.* 98 Bidez (to Libanius); Amm. Marc. XXIII.3.2–3; XXV.3.20; XXVI.6.2–3; Zos. IV.4.2.
[114] Marin. *V. Procl.* 38; the other was Plato's *Timaeus*. Synesius' hymns: Cameron and Long, *Barbarians and Politics* 28–35, against Terzaghi.
[115] Cameron, Alan, 'Latin revival'; *subscriptiones*: Zetzel (1981) 211–31.   [116] XXVIII.4, cf. XIV.6.

of the already contentious *Life* of the pagan wonder-worker Apollonius of
Tyana by Nicomachus Flavianus,[117] but Symmachus' famous appeal for
religious toleration in his third *Relatio* may have been more typical of the
pagan stance in the face of authoritarian Christian emperors.

VIII. EPISTOLOGRAPHY AND LITERARY NETWORKS

The late fourth century is remarkable for the intensity of literary and intellectual activity among certain members of the upper class, both Christian
and pagan; for the sheer volume of surviving works, this is surely the
richest period of antiquity. Moreover, while a considerable amount of
material comes, as we have seen, from late-fourth-century Rome, literary
activity was extraordinarily widely distributed geographically, from
Mesopotamia in the east, to Cappadocia and Pontus, Jerome's retreat at
Bethlehem, Antioch and Constantinople, Rome and Milan, Alexandria and
Upper Egypt, from Cyrenaica and Hippo in North Africa to Gaul and
Spain in the west. Contemporary sources are full of references to travel,
despite the warfare and invasion that was also a feature of the period. Even
given the extreme slowness and uncertainty of delivery by modern standards,[118] enough letters survive to make this also one of the major periods
for ancient epistolography. The letters written by the great Christian writers
such as Ambrose, Jerome, John Chrysostom, Paulinus and Augustine tend
to dominate modern consciousness, but letter-writing was shared by
pagans and Christians alike. Most of these letters are hard for modern taste
to digest, for the demands of rhetoric and genre almost invariably take
precedence over moments of personal revelation. From Q. Aurelius
Symmachus nine hundred letters survive, covering the period from the
360s to A.D. 402. In Greek, Libanius has left a collection no less voluminous
– over fifteen hundred, many of which are the letters of recommendation
on which the organization of the late Roman bureaucracy depended.
Significantly, the correspondence of Pliny the Younger was read again in
this period, giving rise to an admiring comparison between Symmachus
and Pliny. Less by direct statement than by their style and subject matter,
Symmachus' letters express the forms and manners of senatorial and
upper-class life in the late fourth century. They were well received and
appreciated in his own day, even allowing for an element of natural as well
as literary exaggeration in his own claims,[119] and are a primary resource for
social, cultural and administrative history; like the letters of Libanius, if in
the context of Rome rather than of the Greek east, they also show the

---

[117] For which see Sidon. *Ep.* VIII.3.1. Flavianus himself seems to have been somewhat exceptional
in this regard; his son, a Christian, copied the text of Livy.

[118] Cf. also the frequent references in the sources to letter-carriers, e.g. *V. Ant.*, pref.

[119] *Ep.* IV.34.64; V.85–6; II.12.48.

functioning of rhetoric as a badge of cultural belonging. Symmachus was of course a pagan, the champion of the pagan senators in the face of the mounting influence of Ambrose and an increasingly aggressive imperial policy towards pagans, but just as there were Christians among Libanius' pupils, so there were Christians among the correspondents of Symmachus, to whom he wrote without evident awkwardness.

It is hardly surprising if Christian and pagan epistolography followed a similar pattern, with an emphasis on letters of recommendation, consolation and encouragement, in accordance with the demands of late Roman *amicitia*. Augustine's circle at the time of his conversion in 386 comprised men not unlike himself, with official positions as provincial governors, lawyers and the like. They often had provincial origins, and were the more dependent for that reason on networks of patronage and social contact. But the Pauline Epistles were also an influence on Christian epistolography, and these too were read and commented upon in the late-fourth-century west; many Christian letters deal with spiritual matters and contain passages of scriptural exegesis. One of the most important exponents of this genre, Paulinus of Nola, came of a landowning family in Aquitaine and was the son of a senator; he well illustrates the ambiguities of late-fourth-century culture, for though he was famous for his renunciation of wealth and his dedication to the ascetic life at Nola, he continued to express himself not only in his highly cultured poems built on classical models, but also in a long series of letters, of which forty-five survive, in which rhetoric and tradition compete with practical, moral and religious content. Paulinus' letters reached correspondents from Gaul to Palestine, including Jerome, Rufinus, Augustine and Pelagius, as well as less well-known bishops, clergy and laymen; a large group was addressed to his friend Sulpicius Severus, a lawyer who adopted a life of literary activity (as the author of the *Life* of Martin of Tours: see p. 699 below) and religious patronage closely comparable to Paulinus' own. Paulinus' friends and contacts included many who like himself belonged to the circles of Jerome and Augustine, such as Melania the Younger. As in the case of his poetry, his letters combine the traditional themes of classical *amicitia* with the newer and evolving Christian patronage. But the Christian letter was by no means as limited as this might suggest. Many of Jerome's letters, in sharp contrast to Paulinus', amount to bravura displays of satirical writing, like the notorious *Ep.* 22, in which he urges Eustochium, the daughter of his friend Paula, to a life of virginity; among other lapses of taste, her mother is congratulated on the prospect of becoming the mother-in-law of Christ. Often, as here, Jerome's letters amount to miniature treatises, like *Ep.* 78, in which he instructs Paula on the meaning of the forty-two stages on the journey of the Israelites from Egypt (Num. 33), or lays down his usually severe instructions for Christian behaviour in answer to unwary friends and acquaintances who had consulted him, as with Furia, a widow sternly warned against remarriage (*Ep.* 54). But it is also because of these letters, and others written by his contemporaries, that it is possible to construct so detailed a picture of personal contacts between certain groups in this period.[120] Jerome was quite unique. Furthermore, he was a great satirist and literary stylist; even the letters advocating humility and renunciation are written in the most sparkling and elegant Latin. A series of hitherto unknown letters from Augustine was recently discovered by J. Divjak, in addition to the more than two hundred already known; they have added a new dimension to the understanding of Augustine's thinking on sexuality, but are perhaps even more important for the light they shed on practical matters – clerical appointments and slave trading among them. The revival of epistolography was destined to continue with the many letters written in ecclesiastical circles in fifth-century Gaul, and the turgid but important *Variae* written in sixth-century Italy by Cassiodorus for Theodoric.[121]

IX. CHRISTIAN WRITING

As we have seen, Christians patronized the same schools and teachers as pagans. Nevertheless, Christians also had access to a different heritage. Roman ladies like the two Melanias and Paula read the scriptures, especially the Psalms, the Hebrew Bible, the works of Origen in the recent translations by Rufinus, and the writings of Plotinus. A few women, like Stilicho's daughter Maria[122] and evidently also Proba, author of a Virgilian cento (see p. 702 below), were well-read in the classical poets, or in philosophy, like Hypatia, but these tended to have family support or intellectual leanings. Their brothers and husbands, often converted at a mature age, and with the full benefit of secular education, were likely to have had a more extensive earlier experience of reading classical authors, as was the case with Marius Victorinus, who turned from commenting on Cicero's rhetorical works and translating Porphyry and Plotinus to writing commentaries on the Pauline Epistles. An earlier example is that of the astrologer Firmicus Maternus, who, having composed a treatise on astrology (the *Mathesis*) in A.D. 337, then wrote an attack on paganism.[123] But some Christians with a high degree of secular culture were also receptive to works of a quite different sort. The *Life of Antony* made a great impression even in professional western circles (see p. 669 above). We have seen how Christians themselves engaged in an energetic project of adapting themselves to the public environment of high culture, matching an acceptable public speech to their new political persona; something similar happened in the literary sphere.

---

[120] For a network analysis see Clark (1992) ch. 1.
[121] See in general, Garzya (1983); letters of Ausonius: Green (1980).
[122] Claudian, *Carm.* x.229–37.   [123] A.D. 343: see Barnes (1991) 346–7.

These were important and well-connected people, often with public positions and networks of contacts. But contemporary Christianity also had a strongly didactic tone, conveyed not only by theological treatises and exegesis, but more directly by oral forms of teaching, such as homilies and scriptural readings. Some homilies, preserved in literary form, offer a highly sophisticated mixture of the theological and the rhetorical, and reflect the interplay of the requirements of the liturgy and the needs of the worshipping congregation: such are, for example, the Easter homilies of Gregory of Nyssa. Homiletic developed alongside and was shaped by the establishment of a regular calendar of liturgical celebration, of which Easter was the high point. In addition, candidates for baptism received catechetical instruction. The surviving catechetical orations of Cyril of Jerusalem (consecrated A.D. 350) are perhaps untypical of the genre; they consist of a set of eighteen pre-baptismal lectures on the Christian faith, which would have been delivered during Lent, a stiff course indeed for the catechumens. The lectures presume an intelligent audience capable of appreciating a relatively sophisticated argument in Greek; they can hardly be a guide to the type of instruction received by the average Christian in a lesser place. The five *Mystagogical Catecheses* which follow (perhaps attributable to Cyril's successor) constitute an important exposition of the meaning of the liturgy, and at the same time an important source of information. Cyril was no ordinary bishop, and the liturgy of Jersualem in the fourth century, described also by the pilgrim Egeria in the diary of her travels (A.D. 384), was naturally exceptional. Nevertheless, as churches and monasteries were built in more and more places, the cultural apparatus of Christianity also obtruded itself into the consciousness of pagans. For converts, fourth-century church membership was a community affair and congregations were exposed to regular moral and spiritual instruction; whatever their individual reasons for conversion, this was an audience whose needs had to be met.

X. BIOGRAPHY, CHRISTIAN AND PAGAN

Christianity benefited from, and contributed to, a growing focus on the individual. This found some expression in the new genre of hagiography; the *Life of Antony* belongs to the mid fourth century, and by the first half of the fifth century the type was well established, with such works as Jerome's *Lives of the Hermits*, written in emulation of the *Life of Antony*, the *Life of Macrina* by Gregory of Nyssa (early 380s), the *Life of Martin* by Sulpicius Severus, those of Melania the Younger (before A.D. 451) and John Chrysostom, and *Lives* of Ambrose, Augustine and others. The degree of realistic detail in such works varies greatly: recent scholarship demonstrates not only their ideological and exemplary aspects but also the complexity of their writing practice. Christians also wrote about scriptural characters, as in Gregory of Nyssa's *Life of Moses*, or John Chrysostom's *Life of Paul*; there are also biographical features in works such as Gregory of Nazianzus' *encomium* on Athanasius, and an attention to family affection in Gregory's orations on his father, his brother Basil, his brother Caesarius and his sister Gorgonia. Different types of biographical material were also incorporated into other Christian works – for instance, the idealized account of Origen in book VI of Eusebius' *Ecclesiastical History* or the biography of Alypius in Augustine's *Confessions* VI. The *Confessions* itself combines a detailed account of Augustine's early life that is fascinating and unique in its phychological realism[124] with philosophical discussion of memory, time and creation. The more literary of the ascetic lives bear a considerable resemblance to the contemporary *lives* written by pagans about philosophers and 'sophists' (teachers and intellectuals), also presented as larger-than-life models, and praised for their conquest of human weakness and refusal of luxury. Their subjects include sages from the distant or more recent past, such as the lives of Pythagoras by Plotinus, Porphyry and Iamblichus, and Porphyry's *Life of Plotinus*, as well as those of contemporary pagans, as in Eunapius' *Lives of the Sophists* (see p. 681 above). Nicomachus Flavianus' Latin translation of Philostratus' *Life of Apollonius of Tyana* falls into this category, and the lives of Neoplatonist sages were to be continued in the late fifth and sixth centuries in the lives of the philosophers Proclus and Isidore by Marinus of Neapolis and Damascius respectively, with their Christian counterpart, the *Life of Severus* by Zachariah of Mytilene.

XI. ASCETIC LITERATURE

But the later fourth century, and especially the fifth, also saw the prominence of the 'holy man' as a social phenomenon and exemplar, and this too is reflected in the literature of the period. Alongside these more literary works there developed a quite different sort of biographical narrative, including the collection of 'lives' of the desert fathers, built from oral material and written down over a long process of redaction. Already in the early fifth century the *Historia Monachorum*, a Latin version of the Greek original by Rufinus of Aquileia, and Palladius' *Lausiac History* testify to the existence of a luxuriant mass of stories and 'sayings'. If the *Life of Antony* was a seminal work, it belonged nevertheless in a context against which it can at least partly be explained. *Lives* of Pachomius, the other great father of Egyptian monasticism (d. 346/7), were written soon after his death, in Greek and in several Coptic versions.[125] Fifth-century Syria produced a

---

[124] For an illuminating brief discussion of its 'biographical' aspects see Clark (1993) ch. 2.
[125] On Greek and Coptic in fourth-century Egypt, see the corrective to previous views in Bagnall, *Egypt* 235–55.

further example in Theodoret's *Historia Religiosa*, a collection of accounts of holy men (and some women) whom Theodoret had himself encountered as bishop of Cyrrhus.

A dense and complex ascetic literature, ranging from the more or less popular to the highly rhetorical, thus developed in the eastern empire from the fourth century onwards, and quickly spread to the west. Here especially we encounter the mixture of styles and literary levels, and the 'shock of the new' experienced by some traditionally educated converts, like Augustine's friends, on encountering the ideas contained in a work like the *Life of Antony*. Rufinus and Palladius, like Theodoret, were highly educated enthusiasts who made stories of monks and ascetics available to their own circles; indeed, it was difficult to restrain the eagerness of aristocratic parties of clerics and ladies who travelled as religious tourists to see the fathers of the Egyptian desert. Ascetic literature also took more didactic forms – for instance, in the treatises on virginity by authors such as Gregory of Nyssa, or in the late-fourth-century writings of Evagrius Ponticus or the so-called 'Macarian' homilies (written in Greek, and attached to the name of Macarius of Egypt, though in fact reflecting a Syrian background). There were many degrees and shades of asceticism; nor was the desert by any means as much populated by simple uneducated monks as some of the surviving 'sayings' like to suggest. Evagrius of Pontus (d. 399) had been ordained in Constantinople by Gregory of Nazianzus and spent time in Jerusalem before going to live at Nitria. The desert fathers were deeply divided on doctrinal matters, and Evagrius was later condemned for his Origenism; yet his voluminous ascetic writings were enormously influential, both in the west, through the intermediary of John Cassian's Latin *Conferences*,[126] and in the east in the continuous tradition of orthodox monastic spirituality. Evagrius' writings established a typology and a vocabulary of ascetic psychology and spiritual progress: key terms are *logismoi* (evil thoughts, temptation) and *apatheia* (absence of passion, ascetic control). Similar, though less formalized, ideas found expression in all sorts of writing, especially from the late fourth century onwards; the very range of ascetic literature and hagiography is enormous, even in the fourth century, from the highly literary, with strong influences from classical rhetoric, to the semi-popular, the oral and apocryphal.[127] New martyrologies of earlier (often legendary) martyrs were soon joined, especially from the fifth century, by appropriate narratives about the saints whose cult centres were now developing. Three fifth-century *Lives*, two Greek, one

---

[126] The impact of eastern ascetic thought and writing on the west is one of the most important themes of the fifth century: see Markus, *End of Ancient Christianity* 163–7; 181–97. Markus, whose focus is on the west, stresses asceticism as producing a closing in of horizons, against the view presented here.

[127] For the difficulties inherent in the term 'popular', and for the interplay of oral and literary, see Cameron, Averil, *Rhetoric of Empire*, especially ch. 3. For asceticism see also ch. 20 above.

Syriac, survive of Symeon the Stylite (d. 459), whose great shrine was at Qal'at Siman, between Antioch and Aleppo, and a further example is the anonymous Greek *Life and Miracles of Thecla*,[128] the wholly fictional but highly popular virginal saint made famous by the late-second-century *Acts of Paul and Thecla* and featuring in such learned fourth-century texts as the *Symposium* of Methodius (d. 312) and the *Life of Macrina* by Gregory of Nyssa; her cult centred on her great shrine at Seleucia in Isauria, visited by Egeria on her journeyings in the east in 384.

Christian literature in late antiquity allowed more space to women – as subjects, even if not as authors. Macrina, Gorgonia and Gregory Nazianzen's mother Nonna are balanced in the west by the two Melanias, the Elder and the Younger, as the subjects of Christian writing, and some 'desert mothers' can be found in the monastic literature; Therasia, the wife of Paulinus, and Augustine's mother Monica are known to us, at least indirectly, as are Jerome's friends Marcella, Paula and the rest, and Olympias, the loyal friend of John Chrysostom. Writings by women themselves are, however, few.[129] One of the best-known is the vivid and highly personal diary which the western pilgrim Egeria wrote about her experiences while visiting the Christian holy places in the east in the early 380s; it records real life in the late fourth century, unencumbered by literary considerations. Egeria was writing to instruct, and in most cases the writing of lives also aimed at providing models for emulation. These works were not just 'literature': they were presented as explicit teaching-aids, providing ideals of behaviour for contemporary Christians to follow. This is why John Chrysostom advocated the reading of the *Life of Antony*, and why that and similar works had such a strong effect. Christian biography was not a matter of psychological analysis or even realistic detail, but of models and types. Eusebius saw in Constantine's banquet for the bishops a type of Christ in heaven with the apostles[130] and Moses as a type for Constantine. Similarly, the subjects of Christian biography, literary or not, were simultaneously types for the average Christian to follow and types of Christ.

XII. THEOLOGICAL WORKS

An enormous number of technical works of theology survive from the period – doctrinal treatises such as Athanasius' *De Incarnatione*, Gregory of Nyssa's *Contra Eunomium* or *De Virginitate*, commentaries on the scriptures,

---

[128] Above, ch. 21, p. 633.

[129] 'Proba' is also said by Isidore of Seville to have written in addition to her cento on the life of Jesus a poem on war dealing with the rebellion of Magnentius against Constantius II; the date is debated, but the attempt by Shanzer (1986) to identify the poet as the wife of the cos. of A.D. 371 rather than as Faltitia Betitia Proba, wife of the *praef. urb.* of A.D. 351 has not found favour (see Barnes (1991) 350–1).   [130] *V. Const.* III.15.

polemical treatises, sermons, letters. Traditionally, they have been thought to fall outside the realm of literature. Yet they too have a claim to be included in any study of late antique culture. Even when they seem to show few direct traces of secular rhetoric, as is the case, for instance, with Athanasius, these works not only have a power and vigour of their own, but also mark the evolution of a distinct categorization of knowledge. In this process, it is difficult to separate the thought from its verbal expression. Many patristic works in both Latin and Greek draw heavily on the long tradition of expressing Christian thought in terms of Platonic vocabulary and categories; this, together with the widespread influence of philosophy noted above, led to the gradual development of a genuinely Christian philosophy, a process in which Augustine led the way.[131]

Taken as a group, the theological writings of the period have a major cognitive importance; they represent a sustained series of attempts to reclassify human and divine knowledge within clear and authoritative categories which will correspond to the increasing social and institutional power of the church. In all their variety of forms, the theological writings constitute a major attempt to reformulate and control human knowledge; their subject matter embraces the nature of God and the nature of man, cosmology and morals. The process of classification and categorization had profound social and intellectual implications; this was the period when the foundations both of medieval and of Byzantine theology were laid down, and when the implications of Christianity as a dominant state religion were first felt. To a considerable degree this was achieved by defining deviance – what orthodox Christianity was not to be – a process to which the *Panarion* of Epiphanius, half fantasy, half demonology, gave a powerful impetus. An intellectual apparatus would be required for times of need. We can perhaps see this period still as one of competition and fluidity, but bishops would soon find it useful, especially from the time of the council of Chalcedon (A.D. 451), to have to hand collections of quotations (*florilegia*) designed to prove a particular case.[132] The process of definition was to go on for centuries. But at least some part of this body of knowledge and, even more important, of this way of thinking was gradually percolating into the general consciousness.

The reception of such ideas does not have to be ascribed only to reading by the general public of literary or theological works whose actual circulation will no doubt have been very limited. Their authors were often leading and active churchmen, whose ideas had a direct oral impact; an individual writer often wrote many different kinds of work, and thus had multiple ways of transmitting ideas; the writers were often known to or connected

---

[131] This, not literary culture, is the theme of Pelikan (1993), which focuses on the Cappadocians.
[132] See above, ch. 19.

with each other, and did not write in isolation; finally, the content of such writing found its way into sermons orally delivered, had practical import through the results of church councils, and found expression in visual art.[133] Looking at the characteristic metaphors, types of argument and themes of this vast mass of literature is an essential step to understanding the process of contemporary cultural change. That so many highly trained individuals in this period chose to devote themselves to this kind of composition rather than to stay within the bounds of traditional secular culture is indicative in itself of the cultural changes that were taking place. Indeed, the internal conflicts within the church thus emerge as one of the most powerful stimulants to literary production in the period.

XIII. CONCLUSION

The term 'literary culture' begs many questions. In particular, it conceals the actual significance during this period of oral communication (I leave visual art for the relevant chapter (pp. 736–61 below), though the same argument holds good there, too). Late antique towns were theatrical places, and churches soon began to compete for the crowds, as preachers railed against the competition from theatres, spectacles and baths. The manner and style of traditional rhetoric were still part of urban life, just as they were part of the law and of all dealings with the administration. The rise to public prominence after Constantine of great Christian orators like Gregory of Nazianzus and preachers like John Chrysostom or Ambrose introduced a different repertoire of images and a different set of assumptions; but they were all the more effective in that they drew on familiar technical models in order to put them across. Preaching is the hidden iceberg of Christian culture in this period. It reached the classes untouched by classical literary culture, until, as an increasing number of members of the traditional literary élite, such as Augustine and his circle, the Cappadocians or Paulinus of Nola, turned their energies away from their own intellectual background, the mental models and categories of society began to change with them. While John Chrystostom was perhaps the most brilliant preacher, as befitted his prominent position in both Antioch and Constantinople, Augustine was the most acutely aware of what preaching implied, and of the mental reversal it might bring. His techniques were carefully thought out, and built on careful consideration of how to fit Ciceronian precepts to Christian needs. He was deeply conscious of the different rhetorical strengths of the scriptures, and the *De Doctrina Christiana* contains an admiring rhetorical analysis of the famous passage in 2 Corinthians 11 where St Paul defends himself against his critics;[134] like

---

[133] See Cameron, Averil (1997a).   [134] *De Doctr. Christ.* IV.13.

Paul, Augustine well understood that the 'foolishness' in the eyes of men could in its reversal of convention be a source of power. The cumulative message of all these sermons, sometimes taken down by stenographers for later circulation, purveyed a powerful image: the conventional assumptions, the cultural models on which contemporary life was based, were to be turned inside out in favour of 'a new song'. 'In order to learn what the new song is we must first learn what the new life is';[135] old systems of understanding were to be replaced by new ones.

Because of the nature of the evidence, we have little or no access for this period to the habitual metaphors and patterns of speech which can chart the course of change in other societies, but we do have an enormous amount of literary material. It is true that by far the greater part comes from a limited social class, and is imbued by the traditional norms of formal rhetoric. However, two facts stand out: first, the sheer quantity of the literary material, not to mention the amount of oratory and preaching which has left no written trace, and second, the strong impression, even within the limits of the surviving material, of variety, conflict and cultural change. Previous discussions of Christianity and classical culture have focused mainly on the formal literary elements, especially genre development and the Christian use or rejection of classical models. The relation of Christian and pagan literature has too often been presented in terms of an assumed 'conflict', when appropriation and assimilation provide better tools of analysis. But just as ancient historians are becoming accustomed to giving importance to the power of images from visual art, so it is opportune now to extend that approach to the role played by literature, cognitive processes and communication in bringing about cultural change.

This survey may appropriately conclude, therefore, by suggesting some ways forward along these lines. The literature of late antiquity shows, on the one hand, a strong sense of continuity with the past, yet it gives on the other hand a powerful impression of change. New metaphors, different explanatory systems and different cultural models were being disseminated – an uncomfortable process at any time, and one that gives rise to uneasy and contradictory responses from contemporaries. The change is obviously related to, but not by any means coterminous with, Christianization. In order to appreciate it better, and to read late antique literature both as a cultural product and an indicator, we would do well to look at such issues as audience and reception, prevailing images or metaphors, the texture of language (not easy, in view of the nature of the available evidence), the preferred explanatory systems and the relation (not necessarily the difference) between popular and educated beliefs and their expression.

One illustration may be enough to indicate the richness of the potential

---

[135] Aug. *Serm.* 34.1.

field for this sort of enquiry. It has long been traditional to present this period in terms of a supposedly growing irrationality, which is linked in turn to an increased religiosity or, to put it more bluntly, superstition. How to avoid these rationalist assumptions? Elusive concepts like irrationality, or even 'spirituality', rest not only on enlightenment rationalism, but also on a particular conception of religion. Yet much of the Christian theological literature of the period was in fact aimed less at changing the consciousness of spirituality than at changing existing patterns of thought. Throughout this period and later, Christian writers composed treatises attacking astrology and fate; it was a theme especially liable to crop up in the many commentaries on the creation accounts in the book of Genesis, like Basil's *Hexaemeron* (commentary on the account of the six days of creation), where he argues against the notion that the heavenly bodies could have any power of their own. The targets of these Christian attacks included both pagan philosophical systems and popular belief; their agenda was to change the prevailing, and strongly held, explanatory system in a very thoroughgoing way. At least in the popular sphere, their arguments and strictures probably had little effect: belief in astrology was still a major concern for the church in the seventh century, and indeed probably at all periods.[136] Nevertheless, this example allows us to see theological writing in cognitive terms as an 'expert system'; even if its precepts were not readily accepted (and they too took various forms), it represented a major attempt to replace prevailing cultural assumptions. In its many varied forms, so did the whole spread of Christian writing.

Two further questions suggest themselves: first, why did classical models continue to be so dominant, and second, what were the cultural implications of this dominance? Given the conservative nature of imperial literary culture in general, the first can be answered simply: *imitatio*, a central principle in classical literature since Hellenistic times, had been greatly reinforced by the Second Sophistic movement, and short of a fundamental change in the educational system itself it was bound to remain so, as indeed it did right through the Byzantine period. It is not the practice of *imitatio* but the deviation from it that has to be explained. The second question is more difficult. Not only does it take us back to the issues of the overlap between what is classical and what is pagan and the inherent élitism of classicizing literature, but it also implies a limitation of subject matter; one could not easily write in classicizing style about subjects outside the repertoire of Virgil or the other great writers, as is shown by the contortions to which some Christian writers were prepared to go in their efforts to fit Christian subject matter into classical moulds. Moreover, while the technical requirements of composition remained so high, the majority of the

<hr/>

[136] See Amand (1945).

population was excluded from literary activity, either as writers or as audience; thus literary expertise, even of a superficial kind, itself constituted a desirable social commodity. A widening of the range would have meant dilution, and there are no signs that any attempts were made in this direction outside Christian circles; on the contrary, as the traditional culture became more difficult to obtain, especially in provinces infiltrated by barbarians, the value attached to technical skill and the degree of actual preciosity correspondingly rose. This apparent preference of form over content has led in the past to a general disparagement of late Roman – not to speak of Byzantine – literature. The same attitude (deep-rooted in our own cultural assumptions) leads to an underestimation of the volume of actual literary activity and to the tendency to evaluate even so powerful a writer as Ammianus within an overall conception of decline. Such is the power of these assumptions that until recently late Roman literature has generally been studied only by specialists and from a historical point of view. Only very rarely as yet, if at all, have any late antique writers been subjected to a genuinely literary-critical approach. Yet this is the challenge that would move the subject on from literary history to the history of culture.

CHAPTER 23*a*

SYRIAC CULTURE, 337–425

SEBASTIAN BROCK

I. INTRODUCTION

Around the turn of the Christian era the Fertile Crescent had witnessed the emergence of a number of local Aramaic dialects in written form: Nabataean (from the second century B.C.), Palmyrene (from mid first century B.C.), an early form of Syriac (Proto-Syriac; from the early first century A.D.),[1] and Hatran (from the first century A.D.). All these dialects are known only from inscriptions (and, in the case of Nabataean and Proto-Syriac, a few documents on papyrus and skin); only in the case of Proto-Syriac is it certain that the dialect was used for literary purposes as well (though the few literary texts from the first to the third century come down to us in the slightly different later form of the language known as Classical Syriac). Some sixty or so short Proto-Syriac inscriptions from Edessa and its vicinity, dating from the first to the third century A.D., have been found, the majority of which are cultic or funerary (the latter often accompanied by mosaic portraits executed in a Parthian style). Of exceptional interest are three Syriac legal documents dating from 240, 242 and 243, the last found at Dura Europos, and the other two associated with a collection of seventeen Greek documents from Mesopotamia dating between 232 and 252.

Since Syriac, the Aramaic dialect of Edessa (modern Urfa),[2] soon became the literary vehicle for Aramaic-speaking Christianity, this dialect (in its Classical form) rapidly spread over a wide area as a literary language, both in the eastern provinces of the Roman empire, and over the border into the Parthian (subsequently Sasanian) empire.

The origins of Syriac literary culture were thus unlike those of Armenian and Georgian, where it was Christianity which provided the initial stimulus for using the spoken language as a vehicle for literature. There is considerable resemblance, on the other hand, with the situation for Coptic: both

---

* Nearly complete bibliographical coverage can be found by consulting Moss (1962), Brock (1973–92). [1] See Jenni (1965).

[2] Ancient writers use a variety of different terms for Syriac, the most precise being 'Edessene' and 'the language of Mesopotamia'. The dialects of Aramaic spoken in Syria I and II to the west of the Euphrates will have been somewhat different.

708

literary cultures have a long ancestry, embodied in earlier forms of the two languages, Aramaic and Egyptian; and in both cultures, it was the adoption of the local written language for literary use by non-Greek-speaking Christians that ensured the success of these two languages – and indeed their survival (albeit in a very attenuated form) to the present day.

The history of Syriac literary culture prior to the fourth century is extremely obscure, with only a small number of texts surviving. Among the rare pagan texts is a philosophical letter from Mara to his son Serapion, variously dated to soon after A.D. 70 to *c.* 260. Original Syriac compositions include the *Book of the Laws of the Countries* (see p. 713 below), the *Acts of Thomas* and (perhaps) the *Apology of Ps. Melito*, all of the third century. Of early translations from Greek, besides the Old Syriac Gospels, there are the *Hypomnemata* of Ambrosius (a recension of Ps. Justin, *Cohortatio ad Graecos*), the *Apology* of Aristides, and the *Sayings* of Menander (unconnected with the Greek Menander tradition).

Only towards the middle of the fourth century does Syriac literature begin to emerge from its initial period of obscurity, thanks to the preservation of quite extensive works by two major writers, Aphrahat writing in the Sasanian empire between 337 and 345, and Ephrem (d. 373) in the Roman empire, based first at Nisibis (until it was ceded to the Sasanians in 363) and then at Edessa. Other extant writings from the period 337–425 are rather few, especially by comparison with the very abundant literary production that has been preserved from the following two centuries prior to the Arab invasions.

From the Sasanian empire we have the *Book of Steps* (*Liber Graduum*), a collection dating from *c.* 400 of thirty ascetic discourses which bear some resemblance to the Greek *Macarian Homilies* (of Syrian or Mesopotamian origin); the earliest acts of Christian martyrs put to death under Shapur II; and the earliest synodical literature (concerning synods of the Persian church in 410, 420 and 424).

From the Roman empire there are the poets Cyrillona (one of whose poems is on the invasion of the Huns in 396),[3] Balai (d. after 436), author of a cycle of twelve narrative poems on the biblical patriarch Joseph (a work later attributed to Ephrem), and Isaac of Amida, who is said to have visited Rome and written poems on the Secular Games held in 404 and on the sack of the city by Alaric in 410.[4] Other shadowy figures survive only in Armenian translation (e.g. 'Aitalaha' and Pseudo-Ephrem, author of an *Exposition of the Gospel*) or in excerpts (e.g. Abba, another disciple of

---

[3] This invasion also provided the setting for the delightful story of Euphemia and the Goth (ed. Burkitt (1913)), which dates from just after the period under consideration.

[4] Ps.-Dionysius of Tel-Mahre, *Chronicle* I (ed. Chabot, *CSCO* 121, pp. 32, 143–4); these are unfortunately not to be found among the many extant poems under the name of Isaac (many of which must belong to two later Isaacs).

Ephrem, and the poet Aswana). The earliest Syriac hagiography dates from this period and includes the acts of the Edessene martyrs Shmona, Gurya and Habbib (probably martyred 309 and 310),[5] the story of the Man of God (see p. 718 below), and the prose and verse panegyrics on Abraham of Qidun (*fl.* 355/6 according to the *Chronicle of Edessa* XXI; both works were later attributed to Ephrem). From the very end of the period comes the *Teaching of Addai*, describing the origins of Christianity in Edessa, based on the apocryphal correspondence between king Abgar the Black and Jesus (which was already known to Eusebius, *HE* 1.13);[6] closely associated with this work are two Edessene martyr acts, equally legendary, of Sharbel and Barsamya, allegedly martyred under Trajan. It is likely that some of the imaginative anonymous works on biblical figures, in both prose and verse, belong to the early fifth century. Translations from Greek of several fourth-century Christian writings were also undertaken (see p. 718 below).

What survives from the period is sufficient to indicate both the multifarious character and the sophistication of Syriac culture. Here it is worth reflecting on the reasons why hardly any pre-fourth-century and comparatively little fourth-century literature survives, for it is clear that what comes down to us is only a fragment of what must once have existed. Syriac literature has been transmitted largely thanks to monastic copyists and libraries, and so the selection of texts copied will reflect the interests and concerns of these scribes and their patrons. One obvious consequence of this was the loss of writings by authors (such as Bardaisan and Mani) whose views were later considered heterodox.[7] But there is a further important consideration – namely, a change in literary taste which evidently took place in the early Arab period, and which we are able to observe thanks to the preservation of a sizeable number of Syriac manuscripts which date from the fifth and sixth centuries: had these not been preserved[8] we would be vastly poorer in our knowledge of pre-sixth-century Syriac literature, for a large number of the texts preserved in these early manuscripts were never subsequently recopied (or, if they were, it was mostly in excerpted form). Thus, for example, but for the survival of nine (often fragmentary) manuscripts of the fifth and sixth centuries, we should have none of the hymn

---

[5] Shmona and Gurya were executed on 15 November, and Habbib burnt on 2 September, but the evidence for the years in question is conflicting; see Burkitt (1913) 29–34.

[6] On this see Brock (1996).

[7] This also applies, *a fortiori*, to pagan religious literature (some excerpts, possibly genuine, from Baba, a third-century pagan prophet of Harran, are preserved at the end of a collection of Greek pagan prophecies (related to the Greek Theosophia), compiled in Syriac *c.* 600: cf. Brock (1983a)). For the scanty remains on papyri of Manichean literature in Syriac, see Burkitt (1925) 111–19; the recent discovery in Egypt of fragments of a Manichean bilingual Syriac-Coptic literary work (see ch. 23(b), p. 735 below) is of great significance for the way in which Manichean texts travelled (a Greek intermediary had previously been considered a *sine qua non*).

[8] Largely thanks to the bibliophile Moses of Nisibis, abbot of the Syrian monastery in the Wadi Natroun, Egypt, in the early tenth century.

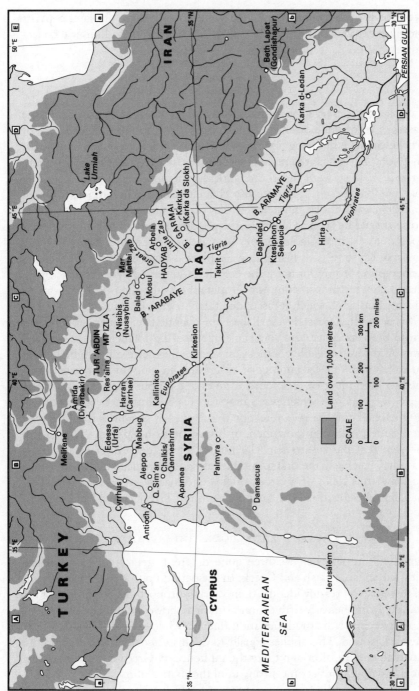

Map 9 Syriac centres in the Middle East

cycles of the most famous of all Syriac authors, Ephrem, for later copyists simply excerpted and abbreviated single hymns for use in liturgical collections.

II. LITERARY GENRES

Two aspects deserve special mention. Several prose writings incorporate passages, often quite extensive, where use is made, for heightened effect, of artistic prose, employing a variety of rhetorical features such as isocola, anaphora, chiasmus, rhyme and assonance. In a few cases (e.g. Ephrem, *Sermo de Domino Nostro*) an entire work is written in this style. It is striking that many of these features are also characteristic of contemporary Greek *Kunstprosa*, but Greek influence in this case is unlikely, for Syriac artistic prose should be seen as a largely independent phenomenon which developed out of earlier traditions of Aramaic prose (examples of which are preserved in some early inscriptions, in biblical Aramaic, and in the Genesis Apocryphon from Qumran): the fact that Greek and Syriac artistic prose share many features in common simply reflects the rhetorical fashions of the time, fashions which transcended the barriers of language.

Syriac metre is based on syllabic, not quantitative, principles. Ephrem wrote both narrative and stanzaic verse; for the former (the *mēmrā*) he employed seven-syllable couplets, and since this metre came to be known under his name a large number of *mēmrē* definitely not by him were attributed to him. Most of Ephrem's large poetic output consists of stanzaic verse (the *madrāshā*, which was sung); for this he employs over fifty different metres (known as *qālē*, referring to the titles of the tunes to which they were sung). Although Sozomen, in his chapter on Ephrem (*HE* III.16), asserted that Bardaisan's son Harmonius, being 'deeply versed in Greek learning', had been 'the first to subdue his native tongue to metres and metrical law', this claim of a Greek origin for Syriac poetry is highly unlikely and should be dismissed as a manifestation of Greek cultural chauvinism.

III. THE THREEFOLD INHERITANCE

Syriac culture was heir to three quite different literary cultures: ancient Mesopotamian, Jewish and Greek. In the period up to 425, elements from all three can be readily identified, in varying proportions, in the extant literature; from the early fifth century onwards, however, the Greek element rapidly becomes the predominant influence, while the other two fade into the background. This applies equally to the history of Syriac culture in the Sasanian empire, although there the influence of Greek culture on Syriac literature does not become strong until the sixth century.

The only ancient Mesopotamian text of non-Jewish provenance to reach

Syriac is the story of Ahiqar; fragments of the earlier Aramaic text from which the Syriac ultimately derives are known from the Elephantine papyri (fifth century B.C.). The Mesopotamian literary genre of precedence-dispute continued to enjoy great popularity in Syriac, normally in verse form; Ephrem already adapts the genre to Christian use, with formal disputes between Death and Satan, and it is likely that several of the delightful anonymous Syriac dispute and dialogue poems go back to the early fifth century.[9] Other traces of the ancient Mesopotamian heritage are chiefly discernible in the transmission of certain ancient religious themes such as the 'medicine of life' (Akkadian *sam balāṭi*, Syriac *sam ḥayyē*) which were Christianized at an early date and so made part of Syriac liturgical vocabulary.[10]

The Jewish heritage is most obviously reflected by the Syriac translation of the Hebrew Bible (Old Testament); this is not a unified work, but it is likely that most books were translated somewhere around the second century A.D. – some, at least, probably by Jews rather than Christians. Certain books (notably the Pentateuch and Chronicles) have some indirect links with an early form of the Jewish Aramaic biblical translations known as the Targums. Jewish influence also came through translations of various non-canonical books, such as the Apocalypse of Baruch (preserved complete only in Syriac) and the Apocalypse of Ezra, or through oral tradition. The latter channel is probably the source of the several striking links with Jewish exegetical tradition which are to be found above all in Ephrem's *Commentary on Genesis*, and in the Syriac compilation, composed in the tradition of the Jewish 'rewritten Bible', known as the *Cave of Treasures* (whose origins seem to go back to the third or fourth century).

It is disputed whether these non-biblical elements of Jewish provenance go back to the earliest stages of Syriac Christianity (implying a sizeable number of early converts from Judaism – the majority view), or whether they are the result of borrowing at a later stage, in the fourth century (thus H. Drijvers, according to whom earliest Syriac Christianity was overwhelmingly of pagan background).

Greek culture had been an effective presence in the Near East for well over half a millennium by the time of Ephrem's birth, *c.* 306, and the first surviving example of Syriac literature, the *Book of the Laws of the Countries*, from the school of Bardaisan (d. 222), consciously adopts the Greek form of the philosophical dialogue and belongs to the Greek intellectual world.

---

[9] E.g. the Dispute of the Months, which successfully combines the Mesopotamian precedence dispute with the Greek *ekphrasis* tradition.

[10] See especially Widengren (1946). Included in the Mesopotamian heritage was also an Iranian component. By the time the local Christian population of Adiabene came to show an interest in their Mesopotamian past (perhaps the sixth century), knowledge of this was by then only accessible to them by way of the Bible and the Greek chronicle tradition.

Thus it is hardly surprising that even the two fourth-century authors who were writing outside the Roman empire, Aphrahat and the anonymous author of the *Liber Graduum*, both show at least some awareness of Greek rhetorical models; in the case of Aphrahat this is reflected in his very choice of the title 'Demonstrations' (i.e. *Epideixeis*), alongside 'Letters', whereas the author of the *Liber Graduum* seems to aim at some sort of fusion between the *genus demonstrativum* and the *genus deliberativum*. One should, however, be wary of trying to fit all Syriac literature of this period into the straitjacket of Greek rhetorical models (there is better justification in the case of late-fifth- and sixth-century writers).

IV. INTERACTION BETWEEN SYRIAC AND GREEK CULTURE

The interaction between Greek and Syriac culture in Syria and northern Mesopotamia was in fact a complex affair, and in the period under consideration the juxtaposition of the two literary cultures resulted in mutual enrichment, as will be seen below (p. 717). There were in fact no clear-cut boundaries between Greek and Aramaic/Syriac speakers in the provinces of Syria I and II, Euphratesia and Mesopotamia; rather, one should think of this as an area of bilingual overlap, where a substantial proportion of the population will have been to some extent bilingual, and where at least a few of the better educated are likely to have been bicultural as well (even though writers normally confined themselves to a single language; an exception, just after the end of the period under consideration, seems to have been Rabbula, bishop of Edessa (see p. 716 below)). In the towns west of the Euphrates, Greek will have predominated as the language of the educated classes, though some dialect of Aramaic was widespread among the lower classes (cf. Lib. *Or.* XLII.31, referring to it as the language of tinkers), and will have been the norm in the countryside.[11]

John Chrysostom, whose parents were both 'of noble family' from Antioch (Socr. *HE* VI.3) probably did not speak the local Aramaic dialect[12] and referred to it as 'barbaric' (*PG* L.646). Theodore (subsequently bishop of Mopsuestia) and Theodoret (subsequently bishop of Cyrrhus), on the other hand, who were also born of wealthy Antiochene parents, were bilingual (Theodoret's mother tongue was probably Syriac: cf. *Hist. Rel.* XXI.15, and he implies that his Greek culture had to be acquired: *Graecarum Affectionum Curatio* v.75). Both men, though they wrote only in Greek, made use of their knowledge of Syriac in their exegetical works. Severian, bishop

---

[11] Thus Theodoret specifies that the peoples of Osrhoene, Syria, Euphretesia, Palestine and Phoinike all spoke dialects of Aramaic (*Quaestio* 19, *in Judices*).

[12] According to Palladius, *Dial.* v, John's father was a *stratelates*. Compare Theod. *Hist. Rel.* XIII.7, where some 'generals' need an interpreter to speak to the ascetic Macedonius when they visited him just outside Antioch after the riots of 387.

of Gabala, despite his renown for learning and eloquence in Greek, never lost his strong Syriac accent (Socr. *HE* VI.1).

Although local dialects of Aramaic clearly provided the everyday language of the countryside of Syria in the fourth and early fifth century, Edessene Syriac appears only rarely to have been used to the west of the Euphrates during this period: the first known Syriac writers who were active west of the river were Balai (Qenneshrin/Chalkis) and John of Apamea, both writing mainly in the second quarter of the fifth century.[13] This picture is borne out by the incidence of Syriac inscriptions west of the Euphrates: these predominantly belong to north Syria and to the sixth century: only a small number are dated to the fifth century or before, the earliest being a fragmentary bilingual Greek–Syriac inscription of 389 (Babisqa, in the Jebel Barisha, *IGLS* 11.555), followed by another bilingual one of 407 (Burj el Qas, in the Jebel Sim'an, *IGLS* 11.373). We thus have a paradoxical situation: in the sixth century, at a time when the prestige of Greek culture was resulting in ever stronger influence on Syriac literature, Syriac was actually gaining ground as a written language to the west of the Euphrates.

In the fourth and early fifth century, Syriac still tended to be despised as 'barbaric' to the west of the Euphrates, but to the east of the river it could hold its own as a literary language alongside Greek. At Zeugma, one of the main crossing points, the ascetic Publius built two adjacent monastic establishments for his followers, one where Greek was used as the liturgical language, the other where Syriac was employed (Theod. *Hist. Rel.* v.5). Compared with the relative abundance of Greek inscriptions found west of the Euphrates, their paucity to the east of the river is striking, though Greek must have been widely used in towns like Edessa which served as administrative centres. Thus at Nisibis when the priest Akepsimas erected a baptistery in 359/60 during the bishopric of Walgash/Volagesias he recorded this in Greek,[14] rather than in the language of Nisibis' renowned poet Ephrem, his exact contemporary. If some authors, like Eusebius, bishop of Emesa (but who originated from Edessa), chose to write in Greek, this was because their parents had been wealthy enough to afford to send their son away to be educated in Greek schools:[15] at the famous 'Persian School' in Edessa (probably already in existence in the early

---

[13] Syriac writers associated with Antioch are very few and all belong after the period covered here (hence Antioch features only in passing in this chapter).

[14] For the inscription, see Jarry (1972) 242–3 (no. 74). On the other hand, Abraham, bishop of Harran (but originally from the region of Cyrrhus), could not understand Greek (Theod. *Hist. Rel.* XVII.9).

[15] Eusebius made use of his knowledge of Syriac in his exegetical writings (he also knew some Hebrew, an exceptional attainment among Christian biblical exegetes of his time). A poem against riches by Isaac, perhaps Isaac of Amida, describes how the wealthy master goes off wandering in discomfort in his search for education while his servants enjoy a restful life at home (*Carmen* 31, ed. Bickell, II, p. 106).

decades of the fifth century) Syriac was the language of instruction.[16] On the other hand, it is significant that Rabbula, who came from a wealthy family in Chalkis, and who is described by his panegyrist as 'highly educated in Greek literature', evidently chose to write in Syriac[17] as well as in Greek, once he had been appointed bishop of Edessa (412–35).

Thus in the areas where Greek and Syriac culture met, there is likely to have been a gradation, running between those for whom Greek was their only language (both written and spoken), those who were bilingual but wrote only in Greek, those who were bilingual but wrote only in Syriac, and those whose knowledge of Greek was minimal or non-existent. This gradation will have run along lines partly social and partly geographical, west to east, with the sharpest divide being provided by the Euphrates. Aphrahat and the author of the *Liber Graduum*, who both lived beyond the boundaries of the Roman empire, will belong to the last category. Thus neither author shows any direct acquaintance even with Christian Greek literature, and though both authors use quite a number of Greek words (Aphrahat just over sixty, the *Liber Graduum* just over seventy), most of these will have been already familiar from the Syriac Bible, while the others belong to the external trappings of Greek civilization.[18] Both in their mode of expression and in the structure of their thought, these two writers belong to an intellectual world that has far more in common with that of the Bible and the ancient Near East than with that of the Greek cultural world.

The case with Ephrem is rather different, for he is clearly much more aware of the contemporary Greek intellectual climate, and he may have read Greek (though Theodoret states that he did not: *HE* iv.29): he knows, for example, of Albinus' *On the Incorporeal* (*Prose Refutations* ii, p. iii), lists a series of opinions on the soul (*Hymns on Faith* i), and alludes on at least two occasions in his hymns to episodes in Greek mythology (*Hymns on Paradise* iii.8 (Tantalus); *Carmina Nisibena* xxxvi.5 (Orpheus – whose portrayal on a mosaic in Edessa he may well have known)). Moreover, it is important to remember that when he speaks of the 'bitterness of the wisdom of the Greeks' (*Hymns on Faith* ii.24), the term 'Greeks' (*Yawnāyē*) has the sense of 'Hellenes', i.e. pagan Greeks, as it does when Athanasius speaks of 'the wisdom of the Greeks being shown to be foolish' (*De Incarnatione Verbi*

---

[16] The Acts of the second council of Ephesus (449) mention only 'Schools of the Armenians, Persians and Syrians' at Edessa (ed. Flemming, 24–5).

[17] The Syriac writings attributed to him probably date from after 427; this certainly applies to his Syriac translation of Cyril of Alexandria's *Oratio ad Theodosium Imperatorem de Fide*.

[18] Among the communities deported from Syria by Shapur I and II and settled at Gondishapur (Syriac Beth Lapat) and elsewhere, there were Greek-speaking Christians who continued to use Greek in the liturgy (e.g. Chronicle of Seert, *PO* iv.222, Rev Ardashir in Persis). Middle Persian was probably not adopted by Christians in the Sasanian empire as an alternative literary language until the sixth century.

XLVI). Ephrem is not opposed to Greek culture as such, but only to the mis-application of 'pagan wisdom' to Christian theology. As far as he himself is concerned, however, he prefers to express his own extremely sophisti-cated theological thought, not in philosophical categories current in the Greek-speaking world of the time, but in poetic ones where symbol and paradox, rather than definition, serve as the basic tools for discourse.

V. SYRIAC INTO GREEK AND GREEK INTO SYRIAC

In the late fourth and early fifth centuries there was a considerable amount of direct exchange between the two languages in the form of translations in both directions.[19] Jerome, writing in 392 (*De Viris Illustribus* 115), had already read in Greek translation a work by Ephrem on the Holy Spirit (unidentified), and such was the renown of Ephrem as a poet that a number of his works, both verse and prose, were soon rendered into Greek (Sozom. *HE* III.16). The Greek translations of Ephrem's narrative verse reproduce the seven-syllable metre of the original. It so happens that very few of the extant Ephrem Graecus texts can be matched with surviving Syriac originals (a notable exception is the long narrative poem (*mēmrā*) on Jonah). It seems likely that these metrical translations gave rise to the use of syllabic metres for narrative poems actually composed in Greek: this probably applies to the Greek poems, attributed to Ephrem, on Abraham and Isaac (Gen. 22) and on Elijah (1 Kings 17), neither of which has any direct relationship to the various Syriac poems on these topics.

Further witness to the very considerable prestige enjoyed by Syriac poetry in the late fourth and early fifth centuries even in the Greek world is provided by Theodore of Mopsuestia, who mentions that Flavian of Antioch and Diodore of Tarsus translated various Syriac liturgical texts in verse into Greek (*apud* Niketas Akominatos, *Thesaurus* v.30, *PG* CXXXIX.1390C).[20]

Although it remains uncertain whether any of Ephrem's many stanzaic poems (*madrāshe*) were translated into Greek,[21] it is very probable that the *madrāshā* form provides the main source of inspiration for the innovative genre in Greek of the *kontakion*, a form of hymn perfected by Romanos in the early sixth century, but for which the oldest examples (anonymous) probably belong to the fifth century. The borrowing is not, however, a

---

[19] Earlier translations from Syriac into Greek include *The Book of the Laws of Countries*, from the school of Bardaisan, excerpts of which are quoted in Ps. Clement, *Recognitions* IX.19–29, and in Eusebius, *Praep. Evang.* VI.10.1–48.

[20] A famous passage in Augustine's *Confessions* (IX.7) witnesses to the influence of oriental hymnody in the west at this time.

[21] George Synkellos' *Ecloga Chronographica* (ed. Mosshammer, p. 15) contains a quotation from Ephrem which has been identified as *Hymns on Paradise* I.10–11, but the correspondence is not at all close.

mechanical one, for the *kontakion* introduces an important new feature, homotony, which is absent from the Syriac model.

A number of hagiographical works composed in Syriac also found their way into Greek. Most influential of these was *The History of the Man of God*, which, once translated into Greek, was expanded and its hero given the name Alexius (in due course the tale was translated back into Syriac in its expanded form). Another work quickly translated into Greek was the history of the ascetic Abraham of Qidun and his niece Mary, wrongly attributed to Ephrem. The Greek versions of both these hagiographies soon found their way into Latin, where they were to enjoy great popularity in the Middle Ages. Knowledge of the Persian martyrs under Shapur II was brought back to the Roman empire by Marutha, bishop of Martyropolis (Maipharqat), who had been sent by Arcadius on embassy to Yezdegerd I in 408. As a result of the publicity brought by Marutha (already reflected in a Syriac manuscript[22] written in Edessa in November 411, where the names of some Persian martyrs have been added to a calendar), many of the Syriac acts of these martyrs were translated into Greek.

Between the fourth and the seventh centuries an impressively large number of Greek texts, mostly of Christian provenance, was translated into Syriac. This process was evidently well under way before the end of the fourth century. Translations which certainly belong to the period 337–425 are Titus of Bostra's *Against the Manicheans* (only parts of which survive in Greek), the *Clementine Recognitions*, and two works by Eusebius, his *Theophania*, of which only fragments in Greek survive, and the long recension (lost in Greek) of his *Palestinian Martyrs*: all these are included in the Edessene manuscript of 411 just mentioned. Eusebius' *Ecclesiastical History*, and perhaps a number of works by Basil (including his *De Legendis Gentilium Libris*)[23] – all preserved in fifth-century manuscripts – may also antedate 425; in the case of Basil's *Homilies* the Syriac translation is remarkably free and expansive. Probably already in the last decades of the fourth century, sporadic attempts were made to revise the Old Syriac Gospels, bringing the translation closer into line with the Greek original; this process, which probably also covered the rest of the Syriac canon of the New Testament (omitting 2 Peter, 2–3 John, Jude and Revelation), seems to have been completed in the early fifth century, and the revision, subsequently named the Peshitta, became the standard Syriac version of the New Testament.

In the fourth century, then, Syriac literary culture belonged to the east of

---

[22] British Library MS. Add. 12150, which has the distinction of being the earliest dated Christian literary manuscript in any language. The elegant format of this vellum codex suggests that it is the product of an already long-established scribal tradition in Syriac.

[23] The earliest Syriac translations of pagan Greek literature are probably from later in the fifth century; most belong to the sixth to ninth centuries.

the river Euphrates: from its original home in Edessa, it had already spread eastwards, with Christianity, into the Sasanian empire, where it existed alongside two other Aramaic literary dialects associated with other religious communities, Babylonian Jewish Aramaic and Mandaean. By contrast, it was only late in the fifth century, and especially in the sixth, that Syriac culture effectively crossed the Euphrates to extend westwards to the Aramaic-speaking areas of the Mediterranean littoral as well. In its own homeland in the fourth and fifth centuries Syriac culture was experiencing what was perhaps to be its finest outburst of literary creativity, witnessed above all in the outstanding religious poetry of Ephrem.

COPTIC LITERATURE, 337–425

MARK SMITH

Egyptian literature of the period A.D. 337–425 consists entirely of texts written in the Coptic script. Of the earlier forms of writing developed by the Egyptians, hieratic seems to have been the first to fall into disuse. The latest known hieratic texts come from the third century. Hieroglyphic and demotic continued to have a restricted use for some time afterwards. The latest known hieroglyphic inscription was written in 394, the latest demotic text in 452. However, neither form of writing was employed for literary purposes during the period under consideration.[1]

The Coptic script uses the Greek alphabet, augmented by characters borrowed from demotic. The language of texts written in this script represents the final stage in the development of the tongue spoken by the ancient Egyptians. So-called Old Coptic texts provide the earliest specimens of both script and language. These are attested from the first century A.D. onwards; all are magical or astrological.[2] The earliest known Coptic texts, properly speaking, date from the third century, and it is with these that our knowledge of Coptic literature may be said to begin.

Throughout Egypt, Coptic was written in a variety of dialects. Experts disagree over the precise number of these, but it is generally accepted that there were six principal literary dialects. They are: (1) Sa'idic, a dialect of uncertain (Theban?) origin which served as the standard literary language everywhere in the Nile Valley during the period under consideration; (2)

---

* *Bibliographical note.* The chief bibliographical aids for Coptic are the following: Kammerer (1951) (covers materials published prior to 1949); Simon (1949–66), Simon and Quecke (1967), and du Bourguet (1971–6), covering the years 1940–76; Biedenkopf-Ziehner (1972–80), covering the period 1967–79; and Orlandi (1982–), which covers the period 1980 to the present. The most important bibliographies devoted specifically to Coptic literature are those of Krause (1980); Orlandi (1970) 59–158; *idem* (1986). There are also bibliographies dealing with specific genres of Coptic literature; these will be cited below under the appropriate headings. A useful starting point for information on this subject is Orlandi's article on Coptic literature in A. S. Atiya (ed.), *The Coptic Encyclopedia* 5 (1991) 1451–60. The *Encyclopedia* itself contains a wide range of articles on specific authors, texts, and groups of texts discussed in this chapter.

[1] For a convenient account of the history of the various forms of Egyptian writing, see Davies (1987) 16–27.

[2] See Kahle (1954) I, 252–6; Quaegebeur (1982); Satzinger (1991).

Bohairic, the dialect of the western delta and Nitria; (3) Fayyumic, that of the Fayyum; (4) Middle Egyptian, current at Oxyrhynchus and its environs; (5) Akhmimic, whose centre of diffusion was Akhmim; and (6) Subakhmimic or Lycopolitan, which may have been the dialect of the region around Assiut.[3] Not all of these dialects are uniform entities. Early Bohairic, for example, is very different from later Bohairic.[4] Some contemporary groups of Subakhmimic manuscripts display such a large number of divergent features that proposals have been made to identify them as representatives of distinct dialects.[5]

The texts that will be cited in the following pages were inscribed, with rare exceptions, in codices with leaves of papyrus or parchment.[6] Normally, these bear no date, although in cases where the binding of a codex has been preserved, inscribed material found within it can provide valuable clues for dating.[7] Otherwise, the age of the MSS. in question must be determined on palaeographical grounds alone. Coptic palaeography is far from being an exact science; consequently, attempting to date Coptic texts within the narrow limits specified in the heading of the present chapter is a somewhat hazardous enterprise. In many cases, the best that one can do is to assign a text to a particular century, without being more exact. Sometimes not even this is possible; hence the virtual absence of precise dates from the account that follows.[8]

Coptic literature of the period A.D. 337–425 was essentially a functional literature. It was composed for a definite purpose, not simply as fine writing intended to be enjoyed for its own sake. This purpose was invariably religious in nature. Texts were written for use in liturgy and ritual, public worship and private devotion, or for instruction and edification. Another notable feature of Coptic literature during the period under consideration is that most of it was originally composed in other languages, chiefly Greek, and translated into Coptic subsequently. For purposes of discussion, this literature may be divided into six categories: magical texts, the Bible and Apocrypha, patristic and homiletic works, monastic texts and martyrologies, the Nag Hammadi library and related tractates, and Manichean writings.

---

[3] Kahle (1954) I, 193–268, provides a comprehensive treatment of the Coptic literary dialects. Some of his conclusions have been modified by others. For a survey of recent opinions, see Kasser in Atiya (ed.), *The Coptic Encyclopedia* 8, 133–41; also articles *ibid.* on the major dialects by various authors.

[4] Cf. Kasser (1958) vii–xii, Shisha-Halevy (1991a) 57–8.

[5] Funk (1985); Nagel (1991a).

[6] For exceptions, see Kahle (1954) I, 275–6; section IV below.

[7] E.g. Shelton in Barns *et al.* (1981) 1–11.

[8] For the nature of the problems involved in dating Coptic texts, see Layton (1985). Kahle (1954) I, 269–78, published a list of MSS. written prior to the sixth century that were known to him in 1953; this is extremely valuable, but now needs updating.

I. MAGICAL TEXTS

Coptic magical texts as a group can hardly be called literary. However, some contain narrative passages, hymns and prayers which merit that description. The only such specimen from the period under consideration occurs in a codex of fourth-century date discovered at Thebes and now in Paris.[9] The spell in question, written in a form of Old Coptic closely allied to Saʿidic and Bohairic, is designed to gain the love of a recalcitrant woman. Its first half consists of a mythological narrative in which the goddess Isis complains to her father Thoth that she has been betrayed by her husband Osiris. Thoth explains how Isis may rekindle Osiris' love by means of an iron spike which she is to dip in her husband's blood. The second half contains the incantation which the magician must recite in order to enchant the object of his desire.

The two halves of the spell are closely related. The narrative provides the environment within which the incantation can take effect. By ritual allusion to or re-enactment of an event from the mythological sphere, the magician seeks to trigger off or actualize a similar event in his own. Spells like this one are of particular interest since, after the triumph of Christianity in Egypt, it was largely through them that the older pagan religious traditions were preserved.[10]

II. THE BIBLE AND APOCRYPHA

Virtually the earliest written evidence for the transmission of the Bible to the native population of Egypt is a Greek–Coptic glossary to Hosea and Amos.[11] This was inscribed on the verso of a land register late in the third century. The dialect is Middle Egyptian. Roughly contemporary are the Coptic glosses found in a pair of Greek manuscripts, one containing Isaiah[12] and the other the Minor Prophets.[13] The glosses in the former are written in an early type of Fayyumic; those in the latter are written in Saʿidic.

Only a single Coptic biblical text may be dated to this period with certainty. A bilingual school tablet found at Thebes is inscribed with eight verses of Psalm 46 in Akhmimic, as well as a Greek paraphrase of the opening lines of the *Iliad* and miscellaneous exercises.[14] Other Coptic biblical MSS. assignable to the end of the third century or slightly later are a

[9] Preisendanz (1928–31) I, 70–6; cf. Meyer (1985).

[10] Cf. the spell of eighth-century date discussed by Kákosy (1961). Additional bibliography on texts of this genre is given by Donadoni (1987) and Vycichl (1991).

[11] Bell and Thompson (1925).

[12] Crum *apud* Kenyon (1937) ix–xii; Vaccari (1951).

[13] Sanders and Schmidt (1927) 46–8.

[14] Crum (1934–7), amended by Lefort (1935). For the dating, cf. Roberts (1979) 67.

Sa'idic version of Ecclesiastes, now in Louvain;[15] a bilingual codex in Hamburg inscribed with the Acts of Paul in Greek, the Song of Songs and Lamentations in early Fayyumic, as well as Ecclesiastes in both languages;[16] a version of Proverbs in a dialect otherwise unattested;[17] and a codex formerly in the possession of the University of Mississippi containing Melito of Sardis on the Pascha, an extract from 2 Maccabees, 1 Peter, Jonah, and an Easter homily, all in Sa'idic.[18]

It is interesting to note the preponderance of texts belonging to the Old Testament among those described so far. The manuscript evidence of the fourth and fifth centuries presents a very different picture. Here, MSS. inscribed with books of the New Testament may be seen to predominate. Even within the aforesaid period a change is apparent, the ratio of New Testament MSS. to those of the Old Testament being higher in the fifth century than in the preceding one.[19]

It is not clear whether the manuscript evidence reflects a genuine shift in interest or emphasis, or simply an accident of preservation. Whatever the case, the period of the fourth–fifth centuries witnessed a number of undoubted developments in the process of transmission of the scriptures into Coptic. Chief among these must be reckoned the completion and standardization of the Sa'idic version of the Bible, which were probably effected before the close of the fourth century.[20] At the same time, translations were being made into the other principal dialects, although it is not known how much of the Bible was rendered into each one. Nor is the relationship of the various versions to one another fully understood.[21]

With respect to the New Testament, which has been studied more extensively than the Old, there is general agreement that the Bohairic version was made independently of the Sa'idic.[22] Some experts believe that the Fayyumic version of this period was derived partially from the Bohairic.[23] Others accord the Fayyumic priority.[24] The relationship of the remaining versions to the one found in Sa'idic is particularly disputed. Some think that the Akhmimic, Subakhmimic and Middle Egyptian renderings were made independently.[25] Others argue that they were translated from the Sa'idic.[26]

---

[15] Lefort (1940) 59–65 with plate 5.   [16] See Diebner and Kasser (1989).

[17] Kasser (1960a); cf. *idem* (1980) 53 note 4.

[18] Willis (1961) 383–9 with plate 5. On the present location of this manuscript, see Goehring (1991) 657–8.

[19] This estimate is based chiefly on the lists published by Kahle (1954) 1, 269–74, supplemented for the New Testament by Metzger (1977) 108–25. The picture is not altered significantly by material published subsequently.   [20] Mink (1972) 181–2.

[21] For literature on this problem, see references cited by Metzger (1991) and Nagel (1991b). Lists of published MSS. of the different versions have been compiled by Vaschalde (1919–33), Till (1959–60) and Nagel (1989).

[22] For the textual affinities of the two, see Metzger (1977) 133–8; Mink (1972) 161–6, 168–77.

[23] Kahle (1954) 1, 279–85.   [24] Layton (1976) 176.

[25] Weigandt (1969); cf. Mink (1972) 177–87.   [26] Kasser (1965) 302–3.

As will be evident from the above remarks, the history of the Coptic Bible, particularly during the crucial years of the period under consideration, is a subject on which a vast amount of research remains to be done. In this branch of Coptic literary studies, the lack of criteria whereby texts may be dated precisely poses problems of an especially difficult nature, perhaps more so than in any other branch. The need for further investigation into the Coptic versions of the Old Testament is particularly acute.[27]

A large quantity of apocryphal literature has been preserved in Coptic.[28] Both Old and New Testament apocrypha are attested. The earliest known specimens occur in MSS. datable to the fourth century, roughly coeval with some of the early MSS. containing translations of the Bible. Here, I shall mention briefly a number of works that are extant in manuscripts securely dated either to that century or to the subsequent one.

An Apocalypse of Elijah is attested by four codices, three in Sa'idic and one in Akhmimic. All were written either in the fourth or the fifth century.[29] The Akhmimic codex preserves a number of leaves of an untitled apocalyptic work as well.[30] One of the Sa'idic codices has a leaf inscribed with a text of similar contents.[31] This includes the words 'Truly I, Zephaniah, saw these things in my vision', and is presumably a fragment of an apocalypse attributed to the prophet of that name. Some authorities think that the Akhmimic leaves are part of this work as well.[32] Others deny that they have any connection with it.[33]

Fragments of the Testaments of Abraham and Job are preserved in a Sa'idic manuscript of fifth-century date.[34] Another text, variously known as the Ascension or the Vision of Isaiah, is attested by two MSS., both of the fourth century. One is Akhmimic, the other Sa'idic.[35] The work consists of an account of the prophet's martyrdom, followed by a description of an apocalyptic vision which he is said to have witnessed. These and the texts mentioned in the preceding paragraph were translated into Coptic from Greek. The originals may have been composed in a Jewish milieu. However, the Coptic versions of some of them show unmistakable signs of adaptation for Christian use.

Among New Testament apocryphal works may be mentioned the Acts of Paul and the Letter of the Apostles. The former is attested by three manuscripts. Two are of fourth-century date, one of them written in the Akhmimic dialect and the other in a dialect variously described as

---

[27] For recent work in this area, see e.g. Diebner (1985); Nagel (1983–4). Cf. also literature cited by the latter (1991b).

[28] Krause (1980) cols. 697–707 provides a full list of texts. Cf. Orlandi (1983); Perez (1991).

[29] Pietersma *et al.* (1981).   [30] Steindorff (1899) 34–65.

[31] *Ibid.* 110–13.   [32] E.g. Wintermute (1983).   [33] Diebner (1978).

[34] Perez (1991) 164.

[35] For the former, see Lefort (1939) 7–10; Lacau (1946). For the latter, see Lefort (1938) 24–30.

Subakhmimic or Saʿidic.[36] The third manuscript has been assigned to the fifth century; it is written in the Subakhmimic dialect.[37] The Letter of the Apostles purports to record the contents of a revelation made by the risen Jesus to his disciples and followers. This is preserved in an Akhmimic codex of the fourth or fifth century.[38] The Coptic versions of both works have been translated from Greek originals. According to Tertullian, the Acts of Paul were composed by a presbyter in Asia Minor.[39] Some believe that the Letter of the Apostles originated there as well. That such texts were translated into Coptic may be evidence of a connection between Asiatic Christianity and a section of the Christian community within Egypt.[40]

Accounts of the martyrdoms of Peter and Paul are preserved in a Saʿidic manuscript of late-fourth- or early-fifth-century date.[41] Several additional apocryphal works have been preserved among the texts discovered at Nag Hammadi. These are discussed below in the paragraphs dealing with that discovery.

III. PATRISTIC AND HOMILETIC WORKS

Patristic literature in Coptic, at least for the period A.D. 337–425, consisted chiefly if not entirely of works translated from Greek. There is no evidence that any of the Fathers of the church, even those such as Athanasius or Cyril of Alexandria, who lived in Egypt and had extensive dealings with Egyptian monks, ever wrote in the language of that country.[42] According to a tradition preserved by Epiphanius,[43] a certain Hieracas (c. 270–360) was the first to write commentaries and other treatises in Coptic. No trace of his work has survived, unless it be an Akhmimic MS. of fourth-century date containing psalms or hymns which some have attributed to him.[44] This being the case, it is difficult to evaluate the tradition critically.

For the purposes of the present discussion, Coptic patristic literature may be divided into two categories: works preserved in manuscripts of the fourth and fifth centuries, and those preserved in manuscripts of later date. Only a few texts fall into the first category. The treatise on the Pascha by Melito of Sardis is attested by three early manuscripts, one Akhmimic and two Saʿidic, as well as a few fragments.[45] One of the Saʿidic MSS., which also contains Jonah, 1 Peter, an extract from 2 Maccabees, and an Easter homily, was written at the end of the third or the beginning of the fourth century. The other Saʿidic MS. and its Akhmimic counterpart are certainly

---

[36] For the former, see Crum (1919–20) 5; for the latter (P. Bodmer XLI, unpublished), see Kasser (1960b); *idem* (1984) 273–5; Robinson (1990) 376–7.   [37] Schmidt (1904), (1905), (1909).
[38] Schmidt (1919).   [39] *De Baptismo* XVII.5.   [40] Cf. Klijn (1986) 168 note 42; Orlandi (1986) 58.
[41] See von Lemm (1890–2).
[42] Arguments to the contrary are unconvincing, e.g. Lefort (1933a); cf. Draguet (1980) 111*–12*.
[43] *Haer.* LXVII.1.2–3.   [44] Lefort (1939) 1–6; Peterson (1947).
[45] See Goehring (1984); Crum and Bell (1922) 47–9.

of fourth-century date. The translation of this work into Coptic has been
seen as further evidence for a connection between Asiatic Christianity and
certain Christian circles within Egypt.[46]

Among other texts, the Shepherd of Hermas is preserved in an
Akhmimic manuscript of the fourth century[47] and a Saʿidic one of the fifth
century.[48] Coeval with the latter is a Middle Egyptian version of the
Didache.[49] The First Epistle of Clement is attested by two Akhmimic
codices, one dating to the fourth century,[50] the other to the fifth.[51] The
latter contains the Gospel of John and the Epistle of James as well. There
are, in addition, miscellaneous letters and sermons preserved in MSS. of
fourth- or fifth-century date. These are mainly fragments and their authors
have yet to be identified.[52]

Thus far, matters are relatively straightforward. For various reasons,
however, the second category of texts is more problematic. A number of
genuine patristic writings are preserved in Coptic MSS. which postdate the
fifth century. Full lists of these have been compiled by Krause[53] and
Orlandi.[54] Among the authors attested are Athanasius, John Chrysostom,
Cyril of Jerusalem, and the Cappadocians, Basil of Caesarea, Gregory of
Nazianzus and Gregory of Nyssa. Unfortunately, with rare exceptions,
there is no way of knowing when the works of these writers were first
translated and, consequently, it is impossible to say whether Coptic versions of them were in circulation during the fourth and fifth centuries. The
point is well illustrated by the four discourses of Gregory of Nazianzus
preserved in Saʿidic and Bohairic MSS. of the eighth–eleventh centuries.[55]
These may have been translated as early as the fifth century, as the editor
of two of them has suggested,[56] but firm evidence that they were is lacking.

The picture is further complicated by a number of late MSS. containing
works that are falsely attributed to one or another of the church Fathers.
Some are genuine patristic writings that have been credited to the wrong
authors. Others are totally spurious, having been composed in Coptic long
after the end of the period under discussion. Examples in the first category
include a homily of John Chrysostom on the Canaanite woman, wrongly
attributed to Eusebius of Caesarea,[57] and an exegesis of a passage from
Paul's Letter to the Romans, written by Basil but credited to Athanasius.[58]
Both are preserved in a Saʿidic codex of seventh-century date. A good
exemplar of the second category is the cycle of homilies ascribed to

---

[46] Orlandi (1986) 59.   [47] Lefort (1952) ii–iv and 1–18.   [48] *Ibid.* viii–ix and 25–6.
[49] *Ibid.* ix–xv and 32–4.   [50] Schmidt (1908).   [51] Rösch (1910) 1–88.
[52] E.g. Crum (1905) nos. 269, 279, 285, 521, 1220; Till (1931).
[53] Krause (1980) columns 707, 710–11.
[54] Orlandi (1970) 69–88, 115–24. Cf. *idem* (1973), (1984).
[55] For bibliography on the editions of the MSS. in question, see Lafontaine (1981) 38–40.
[56] *Ibid.* 43. The same writer expresses a more cautious view at Lafontaine (1980b) 39 and (1980a)
201.   [57] Mercati (1907).   [58] Orlandi (1975) 52–3.

Theophilus, bishop of Alexandria from 385 to 412.[59] Works of this type will not be taken into consideration here.

In general, it can be said that the translators of patristic literature into Coptic were not interested in theological questions as such. Rather, they were influenced by practical concerns. Texts were selected for translation either because they were valuable for liturgical purposes, or capable of providing moral instruction or spiritual edification.[60]

IV. MONASTIC TEXTS AND MARTYROLOGIES

The rise of monasticism in Egypt produced a voluminous literature; however, much of this postdates the period that concerns us.[61] Pachomius (c. 290–346), the founder of the first cenobitic community, was also, on present evidence, the first to write original literature in Coptic.[62] The texts of three letters written by him for the instruction of his followers have survived on leaves dated to the fifth century.[63] These are in Saʿidic, the dialect spoken by their author, as are all the Coptic MSS. described in this and the next four paragraphs. Additional letters are preserved in the remains of a codex of the sixth century.[64] Greek and Latin versions of Pachomian letters are attested as well.[65] The former are of particular interest because of their early date (fourth century). Some of the letters written by Pachomius employ a form of code, which renders them partially unintelligible.[66]

Two further instructions attributed to Pachomius are preserved in codices of the tenth and eleventh centuries.[67] However, many do not accept these as genuine works of his. The same is true of other fragments attributed to him in a further pair of MSS., one of seventh-century date,[68] the other written in the eleventh century.[69] According to tradition, Pachomius was the first to compose a Rule for his followers; it is probably for this that he is best known. In reality, however, he is unlikely ever to have set a particular code of behaviour down in writing. The various Pachomian rules now extant in Coptic and other languages were composed after his death.[70] Because their character is non-literary, they need not be considered here.

---

[59] Orlandi (1985) 103–4; cf. idem (1973).   [60] Orlandi (1986) 71–2.

[61] For details, see Krause (1980) cols. 709–16.

[62] Rousseau, Pachomius, gives a good account of his life and work. For English translations of the writings by and about Pachomius and his followers, see the three-volume collection of Veilleux (1980–2).

[63] Lüddeckens et al. (1968) 69–85 with plates 1–3; see now Quecke (1975a) 41–2 and 112–16.

[64] Quecke (1975a) 42–52 and 111–18; cf. Quecke (1976) 157.

[65] For the former, see Quecke (1975a) 52–5 and 72–110; for the latter, Boon (1932) 77–101, Quecke (1975a) 55–71.   [66] Quecke (1975a) 18–40.   [67] Lefort (1956a) vi–viii and 1–26.

[68] Ibid. xxi–xxii and 80; cf. Quecke (1975a) 44–6.   [69] Lefort (1956a) viii–ix and 26–30.

[70] See Rousseau, Pachomius 48–53 and passim.

The two most prominent successors of Pachomius were Theodore and Horsiesios. The former (d. 368) is claimed as the author of a series of catecheses preserved in two codices of ninth-century date, as well as of fragments of instructions in a codex of the eleventh century.[71] It is not certain that these were actually written by him. Also extant are two letters addressed by Theodore to the Pachomian community. One is attested by two MSS. of fifth- and sixth-century date.[72] The other is preserved only in a Latin translation.[73]

Four further letters are attributed to Horsiesios (d. c. 380). Two occur in a manuscript of fifth- or sixth-century date,[74] the other two in somewhat later papyrus rolls.[75] One of the first pair is addressed to Theodore. Horsiesios is also said to have written a series of instructions and a set of rules.[76] These are preserved in a number of codices ranging in date from the seventh to the eleventh century. Some authorities believe that the instructions are spurious. The style of the rules is more obviously literary than that of the Coptic rules attributed to Pachomius.[77] A final work, the so-called Testament of Horsiesios, is known only in a Latin translation.[78] This, like the other extant Latin versions of Pachomian writings, was made by Jerome near the beginning of the fifth century. Although no Coptic text of the work has survived, it is widely accepted as having been written by Horsiesios. Among other things, it sets out the responsibilities of monastic superiors to those in their charge and explains the duties of ordinary monks towards those who lead them. Two central themes of the Testament are the need for obedience and the evil of withholding one's property from the goods held in common by the community. This, it is known from other sources, caused serious problems for Horsiesios during the time when he was leader of the monks.[79]

A further disciple and contemporary of Pachomius, Karour by name, is credited with an obscure work of prophetic character preserved in two manuscripts of the ninth century.[80] It is uncertain whether this attribution is correct. The earliest Coptic version of the Life of Pachomius occurs in a codex of sixth-century date. But it is widely believed that a form of this Life was in circulation a generation or two after Pachomius' death.[81]

The most important author of original literature in Coptic was the archimandrite Shenoute of Atripe (d. 466).[82] In the course of his long life (over one hundred years), he wrote numerous letters, catecheses and sermons on

---

[71] Lefort (1956a) xii–xvii and 37–62.   [72] Krause (1981); Quecke (1975b).
[73] Boon (1932) 105–6.   [74] Lefort (1956a) xvii–xviii and 63–6.   [75] Orlandi (1981).
[76] Lefort (1956a) xviii–xxx and 66–79, 81–99.   [77] On this development, see Orlandi (1986) 60–3.
[78] Boon (1932) 109–47.   [79] Cf. Rousseau, *Pachomius* 157–8, 184–91.
[80] Lefort (1956a) xxx–xxxi and 100–4. Translation: *idem* (1956b) 100–8.
[81] For the Coptic versions, see Lefort (1933b), *idem* (1925). On the relationship of these with the other versions, see Goehring (1986) 3–23, and literature cited there.
[82] See Timbie (1986).

a range of subjects, including moral questions of all sorts, refutations of heretical doctrines, and condemnations of pagan beliefs and practices.[83] All of his works were composed in the Saʿidic dialect, in some cases tinged with Akhmimic.[84] With rare exceptions, Shenoute's writings cannot be dated precisely, or even to a specific period within his lifetime. Consequently, it is impossible to say how many of them were in circulation before the year 425, the end of the period under consideration, and how many were written afterwards.

The manuscripts which preserve Shenoute's literary output today were inscribed long after his death. In some cases, later scribes attributed works to him of which he was not the author. Fortunately, Shenoute's style is so distinctive that one can recognize such cases without much difficulty. Equally, it is possible to identify writings as his even when no author is named.[85] Shenoute's chief contribution to the development of Coptic literature lies in the fact that he was the first to apply the rules of Greek rhetoric to the production of original works in his native language.[86]

The most important texts written by or about Egyptian monks that circulated in Coptic during the period that concerns us are those composed by Shenoute and by Pachomius and his followers. The contribution in this sphere made by other monastic figures is more difficult to assess. Antony (c. 251–356) is a case in point. Fragments of letters alleged to have been written by him are preserved in a Saʿidic MS. of the eleventh century.[87] However, it is not certain that they are actually his work. If they are, then was their original language Greek or Coptic? If the former, then uncertainty persists regarding the date of their translation.[88] One of the most valuable sources of information about monastic life in the fourth and fifth centuries is the *Apophthegmata Patrum*, a record of the wise sayings of the anchorites who inhabited the settlements of Nitria and Scetis. Although these may have circulated orally during the period under consideration, they were not collected in written form until after the middle of the fifth century, and then only in Greek. The extant Coptic translation must have been made at some point subsequent to that time.[89]

Martyrologies are relatively rare in Coptic MSS. of early date.[90] Only a few have been preserved in codices written in the fourth or fifth centuries. A fragment of one is known from a Saʿidic manuscript written in the fifth

---

[83] For bibliography, see Frandsen and Richter-Aerøe (1981). [84] Shisha-Halevy (1976).

[85] On the distinctive features of Shenoute's Coptic, see Shisha-Halevy (1991b) and literature cited there. For lists of genuine works by him, see Orlandi (1986) 66–9; Shisha-Halevy (1986) 215–20.

[86] Orlandi (1986) 64–70. On the character of Shenoute's writings, see also works cited by Krause (1980) columns 712–13; Shisha-Halevy (1986) 3–5.

[87] Garitte (1955) iv and 11–12, 20–2, 28–9, 41–6.

[88] Cf. Orlandi (1986) 63–4.

[89] See Orlandi (1970) 130–1 and references cited there.

[90] For those of later periods, the standard work is Baumeister (1972). See also Orlandi (1991a).

century.[91] Unfortunately, the name of the martyr is lost. A Middle Egyptian text tentatively dated to the fourth century may be a further specimen of this genre.[92] It describes conditions during the persecution instigated by Septimius Severus and how these were alleviated by a presbyter called John. The text, in its present form, ends abruptly. Originally, it may have served as the introduction to a longer work. It is clear from allusions in contemporary sources that other Coptic martyrologies must have been in circulation at the same time as these.[93] It is probable, however, that such texts were not very numerous. A recent study has drawn attention to the fact that martyrologies are relatively rare in Greek papyri of the fourth and fifth centuries as well.[94] It may be that the paucity of such works from this time reflects the influence of figures like Shenoute, who inveighed against the excessive veneration of martyrs.[95]

V. THE NAG HAMMADI LIBRARY AND RELATED TRACTATES

The Nag Hammadi library is a group of thirteen Coptic codices discovered in 1945 at the Gebel el-Tarif near the city of Nag Hammadi in Upper Egypt. These were inscribed sometime around the middle of the fourth century. Two complete codices and part of a third are written in a form of Subakhmimic. The remainder are in Saʿidic. Each codex contains one or more tractates. There are fifty-two in total, including six that are duplicates. All are translations of Greek originals. These are chiefly, but not exclusively, gnostic in character.[96] Broadly speaking, the texts may be divided into five categories:

(i) *'Classical' or Sethian gnostic works.* This group of texts accords a place of great importance to Seth the son of Adam, as recipient and transmitter of divine revelation, as progenitor of a pure race of gnostic believers, and as saviour of those descended from him. Most of them presuppose an elaborate mythology in which the deity of the Old Testament appears as an evil demiurge.[97] A good example is the tractate titled the Apocalypse of Adam, which relates the history of mankind from the creation of Eve down to the incarnation of the Saviour and the ultimate triumph of Seth's posterity.[98] Related works include the Apocryphon of John,[99] the Hypostasis of the Archons,[100] and the Gospel of the Egyptians.[101] Experts disagree over

---

[91] Crum (1905) 416 (no. 1002).   [92] Alcock (1982) 1–5, with plate 1.   [93] Cf. Horn (1986) 11–25.
[94] *Ibid.* 11 note 58.   [95] *Ibid.* 1–9.
[96] For the relevant literature, see Scholer (1971), with annual supplements in *Novum Testamentum* from 1971 onwards. The codices themselves are published in Robinson (1972–84) (12 volumes). A convenient collection of translations of the tractates is Robinson (1988).
[97] See Layton (1987) 5–22; Layton (ed.) (1981).   [98] Cf. MacRae (1979).
[99] To date, no critical edition of this work has been published; see Layton (1987) 23–51, with references to relevant literature.   [100] Cf. Bullard and Layton (1989).
[101] Böhlig and Wisse (1975).

whether the texts in this category are the product of a single distinct school of gnostic thought, or the work of like-minded but unassociated individuals.[102] Also disputed is the religious and cultural milieu in which they were written. Some think that they were composed in heterodox Christian circles; others ascribe to them a non-Christian, specifically Jewish, origin.[103]

(ii) *Valentinian gnostic works.* This group comprises works written by the philosopher and theologian Valentinus (*c.* A.D. 100–75) and his followers. Valentinus offered an allegorical interpretation of gnostic mythology, making extensive use of New Testament terminology and concepts.[104] Among the Nag Hammadi tractates, the most important work in this category is the Gospel of Truth, which is widely accepted as a genuine writing of Valentinus himself. The text describes the process whereby the elect, through the gnosis imparted by God's son Jesus, are saved and reunited with him.[105] Other Valentinian works, or works with affinities to this school, preserved in the Nag Hammadi library include the Tripartite Tractate,[106] the Treatise on the Resurrection,[107] and the Gospel according to Philip.[108]

(iii) *Works attributed to the apostle Thomas.* Two works of this type were found at Nag Hammadi: the Gospel according to Thomas[109] and the Book of Thomas.[110] Both record sayings or revelations of Jesus said to have been transmitted by the apostle. In both, Thomas is described as the twin or double of Jesus. The texts stress the importance of gnosis for salvation, arguing that knowledge of oneself is the key to knowledge of God. However, there is some disagreement as to whether they are gnostic in the strict sense of the term. These works are believed to have originated among Christian ascetic communities in Mesopotamia.[111]

(iv) *Hermetic works.* Three tractates belong to this category. They are inscribed consecutively in a single codex (no. VI). The works in question are the Discourse on the Eighth and Ninth, a dialogue in which Hermes Trismegistos instructs an initiate about the mysteries concerning the eighth and ninth spheres surrounding the earth, which are the realms of the divine,[112] a Prayer of Thanksgiving,[113] and Asclepius, another dialogue recording revelations made by Hermes Trismegistos.[114] The last two are known from Greek and Latin versions as well.[115]

---

[102] See Wisse (1981) and Schenke (1981).
[103] For the former view, see Layton (1987) 20–1; for the latter, Pearson (1981).
[104] See Layton (1987) 267–75; Layton (ed.) (1980).   [105] Attridge and MacRae (1985).
[106] Attridge and Pagels (1985).   [107] Peel (1985).
[108] Cf. Isenberg and Layton (1989).
[109] See Koester, Layton, Lambdin and Attridge (1989).
[110] See Turner and Layton (1989).   [111] Layton (1987) 359–65.
[112] Dirkse, Brashler and Parrott (1979).   [113] Dirkse and Brashler (1979).
[114] Dirkse and Parrott (1979).   [115] Cf. Mahé (1978–82).

(v) *Miscellaneous works.* In addition to those in the categories enumerated above, the Nag Hammadi library includes a variety of works of other types; some of these are gnostic, others are not. Among them are a crude rendering of a passage from Plato's *Republic*,[116] the Sentences of Sextus, a collection of aphorisms also known in Greek, Latin, Syriac, Armenian, Ethiopic and Georgian versions;[117] the Teachings of Silvanus, a similar collection of maxims and admonitions, portions of which were later attributed to Antony;[118] and works like the Apocryphal Letter of James, which emphasizes the reality of Jesus' Passion and exhorts its audience to follow his example and seek martyrdom.[119]

It is still unclear who assembled the Nag Hammadi library and for what purpose.[120] It does seem certain, however, that the persons responsible regarded the collection of tractates as edifying reading matter. An earlier suggestion that the library may have been assembled by heresiologists for purposes of refutation is now regarded as untenable, since not all of its constituent texts are heretical. Another view, now discredited, is that the library was collected by monks in a nearby Pachomian monastery. This idea, with its implication that the religious beliefs of the said monks were of a heterodox nature, arose from a misinterpretation of several fragments of Greek papyri that were extracted from the bindings of the Nag Hammadi codices, in particular, Codex VII.[121] Gnostic writings have, in fact, been discovered at monastic sites elsewhere in Egypt,[122] but there is no evidence in these Greek fragments to connect the codices with any Pachomian foundation. It seems simplest to assume that the library was assembled by a group of gnostic believers. The presence in it of non-gnostic material is explicable on the grounds that the compilers found this to be congenial to their own point of view, either as read literally or interpreted as allegory.

The gnostic tractates discovered at Nag Hammadi are not the only works of this sort that have been preserved in Coptic. Apart from a number of fragments,[123] there are three further MSS. of particular importance. P. Berolinensis 8502, a Sa'idic codex written in the fifth century, contains four tractates: the Gospel of Mary, the Apocryphon of John, the Sophia of Jesus Christ and the Acts of Peter.[124] The second and third of these occur in the Nag Hammadi library as well. The fourth tractate is not a gnostic work as such, but is susceptible to gnostic interpretation and was probably included with the other three for that reason.

---

[116] Brashler (1979).   [117] Poirier and Painchaud (1983) 12-94.
[118] Janssens (1983); cf. Funk (1976).   [119] Williams (1985).
[120] For a survey of recent research on this subject, see Veilleux (1986).
[121] Veilleux (1986) 278-83.   [122] Cf. Kahle (1954) I, 473-7.
[123] Kahle, *loc. cit.*; Layton (1989).   [124] Till and Schenke (1972).

The Askew Codex, a Saʿidic manuscript of fourth- or fifth-century date, contains a single work, the Pistis Sophia, divided into four books.[125] This purports to be a record of revelations made by the risen Jesus to his disciples concerning the entity mentioned in the title. The last MS. is the Bruce Codex, actually two separate Saʿidic codices bound together, one of fourth- or fifth-century date, the other certainly written in the fifth century.[126] The first of these preserves the Books of Jeu, further gnostic revelations made by Jesus to his disciples. The Jeu of the title, also designated as the true god, is a being who acts to produce emanations of himself under the influence of Jesus' father. These are described in both words and diagrams. The second tractate is of the same type as those works enumerated above under the rubric of 'classical' or Sethian gnosticism.

VI. MANICHEAN WRITINGS

In 1929, several codices written in a form of Subakhmimic Coptic were discovered at Medinet Madi near the Fayyum.[127] All proved to be inscribed with Manichean works. None of them was written originally in Coptic; either they were translated directly from Aramaic (Syriac), or from Greek versions of originals in that language.[128] Estimates of the date of these codices have ranged from the fourth to the fifth century.[129] Soon after their discovery, they were divided up and sold to three different collectors. The bulk of them are now in Dublin and Berlin. Parts of some of the codices which went to Berlin after their purchase were subsequently lost in the aftermath of the Second World War. Several of the texts are still unpublished or only partially published. The contents of the collection are as follows:

(i) Berlin Codex P. 15995. This MS. preserves a commentary on the Living Gospel, one of the seven canonical works written by Mani.[130]

(ii) Berlin Codex P. 15996. This contains the Kephalaia, or Chapters, of the Master, a compendious account of Manichean doctrine. Each chapter is presented in the form of a discourse of Mani with his disciples.[131]

(iii) Berlin Codex P. 15997. This originally preserved an account of Mani's life and the history of the Manichean sect. Unfortunately, all but nine leaves of it were lost in the aftermath of the war.[132]

---

[125] Schmidt (1978a). [126] Schmidt (1978b).

[127] See Schmidt and Polotsky (1933), especially 7–10; Giversen (1988a) vii–viii

[128] Cf. Nagel (1971) 347 note 63; idem (1981).

[129] Schmidt in Schmidt and Polotsky (1933) 35; Polotsky (1934) x note 1.

[130] Böhlig (1968) 185, 222–7. Cf. Beltz (1978) 97.

[131] Polotsky and Böhlig (1940); Böhlig (1966). Cf. idem (1968) 182–3, 228–66; Beltz (1978) 97–8. For additional fragments of the same MS. in Vienna, see Gardner (1988) 53–5.

[132] Böhlig (1968) 183–4; Beltz (1978) 98.

(iv) Berlin Codex P. 15998. This MS., of which all but twenty-eight leaves have been lost, contains a collection of letters written by Mani.[133]

(v) Berlin Codex P. 15999. This MS. was lost before it could be studied properly. The results of a cursory examination made prior to its disappearance suggest that it may have been a collection of sayings (*logoi*) of Mani's followers.[134]

(vi) Chester Beatty Codex A. Psalms used in the Manichean liturgy make up the contents of this MS. These are of several varieties, including psalms attributed to Mani's disciples Thomas and Heracleides, and those used in the feast of the *bema* or tribunal, which commemorated Mani's death.[135]

(vii) Chester Beatty Codex B. The contents of this MS. have yet to be identified.[136]

(viii) Chester Beatty Codex C. This text contains further *kephalaia*, or chapters, setting out Manichean doctrines.[137] There is disagreement among experts as to whether the entire codex is devoted to these or whether its latter part is actually a distinct work which has yet to be identified.[138] Also disputed is the nature of the relationship of the Chester Beatty *kephalaia* with those preserved in Berlin Codex P. 15996. The latter have been ascribed to Mani himself; the former may be the teachings of one of his followers.[139]

(ix) A further codex in the Chester Beatty collection preserves homilies composed by disciples of Mani.[140] The suggestion has been made that this and the now lost Berlin P. 15999 may originally have been parts of the same manuscript.[141]

(x) A single leaf in the same collection is inscribed with what appears to be a historical text.[142] This may be a fragment of the work partially preserved in Berlin Codex P. 15997.[143]

The Coptic texts from Medinet Madi are among the most important Manichean documents yet discovered, chiefly because of their early date. They shed valuable light on the rites and beliefs of this sect during the first century of its existence. The full value of the MSS. will only become apparent when the entire collection has been published and studied. It is to be hoped, for example, that the commentary on the Living Gospel will provide important information about that work, of which only fragments are now extant.[144]

[133] Description as *per* Böhlig (1968) 184. According to Beltz, *loc. cit.*, only eight leaves of the MS. survive.   [134] Böhlig, *loc. cit.*

[135] Giversen (1988a and b); Allberry (1938). Cf. Böhlig (1968) 185; Orlandi (1976) 324.

[136] Giversen (1986b) plates 101–26; Böhlig (1968) 186–7; Orlandi (1976) 324–5.

[137] Giversen (1986a). Cf. Böhlig (1968) 185; Orlandi (1976) 324–5.

[138] Cf. Giversen (1986a) xxi; Orlandi (1976) 325.   [139] Cf. Giversen (1986a) xix.

[140] Polotsky (1934); Giversen (1986b) plates 1–98.   [141] Böhlig (1968) 185–6.

[142] Giversen (1986b) plates 99–100.   [143] Cf. Giversen (1986b) viii–ix; Sundermann (1988) 570.

[144] For these, see Böhlig (1968) 227.

More recently, in 1991–2, additional Manichean texts in Coptic, Greek and Syriac were discovered at the site of Ismant el-Kharab in the Dakhleh Oasis. They were found in a house of which the period of occupation is said to extend from the late third to the late fourth century. Some are bilingual (Coptic–Syriac). At least a few preserve parallel versions of psalms previously known from Chester Beatty Codex A. This material is currently being prepared for publication. It too should add a great deal to our knowledge of early Manicheism in Egypt.[145]

One of the most striking aspects of Coptic literature of the fourth and fifth centuries, including the period 337–425, is its great diversity. As well as biblical, patristic and other categories of text which continued to be read in subsequent periods, it encompasses gnostic, hermetic, and Manichean works, of which no later specimens are known in Coptic. Its diversity is also apparent in the variety of dialects in which it is written. Throughout the period under consideration, Saʿidic was the most important literary dialect. But one is struck by the relatively large number of texts written in Subakhmimic and Akhmimic, particularly in the fourth century. Subakhmimic had special significance as a vehicle for the transmission of heterodox works like those written by the gnostics and Manicheans.

Overall, the fourth and fifth centuries were the most important period in the history of Coptic literature. They witnessed the translation of the entire Bible into Coptic, which did much to accelerate the spread of Christianity in Egypt. They also saw the widest circulation, in that language, of works of gnostic and Manichean origin, sects which posed a major challenge to Christianity. Thus, during the fourth and fifth centuries, Coptic texts provided a further forum for a crucial and ongoing debate. But Coptic literature in these years did not consist solely of translations from other tongues. It was during the fourth and fifth centuries that the first attempts were made to produce original literature in Coptic. These were to culminate in the work of Shenoute, who successfully adapted Greek literary traditions in the process of forging a Coptic prose style that was at once both fresh and vigorous. Innovators like him established the foundations on which all future Coptic authors were to build.

---

[145] For an overview of the Ismant el-Kharab discoveries, see Gardner (1993).

CHAPTER 24

ART AND ARCHITECTURE

JAŚ ELSNER

I. INTRODUCTION

The art of late antiquity embodies one of the great transitions in the history of western art. It marks the first time after the fifth century B.C. when the classical canons of Graeco-Roman forms shifted, over the whole spectrum of the representational arts, towards the less naturalistic and more abstract forms which scholars have held to be characteristic of the art of the Middle Ages. This change is marked by an apparent paradox: the juxtaposition of religious elements (pagan and Christian) and stylistic forms (naturalist and schematic) which normally we might expect to be separate and even antipathetic. The syncretisms of fourth-century art and architecture have been regarded as the visual embodiment of an intellectual and cultural process whose eventual result would be the emergence of Byzantine and Latin Christian culture. This view, which sees the importance of fourth-century art to be its teleological relation to later art, is certainly valid; but perhaps it fails to give due regard to the intrinsic interest of the visual culture of late antiquity.

The fourth and fifth centuries saw the continuation of the great traditions of classical art and architecture as they had been practised for several centuries throughout the Roman empire. At the same time, these traditions were transformed into new, more 'abstract' styles set in a very different religious context. In the period with which this volume deals, A.D. 337–425, colossal statues were still being cast in the tradition of ancient imperial bronzes. Examples include the great bronze of Constantius II (emperor 337–61), now in the Museo dei Conservatori in Rome, and the large fifth-century statue brought by the Venetians to Barletta in the Middle Ages.[1] Imperial statues in marble continued to be made, such as the magnificent Theodosian portraits discovered in Istanbul and Aphrodisias.[2] Triumphal columns were still erected by the emperors; those of Theodosius I (set up

---

[1] On the late bronzes see Kluge and Lehmann-Hartleben (1927) II, 53–8. On tradition and innovation in late antique sculpture generally, see Hannestad (1994).

[2] On the Istanbul image see Kiilerich (1993) 87–9, with bibliography; on the Aphrodisias statue, see *ibid.* 27–30, with bibliography.

in Constantinople in the late 380s) and of Arcadius (erected after 401),[3] emulate the celebrated Roman columns of Trajan and Marcus Aurelius. Imperial arches, like those of Titus in Rome or Trajan at Beneventum, continued to be built; fragments have been found, for instance, of an Arch of Theodosius in Constantinople. Obelisks continued to be raised by the emperors in the tradition of Augustus – like that of Constantius II, set up in the Circus Maximus in 357. A rare fourth-century survival is the base of the obelisk of Theodosius, erected in the Hippodrome in Constantinople in 390, whose four sides represent the emperor at the centre of his state activities.[4] Cameos, such as the Belgrade fragment showing a rider in battle or the sardonyx gem now in Paris probably representing Honorius and his wife Maria (married in 398), continued to be cut, emulating the lavish gems of the earlier empire.[5] Great basilical churches were built, whose forms and techniques looked back to masterpieces of Roman architectural brickwork like the Pantheon, the Macellum of Trajan and the Baths of Caracalla in Rome.[6] Many of these fourth-century monuments or objects do not survive today and are known only from late drawings and engravings. But their existence indicates the continuance of the traditions of imperial patronage and self-advertisement through art which had been so signally established by Augustus' transformation of Rome.

Critics have often seen such continuities with tradition in late antique art as a mark of decline. Fewer monuments and objects appear to have been produced in the traditional media – imperial statues, for instance. And their workmanship has been described as cruder. But there is considerable danger in looking at any one medium in isolation. While fewer large-scale sculptures were produced, late antique artists were making considerable quantities of high-quality ivory reliefs – miniature sculptures, but masterpieces none the less.[7] The decline in the quantity and even quality of large-scale sculpture may represent a transference of taste and patronage to different media rather than any absolute or outright degeneration of quality or skill.

At the same time, the fourth and early fifth centuries saw the entry of a number of innovations into the artistic repertoire of the empire in response to the new patronage of the church and the continued patronage of the aristocracy. These included such features as the expanded use of sumptuous *opus sectile* panels of inlaid coloured marbles to decorate the walls of wealthier edifices; examples are in the secular basilica of Junius

[3] On the columns of Theodosius and Arcadius, see Kiilerich (1993) 50–64, with further bibliography 50, n. 157.

[4] On the Theodosian obelisk base, see Kiilerich (1993) 31–49, with bibliography 31, n. 91.

[5] On the Rothschild Cameo of Honorius, see Kiilerich (1993) 92–4, with bibliography.

[6] On the origins of the Christian basilica, see Ward-Perkins (1954) and Krautheimer (1967).

[7] For a survey of early ivories, see Kiilerich (1993) 136–59.

Bassus, consul 331, from the Esquiline in Rome,[8] and the arcade of the
church of S. Sabina on the Aventine, built in the first half of the fifth
century.[9] Figurative mosaics were introduced into the walls and vaults of
buildings as well as their floors – for instance, in the mid-fourth-century
mausolea of S. Costanza in Rome and Centcelles in Spain. Illumination was
developed to illustrate the new kind of book (vellum codex rather than
papyrus roll) which became predominant in the centuries after the birth of
Christ;[10] the only early-fifth-century illuminated manuscripts surviving are
the Vatican Virgil and the fragmentary Itala of Quedlinburg now in Berlin,
which contains Old Testament texts.[11] On a more domestic level, the
fourth century marked the high point in the production of lavish luxury
tableware, which reached a complexity and sophistication that has rarely
been equalled since.[12] Magnificent late antique collections of silver and
silver-gilt (such as the Sevso Treasure in the collection of the Marquess of
Northampton,[13] or the stylistically related Kaiseraugst Treasure in Basel)[14]
were offset on aristocratic dining-tables by such elaborate objects as cage-
cups, whose glass was often cast in several colours and undercut flamboy-
antly in deep relief (for example, the Lycurgus cup in the British
Museum),[15] or stone vases carved in high relief (like the Rubens vase now
in Baltimore).[16]

Both the changes and the continuities in the art and architecture of the
upper levels of society, in the public and private spheres, indicate the
wealth and artistic vitality of the empire after the death of Constantine.
His successors continued his extensive building projects in Rome, in the
Holy Land and in Constantinople, the city that Constantine founded in
330 but did not live to see completed.[17] The continuity with the patterns
of patronage in the classical past was coupled with the novel process of
Christianization. Now, instead of temples, the emperors were building
churches. In the city of Rome, at any rate, Christianization had a striking
topographic effect. Whereas the ancient temples had been in the centre
of the city, the greatest of the new churches were established on its
peripheries, near the burial sites of the martyrs. Constantine had built St
Peter's on the Vatican hill outside the city walls, the Lateran Basilica just
inside the walls, and S. Agnese fuori le Mura, S. Lorenzo fuori le Mura,

---

[8] On the Basilica of Junius Bassus, see Becatti (1969) 181–215.
[9] On S. Sabina, see Krautheimer (1937–77) IV, 72–98.
[10] See on illumination and the early codex, Weitzmann (1959); Weitzmann (1970); Roberts and Skeat
(1983).   [11] For the Vatican Virgil, see Wright (1993); and for the Quedlinburg Itala see Levin (1985).
[12] For an introduction to late antique silver, see Kent and Painter (1977) 15–76.
[13] For an introduction to the Sevso Treasure, see Mango and Bennett (1994).
[14] On the Kaiseraugst Treasure, see Cahn and Kauffman-Heinimann (1984).
[15] On cage-cups, see Harden (1987) 238–58; and on the Lycurgus cup, *ibid.* 245–9, with bibliography
p. 249.   [16] For the Rubens vase, see Weitzmann (1979) 333–4, with bibliography p. 334.
[17] For a brief survey of Christian architecture in the capitals, see Krautheimer, *Architecture* 45–65.

SS. Marcellino e Pietro and S. Sebastiano all outside the walls. His successors completed these projects and built S. Croce in Gerusalemme just within the walls of Rome and the Basilica of St Paul Outside the Walls.[18] In an age remarkable for its public liturgical processions and urban rituals, the effect of placing such a formidable number of great imperial churches on the periphery of Rome should not be underrated.[19] The new Christian context for artistic patronage created profound changes in the effects of architecture on the environment and experience of the city's inhabitants. Rome, the ancient capital, was rather exceptional in this respect, since the relics of the earliest Christians and martyrs were situated in the graveyards outside and around the city.[20] The peripheral nature of Rome's sacred topography is not emulated in Constantinople or Ravenna, where the patterns of early Christian burial appear to have been different.[21]

Such Christian buildings and monuments became a primary vehicle for the process of Christianization. They constituted the space of Christianity. Churches were built specifically in response to the demands of Christian pilgrims – not only the great campaign of Constantinian churches in Palestine, but also numerous martyria and relic-centres the length and breadth of the empire. At the lower end of the social scale, Christians were not the only religious group to be decorating catacombs, shrines and sacred objects with a wealth of symbolic images which proclaimed their holiness. Jews, followers of the cult of Mithras and initiates in other cults both 'pagan' and 'syncretistic' (soon to be persecuted by the victorious Christians) were equally busy in an age which should be seen as a high point of religious imagery and sensibility.

II. THE MODERN CRITICAL CONTEXT

The art of the fourth century has been studied principally in two ways. One has its roots in the Renaissance and Enlightenment diatribes against the 'decline' and 'degeneracy' supposedly visible in the Arch of Constantine, which juxtaposes fourth-century with second-century imperial relief sculpture. This approach sees the art of the Christian empire as embodying a marked stylistic and formal decline from the apex of classical naturalism

---

[18] On Rome, see Krautheimer, *Rome* 3–58; *idem* (1983) 7–40; Ward-Perkins, *Public Building* 38–48, 51–9 and esp. 236–41.

[19] On urban ritual in Rome, Jerusalem and Constantinople, see Baldovin (1987).

[20] Milan, however, also follows a largely peripheral pattern; see Krautheimer (1983) 68–92 and Monfrin (1991).

[21] On the topography of Constantinople, see Krautheimer (1983) 41–67 and Mango (1985) 23–50; on Ravenna, see Ward-Perkins, *Public Building* 51–83, 241–4 and esp. Deichmann (1989); on the cities of the eastern empire, see Mango (1974) 30–57.

towards the Dark Ages.[22] It interprets the difference between 'naturalistic' and 'abstractionist' styles as being of essential importance.[23] More recently, this view has been refined in a number of directions which do not necessarily or explicitly imply 'decline'. Some have argued, for instance, that the emergence of non-naturalistic styles in the fourth century shows a healthy return to the expressionism long present in Roman art and culture, and only suppressed by the overlay of Greek influence.[24] The end of naturalism is thus interpreted as a response to contemporary needs and social change.[25] All such approaches have a formalist slant in taking their starting-point from exploring the differences that emerge between fourth-century and classical art in a period of crucial change.

The second method of interpretation, concerned less explicitly with form and more with the content and subject matter of images, has seen the art of the fourth century as the cradle for that of the Middle Ages, and in particular for Christian art. This approach focuses more on the continuities between many of the developments in fourth-century art and the medieval Christian future.[26] It observes the breadth of influences on early Christian art, such as the more schematic arts of the Near Eastern provinces of the empire (for example, that of Palmyra),[27] the near-contemporary Jewish images of Dura Europos,[28] even the effects of competition with pagan, Jewish and Manichean art.[29] In this way, the history of images has been tied to the history of Christianization, of supposed pagan revivals and of the settings of early Christian liturgy, such as house-churches and catacombs. More intellectualist versions of this approach have tied the development of late antique 'abstraction' to changes in philosophical, cultural and literary fashions in late paganism and early Christianity.[30]

A third approach has been to blend the two already mentioned, appropriating the 'decline' to a formalist art history of the styles of the early Middle Ages.[31] All the lines sketched above share several assumptions which are worth making explicit. They see their task as interpreting only those images which were produced in the period under discussion, rather

[22] The traditional model of 'decline' is expressed most forcefully and succinctly by Berenson (1954). See also the discussion of Trilling (1987). Note, however, that as early as 1901, Riegl was mounting a powerful argument against the prevailing view of late Roman art as 'decay' in favour of 'progress'; see Riegl (1985) 11–15 and 54–7 on the Arch of Constantine.

[23] Hence, for instance, Rodenwaldt's espousal of 'transcendentalism' or 'expressionism' as formulations for what he none the less sees as a form of decline, in Rodenwaldt (1939) 563–7.

[24] Most notably Bianchi Bandinelli, *Rome* and (1979) 181–223.   [25] See L'Orange (1965).

[26] See, for instance, Grabar (1969).

[27] An approach pioneered by Stzrygowski (1923) 1–46; and upheld by Kitzinger (1940) 8f. and Grabar (1972). See the discussion of Trilling (1987).   [28] See Weitzmann and Kessler (1990).

[29] Suggested by Grabar (1969) 23–30.

[30] On the philosophical influence of Plotinian thought, see Grabar (1967) 288–91 and Walter (1984) 271–6; on literature and imagination, see Onians (1980) and Roberts (1989) 66–121; on magic, see Mathews (1993) 54–91.   [31] See Kitzinger (1977).

than including art made in the past but which was still present in the fourth century or even re-used during it. This is why the critical attack on the Arch of Constantine has not seen the re-use of second-century reliefs as a creative or innovatory way of using images to relate with the past. Art historians have tended not to imagine that re-used second-century sculptures might have an entirely fresh meaning in their new fourth-century context.

Linked with this assumption that the meaning of art is static and frozen in the moment of its production are a number of further reductive expectations. Images with Christian themes are believed straightforwardly to provide positive and factual evidence for the Christianity of the artist or the patron or both. Likewise with pagan and Jewish iconography. Hence single images are presumed to have single meanings which the scholar can simply identify. However, this represents what the anthropologist Ernest Gellner describes as 'the failure to appreciate something which is a commonplace in sociology . . . the difference between single-strand or single-purpose activities, on the one hand, and multi-strand activities on the other. A multi-strand activity [the use of images, in this case], which serves multiple criteria or ends, is treated as if it were a single-strand one.'[32] In other words, the assumption that an image of, say, the sacrifice of Isaac must indicate Christian patrons or artists, is not warranted. On the contrary, it may be a product of Jews, or of pagans drawing syncretistically on Judaeo-Christian mythology. The point is that such an image may have meaning for viewers of all these sects and denominations, no matter who made it or commissioned it.

The approach to fourth- and early-fifth-century art outlined below takes a number of slightly different assumptions from those outlined above as its basis. Changes in style may imply changes in taste, but certainly need not be seen as indices of decline. There is no reason to privilege classical naturalism as in any way a superior regime of representation to any other abstract, schematic or non-naturalist mode. Images are visual symbols which may have a multiplicity of meanings and evocations for different viewers, both at the time they were made and thereafter. In treating of late antiquity, we must look to the whole span of images and monuments, both those surviving into and those created by that period. The meanings of such images may be not only multiple but even contradictory, with different viewers potentially believing different things about the same work of art. Furthermore, an investigation of art and architecture must be sensitive to the different social and cultural levels at which material culture may function. A box used in a liturgical ceremony carries different symbolic evocations from the same object used to hold food in a dinner-party or cosmetics in a toilet set.

[32] Gellner (1988) 42–3, cf. 42–9, 50–3 and 77–9.

Accounts of late antique art have tended to adopt a chronological focus, looking either at the decline of naturalism or the emergence of Christian art, or a topographic approach, looking at developments in the Roman empire province by province, or else have concentrated on style. What follows is, by contrast, a synchronic and thematic approach to topics which are of prime interest to the historian in the art of the fourth and early fifth centuries. This approach is thus biased towards a historical assessment of the contribution of art to understanding the history of the period rather than a strictly art-historical exploration of the forms and styles of monuments.

III. ART AND ARCHITECTURE, 337–425

1. Late antiquity and its past

Describing the entry of Constantine's son Constantius into the city of Rome in A.D. 357, the historian Ammianus Marcellinus writes (XVI.10.13f.):

He stood amazed; and on every side on which his eyes rested he was dazzled by the array of marvellous sights . . . As he surveyed the sections of the city and its suburbs . . . he thought that whatever met his gaze first towered over all the rest: the sanctuaries of Tarpeian Jove so far surpassing as things divine excel those of the earth; the baths built up to the measure of provinces; the huge bulk of the amphitheatre, strengthened by its framework of Tiburtine stone, to whose top human eyesight barely ascends; the Pantheon like a rounded city district, vaulted over in lofty beauty; and the exalted heights which rise with platforms to which one may mount, and bear the likenesses of emperors [i.e. the columns]; the Temple of the City, the Forum of Peace, the theatre of Pompey, the Odeum, the Stadium, and amongst these the other adornments of the Eternal City. But when he came to the Forum of Trajan, a construction unique under the heavens, as we believe, and admirable even in the unanimous opinion of all the gods, he stood fast in amazement, turning his attention to the gigantic complex about him, beggaring description and never again to be imitated by mortal men.

(Trans. J. C. Rolfe, Loeb edn)

This passage from Ammianus is testimony to the extraordinary respect accorded by Romans of late antiquity to the monumental remains of their ancient past.[33] No account of the art of the period can be complete without grounding the developments of the fourth and fifth centuries in this context of near-reverence. It may be objected that Ammianus was a pagan apologist, naturally biased towards the 'sanctuaries of Tarpeian Jove', but in fact Christians and Christian emperors were as enthusiastic about ancient monuments as was their historian in his rhetoric. Constantine and his successors crammed not only the old Rome, but also

---

[33] On ancient statues in late antique Rome, see Curran (1994).

Constantinople, the new Christian Rome, with famous pagan statues culled from the great sites of Greece and Italy.

It is revealing that even at the height of Christian polemic against paganism, even after the prohibition on pagan sacrifices enacted by Theodosius the Great in 391, the sacrificial representations abounding on Rome's monuments were not attacked or destroyed. The relics of the ancient past were allowed to remain, both as testimony to the ancestry of the modern state and as a mark of the difference created by the new Christian dispensation.

The scenes of sacrifice on the arches, on the columns, on the bases of statues and obelisks, represent the kind of ritual which occasions fervent polemic in the majority of our early Christian written sources. If we believe the evidence of such texts to be providing a true sense of attitudes after Constantine's establishment of Christianity as the official religion of the empire, these are the kinds of images which should have been destroyed under the new Christian dispensation. And yet such monuments survive in copious numbers from the ancient buildings of Rome to this day. At no stage were they considered sufficiently offensive to be damaged, whatever the evidence of the more polemical writers might urge us to suppose.

The Arch of Constantine was held by Romans through the fourth and fifth centuries to commemorate a Christian emperor, despite its use of pagan sacrificial scenes and carvings. Another celebrated work of art, explicitly associated with a family of leading pagan aristocrats, is the Symmachorum leaf of an ivory diptych from the late fourth century, now in the Victoria and Albert Museum.[34] It depicts a pagan priestess before an altar under an oak tree. She scatters incense over a small fire, and is accompanied by an attendant holding a bowl of fruit and a *kantharos*. Yet this object with an explicitly pagan theme could well have been made after the Theodosian prohibition against pagan sacrifices in 391. Even during the ascendancy of Christianity, classicizing images not only survived on ancient monuments but were produced. There is no need to resort to theories of a 'pagan' revival in the late fourth century to explain such objects. Rather, they were a natural part of a society which did not necessarily see its classical past (pagan religious associations and all) in direct conflict with its Christian present and future.

The case of Constantinople is still more remarkable than that of Rome. Constantine and his successors appear to have packed the new capital not merely with ancient statues but specifically with some of the most celebrated (and hence execrated) pagan idols. Eighty statues, most of bronze, were gathered into the Baths of Zeuxippus in the city centre and a

---

[34] For a brief and recent discussion of the Symmachorum leaf, with bibliography, see Kiilerich (1993) 144–9.

sumptuous collection of antique masterpieces, including Phidias' chrys-
elephantine Zeus from Olympia and the Cnidian Aphrodite of Praxiteles,
found its way into the Palace of Lausus in the reign of Theodosius II
(406–50). This Aphrodite, we may note, had been the subject of polemic
from such Christian writers as Arnobius and Clement of Alexandria.[35]

To Eusebius, bishop of Caesarea and Constantine's biographer, the
adornment of the city with ancient idols was embarrassing. He wrote in the
Vita Constantini (III.54):

Venerable statues of brass ... were exposed to view in all the public places of the
imperial city: so that here a Pythian, there a Sminthian Apollo excited the contempt of the beholder: while Delphic tripods were deposited in the Hippodrome
and the Muses of Helicon in the palace. In short the city which bore his name
was everywhere filled with brazen statues of the most exquisite workmanship,
which had been dedicated in every province, and which the deluded victims
of superstition had long vainly honoured as gods with numberless victims and
burnt sacrifices, though now at length they learnt to renounce their error, when
the emperor held up these very playthings to be the ridicule and sport of all
beholders.

(Trans. E. C. Richardson, Library of Nicene and Post-Nicene Fathers)

The visual evidence spoke for itself, announcing the high prestige of
ancient art and the new capital's need to ground itself in the imperialist
acquisition of the splendours of the Greek past. But the Christian apologist needs to explain these images away as idols no longer worshipped
because their very display has made them despised. In brief, art and literature provide us with rather different pictures of cultural and religious attitudes.

2. The problems of syncretism: what is Christian art?

This passage from a Christian bishop raises an important point about the
difference between texts and images (at least in this period) as methods for
disseminating meaning. Religious writing in late antiquity tends to establish
self-definition by explicit contrast and polemic (one thinks of Christian
diatribes against heretics and pagans as well as the pagan attacks of Celsus,
Porphyry and Julian against the Christians). Religious images, by contrast,
appear to announce themselves transparently and straightforwardly as
themselves, with little commentary about other or rival programmes of
pictures. There may in fact be an implicit polemical commentary, as in a
recently discovered fourth-century pagan mosaic from the House of Aion,
Nea Paphos, in Cyprus, depicting Hermes seated with the infant Dionysus

[35] For the re-use of antiquities in Constantinople, see Mango (1963) 57–9, and in general: Dawkins
(1924); Saradi-Mendelovici (1990); Bassett (1991); Madden (1992).

(who has a halo) on his lap.[36] This image seems remarkably like Christian representations of the Virgin and Child: whether it represents a peculiar instance of Dionysiac–Christian syncretism or a deliberately anti-Christian Dionysiac use of Christian iconography, we may never know. Usually such images are only implicitly polemical; they do not explicitly state the object of attack or parody.

Christian apologetic texts which were keen to integrate Christianity into the cultural climate of antiquity nevertheless regularly presented the pagan past as at best a pale foreshadowing of the new dispensation. Like the Old Testament, the wisdom of the ancients looked forward to and could only be fulfilled by the incarnation. The extreme Christian polemicists were significantly more brutal about the pagan past. But the visual evidence shows almost no signs of these attitudes. On the contrary, pagan statues remained in the centre of Rome and were placed in prime sites in other cities of the empire like Constantinople; pagan motifs were adopted by and adapted into Christian art, and pagan themes stood side by side with Christian ones throughout the art of the fourth century.

The quality by which an image seemed straightforwardly to stand for itself allowed people to put together several apparently unconnected images to create a new, more complex, work of art. The result was a kind of syncretism or accretion of images which needed to be read through their symbolic connections. Marked accretion is a particular feature of late antique art. This is so not only in the conflations of Christian and pagan themes upon which so much of the scholarship on fourth- and fifth-century art has concentrated, but also in imperial imagery and in the art of the initiate cults. In imperial art, in the bricolage of the Arch of Constantine, original fourth-century sculptures made specifically for the Arch were brought together with earlier second-century reliefs taken as *spolia* from elsewhere.[37] Such a juxtaposition tended to prompt viewers into seeing the emperor directly in the context of his glorious predecessors. His present became a fulfilment of their past, while the activities in which they were represented (hunting, addressing the troops, performing sacrifice and so forth) became a distant prefiguring of the triumphant present. In religious art, the *tauroctony* – the complex image which occupied the cult niche in Mithraic temples and represented the god Mithras killing a bull – blended sacrificial, astrological and biographical information into one coherent image.[38] The high sophistication of the masterpieces of early Christian art, such as the sarcophagus of Junius Bassus in Rome[39] or the ivory reliquary

---

[36] On the images from the House of Aion see Daszewski (1985). For a brief discussion of the pagan–Christian issues, see Bowersock *Hellenism* 49–53.

[37] On the Arch of Constantine, see Pierce (1989) with bibliography. On *spolia*, see e.g. Brenk (1987).

[38] On the *tauroctony*, see Elsner (1995) 210–21.

[39] On the Junius Bassus Sarcophagus, see Malbon (1990), with earlier bibliography.

box known as a *lipsanotheca* from Brescia,[40] with their complex juxtapositions of Old and New Testament themes according to the tenets of patristic typology, represented a Christian artistic appropriation of patterns of
syncretism already common in the art and writing of late antiquity.

The patterns of pagan–Christian syncretism, which are a particular
feature of fourth-century imagery, are part of the same phenomenon. A
pagan text may be inscribed beside a Christian image; for example, there is
gem depicting Orpheus crucified which may have been used as a mystic
token or emblem.[41] Likewise, a Christian invocation can be written on a
pagan representation, as on the celebrated Projecta casket from a collection of treasure discovered on the Esquiline.[42] Here a scene of the Toilet
of Venus has inscribed below it SECUNDE ET PROJECTA VIVATIS IN
CHRISTO ('Secundus and Projecta, may you live in Christ'). Again, pagan
and Christian images can stand side by side; an example is the mosaic
showing Bellerophon and what is probably a portrait of Christ on the
fourth-century Hinton St Mary floor in the British Museum.[43] Such pictures combine to create a new scene which excludes neither pagan nor
Christian themes. In other words, while Christian texts of the period tend
to argue for exclusion (of pagans, of heretics, of illicit practices), the
images, by contrast, suggest a culture of inclusion.

The implications of syncretism are very deep. What happens when one
religious group borrows other groups' motifs, when Christians use
Dionysiac vine scrolls, for instance, which they do ubiquitously on art
objects from all social levels and areas – from Roman catacombs to Coptic
textiles? Such conflations and borrowings ought to prompt questions
which are all too rarely asked in the literature: what makes art Christian?
How can we define Christian art?

It has generally been assumed that Christian art is simply art with a
Christian text or iconography. Syncretistic combinations, like those we have
glanced at just now, tend to be seen as odd and out of line with an ideal of
straightforwardly orthodox Christian iconography. But did such an ideal
exist in the fourth century? Indeed, was there, in the half-century after the
council of Nicaea, a single Christianity which agreed on what was and what
was not orthodox iconography? The extraordinarily fractious history of
the next few centuries of theological dispute suggests the Christians could
not agree on what their most cherished doctrines and dogmas were. When
the Fathers of the church worried deeply about the very language they
should use in describing the relations of the Trinity,[44] why should we

---

[40] On the Brescia Casket, see Watson (1981), with earlier bibliography.
[41] On this syncretistic gem, see Cabrol and Leclercq (1936) vol. 12, p. 2754, fig. 9249. But is it a fake?
[42] On the Esquiline Treasure, see Shelton (1981), and specifically on the Projecta Casket, pp. 72–5.
[43] On the Hinton St Mary floor, see Toynbee (1964).
[44] On language and the Holy Trinity, see e.g. Basil, *De Spiritu Sancto* 1–8, 25–9.

assume there to be any consensus on orthodox imagery? One objection to the approach which so transparently connects Christian iconography with a straightforward and ideal version of Christianity and pagan iconography with some analogous version of paganism is just that it is unhelpfully reductivist. It fails Christian art by applying the exclusiveness we find in texts to a medium which favours inclusion; moreover, it fails to explain both syncretistic juxtapositions and those themes which we might have assumed were straightforwardly pagan.

Let us return to Projecta. A number of spectacular silver items were discovered in the Esquiline Treasure, all apparently part of one set of cosmetic and toiletry paraphernalia and apparently made by the same workshop, probably in the fourth century. The Projecta casket now in the British Museum is the most famous object, because of its inscription. But the iconography is unashamedly pagan and secular – a procession to the baths, a woman (Projecta herself?) at her toilet with servants, the toilet of Venus (who is represented nude on a shell in between sea monsters and erotes), nereids and, on the lid, what appears to be a marriage portrait of Secundus and Projecta in a wreath between erotes. However, the other items of the Treasure have no inscriptions. Their imagery, like that of the casket, is apparently pagan or secular. Let us imagine (as seems not unlikely) that they were all part of one collection of silverware. Are they to be considered Christian or pagan? Obviously Secundus and Projecta considered themselves sufficiently Christian to have the fact inscribed on their gilded silver casket. So the casket at least, despite its iconography including a pagan goddess, is Christian. But what about, say, the patera (or flat dish) with Venus in a cockle shell (from the same treasure, but now in Paris)?[45] We may ask the same question about the flask with cupids and the casket with Muses.[46] It seems absurd to be pushing such questions, based on the form and iconography of the objects, when it is obvious that to Secundus and Projecta, as Christians, none of these items caused offence. The Christianity or paganness of a work of art lay not in its iconography but in how its viewers chose to see it. To Secundus and Projecta the classical theme of the patera may not have been in conflict with their Christianity; to a pagan visitor to their house (or the silversmith who fashioned it) it might have been 'pagan'; to a Christian bishop of fundamentalist tendencies it might have appeared wickedly idolatrous. Indeed to many viewers, whose number did not always include Christian bishops, a 'pagan' theme may simply have evoked the cultural associations of the classical tradition. For such viewers, classical motifs and deities (at least in secular contexts) alluded to the glorious past of Rome in literature, culture and imperial splendour.

---

[45] See, on this patera, Shelton (1981) 78.
[46] The Muse casket, *ibid.* 75–7; flask with cupids, *ibid.* 82–3.

The same questions arise with the splendid Sevso Treasure, probably also from the fourth century.[47] To what extent does the chi-rho monogram on one item of the set make the whole collection 'Christian'?[48] Are apparently pagan scenes such as the iconography of the hunt, of sacrifice, of Dionysus, in some ways appropriable to and not in conflict with a Christian reading? Likewise, does the appearance of a cross and a fish on spoons from the Thetford silver treasure (now in the British Museum and dated to between 350 and 400) allow a Christianizing interpretation for a collection which includes items with images of tritons, Venus, Cupid, Mars, Faunus and other deities?[49]

In other words, if we stress the question 'How do we define Christian art?', can we deny a place in 'Christian art' to those items in any of these collections of silver without Christian inscriptions? But if we are to say that in some sense these treasures, taken to include all their items, are evidence for the kind of art acceptable to Christians in the fourth century, then we need to redefine what we mean by the term Christian art. Moreover, we need to ask in what respect, if any at all, such 'Christian' art was different from other art in late antiquity.

3. Iconography and social function

Before we leave the world of luxury silverware, let us add a further nuance to these questions by considering its function. The silver treasures appear to have been used on the dining-tables or in the boudoirs of wealthy people. They were objects which, despite some Christian elements, were not associated specifically with religion in any sense. They were neither liturgical vessels nor decorations for a liturgical setting, nor funerary objects or adornments. In this sense, they differed from ritually charged examples of Christian art – from the art of the sacred site, of cult enclosure, of private devotion. The primarily social and secular function of such objects may do much to explain the pagan imagery. Secundus and Projecta clearly had no worries about having Venus on their silverware, just as Theodosius II was happy to allow the Aphrodite of Cnidos into the Palace of Lausus. They might all, however, have had rather stronger objections had such explicitly pagan imagery appeared on the walls, ceiling or apse of a church.

In this way, the non-religious function of a great deal of late antique art helps to explain its use of pagan iconography. This is not only true of luxury silverware (to the syncretistic examples discussed above one might add such magnificent, purely pagan items as the Parabiago Plate with

---

[47] On the Sevso Treasure, see Mango and Bennett (1994); Painter (1990); Cahn *et al.* (1991).

[48] The item in question is Sevso's Hunting Plate, see Mango and Bennett (1994) 55–97.

[49] On the Thetford treasure, see Johns and Potter (1983) items 67 and 69; also Watts (1990) 146–58.

Cybele and Attis from Milan,[50] the Corbridge Lanx formerly in the collection of the Duke of Northumberland[51] and the Mildenhall silver dish in the British Museum[52] – although these last two, despite their pagan iconography, were found in caches including objects with Christian inscriptions). It also applies to the great quantity of textiles and tapestries surviving from Egypt with pagan themes,[53] as well as to late antique jewellery.[54] Perhaps the largest repertoire of purely pagan and secular images preserved on a single monument of the period is depicted in the mosaics from the villa at Piazza Armerina in Sicily, probably dating from the early to mid fourth century.[55] The floors of this lavish mansion, which covers some 1.5 hectares, have images of hunting, chariot-racing, sacrifice, fishing, harvesting, lovemaking, the famous dancing girls wearing the late antique version of a bikini and other idealizations of 'daily life'. Mythical elements include pictures of Heracles, Odysseus and Polyphemus, and Orpheus. There are also parodies of some of these themes, including a chariot race and a hunt by erotes. The secular nature of villas like Piazza Armerina means that their imagery cannot exclude the possibility of their having been used by Christian owners, viewers and visitors during their heyday. Like the Projecta casket and other items from the Esquiline Treasure, even a monument so entirely devoid of Christian imagery as the mosaics of Piazza Armerina might have satisfied not only the aesthetic demands of pagans but equally those of Christians, in a non-religious social context. To the mosaics of Piazza Armerina may be added the large numbers of secular mosaic floors excavated in Roman North Africa, whose many Venuses (for instance at Djemila, Setif and the Maison de la Cachette de Statues at Carthage) may have the same relation to Christianity as those from the Esquiline Treasure.[56] It should be added that purely pagan themes continued to decorate secular objects made for the aristocratic or imperial market well into the sixth century. Examples include the Meleager and Heracles plates from Constantinople (now in St Petersburg and Paris respectively)[57] and the floor mosaics from the peristyle of the imperial palace at Constantinople.[58]

Even such religious buildings as mausolea or catacombs often mix explicitly Christian iconography with much more generalized imagery from the Graeco-Roman repertoire, and even with pagan themes. It should be

---

[50] On the Parabiago Plate, see Weitzmann (1979) 185–6, with bibliography, and Kiilerich (1993) 174–7, with bibliography.   [51] On the Corbridge Lanx, see Brendel (1941).

[52] On the Mildenhall Plate, see Painter (1977) 26–8.

[53] On Coptic textiles with pagan themes, see Rutochowscaya (1990) 87–118

[54] For a brief introduction to late antique jewellery, see Weitzmann (1979) 297–329.

[55] On Piazza Armerina, see Carandini, Ricci and De Vos (1982) and Wilson (1983).

[56] On African mosaics, see Dunbabin (1978). On these specific images, *ibid.* 251 (Carthage), 256 (Djemila), 268 (Setif).

[57] For the Meleager plate, see Weitzmann (1979) 163–4; for the Heracles plate *ibid.* 162–3.

[58] On the floor mosaics of the imperial palace, see Trilling (1989), with bibliography.

emphasized that funerary settings such as catacombs, tombs and sarcophagi, while they are both cultic and liturgical, may not have quite the same religious intensity as still more ritually charged locations or objects like temples, churches and icons. In the main cupola of the mid-fourth-century Mausoleum of S. Costanza in Rome (as we know from seventeenth-century drawings) there were mosaics with a good deal of Old and New Testament imagery. On the vault of the ambulatory there is a quantity of generalized Graeco-Roman imagery, vintaging cupids (which are both Christian and 'Dionysiac'), the four seasons and so forth.[59] The same pattern appears in the related imperial mausoleum (probably of Constans) at Centcelles near Tarragona.[60] Specifically religious themes are combined with frankly secular or un-Christian imagery. None of this is explicitly pagan in the way that the Venus on the Projecta casket is an explicitly pagan goddess. The combined evidence of S. Costanza and Centcelles suggests the possibility that the blend of pagan and Christian themes acceptable to Christians on secular objects to be used at home was not the same blend as that acceptable (at least to some kinds of Christian) in places of cult. But even in churches or on Christian sarcophagi, like that of Constantina originally placed in S. Costanza[61] or the Three Good Shepherds sarcophagus from the Lateran collection (both now in the Vatican Museums),[62] generalized themes which were pagan in origin (like putti, vine-harvesting and so forth) were entirely acceptable, even though these continued to carry pagan as well as Christian connotations throughout the fourth century.

To find explicitly pagan images combined with Christian themes in a cultic context, we need to look at the catacombs. The Via Latina catacomb in Rome, for example, discovered in 1955, dates from the mid to late fourth century.[63] It is unusual in being regular in shape and small by the standards of the great catacombs of Rome. Iconographically the picture is rather complex. Some rooms have exclusively Christian and Old Testament cycles. Two are exclusively 'pagan' in imagery – cubiculum N portraying a cycle of the myths of Heracles and cubiculum E an image interpreted as the death of Cleopatra or possibly Tellus, with a gorgon's head in the vault. Others still, namely cubiculum O and the octagonal room I, have syncretistic combinations of images. In the passage to cubiculum O are paintings of Ceres and Proserpina, while in Room I a unique scene of a doctor or philosopher explaining a human body to his

---

[59] The building's two apses are probably later (c. A.D. 400) dating from the Mausoleum's conversion to a church. They contain (unfortunately much restored, indeed remade) dogmatic images, in which Christ appears to give the Law to Peter and Paul and his keys to Peter. See Stern (1958), for general discussion and Hellemo (1989) 65–71 on the apses, with bibliography.

[60] On Centcelles, see Schlunk (1988).

[61] On the sarcophagus of Constantina, see Kleiner (1992) 457–8, with bibliography 464.

[62] On the Three Good Shepherds sarcophagus, see Bovini and Brandenburg (1967) 26–7.

[63] For English discussion see Tronzo (1986) and Ferrua (1990).

students is counterposed symmetrically against an image of Jesus giving the Law to Peter and Paul.

André Grabar writes:

Curiously enough, among the dead interred in this hypogaeum, while the majority were Christians, there were also pagans. With exemplary tolerance they were all buried together, although – judging by the paintings – in different cubicula. Christian and pagan paintings seem to be contemporary; so it is not a case of a pagan family subsequently converting to Christianity.[64]

The conclusion that a mixture of Christian and pagan iconography should be explained by a mixture of actual Christians and actual pagans doing the commissioning, was also reached in the original publication of the catacomb in 1960 and has been underwritten as recently as 1986.[65] But how do scholars know that the people buried here were a mix of pagans and Christians? Only from the iconographical clue that pagan and Christian themes are painted in the catacomb. The unquestioned assumption is that a pagan image must point to a pagan belief and hence to a 'real' pagan who caused it to be put there and was buried beneath it. Likewise with Christian iconography and 'real' Christians. But is this kind of interpretation, with its rigid insistence on a simple correspondence of iconography and doctrine, convincing in the light of the Esquiline Treasure? Why should we assume that iconography points literally to what it appears to represent? Above all, the reductivist assumptions underlying these modern interpretations ignore the wealth of allegorical and exegetic methods of interpretation – not only Christian but also Jewish and pagan – which emerged in the early centuries after Christ.

4. Creative viewing: typology, allegory and the art of reading images

For the Jews, the Pentateuch was the Law; for the Christians it had become the Old Law, which prefigured, was fulfilled in and became redundant because of the New Law (the Law handed by Christ to Peter and Paul, as depicted in so many early Christian representations).[66] This change in relationship to the text of the Bible created a change in the nature of interpretation, and typological exegesis was born. Christian typology essentially involved seeing ancient stories and themes as enigmatic prefigurings of the incarnate truth as revealed in the Gospels. Subjects no longer had a single literal meaning, but might refer allegorically or symbolically to other truths.[67] In the case, for instance, of the beautiful Carrand diptych, the

---

[64] Grabar (1966) 225.   [65] Ferrua (1960) 94 and Engemann (1986) 92.

[66] On the *traditio* of the Law to Peter and Paul, see Hellemo (1989) 65–89 and (for some of its ironies) Sullivan (1994).

[67] On typology and Christian art, see Grabar (1969) 109–48 and Malbon (1990) 42–4, 129–36.

apostolic mission of St Paul is set beside the image of Adam in Paradise before the Fall. The activities of Christian sainthood become visually and typologically related to Paradise, and hence figure the possibility of redemption from sin to a state of prelapsarian innocence.[68]

The Christian allegorical heritage in art owed much to the rich traditions of philosophic and Jewish allegory which were common in the Roman world. The former is perhaps most remarkably exemplified by the *Tabula* of Cebes, an allegorical exegesis of a picture by a pagan philosopher-sage which is presented as a religious initiation and probably dates from the first century A.D. The picture itself does not survive, but its interpretation as transmitted by this text shows the range and sophistication of pagan visual exegesis.[69] The influence of Cebes' text in pagan tradition is marked by several references and even imitations in the writings of Lucian (e.g. *Rhetorum Praeceptor* VI and *De Mercede Conductis* XLII). Jewish allegory, which provided commentary on texts rather than images, reached its apogee in the writings of Philo of Alexandria (a contemporary of St Paul). Philo's texts were to prove particularly influential on the Alexandrine Christian tradition as exemplified by Clement of Alexandria and Origen, and on such fourth-century Platonizing Fathers as Gregory of Nyssa. In the fourth century itself paganism, in the person of the Neoplatonic master Iamblichus of Chalcis, created its own powerful model of allegorical exegesis tied to ritual acts in theurgy, the religious system espoused by Julian. Iamblichus specifically recommended that images be used as ritual symbols in theurgy (*De Mysteriis Aegyptiorum* VII.1–3). Neoplatonic patterns of interpretation were also to prove influential on later Christianity.[70] Intellectually the fourth century was immensely creative and innovative in producing new methods of interpretation and novel patterns of initiation; it was supremely an age of exegesis, particularly of literature and theology. Such exegesis does not deserve to be dismissed as 'a sequence of misplaced discoveries'.[71] On the contrary, it marks a radically new relationship between the present and the past which is of the utmost importance for understanding the conceptual framework within which Christians throughout the Middle Ages interpreted not only their art but everything else in their world.

This exegetic frame of interpretation was not limited only to Old Testament themes. It came to be applied more broadly to many pagan myths and to authors like Homer or Virgil. Hence we find in both art and literature representations of the Christian Orpheus, the Christian Sol, the

---

[68] On the Carrand diptych, see Shelton (1989), with bibliography at p. 126 n. 3.

[69] On the *Tabula* of Cebes, see Fitzgerald and White (1983) and Elsner (1995) 39–46.

[70] On allegory in paganism, see Lamberton (1986) and Dawson (1992) 23–72; on the development of Christian allegory and figural discourse, see *ibid.* 127–240 and Cameron, Averil, *Rhetoric of Empire* 47–88.   [71] Lane Fox (1986) 649–52.

Christian Bellerophon, and the assimilation in Christian iconography of pagan themes such as Hermes Criophorus and Endymion sleeping to Christian subjects like Christ the Good Shepherd and the sleep of Jonah under the gourd.[72] Remarkable examples of such Christianizing interpretations of ancient poems through exegesis include Constantine's fourth-century interpretation of Virgil's Fourth Eclogue as a Christian prophecy,[73] and a remarkable range of allegories of the Homeric theme of Odysseus and the sirens.[74]

It is striking that images of Odysseus and the sirens (assuredly pagan images from pagan contexts) offered the possibility of being interpreted in profoundly Christian ways by Christians who may have seen them. For Basil (*Ad Adulescentes* IV) and Fulgentius (*Fabulae secundum Philosophiam moraliter expositae* II.8), Odysseus was the type of wisdom striving for virtue. For Clement of Alexandria (*Protrepticus* XII) and Jerome (*Capitulationes Libri Josue, praef.*), he is the paradigm of one who passed by the siren-song of death. For Hippolytus of Rome (*Elenchus* VII.13.1–3) the waxed ears of Odysseus' companions are the appropriate response to the 'doctrines of heretics'. Both Clement and Hippolytus create a complex allegory in which the ship of Odysseus is piloted by the Logos, with its mast being the cross itself. Such readings are not the only Christian response to this pagan theme, but they are a possible response, and one exemplified in a number of texts from east and west. They represent the exegetic relationship of Christianity with its past and suggest a range of possible meanings that could be discovered in other pagan themes by a sympathetic Christian.

It should perhaps be added that such allegorical and speculative interpretations seem to have been a popular feature of the more syncretistic areas of late antique religion. There are hints in the Mishnah and in some second-century writers, such as Melito of Sardis and Tertullian, of a Jewish interpretation of Serapis as Joseph.[75] In paganism there were numerous deities with whom Serapis was conflated and identified, including Pluto, Osiris, Dionysus, Apis, Asclepius and Zeus.[76] The non-Christian cults of late antiquity provide us with evidence of soteriological exegesis (for example, in the cult of Cybele and Attis),[77] of the exegesis by one cult of another cult's system (for example, a Neoplatonic Mithras),[78] and of frequent inter-cult syncretism, at least on the artistic level. The Walbrook Mithraeum in London (dating from the mid third to the mid fourth

---

[72] On this imagery, see Huskinson (1974).
[73] On the Fourth Eclogue, see e.g. Lane Fox (1986) 649–51.
[74] On Odysseus and the Sirens, see Rahner (1963) 328–86.
[75] On Serapis as Joseph, see Mussies (1979).   [76] On Serapis syncretized, see Stambaugh (1972) 3.
[77] On soteriology in the cult of Cybele and Attis, see Gasparro (1985) 60–1.
[78] On the Platonic Mithras, see Turcan (1975).

centuries), for instance, yielded sculptures of Mithras, Mercury, Minerva and Serapis.[79]

Let us return to the Heracles cycle in the Via Latina catacomb. In cubiculum N, the lunettes of the two arcosolia show scenes from the Alcestis myth. On the left Alcestis stands at the deathbed of her husband Admetus; on the right she returns to Admetus after having been liberated from death by Heracles, who is holding both his club and Cerberus, the conquered hound of Hell. This theme can be paralleled from other necropolis paintings in antiquity. It is not difficult to recognize its resonance in a funerary location, or its allegorical possibilities, bearing in mind the numerous Christian typological images (such as Daniel in the Lions' Den) in the Via Latina catacomb. By contrast with scholarly assumptions, these images do not imply that pagans occupied this room. Rather, they cry out for exegetic and typological interpretations which could make them no less Christian than the Venus on the Projecta casket. The fact that we possess no texts to support such a Christian exegesis of Heracles is not important. The extent of creative typological reading in the period was an invitation to fourth-century viewers to make such an interpretation. Once such exegesis exists, it is up to different viewers to apply its interpretative possibilities with as much originality as they wish. The room itself, within the Via Latina Catacomb, is evidence that images were creating the possibility for such a Christianizing allegory of Heracles to take place.

On the side walls of the chamber are four further scenes, this time of Heracles' labours. We see his conquests over Antaios and the Hydra, as well as the theft of the golden apples of the Hesperides and a meeting with the goddess Athena. Again, the labours of Heracles can be paralleled in funerary art – for instance, on sarcophagi. Moreover, on the analogy of Odysseus and the sirens or the Christian Bellerophon, one can see how such conquests of the monstrous can be read allegorically in a Christian way.[80] Likewise, the theft of the precious apples and the meeting with one's god can be entirely comprehensible *allegorically* to a Christian viewer. The placing of these images in this context allows for this Christian reading among other possibilities. In effect, the traditions of allegory and typology in viewing images of Old and New Testament themes had an inevitable seepage into similar syncretistic ways of viewing images from sources other than the Christian and Jewish scriptures.

Certainly, typology is a crucial key to understanding the conceptual frame of the fourth century. As one scholar has described it, 'typology perceives patterns; it integrates potentially divergent traditions'.[81] The most

[79] On the Walbrook Mithraeum, see Toynbee (1986).
[80] For a number of pagan heroes in specifically Christian contexts, see Huskinson (1974): examples listed in the appendix, 85–90.   [81] Malbon (1990) 149.

impressive Christian iconographic programmes of late antiquity are those whose multiple images are knit together in an interpretative typological framework. Such programmes include the very grand, such as the mid-fifth-century mosaic cycle (now sadly incomplete) of the nave and triumphal arch of the church of S. Maria Maggiore in Rome[82] or the fifth-century doors of S. Sabina,[83] both of which combine Old Testament, New Testament and apocryphal themes; also they include such relatively humble objects as the late-fourth-century ivory *lipsanotheca* now in Brescia[84] or the small but impressive silver-gilt reliquary found under the high altar of San Nazaro Maggiore in Milan and probably made in the episcopate of Ambrose.[85] Particularly important for their typological programmes are the great Christian sarcophagi of the fourth century, such as the Adelphia sarcophagus in Syracuse (probably made in Rome), the great sarcophagus from Sant' Ambrogio in Milan[86] and that of the Two Brothers in the Vatican.[87] A prime case is the magnificent marble columnar sarcophagus of Junius Bassus (the city prefect and son of the consul) who died newly baptized in A.D. 359.[88] The iconography of this remarkable monument involves a complex typology of Christological, Old Testament and martyrological scenes. In the spandrels of the arches on the lower columns of the sarcophagus are six Old and New Testament themes in which all the figures are represented symbolically as lambs. The high level of biblical knowledge and interpretative ability which such objects demanded of their viewers demonstrates the great complexity and sophistication of meaning which Christian art so quickly developed in the decades after the death of Constantine.

5. Images and power: art, state and church in early Christendom

The toleration of Christianity proclaimed in 313 led to a remarkable transformation in Christian liturgy and its artistic and architectural settings. From house-churches like the third-century baptistery of Dura Europos, Christian ritual moved into huge basilicas in the major cities.[89] From using adapted domestic buildings, Christians found themselves worshipping in new purpose-built churches. From informal journeys by individuals like Melito of Sardis in the second century A.D. to the Holy Land, pilgrimage after the time of Constantine became an institution attracting large

---

[82] On the mosaics of S. Maria Maggiore, see Spain (1979) and Miles (1993).
[83] On the doors of S. Sabina, see Jeremias (1980).
[84] On the Brescia casket, see Watson (1981), with bibliography.
[85] On the San Nazaro reliquary, see Kiilerich (1993) 181–2, with bibliography.
[86] On the Milan city gate sarcophagus, see Sansoni (1969) 3–12.
[87] On the Two Brothers Sarcophagus, see Bovini and Brandenburg (1967) 43–5.
[88] On the Junius Bassus sarcophagus, see Malbon (1990).
[89] On the beginnings of this process, see White (1990).

numbers of the pious.[90] Several first-hand accounts by fourth-century visitors to Palestine like the Bordeaux Pilgrim of A.D. 333 and Egeria, a woman from the western Mediterranean who visited the Holy Land in the 380s, attest to the many pilgrims who thronged the holy places, the existence of facilities to look after them and the interest back at home in their reports.[91] And not only Palestine. Martyria (shrines celebrating the graves and relics of local martyrs) sprang up all over the empire in the fourth and fifth centuries, and these local cults became centres of pilgrimage in their own right.[92] All this religious activity required impressive settings – churches, images and liturgical vessels. Furthermore, visitors to the new multitude of shrines throughout the Roman world demanded souvenirs and relics. By the sixth century, this demand had led to the mass production of amulets, reliquaries, *ampullae* and all manner of small-scale portable paraphernalia, including icons. Comparatively little of this sort has survived from the fourth century, but it is clear that even at that date much must have been produced. The Brescia *lipsanotheca*, a beautiful ivory box whose Christological themes are represented in large scale between smaller borders decorated with Old Testament subjects, is the most impressive reliquary remaining from the period.

The art of church building, of liturgy, of pilgrimage to the tombs of those who died for the faith differs fundamentally from the more secular and syncretistic kinds discussed above. For it is defined by its exclusively Christian and even sacramental nature. A martyrium, for instance, celebrates someone put to death by pagans; it would be unlikely to use pagan iconography for doing this, in the manner of the Projecta casket or the Via Latina catacomb – although it might still make use of classical decorative motifs.

Very little decoration survives today from the many churches built in the fourth century. It has been argued that Constantine was careful to exclude pictorial representations from the great basilicas he constructed in Rome, Constantinople and Jerusalem.[93] Indeed, many in the hierarchy of the early church were hesitant about the use of art or even opposed to images.[94] St Augustine in the west and St Epiphanius of Salamis in the eastern church agreed that images 'lie' (Epiphanius' word in his *Letter to the Emperor Theodosius*), since they are not what they represent. As Augustine put it (*Soliloquies* II.10.18): 'A man in a painting cannot be true, even though he tends towards the appearance of a man.' Others in the fourth century, however, such as Nilus of Sinai (in his *Letter to Prefect Olympiodorus*), argued

[90] On early Christian pilgrimage to the Holy Land, see Hunt, *Holy Land Pilgrimage*, Walker (1990) and Taylor (1993).
[91] On such early Christian pilgrims, see Wilkinson (1971) (with translations of Egeria and the Bordeaux Pilgrim).   [92] Grabar (1946) is the classic study, with Ward-Perkins (1966).
[93] Grigg (1977).   [94] See Kitzinger (1954) and C. Murray (1981).

that images were useful as a way of teaching the illiterate. This was the view which became canonical, at least in the west, after the pronouncements of Gregory the Great on the matter in the sixth century.[95] Certainly as Christianization grew more dominant towards the end of the fourth century, the use of figurative images increased, partly as an aspect of church policy and partly in response to the demands of the laity.

Whatever the theoretical debate about the value of images among theologians, Christian art, including figurative and devotional images, became increasingly popular as an integral part of ecclesiastical, imperial and aristocratic patronage. Already in the mid fourth century there is written evidence that Christian portraits and the kinds of devotional images which were the precursors of icons were being produced. Eusebius refers to paintings of Christ and the apostles (*HE* VII.18.4) and, if his letter to Constantine's sister Constantia is genuine, expressed spirited opposition on theological grounds to her request for a portrait of Christ. The later years of the fourth century in Rome see the dedication of impressive figurative mosaics in the churches. The most distinguished (though somewhat overrestored) survival is the great apse mosaic of S. Pudenziana, dating from the 390s, where Christ is shown enthroned in majesty between the twelve apostles in the heavenly Jerusalem.[96] A number of aristocratic patrons funded decorations for the earlier imperial churches of the city in the same period, mosaics for the façade of St Peter's and apse mosaics for S. Lorenzo fuori le Mura and S. Giovanni in Laterano.[97] Today, very little remains of these first great Christian figurative programmes which were designed as the visual setting for the prime liturgical spaces of the empire's greatest liturgical buildings. But some early mosaics do survive in fragments from elsewhere, such as the late-fourth-century apses of the imperial chapel of S. Aquilino in the church of S. Lorenzo in Milan.[98]

The patterns of patronage vary somewhat through the empire. In Rome, imperial church building (at which we glanced above, pp. 738-9) was exceeded by papal and other local patronage. In the fourth and early fifth centuries the first churches of S. Maria in Trastevere, S. Lorenzo in Damaso and S. Maria Maggiore with its magnificent cycle of mosaics were constructed by the popes.[99] In the same period both wealthy clerics and aristocrats built S. Pudenziana, SS. Giovanni e Paolo, SS. Gervasio e Protasio (now S. Vitale) and S. Sabina.[100] Episcopal and ecclesiastic patronage of church building was strong not only in Rome but also in Italy as a whole,

[95] On Gregory's pronouncements, see Duggan (1989) and Chazelle (1990).
[96] On the mosaics of S. Pudenziana, see Hellemo (1989) 41–63 and Matthews (1993) 92–114.
[97] On these dedications, see Ward-Perkins, *Public Building* 239.
[98] On S. Lorenzo, see Hellemo (1989) 18–19, 29–30, 37–9, with bibliography.
[99] On papal dedications in Rome, see Ward-Perkins, *Public Building* 237.
[100] On these churches, see Ward-Perkins, *Public Building* 239–40.

where the influence of the church became a rival to that of the emperor as early as the dispute between Theodosius and Ambrose in the late fourth century. In Milan, for instance, the site of Ambrose's see, the state appears to have been responsible for S. Lorenzo, perhaps the loveliest of all fourth-century churches to survive into the modern age, with its imperial chapels (or mausolea), S. Ippolito and S. Aquilino, and S. Tecla, the city's original cathedral.[101] Ambrose, the city's bishop, built S. Nazaro in 382, which contains the relics of the local saints Nazarius and Celsus, S. Simpliciano and the church now known as S. Ambrogio, in which he deposited the miraculously discovered relics of the martyrs Gervasius and Protasius.[102]

The miraculous discovery of saints' bodies and their subsequent inclusion in churches (or the building of churches specially for them) began to occur with some frequency in the late fourth and early fifth centuries. This appealed directly to the new passion for pilgrimage and for relics. It made the place of finding the body, and the place to which it was moved, important pilgrimage centres. Ambrose was particularly prolific when it came to this kind of miraculous exhumation; he found the martyrs Vitalis and Agricola in Bologna in 393, some seven years after his discoveries in Milan.[103] His contemporary, pope Damasus, had found 'many saints' bodies' (*Liber Pont.* 1.212) in Rome; and numerous other saints would be discovered, from Toulouse to the Holy Land, in the years between 380 and 415. Such finds gave local churches a certain control over religious charisma and allowed them influence in the building and financing of basilicas.

Nevertheless, in the east the emperors were still the most opulent patrons. In Constantinople they completed Constantine's foundations of Hagia Sophia, Hagia Irene and the Church of the Holy Apostles, which was the imperial mausoleum. A number of other imperial foundations followed, including Chalkoprateia and Blachernae. Hagia Sophia, which had been dedicated in 360, had to be rebuilt and reconsecrated in 415 after fire damage in the riots of 404. Nevertheless, the mid-fifth-century *Notitia Urbis* (an enumerative list of landmarks) indicates only fourteen churches in Constantinople a century after its foundation.[104]

It was in the Holy Land, above all, that the cult of the saints, the demands of pilgrimage and the lavishness of imperial finance combined to produce an extraordinary spate of church building. As Eusebius reports in his *Vita Constantini*, Constantine built the Martyrium or Golgotha basilica on the site of the Holy Sepulchre (Christ's tomb and the place of the Resurrection), the Nativity basilica in Bethlehem, the Eleona church on the Mount of Olives at what was believed to be the site of the Ascension, and the basilica at Mamre near Hebron where Abraham had entertained his

---

[101] On Milan, see Krautheimer, *Architecture* 55–60 and (1983) 68–92.
[102] On these discoveries, see McLynn (1994) 211–17, 220–35.   [103] See *ibid.* 343–50.
[104] On fourth- and fifth-century Constantinople, see Mango (1985) 23–50.

three angelic visitors.[105] To these buildings, extra appendages were rapidly added in succeeding years, such as the Anastasis rotunda at the Holy Sepulchre. In Jerusalem the fourth century saw imperial subsidies for church building in the form of tax exemption by Theodosius, and many more churches were erected, such as the Sion basilica, the Lazarium and the Imbomon.[106] In the first half of the fifth century, Eudoxia, wife of Theodosius II, emulated her royal predecessor Helena in visiting the Holy Land, where she subsequently settled. Her patronage included funds for the martyrium of St Stephen, the monastery of Bassa and other churches.[107]

Ecclesiastical and imperial patronage showed the state, in the form of the governing hierarchy, appropriating Christianity to itself by controlling funding and consequently visual settings. Art and architecture, in the hands of the empire's aristocratic hierarchy both temporal and spiritual, became a means of romanizing Christianity by making it a religion that fitted the social and political needs of the empire. Christian art began to borrow forms for its principal images from the representation of imperial ceremonial.[108] For instance, in the central scenes of the sarcophagus of Junius Bassus, Christ appears in the role of universal emperor seated over a figure of the sky and enters Jerusalem in the form of the imperial *adventus* (compare the Kerch silver dish, now in St Petersburg, showing the *adventus* of Constantius II).[109]

Likewise, imperial art grew iconic, appropriating to itself the abstraction and symbolism of the sacred image as created by the religious cults. In the great silver Missorium (or dish) of Theodosius I, dating to 388 and now in Madrid, the haloed emperor, larger than his symmetrically arranged colleagues, sits gazing full-frontally at the viewer above a representation of the earth. A schematic and hieratic relationship of viewer and viewed is implied, with the emperor far removed from the human level (the viewer's level) to which his icon is addressed.[110] One of the earliest consular diptychs to survive, that of Probus dated to A.D. 406 and now in Aosta cathedral, has the emperor Honorius represented twice in military dress and halo, with a Christian banner prominently displayed.[111] He too is isolated in a niche, with the abstracted gaze of late antique charisma, like the consular portraits of Constantius II and his Caesar Gallus from the celebrated

---

[105] On Constantine's churches, see Hunt, *Holy Land Pilgrimage* 6–27 and Wilkinson (1971) 36–54.

[106] On later-fourth-century church building in Jerusalem, see Wilkinson (1971) 47–54.

[107] On Eudoxia in Palestine, see Holum, *Theodosian Empresses* 217–28.

[108] This view, which has been dubbed 'the Emperor Mystique', has now been systematically attacked by Mathews (1993). I think Mathews rather overstates his case.

[109] On the Junius Bassus images of Christ, see Malbon (1990) 49–54 (Matthews does not discuss this sarcophagus); on the Kerch dish, see Delbrueck (1933) 144–51.

[110] On the Missorium of Theodosius, see Kiilerich (1993) 19–26, with bibliography 19, n. 40.

[111] On the Probus diptych, see Kiilerich (1993) 65–7, with bibliography 65, n. 217.

codex-calendar of A.D. 354, which survives in Renaissance copies and of which the forms prefigure the evangelists' portraits in so many later manuscripts.[112] Such images recall the remarkable verbal portrait of Constantius II which Ammianus draws at XVI.10.10:

As if his neck were in a vice, he kept the gaze of his eyes straight ahead, and turned his face neither right nor left . . . as if he were the image of a man.

(Trans. J. C. Rolfe, Loeb edn)

Likewise one is reminded of Gregory of Nyssa's portrait (written in the late fourth century) of Gregory Thaumaturgus, bishop of Neocaesarea, who astonished observers by entering his home town without his expression or his glance straying. Whether sacred or secular, these accounts and images portray a new kind of charisma fashioned through the intermingling of Christianity with late Roman culture.

Such images and descriptions portray a stratified world in which the charisma of the portrayed, be he saint, emperor or consul, is of a different order from that of both his colleagues and his viewers. Something of this distinction is illustrated in other early consular diptychs, which are themselves secular icons designed to laud the temporal authority of the figure whom they celebrate. The Lampadii ivory leaf, dated to about 415 and now in Brescia, depicts the great man (presumably Lampadius as consul) larger than his two companions and framed in a niche.[113] He appears in the top half of the panel, as a state icon, gazing out and down on to the circus races for which, the image implies, he has paid. The movement and profiles of the lower half of the image contrast markedly with the static enthronement above. In similar vein, the Probianus diptych in Berlin (about A.D. 400) depicts in the upper tier the *vicarius* of Rome seated grandly in an exquisite perspectival niche with two attendants in smaller scale than him.[114] Beneath, two small figures in togas acclaim him. Again, the space is divided into two parts, with the iconic image of authority at the top and the more dynamic image of the populace below.

The ivory diptychs show the Roman state as it wished itself to be seen. They are the visual equivalent of the political theory of Eusebius (in the *Laus Constantini*) in which the secular order imitates the divine order: as God rules the spiritual realm, so the emperor rules the temporal realm. Here, in an abstract iconic language equally suited to the depiction of Christ the universal emperor and Caesar the temporal emperor, art has achieved a fusion of secular and spiritual paradigms, which late antique rulers sought in order to bolster their prestige. In the case of these consular diptychs, the authority of Christ and the emperor is represented by the

---

[112] On the codex-calendar of A.D. 354, see Salzman, *Roman Time*.

[113] On the Lampadii leaf, see Kiilerich (1993) 143–4, with bibliography.

[114] On the Probianus diptych, see Kiilerich (1993) 141–3, with bibliography.

consul whose power is held in both their names. Such images not only depict ceremonial – they are a part of it, used in public display and in private rituals of exchange. In such ceremonies, and in its public appearance on the great buildings of the state, the distinctive art and architecture of late antiquity played its own active and influential part in the transformation of Roman culture.[115]

[115] My thanks are due to Margaret Atkins, Averil Cameron, Robin Cormack and Janet Huskinson for their comments. This chapter was written in 1991 and revised (largely bibliographically) in spring 1994. In the footnotes I refer readers where possible to English-language discussions of monuments, only suggesting foreign publications *in extremis* where no (recent) English discussion exists. In the bibliography, I have cited some fundamental non-English works.

CHRONOLOGICAL TABLE

A.D.	Emperors		The West
337	Death of Constantine (22 May). Constans, Constantine II and Constantius proclaimed emperors (9 September)		
340	Constantine II killed (spring)		
350	Magnentius proclaimed emperor in Gaul. Constans killed (shortly after 18 January)		
351	Gallus, brother of Julian, appointed Caesar; executed 354		
353	Magnentius commits suicide		
		355	Usurpation of Silvanus in Gaul; Silvanus assassinated; Cologne sacked by Franks
		355–9	Julian campaigns in Gaul; besieged at Sens by Alamanni; battle of Strasbourg (357); treaty of federation with Franks (357/8); restoration of Roman fortresses along the Rhine
360	Julian (Caesar 355) proclaimed emperor at Paris		
361	Constantius II died (3 November)		
363	Death of Julian in Mesopotamia while on campaign in the east (26 June). Jovian proclaimed		
364	Jovian dies near Ancyra (17 February). Valentinian I proclaimed (26 February); nominates his brother Valens as co-emperor in the east		
365	Revolt of Procopius in the east		
367	Valentinian's son Gratian proclaimed co-emperor, aged eight	367, 369	Valens leads armies across the Danube
		370–1	Treason trials at Rome; revolt of Firmus in N. Africa
		375	Valentinian I campaigns on lower Rhine and against the Quadi; Milan becomes seat of western court
375	Valentinian I dies after a stroke (17 November). Valentinian II, aged four, proclaimed emperor with Gratian	376	Tervingi allowed to cross the Danube

762

The East	Cultural and Religious
337–50 Early wars of Constantius II against Persia	
	340 Athanasius exiled
343–4 Battle of Singara	343 Council of Sardica
345 Constantius in Nisibis	
346 Second siege of Nisibis	346 Athanasius restored
350 Third siege of Nisibis	350 Death of Pachomius
350–60 Later Persian wars of Constantius II	
	356 Athanasius exiled again
	356 Death of Antony
359 Siege and fall of Amida	
363 Julian at Antioch	
363 Julian's Persian expedition	
364 Jovian's treaty with Persia	
365/6 Constantinople seized by Procopius	
	370–9 Basil bishop of Caesarea
	371–2 Trials at Antioch
	c. 371–97 Martin bishop of Tours
	373 Death of Athanasius
	374–97 Ambrose bishop of Milan

A.D.	Emperors	The West
378	Valens marches west from Antioch against Goths, reaches Constantinople (30 May), killed in battle of Adrianople (9 August)	
379	Theodosius, son of the elder Theodosius, Valentinian's *magister equitum* (executed 375), proclaimed emperor at Sirmium (19 January)	
		382 Peace treaty with Goths
383	Magnus Maximus proclaimed emperor in Britain and invades Gaul; Gratian deserted by his troops and killed (25 August). Magnus Maximus recognized as emperor by Theodosius. Invades Italy 387; Valentinian II and his mother Justina flee to Thessalonica. Arcadius, son of Theodosius, proclaimed emperor in east (19 January)	
388	Magnus Maximus defeated by Theodosius and killed	
392	Valentinian II commits suicide having failed to dismiss Arbogast; Eugenius proclaimed emperor	
393	Honorius, son of Theodosius, proclaimed emperor	
394	Eugenius and Arbogast defeated by Theodosius' army at river Frigidus	
395	Theodosius I dies at Milan. His sons Honorius and Arcadius rule as emperors in west and east respectively	395 The ascendancy of Stilicho
		397–8 Revolt of Gildo in Africa

The East	Cultural and Religious
379 Death of Shapur II of Persia	379 Death of Basil of Caesarea; Gregory of Nazianzus, *Funeral Oration on Basil*
	381 Council of Constantinople
	382 Altar of Victory removed from senate in Rome
	382 Jerome in Rome, forced to leave 384
	383 Gratian drops title of *pontifex maximus*
	384 Symmachus' *Relationes* about the altar of Victory
387 Riot of the Statues, Antioch	
	389–90 Libanius, *For the Temples*
390 Riot and massacre at Thessalonica	
391 Destruction of Serapaeum of Alexandria	391–2 Theodosius I's legislation against paganism
395 Alaric and Goths threaten Constantinople; Gainas and Eastern armies return to Constantinople and assassinate Rufinus	395–430 Augustine bishop of Hippo
396 Alaric and Goths ravage Greece	
397–8 Synesius in Constantinople	397 Augustine's *Confessions*
	398–404 John Chrysostom bishop of Constantinople
399 Revolt of Tribigild and Greuthungi in Phrygia; execution of Eutropius	399 Origenist monks go into exile from Egypt
400 Gainas leaves Constantinople and withdraws to Thrace; massacre of Goths in city; Gainas defeated by Fravitta, killed by Huns December/January 400/401	

A.D.	Emperors		The West
		406	Vandals, Alans, Sueves cross Rhine.
407–13	Series of would-be usurpers in the west, successfully suppressed.		
408	Arcadius dies and is succeeded by his son Theodosius II, aged seven	408	Alaric and Visigoths enter Italy; fall and death of Stilicho
		410	Sack of Rome by Alaric
		410	Revolt of Britain; Honorius writes to cities of Britain
		414	Marriage of Athaulf and Galla Placidia at Narbonne
		418	Goths settled in southern Gaul
421	Constantius, *magister utriusque militiae* in the west since 411, and married to Galla Placidia in 417, declared emperor by Honorius (8 February); not recognized in the east. He dies of an illness after six months (2 September)		
423	Death of Honorius		
425	Honorius' nephew Valentinian becomes emperor as Valentinian III, after a brief period during which John, the *primicerius notariorum*, had been proclaimed		
		429	Vandals cross to Africa
		439	Vandals take Carthage
450	Theodosius II reigns in the east until his death in 450, when he is succeeded by the elderly senator Marcian, his rule reinforced by his marriage to Theodosius' sister the Augusta Pulcheria		

The East	Cultural and Religious
	402 Temples in Gaza destroyed with imperial sanction
	411 Council of Carthage condemns Donatists
	412 Cyril becomes bishop of Alexandria
	413–25 Augustine writing the *City of God*
	415 Hypatia killed by mob in Alexandria
	418 Council of Carthage condemns Pelagianism; Orosius' *History against the Pagans*
	c. 420 John Cassian's *Institutes*
	423 S. Symeon the Elder ascends pillar
	431 Council of Ephesus
	438 Theodosian Code

BIBLIOGRAPHY

ABBREVIATIONS

AASS Maii	*Acta Sanctorum* (May), 71 vols. 1863–1940
ABull	*The Art Bulletin*
AC	*Acta Classica*
ACO	*Acta Conciliorum Oecumenicorum*, ed. E. Schwartz, Berlin
AE	*L'Année Épigraphique*
AJA	*American Journal of Archaeology*
AJAHist	*American Journal of Ancient History*
AJP	*American Journal of Philology*
Amb. Op.	*Opera Omnia di Sant' Ambrogio*, Milan and Rome 1979–
Anal. Boll.	*Analecta Bollandiana*
Annales (ESC)	*Annales (Économies, Sociétés, Civilisations)*
ANRW	*Aufstieg und Niedergang der römischen Welt*, ed. H. Temporini. Berlin 1972–
Ant. Afr.	*Antiquités Africaines*
AP	*L'Année Philologique*
APF	*Archiv für Papyrusforschung und verwandte Gebiete*
ARCA	Classical and Medieval Texts, Papers and Monographs, Liverpool
Arch. Rev. from Cambr.	*Archaeological Review from Cambridge*
ASNP	*Annali della Scuola Normale Superiore di Pisa*
BASOR	Bulletin of the American Schools of Oriental Research
BAGB	*Bulletin d'Association Guillaume Budé*
BAR	British Archaeological Reports
BCH	*Bulletin de Correspondance Hellénique*
BCTH	*Bulletin Archéologique du Comité des Travaux Historiques*
BEFAR	Bibliothèque des Écoles Françaises d'Athènes et Rome
BLE	*Bulletin de Littérature Ecclésiastique*
BMGS	*Byzantine and Modern Greek Studies*
BSNAF	*Bulletin de la Société Nationale des Antiquaires de France*
BSOAS	*Bulletin of the School of Oriental and African Studies*
Bull. Am. Soc. Pap.	*Bulletin of the American Society of Papyrologists*
Byz. Forsch.	*Byzantinische Forschungen*
Byz. Zeit.	*Byzantinische Zeitschrift*

CAH	*Cambridge Ancient History*
CArch	*Cahiers Archéologiques*
CCSL	*Corpus Christianorum Series Latina*
CEFR	*Collection de l'École Française de Rome*
ChHist	*Church History*
Chron. Min.	*Chronica Minora*
CIL	*Corpus Inscriptionum Latinarum*
CJ	*Codex Justinianus*
C&M	*Classica et Mediaevalia*
CPh	*Classical Philology*
CQ	*Classical Quarterly*
CRAI	*Comptes Rendus de l'Académie des Inscriptions et Belles-Lettres*
CS	*Critica Storica*
CSCO	*Corpus Scriptorum Christianorum Orientalium*
CSEL	*Corpus Scriptorum Ecclesiasticorum Latinorum*, Vienna
C.Th.	*Codex Theodosianus*
DOP	*Dumbarton Oaks Papers*
Eccl. Occ. Mon.	*Ecclesiae occidentalis monumenta iuris antiquissima*, ed. C. Turner.
Iur. Ant.	Oxford, 1899–1939
EFR	École Française de Rome
EHBS	Ἐπετηρὶς Ἑταιρείας Βυζαντινῶν Σπουδῶν. Athens
EHR	*English Historical Review*
Entr. Hardt.	Entretiens Hardt
Epigr. Anat.	*Epigraphica Anatolica*
FHG	*Fragmenta Historicorum Graecorum*, ed. C. Müller
FIRA	*Fontes Iuris Romani Anteiustiniani*
GCS	*Die griechischen christlichen Schriftsteller der ersten drei Jahrhunderte.* Leipzig
GRBS	*Greek, Roman and Byzantine Studies*
GWU	*Geschichte in Wissenschaft und Unterricht*
Hist. Zeit.	*Historische Zeitschrift*
HSCP	*Harvard Studies in Classical Philology*
HThR	*Harvard Theological Review*
ICUR	*Inscriptiones christianae urbis Romae*, ed. Degrassi
IEJ	*Israel Exploration Journal*
IG	*Inscriptiones Graecae*
IGLS	*Inscriptions grecques et latines de la Syrie*, Paris
ILCV	*Inscriptiones Latinae Christianae Veteres*, ed. E. Diehl
ILS	*Inscriptiones Latinae Selectae*
IRT	*Inscriptions of Roman Tripolitania*, ed. J. M. Reynolds and J. B. Ward-Perkins. Rome 1952
JAOS	*Journal of the American Oriental Society*
JbAC	*Jahrbuch für Antike und Christentum*
JEA	*Journal of Egyptian Archaeology*
JEH	*Journal of Ecclesiastical History*
JESHO	*Journal of the Economic and Social History of the Orient*
JHS	*Journal of Hellenic Studies*

JJS	*Journal of Jewish Studies*
JöB	*Jahrbuch der österreichischen Byzantinistik*
JQR	*Jewish Quarterly Review*
JRA	*Journal of Roman Archaeology*
JRS	*Journal of Roman Studies*
JS	*Journal des Savants*
JSS	*Journal of Semitic Studies*
JThS	*Journal of Theological Studies*
MAAR	*Memoirs of the American Academy in Rome*
MBAH	*Münsterische Beiträge zur antiken Handelsgeschichte*
MDAI(R)	*Mitteilungen des Deutschen Archäologischen Instituts* (Röm. Abt.)
Med. Hist. Rev.	*The Mediterranean Historical Review*
MEFR	*Mélanges d'Archéologie et d'Histoire de l'École Française de Rome*
MGH, Auct.	
Ant.	*Monumenta Historiae Germaniae, Auctores Antiquissimi*
MH	*Museum Helveticum*
MIOEG	*Mitteilungen des Instituts für österreichische Geschichtsforschung*
Nott. Med. St.	*Nottingham Medieval Studies*
OCA	Orientalia Christiana Analecta
OCP	*Orientalia Christiana Periodica*
OJA	*Oxford Journal of Archaeology*
OLA	Orientalia Lovaniensia Analecta
OLP	*Orientalia Lovaniensia Periodica*
P.Abinn.	*The Abinnaeus Archive*, ed. H. I. Bell and others. Oxford 1962
P.Bodm.	*Papyri Bodmer*, Fondation Martin Bodmer, Geneva
P.Ital.	*Die nichtliterarischen lateinischen Papyri Italiens aus der Zeit 445–700*, ed. J. O. Tjäder. Lund 1955
P.Lond.	*Greek Papyri in the British Museum*, ed. F. G. Kenyon and H. I. Bell. London, 1893–1917
P.Mich.	*Papyri in the University of Michigan Collection*, Ann Arbor 1931–
P.Oxy.	*The Oxyrhynchus Papyri*, ed. B. P. Grenfell and others. London, 1898–
PBA	*Proceedings of the British Academy*
PBSR	*Papers of the British School at Rome*
PCPS	*Proceedings of the Cambridge Philological Society*
PG	*Patrologia Graeca*, ed. J.-P. Migne
PL	*Patrologia Latina*, ed. J.-P. Migne
PLRE i	*Prosopography of the Later Roman Empire* i, ed. Jones, Martindale and Morris, 1971
PO	*Patrologia Orientalis*
PP	*Parola del Passato*
PSI	*Papyri Greci e Latini, Pubblicazioni della Società italiana per la ricerca dei papiri greci e latini in Egitto.* 1912–
QUCC	*Quaderni Urbinati di Cultura Classica*
RAC	*Reallexikon für Antike und Christentum.* Stuttgart
RD	*Revue Historique de Droit Français et Étranger*
RE	Pauly-Wissowa, *Real-Encyclopädie der classischen Altertumswissenschaft*
REA	*Revue des Études Anciennes*

REB	*Revue des Études Byzantines*
RecPhL	*Recherches de Philologie et de Linguistique*, Louvain
RecSR	*Recherches de Science Religieuse*
REL	*Revue des Études Latines*
RFIC	*Rivista di filologia e di istruzione classica*
RH	*Revue Historique*
RHE	*Revue d'Histoire Ecclésiastique*
RIC	*Roman Imperial Coinage*
RIDA	*Revue Internationale des Droits de l'Antiquité*
RIL	*Rendiconti dell'Istituto Lombardo*
Riv. di Arch.	
Cristiana	*Rivista di Archeologia Cristiana*
Riv. di Filologia	*Rivista di Filologia*
RM	*Rheinisches Museum*
ROC	*Revue de l'Orient Chrétien*
Röm. Quart.	*Römische Quartalschrift*
RSA	*Rivista Storica dell'Antichità*
RSI	*Rivista Storica Italiana*
SBAW	Sitzungsberichte der Bayerischen Akademie der Wissenschaften, philologisch-historische Klasse
SChrét.	*Sources Chrétiennes*
SCO	*Studi Classici ed Orientali*
SDHI	*Studia et Documenta Historiae et Iuris*
SEG	*Supplementum Epigraphicum Graecum*
SHA	*Scriptores Historiae Augustae*
SPAW	Sitzungsberichte der Preussischen Akademie der Wissenschaften, Berlin
Stud. Rom.	*Studi Romani*
Stud. Stor.	*Studi Storici*
TAPA	*Transactions of the American Philological Association*
Theol. Zeitschr.	*Theologische Zeitschrift*
T&MByz	*Travaux et Mémoires. Centre de recherches d'histoire et de civilisation byzantines*
TU	*Texte und Untersuchungen*
Vig. Christ.	*Vigiliae Christianae*
YCS	*Yale Classical Studies*
ZPE	*Zeitschrift für Papyrologie und Epigraphik*
ZRG	*Zeitschrift der Savigny-Stiftung für Rechtsgeschichte* (Röm. Abt.)

FREQUENTLY CITED WORKS

Athanassiadi, *Julian*   Athanassiadi, P. (1992) *Julian: An Intellectual Biography.* London. First published as *Julian and Hellenism*, Oxford 1981

Bagnall, *Egypt*   Bagnall, R. S. (1993) *Egypt in Late Antiquity.* Princeton, NJ

Barnes, *CE*   Barnes, T. D. (1981) *Constantine and Eusebius.* Cambridge, MA

Barnes, *NE*   Barnes, T. D. (1982) *The New Empire of Diocletian and Constantine*. Cambridge, MA

Barnes, *Athanasius*   Barnes, T. D. (1993) *Athanasius and Constantius: Theology and Politics in the Constantinian Empire*. Cambridge, MA

Bianchi Bandinelli, *Rome*   Bianchi Bandinelli, R. (1971) *Rome: The Late Empire*. London

Binns, *Latin Literature*   Binns, J. W. (ed.) (1974) *Latin Literature of the Fourth Century* (Greek and Latin Studies, Classical Literature and its Influence). London

Blockley, *Ammianus*   Blockley, R. C. (1975) *Ammiani Marcellinus: A Study of his Historiography and Political Thought* (Collection Latomus 141). Brussels

Blockley, *Foreign Policy*   Blockley, R. C. (1992) *East Roman Foreign Policy: Formation and Conduct from Diocletian to Anastasius* (ARCA 30). Leeds

Bowersock, *Julian*   Bowersock, G. W. (1978) *Julian the Apostate*. London

Bowersock, *Hellenism*   Bowersock, G. W. (1990) *Hellenism in Late Antiquity*. Ann Arbor, MI and Cambridge

Brisson, *Autonomisme*   Brisson, J. P. (1958) *Autonomisme et christianisme dans l'Afrique romaine de Septime Sévère à l'invasion vandale*. Paris

Brown, *Augustine*   Brown, P. R. L. (1967) *Augustine of Hippo: A Biography*. London

Brown, *Religion and Society*   Brown, P. R. L. (1972) *Religion and Society in the Age of Saint Augustine*. London

Brown, *Cult of the Saints*   Brown, P. (1981) *The Cult of the Saints: Its Rise and Function in Latin Christianity*. Chicago and London

Brown, *Society and the Holy*   Brown, P. (1982) *Society and the Holy in Late Antiquity*. London

Brown, *Body and Society*   Brown, P. (1988) *The Body and Society: Men, Women and Sexual Renunciation in Early Christianity*. New York

Brown, *Power and Persuasion*   Brown, P. (1992) *Power and Persuasion in Late Antiquity: Towards a Christian Empire*. (The Curti Lectures, The University of Wisconsin-Madison 1988). Madison, WI

Bury, *LRE*   Bury, J. B. (1923) *History of the Later Roman Empire from the Death of Theodosius I to the Death of Justinian* vol. 1. London

Cameron, Alan, *Claudian*   Cameron, Alan (1970) *Claudian: Poetry and Propaganda at the Court of Honorius*. Oxford

Cameron, Alan, 'Latin revival'   Cameron, Alan (1984) 'The Latin revival of the fourth century', in W. Treadgold (ed.), *Renaissances before the Renaissance* (Stanford) 42–58

Cameron and Long, *Barbarians and Politics*   Cameron, Alan and Long, J. with Sherry, L. (1993) *Barbarians and Politics at the Court of Arcadius*

	(Transformation of the Classical Heritage 19). Berkeley and Los Angeles
Cameron, Averil, *Rhetoric of Empire*	Cameron, Averil (1991) *Christianity and the Rhetoric of Empire: The Development of Christian Discourse.* Berkeley and Los Angeles
Cameron, Averil, *LRE*	Cameron, Averil (1993) *The Later Roman Empire: A.D. 284–430* (Fontana History of the Ancient World). London
Carrié, 'Esercito'	Carrié, J.-M. (1986) 'L'esercito: trasformazioni funzionali ed economie locali', in Giardina (ed.), *Società romana* I, 449–88, 760–71
Carrié, 'Economia e finanze'	Carrié, J.-M. (1993) 'L'economia e le finanze', in A. Schiavone (ed.), *Storia di Roma* III: *L'Età tardoantica* (Rome–Bari) 751–87
Chastagnol, *Préfecture urbaine*	Chastagnol, A. (1960) *La Préfecture urbaine à Rome sous le Bas-empire* (Publications de la Faculté des Lettres et Sciences humaines d'Alger 34). Paris
Chastagnol, *Fastes*	Chastagnol, A. (1962) *Les Fastes de la préfecture de Rome au Bas-empire.* Paris
Chuvin, *Chronicle*	Chuvin, P. (1990) *A Chronicle of the Last Pagans,* Eng. trans. by B. A. Archer of part 1 of Chuvin, *Chronique* (Revealing Antiquity 4). Cambridge, MA
Chuvin, *Chronique*	Chuvin, P. (1990) *Chronique des derniers païens. La disparition du paganisme dans l'Empire romain, du règne de Constantin à celui de Justinien.* Paris (2nd edn 1991)
Clark, *Ascetic Piety*	Clark, E. A. (1986) *Ascetic Piety and Women's Faith: Essays on Late Ancient Christianity* (Studies in Women and Religion 20). Lewiston–Queenston
Courcelle, *Invasions*	Courcelle, P. (1964) *Histoire littéraire des grandes invasions germaniques* Vol. 3. Paris
Courtois, *Vandales*	Courtois, C. (1955) *Les Vandales et l'Afrique.* Paris
Dagron, 'Thémistios'	Dagron, G. (1968) 'L'empire romain d'Orient au IVe siècle et les traditions politiques de l'hellénisme: le témoignage de Thémistios'. *T&MByz* 3: 1–242
Dagron, *Naissance*	Dagron, G. (1974) *Naissance d'une capitale: Constantinople et ses institutions de 330 à 451* (Bibliothèque byzantine, Études 7). Paris
Demandt, *Spätantike*	Demandt, A. (1989) *Die Spätantike: römische Geschichte von Diocletian bis Justinian, 284–565 n. Chr.* (Handbuch der Altertumswissenschaft iii. 6). Munich
Dodgeon and Lieu, *Eastern Frontier*	Dodgeon, M. H. and Lieu, S. N. C. (1991) *The Roman Eastern Frontier and the Persian Wars (A.D. 226–363): A Documentary History.* London and New York

Downey, *Antioch*   Downey, G. (1961) *A History of Antioch in Syria, from Seleucus to the Arab Conquest.* Princeton, NJ

Duncan-Jones, *Structure and Scale*   Duncan-Jones, R. P. (1990) *Structure and Scale in the Roman Economy.* Cambridge

Dvornik, *Political Philosophy*   Dvornik, F. (1966) *Early Christian and Byzantine Political Philosophy: Origins and Background* (Dumbarton Oaks Studies 9). 2 vols. Washington, DC

Fowden, *Egyptian Hermes*   Fowden, G. (1986) *The Egyptian Hermes: A Historical Approach to the Late Pagan Mind.* Cambridge. Corrected reprint Princeton, NJ 1993

Frend, *Donatist Church*   Frend, W. H. C. (1952) *The Donatist Church: A Movement of Protest in Roman North Africa.* Oxford (3rd edn 1985)

Giardina, *Società romana*   Giardina, A. (ed.) (1986) *Società romana e impero tardoantico.* 4 vols. (I: *Istituzioni, ceti, economie*; II: *Roma: Politica, economia, paesaggio urbano*; III: *Le merci, gli insediamenti*; IV: *Tradizione dei classici, trasformazioni della cultura*). Rome–Bari

Goffart, *Barbarians and Romans*   Goffart, W. (1980) *Barbarians and Romans A.D. 418–584: The Techniques of Accommodation.* Princeton, NJ

Harris, *Ancient Literacy*   Harris, W. V. (1989) *Ancient Literacy.* Cambridge, MA

Heather, *Goths and Romans*   Heather, P. J. (1991) *Goths and Romans 332–489.* Oxford

Hendy, *Studies*   Hendy, M. F. (1985) *Studies in the Byzantine Monetary Economy c. 300–1450.* Cambridge

Hoffmann, *Bewegungsheer*   Hoffmann, D. (1969–70) *Das spätrömische Bewegungsheer und die Notitia Dignitatum* (Epigraphische Studien 7: 1–2). Düsseldorf

Holum, *Theodosian Empresses*   Holum, K. G. (1982) *Theodosian Empresses: Women and Imperial Dominion in Late Antiquity* (The Transformation of the Classical Heritage 3). Berkeley and Los Angeles

Hunt, *Holy Land Pilgrimage*   Hunt, E. D. (1982) *Holy Land Pilgrimage in the Later Roman Empire A.D. 312–460.* Oxford

Isaac, *Limits of Empire*   Isaac, B. (1990) *The Limits of Empire: The Roman Army in the East.* Oxford (2nd edn 1992)

Jones, *Greek City*   Jones, A. H. M. (1940) *The Greek City from Alexander to Justinian.* Oxford

Jones, *LRE*   Jones, A. H. M. (1964) *The Later Roman Empire 284–602: A Social, Economic and Administrative Survey.* 3 vols. Oxford; 2 vols. (continuous pagination). Norman, OK

Jones, *Economy*   Jones, A. H. M. (1974) *The Roman Economy: Studies*

	in Ancient Economic and Administrative History ed. P. A. Brunt. Oxford
Jones, *PLRE* I	Jones, A. H. M., Martindale, J. R. and Morris, J. (eds.) (1971) *Prosopography of the Later Roman Empire I: A.D. 260–395.* Cambridge
Jonkers, *Acta*	Jonkers, E. J. (1954) *Acta et Symbola Conciliorum quae saeculo quarto habita sunt.* Leiden
Kaster, *Guardians of Language*	Kaster, R. A. (1988) *Guardians of Language: The Grammarian and Society in Late Antiquity* (The Transformation of the Classical Heritage 11). Berkeley and Los Angeles
Keay, *Roman Spain*	Keay, S. J. (1988) *Roman Spain.* London
Kelly, *Jerome*	Kelly, J. N. D. (1975) *Jerome: His Life, Writings and Controversies.* London
Krautheimer, *Architecture*	Krautheimer, R. (1965) *Early Christian and Byzantine Architecture.* Harmondsworth (rev. edns 1975, 1979, 1986)
Krautheimer, *Rome*	Krautheimer, R. (1980) *Rome: Profile of a City, 312–1308.* Princeton, NJ
Lepelley, *Cités*	Lepelley, C. (1979–81) *Les Cités de l'Afrique romaine au Bas-Empire* (Études augustiniennes). 2 vols. Paris
Liebeschuetz, *Antioch*	Liebeschuetz, J. H. W. G. (1972) *Antioch: City and Imperial Administration in the Later Roman Empire.* Oxford
Liebeschuetz, *Barbarians and Bishops*	Liebeschuetz, J. H. W. G. (1991) *Barbarians and Bishops: Army, Church and State in the Age of Arcadius and Chrysostom.* Oxford
Lieu, *Manichaeism*	Lieu, S. N. C. (1985) *Manichaeism in the Later Roman Empire and in Medieval China.* Manchester (2nd edn. Tübingen 1991)
Luttwak, *Grand Strategy*	Luttwak, E. N. (1976) *The Grand Strategy of the Roman Empire, From the First Century A.D. to the Third.* Baltimore and London
MacCormack, *Art and Ceremony*	MacCormack, S. G. (1981) *Art and Ceremony in Late Antiquity* (The Transformation of the Classical Heritage 1). Berkeley and Los Angeles
MacMullen, *Christianizing*	MacMullen, R. (1984) *Christianizing the Roman Empire (A.D. 100–400).* New Haven, CT and London
MacMullen, *Corruption*	MacMullen, R. (1988) *Corruption and the Decline of Rome.* New Haven, CT
MacMullen, *Changes*	MacMullen, R. (1990) *Changes in the Roman Empire: Essays in the Ordinary.* Princeton, NJ
Maenchen-Helfen, *Huns*	Maenchen-Helfen, O. (1973) *The World of the Huns.* Berkeley and Los Angeles
Marcone, *Colonato*	Marcone, A. (1988) *Il colonato tardoantico nella storio-*

grafia moderna (da Fustel de Coulanges ai nostri giorni). Como

Markus, *End of Ancient Christianity* — Markus, R. A. (1990) *The End of Ancient Christianity.* Cambridge

Marrou, *Éducation* — Marrou, H. (1948) *Histoire de l'éducation dans l'antiquité.* Paris

Matthews, *Western Aristocracies* — Matthews, J. F. (1975) *Western Aristocracies and Imperial Court A.D. 364–425.* Oxford (repr. with a postscript 1990)

Matthews, *Ammianus* — Matthews, J. F. (1989) *The Roman Empire of Ammianus.* London and Baltimore

Mazzarino, *Aspetti sociali* — Mazzarino, S. (1951) *Aspetti sociali del quarto secolo.* Rome

Millar, 'Empire and city' — Millar, F. (1983) 'Empire and city, Augustus to Julian: obligations, excuses and status', *JRS* 73: 76–96

Momigliano, *Conflict* — Momigliano, A. (ed.) (1963) *The Conflict between Paganism and Christianity in the Fourth Century.* Oxford

Musset, *Invasions* — Musset, L. (1975) *The Germanic Invasions: The Making of Europe A.D. 400–600.* London

Patlagean, *Pauvreté* — Patlagean, E. (1977) *Pauvreté économique et pauvreté sociale à Byzance, 4ᵉ–7ᵉ siècles.* Paris

Petit, *Libanius* — Petit, P. (1955) *Libanius et la vie municipale à Antioche au IVᵉ siècle après J.-C.* (Institut Français d'Archéologie de Beyrouth, Bibliothèque archéologique et historique 62). Paris

Piétri, *Roma Christiana* — Piétri, Ch. (1976) *Roma Christiana. Recherches sur l'église de Rome, son organisation, sa politique, son idéologie de Miltiade à Sixte III (311–440)* (BEFAR 284–5). Rome and Paris

Piganiol, *Empire chrétien* — Piganiol, A. (1972) *L'Empire chrétien.* (2nd edn, revised A. Chastagnol, 'Collection Hier'). Paris

Randsborg, *First Millennium* — Randsborg, K. (1991) *The First Millennium A.D. in Europe and the Mediterranean: An Archaeological Essay.* Cambridge

Rich, *City* — Rich, J. (ed.) (1992) *The City in Late Antiquity.* London and New York

Robert, *Hellenica* IV — Robert, L. (1948) *Hellenica. Recueil d'épigraphie, de numismatique et d'antiquités grecques:* IV *Épigrammes du Bas-Empire.* Paris

Roueché, *Aphrodisias* — Roueché, C. (1989) *Aphrodisias in Late Antiquity* (JRS Monographs 5). London

Rousseau, *Ascetics* — Rousseau, P. (1978) *Ascetics, Authority and the Church in the Age of Jerome and Cassian.* Oxford

Rousseau, *Pachomius* — Rousseau, P. (1985) *Pachomius: The Making of a*

	Community in Fourth Century Egypt. (The Transformation of the Classical Heritage 6). Berkeley
Ruggini, *Economia e società*	Ruggini, L. C. (1961) *Economia e società nell'Italia annonaria. Rapporti fra agricoltura e commercio dal IV al VI secolo d.C.* Milan
Ruggini, 'Associazioni'	Ruggini, L. C. (1971) 'Le associazioni professionali nel mondo romano-bizantino', *Settimane di studi del Centro italiano di studi sull'alto Medioevo, Spoleto, 2–8 aprile 1970*
de Ste Croix, *Class Struggle*	de Ste Croix, G. E. M. (1981) *The Class Struggle in the Ancient Greek World.* London
Salzman, *Roman Time*	Salzman, M. R. (1990) *On Roman Time: The Codex-Calendar of 354 and the Rhythms of Urban Life in Late Antiquity* (The Transformation of the Classical Heritage 27). Berkeley and Los Angeles
Schiavone (ed.), *Età tardoantica*	Schiavone, A. (1993) *Storia di Roma, III. L'età tardoantica. I. Crisi e trasformazioni* (Rome–Bari)
Seeck, *Geschichte*	Seeck, O. (1895–1913) *Geschichte des Untergangs der antiken Welt.* 6 vols. Berlin and Stuttgart
Sirks, *Food*	Sirks, A. J. B. (1991) *Food for Rome: The Legal Structure of the Transportation and Processing of Supplies for the Imperial Distributions in Rome and Constantinople.* Amsterdam
Stein, *Bas Empire* I	Stein, E. (1959) *Histoire du Bas Empire* I (2nd edn transl. J. R. Palanque from German 1st edn: *Geschichte des spätrömischen Reiches* I, Vienna 1928). Paris
Tchalenko, *Villages*	Tchalenko, G. (1953–8) *Villages antiques de la Syrie du nord: Le massif du Bélus à l'époque romaine.* 3 vols. Paris
Thompson, *Attila*	Thompson, E. A. (1948) *A History of Attila and the Huns.* Oxford
Thompson, *Visigoths*	Thompson, E. A. (1966) *The Visigoths in the time of Ulfila.* Oxford
Thompson, *Romans and Barbarians*	Thompson, E. A. (1982) *Romans and Barbarians: The Decline of the Western Empire.* Madison, WI
Trombley, *Hellenic Religion*	Trombley, F. R. (1993–4) *Hellenic Religion and Christianization c. 370–529,* 2 vols. Leiden
Van Dam, *Leadership and Community*	Van Dam, R. (1985) *Leadership and Community in Late Antique Gaul* (The Transformation of the Classical Heritage 8). Berkeley and Los Angeles
Vera, 'Forme e funzioni'	Vera, D. (1986) 'Forme e funzioni della rendità

fondiaria nella tarda antichità', in Giardina, *Società Romana* 1. 367–448

Ward-Perkins, *Public Building* — Ward-Perkins, B. (1984) *From Classical Antiquity to the Middle Ages: Urban Public Building in Northern and Central Italy, A.D. 300–850.* Oxford

Whittaker, 'Trade and traders' — Whittaker, C. R. (1983) 'Late Roman trade and traders', in Garnsey, P., Hopkins, K. and Whittaker, C. R. (eds.), *Trade in the Ancient Economy* (London) 163–211. Reprinted in Whittaker, *Land*, chapter 13

Whittaker, *Land* — Whittaker, C. R. (1993) *Land, City and Trade in the Roman Empire.* Aldershot

Whittaker, *Frontiers* — Whittaker, C. R. (1994) *Frontiers of the Roman Empire: A Social and Economic Study.* Baltimore and London

Wightman, *Trier* — Wightman, E. M. (1970) *Roman Trier and the Treveri.* London

Wilken, *John Chrysostom and the Jews* — Wilken, R. L. (1983) *John Chrysostom and the Jews. Rhetoric and Reality in the Late 4th Century.* Berkeley and Los Angeles

Wolfram, *Goten/Goths* — Wolfram, H. (1979) *Geschichte der Goten von den Anfängen bis zur Mitte des sechsten Jahrhunderts.* Munich (Eng. translation (rev. edn) T. J. Dunlap, *History of the Goths.* Berkeley, Los Angeles and London 1988)

PART I: CHRONOLOGICAL OVERVIEW (CHS. 1–4)

Alföldi, A. (1952) *A Conflict of Ideas in the Late Roman Empire: The Clash Between the Senate and Valentinian I.* Oxford

Altheim, F. (1959–62) *Geschichte der Hunnen.* 5 vols. Berlin

Austin, N. (1972a) 'Ammianus' account of the Adrianople campaign: some strategic observations', *Acta Classica* 15: 77–83

Austin, N. J. E. (1972b) 'Julian at Ctesiphon: a fresh look at Ammianus' account', *Athenaeum* 50: 301–9

Austin, N. (1972c) 'A usurper's claim to legitimacy', *RSA* 2: 187–94

Austin, N. (1979) *Ammianus on Warfare: An Investigation into Ammianus' Military Knowledge* (Collection Latomus 165). Brussels

Bagnall, R. S., Cameron, A., Schwartz, S. R., and Worp, K. A. (1987) *Consuls of the Later Roman Empire.* Atlanta

Baldus, H. R. (1984) 'Theodosius d. Gr. und die Revolte des Magnus Maximus. Das Zeugnis der Münzen', *Chiron* 14: 175–192

Baldwin, B. (1978) 'The *Caesares* of Julian', *Klio* 60: 449–66

Barb, A. A. (1963) 'The survival of the magic arts', in Momigliano, *Conflict* 100–25

Barnard, L. W. (1981) 'The emperor Constans and the Christian Church', *RSA* 11: 205–14

Barnes, T. D. (1985) 'Constantine and the Christians of Persia', *JRS* 75: 126–36

Barnes, T. D. (1992) 'Hilary of Poitiers on his exile', *Vig. Christ.* 46: 129–40

Barnish, S. J. B. (1986) 'Taxation, land and barbarian settlement in the western empire', *PBSR* 54: 170–95

Bartholomew, P. (1984) 'Fourth-century Saxons', *Britannia* 15: 169–85

Baynes, N. H. (1910) 'Rome and Armenia in the fourth century', *EHR* 25: 624–43 (=Baynes (1955) 186–208)

Baynes, N. H. (1922) 'Stilicho and the barbarian invasions', *JRS* 12: 207–20 (=Baynes (1955) 326–42)

Baynes, N. H. (1937) 'The death of Julian the Apostate in a Christian legend', *JRS* 27: 22–9 (=Baynes (1955) 271–81)

Baynes, N. H. (1955) *Byzantine Studies and Other Essays.* London

Bichir, G. (1977) 'Les Sarmates au bas Danube', *Dacia* n.s. 21: 167–98

Bidez, J. (1965) *La Vie de l'empereur Julien.* 2nd edn. Paris

Bird, H. W. (1986) 'Eutropius and Festus: some reflections on the empire and imperial policy in A.D. 369–370', *Florilegium* 8: 11–22

Bloch, H. (1945) 'A new document of the last pagan revival in the west, 393–394 A.D.', *HThR* 38: 199–244

Bloch, H. (1963) 'The pagan revival in the west at the end of the fourth century', in Momigliano, *Conflict* 193–218

Blockley, R. C. (1972) 'Constantius Gallus and Julian as Caesars of Constantius II', *Latomus* 31: 433–68

Blockley, R. C. (1977) 'Ammianus Marcellinus on the battle of Strasbourg: art and analysis in the *History*', *Phoenix* 31: 218–31

Blockley, R. C. (1980a) 'Constantius II and his generals', in Deroux (ed.) (1980) 467–86

Blockley, R. C. (1980b) 'The date of the "Barbarian Conspiracy"', *Britannia* 11: 223–5

Blockley, R. C. (1985) 'Subsidies and diplomacy: Rome and Persia in late antiquity', *Phoenix* 39: 62–74

Blockley, R. C. (1989) 'Constantius II and Persia', in Deroux (ed.) (1989) 465–90

Bouffartigue, J. (1992) *L'Empereur Julien et la culture de son temps.* Paris

Brennecke, H. C. (1984) *Hilarius von Poitiers und die Bischofsopposition gegen Konstantius II.* Berlin

Brennecke, H. C. (1988) *Studien zur Geschichte der Homöer.* Tübingen

Browning, R. (1952) 'The riot of A.D. 387 in Antioch: the role of theatrical claques in the later empire', *JRS* 42: 13–20

Browning, R. (1975) *The Emperor Julian.* London

Burns, T. S. (1973) 'The battle of Hadrianople: a reconsideration', *Historia* 22: 336–45

Burns, T. S. (1978) 'Calculating Ostrogothic population', *Acta Antiqua Academiae Scientiarum Hungaricae* 26: 457–63

Burns, T. S. (1979) 'Pursuing the early Gothic migrations', *Acta Archeologica* 31: 189–99

Burns, T. S. (1984) *A History of the Ostrogoths.* Bloomington, IN

Cameron, Alan (1968) 'Gratian's repudiation of the pontifical robe', *JRS* 58: 96–102

Chadwick, H. (1967) *The Early Church* (The Pelican History of the Church 1) London (rev. edn 1993)

Chastagnol, A. (1976) 'Remarques sur les sénateurs orientaux au ive siècle', *Acta Antiqua* 24: 341–56

Chrysos, E. K. (1973) 'Gothia Romana: Zur Rechtslage des Föderatenlandes der Westgoten im 4. Jahrhundert', *Daco-Romania* 1: 52–64

Cochrane, C. H. (1940) *Christianity and Classical Culture*. Oxford

Coleman-Norton, R. P. (1966) *Roman State and Christian Church*. 3 vols. London

Croke, B. (1976) 'Arbogast and the death of Valentinian II', *Historia* 25: 235–44

Croke, B. and Harries, J. (1982) *Religious Conflict in Fourth-Century Rome*. Sydney

Demandt, A. (1968a) 'Die afrikanischen Unruhen unter Valentinian I', in H. J. Diesner *et al.* (eds.), *Africa und Rom in der Antike* (Wissenschaftliche Beiträge d. M. Luther Univ. 6) (Halle–Wittenberg) 277–92

Demandt, A. (1968b) 'Die Tripolitanischen Wirren unter Valentinian I', *Byzantion* 38: 333–63

Demandt, A. (1969) 'Der Tod des älteren Theodosius', *Historia* 18: 598–625

Demandt, A. (1970) 'Magister Militum', *RE* Suppl. 12: 553–790

Demandt, A. (1972) 'Die Feldzüge des älteren Theodosius', *Hermes* 100: 81–113

Demougeot, E. (1951) *De l'unité à la division de l'empire romain, 395–410*. Paris

Den Boer, W. (1960) 'The emperor Silvanus and his army', *AC* 3: 105–9

Deroux, C. (ed.) (1979–92) *Studies in Latin Literature and Roman History* (Collection Latomus Vols. 164, 168, 180, 196, 206, 217). Vol. I (1979); II (1980); III (1983); IV (1986); V (1989); VI (1992). Brussels

Diesner, H.-J. (1982) *The Great Migration: The Movement of Peoples across Europe, A.D. 300–700* (English trans. by C. S. V. Salt). London

Dodds, E. R. (1947) 'Theurgy and its relationship to Neoplatonism', *JRS* 37: 55–69 (repr. as an appendix to *The Greeks and the Irrational*, Berkeley and Los Angeles, 1951)

Drinkwater, J. F. (1983) 'The pagan underground, Constantius II's "secret service", and the survival, and the usurpation of Julian the Apostate', in Deroux (ed.) (1983) 348–87

Duval, Y. M. (1970) 'La venue à Rome de l'empereur Constance II en 357', *Caesarodunum* 5: 299–304

Edbrooke, R. O. (1976) 'The visit of Constantius II to Rome in 357 and its effect on the pagan Roman senatorial aristocracy', *AJP* 97: 40–61

Ehrhardt, A. (1964) 'The first two years of the reign of Theodosius I', *JEH* 15: 1–17

Ensslin, W. (1953) *Die Religionspolitik des Kaisers Theodosius der Grosse*. Munich

Ferrill, A. (1986) *The Fall of the Roman Empire: The Military Explanation*. London

Fontaine, J. (1977) *Ammien Marcellin, Histoire IV* (Collection des Universités de France). Paris

Fowden, G. (1978) 'Bishops and temples in the eastern Roman Empire, A.D. 320–425', *JThS* n.s. 29: 53–78

Fowden, G. (1982) 'The pagan holy man in late antique society', *JHS* 102: 33–59

Fowden, G. (1987) 'Nicagoras of Athens and the Lateran obelisk', *JHS* 107: 51–7

Frend, W. H. C. (1984) *The Rise of Christianity*. London

Frere, S. (1987) *Britannia: A History of Roman Britain.* 3rd edn. London

Gerland, E. (1930) 'Valentinians Feldzug des Jahres 368 und die Schlacht bei Solicinium', *Saalburg-Jahrbuch* 7: 113–23

Gibbon, E. (1913) *The History of the Decline and Fall of the Roman Empire*, 7 vols. (6th edn, ed. J. B. Bury). London

Gleason, M. W. (1986) 'Festive Satire: Julian's *Misopogon* and the New Year at Antioch', *JRS* 76: 106–19

Gottlieb, G. (1985) 'Der Mailänder Kirchenstreit von 385/386', *MH* 42: 37–55

Grasmück, E. L. (1964) *Coercitio: Staat und Kirche im Donatistenstreit.* Bonn

Greenslade, S. L. (1964) *Schism in the Early Church* (2nd edn). London

Grousset, R. (1973) *Histoire de l'Arménie des origines à 1071* (2nd edn). Paris

Grumel, V. (1951) 'L'Illyricum de la mort de Valentinian Ier (375 à la mort de Stilichon (408)', *REB* 9: 5–46

Hadjinicolaou, A. (1951) 'Macellum, lieu d'exile de l'empereur Julien', *Byzantion* 21: 15–22

Haehling, R. von (1977) 'Ammians Darstellung der Thronbesteigung Jovians im Lichte der heidnische-christlichen Auseinandersetzung', in A. Lippold and N. Himmelmann (eds.), *Bonner Festgabe Johannes Straub zum 65. Geburtstag am 18 Oktober 1977* (Bonn) 347–58

Hamblenne, P. (1980) 'Une "conjuration" sous Valentinien?', *Byzantion* 50: 198–225

Hanson, R. P. C. (1988) *The Search for the Christian Doctrine of God.* Edinburgh

Heather, P. (1986) 'The crossing of the Danube and the Gothic conversion', *GRBS* 27: 289–318

Heather, P. and Matthews, J. F. (1991) *The Goths in the Fourth Century.* Liverpool

Hoepffner, A. (1936) 'La mort du "magister militum" Théodose', *REL* 14: 119–29

Homes-Dudden, F. (1935) *The Life and Times of St Ambrose.* 2 vols. Oxford

Johnson, S. (1980) *Later Roman Britain.* London

Kaegi, W. E. (1967) 'Domestic military problems of Julian the Apostate', *Byz. Forsch.* 2: 247–64

Kaegi, W. E. (1975) 'The emperor Julian at Naissus', *L'Antiquité Classique* 44: 161–71

Kaegi, W. E. (1981) 'Constantine's and Julian's strategies of strategic surprise against the Persians', *Athenaeum* 59: 209–13

Kaniuth, A. (1941) *Die Beisetzung Konstantins des Grossen.* Breslau

Kennedy, D. and Riley, D. (1990) *Rome's Desert Frontier from the Air.* London

King, N. Q. (1961) *The Emperor Theodosius and the Establishment of Christianity.* London

Klein, R. (1978) *Kaiser Constantius II und die christliche Kirche.* Darmstadt

Klein, R. (1979a) 'Die Kämpfe um die Nachfolge nach dem Tode Constantins des Grossen', *Byz. Forsch.* 6: 101–50

Klein, R. (1979b) 'Der Rombesuch des Kaisers Konstantius II im Jahre 357', *Athenaeum* 57: 98–115

Klein, R. (1981) 'Kaiser Julians Rhetoren- und Unterrichtsgesetz', *Röm. Quart.* 76: 73–94

Kotula, T. (1970) 'Firmus, fils de Nubel, était-il usurpateur ou roi des Maures?', *Acta Antiqua Academiae Scientiarum Hungaricae* 18: 137–46

Krautheimer, R. (1987) 'A note on the inscription in the apse of Old St Peter's', *DOP* 41: 317–20

Lepelley, C. (1974) 'La préfecture de tribu dans l'Afrique du Bas-Empire', *Mélanges d'Histoire ancienne offerts à William Seston* 285–96. Paris

Lieu, S. N. C. (1989) *The Emperor Julian: Panegyric and Polemic* (Translated Texts for Historians 2). 2nd edn. Liverpool

Lightfoot, C. S. (1988) 'Facts and fiction – the third siege of Nisibis A.D. 350', *Historia* 37: 105–25

Lippold, A. (1965) 'Ursinus and Damasus', *Historia* 14: 105–28

Lippold, A. (1973) 'Theodosios II', *RE* Suppl. 13: 961–1044

Lippold, A. (1980) *Theodosius der Grosse und seine Zeit* (2nd edn). Munich

McCormick, M. (1986) *Eternal Victory*. Cambridge

McLynn, N. (1994) *Ambrose of Milan: Church and Court in a Christian Capital.* Berkeley and Los Angeles

Mango, C. (1990) 'Constantine's Mausoleum and the translation of relics', *Byz. Zeit.* 83: 51–61

Mansi, J. D. (ed.) (1759–98) *Sacrorum conciliorum nova et amplissima collectio.* 31 vols. Florence and Venice

Markus, R. A. (1974) 'Paganism, Christianity and the Latin Classics in the Fourth Century', in Binns, *Latin Literature* 1–21

Matthews, J. F. (1976) 'Mauretania in Ammianus and the Notitia', in R. Goodburn and P. Bartholomew (eds.), *Aspects of the Notitia Dignitatum* (BAR Suppl. series 15) (Oxford) 157–88

Matthews, J. F. (1992) 'The poetess Proba and fourth century Rome: questions of interpretation', in M. Christol *et al.* (eds.), *Institutions, société et vie politique dans l'empire romain au IVe siècle ap. J. C.* (Rome), 277–304

Mattingly, D. J. (1983) 'The Laguatan: a Libyan tribal confederation in the later Roman Empire', *Libyan Studies* 14: 96–108

Mazzarino, S. (1942) *Stilicone: La crisi imperiale dopo Teodosio.* Rome

Millar, F. G. B. (1982) 'Emperors, frontiers and foreign relations, 31 B.C. to A.D. 378', *Britannia* 13: 1–23

Mitchell, S. (1993) *Anatolia: Land, Men and Gods in Asia Minor,* II: *The Rise of the Church.* Oxford

Müller, W. (1973) *Zur Geschichte der Alamannen.* Darmstadt

Neri, V. (1985) 'Ammiano Marcellino e l'elezione di Valentiniano', *Rivista Storica dell'Antichità* 15: 153–82

Nixon, C. E. V. (1991) 'Aurelius Victor and Julian', *CPh* 86: 113–25

Olivetti, A. (1915) 'Sulle stragi di Costantinopoli succedute alla morte di Costantino il Grande', *Riv. di Filologia* 43: 67–79

Oost, S. I. (1968) *Galla Placidia Augusta.* Chicago

Pack, E. (1986) *Städte und Steuern in der Politik Julians: Untersuchungen zu den Quellen eines Kaiserbildes.* Brussels

Palanque, J. R. (1929) 'Sur l'usurpation de Maxime', *REL* 31: 33–6

Palanque, J. R. (1965) *Les Empereurs romains d'Espagne.* Paris

Paschoud, F. (ed.) (1979) *Zosime: Histoire Nouvelle* II (Livre III). Paris

Pavan, M. (1964) *La politica gotica di Teodosio nella pubblicistica del suo tempo.* Rome

Pavan, M. (1979) 'La battaglia di Adrianopoli (378) e il problema gotica nell'impero romano', *Studi Romani* 27: 153–65

Peeters, P. (1920) 'La légende de saint Jacques de Nisibe', *Anal. Boll.* 38: 285–373 von Petrikovits, H. (1971) 'Fortifications in the north-western Roman Empire from the third to the fifth centuries A.D.', *JRS* 61: 178–218

Pieler, P. (1972) 'L'aspect politique et juridique de l'adoption de Chosroes proposée par les Perses au Justin', *RIDA* 3, 19: 399–433

Price, S. (1987) 'The consecration of Roman emperors', in D. Cannadine and S. Price (eds.), *Rituals of Royalty* (Cambridge) 56–105

Richter, W. (1974) 'Die Darstellung der Hunnen bei Ammianus Marcellinus', *Historia* 23: 343–77

Ridley, R. T. (1982) *Zosimus: New History* (Byzantina Australiensia 2). Canberra

Rodgers, B. S. (1981) 'Merobaudes and Maximus in Gaul', *Historia* 30: 82–105

Rubin, Z. (1981) 'The conversion of the Visigoths to Christianity', *Museum Helveticum* 38: 34–54

Ruggini, L. C. (1989) 'Felix Temporum Reparatio', in *L'Église et l'empire au IVe siècle* (Geneva) 179–249

Schmidt, L. (1969) *Geschichte der deutschen Stämme bis zum Ausgang der Völkerwanderung* II: *Die Ostgermanen* (2nd edn). Munich

Seeck, O. (1919) *Regesten der Kaiser und Päpste für die Jahre 311 bis 476 n. Chr.* Stuttgart. Repr. Frankfurt 1964

Solari, A. (1932a) 'I partiti nella elezione di Valentiniano', *Rivista di Filologia* 1: 75–9

Solari, A. (1932b) 'La rivolta Procopiana a Costantinopoli', *Byzantion* 7: 143–8

Solari, A. (1933) 'La elezione di Gioviano', *Klio* 26: 330–5

Stevens, C. E. (1938) 'Magnus Maximus in British history', *Études celtiques* 3: 86–94

Stevens, C. E. (1957) 'Marcus, Gratian, Constantine', *Athenaeum* 35: 316–47

Straub, J. (1952) '*Parens Principum*. Stilichos Reichspolitik und das Testament des Kaisers Theodosios', *Nouvelle Clio* 4: 94–115

Straub, J. (1966) 'Eugenius', *RAC* 6: 860–77

Sulimirski, T. (1970) *The Sarmatians*. London

Szidat, J. (1977) *Historischer Kommentar zu Ammianus Marcellinus Buch XX–XXI*, Teil I: *Die Erhebung Iulians*. Wiesbaden

Szidat, J. (1979) 'Die Usurpation des Eugenius', *Historia* 28: 487ff.

Thévenot, E. (1932) *Autun: cité romaine et chrétienne*. Autun

Thompson, E. A. (1947) *The Historical Work of Ammianus Marcellinus*. Cambridge

Todd, M. (1992) *The Early Germans*. Oxford

Tomlin, R. S. O. (1974) 'The date of the barbarian conspiracy', *Britannia* 5: 303–9

Wardman, A. E. (1984) 'Usurpers and internal conflicts in the fourth century A.D.', *Historia* 33: 220–37

Warmington, B. H. (1956) 'The career of Romanus, Comes Africae', *Byz. Zeit.* 49: 55–64

Warmington, B. H. (1977) 'Objectives and strategy in the Persian war of Constantius II', in *Limes. Akten des XI internationalen Limeskongresses* (Budapest) 509–20

Wirth, G. (1984) 'Jovian. Kaisar und Karikatur', in E. Dassmann and K. Thraede (eds.), *Vivarium: Festschrift Th. Klauser zum 90. Geburtsag* (Münster Aschendorff, 1984) 353–84

Wolfram, H. (1977) 'Die Schlacht von Adrianopel', *Anzeiger der österreichischen Akademie des Wissenschaften. phil.-hist. Kl.* 114: 228–45

Wytzes, J. (1977) *Der letzte Kampf des Heidentums*. Leiden

Zakrzewski, C. (1928) 'Un homme d'état au bas-empire: Anthemius', *Eos* 31: 417–38

Zasetskaja, I. B. (1977) 'The role of the Huns in the formation of the south Russian steppelands in the late fourth and fifth centuries', *Archeologiceskij sbornik* 18: 92–100

Ziegler, J. (1970) *Zur religiösen Haltung der Gegenkaiser im 4 Jr. n. Chr.* Opladen

PART II: GOVERNMENT AND INSTITUTIONS (CHS. 5–8)

Alexander, J. J. G. (1976) 'The illustrated manuscripts of the *Notitia Dignitatum*', in Goodburn and Bartholomew (1976) 11–25

Alföldi, A. (1934) 'Die Ausgestaltung des monarchischen Zeremoniells am römischen Kaiserhofe', *MDAI(R)* 49: 3–118 (=Alföldi (1970) 3–118)

Alföldi, A. (1935) 'Insignien und Tracht der römischen Kaiser', *MDAI(R)* 50: 3–158 (=Alföldi (1970) 121–276)

Alföldi, A. (1952) *A Conflict of Ideas in the Late Roman Empire: The Clash Between the Senate and Valentinian I* (trans. H. Mattingly). Oxford

Alföldi, A. (1970) *Die monarchische Repräsentation im römischen Kaiserreiche.* Darmstadt

Andreotti, R. (1975) 'Problemi del "suffragium" nell' imperatore Giuliano', in *Accademia Romanistica Costantiniana: Atti I° Convegno Internazionale Università degli Studi di Perugia* (Perugia) 1–26

Aricescu, A. (1980) *The Army in Roman Dobrudja*, trans. N. Hampartumian (BAR International Series 86). Oxford

Arnheim, M. T. W. (1970) 'Vicars in the later Roman Empire', *Historia* 19: 593–606

Arnheim, M. W. T. (1972) *The Senatorial Aristocracy in the Later Roman Empire.* Oxford

Arnold, D. W.-H. (1991) *The Early Episcopal Career of Athanasius of Alexandria.* Notre Dame, IN

Austin, N. J. E. (1972) 'Ammianus' account of the Adrianople campaign: some strategic observations', *AC* 15: 77–83

Austin, N. J. E. (1979) *Ammianus on Warfare.* Brussels

Avery, W. T. (1940) 'The *Adoratio Purpurae* and the importance of the imperial purple in the fourth century of the Christian era', *MAAR* 17: 66–80

Bagnall, R. S. (1992) 'Military officers as landowners in fourth century Egypt', *Chiron* 22: 47–54

Baldovin, J. F. (1987) *The Urban Character of Christian Worship: The Origins, Development and Meaning of Stational Liturgy.* Rome

Bardy, G. (1949) 'Pèlerinages à Rome vers la fin du IVᵉ siècle', *Anal. Boll.* 67: 224–35

Barnes, T. D. (1974) 'A law of Julian', *CPh* 69: 288–91

Barnes, T. D. (1985) 'The career of Abinnaeus', *Phoenix* 39: 368–74

Barnes, T. D. (1986a) 'Synesius in Constantinople', *GRBS* 27: 93–112

Barnes, T. D. (1986b) 'When did Synesius become bishop of Ptolemais?', *GRBS* 27: 325–9

Barr, W. (1981) *Claudian's Panegyric on the Fourth Consulate of Honorius* (Liverpool Latin Texts (Classical and Medieval) 2). Liverpool

Barrow, R. H. (1973) *Prefect and Emperor: The Relationes of Symmachus A.D. 384.* Oxford

Baynes, N. H. (1955) *Byzantine Studies and Other Essays*. London

Bell, H. I., Martin, V., Turner, E. G. and Van Berchem, D. (1962) *The Abinnaeus Archive: Papers of a Roman Officer in the Reign of Constantius II*. Oxford

Béranger, J. (1970) 'L'expression de la divinité dans les *Panégyriques Latins*', *MH* 27: 242–54 (repr. in his *Principatus: études de notions et d'histoire politiques dans l'antiquité gréco-romaine*. Université de Lausanne, Publications de la Faculté des Lettres 20 (Geneva 1975) 429–44)

Berger, P. C. (1981) *The Insignia of the Notitia Dignitatum*. New York

Birley, E. (1969) 'Septimius Severus and the Roman army', *Epigraphische Studien* 8: 63–82

Bishop, M. C. and Coulston, J. C. N. (1993) *Roman Military Equipment from the Punic Wars to the Fall of Rome*. London

Blockley, R. C. (1969) 'Internal self-policing in the late Roman administration: some evidence from Ammianus Marcellinus', *C&M* 30: 403–19

Blockley, R. C. (1972) 'The panegyric of Claudius Mamertinus on the Emperor Julian', *AJP* 93: 437–50

de Blois, L. (1986) 'The *Eἰς βασιλέα* of Ps.–Aelius Aristides', *GRBS* 27: 279–88

Blum, W. (1969) *Curiosi und Regendarii: Untersuchungen zur Geheimen Staatspolizei der Spätantike*. Munich

Boak, A. E. R. (1915) 'The Roman *Magistri* in the civil and military service of the empire', *HSCP* 26: 73–164

Boak, A. E. R. (1924) 'The Master of the Offices in the later Roman and Byzantine Empires', in Boak and Dunlap (1924) 1–160

Boak, A. E. R. and Dunlap, J. E. (1924) *Two Studies in Later Roman and Byzantine Administration* (University of Michigan Studies Humanistic Series 14). 2 vols. Ann Arbor, MI (repr. 1972)

de Bonfils, G. (1981) *Il Comes et Quaestor nell'età della dinastia costantiniana* (Pubblicazioni della Facoltà giuridica dell'Università di Bari 62). Naples

de Bonfils, G. (1986) *Ammiano Marcellino e l'imperatore*. Bari (rev. edn 1997)

Born, L. K. (1934) 'The perfect prince according to the Latin panegyrists', *AJP* 55: 20–35

Bowder, D. (1978) *The Age of Constantine and Julian*. London

Bowman, A. K. and Woolf, G. D. (eds.) (1994) *Literacy and Power in the Ancient World*. Cambridge

Bregman, J. (1982) *Synesius of Cyrene: Philosopher-Bishop* (The Transformation of the Classical Heritage 2). Berkeley and Los Angeles

Bréhier, L. (1920) 'Les survivances du culte impérial', in L. Bréhier and P. Batiffol (eds.), *Les survivances du culte impérial romain: à propos des rites shintoïstes* (Paris) 35–73

Bremmer, J. (1988) 'An imperial palace guard in heaven: the date of the vision of Dorotheus', *ZPE* 75: 82–8

Brennan, P. (1972) 'The disposition and interrelation of Roman military units in Danubian and Eastern provincial and field armies in the late third and early fourth centuries A.D.' University of Cambridge, unpublished PhD dissertation

Brennan, P. (1980) 'Combined legionary detachments as artillery units in late-Roman Danubian bridgehead dispositions', *Chiron* 10: 553–67

Brown, P. R. L. (1971) 'The rise and function of the holy man in late antiquity', *JRS* 61: 80–101 (=Brown, *Society and the Holy*, 103–52)

Browning, R. (1952) 'The riot of A.D. 387 in Antioch: the role of theatrical claques in the later empire', *JRS* 42: 13–20

Brunt, P. (1983) '*Principes* and *Equites*', *JRS* 73: 42–75

Bruun, P. (1962) 'The Christian signs on the coins of Constantine', *Arctos* 3: 5–35

Burdeau, F. (1964) 'L'empereur d'après les *Panégyriques Latins*', in F. Burdeau, N. Charbonnel and M. Humbert (eds.), *Aspects de l'empire romain* (Travaux et recherches de la Faculté de Droit et des Sciences Économiques de Paris, série 'Sciences historiques' 1. Paris) 1–60

Burns, T. S. (1973) The battle of Adrianople: a reconsideration, *Historia* 22: 336–45

Bury, J. B. (1910) '*Magistri scriniorum*, ἀντιγραφῆς and ῥεφερενδάριοι', *HSCP* 21: 23–9

Caimi, J. (1984) *Burocrazia e diritto nel de Magistratibus di Giovanni Lido* (Università di Genova Fondazione Nobile Agostino Poggi 16). Milan

Cameron, Alan (1974) 'Claudian', in Binns, *Latin Literature* 134–59

Cameron, Alan (1979) 'The date of the anonymous *De Rebus Bellicis*', in M. W. C. Hassall (ed.), *De Rebus Bellicis I: Aspects of the De Rebus Bellicis: Papers Presented to Professor E. A. Thompson* (BAR 1, 63) (Oxford) 1–10 (repr. in Alan Cameron, *Literature and Society in the Early Byzantine World* (London 1985))

Campbell, J. B. (1984) *The Emperor and the Roman Army, 31 B.C.–A.D. 235*. Oxford

Carney, T. F. (1971) *Bureaucracy in Traditional Society: Romano-Byzantine Bureaucracies Viewed from Within*. Lawrence, KA

Carrié, J.-M. (1976) 'Patronage et propriété militaires au IVᵉ siècle: objet rhétorique et objet réel du discours *Sur les patronages* de Libanius', *BCH* 100: 159–76

Champlin, E. (1987) 'The testament of the piglet', *Phoenix* 41: 174–83

Charlesworth, M. P. (1947) 'Imperial deportment: two texts and some questions', *JRS* 37: 34–8

Chastagnol, A. (1965) 'Les Espagnols dans l'aristocratie gouvernementale à l'époque de Théodose', in A. Piganiol and H. Terrasse (eds.), *Les Empereurs romains d'Espagne. Madrid-Italica, 31 mars–6 avril 1964: Colloques internationaux du Centre National de la Recherche Scientifique* (Paris) 269–92

Chastagnol, A. (1973) 'Le repli sur Arles des services adminsitratifs gaulois en l'an 407 de notre ère', *RH* 249: 34–40

Chastagnol, A. (1975) 'Remarques sur les sénateurs orientaux au IVᵉ siècle', *Acta Antiqua Academiae Scientiarum Hungaricae* 24: 341–56

Chastagnol, A. (1978) *L'Album municipale de Timgad* (Antiquitas 3.22). Bonn

Chastagnol, A. (1982) *L'évolution politique, sociale et économique du monde romain 284–363*. Paris

del Chicca, F. (1984) *Q. Aurelii Symmachi V. C. Laudatio in Valentinianum Seniorem Augustum Prior: Introduzione, commento e traduzione* (Università degli studi di Cagliari, Istituto di filologia latina). Rome

Christiansen, P. G. (1969) *The Use of Images by Claudius Claudianus* (Studies in Classical Literature 7). The Hague

Clark, E. A. (1984) *The Life of Melania the Younger*. Lewiston, NY

Clauss, M. (1980) *Der magister officiorum in der Spätantike (4.–6. Jahrhundert): das Amt und sein Einfluss auf der kaiserliche Politik* (Vestigia 32). Munich

Clauss, M. (1986) 'Heerwesen (Heeresreligion)', *RAC* 13: 1073–1113

Clemente, G. (1968) *La 'Notitia Dignitatum'* (Saggi di Storia e Letteratura 4). Cagliari

Collot, C. (1965) 'La pratique et l'institution du *suffragium* au Bas-Empire', *RD* 43: 185–221

Cosenza, M. E. (1905) *Official Positions after the Time of Constantine*. Lancaster, PA

Costa, E. A. (1972) 'The office of the "Castrensis Sacri Palatii" in the fourth century', *Byzantion* 42: 358–87

Coulston, J. C. N. (1990) 'Late Roman armour, 3rd–6th centuries AD', *Journal of Roman Military Equipment Studies* 1: 139–60

Crawford, M. (1975) 'Finance, coinage and money from the Severans to Constantine', *ANRW* 11.2: 560–93

Creed, J. L. (ed. and trans.) (1984) *Lactantius, De Mortibus Persecutorum*. Oxford

Crump, G. A. (1973) 'Ammianus and the late Roman army', *Historia* 22: 91–103

Crump, G. A. (1975) *Ammianus Marcellinus as a Military Historian*. Wiesbaden

Dagron, G. (1970) 'Les moines et la ville: le monachisme à Constantinople jusqu'au concile de Chalcédoine', *T&MByz* 4: 229–76

Dagron, G. (1977) 'Le christianisme dans la ville byzantine', *DOP* 31: 1–25

Daniélou, J. (1950) 'L'incompréhensibilité de Dieu d'après Saint Jean Chrysostome', *RecSR* 37: 176–94

Dassmann, E. (1975) 'Ambrosius und die Märtyrer', *JbAC* 18: 49–68

Deér, J. (1950) 'Der Ursprung der Kaiserkrone', *Schweizer Beiträge zur allgemeinen Geschichte* 8: 51–87 (repr. in P. Classen (ed.), *Byzanz und das abendländische Herrschertum: Ausgewählte Aufsätze von Josef Deér* (Vorträge und Forschungen 21) (Sigmaringen 1977) 11–41)

Delbrueck, R. (1932) 'Der spätantike Kaiserornat', *Die Antike* 8: 1–21

Delehaye, H. (1933) *Les Origines du culte des martyrs*. Brussels

Delmaire, R. (1989) *Largesses sacrées et res privata: l'aerarium impérial et son administration du IVᵉ au VIᵉ siècle* (Collections de l'École française de Rome 121). Rome

Demandt, A. (1965) *Zeitkritik und Geschichtsbild im Ammians*. Bonn

Demandt, A. (1968) 'Die tripolitanischen Wirren unter Valentinian I', *Byzantion* 38: 333–63

Demandt, A. (1970) '*Magister militum*', *RE* Suppl. 12: 553–790

Demougeot, E. (1946) 'La théorie du pouvoir impérial au début du Vᵉ siècle', *Mélanges de la société toulousaine d'études classiques* 1: 191–206

Demougeot, E. (1975) 'La *Notitia dignitatum* et l'histoire de l'Empire d'Occident au début du Vᵉ siècle', *Latomus* 34: 1079–134

Demougeot, E. (1986) 'Le fonctionnariat du Bas-Empire éclairé par les fautes des fonctionnaires', *Latomus* 45: 160–70

Dillemann, L. (1969) *Haute Mésopotamie orientale et les pays adjacents*. Paris

Dimitrov, D. P. (1962) 'Le système décoratif et la date les peintures murales du tombeau antique de Silistra', *CArch* 12: 35–52

Döpp, S. (1980) *Zeitgeschichte in Dichtungen Claudians* (Hermes Einzelschriften 43). Wiesbaden

Downey, G. (1958) 'Themistius' First Oration', *GRBS* 1: 49–69

Drew-Bear, T. (1977) 'A fourth-century Latin soldier's epitaph at Nakolea', *HSCP* 81: 257–74

Drinkwater, J. and Elton, H. (eds.) (1992) *Fifth-Century Gaul: A Crisis of Identity?* Cambridge

Dunlap, J. E. (1924) 'The office of the Grand Chamberlain in the later Roman and Byzantine empires', in Boak and Dunlap (1924) II, 161–324

Dupont, C. (1967) 'Les privilèges des clercs sous Constantin', *RHE* 62: 729–52

Durliat, J. (1990) *Les Finances publiques de Dioclétien aux Carolingiens (284–889).* Sigmaringen

Dvornik, F. (1955) 'The emperor Julian's "reactionary" ideas on kingship', in K. Weitzmann, (ed.), *Late Classical and Mediaeval Studies in Honor of Albert Mathias Friend, Jr.* (Princeton, NJ) 71–81

Eck, W. (1978) 'Der Einfluss der konstantinischen Wende auf Auswahl der Bischöfe im 4. und 5. Jahrhundert', *Chiron* 8: 561–85

Eck, W. (1983) 'Der Episkopat im spätantiken Africa', *Hist. Zeit.* 236: 265–95

Edbrooke, R. O. (1976) 'The visit of Constantius II to Rome in 357 and its effect on the Pagan Roman Senatorial Aristocracy', *AJP* 97: 40–61

Elliott, T. G. (1978) 'The tax exemptions granted to clerics by Constantine and Constantius II', *Phoenix* 32: 326–36

Ensslin, W. (1943) *Gottkaiser und Kaiser von Gottes Gnaden* (SBAW 6). Munich (pp. 53–83 reprinted in H. Hunger (ed.), *Das byzantinische Herrscherbild* (Wege der Forschung 341) (Darmstadt 1975) 54–85)

Ensslin, W. (1953) *Die Religionspolitik des Kaisers Theodosius d. Gr.* Munich

Ensslin, W. (1954) 'Der Kaiser in der Spätantike', *Hist. Zeit.* 177: 449–68

Farina, R. (1966) *L'Impero et l'Imperatore cristiano in Eusebio di Cesarea: la prima teologica politica del Cristianesimo* (Biblioteca theologica Salesiana 1:2). Zurich

Fitz, J. (ed.) (1976) *Der römische Limes in Ungarn.* Székesfehérvár

Fitz, J. (1983) *L'Administration des provinces pannoniennes sous le Bas-Empire romain* (Collection Latomus 181). Brussels

Foss, C. (1979) 'The *Fabricenses Ducenarii* of Sardis', *ZPE* 35: 279–83

Fowden, G. (1978) 'Bishops and temples in the eastern Roman empire, A.D. 320–435', *JThS* n.s. 29: 53–78

Franchi de' Cavalieri, P. (1928) 'Come andavano vestiti ed armati i "milites" dell' "adparitio"', *Note agiografiche* 7 (Studi e Testi 49) (Rome) 203–38

Frank, R. I. (1967) '*Commendabiles* in Ammianus', *AJP* 88: 309–18

Frank, R. I. (1969) *Scholae Palatinae: The Palace Guards of the Later Roman Empire* (Papers and monographs of the American Academy in Rome 23). Rome

Frézouls, E. (1979) 'Les fluctuations de la frontière orientale de l'empire romain', in T. Fahd (ed.), *La Géographie administrative politique d'Alexandre à Mahomet* (Strasburg) 177–225

Gabba, E. (1974) 'I cristiani nell'esercito romano del quarto secolo d.C.', in his *Per la storia dell'esercito romano in età imperiale* (Bologna) 75–109

Gain, B. (1985) *L'Église au IVe siècle d'après la correspondance de Basile de Césarée (350–379).* Rome

Garnsey, P. and Woolf, G. D. (1989) 'Patronage of the rural poor in the Roman world', in A. Wallace-Hadrill (ed.), *Patronage in Ancient Society* (London) 153–70

Gaudemet, J. (1958) *L'Église dans l'empire romain.* Paris

Gaudemet, J. (1967) *Institutions de l'antiquité.* Paris.

Gaudemet, J. (1986) 'Ordre public et charité chrétienne: la loi du 27 juillet 398', *Studi tardoantichi* 1: 245–64

Giardina, A. (1977) *Aspetti della burocrazia nel basso impero* (Filologia e critica 22). Rome

Giardina, A. (1986) 'Carità eversiva: le donazioni di Melania la giovane e gli equi- libri della società tardoromana', *Studi tardoantichi* 2: 77–102

Giet, S. (1941) *Les Idées et l'action sociales de saint Basile*. Paris

Goffart, W. (1970) 'Did Julian combat venal *suffragium*? A note on *CTh* 2.29.1', *CPh* 65: 145–51

Goodburn, R. and Bartholomew, P. (eds.) (1976) *Aspects of the Notitia Dignitatum: Papers Presented to the Conference in Oxford, December 13 to 15, 1974* (BAR, Supplementary Series 15). Oxford

Goodchild, R. G. (1976) *Libyan Studies* (ed. J. Reynolds). London

Goodenough, E. R. (1928) 'The Political Philosophy of Hellenistic Kingship', *YCS* 1: 55–102

Grabar, A. (1936) *L'Empereur dans l'art byzantin: recherches sur l'art officiel de l'Empire d'Orient* (Publications de la Faculté des Lettres de l'Université de Strasbourg 75). Paris (repr. London 1971)

Graf, D. F. (1989) 'Rome and the Saracens: reassessing the nomadic menace', in T. Fahd (ed.), *L'Arabie préislamique et son environnement historique et culturel* (Leiden) 342–400

Grigg, R. (1979) 'Portrait-bearing codicils in the illustrations of the *Notitia Dignitatum*', *JRS* 69: 105–24

Grigg, R. (1983) 'Inconsistency and lassitude: the shield emblems of the *Notitia Dignitatum*', *JRS* 73: 132–42

Groag, E. (1946) *Die Reichsbeamten von Achaia in spätrömischer Zeit* (Dissertationes Pannonicae 1:14). Budapest

Grosse, R. (1920) *Römische Militärgeschichte von Gallienus bis zum Beginn der byzantini- schen Themenverfassung*. Berlin

Grünewald, T. (1990) *Constantinus Maximus Augustus: Herrschaftspropaganda in der zeit- genössischen Überlieferung* (*Historia* Einzelschriften 64). Stuttgart

Gryson, R. (1979) 'Les élections épiscopales en Orient au IVᵉ siècle', *RHE* 74: 301–45

Gryson, R. (1980) 'Les élections épiscopales en Occident au IVᵉ siècle', *RHE* 75: 257–83

Guilland, R. (1967) 'Études sur l'histoire administrative de l'Empire byzantin à la haute époque (IVᵉ–VIᵉ siècles): remarques sur les titres nobiliaires: egrège- perfectissime-clarissime', *EHBS* 35: 17–40 (repr. in his *Titres et fonctions de l'Empire byzantin* (London 1976))

Gutzwiller, H. (1942) *Die Neujahrsrede des Konsuls Claudius Mamertinus vor dem Kaiser Julian* (Basler Beiträge zur Geschichtswissenschaft 10). Basel

Guyot, P. (1980) *Eunuchen als Sklaven und Freigelassene in der griechisch-römischen Antike* (Stuttgarter Beiträge zur Geschichte und Politik 14). Stuttgart

Haehling, R. von (1978) *Die Religionszugehörigkeit der hohen Amtsträger des Römischen Reiches seit Constantins I: Alleinherrschaft bis zum Ende der Theodosianischen Dynastie (324–450 bzw. 455) n. Chr.)* (Antiquitas 3.23). Bonn

Hansen, M. H. (1993) 'The battle exhortation in ancient historiography: fact or fiction?', *Historia* 42: 161–80

Harmand, L. (1955) *Libanius: Discours sur les Patronages* (Publications de la Faculté des Lettres de l'Université de Clermont-Ferrand 2:1). Paris

Harries, J. (1984) '"Treasure in Heaven": property and inheritance among senators in late Rome', in E. M. Craik (ed.), *Marriage and Property* (Aberdeen) 54–70

Harries, J. (1988) 'The Roman imperial Quaestor from Constantine to Theodosius II', *JRS* 78: 148–72

Harries, J. and Wood, I. (eds.) (1993) *The Theodosian Code: Studies in the Imperial Law of Late Antiquity*. London

Hassall, M. W. C. (1976) 'Britain in the *Notitia*', in Goodburn and Bartholomew (1976) 103–18

Hassall, M. W. C. and Ireland, R. (eds.) (1979) *De Rebus Bellicis* (BAR International Series 63). Oxford

Hawkes, S. C. (1974) 'Some recent finds of late Roman buckles', *Britannia* 5: 386–93

Hawkes, S. C. and Dunning G. C. (1961) 'Soldiers and settlers in Britain, fourth to fifth century: catalogue of animal-ornamented buckles and related belt-fittings', *Mediaeval Archaeology* 5: 41–70

Heather, P. J. (1994a) 'Literacy and power in the migration period', in Bowman and Woolf (1994) 177–97

Heather, P. J. (1994b) 'New men for new Constantines: creating an imperial élite in the eastern Mediterranean', in P. Magdalino (ed.), *New Constantines: The Rhythm of Imperial Renewal in Byzantium, 4th–13th Centuries* (Aldershot) 11–33

Heather, P. J. and Matthews, J. F. (1991) *The Goths in the Fourth Century*. Liverpool

Helgeland, J. (1979) 'Christians in the Roman army from Marcus Aurelius to Constantine', *ANRW* II.23.1: 724–834

Herrin, J. (1990) 'Ideals of charity, realities of welfare: the philanthropic activity of the Byzantine church', in R. Morris (ed.), *Church and People in Byzantium* (Birmingham) 151–64

Hess, H. (1958) *The Canons of the Council of Sardica A.D. 343*. Oxford (rev. edn 1997)

Heurgon, J. (1958) *Le Trésor de Ténès*. Paris

Hirschfeld, O. (1901) 'Die Rangtitel der römischen Kaizerzeit', *SPAW*: 579–610 (repr. in his *Kleine Schriften* (Berlin 1913) 646–81)

Hoffmann, D. (1963) 'Die spätrömischen Soldatengrabschriften von Concordia', *MH* 20: 22–57

Hoffmann, D. (1978) 'Wadomar, Bacurius und Hariulf: Zur Laufbahn adliger und fürstlicher Barbaren im spätrömischen Heere des 4. Jahrhunderts', *MH* 35: 307–18

Holmberg, E. J. (1933) *Zur Geschichte des Cursus Publicus*. Uppsala

Holum, K. (1977) 'Pulcheria's crusade AD 421–22 and the ideology of imperial victory', *GRBS* 18: 153–72

Honoré, T. (1986) 'The making of the Theodosian Code', *ZRG* 103: 133–222

Hopkins, K. (1961) 'Social mobility in the later Roman Empire: the evidence of Ausonius', *CQ* 11: 239–49

Hopkins, K. (1963) 'Eunuchs in politics in the later Roman Empire', *PCPS* 189: 62–80 (=Hopkins (1978) 172–96)

Hopkins, K. (1978) *Conquerors and Slaves* (Sociological Studies in Roman History 1). Cambridge

L'Huillier, M.-C. (1986) 'La figure de l'empereur et les vertus impériales: crise et modèle d'identité dans les *Panégyriques latines*', in *Les Grandes Figures religieuses: fonctionnement pratique et symbolique dans l'antiquité, Besançon 25–6 avril 1984* (Centre de recherches d'histoire ancienne 68, Annales littéraires de l'Université de Besançon 329) (Paris) 529–82

L'Huillier, M.-C. (1992) *L'Empire des mots: orateurs gaulois et empereurs romains, 3ᵉ et 4ᵉ siècles* (Centre de recherches d'histoire ancienne 114, Annales littéraires de l'Université de Besançon 464). Paris

Hunt, E. D. (1981) 'The traffic in relics: some late Roman evidence', in S. Hackel (ed.), *The Byzantine Saint* (London) 171–80

Hunt, E. D. (1982) 'St Stephen in Minorca: an episode in Jewish Christian relations in the early 5th century A.D.', *JThS* 33: 106–23

Hunt, E. D. (1993) 'Christianising the Roman Empire: the evidence of the Code', in Harries and Wood (1993) 143–8

Hurst, A., Reverdin, O. and Rudhardt, J. (1984) *Papyrus Bodmer XXIX: vision de Dorothéos*. Geneva

Huskinson, J. M. (1982) *Concordia Apostolorum: Christian Propaganda at Rome in the Fourth and Fifth Centuries*. Oxford

Isaac, B. (1988) 'The meaning of the terms *limes* and *limitanei*', *JRS* 78: 125–47

James, S. (1988) 'The *fabricae*: state arms factories of the later Roman empire', in J. C. N. Coulston (ed.), *Military Equipment and the Identity of Soldiers: Proceedings of the Fourth Roman Military Equipment Conference* (BAR International Series 394) (Oxford) 257–331

Johnson, S. (1983) *Late Roman Fortifications*. London

Jones, A. H. M. (1949) 'The Roman civil service (clerical and sub-clerical grades)', *JRS* 39: 38–55 (repr. in his *Studies in Roman Government and Law* (Oxford 1960) ch. 10)

Jones, A. H. M. (1953) 'Military chaplains in the Roman army', *HThR* 46: 239–40

Jones, A. H. M. (1963) 'The social background of the struggle between paganism and Christianity', in Momigliano, *Conflict* 17–37

Jones, G. D. B. (1979) 'Invasion and response in Roman Britain', in B. C. Burnham and H. B. Johnson (eds.), *Invasion and Response: The Case of Roman Britain* (BAR British Series 73) (Oxford) 57–70

Kalavrezou-Maxeiner, I. (1975) 'The imperial chamber at Luxor', *DOP* 29: 227–51

Karayannopulos, J. (1956) 'Der frühbyzantinische Kaiser', *Byz. Zeit.* 49: 369–84 (repr. in H. Hunger (ed.), *Das byzantinische Herrscherbild* (Wege der Forschung 341) (Darmstadt 1975) 235–57)

Karayannopulos, J. (1958) *Das Finanzwesen des frühbyzantinischen Staates* (Südosteuropäische Arbeiten 52). Munich

Kelly, C. M. (1994) 'Later Roman bureaucracy: going through the files', in Bowman and Woolf (1994) 161–76

Kennedy, G. A. (1983) *Greek Rhetoric under Christian Emperors*. Princeton, NJ

Kent, J. P. C. (1961) 'The *Comes Sacrarum Largitionum*', in E. C. Dodd, *Byzantine Silver Stamps* (Dumbarton Oaks Studies 7) (Washington, DC) 35–45

Kessels, A. H. M. and van der Horst, P. W. (1987) 'The Vision of Dorotheus (Pap. Bodmer 29) edited with introduction, translation and notes', *Vig. Christ.* 41: 313–59

King, C. E. (ed.) (1980a) *Imperial Revenue, Expenditure and Monetary Policy in the Fourth Century A.D.: The Fifth Oxford Symposium on Coinage and Monetary History* (BAR International Series 76). Oxford

King, C. E. (1980b) 'The *Sacrae Largitiones*: revenues, expenditure and the production of coin', in King (ed.) (1980a) 141–73

Klein, R. (1979) 'Der Rombesuch des Kaisers Konstantius II im Jahre 357', *Athenaeum* 57: 98–115

Klotz, A. (1911) 'Studien zu den *Panegyrici Latini*', *RM* 66: 513–72

Koch, P. (1903) *Die Byzantinischen Beamtentitel von 400 bis 700*. Jena

Kolias, G. (1939) *Ämter- und Würdenkauf im früh- und mittelbyzantinischen Reich* (Texte und Forschungen zur byzantinisch-neugriechischen Philologie 35). Athens

Krause, J.-U. (1987) *Spätantike Patronatsformen im Westen des Römischen Reiches* (Vestigia 38). Munich

Krautheimer, R. (1983) *Three Christian Capitals: Topography and Politics*. Berkeley, CA

Krautheimer, R. (1987) 'A note on the inscription in the apse of Old St Peter's', *DOP* 41: 317–20

Kruse, H. (1934) *Studien zur offiziellen Geltung des Kaiserbildes im römischen Reiche* (Studien zur Geschichte und Kultur des Altertums 19:3). Paderborn

Kunkel, W. (1968) '*Consilium, consistorium*', *JbAC* 11/12: 230–48 (repr. in his *Kleine Schriften: zum römischen Strafverfahren und zur römischen Verfassungsgeschichte*, ed. H. Niederländer (Weimar 1974) 405–40)

Lallemand, J. (1964) *L'Administration civile de l'Égypte de l'avènement de Dioclétien à la création du diocèse (284–382): contribution à l'étude des rapports entre Égypte et l'empire à la fin du IIIe et au IVe siècle* (Mémoires de l'Académie Royale de Belgique 52:2). Brussels

Lancel, S. (1990) 'Évêchés et cités dans les provinces africaines (IIIe–Ve siècles)', in *L'Afrique dans l'occident romain* (Rome) 273–90

Lee, A. D. (1989) 'Campaign preparations in late Roman-Persian warfare', in D. H. French and C. S. Lightfoot (eds.), *The Eastern Frontier of the Roman Empire* (BAR International Series 553) (Oxford) 257–65

Lee, A. D. (1993) *Information and Frontiers: Roman Foreign Relations in Late Antiquity*. Cambridge

Levy, H. L. (1958) 'Themes of encomium and invective in Claudian', *TAPA* 89: 336–47

Liebeschuetz, J. H. W. G. (1986) 'Why did Synesius become bishop of Ptolemais?', *Byzantion* 56: 180–95

Liebeschuetz, J. H. W. G. (1987) 'Government and administration in the late Empire (to AD 476)', in J. Wacher (ed.), *The Roman World*, 2 vols. (London) 1, 455–69

Liebeschuetz, J. H. W. G. (1993) 'The end of the Roman army in the western empire', in Rich and Shipley (1993) 265–76

Liebs, D. (1978) 'Ämterkauf und Ämterpatronage in der Spätantike: Propaganda und Sachzwang bei Julian dem Abtrünnigen', *ZRG* 95: 158–86

Lieu, S. N. C. (1989) *The Emperor Julian, Panegyric and Polemic* (Translated Texts for Historians 2). 2nd edn. Liverpool

Lightfoot, C. S. (1988) 'Facts and fiction – the third siege of Nisibis (A.D. 350)', *Historia* 37: 105–25

Lippold, A. (1968) 'Herrscherideal und Traditionsverbundenheit im *Panegyricus* des Pacatus', *Historia* 17: 228–50

Lizzi, R. (1987) *Il potere episcopale nell'Oriente romano*. Rome

Lizzi, R. (1988) 'Codicilli imperiali e insignia episcopali: un'affinità significativa', RIL 122: 3–13

Lizzi, R. (1989) Vescovi e strutture ecclesiastiche nella città tardoantica. Como

Lizzi, R. (1990) 'Ambrose's contemporaries and the Christianisation of northern Italy', JRS 80: 156–73

Löhken, H. (1982) Ordines Dignitatum: Untersuchungen zur formalen Konstituierung der spätantiken Führungsschicht (Kölner historische Abhandlungen 30). Cologne

Maas, M. (1992) John Lydus and the Roman Past: Antiquarianism and Politics in the Age of Justinian. London

MacCormack, S. G. (1972) 'Change and continuity in late antiquity: the ceremony of Adventus', Historia 21: 721–52

MacCormack, S. G. (1975) 'Latin prose panegyrics', in T. A. Dorey (ed.), Empire and Aftermath: Silver Latin II (Greek and Latin Studies, Classical Literature and its Influence) (London) 143–205

McCormick, M. (1985) 'Analyzing imperial ceremonies', JÖB 35: 1–20

MacMullen, R. (1960) 'Inscriptions on armor and the supply of arms in the Roman Empire', AJA 64: 23–40

MacMullen, R. (1963) Soldier and Civilian in the Later Roman Empire. Cambridge, MA and London

MacMullen, R. (1964a) 'Imperial bureaucrats in the Roman provinces', HSCP 68: 305–16

MacMullen, R. (1964b) 'Social mobility and the Theodosian Code', JRS 54: 49–53

MacMullen, R. (1964c) 'Some pictures in Ammianus Marcellinus', ABull 46: 435–55 (MacMullen, Changes, 78–106)

MacMullen, R. (1980) 'How big was the Roman imperial army?', Klio 62: 451–60

MacMullen, R. (1984) 'The Roman emperor's army costs', Latomus 43: 570–80

MacMullen, R. (1986a) 'Judicial savagery in the Roman Empire', Chiron 16: 147–66 (MacMullen, Changes, 204–17)

MacMullen, R. (1986b) 'What difference did Christianity make?', Historia 35: 322–43 (MacMullen, Changes, 142–55)

Maguinness, W. S. (1932) 'Some methods of the Latin panegyrists', Hermathena 22 [47]: 42–61

Mann, J. C. (1976) 'What was the Notitia Dignitatum for?', in Goodburn and Bartholomew (1976) 1–10

Mann, J. C. (1977) 'Duces and comites in the fourth century', in D. E. Johnston (ed.), The Saxon Shore (CBA Research Report 18) (London) 11–15

Mann, J. C. (1979) 'Power, force and the frontiers of the empire', JRS 69: 175–83

Mann, J. C. (1989) 'The historical development of the Saxon shore', in V. A. Maxfield (ed.), The Saxon Shore (Exeter) 1–11

Mann, J. C. (1991) 'The Notitia Dignitatum – dating and survival', Britannia 22: 215–19

Maraval, P. (1985) Lieux saints et pèlerinages d'Orient. Paris

Martin, A. (1984a) 'Les premiers siècles du christianisme à Alexandrie: essai de topographie religieuse', REA 30: 211–25

Martin, J. (1984b) 'Zum Selbstverständnis, zur Repräsentation und Macht des Kaisers in der Spätantike', Saeculum 35: 115–31

Mathisen, R. W. (1989) *Ecclesiastical Factionalism and Religious Controversy in Fifth-Century Gaul*. Washington, DC

Matthews, J. F. (1971) 'Gallic supporters of Theodosius', *Latomus* 30: 1073–99 (=Matthews (1985) 1073–99)

Matthews, J. F. (1974) 'The letters of Symmachus', in Binns, *Latin Literature* 58–99 (=Matthews (1985) 58–99)

Matthews, J. F. (1976a) 'Gesandtschaft', *RAC* 10: 653–85

Matthews, J. F. (1976b) 'Mauretania in Ammianus and the *Notitia*', in Goodburn and Bartholomew (1976) 157–88

Matthews, J. F. (1985) *Political Life and Culture in Late Roman Society*. London

Matthews, J. F. (1986) 'Ammianus and the eastern frontier in the fourth century: a participant's view', in P. M. Freeman and D. L. Kennedy (eds.), *The Defence of the Roman and Byzantine East* (BAR International Series 297) (Oxford) 549–64

Matthews, J. F. (1992) 'The poetess Proba and fourth-century Rome: questions of interpretation', in M. Christol *et al.* (eds.), *Institutions, société et vie politique dans l'empire romain au IVe siècle après J.-C.* (Rome) 277–304

Matthews, J. F. (1993) 'The making of the text', in Harries and Wood (1993) 19–44

Millar, F. G. B. (1964) *A Study of Cassius Dio*. Oxford

Millar, F. G. B. (1980) 'The *Privata* from Diocletian to Theodosius: documentary evidence', in King (ed.) (1980a) 125–40

Millar, F. (1982) 'Emperors, frontiers and foreign relations, 31 B.C. to A.D. 378', *Britannia* 13: 1–23

Milner, N. P. (trans.) (1993) *Vegetius: Epitome of Military Science*. Liverpool

Mitchell, S. (1993) *Anatolia: Land, Men and Gods in Asia Minor*. 2 vols. Oxford

Mócsy, A. (1962) 'Pannonia', *RE* Suppl. 9: 516–776

Mócsy, A. (1974) *Pannonia and Upper Moesia*. London

Mommsen, T. (1900) 'Das theodosische Gesetzbuch', *ZRG* 21: 149–90 (repr. in his *Juristische Schriften* II=*Gesammelte Schriften* II (Berlin 1905 repr. 1965) 371–405)

Mommsen, T. (1910) 'Das römische Militärwesen seit Diocletian', *Gesammelte Schriften* (Berlin) VI, 206–83

Monks, G. R. (1957) 'The administration of the privy purse: an inquiry into official corruption and the fall of the Roman Empire', *Speculum* 32: 748–79

Monneret de Villard, U. (1953) 'The temple of the imperial cult at Luxor', *Archaeologia* 95: 85–106

Nesselhauf, H. (1938) *Die spätrömische Verwaltung der gallisch-germanischen Länder* (Abhandlungen der Preussischen Akademie der Wissenschaften Philosophisch-historische Klasse 2). Berlin

Nixon, C. E. V. (1987) *Pacatus: Panegyric to the Emperor Theodosius* (Translated Texts for Historians 3). Liverpool

Nock, A. D. (1947) 'The Emperor's divine *comes*', *JRS* 37: 102–16 (repr. in Z. Stewart (ed.) *Arthur Darby Nock: Essays on Religion and the Ancient World*, 2 vols. (Oxford 1972) II, 653–75)

Nock, A. D. (1952) 'The Roman army and the Roman religious year', *HThR* 45: 186–252

Noethlichs, K. L. (1972) 'Zur Einflussnahme des Staates auf die Entwicklung eines christlichen Klerikerstandes', *JbAC* 15: 136–53

Noethlichs, K. L. (1973) 'Materialen zum Bischofsbild aus den spätantiken Rechtsquellen', *JAC* 16: 28–59

Noethlichs, K. L. (1981) *Beamtentum und Dienstvergehen: zur Staatsverwaltung in der Spätantike.* Wiesbaden

Noethlichs, K. L. (1991) 'Hofbeamter', *RAC* 15: cols. 1111–58

Ousterhout, R. (ed.) (1990) *The Blessings of Pilgrimage.* Urbana, IL

Pabst, A. (1989) *Quintus Aurelius Symmachus: Reden* (Texte zur Forschung 53). Darmstadt

Pack, R. A. (1935) *Studies in Libanius and Antiochene Society under Theodosius.* Ann Arbor, MI

Palmer, A.-M. (1989) *Prudentius on the Martyrs.* Oxford

Parker, S. T. (1992) 'Two books on the Eastern Roman frontier: nomads and other security threats', *JRA* 5: 467–72

Parsons, P. J. (1976) 'Petitions and a letter: the grammarian's complaint', in A. E. Hanson (ed.) *Collectanea Papyrologica: Texts published in honor of H. C. Youtie,* (Papyrologische Texte und Abhandlungen 20) (Bonn) II, 409–46

van de Paverd, F. (1991) *St John Chrystostom, The Homilies on the Statues: An Introduction* (OCA 239). Rome

Pedersen, F. S. (1970) 'On professional qualifications for public posts in late antiquity', *C&M* 31: 161–213 (repr. as *Late Roman Public Professionalism* (Odense, 1976))

Petit, P. (1956a) *Les Étudiants de Libanius* (Études prosopographiques 1). Paris

Petit, P. (1956b) 'Recherches sur la publication et la diffusion des discours de Libanius', *Historia* 5: 479–509 (repr. in G. Fatouros and T. Krischer (eds.), *Libanios* (Wege der Forschung 621) (Darmstadt 1983) 84–128)

Petit, P. (1957) 'Les sénateurs de Constantinople dans l'œuvre de Libanius', *L'Antiquité Classique* 26: 347–82

Pflaum, H. G. (1950) *Les Procurateurs équestres sous le haut-empire romain.* Paris

Pichon, R. (1906) *Les Derniers Écrivains profanes* (Etudes sur histoire de la littérature latine dans les Gaules 1). Paris

Piétri, C. (1986) 'Damase évêque de Rome', in *Saecularia Damasiana* (Rome) 29–58

Pitts, L. F. (1987) 'Roman-style buildings in barbaricum (Moravia and SW Slovakia)', *OJA* 6: 219–36

Posner, E. (1972) *Archives in the Ancient World.* Cambridge, MA

Purpura, G. (1973) 'I *curiosi* e la *schola agentum in rebus*', *Annali del Seminario Giuridico della Università di Palermo* 34: 165–273

Reinhold, M. (1970) *History of Purple as a Status Symbol in Antiquity* (Collection Latomus 116). Brussels

Rémondon, R. (1965) 'Militaires et civils dans une campagne égyptienne au temps de Constance II', *JS* 132–43

Rich, J. and Shipley, G. (eds.) (1993) *War and Society in the Roman World.* London

Ritter, A. M. (1965) *Das Konzil von Konstantinopel und sein Symbol.* Göttingen

Roberts, M. (1993) *Poetry and the Cult of Martyrs: The Liber Peristephanon of Prudentius.* Ann Arbor, MI

Roda, S. (1986) 'Polifunzionalità della lettera commendaticia: teoria e prassi nell'epistolario simmachiano', in F. Paschoud (ed.), *Colloque genevois sur Symmaque à l'occasion du mille six centième anniversaire du conflit de l'autel de la Victoire* (Paris) 177–207

Rodgers, B. S. (1986) 'Divine insinuation in the *Panegyrici Latini*', *Historia* 35: 69–104

Roueché, C. (1984) 'Acclamations in the later Roman Empire: new evidence from Aphrodisias', *JRS* 74: 181–99

Rousselle, A. (1977) 'Aspects sociaux du recrutement ecclésiastique au IVe siècle', *MEFR* 89: 333–70

Ruggini, L. C. (1986) 'Poteri in gara per la salvezza di città ribelli: il caso di Antiochia (387 d.C.)', *Studi tardoantichi* 1: 265–90

de Ste Croix, G. E. M. (1954) '*Suffragium*: from vote to patronage', *British Journal of Sociology* 5: 33–48

Saxer, V. (1980) *Morts, martyrs, reliques en Afrique chrétienne aux premiers siècles*. Paris

Schönberger, H. (1969) 'The Roman frontier in Germany: an archaeological survey', *JRS* 59: 144–97

Schubart, W. (1937) 'Das hellenistiche Königsideal nach Inschriften und Papyri', *APF* 12: 1–26 (repr. in H. Kloft (ed.), *Ideologie und Herrschaft in der Antike* (Wege der Forschung 528) (Darmstadt 1979) 90–122)

Schuller, W. (1975) 'Grenzen des spätrömischen Staates: Staatspolizei und Korruption', *ZPE* 16: 1–21

Schuller, W. (1982) 'Prinzipien des spätantiken Beamtentums', in W. Schuller (ed.), *Korruption im Altertum: Konstanzer Symposium, Oktober 1979* (Munich) 201–8

Schweckendiek, H. (1992) *Claudians Invektive gegen Eutrop (In Eutropium): ein Kommentar* (Beiträge zur Altertumswissenschaft 10). Hildesheim

Scorpan, C. (1980) *Limes Scythiae. Topographical and Stratigraphical Research on the Late Roman Fortifications on the Lower Danube* (BAR International Series 88). Oxford

Seager, R. (1986) *Ammianus Marcellinus: Seven Studies in his Language and Thought*. Columbia, MO

Seeck, O. (1906) *Die Briefe des Libanius* (Texte und Untersuchungen zur Geschichte der altchristlichen Literatur 15.1). Leipzig (reprinted Hildesheim, 1966)

Seeck, O. (1919) *Regesten der Kaiser und Päpste für die Jahre 311 bis 476 n. Chr.: Vorarbeit zu einer Prosopographie der christlichen Kaiserzeit*. Stuttgart (repr. Frankfurt am Main 1964)

Seeck, O. (1924) '*Laterculum*', *RE* 12: 904–7

Seibt, W. (1982) 'Wurde die "notitia dignitatum" 408 von Stilicho in Auftrag gegeben?', *MIOEG* 90: 339–46

Selb, W. (1967) 'Episcopalis audientia von der Zeit Konstantins bis zur Nov. XXXV Valentinians III', *ZRG* 84: 162–217

Setton, K. M. (1941) *Christian Attitudes towards the Emperor in the Fourth Century especially as shown in Addresses to the Emperor* (Studies in History, Economics and Public Law 482). New York (repr. 1967)

Sinnigen, W. G. (1957) *The Officium of the Urban Prefecture during the Later Roman Empire* (Papers and Monographs of the American Academy in Rome 17). Rome

Sinnigen, W. G. (1959) 'Two branches of the late Roman secret service', *AJP* 80: 238–54

Sinnigen, W. G. (1962) 'Three administrative changes ascribed to Constantius II', *AJP* 83: 369–82

Sinnigen, W. G. (1964) 'Chiefs of staff and chiefs of the secret service', *Byz. Zeit.* 57: 78–105

Sirks, B. (1993) 'The sources of the Code', in Harries and Wood (1993) 45–67

Sivan, H. S. (1985) 'An unedited letter of emperor Honorius to the Spanish soldiers', *ZPE* 61: 273–87

Sivan, H. (1993) *Ausonius of Bordeaux: Genesis of a Gallic Aristocracy*. London

Smith, J. Z. (1987) *To Take Place: Toward Theory in Ritual*. Chicago

Stancliffe, C. (1983) *St Martin and his Hagiographer: History and Miracle in Sulpicius Severus*. Oxford

Steigerwald, G. (1990) 'Das kaiserliche Purpurprivileg in spätrömischer and frühbyzantinischer Zeit', *JbAC* 33: 209–39

Stein, E. (1920) 'Untersuchungen zum Staatsrecht des Bas-Empire', *ZRG* 41: 195–251 (repr. in his *Opera Minora Selecta*, ed. J. R. Palanque (Amsterdam 1968) 71–127)

Stein, E. (1922) *Untersuchungen über das Officium der Prätorianerpräfektur seit Diocletian*. Vienna (repr. and ed. J. R. Palanque (Amsterdam 1962))

Steinwenter, A. (1950) '*Audientia Episcopalis*', *RAC* 1: 915–17

Stertz, S. A. (1979) 'Pseudo-Aristides, '*ΕΙΣ ΒΑΣΙΛΕΑ*', *CQ* n.s. 29: 172–97

Straub, J. A. (1939) *Vom Herrscherideal in der Spätantike* (Forschungen zur Kirchen- und Geistesgeschichte 18). Stuttgart (repr. 1964)

Straub, J. A. (1962) 'Die Himmelfahrt des Julianus Apostata', *Gymnasium* 69: 310–26 (repr. in his *Regeneratio Imperii: Aufsätze über Roms Kaisertum und Reich im Spiegel der heidnischen und christlichen Publizistik* (Darmstadt 1972) 159–77)

Stroheker, K. F. (1975) *Germanentum und Spätanike*. Zurich

Struthers, L. B. (1919) 'The rhetorical structure of the encomia of Claudius Claudian', *HSCP* 30: 49–87

Sundwall, J. (1915) *Weströmische Studien*. Berlin

Swift, L. J. and Oliver, J. H. (1962) 'Constantius II on Flavius Philippus', *AJP* 83: 247–64

Szidat, J. (1979) 'Die Usurpation des Eugenius', *Historia* 28: 487–508

Taeger, F. (1956) 'Zur Geschichte der spätkaiserlichen Herrscherauffassung', *Saeculum* 7: 182–95

Talbot, R. J. A. (1984) *The Senate of Imperial Rome*. Princeton, NJ

Tassi, A. M. (1967) 'Costanzo II e la difesa della maestà imperiale nell'opera di Ammiano Marcellino', *CS* 6:2: 157–80

Teitler, H. C. (1985) *Notarii and Exceptores: An Inquiry into Role and Significance of Shorthand Writers in the Imperial and Ecclesiastical Bureaucracy of the Roman Empire (from the Early Principate to c. 450 A.D.)* (Dutch Monographs on Ancient History and Archaeology 1). Amsterdam

Testini, P. (1985) 'Note per servire allo studio del complesso paleocristiano di S. Felice a Cimitile (Nola)', *MEFR* 97: 329–71

Thompson, E. A. (1947) *The Historical Work of Ammianus Marcellinus*. Cambridge

Tomlin, R. S. O. (1972) '*Seniores-iuniores* in the late-Roman field army', *AJP* 93: 253–78

Tomlin, R. S. O. (1976) 'Notitia dignitatum omnium, tam civilium quam militarium', in Goodburn and Bartholomew (1976) 189–209

Tomlin, R. S. O. (1979) 'Meanwhile in North Italy and Cyrenaica . . .', in P. J. Casey (ed.), *The End of Roman Britain* (BAR British Series 71) (Oxford) 253–70

Tomlin, R. S. O. (1987) 'The army of the late empire', in J. Wacher (ed.), *The Roman World*, 2 vols. (London) 1, 107–20

Treitinger, O. (1938) *Die oströmische Kaiser und Reichsidee nach ihrer Gestaltung im höfischen Zeremoniell*. Jena (repr. Darmstadt 1956)

Treucker, B. (1981) 'A note on Basil's letters of recommendation', in P. J. Fedwick (ed.), *Basil of Caesarea: Christian, Humanist, Ascetic: A Sixteen-Hundredth Anniversary Symposium*, 2 vols. (Pontifical Institute of Mediaeval Studies) (Toronto) 1, 405–10

Twyman, B. L. (1970) 'Aetius and the Aristocracy', *Historia* 19: 480–503

Valdenburg, V. (1924) 'Discours politiques de Thémistius dans leur rapport avec l'antiquité', *Byzantion* 1: 557–80

Valensi, L. (1957) 'Quelques réflexions sur le pouvoir impérial d'après Ammien Marcellin', *BAGB* (4ᵉ sér.) 16:4: 62–107

Van Dam, R. (1986) 'Emperors, bishops and friends in late antique Cappadocia', *JThS* n.s. 37: 53–76

Van der Meer, F. (1961) *Augustine the Bishop*. London

Vera, D. (1981) *Commento storico alle Relationes di Quinto Aurelio Simmaco: introduzione, commento, testo, traduzione, appendice sul Libro X, 1–2, indici* (Biblioteca di studi antichi 29). Pisa

Verdickt, M. (1968) 'Les proconsulats d'Asie et d'Achaïe aux IVᵉ–Vᵉ siècles après J. C. (à propos de deux chapitres de la *Notitia Dignitatum*)', *RecPhL* 2: 167–208

Vereecke, E. (1975) 'Le corpus des panégyriques latins de l'époque tardive: problèmes d'imitation', *AC* 44: 141–60

Veyne, P. (1981) 'Clientèle et corruption au service de l'état: la vénalité des offices dans le Bas-Empire romain', *Annales (ESC)* 36:3: 339–60

Vogler, C. (1979) *Constance II et l'administration impériale* (Groupe de recherche d'histoire romaine de l'Université des sciences humaines de Strasbourg, Études et travaux 3). Strasbourg

Waas, M. (1965) *Germanen im römischen Dienst im 4. Jh. n. Chr.* Bonn

Walker, P. W. L. (1990) *Holy City, Holy Places. Christian Attitudes to Jerusalem and the Holy Land in the Fourth Century*. Oxford

Wallace-Hadrill, A. N. (1981) 'The emperor and his virtues', *Historia* 30: 298–323

Wallace-Hadrill, A. N. (1982) '*Civilis Princeps*: between citizen and king', *JRS* 72: 32–48

Ward, J. H. (1974) 'The *Notitia Dignitatum*', *Latomus* 33: 397–434

Wardman, A. E. (1984) 'Usurpers and internal conflicts in the 4th century AD', *Historia* 33: 220–37

Warmington, B. H. (1956) 'The career of Romanus, *comes Africae*', *Byz. Zeit.* 49: 55–64

Warren Bonfante, L. (1964) 'Emperor, God and man in the IVth century: Julian the Apostate and Ammianus Marcellinus', *PP* 99: 401–27

Weber, R. J. (1989) 'Albinus: the living memory of a 5th-century personality', *Historia* 38: 472–97

Weiss, P. B. (1975) *Consistorium und Comites Consistoriani: Untersuchungen zur Hofbeamtenschaft des 4. Jahrhunderts n. Chr. auf prosopographischer Grundlage*. Würzburg

Wheeler, E. L. (1993) 'Methodological limits and the mirage of Roman strategy', *Journal of Military History* 57: 7–42, 215–40

Whittaker, C. R. (1980) 'Inflation and the economy in the fourth century A.D.', in King (ed.) (1980a) 1–22

Whittaker, C. R. (1983) 'Trade and frontiers of the Roman empire', in P. Garnsey and C. R. Whittaker (eds.), *Trade and Famine in Classical Antiquity* (Cambridge) 110–27

Whittaker, C. R. (1993) 'Landlords and warlords in the later Roman empire', in Rich and Shipley (eds.) (1993) 277–302

Wilken, R. L. (1992) *The Land Called Holy: Palestine in Christian History and Thought.* New Haven, CT

Wilkes, J. J. (1989) 'The frontier of Noricum', *JRA* 2: 347–52

Wilkinson, J. (1981) *Egeria's Travels to the Holy Land.* rev. edn. Jerusalem

Woods, D. (1991) 'The christianisation of the Roman army in the fourth century', The Queen's University, Belfast, unpublished PhD dissertation

Zecchini, G. (1983) *Aezio: l'ultima difesa dell'Occidente romano.* Rome

PART III: THE EMPIRE: ECONOMY AND SOCIETY (CHS. 9–12)

Alföldi, A. (1970) *Die monarchische Repräsentation im römischen Kaiserreiche.* Darmstadt

Alföldy, G. (1975) *Römische Sozialgeschichte.* Wiesbaden

Anselmino, L. *et al.* (1989) *Il castellum del Nador. Storia di una fattoria tra Tipasa e Caesarea (I–IV sec. d. C).* Rome

Archi, G. G. (1976) *Teodosio II e la sua legislazione.* Milan

Arthur, P. (1991) *Romans in Northern Campania.* London

Balty, J. (ed.) (1984) *Apamée de Syrie. Bilan des recherches archéologiques 1973–1979.* Brussels

Barker, G. and Lloyd, J. (eds.) (1991) *Roman Landscapes.* London

Barnes, T. D. (1974) 'Who were the nobility in the Roman Empire?', *Phoenix* 28: 444–9

Barnish, S. J. B. (1987) 'Pigs, plebeians and potentates: Rome's economic hinterland c. 350–600 A.D.', *PBSR* 55: 157–85

Barnish, S. J. B. (1989) 'The transformation of classical cities and the Pirenne debate', *JRA* 2: 385–400

Bird, H. W. (1984) *Sextus Aurelius Victor: A Historiographical Study* (ARCA 14). Liverpool

Boak, A. E. R. (1955) *Manpower Shortage and the Fall of the Roman Empire in the West.* Ann Arbor, MI

Bowersock, G. (1986) 'From emperor to bishop: the self-conscious transformation of political power in the fourth century A.D.', *CPh* 81: 298–307

Bradley, K. R. (1984) *Slaves and Masters in the Roman Empire* (Coll. Latomus 185). Brussels

Brandes, W. (1989) *Die Städte Kleinasiens im 7 und 8 Jahrhundert.* Berlin

Brown, P. (1961) 'Aspects of the Christianization of the Roman aristocracy', *JRS* 51: 1–11 (=Brown, *Religion and Society*, 161–82)

Brown, P. (1971) 'The rise and function of the holy man in late antiquity', *JRS* 61: 80–101 (=Brown, *Society and the Holy*, 103–52)

Callu, J.-P. (1993) 'I commerci oltre i confini dell'Impero', in Schiavone (ed.), *Età tardoantica* 487–524

Cameron, Alan (1984) 'Probus' praetorian games: Olympiodorus fr. 44', *GRBS* 25: 193–6

Campenhausen, H. von (1929) *Ambrosius von Mailand als Kirchenpolitiker.* Berlin and Leipzig

Camps, G. (1985) 'De Masuna à Koceila: les destinées de la Maurétanie aux VIᵉ et VIIᵉ siècles', in S. Lancel (ed.), *Actes du IIᵉ Colloque International sur l'Histoire et l'Archéologie de l'Afrique du Nord, 1983 (BCTH* 19B) 307–25. Paris

Capogrossi Colognesi, L. (1986) 'Grandi proprietari, contadini et coloni nell'Italia romana (I–III d. C.)', in Giardina, *Società Romana* 1, 325–66

Carandini, A. (1985) *Settefinestre. Una Villa Schiavistica nell'Etruria Romana* 3 vols. Modena

Carandini, A. (1986) 'Il mondo della tarda antichità visto attraverso le merci', in Giardina, *Società romana* III, 3–19

Carlsen, J. and Tvarno, H. (1990) 'The Segermes Valley Archaeological Survey (Region of Zaghouan). An interim report' (typescript)

Carrié, J.-M. (1975) 'Les distributions alimentaires dans les cités de l'empire romain tardif', *MEFR* 87: 995–1101

Carrié, J. M. (1976) 'Patronage et propriété militaire au IVᵉ siècle: objet rhétorique et objet réel du discours "Sur les Patronages" de Libanius', *BCH* 100: 159–76

Cavallo, G. and Giardina, A. (1993) 'L'iconografia delle campagne nel libro antico', in Schiavone (ed.), *Età tardoantica*, 323–48

Cecconi, G. A. (1988) 'Un evergete mancato: Piniano a Ippona', *Athenaeum* 66: 371–89

Cerati, A. (1975) *Caractère annonaire et assiette de l'impôt foncier au Bas-Empire.* Paris

Champlin, E. (1980) 'The Volcei land-register', *AJAHist* 5: 13–18

Charbonnel, N. (1964) 'La condition des ouvriers dans les ateliers impériaux aux IVᵉ et Vᵉ siècles', in Burdeau, F., Charbonnel, N. and Humbert, M. N., *Aspects de l'empire romain* (Paris) 61–93

Chastagnol, A. (1953) 'Le ravitaillement de Rome en viande au Vᵉ siècle', *RH* 210: 13–20

Chastagnol, A. (1960) 'Un scandale du vin à Rome sous le Bas-Empire: l'affaire du préfet Orfitus', *Annales (ESC)* 5: 166–80

Chastagnol, A. (1970) 'L'évolution de l'ordre sénatoriel au III et IVᵉ siècle de notre ère', *RH* 244: 305–14

Chastagnol, A. (1978) *L'album municipal de Timgad.* Bonn

Chastagnol, A. (1992) *Le Sénat romain à l'époque impériale.* Paris

Ciampoltrini, G. (1990) 'Mosaici tardoantichi dell'Etruria settentrionale', *SCO* 40: 369–81

Claude, D. (1969) *Die byzantinische Stadt im 6 Jahrhundert.* Munich

Clauss, M. (1981) *Der magister officiorum in der Spätantike (IV–VI secc.).* Munich

Clemente, C. (1968) *La Notitia Dignatatum.* Cagliari

Consolino, F. E. (1986) 'Modelli di comportamento e modi di santificazione per l'aristocrazia femminile d'Occidente', in Giardina, *Società romana* 1, 273–306

Crawford, J. S. (1990) *The Byzantine Shops at Sardis* (Archaeological Exploration of Sardis, Monograph 9). Cambridge, MA

Dagron, G. (1984) 'Entre village et cité: la bourgade rurale des IVe–VIIe siècle en Orient', in *La Romanité chrétienne en Orient*. London

Deichmann, F. W. (1958) *Frühchristliche Bauten und Mosaiken von Ravenna*. Baden-Baden

Deichmann, F. W. (1969–76) *Ravenna. Hauptstadt des spätantiken Abendlandes*. Wiesbaden

Delplace, C. (1978) 'Les potiers dans la société et l'économie de l'Italie et de la Gaule au 1er s. av. et au 1er s. ap. JC', *Ktema* 3:55–76

Demandt, A. (1980) 'Der spätrömische Militäradel', *Chiron* 10: 609–37

Dentzer, J.-M. (ed.) (1985–6) *Hauran I. Recherches archéologiques sur la Syrie du Sud à l'époque hellénistique et romaine*. 2 vols. Paris

Downey, G. (1958) 'The size of the population of Antioch', *TAPA* 89: 84–91

Drinkwater, J. F. (1992) 'The Bagaudae of the fifth century', in Drinkwater and Elton (eds.) (1992) 208–17

Drinkwater, J. F. and Elton, H. (eds.) (1992) *Fifth Century Gaul: A Crisis of Identity?* Cambridge

Dunbabin, K. M. D. (1978) *The Mosaics of Roman North Africa*. Oxford

Duncan-Jones, R. P. (1976) 'Some configurations of landholding in the Roman empire', in M. I. Finley (ed.), *Studies in Roman Property*, 7–32. Cambridge

Durliat, J. (1990) *De la ville antique à la ville byzantine*. (CEFR 136). Rome

Duval, N. (1982) 'L'urbanisme de Sufetula-Sbeitla en Tunisie', *ANRW* 10:2: 596–632

Ensslin, W. (1943) *Gottkaiser und Kaiser von Gottesgnade* (SBAW 7)

Esmonde Cleary, A. S. (1989) *The Ending of Roman Britain*. London

Euzennat, M. (1989) *Le Limes de Tingitane. La frontière méridionale*. Paris

Farina, R. (1966) *L'impero e l'imperatore cristiano in Eusebio di Cesarea*. Zurich

Février, P.-A. (1964) 'Notes sur le développement urbain en Afrique du Nord. Les exemples comparés de Djemila et de Sétif', *CArch* 14: 1–47

Février, P.-A. (1974) 'Permanence et héritages de l'antiquité dans la topographie des villes de l'occident durant le haut moyen âge', in *Topografia urbana e vita cittadina nell'alto medioevo in occidente, 26 aprile – 1 maggio 1973*. Vol. 1 (Settimane di studi del centro Italiano di studi sull'alto medioevo 21), 41–138. Spoleto

Février, P.-A. (1980) '4. Vetera et nova: le poids du passé, les germes de l'avenir, IIIe–VIe siècle', in P.-A. Février, M. Fixot, C. Goudineau and V. Kruta (eds.), *La Ville antique des origines au IXe siècle (Histoire de la France urbaine* (gen. ed. G. Duby) II) (Paris) 393–493

Février, P.-A. (1981) 'Remarques sur le paysage d'une ville à la fin de l'antiquité: l'exemple d'Aquilée', *Antichità altoadriatiche* 19 (Centro di Antichità Altoadriatiche), 163–212. Udine

Finley, M. I. (1958) Review of Boak 1955, *JRS* 48: 156–64

Finley, M. I. (1980) *Ancient Slavery and Modern Ideology*. London

Finley, M. I. (1981) *Economy and Society in Ancient Greece*, ed. B. D. Shaw and R. P. Saller. London

Finley, M. I. (1985) *The Ancient Economy*. 2nd edn. London

Fontaine, J. (1980) *Études sur la poésie latine tardive*. Paris

Foss, C. (1976) *Byzantine and Turkish Sardis*. Cambridge, MA

Foss, C. (1979) *Ephesus after Antiquity: A Late Antique, Byzantine and Turkish City*. Cambridge

Fowden, G. (1978) 'Bishops and temples in the eastern Roman Empire, A.D. 320–435', *JThS* n.s. 29: 53–78

Foxhall, L. and Forbes, H. (1981) '*Sitometreia*: the role of grain as a staple food in classical antiquity', *Chiron* 12: 41–90

Frank, R. I. (1971) 'Ammianus on Roman taxation', *AJP* 93: 69–86

Frank, T. (ed.) (1933–40) *An Economic Survey of Ancient Rome*. Baltimore

Frantz, A. (1988) *The Athenian Agora* 24, *Late Antiquity: A.D. 267–700*. Princeton, NJ

Franzoni, L. (1987) 'Il territorio veronese', in G. C. Manasse (ed.) *Il Veneto nell'Età Romana*, I–II, 61–105. Verona

Frend, W. H. C. (1969) 'Circumcellions and monks', *JThS* n.s. 20: 542–9

Fustel de Coulanges (1885) *L'Alleu et le domaine rural pendant l'époque mérovingienne*. Paris

Garnsey, P. (1970) *Social Status and Legal Privilege in the Roman Empire*. Oxford

Garnsey, P. (1985) 'Les travailleurs du bâtiment de Sardes et l'économie urbaine du bas-empire', in P. Leveau (ed.), *L'origine des richesses dépensées dans la ville antique, Actes du Colloque Aix-en-Provence 11–12 mai 1984* (Marseilles) 147–60

Garnsey, P. and Saller, R. (1987) *The Roman Empire: Economy, Society and Culture*. London

Garnsey, P. and Woolf, G. (1989) 'Patronage of the rural poor in the Roman world', in A. Wallace-Hadrill (ed.), *Patronage in Ancient Society* (London and New York) 153–70

Gellner, E. and Waterbury, J. (eds.) (1977) *Patrons and Clients in Mediterranean Societies*. London

Giardina, A. (1981) 'Aristocrazie terriere e piccola mercatura. Sui rapporti tra potere politico e formazione dei prezzi nel tardo impero romano', *QUCC* 7: 123–46

Giardina, A. (1983) 'Banditi e santi: un aspetto del folklore gallico tra Tarda Antichità e Medioevo', *Athenaeum* 71: 374–89

Giardina, A. (1986) 'Le due Italie nella forma tarda dell'impero', in Giardina, *Società Romana* I, 1–36. Rome–Bari

Giardina, A. (1988) 'Carità eversiva: le donazioni di Melania la Giovane e gli equilibri della società tardoromana', *Studi Storici* 29: 127–42

Giardina, A. and Grelle, F. (1983) 'La tavola di Trinitapoli: una nuova costituzione di Valentino I', *MEFR* 95: 249–303

Goodburn, R. and Bartholomew, P. (eds.) (1976) *Aspects of the Notitia Dignitatum*. Oxford

Goudineau, C., Février, P.-A. and Fixot, M. (1980) *Histoire de la France Urbaine*, ed. G. Duby. Paris

Gualtieri, M., Fracchia, H. and de Polignac, F. 'Il territorio di Roccagloriosa in Lucania', *MEFR* 95: 345–80

Haldon, J. F. (1985) 'Some considerations on Byzantine society and economy in the seventh century', in J. F. Haldon and J. T. A. Koumoulides (eds.), *Perspectives in Byzantine History and Culture: Dedicated to Father Dr Joseph Gill, S. J.* (Amsterdam) 75–112

Haldon, J. F. (1990) *Byzantium in the Seventh Century: The Transformation of a Culture*. Cambridge

Hannestad, K. (1962) *L'Évolution des ressources agricoles de l'Italie*. Copenhagen

Harmand, L. (1955) *Libanius: Discours sur les Patronages*. Paris

Harries, J. (1992) 'Christianity and the city in late Roman Gaul', in Rich, *City* 77–98

Heather, P. (1994) 'New men for new Constantines: creating an imperial elite in the eastern Mediterranean', in P. Magdalino (ed.), *New Constantines: The Rhythm of Imperial Renewal in Byzantium, 4th–13th Centuries*, 11–33. Aldershot

Herz, P. (1988) *Studien zur römischen Wirtschaftsgesetzgebung: Die Lebensmittelversorgung*. Stuttgart

Heuss, A. (1986) 'Das spätantike römische Reich kein "Zwangsstaat"? Von der Herkunft eines historischen Begriffs', *GWU* 37: 603–18

Higham, N. (1992) *Rome, Britain and the Anglo-Saxons*. London

Hitchner, R. B. (1990) 'The Kasserine Archaeological Survey – 1987', *Ant. Afr.* 26: 231–60

Hitchner, R. B. and Mattingly, D. J. (1991) 'Ancient agriculture', *National Geographic, Research and Exploration* 7.1: 36–55

Hodges, R. and Hobley, B. (eds.) (1988) *The Rebirth of Towns in the West, A.D. 700–1050*. London

Hollerich, M. J. (1982) 'The Alexandrian bishops and the grain trade', *JESHO* 15: 187–207

Hopkins, K. (1961) 'Social mobility in the later Roman empire: the evidence of Ausonius', *CQ* 55: 239–49

Hopkins, K. (1978) 'Economic growth and towns in classical antiquity', in P. Abrams and E. A. Wrigley (eds.), *Towns in Societies* (Cambridge) 35–79

Hopkins, K. (1980) 'Taxes and trade in the Roman Empire', *JRS* 70: 101–25

Hopkins, K. (1983) *Death and Renewal*. Cambridge

Hopkins, K. (1987) *Conquerors and Slaves*. Cambridge

Hurst, H. R. (1993) 'Cartagine, la nuova Alessandria', in A. Carandini, L. Cracco Ruggini and A. Giardina (eds.), *Storia di Roma* (Rome) III.2: 327–37

Isaac, B. (1984) 'Bandits in Judaea and Arabia', *HSCP* 88: 193–203

James, E. (1988) *The Franks*. Oxford

Johne, K.-P. (1988) 'Colonus, colonia, colonatus', *Philologus* 132 308–21

Johne, K.-P., Köhn, J. and Weber, V. (1983) *Die Kolonen in Italien und den westlichen Provinzen des römischen Reiches*. Berlin

Johnson, A. C. (1936) *Roman Egypt*. Vol. II of T. Frank, *Economic Survey of Ancient Rome*. Patterson, NJ

Johnson, S. (1983) *Late Roman Fortifications*. London

Jones, A. H. M. (1971) *Cities of the Eastern Roman Provinces*. 2nd edn. Oxford

Jones, M. (1982) 'Corn production in Roman Britain', in D. Miles (ed.), *The Romano-British Countryside* (BAR 103) 97–108. Oxford

Jongman, W. (1988) *The Economy and Society of Pompeii*. Amsterdam

Jullian, C. (1920–6) *Histoire de la Gaule*. Paris (Rpt ed. C. Goudineau. Paris 1993)

Kabiersch, J. (1960) *Untersuchungen zum Begriff der Philanthropia bei dem Kaiser Julian*. Wiesbaden

Keay, S. J. (1984) *Late Roman Amphorae in the Western Mediterranean* (BAR Ser. Int. 196). Oxford

Kennedy, D. and Riley, D. (1990) *Rome's Desert Frontier from the Air*. London

Kennedy, H. (1985) 'From polis to madina: urban change in late antique and early Islamic Syria', *Past and Present* 106: 3–27

804   III. THE EMPIRE: ECONOMY AND SOCIETY

Kennedy, H. and Liebeschuetz, J. H. W. G. (1988) 'Antioch and the villages of Northern Syria in the fifth and sixth centuries A.D.: trends and problems', *Nott. Med. St.* 32: 65–90

Kohns, H. P. (1961) *Versorgungskrisen und Hungerrevolten im spätantiken Rom.* Bonn

Kolb, F. (1980) 'Finanzprobleme und soziale Konflikte aus der Sicht zweier spätantiker Autoren (Scriptores Historiae Augustae und Anonymus de rebus bellicis)', in W. Eck, H. Galsterer, and H. Wolff (eds.), *Studien zur antiken Sozialgeschichte. Festschrift F. Vittinghoff* (Cologne) 497–525

Kopeck, T. (1973) 'The social class of the Cappadocian Fathers', *ChHist* 42: 443–66

Kraeling, C. H. (1938) *Gerasa: City of the Decapolis.* New Haven, CT

Krause, J.-U. (1987) *Spätantiken Patronatsformen im Westen des römischen Reichen.* Munich

Krautheimer, R. (1983) *Three Christian Capitals.* Berkeley, Los Angeles and London

Krischen, F., Meyer-Plath, B. and Schneider, A. M. (1938–43) *Die Landmauer von Konstantinopel.* 2 vols. Berlin

Lancel, S. (1983) 'L'affaire d'Antonius de Fussala: pays, chose et gens de la Numidie d'Hippone saisis dans la durée d'une procédure d'enquête épiscopale', in C. Lepelley (ed.), *Les Lettres de Saint Augustin découvertes par Johannes Divjak,* 267–85. Paris

Lauffer, S. (1971) *Diokletians Preisedikt.* Berlin

Lepelley, C. (1967) 'Déclin ou stabilité de l'agriculture africaine au Bas-Empire?' *Ant. Afr.* 1: 135–44

Lepelley, C. (1983a) 'Liberté, colonat et esclavage d'après la Lettre 24*: la juridiction épiscopale "de liberali causa"' in C. Lepelley (ed.), *Les Lettres de Saint Augustin découvertes par Johannes Divjak,* 329–42. Paris, 1983

Lepelley, C. (1983b) 'Témoignage et attitude de Saint Augustin devant la vie et la société rurales dans l'Afrique de son temps', *Miscellanea Historiae Ecclesiasticae* 6 (Brussels) 73–83

Lepelley, C. (1987) 'Un aspect de la conversion d'Augustin: la rupture avec ses ambitions sociales et politiques', *BLE* 88: 229–46

Lepelley, C. (1989) 'Peuplement et richesses de l'Afrique romaine tardive', in Morrisson and Lefort (eds.) (1989) 17–30

Lepelley, C. (1992) 'The survival and fall of the classical city in late Roman Africa', in Rich, *City* 50–76

Leveau, Ph. (1989) 'L'organisation de l'espace rural en Maurétanie Césarienne', in Morrisson and Lefort (eds.) (1989) 35–52

Levi, D. (1947) *Antioch Mosaic Pavements.* 2 vols. Princeton, NJ, London and The Hague

Levy, E. (1951) *West Roman Vulgar Law.* Philadelphia

Lewin, A. (1991) *Studi sulla città imperiale romana nell'oriente tardoantico* (Biblioteca Athenaeum 17). Como

Lewit, T. (1991) *Agricultural Production in the Roman Economy, A.D. 200–400* (BAR S 568). Oxford

Liebeschuetz, J. H. W. G. (1992) 'The end of the ancient city', in Rich, *City* 1–49

de Ligt, L. (1990) 'Demand, supply, distribution: the Roman peasantry between town and countryside: rural monetization and peasant demand', *MBAH* 9: 24–56

de Ligt, L. (1991) 'Demand, supply, distribution: the Roman peasantry between town and countryside II: supply, demand and a comparative perspective', *MBAH* 10: 33–77

de Ligt, L. (1993) *Fairs and Markets in the Roman Empire: Economic and Social Aspects of Periodic Trade in a Pre-Industrial Society*. Amsterdam

de Ligt, L. and de Neeve, P. W. (1988) 'Ancient periodic markets: festivals and fairs', *Athenaeum* 66: 391–416

Löhken, H. (1982) *Ordines Dignitatum. Untersuchungen zur formalen Konstituierung der spätantiken Führungsschicht*. Cologne and Vienna

Loseby, S. T. (1992) 'Marseille: a late antique success story?', *JRS* 82: 165–85

MacMullen, R. (1966) *Enemies of the Roman Order: Treason, Alienation and Unrest in the Empire*. Cambridge, MA

MacMullen, R. (1987) 'Late Roman Slavery', *Historia* 36: 359–82

Manfredini, A. D. (1986) 'Les naviculaires et le naufrage', *RIDA* 33: 135–48

Mangin, M. (1985) 'Artisanat et commerce dans les agglomérations secondaires du centre-est de la Gaule sous l'empire', in P. Leveau (ed.), *L'Origine des richesses* 113–32

Mango, C. (1985) *Le Développement urbain de Constantinople IVe–VIIe siècles*. Paris

Maraval, P. (1985) *Lieux saints et pèlerinages d'Orient: histoire et géographie des origines à la conquête arabe*. Paris

Marcone, A. (1981) *L'allestimento dei giochi annuali a Roma nel IV secolo* (*ASNP* series III Vol. 11:1) 105–22

Marcone, A. (1992) 'Il mondo di Paolino di Pella', *De Tertullien aux Mozarabes, Mélanges J. Fontaine* I (Paris) 339–48

Marcone, A. (1993) 'Il lavoro nelle campagne', in Schiavone (ed.), *Età tardoantica*, 823–43

Marrou, H. I. (1970) 'Le dossier épigraphique de l'évêque Rustique de Narbonne', *Riv. di Arch. Cristiana* 46: 331–49

Martino, F. de (1993) 'Il colonato fra economia e diritto', in Schiavone (ed.), *Età tardoantica*, 789–822

Mattingly, D. (1989) 'Farmers and frontiers. Exploiting and defending the countryside of Roman Tripolitania', *Libyan Studies* 20: 135–53

Mazzarino, S. (1973) *L'Impero romano*. 3 vols. Rome and Bari

Mazzarino, S. (1974) *Antico, tardoantico ed era costantiniana* 1. Bari

Meiggs, R. (1973) *Roman Ostia*. Oxford

Mertens, J. (1986) 'Recherches récentes sur le Bas-Empire romain en Belgique', *Studien zu den Militärgrenzen Roms III, 13 internationalen Limeskongress, Aalen 1983*, 192–9. Stuttgart

Mickwitz, G. (1932) *Geld und Wirtschaft im römischen Reich des vierten Jahrhunderts n.Chr.* Helsingfors and Leipzig

Mickwitz, G. (1936) *Die Kartellfunktionen der Zünfte und ihre Bedeutung bei der Entstehung des Zunftwesen, eine Studie in spätantiker und mittelalterlicher Wirtschaftsgeschichte*. Helsingfors

Milano Capitale dell'impero romano (286–402 d. C.). Milan 1990

Mócsy, A. (1974) *Pannonia and Upper Moesia*. London

Morrisson, C. and Lefort, J. (eds.) (1989) *Hommes et richesses dans l'antiquité byzantine* 1. Paris

Neeve, P. W. de (1984) *Colonus*. Amsterdam

Norman, A. F. (1958) 'Gradations in later municipal society', *JRS* 48: 79–85

Ossel, P. van (1983) 'L'établissement romain de Loën à Lixhe et l'occupation rurale au Bas-Empire dans la Hesbaye liègeoise', *Helinium* 23: 143–69

Ossel, P. van (1992) *Établissements ruraux de l'antiquité tardive dans le Nord de la Gaule* (Gallia Supplement 51). Paris

Panella, C. (1989) 'Gli scambi nel Mediterraneo occidentale dal IV al VI secolo', in Morrisson and Lefort (eds.) (1989) 129–41

Parker, A. J. (1980) 'Roman wrecks in the western Mediterranean', in K. Muckleroy (ed.), *Archaeology under Water. An Atlas of the World's Submerged Sites* (New York) 50–1

Parker, A. J. (1989) 'Shipwrecks and ancient trade in the Mediterranean', *Arch. Rev. from Cambr.* 3:2: 99–112

Parker, A. J. (1992) *Ancient Shipwrecks of the Mediterranean and the Roman Provinces* (BAR Ser. Int. 580). Oxford

Paschoud, F. (ed.) (1986) *Colloque genevois sur Symmaque*. Paris

Patrucco, M. F. (1989) 'Tra struttura sociale e prassi ecclesiastica: vescovi e realtà nelle lettere di Agostino', *Agostino d'Ippona 'Quaestiones disputatae'* (Palermo, 1989) 33–48

Patrucco, M. Forlin and Roda, S. (1976) 'Le lettere di Simmaco ad Ambrogio. Vent'anni di rapporti amichevoli', in *Ambrosius episcopus. Atti del Congr. Intern. di Studi Ambrosiani* (Milan) II, 284–98

Patterson, J. (1988) *Samnites, Liguri and Romans*. Circello

Patterson, J. (1991) 'Settlement, city and élite in Samnium and Lycia', in Rich and Wallace-Hadrill (eds.) (1991) 147–68. London

Percival, J. (1959) 'Seigneurial aspects of late Roman estate management', *EHR* 84: 449–73

Persson, A. W. (1923) *Staat und Manufaktur im römischen Reiche*. Lund

Petit, J.-P. (ed.) (1994) *Les Agglomérations secondaires de Gaule Belgique et des Germaines*. (Pré-actes). Metz

Petit, P. (1957) 'Les sénateurs de Constantinople dans l'oeuvre de Libanius', *AC* 26: 347–82

Peyras, J. (1975) 'Le fundus Aufidianus', *Ant. Afr.* 9: 181–222

Pleket, H. W. (1984) 'Urban élites and the economy in the Greek cities of the Roman empire', *MBAH* 3: 3–37

Pleket, H. W. (1988) 'Greek epigraphy and comparative ancient history: two case studies', *Epigr. Anat.* 12: 25–37

Polanyi, K., Arensberg, C. M. and Pearson, H. W. (eds.) (1957) *Trade and Market in the Early Empires: Economies in History and Theory*. Chicago

Potter, T. W. (1979) *The Changing Landscape of South Etruria*. London

Potter, T. W. (1991) 'Towns and territories in Southern Etruria', in Rich and Wallace-Hadrill (eds.) (1991) 191–209

Poulter, A. (1992) 'The use and abuse of urbanism in the Danubian provinces during the later Roman Empire', in Rich, *City* 99–135

Rebuffat, R. (1988) 'Les fermiers du désert', *L'Africa Romana* 5: 33–68

Rebuffat, R. (1989) 'Rapport: citadins, sédentaires, nomades', in Morrisson and Lefort (eds.) (1989) 53–62

Reece, R. (1973) 'Roman coinage in the Western Empire', *Britannia* 4: 227–51

Rich, J. and Wallace Hadrill, A. N. (eds.) (1991) *City and Countryside in the Ancient World*. London

Richmond, I. A. (1930) *The City Walls of Imperial Rome*. Oxford

de Robertis, F. M. (1955) *Il fenomeno associativo nel mondo romano. Dai collegi della republica alle corporazioni del basso impero*. Naples

de Robertis, F. (1974) 'Interdizione dell'usus equorum e lotta al banditismo in alcune costituzioni del Basso Impero', *SDHI* 40: 67–98

Roda, S. (1976) 'Polifunzionalità della lettera commendatricia=teoria e prassi nell'espistolario simmachiano, *Actes du Colloque Symmaque* (Milan) 177–202

Roda, S. (1981) *Commentario Storico al Libro IX dell'Epistolario di Q. Aurelio Simmaco*. Pisa

Roda, S. (1985) 'Fuga nel privato e nostalgia del potere nel IV sec. d. C.: nuovi accenti di un'antica ideologia', in *Le trasformazioni della cultura nella tarda antichità. Atti del convegno* (Catania, 27 sett. – 2 ott. 1982) (Rome) 95–108

Rosafio, P. (1991) 'Studies in the Roman Colonate'. Unpublished PhD thesis, University of Cambridge

Rostovtzeff, M. (1922) *A Large Estate in Egypt in the Third Century B.C.* Madison

Roueché, C. (1993) *Performers and Partisans in Late Roman Aphrodisias*. London

Rougé, J. (1966) *Recherches sur l'organisation du commerce maritime en Méditerranée sous l'empire romain*. Paris

Rubin, Z. (1986) 'The Mediterranean and the dilemma of the Roman Empire in late antiquity', *Med. Hist. Rev.* 1: 13–62

Ruggini, L. C. (1964) 'Vicende rurali dell'Italia antica dall'età tetrarchica ai Longobardi', *RSI* 76: 261–86

Ruggini, L. C. (1969) 'Le relazioni fiscali, annonarie e commerciali delle città campane con Roma nel IV sec. D. C.', *Stud. Rom.* 17: 133–46

Ruggini, L. C. (1976a) 'Collegium e corpus: la politica economica nella legislazione e nella prassi', in *Istituzioni giuridiche e realtà politiche nel tardo impero (III–IV sec. d. c.), Atti di un incontro tra storici e giuristi (Firenze, 2–4 maggio 1974)* (Milan) 63–94

Ruggini, L. C. (1976b) 'La vita associativa nelle città dell'Oriente greco: tradizioni locali e influenze romane', in D. M. Pippidi (ed.), *Assimilation et résistance à la culture gréco-romaine dans le monde ancien* (Travaux du VIe Congrès International d'Études Classiques, Madrid, Sept. 1974) 463–91

Ruggini, L. C. (1983) 'Bagaudi e Santi Innocenti: Un'avventura fra demonizzazione e martirio', in E. Gabba (ed.), *Tria Corda. Scritti in onore di Arnaldo Momigliano* (Como) 121–42

Ruggini, L. C. (1986) 'Poteri in gara per la salvezza di città ribelli: il caso di Antiochia (387 d. C.)', *Studi Tardoantichi* 1: 265–90. (Reprinted in *Hestiasis: Studi di tarda antichità offerti a Salvatore Calderone*, 4 vols. (Messina, 1986–97))

Ruggini, L. C. and Cracco, G. (1977) 'Changing fortunes of the Italian city from late antiquity to early middle ages', *RFIC* 105: 448–75

Saller, R. (1982) *Personal Patronage under the Early Empire*. Cambridge

Sauvaget, J. (1949) 'Le plan antique de Damas', *Syria* 26: 314–58

Scranton, R. L. (1957) *Corinth* Vol. 16, *Medieval Architecture in the Central Area of Corinth*. Princeton, NJ

Seager, A. R. and Kraabel, A. T. (1983) 'The synagogue and the Jewish community', in G. M. A. Hanfmann (ed.), *Sardis from Prehistoric to Roman Times* (Cambridge, MA and London) 168–90

Seyfarth, W. (1969) *Von der Bedeutung der Plebs in der Spätantike.* Berlin

Shaw, B. D. (1981) 'Rural markets in North Africa and the political economy of the Roman empire', *Ant. Afr.* 17: 37–83

Shaw, B. D. (1984) 'Bandits in the Roman empire', *Past and Present* 105: 3–52

Shaw, B. D. (1987) 'The family in late antiquity: the experience of Augustine', *Past and Present* 115: 3–51

Shaw, B. D. (1993) 'The bandit', in A. Giardina (ed.), *The Romans* (translated by C. Zawadzka), 300–41. Chicago and London

Sirks, A. J. B. (1990) 'The size of the distribution in Rome and Constantinople', *Athenaeum* 79: 215–37

Sirks, A. J. B. (1991) 'Late Roman law: the case of *dotis nomen* and the *praedia pistoria*', *ZRG* 108: 187–212

Small, A. M. (1986) 'S. Giovanni di Ruoti (Basilicata). Il contesto della villa tardo-romana. I. La villa e la sua storia', in Giardina, *Società romana* III, 97–113

Spieser, J.-M. (1984) *Thessalonique et ses monuments du IVe au VIe siècle. Contribution à l'étude d'une ville paléochretienne.* Paris

Stevens, C. E. (1933) *Sidonius Apollinaris and his Age.* Oxford

Straub, J. (1972) *Regeneratio Imperii* 1. Darmstadt

Swift, L. J. and Oliver, J. H. (1962) 'Constantius II on Flavius Philippus', *AJP* 83: 247–64

Tate, G. (1989) 'Les campagnes de la Syrie du Nord à l'époque proto-byzantine', in Morrisson and Lefort (eds.) (1989) 63–77

Tchernia, A. (1986) *Le Vin de l'Italie.* Rome

Teall, J. L. (1959) 'The grain supply of the Byzantine Empire 330–1025', *DOP* 13: 87–190

Tengstrom, E. (1974) *Bread for the People: Studies in the Corn-Supply of Rome during the Late Empire.* Stockholm

Thébert, Y. (1983) 'L'évolution urbaine dans les provinces orientales de l'Afrique romaine tardive', *Opus* 2: 99–131

Thomas, C. (1981) *Christianity in Roman Britain to A.D. 500.* London

Toynbee, J. M. C. and Ward-Perkins, J. B. (1956) *The Shrine of Saint Peter.* London

Van Berchem, D. (1937) 'L'annone militaire dans l'empire romain au IIIe siècle', *BSNAF* 80: 117–202

Velkov, V. (1977) *Cities in Thrace and Dacia in Late Antiquity.* Amsterdam

Vera, D. (1981) *Commento storico alle 'Relationes' di Q. Aurelio Simmaco.* Pisa

Vera, D. (1983) 'Strutture agrarie e strutture patrimoniali nella tarda antichità: l'aristocrazia Romana fra agricoltura e commercio', *Opus* 2: 489–533

Vera, D. (1986) 'Enfiteusi, colonato e trasformazioni agrarie nell'Africa Proconsolare del tardo impero', *Africa Romana* 4: 287–93

Vera, D. (1988a) 'Aristocrazia romana ed economie provinciali nell'Italia tardoantica: il caso siciliano', *Quaderni Catanesi di studi classici e medievali* 10: 115–72

Vera, D. (1988b 'Terra e lavoro nell'Africa romana', *Stud. Stor.* 4: 967–92

Veyne, P. (1976) *Le Pain et le cirque. Sociologie historique d'un pluralisme politique.* Paris

Vogler, C. (1979) *Constance II et l'administration impériale.* Strasbourg

Wacke, A. (1980) 'Die "potentiores" in den Rechtsquellen. Einfluss und Abwehr gesellschäftlicher Übermacht in der Rechtpflege der Römer', *ANRW* II, 13, 563–607

Waltzing, J.-P. (1896) *Étude historique sur les corporations professionelles chez les romains depuis les origines jusqu'à la chute de l'empire d'occident.* Louvain

Ward-Perkins, B. (1988) 'The towns of northern Italy: rebirth or renewal?', in Hodges and Hobley (1988) 16–27

Westermann, W. L. (1955) *The Slave Systems of Greek and Roman Antiquity.* Philadelphia

White, K. D. (1984) *Greek and Roman Technology.* London

Whittaker, C. R. (1976) 'Agri deserti', in M. I. Finley (ed.), *Studies in Roman Property*, 137–65 and 193–200. Cambridge (Reprinted in Whittaker, *Land*, chapter 3)

Whittaker, C. R. (1980) 'Inflation and the economy in the fourth century A.D.', in C. E. King (ed.), *Imperial Revenue, Expenditure and Monetary Policy in the Fourth Century A.D.* (BAR Ser. Int. (Oxford) 76: 1–22). (Reprinted in Whittaker, *Land*, chapter 10)

Whittaker, C. R. (1982) 'Labour supply in the later Roman Empire', *Opus* 1: 171–9 (Reprinted in Whittaker, *Land*, chapter 4)

Whittaker, C. R. (1987) 'Circe's pigs: from slavery to serfdom in the later Roman world', in M. I. Finley (ed.), *Classical Slavery* 88–122. London (Reprinted in Whittaker, *Land*, chapter 5)

Whittaker, C. R. (1989) 'Amphorae and trade', in *Anfore Romane storia economica: un decennio de richerche* (CEFR 114: 537–9). (Reprinted in Whittaker, *Land*, chapter 14)

Whittaker, C. R. (1990) 'The consumer city revisited: the *vicus* and the city', *JRA* 3: 110–18. (Reprinted in Whittaker, *Land*, chapter 8)

Whittow, M. (1990) 'Ruling the late Roman and early Byzantine city: a continuous history', *Past and Present* 129: 3–29

Wickham, C. (1988) 'Marx, Sherlock Holmes, and late Roman commerce', review of Giardina, *Società romana*, *JRS* 78: 183–93

Wightman, E. M. (1985) *Gallia Belgica.* London

Wilson, R. J. A. (1990) *Sicily under the Roman Empire.* Warminster

Witherington III, B. (1988) *Women in the Earliest Churches.* Cambridge

Zayadine, F. (ed.) (1986) *Jerash Archaeological Project 1981–1983.* Amman

Zulueta, F. de (1909) *De Patrociniis Vicorum.* (*Oxford Studies in Social and Legal History, I, section II*, ed. P. Vinogradoff). Oxford

PART IV: FOREIGN RELATIONS AND THE BARBARIAN WORLD (CHS. 13–17)

Alföldy, G. (1974) *Noricum*, London

Arrhenius, B. (1985) *Merovingian Garnet Jewellery: Emergence and Social Implications.* Stockholm

Asche, U. (1983) *Roms Weltherrschaftsidee und Aussenpolitik in der Spätantike im Spiegel der Panegyrici Latini.* Bonn

Bachrach, B. S. (1973) *A History of the Alans in the West.* Minneapolis, MN

Barceló, P. A. (1981) *Roms auswärtige Beziehungen unter der Constantinischen Dynastie.* Regensburg

Barnes, T. D. (1976) 'Imperial campaigns, A.D. 285–311', *Phoenix* 30: 174–93

Barnes, T. D. (1980) 'Imperial chronology, A.D. 337–350', *Phoenix* 34: 160–6

Barnes, T. D. (1985) 'Constantine and the Christians of Persia', *JRS* 75: 126–36

Bassett, S. (ed.) (1989) *The Origins of the Anglo-Saxon Kingdoms*. Leicester

Beck, H.-G. (1966) *Christliche Mission und politische Propaganda im byzantinischen Reich* (Settimani di studi del centro italiano di studi sull'alto medioevo 14). Spoleto

Bellamy, A. (1985) 'A new reading of the Namarah inscription', *JAOS* 105: 31–48

Berchem, D. van (1952) *L'Armée de Dioclétien et la réforme constantinienne*. Paris

Bichir, O. (1976) *The Archaeology and History of the Carpi* (BAR Suppl. Series 16). Oxford

Bierbrauer, V. (1980) 'Zur chronologischen, soziologischen und regionalen Gliederung des ostgermanischen Fundstoffs des 5 Jahrhunderts in Südosteuropa', *Denkschriften der Österreichischen Akademie der Wissenschaften in Wien*, Phil-Hist. Klasse 145: 131–69

Bischoff, B. and Koehler, W. (1939) 'Eine illustrierte Ausgabe der spätantiken ravennater Annalen', in W. R. W. Koehler (ed.), *Medieval Studies in Memory of A. Kingsley Porter* (Cambridge, MA) 1, 125–38

Blockley, R. C. (1984) 'The Romano-Persian treaties of A.D. 299 and 363', *Florilegium* 6: 28–49

Blockley, R. C. (1985) 'Subsidies and diplomacy: Rome and Persia in late antiquity', *Phoenix* 39: 62–74

Blockley, R. C. (1987) 'The division of Armenia between the Romans and the Persians at the end of the fourth century A.D.', *Historia* 36: 222–34

Bloşiu, C. (1975) 'La nécrople de Letçani (dép. de Jassy) datant du IVe siècle de n.è.', *Arheologia Moldovei* 8: 203–80

Böhme, H.-W. (1974) *Germanische Grabfunde des 4 bis 5ten Jahrhunderts zwischen unterer Elbe und Loire*. Munich

Böhme, H.-W. (1986) 'Das Ende der Römerherrschaft in Britannien und die angelsächsische Besiedlung Englands im 5 Jahrhundert', *Jahrb. Röm-Germ. Zentralmuseums Mainz* 33: 466–574

Böhner, K. (1958) *Die fränkischen Altertümer des Trierer Landes* (Germanische Denkmäler der Völkerwanderungszeit, Serie B 1), Berlin

Bona, I. (1963) 'Beiträge zur Archäologie und Geschichte der Quaden', *Acta Archaeologica Hungarica* 15: 239–307

Bona, I. (1976) *Der Anbruch des Mittelalters*. Budapest

Borg, K., Nasman, U. and Wegraeus, E. (1976) *Eketorp: Fortification and Settlement on Öland, Sweden*. Stockholm

Bowersock, G. W. (1980) 'Mavia, queen of the Saracens', in W. Eck, H. Galsterer and H. Wolff (eds.), *Studien zur antiken Sozialgeschichte. Festschrift F. Vittinghoff* (Cologne and Vienna) 477–95

Bowersock, G. W. (1983) *Roman Arabia*. Cambridge, MA

Brock, S. P. (1977) 'A letter attributed to Cyril of Jerusalem on the rebuilding of the temple', *BSOAS* 40: 267–86

Brooks, N. P. (1984) *The Early History of the Church at Canterbury*. Leicester

Cajas, H. H. (1972) *Las relaciones internacionales del impero bizantino durante la epoca de las grandes invasiones*. Santiago de Chile

Cameron, Alan (1967) 'Rutilius Namatianus, St Augustine, and the date of the De Reditu Suo', *JRS* 57: 31–9

Campbell, J. (ed.) (1982) *The Anglo-Saxons.* London

Chifflet, J.-J. (1655) *Anastasis Childerici I Francorum Regis.* Antwerp

Christlein, R. (1978) *Die Alamannen.* Stuttgart and Aalen

Christlein, R. (1979) *Der Runde Berg bei Urach III. Kleinfunde der frühgeschichtlichen Perioden aus den Plangrabungen 1967–1972.* Sigmaringen

Chrysos, E. K. (1972) *Tò Βυζάντιον καὶ οἱ Γότθοι. Συμβολὴ εἰς τὴν ἐξωτερικὴν πολιτικὴν τοῦ Βυζαντίου κατὰ τὸν Δ' αἰῶνα.* Thessaloniki

Chrysos, E. (1976) 'Some aspects of Romano-Persian legal relations', *Kleronomia* 8: 1–48

Clarke, G. (1979) *The Roman Cemetery at Lankhills* (Pre-Roman and Roman Winchester, Part II). Oxford

Claude, D. (1987) 'Zur Ansiedlung barbarischer Föderaten in der ersten Hälfte des fünften Jahrhunderts', *Denkschriften der Österreichischen Akademie der Wissenschaften*, Phil.-Hist. Klasse 193: 13–42

Constantinescu, M., Pascu, S. and Diaconu, P. (eds.) (1975) *Relations between the Autochthonous Population and the Migratory Populations on the Territory of Romania* Bucharest

Croke, B. (1977) 'Evidence for the Hun invasion of Thrace in A.D. 422', *GRBS* 18: 347–67

Cunliffe, B. (1976) *Excavations at Portchester Castle* Vol. 2, *Saxon.* London

Demandt, A. (1980) 'Die Anfänge der Staatenbildung bei den Germanen', *Hist. Zeit.* 230: 265–91

Dentzer, J.-M. and Orthmann, W. (eds.) (1989) *Archéologie et histoire de la Syrie.* Saarbrücken

Diaconu, G. (1965) *Tîrgsor.* Bucharest

Dunareanu-Vulpe, E. (1967) *Der Schatz von Pietroasa.* Bucharest

Duparc, P. (1958) 'La Sapaudia', *CRAI* 371–83

Durliat, J. (1988) 'Le salaire de la paix sociale dans les royaumes barbares (Vᵉ–VIᵉ siècles)', in H. Wolfram and A. Schwarcz (eds.), *Anerkennung und Integration* (Vienna) 21–72

Eadie, J. W. (1967) *The Breviarium of Festus: A Critical Edition with Historical Commentary.* London

Eggers, H.-J. (1951) *Der römische Import im freien Germanien.* Hamburg

Engelhardt, C. (1863) *Nydam Mosefund, 1859–63.* Copenhagen

van Es, W. A. (1965) 'Wijster: a native village beyond the imperial frontier, 150–425 A.D.', *Palaeohistoria* 11: 1–595

van Es, W. A. (1973) 'Roman period settlement on the "free Germanic" sandy soil of Drenthe, Overijssel and Gelderland', *Bericht Rijksdienst Oudheidkundige Bodemonderzoek* 23: 273–80

Evison, V. I. (1965) *The Fifth Century Invasions South of the Thames.* London

Ewig, E. (1976) *Spätantikes und fränkisches Gallien.* Munich

Fagerlie, J. (1967) *Late Roman and Byzantine Solidi found in Sweden and Denmark* (Numismatic Notes and Monographs 157). New York

Fleury, M. and Périn, P. (eds.) (1978) *Problèmes de chronologie relative et absolue concernant les cimetières mérovingiens d'entre Loire et Rhin.* Paris

Franken, M. (1944) *Die Alamannen zwischen Iller und Lech.* Berlin

Freeman, P. and Kennedy, D. (eds.) (1986) *The Defence of the Roman and Byzantine East* (Colloquium, Sheffield, 1986). Oxford

French, D. H. and Lightfoot, C. S. (eds.) (1989) *The Eastern Frontier of the Roman Empire* (Colloquium, Ankara, September 1988). Oxford

Garsoian, N. S. (1973–4) 'Le rôle de l'hiérarchie chrétienne dans les rapports diplomatiques entre Byzance et les Sassanides', *Revue des études arméniennes* n.s. 10: 119–38

Gawlikowski, M. (1984) *Les principia de Dioclétien: temples des enseignes, Palmyre* 8. Warsaw

Geiger, J. (1979–80) 'The last Jewish revolt against Rome: a reconsideration', *Scripta Classica Israelica* 5: 250–7

Godlowski, K. (1970) *The Chronology of the Late Roman and Early Migration Periods in Central Europe.* Cracow

Gordon, C. D. (1960) *The Age of Attila: Fifth-Century Byzantium and the Barbarians.* Ann Arbor, MI

Graf, D. F. (1989) 'Rome and the Saracens: reassessing the nomadic menace', in T. Fahd (ed.), *L'Arabie préislamique et son environnement historique et culturel* (Leiden) 341–400

Grohne, E. (1953) *Mahndorf. Frühgeschichte des bremischen Raumes.* Bremen

Grünert, H. (1976) *Römer und Germanen in Mitteleuropa*, 2nd edn. Berlin

Haarnagel, W. (1979) *Die Grabung Feddersen Wierde. Methode, Hausbau, Siedlungs- und Wirtschaftsformen sowie Sozialstruktur.* Neumünster

Hachmann, R. (1970) *Die Goten und Skandinavien.* Berlin

Hagberg, U. E. (1967) *The Archaeology of Skedemosse*, 2 vols. Uppsala

Hagberg, U. E. (ed.) (1972) *Studia Gotica.* Stockholm

Hamerow, H. (1993) *Excavations at Mucking.* Vol. 2. *The Anglo-Saxon Settlements.* London

Hansen, U. L. (1987) *Römischer Import im Norden* (Nordiske Fortidsminder, Serie B 10). Copenhagen

Harhoiu, R. (1977) *The Treasure from Pietroasa, Romania* (BAR Suppl. Series 24). Oxford

Harmatta, J. (1971) 'Goten und Hunnen in Pannonien', *Acta Antiqua* 19: 293–7

Harmon, R. B. (1971) *The Art and Practice of Diplomacy: A Selected and Annotated Guide.* Metuchen, NJ

Härtner, W. (1969) *Die Goldhörner von Gallehus.* Wiesbaden

Haseloff, G. (1973) 'Zum Ursprung der germanischen Tierornamentik – die spätrömische Wurzel', *Frühmittelalterliche Studien* 7: 406–22

Haseloff, G. (1978a) *Die germanische Tierornamentik der Völkerwanderungszeit. Studien zu Salin's Stil I.* Berlin

Haseloff, G. (1978b) 'Römische Elemente in sächsischem Schmuck', in *Sachsen und Angelsachsen* (Hamburg) 153–61

Hassler, H. J. (1983) *Das sächsische Gräberfeld bei Liebenau.* Hildesheim

Häusler, A. (1979) 'Zu den sozialökonomischen Verhältnissen in der Černjachov-Kultur', *Zeitschrift für Archäologie* 13: 23–65

Hawkes, S. C. (1986) 'The Early Saxon Period', in T. Rowley *et al.* (eds.), *The Archaeology of the Oxford Region* (Oxford) 64–108

Heather, P. J. (1986) 'The crossing of the Danube and the Gothic conversion', *GRBS* 27: 289–318

Heather, P. J. (1988) 'The Anti-Scythian tirade of Synesius' *De Regno*', *Phoenix* 42: 152–72

Heather, P. J. (1989) 'Cassiodorus and the rise of the Amals: genealogy and the Goths under Hun domination', *JRS* 79: 103–28

Heather, P. J. and Matthews, J. F. (1991) *The Goths in the Fourth Century*. Liverpool

Hedeager, L. (1979) 'A quantitative analysis of Roman imports in Europe north of the Limes and the question of Roman-Germanic exchange', in K. Kristiansen and C. Paludan-Muller (eds.), *New Directions in Scandinavian Archaeology* (Copenhagen) 191–216

Hedeager, L. (1988) 'The evolution of Germanic society 1–400 A.D.', in R. F. J. Jones *et al.* (eds.), *First Millennium Papers: Western Europe in the First Millennium* (Oxford) 129–44

Hellenkemper, H. (1986) 'Legionen in Bandenkrieg – Isaurien im 4. Jahrhundert', in *Studien zu den Militärgrenzen Roms* III (Stuttgart) 625–34

Helm, R. (1931–2) 'Untersuchungen über den auswärtigen diplomatischen Verkehr des römischen Reiches im Zeitalter der Spätantike', *Archiv für Urkundenforschungen* 12: 375–436

Hewsen, R. H. (1978–9) 'The successors of Tiridates the Great: a contribution to the history of Armenia in the fourth century', *Revue des études arméniennes* n.s. 13: 99–126

Hills, C. M. (1977–87) *The Anglo-Saxon Cemetery at Spong Hill, North Elmham*. Part I: East Anglian Archaeology 6 (1977); Part II: 11 (1981); Part III: 21 (1984); Part IV: 34 (1987)

Hirschfeld, Y. (1992) *The Judean Desert Monasteries in the Byzantine Period*. New Haven, CT and London

Holum, K. G. (1977) 'Pulcheria's crusade A.D. 421–22 and the ideology of imperial victory', *GRBS* 18: 153–72

Honigmann, E. (1935) *Die Ostgrenze des byzantinischen Reiches bis 1071 (Byzance et les Arabes*, ed. A. A. Vasiliev, Vol. 3). Brussels

Hopwood, K. (1986) 'Towers, territory and terror: how the east was held', in Freeman and Kennedy (1986) 343–56

Horedt, K. (1967) 'Quelques problèmes concernant la diffusion de la civilisation de Sintana-de-Mures-Tschernakov en Roumanie', *Studie si cercetari de istorie veche si arheologie* 18: 575–91

Horedt, K. (1982) *Siebenburgen in spätrömischer Zeit*. Bucharest

Horedt, K. and Protase, D. (1970) 'Ein völkerwanderungszeitlicher Schatzfund aus Cluj-Someseni', *Germania* 48: 85–98

Horedt, K. and Protase, D. (1972) 'Das zweite Fürstengrab von Apahida', *Germania* 50: 174–220

Hvass, S. (1978) 'Die völkerwanderungszeitliche Siedlung Vorbasse, Mitteljütland', *Acta Archaeologica* 49: 61–111

Ilkjaei, J. and Lønstrup, J. (1983) 'Der Moorfund im Tal der Illerup-A bei Skanderborg in Ostjütland (Dänemark)', *Germania* 61: 95–116

Ionita, I. (1980) 'Die Römer-Daker und die Wandervölker im donauländischen Karpathenraum im 4 Jahrhundert', *Denkschrift der Österreichischen Akademie der Wissenschaften* 145: 123–54

Isaac, B. (1988) 'The meaning of the terms *limes* and *limitanei*', *JRS* 78: 125–47

Isaac, B. (1995) 'The army in the late Roman East: the Persian Wars and the defence of the Byzantine provinces', in Averil Cameron (ed.), *The Byzantine and Early Islamic Near East* III: *States, Resources and Armies* (Princeton, NJ) 125–55

James, E. (1988) *The Franks.* Oxford

Janssen, W. (1972) *Issendorf. Ein Urnenfriedhof der späten Kaiserzeit und der Völkerwanderungszeit I.* Hildesheim

Jensen, J. (1982) *The Prehistory of Denmark.* London

Jones, M. E. (1987) 'The logistics of the Anglo-Saxon invasions', in *Naval History: The Sixth Symposium of the US Naval Academy, 1983* (Wilmington) 62–9

Jones, M. E. and Casey, J. (1988) 'The Gallic Chronicle restored: a chronology for the Anglo-Saxon invasions and the end of Roman Britain', *Britannia* 19: 367–98

Juster, J. (1914) *Les Juifs dans l'empire romain I–II.* Paris

Kazanski, M. (1982) 'Deux riches tombes de l'époque des grandes invasions au nord de la Gaule: Airan et Pouan', *Archéologie Médiévale* 12: 17–33

Kazanski, M. (1991) *Les Goths (Iᵉʳ–VIIᵉ siècles après J.-C.).* Paris

Keller, E. (1979) *Das spätrömische Gräberfeld von Neuburg an der Donau.* Munich

Kenk, R. (1977) 'Studien zum Beginn der jüngeren römischen Kaiserzeit in der Przeworsk-Kultur', *Bericht der Röm-Germ. Kommission* 58: 161–446

Kennedy, D. and Riley, D. (1990) *Rome's Desert Frontier from the Air.* London

Klose, J. (1934) *Roms Klientel- und Randstaaten am Rhein und an der Donau.* Breslau

Koenig, G. (1980) 'Archäologische Zeugnisse westgotischer Präsenz im fünften Jahrhundert', *Madrider Mitteilungen* 21: 220–37

Krüger, B. (ed.) (1986) *Die Germanen,* 2 vols. Berlin

Lammers, W. (ed.) (1967) *Entstehung und Verfassung des Sachsenstammes.* Darmstadt

Laser, R. (1980) *Die römischen und frühbyzantinischen Fundmünzen aus Mitteldeutschland.* Berlin

Lemant, J.-P. (1985) *Le Cimetière et la fortification du bas-empire de Vireux-Molhain (Ardennes).* Mainz

Leriche, P. (1989) 'Les fortifications grecques et romaines en Syrie', in Dentzer and Orthmann (1989) 267–82

Leube, A. (1975) *Die römische Kaiserzeit im Oder-Spree Gebiet.* Berlin

Lewin, A. (1990) 'Dall' Eufrate al Mar Rosso: Diocleziano, l'esercito e i confini tardo-antichi', *Athenaeum* 78: 141–67

Lieberman, S. (1945/6–1946/7) 'Palestine in the third and fourth centuries', *JQR* 36: 329–70; 37: 43–54

Linder, A. (1987) *The Jews in Roman Imperial Legislation.* Detroit, MI and Jerusalem

Lindner, R. P. (1981) 'Nomadism, Huns and horses', *Past and Present* 42: 1–19

MacAdam, H. I. (1989) 'Epigraphy and the *Notitia Dignitatum* (*Oriens* 37)', in French and Lightfoot (1989) 295–309

Materialy i Issledovniya po Arkheologii SSSR 82 (1960a), 89 (1960b), 116 (1964), 139 (1967)

Matthews, J. F. (1978) 'Gesandtschaft', *RAC* 10: 653–85

Mayerson, P. (1980) 'Mavia, Queen of the Saracens – a cautionary note', *IEJ* 30: 123–31

Metzler, J., Zimmer, J. and Bakker, L. (1981) *Ausgrabungen in Echternach.* Luxemburg

Mildenberger, G. (1970) *Die thüringischen Brandgräber der spätrömischen Zeit.* Cologne and Vienna

Millar, F. (1993) *The Roman Near East, 31 B.C.–A.D. 337.* Cambridge, MA and London

Mitrea, B. and Preda, C. (1966) *Necropole din secolul al IV lea in Muntenia* (French summary 165–88). Bucharest

Mócsy, A. (1974) *Pannonia and Upper Moesia.* London

Mor, M. (1989) 'The events of 351–352 in Palestine – the last revolt against Rome?', in French and Lightfoot (1989) 335–53

Morrisson, C. and Lefort, J. (eds.) (1989) *Hommes et richesses dans l'Empire byzantin*, 2 vols. Paris

Moss, J. R. (1973) 'The effects of the policies of Aëtius on the history of western Europe', *Historia* 22: 711–31

Myres, J. N. L. (1969) *Anglo-Saxon Pottery and the Settlement of England.* Oxford

Myres, J. N. L. (1972) 'The Angles, the Saxons and the Jutes', *PBA* 56: 145–74

Myres, J. N. L. (1986) *The English Settlements.* Oxford

Myres, J. N. L. and Green, B. (1973) *The Anglo-Saxon Cemeteries of Caister-by-Norwich and Markshall, Norfolk.* Oxford

Odobescu, A. (1889–1900) *Le Trésor de Petroasa.* Paris and Leipzig

Oppenheimer, A. (1983) in collaboration with Isaac, B. and Lecker, M. *Babylonia Judaica in the Talmudic Period.* Wiesbaden

Ørsnes, M. (1963) 'The weapon find in Ejsbøl Mose at Haderslev', *Acta Archaeologica* 34: 232–47

Otte, M. and Willems, J. (eds.) (1986) *La Civilisation mérovingienne dans le bassin mosan.* Liège

Oxenstierna, E. (1956) *Die Goldhörner von Gallehus.* Lidingo

Palade, V. (1980) 'Eléments géto-daces dans le site Sîntana de Mureş de Bîrlad-Valea Seacă', *Dacia* n.s. 24: 223–53

Palade, V. (1986) *Nécropole du IVe et commencement du Ve siècles de n.è. à Bîrlad-Valea Seacă* (Inventaria Arch. Roumanie, fasc. 12). Bucharest

Parker, S. T. (1986) *Romans and Saracens: A History of the Arabian Frontier* (BASOR, Dissertation Series)

Parker, S. T. (ed.) (1987) *The Roman Frontier in Central Jordan: Interim Report on the Limes Arabicus Project, 1980–85.* 2 vols. (BAR International series 340). Oxford

Périn, P. and Feffer, L.-C. (1987) *Les Francs.* Paris

Pescheck, C. (1978) *Die germanischen Bodenfunde der römischen Kaiserzeit in Mainfranken.* Munich

Petri, F. (1973) *Siedlung, Sprache und Bevölkerungsstruktur im Frankreich.* Darmstadt

Pirling, R. (1966–74) *Das römisch-fränkische Gräberfeld von Krefeld-Gellep* (Germanische Denkmaler der Völkerwanderungszeit, Serie B 2: Berlin 1966; B 8: 1974)

Pitts, L. F. (1989) 'Relations between Rome and the German king on the middle Danube in the first to fourth centuries A.D.', *JRS* 79: 45–58

Raddatz, K. (1981) *Sörup I. Ein Gräberfeld der Eisenzeit in Angeln.* Neumünster

Randsborg, K. (1990) 'Beyond the Roman empire: archaeological discoveries in Gudme on Funen', *OJA* 9: 355–66

Rau, G. (1972) 'Körpergräber mit Glasbeigaben des 4. nachchristlichen Jahrhunderts im Oder-Wechsel-Raum', *Acta praehistorica et archaeologica* 3: 109–214

Reichstein, J. (1975) *Die kreuzformige Fibel* (Offa-Bücher 34). Neumünster

Roeren, R. (1960) 'Zur Archäologie und Geschichte Südwestdeutschlands im 3 bis

5ten Jahrhunderts n. Chr', *Jahrbuch des Röm-Germ. Zentralmuseums Mainz* 7: 214–94

Röhrer-Ertl, O. (1971) *Untersuchungen am Material des Urnenfriedhofes von Westerwanna.* Hamburg

Roosens, H. (1967) 'Laeti, Foederati und andere spätrömische Bevölkerungsniederschläge im belgischen Raum', *Die Kunde* 18: 89–109

Roques, D. (1983) 'Synésios de Cyrène et les migrations berbères vers l'Orient (398–413)', *CRAI* 660–77

Rouche, M. (1979) *L'Aquitaine, des Wisigoths aux Arabes, 418–781.* Paris

Rougé, J. (1966) 'L'histoire Auguste et l'Isaurie au IVᵉ siècle', *REA* 68: 282–315

Rubin, Z. (1986) 'Diplomacy and war in the relations between Byzantium and the Sassanids in the fifth century A.D.', in Freeman and Kennedy (1986) 677–95

Rubin, Z. (1988) 'The conversion of Mavia, the Saracen queen', *Cathedra* 47: 25–49 (in Hebrew)

Saggau, H. E. (1986) *Bordesholm. Der Urnenfriedhof am Brautberg bei Bordesholm in Holstein. Teil I.* Neumünster

Salway, P. (1981) *Roman Britain.* Oxford

Sartre, M. (1982) *Trois études sur l'Arabie romaine et byzantine.* Brussels

Schach-Dorges, H. (1970) *Die Bodenfunde des 3 bis 6ten Jahrhunderts n. Chr.* Neumünster

Schmidt, L. (1938) *Die Westgermanen.* 2nd edn. Munich

Schmidt, L. (1969) *Die Ostgermanen.* 2nd edn. Munich

Schrier, O. J. (1992) 'Syriac evidence for the Roman–Persian war of 421–2', *GRBS* 33: 75–86

Ščukin, M. B. (1975) 'Das Problem der Černjachov-Kultur in der sowjetischen archäologischen Literatur', *Zeitschrift für Archäologie* 9: 25–41

Ščukin, M. B. (1989) *Rome and the Barbarians in Central and Eastern Europe 1st Century B.C. – 1st Century A.D.* (BAR International series 542) 2 vols. Oxford

Segal, J. B. (1955) 'Mesopotamian communities from Julian to the rise of Islam', *PBA* 41: 109–41

Shahîd, I. (1984a) *Rome and the Arabs: A Prolegomenon to the Study of Byzantium and the Arabs.* Washington, DC

Shahîd, I. (1984b) *Byzantium and the Arabs in the Fourth Century.* Washington, DC

Shahîd, I. (1989) *Byzantium and the Arabs in the Fifth Century.* Washington, DC

Shelton, K. J. (1981) *The Esquiline Treasure.* Oxford

Shepard, J. and Franklin, S. (eds.) (1992) *Byzantine Diplomacy.* Aldershot

Sinor, D. (1977) *Inner Asia and its Contacts with Medieval Europe.* London

Sodini, J.-P. *et al.* (1980) 'Déhès (Syrie du Nord) campagnes i–iii (1976–8), Recherches sur l'habitat rural', *Syrie* 57: 1–301

Soproni, S. (1978) *Der spätrömische Limes zwischen Esztergom und Szentendre.* Budapest

Soproni, S. (1985) *Die letzten Jahrzehnte des pannonischen Limes* (Münchner Beiträge zur Vor- und Frühgeschichte 38). Munich

Stallknecht, B. (1969) *Untersuchungen zur römischen Aussenpolitik in der Spätantike, 306–395 n. Chr.* Bonn

Stemberger, G. (1987) *Juden und Christen im Heiligen Land: Palästina unter Konstantin und Theodosius.* Munich

Stenberger, M. (1933) *Öland under aldre jarnaldern.* Stockholm

Stenberger, M. (1955) *Vallhagar.* Copenhagen

Stenberger, M. (1977) *Vorgeschichte Schwedens.* Berlin

Stern, M. (1974–84) *Greek and Latin Authors on Jews and Judaism,* 3 vols. Jerusalem

Stroheker, K. F. (1965) *Germanentum und Spätantike.* Stuttgart

Syme, R. (1987) 'Isaura and Isauria: some problems', in E. Frézouls (ed.), *Sociétés urbaines, sociétés rurales dans l'Asie Mineure et la Syrie hellénistiques et romaines* (Actes du colloque organisé à Strasbourg (novembre 1985)) (Leiden) 131–47

Synelle, K. (1986) *Οἱ διπλωματικὲς σχέσεις Βυζαντίου καὶ Περσίας ἕως τὸν στ' αἰῶνα.* Athens

Tate, G. (1989a) 'Les campagnes de Syrie du Nord', in Morrisson and Lefort (1989) 53–77

Tate, G. (1989b) 'La Syrie à l'époque byzantine: essai de synthèse', in Dentzer and Orthmann (1989) 97–116

Thompson, E. A. (1952a) 'Peasant revolts in late Roman Gaul and Spain', *Past and Present* 2: 11–23

Thompson, E. A. (1952b) *A Roman Reformer and Inventor: Being a New Text of the Treatise De Rebus Bellicis, with a Translation and Introduction.* Oxford

Thompson, E. A. (1956) 'The settlement of the barbarians in southern Gaul', *JRS* 46: 65–75 (reprinted in Thompson, *Romans and Barbarians* chapter 2)

Thompson, E. A. (1963) 'The Visigoths from Fritigern to Euric', *Historia* 12: 105–26 (reprinted in Thompson, *Romans and Barbarians* chapter 3)

Thompson, E. A. (1965) *The Early Germans.* Oxford

Thrane, H. (1987) 'Das Gudme-Problem und die Gudmeuntersuchung', *Frühmittelalterliche Studien* 21: 1–24

Todd, M. (1987) *The Northern Barbarians.* 2nd edn. Oxford

Tsafrir, Y., Di Segni, L. and Green, J. (1994) *Tabula Imperii Romani. Iudaea, Palestina. Eretz Israel in the Hellenistic, Roman and Byzantine Periods. Maps and Gazetteer.* Jerusalem

Ulbert, T. (1989) 'Villes et fortifications de l'Euphrate à l'époque paléo-chrétienne (IVᵉ–VIIᵉ s.)', in Dentzer and Orthmann (1989) 283–96

van Es, W. A., Miedema, M. and Wynia, S. (1985) 'Eine Siedlung der römischen Kaiserzeit in Bennekom, Provinz Gelderland', *Bericht Rijksdienst Oudheidkundige Bodemonderzoek* 35: 533–652

Varady, L. (1969) *Das letzte Jahrhundert Pannoniens (376–476).* Amsterdam and Budapest

Veeck, W. (1931) *Die Alamannen in Württemberg.* Berlin and Leipzig

Waas, M. (1965) *Germanen im römischen Dienst im 4ten Jahrhundert n. Chr.* Bonn

Wallace-Hadrill, J. M. (1961) '*Gothia* and *Romania*', *Bulletin of the John Rylands Library, Manchester,* 44/1: 25–48 (reprinted in Wallace-Hadrill 1962)

Wallace-Hadrill, J. M. (1962) *The Long-Haired Kings and Other Studies in Frankish History.* London

Warmington, B. H. (1977) 'Objectives and strategy in the Persian war of Constantius II', in J. Fitz (ed.), *Limes: Akten des XI. internationalem Limeskongresses, 1976* (Budapest) 509–31

Waterbolk, H. T. (1979) 'Siedlungskontinuität im Küstengebiet der Nordsee zwischen Rhein und Elbe', *Probleme der Küstenforschung im südlichen Nordseegebiet* 13: 1–21

Welch, M. G. (1983) *Early Anglo-Saxon Sussex* (BAR 112). Oxford
Welch, M. G. (1992) *Anglo-Saxon England*. London
Wenskus, R. (1961) *Stammesbildung und Verfassung. Das Werden der frühmittelalterlichen Gentes*. Cologne and Graz
Werner, J. (1956) *Beiträge zur Archäologie des Attila-Reiches*. Munich
Werner, J. (1962) *Die Langobarden in Pannonien*. Munich
West, S. E. (1985) *West Stow: The Anglo-Saxon Village* (East Anglian Archaeology 24). Norwich
Wightman, E. M. (1985) *Gallia Belgica*. London
Winter, E. (1988) *Die sāsānidisch-römischen Friedensverträge des 3. Jahrhunderts n. Chr. – ein Beitrag zum Verständnis der aussenpolitischen Beziehungen zwischen den beiden Grossmächten*. Frankfurt, Bern, New York and Paris
Wirth, G. (1967) 'Zur Frage der föderierten Staaten in der späteren römischen Kaiserzeit', *Historia* 16: 231–51
Wolfram, H. (1970) 'The shaping of the early medieval kingdom', *Viator* 1: 1–20
Wolfram, H. (1975) 'Athanaric the Visigoth: monarchy or judgeship? A study in comparative history', *Journal of Medieval History* 1: 259–78
Wolski, J. (1980) 'Le rôle et l'importance des guerres de deux fronts dans la décadence de l'empire romain', *Klio* 62: 411–23
Wood, I. (1984) 'The end of Roman Britain: continental evidence and parallels', in M. Lapidge and D. Dumville (eds.), *Gildas: New Approaches*. Woodbridge
Wood, I. (1986) 'Disputes in late fifth- and sixth-century Gaul: some problems', in W. Davies and P. Fouracre (eds.), *The Settlement of Disputes in Early Medieval Europe*. Cambridge
Wood, I. (1987) 'The fall of the western empire and the end of Roman Britain', *Britannia* 18: 251–62
Wood, I. (1990) 'The ethnogenesis of the Burgundians', in H. Wolfram and W. Pohl (eds.), *Ethnogenese unter besonderer Berücksichtigung der Bayern*. Vienna

PART V: RELIGION (CHS. 18–21)

Adshead, S. A. M. and Adshead, K. (1991) 'Topography and sanctity in the north Syrian corridor', *Oriens Christianus* 75: 113–23
Amélineau, E. (1887) *De Historia Lausiaca*. Paris
Armstrong, H. (ed.) (1967) *Cambridge History of Later Greek and Early Medieval Philosophy*. Cambridge
Arnold, D. W. H. (1991) *The Early Episcopal Career of Athanasius of Alexandria*. Notre Dame, IN
Aston, Margaret (1988) *England's Iconoclasts*. Oxford
Bagnall, R. S. (1982) 'Religious conversion and onomastic change', *Bull. Am. Soc. Pap.* 19: 105–24
Bagnall, R. S. (1987) 'Church, state and divorce in late Roman Egypt', in *Florilegium Columbianum: Essays in Honor of Paul Oskar Kristeller* (New York) 41–61
Baldini, A. (1985) 'Problemi della tradizione sulla 'distruzione' del Serapeo di Alessandria', *RSA* 15: 97–152
Bamberger, C. (1968) '*Mnémé-Diathesis*. The psychic dynamisms of the ascetical theology of Saint Basil', *OCP* 34: 233–51

Barnes, T. D. (1986) 'Angel of light or mystic initiate? The problem of the *Life of Antony*', *JThS* n.s. 37: 353–68

Barnes, T. D. (1989) 'Christians and pagans in the reign of Constantius', Entr. Hardt 34: 301–43

Baur, G. (1929–30), *Der heilige Johannes Chrysostomus und seine Zeit*, 2 vols. Munich (Eng. trans. M. Gonzaga, 1959)

Beaucamp, J. (1990) *Le Statut de la femme à Byzance (4ᵉ–7ᵉ siècles)*, Vol. 1: *Le Droit impérial*. Paris

Bell, H. I. (1924) *Jews and Christians in Egypt*. London

Bidez, J. and Cumont, F. (1922) *Iuliani epistulae leges poemata fragmenta varia*. Paris

Blockley, R. C. (1981–3) *The Fragmentary Classicising Historians of the Later Roman Empire*. 2 vols. Liverpool

Blumenthal, H. J. (1990) 'Themistius: the last Peripatetic commentator on Aristotle?', in R. Sorabji (ed.), *Aristotle Transformed: The Ancient Commentators and their Influence* (London) 113–23

Bohlin, T. (1957) *Die Theologie des Pelagius und ihrer Genesis*. Uppsala and Wiesbaden

Bonner, G. (1972) *Augustine and Modern Research on Pelagianism*. Villanova

Brandenburg, H. (1969) 'Christussymbole in frühchristlichen Bodenmosaiken', *Römische Quartalschrift* 64: 76–138

Brennecke, H. C. (1984) *Hilarius von Poitiers und die Bischofsopposition gegen Konstantius II*. Berlin

Brennecke, H. C. (1988) *Studien zur Geschichte der Homöer. Der Osten bis zum Ende der homöischen Reichskirche*. Tübingen

Brogan, O. and Smith, D. J. (1984) *Ghirza: A Libyan Settlement in the Roman Period*. Tripoli

Brown, P. (1963) 'Religious coercion in the later Roman Empire: the case of North Africa', *History* 48: 283–305

Brown, P. (1964) 'St. Augustine's attitude to religious coercion', *JRS* 54: 107–16

Brown, P. (1971) 'The rise and function of the holy man in late antiquity', *JRS* 61: 80–101 (=Brown, *Society and the Holy*, 103–52)

Bruckner, A. (1897) *Julian von Eclanum* (Texte und Untersuchungen 15,3) Leipzig

Budge, E. A. W. (1915) *Miscellaneous Coptic Texts in the Dialect of Upper Egypt*. London

Bunge, G. (1986) 'Origenismus-Gnostizismus. Zum geistesgeschichtlichen Standort des Evagrios Pontikos', *Vig. Christ.* 40: 24–54

Bunge, G. (1988) *Geistliche Vaterschaft*. Regensburg

Burton-Christie, D. (1992) *The Word in the Desert: Scripture and the Quest for Holiness in Early Christian Monasticism*. Oxford

Buschhausen, H. (1991) 'Die Ausgrabungen von Dayr Abu Fana in Mittelägypten', *Ägypten und Levante* 2: 121–46

Carlini, A. (1985) 'Il più antico testimonio greco di Sisto Pitagorico: P. Palau Rib. inv.225v.', *Riv. Fil.* 113: 5–26

Cassin, E. (1973) 'Le semblable et le différent', in L. Poliakov (ed.), *Hommes et bêtes* (Paris) 115–27

Cavalcanti, E. (1976) *Studi Eunomiani*. Rome

Cavallera, F. (1905) *Le schisme d'Antioche*. Paris

Chadwick, H. E. (1959) *The Sentences of Sextus: A Contribution to the History of Christian Ethics*. Cambridge

Chadwick, H. (1976) *Priscillian of Avila, the Occult and the Charismatic in the Early Church*. Oxford

Chadwick, H. (1986) *Augustine*. Oxford

Chadwick, H. (1987) 'Priscillien', in *Dictionnaire de Spiritualité*. Paris

Chapman, J. (1928) *Studies on the Early Papacy*. London

Chitty, D. (1966) *The Desert a City*. Oxford

Clark, E. A. (1992) *The Origenist Controversy: The Cultural Construction of an Early Christian Debate*. Princeton, NJ

Congar, Y. M. J. (1963) *Œuvres de saint Augustin* (Bibliothèque augustinienne 28). Paris

Coüasnon, C. (1974) *The Church of the Holy Sepulchre, Jerusalem*. London

Dagron, G. (1978) *Vie et miracles de Sainte Thècle*. Brussels

Deuse, W. (1973) *Theodoros von Asine*. Wiesbaden

Dodds, E. R. (1965) *Pagan and Christian in an Age of Anxiety: Some Aspects of Religious Experience from Marcus Aurelius to Constantine*. Cambridge

Doignon, J. (1971) *Hilaire de Poitiers avant l'exil*. Paris

Dolbeau, F. (1991) 'Nouveaux sermons de S. Augustin pour la conversion des païens et des donatistes', *REA* 37: 37–77 (=Dolbeau, F. (1996) *Saint Augustin. Vingt-six Sermons au Peuple de l'Afrique*. Études augustiniennes. Paris)

Dörries, H. (1941) *Symeon von Mesopotamien* (Texte und Untersuchungen 55, 1). Leipzig

Dörries, H. (1956) *De Spiritu Sancto* (Abhandlungen der Göttinger Akademie, 3 Folge, 39). Göttingen

Dörries, H. (1978) *Die Theologie des Makarios/Symeon* (Abhandlungen der Akademie der Wissenschaften in Göttingen, phil.hist.Kl. 3 Folge, 103). Göttingen

Drijvers, H. J. W. (1984) 'Conflict and alliance in Manichaeism', in H. Kippenberg (ed.), *Struggles of Gods* (Berlin) 99–124

Dunbabin, K. (1978) *The Mosaics of Roman North Africa*. Oxford

Elm, S. (1991) 'Evagrius Ponticus' *Sententiae ad Virginem*', *DOP* 45: 97–120

Elm, S. (1994) *Virgins of God: The Organization of Female Asceticism in the Fourth Century*. Oxford

Evans, R. F. (1968a) *Four Letters of Pelagius*. London

Evans, R. F. (1968b) *Pelagius: Inquiries and Reappraisals*. London

Evans-Grubbs, J. (1989) 'Abduction marriage in antiquity: a law of Constantine (*CTh* IX.24.1) and its social context', *JRS* 79: 59–83

Ferguson, J. (1956) *Pelagius: A Historical and Theological Study*. Cambridge

Février, P.-A. (1977) 'A propos du culte funéraire: culte et sociabilité', *CArch* 26: 29–45

Février, P.-A. (1984) 'La tombe chrétienne et l'au-delà', in *Le Temps chrétien de la fin de l'Antiquité au Moyen-Age* (Colloques internationaux du CNRS 604) (Paris) 163–83

Foss, C. (1976) *Byzantine and Turkish Sardis*. Cambridge, MA

Foss, C. (1979) *Ephesus after Antiquity: A Late Antique, Byzantine and Turkish City*. Cambridge

Foucault, M. (1982) 'Le combat de la chasteté', *Communications* 35: 13–25

Fowden, G. (1978) 'Bishops and temples in the eastern Roman Empire A.D. 320–435', *JThS* n.s. 29: 53–78

Fowden, G. (1982) 'The pagan holy man in late antique society', *JHS* 102: 33–59

Fowden, G. (1988) 'City and mountain in late Roman Attica', *JHS* 108: 48–59

Fowden, G. (1993) *Empire to Commonwealth: Consequences of Monotheism in Late Antiquity*. Princeton, NJ

Frankenberg, W. W. (ed.) (1912) Evagrius Ponticus, *Antirrhetikos, Abh. Göttingen. Phil.-Hist. Kl. N. F. 13.2*. Berlin

Frantz, A. (1988) *The Athenian Agora* Vol. 24: *Late Antiquity: A.D. 267–700*. Princeton, NJ

Frend, W. H. C. (1984) *The Rise of Christianity*. London

Frezza, P. (1989) 'L'esperienza della tolleranza religiosa fra pagani e cristiani dal IV al V sec. d.c. nell'oriente ellenistico', *SDHI* 55: 41–97

Gardner, I. M. F. and Lieu, S. N. C. (1996) 'From Narmouthis (Medinet Madi) to Kellis (Ismont el-Kharab)', *JRS* 86: 146–69

Garnsey, P. (1984) 'Religious toleration in classical antiquity', in W. J. Shiels (ed.) *Persecution and Toleration* (Studies in Church History 21) (Oxford) 1–28

Gassowska, B. (1982) 'Maternus Cynegius, praef. praet. Orientis, and the destruction of the Allat temple in Palmyra', *Archeologia* 33: 107–23

Gaudemet, J. (1990) 'La législation anti-païenne de Constantin à Justinien', *Cristianesimo nella storia* XI, 448–68

Gauthier, N. (1980) *L'Évangélisation des pays de la Moselle*. Paris

Ginsburg, C. (1992) 'La conversione della Ebrei di Minorca (417–418)', *Quaderni storici* 79: 277–89

Girardet, K. M. (1975) *Kaisergericht und Bischofsgericht*. Bonn

Glucker, C. A. M. (1987) *The City of Gaza in the Roman and Byzantine Periods*. Oxford

Gombrich, R. (1971) *Precept and Practice*. Oxford

Grasmück, E. L. (1964) *Coercitio: Staat und Kirche im Donatistenstreit*. Bonn

Gregg, R. C. and Groh, D. E. (1981) *Early Arianism, a View of Salvation*. Philadelphia, PA

Greshake, G. (1972) *Gnade als konkrete Freiheit*. Mainz

Gribomont, J. (1972) 'Le dossier des origines du messalianisme', in J. Fontaine and C. Kannengiesser (eds.), *Epektasis. Mélanges J. Daniélou* (Paris) 611–25

Griffith, S. H. (1989–90) 'Images of Ephraem: the Syrian holy man and his church', *Traditio* 45: 7–33

Griffith, S. H. (1995) 'Asceticism in the church of Syria: the hermeneutics of Syrian monasticism', in V. L. Wimbush and R. Valantasis (eds.), *Asceticism* (Oxford) 220–45

Grillmeier, A. (1975) *Christ in Christian Tradition* I. 2nd edn. London and Oxford

Grillmeier, A. (1979) *Jesus der Christus im Glauben der Kirche*. Freiburg im Breisgau

Gryson, R. (1973) 'Les élections épiscopales en Orient au IIIᵉ siècle', *RHE* 68: 353–404

Gryson, R. (1979) 'Les élections épiscopales en Orient au IVᵉ siècle', *RHE* 74: 301–45

Gryson, R. (1980) *Scolies ariennes sur le concile d'Aquilée* (SChrét 267). Paris

Guillaumont, A. (ed.) (1958) *Les Six centuries des Kephalaia Gnostica*. PO 28:1

Guillaumont, A. (1962) *Les 'Kephalaia Gnostica' d'Évagre le Pontique et l'histoire de l'origénisme chez les grecs et chez les syriens*. Paris

Guillaumont, A. (1975) 'La conception du désert chez les moines d'Égypte', *Revue de l'histoire des religions* 188: 3–21

Guillaumont, A. and C. (1971) *Évagre le Pontique: Traité pratique ou le moine* (*SChrét.* 170–1). Paris

Guy, J.-C. (1962) *Recherches sur la tradition grecque des Apophthegmata Patrum* (Subsidia Hagiographica 36). Brussels

Hadot, P. (1981) *Exercices spirituels et philosophie antique.* Paris

von Haehling, R. (1978) *Die Religionszugehörigkeit der hohen Amtsträger des römischen Reiches seit Konstantins Alleinherrschaft bis zum Ende der Theodosianischen Dynastie.* Bonn

Hahn, J. (1989) *Der Philosoph und die Gesellschaft.* Wiesbaden

Hajjar, Y. (1985) *La Triade d'Héliopolis-Baalbek. Iconographie, théologie, culte et sanctuaires.* Montreal

Harl, K. (1990) 'Sacrifice and pagan belief in fifth- and sixth-century Byzantium', *Past and Present* 128: 7–27

Harl, M. (1981) 'La dénonciation des festivités profanes dans le discours épiscopal et monastique en Orient chrétien à la fin du ivᵉ siècle', in *La Fête, pratique et discours* (Annales de l'Université de Besançon 262) (Paris) 123–47

Harvey, S. A. (1988) 'The sense of a stylite: perspectives on Symeon the elder', *Vigiliae Christianae* 42: 376–94

Heather, P. J. and Matthews, J. F. (1991) *The Goths in the Fourth Century.* Liverpool

Heinen, H. (1985) *Trier und das Trevererland in römischer Zeit.* Trier

Hirschfeld, Y. (1990) 'Edible wild plants', *Israel, Land and Nature* 16: 25–8

Holl, K. (1904) *Amphilochius von Iconium in seinem Verhältnis zu den grossen Kappadoziern.* Tübingen and Leipzig

Judge, E. A. (1977) 'The earliest use of Monachus for "Monk" (P. Coll. Youtie 77) and the origins of monasticism', *JbAC* 20: 72–89

Kaegi, W. E. (1982) *Army, Society and Religion in Byzantium.* London

Kelly, J. N. D. (1950) *Early Christian Creeds.* Harlow

Kelly, J. N. D. (1958) *Early Christian Doctrines.* London

Kennedy, H. and Liebeschuetz, J. H. W. G. (1988) 'Antioch and the villages of north Syria in the fifth and sixth century A.D.: trends and problems', *Nottingham Medieval Studies* 32: 65–90

Klein, R. (1977) *Konstantius II und die christliche Kirche.* Darmstadt

Kopecek, T. A. (1979) *A History of Neo-Arianism.* Philadelphia, PA

Kotula, T. (1994) 'Julien Auguste et l'aristocratie municipale d'Afrique', *Ant. Afr.* 30: 271–9

Kriss, R. and Kriss-Heinrich, H. (1960–2) *Volksglaube im Bereich des Islam.* Wiesbaden

Landersdorfer, S. (1913) *Ausgewählte Schriften der syrischen Dichter.* Munich

Langenfeld, H. (1977) *Christianisierungspolitik und Sklavengesetzgebung der römischen Kaiser von Konstantin bis Theodosius II.* Bonn

Lepelley, C. (1987) 'Formes païennes de la sociabilité en Afrique au temps de Saint Augustin', *Sociabilité, pouvoirs et société*, Colloque de Rouen (Rouen) 99–103

Liébaert, J. (1951) *La Doctrine christologique de S. Cyrille d'Alexandrie avant la querelle nestorienne.* Lille

Liebeschuetz, W. (1990) *From Diocletian to the Arab Conquest: Change in the Late Roman Empire.* Aldershot

Lietzmann, H. (1904) *Apollinaris von Laodicea und seine Schule*. Tübingen

Linder, A. (1987) *The Jews in Roman Imperial Legislation*. Detroit

Lizzi, R. (1990) 'Ambrose's contemporaries and the Christianization of Northern Italy', *JRS* 80: 151–73

Loofs, F. (1904) 'Pelagius', in *Realenzyklopädie für Protestantische Theologie und Kirche* 15: 747–74

Loofs, F. (1913) 'Pelagius', in *Realenzyklopädie für Protestantische Theologie und Kirche* 24: 310–12

Loofs, F. (1914) *Nestorius and his Place in the History of Christian Doctrine*. Cambridge, MA and New York

Lorenz, R. (1980) *Arius iudaizans?* Göttingen

McLynn, N. (1992) 'Christian controversy and violence in the fourth century', *Kodai* 3: 15–44

McLynn, N. (1994) *Ambrose of Milan: Church and Court in a Christian Capital*. Berkeley, CA

MacMullen, R. (1989) 'The preacher's audience (AD 350–400)', *JThS* n.s. 40: 503–11

Madec, G. (1989) *La Patrie et la voie*. Paris

Maier, J. L. (1987–9) *Le Dossier du Donatisme, Texte und Untersuchungen* 134–35. Berlin

Markschies, C. (1995) *Ambrosius von Mailand und die Trinitätstheologie*. Tübingen

Martin, A. (1985) *Histoire Acéphale et Index Syriaque des lettres festales d'Athanase d'Alexandrie (SChrét* 317). Paris

Martin, A. (1996) *Athanase d'Alexandrie et l'église d'Égypte au IVe siècle (CEFR* 216). Rome

Martroye, F. (1913) *La Répression du Donatisme et la politique religieuse de Constantin et de ses successeurs en Afrique*, in *Mémoires de la société nationale des antiquaires de France*, 8: 3: 23–140

Mathisen, R. W. (1986) 'Ten office-holders: a few *addenda* and *corrigenda* to *P.L.R.E.*', *Historia* 35: 125–7

Matthews, J. F. (1974) 'The Letters of Symmachus', in Binns, *Latin Literature* 58–99

Merkelbach, R. (1986) *Mani und sein Religionssystem*. Opladen

Meslin, M. (1967) *Les Ariens d'Occident 335–430*. Paris

Meslin, M. (1970) *La Fête des kalendes de janvier dans l'empire romain*. Brussels

Metzler, D. (1989) 'Über das Konzept der "Vier grosse Königreiche" in Manis Kephalaia (cap. 77)', *Klio* 71: 446–59

Miller, M. W. (1964) *Rufini presbyteri de fide*. Washington, DC

Mitchell, S. (1993) *Anatolia: Land, Men and Gods in Asia Minor*. 2 vols. Oxford

Monceaux, P. (1912–23) *Histoire littéraire de l'Afrique chrétienne* Vols. 4–7. Paris

Murphy, F. X. (1945) *Rufinus of Aquileia*. Washington, DC

Nau, F. (1929–30) Review of H. Grégoire and M.-A. Kugener, *Vie de Porphyre, ROC* 27: 422–41

Nauroy, G. (1974) 'La méthode de composition et la structure du *De Isaac et beata vita*', in Y. M. Duval (ed.), *Ambroise de Milan* (Paris) 115–53

Nautin, P. (1970) Review of Meslin (1967), *Revue d'histoire des religions* 177: 70–89

Nock, A. D. (1926) *Sallustius: Concerning the Gods and the Universe*. Cambridge

Noethlichs, K. L. (1986) 'Heidenverfolgung', *RAC* 13: 1149–90

O'Donnell, J. J. (1977) 'Paganus', *Classical Folia* 31: 163–9

O'Donnell, J. J. (1979) 'The demise of paganism', *Traditio* 35: 45–88

O'Laughlin, M. W. (1987) 'Origenism in the Desert'. Unpubl. Harvard PhD thesis

O'Meara, D. J. (1989) *Pythagoras Revived: Mathematics and Philosophy in Late Antiquity.* Oxford

Peeters, F. (1941) 'La vie géorgienne de Saint Porphyre de Gaza', *Anal. Boll.* 59: 65–216

Peña, I., Castellana, P. and Fernández, R. (1987) *Inventaire du Jébel Baricha. Recherches archéologiques dans la région des villes mortes de la Syrie du nord.* Milan

Penella, R. J. (1990) *Greek Philosophers and Sophists in the Fourth Century A.D.: Studies in Eunapius of Sardis.* Leeds

Piétri, C. (1984) 'Le temps de la semaine à Rome et dans l'Italie chrétienne', in *Le temps chrétien de la fin de l'Antiquité au Moyen-Age* (Colloques internationaux du CNRS 604) (Paris) 63–97

Plinval, G. (1943) *Pélage, ses écrits, sa vie et sa réforme.* Lausanne

Prestige, G. L. (1956) *St. Basil the Great and Apollinaris of Laodicea*, ed. H. Chadwick. London

Prete, S. (1961) *Pelagio e il pelagianesimo.* Brescia

Puech, H. C. (1949) *Le Manichéisme.* Paris

Raven, C. E. (1924) *Apollinarianism.* Cambridge

Rebenich, S. (1992) *Hieronymus und sein Kreis.* Stuttgart

Rees, B. R. (1991) *The Letters of Pelagius and his Followers.* Woodbridge

Reynolds, J. M. and Ward-Perkins, J. B. (eds.) (1952) *The Inscriptions of Roman Tripolitania.* Rome (with supp. *PBSR* 23 (1955) 124–47)

Ritter, A. M. (1965) *Das Konzil von Konstantinopel und sein Symbol.* Göttingen

Robert, L. (1969–90) *Opera minora selecta. Épigraphie et antiquités grecques.* 7 vols. Amsterdam

Rochow, I. (1978) 'Zu einigen oppositionellen religiösen Strömungen', in F. Winkelmann *et al.* (eds.), *Byzanz im 7. Jahrhundert. Untersuchungen zur Herausbildung des Feudalismus* (Berlin) 225–88

Roques, D. (1987) *Synésios de Cyrène et la Cyrénaïque du Bas-Empire.* Paris

Rose, E. (1979) *Die manichäische Christologie.* Wiesbaden

Rottmanner, O. (1892) *Der Augustinismus.* Munich

Rousselle, A. (1983) *Porneia: de la maîtrise du corps à la privation sensorielle.* Paris

Rousselle, A. (1990) *Croire et guérir. La foi en Gaule dans l'antiquité tardive.* Paris

Rubenson, S. (1995) 'Christian asceticism and the emergence of the monastic tradition', in V. L. Wimbush and R. Valantasis (eds.), *Asceticism* (Oxford) 49–57

Sacks, K. (1986) 'The meaning of Eunapius' History', *History and Theory* 25: 52–67

Saffrey, H.-D. (1976) 'Théologie et anthropologie d'après quelques préfaces de Proclus', in C. Laga (ed.), *Images of Man in Ancient and Medieval Thought, Studia G. Verbeke Dicata* (Louvain) 199–212

Salomonson, J. W. (1979) *Voluptatem spectandi non perdat sed mutet. Observations sur l'iconographie des martyrs en Afrique romaine.* Amsterdam

Savon, H. (1997) *Ambroise de Milan.* Paris

Saxer, V. (1980) *Morts, martyrs, reliques en Afrique chrétienne.* Paris

Schneider, L. (1983) *Die Domäne als Weltbild. Wirkungsstrukturen der spätantiken Bildersprache.* Wiesbaden

Seguí Vidal, G. (1937) *La carta enciclica del obispo Severo.* Palma de Mallorca

Seibt, K. (1994) *Die Theologie des Markell von Ankyra* (Arbeiten zur Kirchengeschichte 59). Berlin

Selb, W. (1967) 'Episcopalis Audientia von der Zeit Konstantius bis zur Nov. XXXV Valentinians III', *ZRG* 84: 167–217

Sellers, R. V. (1940) *Two Ancient Christologies*. London

Shaw, B. (1991) 'The cultural meaning of death: age and gender in the Roman family', in D. L. Kertzer and R. P. Saller (eds.), *The Family in Italy* (New Haven, CT) 66–90

Shaw, G. (1985) 'Theurgy', *Traditio* 41: 1–20

Shils, E. (1975) *Center and Periphery*. Chicago

Souter, A. (1922–31) *Pelagius' Expositions of Thirteen Epistles of St Paul* (Texts and Studies 9). Cambridge

Spanneut, M. (1948) *Recherches sur les écrits d'Eustathe d'Antioche*. Lille

Staats, R. (1984) *Makarios-Symeon Epistola Magna* (Abhandlungen der Akademie der Wissenschaften in Göttingen, phil.hist.Kl. 3 Folge, 134). Göttingen

Stemberger, G. (1987) *Juden und Christen im Heiligen Land*. Munich

Stewart, C. (1991) *Working the Earth of the Heart*.Oxford

Swete, H. B. (1912) *The Holy Spirit in the Ancient Church*. London

Szidat, J. (1979) 'Die Usurpation des Eugenius', *Historia* 28: 487–508

Tengström, E. (1964) *Donatisten und Katholiken*. Gothenburg

Thélamon, F. (1981) *Païens et chrétiens au ive siècle*. Paris

Thomas, C. (1981) *Christianity in Roman Britain to 500 A.D.* Berkeley

Tomlin, R. S. O. (1988) 'The curse tablets', in B. Cunliffe (ed.), *The Temple of Sulis Minerva at Bath* ii. Oxford

Torp, H. (1981) 'Le monastère copte de Baouit', *Acta Instituti Norvegiae Romani* 9: 1–8

Vaggione, R. P. (1987) *Eunomius: The Extant Works*. Oxford

Van Dam, R. (1985) 'From paganism to Christianity in late antique Gaza', *Viator* 16: 1–20

Vatin, C. (1965) 'Delphes à l'époque impériale'. Unpubl. diss., Paris

Veyne, P. (1986) 'Une évolution du paganisme gréco-romain: injustice et piété des dieux, leurs ordres ou "oracles"', *Latomus* 45: 259–83

de Vogüé, A. (1986) 'De la crise aux résolutions: les *Dialogues* comme histoire d'une âme', in J. Fontaine (ed.), *Grégoire le Grand* (Colloques int. du CNRS) (Paris) 305–14

de Vogüé, A. (1991) *Histoire littéraire du mouvement monastique dans l'antiquité*. Paris

Vollmann, B. (1974) 'Priscillianus', in *RE* Suppl. 14: 485–559

Wallis, R. T. (1972) *Neoplatonism*. London

Watts, D. (1991) *Pagans and Christians in Roman Britain*. London

Weigl, E. (1925) *Christologie vom Tode des Athanasius bis zum Ausbruch des nestorianischen Streites, 373–429*. Munich

Wermelinger, I. (1975) *Rom und Pelagius*. Stuttgart

Whitby, Michael and Whitby, Mary (1989) *Chronicon Paschale 284–628 A.D.* Liverpool

Wickham, L. R. (1983) *Cyril of Alexandria: Selected Letters*. Oxford

Widdicombe, P. (1994) *The Fatherhood of God from Origen to Athanasius*. Oxford

Widengren, G. (1961) *Mani und der Manichäismus*. Stuttgart

Williams, D. H. (1995) *Ambrose of Milan and the End of the Arian–Nicene Conflicts*. Oxford

Williams, R. D. (1987) *Arius: Heresy and Tradition*. London

Wimbush, V. L. (ed.) (1990) *Ascetic Behavior in Greco-Roman Antiquity: A sourcebook.* Minneapolis, MN

Wipszycka, E. (1986) 'La valeur de l'onomastique pour l'histoire de la christianisation de l'Égypte', *ZPE* 62: 173–81

Wipszycka, E. (1988) 'La christianisation de l'Égypte aux IVᵉ–Vᵉ siècles. Aspects sociaux et ethniques', *Aegyptus* 68: 117–65

Wytzes, J. (1977) *Der letzte Kampf des Heidentums in Rom.* Leiden

PART VI: ART AND CULTURE (CHS. 22–24)

Alcock, A. (1982) 'Persecution under Septimius Severus', *Enchoria* 11: 1–5

Allberry, C. R. C. (1938) *A Manichaean Psalm-Book* Vol. 2 (Manichaean Manuscripts in the Chester Beatty Collection 2). Stuttgart

Altaner, B. and Stuiber, A. (1980) *Patrologie.* 9th edn. Freiburg-Basel-Vienna

Amand, D. (1943) *Fatalisme et liberté dans l'antiquité grecque.* Louvain (reprinted Amsterdam 1973)

Athanassiadi, P. (1992) 'Philosophers and oracles: shifts of authority in late paganism', *Byzantion* 62: 45–62

Athanassiadi, P. (1993) 'Dreams, theurgy and freelance divination: the testimony of Iamblichus', *JRS* 83: 115–30

Attridge, H.W. (ed.) (1985) *Nag Hammadi Codex I (The Jung Codex)* (Nag Hammadi Studies 22). Leiden

Attridge, H. W. and MacRae, G. W. (1985) 'The Gospel of Truth', in Attridge (1985) 55–122

Attridge, H. W. and Pagels, E. H. (1985) 'The Tripartite Tractate', in Attridge (1985) 159–337

Auerbach, E. (1953) *Mimesis, The Representation of Reality in Western literature.* Eng. trans. Princeton, NJ

Auerbach, E. (1965) *Literary Language and its Public in Late Antiquity and in the Middle Ages.* Eng. trans. New York

Baldovin, J. (1987) *The Urban Character of Christian Worship.* Rome

Balty, J. (1992) 'Les thérapénides d'Apamée', *Dialogues d'hist. ancienne* 18.1: 281–9

Bardy, G. (1948) *La Question des langues dans l'Église ancienne.* Paris

Barnes, T. D. (1976) 'The date and historical setting of Prudentius' Contra Symmachum', *AJP* 97: 373–83

Barnes, T. D. (1978) *The Sources of the Historia Augusta.* Brussels

Barnes, T. D. (1979) 'The date of Vegetius', *Phoenix* 33: 254–7

Barnes, T. D. (1980) 'The editions of Eusebius' *Ecclesiastical History*', *GRBS* 21: 191–201

Barnes, T. D. (1989) 'Jerome and the *Origo Constantini Imperatoris*', *Phoenix* 43: 158–61

Barnes, T. D. (1990) 'Panegyric, history and hagiography in Eusebius' *Life of Constantine*', in R. Williams (ed.), *The Making of Orthodoxy: Essays in Honour of Henry Chadwick* (Cambridge) 94–123

Barnes, T. D. (1991) 'Latin literature between Diocletian and Ambrose', *Phoenix* 45: 341–55 (review of Herzog 1989)

Barns, J. W. B., Browne, G. M. and Shelton, J. C. (1981) *Nag Hammadi Codices: Greek and Coptic Papyri from the Cartonnage of the Covers* (Nag Hammadi Studies 16). Leiden

Bassett, S. G. (1991) 'The antiquities in the Hippodrome of Constantinople', *DOP* 45: 87–96

Baumeister, T. (1972) *Martyr Invictus* (Forschungen zur Volkskunde 46). Münster

Baumstark, A. (1922) *Geschichte der syrischen Literatur.* Bonn

Becatti, G. (1960) *La colonna coclide istoriata.* Rome

Becatti, G. (1969) *Scavi di Ostia, VI.* Rome

Beck, E. (1980) *Ephräms des Syrers Psychologie und Erkenntnislehre (CSCO*, Subsidia 58). Louvain

Beck, H. G. (1959) *Kirche und theologische Literatur im byzantinischen Reich.* Munich

Beckwith, J. (1980) *Early Christian and Byzantine Art.* Harmondsworth

Beggiani, S. J. (1983) *Early Syriac Theology.* Lanham, MD

Bell, H. I. and Thompson, H. (1925) 'A Greek–Coptic glossary to Hosea and Amos', *JEA* 11: 241–6

Beltz, W. (1978) 'Katalog der koptischen Handschriften der Papyrussammlung der Staatlichen Museen zu Berlin (Teil 1)', *Archiv für Papyrusforschung* 26: 57–119

Berenson, B. (1954) *The Arch of Constantine or the Decline of Form.* New York

Beretta, G. (1993) *Ipazia d'Alessandria.* Rome

Bianchi Bandinelli, R. (1979) *Archeologia e Cultura.* Rome

Bidez, J. and Winkelmann, F. (1981) *Philostorgius.* 3rd edn. Berlin

Biedenkopf-Ziehner, A. (1972–80) 'Koptologische Literaturübersicht 1, III–VII', *Enchoria* 2 (1972): 103–36; 4 (1974): 141–55; 5 (1975): 151–79; 6 (1976): 93–119; 8 (1978): 51–72; 10 (1980): 151–83

Biedenkopf-Ziehner, A. (1973) 'Nachtrag zur KLU I (1967/68)', *Enchoria* 3: 81–94

Biedenkopf-Ziehner, A. and Brunsch, W. (1973) 'Koptologische Literaturübersicht II, 1969/70/71', *Enchoria* 3: 95–152

Bleckmann, B. (1991) 'Die Chronik des Johannes Zonaras und eine pagane Quelle zur Geschichte Konstantins', *Historia* 40: 343–65

Blockley, R. C. (1981–3) *The Fragmentary Classicising Historians of the Later Roman Empire*, 2 vols. Liverpool

Boatswain, T. (1988) 'Images of uncertainty: some thoughts on the meaning of form in the art of late antiquity', *BMGS* 12: 27–46

Böhlig, A. (1966) *Kephalaia* 2. Hälfte (Manichäische Handschriften der Staatlichen Museen Berlin 1). Stuttgart

Böhlig, A. (1968) *Mysterion und Wahrheit* (Arbeiten zur Geschichte des späteren Judentums und des Urchristentums 6). Leiden

Böhlig, A. (1987) 'Zur Rhetorik im Liber Graduum', in *IV Symposium Syriacum 1984* (OCA 229) (Rome) 297–305

Böhlig, A. and Wisse, F. (1975) *Nag Hammadi Codices III, 2 and IV, 2: The Gospel of the Egyptians (The Holy Book of the Great Invisible Spirit)* (Nag Hammadi Studies 4). Leiden

Boon, A. (1932) *Pachomiana Latina* (Bibliothèque de la Revue d'Histoire Ecclésiastique 7). Louvain

Bou Mansour, T. (1988) *La Pensée symbolique de saint Ephrem le syrien.* Kaslik, Lebanon du Bourguet, P. (1971–6) 'Bibliographie copte. 20–25', *Orientalia* n.s. 40 (1971): 105*–43*; 41 (1972): 89*–106*; 42 (1973): 79*–97*; 43 (1974): 53*–76*; 44 (1975): 88*–107*; 45 (1976): 88*–117*

Bovini, G. and Brandenburg, H. (1967) *Repertorium der Christlich-Antiken Sarkophage* Vol. 1, *Rom und Ostia*. Wiesbaden

Brashler, J. (1979) 'Plato, Republic 588b–589b', in D. M. Parrott (ed.), *Nag Hammadi Codices V, 2–5 and VI with Papyrus Berolinensis 8502, 1 and 4* (Nag Hammadi Studies 11) (Leiden) 325–39

Brendel, O. (1941) 'The Corbridge Lanx', *JRS* 31: 100–27

Brenk, B. (1977) *Spätantike und frühes Christentum*. Frankfurt

Brenk, B. (1987) 'Spolia from Constantine to Charlemagne: aesthetics versus ideology', *DOP* 41: 103–9

Brennecke, H. C. (1988) *Studien zur Geschichte der Homöer: Der Osten bis zum Ende der homöischen Reichskirche*. Tübingen

Brock, S. P. (1973–92) 'Syriac studies: a classified bibliography', *Parole de l'Orient* 4 (1973): 393–465 (for 1960–70); 10 (1981–2): 291–412 (for 1971–80); 14 (1987): 289–360 (for 1981–5); 17 (1992) 211–301 (for 1986–90); reprinted as *Syriac Studies: A Classified Bibliography (1960–1990)*, Kaslik 1996

Brock, S. P. (1979) 'Jewish traditions in Syriac sources', *JJS* 30: 212–32

Brock, S. P. (1983a) 'A Syriac collection of prophecies of the pagan philosophers', *OLP* 14: 233–5

Brock, S. P. (1983b) 'Towards a history of Syriac translation technique', in *III Symposium Syriacum 1980* (OCA 221) (Rome) 1–14

Brock, S. P. (1984) *Syriac Perspectives on Late Antiquity*. London

Brock, S. P. (1985a) 'A dispute of the months and some related Syriac texts', *JSS* 30: 181–211

Brock, S. P. (1985b) *The Luminous Eye: The Spiritual World Vision of St. Ephrem*. Rome (repr. Kalamazoo 1992)

Brock, S. P. (1985c) 'Syriac and Greek hymnography: problems of origin', *Studia Patristica* 16: 77–81

Brock, S. P. (1989) 'From Ephrem to Romanos', *Studia Patristica* 20: 139–51

Brock, S. P. (1992a) *Studies in Syriac Christianity*. London

Brock, S. P. (1992b) 'Eusebius and Syriac Christianity', in H. W. Attridge and G. Hata (eds.), *Eusebius, Christianity and Judaism* (Detroit), 212–34

Brock, S. P. (1994) 'Greek and Syriac in late antique Syria', in A. K. Bowman and G. Woolf (eds.), *Literacy and Power in the Ancient World* (Cambridge) 149–60

Brock, S. P. (forthcoming) 'Materials for the study of the writings of St Ephrem', *ANRW*

Brock, S. P. (forthcoming) 'Historical fiction in fifth-century Edessa', in D. Bundy (ed.), *Edessa from the Fourth Century to the Arab Conquest*

Browning, R. (1982) 'The later principate', in *The Cambridge History of Classical Literature* Vol. 2 (1982) chapters 35–42. (Also publ. as *The Later Principate*. Cambridge 1983)

Bullard, R. A. and Layton, B. (1989) 'The Hypostasis of the Archons', in B. Layton (ed.), *Nag Hammadi Codex II, 2–7 together with XIII, 2*, Brit. Lib. Or. 4926(1), and P. Oxy. 1, 654, 655* 1 (Nag Hammadi Studies 20) (Leiden) 220–59

Burkitt, F. C. (1913) *Euphemia and the Goth, with the Acts of Martyrdom of the Confessors of Edessa.* London

Burkitt, F. C. (1925) *The Religion of the Manichees.* Cambridge

Cabrol, F. and Leclercq. H. (eds.) (1936) *Dictionnaire d'archéologie chrétienne et de liturgie.* Paris

Cahn, H. A. and Kauffman-Heinimann, A. (eds.) (1984) *Der Spätromanische Silberschatze von Kaiseraugst.* Basel

Cahn, H. A., Kauffman-Heinimann, A. and Painter, K. (1991) 'A table-ronde on a treasure of late antique silver', *JRA* 4: 184–91

Calderone, S. (1985) 'Eusebio e l'ideologia imperiale', in *Le Trasformazioni della cultura nella tarda antichità,* Atti del convegno tenuto a Catania, Università di Studi, 27 sett.–2 ott. 1982 (Rome) 1–26

Cameron, Alan (1964) 'The Roman friends of Ammianus', *JRS* 54: 15–28

Cameron, Alan (1965) 'Wandering poets: a literary movement in Byzantine Egypt', *Historia* 14: 470–509

Cameron, Alan (1966) 'The date and identity of Macrobius', *JRS* 56: 25–38

Cameron, Alan (1977) 'Paganism and literature in late-fourth century Rome', in *Christianisme et formes littéraires,* 1–30

Cameron, Alan (1993) *The Greek Anthology from Meleager to Planudes.* Oxford

Cameron, Averil (1997a) 'Christianity and communication in the fourth century: the problem of diffusion', in H. Pleket and A. Verhoogt (eds.), *Power and Possession: State, Society and Church during the Fourth Century A.D.* (Leiden) 23–42

Cameron, Averil (1997b) 'Eusebius's *Vita Constantini* and the construction of Constantine', in S. Swain and M. Edwards (eds.), *Portraits: The Biographical in the Literature of the Empire* (Oxford) 245–74

Canévet, M. (1983) *Grégoire de Nysse et l'herméneutique biblique. Étude des rapports entre le langage et la connaissance de Dieu.* Paris

Canivet, P. (1977) *Le Monachisme Syrien selon Théodoret de Cyr.* Paris

Carandini, A., Ricci, A. and De Vos, M. (1982) *Filosofiana: The Villa of Piazza Armerina.* Palermo

Chadwick, H. (1983) 'New letters of Saint Augustine', *JThS* n.s. 34: 425–52

Chadwick, H. (1986) *Augustine.* Oxford

Chaumont, M-L. *La Christianisation de l'empire iranien des origines aux grandes persécutions du IVe siècle (CSCO,* Subsidia 80) Louvain

Chazelle, C. M. (1990) 'Pictures, books and the illiterate: Pope Gregory's letters to Serenus of Marseilles', *Word and Image* 6: 138–53

Christianisme et formes littéraires dans l'antiquité tardive en occident (Entr. Hardt 23). Vandœuvres, 1977

Chuvin, P. (1992) *Mythologie et géographie dionysiaques. Recherches sur l'œuvre de Nonnos de Panopolis.* Paris

Clark, Elizabeth A. (1984) *The Life of Melania the Younger: Introduction, Translation and Commentary.* Lewiston, NY

Clark, Elizabeth A. (1992) *The Origenist Controversy: The Cultural Construction of an Early Christian Debate.* Princeton, NJ

Clark, Gillian (1993) *Augustine: The Confessions.* Cambridge

Cochrane, C. N. (1940) *Christianity and Classical Culture.* Oxford

Consolino, F.-E. (1986) 'Modelli di comportamento e modi di santificazione per l'aristocrazia femminile d'occidente', in Giardina, *Società romana* 1, 273–306

Courcelle, P. (1950) *Recherches sur les Confessions de Saint Augustin.* Paris. 2nd edn 1968

Courcelle, P. (1963) *Les 'Confessions' de saint Augustin dans la tradition littéraire, antécédents et postérité.* Paris

Cox, Patricia (1983) *Biography in Late Antiquity.* Berkeley and Los Angeles

Croke, B. (1983) 'The origins of the Christian world chronicle', in B. Croke and A. M. Emmett, *History and Historians in Late Antiquity* (Sydney) 116–31

Crum, W. E. (1905) *Catalogue of the Coptic Manuscripts in the British Museum.* London

Crum, W. E. (1919–20) 'New Coptic manuscripts in the John Rylands Library', *Bulletin of the John Rylands Library* 5: 1–7

Crum, W. E. (1934–7) 'Un psaume en dialecte d'Akhmim', *Mélanges Maspéro* 2 (Mémoires publiés par les membres de l'Institut Français d'Archéologie Orientale du Caire 67) (Cairo) 73–6

Crum, W. E. and Bell, H. I. (1922) *Wadi Sarga* (Coptica 3). Hauniae

Curran, J. (1994) 'Moving statues in late antique Rome: problems of perspective', *Art History* 17: 46–58

Curtius, E. (1953) *European Literature and the Latin Middle Ages.* Eng. trans. by W. Trask. London

Dagron, G. (1969) 'Aux origines de la civilisation byzantine. Langue de culture et langue de l'État', *Revue historique* 241: 23–56. (Reprinted in his *La romanité chrétienne en Orient* (London, 1984), 1)

Dagron, G. (1978) *Vie et miracles de sainte Thècle.* Brussels

Daszewski, W. A. (1985) *Dionysos der Erlöser.* Mainz

Davies, W. V. (1987) *Egyptian Hieroglyphs.* London

Dawkins, R. M. (1924) 'Antique statuary in medieval Constantinople', *Folklore* 35: 209–48

Dawson, D. (1992) *Allegorical Readers and Cultural Revision in Ancient Alexandria.* Berkeley and Los Angeles

Deichmann, F. W. (1989) *Ravenna: Haupstadt des Spätantiken Abendlandes: II Kommentar 3.* Stuttgart

Delbrueck, R. (1933) *Spätantike Kaiserporträts von Constantinus Magnus bis zum Ende des Westreichs.* Berlin and Leipzig

Delehaye, H. (1921) *Les Passions des martyrs et les genres littéraires.* Brussels (repr. 1966)

Delehaye, H. (1927) *Les Légendes hagiographiques.* 2nd edn. Brussels

Den Boer, W. (1972) *Some Minor Roman Historians.* Leiden

Devreesse, R. (1945) *Le Patriarcat d'Antioche depuis la paix de l'Église jusqu'à la conquête arabe.* Paris

Diebner, B. J. (1978) 'Literarkritische Probleme der Zephanja-Apokalypse', in R. McL. Wilson (ed.), *Nag Hammadi and Gnosis* (Nag Hammadi Studies 14) (Leiden) 152–67

Diebner, B. J. (1985) 'Die biblischen Texte des Hamburger Papyrus Bilinguis 1 (Cant, Lam, Co., Eccl Gr. et Co.) in ihrem Verhältnis zum Texte der Septuaginta, besonders des Kodex B (Vat. Gr. 1209). Beobachtungen und methodische Bemerkungen', in Orlandi and Wisse (eds.) (1985) 59–74

Diebner, B. J. and Kasser, R. (1989) *Hamburger Papyrus Bil. 1.* Die alttestamentlichen

Texte des Papyrus Bilinguis 1 der Staats- und Universitätsbibliothek Hamburg (Cahiers d'Orientalisme 18). Geneva

Dihle, A. (1989) *Die griechische und lateinische Literatur der Kaiserzeit von Augustus bis Justinian*. Munich

Dionisotti, A. C. (1982) 'From Ausonius' schooldays? A schoolbook and its relatives', *JRS* 72: 82–125

Dirkse, P. and Brashler, J. (1979) 'The Prayer of Thanksgiving', in D. M. Parrott (ed.), *Nag Hammadi Codices V, 2–5 and VI with Papyrus Berolinensis 8502, 1 and 4* (Nag Hammadi Studies 11) (Leiden) 375–87

Dirkse, P., Brashler, J. and Parrott, D. M. (1979) 'The Discourse on the Eighth and Ninth', in D. M. Parrott (ed.), *Nag Hammadi Codices V, 2–5 and VI with Papyrus Berolinensis 8502, 1 and 4* (Nag Hammadi Studies 11) (Leiden) 341–73

Dirkse, P. and Parrott, D. M. (1979) 'Asclepius 21–29', in D. M. Parrott (ed.), *Nag Hammadi Codices V, 2–5 and VI with Papyrus Berolinensis 8502, 1 and 4* (Nag Hammadi Studies 11) (Leiden) 395–451

Donadoni, S. (1987) 'Testi magici copti', in A. Roccati and A. Siliotti (eds.), *La magia in Egitto ai tempi dei faraoni* (Milan) 331–42

Draguet, R. (1980) *La Vie primitive de S. Antoine conservée en syriaque* (*CSCO* 418. Scriptores Syri 184). Louvain

Drake, H. (1976) *In Praise of Constantine*. Berkeley and Los Angeles

Drijvers, H. J. W. (1966) *Bardaisan of Edessa*. Assen

Drijvers, H. J. W. (1977) 'Hatra, Palmyra und Edessa', *ANRW* 2.8: 799–906

Drijvers, H. J. W. (1980) *Cults and Beliefs at Edessa*. Leiden

Drijvers, H. J. W. (1981) 'Edessa', *Theologische Realenzyklopädie* 9: 277–88

Drijvers, H. J. W. (1984) *East of Antioch*. London

Drijvers, H. J. W. (1985) 'Jews and Christians at Edessa', *JJS* 36: 88–102

Drijvers, H. J. W. (1989) 'Thomasakten', in W. Schneemelcher (ed.), *Neutestamentliche Apokryphen*. 5th edn (Tübingen) 2: 289–367

Duggan, L. G. (1989) 'Was art really the book of the illiterate?', *Word and Image* 5: 227–51

Dunbabin, K. (1978) *The Mosaics of Roman North Africa*. Oxford

Duval, R. (1892) *Histoire politique, religieuse et littéraire d'Édesse*. Paris

Duval, R. (1907) *La Littérature syriaque*. 3rd edn. Paris

Elliott, Alison Goddard (1987) *Roads to Paradise: Reading the Lives of the Early Saints*. Hanover and London

Elsner, J. (1995) *Art and the Roman Viewer: The Transformation of Art from the Pagan World to Christianity*. Cambridge

Engemann, J. (1986) 'Christianization of late antique art', in *The 17th Annual Byzantine Congress: Major Papers*. New Rochelle, NY

Enman, K. (1884) 'Eine verlorene Geschichte der römischen Kaiser und das Buch de viris illustribus urbis Romae', *Philologus*, suppl. 4: 337–501

Farina, R. (1966) *L'impero e l'imperatore cristiano in Eusebio di Cesarea*. Zurich

Fedwick, P. (ed.) (1981) *Basil of Caesarea: Christian, Humanist, Ascetic. A Sixteen-Hundredth Anniversary Symposium*, 2 vols. Toronto

Ferrua, A. (1960) *Le Pitture della Nuova Catacomba di Via Latina*. Vatican City

Ferrua, A. (1990) *The Unknown Catacomb*. London

Festugière, A. J. (1959) *Antioche païenne et chrétienne* (Bibliothèque des écoles françaises d'Athènes et de Rome 194). Rome

Fiey, J.-M. (1970) *Jalons pur une histoire de l'église en Iraq* (*CSCO* Subsidia 36). Louvain

Fiey, J.-M. (1977) *Nisibe, métropole syriaque orientale* (*CSCO* Subsidia 54). Louvain

Fitzgerald, J. T. and White, L. M. (eds.) (1983) *The Tabula of Cebes*. Chico, CA

Fontaine, J. (1980) *Etudes sur la poésie latine tardive d'Ausone à Prudence*. Paris

Fontaine, J. (1981) *Naissance de la poésie dans l'occident chrétien: Esquisse d'une histoire de la poésie latine chrétienne du III*ᵉ *au VI*ᵉ *siècle*. Paris

Fontaine, J. (1986) *Culture et spiritualité en Espagne du IV*ᵉ *au VI*ᵉ *siècle*. London

Fontaine, J. and Piétri, C. (eds.) (1985) *Le Monde latin antique et la Bible* (La bible de tous les temps II). Paris

Fowden, G. (1993) *Empire to Commonwealth: The Consequences of Monotheism in Late Antiquity*, Princeton, NJ

Frandsen, P. J. and Richter-Aerøe, E. (1981) 'Shenoute: a bibliography', in D. W. Young (ed.), *Studies Presented to Hans Jakob Polotsky* (East Gloucester, MA) 147–76

Funk, W.-P. (1976) 'Ein doppelt überliefertes Stück spätägyptischer Weisheit', *Zeitschrift für Ägyptische Sprache* 103: 8–21

Funk, W.-P. (1985) 'How closely related are the subakhmimic dialects?', *Zeitschrift für Ägyptische Sprache* 112: 124–39

Garbsch, J. and Overbeck, B. (eds.) (1989) *Spätantike zwischen Heidentum und Christentum*. Munich

Gardner, I. (1988) *Coptic Theological Papyri 2: Edition, Commentary, Translation* (Mitteilungen aus der Papyrussammlung der Österreichischen Nationalbibliothek N.S. 21). Vienna

Gardner, I. (1993) 'A Manichaean liturgical codex found at Kellis', *Orientalia* n.s. 62: 30–59

Garitte, G. (1955) *Lettres de S. Antoine* (*CSCO* 148. Scriptores Iberici 5). Louvain

Garzya, A. (1983) 'L'epistolografia letteraria tardoantica', in *Il mandarino e il quotidiano* (Naples) 115–48

Gasparro, G. S. (1985) *Soteriology and Mystic Aspects in the Cult of Cybele and Attis*. Leiden

Gellner, E. (1988) *Plough, Sword and Book*. London

Giversen, S. (1986a) *The Manichaean Coptic Papyri in the Chester Beatty Library* I: *Kephalaia. Facsimile Edition* (Cahiers d'Orientalisme 14). Geneva

Giversen, S. (1986b) *The Manichaean Coptic Papyri in the Chester Beatty Library* II: *Homilies and varia. Facsimile Edition* (Cahiers d'Orientalisme 15). Geneva

Giversen, S. (1988a) *The Manichaean Coptic Papyri in the Chester Beatty Library* III: *Psalm Book Part 1. Facsimile Edition* (Cahiers d'Orientalisme 16). Geneva

Giversen, S. (1988b) *The Manichaean Coptic Papyri in the Chester Beatty Library* IV: *Psalm Book Part 2. Facsimile Edition* (Cahiers d'Orientalisme 17). Geneva

Gnilka, C. (1984) *Chresis. Die Methode der Kirchenväter im Umgang mit der antiken Kultur*. Basel–Stuttgart

Goehring, J. E. (1984) 'A new Coptic fragment of Melito's Homily on the Passion', *Muséon* 97: 255–9

Goehring, J. E. (1986) *The Letter of Ammon and Pachomian Monasticism* (Patristische Texte und Studien 27). Berlin

Goehring, J. E. (1991) 'Crosby Schøyen Codex', in A. S. Atiya (ed.), *The Coptic Encyclopedia* 2 (New York) 657–8

Grabar, A. (1946) *Martyrium: Recherches sur le culte des reliques et l'art chrétien antique.* Paris

Grabar, A. (1967) *The Beginnings of Christian Art.* London

Grabar, A. (1969) *Christian Iconography: A Study of its Origins.* London

Grabar, A. (1972) 'Le tiers monde de l'Antiquité à l'école classique et son rôle dans la formation de l'art du Moyen Age', *Revue de l'art* 18: 1–59

Green, R. P. H. (1980) 'The correspondence of Ausonius', *L'antiquité classique* 49: 191–211

Green, R. P. H. (1991) *The Works of Ausonius.* Oxford

Griffith, S. H. (1987) 'Ephraem the Syrian's "Hymns against Julian": meditations on history and imperial power', *Vigiliae Christianae* 41: 238–66

Griffith, S. H. (1989–90) 'Images of Ephrem: the Syrian holy man and his church', *Traditio* 45: 7–33

Grigg, R. (1977) 'Constantine the Great and the cult without images', *Viator* 8: 1–32

Hadot, P. (1971) *Marius Victorinus, recherches sur sa vie et ses œuvres.* Paris

Hadot, P. (1984) *Arts libéraux et philosophie dans la pensée antique.* Paris

Hagiographie, cultures et sociétés, IVe–XIIe siècles, Actes du Colloque organisé à Nanterre et Paris (2–5 mai 1979). Paris, 1981

Hall, S. G. (1993) 'Eusebian and other sources in Vita Constantini I', in *Logos. Festschrift für Luise Abramowski* (Berlin) 239–63

Hannestad, N. (1994) *Tradition and Innovation in Late Antique Sculpture.* Aarhus

Harden, D. B. (ed.) (1987) *Glass of the Caesars.* Milan

Harries, J. and Wood, I. (eds.) (1993) *The Theodosian Code: Studies in the Imperial Law of Late Antiquity.* London

Hassall, M. W. C. and Ireland, R. I. (eds.) (1979) *De Rebus Bellicis* (BAR International series 63). Oxford

Hayes, E. R. (1930) *L'École d'Édesse.* Paris

Hellemo, G. (1989) *Adventus Domini: Eschatological Thought in Fourth Century Apses and Catechesis.* Leiden

Herzog, R. (1966) *Die allegorische Dichtkunst des Prudentius.* Munich

Herzog, R. (1975) *Die Bibelepik der lateinischen Spätantike: Formgeschichte einer erbaulichen Gattung* I. Munich

Herzog, R. (ed.) (1989) *Handbuch der lateinischen Literatur der Antike* (ed. R. Herzog and P. L. Schmidt) Vol. 5: *Restauration und Erneuerung. Die lateinischen Literatur von 284 bis 374 nach Christ.* Munich

Hock, R. F. and O'Neill, E. N. (1986) *The Chreia in Ancient Rhetoric* Vol. 1: *The Progymnasmata.* Atlanta, GA

Holum, K. (1990) 'Hadrian and St Helena: imperial travel and the origins of Christian Holy Land pilgrimage', in R. Ousterhout (ed.), *The Blessings of Pilgrimage* (Urbana and Chicago) 66–81

Horn, J. (1986) *Studien zu den Martyrern des nördlichen Oberägypten* 1 (Göttinger Orientforschungen, iv. Reihe: Ägypten, Band 15). Wiesbaden

Humphrey, J. (ed.) (1991) *Literacy in the Roman World.* Ann Arbor, MI

Hunger, H. (1978) *Die hochsprachliche profane Literatur der Byzantiner*, 2 vols. (Müllers Handbuch XII. 5.1–2). Munich

Hunt, E. D. (1985) 'Christians and Christianity in Ammianus Marcellinus', *CQ* n.s. 35: 186–200

Huskinson, J. (1974) 'Some pagan mythological figures and their significance in early Christian art', *PBSR* 42: 68–97

Huskinson, J. (1993) 'The later Roman empire', in J. Boardman (ed.), *The Oxford History of Classical Art* (Oxford) 297–344

Ihm, C. (1960) *Die Programme der christlichen Apsismalerei vom vierten Jahrhundert bis zur Mitte des achten Jahrhunderts.* Wiesbaden

Innes, D. and Winterbottom, M. (1988) *Sopatros the Rhetor: Studies in the Text of the Diairesis Zetematon.* London

Isenberg, W. W. and Layton, B. (1989) 'The Gospel According to Philip', in B. Layton (ed.), *Nag Hammadi Codex II, 2–7 together with XIII, 2*, Brit. Lib. Or. 4926(1), and P. Oxy. 1, 654, 655* 1 (Nag Hammadi Studies 20) (Leiden) 131–217

Jaeger, W. (1962) *Early Christianity and Greek Paideia.* Cambridge, MA

Janssens, Y. (1983) *Les Leçons de Silvanos* (Bibliothèque copte de Nag Hammadi, Section 'Textes' 13). Quebec

Jarry, J. (1972) 'Inscriptions syriaques et arabes du Tur 'Abdin', *Annales Islamologiques* 10: 207–50

Jenni, E. (1965) 'Die altsyrischen Inschriften, 1.–3. Jahrhundert', *Theol. Zeitschr.* 21: 371–85

Jeremias, G. (1980) *Die Holztzur der Basilica S. Sabina in Rom.* Tübingen

Johns, C. (1990) 'Research on Roman silver plate', *JRA* 3: 28–43

Johns, C. and Potter, T. (1983) *The Thetford Treasure.* London

Judge, E. A. (1979) 'Antike und Christentum: towards a definition of the field. A bibliographical survey', *ANRW* II. 23.1: 3–58

Kahle, P. E. (1954) *Bala'izah*, 2 vols. London

Kákosy, L. (1961) 'Remarks on the interpretation of a Coptic magical text', *Acta Orientalia Academiae Scientiarum Hungaricae* 13: 325–8

Kammerer, W. (1951) *A Coptic Bibliography.* Ann Arbor, MI

Kasser, R. (1958) *Papyrus Bodmer III: Évangile de Jean et Genèse I–IV, 2 en bohaïrique* (*CSCO* 178. Scriptores Coptici 26). Louvain

Kasser, R. (1960a) *Papyrus Bodmer VI: Livre des Proverbes* (*CSCO* 194. Scriptores Coptici 27). Louvain

Kasser, R. (1960b) 'Acta Pauli 1959', *Revue d'histoire et de philosophie religieuses* 40: 45–57

Kasser, R. (1965) 'Les dialectes coptes et les versions coptes bibliques', *Biblica* 46: 287–310

Kasser, R. (1980) 'Usages de la surligne dans le Papyrus Bodmer VI', *Bulletin de la Société d'Égyptologie, Genève* 4: 53–9

Kasser, R. (1984) 'Orthographie et phonologie de la variété subdialectale lycopolitaine des textes gnostiques coptes de Nag Hammadi', *Muséon* 97: 261–312

Kasser, R. (1991) 'Geography, Dialectal', in A. S. Atiya (ed.), *The Coptic Encyclopedia* 8 (New York) 133–41

Kennedy, George A. (1983) *Greek Rhetoric under Christian Emperors.* Princeton, NJ

Kennedy, H. and Liebeschuetz, J. H. W. G. (1988) 'Antioch and the villages of Northern Syria in the fifth and sixth centuries A.D. Trends and problems', *Nottingham Medieval Studies* 32: 65–90

Kent, J. P. C. and Painter, K. S. (eds.) (1977) *Wealth of the Roman World* A.D. *300–700*. London

Kenyon, F. G. (1937) *The Chester Beatty Biblical Papyri* 6. London

Kiilerich, B. (1993) *Fourth Century Classicism in the Plastic Arts*. Odense

Kirsten, E. (1959) 'Edessa', *RAC* 4: 552–97

Kirsten, E. (1963) 'Edessa. Ein römische Grenzstadt des 4. bis 6. Jahrhundert im Orient', *JbAC* 6: 144–72

Kitzinger, E. (1940) *Early Medieval Art*. London

Kitzinger, E. (1954) 'The cult of images before iconoclasm', *DOP* 7: 85–150

Kitzinger, E. (1977) *Byzantine Art in the Making: Main Lines of Stylistic Development in Mediterranean Art, 3rd–7th centuries*. London

Kleiner, D. E. E. (1992) *Roman Sculpture*. New Haven and London

Klijn, A. F. J. (1986) 'Jewish Christianity in Egypt', in Pearson and Goehring (eds.) (1986) 161–75

Kluge, K. and Lehmann-Hartleben, K. (1927) *Die Antike Grossbronzen: Grossbronzen der Römischen Kaiserzeit* Vol. II. Berlin and Leipzig

Koerster, H., Layton, B., Lambdin, T. O., and Attridge, H. W. (1989) 'The Gospel According to Thomas', in B. Layton (ed.), *Nag Hammadi Codex II, 2–7 together with XIII, 2*, Brit. Lib. Or. 4926(1), and P. Oxy. 1, 654, 655* 1 (Nag Hammadi Studies 20) (Leiden) 38–128

König, I. (1987) *Origo Constantini, Anonymus Valesianus* 1. Trier

Krause, M. (1980) 'Koptische Literatur', in W. Helck and W. Westendorf (eds.), *Lexicon der Ägyptologie* Vol. 3 (Wiesbaden) columns 694–728

Krause, M. (1981) 'Der Erlassbrief Theodors', in D. W. Young (ed.), *Studies Presented to Hans Jakob Polotsky* (East Gloucester) 220–38

Krautheimer, R. (ed.) (1937–77) *Corpus Basilicarum Christianarum Romae*, Vols. I–V. Vatican City

Krautheimer, R. (1961) 'The architecture of Sixtus III: a fifth-century renaissance?', in M. Meiss (ed.), *De Artibus Opuscula XL: Essays in Honor of E. Panofsky* (New York) 291–302

Krautheimer, R. (1967) 'The Constantinian Basilica', *DOP* 21: 117–40

Krautheimer, R. (1983) *Three Christian Capitals: Topography and Politics*. Berkeley and Los Angeles

Labourt, J. (1904) *Le Christianisme dans l'empire perse sous la dynastie sassanide*. Paris

Lacau, P. (1946) 'Fragments de l'Ascension d'Isaie en copte', *Muséon* 59: 453–67

Lafontaine, G. (1980a) 'La version copte bohaïrique du discours "Sur l'amour des pauvres" de Grégoire de Nazianze', *Muséon* 93: 199–236

Lafontaine, G. (1980b) 'La version copte sahidique du discours "Sur la Pâque" de Grégoire de Nazianze', *Muséon* 93: 37–52

Lafontaine, G. (1981) 'La version copte des discours de Grégoire de Nazianze', *Muséon* 94: 37–45

Laistner, M. L. W. (1951) *Christianity and Pagan Culture in the Later Roman Empire*. Ithaca, NY

Lamberton, R. (1986) *Homer the Theologian*. Berkeley and Los Angeles

Lane Fox, R. (1986) *Pagans and Christians*. London

Lawrence, M. (1961) 'Three pagan themes in Christian art', in M. Meiss (ed.), *De Artibus Opuscula XL: Essays in Honor of E. Panofsky* (New York) 323–34

Layton, B. (1976) 'Coptic language', in *The Interpreter's Dictionary of the Bible*, supplementary volume (Nashville) 174–9

Layton, B. (ed.) (1980) *The Rediscovery of Gnosticism* I: *The School of Valentinus* (Studies in the History of Religions [Supplements to *Numen*] 41). Leiden

Layton, B. (ed.) (1981) *The Rediscovery of Gnosticism* II: *Sethian Gnosticism* (Studies in the History of Religions [Supplements to *Numen*] 41). Leiden

Layton, B. (1985) 'Towards a new Coptic palaeography', in Orlandi and Wisse (eds.) (1985) 149–58

Layton, B. (1987) *The Gnostic Scriptures*. New York

Layton, B. (1989) 'Treatise Without Title on the Origin of the World: the British Library Fragments', in B. Layton (ed.), *Nag Hammadi Codex II, 2–7 together with XIII, 2*, Brit. Lib, Or. 4926(1), and P. Oxy. 1, 654, 655* 2 (Nag Hammadi Studies 21) (Leiden) 96–134

Lefort, L. T. (1925) *S. Pachomii vita bohairice scripta* (*CSCO*: Scriptores Coptici. Series tertia, Tomus 7). Paris

Lefort, L. T. (1933a) 'S. Athanase, écrivain copte', *Muséon* 46: 1–33

Lefort, L. T. (1933b) *S. Pachomii vitae sahidice scriptae* (*CSCO*: Scriptores Coptici. Series tertia, Tomus 8). Paris

Lefort, L. T. (1935) Review of Crum (1934–7), *Muséon* 48: 234–5

Lefort, L. T. (1938) 'Coptica Lovaniensia', *Muséon* 51: 1–32

Lefort, L. T. (1939) 'Fragments d'apocryphes en copte-akhmîmique', *Muséon* 52: 1–10

Lefort, L. T. (1940) *Les Manuscrits coptes de l'Université de Louvain* I. Louvain

Lefort, L. T. (1952) *Les Pères apostoliques en copte* (*CSCO* 135. Scriptores Coptici 17). Louvain

Lefort, L. T. (1956a) *Oeuvres de S. Pachôme et de ses disciples: Textus* (*CSCO* 159. Scriptores Coptici 23). Louvain

Lefort, L. T. (1956b) *Oeuvres de S. Pachôme et de ses disciples: Versio* (*CSCO* 160. Scriptores Coptici 24). Louvain

von Lemm, O. (1890–2) 'Koptische apokryphe Apostelacten II', *Mélanges asiatiques tirés du Bulletin de l'Académie Impériale des Sciences de St.-Petersbourg* 10: 293–386

Lepelley, C. (ed.) (1983) *Les Lettres de saint Augustin découvertes par Johannes Divjak* (Communications présentées au colloque des 20 et 21 Septembre 1982). Paris

Levin, I. (1985) *The Quedlinburg Itala*. Leiden

Lewy, H. (1978) *Chaldaean Oracles and Theurgy: Mysticism, Magic and Platonism in the Later Roman Empire*, ed. M. Tardieu, 2nd edn. Paris

Liebeschuetz, Wolfgang (1992) 'Hochschule', *RAC* 15, 858–911. Stuttgart

Louth, A. (1990) 'The date of Eusebius's *Historia Ecclesiastica*', *JThS* n.s. 41: 111–23

Lüddeckens, E., Kropp, A., Hermann, A. and Weber, M. (1968) *Demotische und koptische Texte* (Wissenschaftliche Abhandlungen der Arbeitsgemeinschaft für Forschung des Landes Nordrhein-Westfalen, Sonderreihe – Papyrologica Coloniensia 2). Cologne and Opladen

McCullough, W. S. (1982) *A Short History of Syriac Christianity to the Rise of Islam*. Chico, CA

McLynn, N. B. (1994) *Ambrose of Milan: Church and Court in a Christian Capital*. Berkeley, CA

MacMullen, R. (1962) 'Roman bureaucratese', *Traditio* 18: 364–78

MacMullen, R. (1964) 'Some pictures in Ammianus Marcellinus', *Art Bulletin* 46: 435–55

MacMullen, R. (1976) *Roman Government's Response to Crisis, A.D. 235–337.* New Haven, CT

MacMullen, R. (1981) *Paganism in the Roman Empire.* New Haven, CT

MacMullen, R. (1989) 'The preacher's audience (A.D. 350–450)', *JThS* n.s. 40: 503–11

MacRae, G. W. (1979) 'The Apocalypse of Adam', in D. M. Parrott (ed.), *Nag Hammadi Codices V, 2–5 and VI with Papyrus Berolinensis 8502, 1 and 4* (Nag Hammadi Studies 11) (Leiden) 151–95

McVey, K. E. (1989) *Ephrem the Syrian: Hymns.* New York

Madden, T. F. (1992) 'The serpent column of Delphi in Constantinople: placement, purposes and mutilations', *BMGS* 16: 111–45

Mahé, J.-P. (1978–82) *Hermès en Haute-Égypte*, 2 vols. (Bibliothèque copte de Nag Hammadi, Section 'Textes' 3 and 7). Quebec

Malamud, M. A. (1989) *A Poetics of Transformation: Prudentius and Classical Mythology.* Ithaca, NY

Malbon, E. S. (1990) *The Iconography of the Sarcophagus of Junius Bassus.* Princeton, NJ

Mango, C. A. (1963) 'Antique statuary and the Byzantine beholder', *DOP* 17: 55–75

Mango, C. A. (1974) *Byzantine Architecture.* New York

Mango, C. A. (1985) *Le Développement urbain de Constantinople (IVe–VIIe siècles).* Paris

Mango, C. A. (1986) *The Art of the Byzantine Empire 312–1453.* Toronto

Mango, C. A. (1993) *Studies on Constantinople.* Aldershot

Mango, M. M. and Bennett, A. (1994) *The Sevso Treasure.* Part 1 (*JRA* Supplement 12). Ann Arbor

Marriott, I. (1979) 'The authorship of the Historia Augusta: two computer studies', *JRS* 69: 65–77

Marrou, H. I. (1938) *Saint Augustin et la fin de la culture antique.* Paris

Marrou, H. I. (1949) *Saint Augustin et la fin de la culture antique. Retractatio.* Paris

Mathews, T. F. (1993) *The Clash of the Gods: A Reinterpretation of Early Christian Art.* Princeton, NJ

Mathison, R. (1981) 'Epistolography, literary circles and family ties in late Roman Gaul', *TAPA* 111: 95–105

Mathison, R. (1989) *Ecclesiastical Factionalism and Religious Controversy in Fifth-Century Gaul.* Washington, DC

Matthews, J. F. (1974) 'The letters of Symmachus', in Binns, *Latin Literature* 58–99

Mercati, G. (1907) 'A supposed homily of Eusebius of Caesarea', *JThS* 8: 114

Meredith, A. (1976) 'Asceticism – Christian and Greek', *JThS* n.s. 27: 313–22

Metzger, B. M. (1977) *The Early Versions of the New Testament.* Oxford

Metzger, B. M. (1991) 'New Testament, Coptic Versions of the', in A. S. Atiya (ed.), *The Coptic Encyclopedia* 6 (New York) 1787–9

Meyer, M. W. (1985) 'The love spell of *PGM* IV, 94–153: introduction and structure', in Orlandi and Wisse (eds.) (1985) 193–201

Milburn, R. (1988) *Early Christian Art and Architecture.* Aldershot

Miles, M. R. (1985) *Image as Insight: Visual Understanding in Western Christianity and Secular Culture.* Boston, MA

Miles, M. R. (1993) 'Santa Maria Maggiore's fifth-century mosaics: triumphal Christianity and the Jews', *HThR* 86: 155–75

Millar, F. G. B. (1992) 'The Jews of the Graeco-Roman diaspora between paganism and Christianity, A.D. 312–438', in J. Lieu, J. North and T. Rajak (eds.), *The
Jews among Pagans and Christians in the Roman Empire* (London) 97–123

Millar, F. G. B. (1993) *The Roman Near East, 31 B.C.–A.D. 337.* Cambridge, MA

Milner, N. P. (trans.) (1993) *Vegetius: Epitome of Military Science.* Liverpool

Mink, G. (1972) 'Die koptischen Versionen des Neuen Testaments. Die sprach-
lichen Probleme bei ihrer Bewertung für die griechische Textgeschichte', in
K. Aland (ed.), *Die alten Übersetzungen des Neuen Testaments, die Kirchenväterzitate
und Lektionare* (Arbeiten zur Neutestamentlichen Textforschung 5) (Berlin)
160–299

Momigliano, A. (1963) 'Pagan and Christian historiography in the fourth century
A.D.', in Momigliano, *Conflict* 79–99

Momigliano, A. (1971) 'Popular religious beliefs and the Late Roman historians',
Studies in Church History 8: 1–18

Momigliano, A. (1974) 'The lonely historian Ammianus Marcellinus', *Ann. Scuola
Normale di Pisa* III. iv. 4: 1393–1407

Momigliano, A. (1985) 'The Life of St. Macrina by Gregory of Nyssa', in J. Ober
and J. W. Eadie (eds.), *The Craft of the Ancient Historian* (Lanham, MD) 443–58

Momigliano, A. (1991) *The Classical Foundations of Modern Historiography.* Berkeley
and Los Angeles

Mondésert, A. (ed.) (1984) *Le Monde grec ancien et la Bible* (La Bible de tous les temps
I). Paris

Monfrin, F. (1991) 'A propos de Milan chrétien: siège épiscopal et topographie
chrétienne IVᵉ–VIᵉ siècles', *Cahiers Archéologiques* 39: 7–46

Morey, C. R. (1942) *Early Christian Art.* Princeton, NJ

Moss, C. (1962) *Catalogue of Syriac Printed Books and Related Literature in the British
Museum.* London

Murphy, J. J. (1972) *A Synoptic History of Classical Rhetoric.* New York

Murray, C. (1981) *Rebirth and Afterlife: A Study of the Transmutation of Some Pagan
Imagery in Early Christian Funerary Art* (BAR 100). Oxford

Murray, R. M. (1975) *Symbols of Church and Kingdom: A Study in Early Syriac Tradition.*
Cambridge

Murray, R. M. (1977) 'Some rhetorical patterns in early Syriac literature', in R. H.
Fischer (ed.), *A Tribute to A. Vööbus* (Chicago) 109–31

Murray, R. M. (1982) 'Ephraem Syrus', *Theologische Realenzyklopädie* 9: 755–62

Mussies, G. (1979) 'The Interpretatio Judaica of Sarapis', in M. J. Vermaseren (ed.),
Studies in Hellenistic Religion (Leiden) 189–214

Nagel, P. (1971) 'Die Einwirkung des Griechischen auf die Entstehung der koptischen Literatursprache', in F. Altheim and R. Stiehl (eds.), *Christentum am
Roten Meer* I (Berlin) 327–55

Nagel, P. (1981) 'Zographein und das "Bild" des Mani in den koptische-manichai-
schen Texten', in H. Golz (ed.), *Eikon und Logos* (Halle) 199–238

Nagel, P. (1983–4) 'Studien zur Textüberlieferung des sahidischen Alten
Testaments', *Zeitschrift für Ägyptische Sprache* 110: 51–74; 111: 138–64

Nagel, P. (1989) 'Editionen koptischer Bibeltexte seit Till 1960', *Archiv für
Papyrusforschung* 35: 43–100

Nagel, P. (1991a) 'Lycopolitan', in A. S. Atiya (ed.), *The Coptic Encyclopedia* 8 (New
York) 151–9

Nagel, P. (1991b) 'Old Testament, Coptic Versions of the', in A. S. Atiya (ed.), *The Coptic Encyclopedia* 6 (New York) 1836–40

Neusner, J. (1971) *Aphrahat and Judaism: The Christian–Jewish Argument in Fourth-century Iran* (Studia Post-Biblica 19). Leiden

Norden, E. (1909) *Der antike Kunstprosa vom VI. Jahrhundert v. Chr. bis in die Zeit der Renaissance*, 2 vols. Leipzig

O'Meara, D. J. (1989) *Pythagoras Revived: Mathematics and Philosophy in Late Antiquity*. Oxford

Onians, J. (1980) 'Abstraction and imagination in late antiquity', *Art History* 3: 1–24

Onians, J. (1988) *Bearers of Meaning: The Classical Orders in Antiquity, the Middle Ages and the Renaissance*. Princeton, NJ

L'Orange, H. P. (1965) *Art Forms and Civic Life in the Late Roman Empire*. Princeton, NJ

L'Orange, H. P. and Nordhagen, P. J. (1966) *Mosaics*. London

Orlandi, T. (1970) *Elementi di lingua e letteratura copta*. Milan

Orlandi, T. (1973) 'Patristica copta e patristica greca', *Vetera Christianorum* 10: 327–41

Orlandi, T. (1975) 'Basilio di Cesarea nella letteratura copta (appendici di J. Gribomont)', *Rivista degli studi orientali* 49: 49–59

Orlandi, T. (1976) 'Les manuscrits coptes de Dublin, du British Museum et de Vienne', *Muséon* 89: 323–38

Orlandi, T. (1981) 'Due rotoli copte papiracei da Dublino (Lettere di Horsiesi)', in R. S. Bagnall, G. M. Browne, A. E. Hanson and L. Koenen (eds.), *Proceedings of the Sixteenth International Congress of Papyrology, New York, 24–31 July, 1980* (American Studies in Papyrology 23) (Chico, CA) 499–508

Orlandi, T. (1982–) *Coptic Bibliography*. Rome

Orlandi, T. (1983) 'Gli apocrifi copti', *Augustinianum* 23: 57–71

Orlandi, T. (1984) 'Le traduzioni dal greco e lo sviluppo della letteratura copta', in P. Nagel (ed.), *Graeco-Coptica: Griechen und Kopten im byzantinischen Ägypten* (Halle) 181–203

Orlandi, T. (1985) 'Theophilus of Alexandria in Coptic literature', in E. Livingstone (ed.), *Papers Presented to the Seventh International Congress on Patristic Studies* 1 (Studia Patristica 16. Texte und Untersuchungen zur Geschichte der altchristlichen Literatur 127) (Berlin) 101–4

Orlandi, T. (1986) 'Coptic literature', in Pearson and Goehring (eds.) (1986) 51–81

Orlandi, T. (1991a) 'Hagiography, Coptic', in A. S. Atiya (ed.), *The Coptic Encyclopedia* 4 (New York) 1191–7

Orlandi, T. (1991b) 'Literature, Coptic', in A. S. Atiya (ed.), *The Coptic Encyclopedia* 5 (New York) 1451–60

Orlandi, T. and Wisse, F. (eds.) (1985) *Acts of the Second International Congress of Coptic Studies*. Rome

Ortiz de Urbina, I. (1965) *Patrologia Syriaca*, 2nd edn. Rome

Painter, K. (1977) *The Mildenhall Treasure*. London

Painter, K. (1990) 'The Sevso Treasure', *Minerva* 1: 4–11

Palmer, Anne-Marie (1989) *Prudentius on the Martyrs*. Oxford

Parkes, J. (1934) *The Conflict of the Church and the Synagogue*. New York

Pasquali, G. (1910) 'Die Composition des Vita Constantini des Eusebius', *Hermes* 46: 369–86

Pearson, B. A. (1981) 'The figure of Seth in gnostic literature', in Layton (ed.) (1981) 472–504

Pearson, B. A. and Goehring, J. E. (eds.) (1986) *The Roots of Egyptian Christianity.* Philadelphia, PA

Peel, M. L. (1985) 'The Treatise on the Resurrection', in Attridge (ed). (1985) 123–57

Peeters, P. (1950) *Orient et Byzance. Le Tréfonds oriental de l'hagiographie byzantine* (Subsidia Hagiographica 26). Brussels

Pelikan, J. (1993) *Christianity and Classical Culture.* New Haven, CT

Perez, G. A. (1991) 'Apocryphal literature', in A. S. Atiya (ed.), *The Coptic Encyclopedia* 1 (New York) 161–9

Peterson, E. (1947) 'Ein Fragment des Hierakas(?)', *Muséon* 60: 257–60

Petit, P. (1956) *Les Étudiants de Libanios.* Paris

Pierce, P. (1989) 'The Arch of Constantine: propaganda and ideology in late Roman art', *Art History* 12: 387–418

Pierre, M.-J. (1988–9) *Aphraate le sage persan. Les Exposés* I–II. Paris

Pietersma, A., Comstock, S. T. and Attridge, H. W. (1981) *The Apocalypse of Elijah* (Society of Biblical Literature Texts and Translations 19, Pseudepigrapha Series 9). Chico, CA

Poirier, P.-H. and Painchaud, L. (1983) *Les Sentences de Sextus-Fragments-Fragment de la République de Platon* (Bibliothèque copte de Nag Hammadi, Section 'Textes' 11). Quebec

Polotsky, H. J. (1934) *Manichäische Homilien* (Manichäische Handschriften der Sammlung A. Chester Beatty 1). Stuttgart

Polotsky, H. J. and Böhlig, A. (1940) *Kephalaia* 1. Hälfte (Manichäische Handschriften der Staatlichen Museen Berlin 1). Stuttgart

Preisendanz, K. (1928–31) *Papyri Graecae Magicae,* 2 vols. Leipzig and Berlin

Quaegebeur, J. (1982) 'De la préhistoire de l'écriture copte', *Orientalia Lovaniensia Periodica* 13: 125–36

Quasten, J. (1950) *Patrology* Vols. III–IV. Westminster, MD. (Repr. 1986)

Quecke, H. (1975a) *Die Briefe Pachoms* (Textus Patristici et Liturgici 11). Regensburg

Quecke, H. (1975b) 'Ein Brief von einem Nachfolger Pachoms (Chester Beatty Library Ms. Ac. 1486)', *Orientalia* n.s. 44: 426–33

Quecke, H. (1976) 'Die griechische Übersetzung der Pachombriefe', *Studia Papyrologica* 15: 153–9

Rahner, H. (1963) *Greek Myths and Christian Mystery.* London

Reinink, G. J. and Vanstiphout, H. L. J. (1991) *Dispute Poems and Dialogues in the Ancient and Mediaeval Near East* (Orientalia Lovaniensia Analecta 42). Louvain

Riegl, A. (1985) *Late Roman Art Industry.* Rome (trans. R. Winkes from the first edition of 1901)

Roberts, C. H. (1979) *Manuscript, Society and Belief in Early Christian Egypt.* London

Roberts, C. H. and Skeat, T. C. (1983) *The Birth of the Codex.* London

Roberts, M. (1985) *Biblical Epic and Rhetorical Paraphrase in Late Antiquity.* Liverpool

Roberts, M. (1989) *The Jeweled Style: Poetry and Poetics in Late Antiquity.* Ithaca, NY, and London

Roberts, M. (1993) *Poetry and the Cult of the Martyrs: The Liber Peristephanon of Prudentius.* Ann Arbor, MI

Robinson, J. M. (ed.) (1972–84) *The Facsimile Edition of the Nag Hammadi Codices,* 12 vols. (published under the auspices of the Department of Antiquities of the Arab Republic of Egypt in conjunction with the United Nations Educational, Scientific and Cultural Organization). Leiden

Robinson, J. M. (ed.) (1988) *The Nag Hammadi Library in English*. 3rd edn. Leiden

Robinson, J. M. (1990) 'The first Christian monastic library', in W. Godlewski (ed.), *Coptic Studies: Acts of the Third International Congress of Coptic Studies, Warsaw, 20–25 August, 1984* (Warsaw) 371–8

Rodenwaldt, G. (1939) 'The transition to late-classical art', *CAH* XII¹ 544–70

Rösch, F. (1910) *Bruchstücke der Ersten Clemensbriefes nach dem achmimischen Papyrus der Strassburger Universitäts- und Landesbibliothek mit biblischen Texten derselben Handschrift*. Strasburg

Rubenson, Samuel (1990) *The Letters of St Antony*. Lund

Ruether, R. Radford (1969) *Gregory of Nazianzus, Rhetor and Philosopher*. Oxford

Ruggini, L. C. (1977) 'The ecclesiastical histories and the pagan historiography: providence and miracles', *Athenaeum* n.s. 55: 107–26

Ruggini, L. C. (1981) 'Il miracolo nella cultura del tardo impero: concetto e funzione', in *Hagiographie, cultures et sociétés, IVᵉ–XIIᵉ siècles*. Actes du colloque organisé à Nanterre et à Paris (2–5 mai 1979) (Paris) 161–202

Rusch, W. (1977) *The Later Latin Fathers*. London

Russell, D. and Wilson, N. (1981) *Menander Rhetor*. Oxford

Rutschowscaya, M.-H. (1990) *Coptic Fabrics*. Paris

Sanders, H. A. and Schmidt, C. (1927) *The Minor Prophets in the Freer Collection and the Berlin Fragment of Genesis* (University of Michigan Studies, Humanistic Series 21). New York

Sansoni, R. (1969) *I sarcofagi paleocristiani a porte di città*. Bologna

Saradi-Mendelovici, H. (1990) 'Christian attitudes towards pagan monuments in late antiquity', *DOP* 44: 47–61

Satzinger, H. (1991) 'Old Coptic', in A. S. Atiya (ed.), *The Coptic Encyclopedia* 8 (New York) 169–75

Saxl, F. (1957) 'Pagan and Jewish elements in early Christian sculpture', in *Lectures* Vol. I (London) 45–57

Schall, A. (1960) *Studien über griechische Fremdwörter im Syrischen*. Darmstadt

Schenke, H.-M. (1981) 'The phenomenon and significance of gnostic Sethianism', in Layton (ed.) (1981) 588–616

Schlunk, H. (1988) *Die Mosaikkuppel von Centcelles*. Mainz

Schmid, W. and Stählin, O. (eds.) (1924) *Wilhelm von Christs Geschichte der griechischen Literatur*, 6th edn, 7.2.2, *Die nachklassische Periode der griechischen Literatur, 100–530 A.D.* Munich

Schmidt, C. (1904) *Acta Pauli aus der Heidelberger koptischen Papyrushandschrift Nr. 1*, 2 vols. (Veröffentlichungen aus der Heidelberger Papyrus-Sammlung 2). Leipzig.

Schmidt, C. (1905) *Acta Pauli aus der Heidelberger koptischen Handschrift Nr. 1*, Zusätze zur ersten Ausgabe. Leipzig

Schmidt, C. (1908) *Die Erste Clemensbrief in altkoptischer Übersetzung* (Texte und Untersuchungen zur Geschichte der altchristlichen Literatur 32. Band, Heft 1). Leipzig

Schmidt, C. (1909) 'Ein neues Fragment der Heidelberger Acta Pauli', in *Sitzungsberichte der königlich preussischen Akademie der Wissenschaften* (Phil.-hist. Klasse) 216–20

Schmidt,C. (1919) *Gespräche Jesu mit seinen Jüngern nach der Auferstehung*. Leipzig

Schmidt, C. (1978a) *Pistis Sophia*, trans. V. MacDermot (Nag Hammadi Studies 9). Leiden

Schmidt, C. (1978b) *The Books of Jeu and the Untitled Text in the Bruce Codex*, trans. V. MacDermot (Nag Hammadi Studies 13). Leiden

Schmidt, C. and Polotsky, H. J. (1933) 'Ein Mani-Fund in Ägypten', in *SPAW* (Phil.-hist. Klasse) 1: 4–90

Scholer, D. M. (1971) *Nag Hammadi Bibliography 1948–1969* (Nag Hammadi Studies 1). Leiden. Annual supplements in *Novus Testamentum* from 1971 onwards

Seager, R. (1986) *Ammianus Marcellinus: Seven Studies in his Language and Thought*. Columbia, MO 1986

Segal, J. B. (1955) 'Mesopotamian communities from Julian to the rise of Islam', *PBA* 41: 109–39

Segal, J. B. (1970) *Edessa, 'The Blessed City'*. Oxford

Shelton, K. (1981) *The Esquiline Treasure*. London

Shelton, K. (1989) 'Roman aristocrats, Christian commissions: the Carrand Dyptych', in F. M. Clover and R. S. Humphreys (eds.), *Tradition and Innovation in Late Antiquity* (Madison, WI, and London) 105–27

Shisha-Halevy, A. (1976) 'Akhmîmoid features in Shenoute's dialect', *Muséon* 89: 353–66

Shisha-Halevy, A. (1986) *Coptic Grammatical Categories* (Analecta Orientalia 53). Rome

Shisha-Halevy, A. (1991a) 'Bohairic', in A. S. Atiya (ed.), *The Coptic Encyclopedia* 8 (New York) 53–60

Shisha-Halevy, A. (1991b) 'Shenutean idiom', in A. S. Atiya (ed.), *The Coptic Encyclopedia* 8 (New York) 202–4

Simon, J. (1949–66) 'Bibliographie copte. 1–18', *Orientalia* n.s. 18 (1949): 100–20, 216–46; 19 (1950): 187–201, 295–327; 20 (1951): 291–305, 423–42; 21 (1952): 339–57; 22 (1953): 39*–63*; 23 (1954): 70*–97*; 24 (1955): 54*–76*; 25 (1956): 49*–73*; 26 (1957): 116*–39*; 27 (1958): 48*–67*; 28 (1959): 91*–114*; 29 (1960): 45*–69*; 30 (1961): 62*–88*; 31 (1962): 51*–77*; 32 (1963): 114*–36*; 33 (1964): 124*–45*; 34 (1965): 215*–52*; 35 (1966): 139*–71*

Simon, J. and Quecke, H. (1967) 'Koptische Bibliographie. 19', *Orientalia* n.s. 36: 157*–211*

Sivan, H. (1993) *Ausonius of Bordeaux: Genesis of a Gallic Aristocracy*. London

Smith, R. R. R. (1985) 'Roman portraits: honours, empresses and late emperors', *JRS* 75: 209–21

Sorabji, R. (1990) *Aristotle Transformed: The Ancient Commentators and their Influence*. London

Spain, S. (1979) '"The Promised Blessing": the iconography of the mosaics of Sta Maria Maggiore', *Art Bulletin* 61: 518–40

Spira, A. (ed.) (1984) *The Biographical Works of Gregory of Nyssa*. Philadelphia, PA

Spira, A. (1985) 'Volkstümlichkeit und Kunst in der griechischen Väterpredigt des 4. Jahrhunderts', *JöB* 35: 55–73

Stambaugh, J. (1972) *Sarapis under the Ptolemies.* Leiden

Steindorff, G. (1899) *Die Apokalypse des Elias, eine unbekannte Apokalypse und Bruchstücke der Sophonias-Apokalypse* (Texte und Untersuchungen zur Geschichte der altchristlichen Literatur. Neu Folge, Band 2, Heft 3a). Leipzig

Stern, H. (1958) 'Les mosaïques de l'église de Sainte-Constance à Rome', *DOP* 12: 157–218

Stevenson, J. (1978) *The Catacombs.* London

La storiografia ecclesiastica nella tarda antichità. Atti del convegno tenuto in Erice (3–8 xii 1978). Messina, 1980

Stzrygowski, J. (1923) *The Origin of Christian Church Art.* Oxford

Sullivan, R. W. (1994) 'Saints Peter and Paul: some ironic aspects of their imaging', *Art History* 17: 59–80

Sundermann, W. (1988) Review of Giversen (1986a, 1986b), *BSOAS* 51: 569–70

Syme, R. (1968) *Ammianus and the Historia Augusta.* Oxford

Syme, R. (1971a) *Emperors and Biography.* Oxford

Syme, R. (1971b) *The Historia Augusta: A Call of Clarity.* Bonn

Taylor, J. E. (1993) *Christians and the Holy Places: The Myth of Jewish-Christian Origins.* Oxford

Teixidor, J. (1990) 'Deux documents syriaques du III siècle après J.-C. provenant du Moyen Euphrate', *CRAI*: 146–66

Teixidor, J. (1993) 'Un document syriaque de fermage de 242 après J-C', *Semitica* 41/2: 195–208

Thraede, K. (1965) *Studien zur Sprache und Stil des Prudentius.* Göttingen

Till, W. (1931) *Osterbrief und Predigt in achmimischem Dialekt* (Studien zur Epigraphik und Papyruskunde, Band 11, Schrift 1). Leipzig

Till, W. (1959–60) 'Coptic biblical texts published after Vaschalde's lists', *Bulletin of the John Rylands Library* 42: 220–40

Till, W. and Schenke, H.-M. (1972) *Die gnostischen Schriften des koptischen Papyrus Berolinensis 8502.* 2nd edn (Texte und Untersuchungen zur Geschichte der altchristlichen Literatur 60). Berlin

Timbie, J. (1986) 'The state of research on the career of Shenoute of Atripe', in Pearson and Goehring (eds.) (1986) 258–70

Toynbee, J. M. C. (1964) 'A new Roman mosaic pavement found in Dorset', *JRS* 54: 7–14

Toynbee, J. M. C. (1968) 'Some pagan motifs and practices in Christian art and ritual in Great Britain', in M. W. Barley and R. P. C. Hanson (eds.), *Christianity in Britain 300–700* (Leicester) 177–92

Toynbee, J. M. C. (1986) *The Roman Art Treasures from the Temple of Mithras.* London

Toynbee, J. M. C. and Ward-Perkins, J. B. (1956) *The Shrine of St Peter and the Vatican Excavations.* London

Trilling, J. (1987) 'Late antique and sub-antique or the "decline of form" reconsidered', *DOP* 41: 468 76

Trilling, J. (1989) 'The soul of the empire: style and meaning in the mosaic pavement of the Byzantine imperial palace in Constantinople', *DOP* 43: 27–72

Tronzo, W. (1986) *The Via Latina Catacomb.* Philadelphia, PA

Turcan, R. (1975) *Mithras Platonicus.* Leiden

Turner, J. D. and Layton, B. (1989) 'The Book of Thomas the Contender Writing to

VI. ART AND CULTURE

the Perfect', in B. Layton (ed.), *Nag Hammadi Codex II, 2–7 together with XIII, 2*, Brit. Lib. Or. 4926(1), and P. Oxy. 1, 654, 655* 2 (Nag Hammadi Studies 21) (Leiden) 173–205

Vaccari, A. (1951) in M. Norsa and V. Bartoletti (eds.), *Papiri Greci e Latini (PSI 12)* 107–10 (no. 1273) Florence

Van Rompay, L. (1990) 'Palmyra, Emesa en Edessa', *Phoenix* (Leiden) 36: 73–84

Vaschalde, A. (1919–33) 'Ce qui a été publié des versions coptes de la Bible', *Revue Biblique* 28 (1919): 220–43, 513–31; 29 (1920): 91–106, 241–58; 30 (1921): 237–46; 31 (1922): 81–8, 234–58; *Muséon* 43 (1930): 409–31; 45 (1932): 117–56; 46 (1933): 299–313

Veilleux, A. (1980–2) *Pachomian Koinonia*, 3 vols. (Cistercian Studies Series 45–7). Kalamazoo, MI

Veilleux, A. (1986) 'Monasticism and gnosis in Egypt', in Pearson and Goehring (eds.) (1986) 271–306

Vessey, M. (1991) 'Patristics and literary history', *Journal of Literature and Theology* 5: 341–54 (discussion of Herzog)

Volbach, W. F. (1976) *Elfenbeinarbeiten der Spätantike und des frühen Mittelalters.* Mainz

Volbach, W. F. and Hirmer, M. (1961) *Early Christian Art.* London

Vööbus, A. (1958–88) *History of Asceticism in the Syrian Orient.* 2 vols. (*CSCO*, Subsidia 14, 17, 81). Louvain

Vööbus, A. (1965) *History of the School of Nisibis* (*CSCO*, Subsidia 26). Louvain

Vycichl, W. (1991) 'Magic', in A. S. Atiya (ed.), *The Coptic Encyclopedia* 5 (New York) 1499–1509

Walker, P. W. L. (1990) *Holy City, Holy Places: Christian Attitudes to Jerusalem and the Holy Land in the Fourth Century.* Oxford

Walter, C. (1984) 'Expressionism and Hellenism', *Revue des études byzantines* 42: 265–88

Ward-Perkins, J. B. (1954) 'Constantine and the origins of the Christian Basilica', *Papers of the British School at Rome* 22: 69–90

Ward-Perkins, J. B. (1966) 'Memoria, martyr's tomb and martyr's church', *JThS* 17: 20–37

Watson, C. J. (1981) 'The program of the Brescia Casket', *Gesta* 20: 283–98

Watts, D. (1990) *Christians and Pagans in Roman Britain.* London

Weigandt, P. (1969) 'Zur Geschichte der koptischen Bibelübersetzungen', *Biblica* 50: 80–95

Weitzmann, K. (1959) *Ancient Book Illumination.* Cambridge, MA

Weitzmann, K. (1970) *Illustrations in Roll and Codex.* Princeton, NJ

Weitzmann, K. (1977) *Late Antique and Early Christian Book Illumination.* New York

Weitzmann, K. (ed.) (1979) *The Age of Spirituality: Late Antique and Early Christian Art. Third to Seventh Century.* Princeton, NJ

Weitzmann, K. (ed.) (1980) *The Age of Spirituality: A Symposium.* Princeton, NJ

Weitzmann, K. and Kessler, H. (1990) *The Frescoes of the Dura Synagogue and Christian Art.* Washington, DC

White, L. M. (1990) *Building God's House in the Roman World.* Baltimore and London

Widengren, G. (1946) *Mesopotamian Elements in Manichaeism.* Uppsala and Leipzig

Wiessner, G. (1967) *Untersuchungen zur syrischen Literaturgeschichte* Vol. 1 *Zur*

Märtyrerüberlieferung aus der Christenverfolgung Schapurs II (Abh. Ak. Wiss. Göttingen, phil.-hist. kl. III.67). Göttingen

Wilkinson, J. (1971) *Egeria's Travels*. London (rev. edn, *Egeria's Travels to the Holy Land*, 1981, Jerusalem)

Williams, A. L. (1935) *Adversus Iudaeos: A Bird's Eye View of Christian Apologetics*. Cambridge

Williams, F. E. (1985) 'The Apocryphon of James', in Attridge (ed.) (1985) 13–53

Willis, W. H. (1961) 'The new collections of papyri at the University of Mississippi', in L. Amundsen and V. Skånland (eds.), *Proceedings of the IX. International Congress of Papyrology* (Oslo) 381–92

Wilson, R. J. A. (1983) *Piazza Armerina*. St Albans

Winkelmann, F. (1990) 'Kirchengeschichtswerke', in Winkelmann and Brandes (1990) 202–12, with 365–6

Winkelmann, F. and Brandes, W. (eds.) (1990) *Quellen zur Geschichte des frühen Byzanz (4.–9. Jahrhundert)*. Berlin

Wintermute, O. S. (1983) 'Apocalypse of Zephaniah', in J. H. Charlesworth (ed.), *The Old Testament Pseudepigrapha* 1 (London) 497–515

Wipszycka, E. (1984) 'Le degré d'alphabétisation en Égypte byzantine', *REA* 30: 279–96

Wisse, F. (1981) 'Stalking those elusive Sethians', in Layton (ed.) (1981) 563–76

Witke, C. (1971) *Numen Litterarum: The Old and the New in Latin Poetry from Constantine to Gregory the Great*. Leiden

Wright, D. H. (1993) *The Vatican Vergil: A Masterpiece of Late Antique Art*. Berkeley and Los Angeles

Young, F. (1983) *From Nicaea to Chalcedon: A Guide to the Literature and its Background*. London

Zetzel, J. (1981) *Latin Textual Criticism in Antiquity*. New York

INDEX

References in italics are to maps (by map number) and illustrations (by page number).

Arrangement of material within entries is predominantly chronological, though some material of a topical nature is alphabetically ordered; all dates are A.D.

Footnotes are referred to only where the subject is not mentioned in the corresponding page of text.

Aba (lady of Seleucia, Cilicia) 633
Abba (Syriac author) 709–10
Abinnaeus, Flavius 227n103, 230, 231
Ablabius, Flavius (praetorian prefect) 4, 40
Abora, river 74
Abraham, bishop of Harran 715n14
Abraham, Testament of (Coptic) 724
Abraham of Qidun 710, 718
Abundantius (*magister*) 115
Acacius, bishop of Amida 435
Acacius, bishop of Caesarea 36, 37
Acacius, St 401
Academy at Athens 680, 682
Acholius, bishop of Thessalonica 579n40
Acts, apocryphal *see under individual saints' names*
Ad Salices *3 Eb*, 99, 508
adaeratio (conversion of tax payment to cash) 317, 318
Adam, Apocalypse of (Coptic) 730
Addai, Teaching of (Syriac) 710
adiectio sterilium 282
administration: barbarian kingdoms 537; bishops' functions 262–3, 341, 400; cities maintain role 373, 375, 409; civilian dominance in east 112, 115, 117, 430, 435; emperors' power over 352; Julian's decentralization 64–5, 66; military ethos 168–9; *see also* bureaucracy; centralization; provinces
Adonis, Antiochene cult of 69, 393
Adrianople (Hadrianopolis), battle of *3 Eb*, 99–101, 391, 412, 425–6, 509, 517, 575, 764; aftermath 102, 279, 280, 448; reasons for Roman defeat 233; Roman losses 221–2, 223, 234
Adriatic islands, ascetics on 616
adscripticii 288, 292, 293, 296, 357
adventus, imperial 60, 142–3, 150–1, 186, 759; Constantius II's at Rome 142–3, 150, 687, 742, 760

Aedesius (Neoplatonist) 46, 543–4, 607, 680
Aegeae *5 Ba*, 540–1
Aela (Aqaba) *6 Cd, 8 Bb*, 457
Aequitius (*curator palatii*) 100, 101
Aequitius (*magister militum per Illyricum*) 81, 90
Aetius (deacon at Antioch) 33, 47, 570, 572
Aetius, Flavius (*magister utriusque militiae*) 36, 229, 432; and John's usurpation 136, 436, 534; command against Goths 136, 137, 533; rivalry with Boniface and Felix 533, 534, 536; barbarian settlements during ascendancy 519–20, 533–7; reliance on barbarian troops 234, 436, 505, 506, 519, 534, 535, 536; death 528, 536
Afghanistan 39
Africa *1 Dc, 7*; third-century disruption 278; under Constans 4, 5, 9–10; support for Magnentius 15; Constantius recovers from Magnentius 22; Constantius pre-empts Julian's gaining control of 42; barbarian invasions after death of Julian 424; unrest under Jovian 87, 424; Romanus' corruption 87–8; Firmus' rebellion 88, 303, 658, 762; Gildo's revolt 115, 303, 429, 430, 764; Alaric and Attalus try to take 126–7; Heraclian's revolt 131; Bonifatius' activities 136, 137, 533, 536; Vandal invasion *see under* Vandals; migrations of Berbers and Austurians 450
  agriculture 115, 286, 294, 303, 360; army 216; Church 241–2, 252, 260–1, 290–1, 526 (*see also* Donatism); cities 379–80, 389, (prosperity) 303, 404–5, 407, 408, (size) 327, 373, 404–5, (walls) 389, 405; countryside 285–6, 303, 306, 599; euergetism 379–80; governorship 166, 191, 354; land 202, 283–4, 298, 523, 525; monetary system 278; mosaics 303, 749; paganism 599; prosperity 303, 380, 404–5, 407, 408; refugees from Italy 259, 402; trade 315; travel time from Rome 157; see also *circumcelliones*; Donatism; *and under* grain

agentes in rebus 65, 66, 159–60, 165, 176, 181; length of service 196; numbers 189; and religious laws 274; retired *agens* denounces bishop 656; seconded as *principes officii* 170–1

Agedincum *see* Sens

Agilo (general) 62, 90, 91

Aginatius (vice-prefect of Rome) 83

Agonistici (Donatists) 585

Agri Decumates 278

agri deserti 281–5, 519, 525

Agricola, St 758

agriculture 277–87, 305–7, 312, 316, 336; domanial farming 295, 296, 306–7; estate management 305–7; Germanic tribes 285, 286, 473, 479–80, 493, 506; harvest productivity 312, 336, 357–8; labour and property-owners 287–304 (see also *coloni*); marginal land 304; slaves 284, 285, 287, 295–6, 304, 305, 306–7; surpluses 330, 336, 506; technology and development 285–7; *see also under individual regions*

Ahai, *catholicos* of Persia 435

Ahiqar, story of (in Aramaic and Syriac) 712–13

Airan, Calvados; Germanic rich burial 465, 467

'Aitalaha' (Syriac author) 709

Akamatios of Baalbek (diviner) 613–14

Akatziri tribe 506

Akepsimas (priest of Nisibis) 715

Akhmim (Panopolis) *8 Bb*, 601, 602

Alamanni *1 Db-Eb*, *462*; Constantine takes into Roman army 419; Constantine II defeats 5; under Constans 6, 420; and rebellion of Magnentius 22, 236, 421–2; Constantius' campaigns 24, 29, 217, 421–2; Julian's campaigns under Constantius 40, 42, 49, 50–1, 54, 55, 58–9, 422, 762; invade after death of Julian 424; Valentinian I's campaigns 83–5, 217, 424–5; threat to Gaul 101; Gratian's campaigns 105; invasion of Upper Germany (407) 122, 133, 431; Constantine III recruits 528; support Jovinus 130

and Burgundians 516; settlement in empire 84, 280, 470–1

Alans *462*; origins *1 Gb-Hb*, 418, 425; and Huns 425, 500, 503; alliance with Goths against Rome 99, 425, 508; settled on Danube lands after Adrianople 483–4; raids into empire 120, 427, 430; invade Italy under Radagaisus 431; Rhine crossing (406) 122, 236, 431, 505, 518, 766; pass into Spain 129, 132, 432, 518, 528–9; support Jovinus 130; defeated by Goths 515, 518, 519, 521, 530, 536; Aetius settles in Gaul 519, 520, 523, 524, 525, 533–4

nomadism 518; in Roman army 105, 121, 412, 430

Alaric (leader of Goths): rise 113; leads revolt of Goths 114, 429, 430, 431, 511–13; plunders Greece 115, 527, 538; withdraws to Epirus 115, 118, 429, 430, 431; attack on west 118, 120, 430–1, 512, 765; Stilicho commissions to seize Epirus 121; plan fails, Alaric compensated 122–3, 513; invasion of Italy 125–8, 380, 463–4, 513, 518, 521, 522, 766, (upper classes flee) 259, 380, 391, 589; and Attalus' usurpation 126–7, 529; sack of Rome 112, 127–8, 328, 432, 464, 513, 518, 522, 527, 589, 766, (religious reactions) 538, 691; Constantine III avoids confrontation 129; death 127, 513

benefits from east–west rift 512, 513, 518; imperial misjudgements of 527; out of emperor's control 428; respects traditions of empire 529; and Stilicho 233, 236, 511, 512, 513, (Stilicho's failure to destroy) 114, 115, 120, 124, 430–1, 527; wish for Roman generalship 115, 511, 512, 513, 537

Alatheus (leader of Greuthungi) 100, 484, 494; entry to empire 500, 507, 508; disappears 509, 510, 511

Alavivus (leader of Tervingi) 95, 98, 494, 500, 507, 517

Albina (Christian noblewoman) 347

Albinus, Caeionius Caecina 347

Albinus, Caeionius Rufius 347

Aleppo (Beroea) *6 Cb, 9 Ba*, 404, 449, 455, 541–2, 695

Alexander the Great, king of Macedon; Julian's emulation 73, 76, 439

Alexander, bishop of Alexandria 564, 565, 566

Alexander, governor of Syria 644

Alexandria, Egypt *1 Fc, 6 Bc, 8 Aa*; Church 251, 329, 554, 576, (Arianism) 564, 565, 566, (bishops *see* Athanasius; Cyril; George; Gregory; Peter; Theophilus), (buildings) 251, (Christological debate) 596–8, (intellectual tradition) 667, 752, (precedence of see) 104, 245–6, 247, 248, 400, 579, (synods) 573, 574; education 673, 676, 683; and emperors 390; Jews 134, 648, 752; paganism 134, 550, 553, 554 (see also Serapeum *below*); philosophy 544, 556, 681–2, 767; Serapeum 394, 551, 553, 596, 634–5, 646, 765; size 336, *372*, 373; supply and distribution 71, 329; travel time from Constantinople 157

Alexandrovka; Černjachov culture *489*

Alica (leader of Tervingi) 496

allegory in art 751–5

Allobich (*magister equitum*) 129

Allortheus (Gothic leader) 102

Alypius, bishop of Thagaste 179, 344, 384, 591, 622, 700

Amantius (court eunuch) 180

Ambiani *1 Db*, 122

Ambrose (Ambrosius), bishop of Milan:
appointed bishop 266, 268, 580, 655, 656, 763;
and Valentinian II 106, 146–7; and
Theodosius 107–8, 264, 758; and usurpers
105, 109
and altar of Victory 199, 560; asserts
authority of see 249–50, 400, 579; and
Augustine 384; basilicas, issue of 581–2, 612;
condemns feasting at graves 661; and
countryside evangelization 670; and emperors
104, 106, 146–7, 264, 268, 612, 758; funeral
orations on emperors 110, 146–7, 675, 678;
introduces hymn-singing 693; and Jews 108,
394; *Lives* of 699; and Neoplatonism 680; and
non-Nicenes 580, 581–2; political
involvement 350; public speaking 560, 679,
704; brings relics to Milan 252, 254, 349, 401,
755, 758; sainthood 401; social comment 293,
299, 334, 335, 340, 343, 358; social
background 266, 365, 402, 670; and
Symmachus 194, 355; on women ascetics 345;
writings 666, 693, 696, 709
Ambrosius (praetorian prefect, father of above)
6
amicitia (friendship) 654, 694, 697
Amida (Dyarbekir) *1 Hc, 6 Db, 9 Ca*, 217, 419,
437; Persian siege and capture of 39–40, 41,
221, 412, 423, 438, 763, (Ammianus
Marcellinus' description) 212, 686–7,
(effectiveness of Roman army) 220, 229,
236
Amiens (Samarobriva) *2 Cb*, 83
Ammianus Marcellinus (historian) 200, 414,
686–7; aristocratic bias 200, 339–40; on army
211, 212–13, 232–3; on Constantius' *adventus*
142–3, 150, 687, 742, 760; emperors'
addresses to troops 224–5; and Eunapius of
Sardis 688; on Goths 487, 488, 491, 492; on
Huns 488; on Julian 686, 687; military career
25, 27, 39; on religion 685, 687, 688, 689; on
Roman élite 192–3, 200, 687; on siege of
Amida 212, 686–7; and Ursicinus 25, 27, 39,
212, 687
Ammonius (Egyptian hermit) 267n130
Ammonius of Alexandria (poet) 694
Amphilochius, bishop of Iconium 179, 576, 579
amphorae 493, 496
Anastasius, emperor 453
Anatolius (*magister officiorum*) 76
Anatolius (praetorian prefect) 152, 539
Ancaster 477
Ancyra (Ankara) *1 Gc, 6 Bb*, 68, 80, 90; council of
33
Anderitum (Pevensey) *2 Ca*, 7
Andrew, relics of St 38
Andronicus, governor of Cyrenaica 269
Andronicus of Caria (philosopher) 93n43

Anicetus (praetorian prefect) 15
Anicii, family of 345, 362, 591
Ankara *see* Ancyra
annona 220–1, 277, 319–21, 328–9
Anomoeans (anti-Nicene group) 33, 34, 570
Anonymus Valesianus 487, 496
Anthemius (praetorian prefect) 123, 133, 513;
administration 112, 128–9, 430, 433;
diplomacy 123, 434
Antinooupolis 602
Antioch *1 Gc, 6 Cb, 9 Ba, 372*; and Constantine
11–12, 186, 567; Constantius II in 8, 11, 12,
13, 37, 42, 69, 567; under Gallus 17, 24–5, 39,
45, 46, 55, 71–2, 329, 334, 421, 453; Julian in
66, 67–73, 358, (and Church) 69–71, 254,
392–3, 541, (and economy) 65, 69, 71–2, 231,
281–2, 329, 334, 336; Jovian's visit 79–80;
under Valens 92–3, 575; under Theodosius I
107, (Riot of the Statues) 107, 154–5, 201,
373, 402, 646, 679, 765; Huns invade 443
Adonis cult 69, 393; arms factory 456;
army presence 71–2, 329, 456; St Babylas'
shrine 45, 70, 251–2, 254; centrality 455–6;
Church 392–3, 654, (ascetics) 541, 620,
(bishops) 246, 247, 400 (*see also* Eudoxius;
Eustathius; Euzoius; Flavian; Meletius;
Paulinus), (charity) 257, 332, 402, (councils *see
below*), (factions) 42, 80, 104, 107, 265, 268,
393, 566, 571–3, 575, (and paganism) 347, 541,
645–6, (wealth) 261, 402; Church buildings
11–12, 45, 70, 251–2, 254, 567; coinage 186;
councils of bishops, (327) 240, 242, (338) 11,
(341) 33, 567, 569, (352) 23, 569, (363) 80,
(379) 573, 577–8, (380) 103; Daphne 69–71,
303, 392–3, education 676; extent and
population 373; finance 107; food supply 25,
69, 71–2, 107, 312, 329, 334, 336; forward
location 390, 391; hinterland 309, 541; houses
303, 388, 406; imperial presence 11, 37,
375–6, 386, 388, 456; Jews 393, 648, 679; land
281–2, 283, 300; landowners 303, 334;
language use, Syriac and Greek 714, 715n13;
Libanius' influence 679, 682; lower classes
358; magic, trials for 92–3, 763; new men 356;
paganism 69–71, 271–2, 347, 392–3, 541,
645–6; patronage 175–6, 177–8, 310; remains
405, 406; size 336, *374*; supply and distribution
329, 336; temples 69–71, 271–2, 541; travel
time from Constantinople 157; upper classes
303, 334, 356; villas 303; vitality 326, 351–2
antiquitas 663, 664
Antonine Itinerary 308
Antony (Egyptian monk) 601, 602, 614, 763;
writings attributed to 729, 732
Antony, Life of 669, 670, 698, 699, 700; reception
601, 698, 701; Syriac version 604
Apahida, near Cluj; rich burials 485

Apamea, Syria *6 Cb, 9 Ba, 372*; expansion 455;
 Jews 679; remains 405, 406, 681; Zeus-Belus,
 cult of 541, (temple destroyed) 551, 634
Aphaca; sanctuary of Aphrodite 540–1
Aphrahat (Syriac author) 12, 714, 716, 709
Aphrodisias, Caria *6 Ab, 372, 374, 379*, 405, 541,
 736; local government 204, 208, 379
Aphrodite: Cnidian (statue) 744, 748; cult of
 540–1, 545
Aphthonius' treatise on *progymnasmata* 674
apocalyptic literature, Syriac 713
Apocrypha, Coptic 724–5
Apollinarii; recast scriptures into classical
 literary forms 671
Apollinaris, bishop of Laodicea 103, 572–3,
 574–5, 576, 579, 595, 597
Apollo, shrines of 69–71, 540, 557
Apollonius of Tyana 646; *Lives* of 695–6, 700
Apophthegmata Patrum 606, 622, 729
apostasy, Church's attitude to 575, 659
Apostles, Letter of the (Coptic) 724–5
apostolic tradition 38–9
apotheosis of emperors 140
appointment, letters of (*probatoriae*) 165, 170
Apronianus (senator) 613
Apulia *1 Eb*, 368
Aqaba (Aela) *6 Cd, 8 Bb*, 457
aqueducts 167, 379, 386, *387*
Aquila, version of Old Testament by 671, 679
Aquileia *1 Eb, 3 Ba, 4 Ca*, 21, 59, 107, 136, 310,
 563n3; council of bishops 581
Aquincum (Budapest) *1 Eb, 3 Ca*, 85
Aquitaine (Aquitania) *1 Cb-Db, 2 Bb-Cb*, 122;
 Visigothic settlement 112, 131, 132, 133, 223,
 514–15, 518–19, 520, 530–2, 766, (little
 toponymic evidence) 464, 524
Arabs and Arabia *1 Gc-d*, 444–52; Constantius'
 diplomacy 420; conversion to Christianity
 419, 447, 448, 449, 450–1, 460; federations
 444, 448; marginal areas controlled by 455,
 459, 460; migrations 450; nomads' relations
 with settlers 451; Persian allies 75, 76, 135,
 443; phylarchs 449, 450, 451; raiding and
 guerrilla warfare 413, 436, 444–5, 446, 449; in
 Roman army 102, 412; and Roman–Persian
 relations 135, 419, 421, 435, 444–7, 451, 455,
 460; sources on 451; subsidies 446, 447, 449;
 under Mavia (Maouia) 102, 447–9, 451
Aramaic language: artistic prose 712; dialects
 708, 714, 715, 719; *see also* Syriac culture
Aravah 458
Arbitio, Flavius (*magister equitum*) 24, 25, 62, 91
Arbogast (Frankish *comes*) 108–9, 146, 229, 428,
 467, 764
Arborius, Aemilius Magnus 3
Arcadius, emperor 111, 113–18, 123–4, 429–30,
 764, 766; Anthemius' ascendancy *see separate*

entry; and army 229; builds basilica in Rome
 390; civilian administration consolidated 112,
 169–70, 171; division of empire with
 Honorius 111, 113, 164, 429, 512, 764; and
 Goths 512, 518; marriage to Eudoxia 113–14;
 monuments 140, 737; peace with Persia 112,
 430; and religious affairs 118, 160–1, 390, 554,
 657; Rufinus' influence 113–14; Stilicho
 claims guardianship over 113, 114, 175;
 Synesius of Cyrene attacks 146; warfare and
 diplomacy 429–30
archaeology: on agriculture 285; on cities 403–4;
 on Germanic peoples 461, 463–4
archers 102, 105
arches, imperial 398, 737; *see also under* Rome
archiatri (state doctors) 174, 683
architecture: classical tradition 736–7, 742–3;
 education in 683
Ardaburius (general) 136, 435, 436
Ardashir (Artaxerxes) I, king of Persia 416
Ardennes 297
areani (couriers) 7
Arelate *see* Arles
Areobindus (general) 435
Arethusa 71
Argentorate *see* Strasbourg
Arianism: under Constantine 564–5, 566, 595
 (*see also* Nicaea (council of)); under
 Constantius 81 (*see also* Ariminum (council
 of); *homoousios*/*homoiousios* controversy;
 Seleucia (council of)); Valens supports 81, 95;
 council of Constantinople anathematizes
 104; Theodosius I opposes 112, 274, 549,
 559, 575, 578, 579, 580, 582
 in Alexandria 564, 565, 566; and army 106;
 Augustine and 587; barbarians 112, 118, 526,
 581, 587; beliefs 555, 595, 598–9; episcopal
 hierarchy 581
Ariaricus (leader of Tervingi) 496
Arimer (Gothic king) 503
Ariminum (Rimini) *1 Eb, 4 Ca*, 126; council of
 bishops (359) 34, 35–6, 81, 260, 262, 570–1,
 580, (creed) 35, 106
Arintheus (*magister peditum*) 78, 92
Aristarchus of Seleucia (rhetor) 633
Aristides; *Apology* in Syriac 709
aristocracy 354–6; ascetics 612–13, 614; and
 Church 82, 272–3, 399, 655, 657, 670;
 common culture 377, 384–6, 646, 651, 665;
 conspicuous consumption 335; empire-wide
 networks 384–6; old and new 352, 356;
 religious ambiguity 646, 653; retirement to
 countryside 313, 612; sources biased towards
 339–40; *see also* bureaucracy; euergetism;
 landowners; patronage; senatorial order
Aristotelianism 540, 544, 556
Arius 555, 564, 565, 566; *see also* Arianism

Arles *1 Db, 2 Cc, 372*; Constantius II celebrates *tricennalia* 22, 23; Constantine III at 129, 130, 202, 432; Constantius at (414) 131; Visigothic siege 136, 535

    bishop's precedence 245, 250; council of bishops 23–4, 26; council of seven Gallic provinces 202–3; cultural efflorescence 133; St Trophimus and 245, 250

Armenia *1 Gc-Hc, 6 Db*; client rulers under Hadrian 416; Galerius gains suzerainty 418, 437; diplomacy and conflict under Constantine 419, 437; Constantius II and 5, 12–13, 39, 40, 420, 423, 437; Julian and 74; Rome cedes eastern part to Persia and gives up support of Arsak III (363) 79, 424, 442; Valens' diplomacy over Persian interference 91–4, 425; civil war 426; partition between Rome and Persia (386) 106, 426, 442; Huns invade 116, 429, 443; Roman advance into (421) 134; settlement between Rome and Persia (428) 426

    Chrysostom exiled in 118; Church under Persians 134, 434; literary culture 416, 666, 708

armies, private 311; *see also* militias

armour 232

arms manufactories, imperial (*fabricae*) 165, 313, 316, 456

army 211–37; armour 232; *auxilia* 223, 224, 458, (élite) 214, 215; barbarians in 102, 111, 222–4, 365, 412, 413, 419, 423, 433, (*auxilia*) 214, 223, 224, 412, 417, (cavalry) 223, 224, 417, (federates) 103, 124, 223, 280–1, 413, 427, 428, 431, 497, 499, 509, under Honorius 114, 115, 118, 120, 121, under Aetius 234, 534, 535, 536, revolts 510–11, (Germans) 111, 214, 365, 412, 464, 465, 469–70, 472, 478, high-ranking 413, 430, 435, 436, 469, (*laeti, dedicitii, tributarii*) 279–80, (loyalty) 120, 224, 226, 428, (massacre of families, 408) 125, 432, (*see also under individual peoples*); billeting 230, 524–5; cavalry 214, 223, 224, 412, 413, 416, 417, 418; Church and 226–7, 228, 265, 438, 443, 451, 460, 656; cities and 375, 409–10; and civil government 168, 229; civilian relations 229–32; *collegiati* banned from 324; *coloni* in 296; *comitatus* (élite praesental field army) 213–14, 215, 216, 412, 417, 421, 455–6; communications 417, 458–9; conscription 101–2; Constantine's reforms 213–14, 226, 417, 457; construction work 230; defensive nature 413; desertion 308, 311, 367; under Diocletian 213, 219, 417, 457, 459; discipline 232–3; donatives 225, 228; *duces* 214, 217, 236, 263, 412, 456, 460; and economy 211, 219, 231, 329, 456; and emperors 218–19, 224–6, 228–9, 352, 365, 411–12, 421, 427 (*see also under individual emperors*); financial

administration 167, 211; frontier forces 213–14, 217–18, 389, 412, 417, (dispersal of western) 237, (see also *limitanei; ripenses*); intelligence 218, 219; Jews banned from 228; *labarum* 226, 227; land allotments on retirement 234; legionary bases 457–8; *limitanei* 214, 216–18, 230–1, 234–7, 456, 460; *magistri* 213, 215–16, 412, 455–6; manpower 101–2, 120, 121, 220, 221–4, 228; under Marcus Aurelius 416; military effectiveness 220, 229, 232–7; oath 227; organization and deployment 213–19; 'palatine' units 215; *patrocinium* 231–2, 310, 363; pay 220–1; planning and strategy 218–19, 233; policing role 230; and politics 211, 224–9; praesental, see *comitatus* above; Praetorian Guard 214; praetorian prefects' responsibility 54–5, 167; promotion 364–5; protection of peasants 231–2, 310, 363; *pseudocomitatenses* 236; recruitment 101–2, 120, 121, 220, 221–4, 228; regionalization 215–19; religion 106, 226–8, 542, 656; resources 219–21; revolts 211, 224, 510–11; *scholae* (bodyguard) 165, 170, 214; size 211, 219–20; slave recruitment 121; social mobility 188, 194, 195, 364–5, 369; and society 229–32, 417, 456; sources on 211–13, 232–3, 456, 535 (see also *Notitia Dignitatum*); specialization 214–15, 412; under Stilicho 121, 216, 233–4; supply 54–5, 215, 220–1, 229, 285, 316, 317, 360; and tax collection 230, 231–2; taxes finance 220, 221, 277, 375; under tetrarchy 457; unit size and types 214–15; *seniores* and *iuniores* 222; versatility 412; veterans 234, 359

Arnobius (Christian writer) 744

Arrabanes (Persian governor of Armenia) 91, 92

Arsak (Arsaces) III, king of Armenia: accession 437; Constantius II and 40, 41, 430, 423; and Julian's campaign against Persia 74; Jovian promises Persians not to help 79; death 91

Arsak (Arsaces) IV, king of Armenia 426

art, visual: abstraction and naturalism 736, 740, 759; allegorical reading 751–5; and Byzantine art 736; in catacombs 739, 749–51, 754; Christians and 667, 677, 704, (acceptance of classical tradition) 742–4, (attitudes to pagan art) 649–51, 743–4, 745, 746–8, 748–51, 756, (in Church buildings) 672, 756–7; classical tradition 742–4; countryside depicted 304; decline, alleged 737, 739–40; Dionysiac motifs 746, 748; emperors in 30, 759; imperial imagery 745, 759; inclusive definition of Christian 746–8; ivory reliefs 737; Jewish 739, 740; Manichean 740; Middle Ages 736, 740; Mithraic 739, 745; modern critical context 739–42; multiplicity of meanings and evocations 741; pagan/Christian juxtaposition 736, 745, 746, 748, 749–51; and power 755–61; sarcophagi 750, 755; social function 748–51; statues of gods preserved as works of art 650–1; syncretism 736, 739, 744–5, 745–6; typology 751–5; *see also* metalwork (iconography)

Artaxata *6 Db*, 443

Artaxerxes *see* Ardashir

artisans: in countryside 308, 313, 333, 408; ordained 263–4; status, extent of state control 318–22

Artogerassa, Armenia 91

Arvandus (Gallic senator) 203

Arzanena 79

asceticism, Christian 601–31; *anachōrēsis* 618; appearance of ascetic 601, 604, 616; Augustine 622, 628–30; and authority 630–1; Basil and 622, 625–6, 668; body's role 622, 624–6; and class 258, 605–6, 612–13, 614; competitive ethos 604–5; dependence on others 630, 631; desert, myth of 614–16, 617, 618, 619–20, 622, 627; discipline 603–4; diversity 605, 606; energy 624; Evagrius of Pontus 622, 626–8, 630; Great Old Men of Egypt 626–8, 630; households of ascetics 601, 613; intensification of normal renunciations 616–18; literary culture 700–2; localism 606; lower levels of consciousness 625, 626–8; Manichean connection 582–3; Mesopotamia 579–80, 621; Messalians 579–80; philosophical sub-culture 613–14; and political power 610–12; seclusion 620; self, notion of 604, 622–31; and sexuality 610, 619; sources 602, 606; Syria 348, 541, 619–20, 621, 709; and time 609, 610; transformation 603–5, 624–5, 626–8; view of polytheistic ascetics 601–2; in west 582–3, 701; women 258–9, 345–6, 347, 607–8, 613, 620, 670, 702

asceticism, polytheistic 607–12, 622–3, 630; autonomy of individual 630; and body 608–9, 623, 625; and class 612, 614; courage in face of temporal power 610–12; Julian's 63, 64, 72, 150; learning, tradition of 623; lower levels of consciousness 608–9; Neoplatonist 622–3, 623–4; philosophy as form of spiritual exercise 602–3; and political power 610–12, 614, 630; renunciations 622; and sexuality 609; vegetarianism 608; view of Christian ascetics 601–2; women 607–8

Asclepiades, bishop of Chersonesus 276

Asclepigeneia (Athenian theurgist) 557

Asclepius; sanctuary at Aegeae 540–1

Asia, provincial governor of 166

Asiana (diocese) 167, 248

Aspacures (Iberian ruler) 92

Aspar (general) 136, 436

Aspebetos (Arab phylarch) 450–1

Asterius (*comes Hispaniarum*) 519

astrology 274, 655, 706

Aswana (Syriac author) 710

Ataulf *see* Athaulf

Athanaric, leader of Tervingi: agreement with Rome 94; and Huns 95, 500, 511; nature of leadership 495–6, 498, 516–17; reception in Constantinople, and royal funeral 102, 427; supporters establish kingdom 502–3

Athanasius, bishop of Alexandria: becomes bishop 267, 268, 566; opposes Arius at Nicaea 566; deposed by council of Tyre 566–7, 569; western bishops defend 567, 568; restoration 5, 7, 11; exile in west (340) 7–8, 8–9, 11–12, 763; restoration 9, 12, 568, 763; Magnentius' approach to 16, 26, 140, 569; continuing controversy 23–4, 25–7, 569; expelled (356), restored on death of Constantius 27, 574, 763; Julian expels 70–1; Jovian restores 80, 571; death 576, 763 Christology 569, 595–6, 599; and Constantius II 8, 11–12, 248–9, 568, 569; on emperors and Church 34, 140, 239; exile of supporters 7–8, 569; and grain distribution 260, 329; Gregory of Nazianzus' *encomium* 700; power-base 245; writings 666, 702, 726, (spurious) 573

Atharid (Gothic noble) 494

Athaulf (leader of Goths): with Alaric in Italy 125, 126, 513–14, 529; leads Goths into Gaul 127, 130, 432, 513; and Jovinus 130, 513, 529; marriage to Galla Placidia 131, 514, 519, 529–30, 766; death 132, 514, 519, 530; respect for traditions of empire 529, 537

Athena, goddess 538

Athenagoras (Christian apologist) 595

Athens *1 Fc, 5 Bb*; Alaric attacks 538; Academy 680, 682; Julian and 25, 47–8, 60; learning 25, 47–8, 544, 556–7, 676, 677, 680, 682; paganism 538, 539, 557; remains 405, 406

Atrans *3 Ba*, 20

Atripe *8 Bb*

Attacotti 424

Attalus, Priscus (usurper) 126–7, 130, 131, 513–14, 529, 530

Attiaena, Aurelia; repudiates husband 659

Attila (leader of Huns) 436, 506, 534

Attis, myth and cult of 545, 546, 753

Augila, Sahara 558

Augusta Taurinorum (Turin) *4 Aa*, 244–5, 250

Augusta Treverorum *see* Trier

Augustine, St, bishop of Hippo 586–93, 765; and Alypius 591, 700; Ambrose's influence 384; asceticism 622, 628–30; background and early life 261–2, 582, 669, 701, (education) 197, 365–6, 676–7, (teacher of rhetoric) 384, 668, (ordination) 349, 655; baptism 618;

Augustine, St, bishop of Hippo (*cont.*)
    bishop's duties 252, 259, 262, 271, 272; on
    Church wealth 261–2, 343; and classical
    tradition 589, 592, 629, 668, 669, 691, 703,
    704; contacts at court 384, 591; and Donatism
    562, 583, 586; educational theory 681; and
    entertainments 380, 399; on grace 588, 592–3,
    604; and heresy 586–93, 639; on images 756;
    on *laetitia* 661; *Lives* of 699; on lower spirits
    636–7; Manicheism 582, 613; Neoplatonism
    582, 628–9, 680; on original sin 590, 592; and
    pagans 526, 635; Paulinus' letters to 697; and
    Pelagians 179, 589–90, 591–2; political
    theology 352; preaching 670, 704–5; on
    predestination 592–3; and Priscillianism
    582–3; self, notion of 629, 631; on women in
    Church 345
        WRITINGS 606, 666; *City of God* 663, 668,
    691, 767; *Confessions* 582, 692, 700; *De Doctrina
    Christiana* 669, 681, 704–5; *De Magistro* 681;
    De Ordine 681; letters 340, 344, 696, 697, 698
Augustobona (Troyes) *2 Cb*, 49
Augustodunum *see* Autun
Augustonemetum *see* Clermont-Ferrand
Augustus, emperor 411
Aurelian, emperor 416
Aurelian (praetorian prefect) 116, 117, 133, 134,
    512
Aurelius, bishop of Carthage 589
Ausonius, Decius Magnus (poet): and Bordeaux
    327, 381; career 156, 366, 673; compares
    emperor with God 139; and Gratian 105, 366,
    673; life in city and countryside 299–300, 302,
    327, 350; patronage 152; poetry 415, 381, 692
Austuriani 87, 236, 450
Autessiodurum *see* Auxerre
authority, civility in exercise of 644
Autun (Augustodunum) *1 Db, 2 Cb*, 10–11, 49;
    panegyrist of 280, 282
Auxentius, bishop of Milan 106, 526, 578, 580,
    581
Auxerre (Autessiodurum) *2 Cb*, 49
Auxonius (praetorian prefect) 221
Avitus, emperor 203, 535
axes, Germanic throwing- 469
Azraq, Arabia 458

Baalbek *see* Heliopolis
Baba (pagan prophet of Harran) 710n7
Babisqa, Jebel Barisha, Syria 715
Babylas, St 24, 45, 70, 252, 254
Baeterrae (Béziers) *2 Cc*, 29
Baetica *1 Cc*, 132
Bagai *7 Bb*, 9–10, 585–6
Bagaudae 133, 281, 308, 367–8, 431; and
    barbarian settlements in Gaul 531–2, 534
bakers 318–19, 320, 328

Balai (Syriac poet) 709, 715
Baldingen 472
Baltic, western 478–82, 484
banditry 218, 284, 308, 366, 368, 446, 449;
    Isaurian 368, 433, 436; *see also* Bagaudae
baptism 70–1, 618, 640, 657–8; of emperors 1, 7,
    11, 42, 43, 102
baptisteries 251, 252, 400, 715, 755
barbarians 516–37, 663; under Marcus Aurelius
    416; Valentinian I's successes against 424–5;
    Huns force other groups westwards 95, 98,
    425, 428, 487, 500–3, 505, 517; Goths
    accepted into empire 516–17; Theodosius I's
    federate settlements 112–13, 223, 280–1,
    427–9, 483–4; attacks on west (400–8)
    118–23, 504, 518; great Rhine crossing (406)
    122, 431, 505, 513, 515, 518, 766; movement
    into Spain 129, 131, 132, 391, 432, 518, 524,
    528–9; settlements in west, fifth-century
    129–33, 432, 519–20, 522–5, 533–7; Aetius'
    use of 234, 436, 505, 506, 519, 534, 535, 536
    acculturation of Romans and 304, 464,
    537, 665; capitals moved from frontier zones
    in face of 202, 391; Christianization 526;
    confederacies 418, 516; effect on countryside
    279–81, 308; effect on Roman populations
    112, 201–3, 256, 297, 391–2, 665; ethnic
    consciousness undeveloped 224; imperial
    priorities and misjudgements 526–8, 529, 530;
    loyalty to person of emperor 428, 510–11,
    518, 536; military resources and technology
    413; nature of settlements 522–5; political
    involvement in east 116, 117, 369–70; and
    Roman senate 126, 201–3, 204; and Roman
    traditions 529–30, 537; and social change 369,
    675; social stratification 525; subsidies 427,
    429, 523–4, 525; and usurpers 130, 527–8,
    528–9; *see also individual peoples and under
    individual regions and* army
Barbatio (*magister peditum*) 51, 220
Barcelona (Barcino) *1 Db*, 131, 519, 530
Barchalba (tribune under Procopius) 91
Barcino *see* Barcelona
Bardaisan (Syriac writer) 710; school of; *Book of
    the Laws of Countries* 709, 713, 717n19
Barnabas (priest of Hippo) 295
Barsamya, Acts of (Syriac) 710
Baruch, Apocalypse of (Syriac) 713
Basil of Ancyra 37, 161, 568, 654; leads
    homoiousios faction 33–4, 34–5, 36, 568, 570,
    571
Basil of Caesarea 575–8, 763, 765; and
    Apollinaris 576; asceticism 622, 625–6, 668;
    background 303, 365; builds charitable
    institutions in Caesarea 252, 257, 260; career
    575–8; classical literary culture 573, 668, 704,
    753; education 48, 573, 667; feud with bishop

of Tyana 244; financial administration 262;
  Gregory of Nazianzus' funeral oration 668,
  765; on lower clergy 263–4; and political
  power 178–9, 270, 612–13; social comment
  299; on Trinity 576–7; and Valens 576
    WRITINGS 598, 666, 718, 726; *florilegium*
  genre 577; *Hexaemeron* 706; *On the Holy Spirit*
  576–7; letters 340, 576; *Rules* 622, 625
Basilicata; villa of S. Giovanni di Ruoti 306
basilikos logos 689–90
Basilina (mother of Julian) 44
Basmachka; Černjachov culture settlement 489
Bassa, monastery of 759
Bassus, Junius, sarcophagus of 737–8, 745, 755,
  759
Batavi (army unit) 100–1, 233n137
Bath, Avon 632
baths *see under* Constantinople; Rome
Batnae 6 Cb, 24, 542, 695
Bauto (Frank, adviser to Valentinian II) 108
Beer Sheva 6 Bc, 456
Beirut (Berytus) 1 Gc, 6 Cc, 542, 676, 683
belts: military 464, 467, 468, 472, 475; of office
  168–9
benefactions *see* euergetism; patronage
Bennekom, Gelderland, Holland 473–4
Beograd (Singidunum) 3 Db, 33
Berbers 368, 450
Beroea (Aleppo) 6 Cb, 9 Ba, 404, 449, 455,
  541–2, 695
Bertha (Kentish Christian queen) 478
Berytus *see* Beirut
Beth Lapat (Gondishapur) 9 Db, 716n18
Bethlehem 6 Cc, 258, 345, 758
Bezabde 6 Db, 437, 458; Persian acquisition 41,
  42, 43, 74, 423, 439, 460
Béziers (Baeterrae) 2 Cc, 29
Bible 671–3; allusions in literature 671, 672;
  Coptic 722–4, 725, 726, 735; exegesis 672, 751;
  Genesis 672–3, 691; Gothic 487, 491, 581;
  Latin 671–2; Pauline Epistles 697; Song of
  Songs 671, 672; Syriac 713, 716
Bigelis (Gothic leader in Hunnic empire) 503
billeting, military 230, 524–5
biography 699–700; *see also* hagiography
Bîrlad-Valea Seacă; Černjachov culture 489, 493
bisextum, intercalated 81
bishops: administrative functions 257, 262–3,
  332, 341, 400; Arian hierarchy 581; authority
  of councils 562, 563; and community 263,
  269–72; city-based 241–2, 263, 400, 402, 409,
  600; at court 7n20, 239, 264, 265, 269, 270,
  275–6, 384; use *cursus publicus* 35, 36, 238, 239,
  256, 262, 276, 563n4; diplomacy 270, 434–5;
  Donatist 241–2; *episcopalis audientia* 273, 275;
  euergetism 342; exile 8, 11, 240, 290–1, 563,
  565, 567, 574, 612; food relief 336; and heresy

274, 562; hierarchy 400–1; judicial role 271–2,
  272–6, 639, 658–9; laymen appointed 265–7;
  mediation 269, 270, 348–50, 402, 639; military
  role 12, 269–70, 438, 444; monastic life
  incompatible 267, 349–50; patronage 264,
  269, 342, 349, 350, 757–8; perception in
  worldly terms 265–7; political role 263,
  269–70, 349–50, 369–70; power base 409,
  600; precedence 242, 244–50; in public life of
  empire 238–40; rural (*chorepiscopi*) 242; social
  rank 272–3, 342, 349, 365, 402, 576, 670;
  suppression of paganism 551, 554; translation
  104, 241, 268, 578; violence over elections
  267–8, 599–600 (*see also under* Antioch;
  Constantinople; Rome); *see also* councils of
  bishops; metropolitans; Synods
Bitburg 468
Bithynia 6 Ab-Ba, 90, 557
body, attitudes to 608–9, 622, 623, 624–6
bodyguard, imperial (*scholae*) 214
bogs, Scandinavian peat 481–2
Bologna (Bononia) 4 Ba, 124
Boniface (Bonifatius, *comes Africae*) 135, 136, 137,
  532–3, 534, 536
Boniface, pope 249, 267–8
Book of the Laws of Countries (Syriac) 709, 713,
  717n19
book production 677, 738
booty, barbarians and 95, 102
Borbetomagus (Worms) 2 Db, 122, 133
Bordeaux (Burdigala) 1 Cb, 2 Bc, 131, 381, 673,
  674; *Itinerarium Burdigalense* 256–7, 346, 756
Boseth, Medjerda valley 635
Bostra 6 Cc, 71, 457, 458
boulai, civic 371, 373
bread 139; state distribution 167, 318–19, 328,
  329
Brescia *lipsanotheca* 745–6, 755, 756
bridges 260, 419
brigandage *see* banditry
Brigetio 1 Eb, 3 Ca, 85
Brisigavi 24
Britain 1 Ca, 2 Ba-Ca; under Constantine II 4;
  Constans' visit 6–7, 420; and Magnentius 15,
  23; Lupicinus in 57, 58; barbarian invasions
  424; Theodosius' campaigns 86–7; Maximus'
  usurpation *see* Maximus, Magnus; Stilicho
  withdraws units 120; revolts of Marcus,
  Gratian and Constantine 122, 431–2, 527;
  Honorius abandons defence 132–3, 432, 766
    administration 112, 375; agriculture 54,
  285, 294, army 112, 120, 216 17, 428, 431,
  531; Church 35, 262; cities decline 375, 396,
  406, 409; Germanic presence 112, 432, 473,
  474–8, 476, 519, 520, 521, 531; Hadrian's Wall
  216; loss of tax revenues to Rome 234, 535;
  magnates 375, 475; market-settlements 408;

Britain (*cont.*)
  militias 475; pottery 473, 475, 477; Saxon
    shore 7, 216–17; settlement pattern 309, 408;
    villas 278, 294, 297, 302, 408, 475
brooches 464–5, 467, 469, 472, 475, 481
Brumath 49
Budapest (Aquincum) *1 Eb, 3 Ca,* 85
Budeşty 493
buildings, public: abandonment or adaptation
    380, 395; euergetism 330, 332, 342, 362, 377,
    378, 379; maintenance 167; *see also* church
    buildings; temples; *and under individual cities*
Bulla Regia *7 Bb, 372,* 380, 392, 410, 658
Burdigala *see* Bordeaux
bureaucracy 162–80; and army 54–5, 167, 229,
    418, 430; codicils 152, 163, 166; corruption
    175–80; court officials 159, 165–6; *curiales* 324,
    376–7, 378, 381, 384–5; *dignitates* 188, 195–6,
    206; education 197, 675, 683; and emperors
    138, 139, 151–3, 159, 161, 169–75, 182–3, 352;
    groups excluded from 324, 554; immunity
    from civic duties 376; legal profession 683;
    length of tenure 153, 181, 192, 194, 206;
    offices 162–9; overlapping responsibilities
    169–70, 170–1, 174–5, 182; payment in kind
    329; power and status 169, 376–7, 378, 430;
    in provinces 160, 166–8; purges 61–2, 152–3;
    selection, appointment and promotion
    171–3, 173–4, 175–80, 182, 353–4, 364; and
    senatorial order 184, 188, 189–90, 195–7,
    204–9, 364, 369; supernumeraries 196, 675;
    tactical possibilities 138, 180, 183; wealth 388;
    see also *agentes in rebus; notarii;* prefects
Burgundians *1 Ea, 462, 504;* fight with Rome
    against Alamanni 516; and Valentinian I 84;
    invasion of Upper Germany 122, 431;
    support Jovinus 130, 432; settled in eastern
    Gaul 112, 130, 133, 464; Aetius' campaign and
    settlement in Sapaudia 519–20, 522–3, 524,
    533, 534; seize part of Gaul (456) 536
        Christianity 526; and Danube lands 483;
    Liber Constitutionum 522–3, 525; numbers 521;
    social stratification 525
burials: Christian ceremonies 1–2, 273–4, 656–7,
    660–1, 662; Germanic tribes 464, 465, *466, 476,*
    484; *see also* cemeteries
Burj el Qas, Jebel Sim'an, Syria 715
bush, Moses' burning 449
Butheric (garrison commander of Thessalonica)
    108
Byzantine era: art 736; diplomacy 112, 414, 436;
    emperors' remoteness 150; Scandinavian
    contacts 481; theology 703
Byzantium *see* Constantinople

Caecilian, bishop of Carthage 583
Caecilianus, Alphius (duumvir of Abthungi) 359

Caesarea, Cappadocia *1 Gc, 6 Cb,* 41, 68, 244,
    667; 'new city' of charitable institutions 252,
    257, 260
Caesarea (Cherchel), Mauretania 285, 303
Caesarea Maritima, Palestine *1 Gc, 6 Bc,* 244, *372,*
    405, 455, 679
Caesarius (Aurelian's brother) 512
cage-cups 738
Cagliari (Calaris) *4 Bc,* 26
Caister-by-Norwich 477
Calama *7 Bb, 372,* 392
Calaris (Cagliari) *4 Bc,* 26
calendar: Church, of liturgical celebration 699;
    codex-calendar of A.D. 354 542, 759–60;
    Edessene Syriac, of 411 718; Roman 81,
    252–3; *see also* festivals
Callinicum (Raqqa) *6 Cb,* 74, 107–8, *372,* 443,
    447; religious violence 107–8, 394, 642, 646,
    647
Calvisiana, Sicily 308
Cambridge 477
cameos 737, 746
Campania *1 Eb, 4 Cb,* 287, 362, 381
Candidianus (general) 136
Canterbury 478
Capella, Martianus 681
Cappadocia *1 Gc, 6 Bb-Cb,* 443
Cappadocian fathers 207, 208; *see also* Basil of
    Caesarea; Gregory of Nazianzus; Gregory of
    Nyssa
Capua 8, 310
Caputvada *7 Cb,* 373
Carmen de Providentia (anon.) 526
Carpi 491, 497
Carrand diptych 751–2
Carrhae *see* Harran
Carthage *1 Ec, 372;* bishops' councils 586, 591,
    767; churches 252, 253, 256, 405; clergy 263,
    305, 400; Cyprian, cult of St 252, 253, 256;
    Donatism 9, 586; and emperors 390; housing
    405; mosaics; Maison de la Cachette de
    Statues 749; paganism 550, 554; Paul and
    Macarius in 9; precedence of see 246, 400;
    procuratores 305; size 336, 373, *374,* 405; student
    unruliness 676–7; supply 329, 336; UNESCO
    project 405; Vandal capture 519, 520; walls
    391, 405
casarii, casati (cottagers) 295
Cassian, John 606, 622, 626, 630–1, 701, 767
Cassianus (*dux Mesopotamiae*) 422
Cassiodorus 520; *Variae* 698
Castagna, Sicily; villa 300
Castinus (*magister utriusque militiae*) 135, 136, 519
Castra Martis *3 Db,* 99, *504*
Castra Maurorum *6 Db,* 79
castrenses (court eunuchs) 165, 239n6
Castrum Rauracense *see* Kaiseraugst

catacombs 739, 749–51, 754
Catalauni (Châlons-sur-Marne) 83
Catalaunian Plains 2 *Cb*, 534–5, 536
catechumens 658
cattle-rearing 307, 479
Caucasus Mountains *1 Hb*, 429, 434, 442, 443, 501, 502
Cave of Treasures (Syriac compilation) 713
Cebes; *Tabula* 752
Celestine, pope 598
Celestius (disciple of Pelagius) 589
Celsinus Adelphius (prefect of Rome) 21
cemeteries, Germanic: in Britain 475, *476*, 477, 478; Černjachov culture *489*, 490; in Gaul 464–8; in Germany 468, 470, 472; Przeworsk culture 482; in Saxon lands 472–3
Centcelles, Spain; imperial mausoleum 738, 750
centralization: and cities 205, 209, 330, 377; and emperors 138, 151, 155, 161, 181–2, 183; Julian reverses 64–5, 66; *patrocinium* weakens 363
Centumcellae (Civita Vecchia) *4 Bb*, 580
Cepha 458
Cercesium *6 Db*, 74, 457
ceremonial, imperial 142–3, 145, 180–1, 352, 759
Černjachov culture 483, 484, *489*, 490, 493, 496; cemeteries and settlements *489*, 490; and Goths 483, 487, 488, *489*, 490–1, 491–2, 493
Chalcedon *6 Aa*, 61–2, 89, 90, 647; council of 112, 401
Chalcidius (Neoplatonist) 680
Chaldaean Oracles 680, 695
Châlons-sur-Marne 2 *Cb*, 83
Chamavi 54, 422
Charietto (*comes per utramque Germaniam*) 83
chariot-racing 139
charity, Christian 257, 327, 331, 332, 337, 341–4, 402; bishops administer 257, 332, 341; institutions 251, 252, 257, 260; Constantine's scheme 329; Constantinople 252, 262–3, 369; Jerusalem 261; Julian emulates 68–9, 256, 260, 402, 547; state funding 260
chartularii (officials) 167
Cherchel (Caesarea), Mauretania 285, 303
Chersonesus *1 Gb*, 276
Childeric, ruler of Gaul 467
child-rearing in countryside 308
Chionitae 39
Chnodomarius (Alamannic leader) 24, 40, 51, 54
Christ, second coming of 142
Christianity *see* asceticism, Christian; bishops; Church; theology
Christmas 253
Christology 561, 572–3, 574–5, 588, 595–9 (*see also* Arianism; *homoousios/homoiousios*)

chronicles 415; Christian 689, 690; Syriac 416; *of 452* 520, 523, 532, 533; *of 511* 520, 524
Chrysanthius of Sardis 68, 544, 547, 550, 610–11, 612
Chrysanthus, Novatian bishop of Constantinople 266
Chrysostom, John: in Antioch 154, 679; bishop of Constantinople 116, 248, 252, 262–3, 268, 765; conflict with Eudoxia and faction 117–18, 121, 161, 248, 429, 261, 263, 563; exile and death 118, 595, 596
    charitable institutions 252, 261, 262–3; choice of ecclesiastical life 350; on city of God 141–2; and classical tradition 668–9; Coptic translation 726; on emperor and divine 150; and Ephesus 248; and Eutropius 116, 153; homilies 670, 704; and Jews 393, 643, 671; letters 696; Libanius teaches 668, 671; moral teaching 117–18, 343, 399, 671; and Origenist controversy 595; and Phoenician paganism 557; on poor tenant farmers 293, 305, 358; and Porphyry of Gaza 180; social background 265, 714; writings 666, 699, 700
Church 238–76, 561–600; Diocletian's persecution 559; under Constantine (Constantine's support), 257, 301, 304, 329, 558–9, (doctrine) 33, 239, 272, 562–3, 564–7, (Donatism) 583, (involvement in warfare) 438, 460, (*see also* Nicaea, council of); Constans and 7–8, 8–9, 12, 258, 567; under Constantius II 8, 11–12, 17, 20, 24, 32–7, 62, 63, 238, (doctrine) 12, 33, 539, 567–71, (*see also councils of* Ariminum; Serdica; Seleucia); under Julian 46–7, 62–3, 65, 77, 585, (in Antioch) 69–71, (and Christian teachers) 66–7, 547, 688, (conformity before accession) 45, 47, 58, 60–1, 545, 547, (emulates institutions) 68–9, 545, 547, 548; under Jovian 80; under Valentinian and Valens 81, 95, 258, 259, 268, 390, 549, 571–3, 611, (Damasus' accession as pope) 82, 369; under Theodosius I 103–4, 106, 107–8, 112, 581, (Nicene orthodoxy imposed) 112, 274, 549, 559, 575, 578, 579, 580, 582; under Honorius and Arcadius 117–18, 123; under Theodosius II 134, (and war against Persia) 443, 451
    administration 327, 400, 408; apostasy 549, 659 (*see also under* Julian); apostolic tradition 38–9; Aramaic speakers 708; aristocracy and 82, 399, 612–13; and army 226–7, 228, 265, 438, 443, 451, 460, 656; art 667, 672, 676, 677, 704, 742–5, 746–8, 756–7; asceticism *see* asceticism, Christian; austerity 616–18; authority in 272, 562, 563–4, 567, 599–600, 644; baptism *see separate entry*; barbarian conversions *see under* Arabs; Germanic

Church (*cont.*)

peoples; bishops *see separate entry*; body, view of 622, 624–6; book production 677; burial 656–7, 660–1, 662, 675; calendar 699; catechumenate 618, 658; in cities 241–2, 308, 323, 332, 392–403, 409–10, 540, 642, (bishops' power base) 409, 600, (difficulty of Christian life in) 618, (house churches) 251, 755, (local saints) 253, 381, (transfer of relics) 254–5, (and vitality of city life) 304, 327, 332, 352, 403, (and wealth) 261, 327, 401–2, 408; and classical tradition 349–50, 663–4, 665, 675, 695, 705, 742–4; and countryside 242, 308–9, 399, 400, 612, 618, (conversion) 348, 392, 670; creed-making *see separate entry*; cultural *koinē* 606; deacons 262, 341; decline, myth of 662; degrees of Christianization within 651, 655–8, 661; discipline 273; dissension within 62–3, 369, 393, 599–600, 687 (*see also under* Antioch; Constantinople; Rome); *districtiores Christiani* 661; east–west differences 241, 249, 563, 567–8, 578, 579, 663–4, (western support for eastern dissidents) 7–8, 8–9, 11–12, 121, 567–8; and education 66–7, 547, 555, 657, 664, 667–73, 676, 683, 688, 702, 757; emperors and, (authority) 26, 34, 239–40, 352, 563–4, 591–2, 638, 639, (benefactions and favour) 239–40, 257, 301, 304, 633, 738, (and councils) 34, 112, 238, 239, 256, 563, 570–1, (divine aspects) 1, 2, 138, 139–42, 143, 145, 150, 154, 158, 181, 352, 552, 759, 760–1; and entertainments 399; environment influenced by 250–7; epistolography 697–8; estates 260, 301, 304–5, 322, 327, 392; euergetism 257–8, 327, 332, 342–3, 381, 402 (*see also* charity; Church buildings); excommunication 269; festivals 252–3, 253–4, 255, 399, 400, 542, 659–60; *fideles* 657; finance 261–2, 262–3, 332, 341, 400, 401–2; food relief 336; histories, ecclesiastical 415; as institution 238–76, 403, 639; intellectual tradition 667; Islam and 641; and Jews 393, 394, 633, 639, 640–1, 642–3, 646, 648–9, 671, 752; justice 238–9, 248, 271–2, 272–6, 658–9; laws enforcing orthodoxy 638–40; and literacy 677–8; and literary culture 633–7, 665–6, 669–71, 671–3, 698–9, 702–5; lower classes 670; and Magnentius 23; and Manichees 582–3; mediation of Christ 637; metropolitans 239, 242–4, 247, 400, 562; Monophysitism 598; networks 654, 655; Nicene and non-Nicene hierarchies in west 581; oratory 675, 678, 704; organization and hierarchy 240–50, 400–1; Origenist controversy 594–5; and paganism, (ambiguity between cultures) 664, 667, (ascendancy of Christianity) 559–600, 632–3, 633–4, 636, 640, 643, 664, 667, (attacks on)

394, 646, 649–50, 667, 671, 706, (attitudes to art) 649–51, 743–4, 745, 746–8, 748–51, 756, (change in calendar) 399, (collocation of shrines) 633, (mixed marriages) 347, (persistence of pagan habits) 662–3, (polytheism adopts features of Christianity) 641, (shared moral culture) 606, 612–13, (syncretism) 393–4, 542, (tolerance) 641, 642 (*see also under* Neoplatonism); patronage 251, 264, 737, 757–8; persecution, compromise of faith in 562, 583; and philosophy 555, 613–14, 680, 681, 703, 706, 752; political and social power 263, 560, 612; political theology 140–1, 352; and popular beliefs 706; preaching *see* homilies; precedence of sees 104, 247–8, 249, 400–1, 562, 563, 579; primary groups 654–6, 661; provincial structures 207, 242, 244, 400; and public rituals 659; redemption, doctrine of 598, 599; representation of Christianization 633–7, 662, 664; schism 562, 564 (*see also* Donatism); self-regulation 656–7, 658–9, 660–1; and sexuality 610, 617, 618, 619, 656; and slavery 273, 294, 347; and social change 365, 369; and state 1–2, 7, 36, 108, 238–40, 260, 665, 703, (organization based on state) 240–1, 242, 244, 245, 247, 249; symbols 653; tax exemption 260; Theodosius I imposes Nicene orthodoxy 112, 274, 549, 559, 575, 578, 579, 580, 582; time, concept of 634–5, 690; Trinity, doctrines of 565, 566, 567, 568, 570–1, 573–5, 576–7, 577–8, 581–2, 587; triumphalism 634, 640, 643, 664; universality 606; violence, (against pagans) 541, 649–50 (*see also under* temples), (internal) 37, 62–3, 267–8, 369, 393, 394, 599–600, 647–8, 687; and warfare 226–7, 228, 438, 443, 451, 460; wealth 257–62, 401–2, 403; *see also* bishops; charity, Christian; clergy; councils of bishops; heresy; hymns; miracles; missionaries; pilgrimage; relics; saints; theology; women (Christian)

Church buildings 250–2, 327, 394–9, 406, 755; art 756–7; charitable establishments 251, 252, 257, 260; in cities 250–2, 254, 394–9, 406, 755, (on outskirts) 251, 252, 254, 398, 738–9; Donatist 252; in east 406; emperors' 11–12, 257–8, 737, 738 (*see also under* individual emperors); estate churches 309, 392; euergetism 258, 332, 342, 343, 381; in Holy Land 258, 758–9; for martyrs' relics 254; monastic 251; orations on 678; on pagan temple sites 551, 554; sanctuary in 273; state-financed 260; *see also* baptisteries *and under individual cities and patrons*

Cicero, M. Tullius 589, 592, 680

Cilicia *1 Gc, 6 Bb-Cb*, 368, 540–1; *see also* Isauria

cingulum (belt of office) 168–9

circumcelliones 9, 281, 585, 360, 368

circus 330, 660

cities 371–410; administrative role 373, 375, 407–8, 409; archaeology 403–4; barbarian invasions and 202, 391–2; bishops and 241–2, 263, 400, 402, 409, 600; *boulai* 371, 373; capitals 328–9, 381, 386, 388, 406, 407, 409, (forward location) 202, 389–90, 390–1, 409; *civitas* defined 371–3; classical townscape 381–2, *383*, 388, 404; colonnaded streets 382, *383*, 404; as consumers 316, 335; and countryside 308, 309, 349–50, 368, 408–9; decline, alleged 205–6, 301–4, 313, 323–5, 326–8, 381, 408; distribution systems 312, 329–30, 333; in east 326–7, 356, 378, 388, 404–6, 407, 409, 455; economy 316, 326–8, 328–35; education based in 676; emperors and 329, 389–90, 390–1 (see also *adventus*); extramural settlements 406; festivals 399, 652; fortified 217, 417, 420, 433, 437, 438, 455, 459–60; in frontier regions 202, 389–90, 390–1, 406, 409; Greek heritage 377; industry 313, 408; under Julian 64–6, 68, 72, 375; landowners resident in 301–4, 327, 328, 335–6; liturgies 330, 331; lower classes 355–6, 356–7, 358–9, 368–9; magistracies 330, 331; military needs 389–92; military role 375, 409–10; natives' sense of citizenship 381; non-market redistribution 330–2, 337 (*see also* euergetism); northern provinces 375, 396, 404, 406, 409; paganism 68, 254, 395, 540, 542, 550, 558; patronage, municipal 330–1, 337, 361–2; philosophers and 607, 611; political role 409–10; rituals 542, 661–2; saints 253–4, 410; similar settlements of lower category 373; size and wealth 403–9; slaves in 294; social marginalization 368–9; southern provinces 404–6, 409; state control 205, 209, 330, 375–6, 379, 380; supply and distribution schemes 329–30; and taxation 205, 330, 375, 376, 409; territories 371, 371, 373; townscape, (classical) 381–2, *383*, 388, 404, (religious) 250–1, 254, 395–9, 410; in west 241, 327, 351, 404–5, 406–7, 409; *see also* civic duties; *curiae, curiales*; entertainments; euergetism; walls, city; *and under* Church; Church buildings; walls, city; *and individual areas*

civic duties: *collegia* and 317; *curiales* and 324, 376, 380; exemptions 178–9, 205, 263, 264, 275, 365, 376, 384, 676, (restricted) 64, 65, 206

civil service *see* bureaucracy

civility 644, 646

Civita Vecchia (Centumcellae) *4 Bb*, 580

civitas 371–3

Civitas Leucorum *see* Toul

Civitas Mediomatricum *see* Metz

Civitas Petrocoriorum (Périgueux) *372, 374*

clarissimi (senatorial grade) 190

class, social: and asceticism 258, 605–6, 612–13, 614; and education 197, 365–6, 676, 677; and punishments 291, 359–60, 647; *see also* aristocracy; *coloni; curiae, curiales*; equestrian order; lower classes; senatorial order

classical tradition: architecture 736–7; art 742–4; Christianity and 349–50, 606, 612–13, 663–4, 665, 667, 675, 695, 705, 742–4; literary culture 665–6, 675, 695, 704, 705, 706–7; townscape 381–2, *383*, 388, 404

Claudian 488, 527, 673, 692–3; on emperors 139, 140, 411; invective 175, 176–7, 415; praise of Stilicho 114, 115, 175, 176–7, 415, 527

Claudius Gothicus, emperor 361

Clement of Alexandria 625, 744, 752, 753

Clement of Rome 577; First Epistle (Coptic) 726

Clementine Recognitions (Syriac) 718

clergy, Christian: and army 226–7, 265, 438; career in 262–8, 327, 350, 655; civic exemptions 263, 264, 275, 365; *collegiati* banned from 324; diplomacy 270, 434–5; exemplary behaviour expected of 655–6; expansion strengthens Christian primary groups 655; hierarchy 263–4, 275, 327, 400–1, 655; medical skills 434–5; numbers 263; patronage 264; schemes for support of 329; *see also* bishops; metropolitans

Clermont-Ferrand (Augustonemetum) *2 Cb*, 350

clientes 292–3

clothing: ascetics' 601, 604, 616; dress codes 336, 604; mass-produced 313; philosopher's 601, 604, 613, 643

Cluj-Someseni gold hoard 485

Clysma (Suez) *6 Bc, 8 Ba*, 449

coastline, change in 279, 463, 474

Codex Gregorianus 682

Codex Hermogenianus 682

codices, illuminated 738

codicils of appointment 152, 163, 166

cognitive processes and cultural change 705–7

cohortales 204–5

coinage 523–4; *adventus* 186; Constans, FEL TEMP REPARATIO 6; Constantine 2, 186, 497; Constantius II 17; copper 307, 313n3; Eugenius 109; Germanic tribes' import of Roman 469, 472, 480–1, 484, 493; Magnentius 16; Victory on 411; *see also* mints

collatio lustralis (trade tax) 263, 264, 309, 314, 321, 325, 337

collegia 290, 302–3, 318–22, 324–5; state control 289, 313, 317, 318–22, 324–5, 337

Cologne (Colonia Agrippinensis) *1 Da, 2 Da*, 8, 29, 49, 422, 465, 467

coloni (peasant farmers) 285, 287–94, 304, 306–7; army service 296; and *conductores* 285, 305, 306–7; 'free' 292; fugitives 288, 291, 292, 293–4, 296; grades 370; imperial 290, 291;

coloni (peasant farmers) (*cont.*)
land tenure 283; laws on 282, 288–9, 290, 357; near-servile status 288, 357–8, 370; in private armies 311; protection by powerful 309–10, 362–3; punishment 290–1, 360; taxation 284, 289, 290; tied to land of origin 282, 288, 289, 296, 357

Colonia Agrippinensis *see* Cologne

colonnades; evolve into souks 382, *383*, 404

Colt Papyri 456

columns, triumphal 736–7

combs, Černjachov culture bone 493

comedy; *Querolus* (anon.) 367, 531–2

comes, title of 215, 353; *Orientis* 166, 455–6; *rei militaris* 215, 353; *rei privatae* 166; *sacrarum largitionum* 165–6, 168, 353

comets 2, 80, 85

comitatus (field army) 213–14, 215, 216, 412, 417, 421, 455–6

comitiva, emperor's 353

commentarius (official) 167, 168

communications 157, 161, 181, 417; see also *agentes in rebus*; *cursus publicus*; roads; seafaring

competitive ethos 604–5

Comum *4 Ba*, 25, 47

Concordia *1 Eb, 4 Ca*, 228n109

conductores (lessees of estates) 283–4, 290, 298, 300, 304; and *coloni* 285, 305, 306–7

conformity, social 644

coniuratio Marcelliana 203

conscription 101–2

consensus, Christian/pagan cultural 646, 667

Consentia *1 Ec*, 127

consistorium (emperor's council) 151, 275

Constans, emperor: Caesar (333) 2; accession as Augustus 2, 3, 762; share of empire 4; Constantine II fails to depose 5, 215, 762; rule in west 5–11; disaffection from 10, 15; Magnentius' coup against 10–11; death 11, 421, 762

Alamannic campaigns 6, 420; army under 10, 215; and Athanasius 8–9; baptism 7; in Britain (343) 6–7, 420; and Church 7, 8–9, 12, 258, 567; coinage; FEL TEMP REPARATIO 6; and Constantius II 8–9, 12; and Franks 6, 8, 420; law against pagan cults 7; Olympias betrothed to 40; in Rome 6; Sarmatian campaign (338) 5, 420; Trier as capital 6

Constans, son of Constantine III 129, 528

Constantia (Maiumas) *6 Bc*, 241, 392, 542, 555

Constantia (Tella de-Mauzelat) 419

Constantia Postumia, daughter of Constantius II 85, 90

Constantina, daughter of Constantine I 3, 16, 17, 24–5

Constantina (legionary base) 458

Constantine I, emperor 762; *adventus* 186; anniversary celebrations 185, 566, 678; and

army 213–14, 226, 417, 457; baptism 1, 11; and bureaucracy 171; and Church 342, (doctrine) 33, 239, 272, 562–3, 564–7, 583, (financial and material support) 257, 301, 304, 329, 558–9, (honour after death) 1, 2, (management of councils) 239, 240; church building 11–12, 31, 257, 401, 738, 758; coinage 2, 186; *comites* 353; and Constantinople 677, (building projects) 1, 38–9, 401, 738, 758; (creates senate) 185–6, 364; death 1, 2, 567, 762; diplomacy 419; discourses 678; Eusebius' encomium 678; finance 186; frontiers under 417, 419, 495, 497; funeral 1–2; and Holy Land 666, 738, 758–9; house of, as focus of loyalty 15, 16, 22, 28, 30, 225; Julian's criticism of 64, 73; laws 64, 288, 325, 357, 361; Licinius' defeat 185–6, 418; and Maiumas 542; mausoleum 1, 38–9; and paganism 30, 539, 540–1, 545, 644–5; and Persia 12, 13, 14, 419, 437–8, 460; posthumous rule 1, 3; prayer before battle 227; as precedent 7, 17, 26; propaganda 186; and Rome 30, 185, (buildings) 31, 185, 390, *397*, 398, 402, 738; succession to 1–5; taxation 186, 282, 314, 325; on Virgil 753

Constantine II, emperor: accession as Augustus 3, 762; succeeds to share of empire 2, 4; secures Athanasius' restoration (337) 5, 7, 11; victory over Alamanni (338) 5; war against Constans, death 5, 215, 762; patronage of churches in Jerusalem 258

Constantine III, emperor 122, 123, 126, 129–30, 431–2, 527–9; and Gallic Church 250; and Honorius and family 126, 129, 130, 311, 513; impact on border defences 428, 529; remnants of supporters 532

Constantinople *1 Fb, 3 Eb, 5 Da, 6 Aa*, 372, *387*; as capital 112, 117, 351, 390, 391, 666; Constantine and 677, (building projects) 1, 38–9, 401, 738, 758, (creates senate) 185–6, 364; Constantius II and 37–9, 61, 401; emperors' presence 268, 386, *387*, 388; excavations 405; food supply *see* supply and distribution *below*; Gothic threats 102, 448, 509, 765; harbours 386, *387*; Jews 640–1; Julian in 45, 60–7; learning 37, 45, 676, 682, 683; lower classes 358, 369; *Notitia Urbis* 758; pagan attitudes 645–6; praetorship(s) 185, 192; prefect 38, 167; relics 38–9, 134, 254, 386, 388, 401; size 336, *374*, 388; supply and distribution 37, 129, 167, 328–9, 336, 386; Themistius as proconsul 540; triumph (386) 106; Valens and 82, 89; *see also under* senates

BUILDINGS AND WORKS OF ART: Arch of Theodosius 737; baths, (of Constantius) 37–9, (of Zeuxippus) 743–4; churches 38–9, 252, 401, 738, 758, (Holy Apostles) 60, *387*, 758, (St Irene) 38, *387*, 758, (St Sophia) 38,

116, 263, *387*, 571, 758; column of Theodosius
I 106, 736–7; Hippodrome 25, *387*, 737; library
37; mausoleum of Constantine 1, 38–9;
monasteries 252, 259, 345; mosaics 749;
palace 749; statues 2, 386, 388, 736, 743–4,
745; walls 37–9, 102, 129, *387*, 391–2; water
supply 386, *387*

    CHURCH: Arian congregation 578;
bishops 268, 369–70, 400–1, 578–9 (*see also*
Chrysostom, John; Demophilus; Eudoxius;
Eusebius, bishop of Nicomedia; Gregory of
Nazianzus; Macedonius; Maximus; Nectarius;
Nestorius; Paul); charity 252, 262–3, 369;
clergy 263; Constantius and 38–9; councils of
bishops, (360) 37, 571, 581, (381) 103–4,
246–7, 274, 562–3, 573, 578, 579, 765;
factional unrest 37, 62–3, 117–18, 123, 267;
and Jews 640–1; Novatian congregations 266,
648; precedence of see 247–8, 249, 401, 579;
wealth 261; women 654
Constantius II, emperor: becomes Caesar as
child 37; marriage 2, 4; sent to east 419;
accession as Augustus 1, 2, 3, 762; and
murders of family of Theodora 3–4, 11; part
of empire allocated to 4; Constans'
estrangement from 8–9; and Athanasius 8,
11–12, 248–9, 568, 569; and Persia (337–50)
5, 8, 11–14, 16, 420, 421, 763; Magnentius'
usurpation 14, 16, 17, 20–2, 26, 30, 31, 419,
421–2, 762; becomes sole ruler 22; campaigns
against Alamanni 24, 29, 217, 421–2; deposes
Gallus 24–5, 47, 50, 56, 161, 422, 762; and
Silvanus' rebellion 27–8, 762; appoints Julian
Caesar in Gaul 28–9; military collaboration
with Julian 29, 49–51, 54–5, 55–6, 422; court
at Sirmium, and creed-making (357–9) 32–7;
Danube campaigns 32, 35, 54, 422; Persian
campaign (360–1) 39–43, 423, 763; calls for
reinforcements from Julian 40, 56–7, 58, 423;
Julian's usurpation 3, 40, 41, 42, 43, 57–60,
144, 221, 423; death 43, 763; burial 22, 60–1,
678; Julian's succession to 43, 60, 423, (purge
of Constantius' court) 63, 152–3

    and Antioch 8, 11, 12, 13, 37, 42, 69, 161,
252, 567; and Armenia 5, 12–13, 39, 40, 41,
420, 423, 437; and army 4, 215, 225, 227, 421;
baptism 42, 43; bureaucracy 63, 152–3, 159,
171, 188, 190, 196; and Church 8, 11–12, 17,
20, 24, 32–7, 62, 63, 238, 567–71, (and
Athanasius) 8, 11–12, 248–9, 568, 569,
(building) 3, 31, 205, 257, 258, (theological
interest) 12, 33, 36, 539, 559; coinage, HOC
SIGNO VICTOR ERIS 17; and
Constantinople 37–9, 61, 401; diplomacy 32,
41, 42, 420; imperial majesty 30, 142, 143, 150,
687, 760; marriages 2, 4, 42; at Milan 21, 24,
46, 48; and paganism 31, 539–43, 545, 549,
559; portraits 30, 736, 759–60; and senates

187–8, 190, 196–7, 200; *see also under* Persia;
Rome
Constantius III (Flavius Constantius, *magister
utriusque militiae*) 130, 131–2, 135, 249, 766;
campaigns and settlement of barbarians
131–2, 234, 432, 506, 514, 519, 530–2
Constantius (eastern general) 443
construction industry 321–2, 326
consuls: barbarian *see* Nevitta; and council of
Ariminum 34; diptychs 759, 760–1; eastern,
of humble origins 196; emperors 9, 29, 72,
80, 82; Eutropius' nomination 116; emperors'
installation ceremony 64; Symmachus 191,
192; usurpers 11, 107
consumption: by cities 335; conspicuous 335,
343, 355; by landowners 337
contracts, land 291, 292
Coptic literature 666, 720–35; Apocrypha 724–5;
biblical texts 722–4, 725, 726, 735; bilingual
Syriac-Coptic manuscript 710n7, 735; dating
721, 724; dialects 720–1, 735; diversity 735;
gnostic works 730–3, 735; homiletic works
723, 725–7, 734; magical texts 722; Manichean
works 733–5; martyrologies 729–30; monastic
texts 700, 727–9; Nag Hammadi library and
related tractates 725, 730–3; Old Coptic 720,
722; original literature 729, 735; origins 708–9;
patristic works 725–7; script 720
copying of texts 670, 677
Corbridge Lanx 749
Corduba (Cordova) *1 Cc*, 8, 10, 157
Corduene *6 Db*, 39, 79
Corinth *5 Bb*, 249, *372*, 390, 401, 405
corn *see* grain
cornicularius (official) 167, 168
corruption 175–80, 209–10, 320, 360–1
corvée labour services 306, 317, 324–5
council, emperor's (*consistorium*) 151, 275
council of the seven Gallic provinces 133,
202–3, 204, 532
councils of bishops: annual provincial 207, 242;
authority 238–9, 562, 563; imperial
involvement 34, 112, 238, 239, 256, 563,
570–1; *see also* creeds; synods; *and under*
Ancyra; Antioch; Aquileia; Ariminum; Arles;
Béziers; Carthage; Chalcedon;
Constantinople; Ephesus; Milan; Nicaea;
Rome; Seleucia; Serdica; Sirmium; Tyre
countryside 277–311; in Africa 285–6, 306; *agri
deserti* 281–5; artistic depictions 304; artisans'
alleged flight to 308, 313, 333, 408; ascetics
348, 601, 607–8; banditry 308, 368, barbarian
invasions affect 279–81, 308; child-rearing
308; Christianity 242, 308–9, 348, 392, 399,
400, 612, 618, 670; and cities 308, 309,
349–50, 368, 408–9; depopulation, third-
century 278; development 285–7; estate
management 305–7; fairs 308, 309n120;

countryside (*cont.*)
  feudalism 363; fugitives in 308, 366–7; labour
  and property-owners 287–304; lower classes
  365–7, 357–8; manpower 282; marginal
  elements in 366–7; northern frontier, some
  abandonment 279; organization of 304–11;
  paganism 271–2, 308, 550, 553–4, 557–8, 599;
  philosophers in 607–8; poverty 308;
  production 277–87, 304–5; protection of
  poor by powerful 308, 309–11, 3¿2–3;
  rebellions 367–8; ruralization 307–9; security
  308, 309–11, 362–3, 366–7; senatorial order
  in 301–4, 313, 408, 612; slavery 294–7;
  taxation 281–5; war damage 278–9;
  warlordism 308, 311; *see also* agriculture; *coloni*;
  villages; villas
couriers (*areani*) 7
court: bishops' lobbying 239, 264, 265, 269, 270,
  275–6, 384; doctors 683; emperors and 63, 64,
  160–1, 162, 181–2, 533; fall of high officials
  152–3; in forward-located capitals 390–1;
  poetry 694; and provinces 208
crafts: Germanic tribes 473, 479, 493; *see also*
  artisans
creeds 12, 33; Antioch (341) 567, (363) 80, (379)
  577–8; Ariminum 580; Constantinople (381)
  104, 274, 562–3, 579; Nicaea 562–3, 565–6;
  old Roman 567; Serdica 568; of Ulfilas 581
Cross, relics of 255
Croydon; Germanic burials 475
Ctesiphon *6 Dc, 9 Cb*, 75, 424, 439
Cuicul (Djemila) *7 Bb, 372, 374*, 405, 749
culture: barbarian/Roman acculturation 304,
  464, 537, 665; homogeneous Christian 606;
  upper class 377, 384–5, 646, 651, 665; *see also*
  classical tradition; literary culture
curiae, curiales 371, 373; and bureaucracy 324,
  376–7, 378, 381, 384–5; in cities 323–4; and
  civic duties 66, 324, 376, 380; clerical careers
  263, 264; decline 205–6, 331–2, 339, 360,
  373–82, 393, 409; euergetism 377–8;
  impoverishment of lower 299, 324, 327,
  331–2; Julian and 65, 66; and paganism 551;
  and *potentiores* 360–1; *principales* 299, 300, 356;
  punishments 376; replaced in civic power
  structures 382–8; state control 338, 376, 380;
  and taxation 299, 375, 376
curse tablet, leaden 632
cursus honorum 191–5
cursus publicus 65, 165, 167, 170; bishops' use 35,
  36, 238, 239, 256, 262, 276, 563n4
Cybale *3 Eb*, 99
Cybele, Mother of Gods, cult of 68, 552, 753
Cylaces (governor of Armenia) 91, 92
Cynegius, Maternus (praetorian prefect) 106,
  551, 553, 646, 647
Cynics 544

Cyprian, St 252, 253, 256, 586
Cyprus *6 Bc*, 116, 681, 744–5
Cyrenaica *7 Cb*, 236, 245, 433
Cyrene *1 Fc, 7 Db*, 266, 269
Cyril, bishop of Alexandria 134, 596–8, 599, 648,
  767
Cyril, bishop of Jerusalem 261, 699, 726
Cyril, bishop of Scythopolis 450
Cyrillona (Syriac poet) 709
Cyrrhus *6 Cb, 9 Ba*, 298, 455
Cyzicus *1 Fb, 5 Ca*, 71, 366

Dacia *1 Eb-Fb, 3 Da-b*, 121, 278; Goths in 103,
  509, 517–18
Dadastana *6 Ba*, 80
Dadišo (*catholicos* in Persia) 135
Dagalaifus (*magister equitum*) 78, 81
Dakhleh Oasis, Egypt; Manichean texts 710n7,
  735
Dalmatia *1 Eb, 3 Cb*, 126
Dalmatius, Flavius (Caesar) 2, 3, 4, 215
Damascius; *Life of Isidore* 613–14, 700
Damascus *1 Gc, 6 Cc, 9 Bb*, 404, 456
Damasus, pope: appointment contested 82,
  267–8, 648; condemns Apollinarians 573; and
  eastern Church 104, 577, 578, 579; epigrams
  691; Petrine basis of authority 249; publicizes
  martyrs in Rome 253, 758; statements of
  orthodoxy 103, 274
Danaba *6 Cc, 417–8*
Danube region 3, *372*; barbarian threat under
  Marcus Aurelius 416; unrest after Diocletian
  418; Constantine's policy 419; Constans'
  operations 5, 420; Constantius II's campaigns
  32, 35, 54, 422; Magnentius' attempt to
  control 15; Julian strengthens defences 235;
  Julian's advance against Constantius 59;
  barbarian invasions 424; Valentinian I and
  85–6; Valens and Goths 94–101; under
  Honorius 431; Theodosius II rebuilds
  defences 435
      army 217, 227, 235–6; barbarian
  confederacies 418; barbarian raids 413; bridge
  across river 419; cities 406; effect of
  admission of barbarians to empire 428, 463;
  fleet on river 129, 139, 433; Germanic
  settlement outside empire 465, 483–6, 491–2,
  503, 506; Roman strategy 217, 419, 428; rural
  development 286
Daphne, Antioch *6 Cb*, 69–71, 303, 392–3, 406
Darial Pass 442
De Rebus Bellicis (anon.) 158, 367, 415, 535, 685–6
De Viris Illustribus 684
deacons 262, 341
Decentius (Magnentius' Caesar) 17, 22, 24, 40,
  56
declamation 674–5, 682

decuriones see *curiae, curiales*
dediticii 280, 290
defence in depth 428, 458
defensores civitatis 273
defensores plebis 361
Delphi *5 Bb*, 540
Demeas (Ephesian magistrate) 642
Demeter, cult at Eleusis 46
Demetrias (female ascetic) 345
demonetization 313
demons 627–8, 632
Demophilus, bishop of Constantinople 103, 268, 575, 578
Denmark; votive offerings in bogs 481–2
deportment, codes of 604
desert, myth of, and asceticism 614–16, 617, 618, 619–20, 622, 627
Dibio (Dijon) *2 Cb*, 373
Didache (Coptic) 726
Didymus (teacher in Alexandria) 594
Dieulouard (Scarpona) *2 Db*, 83
dignitates (high government posts) 188, 195–6, 206
Dijon (Dibio) *2 Cb*, 373
Dio Chrysostom 680
Diocaesarea *6 Cc*, 453
dioceses 166, 246–7, 364, 375
Diocletian, emperor: abdication 418; army under 213, 219, 417, 457, 459; bureaucracy enlarged 364; Edict on Prices 332–3, 333–4, 336, 673; *fabricae* expanded 313; persecutes Christians 559; and Persia 12; provinces 364; in Rome 30; social reforms 340–1, 361; taxation 220, 277, 282, 289; tetrarchy 351, 418
Diodore, bishop of Tarsus 572, 573, 579, 717
Dionysias *8 Bb*, 178, 230, 231
Dionysius, bishop of Alexandria 577
Dionysius, bishop of Milan 26, 569
Dionysus, cult of 744–5, 746, 748
Diospolis (Lydda) *6 Bc*, 453, 590
diplomacy 411–36; with barbarians 32, 428–9, 433, 536; by clergy 270, 434–5; development 413–14, 415–16, 433–6; foundation of Byzantine 112, 414, 436; by *notarii* 159; to contain Persia 42, 419, 420; with Persia 42, 91–4, 112, 414, 420, 425, 434–5, 438; sources 414–16; over usurpations 16, 41, 59–60; warfare combined with 428–9, 436; warfare replaced by 413, 414, 428–9
diptychs, consular 759, 760–1
Diran, king of Armenia 437
dispute genre 713
dissent 146, 157–8, 290, 308, 311
Dissimilarians 570
distribution systems 215, 312, 333; *see also under* grain *and individual cities*
districtiores Christiani 661

divination 31, 78, 539, 545, 549, 637
Divitenses (army corps) 89
divorce 654
Diyarbekir *see* Amida
Djemila *see* Cuicul
doctors 174, 655, 683
Domitianus (praetorian prefect of the East) 25, 196
Donatism 9–10, 242, 252, 583–6; beliefs 562, 583, 599; Constantine and 564, 583; origins 246, 583; repression 9, 274, 309, 360, 585, 586, 642, 767; see also *circumcelliones*
donatives 57, 166, 228
Donatus (*grammaticus*) 674
Donk 469
Dorchester-on-Thames 475
Dorotheus, vision of 141
Dover (Portus Dubris) *2 Ca*, 477
Dregsted, Jutland 479
Drepanius, Latinus Pacatus 148–9, 150
duces see *dux*
Dulcitius (proconsul of Asia) 196
Dumata (Jawf) 458
Dunkerque II Transgression 279
Dura Europus *6 Dc*, 78–9, 708, 740, 755
Durocatalaunum (Châlons-sur-Marne) *2 Cb*, 83
Durocortorum (Rheims) *1 Db*, *2 Cb*, 49, 122
Durostorum (Silistra) *3 Eb*, 168–9
dux, duces 214, 217, 236, 363, 412, 456, 460
Dyarbekir *see* Amida

earthquakes 36, 118, 645–6
east and west: Church relations 241, 249, 563, 567–8, 578, 579, 663–4, (western support for eastern dissidents) 7–8, 8–9, 11–12, 121, 567–8; civilian and military roles in administration 111, 112, 115, 117, 430, 435; cultural change on division 665; inequalities of wealth 241, 326–7, 351–2, 357, 404–7, 409; rift under Arcadius and Honorius 111, 115, 117, 121, 128, 175, 429, 431, 518
East Anglia 475, 477
Easter 253, 657, 699
Echternach, Luxemburg 467–8
economy 312–37; army and 211, 219, 231, 329, 456; cities 316, 326–8, 328–35; command economy 328–30; demonetization 313; Germanic tribes 493; non-market redistribution 307, 315–16, 323, 330–2, 336, 337; sources 314–15; state intervention and its limits 316–22; supply side 333–5; *see also* agriculture; industry; trade
Edessa (Urfa) *1 Gc*, *6 Cb*, *9 Ba*; arms factory 456; banditry in area 449; calendar of 411 718; Christianity 71, 263, 542, 555, 667, 679, 710; *collatio lustralis* 314; Constantius II's muster 41, 42–3; Ephrem at 619, 679, 709; Hunnic

Edessa (Urfa) (*cont.*)
    invasion 443; learning 667, 679, 715–16;
    mosaics 708, 716; porticoes 388; Proto-Syriac
    inscriptions 708
edicts, imperial 143–4, 157; *see also under*
    Diocletian
Edobich (general) 528
education 667–84; in Asia Minor 45, 46;
    advancement through 673–9, 683; in
    architecture 683; art as means 672, 757;
    bureaucrats' 197, 675, 683; Church and 66–7,
    547, 555, 657, 664, 667–73, 676, 683, 688, 702,
    757; city-based 676; content of traditional
    673–4; in Edessa 679, 715–16; emperors and
    676; in engineering 683; expense 197, 365–6,
    676, 677; importance 365–6; Julian restricts
    Christians' teaching 66–7, 547, 668, 676, 688;
    in law 667, 682–3; in mathematics 675–6; in
    medicine 683; medieval 681, 683–4;
    Neoplatonist 46, 681–2; pagan teachers
    banned under Justinian 558; in philosophy 46,
    543, 667, 675–6; *progymnasmata* 674; for public
    life 197, 364, 673–9, 683; in rhetoric 665,
    667–73, 682, 683–4, 686; and shared culture
    of upper classes 665; teachers 673–4; travel to
    centres of 45, 676–7, 680–1, 682; women's 44
Egeria (pilgrim) 256, 261, 449, 699, 702, 756
Egypt *1 Gc-d, 8*; administration 166; Arab raids
    433, 447; army 218, 221, 230, 231; ascetics
    594, 602, 606, 619, 622, 626–8, 630, 727–9 (*see
    also* Antony); Asia Minor, possible links
    between churches 725, 726; *coloni* 231–2, 357,
    363; grain exports 329, 386; landowners 204;
    literacy 677; Nicene Christians persecuted
    576; poetry 694, 695; protection of peasants
    231–2, 363; scripts 720; taxation 231–2, 282;
    textiles, pagan themes 749; *see also* Coptic
    literature *and individual places*
Ejsbol, Denmark 482
Eketorpsborg, Öland 480
Elbe-Weser region 472, 474, 475, 477
Elephantine papyri 713
Eleusis mystery cult *5 Bb*, 46, 552
Eleusius, bishop of Cyzicus 71, 265
Elijah, Apocalypse of (Coptic) 724
élite *see* aristocracy; bureaucracy; euergetism;
    landowners; patronage; senatorial order
Elna 11
Elsham, Lincs. 475
Emesa *1 Gc, 6 Cc,* 20, 455, 541
emperors 139–62, 352–4; barbarians' loyalty to
    person 428, 510–11, 518, 536; and bureaucrats
    and officials 138, 139, 151–3, 159, 161,
    169–75, 182–3, 352; Byzantine 150; capitals *see
    under* cities; and centralization of power 138,
    150–6, 161, 181–2, 183; ceremonial 142–3,
    145, 180–1, 352, 759; citizen-king image
    147–8, 150; clemency 154–5; *comitiva* 353; and

court 63, 64, 160–1, 162, 181–2, 533; danger
    of offending 157–8, 181–2; distance from
    subjects 143–4, 149–50, 351, 355–6; divine
    aspects 1, 2, 138, 139–42, 143, 145, 150, 154,
    158, 181, 352, 552, 759, 760–1; edicts 143–4;
    empresses' influence 160–1; and eunuchs 161,
    351; finance 352; foreign policy 139; ideology
    145; image of 2, 30, 63, 64, 142, 143, 148, 150,
    687, 759, 760; isolation 138, 181; and justice
    291, 352; landowners 301; and law 139, 141,
    352; limits on power 157–62; oratory on
    147–9, 150; pagan view of divinity 2, 138,
    139–40, 141, 181, 552; patronage 258, 390,
    736–7, 738, 757–8; petitions to 155–6, 201; as
    pontifex maximus 68, 104, 352, 550; and
    provinces 153–6, 375–6; proximity to 151,
    152, 156, 160–1, 181, 247, 351, 353; purple
    144, 352; range of perspectives,
    contemporary 149–50; representation and
    perceptions of power 138, 139–50, 180–1;
    rewards from 155, 181–2; and Rome 148, 185,
    198, 200, 342, 369, 390; and senates 198,
    199–200, 201, 204, 352, 355–6; statues
    venerated 143, 154, 652, 661; and taxation
    139; virtues and vices, catalogues of 145–6,
    150; *see also* intelligence service *and under*
    army; Church; Church buildings; cities
emphyteutic (quasi-permanent) leases 281, 283,
    289–90, 292, 298, 304; on imperial land 283,
    284, 290, 300, 301, 304
encomia 668, 675, 678
Enmann's *Kaisergeschichte* 684
Enna 305
entertainments, public secular 167, 330, 377, 378,
    380, 388, 399; *see also* games; races
environmental change 279, 463, 474
Ephesus *1 Fc, 5 Cb, 372*; Church 248, 401, 641–2,
    664; council of (431) 598, 767; and emperors
    390; inscription on Flavius Philippus 353;
    Julian studies at 543, 544; philosophy 543,
    544, 607; prosperity 326, 406; remains 378,
    405, 406; size, and supply 336
Ephraem *see* Ephrem
Ephrem (Syriac poet) 619–20, 637, 679, 709, 719;
    artistic prose 712; and Greek culture 716–17;
    Jewish influence 713; dispute genre 713;
    hymns 619, 710, 712, 716; panegyric 710;
    translation into Greek 619, 717
Ephrem, Pseudo- 709
epibole 282
epideictic rhetoric 675, 682
Epiphanius of Salamis 586, 594, 639, 671, 703,
    756
Epirus *1 Eb-Fb, 5 Bb,* 115, 118, 122–3, 429
episcopalis audientia (bishop's jurisdiction) 273,
    275, 658–9
epistolography *see* letters
epitomes 415, 684; *E. de Caesaribus* 415, 439, 684

equestrian order 205, 359; demise 339, 352, 369; perfectissimate 189, 190
Erice, Sicily 1 Ec, 305
Eriulf (Gothic leader) 512
Ermenaric, leader of Greuthungi 491, 492, 500, 502, 511, 517
Erythrum, bishopric of 269
Esquiline treasure 464, 746, 747, 748
estates: buildings 306; of Church 322; churches on 309, 392; expansion of private 322–5; imperial 44–5, 71, 166, 322; Julian restores to cities 65
Ethiopia 419, 436
Etruria 4 Bb, 286, 287, 307; diviners 545, 548
Eucherius (son of Stilicho) 120, 124, 125
Eudaimon (Egyptian poet) 694
Eudoxia (wife of Arcadius) 113–14, 116, 117–18, 123; and Church 117–18, 160, 161, 180, 258
Eudoxia (wife of Theodosius II) 135, 694, 695, 759
Eudoxia, Licinia (daughter of Theodosius II) 136
Eudoxius, bishop of Antioch, later of Constantinople 38, 241, 247, 570, 571, 575
euergetism 330, 331–2, 337, 341–2, 377–80; Christian 257–8, 327, 332, 342–3, 381, 402; see also patronage
Eugenius (Constans' magister officiorum) 10
Eugenius, Flavius (usurper) 109, 146, 228, 510–11, 552, 764; cost of suppression 113, 428, 510–11
Eulalius, bishop of Chalcedon 647
Eulalius, candidate for bishopric of Rome 267–8
Eunapius of Sardis 606, 687–8; history 527, 685; Lives of the Sophists 680, 681, 700; Zosimus preserves 414, 685, 687
Eunomian church history, Philostorgius' 689
Eunomius, bishop of Cyzicus 33, 366, 570, 572, 576
Eunomius, bishop of Theodosiopolis 444
eunuchs, court 161, 165, 176, 350–1; see also Eutropius
Euphemitai (Phoenician pagan sect) 641
Euphrates, bishop of Cologne 8
Eupraxius, Flavius 157–8
Euric, Code of 522, 523
Eusebia, empress 25, 30, 47, 48–9, 50, 548
Eusebius, bishop of Caesarea: and classical culture 671, 680, 744; and Nicene creed 565–6; political theology 140, 240, 352, 689
   WRITINGS 689–91; Chronicle 689, 690; Ecclesiastical History 688, 689, 690, 700; Life of Constantine 1–2, 671, 689–90; Onomasticon 456; other works 567, 678, 690–1; translations of 690, 718
Eusebius, bishop of Emesa 20, 715

Eusebius, bishop of Nicomedia 33, 44, 565, 566, 581; translation to Constantinople 11, 241, 247, 268
Eusebius, bishop of Vercelli 26, 569
Eusebius, chamberlain to Constantius II 61
Eusebius, town-councillor of Apamea 644
Eusebius of Myndus 544
Eustathius, bishop of Antioch 566, 595
Euthymius (bishop) 450
Eutropia (Roman aristocrat) 15
Eutropius (epitomator) 415, 684
Eutropius (praepositus sacri cubiculi): ascendancy 114–15, 116, 268, 429, 512; Claudian's attacks on 175, 176–7, 415, 692–3; fall 116, 153, 351, 765
Euzoius, bishop of Antioch 42, 43, 80, 571–2, 575
Evagrius (comes rei privatae) 61
Evagrius, candidate for bishopric of Antioch 265
Evagrius of Pontus (ascetic) 594, 606, 622, 626–8, 701; intellectualism 555, 629, 669; and praktikoi 626–8, 630
Evodius, bishop of Uzalis 265n122
exceptores (officials) 167, 168, 171
exchange see gifts
excommunication 269
exegesis, typological 752–3
exorcism 348, 634
Expositio Totius Mundi 544–5
Exsuperantius (military officer) 531, 532
extramural settlements 406
Ezra, Apocalypse of (Syriac) 713

Fabiola (Roman aristocrat) 659
fabricae (state factories) 165, 166, 170, 232, 313, 316, 456; workers 318, 319, 322
Faesulae (Fiesole) 4 Bb; battle of 121, 234, 518, 431
fairs 300–1, 308, 309n120, 333
Famechon, Picardy 279
family 506, 659
famine 25, 125, 129
farms, fortified 278, 285, 417
Farnobius (Gothic noble) 494
Faustina, empress 42
Faustus of Byzanta 416
Feddersen Wierde 473, 477
Felicianus, Flavius (priest of Apollo at Delphi) 540
Felix (magister utriusque militiae) 137, 533, 536
Felix, pope 31
Felix of Abthungi, trial of (313–14) 359
Felix of Nola, St 253, 254, 255, 256, 350, 660; Paulinus and 258, 660, 693–4
festivals: Christian 252–3, 253–4, 255, 399, 400, 542, 659–60; pagan 399, 542, 585, 652
Festus (epitomator) 415, 684

feudalism 363
Fidustius (governor of Antioch) 92
Fiesole *see* Faesulae
finance, administration of: army 167, 211;
  Church 261–2, 262–3, 332, 341, 400, 401–2;
  imperial 129, 166, 167, 168, 234, 352,
  (centralization) 205, 330
Firmus, bishop of Caesarea 598
Firmus, chieftain of Iubaleni; rebellion 88, 303,
  658, 762
fish-sauce 315
Flavian, bishop of Antioch 270, 271–2, 579, 580,
  717
Flavianus, Virius Nicomachus 172, 194, 551, 552;
  writings 685, 695–6, 700
fleets 22, 54, 75–6; Danube 129, 139, 433
Flögeln 473
flooding, marine 279, 463, 474
Florence (Florentia) *4 Bb*, 121
Florentius (*magister officiorum*) 61
Florentius (praetorian prefect) 54–5, 56–7, 58,
  61
Florentius (Procopius' commander in Nicaea)
  91
florilegia 577, 703
food supply: for army 285; barbarians and
  530–1; Church aid 336; in Constantinople
  129, 167; euergetism 330, 342; monopolies
  321–2; profiteering 71, 72, 312, 331, 334–5;
  riots over 71, 312, 329, 358; in Rome 115, 167,
  307, 355, 390; state intervention in market
  336; storage 312; trade 315; see also *annona*
foreign relations 411–36; *see also individual
  countries and* diplomacy; warfare
foreign residents 341, 342
fortifications: block-houses, Cyrenaica 236; cities
  and towns 217, 417, 420, 433, 437, 438, 455,
  459–60; farms 278, 285, 417; frontier 84, 213,
  214, 217, 425, 428, 432–3, 497; private, in east
  443, 444; villages in Gaul 309; *see also* walls,
  city
forts, military 214, 217, 456–7
Foz de Lumbier, near Pompaelo 302
Franks *1 Da, 462*; Constantine admits to Roman
  army 419; Constans' campaigns 6, 8, 420;
  Julian's campaigns 29, 49, 51, 54, 58, 280, 422,
  467, 762; fail to stop barbarian crossing of
  Rhine (406) 122, 431; support Jovinus 130
    Christianity 112; metalworking 481; raids
  into Gaul 101, 279, 516; in Roman army 14,
  15, 419, 475, 528; settlements in Rhineland
  and Gaul 280, 420, 465, 467–70, 472; usurpers
  14, 15
Fravitta (*magister militum*) 116, 117, 430, 511, 512,
  765
friendship 654, 694, 697
Friesland *2 Da*, 472
Frigideius (general) 98–9

Frigidus, river *3 Ba, 4 Ca*; battle of 109, 114, 227,
  228, 510, 511, 764
Frisii *462*
Fritigern (leader of Tervingi) 98, 100, 102, 494,
  509–10, 511; admission to empire 500, 507,
  517
frontier regions: bishops' role in defence 12,
  269–70, 438, 444; cities 202, 389–90, 390–1,
  406, 409; frontier society emerges 469–70;
  limes 55, 456, 460; *see also under* army;
  fortifications
fugitives 362, 366–7; *coloni* 288, 291, 292, 293–4,
  296
Fulgentius 753
fundus Aufidianus, Africa 298, 304
funerals *see* burials
Fürstengräber 468
Fyn island, Denmark 480–1

Gabinius, king of Quadi 85
Gainas (*comes*) 114, 118, 229, 512n42, 765; revolt
  and death 116–17, 234, 429, 430, 765
Gaiseric, king of Hasding Vandals 137, 519,
  521–2, 526, 536, 537
Gaiso (consul) 11
Gaius (jurist) 682
Galatia *1 Gc*, 68–9, 89
Galerius, emperor 12, 418
Galicia (Gallaecia) *1 Cb*, 132, 524
Galilee *6 Cc*, 24, 452
Gallaecia *1 Cb*, 132, 524
Gallehus, Denmark; golden horns 486
Gallia ulterior, Alan settlement in 519, 520, 523,
  524, 525, 533–4
Gallienus, emperor 155–6, 213
Gallo-Romans 112, 130, 133
Gallus (brother of Julian): early life 3, 4, 17, 44,
  45; Caesar in Antioch 24–5, 39, 46, 55, 421,
  453; and unrest over food prices 71, 329, 334;
  deposition and execution 47, 56, 161, 187–8,
  422; effect on Julian 47, 50
    and Church 24, 45, 70; portrait 759–60
Gamaliel VI, Jewish patriarch 454, 646
games: government provision 167, 388;
  euergetism 185, 342, 355, 378; importance to
  lower classes 358; proposed Oly:.~pic, at
  Chalcedon 647
garnet cloisonné work, Germanic 467
garum 286
Gaudentius (*notarius*) 42
Gaul *1 Cb-Db, 2*; under Constantine II 4; under
  Constans 6, 215; Magnentius' usurpation 15
  (*see also separate entry*); Constantius' recovery
  28, 29; Julian as Caesar 28–9, 48–9, 49–56,
  217, 279, 280, 298, 422, 424, 762; Constantius
  calls for reinforcements from 40, 56–7, 58,
  423; Julian's usurpation 56–60; barbarian
  invasions after death of Julian 74, 424;

defences weakened after Valentinian I 428; administrative disengagement 120, 133, 432, 535; barbarian invasion (406) 122, 431, 505, 513, 515, 518, 766

agriculture 285, 294; army 215, 216, 225–6; Bagaudae 281, 308, 367–8, 531–2, 534; Church 23–4, 29, 244–5, 311, 698; cities 302–3, 327, 371, *374*, 404, 406–7; council of the seven provinces 133, 202–3, 204; fortified settlements 309; Gallo-Roman élite 112, 130, 133; Germanic tribes in 112, 132, 223, 280, 297, 391, 464–70, 473, 528–9, 536 (*see also individual tribes*); imperial tradition 28, 50; literary culture 683, 698; paganism 367; pottery 279; prefecture 166; rural development 286; schools 674, 676, 683; senators 300; taxation 54, 55, 234, 298; villages 309; villas 279, 294, 297, 302, 467–8, 472; war damage 279; warrior burials 465, *466*; *see also individual places*

Gaza *6 Bc, 8 Ba, 372*, 542; temple of Marnas destroyed, church built on site 180, 258, 392, 394, 410, 554, 767

Gebel el-Tarif, Egypt; Nag Hammadi library 730

Geiseric *see* Gaiseric

Gelani 39

Gelasius of Caesarea 689

Gelbe Burg, near Dittenheim 472

Gelduba (Krefeld-Gellep) *2 Da*, 468, 470

Gelimer (king of the Vandals) 521

Genesis, Book of 672–3, 691

Genesis Apocryphon 712

geographical knowledge 218, 219

George of Cappadocia 23, 45, 394, 569, 570

Georgian literary culture 666, 708

Gepids 490, 503n28

Gerasa (Jerash) *6 Cc, 372, 374*, 396, 404, 406

Germanic peoples 2, 6, 118–25, 461–86; agriculture 285, 286, 473, 479–80, 493, 506; in army 111, 214, 365, 412, 464, 465, 469–70, 472, 478, (high-ranking officers) 413, 430, 435, 436, 469; in Baltic 478–82; in Britain 474–8; brooches 464–5, 467, 469, 475, 481; burials 464–8, *466*, 469, 472–3, 475, *476*, 484; Christianity 112, 496, 497, 499, 526, 581, 587; coastal region 472–3, 474; confederacies 418, 461; cultural adaptation 304, 464; in Danube lands 463, 465, 467, 483–6; demographic pressure 472; display 484–5; eastern territories 482–3; environmental change affects 463, 474; ethnic self-consciousness 224; in frontier zone 463, 469–70; Gainas and followers destroyed 430; in Gaul, the Germanys and Raetia 464–71; hill-top strongholds 468–9, 472; in Holland 473–4; jewellery 464–5, 467, 469, 475, 481, 482; legendary origins 517; metalwork, fine 464, 465, 467, 475, 480–1, 482, 484–6, (supply of gold for) 472, 480–1, 484–5; military equipment and fittings 464, 467, 468, 472, 475, 481; mobility 474; pottery 481; Rhine crossing (406) 122, 431, 505, 513, 515, 518, 766; in Rhineland 467–70; in Scandinavia 478–82, 486, 517; settlement patterns 463, 479, 480; settlements in empire, legalized 112, 280, 463; ships 481–2; sources on 461, 463–4; state formation 461, 481; strongholds, walled (Scandinavia) 480; trade and contacts 465, 467, 473, 480, 481, 484, 486, (Goths) 425, 493, 496, 497; votive deposits in bogs 481–2; Wielbark culture 490; *see also individual peoples, notably* Alamanni; Černjachov culture; Goths; Huns

Germanus, bishop of Auxerre 534

Germinius, bishop of Sirmium 32–3

Gerontius (usurper) 129–30, 432, 527–8, 532

Gervasius, St 251, 254, 349, 758

Ghadamès 558

Ghassanids 446

Ghirza 285, 557, 558

gifts and gift exchange 186, 307, 315, 323; payments to Goths 497, 498, 499

Gildo (count of Africa), revolt of 115, 303, 429, 430, 764

glass manufacture, Germanic 480, 493

gnosticism, Coptic works on 730–3, 735

Goar (Alan chief) 529, 534

goldworking, Germanic 467, 472, 480–1, 482, 484–6

Gomoarius (general) 90, 91

Gondishapur (Beth Lapat) *9 Db*, 716n18

Gorgonia, sister of Gregory of Nazianzus 700, 702

Gospel of the Egyptians (Coptic) 730

Gospels, Old Syriac 718

Goths 94–101, *462*, 496–515; early relations with Romans 496–9, 516; threaten Thrace 89; Valens' campaigns (367–9) 90, 94–5, 217, 221, 235, 425, 497, 498, 508–9, 762; pressed by Huns, admitted to empire 95, 98, 201, 425, 463, 487, 500–3, 507–8, 517; Valens' fights in Thrace 94, 97–101, 425, 509, 517 (*see also* Adrianople, battle of); fail to capture Constantinople after battle 102, 448, 509; massacre of group near Constantinople 101; Theodosius' campaigns 102–3, 234, 426–7, 428, 509–10, 517–18, 764; Theodosius' federate settlements 103, 113, 223, 234, 280 1, 427–8, 483–4, 487, 510–11, 517–18; attack on Thrace foiled (386) 106; revolts of federates (390s) 399, 510–11, 512, (Alaric's revolt) 114, 429, 511–13, 518; lynching and massacres in empire 510, 513; invasion of Italy 125–8, 346, 380, 391, 463–4, 513, 518, 521, 522, 766; Radagaisus' invasion of Italy (405) 121, 123, 431, 505, 513, 518; federates

Goths (*cont.*)
help resist Rhine crossing (406) 515; sack of
Rome 112, 127–8, 328, 432, 464, 513, 518, 522,
527, 589, 766, (religious reactions) 538, 691;
Athaulf leads into Gaul 127, 130–1, 432, 513;
and Attalus' usurpation 131; Constantius
destabilizes 131–2, 514; fight for Rome
against other barbarians in Spain 132, 515,
518, 519, 521, 530, 536, 537; settlement in
Aquitaine 112, 131, 132, 133, 223, 464,
514–15, 518–19, 520, 524, 530–2, 766; Aetius'
campaign against force attacking Arles 136,
137, 533, 534, 535, 536; under Theodoric I
514
Alaric unites Tervingi and Greuthungi
511–12; army service with Rome 121, 223,
281, 417, 423, 496, 497, 499, 509, 536, 537,
(high-level officers) 113, (revolts over)
510–11, 512; and Černjachov culture 483, 487,
488, *489*, 490–1, 491–2, 493; Christianity 496,
497, 499, 526, 581, 587; in Danube lands 106,
411, 483–4, 491–2, 509; economy 493;
'Gothic cultural stream' theory 485; and Huns
95, 98, 99, 425, 428, 487, 499–507, 508, 517,
534; language 487, 491; leaders' wish for
recognition by Rome 509–10, 511; military
effectiveness 498; nobles 494, 495, 496, 498;
Ostrogoths 491; personal allegiance to
emperors 511, 518; relations with other
Germanic groups and with indigenous
populations 490–1; Roman prisoners-of-war,
descendants of 496; rulers 495–6, 517; social
and economic organization 493–6; sources
487–8; subdivisions 491–2; subsidies 497,
498, 499, 511, 513; trade 425, 493, 496, 497;
villages 493, 494–5; Visigoths 491, 514; *see also*
Alaric; Athaulf; Greuthungi; Tervingi; Wallia
Gotland 479–80, 481
government *see* administration; bureaucracy;
centralization; emperors; governors
governors, provincial 166, 191, 194, 207, 208,
354; judicial role 238; patronage 361, 379, 399;
staff 168, 205
Gråborg, Öland 480
grace, divine 588, 592–3
grain: African/Egyptian export 71, 115, 329,
386; bureaucrats part-paid in 329; Christian
charitable distribution 260, 329; Italian 307;
northern production 115, 285, 479;
profiteering 71, 72, 312, 331, 334–5; supply
and distribution in capitals 37, 71, 107, 115,
167, 328–9, 386; trade, dearth of evidence
315; Visigoths' need for 530
grammatici (teachers of grammar) 45, 674, 676
Gratian, emperor: becomes Augustus 83–4, 144,
678, 762; marriage to Constantia 85; accepts
accession of Valentinian II 86; campaigns

against Goths 98–9, 508–9; takes Theodosius
as joint emperor 101, 121; Alamannic
campaigns 105; death 105, 764
and altar of Victory 104, 552; and
Ausonius 139, 366, 673; and Church 104,
580–1; conciliates senatorial order 199; laws
207, 359; and paganism 104, 550, 552, 765;
restricts numbers of embassies 155; and
Sapores 426
Gratian (usurper) 122, 527
Gratian the elder 10
Greece 5; Alaric ravages 115, 428, 429, 527, 765;
cities 377, 408; cultural influence in empire
666, 676; governorship 191, 354; mystery
cults 549; slavery 294, 295; and Syriac literary
culture 712, 713–14, 714–17
Greek language: inscriptions in verse 192, 377,
677, 691, 694; poetry 691, 717; prose, artistic
712; in Syria 714–16; teaching in west 674,
676
Gregory I, pope (the Great) 301, 340, 370, 631,
757
Gregory, bishop of Alexandria 9, 11
Gregory of Nazianzus: bishop of Sasima 633;
bishop of Constantinople 103, 104, 268,
578–9; Christology 596; classical literary
culture 657, 668, 704; Coptic translation 726;
education 48, 657, 667; on Julian 45, 46, 67,
415; and Neoplatonism 680; oratory 668, 679,
700, 704, 765; poetry 692, 694; on social
inequalities 370; social rank 208, 365; on
Trinity 577; writings 666, 700; *see also*
Gorgonia; Nonna
Gregory of Nyssa 103; on bishops 266; classical
literary culture 667, 668, 704; Coptic
translation 726; on Gregory Thaumaturgus
760; and Jewish allegory 752; *Life of Macrina*
610, 680, 702; and Messalians 580;
Neoplatonist influence on 610, 668, 680; on
Trinity 577, 579; writings 666, 699, 700, 701,
702
Gregory of Tours 373, 526
Gregory Thaumaturgus, bishop of Neocaesarea
577, 760
Greuthungi: Valens' campaigns 94; and Huns'
advance 95, 500, 502; excluded from empire
95, 507, 508; enter Thrace secretly 98;
collaborate with Tervingi and other Goths
100, 491, 508, 511–12; in Danube lands 106,
411, 509; revolt under Tribigild in Phrygia
116, 765; society 492, 494, 495; *see also*
Alatheus; Saphrac
Grubenhäuser 469, 472, 477
gsurs (Libyan fortified farms) 278, 285
Gudme, Denmark 480–1
Gundomadus (Alamannic leader) 24
Guntiarius (Burgundian chief) 529

Günzburg 470
Gurya, Acts of St (Syriac) 710

Habbib, Acts of St (Syriac) 710
Hadrian, emperor 416
Hadrian's Wall 216
Hadrianopolis *see* Adrianople
Haemus mountains *1 Fb, 3 Db-Eb*, 98
hagiography 451, 487, 675, 690, 699–70; Syriac 710, 718
Halani 95
halls, Germanic 469, 477
Hannibalianus (proclaimed king of Armenia) 2–3, 419, 437
Harff, Belgium 280
Harmonius, son of Bardaisan (Syriac poet) 712
Harpocration (Egyptian poet) 694
Harran (Carrhae) *6 Cb, 9 Ba*, 74, 460; paganism 542, 554–5, 557, 695; Baba, prophet of 710n7
haruspices, see divination
Hasta *4 Ba*; battle of 120, 431
Hatra *6 Db*, 79, 708
Hawran 455
healing, magic 633, 637
heaven, perceptions of 141–2
Hecebolius (sophist) 45–6, 542–3
Helena, mother of Constantine 566
Helena, daughter of Constantine and wife of Julian 29, 30
Heliodorus (Antiochene expert in horoscopy) 92
Helion (*patricius et magister officiorum*) 136, 436
Heliopolis (Baalbek) *6 Cc*, 540–1, 545, 554
Helladius of Alexandria (poet) 694
Helladius of Caesarea 370
Hellenism 64, 66, 665–6, 679; *see also* classical tradition
Helpidius (praetorian prefect) 196
Heracles 754; statue at Sufes 650
Heracles plate 749
Heraclian (governor of Africa) 126–7, 131
Heraclius, emperor 640
Herculani (regiment) 10
heresy: Augustine and 586–93; Christian literary invective against 671; in countryside 366–7; definition and contemporary perceptions 559, 561–2, 639, 703; Epiphanius' catalogue 671; suppression 81, 273–4, 559, 638, 639; women's role in 344; *see also individual heresies*
Hermetic works, Coptic versions 731
Hermogenes (*magister equitum*) 37, 267, 674
Hermopolis, Egypt *8 Bb*, 301
Heruli 490, 503n28
Hesperius (son of Ausonius) 152
hesychasts 580
Hesychius (*castrensis*) 239n6
Hibaldstow, Lincs. 475

Hieracas (Coptic author) 725
Hierapolis *6 Ab*, 43, 695
Hierocles (Platonist) 326, 556
Hilarion, St 449
Hilarius (palace official in Antioch) 92
Hilarius of Phrygia (philosopher) 93n43
Hilary, bishop of Narbonne 250
Hilary, bishop of Poitiers 29, 308, 569, 570, 571, 595
hill-top strongholds, Germanic 468–9, 472
Himerius (sophist) 682
Hinton St Mary mosaic 746
Hippo *1 Dc, 7 Bb*, 368, *372*, 380, 519; church 252, 259, 271, 272, 344
hippodromes and races 25, 59, *387*, 662, 737
Hippolytus of Rome 255, 753
al-Hira 444, 446, 450
Historia Augusta 234, 685
Historia Monachorum 700
historiography 414–15, 416, 633–4, 684–91; Church/classicizing division 415, 688–9; *see also individual historians*
Histria *4 Ca*, 310
hoards, gold 480–1, 485
Hodde, Jutland 478, 479
Holheim villa 472
Holland 473–4
Holy Land: Church buildings 738, 758–9; pilgrimages 253, 255–6, 261, 346, 449, 566, 666, 755–6; relics from 254–5; *see also* Jerusalem; Palestine
holy men 348, 700
homilies 153, 340, 343, 653–4, 670, 678, 699, 704; Coptic 723, 725–7, 734; 'Macarian' 701; Manichean 734; stenography 678, 705
'hommes de corps', medieval 292–3
homoousios/homoiousios controversy: council of Antioch 12; council of Sirmium 32–7, 569–72; under Valens 575; victory of *homoousios* 103–4, 274, 575, 579, 580; Neoplatonist terminology 573
honestiores 291, 339, 359–60
honorati 206–8, 327, 356, 378, 384
Honoratus (urban prefect of Constantinople) 36, 38
Honorius, emperor 111–12, 430–3, 764, 766; youth 107, 109–10, 411; accession 111, 764; rule 111–12; division of empire with Arcadius 111, 113, 164, 429, 512, 764; Stilicho's guardianship 110, 113, 114, 115; and John Chrysostom 118, 121; withdraws court to Ravenna 120; fall of Stilicho 123, 124; and Alaric 112, 125, 126, 128, 512; and Constantine III 126, 129, 130, 135, 249, 528; dealings with barbarians (412–16) 112, 130–1, 132, 528; last years and death 135–6, 435, 766

Honorius, emperor (*cont.*)
and army 111, 229; and Church 112, 179,
249, 268, 273–4, 275; Claudian's panegyric
139, 411; division of empire with Arcadius
111, 113, 164, 429, 512, 764; provides
entertainments 399; frontiers, withdrawal 112,
120, 132–3, 428, 429, 431, 432, 535; *magistri
utriusque militiae* control 111, 135; marriages
115, 123; on officials 171; and paganism
273–4, 550, 554; personal ineffectiveness 429;
portraits 140, 737
Hormizd (Hormisdas) II, king of Persia 418
Hormizd (Hormisdas, brother of Shapur II)
424, 439
horses 139, 479, 482, 507
Horsiesios (Egyptian monk) 728
hospitalitas (military billeting) 230, 525
hospitals, Christian 251, 257, 262
hostels, charitable (*xenodocheia*) 68–9, 251, 256–7,
258, 260
house-churches 251, 755
housing 334, 381, 388, 405; barbarian settlers'
524–5
humiliores 291, 359–60
Hunerich (Vandal leader) 290–1
Huns *1 Fb-Gb*, 499–507, *504*; origins 499–500;
pressure on Goths 95, 98, 425, 428, 487,
500–3, 517; alliance with Goths against
Valens 99, 508; invade Asia Minor and Syria
114, 116, 234, 429, 434, 442–3, 460, *501*, 502,
504; pressure on Radagaisus 505; and Rhine
crossing (406) 505; Uldin's Balkan campaign
128, 433; Olympiodorus' embassy to *504*, 505,
506; Constantius uses 506; invade Thrace 135,
435, 436; alliance with Aetius 136, 436, 505,
506, 519, 534; later wars against Rome 506–7,
534
Christianity 526; on middle Danube 483–4,
487, 503, 505–6; plunder 95, 507; in Roman
army 121, 126, 412, 506; and Roman–Persian
relations 435, 443; Sciri 280; social and
economic structure 500, 506, 507; sources
487–8
Hydatius 520, 523, 524, 532, 533
hymns 678; Coptic magical 722; Ephrem the
Syrian 619, 710, 712, 716; *kontakion* form
717–18; pagan 641, 695; Prudentius' 693; *and
see* Ambrose
Hypatia (Alexandrian Neoplatonist) 134, 556,
602, 611–12, 681–2, 698, 767
Hypatius (abbot near Chalcedon) 557, 647
hypostasis (theological term) 565–6, 567, 568, 569,
572, 573–4, 577
Hypostasis of the Archons (Coptic) 730

Iamblichus (Neoplatonist) 46, 543–4, 556–7,
680; biographical writing 700; educational
theory 681; on theurgy 541, 623, 752

Iberia *1 Hb, 6 Ea*; religion 434, 558; Roman
suzerainty 418, 437; Valens' intervention 92,
93, 425, 442
Iconium (Konya) *1 Gc, 6 Bb*, 179
iconoclasm 649–50
icons, precursors of 757
Igmazen, king of Isaflenses 88
Illerup, Denmark 482
illustres (grade of senator) 190–1
Illyricum *1 Eb*; under Constans 4, 215; Julian
occupies 42, 59; Valentinian I and Quadi
85–6; Gothic presence (370s) 99, 509, 580–1;
division between Arcadius and Honorius
164n138; Stilicho attempts to control whole
of 114, 121, 429, 431, 513, 527
army 215, 216, 226; Church 249, 580–1;
coloni 289, 357; praetorian prefects 152, 166,
194
images, devotional 757
imitatio, literary 691–2, 706
imperial family 15, 16, 22, 28, 30, 225
Imru'l-qais (Arab phylarch) 444
Independenţa; Černjachov culture *489*
industry 312–37; in cities 313, 408; mass-
production 313; possible decline during
fourth century 313–16; state intervention
316–22, 336–7; see also *collegia*
influence (*suffragium*) 138, 172, 173, 179, 194
information *see* intelligence
Ingentius (scribe, of Abthungi) 359
Innocent I, pope 244, 251, 264, 562, 563n3, 591;
and Alaric's invasion 538, 589; and John
Chrysostom 118; and Pelagius 591, 592
inquilini (type of *coloni*) 288, 290, 292, 304
inscriptions: Aramaic artistic prose 712; decline
in number 377, 677; on euergetism 377–8;
Greek verse 192, 377, 677, 691, 694; on
senates 200; Syriac 708, 715
intelligence service, imperial 157, 158, 161, 162,
181, 218, 219; *agentes in rebus* 159–60, 170–1
Irenaeus, bishop of Lyons 577, 583, 599
Irenopolis, Cilicia *6 Bb*, 456
iron-working, Černjachov culture 493
irrigation works 75, 233
Isaac of Amida 709, 715n15
Isaac, bishop of Seleucia-Ctesiphon 128, 435
Isaiah, Ascension or Vision of (Coptic) 724
Isauria *1 Gc, 6 Bb*, 218, 368, 433, 436, 452–3, 460
Isidore of Pelusium 634
Isis, temple at Philae 558
Islam 641
Ismanstorpborg, Öland 480
Ismant el-Kharab Syriac-Coptic manuscript
710n7, 735
Isocasius (sophist) 633
Issendorf: Saxon cemetery 472
Itala of Quedlinburg 738
Italy *4*; under Constans 4, 5, 6; support for

Magnentius 15; Constantius II recaptures 21; western government withdraws into 112, 120, 125, 433; barbarian invasions *see under* Alaric; Radagaisus
  agriculture 289, 294, 295, 296, 307; Alamannic settlements 84, 280; army brings prosperity 231; banditry 368; cities 327, 373, 404, 406–7, 409; euergetism 378, 380; prefecture 166; rural development 286–7; senatorial class 202; taxation 282; villages 309; *see also individual places*
Itinerarium Alexandri 14
Itinerarium Burdigalense 256–7, 346, 756
Iubaleni 88
Iuthungi 533
ivory-carving 737, 743, 745–6, 755, 756, 760
Izvorul; Černjachov culture *489*

Jacob, bishop of Nisibis 12
Jacob of Sarug 634n4, 661
James, Apocryphal Letter of (Coptic) 732
Januarius (potential successor to Jovian) 80–1
January, Kalends of 652
Jawf (Dumata) 458
Jerash *see* Gerasa
Jericho *6 Cc*, 450
Jerome 765; allegorical interpretation of Odysseus myth 753; on Burgundians 521; and classical tradition 668, 669, 680; on countryside/city debate 349–50; and Damasus 82; education 674; in Holy Land 256, 258, 345; letters 696, 697–8; on legacy-hunting by Roman clergy 259; and Origenist controversy 594; Paulinus' letters to 697; and Pelagius 590, 591; and rabbinic scholarship 679; reading 669, 679, 680, 717; on sack of Rome 127; social rank 365; translation work 690, 728, (Bible) 671–2; and women 345, 347, 348, 670; writings 666, 669–70, 699
Jerusalem *1 Gc, 9 Bb, 372*; banditry 450, 452; bishops 17, 244, 260–1; charity 261; Church buildings 255, 258, 678, 758, 759; Constantine and 666, 758; expansion 455; Holy Sepulchre church 366, 678, 758, 759; Julian and Temple 453–4; monastery on Mount of Olives 258, 758; pilgrimages 255–6, 261, 346; remains 405–6; supply and distribution 329; tax exemptions 759; tomb of St Stephen 255; walls 452
Jeu, Books of (Coptic) 733
jewellery 464–5, 467, 469, 475, 481, 482, 749
Jews: Alexandrian 134, 648, 752; allegory 752, 753; almsgiving 332; Ambrose and 108, 394; Antiochene 393, 648, 679; army service forbidden 228; art 739, 740; Christian attitude to 393, 394, 633, 639, 640–1, 642–3, 646, 648–9, 671, 752; *coloni* 362–3; in Constantinople 640–1; disorder in Galilee

under Gallus 24, 453; healers 633; Hellenism 679; John Chrysostom and 393, 643, 671; Judaism 530, 635–6; under Julian 453–4; law, status at 454; learning 679; and Nag Hammadi texts 731; patriarchate 454, 679; prosperity in Palestine 642–3, 679; in Spain 640; synagogues 394, 640–1, 642–3, 646, 647; and Syriac literature 712, 713; taxation 454; under Theodosius 108; *synhedria* 454; violence against 640–1, 642–3, 646, 647, 648–9
Job, Testament of (Coptic) 724
Johannes *see* John (*primicerius notariorum*)
Johannites (supporters of John Chrysostom) 123
John (*primicerius notariorum*, usurper) 135, 250, 274, 423–5, 435–6, 534, 766
John, Apocryphon of (Coptic) 730, 732
John of Antioch 533
John of Apamaea 555, 715
John, bishop of Ephesus (Monophysite) 642
John, bishop of Jerusalem 648
John Chrysostom *see under* Chrysostom
John Lydus 171, 219
John Philoponus 555
Jordanes 491, 492, 517, 532–3
Joshua the Stylite 388, 445
Jovian, emperor 78–80, 762; peace with Persia 78–9, 91, 92, 424, 442, 460, 763; religious policy 80, 548, 571, 575n34
Joviani (regiment) 10
Jovii (regiment) 90
Jovinian (heretic) 638
Jovinus (*magister equitum*, usurper) 83, 130, 513, 529
Jovius (praetorian prefect) 121, 126, 127
Judaism 560, 635–6
Julian, emperor 44–77; early life 3, 4, 25, 44–9; education 25, 44, 45–6, 47–8, 543, 544; point of apostasy 46–7; Caesar in Gaul 28–9, 48–9, 49–56, 217, 279, 280, 298, 422, 424, 762, (relations with Constantius) 29, 49–51, 54–5, 55–6, 422; Constantius' demand for troops 40, 56–7, 58, 423; Julian's usurpation, advance to confront Constantius 3, 40, 41, 42, 57–60, 144, 221, 423, 762; accession 43, 60, 423; rule from Constantinople 60–7, 152–3; restoration of paganism 44, 60, 62–3, 68–71, 543–8, 559; prepares for war against Persia 67–8, 72, 423; in Antioch 69–73, 392–3, 763; Persian campaign 13, 73–7, 413, 424, 437, 439, 442, 445–6, 447, 460, 763, (forces) 220, 221, 233, 236; death 76–7, 89, 424, 547, 762; Jovian succeeds 78, 762
  administration 64–5, 66; Alamannic campaigns 40, 42, 49, 50–1, 54, 55, 58–9, 422, 762; emulates Alexander 73, 76, 439; and Antioch, *see separate entry*; and Arabs 445–6, 447; army under 61, 62, 74, 77, 216, 220, 226,

Julian, emperor (*cont.*)
227–8; asceticism 63, 64, 72, 150; charity 68–9, 256, 260, 402, 547; and Church 62–3, 65, 77, 347, 616, 652, (apostasy) 29, 46–7, 58, (Christian heritage) 45, 47, 545, 547, (edict on Christian teachers) 66–7, 547, 668, 676, 688, (emulates organization) 68–9, 256, 260, 402, 545, 547, 548, (and internal conflicts of) 70–1, 574, 585, 591; and cities 64–6, 68, 72, 375; on Constantine I 64, 73; on Constantius II 21, 73–4, 415, 678; edict on education 66–7, 547, 668, 676, 688; and Etruscan diviners 545, 548; Eusebia protects 47, 48–9, 50; Eusebius as mentor 44; fleets 54, 75–6; frontier defences 40, 55, 235, 762; and Goths 94; Hellenism 64, 66, 543; and imperial dignity 63, 64, 72, 76, 142, 150; inner circle 56, 58, 62, 89; and Jerusalem 453–4; and justice 61, 676; laws 64, 65, 66, 172; Libanius' panegyric 63, 148; and Maximus of Ephesus 46, 63, 544, 547, 601, 680; military tactics 422, 424; paganism 58, 543–8, 559, (in army) 226, 227–8, (personal beliefs) 46–7, 62, 543, 545–6, 652, (restoration) 44, 60, 62–3, 68–71, 72, 241, 541–2, 543–8, 559; philosophy 44, 45–8, 148, 543, 544, 545–6, 680; physical appearance 72, 144; propaganda 57–8, 58–9, 59–60; relieves taxation 54, 55, 64, 65, 298; at Troy 393–4, 542
    WRITINGS: *Letter to the Athenians* 415; *Caesars* 73–4, 685; *Against the Galilaeans* 73, 546; hymns 695; *To King Helios* 546; *Misopogon* 72, 541; *To the Mother of the Gods* 546; panegyric on Constantius 21, 415
Julian, bishop of Eclanum 592
Julian (*comes Orientis*) 69
Julian (son of Constantine III) 130
Julianus, Rusticus (*magister memoriae*) 83
Julius I, pope 8, 239, 249, 251, 567, 573
Julius (father of Ausonius) 152
Julius (*comes* and *magister equitum et peditum*) 90, 101
Julius Constantius 3
Julius Nepotianus 15
justice: administration 166; Church 238–9, 248, 271–2, 272–6, 639, 658–9; emperors and 61, 291, 352, 676; payment for 162, 178; provinces 157, 166, 167, 207, 238; scribes 677; social inequalities 291, 339, 359–60, 647; trials for sorcery 82–3, 92–3, 199, 200, 549; *see also* laws; punishments; torture
Justin, Ps.; *Cohortatio ad Graecos* 709
Justin Martyr 595
Justina, empress 106, 581–2, 764
Justinian, emperor 357, 373, 558, 595, 640
Justinian, Code of 362, 415
Jutes *462*
Jutland peninsula 472, 478–9

Kabylie mountains 303, 311
Kaiseraugst (Castrum Rauracense) *2 Db*, 24, 51, 58, 59; treasure of 738
Karour (disciple of Pachomius) 728
Kasserine, Tunisia 285, 298, 306
Kent 477
Kephalaia of the Master (Coptic) 733, 734
Kerch silver dish 759
Khorenats'i, Moses 416
Khusro III, king of Armenia 426
kingship treatises 146
Kirkesion (Cercesium) *6 Db, 9 Ca*, 74, 457, 458
Kirmington, Lincs. 475
Kobuska 493
Komarov 493
Komrat 493
kontakion (hymn form) 717–18
Konya (Iconium) *1 Gc, 6 Bb*, 179
Korykos, Cilicia *6 Bb*, 326
Kosanovo; Černjachov culture *489*
Krefeld-Gellep (Gelduba) *2 Da*, 468, 470

labarum (military standard) 226, 227
labour 287–304; see also *collegia; coloni;* slavery; workforce
laeti (barbarians settled in empire) 280, 290, 465
laetitia (good cheer) 652, 660, 661
Lakhmid dynasty of al-Hira 444, 446, 450
Lambaesis *1 Dc, 7 Bb*, 372, 379
Lampadii ivory leaf 760
Lampadius (Roman senator) 123, 343
land: army veterans' 234; cities and public 65, 205; marginal, in east 455, 459, 460, 500; tax on 277, 282; tenure *see* leases; uncultivated 281–5, 519, 525
landowners: absenteeism 284, 291, 301–4, 323–4, 327, 328, 333–6; Church 260, 301, 304–5, 322, 327, 392; consumption 337; Egyptian *cohortales* 204; emperors 301; middle and present 297–9; patronage 309–11, 337; private armies 311; profiteering 71, 72, 312, 331, 334–5; protection of peasants 221n58, 309–11; rich 184, 186, 197, 283, 299–304, 309–11, 357, 360; size of holdings 299–301, 304–5, 357; smallholders 297, 298–9, 305, 309; taxation 298–9
Langobardi (Lombards) *462*, 483, 517
Laodicea *6 Cb*, 107
lares and *penates* 108, 553
largitionales (bureaucrats) 189, 196
Latin language 672, 683, 691
latrocinium (illegal force) 647, 649
Lauricius (*comes*) 36
laws: on bureaucracy 65, 66, 168, 172, 173–4; Church and 272–6, 639; conscription 101–2; on country life 282, 283, 288–9, 290, 357; on Donatism 360; drafting of 166; education in

667, 676, 682–3; emperors as source of 139, 141, 352; on family 659; on heresy 273–4, 638, 639; Jews' status in 454; Latin language 683; legal profession 204, 682–3; on monopolies 321–2; against paganism 7, 31, 108, 273–4, 667; *potentiores* limited by 360–1, 369; on praetorship 190–1; private 682; and provinces 157, 167, 207; and Roman identity 112; on senate membership 190–1; social distinctions in 360; on tradesmen 325; *see also* Theodosian Code; justice; *and under individual emperors*
learning: Jewish 679; *see also* education; literary culture; philosophy
leases *see* emphyteutic leases; *locatio-conductio*
legacies to Church 259, 262
legal profession 204, 682–3
Leicester 477
leisure, cultured 193, 349–50, 604, 612
Lejjun *6 Cc*, 457, 458
Lentienses 24, 99
Leonas (*comes*) 36, 41
Leontius (city prefect of Rome) 27
Leontius (city prefect of Constantinople) 647
Leotius (Antiochene official) 303
Lepcis Magna *1 Ec, 7 Cb*, 87–8, 140, 158, 552
Leporius (Gallic monk) 588
Leta (noble Christian woman) 347
Letçani: Černjachov culture *489*, 490
letters 696–8; and *amicitia* 697; of Mani, Coptic 734; monastic, Egyptian 727, 728, 729; Paulinus of Nola 694; philosophical, of Mara 709; professional scribes write 677; of recommendation 696, 697; as source on society 340; *see also under individual writers*
Libanius: at Antioch 73, 154, 333, 334, 679, 682; on bureaucrats 159, 192, 377, 388; civic exemption 384; on civility in exercise of authority 644; at Constantinople 682; estates 303; friends and pupils of other religions 646, 668, 669; and Julian 45–6, 46–7, 63, 72, 73, 148, 543; letters 696; on monkish bands 271, 647; at Nicomedia 45–6, 682; orations 679, 682, 765; panegyric 5, 63, 148, 415; as patron 179, 198–9, 382, 384; *On Patronage* 175–6, 177–8, 310, 362–3; pupils 45–6, 668, 669, 671, 677; and Riot of the Statues 73, 154, 679; on social mobility 196, 356, 370; as source 192, 196, 233, 326; on student life in Athens 677
Liber Constitutionum 522–3, 525
Liber Graduum (Syriac) 709, 714, 716
Liber Pontificalis 261, 301
Liberius, pope 251; and Athanasius 26–7, 31, 249, 569; violence over succession to 82, 267–8
libraries 37–9, 45
Libya *1 Fc, 7 Db*, 278, 285
Licentius (protégé of Augustine) 384

Licinius 185–6, 418, 564
Liebenau: Saxon cemetery 472, 473
lignum crucis (relic of Cross) 255
limes (frontier region) 55, 456, 460
Limigantes 32, 422, 423
limitanei (frontier troops) *see under* army
Limonum (Poitiers) *2 Cb*, 29, 308
Lincoln *1 Ca*, 478
Lincolnshire 475
lipsanotheca, Brescia 745–6, 755, 756
literacy 677
literary culture 664–7, 684–707; ascetic literature 700–2; biography 699–700; Christian 633–7, 665–6, 669–73, 698–9, 702–5; classical tradition 665–6, 675, 695, 704, 705, 706–7; copying of texts 670; and cultural change 705–7; *florilegia* 577, 703; high literary culture 691–6; *imitatio* 691–2, 706; Neoplatonism 680–2; networks 696–8; patronage 683; theology 702–4; women's writings 702; *see also* hagiography; historiography; letters; poetry
Litorius (*magister*) 228n112
liturgies, civic 317, 325, 330, 331, 337
liturgy, Christian 694, 717
Living Gospel, Commentary on (Coptic) 733, 734
Lixhe, Belgium 280
locatio-conductio leases 283, 288, 289–90, 291, 292
Loire valley: ascetics' dwellings 616
Lollianus, teacher in Oxyrhynchus 155–6
Lombards (Langobardi) *462*, 483, 517
London *1 Da, 2 Ba*, 477, 753–4
long-houses, Germanic 473, 478, 479
lower classes 339, 356–8; Church and 670; in cities 312, 334, 342, 355–6, 356–7, 358–9, 368–9, 385; in countryside 356–7, 357–8 (see also *coloni*); emperors and 355–6; sources on 339–40; *see also collegia; coloni*; poverty; slavery
Lucian 752
Lucifer, bishop of Calaris (Cagliari) 26, 564n6, 569, 572
Lugdunum (Lyons) *1 Db, 2 Cb*, 22, 105, 301
Luke, relics of St 38
Lundeborg, Fyn, Denark 481
Lupicinus (*magister*) 57, 58, 90, 98, 507–8
Lusitania *1 Cb-c*, 132
Luxembourg region 279
Luxor *8 Bb*, 169
luxury goods 313; *see also individual types*
Lydia *1 Fc, 5 Cb*, 68
Lyons (Lugdunum) *1 Db, 2 Cb*, 22, 105, 301

Macae 450
Macarius (imperial official) 9, 585
Macarius, bishop of Tkow 649–50
'Macarius, Homilies of' 580, 701

Macedonia *1 Fb, 3 Db, 5 Ba*, 121, 327; Goths and 102, 103, 114, 427, 429
Macedonius, bishop of Constantinople 252, 267, 574
Macedonius (Syrian ascetic) 714n12
Macellum, Cappadocia 44–5
Macrianus, king of Alamanni 55, 84–5
Macrina (Christian ascetic) 608, 610, 620, 668, 702
Macrobius 680; *Saturnalia* 193, 674, 695
Madauros *7 Bb, 372*, 395
madrāshā (Syriac stanzaic verse) 712, 717–18
Maeander, Asia Minor 301
magic: Coptic texts 722; healers 633, 637; theurgy 46, 540; trials 81, 82–3, 92–3, 199, 200, 549
magister officiorum 115, 159, 165, 169–70, 214, 353
magistracies, civic 330, 331; elections 267; short tenure 354
magistri, military 213, 215–16, 412; Germans 430; political influence in west 111, 229
Magna Mater, rituals of 398
Magnentius, Flavius Magnus, usurpation of 10–11, 14–22, 421–2, 762; and Africa 15, 22; Alamannic invasion facilitated by 236, 421–2; approaches Athanasius 16, 26, 569; background 14; coinage 16; Constantius' victory over 14, 16, 20–2, 26, 30, 31, 421–2; diplomacy 16; and Gallic church 23; Nepotianus' rebellion 15, 21, 225; Philippus' alleged complicity 171; and Rome 30, 31, 200; Silvanus deserts 15, 20, 27; Vetranio used to contain 15, 16, 17
Magnus of Nisibis (doctor) 694
Mahndorf: Saxon cemetery 472
Mahon, Minorca: destruction of synagogue 642, 648–9
Main (Moenus), river 84
Mainz (Moguntiacum) *1 Db, 2 Da*, 122
Maiuma (Constantia) *6 Bc*, 241, 392, 542, 555
Malechus (Arab phylarch) 445–6
Mamas, St 45
Mamertinus, Claudius (*cos.* 362) 59, 61–2, 63, 64, 65, 148, 201
Mamre, near Hebron 758–9
Man of God, History of the (Syriac) 710, 718
Mani 710, 734; *Life of* (Coptic) 733
Manicheism 308, 582–3, 588, 598, 621–2, 740; Augustine's 582, 613; literature 710n7, 733–5
manpower: alleged shortage 282, 322, 326; *see also* slavery; workforce *and under* army
mansiones 35, 43
manufactories see *fabricae*
Maouia *see* Mavia
Mara, philosophical letter of (Syriac) 709
Maratocupreni (Syrian bandits) 308
marbles, inlaid coloured (*opus sectile*) 737–8
Marcella (Roman Christian lady) 67, 702

Marcellinus (Magnentius' *magister officiorum*) 10, 15, 21
Marcellinus (pagan *magister, fl.* 460s) 228n112
Marcellinus (*notarius, fl.* 411) 586, 590
Marcellus (*magister equitum*) 49, 50, 29
Marcellus, bishop of Ancyra 17, 566, 595; sympathizers 17, 567, 568, 571, 575
Marcellus, bishop of Apamea 551
Marcian, emperor 190–1
Marcianopolis *1 Fb, 3 Eb*, 98
Marcomanni *1 Eb*, 483
Marcus (usurper) 122, 527
Marcus, bishop of Arethusa 71
Marcus Aurelius, emperor 416
Mardonius (eunuch) 44, 45
Maria, empress 115, 123, 698, 737
Marina (Christian lady of Alexandria) 650
Marinus of Neapolis 700
Marius of Avenches 523
Mark the Deacon 180
markets: cities as 332–5; on country estates 300–1, 308, 309n120; Mesopotamian regulation 443; smaller 308, 332–3, 408
Marnas, temple of *see under* Gaza
marriage: laws 659; mixed Christian/pagan 347; religious views of 609, 610, 618; Roman/Arab dynastic 447, 448
Marseilles (Massilia) *1 Db, 2 Dc*, 131, 372, 407; Proculus as bishop 244–5, 250
Martin, bishop of Tours 258, 265, 267n130, 308–9, 367, 654, 763; appearance 601, 616
Martin of Brive 309
Martyropolis (Mayafarquin) *6 Db; see also* Marutha
martyrs: Coptic martyrology 729–30; Donatist 585; Edessene 710; festivals 659–60, 661, 662, 756; under Julian 575; local shrines 739, 756; Persian 709, 718; Prudentius' poems on 693; at Rome 82, 253, 739
Marutha, bishop of Martyropolis 123, 128, 435, 718
Mary, as Theotokos 596
Mary, Gospel of (Coptic) 732
Mary, niece of Abraham of Qidun 718
Mascezel (brother of Gildo) 115
Massilia *see* Marseilles
Maternus, Firmicus 7, 539, 555, 698
Matrona, St 654
Mauretania *1 Cc-Dc, 7 Ab*, 88, 218, 278, 583, 585
Mauri (Moors) *1 Cc-Dc*, 303, 311, 424
Maurice, emperor 424
mausolea 38–9, 738, 749–50
Mavia (Maouia), queen of Saracens 102, 447–9, 451
Maximian, emperor 79, 80, 214, 418
Maximin, bishop of Goths 587
Maximinus, bishop of Trier 8

Maximinus, prefect of the *annona* 82
Maximus, bishop of Constantinople (the 'Cynic') 246, 578, 613
Maximus, son of Gerontius (usurper) 129, 130, 432, 527–8
Maximus, Magnus (*comes Britanniarum*); usurpation 105, 107, 194, 279, 527–8, 582, 764; impact on army 428, 510, 511
Maximus, Petronius 202
Maximus of Ephesus 29, 77, 549, 609, 624; and Julian 46, 60, 63, 544, 547, 601, 680; exile and death 81, 93n43
Mayafarquin *see* Martyropolis
meat supply 167, 307, 321, 328, 329
mediation: social 269, 270, 348–50, 351, 355–6, 361, 402, 639; supernatural 598–9, 637
medicine 174, 434–5, 683
'medicine of life' theme 713
Medinet Madi, Egypt 733–4
Mediolanum *see* Milan
Melania the elder 258, 345, 346, 698, 702
Melania the younger 256, 300, 309, 346–7, 697, 698; asceticism 258–9, 346; *Lives* of 699, 702; slaves 294, 295, 305; in Thagaste 259, 402
Meleager plate 749
Meletius, bishop of Antioch: and bishopric of Antioch 42, 80, 571–2, 573, 577–8; leading pro-Nicene 573, 575, 577, 578; presidency over council of Constantinople and death 579; shrine to St Babylas 252, 254
Meletius of Lycopolis 566
Melitene *1 Gc, 6 Cb, 9 Ba,* 458
Melito, Apology of Ps. (Syriac) 709
Melito of Sardis 723, 725–6, 753, 755
mēmrā (Syriac narrative verse) 712, 717
Menander Rhetor 147, 668, 675, 689–90, 709
Merobaudes (*magister militum*) 86, 105
Mesopotamia *1 Gc-Hc, 6 Cb-Dc*; under Hadrian 416; Galerius gains eastern 418, 437; Constantius' defence 12, 13–14, 39, 40–2, 420; Julian's campaign, Jovian's cessions to Persia 73–7, 79, 233, 424, 437, 442; Hunnic invasion 443; Persian invasion of Roman 435, 437
  Arabs 448; army deployments 217–18, 458; asceticism 579–80, 621; fortified cities 217, 420, 437, 459–60; inscriptions 715; irrigation works 75, 233; literature 712–13, 731; markets 443; population expansion 455
Messalians 579–80, 621
metalwork: fine 464, 465, 467, 475, 480–1, 482, 484–6, 490, 738, (iconography) 746, 747–9, 759; mass-produced 313
Methodius, *Symposium* 702
metropolitans, ecclesiastical 239, 242–4, 245–6, 247, 400, 562
Metz (Civitas Mediomatricum, Divodurum, Metti) *1 Db, 2 Db, 372, 374, 465*

Meuse, river *2 Da,* 465
Middle Ages: art 736, 740; education 681; theology 703; society 306, 311, 363; *see also* Byzantine era
Milan (Mediolanum) *1 Db, 2 Db, 4 Ba, 372*; Constans in 8; Constantius' court 21, 24, 46, 48; Valentinian I makes capital 82, 351, 762; Gratian in 104, 580–1, 612; Valentinian II in 106; Maximus in 107; Theodosius I in 107, 109–10; Honorius' capital 113; capital withdrawn to Ravenna 120, 391
  Augustine in 582, 669; basilicas, Ambrose and issue of 581–2, 612; bishops 249–50, 400, 563n3 (*see also* Ambrose; Auxentius); Church buildings 106, 252, 254, 349, 401, 757, 758; coinage 109; councils of bishops 26, 568; imperial patronage 386, 563n3, 757, 758; forward location 390; luxury goods trade 313; relics 252, 254, 349, 401, 755, 758; Sant' Ambrogio sarcophagus 755; size *374*; wealth 351, 407
Mildenhall silver dish 749
milestones 457, 653
Milev (Milevis) *7 Bb,* 591
Militants (Donatist) 585
militarization of society 417, 460
militias, private 308, 311, 475
millennialism, circumcellions' 585
mills, water- 285
Milton, Kent: Germanic burials 475
Minervius (senator) 200
mines 166, 319, 325, 435
mints, state 166, 168, 289
miracles 17, 20, 46
Mishnah 753
missionaries: Christian 419, 526; Manichean 582–3
Missorium of Theodosius 151–2, 759
Mithras 546, 552, 739, 745, 753–4
Mitrovica *see* Sirmium
mobility: limits on personal 282, 288, 289, 293–4, 296, 324, 325, 357; social 338, 363–6, 369–70, 673–9, 683
Mocius, St 401
Modares (general) 427, 511
Modena (Mutina) *2 Ec, 4 Ba,* 99, 265
Modestinus: collection of private law 682
Modestus (praetorian prefect) 162, 270
Moenus (Main), river 84
Moesia *1 Eb-Fb, 3 Db-Eb*; barbarians in 101, 103, 128, 427–8, 433
Mogoşani: Černjachov culture *489*
Moguntiacum (Mainz) *1 Db, 2 Da,* 122
Moldavia 487
monasticism: in Antioch 271–2, 402; bands of militant monks 134, 271–2, 282, 543, 550, 551, 557, 601, 647; bishop's calling as incompatible 267, 349–50; and Christian primary groups

monasticism (*cont.*)
655; Church buildings 251; clothing 604; education 667; Egypt 594, 602, 606, 619, 727–9; judicial punishments 647; literature 669, 710, 727–9; Messalian 579–80, 621; women 259, 345–6
Monaxius (praetorian prefect) 133
Monica, mother of Augustine 582, 702
Monophysitism 598
monopolies 144, 321–2, 337
Montius (quaestor) 25
Moors *see* Mauri
Mopsucrenae 43
Mopsuestia *6 Cb*
mosaics: African 303, 749; Apamea 681; Carthage 749; Christian symbols 653, 681, 746; in churches 677, 750, 755, 757; Constantinople, imperial palace 749; Edessa 708, 716; figurative 738; Hinton St Mary 746; New Paphos, Cyprus 681, 744–5; Piazza Armerina, Sicily 749; Rome 750, 755, 757
Moses (Saracen monk, bishop) 447
mounds, Germanic settlement (*terpen*) 473, 474
Moxoeona *6 Db*, 79
Mucking, Essex 475, 477
Mundhir I of al-Hira 443, 450
munera, civic 64, 65, 66, 676; *sordida* 206–7, 260, 290, 317
Mursa (Osijek) *3 Ca*, 15–16, 568; battle (351) 20, 21, 221, 227, 422, 569
Musonianus, Strategius (praetorian prefect) 39, 239n6, 422–3
Mutina (Modena) *2 Ec*, *4 Ba*, 99, 265
Mygdus *5 Da*, *6 Ba*, 90
mystery cults, Greek 549, 552
mythology, Christian interpretation of 752–3, 754

Nabataean dialect 708
Nacoleia *6 Bb*, 91, 222n63
Nador, Algeria 300, 303
Nag Hammadi *8 Bb*; library 725, 730–5
Naissus (Niš) *1 Fb*, *3 Db*, 16, 43, 59–60
Nakolea *see* Nacoleia
Namara 444
Namatianus, Rutilius 202, 531, 532
Naples (Neapolis) *1 Eb*, *4 Cb*, 580
Narbo (Narbonne) *1 Db*, *2 Cc*, 131, 250, 535
Narses, son of Shapur II of Persia 13
navicularii (shippers) 319–20, 320–1, 328
navy *see* fleets
Nazianzus *6 Bb*
Nea Paphos (New Paphos) *6 Bc*, 681, 744–5
Neapolis *see* Naples
Nebridius (praetorian prefect) 41n146
Nectarius, bishop of Constantinople 104, 266, 268, 579
Neerharen-Rekem 469, 470

negotiatores 360
Nemesius of Emesa 555, 683
Neocaesarea, Pontus *6 Ca*, 91
Neoplatonism 556–7, 622–3, 623–4, 680–2; asceticism 622–3, 623–4; Augustine and 582, 628–9, 680; Christianity influenced by 541, 555, 566, 573–4, 610, 668, 681, 703, 752; educational theory 681–2; hymns and prayers 695; Julian and 46, 680; *Lives* of philosophers 700; patterns of interpretation 752; succession (*diadochē*) 556; terminology 623, 703; *see also* Hypatia; Iamblichus; Maximus of Ephesus; theurgy
Nepos, Julius 111
Nepotianus, Julius 15, 21, 225
Nerseh, king of Persia 418
Nessana *6 Bc*, 456
Nestorius (Athenian hierophant) 557
Nestorius, bishop of Constantinople 596–8, 599, 679
Neuburg: Alamannic cemetery 470
Nevitta (consul) 59, 64, 78, 419
new men 196, 364
New Paphos *6 Bc*, 681, 744–5
New Testament, Syriac version of 718
Nicaea *1 Fb*, *6 Aa*, 80–1, 90, 326; council of 104, 239, 240, 242, 274, 566, (on authority of metropolitans) 245–6, 400, 562, (creed) 562–3, 565–6
'Nicenes, New' 80
Nicomachi family of Erice, Sicily 305
Nicomedia *1 Fb*, *5 Da*, *6 Aa*, 1, 36, 186, 248; schools 45–6, 47, 682
Nike, Thrace 35
Nilus of Sinai 756–7
Niš *see* Naissus
Nisibis (Nusaybin) *1 Hc*, *6 Db*, *9 Ca*; Rome acquires 418, 437; unsuccessful Persian sieges, (337) 12, 419–20, 438, (346) 12, 13, 438, 763, (350) 12, 14, 421, 438, 763; Persian advance bypasses (360) 41; Romans cede to Persians 79, 424, 442, 460, 679; Roman siege (421) 134, 435, 443
army in 236; baptistery 715; bishops organize defence 12, 438; Christian intellectual tradition 667; defensive role 217; Ephrem the Syrian in 619, 679, 709; language use 715; market 443
Nitria *8 Ba*, 729
nobiles 355, 356
Nohodares (Persian satrap) 24
Nola *4 Cb*; cult of St Felix 253, 254, 255, 256, 258, 660
nomads: Alans 518; Arabs, relationship with settlers 451; Huns 500, 506; and marginal land 455, 459, 460, 500; and Persia 421; north Africa 269, 433; transhumance 445

non-market redistribution 307, 315–16, 323, 330–2, 336, 337
Nonna (mother of Gregory of Nazianzus) 694, 702
Nonnus (Egyptian poet) 555
Nori, Aetius' campaign against 533
Noricum *1 Eb, 2 Eb, 3 Ba*; Julian's advance through 59; Stilicho's operations 114, 120; Alaric in 122, 126; Vandal and Alan raids 430; Roman loss of control 237; Germanic tribes' contact with Roman province 483
North Sea 418
northern provinces, cities of 378, 404, 406, 409
notarii 159–60, 166, 176, 181, 189
Notitia Dignitatum 116, 211, 340, 415; on army 211–12, 215–16, 219, 236, 456, 535; on bakers 320; on bureaucracy 163–5; on *fabricae* 232
Notitia Urbis of Constantinople 758
Novatians 266, 643, 648
Novempopulana *2 Bc-Cc*, 132, 133
Novie Gorodok: Černjachov settlement *489*
Noviomagus (Speyer) 122
Nubians, conversion of 558
nucleated sites, Libya 278
Numidia *1 Dc, 7 Bb*; *ordo salutationis* 207, 369; religion 246, 550, 583
Nusaybin *see* Nisibis
Nydam 481–2
Nyssa *6 Bb*

obelisks 31, 390, 737
occupations, hereditary 282, 288, 289, 293–4, 296, 324, 325, 357, 364
Odotheus, leader of Greuthungi 502, 512n42
Odovacer (*patricius*) 111
Odysseus myth 753
officials *see* bureaucracy
oil, olive 286, 303, 315; state distribution 167, 321, 329
Öland 480, 481
Old Testament: Aquila, Version of 671, 679; Syriac translation 713
oligarchy 331
Olives, Mount of 258, 345, 758
Olteni: Černjachov culture *489*
Olybrias of Ravenna 283, 295
Olybriones 534
Olympia: Phidias' statue of Zeus 744
Olympiad dates 520
Olympias (benefactress of church in Constantinople) 259, 261, 345, 369, 655, 702
Olympias (Constans' betrothed) 40
Olympias, queen of Armenia 40, 423
Olympias (senator living in Antioch) 187
Olympiodorus of Thebes: embassy to Huns *504*, 505, 506; *History* 314, 414, 688, (on wealth of senatorial class) 300, 323, 355

Olympius (*magister officiorum*) 123, 124, 125, 126
operae (corvée labour) 306
Optatianus, Porfyrius (poet) 692
Optatus of Milev 583
opus sectile 737–8
oral tradition 704–5, 713
oratory: Christian 675, 678, 704; on emperors 147–9, 150; epideictic 682; eulogistic 147; funerary 668, 675, 678; *see also* panegyric; rhetoric
ordination ritual 349
ordo salutationis of the *consularis Numidiae* 178, 369
Oresa 458
Orestes, prefect of Egypt 134
Orfitus, Memmius Vitrasius (urban prefect) 22, 30, 31, 200
Oribasius 49, 56, 58, 76
Orientius 526
Origen: and Christian learning 665; commentary on Song of Songs 672; Eusebius on 700; Evagrius of Pontus and 626, 627; influence of Jewish allegory on 752; influence on *Life of Antony* 670; Logos theory 680; Origenist controversy 565–6, 594–5, 765; Pelagian controversy refers to 594; and philosophy 555, 566, 680; Rufinus' translation of 628, 698; on Trinity 565–6, 594–5
originarii (type of *coloni*) 288, 292
Origo Constantini 684–5
Origo Gentis Romanae 684
Orosius, Paulus 255, 590, 685; *Historia Adversus Paganos* 415, 691, 767
orphans 332
Orpheus 746
Orphic hymns 695
Osijek *see* Mursa
Ossius, bishop of Cordova 8, 10, 239, 240, 275, 569–70
Ostia *4 Cb*, 139, *372*
Ostrogoths *see* Goths
otium (leisure) 193, 349–50, 604, 612
ousia (divine substance) 565, 569, 570, 573, 574, 576, 577
Oxyrhynchus *8 Bb*, 155–6, 336, 602, 613, 659

Pacatus Drepanius, Latinus 148–9, 150
Pachomian monasticism 618
Pachomius, St 729, 763; *Lives* of 700, 728
Paeonius (Gallic senator) 203
paganism 538–60; under Constantine 30, 539, 540–1, 545, 644–5; Constans condemns 7; under Constantius II 31, 539–43, 545, 549, 559; Julian's restoration 44, 60, 62–3, 68–71, 72, 241, 541–2, 543–8, 559; Jovian to Theodosius II 80, 548–58; under Valens 93n43, 548–9; under Valentinian I 81, 82–3, 548–9, 645; under Gratian 104, 550, 552, 765;

paganism (*cont.*)
under Theodosius I 106, 108, 549–50, 553–4, 559, 646, 667, 765; Eugenius and 109; Justinian's measures against 558
  in army 226, 227–8; and Christianity *see under* Church; in cities 540, 550, 558; in countryside 271–2, 308, 550, 553–4, 557–8, 599; *curiales'* vested interest 551; elusive and plural nature 543, 632–3, 666–7; on emperors' divinity 2, 138, 139–40, 141, 181, 552; epistolography 696–7; exclusion from public office 554, 558; festivals 399, 542, 585, 652; funeral rites 273–4; gods' presence in landscape 632–3; Greek poetry and 694–5; as 'Hellenism' 543, 665–6; heresy troubles Church more 559; household observances 62, 108, 553; initiation 46, 48; intellectuals and 135, 543, 555, 599; laws suppressing 7, 31, 108, 273–4, 667; local character 543, 558, 559, 632; loses patronage 392, 393; personal piety 553; policy and practice inconsistent 540; and poor relief 256, 260, 331, 332, 402, 547; priesthoods 68, 104, 352, 542, 550, 655; propaganda 695–6; and state 538; statues of gods 649–51, 743–4; syncretism, inter-cult 753–4; univeralism 545, 546, 552, 559; upper-class culture based on 651; use of term 'pagani' 308, 639; *see also individual gods*; asceticism, polytheistic; sacrifice; temples; theurgy; *and under* art, visual; Church; cities; Rome (SOCIETY) *and individual cities*
pagi (rural districts) 309
paintings, wall 168–9; *see also* catacombs
Palaebisca, Cyrenaica 269
Palestine *1 Gc, 6 Cc*; Arab raids 447; army deployments 218, 459; *coloni* 357; prosperity 455, 679; unrest 452, 453–4; *see also* Holy Land; Jerusalem
Palladas of Alexandria 650, 694
Palladius (Antiochene poisoner) 92
Palladius, bishop of Ratiaria 581, 587
Palladius, *Lausiac History* 606, 700, 701
Palladius (*notarius*) 87, 88, 158, 162
Palladius (praetorian prefect) 160
Palmyra *9 Bb*, 278, 458, 708, 740
Palmyrene dialect 708
Pammachius (Christian senator) 251, 256n78, 342–3
pamphlets 146, 158
panegyric 200–1, 415; *see also under* Autun; Constantius II; Julian; Libanius; Pacatus Drepanius; Themistius
Panegyrici Latini 147, 415
panis aedium 328, 329
Pannonia *1 Eb, 3 Ca*; Germanic tribes' contacts with 483; Magnentius in 20; Constantius II moves court to 32; Julian in 59; barbarian invasions 424, 509; Gratian subdues Goths

and settles as federates 102, 427; under Stilicho 114, 121; defences abandoned 428
Panopolis (Akhmim) *8 Bb*, 601, 602
Pap(a), king of Armenia 91, 92, 93, 425
Paphnutius (Egyptian hermit) 602
Papinian: collection of private law 682
papyri 456, 602, 677, 713
parabalani (followers of Cyril of Alexandria) 134
Parabiago Plate 748–9
Paris (Lutetia Parisiorum) *2 Cb*, 54, 57–8, 372
Parisii *1 Db*
Parma *4 Ba*, 99, 580
Parmenian, bishop of Carthage 585
party politics 117
Patiens, bishop of Lyons 301
patriarchate, Jewish 454, 679
patricii 111, 116, 127
Patricius of Lydia (philosopher) 93n43
patristic works, Coptic 725–7
patrocinium, see protection
Patroclus, bishop of Arles 250
patronage 361–3; army and 231–2, 310; bishops 264, 269, 342, 349, 350, 757–8; building 362, 736–7, 757–8; changing patterns 737, 757–8; Christian private 251, 254, 697; Church 251, 264, 737, 757–8; Church building 251, 254, 258, 738, 757; in countryside 309–11; imperial 258, 390, 736–7, 738, 757–8; landowners, of artisans and traders 337; Libanius and 175–6, 177–8, 310, (protégés) 179, 198–9, 382, 384; literary 670, 683, 694; municipal 330–1, 337, 350, 361–2, 379; non-market redistribution 336, 337; officials 310; paganism loses civic and imperial 392, 393; *patrocinium, see* protection; private 207, 251, 254, 361–2, 377–8, 737, 757–8; reciprocity 323, 331; traditional system 361–2, (undermined) 231–2, 310, 362–3; *see also* euergetism; protection; *suffragium; and under* governors
Patti Marina, Sicily 300
Paul, apocryphal Acts of 723, 724–5
Paul, bishop of Constantinople 8, 267
Paul, *notarius* 9, 23, 585
Paul, St; commemoration in Rome 253, 254, 255, 258; Epistles of 697, 698
Paul, Sentences of 288
Paul the Deacon 517
Paula (Christian benefactress) 258, 345, 347, 698, 702
Paulina, Fabia Aconia (wife of Praetextatus) 552
Paulinus, bishop of Antioch 80, 104, 571, 572, 577; western support 575, 578, 579
Paulinus of Nola 254, 255, 258, 343, 670; and St Felix 254, 350, 660; writings 612, 693–4, 696, 697, 704
Paulinus of Pella 366, 524
Paulinus, bishop of Trier 24, 24
Paulinus, Meropius Pontius *see* Paulinus of Nola

Paulus: collection of private law 682
payments to bureaucrats and judiciary *see* purchase
Pegasius, bishop of Troy 393–4, 542
Pelagius and Pelagianism 179, 588–92, 598, 599, 697, 767
Pella, Palestine *372*, 406
penates 108
Pentapolis 245
perfectissimate 189, 190
Pergamum *5 Cb*, 46, 543, 607, 624, 680
Périgueux (Civitas Petrocoriorum) *372*, *374*
periphery and centre 386
Persia *1 Hc*, 437–44; to death of Constantine 12, 13, 14, 416, 418–19, 437–8, 460; Constantius II and 437, 438–9, (337–50) 5, 8, 11–14, 16, 419–21, 438, 763, (holding-operation policy) 13–14, 40, 420, 421, 438, (Musonianus' approach to) 422–3, 438, (Shapur's destruction of Amida) 39–40, 423, (campaigns) (360–1) 39–43, 56–7, 58, 423, (Persian withdrawals) (351) 14, 421, (361) 43, 423, 439; Julian's invasion 13, 73–7, 413, 424, 437, 439, 442, 460, 763, (preparations) 67–8, 72, 231, 329, 423, 545, 548, (role of Arabs) 445–6, 447, (Roman forces) 220, 221, 233, 236; Jovian's treaty 78–9, 91, 92, 424, 442, 460, 679, 763; Valens' dealings 91–4, 98, 425, 426, 508; instability after death of Shapur II 426; Theodosius' division of Armenia with 106, 426, 442; period of peace 112, 123, 128, 430, 433–5, 443; war (421–2) 134–5, 234, 434, 435, 437, 443–4, 451
    and Arabs 75, 76, 135, 419, 421, 435, 443, 444–7, 451, 455, 460; Church 128, 434, 435, 438, 451, 460, 709, 716n18, (persecutions) 134, 443, 718; defence of Caucasus 443; diplomacy 42, 91–4, 112, 414, 420, 425, 434–5, 438; goldwork 486; irrigation works 75, 233; military resources and technology 413; Roman army dispositions against 217–18; siege warfare 438, 459–60; Syria suffers in wars 278; Syriac culture in empire 708, 709, 712, 719; trade 443; Zoroastrianism 433, 434, 602, 636; *see also* Shapur I *and* II
Peshitta (Syriac version of New Testament) 718
Pessinus *6 Bb*, 68
Peter, apocryphal Acts of (Coptic) 732
Peter, bishop of Alexandria 103, 274, 578, 579
Peter, Martyrdom of (Coptic) 725
Peter, St 245; commemoration in Rome 239, 248, 249, 253, 254, 255
petitions to emperor 155–6
Petrikany 493
Petros, 'bishop of those in the encampment' 450
Petulantes 57
Pevensey (Anderitum) *2 Ca*, 7

Pharan, Sinai 449
Pharandzem, queen of Armenia 91
Phidias (sculptor) 744
Philae *8 Bc*, 558
Philagrius (prefect of Egypt) 239n6
Philip, Gospel according to (Coptic) 731
Philippus, Flavius (praetorian prefect) 20, 171, 196, 353
Philo of Alexandria 752
philosophers and philosophy: allegory 752; asceticism 602–3, 607–12, 613–14, 622–3, 630; and Christianity 555, 613–14, 680, 681, 703, 706, 752; and cities 607, 611; clothing 601, 604, 613, 643; in countryside 607–8; education in 46, 543, 667, 675–6; embodiment of divine soul 608, 623, 630; executions under Valens 93n43; Julian and 44, 45–8, 148, 543, 544, 545–6, 680; and leisure 604; non-élite 613–14; and public life 611–12, 630; recruitment to clergy 655; teaching of rhetoric 607; tradition 543–4, 602–3, 623, 630; universality 606; and wealth 611; in west 544; women 607–8, 611–12, 698; *see also individual philosophers and schools, especially* Aristotelianism; Neoplatonism
Philosophiana, Sicily 308
Philostorgius 488, 524, 689
Philostratus, *Life of Apollonius of Tyana* 700
Phoenicia *1 Gc*, 447, 452, 557, 641
Photinus, bishop of Sirmium 568, 595; and council of Sirmium 17, 20, 33, 35, 569
Photius, patriarch: *Bibliotheca* 414, 488
Phrygia *1 Gc*, 91, 116
phylarchs 444, 445, 446, 449, 450, 451
Piazza Armerina, Sicily 300, 749
Picardy *2 Ca*, 297
Picts *1 Ca*, 216, 424
Pietroasa *489*; treasure of 485–6
pig-rearing 307, 479
pilgrimage 255–7, 346, 633, 739, 755–6; women 346, 449, 566, 620, 756 (*see also* Egeria); *see also* hostels *and under* Holy Land
Pinianus, Valerius (Christian benefactor) 258–9, 294, 344, 346–7, 402
Pirus, Mount (Spitzberg), near Rottenburg 84
Pistis Sophia (Coptic) 733
place name evidence 464, 524
Placidia, Galla: prisoner of Visigoths 127, 131; marriage to Athaulf 131, 514, 519, 529–30, 766; returned to Honorius 530; marriage to Constantius 132, 135, 766; as Augusta 135–6, 766; regent for Valentinian III 136, 137, 533
plague 125
Plas, Aurelius, of Dionysias in Egypt 178
Plato 680; Coptic version of *Republic* 732
Platonism *see* Neoplatonism
Plintha (Goth, *magister militum in praesenti*) 430
Pliny the Younger 147, 696

Plotinus (Neoplatonist) 46, 544, 573–4, 629, 680, 698, 700
Plutarch 556–7
Po valley 84, 280, 287, 371
Podosaces (Arab phylarch) 445–6
Poetovio *1 Eb, 3 Ca*, 25
poetry 691–5; and *amicitia* 694; court 694; in Egypt 694, 695; Greek language 677, 691, 694–5, 717; *imitatio* in 691–2; Latin language 691; and paganism 694–5; Syriac 712, 717–18; 'wandering poets' 694; *see also individual poets*, panegyric *and under* inscriptions
Poitiers (Limonum) *2 Cb*, 29, 308
Poland 482–3, 490
policing 230, 457
politics: army and 211, 224–9; ascetics and 610–12, 614, 630; Church and 140–1, 207, 208, 263, 349–50, 352, 560, 612; cities and 409–10; local 204–9; lower classes' significance 358; personal ambition in 117; senatorial class 197–204, 204–9, 411; theory of 689, 760–1
Pollentia *4 Aa*; battle of 120, 233, 431, 512, 693
polytheism *see* paganism
Pompaelo, Spain; Foz de Lumbier villa 302
Pontica, diocese of 167, 248
pontifex maximus 68, 104, 352, 550, 765
Pontii Leontii (Gallic family) 302
population density 455, 472, 479
pork 307, 321, 329, 479
Porphyry (Neoplatonist) 46, 544, 680, 681, 700; and Augustine 592, 629; *ousia* and *hypostasis* 573, 574
Porphyry, bishop of Gaza 180, 554, 555
portents 80, 85–6, 118
porticoes 382, *383*, 388, 404
postal system *see cursus publicus*
potentiores (strong men) 360–1, 362–3, 370
Potentius (tribune of *promoti*) 101
pottery 315, 336; in Baltic region 480, 481; in Britain 473, 475, 477; Černjachov culture 484, 493; Danubian burnished ware 484; Feddersen Wierde type 473, 477; in Gaul 279; Gothic local manfacture 493; Tunisian fine polished 286
Pouan, Aube 467
poverty 331, 332, 340–4; in cities 368–9; Christian charity 331, 332, 341–4, 402; Constantinople 369; in countryside 308; and crime 308, 367; Julian's charitable schemes 68–9, 256, 260, 402, 547; tax burden 282–3, 298–9
praefectus Augustalis 166
praepositus sacri cubiculi 165
Praetextatus, Vettius Agorius 193, 549, 551–2; career 191, 194, 200; on clergy 260, 365
Praetorian Guard 214
praetorian prefects 54–5, 166–7; of East 38, 115,

167, 169–70; senatorial 194; staffs 54–5, 167, 205; supply army 54–5, 220; tenure of office 153, 194, 196
praetors 38, 185, 190–1, 192
praktikoi (ascetics) 626–8, 630
Praunheim villa 472
Praxiteles: Cnidian Aphrodite 744
prayers 693, 695, 722
preaching 670, 672, 677, 704–5
precedence-dispute genre 713
predestination, divine 592–3
prefects and prefectures 166–7, 364, 375; *see also* praetorian prefects; urban prefects
prices 71; Diocletian's Edict (301) 332–3, 333–4, 336, 673
priests: Christian *see* clergy; pagan 68, 542, 655 (see also *pontifex maximus*)
primicerius notariorum 163, 166, 211
primicerius sacri cubiculi 351
primiscrinius 167
princeps officii 168, 170–1
principales (leading curiales) 299, 356
Priscillian of Avila 582–3
Priscus (Julian's mentor) 48, 77, 547
Priscus of Panium 436, 488, 506
prisoners 257, 273; -of-war 222, 282, 288, 290, 341, 496
privatiani (officials) 189, 196
Proba, Faltonia Betitia (poetess) 698
probatoriae (letters of appointment) 165, 170
Probianus diptych 760
Probus, Petronius (praetorian prefect) 193, 194, 198, 300, 310, 580; consular diptych 759
processions, public liturgical 739
Proclus (Neoplatonist) 552, 557, 682, 695
Procopius (historian) 521–2, 532–3, 688
Procopius (son-in-law of Anthemius) 135
Procopius (usurper): on Persian expedition 74, 75, 76, 79, 89; usurpation 83, 89–91, 144, 762; army supports 225, 228; Goths support 90, 94, 425, 495, 498
Proculus, bishop of Marseilles 244–5, 250
procuratores (estate managers) 305, 306
production 215, 312
professions 360, 364
profiteering 71, 72, 312, 331, 334–5
progymnasmata (educational exercises) 674
Prohaeresius (sophist) 67, 680, 682
Projecta casket 746, 747, 748
Promotus (*magister militum*) 106, 114, 234, 428
propaganda: over admission of Goths to empire 498, 499, 507, 510; Constantine's 186; Julian's 57–8, 58–9, 59–60; Magnentius' 16; pagan 695–6; Themistius' 201, 498, 499, 510
prose, artistic 712
Prosper (*pro magistro militum per Orientem*) 422
Prosper of Aquitaine (historian) 520, 523, 532, 533

Protadius (Gallic landowner) 202

Protasius, St 251, 254, 349, 758

protection of peasants (*patrocinium*) 308, 309–11, 361, 362–3; by army officers 231–2, 310, 363; from army call-up 221n58; of fugitives 288, 291, 293–4, 362; rackets in Near East 308, 449; from taxation 231–2, 284, 300, 310, 314, 362–3; usurpation of land though 300

provinces, administration of 166–8; army finance and supply 54–5, 167, 360; bureaucracy 160, 166–8; Church organization 207, 242, 244, 400; communications and 157, 161, 181; dioceses 166; finance 166, 167, 168; games and entertainments 388; *honorati* 206–8, 356; imperial control 153–6, 375–6; justice 157, 166, 167, 207, 238; number of provinces 364; prefectures 166; separation of military and civilian responsibilities 214; taxation 54, 167, 168; *vicarii* 166, 194, 205; *see also* governors, provincial

proximi (high office-holders) 151

Prudentius (poet) 253, 693, 695

Prusa *6 Aa*, 17

Przeworsk culture 482–3

Psalms 678, 698; Manichean 734, 735

psogos (invective) 671

Ptolemais *6 Cc, 7 Db, 8 Bb*, 245

Publius (ascetic, of Zeugma) 715

Pulcheria, empress 133–5, 443

punishments: death penalty 656; class distinctions 291, 359–60, 647; colonate status as 290–1; of *curiales*, for failure to raise taxes 376

purchase of office or influence 172–3, 173–4, 175–80

purple cloth 144, 169, 352

Puteoli *4 Cb*, 329, 580

Pythagoreanism 541

Quadi *1 Eb-Fb*, 32, 85–6, 422, 424, 431, 483, 762

quaestorships 166, 191

quarries 166

Querolus (anon. comedy) 367, 531–2

quietists 580

Qumran: Genesis Apocryphon 712

quotations, collections of (*florilegia*) 577, 703

Rabbula, bishop of Edessa 648, 714, 716

races and hippodromes 25, 59, *387*, 662, 737

Radagaisus (Gothic leader): invasion of Italy 120–1, 431, 503, *504*, 505, 518; defeat 121, 233–4, 431, 505, 518; and Huns 503, 505; postpones western plans in Balkans 123, 513; and Visigothic confederacy 491

Raetia *1 Eb, 2 Eb*, 59, 120, 221, 513; barbarian raids 58–9, 99, 422, 430, 470–1

ranks, unitary system of 188

Raphaneae *6 Cc*, 458

Raqqa *see* Callinicum

Ravenna *1 Eb, 4 Ca, 372*; court withdraws to 120, 125, 386, 391; death of Stilicho 124; during Alaric's invasion 127, 589

Church buildings 386; rent rolls of Church 305, 306, 307; sarcophagi 386; size *374*; wealth 407

Ravenna Annals 528, 529

reaper, Gallic 285

reciprocity 307, 315, 331

Reculver, Kent 477

redistribution, non-market 307, 315–16, 323, 330–2, 336, 337

regalia, imperial 144

Regium *4 Ba*, 99, 127

Rehimena *6 Db*, 79

relics, saints' 254–5, 648–9, 756; *see also under* Constantinople; Milan; Rome

religion: in army 106, 226–8, 542, 656; diversity of climate 632–3; and education 67; universe, concept of 636–8; upper-class ambiguity 646, 653; *see also* asceticism; Church; paganism

reliquaries 745–6, 755, 756

Remi *see* Rheims

Remigius (Romanus' agent at court) 88, 158

requisitioning, army 317, 360

res privata (imperial estates) 322

Resaina (Theodosiopolis) *6 Db, 9 Ba*, 435, 443, 444

Resapha *6 Cb*, 459

Resurrection 624

Resurrection, Treatise on the (Coptic) 731

rewards in public life 155, 181–2

Rheims (Remi, Durocortorum) *1 Db, 2 Cb*, 49, 122

rhetoric 697, 705; Christian 'simplicity' and classical 669–71; Coptic 729; education 45, 607, 665, 667–73, 682, 683–4; epideictic 675; invective 671; *see also* oratory

rhetors (teachers) 676

Rhine frontier *2, 372*; under Marcus Aurelius 416; unrest after Diocletian 418; barbarians forming confederacies 418; under Constantine 129, 419; Constans' operations 420; under Constantius II 421–2; Julian rebulds forts 40, 55, 424, 762; barbarian invasions 424; Valentinian I's fortifications 84, 425; gradual abandonment 120, 125, 431; great crossing by barbarians (406) 122, 431, 505, 513, 515, 518, 766; Constantine III secures 432

army 217, 227, 285, 469; barbarian federate settlers 428, 463, 470, 473; barbarian raids 413; cities 406; frontier society 469–70

Rhineland 279, 467–70, 480; *see also individual places, notably* Cologne

Rhodanus, bishop of Toulouse 29

Richborough (Rutupiae), Kent *2 Ca*, 477
Richomer (*comes domesticorum*) 98–9, 100
Rimini *see* Ariminum
ripenses (army units) 214
roads: pilgrims', across Asia Minor 256; repair
   260; security 449, 450, 455, 457, 458–9; Strata
   Diocletiana *6 Cb-c*, 217–18
Romanus (*comes per Africam*) 87–8, 162, 158
Rome *1 Eb, 4 Cb, 372*; Constantine I and 30, 31,
   185, 390, *397*, 398, 402, 738; Constans and 6;
   under Constantius II 15, 21–2, 257, 390,
   (Constantius' *vicennalia*) 29–32, 37, 142–3, 148,
   150, 687, 742, 760, (and Magnentius) 15,
   21–2, 30, 31; Julian and 60; sorcery trials
   82–3; Theodosius I and 107, 108, 148, 390;
   Stilicho and senate 115; walls repaired 120;
   Alaric besieges (408) 125; alliance with Alaric
   against Honorius 126; Alaric sacks (410) 112,
   127–8, 328, 432, 464, 513, 518, 522, 527, 538,
   589, 691, 766; Gaiseric sacks (455) 536
   BUILDINGS AND WORKS OF ART *397*;
   arch of Constantine *397*, 398, 739, 741, 743,
   745; arches on road to St Peter's 398; basilica
   of Junius Bassus 737–8; basilica of Maxentius
   397, 398; baths of Constantine 390, *397*, 398;
   catacombs 739, 749–51, 754; churches 251,
   257–8, 396, *397*, 398, 402, 738–9, (S. Agnese
   fuori le Mura) 396, *397*, 738, (S. Croce in
   Gerusalemme) 396, *397*, 739, (SS. Gervasio e
   Protasio (now S. Vitale)) 251, 757, (S.
   Giovanni in Laterano) 31, 396, *397*, 738, 757,
   (SS. Giovanni e Paolo) 251, 757, (S. Lorenzo
   fuori le Mura) 396, *397*, 738, 757, (S. Lorenzo
   in Damaso) 757, (SS. Marcellino e Pietro) 396,
   397, 739, (S. Maria Maggiore) 398, 755, 757, (S.
   Maria in Trastevere) 251, 757, (S. Paolo fuori
   le Mura, on Ostian Way) 251, 390, *397*, 398,
   739, (S. Pietro) 31, 257, 342–3, 396, *397*, 398,
   738, 757, (S. Pudenziana) 757, 757, (S. Sabina)
   738, 755, 757, (S. Sebastiano) 397, 739; Circus
   Maximus 31, 737; classical tradition 742–3;
   Esquiline treasure 464, 746, 747, 748;
   mausoleum of S. Constanza 738, 750; mosaics
   755, 757; obelisks 31, 390, 737; sarcophagi, (of
   Junius Bassus) 745, 755, (Two Brothers) 755;
   statues 742–3, 745; temples 7, 108, 395, *397*,
   398, 551; walls 120, *374*, 390, 391, *397*
   CHURCH: aristocracy and 82; and
Athanasius 8, 26–7, 31; charity 257; clergy
   numbers 263; councils of bishops 578, 598;
   and eastern Church 103, 104, 249, 567, 568,
   578; factional strife 82, 267–8, 369, 394,
   591–2, 599, 648; martyrs commemorated 82,
   253, 255, 401, 739; precedence of see 238–9,
   246, 248–9, 400, 562, 563, 567, 568, 591; relics
   401; wealth 260, 261, 301, 401–2; *see also*
   individual popes, viz: Boniface; Celestine;

Damasus; Felix; Gregory I; Innocent I; Julius
   I; Liberius; Zosimus
   SOCIETY: *Calendar of 354* 252–3; education
   676, 683; emperors' relations with 148, 185,
   198, 200, 342, 369, 390; festival of SS Peter
   and Paul 253, 254, 255; food supply 115, 167,
   307, 355, 390; games 30; as heart of empire
   390; loses pre-eminence 386; paganism 21–2,
   31, 125, 398, 550, 551–2, (Theodosius I and)
   108, 550, 553; pilgrimage to 255, 256n78;
   plebs 342, 358, 369, 385, (violence) 312, 334;
   senatorial order, (*cursus honorum*) 191–2,
   (euergetism) 378, 757, (literary culture) 695,
   (non-Italians) 184, (religion) 82, 347, 538,
   551–2, (and urban poor) 369, (wealth) 334,
   335; size 336, *374*, 407; student unruliness 677;
   supply and distribution 115, 167, 307, 312,
   328–9, 334, 336; urban prefect 21, 167, 169,
   191–2, 198, 200, 354, 358; wealth 334, 335,
   351, 401–2, 407; *see also* senates (ROME)
Rothesteos (Gothic noble) 494
Rouen (Rotomagus) *1 Db, 2 Cb*, 254
Rufinus, Flavius (praetorian prefect) 113–14,
   170, 300, 429, 765; and Alaric 114, 527;
   Claudian on 415, 692–3
Rufinus, Vulcacius (praetorian prefect) 16, 23
Rufinus of Aquileia 256, 345, 697; and Origenist
   controversy 594; translations by 612–13, 628,
   689, 698, 700, 701
Rufinus the Syrian; *On the Faith* 589
Rugi 483
Rumarov: Černjachov culture *489*
Runder Berg, Urach 472
Ruricius, *praeses* of Africa Tripolitania 88
Rusticus Julianus (*magister memoriae*) 83
Rusticus of Narbonne 343
Rutupiae *see* Richborough

Saba, *Passion of St* 487, 494, 499, 516
Sabellius and Sabellianism 565, 566, 588
Sabina: rural development 286
Sabinianus (general) 423
sacra scrinia (officials) 189
sacramentum (military oath) 227
sacrifice: artistic representations 743; bans on
   31, 108, 539–40, 548–9, 553, 554, 644–5, 652;
   Jovian's use 78; Julian reinstates 62, 69, 72,
   546; pollution 645; in Rome 551; in western
   Baltic 482
Sahara desert 557–8
saints, cult of 253–4, 349, 399, 401, 410; *see also*
   relics
Sakrau (Zakrzow), Silesia 482–3
Salia, Flavius (general) 8
Salices, battle of *3 Eb*, 99, 508
Salih (Arab people) 446
Sallustius (consul, 363) 74

Salonae *3 Cb*, 136
Salutius, Saturninus Secundus (praetorian
    prefect) 61, 76, 78, 546, 547, 559
Salvian of Marseilles 399, 526; on social
    conditions 293, 297, 310, 362, 363, 368
Samarobriva *see* Amiens
Samarra, battle of 76
Samosata *1 Gc*, *6 Cb*, 458
San Giovanni di Ruoti 307
sanctuary 273
Sapaudia *2 Db*, 519–20, 524, 533
Saphrac (leader of Greuthungi) 494; requests
    admission to empire 500, 507; at Adrianople
    100; in Pannonia 102, 484, 509; disappearance
    510, 511
Sapor I and II, kings of Persia *see under* Shapur
Sapores (*magister militum*) 426
Saracens *see* Arabs
Saragossa 253n56
Sarapion (philosopher) 602, 607, 613
sarcophagi 386, 745, 750, 755, 759
Sardica (Sofia) *see* Serdica
Sardis *1 Fc*, *5 Dc*, *6 Ab*, *372*; buildings 326, 388,
    405, 406; expansion and prosperity 326; Jews
    394, 679; philosophy 607; religion 550
Sarmatians *1 Eb-Fb*, 416, 418, *462*, 483, 491,
    503n28; Roman campaigns 5, 32, 85–6, 420,
    422, 424, 497; in Roman army 412, 417
Sarpedon's tomb at Seleucia, Cilicia 633
Sarus (Gothic federate chieftain) 121; and
    Constantine's revolt 122, 123, 129, 431; and
    Visigothic invasion 125, 127, 130
Sasanian empire *see* Persia
Sasima *6 Bb*, 103, 104, 633
Satala *6 Ca*, 458
Saturninus (*magister militum*) 102
Sauromaces, king of Iberia 92
Savia *1 Eb*, 102
Saxon shore, Britain 7, 216–17
Saxons *1 Da*, *462*, 465, 472; invasions 279, 418,
    424, 432, 516, 520, 521; in Roman service 465,
    475, 477, 519, 531; society 516–17
Scandinavia 478–82, 484, 486, 517
Scarpona (Dieulouard) *2 Db*, 83
Scetis *8 Ba*, 729
schism, ecclesiastical 562
scholae (imperial bodyguard) 165, 170, 214
Scholastica (benefactress of Ephesus) 378
school tablet, Coptic/Greek bilingual 722
Sciri (Huns) 280, 290
Scots *1 Ca*, 424
scribes, professional 677
scrinia (secretariats) 66, 165, 196
scriptorium of imperial library 37
scripts, Egyptian 720
sculpture *see* statues
Scythia *1 Fb*, *3 Ea-Fa*, 241

Scythopolis *6 Cc*, *372*, 405
seafaring 157, 418, 420, *504*, 505
sea-level, rise in 279, 463, 474
Sebastianus, brother of Jovinus 130, 529
Sebastianus, *comes*. in Persian campaign 74, 75,
    79, 89; and succession to Valentinian I 86;
    killed at Adrianople 100, 101; tactics 426
Secundianus, bishop of Singidunum 581
Seine basin 465
Seleucia in Isauria (Silifke) 557, 633, 654, 702;
    councils of bishops 36, 81, 435, 570
Seleucus, Mons; battle of 22
self, notions of 604, 622–31
self-sufficiency, economic 313
senates 184–210; and emperors 198, 199–200,
    201, 204, 352, 354, 355–6; formal powers 184,
    198, 203, 209; geographical division 187;
    institutional change 184–91; formal powers
    184, 198, 203, 209; local, see *curiae, curiales*;
    political role 197–204, 209; senators residing
    in provinces 199, 206; sources 200
  CONSTANTINOPLE 184–91;
    Constantine's creation 184, 185–6, 364;
    Constantius II's expansion 37–8, 187–8,
    196–7; under Valentinian, Valens and later
    emperors 89, 188–91; and emperor 198, 354;
    formal powers 198, 203, 209; membership
    190–1, 352, 356; political role 198–200, 200–1;
    sources' limitations 192, 200; status *vis-à-vis*
    Roman 185, 187; and Stilicho 115
  ROME 22, 184; under Constantine 185,
    187, 398; and Constantius II 30, 200; and
    Julian 60; and Valentinian I 199, 200; and
    Gratian 104; and Stilicho 115; and Alaric 126;
    aristocratic ethos 352–3; and barbarian
    invasions 126, 201–3, 204; and emperor 198,
    200, 201, 355–6; political role 187, 198–200,
    202, 203; social role 354–6, 687; *see also*
    Victory, altar of
senatorial order 184–210, 354–6; ascetics 258;
    bureaucrats admitted to 184, 188, 189–90,
    204–9; careers 191–7; in cities 313, 333–5,
    381, 408; civic immunities 205; commerce
    333–5; and Constantius II 187, 188, 190,
    196–7; geographical division 187; corruption
    209–10; *cursus honorum* 191–5; *dignitates* as
    route to 188; eastern 352, 356; and emperors
    352, 411; equestrian order absorbed into 339,
    352, 369; euergetism 258, 355, 378, 381, 757;
    growth 184, 188, 189–90, 196, 204–9, 352;
    landowners 184, 186, 197, 221n58, 283, 3??;
    literary culture 193; mediatory role 355–6,
    369; *nobiles*, old aristocracy 355, 356;
    patronage 361; political role 197–204, 411,
    (local politics) 204–9; in provinces 199, 202,
    204–9; three grades 184, 190–1, 192, 356;
    torture 92, 199, 200; unifying factor 209;

senatorial order (*cont.*)
  wealth 181, 184, 300, 314, 334, 335, 401–2;
  western 351, 352–3; *see also* aristocracy
Sens (Agedincum) *2 Cb*, 29, 49, 50, 762
Sepphoris: Jewish academy 679
Septuagint 671
Serapion, bishop of Thmuis 574
Serapis (god) 552, 753; Alexandrian temple 394,
  551, 553, 596, 634–5, 646, 765
Serdica (Sofia) *1 Fb, 3 Db*, 16, 157; council of 8,
  26, 32, 238–9, 241, 265–6, 567–8, 763,
  (east/west dissension) 8, 13, 248, 567–8, (and
  episcopal visits to court) 7n20, 275
Serena (wife of Stilicho) 113, 125, 347
Sergeric, king of Goths 514
Sergiopolis *6 Cb*, 455
sermons *see* homilies
Servius, commentary on Virgil 674, 695
Setif, North Africa 749
Severian, bishop of Gabala 714–15
Severus, bishop of Mahon 648–9
Severus (*magister equitum*) 49, 50
Severus (*magister peditum*) 83
Severus, Libius (senator) 202
Severus, Septimius, emperor 213
Severus, Sulpicius (writer) 670, 697, 699
Sevso Treasure 738, 748
Sexio (governor of Calabria) 172
Sextus, *Sentences* 612–13; *Sentences of* (Coptic) 732
sexuality 592, 609, 610, 617, 619, 656
Shapur (Sapor) I, king of Persia 416, 716n18
Shapur (Sapor) II, king of Persia 418–19; and
  Constantine I 437; and Constantius II 12–14,
  43, 421; Julian's campaign against 73–7; peace
  with Jovian 79; death 426, 765; deportations
  716n18; persecution of Christians 709
Sharbel (Edessene martyr) 710
Shenoute of Atripe 637, 650–1, 728–9, 730, 735
Shepherd of Hermas (Coptic) 726
shepherds 308
shippers of *annona* 319–20, 320–1, 328
ships in Nydam peat bog 481–2
shipwrecks 315, 320
Shmona, St 710
shops 382, *383*, 388
Sicily *1 Ec*, 287, 296, 300, 304–5, 308, 309
Sidonius Apollinaris, bishop of Clermont-
  Ferrand 203, 302, 327, 350, 524
siege warfare 413, 418, 438, 459–60
Sigeric, brother of Sarus, king of Visigoths 132
Silchester 478
Silifke *see* Seleucia
Silistra (Durostorum) *3 Eb*, 168–9
silk textiles 336
Silvanus (*magister*, usurper): deserts Magnentius 15,
  20, 27; revolt 14–15, 27–8, 46, 229, 422, 762
Silvanus, Teachings of (Coptic) 732

silver ware 747–9; Esquiline Treasure 464, 746,
  747, 748; Kerch silver dish 759; Missorium of
  Theodosius 151–2, 759; treasure of Pietroasa
  485, 486; Vermand spear-fittings 465
Simitthus *7 Bb*, *372*, 380
Simocatta, Theophylact 688
sin, original 590, 592, 624
Sinai *8 Bb*, 449
Singara *1 Hc, 6 Db*; Roman control 437, 458;
  'night-battle' near 13, 421, 763; Persian siege
  41, 423, 438; Rome cedes to Persia 79, 442,
  459–60; defensive role 217
Singeric, king of Goths 530
Singidunum (Beograd, Belgrade) *3 Db*, 33
Sîntana de Mureş *489*
Sîntana de Mureş-Černjachov culture *see*
  Černjachov culture
Sintula (general) 57, 58
Sirmium (Mitrovica) *1 Eb, 3 Ca, 372*; Constantius
  II in 17, 32–7; Julian in 59; portent of
  Valentinian I's death 85; Theodosius crowned
  at 101; bishops 32–3, 568; councils of 17, 20,
  569–70; forward location 390, 391; imperial
  presence 386, 406
Siscia (Segesta) *1 Eb, 3 Ca*, 20
Sitifis *1 Dc, 7 Bb*, 88, *372*
Skedemosse, Öland 482
slaves 294–7; agricultural 284, 285, 287, 295–6,
  304, 305, 306–7; in armies 121, 311; *casarii,
  casati* (cottagers) 295; Christians and 273, 294,
  347; collar 653; decline 285, 322; domestic
  294; free poor effectively enslaved 288, 357–8,
  370; manumission 273, 294, 347; masters'
  provision of food 331; as overseers and
  managers 294; punishments at law 360;
  runaways join Alaric 522; some prefer slavery
  to freedom 296–7; trade 493, 496
smallholders 297, 298–9, 305, 309
society 338–70; army's impact 229–32, 417, 456;
  ascetic attitudes to 609, 610, 630; in barbarian
  kingdoms 537; Christianization and 324, 348,
  369, 639; civility 644, 646; conformity 644;
  dress codes 336, 604; east/west distinction
  351–2; emperors 352–4; eunuchs 350–1;
  fourfold categorization by beliefs 639; Goths'
  494–6; *honestiores/humiliores* distinction 291,
  339, 359–60; inequality as basis 370;
  marginalization 366–9; militarization 417,
  460; power structure 339; sources 339–40;
  state coercion 338, 340–1, 363–4, 369;
  verticality 338, 352, 370; *see also* aristocracy;
  class; lower classes; patronage; *potentiores*;
  poverty; protection; senatorial order; women;
  and under mediation; mobility
Socrates (church historian) 643, 689
Sofia *see* Serdica
Sol, cult of 546, 552

Somme basin 465
Song of Songs 671, 672
Sontheim, Stubental 472
Sopater (philosopher) 540, 674–5
Sophia of Jesus Christ (Coptic) 732
Sophistic Movement, Second 706
sorcery *see* magic
Sosipatra (pagan ascetic) 608, 609
souks 382, *383*, 404
southern provinces 404–6, 409
Sovari: Černjachov culture *489*
Sozomen (church historian) 488, 689, 712
Spain *1 Cb-c*; under Constantine II 4; and
    Magnentius 15, 22; defences weakened after
    Valentinian I 428; and Constantine III 129,
    528–9; barbarian settlements 112, 129, 131,
    132, 391, 432, 518, 524, 528–9; Visigothic
    campaigns against barbarian settlers 132, 515,
    518, 519, 521, 530, 536, 537; Visigothic
    kingdom 640
        army 216; cities 253, 278, 404, 406–7;
    countryside 294, 302, 306–7, 311; impact of
    barbarian invasions on Roman population
    112; Jews 640; private armies 311; tax
    revenues reduced 234, 535
Spanţov: Černjachov culture *489*
spectabiles (senatorial grade) 190
speeches, public 147–9, 415
spell, Old Coptic 722
Speyer (Noviomagus) 122
Spitzberg, near Rottenburg (Mount Pirus) 84
state control: and cities 205, 209, 330, 375–6,
    379, 380; economic intervention 316–22,
    336–7; fragmentation 281; social coercion
    338, 340–1, 363–4, 369; *see also* bureaucracy;
    centralization; emperors; taxation
state formation by Germanic peoples 461, 481
statues: Christian attitudes to pagan 649–51,
    743–4, 745; colossal 736, 737; maintenance
    167; reverence for emperors' 143, 154, 652,
    661 (*see also* Antioch (Riot of the Statues)); *see
    also under* Constantinople
stenographers 678, 705
Stephen, St 255, 648–9, 759
Steps, Book of (*Liber Graduum*) (Syriac) 709
Stilicho (*magister utriusque militiae*) 111, 124–5,
    430–3, 764; rise 110, 113, 354; guardian to
    Honorius 110, 113, 114, 115; claims
    guardianship over Arcadius 113, 114;
    campaigns against Alaric (395) 114, 430, (397)
    115, 430; senate at Constantinople declares
    public enemy 115; height of power 118, 764;
    campaign against Alaric (402) 120, 431;
    abortive plan for campaign in Illyricum 121,
    122, 123, 429, 431, 513, 527; defeats
    Radagaisus 233–4; rift with Honorius 123,
    124; death 124, 125, 128, 432, 433, 513, 766

and Alaric 233, 236, 511, 512, 513, (failure
    to destroy) 114, 115, 120, 124, 430–1, 527;
    and Anthemius 513; army under 121, 216,
    233–4; assessment 124–5; and barbarian
    federates 121, 124–5, 506, 513, 527; Claudian's
    panegyrics 114, 115, 175, 176–7, 415, 527;
    comes of Theodosius 354; frontier defences
    neglected 125, 236, 428; legitimism 114, 124,
    430; marriage ties with imperial family 113,
    115, 123; political role 229; and Symmachus
    355; and unification of empire 113, 114, 121,
    124, 128, 164, 175, 431, 512
Stoicism 625
storage facilities 312, 494
Strasbourg (Argentorate) *1 Db, 2 Db*; battle
    of 40, 51, 54, 212, 220, 232–3, 422, 762
Strata Diocletiana *6 Cb-c*, 217–18, 457, 458, 459
streets, porticoed 382, *383*, 388, 404
strongholds, Scandinavian walled 480
Subicara 88
substance (*ousia, substantia*; theological concept)
    33–4, 35, 565, 569, 570, 573, 574, 576, 577
Succi, pass of, Thrace 43, 59
Suevi (Suebi, Sueves) *1 Eb, 504*; Constantius II's
    campaigns 32, 422; Rhine crossing (406) 122,
    236, 431, 505, 518, 766; settle in Spain 129,
    132, 432, 518, 519, 524, 528–9; Christianity
    526; and Huns 503n28
Sufes *7 Bb*, 650
Sufetula *7 Bb*, 405
suffragium (influence) 138, 152, 172, 173, 179, 194,
    697
supply: military 54–5, 215, 220–1, 229, 285, 316,
    317, 360; supply side of urban economy
    333–5
Sura *6 Cb*, 458
Surena (senior Persian minister) 79, 94
Svear *462*
Sweden, southern 480
Symeon the Stylite, St 701–2, 767
Symmachorum leaf (of ivory diptych) 743
Symmachus, Q. Aurelius, the elder 60, 312, 334
Symmachus, Q. Aurelius, the younger: and altar
    of Victory 106, 199, 552, 560, 765; and
    Ambrose 355; on citizen-king 147; *comes* 152;
    as landowner 282, 284, 294, 302, 306, 334;
    letters 340, 696–7; and Maximus 107, 194;
    patronage 172, 194, 361, 362; and religion
    551, 552, 646, 696; senatorial career 158, 174,
    191–2, 194, 200, 209, 355; and Stilicho 355;
    urban prefect 174, 191–2; on woman's place
    345
synagogues 394; destruction of 640–1, 642–3,
    646, 647
syncretism: in art 736, 739, 744–5, 745–6;
    Christian–pagan 393–4, 695; pagan inter-cult
    753–4

Synesius of Cyrene, bishop of Ptolemais: as bishop 245, 266, 269, 765; on Goths in empire 488; hymns 695; *On Kingship* 117, 140–1, 162–3, 512; pamphlet attacking Arcadius 146; Platonism 555, 556, 602, 613, 623, 680, 682, 695

synhedria, Jewish provincial 454

Synkellos, George 717n21

synods: *endēmousai* 248; of the Oak 263n111; Persian synodical literature 709; *see also* councils of bishops

Syracuse *1 Ec*, 755

Syria *1 Gc*, *9 Ba*; and Arabs 135, 448; army presence 215, 231, 459; ascetics 348, 541, 619–20, 621, 709; countryside 278, 282, 286, 298, 308, 714, 715; Hunnic incursion 114, 429, 443; language use 714, 715; monkish bands 282, 550, 646, 647; paganism 540–2, 550, 646, 647; Persian wars 135, 278, 416; *see also* Antioch; Syriac culture

Syriac culture *9 Db*, 708–19; Bible translation 713, 716; bilingual Syriac-Coptic work 710n7, 735; chronicles 416; Coptic translations 733; distribution 714–16; and Greek culture 666, 712, 713–14, 714–17, (translations) 717–19; hagiography 701–2, 710, 718; hymns 619, 710, 712, 716; inscriptions 708, 715; Jewish influence 712, 713; legal documents 708; literary genres 712, 713; liturgical works 713, 717; Manichean works 733; Mesopotamian influence 712–13; origins of literary culture 708–9; poetry 712, 717–18; prose, artistic 712; Proto-Syriac dialect 708; in Sasanian empire 708, 709, 712, 719

Syrianus (military commander) 27

Syrianus (Platonist) 557

tableware, luxury 738, 746, 747–9

Taifali 99

talismans 645–6

Talmud 453; Jerusalem or Palestine 454, 679

Tamsapor (Persian *marzban*) 423

Tanūkh (Arab allies of Rome) 446

Targums (Jewish Aramaic biblical translations) 713

Tarracina *4 Cb*, 329

Tarsus *1 Gc*, *6 Bb*, 73, 89, 93

Taurus, Fl. (praetorian prefect, consul) 35, 61, 196

taxation: and agriculture 281–5; *adaeratio* 317, 318; administration 166, 168, 182, 230, 289, 309, 375, 376; army funded by 166, 220, 221, 277, 375; barbarian settlements 494, 523–4, 525; cities affected by 205, 330, 375, 376, 409; *coloni* and 284, 289, 290; under Constantine 186, 282, 314, 325; under Diocletian 277, 282; donatives funded by 166; emperors' power 139; equalizations 208; evasion by powerful

314; exemptions 206–7, 260, 275, 328, 759; in Gaul 54, 55, 282, 535; 'gold and silver', on tradesmen 65; Goths 494; increasing burden 313, 331, 357; indirect 166; of Jews 454; Julian reduces 54, 55, 64, 65; in kind 313, 316–17, 317–18; land- 277, 282; loss of northern provinces' 535; and the poor 282–3, 298–9; protection of peasants against 231–2, 284, 300, 310, 314, 362–3; provincial administration 54, 167, 168; records 314–15; and rural production 281–5; and smallholders 297, 298–9; tax–trade relation 317–18; trade tax, see *collatio lustralis*; *vectigalia*; see also *annona*; *collatio lustralis*

teachers 673–4, 676; Augustine as 384, 668; Julian's edict on Christian 66–7, 547, 668, 676, 688

Tella de-Mauzelat 419

temples: churches built on sites of 551, 554; closure 108, 160–1, 395, 539, 550, 554; destruction 395, 539, 541, 553, 554, 634–5, 646, 647, (under Constantius) 31, 575, (by monkish bands) 550, 551, 557, 601, 647, (under Theodosius) 106, (*see also* Alexandria (Serapeum)); estates 65, 68, 548; Julian's restoration 62, 65, 68, 546; restoration in Sardis 550; reuse of building materials 395; Rome 7, 108, 395, *397*, 398, 551; survivals into fifth century 7, 551, 557–8

tenuiores 360, 370

Terebon, son of Aspebetos (Arab chief) 450

Terebon III, great-grandson of Aspebetos 450

Terentius (*dux Armeniae*) 91, 92, 93

terpen (settlement mounds) 473, 474

Tertullian 344, 753

Tertullus (urban prefect) 358–9

Tervingi 491, 492; Roman relations to *c.* 370 94, 495, 497–9; pressed by Huns 95, 500, 502–3, 517; admitted to empire 95, 500, 507, 521, 762; revolt 507–8; under Theodosius 102, 509; co-operate with Greuthungi 508, 511–12

    Christianity 495, 497, 499, 526; society 494, 495–6, 516–17; subsidies 497, 498, 499; trade 497; *see also* Alavivus; Athanaric; Fritigern

Testamentum Porcelli 230

tetrarchy 351, 418, 457, 497

textiles 336, 749

Thagaste *7 Bb*, 259, 344, *372*, 384, 402

Thalassius (praetorian prefect) 24, 198–9

Thamugadi (Timgad) *7 Bb*, 178, *372*, 384, 405

thaumaturges 348

theatres 71, 143–4

Thebes, Egypt (Diospolis Magna) *1 Gd*, *8 Bb*, 722

Thecla, St 557, 633; *Life and Miracles of* 702

Themistius (philosopher): appearance 611, 643; on army 235; on emperor 141, 159; on Goths 487, 488, 495–6, 498, 499, 510; paganism 540,

543; panegyric 17, 37; philosophy 540, 544, 643, 680; Praetextatus' translation of 193; proconsul of Constantinople 540; propaganda 201, 498, 499, 510; public oratory 201, 678; and senate of Constantinople 38, 187, 197; source on warfare and diplomacy 415; traditional values 678–9; and Valens 611

Theoderic *see* Theodoric

Theodora, empress of Constantine I; descendants of 2, 3–4

Theodora, empress of Justinian 558

Theodore of Asine 544, 728

Theodore of Mopsuestia 596, 597, 669, 714, 717

Theodoret of Cyrrhus 298, 563, 639, 714; *Religious History* 348, 689, 700–1

Theodoric I, king of Goths 132, 514; Edict of 294

Theodorus (*notarius*) 92, 93

Theodorus, bishop of Mutina 265

Theodosian Code 139, 157, 166, 167, 369, 682, 767; on army 456; on *coloni* 288; on *curiales* 65; on emperors' sanctity 143–4; on episcopal judgements 272; on Eutropius' punishment 351; on Jews 454; on officials and bureaucracy 139, 163, 188, 364; on *patrocinium* 362; on religion 7, 254, 639; on torture of Isaurians 452; value as source 340, 341, 360, 415

Theodosiopolis (Resaina) *6 Db*, 435, 443, 444

Theodosius (*magister equitum*) 84, 85, 88, 764

Theodosius I, emperor: accession 101, 764; Gratian gives Illyricum to 121; new conscription laws after Adrianople 101–2; Gothic campaigns and treaty 102–3, 234, 426–7, 428, 509–10, 517–18, 764; recognizes Maximus 105, 764; peace with Persia 106; and Riot of the Statues in Antioch 107, 154–5, 270, 373; deposes Maximus 107, 428, 764; and Eugenius 109, 428, 764; retirement 109–10; death 110, 678, 764
   accessibility 149, 150; Ambrose and 107–8, 110, 675, 678, 758; and bakers 318–19; barbarian federate settlements 103, 112–13, 223, 234, 280–1, 427–9, 483–4, 487, 510–11, 517–18; barbarians' personal ties with 428, 510–11, 518; baptism 102; bureaucracy under 168, 171, 172; and Church 103–4, 107–8, 227, 258, 268, (imposes orthodoxy) 112, 274, 549, 559, 575, 578, 579, 580, 582; Claudian on 140; consistory minutes 275; dynastic sense 113; laws 101–2, 108, 168, 172, 360–1, 667; Missorium of 151–2, 759; Pacatus' panegyric 148–9, 150; and paganism 106, 108, 549–50, 553–4, 559, 646, 667, 765; restricts embassies 155; and Rome 107, 148, 390; sculptures 736–7; Stilicho continues policies 125; warfare and diplomacy 426–9

Theodosius II, emperor 111, 112, 766; education

133–4; early years of rule 128–9, 164, 433 (*see also* Anthemius); war against Persia 134–5, 234, 434, 435, 437, 443–4, 451; marries Eudoxia 135; and accession of Valentinian III 136
   and army 229; and Church 134, 247, 249, 258, 638; diplomacy 433–6; laws 173–4, 361, 638; and learning 676; and Persia 112, 433–5, 437, 443, 451; stability of government 111, 112, 433, 435; statue collection 744, 748; and Vandals in Africa 519

Theodosius, son of Athaulf and Galla Placidia 131, 132

theological writings 699

theology 561–600, 702–4; *see also* Christology; heresy; *homoousios*; *hypostaseis*; substance; Trinity

Theon (Alexandrian, father of Hypatia) 556

Theophilus, bishop of Alexandria 118, 245, 248, 343, 596, 726–7; and destruction of Serapeum 551, 635; and Origenist controversy 594–5

Theophilus, governor of Syria 329

Theotokos, Mary as 596, 597

Therasia, wife of Paulinus of Nola 693–4, 702

Thermantia, empress 123

Thessalonica *1 Fb, 5 Ba, 372*, 405; Theodosius I's base 102, 509; Valentinian II flees to 107; riot and massacre 108, 646, 765; bishopric 249

Thessaly *1 Fc, 5 Bb*, 102, 114

Thetford silver treasure 748

theurgy 541, 557, 623–4, 625, 680, 752; Julian and 29, 46, 544

Thilsaphata *6 Db*, 79

Thomas, Acts of (Syriac) 709

Thomas, Book of (Coptic) 731

Thomas, Gospel according to (Coptic) 731

Thorsbjerg 481

Thrace *1 Fb, 3 Db-Eb*; under Constantius II 4, 215, 216; Julian reduces taxes 65; Gothic threat (365) 89; Goths allowed to enter (376) 95, 98; Roman campaigns against Goths 98–101; Gothic settlements under Theodosius 103, 234, 517–18; Gothic attacks 106, 114, 116, 428, 429; Gainas defeated in 116, 765; Hunnic invasions 128, 135, 433, 435, 436
   army 215, 216; cities 327; *coloni* 289; diocese 167, 248

Three Good Shepherds sarcophagus 750

Thuringi 483

Thyatira *5 Cb*, 91

Tibatto, rebellion of 534

Tiberias *6 Cc*, 453, 454, 679

Ticinum (Ticino) *1 Db, 4 Ba*, 21, 124, 125

Timasius, Fl. (*magister*) 115, 194

Timavus, battle of river 120

time, conception of 609, 610, 634–5, 690

Timgad (Thamugadi) 7 Cb, 178, 372, 384, 405
Timothy, bishop of Alexandria 579
Timothy, St: relics 38
Tingitania 1 Cc, 216
Tirgşor: Černjachov culture 489
Titianus, Fabius 6, 10, 15
Titus of Bostra 718
Tofting 473
tolls, local (vectigalia) 205
Tolosa see Toulouse
tombs 139, 168–9, 551–2
Tomi 3 Eb, 241, 613
toponymy 464, 524
torques, gold 467, 486
torture, judicial 89, 153, 452, 656; of clergy 263,
    275; of senators 92, 199, 200
Toul (Tullum, Civitas Leucorum) 2 Db, 372, 374
Toulouse (Tolosa) 1 Db, 2 Cc, 29, 372, 407
Tournai (Turnacum) 2 Ca, 465, 467
towns: market 333; see also cities
townscapes: classical 381–2, 383, 388, 404;
    religious 250–1, 254, 395–9, 410
Toxandria 280, 420
trade 312–37; administered, non-market
    transference 307, 315–16, 323, 330–2, 336,
    337; decline or continuation 313–16, 336;
    Germanic tribes 465, 467, 473, 480, 481, 484,
    486, (Goths) 425, 493, 496, 497, (Scandinavia
    and west Baltic) 480; luxury goods 313;
    monopolies 321–2; Persian 443; Scandinavia
    480, 481, 484, 486; sources on 315; state
    intervention 316–22, 336–7; tax and 316–17,
    317–18; see also collatio lustralis
tradesmen 65, 318–22; see also collegia
Trajan, emperor 73
Trajanus (general) 92, 93, 101
transhumance 445
translation: Bible, (into Latin) 671–2, (into
    Syriac) 713; into Coptic 666, 721, 730;
    Greek–Syriac 666, 717–19; Greek–Latin 666,
    680, 695, 700
transport: speed 157, 161, 181, 417; state,
    compulsory duty 293; see also cursus publicus
Trapezus 1 Gb, 6 Ca, 458
travellers, charity towards 257; see also hostels;
    pilgrimage
treason trials 187–8, 359, 762
treasury, imperial 165–6
Treveri, Trèves see Trier
Tribigild (Gothic leader) 116, 512n42, 765
tributarii 280, 290
Trier (Treveri, Augusta Treverorum) 1 Db, 2 Db,
    372, 385; Constans' capital 6; under Valentinian
    I 84, 200, 351; Eugenius and 109; capital
    moved to Arles 202; falls to barbarians 122,
    467; possible core of Germanic kingdom 465
        Athanasius' exile 567; Ausonius in 673;

bishops 8, 24; as capital city 385, 386, 410;
    coinage 109; depopulation 278; forward
    location 390, 391, 202; and house of
    Constantine 22; imperial patronage 386, 406,
    409; religion in region 550, 601; size 374
Trinitapoli, near Foggia 309, 310
Trinity, doctrine of 565, 566, 567, 568, 570–1,
    573–5, 576–7, 577–8, 581–2, 587
Tripartite Tractate (Coptic) 731
triumphs 106, 421
Trophimus, St 245, 250
Troy 5 Cb, 393–4, 542
Troyes (Augustobona) 2 Cb, 49
Truth, Gospel of (Coptic) 731
Tungricani (army corps) 89
Tunisia 286, 298
Tür 'Abdin 6 Db, 9 Ca, 455
Turcii (family of Volcei, Lucania) 299
Turin (Augusta Taurinorum) 4 Aa, 244–5, 250
Turnacum (Tournai) 2 Ca, 465, 467
Tyana 6 Bb, 80, 244
Tyconius (Donatist theologian) 585
typology 751–5
Tyre 6 Cc, 678; council of 33n111, 566–7, 569
Tyrrhenian islands 616
Tzani of Iberia 558

Udruh 457
Ukraine 483, 487, 493
Uldin, king of Huns 117, 503, 504; in Stilicho's
    army 121, 506; Balkan campaign 128, 433
Ulfila (general) 130
Ulfilas, bishop to Tervingi 496, 497, 526, 581;
    expulsion 495, 497, 499; Gothic Bible 487,
    491, 581
Ulpian: collection of private law 682
UNESCO, Carthage project 405
uniforms 168–9
unity of empire 124, 136–7, 209
universe, concept of 636–8, 645–6, 652
universities 364
upper classes see aristocracy; curiae, curiales;
    senatorial order
Ur 6 Db, 79
urban prefects 153, 167, 205; see also under
    Constantinople; Rome
Urfa see Edessa
Ursacius, bishop of Singidunum 33, 568,
    569–70, 580
Ursatius (magister officiorum) 83
Ursicinus (general): eastern magister equitum 24,
    453; under suspicion in Milan 25, 27; deals
    with Silvanus' usurpation 27–8; in Gaul with
    Julian 49; operations against Persia 39, 40,
    422, 423; Ammianus Marcellinus and 212, 687
Ursinus (contender for papacy) 82, 267–8
Ursulus (comes sacrarum largitionum) 61, 220, 229

usurpations: and army 14, 225–6, 535; barbarian support 130, 527–8, 528–9; diplomacy 16, 41, 59–60; priority accorded to suppression 528, 529, 532; statues mutilated 143
Uzalis, bishop of 265n122

Vadomarius, king of Alamanni 24, 42, 58–9, 92
Vagabanta, battle of 92
Vahram, king of Persia see under Varahram
Valamer (Gothic leader in Hunnic empire) 503
Valence (Valentia) 2 Cc, 122, 519, 520, 524, 525
Valens, emperor 89–101, 762; accession 81–2, 762; Procopius' usurpation 83, 89–91, 144, 762; campaigns against Goths 90, 94–5, 217, 221, 235, 425, 497, 498, 508–9, 762; accepts accession of Valentinian II 86; diplomacy with Persia 89, 91–4, 94–5, 98, 508; admission of Goths to empire 95, 98, 507–8; campaign against Goths, defeat and death at Adrianople 94, 97–101, 233, 426, 508–9, 517, 764
   army organization 222; and Church 81, 95, 571, 575, 576, 611; character 92, 162, 233, 611; and paganism 93n43, 548–9; plots against 92–3, 153; relaxes financial control of cities 205, 375; sale of judicial verdicts under 162; and senate at Constantinople 89, 188–91; Themistius' influence 611; unpopularity 89, 92–3
Valens, bishop of Mursa 20, 241, 568–9, 580; and battle of Mursa 20, 569; and Athanasius 26, 568; and creed-making 33, 34, 35, 36, 569–70
Valentia see Valence
Valentines: Germanic burial 464
Valentinian I, emperor 83–8; accession 80–2, 762; division of responsibilities with Valens 82, 762; and magic trials 82–3, 200; Alamannic war 83–5, 217, 424–5; unrest in Africa 87–8, 162, 158; Gratian appointed Augustus 83–4, 144, 762; Theodosius' campaigns, (in Britain) 86–7, (in Africa against Firmus) 88; campaign in Illyricum 85–6, 762; death 85–6, 199, 762
   army organization 216, 222; on bureaucrats 364; capitals 82, 351, 762; and Church 81, 258, 259, 268, 390, 571, 580; cities' revenues 205, 375, 379; and paganism 81, 82–3, 548–9, 645; Pannonians favoured by 152; quinquennalia 200; rages 86, 157–8, 611; and senate 188–91, 199, 200; social measures 310, 361, 369; speech to army 678
Valentinian II, emperor: accession 86, 194, 762; Maximus' usurpation see Maximus, Magnus; restored by Theodosius I 107, 108; death 108–9, 146–7, 764

and Ambrose 105, 106, 146–7; and Arbogast 108–9, 229; and Church 106, 258; on emperor and divine 158; Probus and 194; restricts embassies 155
Valentinian III, emperor: accession 136–7, 436, 766; and army 229; and barbarians 536, 537; bureaucracy under 173–4; court rivalries 533; death 536
Valentinus (heretic) 108, 731
Valeria (province) 102
Valerian, emperor 155–6, 416
Valerianus (curator stabuli) 101
Valerius, bishop of Hippo 179, 613
Vallhagar, Gotland 479–80
Vallia, king of Goths see Wallia
Vandals 462; and Przeworsk culture 482; in Raetia and Noricum 120, 430, 504; in Radagaisus' force 431; Rhine crossing (406) 122, 391, 431, 505, 518, 766; pass into Spain 129, 391, 432, 518; occupation of Spain 132, 524; Roman and Gothic campaigns against 515, 518, 519, 528–9, 530, 536; conquest of Africa 112, 137, 391, 436, 519, 531, 536, 766, (and cities) 379, 380, 405, (court rivalries facilitate) 532–3, 536, (ends euergetism) 379, 380, (fall of Carthage) 391, 405, 520, 766, (land holdings) 202, 523, 525, (refugees) 202, (religious policy) 290–1, 526, (size of force) 521–2; sack of Rome (455) 536; (H)asding 122, 132, 518, 519, 524; Siling 122, 132, 518, 519, 521–2, 524
Varahram V, king of Persia 134, 135, 434, 435, 443–4
Varazdat, king of Armenia 425, 426
Varronianus (father of Jovian) 78
Varronianus (son of Jovian) 80
vases, high-relief carved stone 738
vectigalia (local taxes) 205
vegetarianism 608
Vegetius 415, 686
Veke 493
Venetia 126, 310, 513
Venustus (senator) 200
Verecundus (friend of Augustine) 618
Verenianus (relative of Honorius) 311
Vermand: Germanic cemetery 465
Verona 1 Eb, 4 Ba, 293, 310, 372, 374; battle of 120, 233, 431, 512
Verulamium (St Albans) 477
vestales 104
Vestina (Roman widow) 251
Vetranio (usurper) 15–17, 225, 422
Vibianus, T. Flavius, of Lepcis Magna 552
vicarii 166, 170, 194, 205
Victor (general, fl. 363) 78
Victor (general, son-in-law of Mavia) 447
Victor (grammarian in Numidia) 359

Victor (*magister equitum* to Valens) 98, 99–100

Victor, Aurelius 277, 365, 415, 545, 684

Victor of Vita 521

Victores (legion) 90

Victorinus (Gallic landowner) 202

Victorinus, Marius 67, 574, 676, 680, 698

Victory, altar of, in Roman senate house:
Constantius removes 31, 540; Gratian
removes 104, 552; Theodosius refuses
reinstatement 105–6, 107, 198, 199, 560;
Eugenius restores 109
  Ambrose and 105–6, 199, 560;
Symmachus and 198, 199, 552, 560, 765;
Prudentius on 693

Victricius, bishop of Rouen 254, 265

Viderich, king of Goths 102

Vienna *see* Vindobona

Vienne (Vienna) *1 Db, 2 Cb*, 49, 57, 58, 109, 129,
245

villages 309; Africa 303; east 455; fortified 468,
472; Gaul, 'small agglomerations' 286;
Germanic 468, 469, 470, 472, 493, 494–5, 516;
Italy 309; on large estates 300–1; pagan
sanctuaries 550; Sicily 309; Syria 282, 298;
west 297–8

villas 328; Africa 285, 300, 303; Antioch 303;
artisans working at 313, 333; Britain 278, 294,
297, 302, 408, 475; buildings 306; decline of
Catonian system 284, 285, 296; Gaul 279, 294,
297, 302, 467–8, 472; Italy 306; northern
frontier 297; retirement of élite to 302, 313;
Sicily 300, 749; Spain 302, 306–7, 311

Vimose 481

Vincentius, bishop of Capua 8

Vincentius, praetorian prefect of Gauls 324

Vindobona (Vienna) *1 Eb, 3 Ca*

Vireux-Molhain 468–9

Virgil 738, 753

virgins 134, 257, 329, 344, 345, 402

virtues and vices, catalogues of imperial 145–6,
150

Visigoths *see* Goths

Vitalis (disciple of Apollinaris) 573

Vitalis, St 758

Vitheric, king of Greuthungi 500

Vithicabius, king of Alamanni 84

Vithimer, king of Greuthungi 500, 502, 511

Volcei, Lucania 299

Vorbasse, Jutland 478–9

votive deposits in Baltic peat bogs 481–2

Vulfolaic the Lombard, St 550

Vulgate 671

Wallia (Vallia), king of Goths 132, 514, 518, 519,
521, 530, 537

walls, city 327, 389, 409; Carthage 391, 405;
Constantinople 37–9, 102, 129, *387*, 391–2;

Jerusalem 452; Rome 120, *374*, 390, 391, *397*;
size of areas enclosed by *374*, 406

war damage 278–9

warfare 411–36; Arab guerrilla techniques
444–5, 446; battles 413, 424, 498; Church and
12, 226–7, 228, 269–70, 438, 443, 444, 451,
460; Constantius II's policy towards Persia
13–14, 40, 420, 421, 438; counterattack,
Julian's use of 422, 424; diplomacy combined
with 428–9, 436; diplomacy replaces 413, 414,
428–9; emperors' role 411–12, 421, 427; hit-
and-run tactics 426; siege warfare 413, 418,
438, 459–60; sources 414–16; technology 413,
416; *see also* army; prisoners (-of-war) *and
individual wars, leaders and peoples*

warlordism 281, 311, 433

water mills 285

water supply to Constantinople 386, *387*

wealth: Church 257–62, 401–2, 403;
concentration into fewer hands 334–5, 337,
357; *curiales*' modest 339, 360; philosophers'
attitude to 611; polarization, rich/poor 327,
334–5, 337, 351, 357; Rome 260, 261, 301,
401–2; senatorial class 181, 184, 300, 314,
334, 335, 401–2; *see also under* east and
west

weapons: Germanic tribes' 316, 464, 468, 475,
481; siege 418

west *see* east and west

West Stow, Suffolk 477

Westerwanna: Saxon cemetery 472

widows: Christian charity for poor 257, 329, 332,
341, 344, 402; rich 259, 348, 369

Wielbark culture 490

Wijster, Holland 473

wills 582

Winchester: Lankhills cemetery 478

wine: production and trade 307, 315, 334; state
distribution 167, 321, 329

Winguric (Gothic noble) 494

winter solstice 253

Wittislingen 472

women 344–8; Christian 344–8, (asceticism)
258–9, 345–6, 347, 607–8, 613, 620, 670, 702,
(baptism) 70–1, (networks) 654, (pilgrims)
346, 449, 566, 620, 756, *see also* Egeria; (rich)
70–1, 259, 345–6, (*see also* virgins; widows);
education 44, 670, 698; heretic 344; and
monasticism 259, 345–6; philosophers 607–8,
611–12, 698; writings 702

workers' associations 326, 337; see also *collegia*

workforce: agricultural 282, 289, (slaves) 284,
285, 287, 295–6, 304, 305, 306–7, (see also
coloni); regulation of 282, 288, 289, 293–4, 296,
324, 325, 338, 341, 357; *see also* manpower

xenodocheia (hostels) 68–9, 251, 256–7, 258, 260

Yezdegerd I, king of Persia 433–5; relations with
    Rome 112, 123, 128, 430, 433, 443, 718;
    persecution of Christians 134, 434
Yorkshire 475

Zabdicene 6 Db, 79
Zachariah of Mytilene 700
Zagajkany 493
Zaghouan, Tunisia 285
Zakrzow (Sakrau), Silesia 482–3
Zealand, Denmark 481
Zeno, bishop of Verona 293

Zeno, emperor 321–2, 453
Zenobia (city) 455
Zenophilus (governor of Numidia) 359
Zeugma 458, 715
Zeus: -Belus, cult at Apamea 541; Phidias'
    chryselephantine statue 744; temple at
    Antioch 70
Zizais, prince of Sarmatians 32
Zokomos (Saracen phylarch) 449
Zoroastrianism 433, 434, 602, 636
Zosimus (historian) 414, 488, 685, 687
Zosimus, pope 250, 267–8, 591, 592